Social Psychology

The Science of Everyday Life

Prejudice and Discrimination and Digital Update

3e

Social Psychology
The Science of Everyday Life

Prejudice and Discrimination and Digital Update

Jeff Greenberg
University of Arizona

Toni Schmader
University of British Columbia

Jamie Arndt
University of Missouri

Mark Landau
University of Kansas

worth publishers
Macmillan Learning
New York

Senior Executive Program Manager: Christine Cardone

Senior Development Editor: Valerie Raymond

Assistant Editor: Olivia Madigan

Executive Marketing Manager: Katherine Nurre

Associate Director, Digital Content, Social Science: Anna Garr

Senior Media Editor: Karissa Venne

Senior Media Project Manager: Eve Conte

Senior Director, Content Management Enhancement: Tracey Kuehn

Executive Managing Editor: Michael Granger

Manager, Publishing Services: Ryan Sullivan

Senior Lead Content Project Manager: Won McIntosh

Assistant Director, Process Workflow: Susan Wein

Production Supervisor: Lawrence Guerra

Senior Photo Editor: Sheena Goldstein

Photo Project Manager: Richard Fox, Lumina Datamatics, Inc.

Director of Rights & Permissions: Hilary Newman

Director of Design, Content Management: Diana Blume

Senior Design Manager: Natasha A. S. Wolfe

Cover Design: John Callahan

Interior Design: Lumina Datamatics, Inc.

Art Manager: Matthew McAdams

Composition: Lumina Datamatics, Inc.

Printing and Binding: King Printing Co., Inc.

Library of Congress Control Number: 2023934892

ISBN 978-1-319-54559-8 (paperback)
ISBN 978-1-319-54555-0 (Loose-leaf Edition)
ISBN 978-1-319-54654-0 (International Edition)

Printed in the United States of America

1 2 3 4 5 6   28 27 26 25 24 23

Worth Publishers
One New York Plaza
Suite 4600
New York, NY 10004-1562
www.macmillanlearning.com

We dedicate this book to

Liz, Jonathan, Camila, Murray, Edie, Debbi, Dave, David, Michael, Mitzie, and Dick for their love and support.
J.G.

Matt, Hazen, and Ivy for adding to the sheer joy of everyday life.
T.S.

Stephanie, Nick, and Alexis for their love and support, and my mom and dad for instilling the value of education.
J.A.

To my daughter Colette; may you always be curious.
M.L.

ABOUT THE AUTHORS

Jeff Greenberg

Jeff Greenberg, Ph.D., is a Regents Professor of Psychology and a College of Science Fellow at the University of Arizona. As a small child growing up in the Bronx, he was very curious about the human propensities for vanity and prejudice. Jeff majored in psychology at the University of Pennsylvania, but it wasn't until he took social psychology in his final semester that he found a field where people were asking the questions he thought should be asked. Soon after starting a master's program in social psychology at Southern Methodist University, he knew this was what he wanted to spend his life studying and teaching. After receiving his M.A., Jeff completed his Ph.D. at University of Kansas in 1982, under the mentorship of Jack Brehm. He has since received numerous research and teaching awards, including Lifetime Career Awards from the International Society for Self and Identity, the Society for Personality and Social Psychology, and the International Society for the Science of Existential Psychology. His research has contributed to understanding self-serving biases, how motivation affects cognition, the effects of ethnic slurs, the role of self-awareness in depression, cognitive dissonance, and how concerns about death contribute to prejudice, self-esteem striving, and many other aspects of social behavior. Jeff has coauthored or coedited six other books, including the *Handbook of Experimental Existential Psychology* and *The Worm at the Core: The Role of Death in Life*.

UBC Department of Psychology

Toni Schmader, Ph.D., is a Canada Research Chair in Social Psychology at the University of British Columbia. She received her B.A. from Washington & Jefferson College in Pennsylvania before completing her Ph.D. at the University of California, Santa Barbara. Before moving to Canada in 2009, Toni taught at the University of Arizona for 10 years. For her research, she has been awarded the Killam Prize and Theoretical Innovation Prizes from the Society for Personality and Social Psychology and the European Association of Social Psychology. For excellence in teaching, she received the Magellan Prize from the University of Arizona. Toni has served on the executive committees of the Society for Personality and Social Psychology and the Society of Experimental Social Psychology and as an associate editor at the *Journal of Personality and Social Psychology* and *Personality and Social Psychology Bulletin*. She was drawn to research in social psychology for its ability to take a systematic empirical approach to examining important social issues and to teaching for the opportunity to share those insights with others. Her research examines how individuals are affected by and cope with tarnished identities and negative stereotypes. Toni has published work on topics of social identity threat, stigma and identity, stereotyping and prejudice, self-conscious emotion, and gender roles.

Jamie Arndt

Jamie Arndt, Ph.D., is Professor and Associate Dean of Graduate Studies and Strategic Initiatives at the University of Missouri (MU). After attending Skidmore College in the eastern United States for his B.A. and the University of Arizona in the western United States for his Ph.D., he settled in the middle, accepting a position at MU in 1999. During his time at MU, he has received the Robert S. Daniel Junior Faculty Teaching Award, the Provost's Junior Faculty Teaching Award, the International Society for Self and Identity Outstanding Early Career Award, the University of Missouri Chancellor's Award for Outstanding Research and Creative Activity in the Social and Behavioral Sciences, and the Frederick A. Middlebush Professorship. Jamie is a founding member of the Social Personality and Health Network and former chair of the Society for Personality and Social Psychology Training Committee, and he has served on the editorial boards of various journals in the field. He has authored or coauthored scholarly works pertaining to the self, existential motivation, psychological defense, and their implications for many topics, most notably health decision making, creativity, and legal judgment.

Omri Gillath

Mark Landau, Ph.D., is a Professor of Psychology at the University of Kansas. Mark received his B.A. from Skidmore College, where he became interested in the intersection of experimental psychology and existential philosophy. He continued his education at the University of Colorado, Colorado Springs, and then at the University of Arizona, where he received his Ph.D. in 2007. Mark's research explores how existential concerns motivate social behavior and the use of metaphor to understand social ideas. He has received a number of awards recognizing his research, including the Theoretical Innovation Prize from the Society for Personality and Social Psychology, the Outstanding Early Career Award from the International Society for Self and Identity, and the Early Career Award from the APA. Mark is a founding member of the International Society for the Science of Existential Psychology. He has authored or coedited two other books, including *Conceptual Metaphor in Social Psychology: The Poetics of Everyday Life*. For many years, Mark has enjoyed helping students appreciate the relevance of social psychology to their personal lives and the issues facing society.

BRIEF CONTENTS

CONTENTS

5 The Nature, Origins, and Functions of the Self 157

6 The Key Self-Motives: Consistency, Esteem, Presentation, and Growth 195

13 Prosocial Behavior 475

14 Interpersonal Attraction 511

PREFACE

We are truly excited and honored to be able to offer students an updated edition of our textbook. As we are finishing up this new edition, social psychological knowledge is needed more right now than ever before. The entire world has been trying to cope with the global COVID-19 pandemic, which has brought to the fore a combination of the existential threat of death, economic problems, health disparities, political polarization, issues of freedom versus security, and social isolation. In the face of this crisis, we have also seen the resilience of communities and extraordinary acts of cooperation. During these already tense and anxious times, the United States is also reeling from a new series of racial injustices caught on camera or otherwise brought to light. In particular, the horrific killing of George Floyd by a Minneapolis police officer ignited a wave of peaceful protests around the globe, but in the United States it has also brought looting, vandalism, and clashes with police. These events have reinvigorated focus on the need for major police reforms and greater social justice throughout American society. These are extraordinary historic moments that reveal facets of human psychology that the theories and research programs in this textbook can help us understand.

When we first introduced this textbook in 2015, it was important to us to have two chapters on prejudice, a feature some reviewers at the time questioned. We believed then, as we still do, that this is the most pressing social psychological problem out in the world. Not coincidentally, prejudice is also the topic in our field that has generated the largest body of valuable research. More than ever before, the knowledge and insights provided by social psychology are urgently needed to inform the problems we are all facing and shape this period of social upheaval and change toward a better future.

Our unique coverage of prejudice is thus a major step in helping students appreciate the relevance of social psychology for getting a handle on the major issues facing our society. In the same spirit, we worked hard to speak to pressing social and political events in this updated edition. We updated the text with regard to not only the coronavirus, racial inequality, and social justice, but also the #MeToo movement and growing efforts to root out sexual violence, the civil rights struggles of the LGBTQ+ community, and the decades-long struggle to combat climate change.

Of course, we also have included the latest theories and research findings in the field (more on this later). This edition also provided us with an opportunity to listen to feedback from instructors, students, and peer reviewers and improve the book in several ways. We are gratified that most of the feedback has been quite positive, and so this third edition is built on the same guiding principles and organizational decisions we developed in first preparing this textbook.

The Science of Everyday Life

Since our own days as undergrads, we've been excited by how the science of social psychology helps us understand everyday life. Our goal in this book is to generate this excitement for a new generation of students—by presenting the best, brightest, and most current ideas and findings the field has to offer in a conceptually coherent and lively narrative. We want students to appreciate that social psychology is, first and foremost, the science of all of us. We aimed to write an inclusive book that all students, regardless of their backgrounds, social identities, and career interests, will find enriching and enjoyable.

There's only one good reason to spend many years bringing a new social psych text into the world: to present the field's body of knowledge in a more compelling and appealing way than any of the texts that are currently available. We have tried to do this primarily through a lot of hard work, digging into literatures both from within the traditional bounds of the field and from related disciplines, thinking creatively, staying abreast of the latest developments, and discussing and debating what to present and how best to do it. Indeed, every chapter involved a close collaboration among the four of us, resulting in a consistent voice that conveys our almost 100 years of collective knowledge, experience, and insight. We think this consistent voice and cumulative approach, in which each chapter builds on theory and research established by prior chapters, contrasts with the piecemeal approach taken by most contemporary social psychology textbooks.

Connecting Theory, Research, and Application

This textbook presents social psychology in a more coherent way than prior texts have done. As teachers of introductory social psychology, we have long been struck by the tendency of textbooks to treat each topic as a distinct form of human behavior. We set out to present a more integrative picture of human social behavior, and for 10 years we've continually refined the text to realize that vision.

One strategy we use to accomplish this more integrated vision is to underscore the power of theory. In our teaching, we find that what sticks with students is rarely a single experiment or definition from the field's vast landscape of knowledge. Instead, students most value learning the broader theories that help them gain insight into human nature and how to better people's lives. For instance, Kevin, one of our former students, now working in finance, says he continually benefits from theories in social cognition that explain how habits of thought can bias our judgments and decisions. Anna, now a graduate student, says she can better grasp what's happening in the news after learning about existential theories of people's quest for meaning and self-worth. (We were actually inspired by these students' reactions to create a new feature we will describe a bit later.) We therefore cover a variety of theories in greater depth than other texts, including action identification, attachment, cognitive dissonance, conceptual metaphor, construal level, objectification, reactance, regulatory focus, self-affirmation, self-determination, self-perception, social learning, symbolic self-completion, system justification, terror management, and thought suppression.

Another strategy is to highlight the rich connections between, on the one hand, theory and research discoveries and, on the other, the experiences and issues that matter in the real world. We have woven together theories and findings, practical applications, and examples from history, popular culture, and daily life into an integrated narrative.

A third strategy is to help students appreciate the challenges inherent in studying human behavior. We recognize that social psychology is undergoing a period of self-examination, with many of the field's methods, assumptions, and findings coming in for questioning. Even an introductory text, we feel, should touch on these controversies and their significance for learning outcomes. In every chapter, we point to cases where researchers have raised concerns about the replicability of research findings. We don't want to confuse students or overwhelm students with uncertainty. So we raise these issues in ways that inform them about the original findings and issues that have arisen regarding them and that encourage them to think critically about these issues and consider new ways to gain reliable knowledge of social processes.

Here are seven features we use throughout the book to enact these strategies. The first five were also in the second edition, and the last two are new features we have been excited to add to this third edition:

Integrated Applications

While maintaining the narrative flow, we integrate Application sections with a simple icon. These passages apply research findings to issues in health, law, politics, sustainability, social justice, education, fashion, and a variety of other topics that matter to students' lives. For convenient reference, the Application icons also appear next to each application heading in the detailed table of contents.

Social Psych Out in the World

To further reinforce how social psychology can illuminate the world we all live in, we highlight in feature boxes how the field's knowledge can be applied to understand historical and personal events.

Social Psych at the Movies

Culture and the arts mirror our inner nature as well as the major issues facing society. Over the history of cinema, filmmakers have captured important elements of social behavior in ways that can bring scientific theory and findings to life. In each chapter we analyze a classic or contemporary film that connects the field's theories and findings to human behavior in vivid ways.

THINK ABOUT ▶

[Ann Hermes/The Christian Science Monitor via Getty Images]

Does the self-concept remain pretty much the same as people move from one social context to another? Or does it change? Research supports both possibilities. Some aspects of the self-concept are relatively stable, like the attributes we view as most important for defining our sense of self. Intelligence or athletic ability, for example, might be most central to who someone is as a person, whereas other attributes may be descriptive but not so self-defining. Take a moment to think about your own self-defining attributes. What aspects are central to who *you* are?

According to Hazel Markus (1977), people's knowledge about self-defining attributes are mentally organized as a **self-schema**: an integrated set of memories, beliefs, and generalizations about an attribute that is cen-

Think Abouts

To help students relate concepts to their own lives and to think critically, we engage them by asking specific questions throughout the text, often highlighted as Think About features. Here is one such question, in blue type and accompanied by a photo, that invites students to connect directly to the text.

Enhanced Student Learning Tools

Learning Outcomes, found at the start of each major section of a chapter, focus students on the key concepts in the section they are about to read. These concepts are then briefly summarized in a *Section Review*. This structure provides a useful study tool and a double-check to make sure the material is understood. The Learning Outcomes are also a tool to facilitate syllabus building.

New! Critical Learning Exercises

To get students to more fully engage with the material, at the end of each chapter we pose four questions that ask students to think more deeply about theories and findings and to connect them to their own lives and to social issues. These could be used to generate essays from the students, as questions to pose for class discussions, or as group discussion assignments.

New! Social Psych in Everyday Life

We asked current and former introductory social psychology students to write brief stories about how they have used particular theories or findings from social psychology in their lives—to work smarter, maintain happier relationships, and have healthier lives. For each chapter we added a marginal note next to the relevant section to indicate where the reader can learn about how a former student used the theory or findings just described (www.macmillanlearning.com). We were gratified to have received many interesting stories that illustrate quite well how social psychological knowledge can be applied in people's lives and the value it can have for them.

Achieve
Social Psych in Everyday Life:
Abhay

Overarching Perspectives

A final aspect of this textbook's overarching integrative vision is to utilize five broad perspectives that serve as recurring motifs: culture, evolution, social cognition, social neuroscience, and existential psychology. These perspectives provide thematic continuity both within and across chapters. Of course, social psychology is a diverse field that is not constrained by one single perspective or one small set of perspectives. Instead, the field's accumulated knowledge has benefited from researchers seeking to understand behavior from many different points of view and levels of analysis. We think that's one of the most exciting aspects of our field that we want to communicate to our students. With this goal in mind, we have ensured that our organization of each chapter is not guided in a formulaic, rigid, or repetitive way by the five perspectives but by our desire to provide a conceptually coherent, comprehensible, and memorable discussion of the best and most useful theories and findings pertinent to that topic.

Overview of the Text's Organization

Chapter 1 begins with a brief consideration of the roots and history of social psychology. We then lay out five perspectives that guide much of the contemporary research in the field and the four fundamental assumptions of the field. The second half of the chapter is devoted to introducing students to the scientific methods used by social psychologists to investigate human behavior. We focus on the cyclical interplay of theory and research, correlational and experimental methods, strengths and limitations of different methods, as well as best practices to increase the replicability and insights of the science. We conclude with a consideration of ethics in research.

Chapter 2 considers cultural and evolutionary perspectives in more detail. Our treatment aims to give equal weight to both perspectives, each of which helps set the stage for understanding the fundamental motivations and cognitive architecture that underlie human behavior. Culture profoundly influences human experience. Most social psychology texts refer to culture primarily to explain cultural differences in gender roles, prevalence of the fundamental attribution error, and so forth. In our view, culture reveals at least as much about how people are similar to each other as it does about how they are different. Thus, unlike other textbooks, chapter 2 carefully considers what culture is, how cultures are structured, and the psychological functions they serve. Similarly, evolutionary processes didn't merely produce domain-specific adaptations that may help explain isolated phenomena such as sex differences in aggression or attraction. The evolution of our species also produced the basic sociability, cognitive capacities, potential for learning and growth, motivations, and emotions that contribute to all of our experiences and behaviors. By explaining the joint and interactive roles of culture and evolution in shaping the core proclivities of our species, we aim to provide students with a richer and more balanced framework for understanding and evaluating the ideas and findings they encounter in later chapters.

Following up on these broad aspects of human behavior, chapters 3 and 4 review the important insights that have come from understanding social cognition, including cutting-edge research from social neuroscience that examines brain regions and neural processes associated with particular aspects of thought, emotion, and judgment. Typically, traditional topics in social cognition, such as heuristics and biases, are presented in a list-like, piecemeal fashion. We instead begin with the motives that guide perception, memory, and decision making. This discussion is informed by the fifth overarching perspective of the book, an existential perspective that emphasizes how social life is shaped by core aspects of the human experience, including the needs for meaning, belonging, security, and growth.

After covering how people view others and the world around them, we focus on the self in chapters 5 and 6. These chapters cover the structure and functioning of the self and set the stage for subsequent chapters by illustrating the mutual constitution of self and social reality. The self-concept is largely the product of social and cultural influences; at the same time, individuals' self-regulatory capacities and motives for consistency, esteem, self-presentation, and growth inform their construal of self, other people, and social events.

Chapters 7 through 9 focus on the rich topics of social influence, persuasion, and group processes. Together, these chapters show how individuals' motives, beliefs, attitudes, and behavior influence, and are themselves influenced by, interactions with other people. In addition to covering classic theories and research, these chapters describe more recent developments and debates around issues such as social priming and mimicry, regulatory focus and control, implicit attitudes, and system justification.

Having examined the person's core needs, desires, cognitive capacities, self-motives, and relationships to the social world, we proceed in the final six chapters to focus on specific forms of social thought and behavior. The first three cover the darker side of human behavior. Chapters 10 and 11 (now updated with new research and examples) examine prejudice, stereotyping, and discrimination—their determinants, their consequences for those targeted by such biases, and potential ways to counteract these effects. These two chapters help students understand why prejudice is so prevalent and breeds so much injustice. Chapter 11 specifically offers evidence-based ways we, as societies and individuals, can work to reduce prejudice, stereotyping, and discrimination. Chapter 12 takes up the complex problem of interpersonal aggression. We discuss the consequences of aggression, its individual- and societal-level causes, and practical ways to move toward less violent societies.

The final three chapters focus on the more positive aspects of human experience: prosocial behavior (chapter 13), interpersonal attraction (chapter 14), and close relationships (chapter 15). We end with these topics for two main reasons. First, they cast a much-needed hopeful, upbeat light on human behavior and possibilities. Second, although all the topics in social psychology are relevant to everyday life, few are more pertinent to students' everyday experiences than those concerning the human desire for and experience of community and close relationships.

Our Approach to Preparing This Edition

Our first principle in revising was: If it's not broken, don't fix it. We retained the many aspects of the original text that worked. The primary criticism we received was that there was too much information. In response, we worked very hard to tighten up the writing and shorten the coverage considerably. As a result of these efforts, we reduced the number of words in each and every chapter. Here are other revisions and updates we've made to this third edition:

■ **Updated key research.** We wanted this book to present the latest developments in the field as well as the classic work. So we scoured the journals and added 399 new references to valuable research, with an additional 42 added for the Achieve update, all while reducing the overall text length. We also address head-on some of the methodological issues regarding replication and transparency that have become so important to the progress of our field. We've done this in part with a more elaborate section reviewing current perspectives on replication and scientific best practices in chapter 1. In addition, whenever a set of findings has been the subject of replication and/or debate in peer-reviewed publications, we have included these latest developments so that students can be made aware of issues and complexities regarding particular findings, limitations of current knowledge, and the ongoing nature of progress of knowledge through research.

■ **Expanded real-world relevance.** As we discussed previously, we updated the examples to highlight the major issues and events happening in the world today. In the first edition, we were very concerned with being inclusive and attending to issues of cultural diversity and social justice. But given our own backgrounds and built-in biases, there is always room for broadening our scope further. That's why, in this third edition, with the help of new reviewers' insights, we have improved our inclusiveness and coverage of diverse perspectives, social issues, and examples even further. We have also placed greater emphasis on how theories and research findings apply to today's pressing social issues.

Our hope is that this is an improved new edition, one that retains the strengths of the second edition but is an even better read and better resource for learning. We aimed to create a book that appeals to both those who have used the first or second edition and those who have been looking for an integrative, engaging, and up-to-date text to share the science of everyday life with their students. Of course, it's up to all of you to decide if we have succeeded, so please let us know how we did, one way or the other. We would love to hear from you. Here are our e-mail addresses:

Jeff:	jeff@u.arizona.edu
Toni:	tschmader@psych.ubc.ca
Jamie:	arndtj@missouri.edu
Mark:	mjlandau@ku.edu

Acknowledgments

The production of this book, spanning over a decade, was very much a large-scale team effort, including not just the four of us but many colleagues in our field and an entire team of talented people at Worth. If it takes a village to raise a child, it takes a small city to write a textbook!

First, we would like to thank the leader of the Worth team, Chris Cardone, Worth's Senior Executive Program Manager for psychology. We greatly appreciate her passion for this project, her dedication to making it a success, and her wise guidance throughout the process. Although Chris has overseen the bulk of development and production of this book, we also owe a debt of gratitude to prior editors, Marge Byers, who energetically first set us on the path toward this book, and Erik Gilg, who kept the ball rolling until Chris took over.

A critical moment in the progress of this book occurred when Valerie Raymond graciously agreed to become our development editor. She enthusiastically embraced our vision for this book and has in our view done a great job helping to turn our presentations of the field's knowledge into a pedagogically sound textbook. Valerie has been a sheer pleasure to work with, and we wouldn't have wanted anyone else helping us cut our chapter drafts in half!

We have worked extensively with a number of other helpful, always pleasant, and hardworking people at Worth who have had a hand in sculpting this textbook. Thanks to the very talented copy editor Kitty Wilson for improving our sentences, catching our typos, and making sure our citations are all accompanied by the proper references in our reference section. Thanks to Project Managers Won McIntosh, Valerie Brandenburg, and Valarmathy Munuswamy for overseeing the transformation from Word documents into beautifully laid out textbook pages. Thanks to Senior Photo Editor Sheena Goldstein and Photo Project Manager Richard Fox for the great work they have done assisting with the visual highlights of the book.

Beyond these individuals, with whom we worked directly, many other people at Worth have helped with the production or marketing of the book. Thus, our thanks go out to Senior Workflow Manager Jennifer Wetzel, Media Editor Stefani Wallace, Director of Media Editorial and Assessment Noel Hohnstine, Director of Rights and Permissions Hilary Newman, Permissions Manager Jennifer MacMillan, Executive Marketing Manager Kate Nurre, Art Manager Matt McAdams, Assistant Editor Dorothy Tomasini, and Consulting Media Editor Lauren Samuelson.

In our professional lives, our efforts in writing this book have been supported and improved by many people along the way. This book's emphasis on conceptual organization and the fundamental motives that guide human behavior reflects the influence of Jack Brehm. Our vision for the book, and especially the first two chapters, were helped substantially by the input of our colleagues Sheldon Solomon and Tom Pyszczynski. Many thanks also to Uri Lifshin for his excellent work helping us put together the massive references section. Sincere thanks as well to Tyler Jimenez, Andrew Christy, Jason Martens, Matt Isaak, and Kevin Zabel for their high-quality help with supplementary materials for this edition. We also want to thank Theresa DiDonato, Josh Hicks, Vicki Ritts, Clay Routledge, Daniel Sullivan, and Meg Kozak Williams for their contributions to the previous editions' supplementary materials. Many others, too numerous to mention here—mentors, collaborators, faculty colleagues, and our own former and current graduate students—have contributed to our understanding and knowledge of social psychology and have enhanced our careers and our ability to produce this book. Thanks to all of them for the positive impact they have had on this textbook.

In addition, we would like to thank the faculty and staff at the institutions that provided the foundation of our development as social psychologists and the schools that currently support our work (in alphabetical order): Skidmore College; Southern Methodist University; the State University of New York at Buffalo; the University of Arizona; the University of British Columbia; the University of California, Santa Barbara; the University of Colorado, Colorado Springs; the University of Kansas; the University of Missouri; the University of Pennsylvania; and Washington & Jefferson College.

And before we entered the halls of colleges and universities, the loving support and encouragement of our parents were instrumental for each of us in our pursuit of scholarly careers. So we wish to express our deep and sincere thanks to Murray and Edith Greenberg, Mary Alice and Len Schmader, Charles and Melinda Arndt, and Sara Landau.

Finally, we would like to thank the faculty who reviewed this new edition or graciously participated in prior edition reviews and focus groups:

Daria Bakina, State University of New York, Oswego
Shane Bench, Washington State University
Darren Bernal, University of West Florida
Joshua Bias, University of Mary Hardin-Baylor
Kenneth Bordens, Indiana University–Purdue University, Fort Wayne
Lauren Brewer, Stephen F. Austin State University
Coral Bruni, Palomar Community College
Kelly Cate, University of Northern Georgia
Benjamin Cheung, University of British Columbia
Kyle Conlon, Stephen F. Austin State University
Alex Czopp, Western Washington University
Jenny Davis, James Madison University
Lisa DiDonato, Frederick Community College
Beth Dietz, Miami University
Lori Doan, University of Manitoba
Elliot Entin, University of Massachusetts, Lowell
Jennifer Feenstra, Northwestern College
Elizabeth Focella, University of Wisconsin, Oshkosh
Madeleine Fugere, Eastern Connecticut State University
Joshua Guilfoyle, York University
Jana Hackathorn, Murray State University
Lauren Hawthorne, University of Maine
Amy Heger, University of Tennessee
Robert Hessling, Iowa State University
Joe Hilgard, Illinois State University
Robert Hoople, SUNY Oneonta
Kristina Howansky, Rutgers University
Ann Marie Howard, Montreat College and Point University
Kerry Kawakami, York University
Taylor Kohut, Western University
Shanhong Luo, University of North Carolina, Wilmington
Jason Martens, University of British Columbia
Rusty McIntyre, Eastern Michigan University
Heather Moeck, Coastline Community College
C. David Navarrete, Michigan State University
Vicki Ritts, St. Louis Community College, Meramec
Courtney Rocheleau, Metropolitan State University of Denver
Lindsey Rodriguez, University of South Florida-St. Petersburg
Brock Rozich, University of Texas at Arlington
Maria Shpurik, Florida International University
Carrie Veronica Smith, University of Mississippi
Lyra Stein, Rutgers University
Melissa Streeter, University of North Carolina, Wilmington
Heather Terrell, University of North Dakota
Jessica Tomory, University of Alberta
Matthew Vess, Montana State University
Kim Winford, Blinn College-Brenham
Chrysalis Wright, University of Central Florida
Carrie Wyland, Tulane University

Most sincerely,
Jeff, Toni, Jamie, and *Mark*

CHAPTER 1

The Revealing Science of Social Psychology

New knowledge can be both liberating and useful. It deepens our appreciation of life and gives us more information for better decisions. However, it also comes at a cost. This theme is central to the classic sci-fi film *The Matrix* (Wachowski & Wachowski, 1999). In the film, the prophet Morpheus offers the protagonist, Neo, the choice between a blue pill and a red pill. If Neo takes the blue pill, he will stay inside a safe, familiar world, a computer program created for him that is the only reality he has ever known. But if he takes the red pill, Neo will be pulled out of that virtual reality into a more authentic and complex view of himself and the world around him.

Learning about social psychology will be like swallowing that red pill. As a blue-piller, you live day to day, absorbed in a world of classes, jobs, relationships, sports, parties, Snapchat, YouTube, Instagram, and Twitter. When you think of the future, perhaps you're thinking about grad school or starting your career. Maybe you're involved in student government or environmentalism, or supporting the troops, or helping fight poverty. This is the "programmed" world in which we all live, established by our culture and internalized by us through the socialization process. Although each of us plays a unique role within this reality, we're both part of it and constrained by it. Social psychology, like the red pill, can take you outside the ordinary reality you live in to a more enlightened and sometimes more disturbing vantage point, one that reveals that each of us is a complex but vulnerable animal striving to satisfy basic needs and desires within the cultural matrix. By taking an occasional foray beyond the comfort of our culturally constructed reality, we can better comprehend ourselves and the world around us. **Social psychology** is the scientific study of the causes and consequences of people's thoughts, feelings, and actions regarding themselves and other people. It is a set of concepts and discoveries that together represent the science of everyday life. In this first chapter we'll consider:

■ The historic origins of the field

■ The core assumptions of the study of human behavior in a social context

■ The ways in which all of us, as intuitive scientists, draw inferences about human behavior

■ The scientific methods used to isolate and understand human behavior

■ The ethical considerations at the heart of any social psychological study

▲ In the film *The Matrix*, Morpheus offers Neo the choice of either the blue pill, which maintains his current view of reality, or the red pill, which, like social psychology, provides a more revealing and complex view. Which would you choose? Why?
[© Warner Bros/Photofest]

Social psychology The scientific study of the causes and consequences of people's thoughts, feelings, and actions regarding themselves and other people.

Learning Outcomes

- Describe the three early prominent explanations for human social behavior.
- Describe each of the five perspectives of modern social psychology.

The Roots of Social Psychology

All human beings have wondered, at one time or another, about themselves and the social world, which makes us all amateur social psychologists at heart. Although social psychology is a relatively young field, the concerns this science addresses go back to the dawning days of humankind. The very earliest discovered written texts, such as the 5,000-year-old Sumerian *Epic of Gilgamesh*, focused on basic questions about what it means to be human and how humans come to behave the way they do. Since then, philosophers, poets, playwrights, and novelists have all tried to understand the psychological forces responsible for human social behavior. It wasn't until the 20th century that these questions were put under the lens of scientific inquiry. Let's take a quick tour through several broad perspectives that informed the origins of social psychology.

An Instinct-Based View of Human Behavior

In the 19th century, British sociologist Herbert Spencer extended Charles Darwin's theory of evolution by natural selection from the biological realm to the psychological. Spencer argued that properties of the mind that produce social behavior are inherited through a process of evolution. Spencer's views influenced William McDougall when he published the very first social psychology textbook, *An Introduction to Social Psychology*, in 1908. This textbook proposed that for humans, most behavior is instinctively determined, just as it is for spiders that spin webs and beavers that build dams. McDougall's (1923) conception of instinctual human behavior stood in sharp contrast to the two most dominant schools of thought in psychology during the first half of the 20th century: psychoanalysis and behaviorism.

Psychoanalytic Theory: The Hidden Desires That Guide Behavior

Inspired partly by Darwin's concept of the "struggle for existence," Sigmund Freud claimed that human behavior is directed primarily by aggressive and sexual drives (Freud, 1920/1961). Aggressive behavior is critical for warding off predators and effectively competing for scarce resources; sexual behavior is critical for reproducing and perpetuating genes. However, unbridled aggression and sexuality undermine social cooperation. In his psychoanalytic theory, Freud proposed that human beings' desires for sex and aggression are kept unconscious by repression until they are transformed in ways that allow them to be consciously expressed in a socially acceptable fashion. According to Freud, a substantial proportion of human mental activity is unconscious, and what we are conscious of is rarely a direct reflection of the motivational underpinnings of what we're doing because the true intent of our behavior is generally hidden from us.

Behaviorism: Behavior Is Shaped by Experience

In direct opposition to psychoanalysis, early behaviorists such as John Watson (1930) argued that psychology should focus only on overt behavior because it can be directly observed and measured. The behaviorists argued that feelings and unconscious processes are unobservable fictions invented to explain behavior and that the instincts studied by McDougall are most likely learned, rather than innate, responses. Behaviorists proposed that most human behavior is learned in response to the demands of the environment. Quite simply, behaviors followed by desirable outcomes are likely to reoccur, whereas behaviors followed by undesirable outcomes are not. These behaviorist ideas persuaded many early 20th-century research psychologists to confine their investigations to readily observable behavior.

The Emergence of Modern Social Psychology

What, then, causes human behavior? Is it instinct, unconscious drives, or learning? Social psychology emerged as a new field that would come to address these very questions. Two important and integrative books published in the 1920s sparked its early growth.

In 1922, John Dewey published *Human Nature and Conduct: An Introduction to Social Psychology*, a seminal work that set the agenda for a mature social psychology. Dewey felt strongly that human behavior is determined by both instinct (nature) and experience (nurture) and that the key is to identify how they interact. He also insisted that by recognizing that both unconscious and conscious processes are important determinants of human activity, humans could gain greater influence over what happens to them in the future. Finally, Dewey stressed the uniquely existential concerns of human beings: How do self-conscious, finite creatures find meaning in a world of seemingly infinite possibilities?

The other influential book of the 1920s was Floyd Allport's *Social Psychology*, published in 1924 as an attempt to integrate the study of consciousness, behaviorism, psychoanalysis, and evolutionary theory. Like Dewey, Allport was interested in how humans can apply what we learn about ourselves to promote constructive individual and social change. *Social Psychology* became the classic text in the field for years and inspired a burst of empirical research, including the 1937 publication of *Experimental Social Psychology*, by Gardner and Lois Murphy and Theodore Newcomb. Besides promoting the promise of experimental approaches to studying social psychological phenomena, this intellectual duo stressed the fundamental role of culture in determining human activities and emphasized the need for social psychologists to investigate carefully the nature and function of culture.

World War II had a profound influence on the field by motivating a desire to understand how individuals in a society could nearly annihilate a portion of their population. Events on the scale of the Holocaust demanded explanation, and social psychologists began testing theories of power and social influence. As research in social psychology grew in the 1950s and '60s, the field's concern with understanding important social problems and unsavory forms of behavior contributed to a shift in focus from broad conceptions of human social behavior to relatively specific, topic-based theories about particular phenomena, an emphasis that is still prominent today.

During the 1970s and '80s, a cognitive revolution took hold in psychology. Social psychology was swept up in a shift toward understanding the mental processes that underlie behavior. Grounded in the metaphor of the human being as an information processor, the **social cognition perspective** formed to understand how people perceive, remember, and interpret events and individuals in their social world, including themselves. This focus remains strong to the present day and has expanded to include newer techniques to measure the neural underpinnings of thought and emotion (Doré et al., 2015; Gawronski & Bodenhausen, 2015).

Social cognition perspective A view that focuses on how people perceive, remember, and interpret events and individuals, including themselves, in their social world.

Toward an Integrated Perspective on Human Behavior

Evolutionary perspective A view that humans are a species of animal and that their social behavior is a consequence of particular evolved adaptations.

Cultural perspective A view that focuses on the influence of culture on thought, feeling, and behavior.

Cultural animals A description of humans as viewing reality through a set of symbols provided by the culture in which they are raised.

Existential perspective A view that focuses on the cognitive, affective, and behavioral consequences of basic aspects of the human condition, such as the knowledge of mortality, the desire for meaning, and the precarious nature of identity.

Today, four perspectives that hark back to the roots of the field have combined forces with the *social cognitive perspective*, leading to a renewed focus on answering the core questions from the field's origins (**FIGURE 1.1**).

The first perspective, the **evolutionary perspective**, is an effort to view humans as a species of animal and their social behavior as a consequence of the same physical laws and evolutionary processes as all other forms of life. This suggests that a proper understanding of human activity requires recognizing uniquely human adaptations in addition to those we share with other creatures.

The second perspective, the **cultural perspective**, emphasizes the central role of culture in just about everything people think and do. Many species (including dogs, bees, and humans) are inherently social, having evolved propensities to exist in proximity to, and to coordinate with, other members of their own species. But unlike other species, humans are **cultural animals**: Only humans create their own symbolic conception of reality. This creation is *culture*. Culture gives meaning to life, and it is taken to be a true representation of reality by those who share the same cultural background, despite the fact that it is often clear, even to the casual observer, that people from different cultures can have different beliefs about the nature of reality.

The third perspective, the **existential perspective**, examines basic questions about existence and human nature regarding matters such as meaning, identity, the body, and free will. Social psychologists are increasingly using an

Figure 1.1

The Five Perspectives

There are five influential perspectives in social psychology: social cognitive, evolutionary, cultural, social neuroscience, and existential.

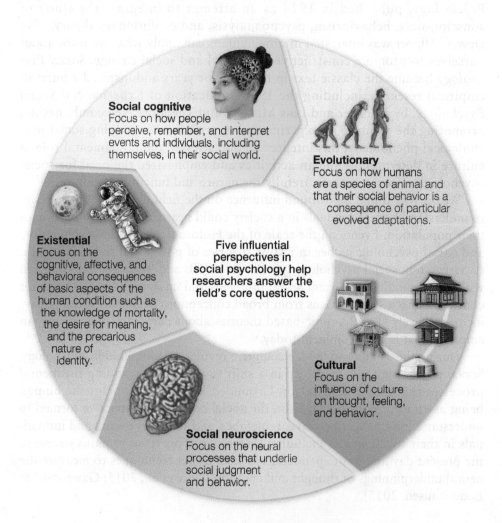

Social cognitive
Focus on how people perceive, remember, and interpret events and individuals, including themselves, in their social world.

Evolutionary
Focus on how humans are a species of animal and that their social behavior is a consequence of particular evolved adaptations.

Existential
Focus on the cognitive, affective, and behavioral consequences of basic aspects of the human condition such as the knowledge of mortality, the desire for meaning, and the precarious nature of identity.

Five influential perspectives in social psychology help researchers answer the field's core questions.

Cultural
Focus on the influence of culture on thought, feeling, and behavior.

Social neuroscience
Focus on the neural processes that underlie social judgment and behavior.

existential perspective to examine human behavior. They devote considerable attention to understanding the basic nature of the self, authenticity, and the core human motives: the needs for meaning, social connections, and the ways in which people cope with the possibilities of trauma and loss, as well as the inevitability of death.

The fourth perspective, the **social neuroscience perspective**, is increasingly gaining momentum as technological advances enable us to understand better what is going on inside the brain when people engage in social thought and behavior. Social neuroscience utilizes assessments of activity in the brain to examine the neural processes that underlie social judgment and behavior. In so doing, researchers can enhance knowledge of the roles of various cognitive, emotional, and motivational processes in social phenomena.

Social neuroscience perspective A view that focuses on understanding the neural processes that underlie social judgment and behavior. Neuroscience involves assessments of brain waves, brain imaging, and cardiovascular functioning.

SECTION REVIEW   The Roots of Social Psychology

Social psychology is a relatively young science, though humans have long been amateur social psychologists at heart.

Roots

- Herbert Spencer extended Darwin's theory of evolution by natural selection to argue that social behavior of humans is also the product of evolutionary processes.
- Freud claimed that human behavior is driven by aggressive and sexual drives that are largely hidden from our conscious experience.
- Behaviorists argued that only overt behavior can be directly observed and measured. They discounted the study of such things as feelings, wishes, and unconscious processes.
- The stage for modern social psychology was set by the integrative efforts of John Dewey, Floyd Allport, and Gardner and Lois Murphy.

Perspectives of Modern Social Psychology

- The social cognition perspective focuses on how we perceive, remember, and interpret events and people.
- The evolutionary perspective is a reinvigorated view of humans as a species of animal and of social behavior as a consequence of evolutionary adaptations.
- The cultural perspective underscores the effect of culture on thinking and behavior.
- The existential perspective focuses on basic human concerns such as mortality, meaning, and connection.
- The social neuroscience perspective focuses on understanding the neural processes that underlie social thought and behavior.

The Four Core Assumptions of Social Psychology

I am human and let nothing human be alien to me.

—Terence, ancient Roman playwright (195/185–159 BC)

The central question that social psychologists attempt to answer is: Why do people behave the way they do? From this general question, we can derive more specific ones that focus on problems we would like to remedy. Why can't people get along with each other better? Why do people care so much about what others think of them? Why do people sometimes conform but other times struggle to stand out from the crowd? How is it possible that the same species that created the Taj Mahal, penicillin, and democracy also produced slavery, the Crusades, and the Holocaust?

Typically, social psychologists try to answer these broad questions by focusing on more specific aspects of human behavior. How do stereotypes affect the ways people view others? Do people have an accurate view of themselves? Does

 Achieve
Video: What Is Social Psychology?

watching violent media encourage violent behavior? Do people's attachment to their parents shape their adult romantic relationships? In answering questions like these, contemporary social psychology builds on four core assumptions.

1. Behavior Is a Joint Product of the Person and the Situation

One core assumption is based on an idea proposed by Kurt Lewin (1936), who is generally considered the father of modern social psychology: Any given behavior is determined by the combined influences of individual features of the person and specific aspects of the situation.

To grasp Lewin's idea fully, we first need to appreciate that a person's immediate environment profoundly influences how the person thinks, feels, and acts in social life. This idea of the power of the situation—sometimes referred to as the "great lesson of social psychology" (Jones & Nisbett, 1971)—means that certain situations elicit very similar behavior from people, regardless of how those people differ from each other. Some of your classmates are very extraverted and talkative, whereas others are quieter and more reserved—and yet all of them are quiet while the instructor lectures. Why? Because the situation tells them that, in a classroom, this is how you behave. In fact, situations can be so powerful that they lead people to do things they normally would not otherwise do. This was vividly demonstrated in Stanley Milgram's (1974) famous studies of obedience. As we'll discuss in more detail in chapter 7, participants in these studies were remarkably compliant when ordered by an authoritative experimenter to administer what appeared to be potentially lethal electrical shocks to an innocent victim.

And yet, each of us is a unique individual, with a constellation of personality traits, values, attitudes, beliefs, and memories that sets us apart from every other person. The genes that we inherit from our biological parents, combined with the experiences we have had over the course of our lives, lead us to develop **dispositions**: consistent preferences, ways of thinking, and behavioral tendencies that influence us across varying situations and over time. Personality psychologists focus on describing these dispositions or traits and documenting their influence on behavior. Indeed, people show a good deal of consistency in behavior across diverse situations and across the life span (Costa & McCrae, 1994). Dispositions powerfully guide how we think, feel, and act in social life. If we go back to your classmates, chances are that a few students *do* talk while the instructor lectures; their dispositional extraversion overrides the power of the situation. And even in the classic Milgram study, 35% of the participants refused to continue shocking the victim prior to the final command to do so.

Now that we've recognized the power of the situation and the influence of the person's dispositions, we might be tempted to argue about which is more important. For many years, psychologists have debated the relative importance of personal and situational forces on predicting behavior. Today, most social and personality psychologists agree that dispositions and situational factors *interact* to determine our thoughts, feelings, and actions. Therefore, throughout this book, we consider the influence of the person's situation, unique personality, attitudes, and values, as well as the ways in which these factors interact.

2. Behavior Depends on a Socially Constructed View of Reality

A second assumption of social psychology is that virtually all thoughts, feelings, and actions are social in nature. From birth on, we learn the language,

Dispositions Consistent preferences, ways of thinking, and behavioral tendencies that manifest across varying situations and over time.

ways, and values of our culture. Throughout life, we routinely encounter and interact with other people. Even when we're completely alone, people occupy our thoughts. As a result, our view of reality is shaped by our connections to others.

Imagine, for example, a student named Carly who lives alone and is startled from sleep by the piercing sound of her alarm clock. She awakens to thoughts of the Western civilization class she has in an hour and what a bore Professor Drone is. She worries a bit about an upcoming exam and whether she is smart enough to do well in the class. Gazing at the clock, Carly thinks of her younger sister, Jen, who gave the clock to her the day she left for college. Then she wonders why she let her friend Megan talk her into taking an 8:00 a.m. class together. As she gets out of bed, Carly notices the Monet painting of a bridge in a garden on the calendar hanging from her closet door. She opens Spotify on her tablet and hears an old Drake song. Then Carly lays out her clothes, thinking about what would be the right look for her lunch date with Dwayne. She jumps in the shower and starts singing her favorite Billie Eilish single—quietly, so Nick, her neighbor in the next apartment, won't be disturbed. So in the course of a mere half hour alone with her thoughts, Carly's inner world has been populated by internal representations of eight other people: Professor Drone, her sister Jen, her friend Megan, Claude Monet, Drake, her lunch date Dwayne, Billie Eilish, and her neighbor Nick.

These and many other people fundamentally shape the way Carly views the world and her place in it. Take, for example, her insecurity about her Western civilization class. How does she know if she is smart enough? Certainly her current grade in the class provides some information. But that grade is feedback from the instructor. In addition, on receiving a grade, most students wonder how everyone else did. These social comparisons are essential to how we understand ourselves (Festinger, 1954). We get a sense of the right or wrong way to act, what is good or bad, and what is true or not true by examining what other people do or say. Whether it's Carly's aptitude for history or her choice of appropriate attire for a lunch date, her knowledge and consequent behavior are products of the social reality in which she lives.

▲ Are you tall? For many judgments we make about ourselves, we rely on social comparisons with others.
[Zurijeta/ESB Professional/Shutterstock]

3. Behavior Is Strongly Influenced by Our Social Cognition

If our view of reality is shaped by our social connections, then the third assumption, that *social cognition* shapes behavior, should come as no surprise. This assumption is based on the work of another pioneering figure in social psychology, Fritz Heider (1958). Heider emphasized how people's own understanding of the causes and consequences of other people's actions play an important role in determining their behavior. Because people play such a major role in our daily existence, we spend a great deal of time and energy thinking about them, trying to understand them, and struggling to make sense of what they say and do. The way each individual understands other people, whether the understanding is accurate or not, has a powerful influence on that individual's social behavior. And different understandings can lead to vastly different judgments and behavior. Can you think of a time when you and a friend or family member had different explanations for someone's behavior? Did that lead you to different judgments or actions regarding that person?

THINK ABOUT
[CSP_JackF/Fotosearch LBRF/AGE Fotostock]

4. The Best Way to Understand Social Behavior Is to Use the Scientific Method

Scientific method The process of developing, testing, and refining theories to understand the determinants of social behavior.

The final core assumption of social psychology, also inspired by Kurt Lewin, is that science gives us the best way to understand the causes and consequences of the thoughts, feelings, and behaviors of social life. Many fields attempt to understand human affairs. Social psychology can be distinguished by its emphasis on the **scientific method**, and especially the use of experiments, as a way of developing, testing, and refining theories to understand the determinants of social behavior. The field developed as a way of refining intuitive thinking, to help us get closer to the truth by providing more accurate conceptions of the way the world really is. The scientific method provides the basis for how social psychologists accumulate knowledge regarding the determinants of human thoughts, feelings, and actions. However, before we describe the specifics of the scientific method, we need a brief overview of how people intuitively come to comprehend the world around them and the people who inhabit that world.

SECTION REVIEW   The Four Core Assumptions of Social Psychology

Social psychology is based on four core assumptions.

• Behavior is determined by the combined influence of specific aspects of the person and the situation.	• Virtually all human thoughts, feelings, and actions involve other people and are social in nature.	• To understand behavior, we must learn how people think about themselves and their social world.	• The scientific method offers the best route to accurately understanding social behavior.

Learning Outcomes

- Identify why people can be inaccurate when explaining their feelings and behavior using introspection.
- List and summarize why intuitive observations of people's behavior can lead to inaccurate conclusions.

Cultural Knowledge: The Intuitive Encyclopedia

How do we know what we know? According to Heider's (1958) **attribution theory**, people are intuitive scientists. Like scientists, ordinary people have a strong desire to understand what causes other peoples' actions. We act as intuitive scientists when we observe other people's behavior and try to figure out why they acted the way they did. Heider labeled these explanations **causal attributions**. These attributions are shaped by **cultural knowledge**, a vast store of information accumulated within a culture that explains how the world works and why things happen as they do. This process of observing and explaining is such an integral part of our daily lives that we usually don't even notice that we are doing it.

Think about the last time you caught a cold. How did you explain your illness? You probably tried to remember if you came into contact with other sick people because our culture, informed by medical science, tells us that colds are transmitted by a virus carried by other people suffering from colds. But the explanation would be different in other cultures and at other times. Your grandparents might have thought back to instances in which they were caught in the rain. Someone living in ancient Greece might have wondered about whether the various humors of her body were out of balance. And members of many traditional cultures would consider the possibility that they had offended the spirits.

Cultural wisdom is shared by individuals within cultures. Sometimes, when the answers we seek aren't part of our readily available cultural cupboard of knowledge, we consult experts: wise men, priestesses, or shamans in ancient times; physicians, ministers, psychotherapists, or online sources and blogs in modern times. In other words, a good deal of our understanding of the world comes from widely shared cultural belief systems and the words of authority figures who interpret that knowledge for us.

Explaining Behavior Through Introspection

When trying to explain the actions of specific people, expert opinions are not always helpful. In these circumstances, you might think that the best approach is simply to ask the person "Why did you do that?" or "What were you thinking?" We ask these questions because we believe people can reveal things about themselves that no one else can know. After all, people have rich memories of their personal histories and awareness of their thoughts, feelings, and other private experiences. Despite having unique access to this inner world, people's explanations for their own behavior can sometimes be misleading—for a couple reasons.

People Don't Always Tell the Truth

We do not deal much in fact when we are contemplating ourselves.

—Mark Twain, "Does the Race of Man Love a Lord?" (1902)

Often, people are not honest about why they acted a certain way. Because we depend on other people for so many of the things we need in life, we care a great deal about the impressions they form of us. Although people may be forthright when asked to report their hometown or college major, they may be less candid when answering questions about their attitudes, GPA, or sexual proclivities. As we'll see in later chapters on the self and interpersonal relations, people have a variety of motives for not telling the truth. For example, our motivation to protect self-esteem can bias how we explain our own actions.

People Often Don't Really Know What They Think They Know

Our accounts of our own behavior can be inaccurate because people often do not know why they do what they do or feel the way they feel. In a classic paper published in 1977, Richard Nisbett and Tim Wilson (1977b) noted that although people can readily answer questions about their moods or preferences, and why they have those feelings, their explanations are often incorrect. This is because people lack direct internal access to the true causes of their thoughts and behaviors. Instead, their explanations are often based either on *a priori* (i.e., preexisting) causal theories acquired from their culture or on other potential explanations that are easily brought to mind.

To test these ideas, Nisbett and Wilson designed some simple studies. In one study, female shoppers at a large department store were shown four pairs of stockings arrayed in a row across a table and asked to select their favorite and then explain why they preferred it over the others. In fact, the stockings were identical except for slight differences in scent and displayed in a random order for each new shopper. As marketing experts know, all other things being equal, people prefer products they evaluate last. In this study, 71% of the participants

Attribution theory The view that people act as intuitive scientists when they observe other people's behavior and infer explanations about why those people acted the way they did.

Causal attributions Explanations of an individual's behavior.

Cultural knowledge A vast store of information, accumulated within a culture, that explains how the world works and why things happen as they do.

▲ When are you not honest with yourself? For many weight-conscious people, it may be when they are weighing themselves.

[Bodrov Kirill/Shutterstock]

chose the stockings on the right side of the table, regardless of which pair of stockings was in that position. The women explained their choices by describing perceived differences in color or texture, but not a single one of them suggested that her choice was determined by where the stockings were positioned on the table. Yet this was clearly the most influential determinant of most of the women's choices!

Other research reveals similar inaccuracies in explaining a range of behaviors and experiences. For instance, people are inaccurate even in judging what determines their day-to-day fluctuations in mood or the ability to think clearly, often assuming that the weather or last night's sleep has a larger influence than it actually does (Draganich & Erdal, 2014; Lucas & Lawless, 2013; Wilson et al., 1982). Why are people so likely to give inaccurate explanations of their preferences and feelings? Nisbett and Wilson argued that the human capacity for introspection—looking inward and observing our own thought processes— is actually quite limited. Although we generally have clear access to the *products* of these processes, we typically have little or no access to the *processes* that generate our preferences.

To get an intuitive sense of this, think of a time you had a craving for some food, say a burrito from your favorite Mexican take-out restaurant. You are clearly aware of the thought "A burrito sure would taste good about now," but where did that thought come from? How did it come to you? And why is it a burrito rather than a slice of pizza you crave? Complete mysteries, right?

THINK ABOUT ▶

[Sam Diephuis/The Image Bank/Getty Images]

Cognitive misers A term that conveys the human tendency to avoid expending effort and cognitive resources when thinking and to prefer seizing on quick and easy answers to questions.

Explaining Behavior Using Intuitive Observation

If people often don't know why they do and feel things, it's not surprising that they are also limited in their knowledge of why other people do and feel things. In fact, most of the time, we tend to be a bit lazy when it comes to thinking and reasoning. This tendency has led some social psychologists to suggest that people are **cognitive misers** who avoid expending effort and cognitive resources when thinking and prefer to seize on quick and easy answers to the questions they ask. If we think an explanation makes sense, we tend to accept it without much thought or analysis.

However, when events are important to us or unexpected, we take greater care to make inferences about how the world works and why the people around us are behaving the way they are. We might even go to the trouble of verifying our inferences with other people. Having decided what caused an event or another person's actions, we use these causal attributions to direct our own behavior. Even when we put in the effort, some major pitfalls can lead us to accept faulty conclusions about ourselves, other people, and reality in general.

Our Observations Come from Our Own Unique and Limited Perspective   One problem occurs when we make inferences based on observation of only part of an event or of an event viewed from a limited perspective. Imagine that you are a clinical psychologist doing a psychological assessment of a new client. You drive up to your client's house to meet him for the first time and observe him in a rather ferocious verbal dispute with a man in his front yard. From this observation, you infer that your client is a hostile and aggressive man. However, suppose that minutes before you arrived, the normally docile and peaceful client happened to discover this man running from the house with the client's laptop under his arm. Seeing a broader range of your client's behavior would almost certainly alter your judgment of his personality.

Our Reasoning Processes May Be Biased to Confirm What We Set Out to Assess   A fundamental problem is that we rarely are objective observers and interpreters of the world around us. Everything we observe, through all of our senses, is influenced by our desires, prior knowledge and beliefs, and current expectations. This leads to a **confirmation bias,** a tendency to seek out information and view events and other people in ways that fit how we want and expect them to be (Lord et al., 1979; Sude et al., 2019).

In an early demonstration of confirmation bias (Lord et al., 1979), students in an introductory psychology class were recruited into a study based on an earlier survey that identified them as having strong feelings either in favor of or opposed to capital punishment. They were unaware that the study was connected to the earlier survey that assessed their feelings about capital punishment. The students read summaries of two studies on capital punishment as a crime deterrent: One concluded that capital punishment reduced crime, and the other concluded that capital punishment is ineffective as a deterrent to crime. After reading the two studies, the students were asked to evaluate how well or poorly each study had been conducted and how convincing the studies' conclusions were. Finally, everyone in the study reported their current attitude about capital punishment.

> **Confirmation bias** A tendency to seek out information and view events and other people in ways that fit how we want and expect them to be.

If perception is a direct reflection of reality, then all the students in the study should have agreed about the quality of the research they read because they were all exposed to exactly the same materials. But this was not the case. Students originally in favor of capital punishment found the study demonstrating its effectiveness for reducing crime more convincing, whereas opponents of capital punishment were much more convinced by the research showing the ineffectiveness of capital punishment (see **FIGURE 1.2**). Regardless of their position on the issue, they found the study that confirmed their belief to be of higher scientific quality. In addition, after their biased reading of the evidence, students who favored capital punishment became even more favorable toward capital punishment, whereas those who opposed capital punishment became even more opposed. In other words, the students' judgments of the same "reality" (the two studies) were dependent on their initial attitudes (for or against capital punishment), and the same "reality" caused them to change their attitudes in different directions (becoming more supportive of or opposed to capital punishment).

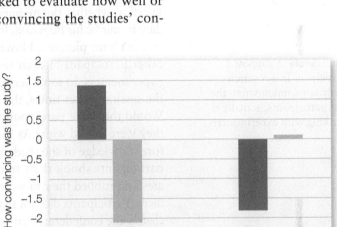

Figure 1.2

Confirmation Bias

When presented with evidence for and against capital punishment, people were more convinced by the evidence that supported their initial attitude.

[Data from Lord et al., 1979]

 APPLICATION

Confirmation Bias in Politics

Confirmation bias can be a problem in science but also occurs with all sorts of social and political issues (Sude et al., 2019). For example, in the summer of 2019, former U.S. President Trump indicated in a phone call to President Zelensky of Ukraine that he would release aid to Ukraine only if President Zelensky would publicly announce investigations into corruption. Democrats in the U.S. House of Representatives and Senate believed this was an impeachable act because the former President was using his power of office to derail the campaign of key political opponent Joe Biden. Consequently, House Democrats instigated impeachment hearings. Republicans, on the other hand, did not agree and viewed the impeachment hearings of Trump as being politically motivated. Confirmation bias led Democrats and Republicans in the House and Senate to view the same information very differently. The Democrats had the majority in the House, and on December 18, 2019, the House of Representatives indeed voted to impeach Trump—with all but four Democrats voting for impeachment but no Republicans at all voting for it. But in the Senate, Republicans had the majority and voted on February 5, 2020 to acquit Trump. ■

The Act of Observing May Change the Behavior We Seek to Explain In addition to the pitfalls just described, one final problem is that people often change their behavior, sometimes unconsciously, when they are being observed by or are interacting with others. Consider a human resources manager for a large company who is reluctant to hire a job candidate who appeared fidgety at her interview. Based on a clever study by Tanya Chartrand and John Bargh (1999), we might question whether the manager's own inability to sit still actually led the job candidate to mimic his fidgeting. In this study, people were paired together to make judgments about pictures. However, unknown to the real participants, the supposed other participant in each session was a **confederate**, someone working with the experimenters. In some sessions, the confederate rubbed his or her face throughout the session; other times, the confederate shook a foot repeatedly during the task. Would the naive participants mimic these nervous behaviors of the confederates they were paired with? As shown in **FIGURE 1.3**, they did. Impartial judges with no foreknowledge of the study coded videotapes of the pairs and found that the real participants shook their feet more when paired with the foot-shaking confederates and rubbed their faces more when paired with the confederates with the itchy faces. Participants did not realize the effects of their partners on their behavior, but clearly the confederates influenced how fidgety they seemed.

This all boils down to a simple conclusion: Basing psychological inferences on one's own observations is a tenuous proposition. Sometimes we have a limited perspective and don't see enough of an event to make a complete judgment. Sometimes our desires, prior beliefs, and expectations bias our perception. Sometimes our observations match reality reasonably well, but we're partly responsible for what we've observed. Does this mean we should abandon observation as a way to learn about ourselves and the world around us? Quite the contrary: Careful observation is an essential aspect of scientific inquiry. We should take great pains to focus on what is happening in the world around us, but we can become better observers by understanding when and how our observations might be suspect and by using the scientific method to minimize the influence of these biases.

Confederate A supposed participant in a research study who, unknown to the real participants, actually is working with experimenters.

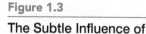

Figure 1.3

The Subtle Influence of Others

Number of times participants rubbed their faces and shook their feet per minute when with a confederate who engaged in that behavior.

[Data from Chartrand & Bargh, 1999]

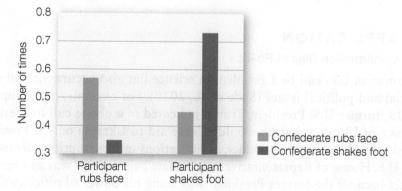

SECTION REVIEW   Cultural Knowledge: The Intuitive Encyclopedia

People's intuitive understanding of much of what happens in the world is derived from cultural knowledge.

Introspection has limitations.	**The intuitive mode of observing and reasoning is faulty.**
• People don't always tell the truth about themselves. • People often don't know the truth.	• We often prefer quick and easy answers. • Our inferences often are based on our own limited perspectives and preexisting expectations. • We may be biased to confirm what we prefer to believe. • Observation itself may change a person's behavior.

The Scientific Method: Systematizing the Acquisition of Knowledge

Learning Outcomes

- Outline the steps in the cycle of theory and research.
- Explain why correlation does not mean causation.
- Distinguish between the correlation and experimental methods.
- Explain the importance of random assignment.
- Identify strengths of field research and quasi-experimental methods.

Theory An explanation for how and why variables are related to each other.

Research The process whereby scientists observe events, look for patterns, and evaluate theories proposed to explain those patterns.

⏀ Achieve
Video: Research Methods

SCIENCE: We must recognize that there are many ways of knowing, but . . . in the entire course of prehistory and history only one way of knowing has encouraged its own practitioners to doubt their own premises and to systematically expose their own conclusions to the hostile scrutiny of nonbelievers.

—Marvin Harris, *Cultural Materialism* (1979/2001)

Over thousands of years, humans have refined everyday thinking to make it less susceptible to bias. The result is the scientific method. Just like everyone else, scientists are interested in explaining how or why things happen as they do. These explanations are called **theories**. **Research** is the process whereby scientists observe events in the world, look for consistent patterns, and evaluate theories proposed to explain those patterns. Research and theory are simply scientific refinements of the more casual observations and explanations we make every day. Whereas ordinary intuitive thinking typically leads us to accept explanations relatively uncritically (especially if they are consistent with our expectations and desires), generating a plausible account of our observations is just the beginning of scientific inquiry.

The Cycle of Theory and Research in Social Psychology

As Lewin put it, "There is nothing so practical as a good theory" (1952, p. 169). Theories tell us about causal factors that influence particular kinds of behavior. This knowledge can help us alter behavior in beneficial ways. For example, if theories specify factors that lead to bad things such as child abuse and good things such as charitable giving, we can design ways to alter these factors to reduce bad behaviors and increase good behaviors. Research tells us whether our theories provide the right explanations.

The concept of theory is often misunderstood: In grade school, some are taught to distinguish theories from facts. From this they might get the impression that a theory is a weaker or unproven version of a fact and therefore shouldn't be taken all that seriously. But in scientific thinking, the concepts of fact and theory play different roles in the process of doing science. A fact is the *content*

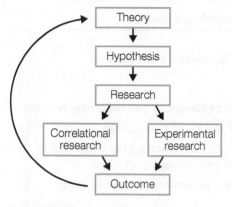

Figure 1.4

The Cycle of Theory and Research

Theories lead to hypotheses, which are then tested. The outcomes of these tests influence views and revisions of the theory.

Hypothesis An "if-then" statement that follows logically from a theory and specifies how certain variables should be related to each other if the theory is correct.

of research observations that have been replicated—that is, verified by multiple researchers. A theory, on the other hand, is an *explanation* for the facts. Although a theory may be our current best explanation for how or why things happen as they do, it is not—and is not expected to be—an entirely complete or accurate explanation in any absolute sense. The history of science shows us that a theory accepted as useful scientific truth in one era often is viewed as a quaint but misguided *mis*understanding centuries or sometimes just decades later. Scientific knowledge is continually evolving, moving toward a more and more useful understanding of reality.

To assess the validity of a theory, a scientist starts by deriving testable hypotheses from the theory (see **FIGURE 1.4**). A **hypothesis** is an "if-then" statement that follows logically from a theory and specifies how certain variables (characteristics that vary and that can be measured) should be related to each other if the theory is correct. Hypotheses are the bridges that scientists use to move from a theory, which explains how or why something happens as it does, to research, in which new observations are made and checked to see if they support the hypothesis.

Typically, a theory generates numerous hypotheses. Once a theory is tested, it is either accepted as it is or revised or replaced in light of the research findings. The reformulated theory (or new theory) is then used to generate additional hypotheses, which are then tested, and the cycle continues. In this way, through the ongoing interplay between theory and research, the process spirals toward more sophisticated theories that provide increasingly accurate explanations of observations and programs of research that probe increasingly refined questions about these processes. Let's consider the cycle of theory and research using the example of the development of stereotype threat theory, a topic we will cover more fully in chapter 11.

Stereotype Threat: Case Study of a Theory

Stereotype threat theory was inspired by the consistent observation that members of socially devalued groups (non-majority groups within a culture that are viewed negatively in some way) often perform less well on average than members of the advantaged or majority group. For example, although it is impossible to predict performance from knowing only a person's self-defined race, persistent racial gaps in intellectual test performance beg for some explanation. In the 1990s, the theories that attempted to explain these gaps were hotly debated and controversial. They ranged from locating a cause in nature (the most contentious being a presumption of genetic inferiority) to pointing to systemic inequalities in environment (patterns of poverty or discrimination in society).

In 1995, Claude Steele and Joshua Aronson proposed stereotype threat theory as a uniquely social psychological explanation for poor performance by members of stigmatized groups. The basic idea is that if you are a member of a group that is negatively stereotyped (e.g., thought to be intellectually inferior to other groups), engaging in behavior that is relevant to those negative beliefs puts you in a doubly threatening situation. Not only will you be judged as an individual but your performance will be taken as evidence of the ability of your entire group. When taking a test of verbal intelligence, an African American male might worry that a low score will be viewed as evidence of his entire race's alleged deficiencies in intelligence, whereas a White male might only see his performance as an indication of his own ability. According to the theory, this resulting experience of *stereotype threat* is at least part of the reason for gaps in academic performance between members of different racial or ethnic groups. Other research has applied stereotype threat to understand why women sometimes perform more poorly than men on standardized tests of mathematical ability (Spencer, Logel, & Davies, 2016). The theory further suggests that, because of the prevailing negative stereotypic beliefs about their group, the situation itself—having to take a test believed to assess one's true ability—arouses stereotype threat and reduces stigmatized individuals' ability to perform up to their potential. Stereotype threat theory thus proposes that conditions that bring the stereotype to mind contribute to poor performance among members of various stigmatized groups.

This, of course, is a very different explanation from one that assumes that differences in the abilities and potential of particular groups result from *either* genetic inferiority *or* a lifetime of experience with poverty or discrimination. If true, stereotype threat theory would demonstrate how understanding basic social psychological processes can shed new light on important personal and social issues. But to have any scientific credibility, this theoretical explanation must be tested. How would a social psychologist use the scientific method to assess the validity of stereotype threat theory? To do so, the researcher would have to generate hypotheses from the theory and then test those hypotheses with research. Consider these two hypotheses that have been generated from the theory of stereotype threat:

▲ Simone Manuel, who, in 2016, became the first African American woman to win an Olympic gold medal in an individual swimming event, describes how it feels to be under stereotype threat. "The title 'black swimmer' makes it seem like I'm not supposed to be able to win a gold medal or I'm not supposed to be able to break records and that's not true because I work just as hard as anybody else" (BBC News, 2016).

[Adam Pretty/Getty Images]

1. The more people are conscious of the negative stereotype of their group, the worse they will perform in areas related to the stereotype.
2. Situations that make a negative stereotype of a person's group prominent in the person's mind will lead to worse performance than situations that do not.

Hypothesis 1 proposes an association between two variables that can be assessed with correlational research. Hypothesis 2 posits that one variable has a causal influence on the other and can be assessed only through experimental research. We will discuss each of these two primary approaches to research in social psychology and how they were used to test these hypotheses derived from stereotype threat theory.

Research: The Correlational Method

One of the most widely used approaches to doing research is the **correlational method,** whereby two or more preexisting characteristics (the variables) of a group of individuals are measured and compared to determine whether and/or to what extent they are associated. If the variables are associated, then knowing a person's standing on one variable predicts, beyond chance levels, that person's standing on the other variable. If this is the case, we can say that the variables are correlated. To test stereotype threat hypothesis 1, we might (1) measure the extent to which particular members of a given group are conscious of their stereotyped status and (2) assess each person's performance on stereotype-related dimensions.

Liz Pinel and colleagues (2005) tested this very hypothesis. They first measured the *stigma consciousness*—the tendency to be highly conscious of one's stereotyped status and to believe that these stereotypes shape how one is viewed by others—of academically stigmatized students (specifically, African Americans and Hispanic Americans) and nonacademically stigmatized students (specifically,

Correlational method Research in which two or more variables are measured and analyzed to determine to what extent, if any, they are associated.

Correlation coefficient A positive or negative numerical value that shows the direction and strength of a relationship between two variables.

European Americans and Asian Americans). Then, they obtained information about their participants' GPAs. To assess whether stigma consciousness is correlated with GPA, the researchers computed **correlation coefficients**. Pinel and colleagues found a moderate negative correlation between stigma consciousness and GPA. Let's briefly consider what this statistic can tell us about how two variables are related.

The Correlation Coefficient The correlation coefficient (typically indicated by r) gives us two vital pieces of information about a relationship—the direction and the strength of the relationship (**FIGURE 1.5**):

■ The sign, positive (+) or negative (−), tells us the *direction* of the relationship. A positive correlation occurs when a high level of one variable tends to be accompanied by a high level of another variable. A negative correlation exists when a high level of one variable is accompanied by a low level of the other variable. If Pinel and colleagues had found that the higher a person scores on stigma consciousness, the better her GPA, they would have found a positive correlation. The negative correlation that they actually found tells us that the *higher* a person's level of stigma consciousness, the *lower* that person's GPA. This negative correlation provides some evidence for stereotype threat hypothesis 1.

■ The numerical value tells us the *strength* of the relationship. The strength of a correlation refers to how closely associated the two variables are—that is, how much knowing a person's standing on one variable tells us about or enables us to predict the person's standing on the other variable. If knowing a person's level of stigma consciousness enables us to predict test performance with

Figure 1.5

Correlation Coefficient

The correlation coefficient (signified by the letter *r*) is a measure of the relationship between two variables. These graphs represent the three kinds of correlations between variables X and Y: positive, negative, and no correlation. The sign of *r* (+ *or* −) tells us whether the relationship is positive or negative. The absolute value of *r* tells us the strength of the relationship. The stronger the correlation, the more confidently we can predict the value of one variable from the value of the other.

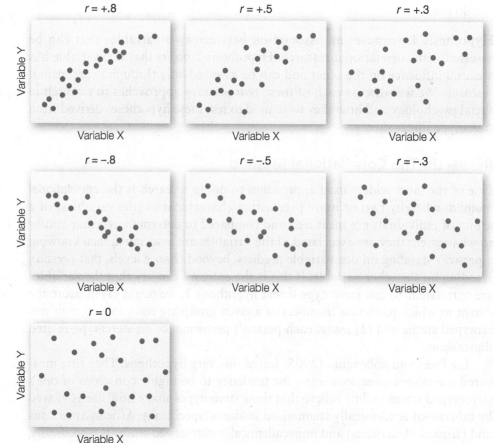

absolute certainty, the two variables are perfectly correlated, and the correlation coefficient equals −1.0 (or +1.0 in a positive relationship). Perfect correlations occur only when the two variables are different measures of the same underlying conceptual variable. For example, temperature as measured on Fahrenheit and Celsius thermometers will be perfectly correlated as long as the thermometers are operating correctly. On the other hand, we would find a correlation of 0 if the two variables were completely unrelated; this means that knowing something about a person's standing on one variable tells you nothing whatsoever about where the person stands on the other. According to stereotype threat theory, knowing a person's level of stigma consciousness should relate to GPA only if the person is a member of an academically stigmatized group. Sure enough, Pinel and colleagues observed no correlation between stigma consciousness and GPA for academically nonstigmatized groups.

It's important to be clear that although the sign of a correlation coefficient tells you whether two variables are positively or negatively correlated, it tells you nothing at all about the strength of that relationship. Thus, a correlation of −0.60 reflects a stronger relationship than a correlation of +0.35.

Pinel and colleagues' finding of a moderate negative correlation between stigma consciousness and GPA tells us that knowing how sensitive people are to stereotypes about their group gives us some basis for predicting how well they are likely to score on measures of academic performance. However, we couldn't predict a person's performance with absolute certainty or precision. Clearly, many variables other than stigma consciousness influence college GPA. And imperfections in our two measures would also reduce the size of any correlation we observe. Nonetheless, the negative correlation between stigma consciousness and test performance tells us that these two variables are indeed related, which is consistent with the hypothesis deduced from stereotype threat theory.

Correlation Does Not Imply Causation   Scientists usually are interested in understanding why variables are correlated. But finding a negative correlation between stigma consciousness and test performance does not allow us to conclude that fear of confirming stereotypes about one's group *causes* poorer performance. Correlation does not prove causality. There must be a correlation between the two variables if one variable causes the other, but there are two major reasons that correlation does not enable us to infer causation.

First, although it is certainly possible that stereotype threat causes poorer test performance, it is also possible that the causal relationship runs in the other direction: Doing poorly on tests makes people especially sensitive to the stereotypes about their group and, perhaps, fearful about contributing to these stereotypes. This problem, known as the **reverse causality problem**, arises because correlations tell us nothing about which of two interrelated variables is the cause and which is the effect.

The second major reason that we cannot draw causal inferences from correlations is referred to as the **third variable problem**, in which the two variables are correlated, but it is still possible that neither exerts a causal influence on the other. It may be that some third variable—for example, a general tendency to be self-conscious and anxiety prone—is responsible for the correlation found between stigma consciousness and performance. Being self-conscious and nervous might make people concerned about how others view their group and at the same time may interfere with test performance. Such correlations between anxiety proneness and stigma consciousness and between anxiety proneness and test performance would create a correlation between stigma consciousness and

Reverse causality problem The possibility that a correlation between variables *x* and *y* may occur because one causes the other, but it is impossible to determine whether *x* causes *y* or *y* causes *x*.

Third variable problem The possibility that two variables may be correlated but do not exert a causal influence on one another, and both are caused by some additional variable.

test performance even if there were no causal relationship between the latter two variables. Taken together, the reverse causality and third variable problems make it impossible to be conclusive about causality from correlational findings.

Longitudinal studies Studies in which variables are measured in the same individuals over two or more periods of time, typically over months or years.

Longitudinal Studies   In **longitudinal studies** two variables are measured at multiple points in time. By examining correlations between one variable at time 1 and another variable at time 2, such studies can make us more confident about likely causal order. For example, one classic study of aggression (see Huesmann, Lagerspetz, & Eron, 1984) found that the amount of violent television watched in childhood correlated positively with the amount of aggressive behavior in adulthood. In contrast, aggressiveness in childhood did not correlate with the amount of violent television watching in adulthood. The result of this longitudinal study suggests that childhood television watching affected later aggression rather than childhood aggressiveness affecting later television viewing. However, such studies are not definitive about causation because the third variable problem remains. For example, it could be that neglectful parents both allow their children to watch a lot of violence and for other reasons produce adult offspring with aggressive tendencies.

Research: The Experimental Method

Experimental method A study in which a researcher manipulates a variable, referred to as the **independent variable**, measures possible effects on another variable, referred to as the **dependent variable**, and tries to hold all other variables constant.

Fortunately, there is an approach to research that lets us draw conclusions about cause and effect: the **experimental method**. This method is extremely popular among social psychologists. An *experiment* is a study in which the researcher takes active control and manipulates one variable, referred to as the **independent variable**, measures possible effects on another variable, referred to as the **dependent variable**, and tries to hold all other variables constant. The independent variable is manipulated because it is being investigated as the possible cause. The dependent variable is the one that is then measured to assess the effect. An experiment can tell us if the dependent variable *depends* on the independent variable. An experiment would be needed to test stereotype threat hypothesis 2: that conditions which increase the individual's awareness of the negative stereotype of that person's group (and thereby increase stereotype threat) will lead to lower test performance. Such an experiment must involve:

1. Manipulating research participants' focus on the negative stereotype of their group, creating two or more conditions differing in the level of the independent variable: stereotype threat
2. Assessing participants' performance on a test that is relevant to that negative stereotype, providing a measurement of the dependent variable
3. Holding everything else constant within the setting

Internal validity The judgment that for a particular experiment it is possible to conclude that the manipulated independent variable caused the change in the measured dependent variable.

When all the requirements of the experimental method are met, the study has **internal validity**, which means it is possible to conclude that the manipulated independent variable caused any observed changes in the measured dependent variable. Let's translate that into a real example.

Steele and Aronson (1995) conducted a series of experiments that provided the first evidence that stereotype threat caused reduced performance among members of stigmatized groups. In one study, African American and White college students were given a challenging test of verbal ability that consisted of sample items from the verbal portion of the Graduate Record Exam. Performance on the test was the dependent measure. To manipulate stereotype threat, the researchers simply asked half of the participants to indicate their race on the answer form prior to beginning the test; this simple act of indicating race was meant to bring to mind the stereotypes about how each participant's group was supposed to perform on such tests. The other half of the participants, the control group, took the test with no mention being made of race, so they were much less likely to be thinking about stereotype-related issues while taking the test. Whether or not race was mentioned was the independent variable.

The racial identity of the participants was the second variable that the experimenters expected to play a causal role. We should note that demographic variables such as race, age, and gender are commonly treated as independent variables, even though the experimenter cannot manipulate them. The caveat to interpreting these variables is to keep in mind that there are lots of different ways that Blacks and Whites might differ from each other (e.g., cultural beliefs, socioeconomic status) that could underlie any racial differences observed. Indeed, in this research, African Americans had lower scores on the SAT than their White peers, and because of this, the researchers statistically controlled for these prior performance differences in their analysis.

As stereotype threat hypothesis 2 predicts, when participants were reminded of their race, there was a significant drop in the performance of African American students but not in the performance of White students (see **FIGURE 1.6**). This pattern of results is referred to as an **interaction**, which occurs when the effect of one independent variable on the dependent variable depends on the level of a second variable. In this study, the effect of the reminder of race depended on whether the participant's racial identity was African American or White. For African American students, the reminder of racial identity led to lower performance; for White students, however, it had no effect. Thus, even though we cannot randomly assign a person's race, the fact that a reminder of race influenced Blacks and Whites differently suggests that racial identity is what mattered here.

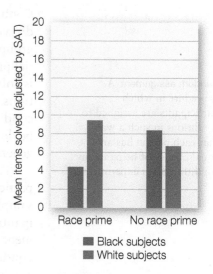

Figure 1.6

Stereotype Threat
Black students performed more poorly on a test when reminded of their race. White students were unaffected by such a reminder.
[Data from Steele & Aronson, 1995]

Interaction A pattern of results in which the effect of one independent variable on the dependent variable depends on the level of a second independent variable.

How Experiments Make Causal Inference Possible   The experimental method overcomes the limitations of the correlational method so that causal inferences are possible. As we previously noted, the first major obstacle to drawing causal inferences from correlational studies is the reverse causality problem because you typically can't tell which variable is the cause and which is the effect. In an experiment, because the researcher determines whether participants are exposed to the experimental condition (race reminder) or the control condition (no race reminder) and subsequently measures performance, it is impossible for the participants' poor test performance to have caused them to be reminded of their race. Causes must come before effects. Consequently, the causal sequence problem is eliminated.

What about the third variable problem? Recall that in an experiment, the only thing that differs between conditions is the independent variable. Everything else is held constant. The researcher treats participants in the various conditions in identical ways: The same instructions are given; the physical setting is the same; and, aside from what is to be manipulated between conditions (the independent variable), any written, audio, and video materials are identical. All this is done so that if there is a difference between conditions, we can be confident that the cause is the independent variable. By holding constant everything across the various conditions in the experiment except the independent variable, the experimenter solves the third variable problem.

Random assignment A procedure in which participants are assigned to conditions in such a way that each person has an equal chance of being in any condition of an experiment.

Controlling the Impact of Individual Differences by Random Assignment How do we know that the participants in the experimental group and the control group didn't simply differ on the dependent measure to begin with? The potential problem of preexisting differences among participants in the two conditions is solved by **random assignment**, in which participants are assigned to conditions in such a way that each person has an equal chance of being in either condition (**FIGURE 1.7**). Deciding which treatment to give each participant can be done by tossing a coin, pulling names from a hat, or using a random number generator to put individuals into treatment conditions.

Random assignment is an essential component of all experiments in which participants are put in different conditions. It ensures that, if a sufficiently large sample is used, no systematic average differences will exist among the participants in the various experimental conditions. This is because random assignment evenly distributes people, and all the ways they may vary, across all the conditions of the experiment. For example, if a sample of 200 people were randomly divided into two groups of 100, the mean height, weight, level of self-esteem, and verbal GRE performance of the two groups would be virtually identical. Random assignment thereby controls for individual differences that might otherwise vary between the experimental and control groups and is thus essential for eliminating the third variable problem. We can draw causal inferences from experiments because the experimental method eliminates both the causal sequence and third variable problems.

Experimental and Correlational Research in Concert Because the experimental method enables us to infer causes for behavior, it is generally the preferred approach, but in some situations, experimental methods cannot be applied. Many of the variables that social psychologists are interested in cannot be manipulated. There are many important questions about the effects of variables such as gender, age, race, and sexual preference, but people can't be randomly assigned to be male or female, old or young, Black or White, or straight or gay. Furthermore, many of the questions of interest to social psychologists deal with long-standing personality dispositions, attitudes, values, and other individual differences. Using correlational methods that examine relationships between preexisting differences among people is the only way to address questions such

Figure 1.7

Random Assignment

Even though individuals differ from each other, when they are randomly assigned to groups, the groups' averages are largely the same.

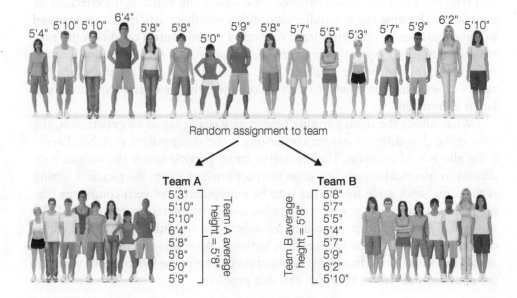

Random assignment to team

Team A
5'3"
5'10"
5'10"
6'4"
5'8"
5'8"
5'0"
5'9"
Team A average height = 5'8"

Team B average height = 5'8"
Team B
5'8"
5'7"
5'5"
5'4"
5'7"
5'9"
6'2"
5'10"

as these. Correlational methods also have the advantage of examining the relationship between variables as they naturally occur in the real world. Experimental methods, by definition, involve observing the effects of variables that are created by researchers; consequently, there is always some question as to how well these experimentally created variables mirror the forces that operate on us in real life. For all these reasons, correlational methods are also important tools for social psychologists.

In fact, the correlational method and the experimental method provide complementary information about how or why people behave the way they do. Let's go back to the example of research-testing hypotheses derived from stereotype threat theory. The experimental research by Steele and Aronson (1995) provides evidence that stereotype threat is at least one of the factors that cause poorer performance by members of stigmatized groups; on the other hand, the correlational research by Pinel and colleagues (2005) suggests that some students will be more vulnerable to these effects than others. When applied together, these two research strategies enable social psychologists to document the role that both individual differences and situational forces play in leading people to behave the way they do. Such evidence fits the first core assumption of social psychology: that behavior is a function of a combination of the features of the person and the situation.

Field Research and Quasi-Experimental Methods Because social psychologists ultimately want to understand the forces that operate on us in real life, another important type of research is **field research.** This type of research occurs outside the laboratory, such as in schools, in office buildings, in medical clinics, at football games, or even in shopping malls or on street corners. Field research is not wedded to an experimental or correlational approach; it can be either. It also often utilizes **quasi-experimental designs.** In a quasi-experimental design, groups of participants are compared on some dependent variable, but for practical or ethical reasons, the groups are not formed on the basis of random assignment. Note that the stereotype threat study described earlier can be considered partly quasi-experimental because participants were not randomly assigned to race.

We can also use research on stereotype threat to highlight an example of field research. Greg Walton and Geoff Cohen (2007, 2011) applied stereotype threat theory to design an intervention that would reduce racial differences in students' actual academic achievement. Walton and Cohen reasoned that for many, if not most, college students, the transition to college can be stressful as students adjust to more rigorous work and are perhaps living on their own and trying to make new friends. For students from minority backgrounds, a lack of racial diversity in faculty they see in their classes or students on campus can itself lead to stereotype threat or heightened feeling that they don't belong. Walton and Cohen wanted to see if shoring up feelings of belonging at college would reduce stereotype threat and improve academic performance for racial minorities.

To do this, they randomly assigned a sample of White and Black first-year college students to one of two conditions. In the intervention condition, students read testimonials the researchers had compiled from more senior students:

> Freshman year even though I met large numbers of people, I didn't have a small group of close friends. . . . I was pretty homesick, and I had to remind myself that making close friends takes time. Since then . . . I have met people some of whom are now just as close as my friends in high school were. (WALTON & COHEN, 2007, P. 88)

Field research Research that occurs outside the laboratory, such as in schools, in office buildings, in medical clinics, at football games, or even in shopping malls or on street corners.

Quasi-experimental designs A type of research in which groups of participants are compared on some dependent variable, but for practical or ethical reasons, the groups are not formed on the basis of random assignment.

Figure 1.8

Belonging and School Performance

A racial gap in achievement observed between European American and African American students was reduced when first-year students received an intervention to bolster feelings of belonging.

[Data from Walton & Cohen, 2011]

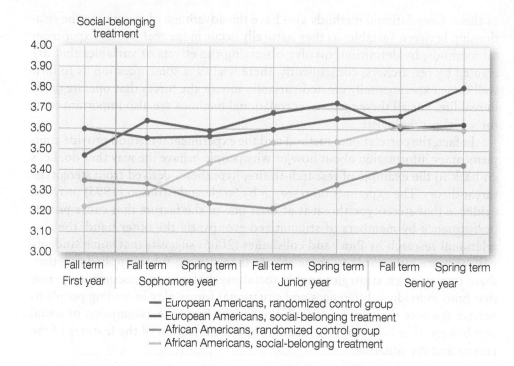

These testimonials from students of different racial, gender, and ethnic backgrounds send the message that stress is a pretty normal and understandable part of *all* students' experience. Students in the control condition read similar testimonials about how students' political attitudes had changed. Then the researchers proceeded to follow both groups of students for the next three years (**FIGURE 1.8**).

Among students in the control group, Black students earned GPAs that were significantly lower than those of their White peers. But for those students who received the intervention and learned that stress is a part of everyone's experience at university, this racial gap in achievement was cut in half over the next three years. Whereas learning about how stressed other students are did not matter too much for White students, it significantly boosted how Black students performed in their courses, and it did so by helping students see that their experience of stress and adversity at college in no way meant that they didn't belong there.

A core strength of field research is to capture social behavior as it occurs out in the world. This is important because, as you well know, the world is a complex place, and researchers need to study that complexity. The chief weakness of field research is that researchers lose a lot of the control they have in the laboratory in terms of what participants are exposed to, and thus they don't always have the clearest manipulation or measurement of the variables they want to study. Although the Walton and Cohen study showed effects of their manipulated variable on real outcomes, we cannot be sure it was because it reduced stereotype threat or because it increased students' sense of belonging.

Quasi-experimental designs have an additional weakness. Because the researchers are not randomly assigning participants to the levels of the independent variable, there is an increased chance that participants may differ on some other potentially important characteristic. So although the researchers may be able to overcome the reverse causality problem of correlational designs, it is more difficult to overcome the third variable problem. None of these methods is perfect, but each has its own strengths and weaknesses, and each plays a useful role in helping social psychologists understand human behavior.

SECTION REVIEW   The Scientific Method: Systematizing the Acquisition of Knowledge

Science is a method for answering questions that reduces the impact of human biases.

Correlational Method	Experimental Method
• Two or more variables are measured and analyzed to determine whether they are related.	• This process seeks to control variables so that cause and effect can be determined.
• A relationship between variables does not mean that one caused the other.	• The independent variable is manipulated, and its effect on the dependent variable is observed.
	• Participants must be randomly assigned to conditions to ensure that observed differences between conditions can only be explained by the manipulation.

Theory Building: The Engine of Scientific Progress

Learning Outcomes

The ultimate function of a good theory is to be *useful* by moving the ongoing cyclical process of science forward. It should advance our understanding of how and why people behave the way they do and facilitate efforts to make the world a better place. Our experiences in applying our newfound knowledge to issues of real human importance ultimately come back to tell us how well our theoretical understanding fits the world in which we live.

- Outline the features of a good theory.
- Define internal validity and external validity.
- Explain the importance of replicability.
- Describe the limitations of science.

What Makes for a Good Theory in Social Psychology?

A useful theory has the characteristics described in the following sections.

Organizes Observations   A theory should organize the observations, or facts, that come out of the research process. Theories create order out of chaos and provide more abstract and general ways of describing the nature of reality. For example, Steele's stereotype threat theory summarizes and simplifies results from other studies that have shown that members of stigmatized groups perform worse when very few other members of their group are present, when they believe the researcher expects their group to do worse, and when the test is presented as one on which the group tends to perform poorly (Grover et al., 2017; Picho & Schmader, 2017). This rather disparate set of facts coheres within the broader theory that performance is impaired when conditions make it likely that people will think of a relevant negative stereotype about their group. Generally speaking, the broader the range of observations that a theory can make sense of, the better. Theories that are able to account for a wide variety of observations are said to have *conceptual power*.

Explains Observations   Theories do much more than simplify and organize knowledge. A good theory also provides insight into how or why things happen. To do this effectively, a theory must be conceptually coherent and logically consistent. It should specify clear relationships between variables that help us understand the processes through which particular events in the world occur. To be truly useful, a theory should provide us with understanding that goes beyond what we already know. It should shed new light on what we observe happening within and around us, giving us a sort of "aha, now I get it" experience. Stereotype threat theory provided an entirely new way of thinking about group differences in academic achievement, and it did so in a coherent and logically consistent way. It is also a relatively simple idea that fits well with our understanding of basic psychological processes. In this sense, stereotype threat theory is highly *parsimonious*: It explains a wide range of observations with a relatively small number of basic principles. Einstein's theory of relativity and Darwin's theory of evolution are two of the most parsimonious theories in the history of science in that both explain extremely diverse sets of observations with just a few relatively simple principles.

Provides Direction for Research   A good theory should inspire research. It should enable us to deduce clear and novel hypotheses that follow logically from its propositions, hypotheses that in turn lead to research that tells us how well the theory fits with reality. Stereotype threat theory has inspired a great deal of research that has both supported its core propositions and led to refinements in our understanding of how stereotype threat undermines performance (Spencer, Logel, & Davies, 2016). Many potentially interesting ideas about why people behave the way they do have been discussed over the millennia; some of these ideas might be quite accurate. But unless a theory produces hypotheses that can be used to assess its fit with reality, it is not scientifically useful. That's not to say that a useful theory must be easy to test, or that it must be testable immediately on its development. An intriguing new theory that seems at first to defy scientific testing often provides the impetus for the development of new technologies that can be used to test the theory's core propositions. For example, research taking a social neuroscience perspective revealed many years after the theory was first proposed that during stereotype threat, neural signatures of attention suggest that people become more vigilant toward any errors they make that might confirm the feared stereotype of their group (Forbes & Leitner, 2014; Forbes et al., 2018).

Generates New Questions   In addition to inspiring research, a good theory should shed light on phenomena beyond what the theory was originally designed to explain. In other words, a good theory should be generative, providing new theoretical insights in other domains. When we combine a good theory with other ideas, new ideas should spill out. Stereotype threat theory has been generative in the sense that it has led to new ideas about performance deficits in a wide range of areas and among a wide variety of different groups of people. It has also led to finer-grained ideas about the processes through which fear of confirming negative stereotypes of one's group undermines successful performance.

Has Practical Value   A good theory should have practical applications that help us solve pressing problems and improve the quality of life (Walton & Wilson, 2018). In recent years, stereotype threat theory has been used to inform interventions applied in schools and on college campuses (Walton & Spencer, 2009). For example, the theory implies that remedial programs to help negatively stereotyped minority-group students may backfire because they continually remind the students of the negative stereotype of their group. Typically, practical applications of social psychological theories take time to emerge. One of the earliest theories about how to reduce prejudice, developed by Gordon Allport in his classic book *The Nature of Prejudice* (1954), led to what is known as the *contact hypothesis*. The idea is that specific forms of contact between groups can break down stereotypes and negative feelings and thus reduce prejudice and intergroup conflict. In 1961, Muzafer Sherif and colleagues (1961) conducted a famous study at a Boy Scout camp in Oklahoma that supported this hypothesis and led to myriad practical applications. For example, Elliot Aronson and colleagues (1978) used ideas from Allport and supported by the Sherif study to reduce interracial conflict in Austin, Texas, public schools that had recently been desegregated. Their jigsaw classroom technique promotes the kind of contact that Sherif and colleagues had found effective in their summer-camp study. We cover all these examples in greater depth later in the text, and we highlight examples of practical applications of theories throughout.

Assessing Abstract Theories with Concrete Research

Theories deal with the world of abstract conceptual variables, such as attitudes, self-esteem, anxiety, attraction, and conflict. They specify relationships among these variables in attempts to explain important aspects of human behavior. For example, one explanation for why stereotype threat undermines performance is that it creates anxiety that people try to regulate and control, saddling minority students with an extra cognitive task that nonstigmatized students don't have to worry about (Schmader et al., 2008). Anxiety is a conceptual variable that most psychologists define as a vague, undifferentiated feeling of unease, tension, or fear. Anxiety can also involve various bodily or physiological reactions: sweaty palms, racing heart, and butterflies in the stomach. Different people experience anxiety in somewhat different ways and exhibit a rather wide range of symptoms or signs that they are experiencing it. The abstract concept of anxiety refers to the essential underlying phenomenon that is indicated by these various signs and symptoms. So how would we as scientists conduct research on—that is, make observations of—something so abstract and diffuse as the concept of anxiety?

To conduct research on any conceptual variable, we first must develop an operational definition of that concept. An **operational definition** entails finding a specific, concrete way to measure or manipulate a conceptual variable. For example, cardiovascular measures (of the heart and blood vessels) have been used to assess the kind of anxiety people might experience during stereotype threat (Flores et al., 2019). Ideally, an operational definition will capture a typical instance of the conceptual variable that illustrates its core meaning or essence. In reality, any conceptual variable can be operationalized in a variety of ways, so that no single operational definition is likely to provide the perfect or only instance of the concept.

Operational definition A specific, concrete method of measuring or manipulating a conceptual variable.

Measuring and Manipulating What We Intend Let's examine how researchers operationalize variables. Operationalizing a dependent variable refers to specifying precisely how it will be measured in a particular study. For example, a researcher might operationalize the conceptual variable anxiety in the following ways:

▲ These people are reacting with concern and anxiety to the 2001 attack on the World Trade Center in New York City. Social psychologists access anxiety by self-report, facial expressions, overt behavior, and psychological measures.

[Jennifer S. Altman/WireImage/Getty Images]

1. Scores on a self-report survey of the subjective feeling of anxiety (e.g., tension, apprehension, uneasiness, self-doubt)
2. Overt behaviors that are thought (on the basis of a theoretical conception) to be indicators of anxiety (e.g., fingernail chewing, rapid foot tapping, twitching eyelids)
3. Physiological measures that assess bodily symptoms or signs that are thought (again, on the basis of a theoretical conception) to be indicators of anxiety (e.g., rapid heart rate, sweaty palms, exaggerated startle response)

These various operationalizations tap into different aspects of the concept of anxiety. It's important for multiple operationalizations of a given conceptual variable to be highly correlated with each other so that we can be confident that the various operationalizations are all tapping into the same underlying conceptual variable. Operationalizing an independent variable refers to precisely the procedures and stimuli that will be used to manipulate some variable of interest.

Construct validity The degree to which a dependent variable assesses what it intends to assess or an independent variable manipulates what it intends to manipulate.

Construct validity is the degree to which a dependent variable measures what it intends to measure or an independent variable manipulates what it intends to manipulate. Often researchers assess the construct validity of an independent variable by including a manipulation check, which is a measure that directly assesses whether the manipulation created the change that was intended. For dependent variables, if different operationalizations of a given conceptual variable are not strongly related to each other, they may actually be tapping into two different conceptual variables. An experiment that lacks construct validity for either the independent variable or the dependent variable does not have internal validity. No clear conclusions can be drawn from the results of such an experiment.

Problems with the construct validity of independent variables are particularly common in social psychological research. Sometimes a manipulation of one construct might have an inadvertent effect on a second conceptual variable. For example, if we manipulate stereotype threat by informing our research participants that it is widely believed that their group performs poorly on a particular task, this may well increase their concern that their poor performance might confirm a negative stereotype, just as our conceptual definition of stereotype threat would suggest. But it may also do other things. Maybe it just creates a general increase in fear of failure that has little to do with concerns about stereotypes. It might even create anger at the thought that some people view one's group as inferior. How can we know if the effect of our independent variable is due to concerns about stereotypes, performance anxiety, anger, or any number of other possible consequences of our manipulation? This is a crucial question for determining whether a study has internal validity.

Confound A variable other than the conceptual variable intended to be manipulated that may be responsible for the effect on the dependent variable, making alternative explanations possible.

When more than one conceptual variable differs across conditions in an experiment, the independent variable is confounded. **Confounds** cloud the interpretation of research results because a variable other than the conceptual variable we intended to manipulate may be responsible for the effect on the dependent variable, making alternative explanations possible. Alternative explanations make it unclear which conceptual variable really is responsible for the changes in the dependent variable that occur. Confounds and alternative explanations are thus major problems in any experimental research.

Researchers do their best to avoid confounds in their studies. Ideally, researchers carefully consider potential confounds and alternative explanations when planning a study. For example, they might include a control group that exposes participants to a possible confounding variable without exposing them to the variable hypothesized to be the true cause. To control for possible confounds in experiments of stereotype threat on test performance, we might include control conditions in which participants are threatened, distracted, or angered in ways unrelated to stereotypes of the groups to which they belong. If the stereotype threat group shows worse performance than an anxious, distracted, or angered control group, we can confidently rule out performance anxiety, distraction, and anger as alternative explanations for our findings. When we rule out alternative explanations, we increase our confidence that stereotype threat is, in fact, causing the poorer performance.

The problem of confounds can also be minimized by replicating our studies with different operationalizations of the key variables—a process known as **conceptual replication.** If different studies, each flawed in one way or another, with possible confounds operating, yield consistent results, the probability that an alternative explanation is responsible for the results is reduced. Science is thus a cumulative process, and scientific knowledge depends heavily on ongoing conceptual replications of findings to rule out any confounds that might be affecting our results (Crandall & Sherman, 2016).

Conceptual replication The repetition of a study with different operationalizations of the crucial variables but yielding similar results.

Can the Findings Be Generalized?   As you can see, establishing the construct validity of an experiment's independent and dependent variables is essential to the internal validity of the experiment. Once internal validity has been established, we can then ask, What does this tell us about other people, in other settings, at other times? This is the basic question regarding **external validity**, the ability to generalize one's findings. Can we generalize beyond the group of people studied at a particular time and place?

External validity The judgment that a research finding can be generalized to other people, in other settings, at other times.

In the case of stereotype threat, one way to determine external validity would be to find out whether these effects are limited to African Americans and intellectual testing or whether they extend to other stigmatized groups. For example, would women perform worse on a challenging math test after being reminded of the stereotype that women supposedly have poor mathematical ability? Would older adults show greater lapses of memory if reminded of the stereotype that age impairs memory? Meta-analyses, studies that combine effects across many different studies, suggest that the answer to both questions is "yes" (Armstrong et al., 2017; Doyle & Voyer, 2016).

▲ Social psychology studies rely heavily on readily available college student samples. But how can we know if findings from such studies can be generalized?
[Diego Cervo/Shutterstock]

Other research suggests that effects do not generalize just to different stigmatized groups but also to groups that are typically in the majority. For instance, one study tested whether the athletic performance of American White males would be diminished by reminding them of the stereotype that "White men can't jump" (Stone et al., 1999). In this study, the researchers reasoned that Whites would feel stereotype threat during a golf putting task when they were led to believe that the task measured athletic ability but that Blacks would experience stereotype threat when the task was framed as a measure of sports intelligence. These hypotheses were supported: Whites performed poorly when the task was described as a measure of athletic ability, and Blacks performed poorly when it was described as a measure of sports intelligence. Other work has found that women also experience stereotype threat during athletic skills testing when they know they will be compared to men (Gentile et al., 2018). Over the years, the results of many studies have shown that the problem of stereotype threat is indeed a general one that, depending on the performance domain, can affect members of a number of different groups that are negatively stereotyped.

These examples illustrate that if we are really to have confidence in the external validity of the findings of psychological research, the research needs to be replicated with other types of operationalizations and other participants from varying cultures, geographic regions, and socioeconomic levels. Social psychological research has been criticized for its heavy use of college students as research participants and for participants who might be described as WEIRD (that is, from countries that are Western, educated, industrialized, rich, and democratic; Henrich et al., 2010; Muthukrishna et al., 2020). This is not surprising because most of the research has been conducted by scientists who are themselves WEIRD. However, some have wondered whether we are simply piling up knowledge about the middle class in WEIRD nations but are learning little about other North Americans, Europeans, Australians, and people from other continents. This narrow choice of participants is a problem because if culture does exert a powerful role in shaping our view of ourselves and the world around us, then building a science of human behavior largely drawn from only a limited slice of human diversity is likely to skew the conclusions we draw.

The ideal solution to this problem would be to randomly sample people from the entire population of the earth. Of course, such random sampling is never possible. Although the rare cross-national survey study might be able to recruit samples that are broadly representative of people from diverse racial, ethnic, national, geographic, and economic constituencies, they are still not representative of people they cannot reach or those who are unwilling to fill out the survey. Most studies that take place in laboratories are forced to rely on samples of convenience—typically college students much like yourself. Increasingly research is carried out using online survey samples that are easy to access in large numbers but also unrepresentative of adults in general and dissimilar in other ways from student samples that are so often studied (Anderson et al., 2019; Yeager, Krosnick et al., 2019). Using online samples also leads to other issues, such as people deciding to stop participating in a study partway through. When people can self-select into or out of the experimental condition to which they have been assigned, the internal validity of the study is called into question (Zhou & Fishbach, 2016).

Fortunately, more and more research is being done around the globe to replicate findings in new cultural contexts. Because cultures vary, however, effects might not always look quite the same (Pettigrew, 2018). For example, research has found evidence that stereotype threat can lead to gender differences in math performance among children in Uganda (Picho & Schmader, 2017). But those differences depended on what children believed the stereotypes were; girls performed worse if they believed the stereotypes favored boys, but boys performed worse if they believed the stereotypes favored girls. Although these true tests of generalizability sometimes confirm the universal nature of phenomena, they might also reveal important cultural differences in how we think and feel about ourselves and others. Throughout this text, we highlight some of the research that has already revealed such interesting cultural variations.

Can the Findings Be Replicated?   A defining characteristic of the scientific process is not simply identifying interesting and important effects but showing that those effects can be repeated by **direct replication**, attempting to use the same methods and measures used by the original researchers. In recent years, there has been growing interest in establishing the replicability of scientific findings, sparked by several high-profile examples where findings could not be replicated. For example, when a large network of psychologists tried to replicate 100 experiments that had been published in top scientific journals, fewer than half of the original effects were replicated (Open Science Collaboration et al., 2015; as indicated by the red dots in **FIGURE 1.9**). The challenge of replicating results is not unique to psychology. In a 2016 survey, more than 50% of chemists, biologists, physicists, medical scientists, and engineers reported having at some point failed to replicate someone else's or their own results (Baker, 2016).

Direct replication The process of reproducing a scientific finding by repeating the same methods and measures used in the original research study.

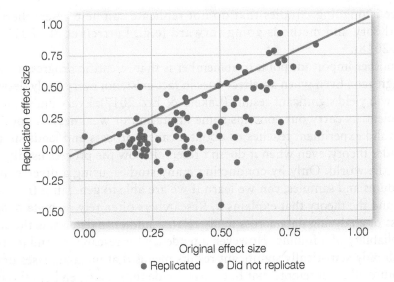

● Replicated ● Did not replicate

Figure 1.9

Replication

In 2015, a team of researchers (Open Science Collaboration, 2015) undertook an ambitious endeavor to replicate 100 published findings in the psychological literature. Among studies that were replicated (blue dots), those with larger effects (e.g., bigger differences between conditions) in the original study (on the x-axis) also had larger effects in the new version (on the y-axis). Among those that were not replicated (in red), there was no relationship between the effect size in the original study and in the new study.

Reports like these can lead to a crisis of confidence in science, but they have had the benefit of spurring researchers to reexamine and adjust scientific practices to increase the replicability of effects. Social psychologists have been at the forefront of these efforts (Asendorpf et al., 2016; Finkel, Eastwick, & Reis, 2015). Findings from a study are more likely to be reproduced when the sample is large, the manipulation is strong, and the measures are reliable. Social psychologists now routinely use a statistical technique called *power analysis* to determine the size of the sample needed to make it highly likely that the results of a study can be replicated. Many researchers also preregister their hypotheses on public online databases, such as the Open Science Framework, so that others can later verify that they did in fact formulate their hypotheses prior to analyzing their data (Nosek et al., 2018). To reinforce some of these best practices, some journals uses badges like those shown in **FIGURE 1.10** to indicate when an article has used preregistered hypotheses and has made materials and data easily accessible so that others can replicate the methods or analyses.

Even when researchers follow these methodological best practices, social psychology's emphasis on how situations affect thought and behavior can make it difficult to replicate findings across different samples, cultures, locations, and time (van Bavel et al., 2016). This is where the cycle of science can be important for identifying **moderator variables** that theoretically explain when, where, or for whom effects are most likely to occur (Noah et al., 2018; Yeager, Krosnick et al., 2019). Humans and life are complex, and the effect of almost any variable is likely to be different across different types of individuals and different kinds of situations. For example, stereotype threat only impairs performance of minority students who are personally invested in doing well academically (Nguyen & Ryan, 2008).

As research progresses, more moderators are discovered, but some might still be unknown. Because of these complexities, Luttrell and colleagues (2017) proposed that informed replication, which takes into account known moderating variables and societal changes, should be the approach when planning replications of older studies. They showed that a classic finding did not replicate when these moderating conditions were ignored but did replicate when the original procedures were adapted to be consistent with known moderating conditions. The important lesson to learn from all this is that the process of

Moderator variables Variables that explain when, where, or for whom an effect is most likely to occur.

Figure 1.10

Open Science

Some journals use badges like these to indicate when an article reports studies that were preregistered and that make their data and their materials available online.

Center for Open Science, https://cos.io/our-services/open-science-badges/

science is ongoing. Studies that do not replicate can help researchers refine both theory and methods going forward (e.g., Luttrell et al., 2017; Noah et al., 2018).

Another important point to remember is that scientific progress is made in the aggregate. Even when an effect does in fact exist, not every study designed to test it will yield significant results (Lakens & Etz, 2017). Every individual study that scientists carry out contains some limitation or weakness. A good, internally valid experiment teaches us about a causal process and lends support to a broader theory, even when it doesn't resemble how the process usually occurs out in the world. Only by conducting many studies, using a diverse array of procedures and samples, can we learn if we are able to generalize from a given effect and the theory that explains it. Researchers often rely on **meta-analysis**, a process of analyzing data across many related studies to determine the strength and reliability of a finding. However, a tendency for researchers and journals to publish only statistically significant results means that meta-analyses often fail to capture all the attempts that have been made to test a given hypothesis. Current efforts to provide more open access to research results aim to remedy this problem (Nosek et al., 2015).

The replicability of stereotype threat has itself been a topic of debate in recent years. On the one hand, meta-analyses show small to medium stereotype threat effects for minorities on intellectual tests, women on math and spatial tests, women in sports, and older adults on memory tests (Armstrong et al., 2017; Doyle & Voyer, 2016; Gentile et al., 2018; Nadler & Clark, 2011; Picho et al., 2013). However, the conclusions from these and other meta-analyses are limited by the fact that studies that fail to show significant effects are seldom published (Flore & Wicherts, 2015; Shewach et al., 2019; Zigerell, 2017). To guard against these publication biases, some journals now agree to publish the results of replication attempts just on the basis of the methods and before the results are known. Interestingly, in 2014, two such **registered reports** attempted to replicate stereotype threat effects on women's math performance. One study replicated the effect, but the other did not (Gibson et al., 2014; Moon & Roeder, 2014). Together, these mixed results suggest that there are still moderators of stereotype threat to be discovered or that stereotype threat has a weaker and more variable effect than researchers first assumed.

The Limitations of Science

By providing a way of assessing the merits of competing claims about the nature of reality, science has enhanced our understanding of the world we live in, ourselves, and how we fit into that world. By applying the knowledge gained from scientific inquiry, humankind has solved many problems that plagued us for millennia. However, the knowledge science has given us has also created many problems, such as the potential to kill each other by the millions and to use up or poison the natural resources we rely on for survival. These are very real problems that must be faced. Social psychology can help us grapple with them by providing the knowledge needed to get people to look beyond their immediate personal benefits to see the long-term consequences of their decisions for others and to put aside age-old ethnic and religious rivalries and realize that our mutual survival depends on sustainable practices of consumption and our ability to coexist peacefully with each other. However, despite its enormous utility, science has some important limitations.

Meta-analysis A process of analyzing data across many related studies to determine the strength and reliability of a finding.

Registered report A study that is accepted for publication on the strength of the methods and importance of the question but before results are known.

First, *there are aspects of reality that we humans cannot know.* Our knowledge of the world originates in the information provided to us by our sense organs. Unfortunately, human sense organs are capable of registering only a tiny fraction of the things that are actually happening in the world. For example, our hearing is limited to a relatively narrow range of sound frequencies. Dogs can hear many sounds we have no hope of perceiving. Although we often use the knowledge that science gives us to develop technologies that enable us to assess things that our raw sense organs cannot perceive, the fact that we are capable of perceiving only part of what is happening in the world makes gaining a complete understanding of all aspects of reality an elusive goal.

Second, *although the scientific method may be objective, the human beings who apply it are not.* The scientific method was developed to provide a more objective way of answering questions. But science remains a human endeavor. Scientists may try their best to put their biases aside, but human nature makes a complete elimination of individual bias impossible. Part of the difficulty in replicating scientific effects might sometimes stem from scientists' own overconfidence in their theories that bias their data analyses toward finding evidence for statistical significance for an effect that does not actually exist (Simmons et al., 2011). Replication attempts can also be hampered when researchers modify procedures in the name of expediency, as when carefully controlled studies originally done in person fail to replicate when translated into online anonymous surveys (see, e.g., Luttrell et al., 2017). Scientists—social psychologists included—often stake their reputations, careers, and ultimately their self-esteem on the ideas they espouse, and this is true both for those supporting the validity of a theory and those seeking to challenge the validity of a theory (Bryan et al., 2019). Fortunately, the scientific method and the communal nature of the scientific enterprise typically weed out these biases in the long run. But it is important to realize that scientists are subject to the same needs, desires, and expectations that produce bias in all other humans.

Third, *not all questions can be answered scientifically.* Many of the most pressing crises facing us today involve questions of values, morality, and ethics. Science cannot tell us which values are the right ones to invest in. Is safety more important than freedom? Are the rights of the individual more important than the welfare of the group? Should scientific knowledge be used to restrict behaviors that are injurious to the people who engage in them? Although science can help us understand the consequences of different courses of action, it cannot tell us which consequences are more important than others and which values we should use to guide our decisions.

Fourth, *human values exert a powerful influence on the way science is conducted.* The questions we choose to ask—or, perhaps more importantly, choose not to ask—are often determined by nonscientific political, religious, and/or economic factors (Duarte et al., 2015). For example, studies of the genetic underpinnings of behavior were actively discouraged in the Soviet Union during most of the 20th century because communist ideology claimed that all differences among individuals result from environmental influences. Similarly, questions pertaining to women's contributions to science and politics are unlikely to arise in cultural milieus where females are regarded as uneducable subordinates. Sometimes the values of a society limit the search for truth that is the ultimate goal of the scientific method. But human values also direct scientific inquiry toward questions that serve constructive aspirations and steer scientific research away from practices that would violate these values.

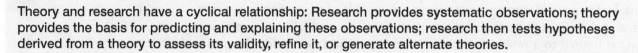

SECTION REVIEW   Theory Building: The Engine of Scientific Progress

Theory and research have a cyclical relationship: Research provides systematic observations; theory provides the basis for predicting and explaining these observations; research then tests hypotheses derived from a theory to assess its validity, refine it, or generate alternate theories.

Features of a Good Theory	Internal and External Validity	Limitations of Science
• Organizes the facts. • Explains observations. • Inspires new research. • Generates new questions. • Has practical applications.	• Abstract ideas need to be made specific and quantifiable to be manipulated and measured properly. • Studies should be able to be replicated using the same and different operationalizations of variables.	• Human knowledge is limited. • Humans are biased. • Some questions are outside the scope of science. • Human values influence the questions asked.

Learning Outcomes

- List the three important ethical safeguards to protect research participants.
- Explain how the safeguards are enacted.

Ethical Considerations in Research

The ultimate goal of psychological research is to advance our understanding of the human condition in order to make life better for people, so we certainly wouldn't want to undermine the quality of life for our research participants. Accordingly, social psychologists devote considerable attention to ethical concerns. Because many of the issues of interest to social psychologists pertain to the dark and distressing side of human nature and behavior, social psychologists are compelled to include these unpleasant aspects of existence in their research. To study fear, it is often necessary to make people afraid; to study egotism and prejudice, people must be put in situations where these unbecoming characteristics become manifest. Social psychologists must continually ask whether the value of the research findings is worth the distress that participants might experience.

Harming Research Participants

Obviously, some practices are ethically unacceptable under any circumstances. Clearly inhumane treatment could never be justified under any circumstances. Examples of such treatment include the horrible experiments conducted by Nazi doctors in the concentration camps during World War II, such as injecting pregnant women with toxic substances to refine abortion and sterilization techniques (Lifton, 1986). Another heinous example is the Tuskegee syphilis experiment, conducted between 1932 and 1972 by the U.S. Health Service. In this experiment, in order to study the progression of syphilis, scientists did not tell African Americans infected with syphilis that they had the disease and did not give them penicillin (Jones, 1981). In general, anything that could cause permanent, long-term damage to human participants is clearly out of bounds for research purposes.

What about experiments that produce temporary discomfort and stress? Milgram's (1974) classic studies of obedience to authority, in which participants believed they were giving a middle-aged man extremely painful and potentially lethal electric shocks, are perhaps the most famous example of social psychological research that put participants in an extremely stressful situation. Some observers thought Milgram's studies were ethically unacceptable, but it would be hard to argue that this research did not produce important findings. Was the stress that participants endured worth the knowledge we gained? Some might argue that no one was really hurt by the shocks that participants thought they were giving and that the participants themselves decided to deliver the shocks. Critics have argued that the problem with this study is that participants were forced to face some very upsetting truths about themselves: They were capable of causing great pain to and potentially killing another human being when ordered to do so by an experimenter.

▲ The Milgram studies sparked debate about ethics in social psychological research.

[Screenshot from Film "*Obedience.*" Rights held by Alexandra Milgram]

Debate about the ethics of the Milgram studies will probably continue for years, and we will discuss these studies in greater detail in chapter 7. Currently, the American Psychological Association (APA) does not allow researchers at American colleges to replicate these studies exactly as they were originally done. However, the results of these studies are considered highly valuable and are taught in virtually every college in North America and in those of many other countries as well. Whether the value of what we learned about obedience to authority outweighs the risks to participants is ultimately a personal judgment that we must all make for ourselves.

Deceiving Research Participants

Social psychologists often mislead the participants in their studies about the true purpose of their research. They do this to create the psychological states they wish to study. Indeed, social psychologists use deception in their research more than any other scientists do. In his obedience studies, Milgram told participants that they were in a study of learning and that their role was to deliver increasingly high-voltage electric shocks to another participant with a heart condition. This was a powerful deception and, as already noted, one that many people believe stepped beyond ethical bounds.

Most social psychological experiments involve some level of deception, but the vast majority of these studies use relatively minor deception by offering a **cover story,** an explanation of the purpose of the study that is different from the true purpose. But some researchers have staged emergencies, told participants they did poorly on intelligence tests, frustrated participants, and given them false information about their personalities.

Cover story An explanation of the purpose of a study that is different from the true purpose.

There are two primary reasons for the use of deception. First, if participants know the true purpose of the research, their responses are likely to be affected by their knowledge of that purpose. But participants need not even be accurate in their suspicions about the purposes of a study for those suspicions to taint the study's findings. A substantial body of research has shown that if people know (or think they know) the purpose of a study, it puts a demand on them to behave in a certain way (Orne, 1962). Aspects of a study that give away a purpose of the study are called **demand characteristics.** Studies with demand characteristics are inconclusive because the possibility that the participants were affected by their knowledge of the purpose introduces an alternative explanation for the results of the study.

Demand characteristics Aspects of a study that give away its purpose or communicate how the participant is expected to behave.

One source of demand characteristics can be an experimenter's expectations of how participants are supposed to behave. As noted earlier, researchers are people with their own desires and biases, which can affect how they treat participants even if the researchers themselves are not aware of it. This is

Experimenter bias The possibility that an experimenter's knowledge of the condition a particular participant is in could affect her behavior toward the participant and thereby introduce a confounding variable to the independent variable manipulation.

THINK ABOUT ▶

[Masterchief_Productions/Shutterstock]

known as **experimenter bias**. To eliminate this bias whenever possible, experiments should be designed so that the researchers are "blind" to experimental conditions—that is, so they don't know which condition a particular participant is in. That way, there is no way for them to systematically treat any participant differently depending on the condition the participant is in.

Second, researchers often use deception to create the conditions necessary to test a hypothesis. For example, if the hypothesis is that frustration leads to aggression, a social psychologist might manipulate level of frustration and then measure aggression to test this hypothesis. The manipulation of the independent variable, frustration, would require staging some sort of frustrating experience. For example, one study (Geen, 1968) tested the frustration–aggression hypothesis by having participants try unsuccessfully to solve a puzzle that was rigged to be impossible.

Although it is clear that deception is a useful practice for conducting research, the question remains whether this kind of deliberate misrepresentation is justified. Some argue that deception is never defensible because it betrays the trust that should exist between a researcher and a research participant. Others argue that using deception often is the only way to study many important psychological states and that the knowledge gained through the use of deception in research justifies the potential distress. Where do you stand?

We, like the vast majority of other social psychologists, embrace the latter position. So do the APA and other legal and professional organizations that govern research in the countries where social psychology flourishes.

Ethical Safeguards

To provide guidance on these matters, the APA established a Code of Ethics that all psychological researchers in the United States must abide by. Most other countries have similar principles of research ethics in place. First, the ethical implications of all studies must be carefully considered and approved, both by the investigators conducting the research and by ethical review boards at their institutions. These ethical review boards judge whether the potential benefits of the research outweigh the research's potential costs and risks to the participants. Second, participants must give their informed consent to take part in any study after they are provided with a full disclosure of procedures they are to undergo and the potential risks that participation might entail. Participants must also have the right to ask questions and to withdraw from the study at any time, even after the study begins. Finally, participants must be assured that adequate steps will be taken to protect their confidentiality and that their identities will not in any way be linked to their responses without their explicit consent.

Debriefing At the end of a study, the procedure in which participants are assessed for suspicion and then receive a gentle explanation of the true nature of the study in a manner that counteracts any negative effects of the study experience.

These safeguards are very important, but when deception is used, the informed consent cannot be fully informing. To minimize any potential negative effects of deception, at the conclusion of a study, the experimenter conducts a **debriefing**. In the debriefing, the experimenter probes for suspicion about the true purpose of the study, gently reveals any deceptions, clarifies the true purpose of the study, and explains why the deception was necessary to achieve the goals of the research. For example, in Milgram's studies of obedience, all participants were fully debriefed, and many were quite relieved to meet and shake hands with the person whom they believed they had been shocking. When properly done, the debriefing should be informative, comforting, and educational, not only alleviating any negative feelings and misconceptions the participants had about the study or their actions in the study but also providing a peek behind the curtain of social psychological research. Research shows that properly done debriefings do indeed achieve these goals (Sharpe & Faye, 2009).

SECTION REVIEW   Ethical Considerations in Research

Any research involving human participants must be conducted in accordance with ethical principles based on a cost–benefit analysis.

Harm	Deception	Ethical Safeguards
• No lasting physical or psychological harm must be caused.	• The use of deception must be justified in any study, and its potential for any harm must be minimized.	• The APA has established a Code of Ethics. An ethical review board assesses whether each study meets these ethical standards. • Informed consent is an important protection, although it is limited in studies that use deception. • Debriefings that are reassuring and educational are crucial to ensure the ethicality of deception research.

CRITICAL LEARNING EXERCISES

1. Think about the five broad perspectives of social psychology: evolutionary, social cognition, cultural, existential, and neuroscience. Think about some recent significant event in your life using each of these perspectives. How was your reaction to the event possibly shaped by each?

2. Confirmation biases can lead us to disregard evidence that might disagree with our intuitions. The scientific method, when applied properly, can provide a more objective way to collect and analyze data. Can you think of a time when you learned the results of a scientific study that disconfirmed what you had assumed to be true? Did you stick with your intuition, or change your beliefs in light of the scientific findings?

3. How would you design an experiment to test the hypothesis that violent video content increases aggression? Be specific about your procedures, cover story, the independent variable, and the dependent variable. How would you try to reduce any confounds in your design and make sure that you chose variables that have construct validity?

4. Social psychologists are increasingly trying to test hypotheses with participants who are not university students living in the Western world. Why is this important? If you could examine a question of everyday human behavior, where would you most want to study it and why? What two places would make for an interesting comparison?

Don't stop now! Check out our videos and additional resources located at: www.macmillanlearning.com.

CHAPTER 2

Fundamentals of Social Behavior

Human beings have resulted from a lengthy and by no means inevitable historical process that began with earth's original life-forms. Our species has inherited a set of biological, behavioral, and psychological characteristics that have evolved over billions of years through natural selection. Think about it. Trillions of life-forms have struggled for billions of years to survive and reproduce in inhospitable and often hostile environments, and the fruit of their labor is, well, *you*.

Many of our inherited characteristics also can be found in other species, but the human mind works in ways that set our species apart. The unique evolution of the human brain enables us to construct and maintain *culture*. This was an enormous leap because culture allows us to create styles of living that no other species can fathom—although not all of these styles of living have been good for us or the planet.

As outlined in chapter 1, the evolutionary and cultural influences on social life are two of the perspectives we'll explore throughout this book. This chapter sets the stage by discussing how, at a fundamental level, evolution and culture make humans the types of creatures we are:

- We trace the evolutionary origins of uniquely human mental capacities, motives, and emotions.

- We look at how these evolved tendencies continue to influence how we modern humans think, feel, and act in everyday life.

- We explore vital aspects of culture: its nature, its functions, and its profound influence on all of our lives.

- Explain the role of variability and competition in the process of evolution by natural selection.

- Describe the role of the environment as it relates to "survival of the fittest."

Evolution: How Living Things Change over Time

Probably all the organic beings which have ever lived on this earth have descended from some one primordial form, into which life was first breathed. . . . [W]hen we regard every production of nature as one which has had a history . . . every complex structure and instinct as the summing up of many contrivances, each useful to the possessor . . . how far more interesting . . . will the study of nature become! . . .

In the distant future I see open fields for far more important researches. Psychology will be based on a new foundation.

—Charles Darwin, *The Origin of Species* (1860)

To get to the roots of human nature, let's begin, well, at the beginning. Planet Earth arrived on the galactic scene roughly 4.6 billion years ago. Within a billion years after that, conditions were ripe for the appearance of an unprecedented form of matter—LIFE! Single-celled creatures were the first on the scene, but fast forward a few millennia, and we find the fantastic variety of creatures that have inhabited and continue to inhabit our planet. How did all this come about? **Evolution**, the idea that species change over time and are descended from common ancestors, goes back at least to the ancient Greek philosopher Anaximander (610–546 BC). Charles Darwin's genius was to propose the theory of **natural selection** to explain the *process* through which evolution occurs.

Evolution The concept that different species are descended from common ancestors but have evolved over time, acquiring different genetic characteristics as a function of different environmental demands.

Natural selection The process by which certain attributes are more successful in a particular environment and therefore become more represented in future generations.

Natural Selection

There are two key ingredients in the recipe for evolution by natural selection:

1. The processes of reproduction cause *variability*, which has two primary sources:

   ■ *Mutation*: As strands of DNA are read to create an organism, random mistakes occur that result in slightly different variations. Most variations were maladaptive, leading to an almost immediate end to the organism's life. However, some were adaptive, which means they improved the organism's chances of surviving and reproducing—even if just a little.

   ■ *Sexual recombination*: When a new creature is produced, it does not have exactly the same genetic makeup as the creatures that produced it. Instead, it has a unique combination of its parents' genes.

2. The second key ingredient is *competition*. In a world of limited food, mating partners, and other resources, even tiny variations might help an individual compete more effectively with other creatures vying for the same resources.

Adaptations Attributes that improve an individual's prospects for survival and reproduction.

Variability and competition in particular environments determine which genes are passed along to subsequent generations through reproduction. These genes influence each individual organism's physical and behavioral attributes. Creatures which possess attributes that improve their prospects for survival and reproduction, as well as the survival of their offspring, are more successful in passing along their genes. As a result, those attributes—known as **adaptations**—become represented more widely in future generations. Over time, individuals with the most successful adaptations outnumber and eventually replace less-well-adapted versions of the creature.

Survival of the Fittest: Yes, but What Is Fittest?

The process of evolution by natural selection has often been characterized as the *survival of the fittest* (a phrase coined by Darwin's contemporary Herbert Spencer in 1864). However, "fittest" does not mean strongest or most aggressive. If it did, *Tyrannosaurus rex* would still be roaming the planet instead of merely posing in fossilized form for museum patrons. What is "fittest" depends entirely on the natural environments in which particular organisms reside. Creatures adapted for warmth would not be fit in cold environments, and vice versa, which is why you don't find iguanas in Alaska or penguins in Panama (except in zoos!).

As new variants on a life-form emerge, with new ways of exploiting an environmental niche for survival and reproduction, the benefits and costs of attributes may shift. For example, if mutations cause individuals of an aquatic species to develop new ways of obtaining oxygen so that they can survive on dry land, what was functional for their ancestors (e.g., gills) may become worthless. However, new variations—such as body protuberances that make it possible to move around on land (rudimentary legs)—may now become advantageous. So the process of evolution depends on changes in both the external environment and the characteristics of the organisms in that environment.

Depictions of evolution in popular culture often describe "Mother Nature" as calling the shots, but the process of natural selection *just happens*; it has no intention and strives toward no goal. Variability and competition are simply facts of life, and a fairly random mixture of characteristics of environments and organisms determines which forms of variability make an organism more competitive. Like much else in life, evolution is a series of trade-offs, and even attributes that were beneficial enough to be passed down over generations can also come with certain costs. Stop and think about what some of these might be. Bipedalism (standing up on two legs) gave early humans significant benefits, such as freeing up their hands for using tools, but it has downsides, including slipped disks, fallen arches, and shin splints. Environments can also change, making some adaptations significantly less adaptive than they once were (Li et al., 2018). For example, our predilection for sweet food was likely adaptive as it led us to consume healthy nutrients like fruits and berries. Now, with a proliferation of soda and candy bars at every grocery checkout line, this fondness can get us into trouble. Keeping this in mind, we'll want to avoid making the **naturalistic fallacy**, whereby we assume (quite incorrectly) that the way things *are* is necessarily how they *ought* to be (Ismail et al., 2012).

▲ New species of amphibians evolved from fish as random mutations allowed for movement and survival out of the water.

◄ **THINK ABOUT**

[Charles Stirling/Alamy]

Naturalistic fallacy A bias toward believing that biological adaptations are inherently good or desirable.

SECTION REVIEW   Evolution: How Living Things Change over Time

Evolution is the idea that species change over time and are descended from common ancestors.

- Evolution occurs through the process of natural selection, which is a consequence of variability and competition.
- Some random mutations eventually result in adaptations: attributes that improve the organism's prospects for survival and reproduction in its current environment.
- What is adaptive depends on the interaction between the environment and the attributes of the organism.
- Adaptations are trade-offs. Evolution is not guided by any purpose or goal. Do not infer that an attribute is "more natural" or "better" just because it evolved.

General Adaptations of the Cultural Animal

- Outline different ways that sociability contributes to human evolution.

- Describe how symbolic intelligence is essential for understanding both the self and the wider world.

- Give examples of the hierarchy of goals.

- Explain how emotions are involved with regulating and communicating our motivations.

Domain-specific adaptations
Attributes that evolved to meet a particular challenge but that are not particularly useful when dealing with other types of challenges.

Domain-general adaptations
Attributes that are useful for dealing with various challenges across different areas of life.

With an overview of evolutionary theory in place, we can look at what adaptations characterize human beings. Some psychologists focus on **domain-specific adaptations**, attributes that evolved to meet a particular challenge but that are not particularly useful when dealing with other types of challenges (Barkow et al., 1992). For example, photosensitive cells in our eyes evolved because they helped us to see color, but they are useless when it comes to, say, digesting proteins. As we'll see throughout this book, focusing on domain-specific adaptations can help us understand some behaviors, such as dating preferences (Neuberg et al., 2010).

In contrast, **domain-general adaptations** are attributes that are useful for dealing with various challenges across different areas of life. For example, the human capacity for learning can help you build a shelter, find food, and avoid a saber-toothed tiger. According to the archaeologist Stephen Mithen (1996, 1998), the flexibility of these domain-general adaptations is what most clearly distinguishes humans from other primate species. It also made it possible for humans to proliferate across the earth's diverse natural environments, from tropical forest to frozen tundra. Next we'll see how four of these domain-general adaptations shape virtually all forms of human behavior.

Humans Are Social Beings

As you'll recall from chapter 1, a core assumption of social psychology is that *behavior depends on a socially constructed view of reality*. Behind this assumption is an even more basic idea: Humans are *social* creatures. Unlike tigers, who live largely on their own, we cannot survive without extensive relationships with other human beings. As infants, we need caretakers to feed, protect, and comfort us; as adults, virtually everyone desires and depends on friends and lovers, as well as the extended communities that help us meet our basic needs. Even Henry David Thoreau, the American writer who famously wrote of his solitary time at Walden Pond, hung out with his friend Ralph Waldo Emerson and took his dirty laundry to his mother!

Darwin recognized that in many species, the prospects for survival and gene perpetuation are vastly improved for those who get along well with other members of their species. The human brain has thus evolved several tools that reflect the adaptive value of sociability and social sensitivity. Here are a few examples:

- An area in the brain called the *fusiform face area* functions specifically to recognize human faces (**FIGURE 2.1**) (Kanwisher et al., 1997). This is useful because faces are unique and convey important information, making it possible not only to recognize individuals and recall information about them (*"that's* the guy who loaned me an ax") but also to interpret what they might be thinking and feeling.

- When social rejection or exclusion occurs, it triggers a strong negative reaction in the brain. In fact, social exclusion activates an area of the brain responsible for generating feelings of physical pain (Eisenberger et al., 2003). To avoid these painful experiences, we try hard to fit in.

- Like the brains of other primates, the human brain is equipped to categorize people in ways that help social interactions go smoothly (Boehm, 1999;

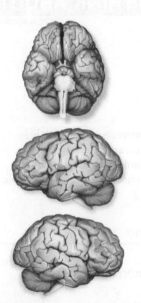

Figure 2.1

Fusiform Face Area

The fusiform face area allows us to recognize the faces of people we know.

[Research from Mansouri et al., 2009]

de Waal, 1996). We quickly categorize others as friend or foe, which tells us immediately whether we can expect good things or bad things from them. We also categorize others' power or rank within a group so that we can determine the most appropriate way to interact with them.

■ The same areas of the brain that are active when we rest are also involved in how we think about the social world. The parallel activity in the medial frontoparietal network suggests that the resting brain is preparing to think about others or consolidating information about others (Meyer, 2019).

The social nature of the human animal is also reflected in **socialization**—the lifelong process of learning from others what are desirable and undesirable styles of living. This learning occurs in our relationships with our parents, siblings, friends, teachers, and many others over the course of our lives.

Socialization Learning from parents and others what is desirable and undesirable conduct in a particular culture.

Why does socialization have such a strong influence on human psychology? Unlike some species that strike out on their own shortly after birth, human infants are born helpless and require years of care if they are to have any chance of survival. This extended period of immaturity and helplessness allows children to learn how to function well in the specific environment in which they develop. Our relative immaturity provides added flexibility to our species and helps to account for the incredible diversity that we see among people.

Humans Are Very Intelligent Beings

Who is smarter: dogs or cats? Questions like these are fun (Mark says cats for sure), but they're based on a poor grasp of evolution by natural selection. All living things are intelligent in the broad sense that they have their own ways of reading their environment and responding in ways that help them to stay alive and reproduce. A bird called the Clark's nutcracker can remember the precise locations of 20,000 tiny seeds that it buried in the forest nine months ago, whereas most of us can't remember what we ate for breakfast. That said, *Homo sapiens* are said to have the smarts—after all, *sapiens* means "wise."

Imagination   Humans have the greatest intelligence in terms of their capacities for imagination, and, consequently, altering their environment to better suit their visions (for better and worse). That's why *there are* iguanas in Alaska and penguins in Panama. Remember when you first moved to a new house, dorm room, or apartment? You looked around and imagined where stuff would go and what kinds of activities you'd do tomorrow and next month. No other species can create entire worlds in their heads.

Symbolic Thought and Language: The Great Liberators   What does a red light have to do with stopping, other than being a socially agreed-on symbol for "Stop"? Most symbols bear no obvious relationship to the objects or ideas they represent. Nonetheless, this connection of specific meanings to arbitrary symbols enables humans to consider a wide variety of concepts and to communicate these ideas to other humans.

The most important result of our symbolic thinking is that it makes language possible. The emergence of language allowed a quantum leap in the flexibility and adaptability of the human species. It enables people to think and communicate about other people, objects, and events that are not in their current environment (**FIGURE 2.2**). Language vastly increases the sources of information that people can use to make decisions and plan action. To illustrate: Coyotes coordinate attacks on prey through the use of a variety of barks, yips, and howls, but only humans can sit back and discuss their plans, recount prior military actions, and debate on nationwide call-in talk shows the pros and cons of a future attack.

The Self

And then an event did occur, to Emily, of considerable importance. She suddenly realized who she was.

—Richard Hughes, *A High Wind in Jamaica* (1929/2010, p. 135)

Our evolved symbolic intelligence not only expands our perspective on the world "out there," it also allows us to experience the fact that we are experiencing it: *I am, and I know that I am, and I know that I know that I am.* Being self-conscious and able to represent the *self* symbolically as an "I" or a "me" enables people to think about the meaning of their experiences (Rochat, 2018). A deer confronted by a pack of wolves may experience fear, but only humans can consciously contemplate the fact that *I am very afraid right now* and ponder the meaning of this feeling. Only humans can feel foolish or embarrassed about their fears or even fear that they might become afraid. Only humans can fear things that don't exist (e.g., ghosts, witchcraft) or that may or may not happen in the future, such as a relationship falling apart or a nuclear holocaust destroying the planet. (We didn't say that self-awareness is always *pleasant.*)

Having a self also makes it possible to evaluate one's actions, feelings, thoughts, or overall sense of identity in light of one's values, ambitions, and principles ("Am I the person I aim to be?") and then to modify one's thoughts and behaviors to bring them in line with those standards. Being able to think about the self symbolically also enables people to mentally simulate future events and to imagine various possibilities for their lives. We can mentally simulate a visceral state such as being cold and take appropriate action, such as packing a hat and gloves (Steinmetz et al., 2018). But people can also delay a habitual response to a situation and consider alternative responses, to ponder the past and anticipate the future, and to ask "Why?" and "What if?" questions. (Imagine the person who invented the hat and gloves.) In a nutshell, having a concept of self that connects past, present, and future is adaptive because it vastly improves our ability to monitor and change our behavior, ultimately increasing our chances that things will go our way. Having a self gives humans freedom and flexibility in their behavior unlike that found in any other known living thing.

Conscious and Nonconscious Aspects of Thinking Although humans are quite capable of being self-aware, think of how much we often don't think. You don't have to think about sweating when the temperature rises; you don't have to think about moving when a car is coming toward you unexpectedly;

Figure 2.2

Symbolic Thought and Language

By simply talking, we humans can create entire worlds in thin air.

you don't have to think about smiling when you recognize a beloved face in a crowd. And very often people are not consciously aware of the factors affecting their behavior, as Freud emphasized in the early 20th century. Contemporary research has extensively examined the role of nonconscious processes, as when people's judgments are influenced by exposure to subliminal stimuli they are not even aware they have seen. For example, super-quick (28-millisecond) subliminal flashes of words associated with aggressiveness can lead people to judge others as being more aggressive (Todorov & Bargh, 2002).

The psychologist William James (1890) pointed out that an action that initially required conscious control can become habitual, such that conscious thought is no longer needed to perform it. For example, learning to play a musical instrument requires rigorous conscious attention over long hours of repetitive practice. Once musical skills have been acquired, however, playing the instrument becomes quite automatic. In fact, once these skills become habits, consciously thinking about them (e.g., thinking about each finger's placement on a flute) can interfere with smooth action (Beilock, 2011).

The process by which a task no longer requires conscious attention is referred to as *automatization*. Can you see how automatization would be quite adaptive? For one thing, it allows people to get stuff done without actively thinking about the actions they are performing, freeing their minds to concentrate on other tasks. As a result of automatization, many behaviors result from unconscious **automatic processes**, while responses to more novel, complex, and challenging situations involve more conscious **controlled processes** (discussed further in chapter 3). Of course, many behaviors combine both types of processes.

This points to a more general picture of the mind as composed of two mental systems (Epstein, 1980). One is an *experiential* system of thought and decision making that relies on emotions, intuitions, and images processed in the brain's evolutionarily older regions, including the limbic system. Automatic processes often happen within this system (**FIGURE 2.3**). The other is a *rational* system that is logical, analytic, and primarily linguistic. This system involves greater activity from the more recently evolved frontal lobes of the cerebrum and supports controlled processes. It takes over when people have sufficient time, motivation, and attention to think carefully about their situation and themselves.

Automatic processes Human thoughts or actions that occur quickly, often without the aid of conscious awareness.

Controlled processes Human thoughts or actions that occur more slowly and deliberatively and that are motivated by some goal that is often consciously recognized.

Motivation The process of generating and expending energy toward achieving or avoiding some outcome.

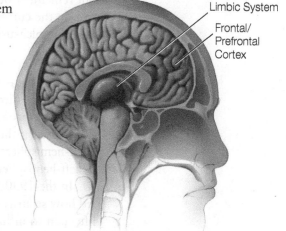

Limbic System

Frontal/
Prefrontal
Cortex

Humans Are Motivated, Goal-Striving Beings

The process of natural selection resulted in systems that energize, direct, and regulate behaviors that help people survive and prosper. In psychology, the concept of **motivation** refers broadly to generating and expending energy toward achieving or avoiding some outcome. Motivation can vary in strength (low to high) and in direction (toward one end state or another). Strength and direction of motivation vary from individual to individual and from situation to situation. For example, some people are motivated to lose weight, while others seek to gain weight; and among those who want to lose weight, some are highly motivated and others much less so. An upcoming high school reunion may increase a person's motivation to lose weight much more than a pie-baking competition at next summer's county fair.

Figure 2.3

Limbic System and Frontal Cortex

Our experiential and rational systems take place in different regions of the brain that support different types of thought processes. Yet these systems are neurally connected and work together in producing thought and behavior.

Needs Internal states that drive action that is necessary to survive or thrive.

Goals Cognitions that represent outcomes that we strive for in order to meet our needs and desires.

Hedonism The human preference for pleasure over pain.

Needs and Goals Humans direct their behavior toward the satisfaction of needs and goals. **Needs** are what is necessary for the individual not just to survive but also to prosper. For example, self-determination theory (Deci & Ryan, 2000) argues that, in order to flourish, people need *competence* (being able to do things successfully), *relatedness* (having close connections with other people), and *autonomy* (being in control of one's life). When these psychological needs are not met, people do not function as well as they could.

Goals, on the other hand, are what people strive for to meet their needs. To meet your need for nutrition, you may decide to pursue the goal of getting a pizza. To meet your need for relatedness to other people, you might choose the goal of striking up a conversation with the person sitting across from you.

Just as human intellectual capacities operate beneath conscious awareness, people are not always aware that their behavior is directed toward a particular goal or what underlying need their current goals ultimately serve. Right now you are probably not consciously thinking about the goal that reading this book is serving (at least you weren't until we just brought it up).

Hedonism: Approaching Pleasure, Avoiding Pain For a life-form to survive and reproduce into future generations, it must be inclined to approach what is good for it and avoid what is bad for it. Humans have thus evolved tendencies to experience displeasure, pain, and negative emotions in response to harmful stimuli; and pleasure, satisfaction, and positive emotions in response to beneficial stimuli. These basic tendencies gave rise to one of the most basic aspects of human motivation: **hedonism**, the motivation to approach pleasure and avoid pain. Hedonism was adaptive for the better part of human evolution because things that brought pleasure were generally good for survival and reproduction. But remember our point that as environments change, so too does what is adaptive. In the current environment, seeking pleasure can get us into trouble, while avoiding pleasure can get us ahead.

The Two Fundamental Psychological Motives: Security and Growth The concept of hedonism suggests that it can be useful to think of two basic motivational orientations that guide human behavior: *security* (avoiding the bad) and *growth* (approaching the good). Neuroscience research supports the distinction between these motivational systems: Avoidance motivation involves more right-hemisphere activity, whereas approach motivation tends to involve primarily left-hemisphere activity (Harmon-Jones, 2003; Harmon-Jones & Allen, 1998).

In the 1930s, Otto Rank (1932/1989), a theorist mentored by Freud, studied how security and growth motives develop and interact over the course of the life span to influence a person's thinking and behavior. He noted that children frequently are distressed and anxious and seek relief from these negative feelings through the nourishment, safety, and comfort provided by their parents. This means that children avoid negative emotions by establishing and sustaining a secure relationship with their loving and protective parents. This desire for security is one side of Rank's analysis of human motivation.

The other side emerges when children are able to maintain that sense of security and, as a result, begin to explore their surroundings in ways that expand their physical, cognitive, emotional, and interpersonal capabilities. This is the growth-oriented side of human motivation. Think of a curious toddler running around a room, opening closet doors, pulling out whatever looks interesting, and trying to play with anyone who offers a smile. Over the years, other theorists have echoed these ideas, proposing that, throughout their lives, people simultaneously seek to feel secure while also seeking stimulation and growth (Lewin, 1935; Scholer & Higgins, 2013).

Whenever we want to understand why people behave the way they do, regardless of the specific social context, it is informative to consider the influence of these two motivational orientations. For example, people want careers that provide financial security, stability, and prestige but that are, at the same time, interesting and challenging. Similarly, people seek relationships with those they can trust and rely on but whom they also find exciting and fun. We even want cars that are safe and dependable *and* that go *zoom zoom*!

To make sense of behavior, it also helps to consider how these motivational orientations interact with each other. Rank noted that there is a complex interplay between security and growth tendencies, such that they can at times pull a person in opposite directions. In childhood, authentic desires for stimulation and new experiences often conflict with what a child's security-providing parents demand. Hence, toddlers throw fits during the "terrible twos," and teenagers rebel against their parents as they seek to create their own adult identities. In adulthood, we often feel tension between competing desires to fit in with our group, which strengthens security, and to stand out and assert our unique self, which supports growth. Should you choose the safe, reliable job, car, and relationship partner? Or should you look for more exciting and challenging alternatives?

▲ Children's active and curious exploration of the world reflects a fundamental psychological motive for growth.

[Hill Street Studios/Blend Boost/AGE Fotostock]

Rank's analysis suggests two broad tendencies that have been highly supported by social psychological research over the past 60 years, much of which we will describe over the course of this book:

■ To sustain security-providing feelings of acceptance and self-worth, people are inclined to follow the crowd, obey authority, and accept the values held by their culture.

■ However, as part of their striving for growth, people exhibit a need for uniqueness, want to express their personal views and preferences, and assert their personal freedoms when they are threatened.

APPLICATION
An Example of the Hierarchy of Goals: Rita and Her Shoelaces

How do we turn our abstract goals into actions? To answer this question, we need to understand that any given activity can be thought of as serving many goals at the same time. Also, these goals fit into a sort of psychological hierarchy of abstraction (Carver & Scheier, 1981; Powers, 1973). This means that any goal can be understood as helping the person to achieve another goal that is more abstract—that is, higher up in the hierarchy. For example, think about a young woman who is tying her shoe; let's call her Rita. Why is Rita doing that? Well, one obvious possibility is that she just noticed that her shoe was untied, and she wanted to avoid tripping on the laces. So that's why Rita tied her shoe—and perhaps that's all there is to it (**FIGURE 2.4**).

But why is Rita concerned about tripping? Let's suppose that Rita tied her shoe in order to run faster in a 5K race that day. She wanted to win the race to get a college scholarship in order to have better job prospects than her immigrant

Figure 2.4

Rita

Goals and the actions of which they are composed can be represented hierarchically in terms of being more or less concrete or abstract. This figure shows how the act of tying a shoe can be connected to both coordinated muscle activity and to being remembered for societal contributions.

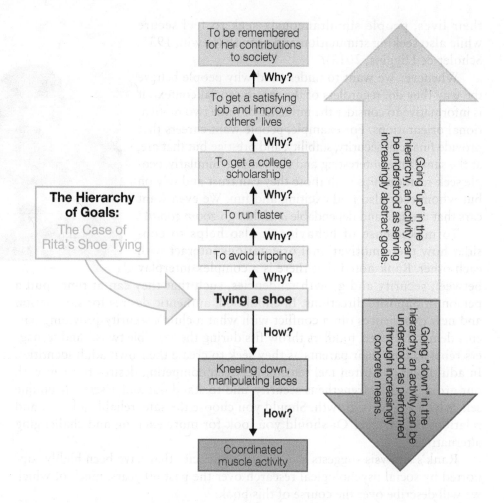

The Hierarchy of Goals:
The Case of Rita's Shoe Tying

To be remembered for her contributions to society

↑ **Why?**

To get a satisfying job and improve others' lives

↑ **Why?**

To get a college scholarship

↑ **Why?**

To run faster

↑ **Why?**

To avoid tripping

↑ **Why?**

Tying a shoe

↓ **How?**

Kneeling down, manipulating laces

↓ **How?**

Coordinated muscle activity

Going "up" in the hierarchy, an activity can be understood as serving increasingly abstract goals.

Going "down" in the hierarchy, an activity can be understood as performed through increasingly concrete means.

Hierarchy of goals The idea that goals are organized hierarchically from very abstract goals to very concrete goals, with the latter serving the former.

parents, who had to work right out of high school. And Rita wanted to attend college mainly so she could go into politics, in the hope of changing immigration laws, so people like her parents would have more productive and dignified lives. She even had hopes of becoming the first female president, winning a Nobel Peace Prize for her humanitarian efforts, and ultimately being remembered for hundreds or, better yet, thousands of years. So that's why Rita tied her shoe: to win the race to go to college on an athletic scholarship to initiate legislation to become president and win the Nobel Prize and make the world a better place and be remembered by others for a *very long time*! Of course, the details of this story don't matter. What is important is that each goal Rita pursues is a means to the end of achieving another, more abstract goal. And you can interpret any action—your own or others'—as situated in such a **hierarchy of goals.**

What is at the top of this hierarchy? What is Rita ultimately trying to do? There are many interesting answers to that question, and we encourage you to come up with your own. One useful answer, which comes from the existential perspective introduced in chapter 1, is that Rita is ultimately trying to maintain a sense of personal value, identity, and purpose that helps her to deal with unpleasant facts of life.

When we take the role of observers of human behavior, we can use the idea of a goal hierarchy to appreciate how a given action serves several goals at the same time. Rita's shoe-tying, for example, can be understood as getting her to the race on time *and* becoming a philanthropist. And when we are reflecting on our own actions, the hierarchy idea helps us to make sense of what we are doing, how successful we are, and why we're doing it (discussed in chapter 5).

Robin Vallacher and Dan Wegner's (1987) action identification theory suggests that the challenges people face in the moment also affect how they are likely to describe their actions. For example, you may describe your goal at this moment as getting your social psych reading assignment done rather than describing it more concretely as moving your eyes across the page or more abstractly as progressing toward a professional career. But when action bogs down because of challenges, people often shift to more concrete descriptions of their action. For example, if Rita fumbles with getting her shoe tied, her attention shifts down the goal hierarchy so that she can make the appropriate adjustments to her shoe-tying behavior rather than be distracted by grandiose visions of a Nobel Prize. ■

Humans Are Very Emotional Beings

A key component of the motivational system is emotion. Darwin (1872) asserted that emotions signal important changes in bodily states and environmental circumstances. Consequently, both the experience and, perhaps even more frequently, the anticipation of emotions play critical roles in motivating behavior (DeWall et al., 2016).

Positive emotions (such as happiness) reinforce one's own successful actions and the actions of others that benefit the self. They provide motivation and energy directed toward improving one's efforts to learn, achieve, help others, and grow (Fredrickson, 2001). At the very least, we want to sustain them, as when we have the aesthetic emotional experience of appreciating a particularly engaging work of art (Menninghaus et al., 2019). Negative emotions (such as fear) and the expectation of them motivate a person to avoid actions and others that could be harmful.

In addition, perceiving that the self has fallen short of an important goal or standard generates negative emotion, spurring the individual to engage in actions to alleviate that negative emotion. In these basic ways, emotions serve the important function of motivating action by kicking us into gear when something needs to be done to reach our goals and, ultimately, satisfy physical and psychological needs. Emotions are not just private experiences. By expressing them with our faces and bodies, we can better communicate how we feel with others. This can help us clarify our understanding of the world and organize collective action (Kraut & Johnston, 1979; Shariff & Tracy, 2011).

The Wide-Ranging Palette of Emotions   What emotions do humans experience? What triggers these emotions? Contemporary researchers generally distinguish several categories of emotions. For example, the neurologist Antonio Damasio (1999) proposed a three-part division of emotions—*background emotions*, *primary emotions*, and *secondary emotions*—all of which can occur at varying levels of consciousness, from complete unconsciousness to dim awareness to profound domination of our conscious experience.

Background Emotions: Background emotions make up an individual's general affective tone at a given moment. These background feelings are what we typically refer to when we say we are in a good mood or bad mood. Most people's resting state is generally with a *positive mood offset*—that is, a mild positive background mood even in the absence of specific emotional events (Diener et al., 2015).

Primary Emotions: Whereas mood tends to be a general feeling that is often not the focus of our attention, at other times we are acutely aware of feeling a specific emotion. Research suggests that there are six primary emotions: happiness, sadness, fear, anger, surprise, and disgust.

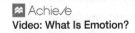
Achieve
Video: What Is Emotion?

Figure 2.5

Cultural Similarities in Emotional Expression

Evidence that people across diverse cultures recognize the same emotional expressions suggests that at least some emotions are universally experienced.

[Paul Ekman, Ph.D./Paul Ekman Group, LLC]

Cognitive appraisal theory The idea that our subjective experience of emotions is determined by a two-step process involving a **primary appraisal** of benefit or harm and a **secondary appraisal** that provides a more differentiated emotional experience.

There are three reasons to think that all humans are born with the capacity to experience these basic emotions. First, for people around the world, these emotions tend to be triggered by the same types of stimuli in physical and social environments (Lazarus, 1991; Mesquita & Frijda, 1992; Rozin & Fallon, 1987). For example, humans typically experience sadness when a loved one dies and disgust when confronted with a rotting animal carcass. Second, the experience of these emotions involves brain structures, such as the amygdala and the anterior cingulate cortex, that developed very early in human evolution (Ekman & Cordaro, 2011; Lindquist et al., 2012).

Third, these emotions are associated with distinctive facial expressions recognized easily by people the world over, even in groups geographically isolated from Western cultures (Ekman, 1980; Izard, 1977; **FIGURE 2.5**). This point is controversial, however. More recent research indicates that facial expression may universally convey information about affective feelings (pleasant or unpleasant), but (at least) adolescents in geographically isolated groups are not so good at identifying which emotions people from Western culture are experiencing based on their facial expressions alone (Crivelli et al., 2016; Gendron et al., 2018). Thus, our capacity to experience primary emotions is innate, though how we express and recognize those emotions is shaped by our culture. We'll explore the powerful effects of culture shortly.

Secondary Emotions: We often experience secondary emotions that are variations on the six primary emotions. For example, joy, ecstasy, and delight are variations of happiness; gloom, misery, and wistfulness are variations of sadness; panic, anxiety, and terror are variations of fear. Another group of secondary emotions includes the social emotions, which depend on even more recent brain structures, specifically the frontal lobes (see Figure 2.3). These include sympathy, embarrassment, shame, guilt, pride, jealousy, envy, gratitude, admiration, indignation, and contempt.

Social emotions regulate social behavior by drawing the person's attention to socially inappropriate behavior, reinforcing appropriate social behavior, and helping to repair disrupted social relationships. For example, feelings of guilt signal that one may have harmed a relationship, and the person may try to reduce that unpleasant social emotion by taking steps to make things right with that person (Tracy & Robins, 2004).

How Cognitions Influence Emotions Primary emotions involve rather general and diffuse activation of specific bodily systems, including specific brain regions, the autonomic nervous system, and facial muscles (Lazarus, 1991; Lazarus & Folkman, 1984; Mandler, 1984; Schachter & Singer, 1962). However, the various subtle shades of emotional experience depend on higher-level cognitive processes and interpretations (Greenaway et al., 2018). **Cognitive appraisal theory** (Lazarus, 1991) proposes that people's subjective experience of emotions is determined by a two-step process involving a very fast primary appraisal that is often followed by a more careful and thoughtful secondary appraisal (**FIGURE 2.6**). The **primary appraisal** often takes place before people are consciously aware of what happened in the outside world to produce it; it signals whether something good or bad is happening. This process involves evolutionarily older brain structures in the limbic system, particularly the thalamus, which responds to the environment with physiological arousal and an initial experience of emotion (LeDoux, 1996) (see Figure 2.3).

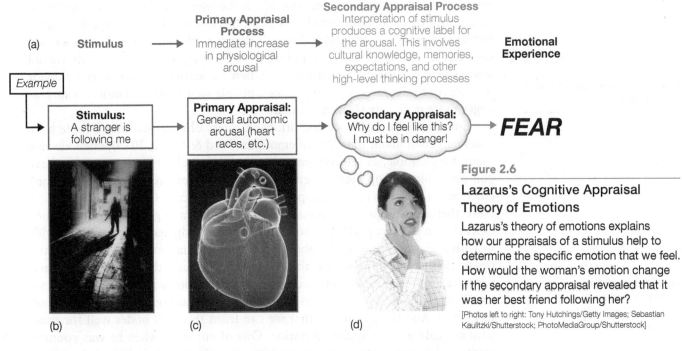

(a) Stimulus → **Primary Appraisal Process** Immediate increase in physiological arousal → **Secondary Appraisal Process** Interpretation of stimulus produces a cognitive label for the arousal. This involves cultural knowledge, memories, expectations, and other high-level thinking processes → **Emotional Experience**

Example

Stimulus: A stranger is following me → **Primary Appraisal:** General autonomic arousal (heart races, etc.) → **Secondary Appraisal:** Why do I feel like this? I must be in danger! → **FEAR**

(b)　　(c)　　(d)

Figure 2.6

Lazarus's Cognitive Appraisal Theory of Emotions

Lazarus's theory of emotions explains how our appraisals of a stimulus help to determine the specific emotion that we feel. How would the woman's emotion change if the secondary appraisal revealed that it was her best friend following her?

[Photos left to right: Tony Hutchings/Getty Images; Sebastian Kaulitzki/Shutterstock; PhotoMediaGroup/Shutterstock]

Once we experience arousal and an initial emotional response, we are likely to engage in a **secondary appraisal** to interpret what's happening. This secondary appraisal often leads to a refinement, a modification, or even a change in the nature of the emotion people experience. The rational processing system described earlier shapes secondary appraisals by bringing up memories, cultural influences, and thoughts of future ramifications. This deeper interpretation engages the prefrontal lobes, a part of the brain associated with consciousness and high-level cognitive functioning such as language (LeDoux, 1996). Indeed, language actually helps to construct our emotional experience. When a particular emotion word, say *anger*, is especially salient, people are more likely to experience that emotion compared to when they are no longer appreciating the meaning of the word (Lindquist et al., 2015).

One of our colleagues recently experienced this two-step appraisal process rather vividly. He walked into a dark room, the lights were suddenly turned on, and a host of people were screaming at him. The primary appraisal initially led to arousal and a mixed state of surprise and fear. When the secondary appraisal process sized up the situation, he recognized that the screaming people were his friends. It was a surprise birthday party, which resulted in an outburst of unmitigated joy. But if the secondary appraisal process instead led him to interpret the people as thieves robbing his home, fear and anger would have been the resulting emotions.

How Emotions Affect Cognition Just as cognition influences emotions, emotions also affect cognitions. When people are in a good mood—after watching a funny video, for example—they make more positive judgments about themselves, other people, and events; they make more optimistic predictions about the future; and they find it easier to recall positive memories. In contrast, bad moods lead people to view things more negatively, to recall negative memories, and to have more negative expectancies (Bower & Forgas, 2000; Isen, 1987).

In addition, people in a good mood rely on their preexisting knowledge in making judgments and don't analyze things too much. In contrast, people in

▲ Discovering that someone is in your apartment will elicit an immediate jolt of arousal, but the realization that it's a surprise party for your birthday will engage a secondary and more positive emotional response.

[MASSIVE/Stone/Getty Images]

negative moods think more intensely about themselves and their environment in an attempt to understand what they are experiencing. Presumably, this occurs because whereas a positive mood signals that everything is fine, a bad mood signals that something is not right and needs to be rectified. But bad moods are not always seen negatively. Sometimes, as when we learn that aggressive behavior can improve outcomes (e.g., in a game), people view negative emotions such as anger more positively (Netzer et al., 2015).

Emotions also influence cognitions in a less obvious manner. People have different beliefs about the value of emotions (Ford & Gross, 2019), often viewing them, for example, as impediments to rational thought. How many times have you been told to stop being so emotional and be "reasonable"? Indeed, strong emotions can at times makes it impossible to think logically (Zillmann et al., 1975). Nevertheless, emotions are necessary for rationality and good decision making, especially in matters pertaining to complex social judgments. Emotions provide us with important information about how a given situation affects our needs and desires. In fact, the more we are able to make fine-grained distinctions in the emotions we are experiencing, referred to as **emotion differentiation**, the better off we are (Kashdan et al., 2015). We can better regulate toward our goals and as a result feel better. And the possibility that we can learn this skill bodes well for those who struggle with such differentiation. One of our sons, when he was younger, responded to any negative experience with anger. This made it difficult for him to realize what he needed, and he sometimes pushed people away rather than leaning on them for support.

Achieve
Video: Paul Ekman on Mastering Your Emotions

Emotion differentiation The skills of recognizing fine-grained distinctions between different emotions.

SECTION REVIEW General Adaptations of the Cultural Animal

Over the course of evolution, human beings inherited four domain-general adaptations. Each is important for understanding human thought and behavior.

Humans are:

Social Beings	Very Intelligent Beings	Motivated, Goal-Striving Beings	Very Emotional Beings
• Our evolved mind/brain is oriented to seek connection and avoid exclusion. • People are sensitive to faces, social exclusion and rejection, group membership, and status hierarchies. These capacities help them to get along with one another. • People are profoundly shaped by socialization throughout their lives.	• Humans have unique capacities to imagine things that do not exist, think and communicate about the world using symbols and language, conceive of themselves and their experiences across time, and monitor and regulate their behavior in sophisticated ways. • People think using a combination of two systems: an experiential system (intuitive, nonconscious, automatic) and a controlled system (rational, conscious, effortful).	• Needs are necessary for survival; striving for goals is how people meet their needs. Both can influence behavior without awareness. • Hedonism is the motivation to approach pleasure and avoid pain. It is reflected in two fundamental human motivations: growth and security. • Humans can arrange goals in a hierarchy, from concrete to abstract, allowing flexibility in self-regulation and planning.	• Emotions help people self-regulate to achieve goals and to communicate internal states to other people. • Humans have background, primary, and secondary emotions. • The experience of emotions is influenced by an initial rapid physiological response, followed by a secondary appraisal of the situation. • Emotions and cognitions affect each other.

Culture: The Uniquely Human Adaptation

Culture and history and religion and science [are] different from anything else we know of in the universe. That is fact. It is as if all life evolved to a certain point, and then in ourselves turned at a right angle and simply exploded in a different direction.

—Julian Jaynes, *The Origin of Consciousness in the Breakdown of the Bicameral Mind* (1976, p. 9)

Our depiction of human beings up to this point is already fairly complex, but it is a one-dimensional depiction of three-dimensional beings. Every individual has three primary psychological dimensions: the *universal*, the *individual*, and the *cultural*. So far we have focused on the universal dimension—the evolved characteristics shared by all human beings. A second dimension of the person is the individual dimension: a person's personality, values, attitudes, and beliefs that result from that person's unique genetic makeup and life experiences and that help distinguish one from all others.

The third dimension is the cultural, which includes the aspects of a person that have been shaped by the particular culture in which that person was socialized and lives. To round out our psychological depiction of humankind, we now turn to a profoundly influential aspect of human life that makes us not just animals but uniquely *cultural animals*.

What Is Culture?

The scheme of things is a system of order. . . . It is self-evidently true, is accepted so naturally and automatically that one is not aware of an act of acceptance having taken place. It comes with one's mother's milk, is chanted in school, proclaimed from the White House, is insinuated by television, validated at Harvard. Like the air we breathe, the scheme of things disappears, becomes simply reality, the way things are.

—Allen Wheelis, *The Scheme of Things* (1980, p. 69)

Consider the present moment, right now, as you read this sentence. This is a moment of your conscious experience of life. It is a moment you will never experience again (perhaps thankfully). Now it's gone, and you are on to another fleeting moment. Your conscious life consists of a continual sequence of such moments, interspersed with sleep, until your death. But is that generally how you conceive of time? Probably not.

Instead, we think of time in terms of minutes, hours, days, years, and so forth. Perhaps right now it's 9:00 p.m. Well, there is another 9:00 p.m. each day. And perhaps it's Wednesday—there'll be another one next week, and maybe you make a plan to meet up with a friend by saying, "See you next Wednesday." This is our culture at work, giving people a convenient and comforting scaffolding for their stream of consciousness. Someone raised in a different culture might experience time in a distinctly different manner. People in India, for example, recognize elaborate cosmic cycles called *yugas*, which consist of 12,000-year *mahayugas*; there are 1,000 *mahayugas* in a *kalpa* and 14 *kalpas* in a *manvantara*, after which a new *yuga* is initiated (Eliade, 1959). Take away culture, and there is no "next Wednesday" or "next *kalpa*"— merely a sequence of lived moments. This is just one of many ways that culture determines how we think about aspects of our lives that we often take for granted.

THINK ABOUT ▶

Culture A set of beliefs, attitudes, values, norms, morals, customs, roles, statuses, symbols, and rituals shared by a self-identified group, a group whose members think of themselves *as* a group.

What sets humans apart from other animals is that they spend the bulk of their waking hours (and even some of their time sleeping) embedded in a world of ideas and values that gives life meaning, significance, purpose, and direction. Think about what really matters to you—the things you aspire to, dream about, and probably sometimes worry about. For some, it's making the grade in school; for others, it's that new car that would feel so incredibly cool to drive. Some are obsessed with music, movies, or the arts, whereas others are wrapped up with nightlife and the club scene. Maybe spiritual values and the fate of the soul capture your attention, or maybe you spend a lot of time thinking about how the goings-on in Washington and around the globe are affecting the future of the world. All of these uniquely human concerns are rooted in culture.

Culture is a set of beliefs, attitudes, values, norms, morals, customs, roles, statuses, symbols, and rituals shared by a self-identified group—a group whose members think of themselves *as* a group. Cultures are perpetuated when they are passed from generation to generation, yet they continually change in response to influences from the environment, the needs of their members, and contact with other cultures.

The Common yet Distinctive Elements of Culture All cultures have certain basic elements. The similarities among cultures are not surprising, given that, as we have noted, people everywhere have the same basic motivations, emotions, and cognitive capabilities and must contend with the same basic realities of life

---

 SOCIAL PSYCH OUT IN THE WORLD

Food for Body, Mind, and Soul

One of the ways that culture influences you in your everyday life is the food you eat. Think about what you have eaten so far today. How would the food you eat be different if you had grown up in Chicago, Berlin, Tokyo, Marrakech, or Chiang Mai? Not only do cultural adaptations dictate how we obtain sustenance, but all cultures have particular ways of preparing and serving foods that embody their unique identities as groups and help to define the social environment. Whether it's hot dogs in the United States, schnitzel in Germany, sushi in Japan, tagines in Morocco, or panang curry in Thailand— you get the idea, and we're getting hungry!—specific food preparations help define a culture. People in that culture are especially likely to eat those foods at times when they want to commemorate particular past events that serve to affirm their cultural identity. Just as most Americans eat turkey on Thanksgiving, other cultures also have specific dishes that are eaten on days of particular historical and symbolic importance. As a result, food is a delicious representation of a culture.

Cultures also specify ritualistic ways in which meals are to be consumed. This includes prayers ("Thank you, Lord, for this food we are about to share") and other utterances that precede meals ("Bon appétit!"), utensils that should be used

(forks, chopsticks, fingers), rules for exactly how the utensils should be held, and customs for the order in which different courses are served. If you have ever watched the late culinary explorer Anthony Bourdain on television, perhaps you've caught a glimpse of some of the food customs of far-flung places around the world.

The echoes of cultural adaptation on how we eat don't stop at the social environment; they extend to the metaphysical. The physical necessity of eating is transformed into an

▲ The late Anthony Bourdain built a reputation for hosting television programs that introduce viewers to the food and eating customs of far-flung cultures.
[Tannis Toohey/Getty Images]

on this planet. At the same time, different groups inhabit different physical environments and different cultural histories. As a result, each culture's version of the basic elements is unique. These differences make meeting and learning about people from other parts of the world interesting but are also sometimes confusing or disturbing. Let's briefly consider each of these elements and how they are similar and different across cultures:

■ *Beliefs* are accepted ideas about some aspect of reality. The idea that the earth revolves around the sun is a belief. Within a culture, many beliefs are virtually never disputed. These ideas are so unquestioned that they are often referred to as *cultural truisms*. Such beliefs create expectations that structure our experience and help us navigate through the world (Lin et al., 2019). Some beliefs seem self-evidently true to one culture but may be vigorously disputed or rejected outright in another. For example, in some cultures, belief in an afterlife is widely accepted, whereas in others, it is not.

Beliefs are generally taken on faith and based on learning from parents, teachers, and other cultural authorities rather than being derived through specific personal experience. After all, if we relied only on personal experience, all but a few scientists and astronauts would believe that the sun revolves around the earth, as the vast majority of people once did. That we hold these and thousands of other beliefs on *faith* is an example of how culture helps people in a group to create a shared sense of reality.

event of not just social significance (e.g., the business lunch) but also spiritual significance, whether it is the Jewish Seder, the wedding rehearsal dinner, or the Irish wake. Further, all cultures imbue life-sustaining food substances with spiritual power or group identity. In many cultures, certain foods are deemed sacred and others unclean. Whereas devout Jews and Muslims refuse to eat pork because it is viewed as unclean and insulting to their conception of God, Hindus avoid beef because cows are viewed as sacred and killing them as immoral. Many vegetarians and vegans eschew all animal meat and/or products because their belief that animals are intelligent makes it disgusting and immoral even to consider eating them (Ruby & Heine, 2012). Culture often infuses the very basic biological need for nutrition with sacred meaning.

Finally, because we associate food with different cultures, we can realize our desire to adapt to or affiliate with a culture by embracing the food customs we associate with that culture. So if you emigrated from China to the United States and you want to become acculturated quickly, you'll not only start learning the language and adopting the clothing styles, you also will start eating what seems like American food. The problem, from a health point of view, is that you might also begin gaining too much weight because American food is typically high in fat and sugar. In one clever study, when Asian American college students were told by an experimenter that they didn't look American, they were more likely to choose American food for their lunch. The meal they chose had 182 calories more than the meal chosen by Asian American participants whose identity as Americans was not called into question (Guendelman et al., 2011). People use the food they eat to signal to themselves and others their cultural identity.

▲ When we eat food, we express our cultural identity through the food choices we make.

[Hill Street Studios/Blend Images/Getty Images]

■ Members of a culture tend to share similar *attitudes*, which are preferences, likes and dislikes, and opinions about what is good and bad. Attitudes are closely linked to beliefs, but they refer more specifically to people's evaluations of something as good or bad. For example, a group of people may share the belief that abortion is legal in the United States, but their attitude toward the legalization of abortion could be favorable or unfavorable.

■ A culture's *values* reflect its members' guiding principles and shared goals. According to Shalom Schwartz and colleagues (e.g., Schwartz, 1992), all cultures tend to recognize the same 10 values—but to varying degrees (**TABLE 2.1**). These values can be viewed as stemming from the two basic motivational orientations mentioned earlier in this chapter: security and growth. The values *security*, *tradition*, *conformity*, *benevolence*, and *universalism* reflect a desire to sustain safety, order, harmony, meaning, connection, and approval. In contrast, the values *self-direction*, *stimulation*, *hedonism*, *achievement*, and *power* involve freedom, choice, excitement, enjoyment, accomplishment, and influence over others. Across more than 50 different cultures, there is remarkable agreement in the importance people give each of these value types. *Benevolence*, the desire to be a good person, ranked first; *self-direction*, the desire for personal freedom, and *universalism*, the desire for a just, meaningful, and peaceful world, were a close second and third. Presumably, the high level of consensus regarding these values

Table 2.1 Ten Cross-Cultural Values, Ranked by Importance

1. **Benevolence.** Preserving and enhancing the welfare of those with whom one is in frequent personal contact; being helpful, honest, forgiving, and responsible.

2. **Self-direction.** Independent thought and action; choosing one's own goals; the freedom to create and explore.

3. **Universalism.** Understanding, appreciation, tolerance, and protection of the welfare of all people and of nature. Advocating for justice, peace, and respect for other people and the environment.

4. **Security.** Safety, harmony, and stability of society, of relationships, and of self. Maintaining social order; establishing trust and reciprocation with others.

5. **Conformity.** Restraint of actions, inclinations, and impulses likely to upset or harm others and violate social expectations or norms. Obeying authorities; being polite. Self-discipline; honoring parents and elders.

6. **Achievement.** Personal success through demonstrating competence according to social standards. Being ambitious and feeling competent.

7. **Hedonism.** Pleasure and sensuous gratification for oneself. Enjoying life.

8. **Stimulation.** Excitement, novelty, and challenge in life.

9. **Tradition.** Respect, commitment, and acceptance of the customs and ideas that traditional culture or religion provide the self. Accepting one's role and observing cultural norms, customs, and rituals. Being devout and humble; accepting one's portion in life.

10. **Power.** Social status and prestige; control or dominance over people and resources. Seeking authority, wealth, and public esteem.

[Research from Schwartz & Bardi, 2001. © 2001 SAGE. Reprinted by permission.]

reflects their psychological importance in serving the basic motives of security and growth. Nevertheless, cross-cultural differences in values also play important roles in various aspects of life (Schwartz, 1992; Schwartz et al., 2014).

- *Norms* are shared beliefs about what is appropriate or expected behavior in particular situations. Every culture has situations that involve very clear, or *strong*, norms (Mischel, 1977), such as court proceedings in the United States. Yet there are also *weak situations*, such as hanging out with friends, where the norms are less clear.

- *Morals* are beliefs about what constitutes good and bad behavior. There are different perspectives on the most important types of morals. For example, there are differences between *community morals* (concerning relationships), *autonomy morals* (concerning individuals' rights and freedoms), and *divinity morals* (concerning what is sacred and pure) (Shweder et al., 1997). Moral foundations theory further distinguishes community morals reflecting ingroup loyalty and respect for authority from autonomy morals reflecting harm/care and fairness/reciprocity (e.g., Haidt & Kesebir, 2010). Other perspectives, such as the theory of dyadic morality, argue that all violations of morals fundamentally involve an individual (or group) harming another in some way (Schein et al., 2015).

Although there are different perspectives on the types of morals that are important, there are two points to emphasize here. First, people can experience different emotional reactions based on which morals they think are threatened. For example, violations of community morals usually evoke feelings of contempt; violations of autonomy morals evoke anger; and violations of divinity morals evoke disgust (Rozin, Lowery et al., 1999). Second, different cultures emphasize different moral domains (Graham et al., 2009). Moral judgments depend on many cultural factors, including religion (Cohen, 2015), political orientation (Davis et al., 2016; Haidt & Kesebir, 2010), and values. For example, a culture that places high value on conformity (e.g., China) is likely to emphasize community morals; a culture that values self-direction highly (e.g., the United States) is likely to emphasize autonomy morals; and a culture that highly values tradition (e.g., Yemen) is likely to emphasize divinity morals (Shweder et al., 1997). Each culture's laws and prescribed punishments are likely to reflect that culture's value-driven moral emphases.

- *Customs* are specific patterns or styles of dress, speech, and behavior that, within a given culture, are deemed appropriate in particular contexts (**FIGURE 2.7**). For example, in the United States, it is customary to clap after watching actors perform an enjoyable play. In Japan, it is customary to burp after an enjoyable meal. In Navajo culture, the first person who sees a baby smile, which typically doesn't

Achieve
Social Psych in Everyday Life: Haley

Figure 2.7

Ornamentation

All cultures share certain elements but put a distinctive mark on them. For example, people in virtually every culture use jewelry, tattooing, and other techniques to adorn their bodies and advertise their status. The particular style of ornamentation, however, differs greatly from culture to culture.

[Left to right: uniquely india/Getty Images; Angelo Giampiccolo/Shutterstock; WILL OLIVER/Getty Images; Frederick M. Brown/Getty Images]

happen until about six weeks after birth, is expected to throw a party to celebrate it. Perhaps not surprisingly, people are just as likely to try to avoid that honor as to try to be the lucky host. Customs are widely followed but not always happily.

■ All cultures have *social roles*, positions within a group that entail specific ways of acting and dividing labor, responsibility, and resources. The enactor of a role usually communicates that role through certain forms of conduct, appearance, and demeanor that are recognized by other group members. Some roles, such as those defined by gender, can inform the person's thoughts and actions across a wide range of situations. Other roles, such as orchestra conductor, dictate action in a particular situation.

■ *Cultural symbols* represent either the culture as a whole or beliefs or values prevalent in the culture. In cultures where members share a nationality, flags often symbolize the culture's meaning, history, and values (Callahan & Ledgerwood, 2016). Cultures defined around religious beliefs often create and recognize sacred symbols and artifacts, such as crucifixes and masks. Symbols are seen as embodiments of cherished beliefs, ideals, and other aspects of cultural identity.

■ Cultural symbols are central aspects of a culture's *rituals*, which are patterns of actions performed in particular contexts that reinforce cultural beliefs, values, and morals. A ritual may signal a change associated with the end or beginning of something of biological, historical, or cultural significance (e.g., birth, puberty, marriage, the founding of one's nation, annual holidays). Funerals, weddings, tea ceremonies, maturation-related ceremonies (e.g., confirmations, bar and bat mitzvahs, *quinceañeras*), birthday parties, and bridal showers are typical rituals. Another common ritual in universities and colleges is the commencement ceremony (**FIGURE 2.8**). Rituals serve a number of psychological functions, including helping to solidify social cohesion of the group (Watson-Jones & Legare, 2016). Think about the rituals that your culture values. Does standing during the national anthem come to mind? It certainly seems to be an important one to many in the United States. To appreciate the importance of this cultural ritual, consider the uproar that National Football League quarterback Colin Kaepernick unleashed in 2016 when he protested racial treatment by refusing to stand for the national anthem before games.

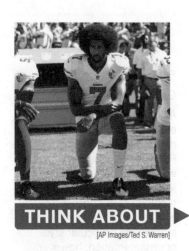

THINK ABOUT

Figure 2.8

Rituals

Universities and colleges around the world hold commencement ceremonies—rituals that mark the beginning of the graduates' entrance into the "real world." Like many other rituals, commencement ceremonies vary in distinctive ways from one institution to another. At the University of Kansas, for example, graduates walk through the doors of a large bell tower and down a big hill to the stadium, where the formal ceremony takes place. At the University of Hawaii at Manoa, graduates are ushered into the ceremony by selected male and female students, each carrying a *koʻo*, or ceremonial wand, that symbolizes complementary male and female energies.

Culture as Creative Adaptation

Culture provides a uniquely advantageous means for adapting to environmental change. Cultural innovations can accumulate far more rapidly than genetic mutations, and good ideas can spread horizontally across populations as well as vertically between generations. This strategy of cultural adaptation, more than anything else, has enabled our species to transform itself from a relatively insignificant large African mammal to the dominant life form on Earth.

—Richard Klein & Blake Edgar,
The Dawn of Human Culture (2002, p. 26)

Culture is a creative adaptation that a group develops to serve its needs and desires in its particular environment. According to the anthropologist Weston La Barre (1954), **cultural evolution** can occur quickly as a group develops new technologies and revises belief systems to provide flexible adaptation in meeting the demands of a changing environment. Cultures can change within a single generation and sometimes almost virtually overnight. Just think of how much music, fashion, politics, and social norms have changed in the very few years that you've been alive. It seems unimaginable, but when your parents were growing up, there was no Internet! How did people back then get information and music? How did they socialize?

Cultural evolution The process whereby cultures develop and propagate according to systems of belief or behavior that contribute to the success of a society.

Cultural Diffusion: Spreading the Word   The transfer of inventions, knowledge, and ideas from one culture to another—a process that the anthropologist Ralph Linton (1936) labeled **cultural diffusion**—is made possible by the human capacity for communication and learning, combined with the urge to explore and grow. This diffusion often occurs through friendly contact, business and trade, mass communication, and immigration, but it also commonly results from conquest and colonization. For example, many aspects of Roman culture were diffused throughout Europe as the Roman Empire spread its domination across Europe and beyond, often by means of extreme violence.

Cultural diffusion The transfer of inventions, knowledge, and ideas from one culture to another.

Through cultural diffusion, a culture can benefit from knowledge, skills, and inventions developed by other cultures to meet the adaptive challenges of the environment. For example, Europe's location and sea-travel-friendly coastlines allowed its evolving cultures to benefit extensively from cultural diffusion in terms of technological innovation and development (Diamond & Bellwood, 2003). Italians brought back pasta from China during the 13th century, and Portuguese missionaries who went to Sri Lanka in the 16th century brought back Buddhist religious texts.

An oft-overlooked consequence of cultural diffusion is that all but the most isolated of cultures are actually hybrid products of many cultures (Linton, 1936). To mention a few examples: Americans often think of horses and cows as prototypical symbols of the American West, but they were first domesticated in Southwest Asia. Windmills and wooden shoes, so closely associated with Holland, originally appeared in Persia (now Iran). The use of eggs to symbolize the Christian Easter celebration dates back to pagan fertility ceremonies as well as to Egyptian traditions 5,000 years ago. The general point is that much of what people consider central characteristics of their own culture are actually elements borrowed from other cultures and subsequently elaborated on (Rosenthal & Levy, 2013). Cultural diffusion can make evaluating the authenticity of a cultural product, be it pizza or windmills, quite challenging (Kreuzbauer & Keller, 2017). Thus, cultures are amazingly complex and useful adaptations, best viewed as cumulative

▲ Some contemporary cultural traditions, such as the Easter egg hunt, are rooted in cultural practices from different eras and countries, such as pagan and Egyptian rituals. This is just one colorful example of cultural diffusion.

[Left: Taurus/mauritius imagesAGE Fotostock; right: Spain, Painted ostrich eggs/DE AGOSTINI EDITORE/Bridgeman Images]

Cultural transmission The process whereby members of a culture learn explicitly or implicitly to imitate the beliefs and behaviors of others in that culture.

collaborative products of the ingenuity of the entire human species, and hence should be sources of pride for us all rather than only for members of particular groups.

Cultural Transmission   Cultural innovation and diffusion across generations requires a specific kind of social interaction between experienced teachers and youngsters open to learning through formal instruction or imitation. Although other animals, especially higher primates, learn a great deal by observing the behavior of others, human adults routinely engage in **cultural transmission**: explicit and implicit efforts to teach children knowledge and skills, largely with the help of language (Hobson, 2004). And human children, regardless of the extent of their formal schooling, spend a considerable proportion of their early years as beneficiaries of direct efforts to inculcate them into the cultural universe of their compatriots.

SECTION REVIEW   Culture: The Uniquely Human Adaptation

Culture is a set of psychological and social elements shared by members of a group and passed from generation to generation.

Elements of Culture

- All cultures have the same basic elements—beliefs, attitudes, values, norms, morals, customs, social roles, symbols, and rituals—but each culture's version of them is unique.

Cultural Evolution

- Culture enables people to flexibly and rapidly adapt their biological and psychological capacities to thrive in diverse and changing environments. This flexibility is made possible by the transmission of cultural elements among cultures and over generations within a culture.

Learning Outcomes

- Describe how culture influences the way people adapt to the physical, social, and metaphysical environment.

How Culture Helps Us Adapt

What does culture *do* for individuals and groups? One insightful answer comes from the social anthropologist W. Lloyd Warner (1959), who proposed that culture helps people adapt to three aspects of their environment:

■   The *physical environment*, through the development of skills and tools that help people meet their basic biological goals of survival and reproduction

- The *social environment*, through the development of social roles, relationships, and order
- The *metaphysical environment*, through the development of cultural world-views that provide answers to the big questions that have concerned humans throughout time: Who am I? Where did we come from? Why are we here? What makes for a good life? What happens to us after death?

Let's look more closely at each aspect.

Culture and the Natural Environment

Imagine what life would be like if you had to sleep outdoors and nourish and defend yourself with your bare hands, fortified by an occasional rock or stick! Our primate ancestors made do with this state of affairs for millions of years until the development of the first stone tools 2 million years ago, followed a few hundred thousand years later by hand axes, control of fire, and basic shelters. These momentous developments marked the earliest beginnings of our history as cultural animals. Survival became increasingly dependent on living in groups and learning how to do things that were first invented or discovered by others.

Living in groups had many advantages. As group size increased, so did the number of humans available to learn from and the resulting stock of shared knowledge. This promoted more rapid development, initially of tools and later of symbols, rituals, and other aspects of culture. These developments enhanced our capacity for symbolic thought and language, which made possible even more sophisticated cultural developments.

As mind and culture mutually built on each other, our species found ways of thriving in different natural environments (Sng et al., 2018). Groups living in areas with rich supplies of plants were especially likely to develop technologies for harvesting fruits and nuts; those in areas with large concentrations of animals developed effective means of hunting and trapping; those living near water developed techniques for fishing. In this way, the physical environment that groups inhabited shaped the sorts of technologies they developed.

⌾ APPLICATION
Cultural Ripples of Environmental Change

One implication of the interdependence between the natural environment and culture is that as the natural environment changes, so too does the culture that adapts to that environment. This is an especially pressing issue as the world increasingly faces consequences of global climate change. Adger and colleagues (2013) describe a few of the many cultural ripple effects that could result from changes to the natural environment. For example, as areas of the world that rely on raising livestock face more and more drought, this will change the traditions and social structure of herding cultures. Or for those of you who enjoy the thrill of downhill skiing, consider that the culture surrounding such activities will need to adjust as the snow cover at high altitudes continues to diminish. Signs of this retreat and cultural adjustment are already evident in North America, Europe, Australia, and Peru. ■

▲ Environmental changes spur cultural changes. Consider how climate change might impact cultures that rely on winter and snow oriented activities.
[Top: Bildagentur-online/Universal Images Group/Getty Images; bottom: Frank Bienewald/Getty Images]

- Explain why socioeconomic development may push a society toward greater individualism.
- Identify ways that people cope with the knowledge of their own mortality.

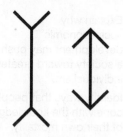

Figure 2.9

Müller-Lyer Illusion

Is one line longer than the other? Your ability to answer this question correctly depends on the culture in which you were raised.

Culture, Cognition, and Perception How a given culture adapts to its physical surroundings has a profound, and in some cases surprising, influence on people's basic perceptions and thought processes. For example, people from hunter-gatherer cultures are especially strong in visual and spatial abilities (Berry, 1966; Kleinfeld, 1971), presumably because they must be able to visually organize and recall the vast amounts of natural territory they explore. Consider the Inuit of Canada and Alaska: In order to hunt, they must navigate a white-dominated terrain by using only the subtlest of visual cues (Nelson, 1969). And the vocabulary of the Eskimo language reflects and reinforces these spatial abilities by including words that make very elaborate spatial and geometric distinctions (Berry, 1966).

Although spatial location is critical for survival in such cultures, the ability to quantify things precisely is less important. For example, although traditional Australian Aborigines do very well in spatial memory tasks, they do not do well in quantitative tasks. Indeed, when speaking their native language, traditional Aborigines generally refer to quantities greater than five simply as "many" (Dasen, 1994). In contrast, people from predominantly sedentary agricultural cultures, such as the Baoule of Côte d'Ivoire (the Ivory Coast) in West Africa, are not so skilled in visual–spatial tasks but are stronger in quantitative tasks (Dasen, 1994).

Culture affects not only the development of cognitive skills but also susceptibility to tricks of visual perception. Consider the well-known Müller-Lyer illusion, depicted in **FIGURE 2.9**. Does the line on the right with the closed-angle arrowhead ends look shorter to you than the line on the left with the open-angle ends? In fact, the lines are same the same length, as a ruler clearly shows.

Cross-cultural research has shown that the more a culture relies on the cultural innovation of carpentry (with extensive use of straight edges and right angles), the more its members fall prey to this illusion (Gregory, 1968; Segall et al., 1963; Stewart, 1973). Some cultural groups, like North Americans, live in physical environments containing many straight lines and right angles. This leads them to view the lines three-dimensionally, such that the right line looks like an "outside" corner protruding toward them, and the left line looks like an "inside" corner farther away. Other cultural groups, such as rural Zambians from the Zambezi Valley, inhabit environments that have less carpentered structures, and so they are rarely exposed to straight lines and sharp angles. Members of these cultures tend to view the lines as two-dimensional patterns, not three-dimensional spaces, so they don't have the illusion that the lines are different in length.

Consider this exchange:

A: "Can you *spare* an hour today? I thought we could *put aside* some time for coffee."

B: "Sorry but I didn't *budget* my time well. I *spent* 45 minutes at the pet store; I thought it would be *worth it*, but it *cost* me the afternoon."

These common expressions reflect a metaphor that treats time as money—that is, as a quantifiable resource that can be wasted, saved, borrowed, spent, given, and invested. As obvious as it may seem, this metaphor is not as prominent in other languages as it is in American English (Kövecses, 2005). Why does English have a more full-blown version of this metaphor? Some theorists say it's because English-speaking cultures are obsessed with money (Hall, 1984; Lakoff & Johnson, 1980). This suggests that some cultural practices—like its economy—can percolate up by means of metaphor to shape how people perceive something as basic as time.

Culture and the Social Environment

All groups of people, if they are to prosper, have to get along with each other, cooperate to achieve mutual goals, and minimize disruptive conflicts within the group. As societies grew in size from small bands of 100 or so people to thousands of people living in close proximity, challenges in social organization arose, as did different solutions. Indeed, some scholars suggest that these complexities of group living put a premium on religious conceptions of God that helped people to coordinate increasingly intricate social affairs (Laurin, 2017).

The Uncertainties of Group Living   One problem people in all cultures face lies in knowing what they *should* do and what they are *allowed* to do. In most modern societies, people interact with strangers on a daily basis. Because they cannot always be sure that the strangers view the world exactly as they do, they may be uncertain about what they should do in a situation, where they fit in, and how they should treat others. Consider your own awkward moments of wondering, for example, if you should call your friend's mom by her first name.

Michael Hogg's (2007) *uncertainty-identity theory* explains how, to reduce this uncertainty, people identify with culturally defined groups that have clear guidelines for behavior. For example, your current author is a member of a culturally defined group of professors, and this group gives him a certain role to play. That role entails how he should act and also how other groups (e.g., students) should act toward him. Supporting this theory are studies showing that when people are led to feel uncertain about who they are, they are more likely to identify with their cultural group, especially if that group has a clear sense of boundaries, expectations, and cohesion (Hogg et al., 2007; chapter 9).

How Individuals Relate to Each Other: Individualism/Collectivism   A second problem that people in all cultures face is figuring out how to orient themselves toward their relationships—that is, how to think about the relationship between self and other. Through study of cultures around the world, Alan Fiske (1990) proposed that there are four basic patterns of social relations:

1. *Community sharing*, in which cooperation and self-sacrifice are prevalent and, as in a family, "What's mine is yours"
2. *Authority ranking*, in which one person gives orders and the other follows him or her, like a sergeant and a private in the army
3. *Equality matching*, in which everyone is treated equally and has the same rights, as is typical in friendship
4. *Market pricing*, in which relationships follow economic principles, as is typical in business relationships

All four of these relationship patterns can be found in every known culture, but their prevalence varies considerably across cultures. The cross-cultural psychologist Harry Triandis (1994) noted that more traditional, ethnically homogenous cultures stress community sharing and authority ranking, and they can be characterized as collectivistic. In **collectivistic cultures**, the emphasis is on interdependence, cooperation, and the welfare of the group over that of the individual. People in such cultures—for example, Korea, Japan, and Pakistan—are expected to fit in with the group, obey authority figures, be part of the whole, and be especially sensitive to how their actions affect others within the group.

More ethnically heterogeneous cultures—such as the United States, Canada, Australia, and Germany—emphasize equality matching and market pricing and

Collectivistic culture A culture in which the emphasis is on interdependence, cooperation, and the welfare of the group over that of the individual.

Table 2.2 Characteristics of Individualism and Collectivism

High levels of collectivism in a culture are associated with . . .	High levels of individualism in a culture are associated with . . .
valuing group membership.	valuing independence, uniqueness, and autonomy.
valuing group harmony, even if it means silencing one's personal views.	general encouragement to express one's personal views, even at the cost of disrupting social harmony.
tolerance for inconsistencies in descriptions of the self across different role contexts.	preference for consistency of the self across different role contexts.
fostering of an *interdependent self-construal* that defines the self in relation to others versus evaluating the self in comparison to others.	fostering of an *independent self-construal* that defines and evaluates the self as distinct from others.
a clear distinction between ingroup and outgroup, coupled with a marked preference for the ingroup over the outgroup.	a tendency to regard others as individuals, not as members of groups, and to treat people the same regardless of group membership.
cognition that tends toward a holistic style that looks for relations between parts; sensitivity to connection and context.	cognition that tends toward an analytic style that looks for parts of the whole; sensitivity to separation and contrast.

[Here are a few of the many excellent papers on the extensive implications of this cultural difference: Cross et al., 2010; Gardner et al., 2004; Markus & Kitayama, 1991; Morelli & Rothbaum, 2007; Shweder et al., 1997; Singelis et al., 1995; Suh, 2002.]

Individualistic culture A culture in which the emphasis is on individual initiative, achievement, and creativity over maintenance of social cohesion.

are referred to as individualistic. In **individualistic cultures**, individual initiative, achievement, and creativity are highly encouraged, and people look primarily after their own interests and those of their immediate families. **TABLE 2.2** lists the primary distinguishing characteristics of collectivistic and individualistic cultures.

You'll see in that table that individualism and collectivism reflect core human values. All cultures encourage some collectivistic and some individualistic tendencies. Thus, it would be inaccurate to portray members of cultures such as Japan and China, or the United States and Great Britain, as either mindless automatons expressing only the collective will of the group or self-absorbed nonconformists with no concern for their relationships and groups. Nevertheless, the broad distinction between individualistic and collectivistic cultures does help account for a variety of interesting psychological differences among typical members of the two types of cultures.

Interdependent self-construal Viewing self primarily in terms of how one relates to others and contributes to the greater whole.

Independent self-construal Viewing self as a unique active agent serving one's own goals.

The Nature of the Self Hazel Markus and Shinobu Kitayama (1991) point out that in collectivist cultures, people tend to have a more **interdependent self-construal.** They view themselves primarily in terms of how they relate to others and contribute to the greater whole. When these researchers asked people to complete the sentence "I am . . . ," those raised in collectivistic cultures tended to fill in the blank with responses indicating their social relationships (e.g., a daughter) and group identifications (e.g., Malaysian). In contrast, people inhabiting individualistic cultures exhibit a more **independent self-construal.** They view themselves as unique individuals who should stand out from the crowd and "do their own thing." Thus, when asked to complete the sentence "I am . . . ," they tended to fill in personal traits (e.g., honest) and feelings (e.g., happy).

Fitting In and Sticking Out   In collectivistic cultures, behaving in a manner that fits expectations and sustains social harmony is more important than expressing one's personal attitudes or preferences or outperforming others. It is not that members of collectivistic cultures don't have personal opinions; they just don't view them as more important than adhering to norms of appropriate behavior. The sense of social obligation—to fulfill one's duty—is much more closely aligned with a sense of choice and agency (Buchtel et al., 2018). In individualistic cultures, in contrast, people strongly value freedom of speech and are generally encouraged to express their personal views, even if they cause debate or dissension (Gardner et al., 1999; Triandis, 1994). Perhaps for these reasons, whereas those from Eastern cultures generally prefer to be small frogs in big ponds (i.e., be less individually successful in a more prestigious group), those from Western cultures often prefer to be big frogs in small ponds (Wu et al., 2018). Also, members of collectivistic cultures strongly dislike people who violate group norms because the cultural ideal is to live up to one's social role and maintain group harmony. But in individualistic cultures, where the cultural ideal is to express one's uniqueness and act freely, people who break the rules can seem powerful (Stamkou et al., 2019).

▲ In Western culture, rock bands and other such artists that break with convention and flaunt more uninhibited self-expression are often celebrated and widely popular, reflecting the more individualistic orientation of their culture.
[Gonzales Photo/Alamy]

Emotion   Individualistic and collectivistic cultures also differ in the way members experience and display their emotions (Tsai & Lu, 2018). The collectivistic emphasis on harmony prioritizes social cohesion over the freedom to broadcast one's emotional reactions. In one study, American and Japanese students viewed a graphic film of a circumcision ritual (Ekman et al., 1972). When viewing it alone, they displayed the same negative facial expressions. However, the Japanese participants inhibited such negative expressions when viewing the film in the presence of an experimenter, suggesting that individuals raised in collectivistic cultures feel less comfortable displaying their emotional reactions.

Such cultural differences in emotional norms and displays have important implications, particularly when people from different cultures interact. For example, in medical contexts, differences in cultural norms for emotion might lead American doctors to view Asian patients as less excited about, and thus receptive to, medical treatment (Tsai, 2007). As a result, the doctors may treat the Asian patients differently, not recommending some treatments as strongly as they do for American patients.

Modernization and Cultural Values   The spectrum between individualism and collectivism is one general way to characterize a culture's norms and values. It helps us to understand how that value profile influences social relationships and provides social order. An important factor in how cultures evolve to meet these needs is modernization. Over the past 500 years, there has been a general trend toward increased *socioeconomic development*; industrial, technological, and economic advancements; and *democratization*. How might these changes have influenced the values that people hold?

Overall, such trends may lead to a rise in individualistic values (Santos et al., 2017). We live in increasingly diverse societies because social policies allow for immigration, and technology makes it easier to travel far from home while still maintaining connections with family. Triandis (1989) proposed that as cultures become more heterogeneous, they tend to become more individualistic and less collectivistic. An analysis of pronoun use in American books published between 1960 and 2008 revealed a 10% decrease in the use of words such as "we" and "us" alongside a 42% increase in "I" and "me" (Twenge et al., 2013). Even the already individualistic United States might be becoming even more individualistic over time.

This rise in individualism might also result from people's increasing mobility. Shigehiro Oishi and colleagues (2009) find that as people move around from place to place, forgoing their roots in a single, long-standing community to increase their personal opportunities in a new place, they adopt more individualistic values. Those who have moved around a lot see their social group memberships as being less central to how they view themselves and feel less obligated to their friends (Oishi, 2010). They are even more likely to be fair-weather fans of their local baseball team, only attending games when the team is winning (Oishi & Kisling, 2009).

▲ In cities that have a low proportion of lifelong residents, such as Miami, fans are less likely to remain loyal when their team is having a losing season. The Miami Marlins, for example, have seen considerable variability in attendance at their games over the years.

[J Pat Carter/AP Images]

As societies become more mobile, they become increasingly diverse and tend to value their diversity as well as other progressive belief systems. A study of 42 countries from 1988 to 1994 found that as cultures modernized or embraced democracy, they increasingly prioritized new ideas, individual initiative, personal worth, equality, and status judgments based on achievement rather than on tradition (Schwartz & Sagie, 2000). As socioeconomic development increased, so did the importance of the values of self-direction, stimulation, and hedonism. In fact, socioeconomic development is one of the best predictors of cultural movement toward individualism. As socioeconomic development has increased in the United States over the past 150 years, so too have different indicators of individualism, such as the uniqueness of baby names, divorce rates, uniqueness themes in books, smaller family size, and solitary living (Grossman & Varnum, 2015).

Culture and the Metaphysical Environment

Happy the hare at morning, for she cannot read
The hunter's waking thoughts, lucky the leaf
Unable to predict the fall, lucky indeed
The rampant suffering suffocating jelly
Burgeoning in pools, lapping the grits of the desert.
But what shall man do, who can whistle tunes by heart,
Knows to the bar when death shall cut him short like the cry of the shearwater,
What can he do but defend himself from his knowledge?

—W. H. Auden, "The Cultural Presupposition," in
Collected Shorter Poems (1950)

In addition to helping people adapt to their physical and social environments, culture helps them adapt to their metaphysical environment, by which we mean gain an understanding of the nature of reality and the significance of our lives within the cosmic order of things. But why are people the world over preoccupied with understanding their place in the metaphysical environment? To answer this question, we have to recognize that humans' sophisticated intellectual abilities are a mixed blessing. On the one hand, our ability to think symbolically about time and space is tremendously adaptive; as we've seen in this chapter, it allows us to imagine possibilities and communicate with each other in complex ways. But this intelligence has some problematic consequences. According to the cultural anthropologist Ernest Becker, writing in books such as *The Birth and Death of Meaning* (1971) and *The Denial of Death* (1973), the most chilling result of our species' vast intelligence is the awareness that the only truly certain thing about life is that it will end someday. We know that death is inevitable and inescapable and that it could come at any moment from any number of causes. Awareness of the fragility of life and the inevitability of death in an animal that seeks survival creates the potential for paralyzing terror. Becker proposed that such terror simply would be too much for a self-conscious animal to bear, leaving us quivering piles of biological protoplasm quaking in fear and unable to act effectively unless we do something to manage this potential terror.

In the mid-1980s, Sheldon Solomon, Tom Pyszczynski, and Jeff Greenberg synthesized Becker's ideas into **terror management theory,** or TMT (Greenberg et al., 1986; Solomon et al., 2015). Terror management theory proposes that humans have fashioned a partial solution to this existential dread, using the same cognitive abilities that made them aware of mortality to manage this terror. As our hominid ancestors' cognitive capacities increased, they began to wonder how the world works and how to do the things necessary to survive; eventually, they began to ask more difficult questions about where they came from, what happened when they died, and what life is all about. In order to feel secure in a threatening world, each cultural group has created answers to these questions. We call these answers **cultural worldviews**—human-constructed symbolic conceptions of reality. The more effective a cultural worldview was at helping individuals manage their mortality fears, the more likely it was to be accepted and transmitted among members of that culture and from one generation to the next.

In this way, cultural worldviews emerged to give life meaning, order, value, and promises that life will continue in some manner beyond the point of physical death. To specify, all cultural worldviews consist of:

1. A theory of reality that provides answers to basic questions about life, death, the cosmos, and one's place in it
2. Institutions, symbols, and rituals that reinforce components of that worldview
3. A set of standards of value that prescribe what is good and bad and what it means to be a good human being
4. The promise of actual or symbolic immortality to those who believe in the worldview and live up to the standards of value that are part of it

By imposing meaning on the subjective experience of reality and creating a sense of enduring significance for the self, cultural worldviews help people maintain the belief that they are more than transient animals in a purposeless universe. A person can view him- or herself as a unique person with a rich history, family heritage, group memberships, and social roles that give life value.

Terror management theory A theory which says that to minimize fear of mortality, humans strive to sustain faith that they are enduringly valued contributors to a meaningful world and therefore transcend their physical death.

Cultural worldview Human-constructed shared symbolic conceptions of reality that imbue life with meaning, order, and permanence.

Achieve
Video: Flight from Death: The Quest for Immortality

We identify as students, professors, doctors, lawyers; as Malaysians, Guatemalans, Americans, Italians; as members of the Communist Party or the local bowling club. We cling to these cultural worldviews every day to feel secure in the world. Rarely do we stop to realize that the cultural worldview is ultimately of our own collective creation!

Although all cultural worldviews address basic existential concerns, they vary considerably in the specific beliefs and values they employ. In the following sections, we will consider both the similarities and the differences among cultures in the aspects of their worldviews central to terror management: creation stories, cultural institutions, symbols and rituals, bases of self-worth, and modes of striving for immortality.

Creation Stories   Where did we come from? How did life begin? How do we humans fit into the grand scheme of things?

- In Mali in West Africa, the Fulani (**FIGURE 2.10a**) believe the world was created from a giant drop of milk, from which the god Doonari emerged and created stone. The stone created iron, iron created fire, fire created water, and water created air.
- The Aztecs' world was initiated when Coatlicue (**FIGURE 2.10b**), the Lady of the Skirt of Snakes, was created in the image of the unknown. She was impregnated by an obsidian knife and gave birth to female and male offspring who became the moon and the stars.
- In the Judeo-Christian tradition that has dominated much of the Western world for the past three millennia, God created the universe in six days and rested on the seventh. Shortly thereafter, he made Adam, the first man (**FIGURE 2.10c**). Because Adam was lonely, God took a rib from his body while he was sleeping to create the first woman, Eve, who became his companion. Eve was tempted by a serpent and convinced Adam to disobey God's command. After eating the forbidden fruit of the Tree of Knowledge, Adam and Eve were expelled from the idyllic Garden of Eden and became mortal.

These examples were gleaned from David and Margaret Leeming's (1994) *A Dictionary of Creation Myths*. The Leemings acknowledge the tremendous variation in the details but note the common themes:

> The basic creation story, then, is that of the process by which chaos becomes cosmos, no-thing becomes some-thing. In a real sense this is the only story we have to tell....
> It lies behind our attempts to "make something" of our lives, that is, to make a difference. (p. viii)

Figure 2.10

Creation Stories

All cultures have stories about the creation of the world and the people in it: (a) members of the Fulani tribe from West Africa; (b) figurine of Coatlicue, the Aztec goddess; (c) *The Expulsion from Paradise*, 1740, painting depicting the Judeo-Christian God with Adam and Eve.

[Left to right: AfriPics.com/Alamy; DEA/ G. DAGLI ORTI/Getty Images; © The Metropolitan Museum of Art/Art Resource, NY]

(a)

(b)

(c)

Perhaps it has occurred to you that the big bang theory of the origin of the universe and the theory of evolution by natural selection are contemporary examples of creation stories.

Institutions, Symbols, and Rituals: Worldview Transmission and Maintenance Cultural worldviews must be transmitted from generation to generation and must be continually reinforced so people can sustain faith in them and avoid the realization that they are essentially fictional accounts of reality. Such faith is nurtured by myriad sources, from the teachings of churches, mosques, and synagogues that convey the religious aspects of worldviews, to the holidays and rituals that celebrate culturally significant events and values, such as Independence Day, Cinco de Mayo, and Eid al Fitr (the end of Ramadan), to the educational systems. For example, in the United States, the elaborate public education system teaches children the history of the United States in terms of names, events, and dates. Similar names, events, and dates might be taught in another culture, but the tone of those lessons might be quite different, conveying that particular culture's current view of those historical people and events. For example, whereas Americans view the December 7, 1941, attack on Pearl Harbor as an unjustified, egregious sneak attack, the Japanese view it quite differently. In the context of their worldview, the United States had acted aggressively toward Japan by imposing an embargo that threatened its national security. The embargo blocked Japan's access to the South Pacific's oil and natural resources, which were critical to the survival of the Japanese way of life.

Bases of Self-Worth: Standards, Values, Social Roles, and Self-Esteem Beyond providing and maintaining a meaningful explanation of reality, all cultures give their members standards of value, specifying which personal characteristics and behaviors are good and which are bad. Living up to these cultural standards of value provides a sense of **self-esteem**, which refers to the person's evaluation of his or her self-worth. People with high levels of self-esteem view themselves as valuable members of a meaningful universe and thus have a protective shield against the potential for terror inherent in the human condition. Self-esteem is thus one of the most basic psychological mechanisms by which culture fulfills its anxiety-managing function (Pyszczynski et al., 2004).

Self-esteem A person's evaluation of his or her value or self-worth.

All cultures provide a wide range of benefits to those who meet or exceed the cultural standards of value—for example, money, better health care, awards and prizes, and good mating prospects. These benefits contribute to individuals' hope that they will continue, in some way, beyond physical death. Reinforcing the connection between goodness and good outcomes, all cultural worldviews convey that good things will happen to the worthy and bad things will happen to the unworthy. Melvin Lerner labeled these ideas **just world beliefs** and, with colleagues, has shown that people are highly motivated to maintain faith in such beliefs (e.g., Lerner & Simmons, 1966). For example, people look for ways to believe that victims of misfortune must have done something to deserve their fates (Hafer & Bègue, 2005).

Just world beliefs The idea that good things will happen to the worthy and bad things will happen to the unworthy.

Although the need for self-esteem is universal, the standards that one must meet to attain self-esteem are specified by one's cultural worldview (Sedikides et al., 2003). In a traditional tribal culture, one person might acquire self-worth as a shaman, another as a warrior, another as a skilled pot maker. For example, according to the anthropologist Walter Goldschmidt (1990):

- Tlingit Indians are valued in proportion to how many blankets and other objects they have accumulated and then either given away or destroyed.

▲ Status symbols: Standards for self-esteem vary across and within cultures. Some American men base their self-esteem on the ability to afford a sweet ride and a nice house.

[Digital Vision/Photodisc/Getty Images]

Literal immortality A culturally shared belief that there is some form of life after death for those who are worthy.

Symbolic immortality A culturally shared belief that, by being part of something greater and more enduring than our individual selves, some part of us will live on after we die.

Contrast that with:

- American men are highly valued if they can hit a spherical object with a wooden stick effectively 3 out of every 10 times that such an object is hurled at them.

Standards for obtaining self-esteem also vary considerably for individuals within each culture, depending on family, gender, and age. In the United States, a small waistline and making the school volleyball team might garner self-esteem for a teenage girl, whereas a middle-aged male might base his self-worth on his ability to afford a Mercedes and a large house in the suburbs.

Striving for Immortality   For those who reach the cultural standards and attain that sense of value, cultural worldviews also provide the prospect of either literal or symbolic immortality. **Literal immortality** is afforded by aspects of the cultural worldview that reassure a person that physical death is not the end of life and promise some form of life after death to those who are worthy. **Symbolic immortality** is the sense that, by being part of something greater and more enduring than one's individual self, some part of the self will live on after the body dies.

Even a passing glance at past and current cultures the world over reveals that the hope of literal immortality has been central to most cultures and organized religions. Archaeological excavations reveal that elaborate ritual burials begin abruptly and appear regularly with the emergence of modern humans, suggesting that concerns about death have been with us from the earliest days of our species (Mithen, 1996; Tattersall, 1998). Indeed, the oldest-known written story—the Sumerian *Epic of Gilgamesh*—concerns the protagonist's fear of the prospect of his own death and his quest to obtain immortality. This quest was also central to ancient Egyptian, Chinese, and Greek cultures.

Virtually all major contemporary religions promise some form of afterlife. Recent surveys suggest that most people around the world believe in some form of afterlife: 51% say yes, 26% say probably but not certain, 23% say no. Confidence in the afterlife is even higher in the United States and Canada: About 69% say absolutely yes, and only 11% say that you simply cease to exist after death (Ipsos/Reuters, 2011; Todd, 2011).

Consider different cultures' contemporary conceptions of the afterlife (Panati, 1996). Many Jews believe that the righteous are resurrected in *Olam Ha-Ba*, the World to Come. Christians believe that everyone has the gift of eternal life. The body dies, but the soul lives forever. Heaven is also central to Muslim conceptions of the hereafter. Hindus believe there is an eternal, changeless core of the self, the *atman*, entrapped in the world of *samsara*, an endless cycle of death and rebirth. For traditional Australian Aborigines, death marks only the end of the physical life, and the spirit is released to rejoin the spirits of ancestors and become a part of the land itself. In sum, a central component of cultural worldviews in almost all times and places has been the prospect of physical immortality.

In addition to the prospect of literal immortality, cultures offer routes to symbolic immortality. In symbolic immortality, humans transcend death by being part of, or by contributing something to, an entity greater than the self that will continue after physical death. The psychohistorian Robert Jay Lifton (1979) proposed that cultures provide (in varying degrees) different modes of symbolic immortality. For example, with *biosocial immortality*, people live on through their children (and their children's children and so on in perpetuity) and identify with larger collectives such as nations that are presumed to continue indefinitely. *Creative immortality* results from contributions to one's culture, such as heroic acts or noteworthy leadership or highly regarded scientific and artistic accomplishments. *Natural immortality* results from strongly identifying with nature and the coincident recognition that an eternal part of one's self will persist over time. Finally, *experiential immortality* results from "peak experiences," described by Abraham Maslow (1964) as quasi-mystical experiences that fill the individual with a timeless (no time = no death!) sense of wonder and awe. Experiential transcendence is often aided by altered states of consciousness and found in combination with one of the other modes of transcendence, such as a grandpa down on the floor playing with a grandchild, a musician lost in her performance, or a hiker communing with nature at the summit of Pike's Peak.

▲ According to Abraham Maslow, peak experiences can allow us to transcend our mortal selves.

[Jose Luis Pelaez Inc/Getty Images]

Extensive lines of research have examined how cultural conceptions of immortality help people adapt to the metaphysical world generally and with their awareness of death specifically. Some studies show that reminders of mortality—such as a major trauma or even an incidental reminder—motivate people to cling to their religious beliefs (Mercier et al., 2018; Trainor et al., 2019; Vail et al., 2010). For example, Pelham and colleagues (2018) documented that, across 16 different countries, when people searched Google about life-threatening diseases, they later searched for information about God and religion. Other studies show that when people have a strong belief that immortality is possible, they are less afraid of death and suffer less anxiety in their everyday life (Florian & Mikulincer, 1998).

The Essential Role of Social Validation   TMT proposes that people protect themselves from the uniquely human fear of death by immersing themselves in the world of symbols and ideas provided by their culture. This might seem a rather flimsy defense against the biological reality of death. In a sense, it *is* flimsy. But people work very hard to sustain unwavering faith in the absolute validity of their cultural worldview and their sense of self-worth within it to defend against that reality.

Confidence in the absolute correctness of our own beliefs and values, and of our own value, is bolstered primarily through *social consensus* and *social validation*. The idea that people rely on others to help them verify the validity of their own perceptions and beliefs has a long history in social psychology that we briefly touched on in chapter 1. According to Festinger's *social comparison theory* (1954), people constantly compare themselves, their performance, and their attitudes with those of others around them. Other people sharing the same beliefs or values bolsters the idea that those beliefs and values are correct.

Significant others are an important source of belief verification. By having similar beliefs and worldviews, significant others help to create a shared reality. In fact, this desire for a shared reality is so potent that when we meet new people who resemble significant others in our life in some way, this new acquaintance

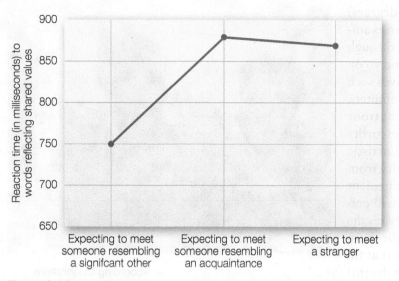

can lead us to implicitly think about the worldview that we share with those they resemble. Przybylinski and Andersen (2015) studied this type of scenario. As shown in **FIGURE 2.11**, when participants expected to meet someone who resembled a significant other with whom they shared a particular worldview (e.g., protecting the environment), this worldview became more accessible than if they expected to meet a non-significant other or did not know who they would meet. Thus, other people play a vital role in helping us to sustain faith in our worldviews.

Figure 2.11

Significant Others and Shared Worldviews

We share systems of meaning with significant others in our life. In this study, expecting to meet a new person who resembled the participant's significant other activated the worldview the participant shared with their significant other.

[Data from Przybylinksi & Andersen, 2015]

The flipside of this is that when other people hold different beliefs and values, it raises the possibility that someone is mistaken. When cultures collide, worldviews are threatened.

The Threat of Other Cultures: A Root Cause of Prejudice   TMT has generated research into a variety of topics we will explore throughout this book, such as self-esteem, leadership, and relationships (Routledge & Vess, 2018). Here we will focus on the cultural worldview-related research. As we have seen, cultures vary greatly in their beliefs about human origins, bases of self-esteem, and beliefs about spirituality and transcending death. Therefore, learning about another culture, especially one with very different versions of these beliefs, suggests that perhaps our views, even though socially validated within our culture, may not be absolutely true. People must therefore minimize the threat to their cultural worldview posed by alternative cultural worldviews. From a TMT perspective, the efforts to do so play a central role in prejudice and intergroup conflict. This idea was a primary focus of early research to test hypotheses derived from TMT.

One basic hypothesis was: *If cultural worldviews function to alleviate anxiety associated with the awareness of death, then reminding people of their mortality* (**mortality salience**) *should increase their need for the protection provided by such beliefs.* The strategy for testing this hypothesis was to get people to think about their own death and then make judgments about others who either violate or uphold important aspects of their cultural worldviews. If cultural worldviews protect the person from concerns about mortality, thinking about death should make people especially prone to derogate those who violate important cultural ideals and to venerate those who uphold them, a general tendency called **worldview defense.**

Mortality salience The state of being reminded of one's mortality.

Worldview defense The tendency to derogate those who violate important cultural ideals and to venerate those who uphold them.

Defending the Worldview   In the initial test of the mortality salience hypothesis (Rosenblatt et al., 1989), municipal court judges were told that they were participating in a study examining the relationship among personality traits, attitudes, and bond decisions. (A bond is a sum of money that a defendant must pay after arrest to be released from prison prior to the trial date.) Embedded in the questionnaire packets for half of the judges, who were chosen by random assignment, were questions that asked them to think briefly about their mortality. The other judges were the control group and did not receive this questionnaire.

All of the judges were then presented with a hypothetical legal case brief that provided information about the defendant, who was charged with prostitution, and the circumstances of her arrest. The judges then set bond for the defendant. Because prostitution violates a moral stance in the judges' worldviews, the researchers hypothesized that reminders of mortality would motivate the judges to uphold their worldview by being especially punitive toward the prostitute, in the form of setting an especially high bond. As shown in **FIGURE 2.12**, the results supported this hypothesis. Remember that all judges reviewed exactly the same materials, except for the presence or absence of the mortality reminder.

Later studies have highlighted the importance of an individual's version of the cultural worldview and the particular values that person holds. For example, if people are not morally opposed to prostitution or are more open-minded and curious, then a prostitute does not threaten their worldview, and thoughts of death do not affect the way they judge prostitutes (e.g., Boyd et al., 2017). It is also important to also note that heightened awareness of mortality leads to more positive responses toward those who uphold important cultural values. For example, reminders of death led to larger recommendations of monetary reward to a hypothetical person who behaved heroically by risking personal injury to report a suspected mugger to the police (Rosenblatt et al., 1989).

Research has also examined in a number of different cultures how thoughts of death affect reactions to people and ideas that more directly support or challenge one's worldview, be it one's identification with country, political party, or religious group. The general tenor of this research is that being reminded of death increases participants' need for faith in that identification, and participants are especially positive toward people or products that support that identification and especially negative toward those that threaten it. For example, Germans interviewed at a cemetery expressed a greater preference for German culture over other European cultures in terms of features such as travel destinations, cars, and cuisine compared with those interviewed away from a cemetery (Jonas et al., 2005).

The Protective Shield of Cultural Beliefs   Studies on worldview defense showcase some of the ways that reminders of mortality influence people's judgment and behavior. And, of course, we encounter such reminders in a variety of ways, from crimes in our cities to health concerns as we age. These reminders of death that occur as people navigate through the world similarly affect our judgment and behavior. Indeed, when countries are at war (which inevitably features death), their citizens tend to identify more with their religious beliefs (Du & Chi, 2016). Clinging tenaciously to that which supports one's cultural worldview provides protection from thoughts of death. So what might happen when these cultural beliefs are compromised or one's faith in their validity is undermined? If you've been following the logic of TMT, you might suspect that when cultural beliefs are undermined—when the existential shield is weakened—thoughts of death would leak through into a person's conscious mind. This is known as the *death thought accessibility hypothesis*: Threats to people's terror management resources increase how accessible thoughts of death are to consciousness (Hayes et al., 2010; Steinman & Updegraff, 2015).

In a typical study, an individual reads a criticism of her worldview and then is asked to complete a series of word stems, such as coff_ _. Reading a criticism of their worldview makes it more likely that people will complete such word

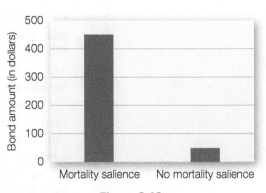

Figure 2.12

Worldview Defense After Mortality Reminders

According to terror management theory, cultural worldviews protect people against mortality fears. Supporting evidence shows that people primed to think about their deaths—that is, in a state of mortality salience—adhere more closely to their cultural worldview. In this study, after being reminded of death, judges imposed more punitive judgments on a prostitute because prostitution violates the cultural worldview's standards for good and bad behavior.
[Data from Rosenblatt et al., 1989]

stems with "coffin" than with the more common "coffee." The more death-related word stems a person completes, the higher death thought accessibility is. Whereas worldview threat increases death thought accessibility, bolstering one's worldview—even, for example, by exposing people to a cherished cultural symbol like the almighty dollar—reduces it (Gasiorowska et al., 2018).

Consider one particularly chilling example of this process. When Christian participants read about how Muslims are gaining dominance in Nazareth, the childhood home of Jesus Christ, thoughts of death became more accessible. But when participants were later exposed to a news story describing how a plane full of Muslims had crashed and all aboard had died, thoughts of mortality were no longer close to awareness (Hayes, Schimel, & Williams, 2008). This study illustrates not only how threats to one's culture can unleash the beast of mortality awareness but that this beast can be recaged through the annihilation of the worldview threat.

Is Death the Factor Responsible for These Findings? The findings just described are important because they help to highlight the direct connection between awareness of death and cultural beliefs. Not only do reminders of death increase investment in culture but threatening that culture increases awareness of death. Of course, death is not the only psychological threat that leads, for example, to more extreme reactions to those who are different. Other threats can and indeed do produce important psychological responses. We have touched on some of these already, such as the threat of uncertainty (Hogg, 2007), and we will discuss others in later chapters. At the same time, thoughts of death do produce unique effects in human judgments and decisions that are not produced by other unpleasant, uncertain, or anxiety-provoking events (Burke et al., 2010).

Table 2.3 Cultural Adaptation

Environment	Human Adaptations
The physical environment: How do people in groups manage the physical environments in which they live?	Technology (skills and tools)
The social environment: How do people in large groups of (mostly) strangers get along with each other?	Shared beliefs systems (e.g., norms, roles, and interaction customs) that reduce uncertainty about the self and one's actions, orient the self toward relationships with others, and establish and maintain social order
The metaphysical environment: How do people in groups manage the awareness of threatening realities inherent to our existence, most notably the fact that it ends in death?	Faith in a meaning-providing cultural worldview combined with a feeling of self-esteem, ensuring psychological equanimity in the face of death

Culture as a Synthesis of Human-Created Adaptations

TABLE 2.3 lists the three human environments we have discussed and summarizes how culture helps people adapt to each of them. However, it is important to recognize that each of these domains of cultural adaptation simultaneously influences and is influenced by adaptations to the other two domains.

For example, the demands of the *physical environment*, such as how specific groups extract a living from it, greatly influence a culture's *social environment*, such as roles and norms. Hunting cultures are generally more individualistic because hunting is a relatively individual activity. In contrast, agricultural cultures are generally collectivistic because large-scale agriculture requires more coordinated actions of larger groups of individuals. The *metaphysical environment* also affects adaptation to the physical environment. Consider that the earliest tools often contain an aesthetic dimension (e.g., ornamental marks on hand axes) that may have lent prestige to the tool maker or owner and enhanced the tool with ritual significance and coincident supernatural power (Kingdon, 1993).

APPLICATION
Culture and Thinking Styles

To appreciate more fully how a synthesis of adaptations to the physical, social, and metaphysical environments determines the character of a culture, let's look at culture's influence on people's thinking styles.

The physical, social, and metaphysical worlds interact to influence some basic aspects of thinking. The most widely studied broad cultural difference in style of thinking about the world concerns East Asian versus Western cultures, but according to Richard Nisbett (2003), East Asian collectivism and European/American individualism are rooted in an even more fundamental cultural difference in the way members of these respective cultures tend to think. Specifically, East Asians tend to think holistically, attending to balance, context, and the complex relationships among things, whereas Westerners tend to think analytically, focusing on stable categories, classification, and logical, linear relationships. Holistic cultures also tend to value moderation over maximization when it comes to the pursuit of desirable goals. Across Australia, Chile, China, Hong Kong, India, Japan, Peru, Russia, and the United States, Hornsey, Bain, and colleagues (2018) found that those from holistic cultures were more constrained when reporting their ideal attainment of outcomes such as health, longevity, happiness, and intelligence.

Nisbett argues that these differences reflect very different metaphysical traditions of philosophical thought that emerged in ancient China (a great influence in the Far East) and ancient Greece (a central influence on Western culture). Ancient China was a relatively ethnically homogeneous, large culture that gave rise to the philosophies of Taoism and Confucianism, which in turn led to a focus on the yin and yang, multiple sides to truth and life, balance, social cohesion and obligation, and harmony with nature. This Chinese tradition encouraged social practices that promoted holistic thinking, which focuses on overall context and relationships among contiguous elements. This type of thinking then reinforced a collectivistic worldview and its associated social practices, as we discussed earlier in this chapter.

Ancient Greece, in contrast, was composed of small, contentious city-states with easy access to the sea in a region of the world where travel and exposure to people of many widely varying cultures was prevalent. In this physical and social environment, a tradition of thought promoted by Aristotle and other philosophers developed. This ancient Greek tradition encouraged social practices that promoted analytic thinking, which focuses on classification of discrete objects and their properties, logic, debate, and individuality. This type of thinking, in turn, reinforced an individualistic worldview and its associated social practices.

Although Nisbett's historical analyses of the genesis of East–West differences is plausible and thought provoking, it cannot be proven definitively. However, a substantial set of research findings do provide clear support for the idea that East Asians are more holistic in their thinking, and Westerners are more analytic. For example, one aspect of the holistic versus analytic distinction is a focus on relationships as contrasted with categories. Chinese and American students were presented with sets of three words, such as *panda*, *monkey*, and *banana*, and asked which two are most closely related (Ji et al., 2004). The Americans generally chose category-based pairs, such as panda and monkey (animals), whereas the Chinese students generally chose relationship-based pairs, such as monkey and banana (monkeys eat bananas).

Nisbett's analysis can also help to explain how such thinking styles might change as environments change. Recall our earlier discussion of how mobility contributes to individualism and undermines collectivism. Mobility can help to foster more analytic versus holistic thinking. San Martin, Schug, and Maddux (2019) found that more relational mobility predicted more analytic thinking across countries as diverse as the United States, Spain, Nigeria, Morocco, and Israel. They also showed that when participants thought about working for a company that frequently mixed up working groups (high relational mobility), as opposed to a company where one repeatedly worked in the same group (low relational mobility), participants performed better on a geometric task that measured their ability to focus attention on a particular object (rather than the relationship between objects). These experimental findings converge with the correlational studies to suggest that relational mobility promotes different styles of thinking. ■

SECTION REVIEW How Culture Helps Us Adapt

Culture simultaneously helps people adapt to the physical, social, and metaphysical environment in which they live.

Culture and the Physical Environment

- Technological innovations and group living have facilitated human adaptation to the natural environment.
- Adaptation to the physical environment depends on the challenges of local environments and the unique needs and values of the cultural groups that occupy them.

Culture and the Social Environment

- People in every culture must adapt to their social environment in terms of uncertainty about what one can and should do and orienting the self toward one's relationships and personal goals.
- Collectivistic cultures emphasize cooperation and group welfare. Individualistic cultures emphasize values such as individual achievement. This distinction has implications for how people conceptualize themselves, experience and display emotions, and form attitudes about outgroup members.
- Modernization has a range of consequences, including increased mobility, that determine which values are most important to members of a culture.

Culture and the Metaphysical Environment

- Cultural worldviews help people understand why they are alive, what they should be doing while they are alive, and what will happen to them when they are dead.
- Both faith in the cultural worldview and the maintenance of self-esteem manage the potential for anxiety stemming from the awareness of mortality. Because these are symbolic constructs, maintaining faith in them depends primarily on social consensus and validation. As a result, people defend them vehemently when threatened by others who challenge their views.
- Tests of terror management theory support the hypothesis that reminding people of their mortality increases protection of their worldviews and that undermining the worldview increases thoughts about death.

Culture as a Synthesis of Human-Created Adaptations

- Humans adapt to each of the three environments simultaneously because each is heavily influenced by adaptations in the other two domains.
- Cultures can be defined as either holistic or analytic, on the basis of different metaphysical traditions.
- Many aspects of a given culture reflect its adaptation to all three environments.

Culture in the Round: Central Issues

- Describe why culture has both beneficial and harmful effects for people.

There is no domain of human thought or activity that is not influenced by a culture's particular combination of adaptations to the physical, social, and metaphysical world. Given culture's importance in human behavior, let's consider some big questions about it.

Does Culture Illuminate or Obscure Reality?

Culture is a uniquely human form of adaptation. Some theorists (e.g., Harris, 1979/2001) view it as a body of knowledge that developed to provide *accurate* information to people that helps them adjust to the many demands of life, such as obtaining food and shelter and defending against rival outgroups. Culture also tells us how groups of people work together to achieve mutually beneficial goals and how to live our lives so that others will like and accept us—and maybe even fall in love with us. So if adaptation to physical and social environments were all that cultures were designed to facilitate, perhaps cultures would always strive toward an accurate understanding of the world.

However, adaptation to the metaphysical environment suggests that people do not live by truth and accuracy alone. Sometimes it is more adaptive for cultural worldviews to distort the truth about life and our role in it. Some things about life are too emotionally devastating to face head on, such as the inevitability of death. Because overwhelming fear can get in the way of many types of adaptive action, it is sometimes adaptive for cultures to provide "rose-colored glasses" with which to understand reality and our place in it. From the existential perspective, the adaptive utility of accurate worldviews is tempered by the adaptive value of anxiety-buffering illusions. As you will see throughout this textbook, compromise between accurate and pleasing perceptions of ourselves and the world pervades many aspects of everyday social life.

Is Culture a Good or Bad Thing?

Culture is a necessary part of being human. Building on generations of accumulated wisdom and innovation culled from many cultural influences, our own culture helps us enjoy our lives, answer our toughest questions, and keep our deepest fears at bay. It provides tried-and-true forms of cuisine, entertainment, and technology. It gives us ways to feel connected, protected, and valuable. A human lacking or stripped of culture would be psychologically (and probably physically) naked, fearful, hard pressed to survive, and barely recognizable as a member of our species.

Cultures other than one's own are important as well because through cultural diffusion, cultures share innovations that mutually enhance people's lives, offering them novel cuisines, technologies, music, and art. Imagine visiting Oslo, Prague, Rio, or Beijing and finding only strip malls full of the same fast-food restaurants and big-box stores you have in your hometown!

Although we can't go about stripping individuals of their culture in a laboratory experiment to assess these functions of culture directly, anthropologists and psychologists have detailed many tragic historical examples of cultural disruptions, some of which have led to complete cultural disintegration. The documented effects of these **cultural traumas** seem to provide clear evidence of the psychological importance of culture.

Cultural traumas Tragic historical examples of cultural disruptions, some of which have led to complete cultural disintegration.

Figure 2.13

Cultural Trauma

Culture makes us human, providing us with a basis for making meaningful sense of our lives and feeling valuable. Forcibly stripping a group of their cultural heritage can be devastating. For example, the forcible removal of the people living on Bikini Island for the purpose of conducting nuclear testing has had severe negative consequences for the Bikinians' psychological functioning and health.

[AP Photo]

A dramatic and sudden example of cultural trauma befell the inhabitants of Bikini Island in the South Pacific. The Bikinians were removed from the island by the U.S. government, which used the island to conduct 67 nuclear tests between 1945 and 1958 (**FIGURE 2.13**). The result was severe demoralization and stress among the Bikinian people, problems with which their descendants are still coping today. Similarly, research on children displaced by war or natural disaster consistently shows that children whose cultural base has been disrupted by traumatic events are likely to develop posttraumatic stress disorder, whereas those who retain a strong cultural base cope much better (Beauvais, 2000).

Over the course of history, cultural traumas have been experienced by indigenous tribal cultures throughout the world, as their ways of life and belief systems have been abruptly or gradually altered—and sometimes completely undermined—by intrusions from more technologically advanced cultures. The best-documented cases of these cultural traumas were set in motion by European explorers, missionaries, traders, and armies. The cross-cultural counseling psychologist Mike Salzman (Salzman & Halloran, 2004) has argued that the long-term consequences of such traumas have been remarkably similar around the globe, even though the victimized groups have often been genetically, geographically, and culturally quite different. Many of the descendants of these traumatized cultures, largely stripped of their traditional ways and beliefs and not embraced by or able to embrace the dominant colonizer culture, have had difficulty sustaining a sense that they are valuable contributors to any meaningful world. Consequently, they suffer a high prevalence of debilitating anxiety, resulting in poverty, physical health problems, anxiety disorders, depression, and abuse of alcohol and other drugs. All these

 SOCIAL PSYCH AT THE MOVIES

Black Robe

Black Robe, directed by Bruce Beresford (Beresford, 1991) with the help of Native American consultants, is a fictionalized but realistic account of historical events. In the 1600s, Jesuit priests travel from France to what is now Québec to help convert the Huron tribe to Christianity. Algonquin tribe members are given gifts such as metal tools in exchange for helping Father La Forgue and his assistant Daniel reach the Huron mission. The film emphasizes both the commonalities and the differences between the French and Algonquin cultures.

Early in the movie, we see the Algonquin chief, Chomina, and Samuel de Champlain, the leader of the French, getting dressed in garb that connotes their high status. Every culture uses clothes and ornaments for this purpose. Both the French and Algonquin play music and dance. They both ingest consciousness-altering substances—tobacco for the Algonquin, alcohol for the French. At first, La Forgue doesn't realize that the Algonquin have a viable worldview of their own. As the film progresses, we see clearly that, consistent with terror management theory, each culture has a belief in

an afterlife, and the members of both strive for self-esteem. The Algonquin men try to maintain their value as warriors and hunters. As Chomina approaches death, he questions whether he has been a great enough warrior. La Forgue sees his mission as a heroic effort to bring the Huron from outer darkness to qualification for the protection and salvation of

▲ [Samuel Goldwyn Company/Photofest]

unfortunate phenomena, taken together, make a strong case for the positive psychological value of an intact, functioning culture.

On the other hand, even cultures that are working well for their members have negative sides. Each culture limits the way its people think about themselves and the world and creates divides between its people and others within and outside the culture. We humans have great potential for freedom of thought and choice because of our reduced reliance on instinctual patterns of behavior and our flexible intelligence. But culture imposes preferred beliefs, attitudes, values, norms, morals, customs, and rituals on us, often leading us to internalize these worldviews long before we have the cognitive or physical capabilities or independence to question them or develop and institute alternative ways of thinking and behaving. Indeed, Becker (1971) argued that each culture is like a shared neurosis—a particular, peculiar, and limited way of viewing the world and acting in it. Consequently, those outside the culture are likely to view the behavior of those within it as odd, if not outright crazy.

Culture affects how people treat those of lower status within the culture as well as those outside the culture. This has contributed greatly to social problems within cultures and egregious conflicts between cultures, often leading to the tragic cultural traumas we have already noted. This aspect of culture is what makes James Joyce's (1961, pp. 22–23) pronouncement that "History . . . is a nightmare from which I am trying to awake" so apt.

All these very real negatives notwithstanding, culture is with us and in us and always will be, at least in some form. As we proceed through this textbook, we will continually consider the specific ways cultures contribute both positively and negatively to human functioning. We will leave it to you to ponder whether some cultures and aspects of culture provide a better ratio of benefits to costs than others.

THINK ABOUT

[Chris Hondros/Getty Images]

Jesus. Daniel eventually betrays La Forgue so that he can be with Annuka, Chomina's daughter, with whom he has fallen in love. But when faced with the prospect of death at the hands of the Iroquois tribe, he shifts his loyalty back to Christianity, La Forgue, and his heroic quest.

We also see what seem, from outside each culture's respective worldview, very strange behaviors. La Forgue self-flagellates with a tree branch after he has lustful thoughts about Annuka. The Algonquin don't understand La Forgue's commitment to celibacy and wonder if he is some sort of demon. In order to decide what to do about La Forgue, Chomina travels out of his way to consult a dwarf covered in face paint who claims to be a shaman from the underworld. La Forgue sees this as one of numerous signs that the Algonquin are being controlled by the devil.

The cultures are different in two principal ways. First, the French culture is more individualistic, the Algonquin more collectivistic. The Algonquin share everything without question and have no sense of private property (communal sharing). They also obey Chomina and the other tribal elders (authority ranking). The French are oriented more toward market pricing,

wanting to trade tobacco for other things rather than share it. And there is more of a sense of equality matching between La Forgue and Daniel. Daniel has no problem disobeying La Forgue and at one point is willing to abandon him to be with Annuka and the Algonquin. Annuka has no thought of ever abandoning her tribe.

Second, French culture is more technologically advanced, an advantage that helped many European nations colonize indigenous tribal cultures. La Forgue eventually reaches the Huron mission and finds the Huron plagued by a deadly disease and desperate. He converts them and holds a large-scale baptism ceremony. In this way, the film depicts the process described by Salzman (2001), whereby Europeans, who had developed immunity to the germs they carried, infected indigenous tribes around the globe when they came into contact with them, leading to the death of up to half the local populations. These mass epidemics led the tribal peoples to question their own worldviews and often to convert to Christianity in the hope of gaining protection from further death. In the case of the Huron tribe depicted in the film, a few decades after converting to Christianity, they were wiped out by rival tribes.

Is There Just One Culture? Beyond a Monolithic View

For presentational purposes in this chapter, we have generally treated culture as a single, largely static entity. However, as we noted at the outset of this chapter, cultures actually are continually evolving. In addition, cultures are often very heterogeneous, consisting of many subcultures. It is important to recognize that members of such subcultures are profoundly influenced by both their subculture and its relationship to the dominant culture.

The tone of this chapter could be taken to suggest that because people are deeply embedded in their cultures, they are mere helpless pawns of their cultural upbringing. But clearly within cultures, people vary greatly in their traits, beliefs, values, preferences, and behaviors. So how much of the person is determined by their culture as opposed to universal or unique characteristics?

APPLICATION
Understanding Cultural Impact Through Immigration

Although there is no basis for putting a number on how much of a person is determined by culture or certain unique or universal characteristics, one way to examine this issue is to consider research on immigrants, people who move from one culture to another. How much of who they are do they keep? How much do they change? How easily can they adapt to the norms and customs of a very different culture? Fortunately, there is a body of theory and research on **acculturation**—the process whereby individuals change in response to exposure to a new culture—that can help answer such questions.

One of our wives has worked with the International Rescue Committee (IRC) to help refugees allowed into the United States to settle into life in America; she has found this to be an incredibly eye-opening experience. In the past decade, many refugees have fled from Sudan, Somalia, and other parts of Africa, where civil war, ethnic cleansing, and genocide have killed many and left many more homeless. Traditional African tribal cultures are generally very collectivistic and technologically primitive, and polygamy, with associated limits on women's rights, is prevalent. For people from these regions, the shift to American culture is a radical one. When they arrive, many of these individuals don't know, for example, what a doorknob or a toilet is or how they work. Many have never walked on a paved road.

Imagine the adjustment to American culture! One caseworker found a group of Somali women sitting in a modern American apartment in a circle on the kitchen floor, cleaning chicken together. This is very odd when seen through American eyes (Why aren't they being hygienic and using the counter?). But it's not so strange if we consider that they had never seen a kitchen counter before and didn't know what it was for—and, more importantly, if we consider that preparing food in this way was a long-standing traditional communal activity in their culture. Yet, despite the radical cultural shift and the steep learning curve necessary to adopt new ways, many African refugees have adapted quite successfully—a testament to the flexibility of human intelligence and the capacity to move beyond the limits of one particular cultural worldview.

Research confirms that, although some level of *acculturative stress* is not uncommon, most immigrants succeed in growing accustomed to their new culture (Berry, 2006; Furnham & Bochner, 1986). Some people gradually shift

Acculturation The process whereby individuals adapt their behavior in response to exposure to a new culture.

◀ Refugees from war-torn nations not only must cope with the stress of upheaval and loss but also must learn quickly to adapt to life in a new and unusual culture.
[Mary Elizabeth Greenberg]

almost entirely from their traditional culture to the beliefs and ways of the new culture, a process known as **assimilation**. As people assimilate, they not only embrace the new culture's ways of dressing, eating, and so on but also begin thinking in ways promoted by the new culture (Berry, 1997; Church, 1982; Kitayama & Markus, 2000).

Most immigrants retain aspects of their former culture while adapting to the new culture in a process known as **integration**. Immigrants who have achieved integration are referred to as *bicultural* because they identify with two cultures simultaneously. It is interesting to note that research on bicultural individuals suggests that they can think and act like members of either culture, depending on which culture's language they are using or which culture's symbols are prominent in their minds. Consider a study set in Hong Kong (Hong et al., 1997), a city of people primarily of Chinese descent and under Chinese control since 1997 but heavily influenced by Western culture because of 100 prior years of British rule. Researchers showed participants a cartoon of one fish swimming in front of a group of other fish. If shown pictures of a cowboy and Mickey Mouse first, they explained the lead fish's behavior in terms of the characteristics of the fish, much as Westerners typically do. However, if first shown pictures of a Chinese dragon and temple, they explained the fish's behavior in terms of the situation the fish was in, as Easterners typically do. This phenomenon further attests to the ability of people to transcend the perspective of one particular cultural worldview and shift to another when exposed to that worldview as well.

Whether individuals with a background in one culture but living in another end up assimilating, integrating, or becoming marginalized depends in part on their own choices, the strength of their initial cultural identification, the compatibility of the two cultures, and how the two cultures meet their psychological needs (Amiot et al., 2018). But it also depends on the attitude of the current culture toward immigrants and those with subcultural identifications (Berry, 2001). Some cultures promote a **melting pot** viewpoint, which assumes that all people will converge toward the mainstream culture; this orientation

Assimilation The process whereby people gradually shift almost entirely from their former culture to the beliefs and ways of the new culture.

Integration The process whereby people retain aspects of their former culture while internalizing aspects of a new host culture.

Melting pot An ideological view which holds that diverse peoples within a society should converge toward the mainstream culture.

Multiculturalism (cultural pluralism) An ideological view which holds that cultural diversity is valued and that diverse peoples within a society should retain aspects of their traditional culture while adapting to the host culture.

more or less forcefully encourages assimilation. Other cultures value cultural diversity and promote **multiculturalism**, or **cultural pluralism**, encouraging integration (Allport, 1954).

In historical terms, American culture could be characterized as having generally had a melting pot orientation with regard to European immigrants while simultaneously having a discriminatory orientation, fostering marginalization, with regard to African Americans, Native Americans, and Hispanic Americans. Currently, the cultural diversity movement, which primarily targets societal orientations toward African Americans, Native Americans, and Hispanics, is attempting to move American culture toward a multicultural orientation. If it succeeds, it may eventually help shift members of these groups from marginalization to integration (Moghaddam, 1988). ■

SECTION REVIEW Culture in the Round: Central Issues

Social psychologists consider broad issues about culture.

Cultures strike a balance between human needs for accurate information and for comforting beliefs that often obscure reality.	Culture serves many vital functions that promote happiness and well-being. Culture also contributes to a variety of social ills in creating divides between people within and outside a culture. Theory and research on cultural traumas reveal the psychological harm that results when one's culture has disintegrated.	Culture is not a single, blanket entity but contains important subcultural differences and influences.	People coming to a new culture can struggle, but they can assimilate to and integrate aspects of the new culture.

CRITICAL LEARNING EXERCISES

1. We saw that the evolved features of our bodies and minds are not designed perfectly. Instead, they are "good enough" solutions that helped people on average to survive and reproduce. With this in mind, consider the feeling of *love* (covered in chapter 15). Love can feel intensely good. Consider the reasons that our ancient ancestors who felt love may have more successfully survived and reproduced—on average—than those who did not. Now consider the flip side: Love can feel horrible; when unrequited or rejected, it can twists your gut in knots. If love is an adaptive emotion, why does it feel so yucky at times?

Might the painful flipside serve an adaptive function, or is this another example of an evolutionary trade-off?

2. Earlier, we took a simple behavior—Rita tying her shoes—and plugged it into a hierarchy of goals. We kept asking *Why* to consider more abstract goals that Rita might be (unconsciously) striving for as she laces up. Try creating a hierarchy of goals for why you are taking your social psychology course. What is the higher-order goal of taking this course? What does *that* goal help you achieve? Imagine a different hierarchy that one of your classmates might create. Why do different people

have different hierarchies? Do you think it's possible for someone to be "wrong"—that is, to be unaware of what goals their behavior is ultimately serving?

3. In 2016 Colin Kaepernick, who was at the time the quarterback for the San Francisco 49ers, began refusing to stand during the national anthem. Given what you've learned about cultural symbols and rituals, as well as the importance of consensual validation of beliefs, why did this action create such an uproar and debate? If you're not familiar with this incident, analyze another event from the past few years that allows you to consider the power of cultural rituals.

4. The news media today tends to report one disaster or trauma after another, from school shootings to hurricanes and tornadoes to the latest geopolitical threats. Meanwhile, we see political groups becoming increasingly polarized. For example, liberals and conservatives often seem unable to reach a common understanding on key issues. Based on what you've learned about terror management theory and other perspectives in this chapter, how might these two trends be related?

Don't stop now! Check out our videos and additional resources located at: www.macmillanlearning.com

CHAPTER 3

The Core Elements of Social Cognition

Think back to your first kiss. You probably remember who you were with and how you felt. But do you remember the day of the week or what you were wearing? Most people would like to think that their memories are like snapshots of the past (maybe with a little Instagram filtering to give them a warm glow). The reality is that recollections of events often lack detail and differ from how they actually occurred.

Like memory, our ordinary sensory perception is riddled with inaccuracies. As just one example, it seems perfectly obvious to see the sun as "rising" and "setting" as it traverses the sky, yet we know that the earth revolves around the sun rather than the other way around. Most of us assume that we take in sensations from our environment and add them to a big pile of knowledge in our head. The whole (i.e., our understanding of the world) is the sum of its parts (impressions of stimuli). But as the examples above suggest, this conventional wisdom breaks down on closer inspection.

In the mid-20th century, psychologists in the *Gestalt* school, such as Kurt Koffka and Max Wertheimer, proposed that people *construct* an understanding of reality. Just as builders construct a house not by simply piling bricks together but by arranging them in orderly ways, the mind actively selects which pieces of information it takes in and organizes those pieces into a network of knowledge. Gestalt psychologists devised a number of visual perception exercises to demonstrate the different ways that the mind actively constructs meaning. One of the most popular and compelling of these exercises is depicted in **FIGURE 3.1**.

After thinking about that first kiss, you might see the image in Figure 3.1 as two faces looking at each other. Look again, and you'll notice that the same image can be seen as a dark vase against a white background. The fact that the same physical stimulus can be viewed in more than one way shows that the perceiver has an active role in what is perceived. The whole is more than the sum of its parts.

If the mind constructs an understanding of even simple stimuli like the image in Figure 3.1, then certainly it must take an active role in shaping how a person makes sense of the people, ideas, and events in everyday life. But how? What are the specific mental processes through which we construct a meaningful understanding of the social world? The research area known as *social cognition* emerged in the 1970s with the goal of answering this question. Its penetrating discoveries are at the heart of

Figure 3.1

Figure and Ground

Do you see a vase or two faces? The mind plays an active part in how we construct reality.

the social cognitive perspective and also the topic of two chapters in this book. In this chapter we focus on:

- The psychological motives behind thinking
- The two ways that people think about the social world
- Schemas as the building blocks of knowledge
- How motives bias thinking and behavior

Learning Outcomes

- Distinguish three different motivations that guide thought and decision making.
- Identify when each of these motives guides thinking.

The "Why" of Social Cognition: The Motives Behind Thinking

When you gaze at the image in Figure 3.1, what is your visual system doing? In essence, it is choosing between two interpretations. In a similar way, our everyday thinking about the social world is largely a matter of choices, many of which are made without our conscious awareness. The difference is that, in our social life, the choices are much more challenging, and the consequences are often more important.

A major challenge to making sense of the social world is the sheer *quantity* of information that is available at any given moment. Imagine that a friend is coming over to watch a movie, and she's asked you to find a "good one" on Netflix. Yikes. Now you're scanning through hundreds of movie titles, most of which you've never heard of. You could learn about each one if you read the plot summary and dozens of online reviews. You might also want to consider your friend's tastes in movies, the nature of your relationship with this person, how long the movie is and what else you'd like to do tonight, and so on. If you were to weigh all of the relevant pieces of information, you would be so immersed in thought that you would die of starvation before you selected a movie (**FIGURE 3.2**).

What's important in this example is not the choice of a movie per se but something more fundamental: the choice of when to stop thinking and reach a conclusion that feels certain . . . or certain *enough*. We make this same basic choice every moment we navigate our social world. Whether we are forming an impression of a stranger or figuring out how we feel about a political issue, there is always more information we *could* consider, but eventually we have to reach a conclusion and move on. According to the *theory of lay epistemology* developed by Arie Kruglanski (1989, 2004), three motives influence this choice:

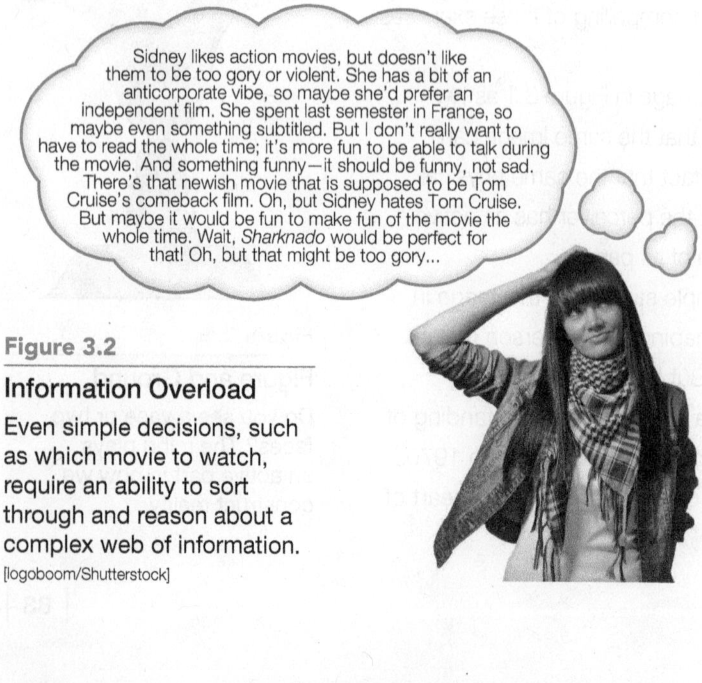

Figure 3.2

Information Overload

Even simple decisions, such as which movie to watch, require an ability to sort through and reason about a complex web of information.

[logoboom/Shutterstock]

- *The need to be accurate*: Sometimes thinking is guided by a motive to achieve an accurate, truthful understanding of a given person, idea, or event. For example, if an employer is looking over a job application, she might be motivated to know for sure whether an applicant is qualified for a job, and so she will invest a lot of time and energy in thinking about the applicant's résumé. Most of us would like to believe that if any force is driving the way we think, it is the motivation to be rational and accurate. But thinking carefully takes time and energy—resources that are in short supply. Further, our motivation to reach closure by making any choice, or by making a certain choice, is sometimes stronger than our motivation to make the most accurate choice.

- *The need to reach closure quickly*: We reach *closure* in our decision making when we stop the thinking process and grab the first handy judgment or decision, quickly and without extensive effort. Can you think of a time when you did not have a strong preference for one conclusion over another but just wanted to reach *a* conclusion—*any* conclusion? When the stakes are low and we just want a decision to be made, people are often content to choose whatever others choose, such as selecting the most popular menu item at a local restaurant or whatever movie is getting the most downloads (Otto et al., 2016).

- *The need to confirm what one already prefers to believe*: This is the motive to reach a conclusion that fits well with the specific beliefs and attitudes that one already prefers. If you held the attitude that *Black Panther* is the greatest movie of all time, and you read just one customer review praising the movie, chances are you'll halt the thinking process right there and confidently declare, "Yup, just as I thought: It's a great movie." In contrast, if you hated that movie and read the same review, you would be more likely to continue reading reviews until you found one that affirms your belief that it stinks.

Which of these three motives influences how a person thinks? It partly depends on his or her situation at the time. The need for accuracy is elevated when there are negative consequences for making a poor decision. If, during a presidential election season, one candidate advocates aggressive military responses while another promises peace, you might be particularly motivated to gain an accurate impression of each candidate before voting because you believe that going to war would affect you and the people you care about.

In contrast, people want to reach closure quickly in situations where thinking is effortful or unpleasant. If you feel that you are under time pressure to make a decision, if you have a lot of things on your mind, or if you are simply exhausted from a long day at work, you will be more inclined to terminate the thinking process early and reach closure on a "good enough" conclusion. The first recommended movie that pops up might be the one you choose to watch.

Finally, people are motivated to validate what they think they already know or prefer to believe when their prior beliefs and values are brought to mind, when those beliefs are central to their sense of meaning in life or personal worth, and perhaps especially when they feel that their beliefs are being challenged by contradictory information. In these cases, people might be motivated to act on information that confirms their worldview, even if it's not very accurate. For example, during recent political elections, people have shared a proliferation of fake news stories on social media without critically examining the accuracy of those stories (Holan, 2016). These stories have heightened distrust in the media, fomented hostility toward politicians, and contributed to political polarization (**FIGURE 3.3**) (Barthel et al., 2016; Gallup, 2018; Pennycook et al., 2018).

Figure 3.3

Confirming What We Believe: Americans Who Share Fake News

People are often motivated to believe information that confirms their existing views. For example, in a 2016 Pew survey, 23% of American adults reported that they had shared a political news article that was fake, although they might not have realized it was fake at the time.

[Data from Barthel et al., 2016]

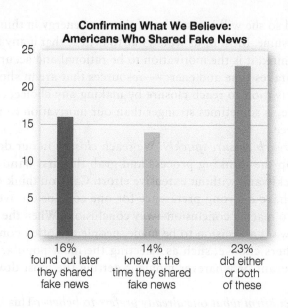

Confirming What We Believe:
Americans Who Shared Fake News

16%
found out later
they shared
fake news

14%
knew at the
time they shared
fake news

23%
did either
or both
of these

Which motive influences a person's thinking also depends on his or her personality traits. Some people have a high need for closure; they seek and prefer simple and clear knowledge and feel especially uncomfortable when confronted with ambiguous or confusing situations (Thompson et al., 2001). By contrast, other people are more tolerant of complexity and ambiguity and are willing to gather more information and deliberate before arriving at a conclusion. In fact, they may view novelty, surprise, and uncertainty to be the very spice of life. If you want to see where you stand on this dimension, consider how you would respond to the survey in **FIGURE 3.4**. Another factor is expertise. As people become expert in a given area, they can come to feel more entitled to have close-minded or dogmatic views (Ottati et al., 2015).

Keep these three motives in mind as you read the rest of this chapter—and indeed, this entire textbook—because you'll see how they influence social thought and behavior in various ways across a wide range of situations.

Figure 3.4

Do You Need Closure?

Complete these six scale items and total your scores to learn whether you have a high need for closure.

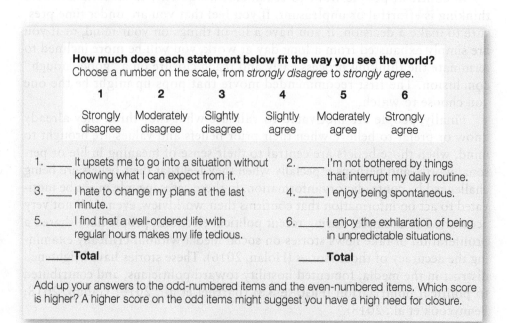

How much does each statement below fit the way you see the world?
Choose a number on the scale, from *strongly disagree* to *strongly agree*.

1	2	3	4	5	6
Strongly disagree	Moderately disagree	Slightly disagree	Slightly agree	Moderately agree	Strongly agree

1. _____ It upsets me to go into a situation without knowing what I can expect from it.

2. _____ I'm not bothered by things that interrupt my daily routine.

3. _____ I hate to change my plans at the last minute.

4. _____ I enjoy being spontaneous.

5. _____ I find that a well-ordered life with regular hours makes my life tedious.

6. _____ I enjoy the exhilaration of being in unpredictable situations.

_____ **Total**

_____ **Total**

Add up your answers to the odd-numbered items and the even-numbered items. Which score is higher? A higher score on the odd items might suggest you have a high need for closure.

SECTION REVIEW   The "Why" of Social Cognition: The Motives Behind Thinking

Three psychological motives influence thinking about the social world.

The Need to Be Accurate	The Need to Reach Closure Quickly	The Need to Confirm What One Already Prefers to Believe
• A desire to achieve an accurate understanding • Activated when being inaccurate could result in undesired outcomes	• A desire for a simple, quick, and clear-cut understanding as opposed to confusion and ambiguity • Activated when thinking is effortful or unpleasant (e.g., when under time pressure)	• A desire to understand something in a way that fits well with previously held beliefs and values • Activated when prior beliefs and values are brought to mind, central to one's sense of meaning in life or personal worth, or threatened by contradictory information

The "How" of Social Cognition: Two Ways to Think About the Social World

Learning Outcomes

As we humans evolved, we developed neocortical structures in the brain that allow for high-level thought processes: consciousness, self-awareness, language, logic, and rationality. Yet we also have older brain structures, such as the limbic system, that we share with birds and reptiles. The result of having a hybrid brain is that social cognition is governed by two systems of thinking: a rational and controlled way of thinking—the **cognitive system**—and an unconscious, intuitive, and automatic way of thinking—the **experiential system** (Epstein, 1994; Kahneman, 2011; Sloman, 1996). Depending on the individual and the circumstances, a person's thought and action can be directed primarily by one system or the other. As an illustration of these distinct systems of thought, consider the rise and fall of facilitated communication as a treatment for autism.

- Compare and contrast the two systems of thinking.
- Explain how and why intuition is sometimes "smart."

Cognitive system A conscious, rational, and controlled system of thinking.

Experiential system An unconscious, intuitive, and automatic system of thinking.

The Strange Case of Facilitated Communication

In the fall of 1991, Mark and Laura Storch were informed that their 14-year-old daughter, Jenny, had accused her father of repeated sexual abuse that her mother had ignored. Their daughter was promptly removed from their home, and her parents spent the next 10 months fighting the charges, which turned out to be false (Berger, 1994). Her stunned parents were not only shocked by the specific allegations, they were dumbfounded because their daughter was severely autistic and had little ability to communicate with others verbally. With no ability to share whatever thoughts she had, how had her teachers and aides tapped into Jenny's inner world? Jenny had apparently told of a history of abuse by using a technique known as facilitated communication, which allows individuals with severe forms of autism to spell out their internal thoughts with the help of an assistant. The assistant, called the facilitator, steadies the autistic person's arm to allow the individual to hunt and peck at letter keys. When first introduced in the United States in the early 1990s, facilitated communication seemed a revolutionary way to unlock the inner world of loved ones who could not otherwise communicate their thoughts.

▲ Although it initially seemed to provide severely autistic children with a method for communicating with others, facilitated communication was eventually discredited after it was discovered that the adult facilitators were unconsciously shaping the messages that the children typed out.

[Andy Cross/The Denver Post via Getty Images]

Facilitated communication quickly aroused skepticism, however, as children such as Jenny began sharing horrific stories of sexual abuse (Gorman, 1999). When the scientific community investigated the technique, study after study suggested that the thoughts being typed out were not those of the autistic child but rather were those of the facilitator (Schlosser et al., 2014). In one experiment, two autistic middle schoolers were shown pictures of common objects and asked to type out what they saw (Vázquez, 1994). The experimenter could not see the pictures on the cards, and in half the trials, the facilitator was also prevented from seeing the cards. But in the other half of trials, the facilitator could see what was shown to the child. When their facilitator knew what the card depicted, both children typed out correct answers on all 10 of the trials. However, when the picture was shown only to the children and not to their facilitator, one child was unable to identify any of the pictures correctly, and the other got only 2 out of 10 correct. On the basis of this kind of evidence, the American Psychological Association passed a resolution in 1994 denouncing the validity of facilitated communication.

The rise and fall of this controversial technique was fraught with heartache and dashed hopes. But it also illuminated something rather interesting about human psychology. In practically all of the cases where communicated messages were deemed written by the facilitator and not the child, the facilitators adamantly and fervently believed that they had not and could not have constructed the thoughts that had been typed out on paper. But the research clearly suggests that they had played an integral role. Although their conscious, cognitive systems produced the belief that they were merely helping pupils control their muscles, the facilitators' unconscious, experiential systems were likely guiding the pupils' fingers toward each letter to spell out meaningful words, phrases, and ideas.

Dual Process Theories

Dual process theories Theories that are used to explain a wide range of phenomena by positing two ways of processing information.

The ideas discussed so far—that thinking is governed by two systems of thought—lie behind several theories you'll encounter in this textbook. These theories are often referred to as **dual process theories** because they posit two ways of processing information, as outlined in **FIGURE 3.5**. Researchers have developed dual process theories to explain wide-ranging phenomena, including attitudes, memories, and thought suppression.

Figure 3.5

Are We of Two Minds?

According to dual process theories, thinking is governed by two systems of thought, each of which recruits multiple interrelated brain reactions.

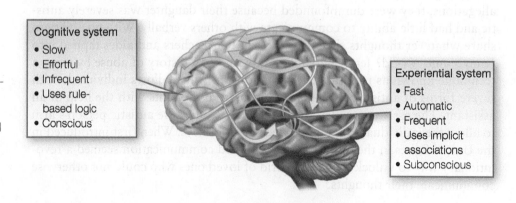

Cognitive system
• Slow
• Effortful
• Infrequent
• Uses rule-based logic
• Conscious

Experiential system
• Fast
• Automatic
• Frequent
• Uses implicit associations
• Subconscious

To appreciate the gist of these theories, let's analyze what you are doing right now. You made a conscious intention to read your social psych textbook, and you're following through with it, pushing distracting thoughts about other matters out of your mind. You are able to consciously think about the concepts and ideas you're reading about, and perhaps you are going further to *elaborate* on that information—that is, think it over, critique it, and compare it with your prior knowledge and experience. In each case, you are using the cognitive system to consciously direct your attention, guide your behavior, and make deliberate decisions.

At the same time that your cognitive system is busy with rational thinking, your experiential system operates in the background, controlling your more automatic thoughts and behaviors. You might read a sentence about a lazy black dog yawning and lying down and find yourself yawning involuntarily, even though you don't feel the slightest bit tired. Or your favorite song might come on and, before you are consciously aware of it, you find yourself in a better mood. It is because these two systems can operate independently of each other that you can focus on the textbook while unconsciously responding to other stimuli around you.

The two systems have different ways of organizing information. The cognitive system uses a system of rules to fit ideas into logical patterns. Much as your intuitive understanding of English grammar tells you that something is wrong with the statement "Store Jane to the goes," your cognitive system uses a type of grammar to detect when ideas fit and don't fit. In this way, it can think critically, plan behavior, and make deliberate decisions. By contrast, the experiential system is guided by automatic or implicit associations among stimuli, concepts, and behaviors that have been learned from experience.

Heuristics Mental shortcuts, or rules of thumb, that are used for making judgments and decisions.

Because the experiential system stores a large collection of well-learned associations, it can be used to make rapid, "good enough" judgments and decisions at times when using the cognitive system's logical style would be too slow and effortful (Epstein, 1990). These mental shortcuts, or rules of thumb, are called **heuristics**. One simple heuristic that people utilize automatically is that "more is better."

Imagine that you could win money by closing your eyes and picking a red marble from a jar filled with many colored marbles. Let's say you can choose to draw a marble from either a small jar with one red marble and nine marbles of other colors or from a large jar with 10 red marbles and 90 marbles of other colors. Which jar would you choose? Intuitively, it seems as if the chances are better with more possible winning marbles, even though statistically, and therefore rationally, this is not true: The chances of winning the money are equal for the two jars. Yet a large majority of people choose the large jar with 10 red marbles rather than the small jar with one, even when they recognize the equal odds of winning (Kirkpatrick & Epstein, 1992; Risen, 2016).

THINK ABOUT

[Cecilia Varas]

Achieve
**Social Psych in Everyday Life:
Ryan**

The marble-choice scenario helps us to see the intuitive appeal of heuristics, but it raises an important question: Do heuristics influence judgment when the real-world stakes are high? The answer is "yes." For example, imagine that a deadly disease is threatening a small town of 600 people, and public health officials are considering two different treatment plans. If Treatment A is adopted, 200 lives will be saved. If Treatment B is adopted, there's a 1/3 probability that all 600 people will be saved and a 2/3 probability that no one will be saved. Which would you choose? If you are like most participants asked this question by the Nobel Prize winner Daniel Kahneman and his collaborator, Amos Tversky (Tversky & Kahneman, 1981), you would probably choose Treatment A. But now consider the following version of the same problem: If Treatment A is adopted, 400 people will die. If Treatment B is adopted, there is a 1/3 probability that nobody will die and a 2/3 probability that all 600 people will die. Would you now prefer Treatment B? If you take a close look at these two framings of the issue, they are statistically identical choices. But people's preferences change dramatically when they are cued to think about what would be lost compared with what might be gained. When the question is framed the second way, in terms of lives lost, the majority of people prefer to take the chance with Treatment B, where there is some chance of avoiding any loss of life. Our experiential minds are more readily swayed by thinking about what we might lose than by thinking about what we might gain. It takes a much closer and more rational consideration of the odds to realize that these choices are the same.

APPLICATION
Two Routes to Engaging in Risky Health Behavior

Dual process theories help researchers to understand a number of important decisions that people make, including those that affect their physical health. The decision, for example, to engage in risky behavior such as smoking or unprotected sex can be influenced by people's conscious intentions ("No way would I have unprotected sex!"), but unfortunately, in the heat of the moment, these conscious intentions can fall by the wayside. Why? Because the experiential system learned to associate those behaviors with attractive images (Gerrard et al., 2005; Gerrard et al., 2008). For example, if adolescents' experiential system associates vaping with a cool rebel image, they are more willing to try vaping when the opportunity arises, even if they are consciously aware of the health risks. ■

▲ Adolescents whose experiential system associates smoking as something that is cool are more likely to try it, even if they are consciously aware of the dangers.
[LEMOINE/BSIP/AGE Fotostock]

Implicit attitudes Automatic associations based on previous learning through the experiential system.

Explicit attitudes Attitudes people are consciously aware of through the cognitive system.

Implicit and Explicit Attitudes Attitudes are emotional reactions to people, objects, and ideas. If we have two systems for thinking, does that mean we have two ways of evaluating something as good or bad? The answer is "yes," according to dual process theories of attitudes (Gawronski & Bodenhausen, 2006; Nosek, 2007). According to these theories, **implicit attitudes** are based on automatic associations that make up the experiential system. Some automatic associations can be passed on genetically through evolution (such as an automatic fear response to snakes; Öhman & Mineka, 2003), but most are learned from our culture (such as a negative attitude toward eating pork or fried ants). By contrast, **explicit attitudes** are the evaluations that we consciously make using the cognitive system (Gawronski & Bodenhausen, 2014).

Because we have no direct conscious access to our experiential system, measuring people's implicit attitudes requires a bit of cleverness. One popular task developed by Tony Greenwald and colleagues is the *implicit association test* (Greenwald et al., 1998; Jost, 2019). This task measures the degree to which people mentally associates two concepts (e.g., "flowers" and "pleasant"), essentially by measuring how quickly they can lump together examples of Concept 1 (rose, petunia, tulip) alongside examples of Concept 2 (happy, lucky, freedom). If you are like the average person (and not an entomologist), you'd probably be quicker to throw these flower and pleasant words in the same mental file folder than to group the same pleasant words with insect names such as *flea*, *locust*, and *maggot*. It's this difference in speed that tells us something about your implicit attitude toward flowers relative to insects, which may or may not be the same as what you would report explicitly on a questionnaire.

If the cognitive and experiential systems can both produce attitudes, and if these two systems operate independently of one another, does that mean that the same person can have different attitudes toward the same thing? The answer, again, is "yes." To illustrate, when volunteers in one study (Nosek, 2005) were asked whether they prefer dogs or cats, what they consciously *said*—that is, their explicit attitude—was that they prefer dogs. But their responses on a reaction-time measure revealed that, at an implicit level, they associated cats with *good* more than dogs with *good* (perhaps because cats seldom have a bad reputation as dangerous animals). People's explicit attitudes toward dogs and cats were correlated positively with their implicit attitudes—but only moderately so.

As shown in **FIGURE 3.6**, some attitudes are pretty similar when assessed implicitly or explicitly (Nosek, 2007; see also Kurdi et al., 2019). For example, in a study on judging political parties, the correlation of about .75 suggests that people's reported party preferences on a questionnaire correlate quite strongly with their automatic evaluations of Republicans and Democrats. Other attitudes can be quite distinct, so the preference people *say* they have for family versus career might be only weakly correlated (about .30) with their implicit attitude for one over the other. People's implicit and explicit attitudes are more likely to align when they feel strongly about the issue in question, have given it a lot of thought, and feel comfortable expressing their attitudes (Nosek, 2007). On the other hand, when people are explicitly

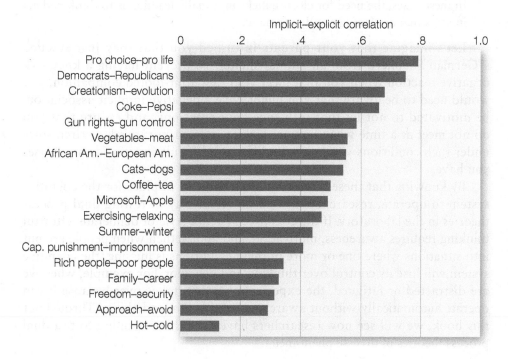

Figure 3.6

Implicit and Explicit Attitudes

On some issues, such as those at the top of this graph, people's implicit and explicit attitudes are highly related; for other issues, the two types of attitudes are quite distinct.

[Data from Nosek, 2007]

undecided about an issue, their implicit attitudes predict their explicit preferences and behavior better than their explicit attitudes (Galdi et al., 2008; Kurdi et al., 2019; Payne & Lundberg, 2014). It seems that our experiential system is a bit of a backseat driver at times, whispering directions when our cognitive system is not sure which way to turn.

Automaticity and Controlled Processes   Implicit and explicit attitudes can kick in under different circumstances to influence how we act. Your explicit attitude toward cats and dogs might dictate which kind of pet you choose to adopt from a local shelter (a very conscious decision), but it's your implicit attitude that probably accounts for the automatic startle response you might have if you encounter a German Shepherd, rather than a tabby cat, in a dark alley. And this is a reaction that even someone who explicitly loves dogs might have. This example of the German Shepherd in the dark alley illustrates that our automatic reactions to cues in the environment can be at odds with our conscious goals, beliefs, or intentions. These automatic associations get learned through repeated exposure to different ideas or to behaviors we carry out routinely. Such automatization of associations and behaviors is highly adaptive because it allows us to react quickly while saving our mental energy. But what if we don't want to react with fear every time we meet a German Shephard? Fortunately, the cognitive system is designed to override the experiential system in these situations, applying controlled processes of reasoning and decision making to solve unexpected problems to help you reach your goals. However, three conditions must be met in order for the cognitive system to successfully override the experiential system:

- We are *aware* that controlled processes are necessary to counteract automatic processes.
- We are *motivated* to exert control over our thoughts and behaviors.
- We have the *ability* to consider our thoughts and actions at a more conscious level, because controlled processes require more mental effort. Sometimes we do not have enough cognitive resources to engage controlled ways of thinking. In these cases, the need for closure kicks in, usually leading us to think and act in ways that are familiar and automatic.

Let's imagine that your parents informed you that they just rescued a German Shepherd from an animal shelter. To prevent having a knee-jerk negative reaction when you first meet your new four-footed companion, you would need to be aware that you might have a negative implicit association, be motivated to not let that influence your reactions, and ensure that you do not meet at a time when you are feeling stressed, surprised, or tired since under such conditions you might find it more difficult to set aside any biases you have.

By knowing that these three conditions must be in place for the cognitive system to operate, researchers have a powerful way of testing dual process theories in the laboratory. If the cognitive system's style of deliberate, effortful thinking requires awareness, motivation, and ability, then when people are put into situations where one or more of these conditions is missing, the cognitive system will lose its control over thinking and behavior. For example, when we are distracted or fatigued, the experiential system takes over because it can operate automatically without awareness, motivation, and ability. Throughout this book, we will see how researchers have used this reasoning to test dual process theories of diverse phenomena.

Five ways the unconscious is smart
1. The motives that guide thinking often operate unconsciously
2. Memory consolidation occurs during sleep
3. Unconscious mind wandering can help generate creative ideas
4. Intuition can facilitate sound decisions
5. Unconscious emotional associations can promote beneficial decisions

The Smart Unconscious

Although it is tempting to view the conscious, rational cognitive system as the essence of human intelligence and the experiential unconscious as more primitive, in actuality, the unconscious is quite smart in at least five ways (**FIGURE 3.7**). For one, the basic motives that we said earlier guide social cognition—the needs to make decisions accurately, quickly, or to confirm our preferred beliefs—often happen with little to no conscious awareness. People rarely seem to be aware that these motivations are influencing their judgments and behavior. Second, during sleep, our cognitive system shuts down, but our unconscious stays busy *consolidating* memories—that is, organizing and solidifying what we've learned and experienced (Diekelmann & Born, 2010). Third, studies of influential artists and scientists show that flashes of creative insight can arise spontaneously from the unconscious (although usually after a period of extensive conscious deliberation on the task at hand; Cattell, 1971; Csikszentmihalyi, 1996; Gable et al., 2019; Wallas, 1926).

Fourth, intuition plays a critical role in good decision making. It was long believed that successful decision making relies on a conscious, systematic process of weighing costs and benefits. In choosing a college, you might have been encouraged to weigh the pros and cons of each school, to scrupulously compare features such as the availability of student aid and the student-to-faculty ratio. You probably weren't encouraged to listen to your gut-level feelings about the different schools. But research suggests that unconscious feelings can steer us toward the best decisions. For example, our unconscious can intuitively sense when information is logically coherent, and it responds with a burst of positive affect (Topolinski & Strack, 2009; Winkielman & Cacioppo, 2001; Winkielman et al., 2007).

▲ People make many tough choices by weighing all the pros and cons, but intuitions also guide good decision making. As Oprah Winfrey said in her commencement speech at Stanford University: "Every right decision I've made—every right decision I've ever made—has come from my gut."

[REUTERS/Kimberly White/Alamy]

In many cases, though, we fail to listen to our unconscious feelings when forming attitudes and making decisions. One reason for this is that we often have difficulty verbalizing—that is, putting into words—why we like or dislike something. In chapter 1 we described a study by Nisbett and Wilson (1977b) that made this point by revealing the factors that influenced shoppers' stocking preferences without their conscious awareness. Because we have very little internal access to what actually determines our emotional reactions, when we are deciding things such as what fruit jam or poster we prefer or even how we feel about a relationship partner or a college, a conscious consideration of what we like or don't like will lead us to focus on factors that are easy to verbalize. And yet those factors may not reflect our feelings deep down.

In fact, when we think consciously about why we hold an attitude toward something, we often come up with a story that *sounds* reasonable but that does a poorer job than our gut feelings at predicting later behavior (Wilson et al.,

1989). In one study (Wilson & Kraft, 1993), some participants were first asked to analyze the reasons they felt the way they did about their current romantic relationship and were then asked to rate their overall satisfaction with the relationship. Another group of participants did not do a reasoned analysis; they just rated their overall satisfaction on the basis of their gut feelings. You might think that the people led to analyze their reasons would figure out how they really felt about the relationship so that their satisfaction ratings would predict whether their relationship stayed together or not. But the results revealed exactly the opposite. It was the people asked to rate their satisfaction based on their gut feelings whose satisfaction ratings predicted whether they were still dating that partner several months later. For the people who thought hard about their feelings, their rated satisfaction did not predict the outcome of their relationship.

A fifth way that the unconscious is smart is that our unconscious evaluations are essential for good judgment. According to Damasio's (2001) **somatic marker hypothesis**, there are certain somatic (i.e., bodily) changes that people experience as emotion. These somatic changes become automatically associated with positive or negative contexts for that emotion. When people encounter those contexts again, the somatic changes become a marker or a cue for what will happen next, helping to shape their decisions even without any conscious understanding of what they are doing.

We can see this when we compare the decisions made by healthy adults with those made by adults who have suffered damage to areas of the brain responsible for social judgments, particularly the ventromedial prefrontal cortex. Let's look at an example of a typical study. (See Simonovic et al., 2019, for a recent meta-analysis and critique of this literature.) Participants are given a gambling task in which their choice of cards from four different decks can either win or lose them money. Two of the decks are risky; they can give big payouts, but choosing from them repeatedly over the course of the game is a losing strategy. The other two decks give more modest payouts, but the losses are milder as well, and a normal participant eventually learns to stick to these less risky options. Patients with damage to the ventromedial prefrontal cortex, however, don't learn to avoid the risky decks. Why do these people continue to make high-risk decisions that will lose them money in the end? Part of the reason is that they don't show any fear that their choices will have negative consequences. Bechara and colleagues (1996) assessed participants' skin conductance as a measure of arousal just before they decided which deck to choose from. Normal participants showed elevated arousal prior to each pick (**FIGURE 3.8**). They were anticipating that their choice could be a bad one, and they were therefore more likely to learn from their mistakes. Ventromedial patients did not show evidence of this increased arousal, and without that somatic marker to warn them against the riskier decks, they chose from them over and over again as their money dwindled away.

Somatic marker hypothesis The idea that changes in the body, experienced as emotion, guide decision making.

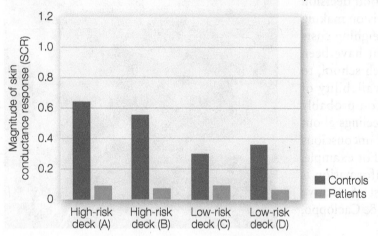

Figure 3.8

Somatic Markers of Risk

After playing a gambling game with both a high-risk deck of cards and a low-risk deck, most people (the controls) exhibit higher arousal just before selecting from the risky deck. Over time, they learn to avoid these risky choices. Patients with ventromedial damage to the prefrontal cortex do not show this arousal and do not learn to avoid the risk.

[Data from Bechara et al., 1996]

We don't need to be consciously aware of how our brains are interpreting our emotional associations for those emotions to aid our decision making. In one study (Bechara et al., 1997), 30% of normal participants were unable to explain why they chose cards from one deck more or less than from another. They had no conscious understanding of the patterns that had shaped their decision making over the course of the task, yet they showed the same pattern of improved performance as the participants who had developed a clear hunch that two of the decks were riskier than the others.

APPLICATION

Can the Unconscious Help Us Make Better Health Decisions?

There is a big push in the health care field to assist patients in making more informed medical decisions. You or someone you know may have encountered new decision aids like the one shown in the accompanying photo. In addition to providing information about the disease and treatment options, such an aid guides you through a series of rational and deliberate questions to help you arrive at a more educated understanding of the choices you can make for your treatment. In short, these aids rely strongly on the conscious processing system.

But is conscious reasoning always the best way to make these decisions? Research suggests that perhaps even medical decisions can benefit from some input from the intuitive processing system (de Vries et al., 2013). One reason may be that the intuitive system is better able to integrate feelings and emotions that can play a key role in treatment adherence. Taken together, research suggests that complex decisions may best be made by integrating conscious and unconscious processes (Nordgren, Bos et al., 2011). ∎

▲ Medical decision aids use a rational approach to guide people through medical treatment options, but some research suggests that the intuitive system can better integrate the role of emotion in decision making.

[Sonda Dawes/The Image Works]

SECTION REVIEW   The "How" of Social Cognition: Two Ways to Think About the Social World

Social cognition is governed by two systems of thinking: a *cognitive system* that is conscious, rational, and controlled, and an *experiential system* that is unconscious, intuitive, and automatic.

The Two Ways of Thinking Influence Attitudes and Behavior

- Implicit attitudes are unconscious, automatic, and based on learned associations (often called *heuristics*). Conscious, explicit attitudes are relatively independent of implicit attitudes. Hence, the same person can hold opposing implicit and explicit attitudes toward the same thing.

- Routine behaviors can become automatic, but in novel situations, the cognitive system takes over to make deliberate, reasoned judgments and decisions.

- The cognitive system requires awareness, motivation, and ability. If these conditions are not met, the cognitive system is interrupted, whereas the experiential system is relatively unimpeded.

The Unconscious Can Be Smart

The unconscious does "smart" things such as consolidating memories and guiding decision making.

Learning Outcomes

- Define *schemas*.
- Explain how priming of schemas influences both our impressions of people and our behavior.
- Define *confirmation bias* and give examples of how it occurs.
- Explain how metaphors can help us understand abstract ideas.

THINK ABOUT
[Dag Sundberg/Getty Images]

Categories Mental "containers" in which people place things that are similar to each other.

Schema A mental structure, stored in memory, that contains prior knowledge and associations with a concept.

The "What" of Social Cognition: Schemas as the Cognitive Building Blocks of Knowledge

So far we've outlined the broad motives and systems that guide *how* we think about the social world. Let's turn now to consider some of the more specific thought processes that underlie *what* people think about. The first thing to notice is how quickly and effortlessly the mind classifies stimuli into categories. **Categories** are like mental containers into which people place things that are similar to each other. Or, more precisely, even if two things are quite different from one another (two unique individuals, for instance), when people place them in the same category ("frat boys"), they think about those two items *as though* they were the same.

To appreciate what categories can do, stop and look around at your surroundings. What do you see? As for this author, I'm sitting at the dining room table in my house. I see my laptop in front of me and a stack of books nearby, along with my half-eaten lunch. There are pictures hanging on the walls, a plant in a corner of the room, and our pet dog near my feet (probably hoping for some of the lunch). Just within this 4-foot radius of my world, things are already pretty complex. I don't have the mental capacity to attend to and process every aspect of the environment, so I group stimuli together into broad categories. For example, although each of these books is unique, for now I lump them into the category *books*; in fact, for added convenience, I can lump the books along with those pens and used tea bags under the broader category *things on my desk that I don't have to deal with at the moment*. If people didn't group things into categories of objects and ideas, they would be overwhelmed by what William James called the "blooming, buzzing confusion" that they first experience as newborn infants before they develop categories (James, 1890, p. 462).

Knowledge Is Stored in Mental Structures Called Schemas

Categorization is an interesting process in its own right, but it is just the starting point of our mind's active meaning making. That's because as soon as people classify a stimulus as an instance of a category, their minds quickly access knowledge about that category, including beliefs about the category's attributes, expectations about what members of that category are like, and plans for how to interact with it, if at all. All this knowledge is stored in memory in a mental structure called a **schema**. For example, while at the library, if you categorize a person behind the desk as a librarian, you instantly access a schema for the category *librarian* that contains beliefs about which traits are generally shared by members of that group (e.g., intelligence), theories about how librarians' traits relate to other aspects of the world (e.g., librarians probably do not enjoy extreme sports), and examples of other librarians you have known. Using schemas, people can interpret ambiguous things they encounter by using prior knowledge to "go beyond the information given" (Bruner, 1957). We can demonstrate this with a simple example. Read the following paragraph:

> The procedure is quite simple. First, you arrange things into different groups. Of course, one pile may be sufficient, depending on how much there is to do. If you have to go somewhere else due to lack of facilities, that is the next step; otherwise you are pretty well set. It is important not to overdo things. That is, it is better to

do too few things at once than too many. At first the whole procedure will seem complicated. Soon, however, it will become just another facet of life. (BRANSFORD & JOHNSON, 1973, P. 400)

You might be scratching your head right now, wondering what these instructions are referring to. If you close your textbook and five minutes later try to remember all of the points in the paragraph, you will probably run into difficulty. What if we tell you that the paragraph is about laundry? Now, reread the paragraph, and you will see that the information makes much more sense to you than it did initially. After five minutes, you might do a reasonable job of remembering each of the steps described. The mere mention of the word *laundry* activated your schema of this process and made it a template for understanding the information you were reading.

Scripts: Schemas About Events Schemas are given special names, depending on the type of knowledge they represent. Schemas that represent knowledge about events are called **scripts**. These types of schemas (like the laundry example) always involve a temporal sequence, meaning that they describe how events unfold over time (first you sort, then you put one pile into the machine, then you add the soap, and so on). Scripts make coordinated action possible. Playing a game of tennis requires that both you and your partner have a schema of the game so that you can coordinate your actions and follow the rules of the game, even though you are playing against one another. They also allow you to fill in missing information. If I told you that I got a sandwich at the student union, I don't need to tell you, for example, that I paid for it. You can fill in that detail because you have the same basic "getting food at a restaurant" script as I do. Our reliance on scripts becomes embarrassingly apparent when we find ourselves without a script for a new situation. Imagine being invited to a Japanese tea ceremony but not knowing where to sit, what to say and when to say it, and how to sip the tea—when everyone else in attendance seems thoroughly acquainted with this very complex ritual of great importance for maintaining respectful social relationships.

Scripts Schemas about an event that specify the typical sequence of actions that take place.

Impressions Schemas people have about other individuals.

Impressions: Schemas About People Schemas that represent knowledge about other people are called **impressions**. Your schema of the actress Felicity Huffman might include physical characteristics (tall, blond, attractive), personality traits (talented, entitled), and other beliefs about her (convicted of fraud for paying $15,000 to have someone take the college entrance exam for her daughter). Similarly, we can also have a schema for a category of people (e.g., celebrities), called a *stereotype*. You can see that your impression of Felicity Huffman contains many traits (e.g., wealthy, talented, entitled) that are also part of your stereotype for celebrities.

▲ Your schema of Felicity Huffman might include aspects of her physical characteristics (blond), personality traits (talented), and beliefs about her life experiences (convicted of fraud in the 2019 college admissions scandal).

[Brian Snyder/REUTERS/Newscom]

You also have a schema about yourself—your *self-concept*. Self-concept is a topic we'll discuss in more depth in chapter 5.

Schemas Can Change Regardless of the type of schema, a schema consists of a pattern of learned associations. These patterns of associations can change and expand over time. You first might have learned about Felicity Huffman from her roles on *Desperate Housewives* or *When They See Us* and only later had to adjust or edit this positive view of her after learning about her illegal efforts to buy a better SAT score for her daughter. Some of our associations with Huffman might be stronger than others because we more frequently think about or hear about her in terms of those aspects.

But it's also important to realize that schemas are not passively filled up with information from the outside. Because of our need to validate and maintain particular beliefs and attitudes, we often tailor our schemas to highlight certain bits of knowledge while pushing others to the edges of the brain. Think about it this way: On your computer you probably have file folders that contain documents, pictures, and sound files that are related in some way, and you label those file folders accordingly, such as "Social Psychology Class" and "Summer Vacation." The schemas stored in your long-term memory are like those file folders in the sense that they contain all the bits of knowledge you have about a given category, from *Nazis* and *pedophiles* to *doorknobs* and *stickers*. But the similarities end there. Computer file folders usually don't magically acquire or lose documents, and they never insist that you open *this* picture and get nervous if you open up *that* picture. But that is exactly what schemas do, even without our conscious awareness. For example, if you are the faithful president of the Felicity Huffman fan club, your schema for her likely will emphasize the bits of knowledge that flatter her and will downplay anything that casts her in a negative light.

Where Do Schemas Come From? Cultural Sources of Knowledge

Let's take a closer look at where we acquire the knowledge that makes up our schemas. In some cases, we come into direct contact with people, events, and ideas and form concepts on the basis of that personal experience. But looking at this from the cultural perspective, we also learn a great deal about our social world indirectly and during childhood, from parents, teachers, peers, books, newspapers, magazines, television, movies, and the Internet. As children learn language and are told stories, they are taught concepts such as *honesty* and *courage*, *good* and *evil*, *love* and *hate*. From this learning, people develop ideas about what people in the world are like, the events that matter in life, and the meaning of their own thoughts and feelings.

As a result of these socializing influences, there are interesting cultural differences in people's schemas. For example, kids who grow up in a rural Native American culture that values connections with nature have a concept of "animal" that is most closely linked to those species that become part of their daily lives (Winkler-Rhoades et al., 2010). In contrast, urban-dwelling European American kids asked to list animals bring to mind exotic species such as elephants and lions that populate their picture books. Although each group has formed a schema for the category "animal," the content of that schema differs in important ways, depending on the values and structure of the group's physical, social, and cultural environment.

Rumors and Gossip   Much of what we learn about other people or events comes from rumors and gossip passed from one person to another. But beware. As people perceive and relay information, it is altered a bit as it is filtered by each person's schemas and motivations. An unfortunate consequence of these storytelling biases is that people hearing about a person or an event, rather than gaining knowledge firsthand, tend to form an oversimplified, extreme impression of that person or event (Baron et al., 1997; Gilovich, 1987).

For example, Robert Baron and colleagues (1997) had a participant watch a videotape in which a young man described unintentionally getting drunk at a party, getting involved in a fight, and subsequently getting

Figure 3.9

Spreading Rumors
People talked about the event depicted in this picture to others, who in turn told the story to still others, and so on. Over the course of several retellings, people's memories of the event became more consistent with racial stereotypes: Eventually the man holding the razor was remembered as Black, not White.

into a car accident. The man noted that this was uncharacteristic of him, that he was egged on by friends, and that he regretted his actions. The participant rated the man on various positive and negative traits. Then the participant, now in the role of storyteller, was asked to speak into a tape recorder while describing the man's story. Listeners who then only heard that audiotape retelling rated the man more negatively than the original storyteller did. These effects seem to result both from a tendency of storytellers to leave out mitigating factors and complexities and a tendency of listeners to attend only to the central aspects of the stories they hear.

In addition to this tendency to tell simplified stories, our stereotypes of groups can also make us biased in our recall and retelling of information. Gordon Allport and Joseph Postman (1947) demonstrated this back in the 1940s. They recruited a sample of White North American participants. Each participant was shown a picture depicting a scene on the New York subway involving a White man standing, holding a razor, and pointing his finger at a Black man (**FIGURE 3.9**). After viewing the picture, that participant was asked to describe the scene to another person who had not seen the picture. That second person then described the scene to a third person, and so on, until the information had been conveyed to a seventh person. More than half the time, that seventh person reported that the scene involved the Black man, rather than the White man, holding the razor. This finding suggests that when information is filtered through lots of people, it is likely to be biased by culturally prevalent schemas, including group stereotypes.

Mass Media Biases   Of course, we don't get information only from having it told to us directly by others; we also learn a great deal from the stories we see and hear in the media, books, and film (Mar, 2018). Just as rumors and gossip can distort the truth, media portrayals seldom are realistic accounts of what life is like, although they do provide vivid portrayals of possible scenarios. Unfortunately, these media offer biased views of many of these matters. For example, they tend to portray romantic relationships and love in oversimplified ways; portray men, women, and ethnic groups in stereotypic ways; and show a lot of violence (Dixon & Linz, 2000). The latter feature may explain why people who watch a lot of television think that crime and violence are far more prevalent in the world than they actually are (Shanahan & Morgan, 1999).

News programming and other descriptions of current and historical events are based on reality, and so people tend to assume that they paint a realistic, accurate, and unbiased picture of events and people. But the news is created at least as much as it is reported. Those who document and describe events in the news choose which events and people to report about and what perspective on the events to provide. These decisions are influenced by concerns about what information will most appeal to audiences and advertisers. Even the content presented in high school

Teenagers in both states will learn about the Harlem Renaissance and debates about the movement's impact on African American life.

But Texas students will read that some critics "dismissed the quality of literature produced."

Figure 3.10

Revisionist History?

Take a look at these two examples of how the same material about the Harlem Renaissance is taught to high school students in California and Texas. Only in the Texas edition of the same textbook are the impacts of the movement on African American culture called into question with a suggestion that the quality of literature produced by Black authors was poor.

Accessibility The ease with which people can bring an idea into consciousness and use it in thinking.

Salience The aspect of a schema that is active in one's mind and, consciously or not, colors perceptions and behavior.

Priming The process by which exposure to a stimulus in the environment increases the salience of a schema.

Associative networks Models for how pieces of information are linked together and stored in memory.

textbooks is described or evaluated differently depending on the audience. Just consider the two different descriptions of the Harlem Renaissance in high school history books for California and Texas (**FIGURE 3.10**). Both books describe the impact that this era of cultural growth had on the development of a positive African American identity. However, in the Texas edition of the book, it is mentioned that some critics have "dismissed the quality of the literature produced." In another example, a Californian history textbook provides a story about a Dominican American family in a chapter about immigration, whereas the same textbook used in Texas instead features the perspective of a Border Patrol agent (Goldstein, 2020).

How Do Schemas Work? Accessibility and Priming of Schemas

Given that people learn a host of schemas, the question becomes Which schemas are used to guide thinking and behavior at any given moment? To answer this question, it helps to introduce some technical terms. **Accessibility** refers to the ease with which people can bring an idea into consciousness and use it in thinking. When a schema is highly accessible, the **salience** of that schema is increased: It is activated in the person's mental system, even if she is not consciously aware of it, and it tends to color her perceptions and behavior (Higgins, 1996). We can now rephrase the question as What factors increase the salience of a schema, making it more accessible for thinking and acting? One answer is that the mind accesses schemas that fit (or seem to fit) with characteristics of the context. If Yana walks by a social gathering and sees people drinking and hears loud music, she'll likely pull up her *party* schema to interpret what is going on and how to relate to it.

Notice that in the above example, seeing the party is what activates Yana's *party* schema. **Priming** occurs when something in the environment activates a schema. This happens because the information that we store in memory is connected in **associative networks** (**FIGURE 3.11**). These networks are tools that psychologists use to describe how pieces of information stored in a person's memory are linked to other bits of information (Anderson, 1996; Collins & Loftus, 1975). These links result both from two concepts having similar meaning (e.g., nice and kind are semantic associations) or from two concepts being experienced together in time or space (e.g., clouds and rain are experiential associations). Because some concepts become linked based on one's personal experiences, different people's associations to the same concept can vary. For a person living in a high-crime area, guns might be experientially associated with violence; for a person living in the rural countryside, guns might be experientially associated with hunting.

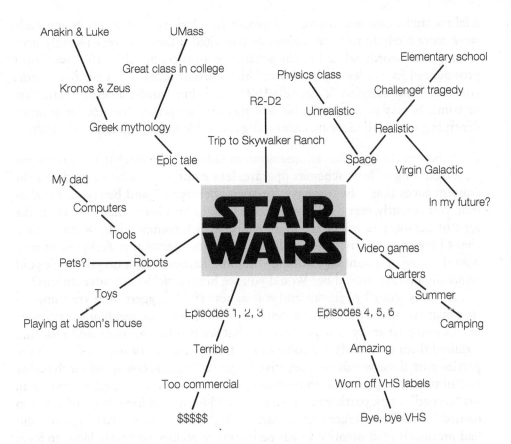

Figure 3.11

Associative Networks

Information is organized in associative networks in which closely related concepts are cognitively linked. Bringing to mind one concept can prime other concepts connected to it, sometimes without the person's conscious awareness.

Through these mental links, priming, or "turning on," one idea will bring to mind other ideas that are closely linked in a person's associative network but will be less likely to bring to mind ideas that are not strongly linked.

In addition to the immediate environment and priming, the person's personality determines how accessible certain schemas are. **Chronically accessible schemas** are schemas that represent information that is important to individuals, relevant to how individuals think of themselves, or used frequently (Higgins, 2012; Markus, 1977). Such schemas are very easily brought to mind by even the subtlest reminder. For example, Mary is really interested in environmental issues, whereas Jason is attuned to contemporary fashion. Mary is more likely to notice an electric car in the parking lot or express disdain over the plethora of plastic cups lying around at a party. Meanwhile, Jason has his fashion radar working and his associated constructs chronically accessible, and he may dislike the tacky cups and be more likely than Mary to notice that Cynthia arrived in last season's designer shoes. Even though they are in the same situation, the differences in what schemas are chronically accessible for Mary and Jason lead to very different perceptions and judgments of the scene.

People are also likely to interpret others' behavior in terms of their own chronically accessible schemas (Higgins et al., 1982). If you read a biography of Steve Jobs, the co-founder of Apple, and if *honesty* is a chronically accessible trait for you, you will be likely to have a good memory for incidents in Jobs's life that pertain to honesty, and your overall impression of Jobs will be largely colored by how honest he appears to have been. On the other hand, if *kindness* is chronically accessible for you, his incidents of kindness or unkindness will be particularly memorable and will influence your attitudes.

Situational and chronic influences on schema accessibility also can work together to influence our perceptions of the world. For example, after witnessing

Chronically accessible schemas Schemas that are easily brought to mind because they are personally important and used frequently.

a fellow student smile as a professor praises her class paper, students in one study were more likely to rate the student as conceited if they had very recently been primed with words related to the schema *arrogance*, but this effect was most pronounced for students who showed high chronic accessibility for the schema *conceitedness* (Higgins & Brendl, 1995). In other words, a certain situation or stimulus may prime particular schemas for one person but not for another, depending on which ideas are chronically accessible to each (Bargh et al., 1986).

Can Priming Change Our Impressions of Others?   Now that we have some understanding of how schemas operate, let's examine in a bit more detail the consequences that schemas have for social perception and behavior. Imagine that you recently met a fellow named Donald. You learn that Donald is the type of person you might see in an energy-drink commercial: He has a penchant for extreme activities—skydiving, kayaking, demolition derby—and he is now thinking of mountain climbing without a harness. What do you think your impression of him would be? Would you see him as reckless or adventurous?

An early study by Higgins and colleagues (1977) suggests that your impression might depend on the traits accessible to you before you met him. Participants in this two-part study first performed what seemed like an unrelated task that required them to identify the color of the font in a series of words. For half the participants, those words were negative adjectives (e.g., *reckless*), and for the other half of the participants, the words were positive adjectives (e.g., *adventurous*). In the "second" study, participants read about and formed an impression of a person named Donald who takes part in various high-risk activities. Participants who had previously read negative words pertaining to recklessness were likely to form more negative impressions of Donald, whereas participants who had previously read positive words pertaining to adventurousness tended to view Donald more positively. Their impressions seemed to be influenced by the different ideas they were primed with before they read about him, suggesting that our impressions of others can be shaped by salient schemas.

One caveat to this research is that a more recent replication of a similar study failed to show reliable effects of subtle primes on impression formation in a much larger sample (McCarthy et al., 2018). Perhaps this is because priming can have quite different effects on impressions for different people or in different situations. One meta-analysis suggested that sometimes primes are *assimilated* into the impressions we form of a person (as when an adventurous prime leads us to see Donald as adventurous). Other times those primes become a point of *contrast* (as when an adventurous prime leads us to see Donald as timid by comparison) (Decoster & Claypool, 2004). Some evidence suggests that very extreme and highly salient primes are more likely to lead to contrast rather than assimilation effects (Higgins, 1996). However, more work is needed to nail down exactly if, when, and how priming a schema affects the impressions we form.

Can Priming Change Our Behavior?   It is one thing to push around people's judgments with simple primes. There has been much debate in the field as to whether priming simple concepts can actually affect behavior. Initially, there seemed to be some good evidence for behavioral priming. In one often-cited study (Bargh et al., 1996), college students were asked to unscramble words to make sentences from four of five words. Unbeknownst to them, several key sentences were designed to prime either a schema of *rudeness* or a schema of *politeness* (e.g., four words would unscramble to make "they usually bother her" or "they usually respect her"). When participants then tried to return

▲ This man is free climbing without a safety harness. Would you describe him as adventurous or reckless? Because of priming, your impression might be influenced by what you were thinking about just before meeting him.

[James Balog/The Image Bank/Getty Images]

their packet of surveys to the experimenter, they found her stuck in a conversation that didn't seem likely to end anytime soon. The researchers reported that only 17% of those primed with politeness-related words interrupted the conversation within a 10-minute time frame, compared with 64% who were primed with rudeness-related words. Those primed with rudeness behaved more rudely.

These and other similar prime-to-behavior studies have garnered a lot of interest, but there has also been intense debate about the strength and reliability of these kinds of findings since several concerted follow-up studies have failed to show clear effects (Earp et al., 2014; Harris et al., 2013; Shanks et al., 2015). One set of studies suggests that experimenters' own expectations have a stronger effect on participants' behavior than subtly primed concepts, suggesting that experimenters themselves might have been unknowingly shaping participants' behavior in these priming studies (Gilder & Heerey, 2018). These critiques highlight the importance of designing studies where experimenters are blind to condition.

On the one hand, there is no question that priming one concept can activate another in someone's mind. In fact, researchers harness the power of priming to measure the automatic activation of attitudes that people might otherwise deny having (Payne & Lundberg, 2014). The question is whether such primes can be powerful enough to alter one's actions. More recent studies offer a few key insights (Weingarten et al., 2016). First, people seem to be especially suggestable to primed information when the right action is ambiguous and they have to act quickly. For example, in a recent study participants had to make a series of very quick betting decisions. In these studies, participants primed with words like *gamble* or *wager* were consistently more likely to place a bet, but only when the cards they were dealt were not obviously good or bad (Payne et al., 2016). When one has to act fast on ambiguous information, priming might be more likely to affect behavior simply because the more rational system is forced to take a backseat to experiential processing.

In addition, a recent meta-analysis of 133 studies suggests that primes have a larger effect on behavior when people are already somewhat motivated to enact that behavior (Weingarten et al., 2016). For example, if Claire is high in achievement motivation, then being primed with success-related words might lead her to persist on a difficult homework assignment. But if she was not already high in achievement motivation, exposure to the same words would likely not affect her behavior (Jonas, 2013; Klatzky & Creswell, 2014; Molden, 2014).

 APPLICATION
Using Priming to Prevent Infection

Recent research finds some evidence that priming can be used to promote public health. Think about this scenario: You come the hospital to visit friend who is in intensive care after being involved in a car accident. As you come to the door of the ICU, there is a hand gel dispenser on the wall, with a sign warning you that you are entering a "hand hygiene zone." Surely, you would stop to sanitize your hands before entering the ICU, right? Maybe not. Research suggests that fewer than 12% of visitors to a hospital comply with such requests to wash the bacteria and germs from their hands before entering the rooms of those most at risk of infection (Birnbach et al., 2012). Can priming cleanliness increase this behavior? Maybe it can. In one study, when researchers added an automated air

THINK ABOUT
[Toey Toey/Shutterstock]

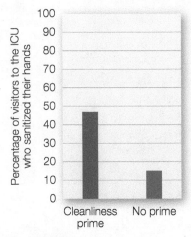

Figure 3.12

Primed to Act

When researchers introduced a clean-smelling citrus scent just outside the entrance to the ICU at a hospital, 47% of visitors stopped to sanitize their hands. This was a large increase from the 15% who cleansed their hands without this cleanliness prime.

[Data from King et al., 2016]

freshener that released a clean citrus scent just at the entrance to the ICU, the percentage of visitors who cleansed their hands increased from 15% to 47% (**FIGURE 3.12**) (King et al., 2016). Such effects might provide key strategies for slowing the spread of infection and dealing with global pandemics like the COVID-19 pandemic in 2020. ■

Confirmation Bias: How Schemas Alter Perceptions and Shape Reality

Schemas and the expectations and interpretations they produce are generally quite useful. Your *party* schema tells you what to expect, how to behave, how to dress, and so forth. Your *mom* schema helps you predict and interpret things your mom will say and do. And the schemas that become active in particular situations are usually the ones most relevant to that situation. However, once we have a schema, we tend to seek out and evaluate new information so that it confirms what we already believe or feel. This is known as *confirmation bias*. In chapter 1 we saw how this bias influenced students' evaluations of an article on capital punishment (Lord et al., 1979). Confirmation bias helps people preserve their worldview by sustaining a stable, consistent set of beliefs and attitudes about the world. In this way, it provides an individual with psychological security. However, confirmation bias also often leads to inaccurate interpretations of new information.

One reason that confirmation biases occur is that schemas activated in our mind can lead us to interpret ambiguous information in a schema-

 SOCIAL PSYCH OUT IN THE WORLD

A Scary Implication: The Tyranny of Negative Labels

In a 2013 episode of the radio program *This American Life*, Ira Glass (Glass, 2013b) described the murder case of Vince Gilmer. In 2006, Gilmer was sentenced to life in prison and described by the judge as a "cold-blooded killer." The evidence was irrefutable and showed that Vince was guilty of strangling his elderly father to death and dumping the body on the side of the road in another state, after chopping off the fingers to make the body harder to identify. Although Vince didn't deny his role in ending his father's life, he maintained that his crime was not the act of a cold-blooded killer. Representing himself in court, he laid out a rather incoherent case for his insanity, built around the idea that his brain was destabilized by low levels of serotonin after he quit his antidepressants cold turkey. Although Vince showed some unusual twitching behavior, severe mood swings, and cognitive problems in the lead-up to his trial, law enforcement officials, a psychiatrist, the judge, and the jury all assumed that he was faking these symptoms. After all, isn't this exactly what you would expect from a cold-blooded killer trying to avoid doing time for his crime?

The good news about human nature is that extremely negative behavior such as Vince's is actually rare. But because

it's so harmful or disruptive to society when people do bad or unusual things, we are quick to slap a negative label on those who commit crimes or who exhibit other abnormal tendencies, and we are very reluctant to peel off such labels. Once someone is labeled a psychopath, as Vince was, his or her every action is interpreted as evidence of psychopathic tendencies. These biases have been confirmed in research in which naive observers and trained clinicians are more likely to interpret drawings from mentally ill patients as revealing signs of the artists' disorders. In fact, the researchers had randomly paired each picture with a given disorder. It was people's schemas for how mental illness should look, not a mental illness itself, that shaped how these drawings were viewed (Chapman & Chapman, 1967, 1969). In the same way, for Vince, his negative or unusual behaviors seem fitting for a psychopath, but of course anything positive or exculpatory seemed like a cunning attempt to charm and manipulate others. If the label is accurate, we tend not to stress about the mental straitjackets we apply to people. But these labels not only leave little room for people to grow beyond or redeem themselves from past wrongs, they also make it nearly impossible for those who have been mislabeled to break free of these binds. In Vince's case, it took someone who was willing to construct an impression or schema of him built around more positive associations to provide a different interpretation of what had happened to confirming manner. For example, in one study, participants watched a silent videotape of a woman being interviewed (Snyder & Frankel, 1976). They were either told that the interview was about sex or that it was about politics, and their job was to assess the woman's emotional state. When participants thought the interview was about sex, they rated her as more anxious than when they thought the interview was about politics. The videotape was the same in both cases, and the woman's reactions were ambiguous. But when participants thought the topic was sex, they *expected* the woman to be anxious over discussing such a personal topic, and they therefore interpreted any fidgeting they saw as indicating anxiety. You've heard the expression "Seeing is believing"; studies such as these suggest that the converse holds true as well: "Believing is seeing"!

 APPLICATION
Confirmation Bias and Climate Change

One reason for confirmation biases is that people tend to pay more attention to information that fits the schemas they already have and ignore information that doesn't fit. As a result of these attentional biases, people can even misremember factual information in ways that support their preferred beliefs. Take, for example, the ongoing political discussion about what can be done to curtail global climate change. With so much at stake, one might hope that only the motive for accuracy guides attention and memory. But studies show that confirmation biases sneak in. In one study, participants watched a documentary detailing the

Vince. You see, before Vince killed his father, he was a beloved and compassionate doctor. The physician who took over Vince's clinic learned about the close and caring relationships he had with his patients and dug into Vince's case in more detail. Eventually, he discovered that Vince had tested positive for Huntington disease, a degenerative condition that could explain every one of the unusual behaviors, mood changes, and violent actions that Vince had been displaying over the past few years. Although Huntington disease is a terminal illness with no cure, and Vince Gilmer remains locked up in a psychiatric facility, Vince could finally feel vindicated that the label of cold-blooded killer might not be the best explanation for his behavior.

Stories like Vince's reveal the power of schemas to influence a person's perceptions and lead to confirmation biases that justify whatever label the person already decided on. Of course, in Vince's case, he had committed an unspeakable crime and was, in fact, exhibiting unusual and dangerous behavior.

Can negative labels be just as confining when inaccurately applied to sane and healthy people? Imagine the following horror film scenario: You wake up one day in a psychiatric institution and learn that you have been labeled schizophrenic. How easy do you think it would be to con-

vince the staff you were not schizophrenic and get them to release you? This was a question asked in a classic but controversial study by David Rosenhan (1973). Rosenhan and seven other people with no actual history of mental illness checked themselves into San Francisco–area mental hospitals, complaining of symptoms consistent with schizophrenia. After they were admitted, they behaved completely normally and never again reported having any symptoms diagnostic of schizophrenia for the two to three weeks they remained institutionalized. Even so, their normal behavior was sometimes interpreted through the lens of their diagnosis. For example, one psychiatrist noted writing in a journal as evidence of "obsessive writing behavior." None of the pseudopatients were ever judged as fakes by the psychiatrists. No amount of positive, everyday, sane behavior was enough to wipe away the original label they had received.

This study caused an uproar (and is still being debated; see Calahan, 2019) partly due to qualms about whether it was ethical but mainly because it illustrated that mental health diagnostic labels become schemas that, once attached to a person, are very hard to disconfirm. Most of the time, people's tendencies to use schemas to categorize and understand other people are helpful, but in cases such as these, labels can become perceptual prisons.

▲ Confirmation biases can cloud people's judgment leading climate deniers to ignore evidence of climate change.

[Giuseppe Manfra/Moment/Getty Images]

scientific evidence for climate change and afterward were tested for their memory of details in the film. Those who had a strong motivation to justify current economic practices and regulations were more likely to misremember evidence as presenting a less severe problem. As a result, they were less likely to believe that climate change is problem that requires economic intervention (Hennes et al., 2016). ■

When Objective Information Is Used to Justify Bias Confirmation bias is so strong that it can distort the meaning of objective information. Darley and Gross (1983) had participants watch one of two versions of a videotape about a nine-year-old fourth-grader named Hannah, showing her playing in a playground, along with scenes of her neighborhood and school. The videotapes made it clear that Hannah had either an upper-class or lower-class background. Darley and Gross reasoned that participants shared the common schema of upper-class kids as academically successful and the common schema of lower-class kids as unsuccessful.

Half the participants (the no performance group) were then simply asked to rate Hannah's academic abilities on a scale ranging from kindergarten to sixth-grade level. The other half (the performance group), before being asked to rate Hannah, watched a second videotape showing Hannah answering intellectual questions ranging from easy to difficult. This video was the same, regardless of the earlier depiction of Hannah's social class. Hannah did well on some problems and not well on others.

Which group do you think was especially likely to be influenced in their ratings by Hannah's socioeconomic status—the no performance group or the performance group? We might expect participants given only class-based schemas to rate Hannah higher if they thought she was upper class rather than lower class. However, one would hope that participants provided with objective evidence of Hannah's academic abilities would rely on that information and ignore the class-based schemas.

And yet the opposite occurred, as we see in **FIGURE 3.13**. The objective evidence *increased* rather than decreased the bias. The group that didn't have the opportunity to see Hannah perform estimated her math abilities to be the same regardless of whether she was upper class or lower class. They seemed to realize that they didn't have much basis for prejudging her abilities after only seeing her on a playground. However, the group that observed Hannah's performance rated her much better if she was upper class rather than lower class.

The point is that the participants didn't interpret the so-called objective evidence objectively; instead, they interpreted it as confirming what they already believed they knew about Hannah's ability based on knowing her social class.

Biased Information Gathering Schema use can bias how people gather additional information, often in ways that confirm prior beliefs and attitudes. Participants in one study had a brief discussion with a conversation partner

Figure 3.13

Schemas Bias Interpretation

When rating the math ability of a little girl, participants were not biased by her social class if they had no opportunity to observe her taking an achievement test. However, those who watched a video of her taking an oral test interpreted her performance more negatively if they believed that she attended a lower-class elementary school.

[Data from Darley & Gross, 1983]

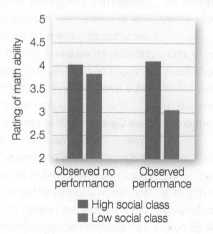

High social class
Low social class

who was described to them as being an extravert or an introvert (Snyder & Swann, 1978). Their job was to assess whether this description was true, and they were given a set of questions to choose from to guide their conversation. Participants tended to ask the conversation partner questions that already assumed the hypothesis was true and would lead to answers confirming the hypothesis. For example, a participant wanting to determine whether the partner was an extravert chose to ask questions such as, "What kinds of situations do you seek out if you want to meet new people?" and "In what situations are you most talkative?" However, if they wanted to determine whether the partner was an introvert, they chose questions such as, "What factors make it hard for you to really open up to people?" and "What things do you dislike about loud parties?" It is important to note here that these are leading questions: When answering a question about how she livens up a party, for example, a person is very likely to come across as extraverted, even if she is not; likewise, even an extravert will look introverted when talking about what he dislikes about social situations. This study shows that people tend to seek evidence that fits the hypothesis they are testing rather than also searching for evidence that might not fit that hypothesis.

Achie√e
Video: Confirmation Bias

The Self-Fulfilling Prophecy Another vivid testament to the power of schemas is evidence that they not only bias our perceptions of social reality but can also *create* the social reality that we expect. More specifically, people's initially false expectations can cause the fulfillment of those expectations, a phenomenon that Robert Merton (1948) labeled the **self-fulfilling prophecy.** To investigate this idea, Robert Rosenthal and Lenore Jacobson (1968) administered tests to students in an elementary school in 1964. After scoring the tests, they gave the teachers the names of some kids in their class who, according to the Harvard Test of Inflected Acquisition, were on the verge of experiencing a substantial leap forward in their general learning abilities. The teachers were told that these kids were "late bloomers" who were about to display an "intellectual growth spurt."

Self-fulfilling prophecy The phenomenon whereby initially false expectations cause the fulfillment of those expectations.

Two years later, the kids labeled as late bloomers actually scored substantially higher than their classmates did on a test of general abilities. However, unknown to the teachers, the list of kids originally labeled late bloomers was a random selection from the class rosters. So the only reason they experienced a dramatic intellectual growth spurt was that the teachers were led to expect that they would!

What accounts for this self-fulfilling prophecy? Years of additional research have revealed that although such effects don't always occur, when they do, it is because teachers' expectations affect their behavior toward the students in ways that improve the students'

▲ Through a process known as the self-fulfilling prophecy, teachers' positive expectations for their students can shape how well those students actually perform.
[Darrin Henry/Shutterstock]

learning (Rosenthal, 2002). For example, kids expected to do well are given more attention and more nods and smiles, are challenged more, and are given more positive reinforcement for their successes (Harris & Rosenthal, 1985; Jussim, 1986). Students tend to respond to such behavior with more engagement and more effort and, consequently, more learning. One study also showed that students' expectations can also change teachers' behavior: If students expect a teacher to be excellent, the teacher performs better (Feldman & Prohaska, 1979).

Since that classic study on teachers and students, self-fulfilling prophecies have been demonstrated in many other contexts as well (e.g., Snyder et al., 1977; Madon et al., 2018). If you expect someone to be friendly and sociable, you are likely to act in ways that elicit such behavior. If you expect someone to be unpleasant and annoying, you are likely to act in ways that provoke that kind of behavior. The more people who hold these expectations, the larger the effect on one's behavior (Madon et al., 2018). Mere expectations won't turn a serial killer into a humanitarian, but most of us are capable of being pleasant or unpleasant, industrious or indifferent. Within a moderate range of variability, perceivers' expectations about others can shift people's behavior toward confirming those expectations.

Limits on the Power of Confirmation Biases   We have beaten the drum for confirmation bias very loudly in this section, and the large body of evidence warrants doing so. However, confirmation bias does not always occur. Why not?

If people's observations clearly conflict with their initial expectations, they will revise their view of particular people and events. This is especially likely if the gap between what people expect and what they observe is extreme. For example, if you play chess with a nine-year-old and don't expect the child to show much skill, and then the kid beats you, you will likely revise your opinion of the child's chess ability. In fact, because your expectation was so different from the outcome, you might even overrate the child's ability. It is interesting, though, that even in such cases, people usually grant the exception but keep the underlying schema. In the chess example, you'd probably think, "This kid's a genius, but most nine-year-olds stink at chess." Of course, if enough nine-year-olds whip you in chess, the schema eventually would give way to the data.

In addition, when people are aware of and concerned about being biased, their cognitive system may kick in to correct the feared bias (Chien et al., 2014; Wegener & Petty, 1995). Another way to think about this correction is to say that people's need for accuracy trumps their need for closure, leading them to think more carefully—or at least to respond in a way that is opposite to what they think is a biased judgment. However, the evidence suggests that this correction process tends to be inexact and sometimes leads people to bend over backward in the opposite direction. However, there is also promising evidence that people (including perhaps you) can be successfully taught what confirmation bias is and how to prevent this bias from influencing decision making (Sellier et al., 2019).

Finally, in the context of self-fulfilling prophecies, if targets of your expectation know you think a certain way about them, they may go out of their way to try to disconfirm your expectation (Hilton & Darley, 1985; Jamieson & Harkins, 2007).

Beyond Schemas: Metaphor's Influence on Social Thought

So far we've discussed how people use schemas to make meaningful sense of the world. This is an intuitive perspective, as we would expect people to think about something in the context of their knowledge about that type of thing. Still, there are likely to be other cognitive tools besides schemas that guide our thinking.

Consider this: If people rely solely on schemas, then why do they commonly talk about social concepts in terms of things that, on the surface, are totally unrelated? For example, why do English speakers commonly say "*Lift* my spirits" when they know that being in a positive mood does not literally lift you up? Why do they say, "Those days *are behind me*" when there are no days piled up like bricks behind them? Or why might Korean speakers say, "애써 그 사람이 그리운 생각을 밀어냈다" (translation: "With much effort I *pushed away* my longing for him"), when they know that a desire for someone is not an object that can be pushed and pulled?

Given that these types of expressions pervade the way we *talk* about social things, the big question becomes Does that tell us anything about the way people ordinarily think? According to *conceptual metaphor theory*, it does. **Metaphor** is a cognitive tool that people can use to understand abstract social ideas in terms of *other types* of ideas that are more concrete and better understood (Kövecses, 2010; Lakoff & Johnson, 1980). For example, when Lisa says, "Christmas is fast approaching," she may be using her knowledge about *moving objects* to conceptualize *time*. Why? Because Lisa may find it difficult to get a clear image of time in her mind (which is not surprising, since physicists aren't sure what time is!). She has a concrete schema for physical objects moving around, and this schema tells her that objects tend to be more relevant as they draw closer. By extending her *objects* schema to think about time, Lisa can make sense of what an "approaching" event means for her (time to buy gifts!), even though there is no such thing as an event moving toward her in space.

How does this perspective enhance what we know about social cognition? It suggests that whereas a schema organizes our knowledge about similar stimuli (like librarians or snowstorms), a metaphor blends our knowledge of one thing with knowledge of a different type of thing. This is especially useful when we're grappling with ideas that are vague or complicated. In fact, good ideas themselves are often framed in terms of metaphors of a light bulb suddenly lit up or a seed beginning to take root and grow (Elmore & Luna-Lucero, 2017). By using metaphor, our minds "borrow" a familiar schema from one concept (a light bulb) to give shape to these abstractions (a good idea) and inform how we think and feel about them, even though the concepts are unrelated at a surface level.

One example of this occurs when people use metaphor to represent an abstract idea in terms of a bodily experience. Research has found some evidence that priming bodily feelings can carry over and influence judgments and decisions about that abstract idea. Have you ever heard someone say, "This is a *heavy* issue that's been *weighing on* my mind; can we deal with something *lighter*?" Of course, an issue is not literally an object with weight. And yet studies show that this link goes deeper than language: In studies in which people were asked to rate something's importance, those who meanwhile held a heavy object (e.g., a bulky clipboard) judged that thing as more important than those who handled a light object. This effect has been reported for ratings of issues at one's university (Jostmann et al., 2009), a job applicant's seriousness (Ackerman et al., 2010), the severity of a

Metaphor A cognitive tool that allows people to understand an abstract concept in terms of a dissimilar, concrete concept.

▲ Which of these two books seems to deal with a more important topic? Metaphors linking weight to importance might lead us to assume that it's the larger book underneath.

[netopaek/Shutterstock]

disease (Kaspar, 2013), and a book's literary significance (Chandler et al., 2012). Taken together, these findings suggest that people's conception of importance may be based on more than a schema; it might also build on their bodily experiences with weight and lightness.

Zestcott et al. (2017) put a further spin on these findings. What happens, they asked, when people become consciously aware of their bodily states? Will they still use that body as a source of information when rating the importance of something? Our discussion of the two systems of social cognition suggests that if something draws conscious attention to what the body is sensing, people will switch to a more analytical and deliberate style of thinking, focusing on the facts and ignoring passing feelings. Consistent with this reasoning, when participants completed a survey about the importance of improving the city's roads, those who completed the survey on a heavy clipboard (2.29 lb.) judged the issue as more important than did students who held a light clipboard (1.45 lb.). But if the experimenter told participants "just to let you know, some people have found the weight of the clipboard to feel heavy," the effect of weight on ratings of importance disappeared. People may use their bodies to think about abstract ideas, but not if something in the context makes them aware that they are doing so.

SECTION REVIEW   The "What" of Social Cognition: Schemas as the Cognitive Building Blocks of Knowledge

The mind typically classifies a stimulus into a category and then accesses a schema, a mental structure containing knowledge about a category. Schemas allow people to "go beyond the information given" and make inferences, judgments, and decisions about a given stimulus. Although generally helpful, schemas can produce false beliefs and limit a person's interpretation of reality.

Sources	Accessibility and Priming	Confirmation Bias	Metaphor
• Schemas come from multiple sources and are heavily influenced by culture. They are also shaped by the need for closure.	• Salient schemas are highly accessible and color thinking and behavior. • Priming occurs when something in the environment activates a schema. • When primed, schemas can influence the impressions we form of others and might sometimes influence behavior.	• People tend to interpret information in a way that confirms their prior schemas. • Objective information may be skewed to fall in line with expectations. • Schema-inconsistent information may be overlooked. • Our expectations may shift another's behavior toward confirming those expectations. • We may revise our views for exceptional cases but retain the underlying schema.	• People use metaphor to understand an abstract concept in terms of another type of idea that is more concrete and easier to grasp.

Returning to the "Why": Motivational Factors in Social Cognition and Behavior

So far, we have focused on the automatic processes involved in how we perceive people and events in the environment. We have not said too much about motivation. This doesn't mean that motivational factors have little influence on when, what, and how we apply schemas to our understanding of the world. As noted at the outset of this chapter, motivational factors are linked to cognitive processes. They are the engine that puts this cognitive machinery into action (Kruglanski, 1996; Kunda, 1990; Pyszczynski & Greenberg, 1987b), and they often operate outside our conscious awareness (Kihlstrom, 2019).

- Explain when a prime such as "thirst" motivates behavior.
- Identify which psychological motive is most likely to come into play when there's a time pressure for a decision.
- Explain the relationship between mood and social judgment.

Priming and Motivation

To see how motivation plays a role in priming, consider the long history of controversial media accounts of subliminal priming. For example, in 1957, a movie theater proprietor claimed to have boosted popcorn and soda sales at concession stands by presenting subliminal messages encouraging patrons to visit the snack bar. This was later discovered to be false because no such messages were actually presented, but the idea certainly raised the ire of many moviegoers at the time. In 1990, the heavy metal band Judas Priest was sued over purportedly presenting in a song subliminal messages that encouraged a young man to commit suicide.

Although these examples turned out to be groundless, modern research gives us a better theoretical grasp of how priming, and even subliminal priming, might influence thought and behavior. We know that information (such as words and pictures) can be presented precisely long enough to activate them in the mind without bringing them into conscious attention. (In most experiments, exposures range from 10 to 100 milliseconds.) We also know that subliminal primes—or any primes for that matter—do not lead people automatically and robotically to do whatever it is they are told to do, such as buy a soda or commit suicide. Rather, subliminal priming makes some ideas more accessible than others. A person's competing or complementary goals and motives can then influence whether and when primes lead to behavior (Weingarten et al., 2016). For example, subliminally priming the idea *thirst* can lead a person to drink more—but only when that person is thirsty; without this motivation to satisfy thirst, the prime has no effect on beverage consumption (Strahan et al., 2002).

In addition, because our motivations can be quite distinct in different environments and with different people, the surrounding context can affect when, why, and whether primes might affect behavior (Gollwitzer & Bargh, 2005; Loersch & Payne, 2011). Cesario and colleagues (2006) illustrated this point by using a priming procedure developed by Bargh and associates (1996). In the original study, participants had to rearrange sets of scrambled words to form grammatical sentences. Embedded within this sentence-unscrambling task were some words related to college students' concept of the elderly (compared to only neutral words in a no-prime condition). After completing the sentence-unscrambling task, participants were told they could leave. Little did they know that the experimenter measured

Achie/e
Video: Priming in the Real World

▲ Priming helps people prepare to act. When primed with the concept of "elderly," for example, people who have positive attitudes toward older adults walk more slowly, perhaps because doing so would allow them to interact with an elderly person more easily.

[Lisa F. Young/Shutterstock]

how long it took them to walk down the hallway to the elevator. Participants primed with the *elderly* schema walked more slowly than those who did not have this schema primed. This was originally interpreted as an "automatic activation" effect in which the *elderly* schema was salient (as a result of being primed) and automatically influenced participants' behavior.

However, Cesario and colleagues argued that being exposed to the prime didn't just make the *elderly* schema accessible but also activated participants' feelings about and motivation to interact with elderly individuals. Some people have positive attitudes about old people, and others have more negative attitudes. For those who have positive attitudes toward the elderly, when the *elderly* schema is activated, so too is the motivation to interact positively with such people. These participants might unconsciously adjust their behavior to have a smoother interaction with an elderly person; this could include walking more slowly, as Bargh and his team had shown.

But when the same schema is primed for those who have negative attitudes toward the elderly, so too is the motivation to avoid them. Therefore, the researchers hypothesized, these participants should walk faster to avoid the elderly and leave them in the dust. This was exactly what they found. When participants had positive attitudes about elderly people, they responded to the *elderly* prime by walking more slowly. However, when participants had negative attitudes about elderly people, they responded to the prime by walking faster! These results support the point that primes do not influence behavior in a simple manner but rather interact with individuals' motivation to determine what they think and do in a given context (Cesario et al., 2010).

Motivated Social Cognition

Clearly, people are not simply automatons, blindly controlled by whatever schemas happen to be accessible in their minds. Indeed, the tools that we use to think serve our needs and goals (Kenrick et al., 2010). As a result, we do not think about the world "out there" as though we were video cameras; rather, our everyday thinking is significantly shaped by the motives and needs that we have at that time and place.

What are those motives and needs? Some stem from our bodies, of course. A hungry person is more likely to think about food than sex and will likely look for, and notice, a restaurant faster than an attractive person who happens to be walking by. Other motives have to do with the kinds of thoughts we want to have about the people, ideas, and events that we encounter in our social environment. Specifically, *what* we think about and *how* we think about it are continually influenced by three psychological motives that we introduced earlier in this chapter: the need to be accurate, to reach closure quickly, and to validate what we prefer to believe (Kruglanski, 1980, 2004). These motives are constantly at work, sometimes below our conscious radar, filtering which bits of information get into our minds, how we interpret and remember them, and which we bring to mind to justify what we want to believe. Let's consider specifics.

The Need for Accuracy The motive for accuracy can lead people to set aside their schemas and focus on objective facts. For example, when a person is motivated to understand who another person really is, perhaps because he is going to work with her on a task, he may be motivated to look past the convenient stereotypes he has for her group and put more thought into her individual personality (Fiske & Neuberg, 1990).

The Need to Reach Closure Quickly What about the need to reach closure quickly? When people are motivated to gain a clear, simple understanding of their surroundings, they tend to see events in a way that wraps up the world in a neat little package. For example, if people know they have to form an impression of someone quickly, they are more likely to seize on the first bit of information they receive and fail to take into account relevant information that they encounter later (known as the *primacy effect*; Kruglanski & Freund, 1983). In contrast, people not under time pressure are more able to consider all the relevant information before reaching a conclusion about what a person is like.

Mental laziness is not the only reason people seek closure on simple, consistent interpretations of the world. Uncertainty, ambiguity, and complexity can also be very unsettling. According to the *meaning maintenance model*, even brief exposure to stimuli that seem out of place or inconsistent with expectations can put people on alert to make sense of their environment or to affirm other moral convictions (Heine et al., 2006; Proulx & Heine, 2008, 2009; Proulx & Inzlicht, 2012). In one study, after simply viewing nonsensical word pairs such as "*turn–frogs*" and "*careful–sweaters*" (compared with sensible word associations), participants were more eager to reaffirm a sense of meaning by acting in line with their moral beliefs (Randles et al., 2011). When unexpected events occur, people have an automatic tendency to restore a sense of meaning, even in unrelated areas of life.

Why, deep down, are inconsistent states of mind threatening? From the existential perspective, maintaining clear, simple interpretations of reality provides people with a psychological buffer against the threatening awareness of their mortality (Landau, Johns et al., 2004) and a broader sense of meaning (Heine et al., 2006). If the world appears fragmented, chaotic, or vague, people may have difficulty sustaining faith that there is anything bigger than themselves—anything that they can rely on to give their life meaning and significance—and so they are left with the possibility that they will simply die and be forgotten. Conversely, the sense that the world is ordered—that people act in consistent ways, for example, and that people generally get what they deserve—buttresses people's faith that they can establish some meaning and personal value that will be remembered after they die (Schimel et al., 1999).

The Need to Validate What We Already Believe Let's turn to the need to validate our prior beliefs. In many cases, people want more than mere certainty: They want to reach conclusions that support their preferred views of the social world. The motive to validate beliefs can lead people to assume that the use of so-called enhanced interrogation practices will yield higher-quality intelligence if they support these practices compared to those who reject them on moral

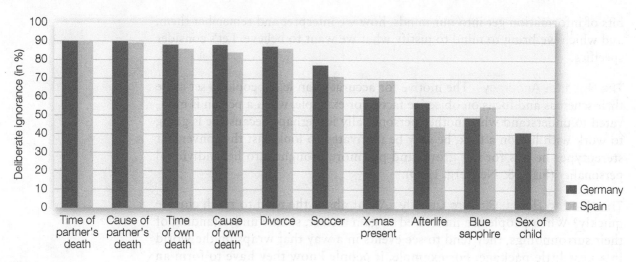

Figure 3.14

Ignorance Is Bliss?

In representative surveys conducted in Spain and Germany, people often showed a preference not to know the truth. For example, nearly 90% of respondents said that they would rather not know the time of their own or their partners' death, and more than 60% said that they would prefer not to know what they are receiving as a present.

[Data from Gigerenzer & Garcia-Retamero, 2017]

grounds (Ames & Lee, 2015). This motive doesn't just bias perceptions of other people and events; it can also bias perceptions of information that is closer to home. When presented with complicated statistical information, many people fail to engage sound reasoning to accurately assess risk. However, if the information is relevant to their own health, they become more accurate at analyzing the same kinds of statistical problems, especially if the answer gives them better odds of good health (Mata et al., 2015).

On the other hand, sometimes people prefer to be ignorant of the truth. In representative surveys conducted in Spain and Germany, nearly 90% of respondents said that they would rather not know the time of their own or their partners' death, and 50 to 60% said that they would prefer not to know what they are receiving as a present or whether that blue sapphire they bought while traveling is in fact a rare gemstone (Gigerenzer & Garcia-Retamero, 2017; see **FIGURE 3.14**). For both positive and negative events, people are not always motivated to have complete knowledge before the fact. Rather, people filter, manipulate, and analyze information to maintain their preferred beliefs and attitudes.

 APPLICATION

"Seeing" the Play

Let's consider one more example of motivated social cognition: how people interpret an athletic event when they attach their feelings of self-worth to the success of one of the teams. If you've ever watched a game with another person and you were each rooting for a different team, you probably noticed that you have very different perceptions of what is happening in the game. With a close play at the plate in the bottom of the ninth, do you think Red Sox and Yankees fans see the attempted tag of the runner in the same way?

Consistent with your likely intuition, a study of fans' impressions of a particularly rough football game between Princeton University and Dartmouth College in 1951 indicates that they would not. Following the game, Albert Hastorf and Hadley Cantril (1954) showed students from both schools a film of it and then asked them how many penalties each team had committed. Princeton students saw Dartmouth players committing many more penalties than Princeton players, whereas Dartmouth students saw their team commit only half the number of penalties that the Princeton students attributed to them. But of course, students from both schools watched the same film! Our motivations—in this example, our investment in our sports team—affect the way in which we perceive events unfolding. We look for what we want to find and come up with justifications for our conclusions ("See—look at that! The receiver was mugged before the ball got there!").

Since this classic study, researchers around the globe have shown in myriad studies the many ways in which people's cognitions are biased by their motivation to maintain preferred beliefs and attitudes. Of course, there are limits to the influence of motives on people's thinking. For people to function effectively in the world,

▲ When people watch competitive sports, their interpretation of controversial plays and penalties is often biased by which team they want to win.
[MEL EVANS/AP Images]

their cognitions must be generally accurate representations of external and social reality. If a young man's company is losing more money than it is bringing in, he cannot sustain a belief that his new business is successful for very long. Instead, a person's understanding of reality is the product of a compromise among three motivations: desire to be accurate, to be certain, and to hold on to valued beliefs (Heine et al., 2006; Kunda, 1990). ■

Mood and Social Judgment

In addition to psychological motives, moods can play an important role in shaping social judgment about a given event or person. A *mood* is a generalized state of affect that persists longer than the experience of an emotion. For example, the happiness a person experiences after finding a dollar bill on the ground lasts a couple minutes, but moods can continue to resonate for much longer. And although emotions usually have clear causes, sometimes we just find ourselves in a bad or good mood, and we cannot quite put our finger on why.

Why might humans have evolved the ability to experience moods in the first place? For one thing, moods may inform a person about the status of things in the immediate environment. Think about this from an evolutionary perspective. Being in a positive mood is a signal that everything is okay, that there are no immediate threats to be concerned with. Negative moods, on the other hand, signal that something is wrong and might be deserving of one's attention. In fact, over the course of human evolution, positive moods might have promoted exploration of the environment, expansion of hunting territories, and openness to unfamiliar foods—behaviors that, when well attuned to cues in the environment, would have facilitated the success of the species. Likewise, negative moods might have promoted greater vigilance against attack, protection of the tribe, and more conservative eating habits—behaviors that would also increase the chance for survival when the threat of danger is real. As a result of these evolutionary pressures, people today may be oriented to use their *mood as information* in their judgments (Schwarz & Clore, 1983, 2003). Whether they realize it or not, they are listening to their moods when making decisions and forming judgments.

THINK ABOUT
[nmedia/Shutterstock]

Pi

π (*Pi*), a surrealist psychological thriller directed by Darren Aronofsky and released in 1998 (Aronofsky, 1998), dramatically illustrates the power of schemas over people's lives. The movie centers on Max Cohen (Sean Gullette), a genius mathematician who lives like a hermit in his apartment, into which he's crammed a sprawling, home-built supercomputer. Max is obsessed with the idea that reality can be understood in terms of numbers. He can state his entire worldview in three assumptions: "1. Mathematics is the language of nature. 2. Everything around us can be represented and understood through numbers. 3. If you graph the numbers of any system, patterns emerge."

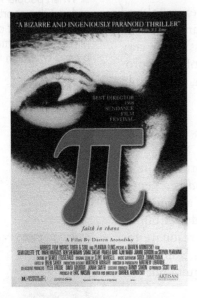

[HARVEST FILM WORKS/Album/Newscom]

For the past 10 years, Max has been trying to uncover the hidden numerical pattern beneath the stock market, a notoriously chaotic system. Max's supercomputer crashes under the strain of his research, but the answer it spits out just before crashing—a 216-digit number—fascinates Max. He starts to believe that this number provides the key to unlock not just the stock market but the very nature of the cosmos and existence.

Let's focus on three aspects of Max's life that connect with ours, albeit usually in less extreme forms:

1. Max sees elusive mathematical patterns everywhere. For him, they pop out of the environment, just as faces or a vase can pop out of Figure 3.1. For example, when we see a city street through Max's eyes, passersby appear as a jittery, undifferentiated mass of bodies, whereas the stock market numbers displayed on a building's LCD monitor are crystal clear. Later, when Max becomes obsessed with spirals (a representation of the mysterious Golden Ratio in math), he sees them in his coffee, the newspaper, and the smoke rolling off a cigarette. He is hunting for order in nature, and he sees it everywhere . . . or does he?

Sol Robeson (Mark Margolis), Max's elderly mentor and only friend, warns Max about his obsession: "You have to slow down. You're losing it. . . . Listen to yourself. You want to find the number 216 in the world, you will be able to find it everywhere. Two hundred and sixteen steps from your street corner to your front door. Two hundred and sixteen seconds you spend riding on the elevator. When your mind becomes obsessed with anything, you will filter everything else out and find that thing everywhere!"

Max is clearly extreme in the way he filters reality through his schemas, but even supposedly normal people like the rest

By this logic, mood states should affect both the content of a person's social judgments and how motivated the person is to engage in effortful processing of information. If people are feeling good while considering whether they like the party they are attending or the person they just met, they are more likely to view each of them positively. If they are feeling lousy, that will color their view of such things negatively. Also, the more thought people put into such judgments, the more their moods color those judgments (Forgas, 1995); the more thinking people do, the more their moods infuse their evaluations of the various aspects of the person or event they are evaluating.

Mood also affects how motivated people are to think extensively about people and events around them. Because positive moods signal that things are okay, individuals who feel good rely on more heuristic or automatic forms of processing when making judgments about people, events, and issues of us prefer interpretations of reality that confirm our schemas. As we've seen, this is *confirmation bias*. Perhaps the only difference is that Max's schemas are idiosyncratic: No one else seems to share them—and Max is perfectly fine with that. The rest of us tend to use schemas that we share with other members of our culture.

2. Just as powerfully as Max's schemas make some features of the environment salient, they downplay whatever does not fit within his precise mathematical worldview. When Max is approached by Devi (Samia Shoaib), his friendly neighbor bearing gifts and offering affection, he resists her. Why? For one thing, Max lacks a *script* for interacting with others—that is, he lacks knowledge of how the give-and-take of normal social interactions unfolds in time. As a result, social interactions are too uncertain and unpredictable for him to manage; hence, they end awkwardly.

    But looking deeper, we also see the *self-fulfilling prophecy* at work. Schemas that other people impose on us alter how they treat us and consequently how we behave. Schemas that we impose on *ourselves* can similarly constrain us. In Max's case, he seems to have convinced himself that he lacks the capacity to establish emotional intimacy; therefore, he doesn't.

3. Finally, Max's character illustrates a simple but important point: People do not simply like order; they actually *need* order because they are threatened by the opposite: disorder and chaos. Sol tries to convince Max that the world is extremely complex and chaotic, but Max's search for order is unrelenting. Driven by purpose, he becomes more restless, disheveled, and paranoid. He is beset with debilitating migraine headaches, hallucinations, and blackout attacks.

Is Max that different from the rest of us? As we've noted in this chapter, people certainly differ in how much they prefer well-structured knowledge to unstructured knowledge. Yet within all of us lies a pit of fear that drives us to search for patterns in the environment, piece things together in coherent and predictable ways, and react negatively toward anything that threatens to unravel the order underlying our experience. We see these tendencies every day: gambling, betting, religious quests, the creation of conspiracy theories, scapegoating a "bad guy" for a hazardous outcome, or simply turning up our noses in disgust at a visually chaotic artwork, such as the movie *Pi* itself!

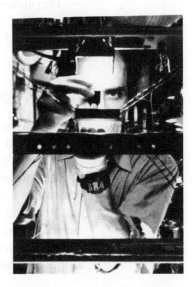

▲ Max's search for mathematical order highlights some aspects of reality and obscures others. The rest of us may not be so fanatical, yet we all use schemas to filter our perception of the social world.
[Live Entertainment/Photofest]

(Bless et al., 1996; Forgas, 1998; Mackie & Worth, 1989). In other words, they rely more on the experiential system of cognition that we introduced at the beginning of this chapter. For instance, people in good moods are especially likely to rely on stereotypes when judging people (Bodenhausen et al., 1994).

On the other hand, negative moods tell a person that something is wrong; they lead the person to think more carefully to figure out what is problematic. Studies show, in fact, that participants experiencing a negative mood focus on relevant details before making a judgment rather than settling on a quick-and-dirty judgment (Bless et al., 1990; Forgas et al., 2005; Gasper & Clore, 2002).

As a demonstration of this idea, Herbert Bless and his colleagues (1990) had students recall a very happy or a very sad event in their lives, a manipulation that reliably induces a positive or negative mood. In a supposedly unrelated study, participants listened to an essay that argued for an increase in student fees at the university. Half of the sample perceived the arguments in the essay as rather weak. But to the other half, the arguments in the essay were quite strong and seemed to include logical claims built on solid evidence. Because most college students are likely to be opposed to a fee increase, the default, or heuristic, response is to pay little attention to how good the arguments are and maintain one's negative attitude toward the proposal. However, if you are processing the information in the essay carefully, paying attention to details, then strong arguments for the proposal could sway your opinion. Bless and colleagues found that the students who were in a happy mood processed the essay more heuristically. Their attitude toward a tuition increase was negative, even when the arguments for the increase were strong. In contrast, participants who were in a negative mood really thought carefully about the essay, and they were persuaded by the strong arguments to believe that the fee increase would be a good idea.

Our intuition might lead us to think that if a friend is in a bad mood, it is not a good time to try to change her opinion on some issue. However, according to this line of research, if your arguments are strong, it is actually the best time to do so!

The Next Step Toward Understanding Social Understanding

In this chapter, we have focused primarily on how we process and are affected by information as it unfolds—how we seek knowledge, how we organize the knowledge we have, how that knowledge can be activated by features of the situations we encounter, and how motivation affects the processing of information. But social understanding involves more than merely processing incoming information. Our cognitive system is highly attuned to rely on memories, infer causation, form impressions of people, and imagine alternative possible outcomes to make sense of people and events. In chapter 4 we will turn to these central aspects of understanding the social world.

SECTION REVIEW   Returning to the "Why": Motivational Factors in Social Cognition and Behavior

Motivation plays a role in shaping which schemas are activated as well as when and how those schemas affect behavior and judgment.

Motivation and Priming	Motivated Social Cognition	Mood Affects Information Processing
Primed ideas can influence thinking and behavior when they are compatible with the person's preexisting motivation.	The three psychological motives introduced in the first part of this chapter—to be accurate, to be certain, and to validate existing beliefs and attitudes—are constantly at work, sometimes subconsciously, influencing which schemas come to mind and how powerfully they influence thinking and behavior.	Mood affects how motivated we are to expend effort on processing information.

CRITICAL LEARNING EXERCISES

1. Although we often try to have an accurate sense of the world around us, we aren't always motivated to seek out the best evidence to inform our decisions. Sometimes we simply want to come to some decision quickly or confirm what we already think we know to be true. What role do you think these two motives play in people's political views? How might they contribute to people's views on either side of the political spectrum being increasingly polarized?

2. When you selected the college or university you would attend, how did you make that decision? Was your judgment influenced more by implicit, automatic associations or by controlled, deliberate processing that involved systematically weighing pros and cons? Do you think that one mode of thinking would result in a better decision than the other? Why or why not?

3. In this chapter, you learned about some of the evidence related to the idea that being primed with one concept can bring to mind other related concepts. The evidence that priming can influence a person's behavior has been more mixed. Based on what you have read in this chapter, do you think that people's behavior can sometimes be influenced by ideas that have been primed? If so, when and for whom are primes most likely to influence our actions?

 Achieve

Don't stop now! Check out our videos and additional resources located at:
www.macmillanlearning.com

TOPIC
OVERVIEW

CHAPTER 4

Thinking About People and Events

Imagine that classes have ended. You are driving, and as you make a left turn, a red sports car in the oncoming lane comes straight toward you at high speed and hits the side of your car. With your mood ruined, you pop out of your car, relieved no one was hurt, but upset and confused. The other driver jumps out of his car and is adamant that you cut him off. You claim he was speeding and that it was his fault. The police are called to investigate what happened.

This situation and the subsequent crime scene investigation would involve four essential ways people typically make sense of the world:

- We rely on our ability to recall events from the past (memory).
- We make inferences about what causes other people's behavior (causal attributions).
- We imagine alternatives to the events we experience (counterfactual thinking).
- We form impressions of other people, often on the basis of limited information (person perception).

An investigation of the fender bender would involve retrieving memories for what happened, making determinations of what or who caused the accident, forming an impression of those involved in the accident, and considering how things might have happened differently.

We use these same cognitive processes every day to make sense of the world around us. And, unlike a police detective, our cognitive system often engages these processes automatically and without any taxpayer expense!

Learning Outcomes

- Explain how memories are formed.
- Describe evidence which shows that memories are often reconstructions rather than objective facts.
- Explain how schemas shape memories and, hence, our view of the world.
- Relate the misinformation effect to the reliability of eyewitness testimony.
- Give an example of how the availability heuristic can distort judgment.

Short-term memory Information and input that is currently activated.

Long-term memory Information from past experience that may or may not be currently activated.

Remembering Things Past

Through our senses, we take in information from the world around us. But we don't just perceive and then act. We are also equipped with the important ability to lay down traces of memory that allow us to build a record of events, people, and objects we have encountered in the past. This record of memory helps us make sense of the present and also allows us to learn from past experience so we can do better in the future. In our everyday understanding, we think about memories as the past record of personal experiences we have had (*that time I almost caught on fire when I sprayed an aerosol can of cooking spray at a lit barbecue grill*). But memory is really much more than that; in fact, there are different types of memory, and a sequence of processes underlie how memories get formed and are recalled. Let's consider how memories are formed so we can then understand how they are influenced by various social factors.

How Are Memories Formed?

On rare occasions—such as when studying for a test—we actively try to store information in memory, but most of the time, laying down memories happens automatically, with little effort on our part. How does this process of memory formation happen?

First, we can make a distinction between **short-term memory** (information that is currently activated) and **long-term memory** (information from past experience that may or may not be currently activated). At every moment, you are attending to some amount of sensory stimulation in your environment, and some of that information will be *encoded*, or represented, in *short-term memory*. Information that is actively rehearsed or is otherwise distinctive, goal relevant, or emotionally salient gets *consolidated*, or stored, in long-term memory for later *retrieval*.

When you are at a party, embarrassed that you cannot remember the name of your roommate's date, you can take some comfort in knowing that the process of remembering can break down for many reasons. Perhaps you were distracted when the name was mentioned and lacked the attention needed to encode the information. Even if you were paying attention, you might not have been motivated to consolidate the name into long-term memory; maybe you thought you wouldn't meet the person again. Or maybe you intended to repeat the name to yourself a few times to remember it but forgot to do so (lack of rehearsal). People, it turns out, are often overly optimistic about how much they will reflect on events they experience (Tully & Meyvis, 2017). Finally, you could have the name stored in memory but may be temporarily experiencing an inability to retrieve it because of distractions at the party.

APPLICATION
Social Media and Memory

Social media is an ever-present strand in the fabric of social life, as evidenced by the 350 million photos uploaded to Facebook per day (Omnicore, 2020) and 8,800 tweets per second (internetlivestats.com, 2020). You've likely noticed that at just about any event, whether a visit to a tourist attraction or a get together with friends, most people seem to be tweeting, snapchatting, or posting. Have you thought about how our pervasive use of social media to preserve and share our experiences might come at a cost of actually encoding those experiences and laying down retrievable tracks in memory?

Tamir and colleagues (2018) considered this very question. They had participants in one study watch a *TED* talk (an educational video lecture). In another study, they recruited participants visiting a museum. In both studies, they had some participants use social media to share their experience and told others not to use social media. Both immediately after the experience and a week later, the researchers assessed participants' memories for the events. Those who had used social media during their experiences showed poorer memory for the event than those who did not. Similar memory impairments have been found to occur if people take pictures of the events they experience (Barasch et al., 2017). Social media is certainly an important and valuable aspect of our world, but dividing your attention between your phone and an experience can impair your ability to recall that experience. ■

▲ Taking photos of our experiences and posting them online can sometimes interfere with our ability to encode events into memory.

[Thomas Barwick/Stone/Getty Images]

How Do We Remember?

Retrieving information from long-term memory seems like it should be a fairly objective process. We experienced some event and then try to retrieve that event from our mind's storage chest of information. However, like our perceptions and encoding of the social world, the process of retrieval is colored by many of the factors discussed in chapter 3: our biases, our schemas, our motives, our goals, and our emotions (Talmi et al., 2019). As the psychologist John Kihlstrom (1994, p. 341) put it, "Memory is not so much like reading a book as it is like writing one from fragmentary notes." When we seek to remember an event, we often have to build that memory from the recollections available to us. We reconstruct an idea of what happened by bringing to mind bits of evidence in much the same way an investigator might interview different sources and pull together several pieces of evidence to create a coherent picture of what happened.

In trying to gather this information, we may intend to seek accurate knowledge. After all, who doesn't *want* to be accurate? But the problem is that motives to reach conclusions that fit with what we expect or what we desire often crash the party. Indeed, among the more potent tools that we use to reconstruct our memories are our schemas. As you might expect from our discussion of schemas in chapter 3, when we try to recall information about an event, our schemas guide what comes to mind.

Memory for Schema-Consistent and Schema-Inconsistent Information   In one study illustrating how schemas shape memory (Cohen, 1981), participants watched a videotape of a woman the researchers described as either a librarian or a waitress. The woman in the videotape noted that she liked beer and classical music. When later asked what they remembered about the woman, participants who believed she was a librarian were more likely to recall that she liked classical music. Those who believed she was a waitress were more likely to remember that she liked beer. Why the difference? Their schema of the woman led the participants to look for, and therefore tend to find and encode into long-term memory, characteristics she displayed that fit their schema of her. Participants exhibited such schema-consistent memory even when interviewed a week later.

Although most of the time it's easier to remember information that is consistent with our schemas, sometimes information that is highly inconsistent with our schemas also can be very memorable (Hamilton et al., 1989). Such information often grabs our attention and forces us to think about how to make sense of it. If you go to a funeral and someone starts tap-dancing on the coffin, it will violate your script for such an event, and you'll probably never forget it. Thus, encountering information that conflicts with a preexisting schema can be quite memorable (Pyszczynski et al., 1987). This is especially true when we are motivated to make sense of schema-inconsistent information, and we have the cognitive resources to notice and think about it (Moskowitz, 2005). When we are very busy or unmotivated, we primarily attend to and encode in memory information that fits our currently activated schemas.

Better memory for schema-consistent information is especially likely when we recall prior experience through the lens of a current schema. Consider two people, Frank and Mike, who each just started dating a new partner in September. Both report being moderately in love. Fast-forward two months, to November, and Mike's relationship has been doing quite well. Frank's relationship, in contrast, has turned sour, and he is having lukewarm feelings. How will their current feelings affect their memories of their initial attraction? Mike will tend to recall being more in love initially than will Frank, even though back in September they were equally in love with their partners (McFarland & Ross, 1987). Our present perceptions can create a schema that biases how we recall (or, actually, reconstruct) events from the past.

Although a schema can color memory in either a positive or negative light, people have a general tendency to show a rosy recollection bias, remembering events more positively than they actually experienced them (Mitchell et al., 1997). This is especially true if people feel positively about their current experience. People also tend to exhibit *mood-congruent memory*. That is, we are more likely to remember positive information when we are in a positive mood and to remember negative information when in a negative mood. Shoppers, for instance, tend to recall more positive attributes of their cars and TVs when they have previously been given a free gift that sparks a good mood (Isen et al., 1978). Such mood-congruent memory effects help explain why depressed persons seem to have such difficulty extracting positive feelings from events they experienced in the past. Because they are typically in negative moods, they tend to recall more negative information from the past (Barnett & Gotlib, 1988).

The cultural perspective, however, offers one caveat to this tendency to attend to and remember schema-consistent information. In individualistic cultures, people prefer to have well-defined concepts that are distinct from each other and stable over time, so consistency is highly valued. In collectivistic cultures, people tend to think of concepts, including other people, as varying over time and situation, and tolerance for inconsistency is greater. Theorists refer to this collectivistic preference as *dialecticism*—a way of thinking that acknowledges and accepts inconsistency (Spencer-Rodgers et al., 2010). These culturally based differences in ways of thinking, in turn, influence how people's memory biases construct stable and consistent schemas of the world and the people in it—including themselves. In one study, for example, when asked to recall aspects of themselves, Chinese participants were likely to remember aspects that implied more inconsistent self-descriptions than were European American participants (Spencer-Rodgers et al., 2009).

The Misinformation Effect   Clearly our memories are biased by our schemas both when we first encode new information and when we later recall it. These biases can even lead us to remember things that didn't actually happen. The process is

best captured by Elizabeth Loftus's work on the **misinformation effect,** a process in which cues given after an event can plant false information into memory. In a classic study by Loftus and colleagues (1978), all participants watched the same video depicting a car accident (**FIGURE 4.1**). After watching, some participants were asked, "How fast was the car going when it *hit* the other car?" Other participants were asked, "How fast was the car going when it *smashed into* the other car?" Participants asked the question with the word *smashed* estimated that the car was going faster than did participants who were asked the question with the word *hit.* Even a simple word such as *smashed* can prime a schema for a severe car accident that rewrites our memory of what we actually saw in the video.

Perhaps more interesting, however, is what happened when participants were later asked if there was broken glass at the scene of the accident. Participants who had earlier been exposed to the word *smashed* were more than twice as likely to say "yes" as were participants previously exposed to the word *hit* (even though there was no broken glass at the scene). The way in which the question was asked created an expectation that led to people remembering something that actually was not there!

 APPLICATION

Eyewitness Testimony, Confessions, and False Memories

The misinformation effect suggests ways in which real-life investigations can be biased. Eyewitness testimony and confessions are the most influential forms of evidence in trials, and thousands of cases have been decided based on such evidence. However, the misinformation effect suggests that leading questions by police investigators and exposure to information after the event in question are capable of influencing witnesses to remember events in ways, or with a degree of confidence, that may not be accurate.

A well-publicized example is the case of Ronald Cotton, falsely convicted in 1984 of burglary and rape based on the eyewitness testimony of the victim,

Figure 4.1

Visualizing the Misinformation Effect

Loftus and her colleagues illustrated how the phrasing of a question can lead someone to remember seeing something, like broken glass, that actually wasn't there.

Misinformation effect The process by which cues that are given after an event can plant false information into memory.

▲ Jennifer Thompson-Cannino's mistaken eyewitness testimony led to Ronald Cotton's wrongful conviction. After his exoneration, Thompson-Cannino and Cotton cowrote a book telling their dramatic stories.

[American Film Foundation/Kobal/Shutterstock]

Achieve
Video: How Reliable Is Your Memory?

Availability heuristic The tendency to assume that information that comes easily to mind (or is readily available) is more frequent or common.

Jennifer Thompson-Cannino. After initially studying a photographic lineup for some time, Thompson-Cannino tentatively identified Cotton, and the detective congratulated her on doing a good job. This affirmation of her tentative identification operated as a form of misinformation that strengthened her false belief. Subsequent and repeated images of the assailant during the course of the investigation and trial reinforced her memory such that her confidence increased over time. After serving 11 years of a life sentence, Cotton was exonerated based on DNA evidence (and the real perpetrator identified). Interestingly, Cotton and Thompson-Cannino have since worked to reform eyewitness identification procedures and cowritten a best-selling book, *Picking Cotton* (Weir, 2016).

Not only can witnesses be led astray, but so too can confessors. Investigators in one study interviewed college-aged participants on three occasions (Shaw & Porter, 2015). They mentioned in the first interview a crime the participant had committed as an adolescent. Although the participant had not actually committed the crime, the investigators claimed that the information had come from the participant's parents. To enhance believability, the investigators wove in some details the participant had actually experienced as a youth. At the first interview, none of the participants recalled such an event having occurred, but by the third interview, 70% of participants falsely remembered having committed a theft or an assault at about age 12. Tempted to think such false confessions rarely occur in actual legal investigations? Think again. About 25% of exonerations (instances in which a convicted individual is later declared not guilty) based on DNA evidence involved false confessions, and, not surprisingly, such false confessions also taint the way other evidence is evaluated (Kassin et al., 2012).

Understanding how false memories are created can help us make sense of controversies about repressed memories of childhood sexual abuse (Otgaar et al., 2019). Some researchers suggest that even such dramatic memories can be falsely reconstructed. This may occur when a person is especially susceptible to suggestion, is suffering from psychological difficulties, and is motivated to understand and get past those problems. In the course of therapy, the seeds of such memories can be planted by leading questions from the therapist (Kunda, 1999; Schacter, 1996). Although it is not clear how often false memories of abuse occur, real memories of such horrific experiences may be initially dismissed because they don't fit the schema most of us have of how adults—whether coaches, priests, or parents—treat children. This phenomenon was portrayed in the award-winning 2015 film *Spotlight* (McCarthy, 2015), which recounts how *Boston Globe* journalists eventually brought to light child sexual abuse that numerous Catholic priests in the Boston area had perpetrated over an extended period of time. ■

The Availability Heuristic and Ease of Retrieval   Clearly, the content of the memories people recall, whether true or false, greatly influences their judgments. But people's judgments can also be affected by how readily memories can be brought into consciousness. Try to make the following judgment as quickly as possible. Which of the two word fragments listed below could be completed by more words?

(1) _ _ _ _ I N G   or   (2) _ _ _ _ _ N _

If your first inclination was to choose option 1, you just exhibited what is referred to as the **availability heuristic** (Tversky & Kahneman, 1973). This is our tendency to assume that information that comes easily to mind (or is readily available) is more frequent or common. It's relatively easy to think of four-letter words that you can add "ing" to, but it is more of a struggle to come up with seven-letter words with N in the sixth position. If we compare the relative difficulty in recalling such words, it's easy to conclude that option 1 could be completed with more words. Of course, on closer examination, you can readily see that option 2 has to be the correct answer. Any word that you could think of that would fit in option 1 would also fit in option 2, and some words, such as *weekend*, fit only option 2.

The availability heuristic has the power to distort many of our judgments. Think for a moment about how you might feel if offered a free trip to a region where there have been terrorist bombings. Does the thought of traveling to this region of the world make you a little nervous? Such a reaction would be understandable because you might be worried about possible suicide bombings. When such attacks occur—for example, in Israel—they make the news. But actually, Israel has a very high fatality rate from car accidents, and when in Israel, you are far more likely to die in a car accident than in a suicide bombing. Similarly, people generally are more afraid of flying in an airplane than of driving their car, yet according to the National Safety Council (2020), the lifetime risk of dying in a motor vehicle accident is 1 in 103, whereas the lifetime risk of dying as an airplane passenger is 1 in 188,364. But every airplane accident attracts national media attention, whereas most car fatalities are barely covered at all. Because airplane crashes are so easily recalled, the availability heuristic makes it seem that they are more prevalent than they really are. If the media covered each fatal car accident with as much intensity, the airline industry would probably enjoy a large increase in ticket sales!

Inspired by research on the availability heuristic, Norbert Schwarz and colleagues (Schwarz, Bless, Strack et al., 1991) discovered a related phenomenon known as the ease of retrieval effect. With the availability heuristic, people rely on what they can most readily retrieve from memory to judge the frequency of events. With the **ease of retrieval effect**, people judge how frequently an event occurs on the basis of how easily they can retrieve a certain number of instances of that event. To demonstrate this, Schwarz and colleagues asked college students to recall either 6 instances when they acted assertively or 12 instances when they acted assertively. You might expect that the more assertive behaviors you remember, the more assertive you feel. But the researchers found exactly the opposite pattern: Participants asked to recall 12 instances of assertiveness rated themselves as *less* assertive than those asked to recall only 6 instances. For most people, coming up with 12 distinct episodes is actually pretty difficult; it's much more difficult than recalling only 6 instances of assertiveness. People thus seem to make the following inference: If I'm finding it difficult to complete the task that is asked of me (recalling 12 acts of assertiveness), then I must not act assertively much, and so I must not be a very assertive person. People asked to recall 6 instances ended up thinking they were more assertive than participants asked to recall 12 instances. Some studies suggest that this ease of retrieval effect occurs only if the person puts considerable cognitive effort into trying to retrieve the requested number of instances of the behavior (e.g., Tormala et al., 2002). Only then do they attend to the ease or difficulty of retrieval and use it to assess how common the recalled behavior is (Weingarten & Hutchinson, 2018).

THINK ABOUT

[Cihan Xinhua/eyevine/Redux]

Ease of retrieval effect The process whereby people judge how frequently an event occurs on the basis of how easily they can retrieve examples of that event.

APPLICATION
What Is Your Risk of Disease?

Ideally, people should objectively determine their estimated risk of disease by considering their actual risk factors. However, peoples' judgments about health risk are strongly influenced by many of the cognitive and motivational factors covered throughout this textbook. One factor is the ease with which people can recall information that makes them feel more or less vulnerable (Schwarz et al., 2016).

The ease of retrieval effect occurs in judgments of health risks such as the risk of contracting HIV (e.g., Raghubir & Menon, 1998). The more easily students could recall behaviors that increase risk of sexually transmitted diseases, regardless of the number of risk behaviors they remembered having actually engaged in, the more at risk they felt. Similarly, participants asked to recall three behaviors that increase the risk of heart disease perceived themselves as being at greater risk than did participants asked to recall eight such behaviors (Rothman & Schwarz, 1998).

But there is an important caveat here, as well as reason for optimism. When Rothman and Schwarz (1998) asked participants who had a family history of heart disease, and thus for whom the condition was quite relevant, to think of *personal* behaviors that increase risk, they estimated themselves to be at higher risk when asked to come up with more, rather than fewer, risky behaviors. This suggests that with greater personal relevance, people can be more discriminating in how they evaluate information, and judgments are less subject to the ease of retrieval effect. This is especially important to keep in mind with our increasing exposure to misinformation about our risk for disease, much of it spread by automated bot Internet accounts that are often indistinguishable from real people (Broniatowski et al., 2018). The spread of erroneous information about what causes cancer, or why vaccines are harmful, and the ease with which we remember such information can have dire consequences. Indeed, the more people are exposed to vaccine misinformation through social media, the less likely they are to get vaccinated (Jolley & Douglas, 2014). This has become such a concern that the World Health Organization has identified "vaccine hesitancy" as a top 10 threat to global health (Yang et al., 2019). ■

SECTION REVIEW Remembering Things Past

We rely on our memory to make sense of the world.

Forming Memories	Remembering
Memories are formed when we encode information and consolidate it into long-term memory for retrieval.	• Our memories are often reconstructions rather than objective facts and are subject to bias. These reconstructed memories are influenced by our schemas, which generally guide us to remember information that is consistent with the most salient schema.
	• The misinformation effect is an example of reconstructed memory because leading questions plant expectations that influence us to remember events differently than they actually occurred.
	• We often base our judgments on how readily information comes to mind (the availability heuristic) and the ease with which we can retrieve it.

Inferring Cause and Effect in the Social World

Now that we have a sense of the role of memory in how we understand people and events, we can move on to a second core process we use to gain understanding. This is the process by which we look for relationships of cause and effect. In our fender-bender example, the investigator involved is charged not only with obtaining a (let's hope accurate) record of what happened but also with identifying what factors *caused* the outcome. In our own interpretation of events, we similarly seek to pair effects with their causes in order to better predict and improve outcomes in the future. When you see that your friend is really upset, you want to know what caused those feelings so that you can effectively console your friend, maybe help fix the problem, and know how to avoid the situation in the future. Fritz Heider pioneered this line of inquiry beginning in the 1930s. At that time, the two dominant views of what causes humans to behave the way we do—psychoanalysis and behaviorism—placed little emphasis on our conscious thoughts. But Heider argued that to understand why people behave the way they do, we have to examine how they come to comprehend the people around them. To this end, Heider (1958) developed a common sense, or naive, psychology: an analysis of how ordinary people like you and me think about the people and events in our lives.

Common Sense Psychology

Working from a Gestalt perspective, Heider assumed the same kinds of rules that influence the organization of visual sensations also guide most people's impressions of other people and social situations. In one early study (Heider & Simmel, 1944), people watched a rather primitive animated film in which a disk, a small triangle, and a larger triangle moved in and out of a larger square with an opening. The participants were then asked to describe what they saw (**FIGURE 4.2**). People tended to depict the actions of the geometric objects in terms of causes, effects, and intentions, such as "The larger triangle chased the smaller triangle out of the room [the larger square]."

This tendency, along with his observations of how people talked about their social lives in ordinary conversation, led Heider to propose that people organize their perceptions of action in the social world in terms of causes and effects. Specifically, people tend to explain events in terms of particular causes. Heider referred to such explanations as **causal attributions**.

Because causal attributions help people make sense of, and find meaning in, their social worlds, they are of great importance. When an employee is late, whether the employer attributes that behavior to the person's laziness or to her tough circumstances can determine whether she is fired or not. If a woman shoots her abusive husband, a jury may have to decide if she did it because she feared for her life or because she wanted to collect on his life insurance. In any given election, your vote is influenced by which political party's policies you view as being responsible for the current state of the country. In nearly every domain of life, causal attributions play a significant role.

Basic Dimensions of Causal Attribution   Heider (1958) observed that causal attributions vary on two basic dimensions. The first dimension is **locus of causality**, which can be either *internal* to some aspect of the person engaging in the action (known as the actor) or *external* to some factor in the person's environment (the situation). For example, if Justin failed his physics exam, you

Learning Outcomes

- Define the two basic dimensions of causal attribution.
- Explain how a particular mind-set can affect behavior.
- Explain when people are most likely to make the fundamental attribution error.
- Identify the types of information people consider when thinking carefully about causal attributions.

Causal attributions Explanations of an individual's behavior.

Achieve
Video: The Heider/Simmel Experiment

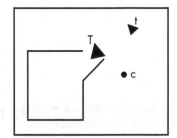

Figure 4.2

Seeing Intention

People tend to perceive actions in the world in terms of cause and effect. In viewing these shapes, subjects perceived the scene as one triangle pushing the other out of the room.

[Information from Heider & Simmel (1994) © 1944 by the Board of Trustees of the University of Illinois]

Locus of causality Attribution of behavior to either an aspect of the actor (internal) or to some aspect of the situation (external).

could attribute his poor performance to a lack of intelligence or effort, factors internal to Justin. Or you could attribute Justin's failure to external factors, such as a lousy physics professor or an unfair exam.

The second basic dimension is *stability*: attributing behavior to either stable or unstable factors. If you attribute Justin's failure to a lack of physics ability, that's a stable internal attribution because people generally view ability as being relatively unchangeable. On the other hand, if you attribute Justin's failure to a lack of effort, that is an unstable internal attribution. You would still perceive Justin as being responsible for the failure, but you would recognize that his exertion of effort can vary from situation to situation. Stable attributions suggest that future outcomes in similar situations, such as the next physics test, are likely to be similar. In contrast, unstable attributions suggest that future outcomes could be quite different; if Justin failed because of a lack of effort, he might do a lot better on the next test if he exerted himself a bit more.

External attributions can also be stable or unstable. If you attribute Justin's failure to a professor who always gives brutal tests or who is an incompetent teacher, you are likely to think that Justin will not do much better on the next test. But if you attribute Justin's failure to external unstable factors such as bad luck or the "love of his life" having broken up with him right before the test, then you're more likely to think Justin may improve on the next exam.

As poor Justin's example suggests, how we attribute a behavior—to internal or external factors and stable or unstable factors—affects both the impressions we form of the actor and the predictions we make about the actor's future behavior.

- An internal attribution for a poor performance or a negative action reflects poorly on the actor, whereas an external attribution tends to let the actor off the hook.
- On the other hand, an internal attribution for a positive behavior generally leads to a positive impression of the actor, whereas an external attribution for a positive action undermines the benefit to the actor's image.
- Attributions to stable factors lead to strong expectations of similar behavior in similar situations, whereas attributions to unstable factors do not.

APPLICATION
School Performance and Causal Attribution

Attributional processes influence how we perceive ourselves. The psychologist Carol Dweck (1975) investigated the causal attributions that elementary school boys and girls made for their own poor performances in math courses. Whereas boys tended to attribute their difficulties to the unstable internal factor of their lack of effort or to external factors such as a bad teacher, girls tended to attribute their difficulties to a stable internal cause: lack of math ability. Dweck reasoned that girls were therefore likely to give up trying to get better at math. What's the point of trying if you simply don't have the ability? But of course, if you don't try, you won't succeed. Accordingly, Dweck and colleagues (1978) developed an attributional retraining program that encourages grade school children to attribute their failures to an internal but unstable factor: lack of sufficient effort. This attribution implies that one can improve by working harder,

▼ Getting children, including girls, to attribute math performance to effort rather than natural ability can improve math performance.
[Ariel Skelley/Blend Images/Getty Images]

and, indeed, the researchers found that students doing so enjoyed substantial improvement in subsequent math performance. ■

Fixed and Incremental Mind-Sets   Inspired by her early work on achievement, Dweck and colleagues (Dweck, 2012; Hong et al., 1995) proposed that intelligence and other attributes need not be viewed with this *fixed*, or entity, *mind-set*— that is, as stable traits that a person can't control or change. Rather, they could be viewed as attributes that change incrementally over time. When we take an *incremental* mind-set, we believe an attribute is a malleable ability that can increase or decrease. Often these mind-sets concern a person's ability to grow or improve. For example, we may see an attribute such as shyness as a quality that, with the right motivation and effort, people can change so they become less shy (Beer, 2002). Take a moment to think about which attributes you think are fixed entities and beyond your control and which attributes you think are changeable.

THINK ABOUT

[Lisa Peardon/The Image Bank/Getty Images]

These mind-sets have implications for how an individual interacts with, and responds to, the social world. Children and adults with fixed mind-sets make more negative stable attributions about themselves in response to challenging tasks and then tend to perform worse and experience more negative affect in response to such tasks. Moreover, they tend to eschew opportunities to change such abilities, even when the abilities are crucial to their success. For instance, exchange students who had stronger fixed mind-sets about intelligence expressed less interest in remedial English courses when their English was poor, even though improving would facilitate their academic goals (Hong et al., 1999). In contrast, those with incremental mind-sets viewed situations that challenged their abilities as opportunities to improve, to develop their skills and knowledge. Our mind-set affects not just what we do for ourselves but how we treat others. Although holding an incremental mind-set can lead one to blame others for their chronic shortcomings (Ryazanov & Christenfeld, 2018), it also makes one more likely to help others improve, as when business managers with stronger incremental mind-sets are more willing to mentor their employees (Heslin & Vanderwalle, 2008).

Although people generally have dispositional tendencies to hold either fixed or incremental mind-sets about human attributes, these views can be changed (Dweck, 2012; Heslin & Vanderwalle, 2008; Kray & Haselhuhn, 2007). For example, convincing students that intelligence is an incremental attribute rather than a stable entity encourages them to be more persistent in response to failure, adopt more learning-oriented goals, and make fewer ability attributions for failure (Burnette et al., 2012; Paunesku et al., 2015). Although there is some debate about the strength of these interventions, with some meta-analyses indicating weak effects (Moreau et al., 2019; Sisk et al., 2018), a recent study of more than 12,000 adolescents found that a 50-minute training in growth mind-sets improved grades among lower-achieving students (Yeager et al., 2019).

Given the importance of these mind-sets for academic achievement and other domains, you might wonder where these different mind-sets come from. Most likely people learn them through the socialization process (see chapter 2), including interactions with their parents. But we don't just adopt whatever mind-set—about intelligence, for example—our parents hold. Haimovitz and Dweck (2016) have argued that mind-sets about traits such as intelligence are often not clearly conveyed to children. Rather, Haimovitz and Dweck have found that it is the parents' mind-set about failure that exerts a potent influence

Figure 4.3

The Development of Entity and Incremental Mind-Sets

Where do our mind-sets come from? Research suggests that parents are part of this origin story (Haimovitz & Dweck, 2016). The way parents react to their children's failures affects the children's perceptions of what the parents prioritize, and this in turn affects the children's mind-sets about intelligence.

on the intelligence mind-set their children develop. As shown in **FIGURE 4.3**, when parents view failure as a statement about their children's ability, the children perceive their parents as focusing on performance as opposed to learning, and this leads the children to develop a mind-set of intelligence as stable. But when parents view failure as an opportunity to learn and grow, the children perceive the parents as focusing on learning as opposed to performance, and this leads the children to develop a mind-set of intelligence as malleable.

Automatic Processes in Causal Attribution

How do people arrive at a particular attribution for a behavior they observe? Like most other products of human cognition, causal attributions sometimes result from quick, intuitive, automatic processes and sometimes from more rational, elaborate, thoughtful processes.

When you ask people why some social event occurred, they can usually give an opinion. However, research has shown that people often don't put much effort into thinking about causal attributions. People make a concentrated effort primarily when they encounter an event that is unexpected or important to them (Jaynes, 1976; Pyszczynski & Greenberg, 1981; Wong & Weiner, 1981). Such events are more likely to require some action on our part and are more likely to have a significant impact on our own lives, so it is more important to arrive at an accurate causal attribution.

Imagine that when you were a child, your mom always had coffee in the morning, and you came into the kitchen one morning and saw your mom put on a pot of coffee. If a friend dropped by and asked you why your mom was doing that, you would readily respond, "She always does that" or "She loves coffee in the morning"—the same knowledge that led you to expect her to do exactly what she did. However, if one morning she was brewing a pot of herbal tea, this would be unexpected, and you'd likely wonder why she was doing that instead of brewing her usual coffee. You would be even more likely to think hard about a causal attribution for her behavior if one morning she was making herself a martini.

Most events in our daily lives are expected; consequently, we don't engage in an elaborate process to determine causal attributions for them. According to Harold Kelley (1973), when an event readily fits an existing *causal schema* (a theory we hold about the likely cause of that specific kind of event), we rely on it rather than engage in much thought about why the event occurred. These causal schemas come from two primary sources. Some are based on our own personal experience, as in the mom-making-coffee example. Others are based on general cultural knowledge. If an American watches another person in a restroom passing a thin, waxed piece of thread between her teeth, little or no thought about *why* is generated because it is a culturally normative form of hygiene known as flossing. But consider our discussion in chapter 2 of cultural differences and think, from this cultural perspective, about how people garner prestige and self-worth. In the same way we might think little of someone flossing in a restroom, a traditional Trobriand Islander wouldn't blink an eye at a man building up a large pile of yams in front of his sister's house and leaving them to rot. In that culture, this behavior is a way that people enhance their status and would not require any explanation. But a Trobriander seeing someone flossing or an American seeing someone "yamming" would require a more elaborate process of determining attribution.

When an event we observe isn't particularly unexpected or important to us but doesn't readily fit an obvious causal schema, we are likely to base our causal attribution on whatever plausible factor is either highly visually salient or highly accessible from memory. This "top of the head phenomenon" was illustrated in a set of studies by Shelley Taylor and Susan Fiske (1975), in which participants heard a group discussion at a table. One particular member of each group was made visually salient. One way the researchers accomplished this was by having only one member of the group be of a particular race or gender. Participants tended to think the visually salient member of the group had the largest effect on the discussion. For instance, when the group included only one woman, she was viewed as most causally responsible for the discussion.

THINK ABOUT

[geographyphotos/Alamy]

The Fundamental Attribution Error   Reliance on visual salience was anticipated by Heider (1958), who proposed that people are likely to attribute behavior to internal qualities or motives of the person because when a person engages in an action, that actor tends to be the observer's salient focus of attention. Edward Jones and Keith Davis (1965) carried this notion further, proposing that when people observe an action, they have a strong tendency to make a **correspondent inference**, meaning that they attribute to the person an attitude, a desire, or a trait that corresponds to the action. For example, if you watch Ciara pick up books dropped by a fellow student leaving the library, you will automatically think of Ciara as helpful. Correspondent inferences are generally useful because they give us quick information about the person we are observing, in terms of either their dispositions or intentions (Moskowitz & Olcaysoy Okten, 2016). Correspondent inferences are most likely under three conditions (e.g., Jones, 1990):

Correspondent inference The tendency to attribute to an actor an attitude, desire, or trait that corresponds to the action.

1. *The individual seems to have a choice in taking an action.*
2. *A person has a choice between two courses of action, and there is only one difference between one choice and the other.* For example, if Sarah must choose between two similar colleges except one is known to be more of a party school, and she chooses the party school, you may conclude that Sarah

is into partying. But you would be less likely to do so if the school she chose was more of a party school but also closer to her home and less expensive.

3. *Someone acts inconsistently with a particular social role.* If a contestant in a game show wins a car but barely cracks a smile and simply says "Thank you," you would be likely to infer that she is not an emotionally expressive person. But if she jumps up and down excitedly after she wins the new car, you would not be as certain what she is like because most people in that role would be similarly exuberant.

Although all three of these factors increase the likelihood of a correspondent inference, this tendency is so strong that we often jump to correspondent inferences without sufficiently considering external situational factors that may also have contributed to the behavior witnessed (e.g., Jones & Harris, 1967). People's tendency to draw correspondent inferences, attributing behavior to internal qualities of the actor and, consequently, underestimating the causal role of situational factors, is so pervasive that it is known as the **fundamental attribution error (FAE)**. The initial demonstration of the FAE was provided by Ned Jones and Victor Harris (1967) (**FIGURE 4.4**). Participants read an essay that was either strongly in favor of Fidel Castro (the longtime dictator of Cuba) or strongly against Castro. Half the participants were told that the essay writer chose his position on the essay. When asked what they thought the essay writer's true attitude toward Castro was, participants, not surprisingly, judged the true attitude as pro-Castro when the essay was pro-Castro and anti-Castro when the essay was anti-Castro. However, the other half of the participants were told that the writer didn't have a choice in whether to advocate for or against Castro; instead, the experimenter had assigned what side the writer should take. Logic would suggest that the lack of choice would make the position advocated by the essay a poor basis for guessing the author's true attitude. However, these participants, despite knowing the essay writer had no choice, also rated his attitudes as corresponding to the position he took in the essay.

Fundamental attribution error (FAE) The tendency to attribute behavior to internal or dispositional qualities of the actor and consequently underestimate the causal role of situational factors.

Many experiments have since similarly shown that despite good reasons for attributing behavior largely, if not entirely, to situational factors, people tend to make internal attributions instead. For example, in a study using a quiz show type format, people thought that those asking trivia questions were more knowledgeable than those answering them (Ross, Amabile, & Steinmetz, 1977), even though it is pretty obvious that coming up with tough questions from your own store of knowledge is a lot easier than answering difficult questions made up by someone else. But the participants did not sufficiently take into account the influence of the situation—the questioner and contestant roles—in making these judgments.

To appreciate the FAE, consider how we often think that actors are like their characters. Actors who play evil characters on soap operas have even been verbally abused in public! Similarly, slapstick comics such as Will Ferrell have expressed frustration that people expect them to be wacky loons in real life. On the one hand, these errors make sense because we know these people only as their fictional characters. On the other hand, they are great examples of the FAE

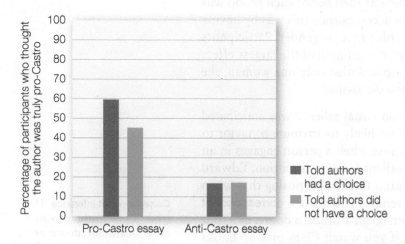

Figure 4.4

The Fundamental Attribution Error

Participants inferred that the author's true attitude matched the position advocated in the essay, even when told the author had no choice in what position he took for the essay.

[Data from Jones & Harris, 1967]

because we know that most of the time actors are saying lines written for them by someone else and are being directed with regard to their appearance, movements, and nonverbal behaviors.

APPLICATION
Judging Others

The FAE has implications for how people judge others—for example, defendants in court—and for how people judge social issues pertinent to individuals and groups. If people are likely to make internal attributions to drug addicts, homeless people, and welfare recipients, they are probably more supportive of treating these groups harshly and less likely to entertain ways to change environmental factors that contribute to these problems. Linda Skitka and colleagues (2002) found that, consistent with this reasoning, American political conservatives seem to be more susceptible to the FAE than liberals and are therefore less sympathetic to those low on the socioeconomic ladder. Likewise, conservatives judging wealthy people are led by the FAE toward attributions to those people's abilities and initiative rather than to their trust funds, connections, or lucky breaks. ■

How Fundamental Is the FAE?   Although the FAE is common when people make attributions for the behavior of others, this is not the case when making attributions for oneself. And if you think about visual salience, you should be able to (literally) see why. When we are observers, the other person is a salient part of our visual field, but when we ourselves are acting in the world, we are usually focused on our surroundings rather than on ourselves. This leads to what has been labeled the **actor–observer effect**: As observers, we are likely to make internal attributions for the behavior of others, but as actors, we are likely to make external attributions for our own behavior (Jones & Nisbett, 1971). When observing others, we attend primarily to them and not to their situation. In contrast, when acting ourselves, we are usually reacting to someone or something in our environment. When that is the case, such external factors are likely to be more salient.

Actor–observer effect The tendency to make internal attributions for the behavior of others and external attributions for our own behavior.

It is interesting that the actor–observer effect can be reversed by shifting the individual's visual perspective. For instance, Storms (1973) replicated the actor–observer effect by showing that when pairs of participants sat across from one another and had a conversation, they generally thought their partners were determining the things they talked about. They attributed the direction the conversation took to the person they could see—their partner. Then Storms demonstrated that if shown a video playback of the conversation from the discussion partner's perspective (now the actors were watching themselves talk), participants were more likely to think that they were the ones steering the direction of the conversation.

There are, however, important qualifications to the actor–observer effect. For one, as actors, we are much more likely to make internal attributions for our successes ("I aced the test because I studied really hard") but external attributions for our failures ("I bombed the test because the instructor is so awful he could not teach someone to tie a shoe") (Campbell & Sedikides, 1999; Dorfman et al., 2019). We will discuss this tendency at greater length when we talk about self-esteem biases in chapter 6. Because of this tendency, the actor–observer difference is stronger for negative behaviors (Malle, 2006). In addition, research indicates that classic actor–observer asymmetries are largest when actors are not focused on a strong motive or intention for their behavior; if actors have a salient intention in mind, they tend to attribute their behavior internally to that intention (Malle et al., 2007).

APPLICATION
Finger-Pointing

The actor–observer effect has clear implications for interpersonal and intergroup relations. When things are going badly in a relationship, whether it is a friendship, a marriage, or an alliance between two countries, each actor is likely to view the external situation that is salient as being responsible for the problems. This means the friend, the marriage partner, or the other country is seen as the cause of the problem. And this, of course, can create and intensify finger-pointing and hostility between individuals and groups. Storms's (1973) work suggests that one way to combat this kind of attributional finger-pointing is to make the other party's perspective on the issues salient. This might defuse tensions by helping the parties see how they themselves are contributing to the problem. ■

▲ The actor–observer effect can contribute to relational struggles when each partner thinks the other is the cause of an argument or a problem. Such struggles can be reduced when each partner considers the other perspective.

[Monkey Business Images/Shutterstock]

Does the FAE Occur Across Cultures? Some social psychologists have proposed that the FAE is a product of individualistic cultural worldviews, which emphasize personality traits and view individuals as being responsible for their own actions (Watson, 1982; Weary et al., 1980). In fact, the original evidence of the FAE was gathered in the United States and other relatively individualistic cultures. And it does seem clear, as we noted in chapter 2, that people in more collectivistic cultures are more attentive to the situational context in which behavior occurs and to view people as part of the larger groups to which they belong. Indeed, when directed to explain behavior, people from more collectivistic cultures (e.g., China) generally give more relative weight to external, situational factors than do people from more individualistic cultures (Choi & Nisbett, 1998; Miller, 1984; Morris & Peng, 1994). Such research suggests that socialization in a collectivistic culture might sensitize people to contextual explanations of behavior.

Evidence of cross-cultural variation in attributional biases doesn't necessarily mean that individuals raised in collectivistic settings don't form impressions of people's personalities by observing their behavior. Douglas Krull and colleagues (1999) found that when participants are asked to judge another person's attitudes or traits on the basis of an observed behavior, people from collectivistic cultures such as China are just as susceptible to the FAE as people from more individualistic cultures such as the United States. Around the globe, when the goal is to judge a person, we judge people by their behavior. But when the goal is to judge the cause of a behavior, there is cultural variation in how much the behavior is attributed to the person or the situation.

Dispositional Attribution: A Three-Stage Model

Although the FAE is common and sometimes automatic, even people from individualistic cultures often take situational factors into account when explaining behavior. When might people consider these situational factors before jumping to an internal attribution?

To answer this question, Dan Gilbert and colleagues (1988) proposed a model in which the attribution process occurs in a temporal sequence of three stages:

1. A behavior is observed and labeled ("That was helpful behavior").
2. Observers automatically make a correspondent dispositional inference.
3. If observers have sufficient accuracy motivation and cognitive resources available, they modify their attributions to take into account salient situational factors.

This model predicts that people will be especially likely to ignore situational factors and to make the FAE when they have limited attention and energy to devote to attributional processing.

Putting this model to the test, Gilbert and colleagues (1988) had participants watch a videotape of a very fidgety woman discussing various topics. The participants were asked to rate how anxious this person generally was. The videotape was silent, ostensibly to protect the woman's privacy, but participants were shown one- or two-word subtitles indicating the topics she was discussing. The videotape was always the same, but the subtitles indicated either very relaxing topics such as vacation, travel, and fashion or very anxiety-provoking topics such as sexual fantasies, personal failures, and secrets.

If observers have sufficient resources, they should initially jump to an internal attribution for the fidgety behavior and view the woman as anxious, but in the condition in which the topics are anxiety provoking, they should make a correction and view the woman as a less anxious person. Indeed, as **FIGURE 4.5** shows, this is what happened under normal conditions. But half the observers were given a second, cognitively taxing, task to do while viewing the videotape. Specifically, they were asked to memorize the words in the subtitles displayed at the bottom of the screen. Under such a high cognitive load, these participants lacked the resources to correct for the situational factor (the embarrassing topics) and therefore judged the anxious-looking woman to be just as prone to anxiety if she was discussing sex and secrets as if she was discussing travel and fashion.

The three-stage model of attribution also helps us to understand how individual differences in the motivation to focus on possible situational causes can influence the kind of attributions people make. For example, Skitka and colleagues (2002) found that liberals generally are less likely than conservatives to view an AIDS victim as an irresponsible person. However, when cognitively busy, the liberals viewed the AIDS patient as just as irresponsible as conservatives did. So when people have the motivation and resources, they often correct their initial leap to internal dispositional attributions, but when cognitively busy, they are less able to make this correction.

Elaborate Attributional Processes

So far we have focused on the relatively quick, automatic ways people arrive at causal attributions: relying on salience, jumping to a correspondent inference, and perhaps making a correction. But when people are sufficiently surprised or

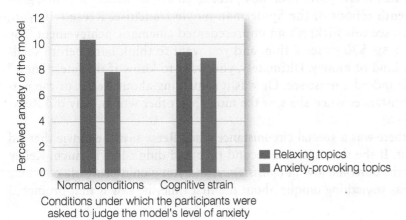

Conditions under which the participants were asked to judge the model's level of anxiety

Relaxing topics
Anxiety-provoking topics

Figure 4.5

On Second Thought

People who are cognitively strained are less likely to correct their dispositional judgments of others. In this study, participants under normal conditions did not perceive an anxious-looking woman as being an anxious person if they knew she was talking about something anxiety provoking. But under cognitive strain, participants did not take into account the topic and judged her as being a dispositionally anxious person.

[Data from Gilbert et al., 1988]

care enough, they put effort into gathering information and thinking carefully before making a causal attribution. Imagine a young woman eager about a first date with a young man she met in class and really liked. They were supposed to meet at a restaurant at 7:00 p.m., but he's not there at 7:00, or 7:05, or 7:15. She would undoubtedly begin considering causal explanations for this unexpected, unwelcome event: Did he change his mind? Was he in a car accident? Is he always late?

Causal Hypothesis Testing Putting conscious effort into making an attribution is like testing a hypothesis (Kruglanski, 1980; Pyszczynski & Greenberg, 1987b; Trope & Liberman, 1996). First, we generate a possible *causal hypothesis* (a possible explanation for the cause of the event). This could be the interpretation we'd prefer to make, the one we fear the most, or one based on a causal schema. A large paw print seems more likely to be caused by a large animal than a small one (Duncker, 1945). The causal hypothesis could also be based on a salient aspect of the event or a factor that is easily accessible from memory. Finally, causal accounts can be based on close temporal and spatial proximity of a factor to the event, particularly if that co-occurrence happens repeatedly (Einhorn & Hogarth, 1986; Michotte, 1963). If Frank arrives late to a party and, soon after, a fight breaks out, it is likely that you'll entertain the hypothesis that Frank caused the melee, especially if the co-occurrence of Frank's arrival and fights happens repeatedly. The tendency of the co-occurrence of a potential causal factor (Frank's arrival) and an outcome (a fight) to lead to a causal hypothesis (Frank causes fights) is called the **covariation principle** (Kelley, 1973).

> **Covariation principle** The tendency to see a causal relationship between an event and an outcome when they happen at the same time.

Once we have an initial causal hypothesis, we gather information to assess its plausibility. How much effort we give to assessing the validity of that information depends on our need for closure versus our need for accuracy. If the need for closure is high and the need for accuracy is low, and if the initial information seems sound and fits the hypothesis, we may discount other possibilities. But if the need for accuracy is higher than the need for closure, we may carefully consider competing causal attributions and then decide on the one that seems to best fit the information at our disposal. What kinds of information would we be most likely to use to inform our causal attributions?

Three Kinds of Information: Consistency, Distinctiveness, and Consensus Harold Kelley (1967) described three sources of information for arriving at a causal attribution when accuracy is important: consistency (across time), distinctiveness (across situations), and consensus (across people) (**FIGURE 4.6**).

Imagine that a few years from now, Reese, an acquaintance of yours, goes to see the tenth reboot of the Spiderman movie franchise. Reese tells you, "You have to see this flick; it's an unprecedented cinematic achievement." By this time, it costs $30 to see a film, and you want to think hard before shelling out that kind of money. Ultimately, you want to know if the latest "new" Spiderman is indeed a must-see. Or was it something about Reese, or the particular circumstances when she saw the movie? In other words, why did Reese love the movie?

Maybe there was a special circumstance when Reese saw the movie that led her to love it. If she then saw it a second time and didn't like it much, Kelley would label the outcome low in *consistency*, and you would probably conclude that there was something unique about the first time she saw it that prompted

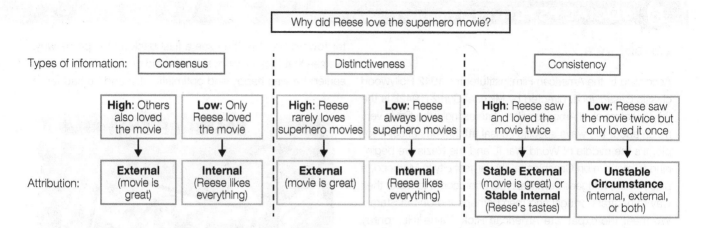

Why did Reese love the superhero movie?					
Types of information:	Consensus		Distinctiveness		Consistency
	High: Others also loved the movie	**Low:** Only Reese loved the movie	**High:** Reese rarely loves superhero movies	**Low:** Reese always loves superhero movies	**High:** Reese saw and loved the movie twice · **Low:** Reese saw the movie twice but only loved it once
Attribution:	**External** (movie is great)	**Internal** (Reese likes everything)	**External** (movie is great)	**Internal** (Reese likes everything)	**Stable External** (movie is great) or **Stable Internal** (Reese's tastes) · **Unstable Circumstance** (internal, external, or both)

her reaction. Maybe she really needed a distraction the first time she saw it. This would be an attribution to an unstable factor that might be very different each time Reese saw the movie. However, if Reese saw the movie three times and loved it each time, Kelley would label the outcome high in *consistency across time*, and you would then be likely to entertain either a stable internal attribution to something about Reese or a stable external attribution to something about the movie. Two additional kinds of information would help you decide.

First, you could consider Reese's typical reaction to other movies. If Reese always loves movies in general, or always loves superhero movies, then her reaction to this specific film is low in *distinctiveness*. This information would lead you to an internal attribution to something about Reese's taste in these kinds of movies rather than the quality of the movie. On the other hand, if Reese rarely likes movies, or rarely likes superhero movies, then her reaction is high in *distinctiveness*, which would lead you more toward an external attribution to the movie.

Finally, how did other people react to the movie? If most others also loved the movie, there is high *consensus*, suggesting that something about the movie was responsible for Reese's reaction. However, if most other people didn't like the movie, you would be most likely to attribute Reese's reaction to something about her. In short, when a behavior is high in consistency, distinctiveness, and consensus, the attribution tends to be external to the stimulus in the situation, whereas when a behavior is high in consistency but low in distinctiveness and consensus, an internal attribution to the person is more likely. Research has generally supported Kelley's model. Recent findings confirm that when distinctiveness is low and consistency is high, observers tend to make trait attributions to the person (Olcaysoy Okten & Moskowitz, 2018).

The presence of other potential causes also influences the weight that we assign to a particular causal factor. For example, some years ago, most of the baseball-watching world was in awe of players such as Barry Bonds and Alex Rodriguez, attributing their remarkable accomplishments to their incredible athletic ability and effort. However, when allegations of steroid use surfaced, many fans discounted the players' skills, attributing some of their accomplishments to an alternative causal factor: performance-enhancing drugs. This tendency is called the **discounting principle**, whereby the importance of any potential cause of another's behavior is reduced to the extent that other potential causes are salient (Kelley, 1971; Kruglanski et al., 1978).

Motivational Bias in Attribution What makes causal attributions so intriguing to social psychologists—and we hope to you as well—is that they are both

Figure 4.6

The Covariation Model

When an attribution is high in consistency, consensus, and distinctiveness, we attribute the behavior (Reese's love of the movie) to an external cause (a great movie).

▲ Although Barry Bonds holds the record for most home runs in a career (762), many people now discount his achievement because they attribute it at least partly to the use of performance-enhancing drugs.

[Doug Pensinger/Getty Images]

Discounting principle The tendency to reduce the importance of any potential cause of another's behavior to the extent that other potential causes exist.

SOCIAL PSYCH AT THE MOVIES

Casablanca

According to the American Film Institute, the 1942 Hollywood classic *Casablanca*, directed by Michael Curtiz (1942), is the third greatest of all American films. Interestingly, the film is very much about the ways specific causal attributions affect people. It's the middle of World War II, and the Nazis are beginning to move in on Casablanca, the largest city in Morocco, a place where refugees from Nazi rule often come to make their way to neutral Portugal and then perhaps the United States. We meet the expatriate American Rick Blaine (Humphrey Bogart), the seemingly self-centered, cynical owner of Rick's Café Américain, where exit visas are often sold to refugees. A well-known anti-Nazi Czech freedom fighter, Victor Lazslo (Paul Henreid), and his wife, the Norwegian Ilsa Lund (Ingrid Bergman), arrive in Casablanca with the Nazis on their trail. Victor and Ilsa hope that Rick can obtain letters of transit to help get them out of Morocco, so they won't be captured by the Nazis. Rick is highly resistant and, it turns out, quite bit-

ter toward Ilsa. We then see a flashback that explains why. We see that Rick was not self-centered or cynical a few years earlier; he was happy and optimistic. Ilsa and he had fallen

[Warner Bros. Pictures/Photofest]

important and ambiguous. They are important because they play such a large role in the judgments and decisions we make about other people and about ourselves. They are ambiguous because we can't really see or measure causality; our causal attributions are based on guesswork because we rarely if ever have direct evidence that proves what caused a given behavior. And if we did, it would probably tell us the behavior was caused by a complex interaction of internal and external factors. For instance, any performance on a test is likely to be determined by a combination of the individual's aptitude, physical and mental health, amount of studying, and other events in the person's life commanding attention, as well as the particular questions on the test, the amount of time allotted for each question, and the quality of instruction in the course. And yet we typically either jump on the most salient attribution or do a little thinking and information gathering and then pick a single attribution, or at most two contributing factors, and discount other possibilities (Kelley, 1967).

As Heider (1958) observed, because causal attributions are often derived from complex and ambiguous circumstances, there is plenty of leeway for them to be influenced by motivations other than a desire for an accurate depiction of causality. Think about how we make attributions for mass killings, an unfortunately all too common event in today's world. Sometimes the intent is clear, but other times it is more ambiguous. What kind of attributions have you made in such ambiguous situations? Noor and colleagues (2019) found that motivations bias people's attributions. When Germans who were anti-immigration read about a violent Syrian refugee, they ascribed terrorist motives. But Germans who were pro-immigration attributed the behavior to mental instability.

THINK ABOUT

[Michael Brochstein/SOPA Images/
LightRocket/Getty Images]

in love in Paris and agreed to meet at a train scheduled to leave the city just days after the Nazis marched into the French capital. However, Ilsa instead sent him a note indicating that she could never see him again. So he left alone on the train in despair, thinking that she had betrayed him. This event and his (as it turns out) incorrect attribution for it made him defensively self-centered and cynical.

As the movie progresses, Rick learns that Ilsa thought that her husband, Victor, had died trying to escape a concentration camp but found out that day in Paris that he was ill but alive and went to meet him. As Rick shifts his causal attribution for her not meeting him, his cynicism gradually lifts, and he ends up trying to help Victor escape. He arranges a meeting with his friend, the corrupt chief of police, Captain Louis Renault (Claude Rains), ostensibly to have Victor captured so he can have Ilsa for himself, a causal attribution quite plausible to Renault because of his own manipulative, womanizing ways. But Rick has a different reason for calling Renault to his café: to force him to arrange

transport out of Casablanca for Victor. In case you haven't seen the film, we won't tell you how things turn out.

The film illustrates the importance of causal attributions not only in altering Rick's outlook on life but in other ways as well. Victor suspects that Rick wasn't always dispositionally the politically indifferent, self-centered character he seems to be because he knows Rick had helped fight imperialism in Ethiopia and fascism in the Spanish Civil War. Victor therefore judges Rick's current behavior to be high in distinctiveness and thus doesn't attribute it to Rick's disposition. Rather, he comes to realize that Rick's resistance to helping him had to do with his feelings for Ilsa and what happened in Paris, not self-centered indifference. In one more example of attribution from the film, when Renault, an unrepentant gambler, is ordered by the Nazis to shut down Rick's café, in order to justify doing so, he uses a convenient external attribution: "I'm shocked, shocked to find that gambling is going on in here!" he exclaims as a croupier hands him his latest winnings.

Our attributions are also biased by our preferred views of the way the world works—our desire to maintain specific beliefs. Recall that people generally prefer to believe the world is just, that good things happen to good people, and that bad things happen to bad people (Lerner, 1980). One way we preserve this belief is to view people as being responsible for the outcomes they get. When people are strongly motivated to believe the world is just, they are especially likely to blame people who have had bad things happen to them, such as those who have contracted STIs, rape victims, battered spouses, and poor people (e.g., Borgida & Brekke, 1985; Furnham & Gunter, 1984; Hafer & Bègue, 2005; Summers & Feldman, 1984). Moreover, because we value people who affirm our preferred way of viewing the world, we tend to like those who buy into the world being just and think they are more likely to be successful. When people proclaim that the world is unjust and has given them a raw deal, we assume they will be less successful even if they are otherwise just as competent as those endorsing just world beliefs (Alves et al., 2019).

Understanding attributions enables us to appreciate their powerful role in how we interact with the world. Attributions lead us to like or blame others and even, at times, to blame ourselves. For example, messages advocating for women's empowerment can lead women to attribute responsibility for gender-based disadvantages to themselves (Kim et al., 2018). The concern here is that a message indicating that women have the power to overcome workplace gender inequalities can also lead them to perceive themselves as being responsible for creating the inequalities.

SOCIAL PSYCH OUT IN THE WORLD

"Magical" Attributions

Imagine that it is time for U.S. citizens to choose another president. Zach is at home on election night, watching as news channels tally up the votes from each state. He hopes and wishes and prays for his preferred candidate to emerge the victor. A couple hours later, Zach's preferred candidate is declared the president-elect. Zach believes that his hoping and wishing and praying played a role in determining the election outcome.

This is an example of **magical thinking**—believing that simply having thoughts about an event before it occurs can influence that event. Magical thinking is a type of attribution. It's a way of explaining what caused an event to happen. But it's a special type of attribution because it goes beyond our modern, scientific understanding of causation. Returning to our example, we know that the election outcome is determined by myriad factors that are external to Zach and not by his wishes transmitting signals to election headquarters. And yet, however unrealistic or irrational magical thinking is, many of us have an undeniable intuition that we can influence outcomes with just our minds. To see this for yourself, try saying out loud that you wish someone close to you contracts a life-threatening disease. Many people find this exercise uncomfortable because some intuitive part of them feels that simply saying it can make it happen.

Why is magical thinking so common? Freud (1913/1950) proposed that small children develop this belief because their thoughts often do in fact seem to produce what they want. If a young child is hungry, she will think of food and perhaps cry. Behold! The parent will often provide that food. Although as we mature we become more rational about causation, vestiges remain of this early sense that our thoughts affect outcomes. As a result, even adults often falsely believe they control aspects of the environment and the world external to the self. Ellen Langer's classic research on the illusion of control demonstrated that people have an inflated sense of their ability to control random or chance outcomes, such as lotteries and guessing games (Langer, 1975). For example, participants given the opportunity to choose a lottery ticket believed they had a greater chance of winning than participants assigned a lottery ticket.

Research by Emily Pronin and her colleagues (2006) has pushed this phenomenon even further. In one study, people induced to think encouraging thoughts about a peer's performance in a basketball shooting task ("You can do it, Justin!") felt a degree of responsibility for that peer's success. In another study, people asked to harbor evil thoughts about and place a hex on someone believed they actually caused harm when that person later complained of a splitting headache.

Magical thinking is not only something that individuals do. We see the same type of causal reasoning in popular

---

SECTION REVIEW Inferring Cause and Effect in the Social World

People tend to explain events in terms of particular causes, referred to as causal attributions.

Dimensions of Causal Attributions	Fundamental Attribution Error	A Three-Stage Model	Effort for Unexpected or Important Events
• Locus of causality refers to whether attributions are made to an internal attribute of the actor or to some external factor in the person's environment. • Stability refers to whether a causal factor is presumed to be changeable or fixed. • People who believe that attributes can change are more likely to seek opportunities to improve in areas related to that attribute.	• We tend to attribute the behavior of others to internal factors. • We generally attribute our own behavior to the situation. • Although the FAE occurs across different cultures, collectivistic cultures often emphasize situational factors more than individualistic cultures do.	• A behavior is observed and labeled. • An internal attribution is made. • Situational factors are considered if there is a motivation for accuracy and if cognitive resources are available.	• When motivated, we make and test hypotheses for causes of the event. • We consider the consistency, distinctiveness, and consensus information regarding an event. • Motivational biases can lead us to adjust our attributions to support our own preferred beliefs.

cultural practices. In religious rituals such as prayer or the observance of a taboo, or when people convene to pray for someone's benefit or downfall, there is a belief that thoughts by themselves can bring about physical changes in the world. Keep in mind, though, that a firm distinction between these forms of magical thinking and rational scientific ideas about causation may be peculiar to Western cultural con-texts. Some cultures, such as the Aguaruna of Peru, see magic as merely a type of technology, no more supernatural than the use of physical tools (Brown, 1986; Horton, 1967). But people in Western cultures are not really all that differ-ent. Many highly popular self-help books and videos such as *The Secret* (see www.thesecret.tv) extol the power of posi-tive thinking, and many Americans believe at least in some superstitions.

Although magical thinking stems partly from our inflated sense of control, it can also be a motivated phenomenon—something that people *desire* to be true. People may feel threatened by the awareness that they are limited in their ability to anticipate and control the hazards lurking in their environ-ment. They realize that their well-being—and even their *being* at all—is subject to random, uncaring forces beyond their con-trol. To avoid this distressing awareness, people apply magical thinking to restore a sense of control. Supporting this account, research has shown that superstitious behavior is displayed more often in high-stress situations, especially by people with a high desire for control (Keinan, 1994, 2002). This is a good example of a broader point we discuss in the main text: Peo-ple's motivation to cling to specific beliefs about the world and themselves can bias how they perceive and explain the world around them.

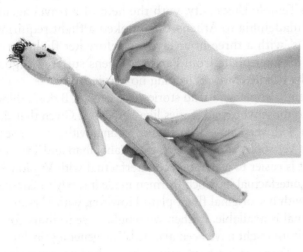

[Africa Studio/Shutterstock]

What If, If Only: Counterfactual Thinking

Learning Outcomes

When we settle on a causal attribution for an event, we also often think about how changing that causal factor could have changed the event. For example, what if we decide that the accident we described at the outset of the chapter occurred because the guy in the red sports car was texting while driving? We might then think if only the person hadn't been looking at his phone, he would have seen you starting to make a left turn and would have slowed down and avoided causing all that damage. This process of imagining how some event could have turned out differently is referred to as *counterfactual thinking* (Roese & Epstude, 2017). Counterfactuals are deeply ingrained in how we react to events; they are asso-ciated with unique patterns of activation of regions of the brain (De Brigard & Parikh, 2019), and they often affect us without our conscious awareness. In fact, the research we are about to present demonstrates that counterfactual thoughts routinely influence how we judge and respond emotionally to events in our lives.

- Explain why the ease of generating a counterfactual influences emotional reactions.
- Differentiate between downward and upward counterfactuals.
- Explain when it is more productive to generate upward than downward counterfactuals.
- Identify four essential ways people make sense of the world, as presented in this chapter.

The More Easily We Can Mentally Undo an Event, the Stronger Our Reaction to It

Consider the following story, based on Kahneman and Tversky (1982), which we'll call Version A: Carmen always wanted to see the Acropolis, so after grad-uating from Temple University, with the help of a travel agent, she arranged to fly from Philadelphia to Athens. She originally booked a flight requiring her

Magical thinking The tendency to believe that simply having thoughts about an event before it occurs can influence that event.

▲ Is every case in which a young woman dies before getting to see the Acropolis equally tragic?

[Chris Warren/AGE Fotostock]

to switch planes in Paris, with a three-hour layover before her flight from Paris to Athens. But a few days before her departure date, her travel agent e-mailed her that a direct flight from Philly to Athens had become available. Carmen figured "Why not?" and so she switched to the direct flight. Unfortunately, her plane suffered engine failure and came down in the Mediterranean, leaving no survivors. How tragic would you judge this outcome for Carmen?

Well, if you are like the students who participated in Kahneman and Tversky's classic study, you would say very tragic. But what if you read a Version B: Carmen always wanted to see the Acropolis, so after graduating from Temple University, with the help of a travel agent, she arranged to fly from Philadelphia to Athens. She booked a flight requiring her to switch planes in Paris, with a three-hour layover before her flight from Paris to Athens. Unfortunately, her plane from Paris to Athens suffered engine failure and came down in the Mediterranean, leaving no survivors.

How tragic does that seem? People who read stories like Version B don't think they are nearly as tragic as do those who read stories like Version A. Given that the outcome is really the same in both versions—Carmen died young, without ever seeing the Acropolis—why does Version A seem more tragic? Kahneman and Tversky explained that it is because it is easier to generate a counterfactual with Version A; it's very easy to imagine a counterfactual in which Carmen made it safely to Greece: All she had to do was stick with her original flight plan! However, with Version B, no such obvious counterfactual is available. Rather, we would have to think for a while about ways her tragic death might have been avoided. The general principle is that if something bad happens, the easier it is to imagine how the bad outcome could have been avoided, the more tragic and sad the event seems. And, as this example illustrates, it is generally easier mentally to undo bad outcomes if they are caused by an unusual action, such as switching flight plans.

Here's another example based on Kahneman and Tversky (1982) that illustrates the pervasive influence of counterfactual thinking on emotional reactions. You go to a basketball game to see your favorite team play. In one version, your team gets trounced by 15 points. This would undoubtedly be upsetting. In the other version, your team loses on a last-second 50-foot buzzer beater. **Now how upset would you be? More upset, right?** Yet, in both cases, the pragmatic outcome is the same: Your team lost the game. So why is the close loss more agonizing? The close loss is more upsetting because it is much easier to imagine a counterfactual in which your team would have won the game: If only that desperation heave had clanked off the back of the rim! If the team lost by 15, it is much harder to mentally undo the loss, so it is less frustrating. In other words, it is easier to undo mentally the close loss than the not-so-close loss, just as it was easier to undo mentally the tragic fate of Carmen if she had changed flight plans than if she had simply taken the flight she had planned to take all along.

APPLICATION
Awarding Damages

Counterfactual thinking has serious consequences in a variety of important areas of life. Consider the legal domain, where we'd like to think that jury decisions are based on rational consideration of the facts at hand. Miller and McFarland (1986) showed how this phenomenon of viewing the negative event that seems easier to undo as more unfortunate could influence trial outcomes. In one study, they described a case in which a man was injured during a robbery. Half the participants read that the injury occurred in a store the victim went to regularly, whereas the other half were told it occurred in a store the victim did not usually go to. All other details were identical, yet participants recommended over $100,000 more in compensation for the injury if the victim was injured at the store he rarely went to because the unfortunate injury was easier to mentally undo in this version: "If only he had gone to the store where he usually shops!" To summarize, negative outcomes resulting from unusual or almost avoided actions are easier to imagine having gone better and therefore arouse stronger negative emotional reactions. ■

▲ The agony of defeat can be that much more agonizing when we imagine how our team might have won.
[Flashpop/Getty Images]

Upward counterfactual An imagined alternative in which the outcome is better than what actually happened.

Upward Counterfactuals

A handy term for a counterfactual that is better than what actually happened is **upward counterfactual**, with "upward" denoting a better alternative than what happened. All the examples we have considered so far have involved the effects of upward counterfactuals. When bad things happen, people often generate such upward counterfactuals, and the more easily they do so, the worse the negative outcomes that actually occurred seem.

So far we have also focused on how we react emotionally to the fortunes of others, but we also generate upward counterfactuals for our own less-than-desired outcomes: "If only I had studied harder"; "If only I hadn't had that last tequila shot"; "If only I had told her how much I care about her"; and so on. Upward counterfactuals generally make us feel worse about what actually happened. In particularly traumatic cases, for example, if a person causes a car accident by driving drunk, that individual may get caught in a recurring pattern of "if only I had" upward counterfactuals that fuel continued regret and guilt over the incident (Davis et al., 1995; Markman & Miller, 2006).

Interestingly, though, studies (e.g., Gilovich & Medvec, 1994) have found that when older people look back over their lives, they tend not to regret actions they did but actions they didn't do: "If only I had gone back to school and gotten that master's degree"; "If only I had spent more quality time with my kids"; "If only I had asked Jessica out when I had the chance." A broad survey of Americans found that their regrets about inaction are most commonly about decisions in the domain of one's love life rather than in other aspects of their lives (Morrison & Roese, 2011). This may be something to keep in mind while you are young. But research suggests that one reason that we regret inactions is that we no longer recall the more concrete pressures and difficulties that kept us from taking those alternative courses of action. For example, when Tom Gilovich and colleagues (1993) asked current Cornell students how much they would be affected by adding a challenging course to their workload, the students focused on the negative impact, such as lower grades, less sleep, and less time for socializing. However, when they asked Cornell alumni how adding a challenging course would have affected them in a typical semester back in the day, the alumni thought the negative impact would have been minor.

If upward counterfactuals—whether contrasted with things we did or with things we didn't do—tend to lead to such negative feelings about the past, why do people so commonly engage in them? Neal Roese and colleagues (e.g., Epstude & Roese, 2008; Roese, 1994) proposed that by making us consider what we could have done differently, upward counterfactuals serve an important function: They can provide insight into how to avoid a similar bad outcome in the future. Supporting this point, Roese found that students encouraged to think about how they could have done better on a past exam reported greater commitment to attending class and studying harder for future exams. Thus, although upward counterfactuals can make us feel worse about what transpired, they better prepare us to avoid similar ills in the future.

Downward Counterfactuals

Downward counterfactual An imagined alternative in which the outcome is worse than what actually happened.

We often also generate **downward counterfactuals**, thoughts of alternatives that are worse than what actually happened. These counterfactuals don't help us prepare better for the future, but they help us feel better about the past (Roese, 1994). By making salient possible outcomes that would have been worse than what actually happened, downward counterfactuals allow us to feel better about what happened. They serve a consolation function. After a robbery, you might conclude that although the thieves took your television, at least they didn't get your laptop. When visiting a friend in the hospital who broke both her legs in a car accident, people might offer consoling comments such as, "You were lucky—you could have had spine damage and been paralyzed for life."

It is worth considering how people use counterfactuals to reframe such bad events. While visiting Los Angeles once, a football player from one of our schools was shot in the leg by a random bullet. The bullet missed the bone, and the newspaper emphasized how lucky the player was, because if the bullet had hit the bone, it would have caused more serious, potentially permanent damage. That makes sense, but the player would have been even luckier if he hadn't been shot at all! So whether he was lucky or not depends on whether you focus on the upward counterfactual of not being shot at all or on the downward counterfactual of the bullet's shattering a bone. When people want to put a positive spin on an outcome, they choose the downward counterfactual.

Retail stores often take advantage of how making a downward counterfactual salient can place actual outcomes in a more positive light. Imagine that you come upon a pair of athletic shoes with a sign indicating a price of $99. You may think, "That's not a bad price." But what if the sign indicated that the shoes were reduced 50%, from $199 to $99? Such a sign essentially makes salient a downward counterfactual: The shoes could have cost $199! Does this downward counterfactual make paying $99 for the shoes more enticing? You might want to keep this in mind next time you shop online.

Upward and Downward Counterfactuals and Personal Accomplishments: The Thrill of Victory, the Agony of Defeat

Counterfactuals affect how we feel about our own achievements. Subjective, emotional reactions of satisfaction or regret are not determined so much by what you did or did not accomplish as by the counterfactuals you generate about those outcomes. In one clever demonstration of this phenomenon, researchers asked participants to judge the happiness of athletes at the 1992 Barcelona Summer Olympics who had won either the silver or the bronze medal by watching silent videotapes of them at the awards ceremony (Medvec et al., 1995). The silver medal, which means the person was the second best in the world at the event, is obviously a greater achievement than the bronze medal, which means the person was the third best in the world. However, on the basis of an analysis of which counterfactuals are most likely for silver- and bronze-medal winners, the researchers predicted that the bronze-medal winners would actually be happier than the silver-medal winners. They reasoned that for silver-medal winners, the most salient counterfactual is likely to be the upward counterfactual that "If only I had gone X seconds faster, or trained a little harder, I could have won the ultimate prize, the gold medal!" In contrast, bronze-medal winners are likely to focus on the downward counterfactual that "If I hadn't edged out the fourth-place finisher, I would have gone home with no medal at all!" In support of this reasoning, Medvec and colleagues found that bronze-medal winners were rated as appearing happier than silver-medal winners on the awards stand. Furthermore, in televised interviews, bronze medalists were more likely to note that at least they received a medal, whereas the silver medalists were more likely to comment on how they could have done better.

▲ Most people would be pretty thrilled to win a silver medal at the Olympics. So why does the American gymnast McKayla Maroney look so glum? Her reaction exemplifies research on Olympic medalists, which finds that athletes who win a silver ("With fewer mistakes, I could have won the gold!") are usually less happy than those who win a bronze ("One more mistake, and I might not have medaled at all!").

[Ronald Martinez/Getty Images]

Is It Better to Generate Upward or Downward Counterfactuals?

The work on counterfactual thinking illustrates how the human capacity for imagining "if only" alternatives to past events plays a central role in our emotional reactions to those events. Now, in light of all this, you might be wondering, is it better to generate upward or downward counterfactuals? That depends on a few factors. If you're down in the dumps and just want to feel better about what happened, downward counterfactuals and imagining a worse outcome can improve how you feel. But that's not always the most productive response. Sometimes we can learn a lot from thoughts that make us feel worse. Indeed, if the outcome pertains to an event that is likely to reoccur in the future, upward counterfactuals can give you a game plan for improvement or avoiding the bad outcome. But it also depends on whether you're able to exert any control over the outcome that you experienced or that you might face in the future (Roese, 1994). Say that you get into a car accident, because—shame on you—you were texting while driving. In this case, assuming that you're reasonably okay, it would be more productive to generate an upward counterfactual, such as "If only I had not been texting, I would not have hit the stop sign." This teaches you to avoid texting while driving, and since you're likely to be driving again, this is a good lesson to learn! But say you were attentively driving when someone ran a stop sign and nailed your rear fender. In this case, the outcome is out of your control, and so you're better off generating a downward counterfactual and thanking your lucky stars that it was just a fender bender, and you're all right.

SECTION REVIEW   What If, If Only: Counterfactual Thinking

Counterfactual thoughts routinely influence how we judge and respond emotionally to events in our lives and those of others.

Easily Undone	If Only . . .	At Least . . .
A close miss is more upsetting because it's easier to imagine a better counterfactual.	Upward counterfactuals—"if onlys"—make us feel worse but prepare us to avoid similar ills in the future. They are best applied when we have the possibility of exerting control over future outcomes.	Downward counterfactuals—"It could have been worse: at least . . ."—are best applied when there is no possibility of future action, or we're unable to exert control over outcomes.

Learning Outcomes ⟩⟩

- Explain why being highly attuned to physical characteristics of people could be an evolutionary advantage.
- Differentiate between "bottom up" and "top down" ways that we form impressions of others.
- Describe three sources of top-down ways of perceiving another person.
- Explain the power of a first impression.

Fusiform face area A region in the temporal lobe of the brain that helps us recognize the people we know.

THINK ABOUT ▶

[Tyler Olson/Shutterstock]

Prosopagnosia The inability to recognize familiar faces.

Forming Impressions of People

Let's return again to the scene of the accident with which we began this chapter. As the investigator, you show up and see the two drivers engaged in animated debate about who was at fault. Very quickly you'll begin to form impressions of each of them. What are the factors that influence these impressions? In this section, we examine some of the processes that guide our impressions.

Beginning with the Basics: Perceiving Faces, Physical Attributes, and Group Membership

When we encounter another person, one of the first things we recognize is whether that person is someone we already know or a stranger. As we mentioned in chapter 2, a region in the temporal lobe of the brain called the **fusiform face area** helps us recognize the people we know (Kanwisher et al., 1997). We see the essential role of the fusiform face area from studies of people who suffer damage to this region of the brain. Such individuals suffer from **prosopagnosia**, the inability to recognize familiar faces, even though they are quite capable of identifying other familiar objects. It seems that the ability to recognize the people we know was so important to human evolution that our brains have a region specifically devoted to this task. Research is beginning to suggest that those with autism show less activation in this brain region, consistent with the notion that autism impairs social perception (Schultz, 2005).

Our brains are also highly attuned to certain physical characteristics of other people (Kramer et al., 2017; Messick & Mackie, 1989). These include a person's age and sex and whether we are related to him or her (Lieberman et al., 2008). Think about the last time you bought a cup a coffee or went through the grocery-store checkout line. What do you remember about the cashier? It wouldn't be surprising if all you can remember about these kinds of quick interactions is that the cashier was an older woman or a man in his 20s.

People may have evolved to detect these cues automatically because they are useful for efficiently distinguishing allies from enemies, potential mates, and close relatives (Kurzban et al., 2001). The idea is that to survive, our ancestors had to avoid dangerous conflicts with others and avoid infection from people who were carrying disease. Individuals who could quickly size up another person's age, sex, and other physical indicators of health, strength, and similarity most likely had better success surviving and reproducing than those who made these judgments less quickly or accurately. We can even detect that someone is sick based on a photo, and when we do, physiological reactions are triggered that cue the immune system to prepare to fend off potential disease (Schaller et al., 2010).

Impression Formation

If you have ever had a roommate, think back to when you first met the person. You were probably thinking, "Who is this person? What will he or she be like as a roommate?" Once we have determined a person's basic characteristics, such as gender and physical attributes, the next step is to form an impression of that person's personality. What are the person's traits, preferences, and beliefs? Knowing what people are like is useful because it guides how you expect them to act. The more accurate you are, the more you can adapt your behavior appropriately. If you think particular people are likely to be friendly, you might be more likely to smile at them and act friendly yourself, whereas if you think some individuals are likely to be hostile, you might avoid them altogether. This interpersonal accuracy and behavioral adaptability, in turn, often lead to more satisfying relationships (Schmid Mast & Hall, 2018).

There are two general ways we form impressions of others: from the bottom up and from the top down.

Building an Impression from the Bottom Up: Decoding the Behaviors and Minds of Others   We build an impression from the bottom up by gathering individual observations of a person to form an overall impression. As we listen and observe, we begin inferring the individual's traits, attitudes, intentions, and goals, largely through the attribution processes we've already described. As we move toward a general impression of the person, there is a *negativity bias*, a tendency to weigh instances of negative behavior more heavily than instances of positive behavior (Pratto & John, 1991). This occurs for two reasons. First, there's a likely adaptive tendency to being particularly sensitive to detecting the negative things in our environment (Ito et al., 1998). Second, most of the time, people follow norms of good behavior, so bad behavior is more attention grabbing and may seem to reveal a person's "true colors." As a consequence, we are particularly likely to remember when someone we thought was good does a bad thing, but we easily overlook when a person we're used to observing do bad things does something good (Bartholow, 2010).

Brief Encounters: Impressions from Thin Slices   We are surprisingly accurate at forming impressions of individuals by observing what they say and do. We can even decode certain personality characteristics based on very thin slices, such as a 30-second video clip, of a person's behavior (Ambady & Rosenthal, 1992). Having more time to observe the person increases accuracy, but not by much (Murphy et al., 2019). Indeed, in one study, the impressions participants formed of a person based on a photograph were remarkably similar to their impressions a month later, after they had met the person (Gunaydin et al., 2017). When it comes to forming impressions, it seems that people ignore the old adage "Don't judge a book by its cover." Part of the reason may be that such judging works pretty well.

In fact, people can accurately perceive the personality traits of others without ever seeing or meeting them, having only evidence of everyday behaviors such as what they post on Facebook (Vazire & Gosling, 2004). Some personality traits, such as being socially extraverted, can be predicted by knowing that a person has a preference for music with vocals (Rentfrow & Gosling, 2006). Other traits, like conscientiousness and openness to new experiences, can be accurately perceived merely by seeing people's office space or bedrooms (Gosling et al., 2002). Check out the exercise in **FIGURE 4.7** to get a sense of what we mean. Finally, as you might expect, some people are better at guessing personalities than others. People who are higher in empathetic understanding and have the ability to adopt another's perspective tend to make more accurate judgments about the personalities of others (Colman et al., 2017).

Figure 4.7

Clues to Personality

What's your impression of the person who lives in the room on the left? What about the person living in the room on the right? Think about how you make these judgments without even seeing or knowing the person.

[Sam Gosling]

Theory of mind A set of ideas about other peoples' thoughts, desires, feelings, and intentions based on what we know about them and the situation they are in.

Mirror neurons Certain neurons that are activated both when one performs an action oneself and when one observes another person perform that action.

Transference A process whereby we activate schemas of a person we know and use the schemas to form an impression of someone new.

▲ If you meet someone who reminds you of Will Smith, you're likely to transfer some of your feelings about this famous actor to the new person.

Theory of Mind Not only can we learn about a person's personality on the basis of minimal information, but we are also pretty good at reading peoples' minds. No, we are not telepathic. But we do have an evolved propensity to develop a **theory of mind**: a set of ideas about other people's thoughts, desires, feelings, and intentions, based on what we know about them and the situation they are in (Malle & Hodges, 2005). This capacity is highly valuable for understanding and predicting how people will behave, which helps us cooperate effectively with some people, compete against rivals, and avoid those who might want to do us harm.

For example, we use facial expressions, tone of voice, and how the head is tilted to make inferences about someone and how the person is feeling (Witkower & Tracy, 2019). If your new roommate comes home with knit eyebrows, pursed lips, clenched fists, and a low and tight voice, you might reasonably assume that your roommate is angry. Most children develop a theory of mind around the age of four (Cadinu & Kiesner, 2000). We know this because children around this age figure out that their own beliefs and desires are separate from others' beliefs and desires. However, people with certain disorders, such as autism, never develop the ability to judge accurately what others might be thinking (Baron-Cohen et al., 2000). Even those with high-functioning forms of autism, who live quite independently and have successful careers, show an impaired ability to determine a person's emotions on the basis of the expression in their eyes or the tone of their voice (Baron-Cohen et al., 2001; Rutherford et al., 2002). As a result, these individuals often have difficulty with social tasks most of us take for granted, such as monitoring social cues indicating that our own behavior might offend or step outside behavioral norms.

To uncover the brain regions involved in this kind of mind reading, neuroscientists have focused on a brain region called the medial prefrontal cortex (Frith & Frith, 1999). This region contains **mirror neurons**, which respond very similarly both when one does an action oneself and when one observes another person perform that same action (Uddin et al., 2007). When seeing your roommate's expressions of anger as described above, you might find yourself imitating those facial displays. But even if your own facial expression doesn't change, mirror neurons in your brain allow you to simulate your roommate's emotional state, helping you to understand what your roommate is thinking and feeling (Iacoboni, 2009).

Building an Impression from the Top Down: Perceiving Others Through Schemas Bottom-up processes describe how we build our impressions of others by observing their individual actions and expressions and drawing inferences about who they are or what they are thinking. In contrast, people also often build an impression from the top down, based on their own preconceived ideas.

Transference We often automatically perceive certain basic characteristics about a person and then infer that the individual will share the features that we associate with similar people. Sometimes this quick inference might result from the person's reminding us of another person we already know. Let's suppose you meet someone for the first time at a party, and your first thought is that she bears some resemblance to your favorite cousin. Research by Susan Andersen and colleagues (Andersen et al., 1996) suggests that because of this perceived similarity, you will be more likely to assume that this new acquaintance's resemblance to your cousin lies not just in appearance but extends to her personality as well. This process was first identified by Freud (1912/1958) and labeled **transference.** Transference is a complex process in psychoanalytic theory, but in social psychological research, it has been more narrowly defined as forming an impression of and feelings for an unfamiliar person using the schema one has for a familiar person who resembles him or her in some way.

False Consensus   Even when a person we meet doesn't remind us of someone specific, we often project onto him or her attitudes and opinions of the person we know the best—ourselves! **False consensus** is a general tendency to assume that other people share the attitudes, opinions, and preferences that we have (Mullen et al., 1985; Ross, Greene, & House, 1977). As we mentioned earlier, in our discussion of theory of mind, most of us can understand that other people do not view the world exactly as we do, and yet often we assume they do anyhow. People who are in favor of gun control think most people agree with them. People who are against gun control think they are in the majority. We are more likely to assume consensus among members of our ingroups than with members of outgroups (Krueger & Zeiger, 1993). After all, our ingroups are more likely to remind us of ourselves. In part because of this tendency, we often assume that, as a group, our friends are more similar to each other than people we don't like are, even though having more information about our friends suggests that we should recognize the differences between them (Alves et al., 2016).

False consensus A general tendency to assume that other people share our own attitudes, opinions, and preferences.

False consensus stems from a number of processes (Marks & Miller, 1987). Among them:

- Our own opinions and behaviors are most salient to us and, therefore, most cognitively accessible. So, they are most likely to come to mind when we consider what other people think and do.

- It is validating for our worldview and self-worth to believe that others think and act the way we do. So, when we feel under attack, we're motivated to think that others share our viewpoint and validate our actions (Sherman et al., 1984). Think of the teenager caught smoking behind the school who explains his actions by saying, "But everybody does it!" Research suggests that this isn't just a cliché; teenagers who engage in behaviors that might be bad for their health actually do overestimate the degree to which their friends are engaging in the same behaviors (Prinstein & Wang, 2005).

- We tend to like and associate with people who are in fact similar to us. If our group of friends really do like to smoke and drink, then in our own narrow slice of the world, it does seem as if *everyone does it* because we forget to adjust for the fact that the people we affiliate with are not very representative of the population at large. We see this happening on the Internet, where our group of Facebook friends or Twitter followers generally validate and share our opinions (Barberá et al., 2015), and the news outlets we seek out package news stories in ways that seem to confirm what we already believe. One of the benefits of having a diverse group of friends and acquaintances and a breadth of media exposure might be to disabuse us of our false consensus tendencies.

Implicit Personality Theories   As intuitive psychologists trying to make sense of people's behavior, we develop our own theories about how different traits are related to each other. Consequently, one way we use our preexisting schemas to form impressions of a person is to rely on our *implicit personality theories*. These are theories that we have about which traits go together and why they do. To clarify what this means, we will consider some examples from research.

Asch (1946) found that some traits are more central than others, and the more central traits affect our interpretation of other traits that we attribute to a person. Asch's participants were asked to consider two people with traits like those described in **TABLE 4.1**. Asch's participants viewed someone like Bob as generous, wise, happy, sociable, popular, and altruistic. They viewed someone like Jason as ungenerous, shrewd, unhappy, unsociable, irritable, and hard headed.

Table 4.1 Asch's Character Traits Description

Bob	Jason
Intelligent	Intelligent
Skillful	Skillful
Industrious	Industrious
Warm	Cold
Determined	Determined
Practical	Practical
Cautious	Cautious

The only difference in the descriptions of the two guys was that *warm* was included in the traits for Bob and was replaced with *cold* for Jason. Yet changing that one trait—which is a metaphor, not a literal description of a person (Bob doesn't radiate more heat than Jason)—greatly altered the overall impressions of them. Combined with "warm," "intelligent" was viewed as "wise." Combined with "cold," "intelligent" was viewed as "shrewd." Warmth and coldness are therefore considered central traits that help organize overall impressions and transform interpretation of other traits ascribed to a person. When Asch replaced "warm" and "cold" with "polite" and "blunt," he did not find similar effects, suggesting that these are not central traits.

While "polite" might not be perceived as especially diagnostic, recent research indicates that morality is a particularly central trait influencing our impressions of others (Goodwin, 2015). Independent of how "warm" people seem to be, how honest and trustworthy we think they are goes a long way in predicting whether we like or dislike them. This may be why morality is such a focus in political campaigns. For example, during the 2016 presidential campaign, then Republican nominee Donald Trump made this a centerpiece of his campaign against Democratic nominee Hillary Clinton, and she responded with her own allegations of immorality. Perceptions of trust are often gleaned quickly and have critical consequences. For example, in both Arkansas and Florida, convicted murderers who have more "untrustworthy" faces are more likely to get a death sentence (versus life in prison), even when trust is not judicially relevant (Wilson & Rule, 2015, 2016).

Another implicit theory many people hold is that how someone behaves in one context is how the person behaves in others. For example, if you have a roommate who is neat and organized in your living quarters, you may infer that she is also a conscientious student or worker. However, it turns out that conscientiousness at home often does *not* extend to the classroom or job (Mischel & Peake, 1982). In short, we tend to assume that people are more consistent in how they behave across situations than they actually are.

People also tend to view positive traits as going together and negative traits as going together. For example, people who are viewed as more physically attractive are also perceived to be more personable, happier, competent, and more successful (e.g., Oh et al., 2019), a finding that has come to be known as the "what is beautiful is good" stereotype (Dion et al., 1972). But this effect is most likely reflective of a broader **halo effect** (Nisbett & Wilson, 1977a; Thorndike, 1920), whereby social perceivers' assessments of an individual on a given trait are biased by their more general impression of the individual. If the general impression is good, then any individual assessment of the person's friendliness, attractiveness, intelligence, and so on is likely to be more positive. The same halo effects can negatively bias our perceptions of the people we dislike, but they tend to be stronger for positive information than for negative information (Gräf & Unkelbach, 2016).

Halo effect The tendency of our assessments of an individual on a given trait to be biased by our more general impression of the individual.

Stereotyping The process just described involves applying a schema we have of a type of people, "attractive people," to judge an individual. This is what we do when we *stereotype* others. Stereotyping is a cognitive shortcut or heuristic, a quick and easy way to get an idea of what a person might be like.

Say you learn that your new roommate is a political science major planning for a future career in politics. Might you use whatever prior schema you have about politicians to make a judgment of what she is like as a person? Some of those impressions might later prove to be accurate (e.g., an abiding interest in current events), and others might not (e.g., a knack for talking eloquently without saying anything of substance), but in both cases, they help you size up your new living partner quickly.

THINK ABOUT ▶

[Evgheni Lachi/Shutterstock]

Stereotyping is an application of schematic processing. Forming a completely accurate and *individualized* impression of a person (i.e., one that is unbiased by stereotypes) is an effortful process. We often fall back on mental shortcuts when the stakes are low ("Does it really matter if I falsely assume that Tom is an engineer?") or we aren't especially motivated to be accurate. But even when the stakes are high and our judgments matter, we can still be biased by our stereotypes when we are tired or fatigued. For example, when participants are asked to judge the guilt or innocence of a defendant on the basis of ambiguous evidence, their decisions are more likely to be biased in stereotypical ways when they are in the off-cycle of their circadian rhythm—such as at 8:00 a.m. when they are normally at their cognitive peak in the evening (Bodenhausen, 1990). In such situations, our tendency toward stereotyping may be cognitively functional, but it can clearly have very damaging social costs.

In this way, general stereotypes about a group of people are often employed to form an impression of individual members of that group. In addition, sometimes we take a bit of information we might know about a person and erroneously assume that the person is part of a larger category merely because he or she seems to map onto our schema of that category. For example, imagine that you've been given the following description of a person chosen from a pool of 100 professionals:

> Jack is a 45-year-old man. He is married and has four children. He is generally conservative, careful, and ambitious. He shows no interest in political and social issues and spends most of his free time on his many hobbies, which include home carpentry, sailing, and mathematical puzzles.

If this is all you knew about Jack, do you think it's more likely that Jack is an engineer or a lawyer? If you are like most of the participants who were faced with this judgment in a study carried out in 1973, you'd stake your bet on engineer. But what if you were also told that of the 100 professionals, 70 are lawyers and 30 are engineers? Would that make you less likely to guess engineer? According to research by Amos Tversky and the Nobel Prize winner Daniel Kahneman (Kahneman & Tversky, 1973), the answer is "no." As long as the description seems more representative of an engineer than a lawyer, participants guess engineer, regardless of whether the person was picked out of a pool of 70% lawyers or 70% engineers!

Such erroneous judgment occurs because people fall prey to the **representativeness heuristic**, a tendency to overestimate the likelihood that a target is part of a larger category if the person has features that seem representative of that category. In this case, "lacking interest in political issues and enjoying mathematical puzzles" seems more representative of an engineer than of a lawyer. But this conclusion depends heavily on the validity of these stereotypes and involves ignoring statistical evidence regarding the relative frequency of particular events or types of people. Even when the statistical evidence showed that far more people in the pool were lawyers than engineers (that is, a 70% base rate of lawyers), the pull of the heuristic was sufficiently powerful to override this information.

Representativeness heuristic The tendency to overestimate the likelihood that a target is part of a category if the person has features that seem representative of that category.

Stereotypes and Individuation   Of course, we don't always rely on stereotypes to judge others. As we get to know a person better, we come to view him or her more as an individual than as a member of a stereotyped group (Kunda et al., 2002). When do people rely on the top-down process (applying a stereotype, or schema for someone's group, to see that person solely as a member of that group), and when do they use the bottom-up process (perceiving the person as a unique individual)?

We are more likely to use a bottom-up approach and perceive a person as an individual unique from social groups when we are motivated to get to know and understand who that person is (Fiske & Neuberg, 1990). Such motivation is often activated when we need to work together with the person on a project (Neuberg & Fiske, 1987) or when we are made to feel similar to them in some way (Galinsky & Moskowitz, 2000). When this happens, rather than lazily rely on stereotypes, we attend closely to the person's specific words and actions and form individualized impressions of the unique individual with whom we are interacting (Kunda et al., 2002).

Changing First Impressions

No doubt you have heard the old adage that you have only one chance to make a first impression. The research reviewed so far suggests that we do form impressions of others quite quickly. As we've already learned, once we form a schema, it becomes very resistant to change and tends to lead us to assimilate new information into what we already believe. What we learn early on seems to color how we judge subsequent information. This **primacy effect** was first studied by Asch (1946) in another of his simple but elegant experiments on how people form impressions (see also Sullivan, 2019). In this study, Asch gave participants information about a person named John. In one condition, John was described as "intelligent, industrious, impulsive, critical, stubborn, and envious." In a second condition, he was described as "envious, stubborn, critical, impulsive, industrious, and intelligent." Even though participants in the two conditions were given exactly the same traits to read, the order of those traits had an effect on their global evaluations of John (**TABLE 4.2**). They rated him more positively if they were given the first order, presumably because the opening trait, "intelligent," led people to put a more positive spin on all of the traits that followed it. When it comes to making a good impression, you really do want to put your best foot forward.

But if we form such quick judgments of people, what happens if we later encounter information that disconfirms those initial impressions? If the disconfirmation is strong enough, our initial impressions can be changed. In fact, our initial evaluations of someone can even change quite rapidly when we are presented with new information about a person (Ferguson et al., 2019; Olcaysoy Okten et al., 2019) as well as if we are prompted to reconsider initially available information (Brannon & Gawronski, 2017). Our schemas exert a strong pressure on the impressions we develop, but they are not so rigid as to be unchangeable. When people do things that are unexpected, our brain signals that something unusual and potentially important has just happened (Bartholow et al., 2001). A broad network of brain areas appears to be involved in this signaling process, spurred by the release of the neurotransmitter norepinephrine in the locus coeruleus (Nieuwenhuis et al., 2005). Because of this increased processing of information, we become more likely to modify our initial impression. However, because of the negativity bias, this is especially true when someone we expect good things from does something bad.

In sum, our processes of remembering events and people, drawing causal attributions for events, generating counterfactuals, and forming impressions have important implications for the way we feel toward the past and act in the future. These processes can help or hinder our efforts to regulate our actions to achieve our desired goals, a theme we will pick up in the next set of chapters, where we focus on the self.

Primacy effect The idea that what we learn early colors how we judge subsequent information.

Table 4.2 Asch's Two Character Descriptions

John's Description: Condition 1	John's Description: Condition 2
Intelligent	Envious
Industrious	Stubborn
Impulsive	Critical
Critical	Impulsive
Stubborn	Industrious
Envious	Intelligent

SECTION REVIEW   Forming Impressions of People

As social beings, we are highly attuned to other people.

The Basics	Decoding Minds and Behavior	Perceiving Through Schemas	Changing First Impressions
• A region in the temporal lobe, the fusiform face area, helps us recognize faces. • We have evolved to quickly size up physical indicators of health, strength, and similarity, perhaps for survival reasons.	• We build an impression from the bottom up when we gather individual observations of a person's actions to draw an inference about who he or she is. • Our impressions are often quite accurate, even with minimal information. • We are also pretty good at understanding what people are thinking.	• We build an impression from the top down when we use a preexisting schema to form an impression of another. • These preexisting schemas are often heuristics that include transferring an impression we have of one person to another, assuming that similar traits go together, and relying on stereotypes. • Such heuristics can lead us to make biased judgments.	• Initial impressions have a powerful influence on interpretations of subsequent information. However, they can change when people act in unexpected ways.

CRITICAL LEARNING EXERCISES

1. Tune in to any news outlet these days, and you're likely to come across allegations of "fake news." Given what you have learned about how memories are formed—and specifically the misinformation effect—do you think our exposure to fake news could lead to the creation of false memories? Now apply what you've learned about the influence of schemas on memory. Do you think fake news might be more likely to lead to the creation of false memories for alleged events that fit our schemas? After you've thought through these questions, check out research by Murphy, Loftus, and colleagues (2019) that inspired this critical thinking exercise.

2. Imagine that you're teaching a class (perhaps even a class in social psychology). As you look out at the room, you watch as a student's eyes start to glaze over, his head nods back, and he begins to snooze. As the instructor, you're now wondering whether your lecture is really that boring or if perhaps the cause is the student. What questions will you consider to determine if it is your lecture or the student that is the cause of the sleeping? If you determine that the student is the cause, what additional information would you need to inform how you could best help the student to do better?

3. Consider the last time you thought about how an event in your life could have turned out differently than it did. Now that you've read about counterfactual thinking, try to identify whether you used an upward or downward counterfactual. Did imagining this alternative outcome make you feel better or worse about what happened? Did imagining this alternative outcome provide you with a plan for how you might act differently in the future?

4. Think about a time when your first impressions of a person turned out to be wrong. Maybe it's a person you first thought was a jerk but ended up being a friend, or maybe it's someone you initially thought would be a friend but who turned out to be a jerk. What were the factors that influenced your first impression? What events transpired that led you to change your first impression?

CHAPTER 5

The Nature, Origins, and Functions of the Self

Every species on this planet has unique adaptations that set it apart from other species. African pixie frogs can hang out for years underground in a self-made sac until a rainy season comes around; octopuses have camouflaging skin that changes color and pattern to blend in with their surroundings; and hippos have their own natural sunscreen that oozes out of their pores. We humans have a pretty cool trick of our own — the ability to focus attention on our own thoughts, moods, behaviors, and experiences. In short, we have a sense of *self*.

In some ways, the self is private. Only you know what it's like from your point of view. Yet the self is also a thoroughly *social* thing. It is continually shaped by social contexts, and it directs how we perceive and relate to others. This constant dialogue between the self and the social world is the subject of this chapter.

A useful starting point is a distinction proposed by William James in his groundbreaking *Principles of Psychology* (1890). James noted that, in one sense, the self is all the knowledge you have about your characteristics and experiences. James labeled this the *Me*, but today we call it the **self-concept**. In another sense, the self is the voice in your head that contemplates, makes decisions, and chooses what courses of action to take — what James and Freud labeled the *I*. Freud originally wrote in German, and his early English translators used the Latin word for "I," **ego**, and that has become the most common term for the aspect of self that controls one's actions. James noted that these two aspects of the self make it a unique topic to study: It is a thing that thinks *and* a thing that is thought about. It's like using your eyes to look at your eyes!

This chapter builds on James's *I/Me* distinction to explore how the self and the social world interact. We will look at:

- How people's cultural and social environments shape the self-concept by determining *what* they know about themselves and *how* they acquire that knowledge

- How the ego regulates a person's thoughts, feelings, and behavior

- People's everyday efforts to pursue goals and why they sometimes succeed and other times fall short

Self-concept A person's knowledge about him- or herself, including one's own traits, social identities, and experiences.

Ego The aspect of self that controls one's thoughts and actions.

- Outline some influences of culture on the self-concept.
- Explain how gender and culture interact to shape the self-concept.
- Describe how shifting social contexts create change in the self-concept.

Social Influences on the Self-Concept

If we imagine the self-concept as the *Book of You*—the ongoing story about your life—then who writes it? Many of us would respond, "I do!" But in reality, your particular life story has plots, themes, and characters that are borrowed from your social environment. Let's consider how culture, gender, and shifting contexts shape the self-concept.

Culture

Our discussion of the cultural perspective in chapter 2 made the point that people's self-concept emerges as they are socialized into the cultural worldview. Culture has a hand in virtually all the ways that people describe themselves. When you are asked the question "Who are you?" your first response is usually your name. If you're like me, your name seems somehow meaningful, not arbitrary: I'm Jeff. I can't think of myself any other way. But your name is not an inherent part of you. It's a label given to you at birth that reflects various cultural influences, such as famous movie stars (in Jeff's case) and the Bible (in Mark's case). In some cultures, such as the Native American Nez Perce culture in Idaho, people's names change over the course of their lives (Cash Cash, 2006).

Consider other ways people might answer the "Who are you?" question: They might highlight being a student, a woman, a friend of Susan, an American citizen, a psychology major, an honest person, a shy person, an amateur photographer, a Gemini, a daughter, a Jew, a Midwesterner. This list illustrates how culture offers a set of socially acknowledged identities (e.g., *woman, American*), roles (e.g., *student, friend of Susan*), traits (e.g., *honest, shy*), and interests (e.g., *photography*). These cultural constructs are not simply things we have, wear, or do; they often feel like essential parts of who we are (Hatvany et al., 2018). Still, despite how real they seem, the building blocks of the self are specific to one's place and time in history. If you are raised in Canada, your self-concept may very well include *hockey player*, but this is rather unlikely if you are raised in equatorial Africa.

Social identity theory The theory that people define and evaluate themselves largely in terms of the social groups with which they identify.

Even within a relatively small geographic region, we see cultural influences on people's sense of self. According to **social identity theory** (Tajfel & Turner, 1979), people define themselves largely in terms of the social groups with which they identify. They come to know what characteristics they have by thinking of themselves in terms of family, race, nationality, and other group memberships. Thus, two people raised in the same geographic region may define themselves in very different ways, depending on their group identifications (Smith & Henry, 1996; Tropp & Wright, 2001).

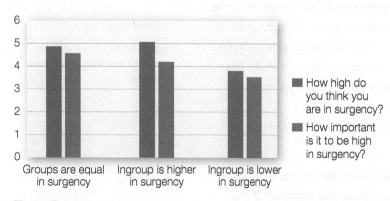

Figure 5.1

Groups and Self-Definition

Students who were told that their group was high in a trait they have never heard of assumed themselves to be high in that trait. People define themselves in terms of their social groups.

[Data from Schmader & Major, 1999]

To see how this works, consider a study by Schmader and Major (1999). College students were told, based on their judgments of abstract paintings, that they tend to have a "figure" orientation or a "ground" orientation (when in fact they were randomly assigned to one of these two groups). The students were next asked to complete a questionnaire measuring a new personality trait called *surgency*. Without learning their own score on the measure, students were told either that both groups tend to be equal in surgency, that "Figures" tend to be higher in surgency, or that "Grounds" tend to be higher in surgency (**FIGURE 5.1**). Although the participants didn't know what surgency was (no one does; it's a fictitious trait!), they assumed that if their ingroup scored higher on surgency, then they probably were high in surgency as well and, furthermore, that surgency was a pretty important trait to have!

In addition to defining the identities, roles, and traits with which people describe themselves, cultures differ in whether they promote an understanding of the self as independent or interdependent (see further discussion in chapter 2). In relatively individualistic cultures—like North America, Australia, and Europe—people are socialized to view themselves as unique individuals, relatively independent from others. Their self-concept tends to center around their own attributes, like "I am artistic." By contrast, people socialized in collectivistic cultures—like China, Japan, India, and Mexico—tend to view themselves as interdependent, defined primarily in relation to other people, like "I am a daughter" and "I am a Buddhist" (Markus & Kitayama, 1991).

Of course, people do not identify with just one cultural group. In North America, the number of people who identify with two or more racial ingroups has increased by more than 25% in the past 15 years. This means that many people are increasingly expected to balance multiple identities—which can be stressful but also has advantages. Multiracial individuals feel pressure to "choose" one of their racial groups; they get embarrassing questions like "What *are* you, anyhow?" and face more discrimination than their monoracial peers. But the ability to switch between multiple racial identities also increases sensitivity to social cues and helps people adapt to their surroundings (Gaither, 2015).

Gender

Popular culture tells us that men and women's minds are wired in totally different ways; you might, for example, remember the bestselling book *Men Are from Mars, Women Are from Venus*. However, men and women are more similar than they are different (Hyde, 2005). Women rate themselves as more trusting, anxious, and slightly more conscientious, whereas men rate themselves as more assertive and a little more open to new experiences. But most of these differences are statistically small, and men and women are nearly identical on other important characteristics, such as extraversion and impulsivity. For example, an American stereotype holds that women talk more than men. Matthias Mehl and colleagues (2007) put this stereotype to the test. They had female and male college students wear a device called the electronically activated recorder (or EAR), which records ambient sound at random times throughout the day (Mehl, 2017). Contrary to the popular stereotype, men and women talked virtually the same amount—about 1,600 words a day.

Not only do we imagine and exaggerate differences between men and women, we also tend to be mistaken about the origin of the differences that do exist. We commonly assume that those differences are *essential* to men and women because they are biologically or genetically based (Hyde, 2005). But people also *learn* from their culture what behaviors and self-views are appropriate for their gender. As Freud (1921/1955) argued, children tend to identify strongly with their same-sex parent and mimic that parent's traits and qualities (Bussey & Bandura, 1999; Perry & Bussey, 1979).

We also learn gendered behavior by simply being told what is appropriate. For example, when preschoolers are told that some unfamiliar toys are for boys and others are for girls, they tend to like the toys described as appropriate for their sex and dislike the other toys (Martin et al., 1995). Through this kind

▲ The electronically activated recorder (EAR; worn by the woman on the right) is a device that enables researchers to record snippets of everyday conversations, revealing a great deal about how people interact with each other.

[Dr. Matthias Mehl]

▲ How does the message of the "Men at Work" sign subtly reinforce gender roles? Why not "People Working" instead? Where do you see similar messages in your culture? Have they influenced what you imagine yourself being or doing?

[dbn/imageBROKER/AGE Fotostock]

THINK ABOUT ▶

[Ann Hermes/The Christian Science Monitor via Getty Images]

Social role theory The theory that gender differences in behavior, personality, and self-definition arise because of a long history of role distribution between the sexes and error-prone assumptions that those roles are essential to the nature of men and women.

Self-schema An integrated set of memories, beliefs, and generalizations about a personally important attribute that defines the self.

Working self-concept A set of self-aspects that are currently activated by situational cues and strongly influence thoughts, feelings, and actions in the moment.

of sex-role socialization, most individuals (although clearly not all) come to develop a sense of themselves and their role in life that is consistent with their culture's sex roles.

Of course, once we say sex differences are partly learned through culture, we're faced with broader questions: Why do cultures promote different roles for females and males? Why do women and men typically conform to gender-appropriate behaviors and preferences? How do gender roles shape people's self-concepts? To address these questions, Alice Eagly (1987) developed **social role theory.** She noted that biological differences in body type and childbearing ability have meant that, across history and culture, men have traditionally taken on physically demanding tasks, while women have had more control over child rearing and managing communal relationships. Eagly made an interesting point about how we interpret those differences: By observing males and females engage in specific roles, people often infer that women do more socially oriented and caregiving behaviors *because that is what they are intrinsically good at* and that men find themselves in positions of leadership and power *because that is what they are intrinsically good at.* To illustrate, one of your authors (Mark) has had his car fixed several times in the past few years, and every mechanic he's interacted with has been male. You can imagine how it would be easy for him to jump to the conclusion that men are *by their nature* better suited than women to fix cars. But step back and see that he'd be basing that inference on no solid evidence about human nature—only a correlation he's observed in his local community.

Context

Does the self-concept remain pretty much the same as people move from one social context to another? Or does it change? Research supports both possibilities. Some aspects of the self-concept are relatively stable, like the attributes we view as most important for defining our sense of self. Intelligence or athletic ability, for example, might be most central to who someone is as a person, whereas other attributes may be descriptive but not so self-defining. Take a moment to think about your own self-defining attributes. What aspects are central to who *you* are?

According to Hazel Markus (1977), people's knowledge about self-defining attributes are mentally organized as a **self-schema:** an integrated set of memories, beliefs, and generalizations about an attribute that is central to one's self-concept. A self-schema for *compassion,* for example, may include memories of specific events ("Last week I helped a duck get out of the road") and more general beliefs about how one typically behaves in various situations ("I always give change to homeless people"). People process information about a self-defining attribute very quickly, remember a lot of specific behaviors that reflect that attribute, and are reluctant to believe information that conflicts with their belief about how much of that attribute they possess.

Although central aspects of the self-concept remain stable, shifting social contexts can call up different aspects of the self-concept, changing how we think and act. At a party, you might be conscious of your identity as Susan's friend (since you came to the party with her), that you are shy (when feeling awkward talking to people), and that you enjoy photography (when admiring several photographs hanging in the house). The term **working self-concept** refers to the portion of a person's self-schema that is currently activated and influences the individual's behavior (Markus & Kunda, 1986). Which aspects of your total self-concept are active in your working self-concept at any given moment can be determined by your social situation, information you've been primed with, and your motivation to think or act in particular ways. If you're in class, situational cues such as books and computers, as well as your motivation to succeed, will likely bring aspects of your "student self" (e.g., *intelligent, industrious*) to the forefront of your consciousness. But those same aspects are less likely to influence your thoughts and behavior in a different context, as when you're playing Frisbee in the park.

Another contextual factor is the people around you. People tend to define themselves in terms of attributes that distinguish them from other people in their current environment. Imagine walking into a classroom on the first day of a new class to find that you're the only person over 40 years old. In this context, your age will likely emerge as a central part of yourself. This is an example of how **solo status**—a sense that one is unique from those in the current environment—highlights certain parts of the individual's working self-concept. In one study, when children were asked to consider who they are, they tended to mention characteristics such as age, gender, and ethnicity if they differed on those characteristics from the majority of their classmates (McGuire et al., 1978).

▲ The brightly dressed woman might view attributes such as spontaneity and cheerfulness as being central to her self-concept. But that might be a temporary result of her solo status among the suits.

[Greg Ceo/The Image Bank/Getty Images]

Solo status A sense that one is unique in some specific manner in relation to other people in the current environment.

SECTION REVIEW   Social Influences on the Self-Concept

People's self-concept is shaped by their cultural and social environments.

Culture	Gender	Context
• Culture shapes virtually all the ways people describe themselves. • People understand and evaluate themselves in terms of the social groups with which they identify.	• Men and women are more similar than they are different. • Children learn from adults and the broader culture how men and women behave. • Social role theory claims that men and women's biological differences favor different social roles, and those roles are often assumed to reflect "natural" limits on what men and women can and should be.	• The self-concept is stable from one occasion to another because people have *self-schemas* for the attributes that are important to them. • At the same time, the self-concept is malleable. Contextual factors, such as solo status, highlight and downplay different parts of the *working self-concept* at any given moment.

How Do We Come to Know the Self?

Learning Outcomes

Know then thyself, presume not God to scan; The proper study of mankind is Man.

— Alexander Pope, *An Essay on Man* (1732–1744/1903)

The idea that the self-concept is created in the context of social life raises a thorny question: How do people do it? How do they figure out what qualities define them and set them apart from other people? Social psychologists have identified three sources of self-knowledge: the appraisals people get from others, their social comparisons, and their self-perceptions. As we examine these sources, observe how they can occasionally lead us to make errors that lead us to think we know ourselves better than we do.

- Apply the concept of reflected appraisals to explain how people come to know and evaluate themselves.

- Differentiate between the influence of upward and downward comparisons on the self-concept.

- Explain how self-perception guides people to use their own behavior and bodily experiences as clues to who they are.

▲ Charles Cooley (left) and George Herbert Mead (right) developed the idea that people learn about and judge themselves on the basis of how other people perceive them.

[Left: Photographer Unknown, c. 1902; right: The Granger Collection, NYC — All rights reserved.]

Symbolic interactionism The perspective that people use their understanding of how others view them as the primary basis for knowing and evaluating themselves.

Looking-glass self The idea that others reflect back to us (much like a looking glass, or mirror) who we are by how they behave toward us.

Appraisals What other people think about us.

Reflected Appraisals: Seeing Ourselves Through the Eyes of Others

Two 20th-century sociologists, Charles Cooley (1902) and George Herbert Mead (1934), examined the social origin of the self-concept from a perspective known as **symbolic interactionism**. They said that people use their understanding of how *other* people view them as the primary basis for knowing themselves. Cooley coined the term **looking-glass self** to refer to the idea that others reflect back to the individual (much like a looking glass, or mirror) who she is by how they behave toward her. Note how the symbolic interactionism perspective flips common wisdom on its head. Whereas you might assume that you have direct insight into who you are, this view says that first you observe how others view you—what are called others' **appraisals** of you—and then you incorporate those appraisals into your self-concept.

People use others' appraisals not only to know their attributes but also to judge themselves and their actions as good or bad. For example, a person might feel bad about the pile of laundry on the floor because she imagines Mom's voice saying, "You are such a slob!" Because people internalize others' appraisals, they evaluate themselves as if those other people were in their heads, observing them act. Cooley also pointed out that a person's self-concept is more likely to develop and change in response to the appraisals of people who are close or admired than in response to the appraisals of strangers.

Based on Mead's and Cooley's insights, Baldwin and colleagues (1990) hypothesized that even unconscious reminders of approval and disapproval from significant others would influence self-evaluations. In one study, the researchers first had Catholic participants read a description of a sexual dream and then subliminally presented them with the scowling face of either the pope or an unfamiliar other, also with a disapproving expression, and finally had them rate themselves on dimensions such as morality, intelligence, and talent. Catholics viewed themselves as less worthy after being exposed to the disapproving face of a significant authority figure but not a stranger (even though they had no conscious awareness that they saw the pictures—they were on the screen for only a few milliseconds). Even at an unconscious level, people carry with them the knowledge of how significant others view them, and they use those appraisals to judge themselves.

Whereas Cooley said that people look to significant others to define themselves, Mead added that they also form a mental image of most people in society—called the *generalized other*—and consider how that collective eye views them. Consistent with this idea, overweight people are significantly less happy if they live in a society that stigmatizes obesity and values thinness than if they live in a society in which obesity is common and accepted (Pinhey et al., 1997).

▲ If you consider Pope Francis to be a significant figure in your life, how do you think being exposed to this image of his scowling expression would make you feel about yourself? What if you had just engaged in some questionable activity?

[FILIPPO MONTEFORTE/AFP/Getty Images]

Errors in Reflected Appraisals Our self-concept doesn't always match up with how other people view us. Which view is more accurate? It depends, says Simine Vazire (2010). When it comes to external characteristics that are easily observed by others, such as being boisterous or charming, others may have more accurate views of us than we do of ourselves. This is especially likely when there is a value judgment placed on those characteristics because, as you'll soon read, we may be biased to see ourselves positively (after all, who wants to be boisterous, and who doesn't want to be charming?). But when it comes to internal characteristics that are not so readily observable, such as being anxious or optimistic, we are often more accurate than others at judging ourselves (Vazire & Carlson, 2011).

Another reason we might have inaccurate self-knowledge is that we can misread the appraisals others are reflecting back onto us (Carlson et al., 2011). Instead of forming a photocopy of how people actually see us, we base our self-views on **reflected appraisals**—what we *think* other people think about us. But these reflected appraisals can be very different from the *actual appraisals* that people have of us (Ichiyama, 1993; Shrauger & Schoeneman, 1979). For example, the average correlation between self-ratings of attractiveness and ratings by romantic partners and friends is only about .24 (Feingold, 1988). That means some people overrate their attractiveness, and other people underrate it. In both cases, people's perceptions of themselves stem from factors other than the appraisals they receive from others.

We also misread how much people like us. After we meet a new person, such as a potential romantic partner or friend, it's common to wonder whether we made a good impression or whether the other person thought we were dull or obnoxious. The problem is that our best guesses typically center on perceived faults: "Ugh, I talked too much again, and I always make that stupid joke." But the other person does not have access to that information and doesn't know about the insecurities we've been dealing with. As a result, we underestimate how much our new conversation partners like us and enjoy our company (Boothby et al., 2018). We're probably liked more than we know.

The gap between reflected appraisals and actual appraisals is partly due to distortions in the feedback that people provide to each other. Others often try to be tactful, softening their feedback—and what they convey is not necessarily what they genuinely think (DePaulo & Kashy, 1998).

Another reason for the gap is that we falsely assume that other people will make sweeping judgments of us based on one or two actions. Imagine that you attempt to bake cookies to bring to a potluck, but they don't turn out very good (you used a *table*spoon rather than a teaspoon of salt). You might think people at the party will negatively judge your cooking skills *in general*, viewing you as someone who is incapable of making anything worthy of human consumption. But research shows that they probably won't go that far. They'll probably judge you on only your *cookie*-making abilities (Moon et al., 2020).

The good news is that there are ways to reduce the gap between reflected appraisals and actual appraisals. With a little effort, people can recognize that they hold unrealistic perceptions of their personality—in both positive and negative directions (Bollich et al., 2015). They can tell you, for example, that they view themselves as more creative or as less kind than the majority of their peers view them. People are even pretty good at perceiving moment-to-moment changes in their personality; they know, for example, when they are being more or less extraverted than usual (Sun & Vazire, 2019).

Let's also appreciate that the individual is not solely responsible for the gap between who she is and who others think she is. Sometimes other people don't get the memo that the individual has changed. For example, between the ages of 14 and 29, individuals report large increases in emotional stability, but other people fail to appreciate these changes, probably because they are so gradual (Rohrer et al., 2018).

Reflected appraisals What we *think* other people think about us.

Social Comparison: Knowing the Self Through Comparison with Others

Social comparison theory The theory that people come to know themselves partly by comparing themselves with similar others.

Downward comparison A comparison of oneself with those who are worse off.

Upward comparison A comparison of oneself with those who are better off.

Leon Festinger (1954) described a second route to self-knowledge in his **social comparison theory**. He pointed out that people often don't have an objective way of knowing where they stand on an attribute. Therefore, they compare themselves with others to figure out who they are.

To illustrate, would you say you're a fast runner? Compared with a four-year-old, you probably are. This is an example of a **downward comparison**, or a comparison with others who are worse off in the dimension at hand. But how does your running speed compare with that of an Olympic runner? Not so well. This is an **upward comparison**, or a comparison with others who are better off.

Who do people usually compare themselves to? Festinger suggested that people look to similar others because they seem to provide the most informative indication of their traits, skills, and abilities. For example, if you think you're fast, you're probably making that judgment relative to other people similar in age who also play the same sports you do rather than to four-year-olds or to Olympic runners. What's more, people are more likely to compare themselves with individuals in their local environment than with large groups, national averages, or other entities that lie outside their familiar day-to-day experience (Zell & Alicke, 2010).

Festinger further suggested that people are particularly likely to make these comparisons when they lack objective indicators of how they're doing and are uncertain of where they stand. Morse and Gergen (1970) created such an uncertain situation to see how social comparisons influence people's views of themselves. College students came to the lab in response to an advertisement for a data-entry position. On arriving, each student and another person were asked to wait in a room and complete some initial personnel questionnaires. In one condition, the other candidate (who was actually a confederate of the research team) was dressed in a suit and carried a briefcase, giving off an air of competence and dependability. In the other condition, the confederate was dressed in wrinkled clothing, his hair was unkempt, and he carried an unorganized stack of papers. Among the questionnaires students completed was a measure of self-esteem. According to social comparison theory, downward comparison with the person who seems like a worse candidate for the job than yourself would make you puff up with pride, whereas upward comparison with the more impressive candidate would be more likely to leave you feeling inferior. This is exactly what the researchers found: The students rated themselves more positively when they sat in the room with Mr. Sloppy compared to when they sat in the room with Mr. Neat.

Upward comparisons can even cause people to get discouraged and give up on goals altogether. When college students enrolled in an online course were asked to peer-review excellent essays written by their classmates, they were more likely to quit the course than those asked to look over lower-quality essays (Rogers & Feller, 2016). Being presented with a "star" peer is meant to motivate us, but it can backfire when it leads us to perceive success or excellence as being out of reach. These and other forms of social comparison are likely pervasive and in fact can influence us without our awareness. In one study (Chatard et al., 2017), women exposed to media images of ultra-thin models for only 20 milliseconds reported being more anxious about their own body image.

Errors in Social Comparison Just as reflected appraisals sometimes are a poor match to what people really think of themselves, the self-knowledge people gain through social comparison is not always accurate. In fact, people consistently make errors in their use of social comparisons to judge their own attributes. These errors can come from over- or underestimating your own attributes or from over- or underestimating the attributes of those you compare yourself with.

One well-documented social comparison error is the **better-than-average effect**, people's tendency to rank themselves higher than most other people on positive attributes (**FIGURE 5.2**; Alicke, 1985). For example, one study found that 42% of engineers thought their work ranked in the top 5% of their peers (Zenger, 1992), and another found that 94% of college professors thought they did above-average work (Cross, 1977). Even people in prison thought they were kinder and more moral than the average person (Sedikides et al., 2014). Of course, if you think about it, many of these individuals can't be accurate. It's statistically impossible for most people to be above average; the average response should be average! As we will discuss in detail in the next chapter, this and other biases in self-perception reflect people's need to maintain a feeling of self-worth.

Why else do people make this common error? One clue comes from David Dunning's observation that the same people who rate themselves above average are the *worst* performers (Dunning et al., 2003). Many people who overestimate their sense of humor, for example, are the least funny, while many people who overestimate their problem-solving ability are the least skilled. Dunning and colleagues offered a simple but interesting explanation for this phenomenon. If you asked people how good they are as writers, for example, most people would rate themselves as better than average. But why would the worst writers do this? Because they lack the knowledge of writing—of grammar, composition, and so on—to realize how bad their writing is! If they had this knowledge, they would probably be better writers! Dunning and colleagues (2003, p. 83) characterized this as a double curse: "The skills needed to produce correct responses are virtually identical to those needed to evaluate the accuracy of one's responses."

In fact, sometimes people are so confident they're experts on a topic that they claim knowledge they cannot possibly have. If you're feeling devious, find someone who boasts a vast understanding of politics and ask them about the "1975 Public Affairs Act." Let them opine for a while before gently informing them the act is a complete fiction (Bishop et al., 1980). In one study, people who claimed to be experts in areas such as personal finance or biology claimed to know about concepts that, unknown to them, were totally made up (Atir et al., 2015). They were so unaware of what they didn't know that they imagined knowing what cannot be known.

Can people be trained to assess their weaknesses accurately, so that they know what they need to do to improve? To find out, Kruger and Dunning (1999) first observed that poor performers on a logic test greatly overestimated their performance. Then the researchers trained some of these poor performers how to distinguish correct from incorrect answers and gave them their tests to

Figure 5.2

The Better-Than-Average Effect

Each of these frogs believes it's the best fly-catcher in the land. Of course, this is logically impossible. The better-than-average effect can distort reality.

Better-than-average effect The tendency to rank oneself higher than most other people on positive attributes.

look over. Their self-ratings now became more accurate. In another ironic twist, they now rated their own logical reasoning ability *lower* than they did before being trained, even though the training probably strengthened that ability.

Thus, ignorance of ignorance is one source of inaccuracy in evaluating the self in comparison to others. As people learn and become aware of their own ignorance, they tend to become more accurate about themselves. Although knowledge of your shortcomings can be humbling, it is often better than remaining blissfully unaware because then you wouldn't be motivated to take steps to improve.

Self-Perception Theory: Knowing the Self by Observing One's Own Behavior

Self-perception theory The theory that people sometimes infer their attitudes and attributes by observing their behavior and the situation in which it occurs.

According to **self-perception theory** (Bem, 1965), we often discover who we are in the same way that we form impressions of other people. In chapter 4, we talked about how you might form an impression of your roommates by observing their behavior. In the same way, we sometimes form impressions of ourselves by observing our own behavior and coming up with stories that explain why we acted that way.

We are most likely to learn about ourselves through this self-perception process when in new or unusual situations. Imagine that a friend invites you to go spelunking with him. You've never been spelunking, but you like the idea of exploring caves and trying something new. You are 30 feet into the cave and navigating a tight corridor when your heart starts racing, your palms start sweating, and you start backing out of the cave. Your friend is perfectly calm, and you had only a single cup of coffee this morning, so what could possibly be causing your behavior? You realize for the first time in your life that you are claustrophobic. This is the sort of self-knowledge that you gain only through self-perception. You found yourself in a new situation where the best explanation for your behavior is something about *who you are* and the traits (or in this case, phobias) you possess.

In a less dramatic way, we often find ourselves relying more on self-perception when we come to transition points in our life. A freshman who just showed up on campus doesn't really know yet what kind of college student she is. If asked whether she is a punctual student, she can remember back to her most recent class and think, "Yeah, I did show up on time to chemistry and was actually 20 minutes early to my Spanish class, so maybe I am punctual." Or she might think about whether she is punctual in other domains, such as her job, and generalize from that. In both ways, she can make a judgment about whether she is a punctual college student, but she must first engage in a self-perception process of reflecting on examples of her own behavior. By her senior year, enough of this experience might have built up so that now when asked if she is a punctual college student, she can give an immediate "yes" or "no," without having to cobble together self-knowledge from observations (Klein et al., 1996).

Using One's Movements to Know the Self   Lift your chin up, drop it down, and repeat this motor movement. This is a subtle movement, and we might not imagine that it would have any power to influence our judgment. But think about when we usually engage the muscles in our head and neck in this way. Often it is when we are signaling our agreement with something. Could this mean that our brain unconsciously uses this same sequence of muscular movements to infer agreement? Research suggests that the answer is "yes."

For instance, Wells and Petty (1980) had participants listen to an audio recording that included an editorial advocating tuition increases. Under the guise of testing the durability of the headphones, participants were asked to move their chins up and down or from side to side while listening to the tape. Afterward, participants were asked how much they thought tuition should be. Those who had been nodding their heads the entire time were in favor of tuition fees that were about 38% higher than those who had been shaking their heads!

Another example comes from work on the **facial feedback hypothesis.** We become so accustomed to expressing our emotional states through our facial expressions that changes in our facial movements become a signal of the emotion we might be feeling. In the first test of this hypothesis, James Laird (1974) attached electrodes to participants' faces and asked them to evaluate a series of cartoons. Before showing the participants each cartoon, he gave them instructions to contract their facial muscles or squeeze their eyebrows together in certain ways, such as, "Use your cheek muscles to pull the corners of your lips outward." Participants were told that the electrodes were measuring the activity of their facial muscles, but in reality Laird was subtly inducing them to make either a smiling expression or a frown. Those induced to make the smiling face rated the cartoons as funnier and reported feeling happier than those induced to frown. You can try this out at home without the fancy electrodes. Try putting a pen or pencil between your teeth as shown in the photo on the left. This activates your zygomaticus major muscles, forcing your lips to draw back as they do when you smile. Now hold the pen or pencil with your lips as shown in the photo on the right. This activates your corrugator supercilii muscles, which you use when you are frowning. Strack and colleagues (1988) used this technique and found similar effects to what Laird found with the electrode approach. Participants seemed unconsciously to infer, "If I am smiling (or frowning), I must be amused (or turned off)."

▲ Facial movements provide signals as to what emotions we might be feeling.
[Mark Landau]

> **Facial feedback hypothesis** The idea that changes in facial expression elicit emotions associated with those expressions.

Research by Maya Tamir and colleagues (2004) built on these findings to show that these inferences are quite flexible because the meaning of a given muscle movement changes depending on the context in which it occurs. For example, in one study participants were led to shake their heads side to side while watching a video (as opposed to nodding their heads)—a movement generally associated with disapproval. If, at the same time, they watched a video of a murderer, head shaking led to more negative judgments of the person, as we might expect. However, if they watched a video of a drug addict who had faced difficult circumstances, the participants inferred from their head shaking that they disapproved of the hardships she had faced, leading them to judge her more positively than the nodding participants. These findings show that the same movement can take on several contextually sensitive meanings, and our minds flexibly integrate those meanings when forming judgments.

It's worth noting that there have been failed attempts to replicate facial feedback effects on emotions (Coles et al., 2019). As you read in chapter 1, findings in social psychology are sometimes difficult to replicate for a number of reasons. Does that mean the effects are not "real"? Perhaps, but Noah and colleagues (2018) made a side-by-side comparison of the methods used in the original studies and the replication attempts. They realized that researchers who failed to find the facial feedback effect told participants they would be observed or video recorded, whereas those who found the effect did not. They hypothesized that being observed might reduce participants' reliance on their facial muscles for information about how they were feeling. Noah then tested this hypothesis and found that without a video camera in the lab, facial feedback effects emerged, but when there was a video camera, they did not. Sometimes failures to replicate ultimately inspire us to learn more about a phenomenon. Here we learned that people use facial feedback when there are not other sources of potential information, such as how others are observing them.

Errors of Self-Perception   The basic idea of self-perception is that we often lack insight into who we are or how we feel, and we look to our own behavior to make inferences about what we are like. However, those inferences can be incorrect when we misjudge how situations affect us. We underestimate the effects of some situational factors and overestimate the effects of others. For example, Nisbett and Wilson (1977b) showed that people liked a movie less if it was out of focus part of the time but were unaffected by a loud noise outside the room where the movie was showing. However, when the researchers asked participants about the factors that influenced their enjoyment, the participants thought the focus problems *did not* affect their liking (underestimating the effect) and that the loud noise *did* (overestimating the effect).

This doesn't mean our beliefs about why we feel and behave the way we do are always wrong; rather, it means that those beliefs are based on an imperfect inference process that sometimes leads to inaccurate or incomplete understanding. If you just found out a close friend died, and you felt very sad, you would probably be right in inferring that this news made you sad. But so would an objective observer who did not have access to your internal feelings. At other times, the cause of negative feelings may not be so obvious. You might erroneously attribute them to particular reasons, such as lack of sleep, when they are really due to something else. In fact, studies comparing daily fluctuations in mood with other things going on in people's day-to-day lives show that people are not very accurate in their beliefs about the factors that affect their moods (Stone et al., 1985).

Using the Self to Know One's Feelings

Two-factor theory of emotion The theory that people's emotions are the product of both their arousal level and how they interpret that arousal based on contextual cues.

Self-perception processes can play an important role in the emotions we feel. Stan Schachter's (1964) **two-factor theory of emotion** proposed that people's level of arousal determines the *intensity* of an emotion, but the specific *type* of emotion they experience is determined by the meaning they give to that arousal. To determine which emotion they're feeling, people often look to what's happening in their current environment. One surprising implication of this theory is that the same arousal can be attributed to one or another emotion, depending on which aspects of their environment people focus on. **FIGURE 5.3** shows an example of how the two-step process can elicit different emotions.

In the first experiment to test this idea, Schachter and Singer (1962) gave participants an injection of epinephrine (also known as adrenaline), which

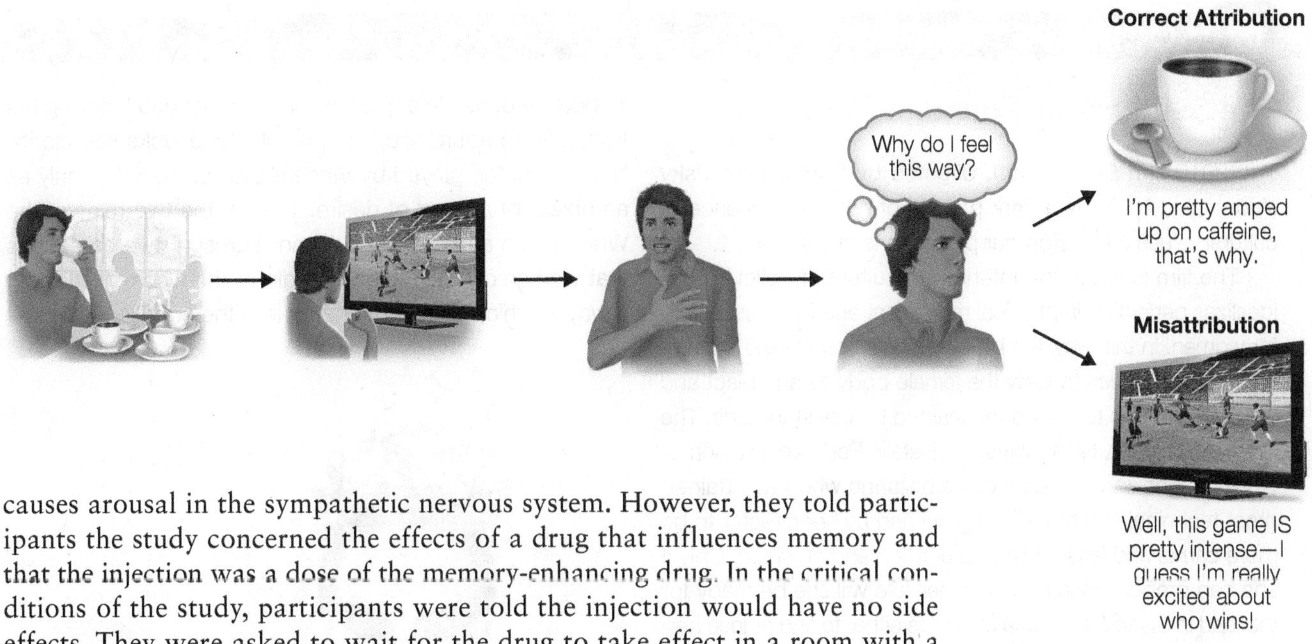

I'm pretty amped up on caffeine, that's why.

Why do I feel this way?

Misattribution

Well, this game IS pretty intense—I guess I'm really excited about who wins!

Figure 5.3

Misattribution of Arousal and Emotion

When we observe our own behavior to figure out why we feel aroused, we can make mistakes about where that arousal came from. As a result, we can experience emotions that are fueled by something else entirely.

causes arousal in the sympathetic nervous system. However, they told participants the study concerned the effects of a drug that influences memory and that the injection was a dose of the memory-enhancing drug. In the critical conditions of the study, participants were told the injection would have no side effects. They were asked to wait for the drug to take effect in a room with a confederate who was either happily shooting balls of paper into a trash can or voicing his anger over what he saw as intrusive questions on a survey he was filling out. Why did Schachter and Singer put participants in the room with different confederates? They wanted to determine if they could alter the participants' emotions by varying the salience of a label for their heightened arousal. As the researchers expected, participants who witnessed the happy confederate reported being happy, whereas those who spent time with the angry confederate reported being angry themselves. In contrast, participants who also were given the injection but were told to expect symptoms of physiological arousal as a side effect were less likely to experience these emotions. This is because they already had an obvious label for their heightened arousal: It was a side effect of the injection. Only participants without such an obvious explanation looked to their environment to figure out why they felt aroused. It's also important to note that the specific emotion to which they attributed their arousal was different—either happiness or anger—depending on the cues provided by the confederate.

This phenomenon, which has become known as **misattribution of arousal**, occurs when we ascribe arousal resulting from one source (in the case of the study just mentioned, an injection) to a different source and, therefore, experience emotions that we wouldn't normally feel in response to a stimulus. Although some emotions are characterized by specific physiological responses (Barrett et al., 2007; Reisenzein, 1983), a state of heightened arousal is often experienced as general and vague. As a result, people's emotions can be influenced by their interpretation of the circumstances of that arousal.

Understanding how people use self-perception to label their emotions can be rather useful. Take the case of insomnia. Storms and Nisbett (1970) asked people suffering from insomnia to take a placebo pill described as arousing before they went to bed: a seemingly paradoxical form of treatment for insomnia! The researchers reasoned that some people have trouble falling asleep because they feel anxious about their lives and frustrated by their inability to fall asleep. Perhaps if they could be led to misattribute some of their anxious arousal to a pill, they would feel more relaxed and restful. This is precisely what happened.

Misattribution of arousal Inadvertent ascription of arousal resulting from one source to a different source.

SOCIAL PSYCH AT THE MOVIES

The Self Lost or Found in *Black Swan*

The 2010 film *Black Swan*, directed by Darren Aronofsky (Aronofsky, 2010), is a dark parable of how the influence of cultural values can distort our perceptions of ourselves.

The film is set in the intense subculture of ballet, which idealizes perfection in physical movement and form, especially for women. In this way, the ballet world represents the broader cultural tendencies to view the female body as an object and pressure women to live up to idealized beauty standards. The film's protagonist, Nina, played by Natalie Portman, is a somewhat uptight and self-conscious ballerina who has attained great technical skill but is being pushed by her director to be more carnal and less repressed both on and off stage. Only if she can properly lose herself in her role will she be ready for the lead in *Swan Lake*. Nina struggles either to find or lose herself in a world where she is defined by the people around her. In one sense, Nina's view of herself is a construction of how others see her, shaped by reflected appraisals.

Nina's overbearing mother, played by Barbara Hershey, resents that she was forced to give up a dancing career to be a mother. She tries to rediscover her own identity either by driving her daughter's dancing ambitions or by obsessively painting her self-portrait. But she also tries to protect the innocence of her little girl, fawning over her and blocking her transition to adulthood. As a result, Nina lacks self-clarity. Nina's director, played by Vincent Cassel, sees her only as an object of art and of desire. To him, the two roles of the White Swan and the Black Swan represent two categories that women can occupy: the virgin or the whore. Reflecting a way in which people often buy into the stereotypical roles

[Fox Searchlight Pictures/Photofest]

Excitation transfer theory The theory that leftover arousal caused by an initial event can intensify emotional reactions to a second, unrelated event.

Studies have similarly used placebo pills to prevent the self-perception process from eliciting fear, anger, sexual attraction, and guilt (Dienstbier et al., 1980; Nisbett & Schachter, 1966).

Of course, outside the confines of the lab, rarely are people unwittingly given injections of adrenaline or placebo pills. This led Dolf Zillmann (e.g., Zillmann et al., 1972) to wonder: Under what conditions does misattribution of arousal occur in everyday life? According to his **excitation transfer theory**, misattribution happens when an individual is physiologically aroused by an initial stimulus and then a short time later encounters a second, potentially emotionally provocative, stimulus. Leftover excitation caused by the first event becomes misattributed or, in Zillmann's terms, *transferred*, to the reaction to the second stimulus, resulting in an intensified emotional response to that second stimulus. This is especially likely to happen if people are not aware of the leftover arousal from the first event or don't connect it to that first event (Reisenzein & Gattinger, 1982).

In one study (Zillmann et al., 1972), half the participants were asked to exercise by riding a stationary bike vigorously for two and a half minutes. The others were seated comfortably at a table and asked to pass thread through discs with holes (not particularly arousing). In the second part of the study, participants were provoked with insults or not provoked by another participant (in actuality, a confederate). Participants then had an opportunity to punish that society offers, Nina seems to accept this duality. Rather than express any unique perspective of her own, she struggles to find the darker drives that will enable her to embody the Black Swan role. And when she is given the role she so desperately wants, she calls her mother and says, "He picked me, mommy!" These four words capture the ways women aspire to standards men define for how women should be. And women themselves, just like Nina's mom, often police these roles and ideals.

In addition to defining herself through these reflected appraisals, Nina is also quite intensely caught up in social comparison. The arrival of Lily, a dancer played by Mila Kunis, marks the beginning of Nina's dark descent into negative self-focus and paranoid delusions. In contrast to Nina's technically perfect but repressed style, Lily is a free spirit who refuses to internalize the constraints that a career in ballet might place on her social life. Nina becomes obsessed with the thought that Lily might take her role, an obsession depicted by disturbing visual imagery. Nina's sense of self is defined in an incredibly narrow manner (success in dancing). Thus, she fixates on that one particular goal, as we might expect on the basis of self-regulatory perseveration theory, which is discussed later in this chapter. Perhaps because of this focus, Nina's grip on her own identity and reality disintegrates. Losing herself in her role

leads her to hallucinate that she is sprouting the feathers of a swan. Nina's intense social comparison with her understudy manifests itself in visions and dreams that Lily is trying to sabotage her performance.

Part of what drives motivation toward any goal is self-awareness of a discrepancy between what we are now and what we would like to become. Throughout the film, when Nina sees her own reflection, she often confronts an image that looks or behaves quite differently than it should. These disturbing moments on screen symbolize how it can be to see oneself carry out actions seemingly out of step with one's internal motivation.

Of course, mirrors also symbolize our own vanity. In the final scenes of the movie (spoiler alert!), Nina's obsession with living up to ideals of perfection reaches the breaking point. Her grasp on reality finally is lost when she imagines pushing her rival, Lily, into a mirror and shattering it during an intermission in the ballet performance. Although she envisions her competitor being destroyed, it is revealed in the next scene — after she dances the Black Swan role perfectly — that her attempt to pursue an ideal imposed on her by others leads only to self-destruction. The shard of glass she imagined having plunged into Lily backstage is actually impaled in her own body.

the other participant by delivering painful electric shocks. As you see in **FIGURE 5.4**, the unprovoked participants were not very aggressive, regardless of whether they exercised. Provoked participants, however, were more aggressive if they had exercised than if they had not, suggesting that they misattributed leftover arousal as anger caused by the provocation.

Leftover arousal can also be misattributed to positive emotion-based responses, including prosocial behavior (Mueller & Donnerstein, 1981), the enjoyment of music (Cantor & Zillmann, 1973), and laughter (Cantor et al., 1974). In a recent study (Adam et al., 2019), participants were introduced to an auction task and instructed to make a bid on rare coins. Just before bidding, one group of participants saw highly arousing images (e.g., a fire, a roller coaster ride) and listened to energetic music; the other group saw neutral images (e.g., Q-tips) and listened to calming music. The aroused participants were more excited about the coins and bid more money, further showing that sources of arousal that have nothing to do with the task at hand can affect people's judgments and perceptions.

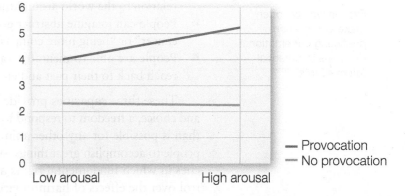

Figure 5.4

Excitation Transfer

Physiological arousal created in one context can be misattributed, intensifying emotional reactions to a subsequently encountered stimulus in an unrelated context.

[Data from Zillmann et al., 1972]

SECTION REVIEW How Do We Come to Know the Self?

Reflections, comparisons, and self-perceptions are three important ways that people learn about themselves during the course of their everyday social interactions.

Reflection	Comparison	Self-Perception
• People learn about the self by assessing how others view them (appraisals).	• People learn about the self by comparing themselves with others, especially those in similar circumstances.	• People learn about the self by observing their own behavior and making inferences about their traits, abilities, and values.
• Others serve as a mirror, or looking glass.	• Upward social comparisons can threaten self-esteem; downward comparisons can enhance it.	• These inferences can be incorrect when behavior has unknown causes.
• Nevertheless, people do not always perceive accurately what others think of them. Reflected appraisals don't always match actual appraisals.	• Comparisons are often biased in the self's favor, sometimes due to ignorance of personal shortcomings.	• A self-perception process also guides the experience of emotions based on one's bodily states (e.g., physiological arousal) and labeling of the current situation.

Learning Outcomes

- Identify the feelings that arise when we fall short of our "ought" self as compared to when we fall short of our "ideal" self.
- Consider an everyday action and apply action identification theory to describe it at concrete and abstract levels.
- Explain why we often make errors when predicting our emotional reactions to potential future events.

Self-regulation A set of processes for guiding one's thoughts, feelings, and behavior to reach desired goals.

Self-awareness theory The theory that aspects of the self—one's attitudes, values, and goals—will be most likely to influence behavior when attention is focused on the self.

Self-Regulation

Now that we've discussed the self-concept (what James called the *Me*), it's time to turn to the ego, the part of the self that motivates and controls behavior (what James called the *I*). We'll focus on **self-regulation**—how people decide what goals to pursue and how they attempt to guide their thoughts, feelings, and behavior to reach those goals.

The ability to self-regulate is based on three key capacities of the human mind that emerged as the hominid cerebral cortex evolved:

- People are self-aware—able to assess their thoughts, feelings, and behavior in relation to the world around them.
- People can imagine abstract goals and hypothetical outcomes such as "curing cancer" or "being more compassionate."
- People are able to mentally travel in time, to pop out of the here and now to reach back to their past and envision the distant future.

These three capacities provide people with a tremendous degree of flexibility and choice, a freedom to respond to a given situation in a much wider range of ways than is possible for any other animal on the planet. This mental flexibility enables people to accomplish great things, such as developing, or at least conceiving of, societies in which fundamental rights are granted to all citizens and getting some control over the effects of harmful viruses, such as the coronavirus (COVID-19) that reached pandemic proportions in 2020. But the same intelligence allows people to do evil things such as plot large-scale violence. Let's examine in more detail the mental capacities that make possible the magnificent and horrific potential of our species.

Self-Awareness and Self-Regulation

Although it's fairly easy to ask people about themselves and thereby study the self-concept, investigating the ego is more difficult because it is the thing in your head doing all the doing. A helpful framework is provided by Shelley Duval and Bob Wicklund's (1972) **self-awareness theory.**

Duval and Wicklund started with the idea that, at any given moment, your attention is focused either inward on some aspect of self—things you need to get done today, your social life, and so on—or focused outward on some aspect of the environment—a building, a dog, a new tune on your phone. When attention is focused inward, you bring to mind aspects of yourself—such as attitudes, values, and goals—that connect to the situation you're in. In the voting booth, for instance, self-awareness would bring to mind your attitudes about political issues, whereas taking an exam in class brings to mind your academic goals.

We saw in chapter 4 that salient information significantly influences behavior. Duval and Wicklund make the same point regarding the self: When attention is focused on the self, the self-aspects that come to mind have a stronger influence on behavior. This is because self-awareness makes us mindful of the gap between what we are doing right now and what we aspire to or feel we should be doing. In Freud's terminology, directing attention onto the self activates the *superego*—the internal judge that compares how we currently are with internalized standards for how we think we should be or want to be. Sometimes, this comparison reveals that we're falling short of our standards. In those cases, we feel bad and are motivated to feel better.

But how can you feel better? One way is to distract yourself from self-focus so that you stop thinking about the discrepancy between how you are and how you want to be. For example, if you found out you bombed on your first social psych test, you might go to a movie or hang out with friends as a distraction from dwelling on your failure. Another, generally more constructive, way is to commit to doing better. In our example, you might commit to studying harder, taking better notes, or getting a tutor.

What determines whether you will avoid self-focus or commit to doing better? If you think you have a good chance of reducing the gap between where you are and where you want to be, then you're likely to strive harder. But if you think your chances of acting in line with your superego's demands are slim, then you're more likely to take the distraction route or perhaps even give up on the goal entirely (Carver et al., 1979). This process is summarized in **FIGURE 5.5.**

Self-Awareness Promotes Behaving in Line with Internal Standards
Self-awareness theory proposes a fairly elaborate process going on inside our heads. So how can researchers test this theory? To do so, they need a way to

Figure 5.5

Self-Awareness Theory
According to self-awareness theory, an internal focus of attention leads relevant standards to become salient. People compare their current state to those standards. If they perceive a gap, they feel bad and are motivated to either reduce that gap (e.g., by trying harder) or escape self-awareness.

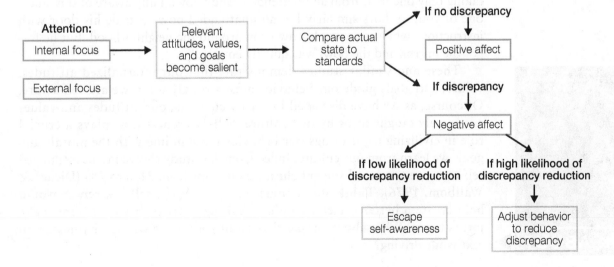

increase and decrease self-awareness and observe the consequences. This is a tricky problem because people's focus tends to shift back and forth between the self and the outside world.

Duval and Wicklund reasoned that some external stimuli cause people to focus inward on themselves. For example, seeing images of themselves in a mirror, particularly in contexts in which they don't expect to, is likely to make people think of themselves. Can you think of an example of this for yourself—say, a time when you were unexpectedly sitting next to a mirror at a coffee shop? In fact, exposing people to mirrors has been the most common way that psychologists have increased self-awareness. They've also had people hear their names or their own voices on an audio recording, pointed video cameras at people, and asked them to write an essay in which they have to use first-person pronouns such as *I*, *me*, and *mine*.

When researchers began randomly assigning people to be in situations that evoke high or low self-awareness, they found that, as the theory proposes, high self-awareness leads people to behave in line with their internal standards. In one classic study, Chuck Carver (1975) recruited participants who had earlier expressed either favorable or unfavorable attitudes toward using physical punishment as a teaching tool. Once they arrived at his lab, participants were given the role of teacher and asked to use electric shock to punish another student (in reality a confederate) when he made errors on a learning task. The participants were allowed to choose the intensity of the shock they would use as the punishment. To test the role of self-awareness, Carver had half the participants deliver shocks while they were in front of a mirror, whereas the other participants delivered shocks with no mirror present. Without the self-focusing mirror, participants' prior attitudes about the use of physical punishment did not predict the intensity level of the shocks they chose to administer. This may seem strange, but it shows how attitudes and behavior don't always line up. When they could see themselves in the mirror, participants who had earlier said they opposed physical punishment chose low shock levels, whereas

▲ A trick-or-treater may be more likely to do the right thing and take one piece of candy if he catches his reflection in the window.
[Jeff Greenberg]

those in favor of physical punishment administered high levels of shock. They acted in line with their attitudes.

In another study, Beaman and colleagues (1979) showed that a mirror can even make Halloween trick-or-treaters more likely to follow the instruction of taking only one treat from an unattended candy bowl. Fully aware of this study, one of your authors similarly left an unattended bowl outside his door with instructions while escorting his own son around the neighborhood. But he forgot the mirror, and the bowl was quickly emptied!

These and similar studies demonstrate that our internalized attitudes, values, and goals guide our behavior most strongly when we are self-aware. Of course, as we have discussed in earlier chapters, our attitudes and values are largely taught to us by our culture. Self-awareness thus plays a crucial role in civilizing us; it brings our behavior more in line with the morals and goals we learn from our culture. Indeed, one lab study showed that heightened self-awareness reduced student cheating on a test from 71% to 7% (Diener & Wallbom, 1976). Think about some ways increasing self-awareness would help create a better society. Would installing mirrors in courtrooms make jurors fairer? What about phones that shout your name whenever you start to text while driving?

APPLICATION
Escaping from Self-Awareness

We've seen that focusing on ourselves can lead us to behave in line with how we want to be. This is especially likely when we feel hopeful about making these changes. But if we're not confident we can change our behavior to meet our standards, we respond by trying to escape from self-awareness. In one study, people who delivered a speech poorly avoided self-awareness if they thought one's speaking ability is fixed for life, but they did not avoid self-awareness if they thought it was possible to improve one's speaking ability (Steenbarger & Aderman, 1979).

Self-awareness research has revealed several ways that people try to escape from self-awareness when they feel incapable of changing. People try to shift attention away from their shortcomings by binge-watching TV (Moskalenko & Heine, 2003) and even causing themselves physical pain (Wilson et al., 2014). People's efforts to escape self-awareness may also contribute to binge eating and drug and alcohol abuse (Heatherton & Baumeister, 1991). This is because these activities tend to reduce self-focus and, therefore, any unpleasant thoughts that the self is falling short of its standards.

But does everyone make equal use of this avoidance strategy? Not really. People who are generally high in self-awareness—who tend to think about their attitudes and feelings a lot—are more likely to seek ways of escaping self-awareness than those who are less likely to introspect.

Hull and Young (1983) examined whether people high in private self-consciousness, the trait of being generally high in self-awareness, would use alcohol as a way to escape from self-awareness. Participants took part in what they thought were two unrelated studies, one on personality and the other on alcohol preferences. (In reality, the studies were related.) Participants first completed the private self-consciousness scale, indicating how much they agreed with statements such as "I'm always trying to figure myself out" (Fenigstein et al., 1975). Then they were told they did either really well or really poorly on an intelligence test. In this way, the researchers introduced a negative discrepancy between some participants' standards of success and their current performance. Believing that the first study was now complete, they walked down the hall to participate in a study on wine-tasting preferences, where they had the opportunity to sample as much wine as they wanted. Did their earlier experiences with the test affect how much alcohol they consumed? Yes. Those participants who were high in private self-consciousness and received failure feedback consumed more wine than the other participants. They were, in effect, "drinking their troubles away." Similar results have been found outside the laboratory. Hull and colleagues (1986) found that, among individuals being treated for alcoholism, those who were higher in private self-consciousness tended to respond to experiences of failure by returning to alcohol use.

How can we avoid this kind of response? A key factor, we're learning, is *hope*, or the belief that one can accomplish future goals. People with high or temporarily increased feelings of hope view obstacles as challenging opportunities for growth rather than as reasons for giving up on life (Kwon et al., 2015). ■

What Feelings Does Self-Awareness Arouse? At a general level, the emotions we feel when we focus internally help to keep the self on track toward meeting goals. If we sense that we are living up to our standards or making rapid progress toward a goal (such as getting an A on a midterm exam), we experience positive emotions that are reinforcing. But when we judge ourselves as falling short or making inadequate progress toward a goal, we experience anxiety, guilt, or disappointment. As we just saw, these emotions can motivate us to do better if that seems possible or to escape from self-awareness if change seems unlikely.

Tory Higgins's (1989) **self-discrepancy theory** provides a more refined understanding of the different types of emotions that self-awareness is likely to evoke. Higgins built on the Freudian notion of the superego, which posits that during childhood, we internalize a set of standards and goals regarding ourselves. Freud proposed that these internalized standards form two clusters. The first cluster is a conscience, which focuses on how you should be. Higgins referred to this as the *ought self*. The second cluster is an ego-ideal, which focuses on how you want to be or what you would like to accomplish. Higgins referred to this as the *ideal self*.

As children, when we fall short of achieving the ought self, we anticipate that our parents might become angry and punish us or withdraw love and protection, and we feel anxious as a result. Imagine being caught gorging on cookies right before dinner. You might feel anxious in anticipation of punishment. Of course, if you refrain from eating the cookies, you are likely to feel calm and secure instead (albeit a little hungry perhaps).

In contrast, when we fall short of the ideal self, we anticipate letting our parents down and so feel discouraged and dejected. Imagine that your parents are watching you as a child playing Little League baseball, and you strike out to end the game with your team down one and the bases loaded. No matter what your parents say, you'll hear disappointment in their voices and see it in their faces. On the other hand, if you hit a game-winning double, they will be proud, and you will feel elation and satisfaction.

Higgins argued that these same feelings arise throughout our lives when we fall short of meeting oughts and ideals. Failing to live up to the ought self elicits anxiety and guilt because, in those situations, we have become used to expecting punishment. In contrast, failing to live up to the ideal self elicits dejection and sadness because, in those situations, our parents reacted with disappointment. These different reactions to the same event are pictured in **FIGURE 5.6**.

Research testing self-discrepancy theory shows these distinct emotional consequences (Higgins, 1989). When college students were led to compare who they were at the time (the actual self) with the person they thought they should be (the *ought self*), they felt calmly secure if the discrepancy was small or nonexistent, and they felt anxious and guilty if the discrepancy was large. But when students were led to compare the actual self with the *ideal self*, small discrepancies were associated with feelings of satisfaction, while large discrepancies increased feelings of rejection and discouragement.

Does it matter which self-guides are regulating behavior and which emotion people feel? Yes. The psychologist Otto Rank (1930/1998) proposed that feelings of guilt arise from *bad behavior* and signal to us that an important social relationship is in trouble. As a result, guilt motivates us to take action to repair the damage we have done. Supporting studies show that people who are likely to experience guilt about their self-discrepancies also feel more empathy for others (Tangney,

Self-discrepancy theory The theory that people feel anxiety when they fall short of how they *ought* to be but feel sad when they fall short of how they ideally *want* to be.

Figure 5.6

What Feelings Does Self-Awareness Arouse?

How we feel about an action depends on whether we compare it to our mental image of who we ought to be or the person we ideally want to be.

"Yesterday in Chemistry I cheated off Trevor's test."

"That conflicts with my **ought self**—the person I know I *should* be."

"That conflicts with my **ideal self**—the person I really *want* to be."

"I feel *anxious* and *guilty* about what I did."

"I feel *sad* about what I did."

1991) and are more motivated to make up for their past mistakes by apologizing to those who are harmed and offering to make the situation better somehow (Tangney et al., 1996). On the other hand, people feel ashamed of themselves when they conclude they are *bad people*. People who experience shame, in turn, show higher levels of depression (Tangney et al., 1992) and are also more likely to turn to drugs and alcohol as a means of escaping painful feelings of self-awareness (Dearing et al., 2005).

Self-guides impact our behavior in other ways as well. People are more likely to persevere and succeed when they frame their goals in terms of living up to their *ideal* self. These are also called "want-to" goals, or autonomous motives, because the person freely chooses them to seek enjoyment or personal benefit or to express their true self. People are less successful attaining goals framed in terms of their "ought" self—also called "have-to" goals because they're driven by feelings of guilt and social pressure (Inzlicht et al., 2014; Sheldon, 2014; Stavrova et al., 2019; Werner & Milyavskaya, 2019).

Staying on Target: How Goals Motivate and Guide Action

Now that we have seen how self-awareness activates our concerns with meeting goals and the emotions linked to oughts and ideals, let's focus on how goals keep our behavior on target. First, let's consider why, at any moment, people choose to pursue some goals over others.

Activating Goals: Getting Turned On   People can activate goals either by consciously bringing them to mind or by being unconsciously cued by the environment. The first route to activation is familiar, and you can easily think of times when you've consciously set a goal for yourself by making a commitment to achieve some desired end state (e.g., "I'm going to get that term paper finished today"). The second route may be less familiar to you. The idea is that we often pursue goals without any conscious awareness that we are doing so. To illustrate, you are reading this book in part to move toward getting a degree and perhaps toward a career in psychology or some other field. But we suspect that you are not consciously dwelling on those long-term goals from moment to moment; indeed, doing so would probably interfere with learning the material and thereby work against accomplishing the very goals the activity is serving. But then what initiates our goal pursuits when we are not consciously thinking of our goals?

Bargh's **auto-motive theory** (Chartrand & Bargh, 2002) proposes that goals are strongly associated with the people, objects, and contexts in which the person pursues them. This means that even subtle exposure to goal-related stimuli in the environment can automatically activate a goal and guide people's behavior without their even knowing this is happening. For example, Sandy's goal to improve her dancing skills is associated with, among other things, her dancing shoes. In a hurry one day, she runs by a store window in which those same shoes are displayed. Without her being aware of why, the goal of improving her dancing may be activated, making it more likely that Sandy will choose to rehearse rather than give in to the temptation to sit on the couch and watch TV.

Goals are also strongly associated with other people. From early childhood, people internalize the standards and values of their parents and the broader culture, and throughout adulthood, these social influences act like internal voices judging one's behavior. For example, perhaps your goal to achieve in school is linked to your mother, who has very high expectations for you, or your grandmother, who worked tirelessly despite hardship to help pay your college tuition. If this is the case, then being reminded of these individuals, even without your

Auto-motive theory The theory that even subtle exposure to goal-related stimuli can automatically activate a goal and guide behavior.

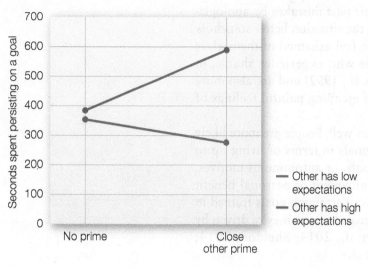

Figure 5.7

Goals Are Unconsciously Linked to Relationships

After being subliminally primed with the name of a close other who expects them to succeed, participants persisted for more time on their goals.

[Data from Shah, 2003]

Action identification theory The theory that explains how people conceive of action—their own or others'—in ways that range from very concrete to very abstract.

realizing it, might prompt you to work harder to achieve their high expectations. In one test of this idea, Shah (2003) asked people for the names of close others who they felt would have high or low expectations of their own academic abilities. Later in the same session, they were asked to solve some anagrams (word puzzles). Meanwhile, half the participants were subliminally primed with the name of a close other. As you see in **FIGURE 5.7**, participants primed with someone thought to have high expectations toiled away on the anagrams for almost twice as long as those primed with someone thought to have low expectations. They also ended up solving almost twice as many anagrams. These findings show that, because people associate goals with other people, reminders of those other people can activate goals outside of conscious awareness (Fitzsimons & Bargh, 2003).

Does this mean that goals are represented in the mind just like every other piece of knowledge? No, goals are unique because they send urgent messages to the ego to act. Whereas simple bits of knowledge—like the fact that a typical golf ball has 336 dimples—tend to fade from memory at a constant rate, goals continue to demand attention at a constant and, in some cases, increasing rate until the end state is attained (Lewin, 1936; McClelland et al., 1953). In fact, when goal-directed action is interrupted, memory of the goal and a state of tension remain strong until the goal is attained, a substitute goal is pursued, or the goal is completely abandoned (Lewin, 1927; Zeigarnik, 1938). Also, when people fall just short of attaining a goal, they feel more motivated and eager for rewards than if they had attained the goal (Wadhwa & Kim, 2015).

Defining Goals as Concrete or Abstract There is an old story of a man who comes across three bricklayers busy at work. He asks the first bricklayer, "What are you doing?" and the bricklayer replies, "What does is look like I'm doing? I'm laying brick." He comes to the second bricklayer and asks him, "What are you doing?" This man replies, "I'm building a wall." Still somewhat unsatisfied, the man approaches the third bricklayer and repeats his question, to which the bricklayer replies, "I am building a cathedral."

This story illustrates how the same action can take on different meaning, depending on how it connects to goals. This idea is central to **action identification theory** (Vallacher & Wegner, 1987), which was introduced briefly in chapter 2. This theory explains how people conceive of action—either their own or others'—in ways that range from very concrete to very abstract. As the story above illustrates, the three bricklayers conceive of their actions in different ways, ranging from the concrete level of stacking bricks layered with mortar to the more abstract end state of building a cathedral. One way to understand the key difference is that a concrete interpretation of an action is about *how* the action is accomplished, while a more abstract interpretation describes *why* the action is performed. Thus, we can say that each bricklayer is building a wall *by* laying bricks (more concrete) and is doing so *because* he wants to build a cathedral (more abstract). In the brick story, each worker has one interpretation, but in reality, any person can interpret the same action at different levels of abstraction. In fact, we can imagine that each person has a mental "hierarchy" of interpretations arranged like a ladder. One can mentally move up the ladder to form broader, more comprehensive conceptions of an action, or down to form concrete conceptions of how that same action is accomplished.

Being able to identify our actions at different levels in the goal hierarchy is very handy. For example, when we run into difficulty in attaining an abstract goal, we can shift to a lower-level interpretation that allows us to focus more attention on specific concrete actions. This is demonstrated in a study (Wegner et al., 1983) in which American participants were asked to perform the fairly routine task of eating the cheesy snack known as Cheetos. However, although some participants were asked to eat the Cheetos in the usual manner (with their hands), other participants were asked to eat the Cheetos with a pair of chopsticks (see **FIGURE 5.8**).

For all but the most adept chopsticks users, this presents some difficulty. (Chopsticks are certainly not the utensil of choice for most Americans who have the munchies.) Participants were then asked to describe what they were doing. Participants using their hands, and not surprisingly performing the task rather well, were more likely to agree with abstract definitions of their actions, such as "eating" and "reducing hunger" (note that those are *why* interpretations). However, participants using the chopsticks, who were having considerably more difficulty, we're more likely to give concrete "how" descriptions of their action, like "chewing" and "putting food in my mouth." When our goal-directed action bogs down, we shift attention toward lower levels of abstraction, defining our actions in concrete terms.

Although this can be effective when we encounter problems, there are benefits to defining our actions at higher, more abstract levels. For one, it provides a way for us to make sense of our experience. For example, when you think that you are reading this textbook as one step in the larger endeavor of trying to complete your degree requirements, this helps to make sense of your (we hope not too dull) activity of staring at words on pages. And by making sense of the nitty-gritty details of our daily experience by framing them in terms of abstract goals, we also stay motivated to achieve those goals (Wegner et al., 1986).

Figure 5.8

Action Identification Theory

Ever try eating Cheetos with chopsticks? Unless you're accomplished at using these utensils, chances are the difficulty you encounter will lead you to shift to a more concrete interpretation of what you're doing.

[Mark Landau]

Self-Regulation and the Psychology of Time

Basing Decisions on Abstract Versus Concrete Ideas   As you prepare for an upcoming semester and consider what courses to take, how much do you think about how interesting the topic is versus the amount of writing that will be involved? Do the factors that influence your decision differ if the course starts next week or next fall? According to Yaacov Trope and Nira Liberman's **construal level theory** (Liberman & Trope, 1998; Trope & Liberman, 2003), when people imagine events in the distant future, they focus more on the abstract meaning of those events—such as their connection with personal growth—than on the concrete details. As a result, they base their decisions more on this abstract meaning. In contrast, when people think about events in the near future, they base their decisions more on the concrete details. Why? People tend to have more concrete information for events that are closer in time. For example, you probably have more information about your entertainment options for this Saturday night than for a Saturday night three months from now. As a result, people get accustomed to having details available for near-future events but only general, abstract ideas available for distant future events. They learn to associate temporally close events with concrete thinking and far-off events with abstract thinking. This association then becomes part of their routine way of thinking about events.

In one illustrative study, students were told they would be doing an assignment either the next week or in nine weeks (Liberman & Trope, 1998). In each

Construal level theory The theory that people focus more on concrete details when thinking about the near future and focus more on abstract meaning when thinking about the distant future.

case, they had to choose either a difficult but interesting assignment or an easy but uninteresting one. When thinking about next week, the students preferred the easy assignment. But when thinking about nine weeks from now, they preferred the interesting assignment. When thinking about the distant future, the concrete detail of difficulty mattered less than the abstract goal of pursuing one's interests.

Predicting How We'll Feel   Imagine that Saturday night is approaching, and you have two options: Are you going to check out that new band at the local club? Or are you going to the party at Maria's house? You'll probably base your decision on some mental calculation of whether you will have more fun at the club or at Maria's. The same thought process lies behind your decisions about what college to attend, what car to buy, whom to date, or even whether to get Cap'n Crunch or Cookie Crisp cereal for breakfast: How will the different options available to you make you feel down the road (DeWall et al., 2016)? This is a sensible strategy insofar as your predictions are accurate, but how accurate are they? Research on **affective forecasting** reveals that people are often bad at predicting, or "forecasting," their emotional reactions to potential future events (Wilson & Gilbert, 2005). This doesn't mean that mental time travel isn't a valuable tool; it totally is. It means that, like a lousy meteorologist, we're often wrong about how we're going to feel later on.

Affective forecasting Predicting one's emotional reactions to potential future events. These predictions are often inaccurate.

Dunn, Wilson, and Gilbert (2003) studied the accuracy of affective forecasting by taking advantage of a naturally occurring experiment that happens on college campuses every year: the random assignment of students to dorms and other housing options. In the spring of their freshman year, college students were presented with a list of dorm and housing options and asked to predict how happy they would be if they were assigned to a desirable housing location or an undesirable housing location. As you might expect, students said they'd be much happier if they were assigned to one of the more desirable houses. However, one year later, students did not differ in their level of happiness, regardless of where they were housed. Their earlier predictions had been inaccurate. Students in the desirable houses had overestimated how happy they would be, and students in the undesirable houses had overestimated how miserable they would be. Similar studies show that when people predict how they will feel after suffering a harsh insult or watching their favorite sports team lose an important game, they anticipate that the painful sting of these unpleasant events will be greater than it is and will last longer than it does (e.g., Gilbert et al., 2004).

Why do these errors in affective forecasting happen? One explanation is that we often overestimate the impact of a salient factor, such as where a given dorm is located on campus or how big the rooms are. In so doing, we don't think about the other factors that will likely influence our future emotions, such as our relationships and health (Schkade & Kahneman, 1998; Wilson et al., 2000). Also, we tend to underestimate how successful we are at coping with negative emotions that arise, and we overestimate how often we'll experience an emotion (Lench et al., 2019).

▲ First-year students moving into their dorm might try to predict how happy they'll be in their new living situation. Research suggests that their predictions may be inaccurate.

[Simon Jarratt/AGE Fotostock]

Our shoddy affective forecasts are more than just bugs in our cognitive system; they matter for how we organize our lives right now. For one, overestimating future negative reactions may stop us from taking chances for fear that things won't work out. We might not ask a potential friend to hang out, for example, because of the anticipated pain of being rebuffed (which probably won't be as agonizing as we predict). We might also deprive ourselves of enjoyment. Research shows that when people do something once, like go to a museum or play a video game, they think they have seen "it," and they underestimate the enjoyment they will get from repeating that experience (O'Brien, 2019). Affective forecasts can even make us more likely to act unethically. Participants given a series of opportunities to cheat, such as lie about the outcome of a private coin flip to get a payoff, were almost three times more likely to cheat at the *end* of that series than earlier (Effron et al., 2015). Why? Because as they realized their cheating opportunities were coming to an end, they forecasted regretting not bending the rules a bit to get ahead ("This is my last chance to sneak a little extra payment!").

Making Better Forecasts   Can we do anything to increase the accuracy of affective forecasting? A good place to start is by encouraging people to think broadly about future events that can influence their affective reactions, rather than to focus narrowly on just one anticipated event. For example, college football fans at the University of Virginia and Virginia Tech were asked to predict how happy they would be for a week after their team won or lost a game between the two schools (Wilson et al., 2000). A subset of these participants was also asked to make a diary planner of their upcoming week (the week after the game) and indicate how much time they would spend on different activities. Students who did not make a diary planner overestimated the duration of their happiness with a win and the extent of their misery with a loss. In contrast, students who indicated their activities over the coming week did not commit this forecasting error. Because they listed all the activities that might also trigger emotions, they were more aware that the outcome of the football game would be only one factor affecting how they would feel down the road.

SECTION REVIEW   Self-Regulation

The ability to self-regulate is fundamentally based on three key capacities of the human mind.

We are self-aware.	We are able to think about overarching goals.	We can mentally time travel.
• Self-regulation requires the ability to think about the self and to compare current behavior with what we aspire to do or be.	• Goals can be brought to mind consciously or cued unconsciously by the environment.	• When an action is thought of as being far in the future, we tend to focus on its abstract meaning. When it's thought of as being in the near future, we focus on the concrete details.
• When current behavior falls short of standards, but we feel we can reach the goal, we may commit to doing better.	• The same goal can be interpreted at concrete levels or more abstract levels. Shifting goal interpretations matter for motivation and self-perceptions.	• We are often poor at predicting our emotional reactions to future events, which can lead to decisions we may regret.
• If reducing that gap seems impossible, we may seek to escape self-awareness, which may contribute to food, drug, and alcohol abuse.		
• Our *ought self* is the internalized idea of who we should be, and our *ideal self* is who we want to be. These different self-representations can lead to different types of affect.		

Learning Outcomes

- Compare and contrast the "cool" and "hot" systems for self-regulation.

- Describe how ironic process theory explains why efforts at willpower can backfire.

- Identify evidence for and against the concept of ego depletion.

- Explain what implementation intentions are and how they help people pursue their goals.

- Explain the interrelationship between self-regulation, self-awareness, and depression.

Achieve

Social Psych in Everyday Life: Jaden

Self-Regulatory Challenges

You may have noticed that regulating thoughts and behavior can be difficult. Have you ever sat down on a Sunday for a long and productive day of schoolwork, but at the end of the day, found that all you had produced was a turkey sandwich? The difficulty of self-regulation also contributes to more serious problems. For example, children who have difficulty with effortful control and regulating their impulses show more school behavioral problems (Atherton et al., 2019), and self-regulation failures play a role in many of the leading causes of death in North America (Mokdad et al., 2004). Why is self-regulation so challenging, and what can we do to get on track to our goals?

Willpower: Running Hot and Cool

One of the keys to effective self-regulation is the capacity for what psychologists variously call effortful control, impulse control, ego control, or ego strength and what everyone else typically calls willpower. Willpower is essentially the capacity to overcome the many temptations, challenges, and obstacles that could impede pursuit of one's long-term goals. For a dieter, the problem may be a chocolate cake; for a premed student, it might be opportunities to party or a tough organic chemistry class; for a loyal spouse, it might be an attractive new acquaintance or a partner's annoying habits.

To understand how people use willpower to self-regulate, Walter Mischel and colleagues built on Freud's concepts of the id and the ego and distinguished between *hot* processes, which are driven by strong emotions, and *cool* processes, which rely more on level-headed reason (Mischel & Ayduk, 2004). The hot system provides the direction and energy to seek out goals. That's because focusing on our emotions orients us to seek out pleasurable outcomes and avoid unpleasant outcomes. The cool system is essential to keep us on track as we traverse a minefield of temptations and difficulties. When our hot system predominates, we tend to be impulsive, caving into these challenges and stalling or completely derailing our progress toward our long-term goals. However, when the cool system rules, we leap over these hurdles rather than being tripped up by them.

You may think that some people seem to have more willpower than others, and you are right. Mischel and Ebbesen (1970) studied people's varying abilities to use their cool system to overrule their hot system, working with children as young as four years old. The core idea was to pit an attractive short-term temptation against a more desired delayed goal that could be attained only if the short-term temptation was resisted. The original task was very simple: A child was told that when the experimenter returned in about 20 minutes, she would get *two* cookies. However, if she didn't want to wait for the two cookies, she could ring a bell, and the experimenter would return and give her *one* cookie. Two cookies are better than one, and if the child delayed gratification, she would get the preferred reward. This procedure gave researchers a precise way of measuring a person's capacity to delay gratification—namely, the amount of time the child waited before ringing the bell. The highest score was obtained by waiting the full 20 minutes for the experimenter to return with the two cookies.

In an amazing finding, performance on this delay of gratification task at age four predicted self-regulatory success up to 30 years later! Additional studies have shown that an ability to resist temptation early in life predicts adults' academic achievements, self-esteem, stress-management skills, and relationship satisfaction (Allemand et al., 2019; Ayduk et al., 2000; Mischel & Ayduk, 2002;

Shoda et al., 1990; Watts et al., 2018). And, of course, people's willpower continues to influence behavior. In adulthood, compared to those who prefer to live in the moment, those high in trait consideration of future consequences are more likely to eat healthily, recycle, put money into savings, and limit their risk of contracting sexually transmitted infections, among many other outcomes (Joireman & King, 2016).

Given that early displays of self-control predict adult outcomes, are we fated to our prepubescent susceptibility to the hot or cool system? Maybe to some extent, but we can certainly take steps to improve our self-control both as children and as adults. As parents, we can teach our kids the benefits of delaying gratification by, for example, showing them how to save their money for a toy they desperately want. In fact, Carlson and colleagues (2018) examined the ability to delay gratification among children born in the 1960s, 1980s, or 2000s using Mischel's original task. They found that children have generally improved their self-control abilities through the decades. Although it is difficult to pinpoint the cause of this improvement, the researchers suggest preschool education may play a role.

APPLICATION
Cool Strategies

In Homer's famous epic *The Odyssey*, the protagonist Odysseus knew he wanted to avoid getting mixed up with the enticing but deadly Sirens during his sailing trip. He could have used brute willpower, steeling himself against the Sirens' calls. But he tried a different strategy: As the ship was approaching the Sirens' hangout, Odysseus ordered his shipmates to leave him tied tightly to the ship's mast so that he couldn't move even if he wanted to. The story's lesson is that effective self-regulation does not require a strenuous effort to control oneself in the face of a temptation. It can also be accomplished by designing one's environment to avoid encountering temptations in the first place (Duckworth et al., 2016; Trope & Fishbach, 2005). Your current author finally learned this lesson after years of overeating at all-you-can-eat buffets. He realized it required great mental effort to subdue his desire for seconds (and thirds). Now, he orders a normal-sized meal off the menu instead.

Another "cool," or calm, self-regulatory strategy is the increasingly popular practice of mindful attention—simply observing one's thoughts as passing mental events rather than chasing after them in the hopes of gaining pleasure or avoiding pain. When study participants were given a choice between healthy snacks and tasty but unhealthy snacks, their hunger level predicted their craving for the unhealthy snacks. Although that might not surprise you, this "hot" craving was absent among participants trained to direct mindful attention at their food thoughts and see them as mere mental events (Papies et al., 2015).

A third "cool" strategy is to trick ourselves into thinking that we don't value a temptation. Participants instructed to think about a temptation and tell themselves "no, not ever" still desired that temptation later on. In contrast, participants who told themselves "you can have that some other time" were better at resisting their temptation even a full week later (Mead & Patrick, 2016). By postponing a temptation in such a general way, this second group convinced themselves that they must not crave it after all. ∎

▼ Sugary snacks and other temptations are all around us. We don't need to strenuously resist them to control our behavior.

[fizkes/Shutterstock]

SOCIAL PSYCH OUT IN THE WORLD

Neurological Underpinnings of Self-Regulation

In the late summer of 1848, Phineas Gage was busy laying railroad track in Vermont, a job that required drilling a hole in a rock and filling it with explosive powder, then running a fuse to it and covering the powder with densely packed sand (Fleischman, 2002). Gage had a custom-made tamping iron, a rod that he used to pack the sand. One day, a spark set off by his tamping iron hit the powder and set off a massive explosion. Gage lay on the ground, blood pouring from a hole where his cheek had been and another on the top of his head. The tamping rod had shot through Gage's head, tearing through his skull and brain tissue. Surprisingly, Gage was not only alive but (after a few minutes of convulsive twitching) conscious and quite alert!

With a doctor's help, the wound eventually healed, but the reason Gage's case has become so interesting to psychologists is that although Gage's intellectual capacities were essentially intact and his motor functioning unimpaired, his personality was radically transformed. Before the accident, Gage had a reputation as an honest, hard-working citizen with a sharp mind. After the accident, he became impatient and susceptible to angry outbursts. He would shout a constant stream of loosely organized ideas, his speech laced with profanity and sexually inappropriate remarks. Further, he had difficulty following any coherent plan of action and had a difficult time planning or controlling his behavior. As one of his peers remarked, "Gage was no longer Gage."

One general lesson we can take away from the case of Phineas Gage is how the brain is involved in those aspects of our self and personality that make us who we are, including the choices we make and the impression we give to others. Gage's case also offers exciting clues about which regions of the brain are involved in self-regulation. Using brain imaging techniques and analyzing Gage's skull fractures, a reconstruction (Damasio et al., 1994) of Gage's lesions showed that the rod destroyed the very front of the frontal cortex in the left and right hemispheres, in a brain region known as the *ventromedial prefrontal cortex* (vmPFC) (see figure on next page). This region of the brain is particularly important in processing emotional information (Banfield et al., 2004). Following damage to the vmPFC, people often have unimpaired intellectual abilities, but they lose the ability to process emotion, and because emotion plays a role in goal pursuit, these individuals also have difficulty forming and carrying through the coherent plans of action needed to accomplish goals.

The ventromedial prefrontal cortex is just one of the regions that are important to social and emotional aspects of self-regulation. In addition:

- The *orbitofrontal cortex* is an area that lies just behind the eye sockets. Jennifer Beer and colleagues (2003) have examined how damage to the orbitofrontal cortex impairs people's ability to regulate their social behavior. For example, when asked to generate a nickname for an experimenter who is an attractive young woman, most people inhibit a tendency to use sexually inappropriate names, but people who have suffered injury to the orbitofrontal region of the brain blurt out

[Warren Anatomical Museum in the Francis A. Countway Library of Medicine. Gift of Jack and Beverly Wilgus.]

THINK ABOUT ▶

Trying Too Hard: Ironic Process Theory Sometimes our mind goes places we don't want it to go. Perhaps you're trying to study but keep getting distracted by a dog barking; perhaps you're having lustful thoughts for someone and feel guilty about it; or perhaps you can't stop thinking about a hurtful conversation from last week. When unwanted thoughts absorb our attention, we often try to shift focus away from those thoughts and back onto the things we want to focus on (such as that upcoming stats midterm). As agents with free will, surely, we should have some say over what we think about. However, mind control—even of our own minds—is not nearly so straightforward. Try closing your eyes for one minute and NOT thinking about white bears.

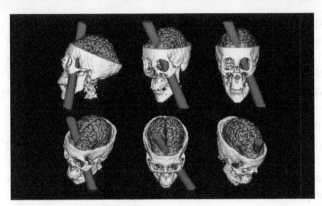

▲ A reconstruction of Gage's injury.

[Patrick Landmann/SPL/Science Source]

the inappropriate nickname (Beer et al., 2003). Whereas most people would feel embarrassed if they said such a nickname aloud, orbitofrontal patients feel proud of how clever they are. Not only are they unable to monitor their thoughts ahead of time and screen out potentially offensive comments, they also aren't able to monitor the negative social feedback they get afterward.

■ The *dorsolateral prefrontal cortex* (DLPFC) is not an anatomical structure but rather an area of the frontal lobes that is responsible for many executive functions. For example, it is involved in planning, inhibition, and regulation of behavior toward an abstract goal (Banfield et al., 2004). As you might imagine, people with damage to this area have difficulty carrying out even simple everyday tasks (Shallice & Burgess, 1991). Consider the case of one frontal-lobe patient, who attempted to purchase soap and discovered that the store didn't carry her favorite brand. Most people in this situation would find an alternative means of achieving the goal, such as purchasing another brand of soap. But the frontal-lobe patient instead gave up altogether on the goal of buying soap.

■ The *anterior cingulate cortex* (ACC) is a region that lies on the medial (inner) surface of the frontal lobes and interacts with areas of the prefrontal cortex. One primary function of the ACC is to signal when some behavior or outcome is at odds with your goals (Banfield et al., 2004). The ACC helps draw your attention to conflicts between what you want and what has just happened. It then communicates with the DLPFC, which steps in to switch plans or change behavior to get you back on track.

Cunningham, Johnson, and colleagues (2004) looked at how the ACC and the DLPFC allow people to monitor and regulate their social biases. Using **functional magnetic resonance imagery (fMRI)**, a technique that provides information about activity in the brain when people perform certain cognitive or motor tasks, Cunningham and colleagues found increased activation in the *amygdala*, a brain region implicated in fear processing, when people were presented very quickly with a Black as opposed to a White face. This neurological signature of an automatic fear response was particularly strong for participants with more negative implicit racial biases. When people had a bit longer to look at a Black face, they showed increased activation in both the ACC and the dorsolateral prefrontal cortex but no longer showed increased amygdala activation. The level of ACC and DLPFC activity was the strongest for people who had not only strong implicit biases but also the goal of being nonprejudiced. The implication is that after an initial fear response, the ACC in these individuals might have signaled that this was not the response they wanted to have to Blacks, and perhaps their DLPFC kicked in to reduce and regulate that immediate, knee-jerk reaction.

Although research that links neurological processes to social behaviors is still in its infancy, results such as these are beginning to shed light on the complex array of cognitive systems that are involved in helping us formulate, enact, monitor, and follow through on our goals and intentions.

Functional magnetic resonance imagery (fMRI) A scanning technique that provides information about the activity of regions of the brain when people perform certain cognitive or motor tasks.

How did you do? Perhaps this task wasn't too difficult, and you were able to focus your attention elsewhere. Many people, however, are surprised to discover that even though they try to keep white bears out of consciousness, the bears keep popping up. This is an example of what Dan Wegner (1994) called **ironic processing,** whereby the more we try *not* to think about something, the more those thoughts enter our mind. In laboratory studies, students who first spent five minutes trying to suppress thoughts of white bears reported having more than twice as many thoughts of white bears by the end of a subsequent five-minute period, compared to students who didn't first try to push thoughts of white bears out of their minds. If it's hard to keep random polar bears out of

Ironic processing The idea that the more we try *not* to think about something, the more those thoughts enter our mind and distract us from other things.

consciousness, you can imagine how difficult it must be to push away troubling thoughts about the low grade you just got on an exam or how badly your date went last weekend!

To explain why thought suppression is so difficult, Wegner (1994) analyzed the mental processes that make it possible. One process acts as a **monitor** that is on the lookout for signs of the unwanted thought. The second process is an **operator** that actively pushes any signs of the unwanted thought out of consciousness. The best way to do this is through distraction, filling consciousness with thoughts of other things.

Most of the time people can engage both the monitor and the operator to successfully keep an unwanted thought out of consciousness. However, once they stop trying to suppress the thought, typically a *rebound effect* occurs: The unwanted thought becomes even more accessible than it was before suppression. Scientists are even able to observe this rebound effect in the brain. Hu and colleagues (2015) asked one group of students to commit a crime: stealing a ring from a faculty member's mailbox. When they were later hooked up to a brain-scanning device and asked to avoid memories of their crime, their brain-wave activity looked no different than that of their peers who were not instructed to suppress criminal memories or who didn't commit the crime in the first place. But about a half-second later, those who consciously suppressed their criminal memories showed a distinctive neural signal of conflict between the monitor and the operator. Unwanted thoughts come back with a vengeance.

Possible Causes of the Rebound Effect

There is still some debate about the cause of the rebound effect. One explanation is that the monitor process has to keep the unwanted thought close to consciousness in order to watch for it, and so when the operator stops actively providing alternative thoughts, the unwanted thought becomes more salient than if there had been no effort to suppress it. For instance, participants who were asked to *not* think about a particular person in their lives right before they went to bed were more likely to dream about the person than were participants who did not receive this request (Wegner et al., 2004).

Another explanation is that the monitor and the operator place different demands on mental energy. The monitor is an automatic process that can search for signs of an unwanted thought without demanding too much mental energy. It's fast and effortless. The operator, in contrast, is a controlled process that requires more mental effort. This leads to a testable prediction about the two components of thought suppression. We would expect that when people have some drain on their cognitive resources, the automatic monitor process will continue searching for instances of an unwanted thought, but the controlled operator process responsible for focusing attention away from that thought will be disabled. Consequently, the undesired thought kept accessible by the monitoring process will become especially likely to pop into consciousness.

This reasoning is supported in several studies examining diverse contexts of thought suppression. Suppressed thoughts return with a vengeance particularly when people are under cognitive load, whether that be from stress, distraction, or time pressure (Ansfield et al., 1996; Wegner, 1994). For example, if people reminisce about sad events and then try to suppress sad feelings, they are generally successful when cognitive load is low, but if meanwhile they're rehearsing a long string of numbers, their efforts to suppress the sad thoughts backfire, and they think about them even more (Wegner et al., 1993).

Monitor The effortless mental process that is on the lookout for signs of unwanted thoughts.

Operator The effortful mental process that pushes any signs of unwanted thoughts out of consciousness.

Minimizing Ironic Processing   There are two basic ways to minimize ironic processing. One is to keep distraction, stress, and time urgency to a minimum when regulating our thought and behavior so that the operator has the energy to do its job. We can, for example, work in a quiet room or start projects far in advance of deadlines. Of course, we can't always avoid mental stressors. The second strategy is simply to stop trying to control your thoughts when cognitive strain is likely to be present. Under such circumstances, relaxing effortful control can eliminate the ironic process. In fact, a form of psychotherapy called paradoxical intervention involves telling clients to stop trying to get rid of their problems. You can't sleep when you go to bed? Stop trying to! It seems to work, at least for some people, some of the time (Shoham & Rohrbaugh, 1997).

Insufficient Energy or Diminished Motivation

Our lack of success with trying to suppress unwanted thoughts highlights the more general point that goal pursuit is often an effortful process. Perhaps you are a strong environmentalist and value recycling, but one day you come home from a long day of work and studying. You barely have enough energy to make yourself dinner. You look at the mess of recyclables and nonrecyclables, say "Forget this!" and toss them all in the trash. Why would you give up so easily on a cherished value?

Muraven, Tice, and Baumeister (1998) argued that the ego is like a muscle. We have a certain amount of ego strength that allows us to regulate and control our behavior. But just as our quadriceps ache after we've run five miles, our ego strength becomes depleted by extended bouts of self-control. This mental fatigue, or **ego depletion**, can make it harder to regulate our behavior, even when the task that depletes our energy is different from the one we are trying to regulate. For example, in one study participants watched a film about environmental disasters that included graphic scenes of sick and dying animals. Some participants were instructed to suppress the emotions they naturally felt in response to the movie, whereas others were instructed to deliberately amplify or exaggerate the emotions they felt. A third group received no instructions about regulating their emotions. Afterward, participants were asked to squeeze a handgrip for as long as they could. Compared with those who had received no instructions, participants who had regulated their emotions—either suppressing or amplifying them—squeezed the handgrip for a shorter amount of time. In a more recent study (Garrison et al., 2019), students asked to control their writing behavior—write a story about yourself, but do *not* use the letters *A* or *N!*—made more mistakes on subsequent tests of attention control compared to students who did not first exercise self-control. These findings suggest that even when tasks look different on the surface, they rely on the same bank of self-regulatory energy.

Although many studies find ego depletion effects, others do not, and there is much discussion about this area of research (Baumeister, in press; Baumeister & Vohs, 2016; Berkman et al., 2017; Friese et al., 2019; Hagger et al., 2016). Further, researchers have made discoveries that raise questions about whether we really have a limited supply of self-regulatory strength. Consider that incentives such as a monetary reward for maintaining effort can dramatically reduce, or even eliminate, the ego depletion effect (Boksem et al., 2006; Muraven & Slessareva, 2003). Not only does offering people money counteract the ego depletion effect, so too does reminding them of their personal values (Schmeichel & Vohs, 2009), as does convincing them that engaging in further self-control will benefit either themselves or others (Muraven & Slessareva, 2003; for a review,

▲ Pursuing a goal, such as sorting waste items in responsible ways, takes energy.
[Antenna/fStop/AGE Fotostock]

Ego depletion The idea that ego strength becomes depleted by extended bouts of self-control.

see Masicampo et al., 2014). If self-control strength is just like a battery charge that can get drained, then it isn't clear how incentivizing people with money, showing them humorous videos (Tice et al., 2007), or reminding them of personal values would restore this resource. These findings have been important in refining social psychology's understanding of self-control because they show that there is more going on than using up a limited resource.

So what else is going on? Inzlicht and colleagues (2014) provided further insight into why exercising self-control at times *seems* to be so limited. They proposed that initial acts of self-control shift people's motivation away from further restraint or impulse control and toward gratification. Put simply, after people have done the work of maintaining self-control, they are less motivated to do any further work. They feel like they are "owed" a break and that they are justified in slacking off. It's as though our minds say, "I've put in the effort, and now I choose not to control myself any further. In fact, it's time for a reward!" Even if you feel like you just controlled yourself in a way that felt hard or draining, shifting to a task that is exciting or important can feel rejuvenating. Self-control feels difficult, and that difficult feeling determines whether we're willing to further control ourselves or to let ourselves go. But despite the sensation of effort and even internal conflict, the researchers say, self-control does not "drain" our energy in the same way that vigorous exercise does (Inzlicht & Berkman, 2015).

In fact, a major factor determining how well we can exert control is our belief about what effort means. When people were led to believe that willpower is an unlimited resource, they did not show the typical ego depletion effect (Job et al., 2010). Or consider the role of cultural beliefs about willpower: Americans believe that exerting self-control drains you, and indeed they show the typical ego depletion effect, but Indians believe that exerting willpower is energizing, and for them self-control *improves* performances (Savani & Veronika, 2017). You could also believe that self-control is a fixed trait—that, essentially, you've got what you've got. With that belief, you're likely to interpret high levels of effort as a sign that you're hitting the limits of your capacity. Alternatively, you could take a *growth mind-set* and believe that self-control is a malleable trait that can be developed with practice. When study participants were trained to take a growth mind-set on self-regulation, they interpreted high levels of effort as an indication that they were working hard to improve their abilities, and rather than feel depleted when the going got tough, they persevered on their goals (Mrazek et al., 2018).

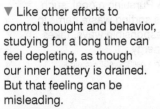

▼ Like other efforts to control thought and behavior, studying for a long time can feel depleting, as though our inner battery is drained. But that feeling can be misleading.

[ColorBlind Images/Getty Images]

Getting Our Emotions Under Control

Imagine that your romantic partner of several months takes you out to dinner. You are expecting a quiet, romantic evening when, over your corn chowder, your partner blurts out that your relationship is now over. Ouch. To maintain your dignity, you try to choke back your surprise, your anger, and your crushing disappointment. But how successful are you likely to be? If you consider what you've just learned about people's mixed success at pushing thoughts out of mind, you'll probably realize that attempting to control your emotions by suppressing them is likely to be ineffective.

Fortunately, there is a better strategy. Building on cognitive appraisal theory of emotion, introduced in chapter 2, James Gross (2001) recommended **cognitive reappraisal**—reexamining the situation so that you don't feel such a strong

Cognitive reappraisal The cognitive reframing of a situation to minimize one's emotional reaction to it.

emotional reaction in the first place. In the example of being dumped, you might excuse yourself to go to the restroom and use that time to think about all of your partner's annoying habits that actually drove you crazy or about the fact that you don't have the time for a relationship anyway. With these cognitions in mind, the sudden breakup might seem a little more like a blessing than a curse.

But can the mind really control the heart through reappraisal? Research suggests that it can (Gross, 2002). Gross (1998) showed people a disturbing film of an arm amputation. He instructed one group of participants simply to watch the film (the control condition). Another group of participants were told to suppress their emotional response so that someone watching them wouldn't be able to tell how they were feeling. A third group was instructed to reappraise the film—for example, by imagining that it was staged rather than real. Compared with the people in the control condition, people who suppressed their emotion did make fewer disgust expressions, but they showed increased activation of the sympathetic nervous system and still reported feeling just as disgusted. In contrast, participants who reappraised the film showed no increase in their physiological signs of arousal and reported lower levels of disgust than participants in the control condition.

Emerging research reveals several other interesting forms of reappraisal that help us control our emotions. One is to view the events that are currently stressing you out from the perspective of a "future you" many years down the road (Bruehlman-Senecal & Ayduk, 2015). How does adopting this distant-future perspective work? It reminds us that our current struggles are impermanent—that "this too shall pass"—which loosens their grip on our emotions. Be careful, though, as reappraisal might feel good in the short run but lull you into not taking any action to improve your situation in the long run (Ford et al., 2019). In addition to using reappraisal, recall from chapter 2 that you can develop a finer-grained understanding of exactly what emotions you're experiencing. For instance, differentiating between feelings of anger and sadness in the aforementioned example of getting dumped can enable you to more productively work through those feelings (Kashdan et al., 2015). You can similarly improve self-control by simply acknowledging, to yourself or to others, how you've fallen short in the past (Lowe & Haws, 2019).

 APPLICATION

What Happened to Those New Year's Resolutions? Implementing and Maintaining Your Good Intentions

What about times when we believe we can achieve our goals and yet we have difficulty actually getting started? Peter Gollwitzer (1999) pointed out that because our attention usually is absorbed in our everyday activities, we often make it through our days without ever seizing opportunities to act on our goals. Imagine that you wake up on New Year's Day, look in the mirror, and make a resolution: "I'm going to be a better friend from now on!" Sounds great, but throughout the day, your attention is absorbed in your usual tasks, and as you fall asleep that night, you think to yourself, "Hey! I never got a chance to be a better friend!" Your goal is stuck as a broad vision, and you haven't specified how you will implement it. A related problem is that planning how we are going to stay on track to reach our goals requires effortful control of thought, and when we've been busy and mentally taxed, we have less mental energy left over to make plans (Sjåstad & Baumeister, 2018).

Gollwitzer claimed that we'll be more successful if we create **implementation intentions**, mental rules that link particular situational cues to goal-directed

Implementation intentions Mental rules reminding us to respond to a cue in a situation with a goal-directed behavior.

behaviors, such as "IF *Situation X* arises, THEN I will perform *Action Y*." In the example of the New Year's resolution to be a better friend, an implementation intention might be something like, "IF I see Stephen, THEN I will ask him how his kids are." Now, rather than taking the time and energy to decide when to get started on a goal and what to do, the person programs herself to respond to aspects of the situation automatically, with goal-directed behaviors. This makes it more likely that effective self-regulation will proceed even in the presence of stressful situations or cognitive distraction. It also frees the mind from having to choose among various means to attain the goal (e.g., asking about Stephen's kids *or* buying him coffee?), which can make the person less confident that any one means will work and less motivated overall (Bélanger et al., 2015).

Forming implementation intentions helps people reach all sorts of goals. A recent meta-analysis of 12 studies showed that implementation intentions helped people to quit smoking (McWilliams et al., 2019). They can also be effective at getting people to exercise. One study (Milne et al., 2002) recruited college students, all of whom had the goal of exercising more. One group of students was randomly assigned to hear about the health risks associated with heart disease. This risk reminder intervention was mildly successful, increasing the percentage of students who exercised regularly from 29% to 39%. Another group of students was reminded of their risk and additionally asked to form implementation intentions—that is, specific rules for when and where to exercise ("As soon as I get up, I'll go for a 3-mile run."). In this condition, 91% of the participants exercised regularly! A similar study encouraging women to get early-detection screening for cervical cancer found that instructions to form implementation intentions increased the percentage of women who got screenings from 69% to 92% (Sheeran & Orbell, 2000).

A similar strategy is to form a habit. Wendy Wood and her colleagues showed that goals and intentions can lead to habit formation by initially motivating us to repeat certain actions in particular contexts. But once the habit is formed, it can run automatically without requiring motivation or effortful control. As a result, even when we're stressed, distracted, or otherwise unmotivated, a habit enables us to respond to situational cues with a repeated behavior without having to drum up intentions or make conscious decisions (Wood & Ruenger, 2016). In fact, if we can put ourselves on autopilot in one area of life, such as setting a morning routine, it helps us regulate our behavior in other areas (e.g., saving money) (Tian et al., 2018). Of course, it's precisely this automatic property that makes *unwanted* habits and routines so hard to break. For example, if a strong habit automatically links the sight of a cookie jar with cookie-grabbing action, a person may end up munching several cookies before his controlled system has a chance to intervene.

To recap, we often fall short of our goals because we don't know when to initiate goal-directed actions and because we have to cope with tempting distractions, bad habits, and competing goals. The upshot is that we have a much better chance of achieving our goals if we create implementation intentions or habits that link specific situational opportunities to specific goal-directed behaviors. In a sense, we "outsource" action initiation to our lived environment.

Another way to ensure that you maintain your New Year's resolutions is to lean on others. Throughout this chapter, we've portrayed the ego as working on its own to keep the person on track toward goals; think of the poor kid trying to resist ringing the bell for a cookie! But people pursue goals in the context of their relationships with spouses, coworkers, parents and children, doctors, and so on (Fitzsimons & Finkel, 2018). They look to close others for information, practical assistance, and encouragement. And whether or not people achieve their goals often depends on how well they coordinate their actions with relationship partners. So whether your goal is to get better grades, recover from a disease, or get a career promotion, sometimes you can make it further as part of a social unit than you would on your own. ∎

When We Can't Let Go: Self-Regulatory Perseveration and Depression

Let's say you choose the goal of signing up online for a philosophy class that would help you complete your degree requirements. But what happens if the online sign-up system doesn't allow you to enroll because you don't meet the prerequisites? Although you have not met your goal, you probably won't spend the rest of the day mindlessly clicking the "Enroll" icon over and over. What would you do instead? Recall our earlier discussion of action identification theory. You'd probably move up the hierarchy to more abstract interpretations and consider the higher-order goal of getting enough credits to graduate. Once you did that, you'd stop fixating on getting into that particular course and consider other courses you could take to get the credits you need. Indeed, people can be quite flexible at compensating for blocked goal pursuit by finding substitute means of satisfying the more abstract goal. This is useful because it allows people to search for alternative lower-level goals that may help them achieve the same higher-level goal.

But sometimes people persist in pursuing a goal long after it's no longer beneficial to do so. The **self-regulatory perseveration theory of depression** (Pyszczynski & Greenberg, 1987a, 1992) proposes that this is one way that people can fall into depression. This theory builds on research on self-awareness. Recall that self-awareness theory claims that directing attention to the self leads people to compare their current state with their ideal state. If they notice a discrepancy and feel they have the means to reduce it, they will alter their behavior to bring it more closely in line with their ideal. But if the chances of reducing this discrepancy are unlikely—for example, if the task is very difficult—the person will disengage, or let go of the goal and divert attention away from the self. And although giving up on goals and avoiding self-awareness can lead to destructive behaviors such as excessive alcohol consumption, letting go of unattainable goals is generally an adaptive response. If you drop a pencil down a gutter, it's pointless to sit all day by the gutter, fishing around with a coat hanger and hoping that your pencil will magically reappear.

Of course, not all goals are as easily abandoned as your favorite pencil. If a goal is a central source of self-esteem, and the person has few other ways of deriving self-esteem, letting go of that goal may be very difficult even after it becomes evident that the goal is lost or probably will never be attained. Pyszczynski and Greenberg proposed that this persistent focus on an unattainable goal results in many of the common symptoms of depression, including elevated negative emotion, a tendency to blame oneself for shortcomings, and decreased motivation and performance in other areas of life. Supporting this theory is evidence that lost and limited bases of self-esteem are precursors of depression, that depressed people tend to be high in self-awareness, and that reducing self-awareness in depressed people tends to reduce their symptoms (Pyszczynski & Greenberg, 1992).

The reason for this escalating pattern of problems is that excessive inward focus on the self magnifies negative feelings, promotes attributing one's problems to oneself, and interferes with attention to the external world, leading to

Self-regulatory perseveration theory of depression The theory that one way in which people can fall into depression is through persistent self-focus on an unattainable goal.

Figure 5.9

The Positive Spiral of Recovery

According to self-regulatory perseveration theory, recovery from depression after a loss involves moving up the goal hierarchy to consider the higher-order goal no longer being served and then considering alternative pathways to achieve that goal.

further failures. The spiral of misery and self-recrimination culminates in a negative self-image. Many of us, for example, have had the misfortune of being dumped by a romantic partner. When this happens, if the relationship was really important to us, we may become depressed as we continually think about how much we wish we were still with that person, what we did wrong, why we're unworthy of love, and so on. We obsess about getting that person back. But it's just not going to happen. We may eventually think that without that person, who previously provided us with such joy, self-worth, and meaning, life really . . . well . . . sucks. A similar negative spiral can begin with other losses in the realms of love and work: the death of a spouse, parent, or child; being laid off; or failing to get a promotion or an opportunity to pursue a desired career. Still, from experiences of adversity, people can experience a major improvement in psychological and social functioning (Mancini, 2019).

The positive spiral of recovery begins by identifying the abstract goal that the now-unattainable goal was serving. In this way, the person can find alternative means of satisfying that abstract goal. As he or she invests time and energy in those alternative means, self-focus on the unattainable goal is reduced. Let's illustrate this positive spiral in the case of a failed relationship (**FIGURE 5.9**). The mourning partner recognizes that the concrete goal of being in a relationship served the more abstract goal of feeling loved and valued. This realization opens up the possibility of other means of establishing personal value. That person may consider other romantic prospects or may recognize that family, friends, or career goals provide a sense of worth. After becoming more involved in those alternative goals, the unattainable relationship seems less important and no longer is a constant reminder of personal shortcomings.

Maintaining a state of optimal well-being, then, requires a delicate balance between self-focused pursuit of some goals and at the same time letting go of goals that are beyond our means. Sometimes our desire to control things makes us less flexible and more frustrated (Uziel, 2018). The ability to know whether a goal is doable, and thus to choose wisely whether to persist or give up and strive for another goal, is itself a skill (Ntoumanis & Sedikides, 2018). It requires accurate answers to questions such as Do I know what needs to be done? How much time and energy will this take? And What social support is available if I get in a pickle? This point brings this chapter full circle to show how the *I* and the *Me* are interrelated parts of the self. As the *I* controls our thoughts, feelings, and behaviors to keep us on track toward our goals, it is constantly referring to the *Me*'s library of self-knowledge. Correcting common errors in self-knowledge, then, is a step toward attaining our goals and, ultimately, to enjoying happier, healthier, and more successful lives.

SECTION REVIEW   Self-Regulatory Challenges

Research has discovered numerous factors that make self-regulation difficult. These findings point to some concrete strategies that people can use to improve self-regulation and achieve their goals.

- Strengthen willpower by avoiding factors that block the "cool" system for staying on track, such as stress, cognitive overload, and alcohol.
- Minimize ironic processing—the intrusion of thoughts we are trying to suppress—by keeping distractions and stress to a minimum or relaxing efforts to suppress thoughts.
- Reappraise difficult situations as a way to avoid feeling strong negative emotions.
- Form "if–then" rules to program yourself to respond to situational cues with specific goal-directed behaviors and monitor goal progress as you go along.
- Rely on relationship partners for resources like time, energy, and encouragement.
- Maintain a balance between self-focused pursuit of some goals and letting go of goals that are beyond reach.

CRITICAL LEARNING EXERCISES

1. Think about the place you have been that is the most different from where you grew up. Would you still be the same you if you had grown up in that different place? If you say "yes," that means you believe that your sense of self and self-concept would be the same as it is now. If you say "no," you believe that your self would be quite different. Try to use what you have learned about the influences on one's self-concept to argue for both sides.

2. Pick a trait—any trait—that has been central to your personality and that sets you apart from others. Perhaps you've always thought of yourself as creative, generous, competitive, or rational. Once you've identified your trait, ask yourself how you know it defines you. When in your past did you begin to identify with it? Is it something that other people, like your parents or teachers, always said about you? Consider the three major routes to self-knowledge we discussed: reflected appraisal, social comparison, and self-perception. Consider how each helped you figure out who you are. Now consider how else you came to know about this trait. Are there other routes to self-knowledge that social psychologists have overlooked?

3. Let's say you're a high school art teacher, and your student Quinn just can't seem to get anything done.

He sits in class playing with his phone and has never followed through on a project. If he keeps this up, he'll fail your class, and you want to help him avoid that. Try to think of three reasons Quinn can't get his act together. That is, try to analyze potential reasons for his lack of progress in self-regulating toward goals. Then, for one of those potential reasons, design an intervention to help him get on track. What are some techniques you could borrow from this chapter?

4. Our discussion of self-regulatory challenges portrays average people as having already selected their goals but struggling to meet them. People know what they want (e.g., to finish homework, eat less sugar) but get off course for various reasons. But might there be times when self-regulation fails because we simply don't know what we want? Consider the feeling of boredom. Imagine that someone complains of boredom, and when others suggest activities, each one sounds unappealing. Does this present a unique challenge to self-regulation? It's not as though the person cannot make progress toward a goal; rather, the person can't identify a meaningful goal. How do you think social psychologists might study this?

CHAPTER 6

The Key Self-Motives: Consistency, Esteem, Presentation, and Growth

Your sense of self—*who you are*—is not something that exists solely in your own head. Instead, it is an active force that interacts with the social world to achieve certain goals. When your current author (Jeff) looks back over his own life, he considers whether his actions always fit his values and beliefs and whether they have summed to a coherent story; he thinks about whether he's had a positive impact through his work and his relationships; he considers the impressions he has made on others; and he ponders how much he has changed and grown over the years. In short, he focuses on four important self-related motives that have guided human behavior across cultures and historical periods:

- We want to view ourselves as a coherent whole.

- We want to see ourselves in a positive light.

- We want to control how others perceive us.

- We want to grow, learn, and improve.

The Motive to Maintain a Consistent Self

Learning Outcomes

People want to perceive consistency among the specific things they believe, say, and do—what we'll call the *micro* level of day-to-day experience. But it's virtually impossible to be consistent all the time. For example, you probably believe in the value of energy and water conservation, but have you ever taken a long, hot shower? Have you ever had a professor urge you to do the assigned readings prior to each lecture, agree that this is a good idea, and still not done it? Cognitive dissonance theory explains how people react to these micro-level inconsistencies in their thoughts and behavior. We begin this section by outlining the theory and research supporting it. Afterward, we'll consider people's efforts to maintain consistency at the *macro* level of their lives as a whole.

Self-Consistency at the Micro Level: Cognitive Dissonance Theory

According to Leon Festinger's (1957) **cognitive dissonance theory,** people have such distaste for perceiving inconsistencies in their beliefs, attitudes, and behavior that they will bias their own attitudes and beliefs to try to deny those

- Explain what conditions cause people to experience cognitive dissonance and factors that affect the magnitude of dissonance experienced.

- Identify the primary ways people reduce their feelings of cognitive dissonance.

- Explain how self-consistency across situations and across time affects the ability to cope with life's challenges.

Cognitive dissonance theory The idea that people have such distaste for perceiving inconsistencies in their beliefs, attitudes, and behavior that they will bias their own attitudes and beliefs to try to deny inconsistencies.

inconsistencies. The basic idea is that when two cognitions (e.g., beliefs, attitudes, perceived actions) are inconsistent with or contradict one another, people experience an uncomfortable psychological tension known as *dissonance*. The more important the inconsistent cognitions are to the person, the more intense the feeling of dissonance and the stronger the motivation to get rid of that feeling. There are three primary ways to reduce dissonance:

1. Change one of the cognitions.
2. Add a third cognition that makes the original two cognitions seem less inconsistent with each other.
3. Trivialize the cognitions that are inconsistent.

Let's consider, as Festinger did back in the 1950s, the example of a cigarette smoker. Serena the smoker has two cognitions: (1) She knows that smoking cigarettes is bad for her health, and (2) she knows that she smokes cigarettes. Because the cognition "Smoking is bad for me" is inconsistent with the cognition "I smoke," Serena often feels tense and conflicted about her smoking. That is, she experiences dissonance. To reduce the dissonance, Serena could change one of the two dissonant cognitions. However, cognitions can be difficult to change. For Serena to decide that smoking is not bad for her, she would have to call into question the judgment of the entire medical community, and this would likely conflict with a host of other beliefs she has, such as the trustworthiness of cultural authorities. Alternatively, Serena could change the cognition "I smoke" by quitting. Most smokers do in fact try to quit, and many eventually succeed, but behaviors are often hard to change once they become habits (Wood & Neal, 2007), particularly if engaging in them creates positive feelings (e.g., a nicotine high) and giving them up creates negative feelings (e.g., withdrawal symptoms).

When it's hard to change either of the dissonant cognitions, people usually add a third cognition that resolves the inconsistency between the original two cognitions (Vaidis & Bran, 2018). Take a minute to think of any additional cognitions that smokers use to try to reduce their dissonance. Now look at FIGURE 6.1, depicting Serena the smoker's thoughts. How many of these rationalizations did you come up with? These added cognitions help to reduce dissonance, but they also make it easier to avoid the difficult but healthy change of quitting.

A third way to reduce dissonance is to *trivialize* one of the inconsistent cognitions (Simon et al., 1995). Let's illustrate this with an example. Suppose you buy a traditional gas-powered car, knowing that a hybrid car would use less fuel and so be better in terms of sustainability. If you were to reduce dissonance by trivializing one of the cognitions, you could think to yourself, "With all the fuel consumption in the United States, the extra fuel my new car will use is a tiny drop in the bucket."

THINK ABOUT ▶

[Aubord Dulac/Shutterstock]

Figure 6.1

Smoking and Dissonance

Smokers often are experts at generating additional cognitions to reduce the dissonance created by doing something they know is bad for their health. How many of these have you heard before—or used yourself, if you're a smoker?

- "I've only been smoking for a short time. I will quit soon."
- "My grandma smoked and lived to be 80, so my genes will protect me."
- "If I don't smoke, I'll get fat and die from that."
- "We'll all die of something. I'd rather live a shorter but more enjoyable life."
- "I prefer to take the suspense out of what kills me."
- "It's just not possible for me to quit."
- "I've cut back to 12 a day."
- "I only smoke at parties or when I'm stressed."

To understand more about the conditions that arouse dissonance and the ways people reduce it, researchers have come up with a number of laboratory situations, or *dissonance paradigms*. Two such situations are the *free choice paradigm* and the *induced compliance paradigm*.

The Free Choice Paradigm   The **free choice paradigm** (Brehm, 1956) is based on the idea that any time people make a choice between two alternatives, there is likely to be some dissonance. This is because all of the bad aspects of the alternative people chose and all of the good aspects of the alternative they rejected are inconsistent with their choice. Hard choices are ones for which there are more of these inconsistent cognitions. So, the harder it is to make a choice, the more dissonance there will be after the choice is made.

How do people cope with this dissonance? They do so by *spreading the alternatives*: After the choice is made, people generally place more emphasis on the positive characteristics of the chosen alternative and the negative aspects of the rejected alternative. For example, if you chose a fuel-efficient small car over a gas guzzling luxury car, you could spread the alternatives by focusing on the value of being green as well as the extravagance and repair costs of the luxury car. But if you had instead chosen the luxury car, you might spread the alternatives by focusing on its comfort and the small car's lousy sound system.

In the first test of this idea, Brehm (1956) asked one group of participants to choose between two consumer items (such as a stopwatch and a portable radio) that they liked a lot (**FIGURE 6.2**). This was a difficult decision. The other group was asked to choose between an item they liked a lot and one they didn't like, which is an easy decision. After participants chose the item they wanted, they were again asked to rate how much they liked them. Brehm reasoned that when the choice was easy, participants would not feel much dissonance, and so they would rate the items pretty much as they had before their decision. But the participants who made a difficult decision would feel dissonance because their cognition "I made the right choice" is inconsistent with their cognition "The item I chose has some negative aspects, and the one I didn't choose has some attractive aspects." Brehm expected these participants to spread the alternatives on their second rating, exaggerating their chosen item's attractiveness and downplaying the other item's value. This is exactly what he found. Related research shows that people also spread the alternatives following a difficult choice by searching for information that supports their choice and avoiding information that calls their choice into question (e.g., Frey, 1982).

The Induced Compliance Paradigm   Dissonance is aroused whenever people make difficult choices. And many of our difficult choices result from our being pulled in opposite directions, as when we're induced to say something we don't truly believe. For example, when your professor asks you whether you liked today's sleep-inducing lecture, you are likely to say, "Oh, it was very interesting." Could the dissonance aroused in such situations change our beliefs? Festinger and Carlsmith (1959) endeavored to find out. They had participants engage

Free choice paradigm A laboratory situation in which people make a choice between two alternatives, and after they do, attraction to the alternatives is assessed.

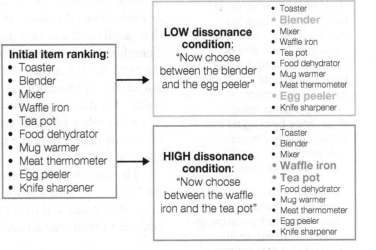

Figure 6.2

Brehm's Free Choice Paradigm

In the free choice paradigm (Brehm, 1956), participants in the high dissonance condition are asked to make a difficult choice between two similarly attractive options. Participants in the low dissonance condition make an easy choice between one attractive option and one unattractive option. After making their choices, participants in the high dissonance condition increase their liking for what they chose and decrease their liking for what they didn't choose, a spreading of alternatives.

[Data from Brehm, 1956]

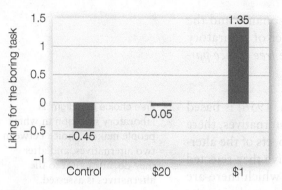

Figure 6.3

Support for Dissonance Theory Using the Induced Compliance Paradigm

When participants told another person that they liked a boring task, those who received $1 later reported liking the task more than those who received $20 and more than those who did not say they liked the task. Lacking sufficient justification for lying, participants in the $1 condition reduced dissonance by bringing their attitude in line with their behavior.

[Data from Festinger & Carlsmith, 1959]

Induced compliance paradigm A laboratory situation in which participants are induced to engage in a behavior that runs counter to their true attitudes.

in an hour of boring tasks, such as turning wooden square pegs one quarter turn at a time. One third of the participants, those in the control condition, were then simply asked how much they liked the tasks. As **FIGURE 6.3** indicates, these participants rated the tasks negatively. The other two thirds were told that the purpose of the study was to investigate the effects of expectations on performance and that they had been given no prior expectations because they were in the control condition. They were also told that the next participant was supposed to be given the expectation that the tasks would be very interesting, but the assistant who usually tells this to the next participant was running late. So the real participants were asked if they would go in the waiting room and tell the waiting participant (actually an experimental confederate) that the tasks were very interesting.

Half of these participants were offered $1 to say the boring tasks were interesting; the other half were offered $20 to do so. All of these participants agreed. Participants in these two conditions had the potential to experience dissonance because they told the confederate something that was inconsistent with their attitude about the tasks. However, receiving $20 provided an added cognition that justified the action and thereby reduced the overall level of dissonance. Therefore, when later asked about their true attitudes, these participants saw the tasks for what they really were—a boring waste of time. In contrast, $1 is not sufficient to justify saying that a boring task is interesting and so does not reduce the dissonance. How, then, did the people in this condition reduce the dissonance they felt? They actually changed their attitude to bring it in line with their statement, rating the tasks more positively than did the participants in the other conditions.

The situation that Festinger and Carlsmith created to arouse dissonance in the lab has become known as the **induced compliance paradigm**. In it, the participants are induced to comply with a request to engage in a behavior that runs counter to their true attitudes.

Factors That Affect the Magnitude of Dissonance Will people always experience dissonance when their behavior is inconsistent? Festinger argued that virtually any action a person engages in will be inconsistent with some cognition the person holds, but he did not think actions will always lead to strong feelings of dissonance. Much of the time people think or act in inconsistent ways without even being aware that they're doing so. Research shows that people feel dissonance primarily when the inconsistent cognitions are salient or highly accessible to consciousness (Newby-Clark et al., 2002; Swann & Pittman, 1975; Zanna et al., 1973). The level of dissonance that is aroused when inconsistent cognitions are salient or accessible depends on a number of factors.

Weak External Justification Dissonance will be high if you act in a way that is counter to your attitudes with only weak external justification to do so. On the other hand, if the external justification is very strong, dissonance will be low. As we saw in the Festinger and Carlsmith study, $1 was a weak justification, so participants changed their attitude to reduce dissonance; $20 was a strong external justification, so participants maintained their original attitude. External justification doesn't have to come in the form of money; it can also be praise, grades, a promotion, or pressure from loved ones or authority figures.

Choice   As the work on the free choice paradigm might suggest, a key factor in creating dissonance in the induced compliance paradigm is perceived choice (Brehm & Cohen, 1962). Just as $20 is an added cognition that reduces the overall dissonance, so too is a lack of choice. If some twisted character held a gun to your head and told you to say your mom is an evil person, you'd probably do it and not feel too much dissonance about it. But neither would you feel you had much choice in the matter, because although the statement would be inconsistent with your love for your mom, it is quite consistent with wanting to stay alive. One study demonstrating the role of choice (Linder et al., 1967) showed that when an experimenter simply ordered students to write an essay in favor of an attitude they did not agree with (known as a counterattitudinal essay)—banning controversial speakers from campus—the cognition "I didn't have a choice; I was just doing what I was told" kept the dissonance low. This is known as a *low choice condition*. On the other hand, when the experimenter asked students to write the counterattitudinal essay but emphasized that it was up to them whether or not to do so, the students were no longer able to justify their behavior by saying, "I didn't have a choice." In this *high choice condition*, the students experienced dissonance and therefore actually shifted their attitude toward supporting the ban on speakers. In the low choice condition, they did not.

Commitment   When people's freely chosen behavior conflicts with their attitudes, the more committed they are to the action, the more dissonance they experience. If the action can be taken back or changed easily, that reduces the extent to which the action is dissonant with one's attitude. A study by Davis and Jones (1960) illustrates this point. They induced participants to help the experimenter by insulting another person and either gave participants a sense of choice in doing so (high choice condition) or did not (low choice condition). In addition, half of the participants thought they would be able to talk to the person later and explain that they didn't really mean what they said and were just helping the experimenter (low commitment as the behavior could be taken back). The other half thought they would not be able to explain themselves to the other person later (high commitment to the behavior). If you're having a rough day and happen to treat someone badly and can't take it back, you might reduce your dissonance by deciding the person deserves the insult. And this is just what happened in the high choice, high commitment condition: The participants rated the person they insulted negatively. This did not occur in the low choice condition, and it also didn't occur in the high choice condition if the insult could be taken back.

A clever field experiment at the track by Knox and Inkster (1968) also supported the role of commitment. They showed that horse-race bettors are more confident their horse will win after they have placed their bets than they are just before doing so. The higher the commitment to a chosen course of action, the more dissonance, and consequently, the more one's beliefs and attitudes are likely to change to justify the actions.

Foreseeable Aversive Consequences   The more aversive the foreseeable consequences of an action are, the more important the inconsistent cognitions are, and thus, the more dissonance. Imagine you wrote an essay arguing that smoking cigarettes is a good thing to do (it's a legal way to get a buzz, it makes you look cool) and either: (*a*) threw it away or (*b*) read it to your 10-year-old cousin. In which case do you think you would experience more dissonance? The cognition "I wrote an essay in favor of smoking that no one read" is inconsistent with your beliefs about smoking, but it has no unwanted consequences and so arouses minimal dissonance. But encouraging a 10-year-old to smoke has foreseeable bad consequences indeed, so more dissonance will be aroused. In fact, research shows that action *b* would lead to a more positive view of smoking than would action *a* (Cooper & Fazio, 1984).

Cultural Influences   Although a consistent sense of self is an important aspect of being human, different situations may arouse dissonance for people who are from different cultures. For East Asians and people from other collectivistic cultures that value interdependence, *public* displays of inconsistency should arouse more dissonance because harmonious connections with others are very important to them. To test this idea, Kitayama and colleagues (2004) had Western and East Asian students engage in a free choice task either in private or with a reminder that others could see them. Whereas Westerners displayed the most spreading of alternatives (to justify their choice) when they completed the task in private, East Asians displayed the most spreading of alternatives when they thought about how others could be watching them.

Applications of Dissonance Theory

Induced Hypocrisy.   Outside the social psychology lab, it can be difficult to get people to engage in counterattitudinal actions and still feel they had a choice. So, in the early 1990s, Elliot Aronson, Jeff Stone, and their colleagues came up with a way to arouse dissonance that could be more easily used to change people's behavior in their daily lives. In this **induced hypocrisy paradigm**, people are asked to publicly advocate a position they already believe in, but, to arouse dissonance, the experimenters remind them of a time when their actions ran counter to that position. In one study, the researchers asked one group of sexually active students to make a short, videotaped speech for high school students about the importance of using condoms to prevent AIDS (Stone et al., 1994). They asked another group to think about such a speech but not to prepare one. Then they asked some participants from both groups to think about times they had failed to use condoms.

Induced hypocrisy paradigm A laboratory situation in which participants are asked to advocate an opinion they already believe in but then are reminded about a time when their actions ran counter to that opinion, thereby arousing dissonance.

The participants who both advocated the use of condoms and who were reminded of times they hadn't used them were in the induced hypocrisy condition and therefore were expected to experience dissonance. The researchers predicted that, to reduce this dissonance, these participants would be motivated to engage in behaviors consistent with the belief they had just advocated. After receiving $4 for taking part in the study, participants were told that the campus health center had made it possible for them to purchase condoms. As the experimenters predicted, 83% of the induced hypocrisy participants purchased at least one condom, whereas participants who either didn't make a pro-condom speech or didn't think about prior failures to use condoms purchased condoms less than 50% of the time. The participants who made a very public declaration of their beliefs but then were reminded of times when they had failed to live up to them felt more dissonance, which they then reduced by reasserting their commitment to safe-sex behaviors. Inducing hypocrisy has also been shown to promote conservation of water and electricity, safe driving, exercising and other health-protective behavior (**FIGURE 6.4**), and volunteering (Dickerson et al., 1992; Fointiat, 2004; Kantola et al., 1984; Stone & Fernandez, 2008; Wilding et al., 2019). Assuming that you could call people in their homes, how would you try to use induced hypocrisy to reduce their water usage in the coming months?

THINK ABOUT ▶

[Jochen Tack/Alamy]

Effort Justification: Loving What We Suffer For. One implication Festinger drew from dissonance theory is that people come to believe in and to love the things they suffer for. In other words, when people choose a course of action that involves unpleasant effort, suffering, and pain, they experience dissonance because of the costs of that choice. They reduce this dissonance by convincing themselves that what they suffered for is actually quite valuable; this phenomenon is known as **effort justification.**

Elliot Aronson and Jud Mills (1959) tested this idea in a study inspired by fraternity initiation practices. They proposed that people who go through these initiations reduce their dissonance in the face of the effort and humiliation that is sometimes involved by becoming fonder of and more committed to those organizations. If this is true, then all other things being equal, the more severe the initiation to gain inclusion in the group, the more the group should be liked.

To test this hypothesis, they solicited female students who expressed some interest in joining a group that met regularly to talk about sex. They manipulated whether there was an initiation required to join the group and, if there was, the difficulty of the initiation. In a control condition, the young women were immediately added to the group. In the mild initiation condition, participants had to read some mildly sexual words, such as *virgin*, in front of the male experimenter to join the group. In the severe initiation condition, they had to read some sexually explicit terms and then read a passage of explicit pornography in front of the experimenter. Imagine how difficult and embarrassing that would have been for young female college students back in 1959. In fact, from a modern perspective, the ethics of this study's methods have been called out as possible sexual harassment in psychological research (Young & Hegarty, 2019).

Regardless of the questionable ethicality of the study, it has been influential, and thankfully, the study thereafter became much more mundane. Once accepted into the group, participants first merely listened in on the group discussion. To their disappointment, it was a dreadfully boring discussion of the sex habits of insects. The women were then asked how much they liked the group discussion and how committed they were to the group. The women who had gone through nothing or only a mild initiation were not impressed with the discussion and also were not highly committed to the group. In contrast, the severe initiation group—those who had gone through a lot to get accepted—justified their effort by rating the discussion and their commitment to the group much more positively.

Children as young as six years old show some evidence of effort justification, finding stickers more valuable if they had to put in considerable effort to earn them (Benozio & Diesendruck, 2015). These findings and others like them have clear implications for both educational practices and organizational loyalty. Could this be why so many groups go out of their way to put new recruits through the wringer?

Might effort justification also play a role in the outcome of psychotherapy? Joel Cooper (1980) investigated whether a sense of choice would make an effortful therapy more effective. He gave participants with a severe snake phobia either a real form of therapy or a bogus one involving exercise, and he gave them either a high or low sense of choice. Compared with those who were not given a choice, participants who felt they freely chose the effortful therapy actually

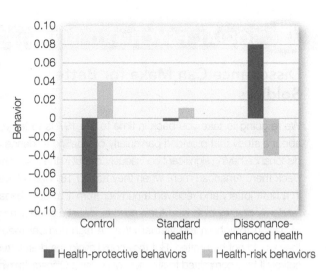

Figure 6.4

Dissonance Made Me Do It

Participants answered questions about an irrelevant topic (control condition) or health behaviors (health conditions). In the dissonance-enhanced health condition, participants read why these health behaviors are important and then answered questions about their current behavior, thereby eliciting dissonance about falling short. As a result, those assigned to this condition engaged in more health-protective behaviors and fewer health-risk behaviors over the next month.

[Data from Wilding et al., 2019]

Effort justification The phenomenon whereby people reduce dissonance by convincing themselves that what they suffered for is actually quite valuable.

SOCIAL PSYCH OUT IN THE WORLD

Dissonance Can Make for Better Soldiers

We're going to take you back in time to the 1970s to tell you about a study that provided particularly compelling evidence of dissonance having significant consequences out in the real world. Back then, American men, when they turned 18, were placed in a draft lottery and received a number from 1 to 365, based randomly on their birthdate. A low number meant a good chance of having to fight in the Vietnam War. A high number meant they would not be drafted. But they could avoid the draft lottery entirely if they committed to six years of Reserve Officers Training Corps (ROTC) service before the draft lottery numbers for their year were announced. This would mean military service, but they would remain in the United States rather than go to war.

The researcher Barry Staw (1974) studied men who chose the ROTC option and how dissonance affected satisfaction with their choice. He reasoned that men who chose to join the ROTC only to learn that they would not have been drafted anyway because of their high lottery number would experience a lot of dissonance about their six-year commitment to the ROTC. After all, they had made this huge time and effort commitment and then found out they would not have gone to Vietnam even if they hadn't joined ROTC. In contrast, Staw reasoned, guys who later learned that they would have been drafted had they entered the lottery should experience little dissonance. They knew that their decision to join the ROTC kept them on U.S. soil.

How did the guys in the first situation reduce the dissonance they felt? Staw predicted that the men who found out

showed reduced phobia: They were able to move 10 feet closer to a snake than those who had the therapy without a sense of having chosen to participate in it. And the bogus therapy worked just as well as the real one; the only thing that mattered was the participants' sense of having chosen to go through the effort. In a sense, to justify the effort, the participants made themselves improve.

Although neither Cooper nor we are suggesting that dissonance reduction is the only reason that psychotherapy can work, it may be one way patients can help themselves. The practical implication is that the client's choice in participating in the therapy may help motivate positive change—and it may explain why court-ordered programs to address such problems as drug addiction and anger management often don't work.

Minimal Deterrence: Advice for Parenting.   In the course of raising children, parents inevitably have to stop them from acting on many of their natural impulses, usually to deter them from doing things that are harmful or socially inappropriate. ("Don't put that in your mouth!" "Stop sitting on your sister!") A typical strategy that parents use to deter a child from misbehaving is to threaten with negative consequences such as spanking or grounding from video games. In these cases, the child has a strong external justification for not doing the behavior ("I don't want to get spanked!"), but this doesn't mean that the child loses the *desire* to do the behavior. A better way to deter the behavior would be to use the minimal level of external justification necessary—that is, to use *just enough* inducement or threat of punishment to prevent the behavior, while allowing the child to feel that she or he *freely chose* not to do that behavior. In these cases, the child has the dissonant cognitions "I'm not doing what I enjoy" and "The punishment for not doing it is pretty mild." To reduce this dissonance, the child may change his attitudes, coming to believe that he is not doing the behavior because he didn't really enjoy it in the first place.

Minimal deterrence Use of the minimal level of external justification necessary to deter unwanted behavior.

To test this idea, Aronson and Carlsmith (1963) developed a way to study the effects of **minimal deterrence.** They had four-year-olds at the Harvard Preschool play with five toys and rank them in order of liking. Each child's their lottery numbers would have been high would reduce their dissonance by liking the ROTC more. In support of this hypothesis, he found that these men increased the value they placed on their ROTC training and became better soldiers (as judged by their commanding officers) than the men who knew that the ROTC kept them from combat in Vietnam. The men who could not justify their commitment to the ROTC by saying, "Well, it's better than going to war" had to find some other way to justify their decision. They did this by becoming happier and better soldiers. Because the draft-lottery numbers randomly assigned these men to low- and high-dissonance conditions, this study capitalized on a natural experiment being conducted by the U.S. government to demonstrate the impact of dissonance and its reduction on people's responses to major life decisions.

[Bettmann/Getty Images]

second-favorite toy was then placed on a table. In the *no-threat* condition, the experimenter told the children he had to leave for a while, picked up the second-favorite toy to take with him, and told them they could play with any of the remaining toys while he was gone. In the *mild-threat* condition, the experimenter said that while he was gone, they could play with any toy except the one on the table: "I don't want you to play with the [toy on the table]. If you played with it, I would be annoyed." In the *severe-threat* condition, he said: "I don't want you to play with the [toy on the table]. If you play with it, I would be very angry. I would have to take all of my toys and go home."

During this temptation period, the children were watched through a one-way mirror. None of the children in the mild- and severe-threat conditions played with the forbidden toy. In the no-threat condition, they couldn't because the experimenter took it with him. When the experimenter returned (with the second-favorite toy in the no-threat condition), he asked the children to re-rank their liking for the five toys. As dissonance theory predicts, the children in the mild-threat condition now liked their formerly second-favorite toy *less* than did the children in the no-threat and severe-threat conditions. Because the mild threat of annoying the experimenter was only a minimal deterrent to not playing with the attractive forbidden toy, the children in the mild-threat condition reduced their liking for that toy to justify not playing with it. The kids in the severe-threat condition also refrained from playing with the toy when forbidden to do so. But they had plenty of external justification—the threats of anger and of having all the toys taken away—so they didn't change their attitudes toward the toy. A later study (Freedman, 1965) showed that this effect was still present 40 days later! So the message for parenting is clear: Using the minimal deterrence necessary to stop a child from engaging in a behavior will make it most likely that the child will internalize that she doesn't want to engage in that behavior anyway.

▼ The best way for parents to deter a child's undesired behavior, such as pulling the dog's tail, is to use the minimal intervention necessary to stop the behavior.

[Design Pics/Ron Nickel/Getty Images]

Dissonance as Motivation. How do we truly know that cognitive dissonance produces negative feelings that motivate changes in attitude and behavior? Evidence shows that engaging in counterattitudinal actions under high choice conditions elevates participants' ratings of discomfort, their levels of physiological arousal, and their neurological signs of motivation to exert control (Elliot & Devine, 1994; Harmon-Jones et al., 1996; Harmon-Jones et al., 2012). These indices of discomfort also predict the degree to which people will change their attitudes. Further, when people are feeling dissonance, they may alleviate the negative affect with other ways to feel better, such as drinking alcohol or increasing their religious faith (e.g., Randles et al., 2015; Steele et al., 1981). Other research suggests a role for *misattribution of arousal* (see chapter 5): When participants are given an alternative explanation for why they might be experiencing tension and discomfort, they no longer adjust their attitudes after engaging in inconsistent behavior (e.g., Higgins et al., 1979; Zanna & Cooper, 1974). Taken together, this evidence provides strong support for the idea that perceived inconsistency arouses negative affect (dissonance), which then motivates attitude change (dissonance reduction). While these findings support Festinger's cognitive dissonance theory, they also provided the first compelling laboratory evidence for a more general idea introduced by Freud at the dawn of the 20th century: that people's motivational concerns—in the case of dissonance, to deny cognitive inconsistencies—lead to psychological defenses that substantially influence people's thoughts and behavior.

Self-Consistency at the Macro Level: Sustaining a Sense of the Self as a Unified Whole

The picture on the left (**FIGURE 6.5a**) is a rendition of Dorothea Lange's classic photograph *Migrant Mother, Nipomo, Calif.* If we squint our eyes or look at the picture from a distance, we can make out a young mother with an expression of deep concern as her children huddle around her. And when we learn that this picture was taken during the Great Depression, we can imagine this woman's life struggle to care for herself and her family. But looking more closely, we discover that the image is made up of hundreds of tiny photographs of assorted aspects of this woman's surroundings, such as a door and a weather vane (**FIGURE 6.5b**). Although these tiny images make up the broader image, none of them captures the emotional significance of this woman's life as clearly as the broader perspective does.

In a similar sense, the question of identity—*Who am I?*—is easy to answer from a distance. We can step back and describe ourselves with broad generalizations such as *family oriented, outgoing, ambitious,* and so on. But up close we see that our lives are made up of thousands of separate memories, behaviors, and other elements of experience that have little meaning of their own. How do we integrate these lived experiences to establish consistency at the *macro* level of our overall self-concept?

Self-Consistency Across Situations If you were to describe yourself, you might say you are an introvert. But you might also be able to think of that time you belted out "Sweet Home Alabama" on karaoke night. Despite such inconsistencies, most people prefer

Figure 6.5

Dorothea Lange's Classic Photo: *Migrant Mother, Nipomo, Calif.*

Dorothea Lange's photograph powerfully captures one woman's struggles during the Great Depression. Many years later, Robert Silvers replicated this iconic image in a photo mosaic built out of Depression-era photographs of the American West. In this way, he conveys how many individual episodes and experiences make up a person's self-concept.

[Photomosaic by Robert Silvers]

self-concept clarity, a clearly defined, internally consistent, and temporally stable self-concept (Campbell, 1990). In fact, individuals with high self-concept clarity report being happier and better equipped to cope with life's challenges. Why? They are less sensitive to the feedback they receive from others, such as insults or nasty looks on the street. In contrast, individuals with low self-concept clarity tend to look to other people's feedback to understand who they are. Their attitudes toward themselves are therefore more likely to fluctuate, depending on whether they perceive that others view them positively or negatively.

One way people sustain a clear self-concept is by seeking out diagnostic information about themselves. People often search for ways to assess their traits and abilities to have an accurate view of themselves (e.g., Sedikides & Strube, 1997; Trope, 1986). They gather others' opinions of them, take personality and ability tests, see how they do on challenging tasks, and compare themselves with others.

People also tend to seek out others and social situations that confirm the way they view themselves, a phenomenon known as **self-verification.** People have a propensity to seek out others who corroborate their self-image, even when that means affiliating with people who don't think all that highly of them (Swann, 1983). Most people report thinking positively of themselves and prefer others who bolster their self-esteem. However, those with negative self-views (e.g., more depressed people) choose to interact with people who have a more negative impression of them (Swann et al., 1992). Although this preference for self-verification can help to solidify a clear and consistent sense of self, the unfortunate cost is that those with low self-esteem might avoid people who would actually help bolster and reinforce a more positive self-view.

Although self-concept clarity has benefits, to some degree, we're all aware that we act differently when we find ourselves in different roles or situations. Perhaps you're laid back and even silly when hanging out with friends, but a couple hours later at the gym you're ambitious and aggressive. The poet Walt Whitman (1855/2001, p. 113) acknowledged and even celebrated contradictions in his own self-concept:

> Do I contradict myself?
> Very well then I contradict myself,
> (I am large, I contain multitudes.)

Research on **self-complexity** examines the degree to which the self-concept is made up of many distinct aspects, including social roles (e.g., student), relationships (e.g., daughter), and activities (e.g., mountain biking). One benefit of high self-complexity is that the person can cope with difficulties in one area of life by drawing strength from others (Linville, 1985). However, self-complexity contributes to stress if the many facets of the self seem to be forced on the person or cause conflicting demands (e.g., Goode, 1960; Hirsh & Kang, 2016; McConnell et al., 2005).

My Story: Self-Consistency Across Time   To tie together separate pieces of experience over time into a coherent whole, each person constructs a **self-narrative,** or life story, in which he or she is the protagonist in a continuously unfolding drama of life, complete with characters, setting, plot, motivation, conflicts, and their resolutions (Bruner, 1990; Erickson, 1968; Gergen & Gergen, 1988; McAdams, 1993, 2001). Self-narratives integrate these various aspects of personal history, everyday experience, roles, and envisioned future into a

Self-concept clarity A clearly defined, internally consistent, and temporally stable self-concept.

Self-verification Seeking out other people and social situations that support the way one views oneself in order to sustain a consistent and clear self-concept.

Self-complexity The extent to which an individual's self-concept consists of many different aspects.

Self-narrative A coherent life story that connects one's past, present, and possible future.

unified, purposeful whole. Why do we need a narrative understanding of ourselves over time?

A clear self-narrative enhances well-being (Adler et al., 2016). It provides a basis for effective action, helping us to gauge what actions we should or should not attempt and what future challenges and obstacles might arise. But making sense of experience does more than facilitate action: It also provides psychological security by connecting separate experiences together into a coherent whole that is more significant and longer lasting than a series of passing moments. For example, you might view the time you overcame a bully in grade school and the time 10 years later that you stood up to an oppressive boss as fitting a theme of "standing up for myself."

Dan McAdams (2006) found that middle-aged and older adults tend to structure their life stories around two story patterns. One is the contamination story, in which the person first experiences good fortune but then experiences tragedy or failure and ends up in a place of bitterness or depression. But much more common is the uplifting redemption story. In this tale, people experience obstacles, challenges, and sometimes even tragedies but then turn their lives around and overcome those difficulties to feel successful in their lives. As you might guess, people who tell redemption stories report greater life satisfaction and well-being than those who tell contamination stories (e.g., McAdams & Guo, 2015). Think about your mom and dad: Which kind of life stories would they tell?

THINK ABOUT ▶

[michaeljung/Shutterstock]

Research supports the idea that a need for psychological security motivates people to integrate their personal past and present into a coherent story. For example, Landau and colleagues (2009) showed that after a reminder of death, participants attempted to restore psychological security by seeing their past experiences as meaningfully connected to the person they are now rather than as isolated events. Related studies show that whereas participants typically saw life as less meaningful after being reminded of death, this was not the case for participants who were prompted to think nostalgically about the past (Routledge et al., 2008). Nostalgia, by increasing the perceived connection of one's past to the present, can bolster people's view that their life has enduring significance (e.g., Sedikides et al., 2008; van Tilburg et al., 2019). Encouraging people to have nostalgic thoughts can also generate positive moods, boost self-esteem, enhance creativity and social connections, and increase meaning in life (e.g., Jiang et al., 2019; Routledge et al., 2011; van Tilburg et al., 2019). However, recent research suggests that nostalgia is a mixed experience, as when people spontaneously think nostalgically in their daily lives, it often is associated with negative rather than positive feelings (Newman et al., 2020).

Because self-narratives fit the past, present, and future into a consistent and meaningful structure, they can also help the person to "work through" the emotional pain caused by stressful events and experiences.

APPLICATION
Stories That Heal

The healing power of working through past traumas was emphasized by psychoanalysts such as Freud and has been supported by experimental studies by Jamie Pennebaker and colleagues. In one such study, people who wrote about an emotionally traumatic experience for four days, just 15 minutes a day, showed marked improvements in physical health (e.g., fewer physician visits for illness) many months later (Pennebaker & Beall, 1986).

How does narrating a traumatic event help with coping? Pennebaker and colleagues (1997) developed a computer program to analyze the language that individuals use while disclosing emotional topics. They found that people who narrated the trauma using words associated with seeking insight and cause-and-effect connections (e.g., *because*) showed the most pronounced health improvements. Thus, narrating can translate vague, negative feelings into a coherent explanation of why the event happened and what it means for the self, which in turn helps the person to cope with the event.

Not only do self-narratives create meaning from the past, they also allow people to view their present self as being on a stable path to future selves that will make a lasting mark on the world. Whereas perceiving the events in the coming week (e.g., picking up business cards) as a series of separate activities offers little meaning to one's actions, seeing the same activities as being tied to one's long-term goals (e.g., advancing my career) helps sustain a conception of one's life as significant (Landau et al., 2011). People with a sense of continuity into the future may even view themselves as literally continuing after their death to eternal life, or they may picture themselves as being symbolically immortalized through their identification with enduring entities and causes (e.g., the nation, the corporation), memories, and cultural achievements in the sciences and arts (Greenberg et al., 2014). ■

 APPLICATION
Educational Achievement

Personal narratives include **possible selves**, vivid images of what the self might become in the future. Some possible selves are positive ("the successful designer me," "the party animal me"), whereas others are negative ("the unemployed me," "the lonely me"). Possible selves give a face to a person's goals, aspirations, fears, and insecurities. For example, your personal goal of succeeding in college probably is not some vague abstraction but more likely takes shape in your mind as a vivid image of a positive possible self, "academic star me," up on stage receiving a prestigious award.

Possible selves help motivate and guide our behavior (Markus & Nurius, 1986) because they make us aware of the actions we need to take to become those selves in the future. In one demonstration, Daphna Oyserman and colleagues (2006) went into low-income urban school districts where failure is depressingly common. The researchers randomly assigned eighth-graders to sit in their regular homeroom period (control) or to take part in an intervention called "School-to-Jobs" twice weekly over a seven-week period. During the early part of this intervention, participants were asked to imagine academic possible selves, at one point identifying photographs of adults that fit their visions of a good future. A couple of weeks later, they were asked to describe specific strategies they need to use to realize their academic possible selves, such as attending class and completing their homework. Students in the intervention condition had fewer classroom behavior problems and better grades even a year later, suggesting that thinking about possible selves in the future, when combined with pragmatic thinking about how to get there, can motivate people to take constructive action in the present. ■

Possible selves Images of what the self might become in the future.

SECTION REVIEW The Motive to Maintain a Consistent Self

People strive make sense of their lives by being consistent at the micro level of day-to-day experience, but consistency from the broader, macro perspective is essential to understanding the whole picture.

Cognitive dissonance theory explains how people minimize inconsistency between their cognitions.

- Research using the free choice paradigm shows that after people choose between two alternatives, they reduce dissonance by emphasizing the positive aspects of the chosen alternative and the negative aspects of the rejected alternative.

- Research using the induced compliance paradigm shows that when people perceive insufficient external justification for choosing to say or do something against their initial beliefs, they change their beliefs to reduce dissonance.

- Dissonance increases with less external justification and more perceived choice, commitment, and foreseeable negative consequences.

- In cultures that value interdependence, public displays of inconsistency arouse more dissonance because harmonious relationships are so valued.

- When faced with an apparent discrepancy between past behavior and a currently advocated position, people engage in behaviors to reassert their commitment to the recently advocated position.

- After working hard for a goal, people justify the effort by convincing themselves that the goal is valuable. When a minimal level of external justification is used to deter behavior, people internalize that they don't want to engage in the behavior anyway.

Self-consistency is an important way that people make sense of their lives as a whole.

- Self-concept clarity is a clear sense of *who one is* from one situation to the next. High self-concept clarity supports psychological well-being.

- A complex self-concept, as defined by many distinct roles and activities, may be a buffer against stress if those aspects of self are freely chosen and controlled.

- Self-narratives are coherent stories explaining how one's past, present, and future cohere into a unified whole. Threats to psychological security increase reliance on self-narratives. Talking or writing about a painful event can help a person cope with stressful experiences.

- Envisioning possible selves can help motivate people to achieve their long-term goals.

Learning Outcomes

- Differentiate self-esteem as a trait and a state.
- Describe the ways that people maintain and defend self-esteem.
- List the functions of self-esteem.
- Explain self-esteem stability and the consequences of high or low stability.
- List important implications of the need for self-esteem.

The Self-Esteem Motive: Establishing and Defending One's Value

Although a consistent self is desired, people also want that view of self to be positive. When your current author (Jamie) was growing up, his brother used to run around the house exclaiming, "I want to be special!" Although few of us may admit it so blatantly, who hasn't dreamed about becoming a world-famous scientist, an admired actor or singer, or a sports superstar? These aspirations reflect something very basic about human beings: We strive to view ourselves as valuable, to bolster feelings of self-esteem, and to defend our positive view of ourselves when it is called into question.

What Is Self-Esteem, and Where Does It Come From?

Self-esteem is the level of positive feeling you have about yourself, the extent to which you value yourself. Self-esteem is generally thought of as a *trait*, a general attitude toward the self ranging from very positive to very negative. Researchers have developed a number of self-report measures to assess self-esteem in both children and adults (e.g., Coopersmith, 1967; Rosenberg, 1965). Using such measures in longitudinal studies, researchers have shown that self-esteem is fairly stable over a person's life span (e.g., Orth & Robins, 2014; Trzesniewski et al., 2003).

Self-esteem The level of positive feeling one has about oneself.

However, self-esteem can also be viewed as a *state*, a feeling about the self that can temporarily increase or decrease in positivity in response to changing circumstances, achievements, and setbacks. In other words, someone whose trait self-esteem is pretty low can still experience a temporary self-esteem boost after getting a good grade. Similarly, someone with normally high trait self-esteem can experience a dip in state self-esteem after having his marriage fall apart.

The fact that self-esteem can remain stable as a trait but vary as a state indicates that a number of factors influence it. The stability of trait self-esteem from childhood to adulthood suggests that the reflected appraisals, social comparisons, and standards of value we experience as children have a lasting impact on our sense of self-worth. Research supports this idea (Harter, 1998). For example, a positive family environment in early childhood predicts higher self-esteem in adulthood (Orth, 2019). Of course, what people base their self-worth upon is often quite different, depending on the culture in which they are raised. In individualistic cultures such as the United States, displaying one's personal qualities and accomplishments garners self-esteem, whereas in more collectivistic cultures such as Japan, displays of modesty and pleasing the family patriarch would better improve self-esteem (Markus & Kitayama, 1991; Sedikides et al., 2003). Cultures also prescribe different standards of value for individuals at different stages of one's life; what made you feel valuable in grade school is likely to be different from what gave you self-esteem in high school, and those standards continue to change throughout adulthood.

▲ Especially in collectivistic cultures, even as an adult, showing respect and caring for one's parents is an important basis of self-esteem.
[MIXA/Getty Images]

In addition, because cultural worldviews offer individuals multiple paths to feeling valuable and successful, individuals raised in the same culture are likely to stake their self-esteem on different types of activities. Crocker and Wolfe (2001) studied these differences and found that whereas one person may base self-esteem on being physically attractive, another person's self-esteem may be tied to academic accomplishments. Other common contingencies are others' approval, virtue, and God's love. People's state self-esteem increases and decreases primarily in response to achievements and setbacks in the areas of life that are most important to them.

Maintaining and Defending Self-Esteem

Imagine this is your first couple of weeks at a new university or college. A group of students is discussing what kind of music they like, and you want to join the conversation. But you're nervous. Will they like you? After a while, you decide to enter the conversation and note your fondness for Gregorian chants. A painful silence in the conversation follows. Your contribution is ignored by

some and ridiculed by others. Wait until they hear about your enthusiasm for ice fishing!

As we navigate through our social worlds, we encounter a seemingly limitless cascade of challenges and events that can potentially threaten our sense of ourselves as persons of worth. Focus on yourself for a moment. What are the soft spots in your self-esteem armor? Of course, it's never easy to admit or think about such things, but the more we understand about ourselves, ultimately the better off we are.

How can we maintain self-esteem in light of all these potential threats? It turns out that people use many strategies to defend self-esteem and enhance it when possible.

Self-Serving Attributions The self-serving attributional bias is to make external attributions for bad things that one does but internal attributions for good things one does. In other words, people are quick to take credit for their successes and blame the situation for their failures (e.g., Snyder et al., 1976), a biased way of viewing reality that helps people maintain high levels of self-esteem (Fries & Frey, 1980; Gollwitzer et al., 1982; McCarrey et al., 1982).

What are the consequences of making self-serving attributions for our behavior? Some research suggests this bias helps support mental health. For example, self-serving attributions seem to work well for preserving self-esteem and are common among well-adjusted people. Individuals suffering from depression tend *not* to make self-serving attributions, viewing themselves as equally responsible for their successes and their failures (Alloy & Abramson, 1979). So some level of self-serving bias in attributions is probably useful for mental health (Humberg et al., 2019; Taylor & Brown, 1988). However, this bias may interfere with an accurate understanding of poor outcomes. This is a problem because understanding the true causes of one's poor outcomes is often very helpful in improving one's outcomes in the future.

Self-handicapping Placing obstacles in the way of one's own success to protect self-esteem from a possible future failure.

Self-Handicapping In a strategy known as **self-handicapping**, people set up excuses to protect their self-esteem from a failure that may happen in the future (Berglas & Jones, 1978). Suppose you decide to go out with friends and stay out late the night before an important exam. How would that be a preemptive strategy to protect your self-esteem? If you fail the test, you can say, "Well, it's because I was celebrating my best friend's birthday the night before." And if you happen to do well, this makes your success all the more remarkable. That way, even though you're doing something likely to hinder (handicap) your own performance, you can attribute your failure to the excuse (e.g., partying) and keep your self-esteem intact.

People self-handicap when they are especially focused on the implications of their performance for self-esteem rather than on getting the rewards associated with success (Greenberg et al., 1984). In addition, Berglas and Jones (1978) showed that self-handicapping stems from uncertainty about one's competence. People who have experienced success in the past but are uncertain about whether they can sustain success in the future are the most likely to self-handicap.

Self-handicapping has been used to explain a wide variety of behaviors in which individuals appear to sabotage their own success: abusing alcohol or other drugs, procrastinating, generating test anxiety, or not preparing for an exam or performance. Indeed, perhaps the most common forms of self-handicapping involve denying one's desire for success and not trying one's hardest (e.g., Reich & Wheeler, 2016). If you don't try your hardest, then you can attribute poor performance to a lack of effort rather than a lack of ability. Psychologists often attribute lack of effort to feelings of helplessness or fear of success. But often instead what people are doing is self-handicapping. How do we know? When people who fear they will not succeed on a task are given a handy excuse for why they might fail (such as the presence of distracting music), they actually perform better (Snyder et al., 1981). The excuse reduces their concern about protecting their self-esteem, which frees them to put in their best effort.

Some individuals are more prone to self-handicapping than others (Eyink et al., 2017; Kimble & Hirt, 2005). In addition, men are more likely than women to self-handicap (McCrea et al., 2008).

THINK ABOUT

[GlowImages/AGE Fotostock]

The Better-Than-Average Effect   Think for a moment about the percentage of the chores you do around your house or dorm. Then ask your roommate what percentage of the chores she thinks she does. We're betting the total will well exceed 100% (Allison et al., 1989). This example illustrates how people often overestimate the frequency of their own good deeds relative to those of others (Epley & Dunning, 2000). In fact, as we described in chapter 5, most people think they are above average on most culturally valued characteristics and behaviors, including their moral virtue (Tappin & McKay, 2017; Taylor & Brown, 1988). Clearly, we can't all be above average on these characteristics, so how do people maintain this perception that they're superior? When people fall short, they tend to overestimate how many other people also would fall short. In contrast, when people do good things, they tend to underestimate how many other people also do good things (e.g., Campbell, 1986). Because of social media, however, there is one domain in which most people in the United States think they are worse than average: They tend to think other people have richer social lives than they do (Deri et al., 2017)!

Projection   Another way people avoid seeing themselves as having negative characteristics is to try to view others as possessing those traits which they fear they themselves possess. For example, if I fear that I'm overly hostile, I might be more likely to see others as hostile. Classic psychoanalytic psychologists (Freud, 1921/1955; Jung & von Franz, 1968) labeled this form of self-esteem defense **projection.**

In one series of studies (Schimel et al., 2003), students were given personality feedback showing that they had high or low levels of a negative trait such as repressed hostility or dishonesty. Participants then read about a person, Donald, whose behavior was ambiguously hostile (or dishonest). Those participants given an opportunity to evaluate Donald saw him as possessing more of the trait they feared they might possess (e.g., hostility). Moreover, after evaluating Donald, they saw themselves as having less of that trait than participants who were not given the opportunity to rate (and thus project onto) Donald. Because they saw the feared trait in someone else, they no longer feared that they had it!

Projection Assigning to others those traits that people fear they possess themselves.

Symbolic Self-Completion   In the early 1900s, Alfred Adler noted that when people feel inferior in a valued domain of life—he called that feeling an *inferiority complex*—they often compensate by striving very hard to improve in that domain (Adler, 1964). This can be a very productive kind of compensation for one's weaknesses. However, the **theory of symbolic self-completion** (Wicklund & Gollwitzer, 1982) suggests that people often compensate for their shortcomings in a shallower way. When people aspire to an important identity, such as lawyer or nurse, but are not there yet and worry they may not get there, they feel incomplete. To compensate for such feelings, they often acquire and display symbols that support their desired identity, even if those symbols are rather superficial.

Theory of symbolic self-completion The idea that when people perceive that a self-defining aspect is threatened, they feel incomplete, and then try to compensate by acquiring and displaying symbols that support their desired self-definition.

Consider a woman who has always wanted to be a doctor but then experiences some kind of setback, such as getting a poor MCAT score or making a mistaken diagnosis while interning. This poses a threat to her view of herself as an aspiring doctor, making her feel incomplete. She compensates by amassing symbols of competence as a premed student, medical student, or doctor, perhaps prominently displaying her medical degree or wearing a lab coat and stethoscope around her neck whenever possible. In one study, male college students given feedback that they were not well suited for their career goals became very boastful regarding their relevant strengths—even when interacting with an attractive female student who they knew did not like boastful people (Gollwitzer & Wicklund, 1985). In contrast, people who are secure in their identity are more open to acknowledging their limitations and do not need to boast of their intentions or display symbols of their worth (Wicklund & Gollwitzer, 1982).

Recent research has focused on individuals who have just acquired a symbol of completeness. For instance, law students who were induced to state publicly their positive intention to study actually acted on this intention less often than students who were made to keep this intention private. Going public with their intention enhanced their symbolic completeness, thus ironically making further striving for their identity goal of becoming successful lawyers less necessary (Gollwitzer et al., 2009). This finding suggests a possible negative consequence of using social media to broadcast one's progress toward goals by posting, for example, calories burned or books read. These symbols might give you a premature sense of having achieved your desired identity. As a result, you may neglect to take concrete steps toward fully achieving your identity goal.

Compensation and Self-Affirmation Early personality theorists such as Gardner Murphy and colleagues (Murphy et al., 1937) and Gordon Allport (1937) noted that people possess considerable flexibility in the way they maintain self-esteem and deal with threats to the self. When self-esteem or self-consistency is threatened in one domain, people often shore up their overall sense of self-worth by inflating their value in an unrelated domain. This has been labeled **fluid compensation**, which essentially allows a person to think, "I may not be achieving success in this domain, but I rule in that other one" (Greenberg & Pyszczynski, 1985a; Randles et al., 2015). For example, when participants were given personality feedback that they were not very socially sensitive, they responded by viewing themselves more positively on unrelated traits (Baumeister & Jones, 1978).

Steele's **self-affirmation theory** (Steele, 1988) has provided the most influential modern account of these phenomena. The theory posits that people need to see themselves as having global integrity and worth but can do so in flexible ways. As a result, people respond less defensively to threats to one aspect of themselves if they first bring to mind another valued aspect of themselves—that is, if they self-affirm.

For example, college students participated in a study immediately after their intramural sports team either won or lost a game (Sherman et al., 2007). Players generally displayed a defensive self-serving bias, taking more responsibility for a win than a loss. However, players who had self-affirmed by writing about something else they valued took equal responsibility for their team's victory or defeat.

Self-affirmation also reduces people's defensiveness when they are faced with threatening information about their health (Epton et al., 2015). For example, whereas smokers tend to respond to cigarette warning labels by denying the

Fluid compensation After a blow to self-esteem in one domain, the process of shoring up one's overall sense of self-worth by bolstering how one thinks of oneself in an unrelated domain.

Self-affirmation theory The idea that people respond less defensively to threats to one aspect of themselves if they think about another valued aspect of themselves.

Achieve
Social Psych in Everyday Life: Abhay

risk or downplaying their smoking habit, these defensive responses are minimized if smokers first affirm core personal values or morals (Harris et al., 2007). Similarly, self-affirmation helps overweight people successfully lose weight and develop healthier lifestyles (Logel et al., 2019; **FIGURE 6.6**). These self-affirmations work by providing a broader and more positive perspective on oneself that makes specific concerns seem less troubling while also activating reward pathways in the brain (Critcher & Dunning, 2015; Dutcher et al., 2016; Sherman, 2013). Although self-affirmation and fluid compensations are useful strategies for indirectly minimizing self-esteem threats, people generally prefer to counteract their shortcomings directly when feasible (Stone et al., 1994). Consistent with symbolic self-completion theory, this is especially true when the threat pertains to an important identity goal (Gollwitzer et al., 2013).

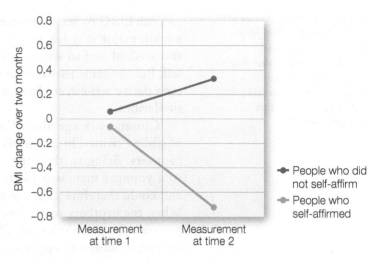

Figure 6.6

Self-Affirmation and Weight Loss

A study of women at least somewhat dissatisfied with their weight showed that for women with a high initial body mass index (BMI), having them affirm their values led to significant weight loss over a two-month period.
[Data from Logel et al., 2019]

Social Comparison and Identification In chapter 5, we noted that social comparison plays a substantial role in how people assess their own abilities and attributes. As a consequence, comparing ourselves with others who are superior to us leads to upward comparisons that can threaten self-esteem, whereas comparing ourselves with others who are inferior leads to downward comparisons that help us feel better about ourselves. Generally, people prefer to compare themselves with others who are a bit less accomplished than themselves, so comparisons can bolster their self-esteem (Wills, 1981). If you're a moderately experienced tennis player, beating a similarly experienced friend in tennis in close matches feels better than either getting beaten by a pro or trouncing a novice.

Although comparison with successful others can hurt self-esteem, affiliating with successful others can help bolster self-esteem when people **bask in reflected glory**, or BIRG (Cialdini et al., 1976). If you're associated with an individual or group that is successful, then that reflects positively on you. Robert Cialdini and colleagues (1976) demonstrated this by observing that college students were more likely to wear school-affiliated apparel on the Monday after their football team had won than they were after it had lost.

Although research on BIRGing shows that people sometimes gain self-esteem by affiliating with very successful others, other evidence suggests that people could lose self-esteem by comparing themselves with more successful others. How can other people's successes trigger opposite effects? Abe Tesser's (1988) **self-evaluation maintenance model** proposes that people adjust how similar they think they are to successful others, both to minimize threatening comparisons and to maximize self-esteem-bolstering identifications. When another person outperforms you in a type of activity that is important to your self-esteem, perceiving the other person as dissimilar makes comparison less appropriate. But when the domain is not relevant to your self-esteem, comparison is not threatening, so

Basking in reflected glory Associating oneself with successful others to help bolster one's own self-esteem.

▲ People often wear the jerseys of very successful sports figures to BIRG. This is why six-time Super Bowl–winning quarterback Tom Brady's jersey was the best-selling jersey of 2019.
Boston Globe/Getty Images

Self-evaluation maintenance model The idea that people adjust their perceived similarity to successful others to minimize threatening comparisons and maximize self-esteem-supporting identifications.

you can BIRG by seeing yourself as similar to the successful other. For example, a math major may feel threatened by comparison with the math department's star student and so will see the math star as a very different person than herself. But the same person won't be threatened by a star music student and may even derive self-esteem from affiliating with that person and focusing on their similarities.

Closeness in age also affects self-evaluation maintenance in the context of sibling rivalry. In one study, Tesser (1980) examined relationships between brothers. Being further apart in age makes comparisons less relevant, and so a younger male was likely to see himself as "just like my older brother" and could therefore gain self-esteem through identifying with him (BIRGing). When the brothers were closer in age (i.e., less than three years apart), comparison was more relevant. This self-esteem threat strained the relationship, leading to more perceptions of difference and more friction. So a key variable that determines whether people identify with or distance themselves from a successful other is whether comparison is or is not relevant. If it is relevant, people distance; if it is not, they identify. Kids and amateur basketball players can safely admire and view themselves as generally similar to LeBron James, but if you were a fellow NBA player, you'd be more likely to think you're very different from him.

APPLICATION

An Example of Everyday Self-Esteem Defenses: Andrea's Day

To summarize this section on self-esteem defenses, let's consider how a fictional college student named Andrea might employ such defenses in a typical day.

Andrea wakes up and sends a text to her brother, telling him that her close friend Megan just won a poetry competition. "I don't know anything about poetry," she writes, "but I'm so proud of her!!" (*basking in reflected glory*). Driving to work, Andrea is appalled at how bad drivers are in this town. "The majority of these people don't have a clue about how to drive," she tells herself (*the better-than-average effect*). She's walking to class when her mother calls her and starts yelling about how Andrea forgot to call Grandma and wish her a happy birthday yesterday. Andrea yells back, "Well, I totally would've if you had just reminded me!!" and hangs up (*self-serving attribution*).

She still has some lingering doubts about her value as a granddaughter, but she reminds herself that her job right now is to do well in school (*self-affirmation*) and that she is an excellent student (*fluid compensation*). After class, a friend approaches Andrea and asks if she wants to come to a free ballroom dance class that evening. She agrees to go to the class but decides to work out at the gym that afternoon. Later, as they are walking to the studio, Andrea tells her friend how tired and sore she is from working out earlier (*self-handicapping*). Andrea is stunned to see what a good dancer her friend is and just how much more graceful her friend is than Andrea could ever hope to be. Andrea then says to herself, "My friend and I are such different people. Dancing is her thing, not mine" (*self-evaluation maintenance*).

She leaves the class to meet up with her boyfriend for dinner. At one point during dinner, Andrea looks out the restaurant window and notices a particularly attractive guy whom she's admired a couple times. A moment later, she looks up and notices her boyfriend glancing at another woman. Instantly she starts berating her boyfriend about being loyal and keeping his eyes off other women (*projection*). That night Andrea posts photos of herself receiving an academic award and vacationing in Europe on Instagram so that everyone can see that she is educated and cosmopolitan (*symbolic self-completion*). She goes to bed, secure in the knowledge that she is a person of value. ■

Why Do People Need Self-Esteem?

Clearly people use a wide range of strategies to defend their self-esteem, but why are they so driven to do so? Do we have an innate need to view ourselves positively? Perhaps, but our needs typically serve some function. The need for food serves the larger purpose of making sure that we get the nutrition we need for survival. But what purpose does self-esteem serve?

Self-Esteem as an Anxiety Buffer   One answer to this question comes from the existential perspective of terror management theory. As we described in chapter 2, this theory starts with the idea that we humans are uniquely aware of the fact that our lives will inevitably end one day. Because this fact can create a great deal of anxiety, people are motivated to view themselves as more than merely material creatures who perish entirely when they die. According to terror management theory, this is precisely the function of self-esteem: to help the individual feel like an enduringly significant being who will continue in some way beyond death. In this way, self-esteem functions as an **anxiety buffer**, protecting the individual from the anxiety stemming from the awareness of his or her mortality. The poet T. S. Eliot anticipated this idea in his eloquent ode on low self-esteem, "*The Love Song of J. Alfred Prufrock*" (1917/1964, p. 14):

> I have seen the moment of my greatness flicker,
> And I have seen the eternal Footman hold my coat, and snicker,
> And in short, I was afraid.

Anxiety buffer The idea that self-esteem allows people to face threats with their anxiety minimized.

Self-esteem serves this anxiety-buffering function over the course of development. As children, we minimize our anxieties by being good because if we are good, our parents love and protect us. As we develop and become more and more aware of our mortality and the limitations of our parents, we shift our primary source of protection from our parents to the culture at large. As adults, we therefore base our psychological security not on being good little girls or boys but on being valued citizens, lovers, group members, artists, doctors, lawyers, scientists, and so forth. We feel high self-esteem when we believe that we have or will accomplish things and fulfill roles our culture views as significant, that we are valued by the individuals, groups, and deities we cherish, and that we are making a lasting mark on the world. In this way, we can maintain faith that we amount to more than mere biological creatures fated only to perish entirely.

If self-esteem protects people from death-related anxiety, then we would expect that when self-esteem is high, people will be less anxious. And this is true. Compared with those low in self-esteem, high-self-esteem people are generally less anxious; less susceptible to phobias, anxiety disorders, and death anxiety; and better able to cope with threat and stress (e.g., Abdel-Khalek, 1998; Hornsey, Faulkner et al., 2018; Lee & Way, 2019). However, because this evidence is correlational, it may mean that high self-esteem buffers anxiety, but it also could mean that functioning well with minimal anxiety raises people's self-esteem.

▲ Many organizations and professions bestow awards and medals on their members to show that they are making valued contributions, thereby validating their self-worth.

[altrendo images/Juice Images/Getty Images]

More compelling evidence that self-esteem buffers anxiety comes from experimental studies. In a study by Greenberg, Solomon, and colleagues (1992), half of the participants were randomly assigned to have their self-esteem boosted by receiving very positive feedback about their personality, supposedly based on questionnaires they had filled out a few weeks earlier; the other half were given more neutral personality feedback. Then participants watched a 10-minute video that was either neutral or depicted graphic scenes of death. Participants then reported how anxious they felt.

When the personality feedback was relatively neutral, participants reported feeling more anxiety after the threatening video than after the neutral video, as you might expect. However, if they had first received the positive personality feedback, participants who watched the threatening video did not report any more anxiety than those who watched the neutral video. The boost to self-esteem allowed them to be calm even in the face of gruesome reminders of mortality. Not only do people report less anxiety after a self-esteem boost, their bodies show fewer signs of it. In two additional studies, participants anticipating receiving electric shocks were less physiologically aroused if they first received a self-esteem boost (Greenberg, Solomon et al., 1992). Self-esteem accomplishes this anxiety buffering by increasing activation of the parasympathetic nervous system, which helps to calm people (Martens et al., 2008), and by increasing cortical control over the amygdala (Yanagisawa et al., 2016).

▲ Zestcott et al. (2016) found that a reminder of mortality improved one-on-one basketball performance among students who valued their playing ability.

[ARENA Creative/Shutterstock]

Another way to assess this function of self-esteem is to find out if reminding people of their own mortality leads them to strive even harder to bolster their self-esteem and to defend it against threats. In the first direct tests of this hypothesis, Israeli soldiers who reported that they derived self-esteem from their driving ability drove more boldly if they were first reminded of their mortality (Ben-Ari et al., 1999). Additional studies have shown that mortality salience also increases strivings in other self-esteem-relevant domains, such as demonstrating one's strength, basketball skill, intelligence, and generosity (e.g., Jonas et al., 2002; Zestcott et al., 2016).

If self-esteem shields us from our fear of death, then our shield should be weakened when our self-esteem is threatened, making us more likely to think about death. Across a series of studies, Hayes, Schimel, Faucher, and Williams (2008) found that when participants experienced a threat to their self-esteem, thoughts of death became more accessible to consciousness. In sum, a substantial body of converging evidence indicates that self-esteem provides protection from basic anxieties about vulnerability and mortality.

Social Functions of Self-Esteem Two other perspectives on the function of self-esteem emphasize its social aspects. First, Jerome Barkow (1989) proposed that people desire self-esteem to maximize their social status, just as monkeys try to maximize their position in a dominance hierarchy. Barkow proposed that those of our ancestors who were most focused on seeking high social status had the most access to fertile mates and resources to nurture their offspring, therefore perpetuating their genes into future generations. To the extent that desiring self-esteem aids in attaining high social status, this desire would have been selected for over the course of hominid evolution.

Second, according to Mark Leary and colleagues' (1995) **sociometer model**, a basic function of self-esteem is to indicate to the individual how much he or she is accepted by other people. According to this model, self-esteem is like the gas gauge in your car. Just as a gas gauge lets you know when the gas is too low

Sociometer model The idea that a basic function of self-esteem is to indicate to the individual how much he or she is accepted by other people.

and you need to fill up, self-esteem is like a *sociometer* that lets you know if you are currently receiving enough social acceptance to satisfy your need to belong. Consequently, the more you perceive yourself to be liked and accepted by others, the higher your level of self-esteem. The sociometer model proposes that when people appear to be motivated to maintain self-esteem, they actually are motivated to feel a sense of belongingness with others. Although both Barkow's status-maximizing perspective and Leary and Baumeister's sociometer model emphasize the social functions of self-esteem, the former emphasizes the desire to stand out and be better than others, whereas the latter emphasizes fitting in with and gaining the acceptance of others. Each perspective captures something true about self-esteem. Barkow's analysis can help explain why people often sacrifice being liked in order to be successful and gain status. The sociometer model can't explain that, but it can help explain why people sometimes sacrifice status and material gain in order to fit in with the group. However, both perspectives have difficulty explaining why people are so likely to bias their judgments to preserve their self-esteem. For example, people often feel they are more worthy than other people think they are. If self-esteem were primarily an indicator of something of evolutionary value, such as social status or belonging, rather than something that buffers anxiety, why do people seem to distort their beliefs to inflate their views of themselves? It would be akin to moving the gas gauge with your fingers to convince yourself you had gas in your tank when you actually did not. Does this disconfirm the Barkow status and Leary sociometer models? Or is there some way to reconcile the models or revise them to fit with the research on self-esteem defenses?

THINK ABOUT

[winnond/Shutterstock]

The Influence of Treatment by Others: Ostracism

Despite their different emphases, terror management theory and the status and sociometer perspectives all suggest that self-esteem is influenced by one's popularity (Reitz et al., 2016) and how one is treated by others. Imagine seeing three kids playing a harmless game of catch, or imagine that you and two friends are outside on a sunny day, tossing around a Frisbee. What if they stopped including you in the game? How would you feel?

Kip Williams and colleagues set up a computerized analog of this situation that they call *cyberball* (Zadro et al., 2004). In cyberball, participants play a virtual game of catch with two other people who are presumably playing from other computer terminals. When you are a participant, your "hand" is shown at the bottom of the screen (see **FIGURE 6.7**). It catches the ball when another

Figure 6.7

Kip Williams's Cyberball Game

In his studies of ostracism, Williams and colleagues (e.g., Zadro et al., 2004) had participants start playing this cyber game of catch with what they believed were two other participants. Soon after, the other two players' avatars stopped throwing the ball to the participant's avatar, thereby creating an intense feeling of being ostracized.

[Courtesy Professor Kipling D. Williams, Purdue University]

participant has thrown it in your direction, and you hit one of several keys to indicate which player you will throw the ball to next. In one condition, the game progresses in this way for several minutes, with everyone getting the ball an equal numbers of times. But in another condition, after a minute or so, the others players stop throwing the ball to you, and your poor little virtual hand is left looking empty and lonely at the bottom of the screen while the others continue the game.

Even this simple five-minute experience of being excluded by people a participant had never met and never would interact with significantly lowered the participant's self-esteem. In fact, even when participants were told that they were the only person playing and that the other figures were controlled by the computer, they felt lower self-esteem when the ball didn't come their way!

Looking at this from a neuroscience perspective, we find evidence that when people are excluded in a situation such as cyberball, they show activation in the *anterior cingulate cortex* (Eisenberger et al., 2003). This brain region is generally responsible for detecting when a given situation isn't meeting our goals. It also is activated when people experience physical pain, suggesting that sticks and stones might break your bones, but words—if they suggest rejection—might be perceived as being just as hurtful. If even a minor slight such as exclusion from cyberball lowers self-esteem, it is not surprising that prolonged experience of social rejection and ostracism can damage both psychological and physical health (Murphy et al., 2015; Williams & Zadro, 2001).

Protecting and Enhancing Self-Esteem: Cultural Differences

As we have seen, a vast array of evidence indicates that self-esteem is of great importance to people. But seen from a cultural perspective, most of this work has been conducted in relatively individualistic cultures. Is self-esteem important in more collectivistic cultures as well?

Some social psychologists have argued it is not. They suggest that people from collectivistic cultures, such as those in East Asia, place more value on group cohesion and the self's connection with others (Markus & Kitayama, 1991). East Asian cultures also value traits such as self-criticism and emotional restraint, which are not embraced so strongly by North American culture. Does this mean that self-esteem is not a driving concern to people from East Asian cultures?

No, it does not. The evidence clearly indicates that people in all cultures strive for self-esteem and get value from it (Kim & Pettit, 2019; Sedikides et al., 2005; Seery & Quinton, 2015). In considering this point, keep in mind our earlier discussion of how self-esteem comes from living up to cultural standards of value and fulfilling culturally sanctioned roles. Self-esteem is pursued universally, but the attributes, values, and roles that lead to feelings of worth vary depending on the individual's culture. Those raised in individualistic cultures tend to derive self-esteem from proving their superior skills and abilities, whereas those raised in collectivistic cultures are more likely to derive self-esteem from sustaining their honor, gracefully performing cultural rituals, and promoting group harmony. For example, one study (Sedikides et al., 2003) found that participants from the United States were more likely to see themselves as better than average on traits that are important to individualistic cultures (e.g., self-reliance), but Japanese participants were not. In contrast, participants from Japan were more likely to view themselves as better than average on traits that are important in collectivistic cultures (e.g., loyalty).

Types of Self-Esteem

Up to this point, we have been talking about self-esteem as if it were a unitary construct. But if two people both report having high self-esteem, does this mean their feelings of worth actually are the same? Early theorists such as Karen Horney (1937) and Carl Rogers (1961) suggested that the answer is no. They pointed out that some people have more secure, authentic feelings of positive self-regard, whereas others may report the same high self-regard but are actually compensating for feelings of inferiority. Furthermore, for some people, self-esteem is durable, but for others, it fluctuates from day to day. Take a moment to think about how you feel about yourself. Is your self-esteem generally the same as it was yesterday? And the day before that?

◀ **THINK ABOUT**

Mike Kernis and colleagues measured self-esteem stability by looking at how much people's responses to self-esteem measures changed over the course of a week (Kernis & Waschull, 1995). People who don't change much have stable self-esteem. People who change a lot have unstable self-esteem. Even when people are equally high in overall self-esteem, people whose self-esteem is more unstable tend to be sensitive to potential threats to their self-esteem. For example, when an acquaintance doesn't return a greeting, a person with unstable self-esteem is likely to be offended, whereas a person with stable self-esteem is more likely to ignore the same event (Kernis et al., 1998).

Why are certain feelings of self-esteem more unstable than others? One important factor is where we get our self-esteem from. As we noted previously, self-esteem can be derived from a variety of sources. Some sources, such as physical appearance, are extrinsic because they provide self-esteem when we meet standards dictated by the external environment. Other sources are intrinsic because they connect feelings of self-esteem to inner qualities that seem more enduring. As a result, when people rely on extrinsic sources, their self-esteem is contingent on feedback from others. Because this feedback can vary in favorability, they have less confidence in their overall value. In contrast, when people base their self-esteem on intrinsic qualities, their feelings of value are less contingent on others' feedback. Research has found that people reminded of positive intrinsic qualities of themselves are less defensive than people reminded of extrinsic sources of self-esteem, such as social approval or personal achievements; those reminded of positive intrinsic qualities are less prone to make downward social comparisons and to engage in self-handicapping (Arndt, Schimel et al., 2002; Schimel et al., 2001).

Researchers have often assumed that self-esteem is a conscious attitude about oneself that people can accurately self-report. But work on implicit self-esteem has called this view into question. Various methods have been developed for tapping feelings about the self in more subtle ways (e.g., Bosson et al., 2000). In one study, implicit self-esteem was measured as the speed at which participants could identify words such as *good* (as opposed to *bad*) after being primed with first-person pronouns such as *I*, *me*, and *myself* (as opposed to neutral primes) (Spalding & Hardin, 1999). Interestingly, these implicit measures of self-esteem are only weakly correlated with people's self-reported feelings about themselves.

Research suggests that it is a high level of implicit self-esteem, rather than self-reported self-esteem, that is most important for anxiety buffering, reduced defensiveness, and more neural activity in the reward-related regions of the brain (Izuma et al., 2018; Schmeichel et al., 2009). Indeed, people who consciously report high self-esteem but are low in implicit self-esteem are likely to have unstable self-esteem and to exhibit narcissistic tendencies and defensive responding (Jordan et al., 2003).

APPLICATION
The Good, the Bad, and the Ugly of Self-Esteem

So far we have discussed what self-esteem is, the sources of self-esteem, the many ways we maintain and defend it, and why people need self-esteem. Let's now consider four important implications of this knowledge.

1. *Self-esteem cannot be easily granted to people.* Children must internalize a meaningful worldview and clear standards for being a valued person. Then they must learn how to self-regulate to meet those standards of value and continue to meet them so that their value is validated throughout the life span. So youth soccer leagues that give every player a trophy are not helping to instill secure, enduring self-esteem. And in adulthood, simply telling someone else or yourself, "You are a good, worthy person" won't do the trick either (e.g., Greenwald et al., 1991). Instead, meeting socially validated standards of self-worth provides the best basis of stable self-esteem, the kind of self-worth that best serves people's psychological needs.

2. *People with either unstable self-esteem or low self-esteem will struggle with psychological problems such as anxiety, depression, and drug dependencies, which often result from attempts to avoid or alleviate these negative psychological feelings.* Such people are also likely to lash out at others, to express hostility, and even to resort to physical aggression. Research has clearly linked narcissism and borderline personality disorder, two psychological profiles in which unstable self-esteem and low self-esteem are prominent, to various forms of aggression (e.g., Bushman & Baumeister, 1998; Kernis et al., 1989; Salmivalli et al., 1999). The same message can be found by examining dramatic examples of mass killings, such as those at Columbine High School in Colorado (1999) and near the campus of University of California, Santa Barbara (2014). Those who engage in them are typically lashing out at specific people or the world in general because they do not feel valued.

3. *People pursue self-esteem in ways that fit with their cultural worldview.* Depending on one's worldview, this can lead to noble actions or ignoble ones. Those who define being good as helping others might pursue self-esteem by combatting poverty or raising money for cancer research. In one study, those who reported deriving self-esteem from being altruistic were the most likely to help a stranger they believed had been injured (Wilson, 1976). But for others, doing good might require eradicating individuals or groups perceived to be evil. Hard as it may be for Americans to believe, the people who committed the suicidal attacks on the World Trade Center in 2001 or the coordinated terrorist attacks in Paris in 2015 did so because they thought it was the right thing to do. What one group calls a terrorist, another might view as a heroic martyr.

[Leo Cullum/Cartoon Collections]

"We lost!"

4. *Striving for self-esteem can have constructive or destructive consequences for the self.* For instance, an emphasis on deriving self-value from appearance can sometimes lead to extreme dieting, restrictive eating, and ultimately anorexia (Geller et al., 1998). But if value is placed on an athletic, healthy body, you can see a more positive health consequence of self-esteem striving. Striving for self-esteem can also be self-destructive if the focus is on risky behaviors such as reckless driving, fighting, binge drinking, or drug use. Reminders of death increase self-esteem striving, and so, depending on the basis of self-esteem the person is trying to bolster, such reminders can either increase risky behavior (e.g., restrictive eating, excessive tanning) or reduce it (e.g., quitting smoking; Arndt & Goldenberg, 2011, 2017). ∎

Should We Stop Caring About Self-Esteem?

Because self-esteem striving can be detrimental in some ways, researchers (e.g., Crocker & Park, 2004) have wondered whether people can simply stop caring about their self-worth. But the theories and research we have reviewed suggest that this is both undesirable and unlikely. First, striving for personal value often leads to accomplishments that contribute positively to society. Second, if we accept the idea that self-esteem is a vital buffer against anxiety, then if we were stripped of self-worth, we would be unable to function effectively. Longitudinal research indicates that high self-esteem contributes to better physical and mental health, more educational and career success, and more satisfying social relationships (Orth & Robins, 2014). In addition, in societies that limit people's avenues for self-worth, clinical depression and dependence on chemical mood enhancers are more prevalent (Kirsch, 2010; Swendsen & Merikangas, 2000). Perhaps the best we can hope for is to fashion, both individually and as a society, more constructive avenues for obtaining self-esteem that are open to all (e.g., Becker, 1971).

Another possibility is to cultivate **self-compassion**, an idea developed from Buddhist psychology (Brach, 2003; Neff, 2011). Compassion involves being sensitive to others' suffering and desiring to help them in some way. You feel it, for example, when you stop to consider your friend's struggle with a painful experience. Rather than judge or criticize her, you look for ways to provide comfort and care. You practice self-compassion when you take the stance of a compassionate other toward the self.

Self-compassion involves three elements. The first is *self-kindness*. When faced with painful situations or when confronting your mistakes and shortcomings, your tendency might be to beat yourself up, but with self-compassion, you would respond with the same kindness toward the self that you would show to a close other. The second element is the *recognition that everyone fails or makes mistakes on occasion* and that suffering and imperfection are part of the shared human experience. The third element, *mindfulness*, means accepting negative thoughts and emotions as they are rather than suppressing or denying them.

Self-compassion lessens the impact of negative life events and is linked to psychological well-being, including more optimism, curiosity, and creativity and less anxiety and depression (Hollis-Walker & Colosimo, 2011; Leary et al., 2007; Sirois, 2014). Most of this research has used trait measures of self-compassion,

Self-compassion Being kind to ourselves when we suffer, fail, or feel inadequate, recognizing that imperfection is part of the human condition, and accepting rather than denying negative feelings about ourselves.

▼ Self-compassion involves reflecting on one's shortcomings in a mindful and forgiving way.
[Plush Studios/Blend Images/AGE Fotostock]

but other researchers also have developed ways to increase self-compassion and look at the effects of doing so. In one study (Shapira & Mongrain, 2010), a group of volunteers wrote a self-compassionate letter to themselves every day for a week; another group wrote letters about personal memories. The self-compassion group showed higher levels of happiness as much as six months later.

Self-compassion offers a way to maintain stable high self-esteem even though you make mistakes and sometimes fall short of your own standards and goals and other people's expectations for you (Neff & Vonk, 2009). This healthier approach to maintaining self-worth should make it less dependent on specific life outcomes and external validation from others.

SECTION REVIEW The Self-Esteem Motive: Establishing and Defending One's Value

Self-esteem is the level of positive feeling one has about oneself. It can be thought of as a trait (a general attitude) or a state (a temporary feeling that is changeable).

Defenses to Protect Self-Esteem	Functions and Influence of Self-Esteem	Self-Esteem Stability	Five Implications of Self-Esteem
• Self-serving attributions • Self-handicapping • Seeing self as better than average • Projection • Symbolic self-completion • Compensation and self-affirmation • Social comparison	• Buffers anxiety about vulnerability and mortality • Indicates one's social status and how accepted one is by others • Influenced by how one is treated by others • Maintained through attributes and behaviors valued by one's culture	• More constant over time and more resistant to feedback from others • Based on intrinsic factors rather than extrinsic factors	• It is not easily granted. • When low or unstable, it contributes to psychological problems. • It depends on a person's worldview. • Striving for it can have constructive or destructive consequences for others and the self. • Self-compassion may be one valuable route for maintaining it.

Self-Presentation: The Show Must Go On

* Describe how theater is a metaphor for behavior in social interactions.
* Identify self-presentation strategies.
* Explain when and why people are motivated to self-present.

Alan: I think we live our lives so afraid to be seen as weak that we die perhaps without ever having been seen at all. Denny, do you ever worry that when you die, people will never have truly known you?

Denny: I don't want them to know me, I want them to believe my version.

—David E. Kelley, *Boston Legal* (2008)

We've been focusing primarily on the individual's private view of her or his own self, but the self is as much a public entity as it is a private one. Life casts people into different social roles (child, student, patient) that are part of their cultural worldview, but those people also help create their own public personas. In fact, the word *personality* derives from the Greek word *persona*, a word originally used to describe the masks that Greek actors wore on stage to represent their characters' emotional state.

The Dramaturgical Perspective

"All the world's a stage, and all the men and women merely players."
—William Shakespeare, *As You Like It*, act 2, scene 7, line 138 (Shakespeare, 1623)

In books such as *The Presentation of Self in Everyday Life* (1959), the sociologist Erving Goffman offered a **dramaturgical perspective** that uses the theater as a metaphor to understand how people behave in everyday social interactions. From this perspective, every social interaction involves self-presentation in which actors perform according to a script. If all involved know the script and play their parts well, then, like a successful play, their social interactions flow smoothly and seem meaningful, and each actor benefits.

People learn their scripts and roles through socialization. Parents, teachers, and the media teach children about weddings, funerals, school, parties, dates, concerts, wars, and so forth long before they experience any of these things firsthand. Kids play at various culturally valued adult roles, such as astronaut, athlete, mother, doctor, teacher, or pop star. As a result of these socialization experiences, in every social situation, there is a working consensus, an implicit agreement about who plays which role and how it should be played.

The power of the situation to define people's roles, perceptions, and behavior was vividly demonstrated when, in 2007, *Washington Post* journalist Gene Weingarten persuaded the internationally acclaimed violinist Joshua Bell to play for nearly an hour in a crowded Washington, DC, Metro station. Three nights earlier, in the impressive setting of a sold-out concert hall, Bell took on the role of virtuoso. The listeners played their role, sitting in their seats (for which they paid $100) and stifling their coughs during the performance. But although he filled the Metro station with the same virtuosity, here Bell took on the role of the panhandler, and passersby played their part by ignoring him. Only seven people actually stopped to listen. Indeed, Bell suddenly found his very identity threatened. He said, "When you play for ticket-holders, you are already validated. I have no sense that I need to be accepted. I'm already accepted. Here, there was this thought: *What if they don't like me? What if they resent my presence?*" (Weingarten, 2007).

Sincere Versus Cynical Performances People encounter so many familiar situations that they often are not consciously aware that they're playing a role or following a script. In a classroom, for instance, you automatically take on the student role. Goffman refers to these well-practiced scripts as *sincere performances*. But when something goes awry, when someone doesn't play a role properly, then people become aware of the implicit rules and norms they've been following automatically all along.

In contrast to sincere performances, *cynical performances* are conscious attempts to perform in a certain way to make a particular impression. People are most likely to engage in such performances when they find themselves in unfamiliar territory or when they want to convey a specific impression. Think back to your first day of college. You probably did a lot of preparation, thinking about what to expect, how to dress, and so on. When you arrived, you were probably fairly self-conscious, thinking about how to act and what to say. Job interviews and first dates also provide good examples of cynical performances. Cynical

Dramaturgical perspective Using the theater as a metaphor, the idea that people, like actors, perform according to a script. If we all know the script and play our parts well, then, like a successful play, our social interactions flow smoothly and seem meaningful, and each actor benefits.

▼ Virtuoso Joshua Bell donned the unfamiliar role of a panhandler while playing his $3 million violin for spare change at L'Enfant Plaza Metro Station.
[Michael Williamson/*The Washington Post*/Getty Images]

performances can turn into sincere performances as they become increasingly familiar and more rehearsed.

Are people always performing? Goffman would say "yes." Even when you wish to be most genuine—for example, when offering condolences to a friend whose father has died—you still rely on scripts to express your true feelings of sympathy and offer comfort. You may end up drawing on phrases you've seen used in movies or read in sympathy cards. So, for Goffman, performing and self-presentation are not primarily done to be phony or manipulative (although sometimes they are), but rather to accomplish the goal that is important to a person in a particular social situation.

Self-Presentational Strategies

Honing an Image. Jones and Pittman (1982) described some common strategies we use to meet our self-presentational goals. To appear competent, we advertise our achievements through self-promotion. But self-promotion can backfire if it comes off as too boastful or involves false modesty (e.g., Sezer et al., 2018; Wosinska et al., 1996), and sometimes people undersell their competence to protect the feelings of or connect with an audience (Dupree & Fiske, 2019). When we simply want people to like us, we often use ingratiation, such as by flattering others, which is generally quite effective (e.g., Jones & Wortman, 1973). We also ingratiate ourselves to others by presenting ourselves as being like them (Gordon, 1996). But sprinkling in a little disagreement can help us come across as more sincere and create a better impression overall (e.g., Jones, 1990; Jones et al., 1963). Finally, in certain situations, people—more often men than women—turn to intimidation to create an image of power and strength (Jones & Pittman, 1982).

Audience Segregation. In their everyday lives, people have to stay in character to uphold a particular public identity with a given audience. Goffman pointed out that people do so in part by keeping different audiences segregated so that they can perform consistently with each audience. If you have ever worked in a restaurant, you know that waitstaff act very differently in the kitchen than they do out on the floor.

But what happens when you have two different audiences present at the same time? Faced with such a multiple-audience problem, sometimes people use

▼ Goffman (1959) pointed out that waiters have to work hard to perform in a deferential and pleasant manner to their audience, the restaurant customers. Because of the strain behaving in this manner creates, they often act very differently backstage, in the kitchen area. The 2005 film *Waiting* humorously portrays this phenomenon, as exemplified here by waitress Naomi (played by Alanna Ubach), who exudes charm and patience out front with the customers but rage and contempt when back in the kitchen.

different communication channels to convey different self-images. For example, you may at some point find yourself flattering someone on the phone while rolling your eyes for a friend who is with you (Fleming & Rudman, 1993). Or you might adopt a compromise position on an issue when two present audiences have opposite views (e.g., Braver et al., 1977). Although people use such strategies, they find multiple-audience situations very difficult, and people are not nearly so effective as they think they are at sustaining different identities simultaneously (Fleming et al., 1990; Van Boven et al., 2000).

Face.   One fundamental goal in self-presentation is to maintain *face*, a person's sense of public value. Every social encounter brings with it the risk of losing face if the person slips up or says or does the wrong thing. People are very concerned with protecting their own face, as one's public image often affects self-esteem. However, when others fall short of their presentational roles, people often tactfully help them save face and maintain a positive self-image. Individuals often minimize threats to someone else's face out of empathy and kindness, but this tactic also helps social interactions flow smoothly and increases the likelihood that such tact will be reciprocated.

Lying.   Because of the importance of protecting face, people often bend the truth. For example, you may assure someone that his presentation went well when in fact it put you to sleep. This perspective suggests that lying is pretty common and often motivated by the need to protect face—our own and others'—rather than intentionally harm or manipulate others. A study by Bella DePaulo and colleagues (1996) found considerable support for these ideas. Participants were given little notebooks and instructed to record any and all lies, and the reasons for telling them, over the course of a week. The participants lied about twice a day and lied to 38% of the people they interacted with over the week. Three quarters of the lies were about face-saving. Half the lies were told to save the participant's own face, and a quarter of them were told to protect someone else's. Women were equally likely to lie for themselves or for someone else. Men, in contrast, were more likely to save their own face than someone else's. What would you write in your notebook if you were recording any and all lies over the course of a week?

◄ THINK ABOUT

[Kongsak/Shutterstock]

 APPLICATION
The Unforeseen Consequences of Self-Presentation

In 2015, among high school students who were sexually active, about 40% reported not using a condom during their last sexual encounter (Kann et al., 2016). Why? One reason is that many people report feeling embarrassed when they buy condoms (Bell, 2009). Those who do have condoms sometimes feel that it might make the wrong impression if they suggest using one during sex (Herold, 1981). These concerns about the impression you are making on a drugstore cashier or a one-night stand can lead you to do something that could leave you with a sexually transmitted and perhaps even life-threatening disease!

Unsafe sex isn't the only risky health behavior that people might adopt for the sake of making a good impression. Those who are more concerned about the impression they make on others are also more likely to put themselves at risk for skin cancer in order to perfect their tans (Leary & Jones, 1993); use or abuse drugs and alcohol as a way to fit in with the "right" crowd (Farber et al., 1980; Lindquist et al., 1979); or engage in unhealthy dieting practices or steroid use to achieve that perfect body (Leary et al., 1994). Studies show that women eat less in front of an attractive man (Pliner & Chaiken, 1990) and when they want to present a more feminine impression (Mori et al., 1987). Based on these lines of research, interventions (e.g., for sun protection or smoking cessation) are starting to focus more on image-based concerns (Mahler et al., 2007). ■

Individual Differences in Self-Presentation

At this point you might be thinking, "Wow, I can really see how much I self-present." Or you might think, "I don't care enough about what other people think to do this kind of stuff." Such varied reactions reflect how people differ both in their sensitivity to how others see them and how motivated they are to put effort into strategic self-presentation. This individual difference is known as **self-monitoring** (Snyder & Gangestad, 1986).

People high in self-monitoring are social chameleons, adjusting their appearance and behavior to fit with the norms and expectations in a given situation. They are better at what we called cynical performances; that is, they are able to change their expression, vocal tone, and mannerisms strategically to convey a certain character (Snyder, 1974). They also tend to have more friends, though these friendships are often less close and more short term, but have fewer long-lasting romantic relationships.

Those low in self-monitoring seem to march to the beat of their own drum, ignoring other people's expectations and doing what feels true to them. They present themselves in a more consistent way, so their behavior stems not so much from what the situation might demand but from their own inner states and desired self-image. This means their behavior is more stable across situations. In fact, low self-monitors are more likely to choose situations where they can just be themselves.

Audience-Monitoring Errors

Does careful self-monitoring ensure that people accurately understand the impression their audience is forming of them? Unfortunately, people often have difficulty getting beyond their own subjective experience when judging how much other people attend to them, an egocentric bias. In one study (Gilovich et al., 2000), a college student wearing the concert T-shirt of 1970s singer Barry Manilow was sent into a room of observers. After being in front of the observers for under a minute, the average participant in this study estimated that close to 50% of the people in the room must have noticed the shirt. In fact, reports by the observers showed that only about 25% actually did. Because the participants were acutely aware of sporting the Barry Manilow attire, they falsely inferred that the rest of the world noticed as well. This is known as the **spotlight effect**—the belief that others are more focused on the self than they actually are. So, when we are very self-conscious of some aspect of self, we are prone to the spotlight effect. But when our attention is shifted away from the self, the opposite may occur

Self-monitoring A personality variable that indicates the extent to which an individual has the desire and ability to adjust their self-presentations for different audiences.

Spotlight effect The belief that others are more focused on us than they actually are.

Illusion of transparency The tendency to overestimate another's ability to know our internal thoughts and feelings.

$30

Heart Shirt – Women's

▲ How would you feel wearing this T-shirt to the next party you attend?

(Macrae et al., 2016). For example, when participants wore the Manilow T-shirts for a while before entering the room of observers (so that it was no longer so salient to them), they underestimated the number of people who would notice. And, in general, when in public, people think they observe others more than other people observe them; the truth is that others observe us much more than we think they do (Boothby et al., 2017).

Such egocentric bias also leads people to overestimate others' ability to know their internal thoughts and feelings. Imagine a situation where you smile politely as you choke down bite after bite of a friend's new, but decidedly vile, recipe. Many of us imagine that the disgust we are so aware of will also be noticed by others. According to Gilovich and colleagues (1998), this is probably only an **illusion of transparency** because people are often better than they think they are at hiding their internal feelings. Keep this in mind the next time you get nervous about giving a speech or doing something in public. In fact, even when people rate themselves as being jittery balls of nerves, those who observe their speeches often rate them as not appearing anxious (Savitsky & Gilovich, 2003).

▲ A chilling portrayal of the illusion of transparency can be found in Edgar Allan Poe's classic short story "The Tell-Tale Heart." In this story, the main character's paranoid fears that a detective can tell what he has buried beneath the floor give away his dark secret. In less dramatic but more everyday terms, we often doubt whether we can keep our thoughts and feelings hidden from others.
[Culture Club/Getty Images]

The Goals of Self-Presentation

Why is self-presentation so prevalent and important? We often use self-presentation to achieve specific goals such as getting a job, impressing a date, and so on. But it also serves three broader goals. One is to convey and protect one's desired self-image. A second goal is to support the meaningfulness of social interactions by properly enacting the culture's scripts and roles. Finally, self-presentation also serves self-improvement and personal growth. Goffman (1959) noted that people often use idealization to convey a best-case view of themselves to others. To quote the sociologist Charles Horton Cooley (1902, p. 352), "If we never tried to seem a little better than we are, how could we improve or 'train ourselves from the outside inward'?"

SECTION REVIEW Self-Presentation: The Show Must Go On

People are motivated to manage how others view them.

Theater as a Metaphor	Self-Presentational Strategies	Application	Basic Motives for Self-Presenting
• People self-present according to a script, like actors in a play. • Sincere performances happen automatically and unconsciously. • Cynical performances are conscious attempts to make a particular impression.	• Honing an image through self-promotion, supplication, ingratiation, and intimidation • Audience segregation • Lying	Concerns about making certain impressions can lead to unhealthful behaviors.	• People high in self-monitoring, highly motivated in how they self-present, are most likely to change for different audiences. • The spotlight effect and the illusion of transparency show how people are often inaccurate in their understanding of the audience's impression of them. • Three broad goals are to protect one's self-image; uphold meaning; and foster self-improvement.

Motives for Growth and Self-Expansion

- What does it mean to feel self-determined, and what conditions foster feelings of self-determination?
- Explain the danger of the overjustification effect.
- Describe factors that help maximize self-growth.

THINK ABOUT

[© 2021 Macmillan]

Self-determination theory The idea that people function best when they feel that their actions stem from their own desires rather than from external forces.

Ideas about self-growth toward optimal fulfillment of one's potential have a long history in Western philosophy, from the Greek philosophers to modern times (Coan, 1977). Otto Rank (1932/1989) proposed that inside each of us is a *life force* that drives us to separate from others and establish the self as a unique individual who determines one's own actions. Erik Erikson (1959, 1963) further proposed that people progress through eight stages of growth. These perspectives contributed to an influential movement in the 1960s known as *humanistic psychology*. One prominent theorist, Carl Rogers (1961), posited that people are naturally motivated to expand and enrich themselves but that conformity to society's expectations often derails this process. Abraham Maslow (e.g., Maslow et al., 1970) similarly proposed that all humans are fundamentally motivated toward self-actualization, or being all they can be, particularly if they have satisfied more pressing needs for food, shelter, belonging, and a secure sense of personal value. These ideas inspired the development of self-determination theory, the most influential contemporary perspective on growth.

Self-Determination Theory

Consider for a moment why you are reading this textbook. Are you doing it because you think you have to, and it's a necessary step to completing this course? Or perhaps you would feel guilty if you didn't? Or maybe you are doing it because you truly enjoy reading and mastering this material?

According to Ed Deci and Rich Ryan's **self-determination theory** (2000), your answers to these types of questions say a great deal about your level of self-determined motivation. People who have low levels of self-determined motivation view their action as being controlled by external forces; this is called *extrinsic motivation*. People who have high levels of self-determined motivation view their action as originating in their own authentic desires; this is called *intrinsic motivation*.

To illustrate, imagine that Nick and Mikalya are in medical school. Both are going to classes, studying for tests, and so on. Nick goes to medical school purely because he feels obligated to fulfill his family's wish that he become a doctor and make lots of money. Nick's behavior is an example of extrinsically motivated behavior. In contrast, Mikalya is going to medical school because being a doctor connects with her core sense of self and her value of helping others maintain their health. Mikalya's behavior is more intrinsically motivated.

Self-determination theory proposes that people are naturally powered by curiosity to explore their environment, master new challenges, and integrate these experiences with a core sense of who they are. However, the social world often tries to control us, moving us away from our natural tendencies for self-determination. Deci and Ryan argue that people feel self-determined in their actions when three basic needs are met:

Relatedness: being meaningfully connected with others
Autonomy: feeling a sense of authentic choice in what one does
Competence: feeling effective in what one does

When people are in social situations that allow for the satisfaction of these needs, they experience their action as more self-determined, authentic, and rewarding. In fact, under these conditions, people can become intrinsically motivated to do activities that they were initially compelled to do for external

◀ The late singer/songwriter and philanthropist Harry Chapin illustrated the value of feeling self-determined in your actions in this anecdote about his then 88-year-old artist grandfather, who told him: "Harry there's two kinds of tired, there's good tired and there's bad tired . . . ironically enough bad tired can be a day that you won but you won other people's battles, you lived other people's days . . . other people's dreams . . . and when you hit the hay at night somehow you toss and turn you don't settle easy. . . . Good tired ironically enough can be a day that you lost but . . . you knew you fought your battles, you chased your dreams . . . and when you hit the hay at night you settle easy. . . . I painted and I painted and I am good tired and they can take me away."

[Keith Bernstein/Getty Images]

reasons. However, when social situations thwart these needs, people see their actions as less self-determined, controlled instead by external forces.

Does it matter whether people feel self-determined? Yes, it makes a big difference. In our medical school example, both Nick and Mikayla may have successful careers as doctors, but according to self-determination theory, Mikayla is more likely to derive real satisfaction from her career and reach her full potential as a doctor. Research backs this up. Across a wide variety of domains—from marriage to academics to weight-loss programs—people who feel more self-determined and authentic perform better and more creatively, are happier, and experience more satisfaction and feel more power in their lives than those who experience controlled forms of regulation (Deci & Ryan, 2002; Gan et al., 2018; Reeve, 2015). For instance, Sheldon and Krieger (2007) investigated students during their three years in law school, a notoriously brutal undertaking. Students who felt that the faculty supported their autonomy (providing a sense of choice and acknowledging their feelings) performed better on the bar exam and experienced greater life satisfaction than those who felt that their autonomy was thwarted. Similarly, people with a high *internal locus of control* view themselves as being in control of their outcomes and are generally more successful than people with an *external locus of control,* who think fate controls their outcomes (Brown & Strickland, 1972; Kraus et al., 2012; Rotter, 1954).

Around the globe, millions of people believe that significant outcomes in their lives, including the courses of their careers and romantic relationships, are determined by the movements of celestial bodies. Recalling what you have learned about self-determination theory, how do you think belief in astrology might influence a person's motivation and ability to grow? What is the appeal of yielding control over one's life to the stars?

Locus of control The extent to which a person believes that either internal or external factors determine life outcomes.

◀ **THINK ABOUT**

[Shutterstock]

The Overjustification Effect: Undermining Intrinsic Motivation What types of social contexts can thwart a person's sense of autonomy? Think about something that you typically enjoy doing for its own sake, such as reading, mountain climbing, or dancing. Now imagine that you started to get paid for this activity. Would you enjoy it more or less? Common sense and behaviorism would suggest that if you liked it already, you'd like it even more if you received extrinsic monetary rewards for doing it. But not so fast. In a seminal study to address this question (Lepper et al., 1973), preschool children were asked to do some coloring, an activity most children find enjoyable. One group of children was promised a "good player" ribbon for their coloring and were given the ribbon; another group was promised no reward. Later, when all the children were given a free choice among a variety of activities, the children who received the promised ribbon reward were *less* interested in coloring.

Why would this happen? Self-perception theory provides the best answer. For the children offered the reward, the external inducement was so salient that they inferred they were coloring *for* the reward and discounted enjoyment as their reason for doing it. Consequently, when no more rewards were offered, these kids no longer saw a reason to color. Psychologists call this the **overjustification effect:** When external factors lead people to attribute the reason, or justification, for their action to an external incentive (such as money, approval, or meeting a deadline), their intrinsic motivation and enjoyment of the task are diminished. Interestingly, the overjustification effect occurs only if the external incentive is seen as the reason for the behavior. Another group of children *unexpectedly* given the same ribbon after coloring continued to be intrinsically interested in coloring.

Because extrinsic inducements are used so often in child rearing, schools, and work settings, research on the overjustification effect has inspired a lot of controversy and interest. It turns out that this effect has been shown in everyone from preschool children to elderly people and in collectivistic as well as individualistic cultures. Overjustification not only reduces interest in the activity but also leads to less effective, less creative performance. More intrinsically motivated kids, students, and employees will do a better job, go the extra mile, and have more satisfaction with their lives at home, in school, and at work (Deci & Ryan, 2002; Gagné & Deci, 2005).

Do rewards always undermine intrinsic motivation? If the reward is viewed as an indicator of the quality of one's efforts, rather than as an inducement to engage in the activity in the first place, it often actually improves performance and intrinsic interest rather than undermining it (Eisenberger & Armeli, 1997). Rewards also can be effective when people aren't aware that the reward is controlling their choices. Furthermore, rewards are effective when given in an atmosphere that generally supports relatedness, autonomy, and competence. A sales manager who is friendly, caring, and appreciative and who doesn't micromanage and scrutinize employees' every move would foster self-determined selling better than would a cold, rigid control freak (Richer & Vallerand, 1995).

Overjustification effect The tendency for salient rewards or threats to lead people to attribute the reason, or justification, for engaging in an activity to an external factor, which thereby undermines their intrinsic motivation for and enjoyment of the activity.

APPLICATION
How to Maximize Self-Growth

Self-determination theory provides a framework for understanding the individual's motivation for self-growth. Research has also uncovered more specific types of experiences and goals that help individuals expand their capacities and enrich their enjoyment of life.

Pursue Goals That Support Core Needs   We've just seen that *why* we pursue a goal is an important factor in our growth; *what* goals we pursue also matters. Some goals strengthen a meaningful relationship or exercise a talent, helping to satisfy personal core needs (Sheldon & Elliott, 1999). Other goals, such as striving to be popular, do so less well. Indeed, people who pursue materialistic goals of fame and fortune tend to have lower levels of life satisfaction than those who pursue more intrinsic goals such as good social relationships and personal growth (Kasser & Ryan, 1993; Sheldon et al., 2004; Werner & Milyavskaya, 2018). And intrinsic goals may facilitate each other, as good social relationships spur people on to pursue personal growth (Lee et al., 2018).

Get in the Zone Have you ever participated in some activity where your sense of time seems to evaporate, you lose all sense of your self, and you are totally focused on the activity at hand? Maslow referred to such instances as "peak experiences," and he felt that they contribute to self-actualization. More recently, Mihaly Csikszentmihalyi (1990) labeled this experience **flow**. From his interviews with surgeons, mountain climbers, and others about their optimal performances, Csikszentmihalyi argued that achieving flow can improve performance and enrich our sense of self.

Flow The feeling of being completely absorbed in an activity that is appropriately challenging to one's skills.

Flow is achieved when the challenge of a situation, person, or task is just above our typical skill level, requiring a full engagement of all our concentration and focus. As you see depicted in **FIGURE 6.8**, when the challenge is too high, we experience anxiety, and when the challenge is too low, we experience boredom. But when skills and challenges match, intrinsic motivation and flow can emerge. This idea helps explain why video games are so popular: They are designed so that once you master a given level, there's another, higher level to challenge you, so you always have a good match for your skill level (Keller & Bless, 2008). Although people cannot be in flow all the time, research suggests that flow experiences can reduce stress and contribute to better physical health (Burton & King, 2004; Sweeney, 2018).

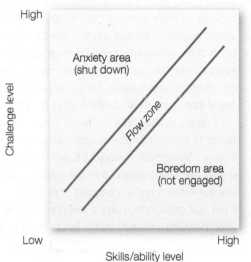

Figure 6.8

Csikszentmihalyi's Concept of Flow

When the challenge level of a task, situation, or role matches well with the person's skills and abilities, he or she experiences an enjoyable and absorbed feeling known as flow.

[Research from Csikszentmihalyi, 1990]

Challenge Versus Threat Another line of research also focuses on the difference between experiences that we feel up to and those we do not. Generally, threatening experiences motivate people to seek out security, driving them to cling to the safe and familiar parts of life and to cut off growth, making them narrower and more rigid in their thinking (e.g., Derryberry & Tucker, 1994; Fredrickson & Branigan, 2005; Landau, Johns et al., 2004; Zillman & Cantor, 1976).

Yet a popular cliché is philosopher Friedrich Nietzsche's famous line: "What doesn't kill me makes me stronger." Indeed, Nietzsche was a strong proponent of the idea that to achieve a more freely determined and satisfying life, the person must face distressing truths and endure hardships. People do indeed very commonly report that they experienced valuable growth after traumatic experiences

◀ Skiing is one example of flow. Good skiers get the rush on the really difficult slopes, whereas novices can experience the exhilaration on much easier slopes. In both cases, though, the challenge demands a full engagement of one's skill.

[Left: Photobac/Shutterstock; right: matthaeus ritsch/Shutterstock]

SOCIAL PSYCH AT THE MOVIES

Blue Jasmine

The 2013 film *Blue Jasmine*, written and directed by Woody Allen, illustrates a woman's struggle with dissonance, self-narrative, self-esteem, self-presentation, and growth. The protagonist, Jasmine, played by Cate Blanchett, who won an Oscar for her performance, is a highly intelligent and once wealthy New Yorker who exudes elegance and was used to the "finer things in life." She arrives penniless to San Francisco to live with her very different working-class sister, Ginger (Sally Hawkins). Jasmine takes a clerical job in a dental office and aspires to finish college through online courses so she can become an interior designer. But it's debatable whether these are genuine attempts to grow as a person or just efforts to restore the social status she was so reliant on as her basis of self-worth.

Eventually she shifts her focus toward marrying a wealthy suitor to regain her status and transform her self-narrative from a contamination story to a redemption story. As events unfold, we see flashbacks to the events that have led to her low self-esteem and consequent high anxiety. Years ago, Jasmine quit college to marry a wealthy investment broker, Hal (Alec Baldwin). Hal violated the law in building their high social status; eventually he was arrested by the FBI. All their assets were seized, and Hal hanged himself while in prison.

Throughout the film, Jasmine is obsessed with trying to maintain face in light of these events. She recounts her humiliation at being seen working in a department store shoe department by a socialite former friend. She presents herself to her sister as ignorant of her husband's shady deals and blameless in his downfall. However, we eventually learn through her own memories that this is not true and that her choices contributed to his downfall.

Part of Jasmine's current struggle stems from her inability to reduce the dissonance caused by these past actions and their foreseeable negative consequences. She feels guilt and shame both about her actions and about having been cheated on extensively by the philandering Hal. His unfaithfulness brought her to initiate his downfall with a call to the FBI. Hal's arrest and subsequent death are not easy things for Jasmine to rationalize. When she meets her future fiancé, her intelligence, charm, and physical attractiveness appeal greatly to him. But instead of being honest about her past and her current situation, she portrays herself as a successful designer and claims that her husband died of a heart attack. When

(e.g., Wozniak et al., 2020). However, a recent meta-analytic review calls into question whether traumatic events have any unique value in promoting growth (Mangelsdorf et al., 2019). Fortunately, there is a line of research that can help us understand when stressful situations are more likely to stifle growth and when they are more likely to facilitate it.

According to James Blascovich and colleagues (Blascovich & Mendes, 2000; Blascovich & Tomaka, 1996), when people face stressful situations such as taking a test or giving a speech, they assess whether they have the resources to meet the demands of the situation. When they conclude that their resources are inadequate, they feel threatened, but when they view their resources as meeting or surpassing the demands, they feel challenged. This feeling of challenge provides an opportunity for growth.

In fact, whether people respond to a stressor with feelings of threat or challenge is reflected in their bodies' physiological responses. When people feel threatened, their heart rate increases, but their veins and arteries don't expand to allow blood to flow easily through the body. People's heart rate similarly increases when they feel challenged, but here the veins and arteries dilate to improve blood flow. And feeling challenged as opposed to threatened can make a difference in performance. Blascovich and colleagues (2004) had college baseball and softball players imagine a stressful game situation at the beginning of the season while their physiological responses were being monitored. Those whose bodies signaled a challenge response actually performed better over the course of the season than those who showed a threat reaction.

Foster a Positive Mood Positive emotions such as happiness and excitement can stimulate creative thought, in part because they tell the person that things are safe, these lies come to light, her engagement and her easy path back to high social status go up in smoke.

Jasmine, stripped of self-esteem and any clear path to regaining it, becomes consumed with anxiety. She hides the broken engagement from her sister. In retrospect, the viewer realizes that Jasmine's struggles were set up by her quitting college to marry the wealthy Hal and her consequent reliance on his shady successes for her social status and opportunities for philanthropy. These became the primary bases of her self-worth, leading her to turn a blind eye to both his shady deals and his extramarital affairs.

In fairness to both the fictional Jasmine and to real women who have made similar choices in their lives, Jasmine was in part a victim of how cultures guide people's ways of seeking and maintaining self-worth. She was raised in a patriarchal culture in which women were reinforced for seeking self-worth through the success of a male partner and in which successful married men often feel they have the right to "sleep around" on the sly. This point is brought home by what happens when Jasmine tries to support herself through her receptionist job with a male dentist as a way to secure an income while she pursues her online studies. Jasmine comes to genuinely embrace this job as a way to become the person of value she desires to be.

However, the dentist begins sexually harassing her and eventually tries to force himself on her. Jasmine promptly quits, and this precipitates her losing faith in building success and self-worth through her own intellectual development and falling back on seeking a successful suitor to restore her self-worth. Perhaps she would have built a truly stable basis of self-worth over time had she not been victimized by this problem—one that women face in the workplace in many contemporary societies.

▲ [Perdido Productions/The Kobal Collection/Shutterstock]

and it's okay to explore novel experiences (Fredrickson, 2001; Lyubomirsky et al., 2005). So positive mood stimulates growth by making it more likely people will think in new ways and find creative solutions to problems. In an illustrative study (Isen et al., 1987), some participants were put in a positive mood by watching five minutes of a funny movie, whereas participants in the control condition watched a neutral movie. Participants were then given the objects in **FIGURE 6.9a**—a box of tacks, a candle, and a book of matches—and were told to come up with a way, using only those objects, to attach the candle to a corkboard on the wall so that it would burn without dripping wax on the floor. After about 10 minutes, only 20% of the participants in the neutral film condition found the correct answer, but participants who had just watched a mere five minutes of funny bloopers found the correct solution 75% of the time. (For the answer, please see **FIGURE 6.9b** on p. 234.)

Act Mindfully   Being mindful—attentive to the present moment in which one is actively involved with one's actions and their meaning—can facilitate growth (Brown et al., 2007; Langer & Moldoveanu, 2000). According to Ellen Langer (1989), **mindfulness** can be understood by contrasting it with its opposite, mindlessness. When we act mindlessly, we habitually engage with our actions and the external world, and we rarely consider novel and creative approaches to life. The self becomes stagnant. But when we're mindful, we open ourselves up to consider the world and ourselves in new, more open, and multidimensional

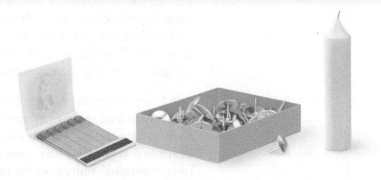

Figure 6.9a

Matches, Tacks, and Candle

One test of creative thinking is to ask a person how to use these objects to attach the candle to a corkboard so it will burn without wax dripping onto the floor. Before turning the page, see if you can figure out the solution.

Mindfulness The state of being and acting fully in the current moment.

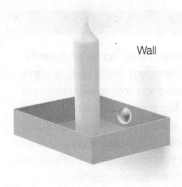

Wall

Figure 6.9b

Solution to Question

Here is how it can be done. The key is being able to view the box containing the tacks in a different way than you usually would.

ways. Research shows that being mindful in our daily lives may reduce our stress and anxiety and improve creativity, concentration, and overall well-being (Brown et al., 2007; Kabat-Zinn, 1990; Sweeney, 2018).

Expand Your Mind: Challenge Yourself and Explore the World Have you ever had a creative idea—such as a different way to approach a term paper or an interpersonal dilemma—pop into your head while hiking in the woods or watching a unique foreign movie? You're not alone. Many physicists, composers, and other creative individuals have hatched their most innovative ideas while climbing mountains, looking at the stars, and taking part in other novel experiences (Csikszentmihalyi, 1996). Both correlational and experimental research show that the more people engage in novel, challenging, and interesting activities, the more their self expands. The result is a broader, more multifaceted self-concept that contributes to better relationships, self-confidence, creativity, and success in accomplishing life goals (Mattingly & Lewandowski, 2014). The idea that exposure to novel experiences can stimulate creativity is also one reason your university or college encourages you to study abroad and why employers often seek to increase cultural diversity in the workplace. In fact, research shows that even brief exposure to a foreign culture can improve creativity. In one study (Leung & Chiu, 2010), European American students first watched a 45-minute slide show. Some participants viewed aspects of either Chinese culture (e.g., food and architecture) or American culture. Others were shown aspects of both cultures intermixed, such as fashion that blends American and Chinese influences. Afterward, participants were asked to interpret the story of Cinderella for Turkish children, and the researchers measured how creative these interpretations were. They found that compared with participants who viewed either Chinese or American culture, those exposed to a mingling of both cultures subsequently wrote more creative Cinderella interpretations. Interestingly, exposure only to reminders of one culture did not boost creativity. This suggests that people gain in creativity when they juxtapose and integrate seemingly incompatible aspects of different cultures.

Can Even Thoughts of Death Promote Growth? When are thoughts of mortality likely to lead to defensiveness? When might they stimulate growth? Thinkers such as Seneca and Martin Heidegger argued that when people think about death in a superficial way, they are more likely to avoid their fear by clinging to conventional sources of meaning and self-esteem—just as most research on mortality salience has shown. But for people very open to new experiences and who view life holistically, brief thoughts of death can lead to appreciation of life and growth (Ma-Kellams & Blascovich, 2012; Vail et al., 2012). In addition, thinking more deeply about death can catalyze authenticity and growth. Why? Recognition of mortality might serve as a reminder that our life spans are limited and prompt us to change what we think of as meaningful so we avoid getting mired in trivial tasks and focus on more intrinsically satisfying goals, such as lasting relationships and enjoyable activities (e.g., Carstensen et al., 1999; Kosloff & Greenberg, 2009). Indeed, research on survivors of near-death experiences finds that many people report growing from the experience, becoming more balanced, more accepting, and better able to appreciate life and all it has to offer (e.g., Blackie et al., 2015). Elderly folks are particularly likely to think about death a great deal, in part because they have generally known more people who have died and are closer to their own end. Research shows that being close to the end has some positive consequences for elderly people (Carstensen et al., 1999). It leads them to want to maximize their enjoyment of life. Elderly people are especially interested in being with those they really care about, and they focus on the positive—how the glass of life is half full rather than half empty (e.g., Livingstone & Isaacowitz, 2015). Indeed, they are wise in another important way: They are consistently happier than younger people (Carstensen, 2009; Yang, 2008).

Why are older people better able to appreciate life and connect to their authentic goals? Perhaps as one approaches the loss of everything, it becomes easier to appreciate those things before one loses them. The poet W. S. Merwin (1970, p. 136) put it this way:

> and what is wisdom if it is not
> now
> in the loss that has not left this place

SECTION REVIEW Motives for Growth and Self-Expansion

People are motivated for personal growth and self-expansion.

Self-Determination Theory

- People thrive and grow when they feel their actions are self-determined rather than controlled by external forces.
- Self-determination is fostered by fulfillment of three basic needs: relatedness, autonomy, and competence.
- An internal locus of control is generally associated with positive outcomes in life.

Overjustification Effect

Behaviors that are initially intrinsically motivated can, if rewarded with external incentives, come to feel extrinsically motivated, with consequent decreases in interest and enjoyment.

How to Maximize Self-Growth

- Pursue goals that support core needs.
- Experience flow.
- Interpret stressful situations as challenges rather than threats.
- Foster a positive mood.
- Act mindfully.
- Explore novel aspects of the world.
- Maximize life's enjoyment in the face of limited time.

CRITICAL LEARNING EXERCISES

1. Say that you are interviewing teenagers to join a summer camp, and you want them to have a strong commitment to the camp when they join. Based on your knowledge of dissonance research, what strategies might you use in telling them about the pros and cons of the camp before they decide whether to join? What strategies might you use after they have joined the camp?

2. Imagine that you are giving advice to a friend who finds herself continually finding ways to avoid studying for her law school entrance exam. Drawing on what you have learned about self-esteem defenses, why is she behaving this way, and how could you help her overcome her problem?

3. Think about ways in which you engage in self-presentation in your everyday life. What goals do these efforts at self-presentation serve? If you think about your behavior when you interact with others as efforts at self-presentation, does this change how you think about yourself?

4. Imagine that some time in the future, you are in a management position in which you have to supervise a team of people. Based on self-determination theory, what policies or procedures would you implement to help maximize their creativity and job satisfaction?

Robert Daly/Ojo Images/AGE Fotostock

CHAPTER 7

Social Influence

Think back to your first couple weeks of college. You likely did not know where to go or what to do or who your new friends might be. How did you get by? How did you move from being an unsure person seeking direction to finding your way? Chances are you relied on other people to help you navigate through this sea of novelty. You learned about the norms and expectations; you used other people as sources of information; maybe you went to some parties to fit in and make friends; you followed the commands of those in authority (e.g., teachers, dorm leaders).

A new situation like college brings to the fore psychological processes of **social influence**, the effects of other people on an individual's beliefs, attitudes, values, or behavior. We have already noted many ways in which we humans are profoundly influenced by the individuals and culture around us. In a sense, the adult human is largely a product of social influences; however, we are never finished products, and we are subject to social influence from childhood throughout the life span.

In this chapter we cover the following aspects of social influence:

- Basic ways in which people learn specific behaviors and views of the world from others

- The formation of social norms and conformity, involving altering one's attitudes or behavior to fit a majority view

- Minority influence: situations in which a single individual ends up influencing the majority

- Compliance techniques, which are strategies one uses to get others to do what one wants them to do

- Obedience—following explicit commands from an authority figure

- The appeal of charismatic leaders

Social influence The effects of other people on an individual's beliefs, attitudes, values, or behavior.

Learning Outcomes

- Explain the factors that increase the likelihood that an observed behavior will be imitated.
- Explain the difference between injunctive and descriptive norms.
- Give an example of social contagion.
- Summarize how our cultural worldviews influence us in ways we may take for granted.

Learning from Others

Like other animals, humans learn by experiencing associations between stimuli (classical conditioning; Pavlov, 1927). If every time we see Tim, we have a good time, our association of Tim with good feelings may lead us to develop a positive attitude toward Tim. We also learn to repeat behaviors that in the past have been followed by favorable outcomes and avoid behaviors that have had unfavorable outcomes (operant conditioning). In addition to these forms of learning, we humans also learn a great deal by getting information from others and from observing others and imitating their behaviors.

Social Learning Theory

Social learning The capacity to learn from observing others.

The old expression "Monkey see, monkey do" captures the basic idea of **social learning**. Plenty of animals besides monkeys learn this way. Birds learn songs from other birds. Untrained dogs learn faster if they are taught behaviors alongside dogs who are already trained (Adler & Adler, 1977). Even octopi are faster at learning how to open a jar to get food if they first have an opportunity to observe another octopus do it (Fiorito & Scotto, 1992). However, we humans are probably the species most reliant on social learning.

From hitting a tennis ball to eating sushi or doing the tango, we learn largely from watching others *model* those behaviors. In fact, we saw in chapter 4 that certain neurons, called *mirror neurons*, are activated both when one does an action oneself and when one simply observes another person perform that action (Uddin et al., 2007). As the neuroscientist Marco Iacoboni notes, "When you see me perform an action—such as picking up a baseball—you automatically simulate the action in your own brain" (Blakeslee, 2006). Moreover, the more we watch something—say a person juggling on YouTube—the more we (erroneously) think we could perform the skill as well (Kardas & O'Brien, 2018). This misperception stems from our failure to appreciate what it takes to perform the steps involved (e.g., actually catching this rotating object is tougher than it looks). But believing you can do something, known as *self-efficacy*, can motivate taking those steps.

Albert Bandura (Bandura et al., 1961, 1963a, 1963b) led seminal studies investigating social learning. In these studies, mildly frustrated nursery school children (between ages three and six) watched a film of a young woman punch and kick a large inflated Bobo doll and hit it with a mallet. Children readily imitated this behavior (see **FIGURE 7.1**) when they were later given an opportunity to play with the Bobo doll; they punched and kicked the doll and hit it with a mallet in a manner eerily similar to the model's behavior, right down to repeating the same aggressive remarks the model had made (e.g., "Pow, right in the nose, boom, boom.").

Figure 7.1

The Bobo Doll Studies

Albert Bandura's classic Bobo doll studies illustrate how we learn our behaviors by watching others. Here we see that the adult's (top panel) aggressive actions are subsequently modeled by both boys and girls.
[Courtesy of Albert Bandura]

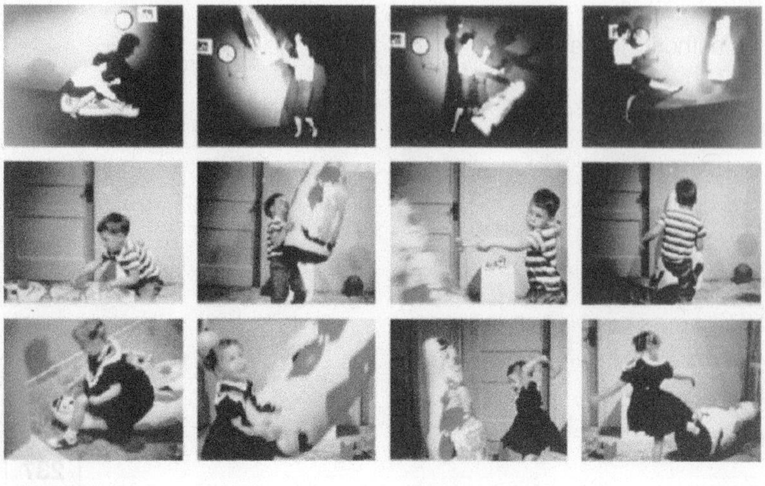

But observing and learning a behavior doesn't necessarily mean we will imitate it. According to Bandura's (1965) social learning theory, we can be encouraged or discouraged to engage in both new and known behaviors, depending on the consequences of the action. Thus, children were more likely to imitate the Bobo doll bashing if the model

was rewarded for the actions (e.g., supplied with a soda and candy) but were less likely to do so if the model was punished for the actions (e.g., a second adult spanked the aggressive model with a rolled-up magazine) (Bandura, 1965). Social learning is also more likely if the behavior observed fits the motivational state of the observer. So kids who were frustrated were more likely to imitate a violent model.

Finally, social learning is more likely when observers identify with the model—that is, when the model is liked and seems similar to the observer. This helps account for the value of role models for members of underrepresented groups in various fields, such as women in STEM fields (science, technology, engineering, and math). This underrepresentation is due to many factors (Stoet & Geary, 2018), such as stereotypes about women's math ability (which we will cover in chapters 10 and 11), but research has shown that it can be combatted by exposing women to successful role models in STEM fields (Dasgupta, 2011). This may be especially important during adolescence, when young women face pressures that turn them away from science-related interests. Indeed, in one study, middle school girls attended a science outreach program (O'Brien et al., 2017). Those randomly assigned to write about their favorite female role models in the program later reported an increased sense of fit in science compared to those not writing about their role models.

Of course, the tendency to learn from others and even imitate them can also be more subtle. The next time you find yourself at a restaurant, look at the people at other tables. How often do you see people mirroring each other's posture, such as two people both leaning in on their elbows? Tanya Chartrand and John Bargh (1999) documented this **chameleon effect**—the tendency to unconsciously mimic the nonverbal mannerisms of someone with whom you are interacting.

In one study, the researchers paired each participant with a partner and videotaped them telling each other a story about a photograph. These partners actually were confederates of the experimenters, trained to rub their faces or shake their feet at certain times during the interaction. As expected, when doing the task with a face-rubbing confederate, participants were more likely to rub their faces; when doing the task with a foot-shaking confederate, participants were more likely to shake a foot. None of the participants reported having any conscious awareness of the other person's mannerisms or that they mimicked them. This chameleon effect occurs mainly when the other person is likable (Cheng & Chartrand, 2003; Lakin & Chartrand, 2003).

This kind of mimicry isn't limited to casual, nonverbal behaviors. People also automatically shift their attitudes toward what they think another person's opinions might be, especially when they are motivated to get along with that person. One study (Sinclair, Lowery et al., 2005) had White participants complete an implicit association test (the IAT, which we introduced in chapter 3) to measure their automatically activated attitudes toward African Americans in the presence of an experimenter who was wearing a T-shirt that either was blank or said "Eracism" (suggesting the eradication of racism). The researchers also had the experimenter act in either a friendly or rude way. When the experimenter wore the Eracism shirt and was likable, participants indeed exhibited more positive attitudes toward African Americans in their IAT responses. But participants did not shift their attitudes when they did not like the antiracism experimenter.

The role of liking suggests that mimicry often happens because most social interactions involve a general goal of trying to get along. Our group-living

▲ Role models, such as social robotics expert Dr. Cynthia Breazeal, can help to increase people from underrepresented groups getting involved in STEM fields.

[The Washington Post/Getty Images]

⚏ Achie/e
Video: Albert Bandura

Chameleon effect The tendency to unconsciously mimic the nonverbal mannerisms of someone with whom you are interacting.

ancestors were probably more successful at propagating their genes by being able to interact with each other smoothly and thereby coordinate behavior to achieve shared goals.

 ## APPLICATION
Helpful and Harmful Media-Inspired Social Learning

Think about some of your favorite TV shows and how you might learn from what you see. In the course of watching a gripping drama, for example, you see characters that you identify with rewarded for certain actions. Might this influence your own behavior? Around the globe, television executives have been creating shows based on the principles of Bandura's social learning theory in an effort to address some of their communities' most pressing social issues. From literacy in Mexico to safe sex and family planning in Tanzania, using characters to convey the value of such things as reading and family planning through their actions has notable impact. For example, one show in Mexico featured a popular actor playing a character who advocated for literacy. The year before the show aired, about 90,000 people were enrolled in a literacy program, but after it aired, enrollment ballooned to over 1 million people (Bandura, 2009).

Although the human aptitude for social learning is generally adaptive, there can be downsides. The sociologist David Phillips (1974, 1979) discovered that media portrayals of celebrity suicides are associated with subsequent increases in suicides and car accidents among the general public. Phillips also showed that the more media coverage suicides get in a particular region of the country, the more people tried the act themselves. Feature films also often inspire unfortunate examples of social learning. The award-winning 1978 film *The Deer Hunter* showed soldiers playing the game Russian roulette (Cimino, 1978). In the following weeks, many instances of teenagers playing this dangerous game were reported. In 1993, another film, *The Program*, had a scene in which teenagers were shown lying down on the median between car lanes (Ward, 1993). Within days of the film's appearance in theaters, numerous teens tried this, sometimes with tragic consequences. We'll examine other unsavory examples of social learning in our coverage of aggression in chapter 12. ∎

Social Priming and the Influence of Norms

Another basic way that people influence us is by priming ideas, values, and norms. As we saw in chapter 3, when concepts are made salient or more accessible, they are more likely to influence our behavior. When other people remind us of the norm to be fair or charitable, for example, often we are more likely to act in accord with those norms. Consider a bunch of drivers at a busy intersection. While stopped at a traffic light, some were approached (or not) by a passerby who asked for directions to a well-known store (Guéguen et al., 2016). The light turned green, but the researchers, positioned ahead of the drivers at the intersection, pretended to stall their car. Those who had been primed with being helpful (i.e., by giving directions to the passerby) were less likely to honk their horn at the stalled driver than were those who had not been asked directions.

Robert Cialdini's (2003) *focus theory of normative conduct* emphasizes the important role that salience plays in enhancing the influence of norms. This theory distinguishes between two types of norms. **Injunctive norms** are beliefs about

Injunctive norm A belief about what behaviors are generally approved of or disapproved of in one's culture.

which behaviors are generally approved of or disapproved of in one's culture. **Descriptive norms** are beliefs about what most people typically do.

Often the two types of norms align and can be responsive to new information from the world. For instance, following the 2015 Supreme Court ruling on same-sex marriage in *Obergefell v. Hodges*, people's perceptions of the injunctive and descriptive norms supporting gay marriage shifted (Tankard & Paluck, 2017). The ruling obviously changed the perception that gay marriage is acceptable (injunctive norm), and it also changed the perception about Americans supporting gay marriage (descriptive norm). However, norms can also diverge. People think others should not litter but believe that most people do.

Descriptive norm A belief about what most people typically do.

APPLICATION
Using Norms to Preserve and Sustain

There are a few tricky aspects to using norms to change behavior. Well-intentioned efforts to get people to do the right thing, such as public service announcements, sometimes make salient a descriptive norm that turns out to be counterproductive (Cialdini, 2003). For instance, in 2000, visitors to the fascinating Petrified Forest National Park in Arizona were greeted by a sign saying, "Your heritage is being vandalized every day by theft losses of petrified wood of 14 tons a year, mostly a small piece at a time." Although this sign surely communicates the injunctive norm that it is wrong to take the wood, it also implies the descriptive norm that many people do take the wood. In such a case, the injunctive and descriptive norms being made salient are working at cross-purposes. Cialdini and colleagues (2006) ran a study in which they created and posted signs at two different spots in the park. One sign emphasized only the injunctive norm: "Please don't remove the petrified wood from the park." The other sign emphasized only the descriptive norm: "Many past visitors have removed the petrified wood from the park, changing the state of the Petrified Forest." The researchers were able to measure theft by tracking the disappearance of subtly marked pieces of wood placed throughout the park. Compared with the park average of just under 3% of the (specially marked) wood being stolen, the injunctive sign led to only 1.67% of the wood being stolen, but the descriptive sign led to a disturbing theft rate of 7.92%. So when you're trying to get people not to do bad things, be careful not to make salient the idea that many or most people do those bad things.

An additional challenge with encouraging sustainable behaviors is that they often require people to change entrenched routines supported by descriptive norms. For example, reports estimate that people generally eat more meat than physicians recommend and that livestock contribute to about 15% of global warming (Gerber et al., 2013). How do we change a behavior in which so many engage? Sparkman and Walton (2017, 2019) hypothesized that highlighting *dynamic norms*—norms about how behavior is changing—might help do the trick. In one of their studies, they asked café patrons waiting in line to complete a brief survey. Some participants received information about the study's interest in food choices; others about a static norm (that 30% of Americans eat less meat than they otherwise would); and yet others about a dynamic norm (that 30% of American are starting to change their eating habits to reduce meat consumption). Participants given information about dynamic norms were actually the least likely to order meat when they got to the café cashier. By anticipating a shift in normative behavior, people were more likely to change themselves. ◼

▲ Dynamic norms that convey how behavior, such as meat consumption, is changing can help promote even more widespread shifts in behavior.

Social contagion The phenomenon whereby ideas, feelings, and behaviors seem to spread across people like wildfire.

Social Contagion

The ideas of both mimicry and social priming may help explain a phenomenon that Gustave Le Bon (1897) labeled **social contagion**: that ideas, feelings, and behaviors seem to spread among people like wildfires. Le Bon noted that people in crowds come to behave almost as if they were of one mind. Since his time, studies have shown that everything from yawns, laughter, and applause to moods, goals, and depression seems to be contagious, spreading easily from person to person (e.g., Aarts et al., 2004; Hatfield et al., 1993; Provine, 2004). Contagion also affects our anticipatory actions. When participants observed another person wrinkling the nose (but not scratching it), they were more likely to scratch their own noses (Genschow & Brass, 2015).

APPLICATION
Psychogenic Illness

One particularly remarkable form of social contagion is called mass psychogenic illness (Colligan et al., 1982). This phenomenon occurs when an individual develops physical symptoms with no apparent physical cause, which then leads other people to feel convinced that they too have the same (psychologically generated) symptoms. Instances of this phenomenon seem to date back to at least the Middle Ages (Sirois, 1982). In one fairly well-documented case that occurred in 1998, a high school teacher in Tennessee reported a gasoline smell in her classroom and developed headaches, dizziness, and nausea. Once the idea of the gas leak and its supposed effects began to spread, more than 170 students, teachers, and staff members searched internally and, thanks to confirmation bias, ultimately found such symptoms in themselves, and the entire school was evacuated. Careful investigation by the Tennessee Department of Health determined that there was no physical cause of the symptoms (Jones et al., 2000). Eventually, the authorities convinced everyone there was no gas leak, and the symptoms disappeared. ■

The Social Construction of Reality

We have seen that our great reliance on social learning and our susceptibility to concepts that are brought to mind make us very open to social influence. Considered from the cultural perspective, these two forms of social influence play a large role in how people are socialized as children into a cultural worldview (see chapter 2). The title of sociologists Peter Berger and Thomas Luckmann's 1967 book *The Social Construction of Reality* nicely captures the point. Many of our beliefs, attitudes, values, and behaviors are taught to us in the first years of our life, when we are virtually totally dependent on our parents for sustenance, security, and knowledge. As we mature, educational, religious, and social institutions further reinforce our own culture's way of viewing the world. The version of the cultural worldview we have internalized over the course of childhood becomes a form of social influence that is both profound and largely taken for granted. The poet Samuel Taylor Coleridge put it this way:

> The great Fundamental . . . doctrines . . . are . . . taught so early, under such circumstances, and in such close and vital association with whatever makes or marks *reality* for our infant minds, that the words ever after represent sensations, feelings, vital assurances, sense of reality—rather than thoughts, or any distinct conception. Associated, *I had almost said identified*, with the parental Voice, Look, Touch, with the living warmth and pressure of the Mother on whose lap the Child is first made to kneel,

within whose palms its little hands are folded, and the motion of whose eyes its eyes follow and imitate . . . from within and without, these great First Truths, these good and gracious Tidings, these holy and humanizing Spells, in the preconformity to which our very humanity may be said to consist, are so infused, that it were but a tame and inadequate expression to say, we all take them for granted. (COLERIDGE & FENBY, 1825/1877, P. 207).

From this cultural worldview, we learn scripts for how to behave in different situations and different social roles.

Culturally Defined Social Situations For an illustration of the influence of culturally defined situations, think of instances in which the norm is to be quiet. You might come up with a library, a tennis match, or a funeral. But this same norm doesn't apply at a playground, a hockey game, or a wedding reception. As a child, you had to learn which norms apply in which situations, but once you've internalized those rules, you don't need to decide consciously to be quiet or loud. Instead, the context itself automatically activates the norm, which then guides your behavior.

To demonstrate this, Aarts and Dijksterhuis (2003) presented participants with a picture of a library or a train station and told them they would be going to that location later in the session. A third group was shown a library but had no expectation of going to a library. Participants then had to make judgments in a lexical decision task (a task in which participants have to decide whether a presented string of letters is a word or a nonword). Only the group that expected to be going to a library showed evidence of activating the concept of silence. Specifically, those participants were faster than either of the other groups to recognize silence-related words as being actual words. In a second study, participants who expected to go to a library also pronounced words more softly in what they thought was an unrelated communication task. For them, the anticipation of entering a library automatically activated a norm of being quiet that then affected their speaking volume even before they left the lab!

As you read this, what also might come to mind are the instances when people break social norms. Have you ever been studying at the library when someone walked in, talking loudly to a friend? Clearly some individuals are more likely to toe the line than others. Does everyone activate the same norms, but the nonconformists merely ignore these cues? Or do they not activate the norms in the first place? Although it's probably a little of both, some research suggests that nonconformists show less automatic activation of norms. When Aarts and colleagues (2003) followed up on the library study just described, they found that nonconformists (those who responded on a questionnaire that adhering to social norms was not very important to them) were less likely even to activate a concept of silence when expecting to visit a library. If people don't have the goal of fitting in, situations might not have the same power to activate norms that influence their behavior.

THINK ABOUT

[PHOVOIR/Alamy]

Culturally Defined Social Roles Along with learning social situations, early in life we also learn social roles and generalized beliefs, or stereotypes, about those roles. We learn about being doctors, lawyers, nurses, firefighters, and so forth. This knowledge is transmitted by our parents, by role models, and by mass media portrayals. Enacting these roles affects our attitudes and behavior.

The effect of social roles was the target of the well-known Stanford prison experiment. Philip Zimbardo and colleagues (Haney et al., 1973) used newspaper ads to recruit young men. The researchers created a mock prison in a basement on the campus of Stanford University. They randomly assigned half the young men to be guards and the other half to be prisoners. Guards were given prison guard–style uniforms, whistles, and nightsticks. Prisoners were dressed in inmate-style clothing. Zimbardo served as prison superintendent and gave the "guards" instructions and routines to follow in maintaining the incarceration of the "prisoners." Zimbardo reported that within days, the guards were treating the prisoners poorly, inflicting punishments that bordered on sadistic. Meanwhile, the prisoners either became rebellious or showed signs of depression. According to Zimbardo, the effects were so powerful that the experiment had to be stopped after only six days for the sake of the participants' well-being.

This Stanford prison experiment was traditionally credited as demonstrating the powerful effect that roles can have on people. In recent years, however, many of Zimbardo's claims about the study have been questioned. Based on archival investigation, it has been argued, for example, that Zimbardo gave clear instructions to the guards to dehumanize the participants and act harshly, that there were strong demand characteristics in the study that participants responded to, and that the frequency of the more egregious acts was exaggerated (e.g., Le Texier, 2019).

These critiques raise important questions about what the Stanford prison experiment teaches us. The study may still show the power of roles, though with some qualifications. Years after the Stanford study, Reicher and Haslam (2006) similarly constructed a situation that resembled a prison and randomly assigned participants to the roles of prisoner or guard. One of their key findings was that people adopted role-consistent behavior when they internalized the social identity of a role. It is not that people blindly took on any role assigned to them. Instead, participants' behavior was likely a result of identifying with their roles and then further committing to their roles to reduce dissonance caused by the behaviors they began engaging in to fulfill those roles (Haslam et al., 2015).

It is also interesting to note that, at least for the "prison guards," the original Zimbardo study may be more of a demonstration of obedience than a demonstration of social roles because the guards were primarily responding to explicit orders for how to behave. We will cover obedience in depth shortly. Here we encourage you to consider what kind of effect you think roles can have. Zimbardo (2007) and others have noted parallels between these studies and real-world cases of taking roles too far, such as when American soldiers overseeing the Iraqi detention center known as Abu Ghraib tortured and humiliated detainees, many of whom may not have been guilty of any crimes.

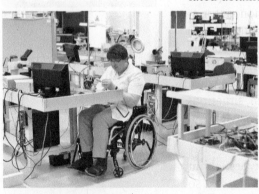

▲ Roles can be powerful forces of productive social change. Occupational roles for those with disabilities can improve their psychological functioning.
[industryview/Alamy]

These examples emphasize the negative influence of social roles, but roles can also be powerful forces for productive social change. For example, in economically developing countries like Sri Lanka, young rural women have gradually taken on a wider range of occupational roles since the late 1970s. As they have, they have become more independent and modern in their thinking and behavior (Attanapola, 2004). As another example, research on people with disabilities has shown that taking on occupational roles improves their sense of social connection, their self-esteem, and their quality of life (Blessing et al., 2012).

Based on this research, along with insights from anthropology and cross-cultural psychology, it is clear that the ways we think about situations and roles—and our views of ourselves and of historical and current events—are influenced by the cultural milieu in which we were raised and in which we live. But does this social influence truly extend to the basic ways we perceive the world? Pioneering work from way back in the 1930s on how conformity influences perception suggests that it does.

SECTION REVIEW Learning from Others

Humans learn a great deal by observing and imitating others.

Social Learning	Social Priming	Social Contagion	Social Construction
• We learn to do something new from watching others model the behavior. • We unconsciously tend to mimic the nonverbal mannerisms of others. • We also shift our attitudes to be similar to those of people we like.	• Reminders of norms and values can influence behavior. • Injunctive norms and descriptive norms can have different influences on behavior.	• Ideas, feelings, and behaviors can spread among people like wildfire.	• Cultures prescribe particular norms for particular situations. • These norms influence our behavior as the situation activates associated schemas. • Similarly, our cultures teach us the generalized beliefs that accompany particular roles.

Conformity

Conformity is a phenomenon in which individuals alter their beliefs, attitudes, or behaviors to bring them in accordance with the behavior of others. Muzafer Sherif (1936) sought to study the possibility that even basic perceptions of events can be affected by efforts to bring one's own perceptions in line with those of others. To do so, he took advantage of a perceptual illusion first noted by astronomers. If a small, stationary point of light is shown in a pitch-black room, it appears to move. This false perception of movement is known as the *autokinetic effect*.

Sherif sought to determine whether other people could influence an individual's perceptions of how much the point of light moves. First, he had people individually judge how much the point of light moved. He got various estimates (see **FIGURE 7.2**). Then he put two or three people together in a dark room and had them call out estimates of how much the light was moving. He made the quite remarkable finding that people started out with varying estimates, but after only a few trials, they came to agree on a particular estimate of how much the light moved. He also showed that a confederate planted in the group who made a particularly large assessment of the distance moved could push the group norm to a higher estimate. Furthermore, if the confederate was replaced by new, naive participants, the remaining group members would sustain the group norm and bring the new participants on board with them (Jacobs & Campbell, 1961). This "tradition" continued over five "generations" of participants.

Of course, it is reasonable to ask whether the participants' agreed-on estimate of the light's movement was just an effort to get along with others rather than a real shift in perception. Did people conform merely to agree with the group, a form of social influence called **public compliance**? Or did their own sense of what they were seeing actually change, a form of social influence referred to as **private acceptance**? Subsequent research has shown that it was the latter. One year after replicating the Sherif study, Rohrer and colleagues (1954) brought people back individually to judge the movement of the light. Those who had come to a group norm about the distance the light moved still viewed

Learning Outcomes

- Differentiate between informational and normative influence.
- List the personality and situational factors that influence our willingness to conform.
- Identify how the brain responds when we fail to conform and, thus, stick out from the crowd.

Conformity The phenomenon whereby an individual alters beliefs, attitudes, or behavior to bring them in accordance with those of a majority.

Public compliance Conforming only outwardly to fit in with a group without changing private beliefs.

Private acceptance Conforming by altering private beliefs as well as public behavior.

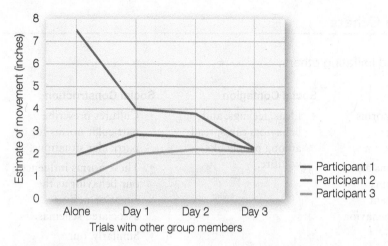

Figure 7.2

Sherif Conformity Studies on Norm Formation

The ambiguity of the estimation task reveals an informational influence on conformity and the formation of a group norm. When participants got into a group, their individual judgments converged to a common norm over the course of three days.

[Data from Sherif, 1936]

Informational influence The process of using others as sources of information about the world.

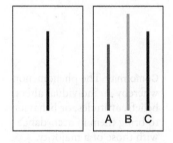

Figure 7.3

Asch Conformity Studies

The lack of ambiguity of the estimation task reveals a normative influence on conformity. Many participants went along with the group judgment even when their senses told them the judgment was incorrect.

[Photo by William Vandivert/Asch, 1955]

the light moving the amount the group had agreed upon a year earlier—a compelling example of the social construction of reality.

This body of research demonstrated conformity to a group norm on the basis of **informational influence**. The participants were not just trying to get along; they were trying to figure out how much the light was moving and used other people's estimates as information. Similar findings have been shown for a wide variety of tactile, perceptual, numerical, and aesthetic judgments (Sherif & Sherif, 1969). Generally, informational influence leads to private acceptance—a genuine belief that the attitude expressed or the behavior engaged in is correct. People most often seek others as information sources when they aren't sure what to think or how to behave. This was clearly the case for the ambiguous task that Sherif gave his subjects. But would people be so influenced by others if the task being judged were less ambiguous? What if they could rely on their own senses to make a judgment? This is what Solomon Asch wanted to find out.

Asch Conformity Studies

Imagine that you show up to a classroom to participate in a psychology experiment on visual judgment. With you are seven other students. As you settle around a table, an experimenter explains that he will display a series of pairs of large, white cards. On one card in each pair are three vertical lines of varying lengths, labeled A, B, and C; the other card shows a single vertical line (see **FIGURE 7.3**). Your task is to state out loud which line length best matches the single line. The first trial begins, and the experimenter starts with the first student to your left. The student says Line C. The next person also says Line C, and so forth, until it's your turn to respond. You respond Line C and quickly settle in to what appears to be a super boring (and totally easy) experiment. After a few such trials, however, something unexpected occurs. On presentation of lines like those displayed in Figure 7.3, the first student responds with Line A. You probably stifle a chuckle and think this person needs to have his eyes checked. But then the next person also says Line A. And so do the next person and the person after that. All of the other seven students say Line A; you begin to think that maybe it is you who needs your eyes checked. What could be going on here? Now it is your turn. How do you think you would respond?

This is the situation students faced in one variant of Asch's (1956) classic conformity studies. In contrast to Sherif, who presented people with an ambiguous situation, Asch was interested in how people would respond in situations where there was little ambiguity about what they perceived. Indeed, when judging these line lengths alone, participants made errors on fewer than 1% of the trials. Thus, Asch (1956) presented each participant with two opposing forces: on the one hand, the evidence of the senses, and on the other, the unanimous opinion of a group of peers (who actually were confederates instructed to respond in a set manner). Would people go with the answer they knew was correct? Or would they deny their own perceptions to agree with the group? Asch discovered that in situations such as the one just described, 75% conformed to the group opinion on at least one trial, and overall, participants conformed on 37% of the trials.

What the Asch Conformity Studies Teach Us About Why People Conform

[photo by William Vandivert/Asch, 1955]

What do you think this study teaches us beyond what we learned from Sherif's work? If you started to think it tells us something different about *why* people conform, you're in the right ballpark. Whereas Sherif's studies show that we are influenced by others to understand events in our world, Asch's studies point to a different— but very potent—pressure toward conformity. Because the stimulus being judged was not ambiguous, participants had sufficient perceptual information to make a confident judgment. It is unlikely that people conformed to others in this study because they were sources of information. Rather, Asch teaches us that people also conform to the norms of a group even if it means discounting what they know to be true. This process, referred to as **normative influence,** can be contrasted with the power of *informational influence,* which we saw demonstrated in Sherif's studies (Crutchfield, 1955; Deutsch & Gerard, 1955). Normative influence occurs when we go along with the group because we want to be liked and accepted by that group or because we want to avoid rejection. Examples of normative influence abound, as when we see teenagers dyeing their hair, getting nose piercings, or pining away for the hot brand of jeans or sneakers simply because that is what everyone else is doing. (Of course, this is not to say that some people don't adorn themselves in these styles as expressions of their individuality.)

But the objecting reader might be thinking, "Wait a minute! How do you know that people in Asch's study were not really convinced by the group? Maybe they did think the others were informing them about the actual lengths of the lines." And indeed, in postexperimental interviews, Asch found that some participants did question their own perceptions and thought that the majority might be correct. Some questioned their viewing angle, others their eyesight. However, they were in the minority. The rest acknowledged that they made choices they didn't believe were right simply to go along with the group. These participants reported feeling anxious, fearing the disapproval of others, and wanting to avoid sticking out. When we stick out, we run the risk of looking foolish, and many people are reluctant to face that possibility (Cialdini & Goldstein, 2004). In probing this issue further, Asch discovered that when people could write down their responses privately after hearing others' judgments, they almost never went along with the group opinion. Thus, publicly going against the group played a pivotal role in participants' tendency to conform.

Did the Asch participants really have a reason to worry about publicly deviating from the group? Nonconformers do in fact risk social rejection and ostracism. A classic study by Stanley Schachter (1951) found that when one confederate planted in a group stubbornly disagreed with the unanimous opinion of the group, that person was taunted, verbally attacked, and rejected. As we discussed in chapter 6, people find social rejection and ostracism highly upsetting. So the negative reaction that nonconformers so frequently receive helps explain why people often submit to the norms of the group.

Asch recognized that not all, or even most, participants were blindly punting away their own individualism to succumb submissively to the group opinion. In postexperimental interviews, many subjects expressed considerable concern for the solidarity and well-being of the group. Thus, the participants' responses can also be interpreted as valuing positive social relationships (Hodges & Geyer, 2006). From

Normative influence The process of using others to determine how to fit in.

Achieve
Video: Social Influence: Conformity

▲ When we stick out, we can risk ridicule and rejection from others.

[Joseph Farris/Cartoonstock]

▼ It's a bird, it's a plane, it's . . . . When we see others gazing upward, we're likely to follow suit. Here people on the streets of Ajmer in India demonstrate this tendency.

[Amos Chapple/Getty Images]

this perspective, then, participants' conformity to the group norm despite their own perceptions can be seen as an adaptive means of productively and harmoniously coexisting with others. Indeed, people who come from more collectivistic cultures, which strongly value group cohesion, generally are more likely to conform than people who come from individualistic cultures, which strongly value unique self-expression (Bond & Smith, 1996).

What Personality and Situational Variables Influence Conformity?

In many contexts, such as deciding whether a defendant is guilty or whether an aircraft design is safe, it would be rather alarming if individuals went along with the group despite what they know to be true from their physical perceptions. From Asch's studies, it's tempting to agree with Mark Twain's comment that "we are discreet sheep; we wait to see how the drove is going, and then go with the drove." But we shouldn't lose sight of the fact that 25% of participants never conformed to the group. These results also provide compelling evidence that some people do resist social pressure.

Unfortunately, not a great deal is known about the personality characteristics of those who tend to conform as opposed to those who do not. Early studies found some indications that people who have traits such as a high need to achieve (McClelland et al., 1953) and a propensity to be leaders (Crutchfield, 1955) are less likely to conform. People who have a greater awareness of self and high self-esteem (Santee & Maslach, 1982) are also less likely to conform because they are more confident in their own judgments and less in need of other people's approval. Intrinsic bases of self-esteem (feelings of self-worth based on who one thinks one really is, as opposed to self-esteem based on achievements that others may value) are especially likely to help people resist conformity (Arndt, Schimel et al., 2002).

For years, psychologists also thought that women conformed more than men, but any such differences are actually quite small. It turns out that people will more readily conform on topics they don't know much about. Thus, whereas women are more likely to conform on stereotypically masculine topics such as sports or cars, men are more likely to conform on stereotypically feminine topics such as fashion or family planning (Eagly & Carli, 1981).

Aspects of a situation also can influence the likelihood of conformity. One such factor is the size of the group exerting the pressure. Larger groups of unanimous opinions elicit more conformity—but only up to a point (Asch, 1956). This effect of diminishing returns for group size also is apparent with more subtle instances of conformity. Imagine walking down the street and seeing someone looking up and maybe even pointing at the sky. It's an almost reflexive response to follow that person's gaze to see what might be so interesting. Stanley Milgram and colleagues (1969) carried out a classic study to capture this simple phenomenon. On Forty-Second Street in Manhattan, research confederates stopped and stared up at a sixth-floor window. The researchers varied the number of assistants, and a key finding was that the greater the number of confederates who looked up, the greater the percentage of passersby who stopped to look up as well. Forty-two percent looked up if only 1 confederate was gazing up at the building. The proportion increased to about 80% with a group of 5 but rose to only about 85% when the number of confederates was 15. Thus, although larger numbers do increase pressure to follow the group, after a certain point, the effect of increasing numbers levels off. Perhaps this analogy will be helpful: Think of the sound of 10 people applauding. It's a lot more rousing than the sound of 3 people applauding. However, the difference between 43 people and 50 people applauding is far less noticeable.

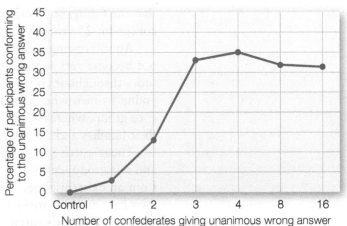

More important than the number of others is their unanimity. Three unanimous confederates creates considerable conformity to wrong answers. (**FIGURE 7.4** shows the percentage of participants who conformed to the unanimous majority in Asch's study.) But even *one* dissenting voice in a group of nine confederates appears to disrupt the pressure of the majority view and decreases conformity such that participants conform to the incorrect group on fewer than 5% of the trials in the line-judging paradigm (Asch, 1956). Interestingly, this other dissenting voice need not indicate the correct answer or appear to be especially competent. As long as one other person breaks from the majority view, participants feel more empowered to express their own view (Allen & Levine, 1969). Many organizations seem to understand this and deal harshly with the first person who steps out of line in order to prevent one dissenting voice from licensing others to buck the majority view.

As you might expect, characteristics of the group and the individual's relationship to that group can also influence conformity. High-status groups tend to inspire more conformity because they promise more social inclusion and self-esteem benefits. For example, when 12- to 15-year-old adolescents responded to different opinion surveys, knowledge quizzes, and video rating tasks, they conformed more to the judgments of high-status peer groups than they did to low-status peer groups (Gommans et al., 2017).

Such influence is not limited to adolescents. In personnel hiring decisions, for example, people may make subtly biased decisions to conform to the prejudices of their boss. When Vail and colleagues (2019) presented participants with hypothetical hiring scenarios, participants were less likely to endorse hiring women when they were given information suggesting that their supervisor was sexist. This disturbing tendency occurred regardless of participants' own beliefs and attitudes and reflected their desire to conform to the organizational culture of the hypothetical company.

In addition, strongly identifying with a large group, known as a **reference group**, is likely to have a substantial influence on an individual's attitudes and behavior (Turner, 1991). Reference groups are generally a source of both informational and normative influence. We trust them more than we trust other groups, and we want their approval more. Theodore Newcomb (1943) conducted a unique longitudinal study of conformity by tracking the political and economic attitudes of new students who enrolled in Bennington College, a private college for women, in the 1930s. The students came from wealthy, conservative backgrounds, but the staff and senior students at the college were quite liberal. He found that most of the students became increasingly liberal over their years at the college. Furthermore, a follow-up study in 1960 showed

Figure 7.4

The Effect of Group Size on Conformity

Conformity is more likely as group size increases from one to three people, but then the influence starts to level off.

[Data from Asch, 1956]

Reference group A group with which an individual strongly identifies.

that the former students had retained the liberal attitudes they had acquired in college for 25 years or more (Newcomb et al., 1967).

An interesting finding was that a minority of the young women who did not become very socially involved on campus retained their conservative attitudes throughout college. Newcomb discerned that the difference was that the young women who became liberal used the campus community as their reference group, whereas the young women who remained conservative maintained their families and friends from home as their reference group.

The research indicating that conformity is affected by our desires for esteem and our group identifications suggests that we can also understand conformity from an existential perspective. The groups people belong to help them to see their lives and the world as meaningful. In this way, conformity can be one strategy of deriving existential security. Research by Moynihan and colleagues (2019) supports this idea. When participants' beliefs in free will were undermined, they reported more meaninglessness, and this meaninglessness in turn was associated with higher tendencies to conform. Moynihan and colleagues suggested that conformity can serve as an escape from our existential burdens and insecurities.

 **APPLICATION**
Conformity in Juries

One context in which conformity probably plays a large role is in criminal jury trials. In the United States, juries typically have 6 to 12 members and usually have to come to a unanimous verdict. If they don't, the result is a hung jury, and the defendant is either released or retried; thus, there is a lot of pressure to go along with the majority verdict. Indeed, research highlights the influence of normative pressure in juror decisions. In a survey study of former jurors from 367 jury trials, Waters and Hans (2009) found that for 38% of the juries, at least one person reported that he or she would have chosen a different verdict if he or she had decided alone! This percentage is strikingly similar to the finding in the Asch study that participants conformed to the wrong answer on 37% of the line-judging trials. In addition, Waters and Hans found that hung juries were more likely when there were two or more private dissenters than when there was only one; this finding is consistent with the Asch finding that having a fellow dissenter makes it much easier to hold one's ground and not conform. This pattern of findings suggests that conforming to the majority due to normative pressure contributes to decisive verdicts that profoundly affect people's lives. ∎

Neural Processes Associated with Conformity

Recall that Sherif's work showed that a majority group opinion sometimes changes the way we actually *perceive* things. Are these changes in perception reflected in how our brain processes perceptual stimuli? Berns and colleagues (2005) scanned participants' brains using fMRI while the participants made judgments about the spatial orientation of three-dimensional geometric figures. Participants were given feedback about how other people who were purportedly in the session thought the figures were oriented. In another condition, participants were given the same type of feedback but were told it was computer generated. When participants conformed to the opinions of others, the areas of the brain implicated in spatial perception (the occipital-parietal areas) were more active. However, this effect did *not* occur when the feedback was said to be from the computer. Berns and colleagues thus suggested that peer opinion exerts an especially potent influence on how we perceive objects in our world.

The research of Berns and colleagues also indicates how the brain responds when we fail to conform and thus stick out. Brain scans of the nonconformists showed increased activation of the amygdala in the brain's right hemisphere, an area commonly associated with fear. This fits with the idea that people conform to avoid the negative feelings of social rejection (Cialdini & Goldstein, 2004).

SECTION REVIEW   Conformity

People conform both to get along with others and because others are sources of information.

The Sherif and Asch Conformity Studies	Personality and Situational Influences	Neural Processes
People often conform to groups. • They want to be right (informational influence). • They want to fit in (normative influence).	The people who are least likely to conform have: • A high need for achievement • Leadership qualities • Confidence in their own judgment • High self-esteem Willingness to conform also depends on: • The number of people in the group and the group's status • Whether even one other person breaks from the majority view • How strongly the individual relates to the larger group	fMRIs provide evidence that: • People are more sensitive to peer opinion than to other kinds of information.

Minority Influence

Learning Outcomes

Social psychologists have long considered how the numerical majority can influence people. But in the mid- to late 1960s, amid the protests surrounding the Vietnam War and civil rights, open dissent became prevalent. Partly as a consequence, this period also saw the dawn of research into how the voice of one could influence the views of the many. Serge Moscovici (Moscovici, 1980; Moscovici et al., 1969) pioneered this work on **minority influence**—the process by which dissenters (or numerical minorities) produce attitude change within a group, despite the extraordinary risk of social rejection and disturbance of the status quo. It's vital to understand these processes, for without this knowledge, we would have little understanding of how social change occurs.

Ralph Waldo Emerson famously wrote, "All history is a record of the power of minorities, and of minorities of one." Indeed, single individuals and small movements have many times profoundly altered the course of history: Plato, Confucius, Moses, Jesus, Muhammad, Nicolaus Copernicus, Galileo, Karl Marx, Charles Darwin, Sojourner Truth, Thomas Edison, Susan B. Anthony, Sigmund Freud, Mahatma Gandhi, Albert Einstein, Adolf Hitler, Rosa Parks, Mother Teresa, Martin Luther King Jr., Cesar Chavez—the list could go on and

- Explain when minority influence can create a more enduring attitude than majority influence.
- List ways to increase influence when in a minority position.

Minority influence The process by which dissenters (or numerical minorities) produce attitude change within a group, despite the risk of social rejection and disturbance of the status quo.

on. Thus, the study of minority influence is a window into the agents of cultural and social changes through scientific or artistic achievements, religion, political movements, horrific wars, advances in racial or gender equality, or other historical trends. Toward the end of this chapter, we'll consider how individuals can influence others by holding a position of authority or rising to a leadership position. But for now, we're going to focus on how individual dissenters can influence the majority even without the advantage of being in a position of authority.

How Minorities Exert Their Influence

In their initial study of minority influence, Moscovici and colleagues (1969) developed their own perceptual judgment paradigm but with some interesting twists. Instead of confronting participants with majority pressure, Moscovici presented them with a minority view and examined how that view influenced their perceptions. In what they were told was a study of color perception, groups of six participants were asked to view slides, all varying shades of blue, and name the color in each. In the control conditions, all participants indicated that the slides were blue. As in the Asch studies, confederates were involved in the experimental conditions. In the *inconsistent* condition, each group had four actual participants and two confederates, who described two thirds of the slides as green and the other third as blue. In the *consistent* condition, the two confederates described all the slides as green. Did this minority view change what the participants reported? It did, but primarily when the minority was consistent. When the confederates were consistent in saying a slide was green, 32% of the participants indicated at least once that they too thought the slide was green, compared with only 8% in the inconsistent condition and less than 1% in the control condition.

Conversion theory The explanation that people are influenced by a minority because the minority's distinctive position better captures their attention.

That a minority can have an influence over the majority was a shocking finding in a field that had previously considered only majority influence. Moscovici also studied how such historical figures as Galileo and Freud succeeded in thwarting the consensus of their times. Moscovici (1980) proposed his **conversion theory** to explain how and why being influenced by a minority differs from being influenced by the majority. According to Moscovici, because people generally want to fit in with the majority group, they often go along with the majority position without deeply considering the message the majority is delivering. They tend just to accept it, especially when they are not invested in the issue. The minority position, however, is by definition more distinctive. Although Moscovici reasoned that people generally don't want to identify with the minority, the distinctiveness of the minority's position better captures their attention. As a result, they tend to consider it more thoroughly; this deeper consideration can lead to a genuine change in attitude (e.g., Crano & Chen, 1998; De Dreu & De Vries, 1993; Maass & Clark, 1983). You may have noticed that the dual processes specified by Moscovici's conversion theory sound quite similar to the dual automatic and controlled processes of social cognition (see chapter 3). If you did, you're right. Can you think of an example where, after initially reacting to a minority opinion negatively, you were eventually influenced by it?

If being convinced by a minority involves more elaborate processing of the message, it should lead to a stronger and more enduring attitude that will be a more potent guide to behavior (Petty & Cacioppo, 1986). In contrast, if being convinced by a majority involves more superficial processing, the resulting attitude should be weaker and have less influence on one's behavior. Findings from

THINK ABOUT ▶

[Buyenlarge/Archive Photos/Getty Images]

Martin and colleagues (2007) support this idea. In their study, students who were initially not really invested in joining the student union were more likely to sign a petition supporting membership fees when they were persuaded of the union benefits by a minority than when they were persuaded by a majority.

Adopting a minority decision is risky (Erb et al., 2015). Among other problems, the minority group or individual courts negative reactions from others (Nemeth, 1979), and those who adopt the minority position may in fact be aware that they are flirting with such disdain. This helps explain the **minority slowness effect**. When people are asked about their attitudes on various topics such as sports, politics, celebrities, and social issues, those who adopt the minority position take longer to express their opinions (Bassili, 2003).

The minority position presents a distinctive and interesting puzzle that people want to figure out. In so doing, people can derive considerable benefits. As people think extensively about the minority's argument, they often think about different perspectives themselves, which allows for the consideration of novel and creative possibilities (Kenworthy et al., 2008; Nemeth, 1986). As one example, Mucchi-Faina and colleagues (1991) had students from Perugia, Italy, try to think of ways to enhance the international reputation of their city. The students were shown pictures of two historic landmarks in Perugia—the Palazzo dei Priori (**FIGURE 7.5a**) and the Arco Etrusco (**FIGURE 7.5b**)—and were told that marketing these sites to enhance the city's reputation was advocated by either a majority or a minority of citizens surveyed. When students were presented with what they thought was the minority opinion on how to enhance the city's reputation (versus what they thought was the majority opinion), they offered more creative and unique ideas about how to do so.

Minority slowness effect An effect that occurs when people who hold the minority position take longer to express their opinions.

Figure 7.5

Minority Opinion

The Palazzo dei Priori (a) and the Arco Etrusco (b) are two historical landmarks in Perugia, Italy. Mucchi-Faina and colleagues (1991) showed that study participants' ideas about how to market these sites to increase tourism were more creative when participants thought that using these sites was advocated by the minority rather than by the majority.

[Part (a): Stuart Robertson/Alamy; part (b): De Agostini Picture Library/M. BORCHI/Getty Images]

(a)

(b)

 APPLICATION

How Minorities Can Be More Influential

Earlier we noted that in addition to conforming for normative reasons, people also conform because of informational influence. We tend to trust others as sources of information. Heading to hear a presidential candidate speaking on campus some years ago, but not knowing where to go, your current author (Jamie) and family followed droves of people making their way to a particular location: They assumed that these other people knew where to go and followed their lead. Of course, the family would have been less likely to follow only a few people heading in a particular direction. This example illustrates the types of issues for which majorities can have greater influence: questions of fact. And indeed, research based on quiz shows that allow contestants to consult an audience suggests that when it comes to facts, majority opinions usually are accurate sources of information (Surowiecki, 2004). Consequently, minorities are not especially influential concerning issues for which there is an objective answer. Rather, minorities tend to have their greatest influence on matters of opinion. In one study, for example, minorities had less influence when Italian students were asked, "From which country *does* Italy import most of its raw oil?" than when the students were asked, "From which country *should* Italy import most of its raw oil?" (Maass, Volpato et al., 1996).

Research also has identified a number of other qualities that enhance the likelihood that a minority can successfully sway the majority. These are important tips to keep in mind the next time you find yourself in a minority position and want to convince others:

■ It is important for the minority to project self-confidence and be consistent in its advocacy (e.g., Moscovici et al., 1969; Wood et al., 1994). When Dr. Martin Luther King Jr. endeavored to convince a nation of the need for racial equality, he did so with unwavering consistency, even though it meant that he was hated by many.

■ Although consistency and self-confidence are important, they can backfire if the minority person or group is perceived as rigid and inflexible. Studies show that a flexible and open-minded behavioral style, indicating a willingness to compromise, is an effective complement to consistency in promoting persuasion by either a minority or a majority (Moscovici et al., 1985).

■ Getting members of the majority to defect, or cross over, and adopt the minority view is one of the most potent ingredients of minority influence. In fact, studies of jury decision making have shown that a minority is more influential when it can achieve a defection from the majority than when it starts with someone already on its side (Nemeth & Wachtler, 1974). Part of the reason that this can lead to a snowball effect and influence the rest of the majority is that it undermines an "us versus them" mentality.

■ Finally, as with all other forms of social influence, the more people identify with the person attempting to persuade them, the more likely they are to be persuaded (Maass & Clark, 1984). ■

SOCIAL PSYCH AT THE MOVIES

12 Angry Men

The classic 1957 film *12 Angry Men* (Lumet, 1957), starring Henry Fonda and directed by Sidney Lumet, portrays in great detail one riveting example of minority influence while also illustrating other factors in social influence. The film opens with 12 jurors who have just heard the murder trial of a boy accused of killing his father. The jurors settle into the deliberation room, muttering that it appears to be an open-and-shut case. Soon after, an initial vote is taken by a show of hands. Ten hands rise in favor of a guilty verdict, quickly followed by another, tentative hand. Immediately, we see elements of both normative and perhaps informational social influence as the initially tentative juror looks to the others for what might be the correct verdict. When the foreman asks for votes of "not guilty," only one hand is raised.

What follows is a compelling portrayal, filmed exclusively in the confines of this one room, of the process by which 1 man succeeds in changing the minds of 11 other jurors. Demonstrating how art can anticipate scientific insight, the film highlights a number of factors that subsequent research

has shown increase the likelihood of minority influence. Fonda's character takes some time to ponder his initial vote but thereafter consistently advocates an open-minded consideration of the evidence. The distinctiveness, flexibility, and

▲ [Mary Evans/ORION NOVAPRODUCTIONS/Ronald Grant/Everett Collection]

SECTION REVIEW   Minority Influence

Despite disturbance of the status quo, minorities can produce attitude change and throughout history have been agents of cultural and social change.

How Minorities Exert Influence	Factors That Increase Minority Influence
• The distinctiveness of the minority position captures attention and prompts deeper consideration. This can lead to lasting attitude change.	• Minority advocates being consistent and confident yet flexible
• Minorities are generally disliked, so those holding a minority position may take longer to express their opinions.	• A defection from the majority
• The majority finds the minority position puzzling, which may lead to original thinking and diversified strategies for figuring out solutions.	• Identifying with the minority advocate

Compliance: The Art and Science of Getting What You Want

Learning Outcomes

• Describe methods people use to get others to do what they want them to do.

• Identify factors that increase our willingness to comply.

Conformity often involves implicit pressure. But there are many situations in which one person's explicit goal is to change another person's behavior. Salespeople want you to buy their product, parents want their kids to do the right things, and so forth. This brings us to *compliance* and *obedience*. In the case of obedience, you simply tell people what to do. It turns out this works quite

firmness of his views ultimately provoke deeper and more thorough reflection in some of the other jurors, which further inspires their own creative thoughts about the issues at hand. They start to see holes in the prosecution's case that even Fonda's character did not notice. This more thoughtful and systematic consideration leads some of the jurors to more sustained attitude change. In contrast, those jurors who were simply agreeing with the majority for superficial reasons show signs of more fleeting opinions, "bouncing back and forth like a Ping-Pong ball."

Henry Fonda's character also has brief personal conversations with some of the other jurors, which helps to break down the walls between them. He no longer seems like an outcast. And as research shows, the more people identify with a minority, the more influential that minority can be.

Three of the more noteworthy performances are by Lee J. Cobb, E. G. Marshall, and Joseph Sweeney. In Lee J. Cobb's character, we see a powerful example of personal bias and stereotypes coloring the way a person processes the information to which he is exposed. The young defendant reminds him of his struggles with his own son, and he is unable to get

beyond the bias and bitterness that seethe in him. In E. G. Marshall's character, a cool, level-headed, and (almost) always composed stockbroker, we see the ultimate example of social influence through informational routes. He rationally sticks to his vote until finally, showing his first trickle of perspiration on this stifling, hot afternoon, he admits that the accumulation of information raises a reasonable doubt. With Joseph Sweeney, an astute and rather observant older gentleman, we see the power of an initial defection. After standing alone in his insistence on continuing to go over the details of the case, Henry Fonda's character takes a gamble, asking for a vote and agreeing to abstain. If everybody else continues to vote guilty, he claims, he will go along with the verdict, adding, "But if one person votes not guilty, we stay here and talk this out." His initial success in converting a lone defector (Joseph Sweeney's character) is subsequently followed by the gradual conversion of the remaining jurors.

After the film was released, each of these tactics was subsequently examined and supported in empirical research on how and when minorities can influence numerical majorities.

well when you have authority over someone else. We hinted at this in discussing the Stanford prison experiment, and we will explore it more deeply in the next section. But without the power of authority over someone, what techniques can you use to gain compliance with requests?

The study of compliance has revealed a handy toolkit of methods to bring someone else's behavior in line with a request. As you learn about these methods, notice how they are used all the time by advertisers, salespeople, and others in the business of influencing your consumer behavior. In fact, many of these methods were discovered when the social psychologist Bob Cialdini spent a few years undercover, going into car dealerships and taking other sales positions to find out which sales techniques are the most effective for getting people to pull out their credit cards (Cialdini, 2006). Of course, methods of compliance are also useful outside the marketplace for changing a range of behaviors, from getting your roommate to do the dishes to getting people to give generously to charities.

Self-Perception and Commitment

According to Bem's self-perception theory (discussed in chapter 5), once we freely engage in a behavior, we often infer that we hold attitudes that are consistent with that behavior (Bem, 1967). This process explains the **foot-in-the-door effect**: People are more likely to comply with a moderate request if they initially comply with a smaller request. If you agree to let a door-to-door salesperson into your home, you may infer that you have some interest in hearing about the product being sold, which makes you more likely to give that product a try.

Imagine that you are participating in the following study by Burger and Caldwell (2003). In one condition, you spend time completing several questionnaires. At the end of the study, you are asked if you would be willing to volunteer a couple of hours the following weekend, helping to sort food donations for a local homeless shelter. If you are like most other participants, you would probably come up with some excuse for why you wouldn't have the time. In this condition, only 32% of the participants volunteered. But now rerun the simulation with the following change: At the very beginning of the session, another participant asks if you might be willing to sign a petition to increase awareness about the plight of homeless people. This is an easy enough thing to agree to, and you add your name to the list. Having done so, you now feel like a champion of the underprivileged. What happens when you are next asked to spend your Saturday afternoon sifting through food donations? In the real experiment, 51% of the participants complied with the fairly substantial larger request if they had first complied with a smaller request (**FIGURE 7.6**). This significant increase in compliance resulted from simply carrying out an initial smaller request.

The foot-in-the door effect happens because when you comply with a small request, you are likely to infer that you are the type of person who helps others or is interested in the particular cause. Because of this shift in self-perception, you become more receptive to the related but larger second request. Indeed, once you have this new view of yourself, refusing the second request would likely arouse dissonance.

This raises an interesting possibility: If you initially comply with a small request for extrinsic reasons, such as a monetary reward, will you be less likely to infer that you are the helping type? Perhaps yes, if you

Foot-in-the-door effect A phenomenon whereby people are more likely to comply with a moderate request after having initially complied with a smaller request.

Figure 7.6

The Effect of Self-Perception Processes on Compliance

Burger and Caldwell's (2003) study shows how self-perception processes can increase compliance. When participants first agreed to a smaller request or were complimented on being thoughtful and caring, they were more likely to agree to a larger request to donate time.

[Data from Burger & Caldwell, 2003]

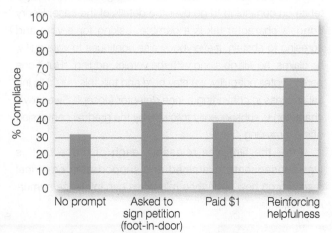

Willingness to volunteer at a homeless shelter

attribute your compliance to the extrinsic factor. In this case, when you are later asked to comply with a larger request, you will feel less pressure to act in ways that are consistent with your self-image. This point was also illustrated in Burger and Caldwell's (2003) study (see **FIGURE 7.6**): When participants were offered a dollar to sign a petition, they were *not* more willing to comply with a second, larger request to volunteer at the homeless shelter. Presumably they inferred that they signed the petition for the dollar and not because of who they were or what they believed. The role of self-perception processes is also illustrated in an additional condition in which, after signing the petition, participants were explicitly told by the requestor what caring and thoughtful people they are. Participants in this condition were much more likely to comply with the large request—65% of them did so—because the compliment reinforced their image of themselves as caring. This might be why we often seek to butter up someone we are about to ask for a favor. By flattering the person for being generous or caring, for example, we validate a self-perception that the person then may be more likely to uphold.

Our motivation to view ourselves as consistent also contributes to a social norm to honor our commitments. This **norm for social commitment** underlies the strong sense of trust that is one of the building blocks of cooperative relationships. Most of the time, behaving in line with such a norm fosters healthy social bonds. Those who renege on their agreements earn a reputation for being untrustworthy. But the norm for social commitment can get you to do things you might not otherwise want to do.

Norm for social commitment A belief whereby once we make a public agreement, we tend to stick to it even if circumstances change.

For example, the norm for social commitment can make you feel trapped in a decision and forced to accept a *lowball offer*. **Lowballing** can take different forms, but the general principle is that after agreeing to an offer, people find it hard to break that commitment, even if they later learn of some extra cost to the deal. Consider this technique in the context of trying to sell someone a car. One of your authors, Jamie, found himself in this very situation just the other day. He and the salesperson agreed on an "out the door" price that included the dealership's $200 service fee. But in the final paperwork, the salesperson had forgotten to include the service fee, and the price Jamie was asked to sign for was $200 higher than he had expected. Although he balked at that price initially, he then found it hard to say "no," and he agreed to split the $200 service fee with the dealership.

Lowballing A phenomenon in which after agreeing to an offer, people find it hard to break that commitment even if they later learn of some extra cost to the deal.

Researchers have studied lowballing in a number of real-life contexts. In one such study (Cialdini et al., 1978), researchers called participants and recruited them to take part in a psychology experiment. When participants were immediately told that the study would be taking place at 7:00 in the morning, only 24% agreed to sign up. But the compliance rate more than doubled (56%) when people were first asked if they wanted to participate in a study and only after they said "yes" were informed that it took place at 7:00 in the morning. Even when given the chance to change their minds, none of them went back on their initial commitment. What's more, 95% of those who agreed actually showed up for the study!

Lowballing is different from the foot-in-the-door request because it requires only an initial commitment that binds one to an agreement with another person, not the enactment of any behavior that changes one's view of oneself. Because complying with an initial foot-in-the-door request leads to a change in self-view, people comply with the second, larger request even if it comes from a different person (Freedman & Fraser, 1966). In contrast, the effect of agreeing to an initial lowball request is specific to that requestor; if someone else springs the added cost on us and asks if we will still follow through, we tend to walk away from the table (Burger & Petty, 1981). When the two strategies are compared, lowballing often gains greater compliance (Brownstein & Katzev, 1985; Cialdini et al., 1978).

Reciprocity

The age-old saying "You scratch my back, I'll scratch yours" reflects another very basic norm of social interaction: reciprocity. Humans across cultures show a very strong norm to reciprocate acts. Reciprocity is seen in nonhuman animals as well—apes, monkeys, even bats! After a successful night of collecting blood, vampire bats regurgitate some of that blood to share with other bats—but not just *any* other bats: Such sharing is more likely to happen with bats that have shared their own blood in the past (Wilkinson, 1990). You cough up some of your blood, and I'll cough up some of mine.

Because the norm of reciprocity is strong, it is often used to induce compliance. If you have ever donated money to an organization after it provided you with a free gift (preprinted address labels, for example), then you have felt the pull of reciprocity. But why do we reciprocate? Is it a built-in instinct, instilled over the course of evolution? Perhaps when someone does us a favor, we just like that person more or we're simply in a better mood, and these factors make us more likely to reciprocate.

A clever experiment by Dennis Regan (1971) provides some answers. Each participant worked on a task alongside a confederate who came across as either very likable or downright rude. In one condition, the confederate returned from a break halfway into the study and, as an unexpected favor, gave the participant a can of Coke. In a second condition, the participant also received a Coke, but this time from the experimenter. In a third condition, the participant did not receive this unexpected gift. At the end of the session, the confederate asked the participant if he would be willing to help him out by purchasing lottery tickets for a fundraiser.

Regan figured that if people help others simply because they like them, then participants in this study would not help the rude confederate, even if he kindly delivered a Coke. Also, if receiving favors increases helping simply because it improves mood, then participants would be more willing to help the confederate if they had been given a free Coke, regardless of whether it came from the confederate or the experimenter. The results did not support either of these hypotheses. Instead, people bought about 75% more tickets when the confederate had given them a Coke compared with the other two conditions, regardless of whether the confederate was generally likable or rude. This suggests that liking or being in a good mood are not essential ingredients of reciprocity. That is, although both positive moods and liking tend to increase compliance, they were not especially influential in this context (Carlson et al., 1988; Isen et al., 1976). Rather, this experiment shows the power of following the norm of reciprocity.

Norms toward reciprocity can also play a role in negotiations. Conventional wisdom might tell you that when you approach your boss about requesting a raise, you might not want to start with a high initial request that could alienate your superior and stop the process before it starts. But such wisdom ignores the powerful role that reciprocity can play. Although your boss might deny your request for a hefty $10,000 raise, the guilt she might experience from turning down your request could lead her to compromise at a $5,000 raise, which might have been the amount you were hoping for all along. This is called the **door-in-the-face effect**; it's the idea that people are more likely to comply with a moderate request after they have first refused a much larger request. (Although this tactic isn't working for Calvin in the cartoon, it often does!) The name of this effect draws on the nature of door-to-door sales, in which making an unreasonable request might initially get the door slammed in your face but might also open the person to considering a compromise offer.

Door-in-the-face effect A phenomenon whereby people are more likely to comply with a moderate request after they have first been presented with and refused to agree to a much larger request.

▲

Consider a classic study that Cialdini carried out with his research team (1975). Members of his team approached students around campus and asked if they would be interested in volunteering their time on an upcoming Saturday to chaperone a group of juvenile delinquents on a trip to the zoo. With no financial incentive and concerns about lacking experience, 83% of those approached refused. But the experimenters first approached another group of students with the offer of spending two hours a week for two full years as counselors to delinquent kids. Not surprisingly, no one was willing to make this extreme commitment of time. However, when their refusal was followed by a smaller request to chaperone for one Saturday afternoon (the same request initially given to the other group of students), half of the students agreed to help out. In other words, the door-in-the-face strategy actually tripled the number of volunteers!

How is reciprocity involved here? When the person being approached with a request views the smaller compromise offer as a concession, that person can become motivated to reciprocate and do her part to maintain good faith in the exchange. This then can lead her to be more likely to accept the compromise offer.

Social Proof

During college, one of your authors (Toni) spent a summer selling educational books door to door. The job entailed trying to meet and talk to every family in a neighborhood. Whenever a family placed an order for books, its name was added to a list of buyers. The list was shown to potential customers as a sort of proof that the product was good. In one community, your author was fortunate enough to have several high school teachers and parents in the local school district purchase the books so that their names adorned the buyer sheet. When she approached the house of the high school's principal, he took just one look at this list and instantly said, "Well then, I guess I have to buy them," and pulled out his wallet without even taking a very close look at what it was he was buying!

This anecdote typifies the powerful effect that **social proof** has on our behavior. This technique capitalizes on our tendency to conform to what we believe others think and do. It is akin to making salient a descriptive norm but emphasizes the special value of information about what similar and respected others have done. As social comparison theory posits, we often look to similar others to provide us with information about what is good, valuable, and desirable. This makes our friends the most effective salespeople we know, and we commonly follow their recommendations for restaurants, movies, and clothing brands.

Social proof A tendency to conform to what we believe respected others think and do.

If consistency means choosing a behavior that conforms to your perception of yourself, and social proof means choosing a behavior that conforms to what others are doing, you can imagine that in some cases these two compliance strategies could pull a person in opposing directions. In fact, there can be cultural variation in which strategy is more effective. For example, in one study, students from a collectivistic culture (Poland) chose to comply with a request based on information about how many of their peers had complied, whereas U.S. students, who are typically more individualistic, were more influenced by considering whether they had complied with similar requests in the past (Cialdini et al., 1999).

Scarcity

In the summer of 2008, record numbers of people lined up for hours, sometimes days, to buy the latest must-have gadget: the first Apple iPhone. Anticipation for the product, with its integrated camera and lightning-speed Internet connection, had been building for months. If Apple wanted to sell products, why hadn't the company's market-research team more accurately estimated the demand for this new toy? The answer might lie in an interesting fact about human psychology: We want . . . no, *need* . . . no, *absolutely must have* things that are scarce. Perhaps because it was selected for back in prehistoric days of feast and famine, we seem to have an innate preference for anything that is in short supply. Consequently, things or even ideas that are scarce or rare are attended to especially carefully (Brock & Brannon, 1992). Another explanation is that our craving for scarce things stems from the feeling that scarcity is an insult to our basic freedom of choice, and that makes us want what is rare even more (Brehm, 1966).

▲ Might the initial scarcity of the original iPhone have contributed to its popularity?

[Chesnot/Getty Images]

Each of these explanations has some support, and research has not definitively favored one over the other. Regardless of the precise reason for valuing what's scarce, stores and manufacturers realize and exploit this little quirk of human nature. You probably have seen countless advertisements declaring that a good deal won't last: *Limited time offer! Sale ends Saturday! Limited quantity!* In fact, sometimes these offers aren't even genuine. Take the example of a Circuit City store that was going out of business and having a "liquidation sale" for a "limited time." Instead of lowering the prices on products, the company charged with orchestrating the liquidation of the store's inventory actually *raised* prices (Glass, 2009)! Many unsuspecting customers who hadn't done their homework flocked to the store and bought up electronics for more than they might have paid online or from a different vendor.

Mindlessness

A final way that we can sometimes get people to comply with requests is to take advantage of the fact that we often go about our daily lives operating on autopilot. Situations bring to mind certain standard scripts of what to do and say. Once these scripts are set in motion, we sometimes fail to stop and think whether what we are actually doing seems reasonable. Imagine that you are standing in line at an automated teller machine when someone approaches and wants to cut in line. Presumably, you would be more likely to comply with this request if she gives a good reason, right? Maybe not.

Ellen Langer and her colleagues did a simple study in which a confederate asked if she could cut in line at a photocopy machine (Langer et al., 1978).

When the confederate explained her request by saying that she was in a rush, 94% of people agreed to let her go ahead of them, compared with only 60% when the person gave no reason whatever and simply asked to use the copy machine. But the interesting condition was one where the confederate asked to use the copy machine "because I have to make some copies." On the surface this *sounds* like a reason and probably activated a schematic impression that the requestor had a good reason, but it was really just a statement of what she planned to do. (Why else would someone use a copy machine?) Yet in a fairly mindless way, a full 93% capitulated to this request. In chapter 6, we introduced the idea that such mindlessness can stunt our creativity and lead us to behave and think in a rather rigid way. As we see here, it can also leave us vulnerable to complying with rather meaningless requests.

Of course, some situations evoke a knee-jerk reaction to say no. When a telemarketer calls during dinner or a panhandler asks for change, our mindlessly scripted response might be to say "no" and go on about our business. So in these types of situations, compliance can be increased by breaking people free of their mindless response (Davis & Knowles, 1999). For example, would you be more likely to give change to a panhandler who (a) asks for a quarter or (b) asks for 37 cents? Almost any economists would say that a rational person would answer (a) because $0.25 is less than $0.37. But Santos and colleagues (1994) found that when passersby were asked if they could spare any change, only 44% complied. When they were asked for a quarter, 66% complied. But in a surprise result, when they were asked for 37 cents, 75% of people dug in their pockets to fish out their coins. Why did this last group comply? Because such a specific request breaks some people out of an automatic tendency to say no while also leading them to think there must be a good reason that the panhandler needs this exact amount. The next time you are hoping to borrow money from your roommate, you might want to remember these little tricks!

▲ How often do you give money to panhandlers on the street? Would it make a difference if instead of asking for $1.00, a panhandler asked for $1.17?

[Spencer Platt/Getty Images]

 ## APPLICATION
Recycling Mindlessness to Enhance Sustainability

Since the 1990s, there has been a growing effort to encourage recycling as a way to offset the enormous costs of processing trash and to protect our environment. From universities to clothing companies, groups create messages designed to promote recycling as an environmentally responsible behavior. Despite these efforts, though, compliance is low. Our foregoing discussion of mindlessness sheds some light on why and points to ways we can improve compliance.

Imagine that you are deciding whether to throw a soda can in the trash or take the extra step to find a recycling bin for it. Would it make a difference whether the can was dented or crushed? It shouldn't. Cans that have lost their shape are just as recyclable as whole cans. But when Trudel and Argo (2013) created this situation, they found that people were more likely to recycle a can if it was whole than if it was crushed. They also found that a whole piece of paper was likely to be recycled, but if the same piece of paper was cut into small pieces, it was more likely to be dropped in the garbage.

Here we see mindlessness in action . . . or inaction. Mindlessness happens when we rely too much on familiar categories. In the case of recycling, we tend to categorize as "garbage" those things that are useless or worthless, whereas

▲ How we design recycling opportunities affects compliance. Having many similar-looking recycling bins (top) for different categories of waste taxes people's minds. They may give up on recycling altogether and throw everything in the trash. But having bins with specialized lids (bottom) makes our decisions obvious and less cognitively taxing, leading to more compliance.

[Top: CSP_sunny_baby/AGE Fotostock; bottom: seaonweb/Shutterstock]

we think of "recyclables" as products that have some future use, like paper that can be written on. When we see a recyclable item that is damaged or misshapen, such as a crushed can, we automatically perceive it to be less useful and hence more typical of garbage. As a result, we are more likely to throw it in a trashcan as opposed to recycling it. But if the same product retains its form, we perceive it to be useful and hence more typical of a recyclable. The problem with these heuristics is that they are wrong, leading us to trash things that should be recycled. Does this mean that shifting people's perceptions of an item's usefulness can change their recycling behavior? The results of one study (Trudel & Argo, 2013) suggest that it can: Participants asked to think of some uses for bits of paper were later more likely to recycle (as opposed to trash) ripped-up paper.

So one strategy for improving recycling compliance is to break people's mindless reliance on familiar categories. Another strategy is to *accept* that people can be mindless automatons and, from there, create recycling conditions and opportunities that demand less thought. For example, you've likely come across those gauntlets of multiple recycling bins for different categories of waste: paper, cardboard, glass, aluminum, paper towels, food waste, batteries, and so on. The design of such recycling opportunities is based on the assumption that the public pays close attention. But many people are likely to get overwhelmed, say "forget it," and go with a default response of tossing recyclables in the nearest trashcan.

Knowing about mindlessness, we can design environments that promote recycling by making it less cognitively taxing. Here's one way: Design recycling bins to have those specialized lids where the shape and size of the holes resemble the type of item they're for, like a hole for cans or a slot for newspapers. The specialized lids are like cues for how to use the containers. Does this really work? Yes. Duffy and Verges (2009) arranged it so that 30 recycling containers placed throughout an academic building were topped with either specialized lids or had no lids on top. They found that the containers with specialized lids increased the rate of recycling by more than 30%. What's more, there was a 95% decrease in the food scraps and other non-recyclable waste incorrectly deposited in these bins.

SECTION REVIEW Compliance: The Art and Science of Getting What You Want

The study of compliance has revealed a toolkit of methods to get people to do what you want them to do.

The Foot-in-the-Door Effect and Lowballing	Reciprocity and Social Proof	Scarcity	Mindlessness
• People are more likely to comply with a moderate request after complying with a smaller one. • People find it hard to break a deal even if they learn later of an extra cost because of the norm to honor commitments.	• People are likely to reciprocate favors and concessions from others. • Reciprocity contributes to the door-in-the-face effect of agreeing to a moderate request after refusing a larger one. • People often choose behaviors that conform with what respected others are doing.	• People value what is scarce.	• People may comply out of mindlessness. • When a mindless tendency to refuse is interrupted, people may comply more because they become open to suggestion.

Obedience to Authority

In this section we look at a set of classic studies concerning **obedience**—doing what someone else tells you to do. This research focuses on how obedience is sometimes behavior with much more serious consequences than being taken in by a slick roommate or an infomercial. Unlike with the pressure of conformity, which can often be rather subtle, the pressure to obey is very direct and explicit. And unlike compliance techniques, which involve requests, obedience involves commands. Yet like conformity and compliance, it is a very common form of social influence—because we live in societies that have a hierarchical structuring of power (Milgram, 1974). Some people, by the nature of their roles in the culture, are given the legitimate authority to tell other people what to do in particular contexts. In families, parents have authority over children; in the classroom, teachers have authority over students; in airplanes, pilots have authority over passengers; in the army, sergeants have authority over privates; and so forth. We even obey people who are not necessarily of higher social status, such as ushers in theaters. And generally in our society, such obedience is encouraged. It is deemed good when children obey their parents, students obey their teachers, employees obey their bosses, patients obey their doctors, and citizens obey the police. Moreover, obedience is sometimes essential to preserve societal health and functioning. A glaring example was seen in the early days of the COVID-19 coronavirus pandemic across the world in 2020. Health and government officials told people to socially distance, and the more they obeyed, the less the virus spread. However, history has taught us that obedience to the wrong authorities has led people to great harm to themselves or others. The most dramatic example is the Nazi Holocaust, the catastrophe that inspired the seminal research on obedience.

Like many other social scientists in the early 1960s, Stanley Milgram wondered about the obedience displayed by the German people during the Nazi era. How did the demented Nazi ideology and the brutality and genocide it spawned come to be embraced by an entire nation? It is not hard to imagine that Adolf Hitler was a disturbed, hateful, narcissistic man because of some combination of genetic predispositions, childhood upbringing, and stressful life experiences. We might conclude the same of members of his Nazi inner circle. But how could the majority of an entire large nation participate in such egregious atrocities? Could millions of people be that deranged or evil?

Milgram did not think that Germany was filled with evildoers, but he did think that perhaps the German people were particularly prone to obedience because they were raised in an unquestioning environment that encouraged obedience to authorities. He speculated that living in this *authoritarian* society might have led citizens down the tragic path of war, genocide, and national disgrace. To understand this mass obedience, Milgram developed a laboratory situation to test people's willingness to harm another just because an authority figure said to do so. Because of the astounding, surprising nature of the findings, these studies have become the best-known, most widely taught research produced by social psychology: the Milgram obedience studies. We refer to these as studies rather than experiments because Milgram actually did not manipulate an independent variable or randomly assign participants to conditions. Rather, he conducted a series of 18 demonstrations that revealed something very fundamental about human nature—something that, before this research was conducted, no one had fully realized.

In his first study, conducted at Yale University, Milgram (1963) recruited 40 ordinary men, ranging in age from 20 to 50, from the New Haven, Connecticut, area to participate in a study of learning. When each man arrived at the lab, he received $4.50 and was told it was for coming to the experiment and was his

- Outline factors that *decrease* obedience to authority.
- Summarize explanations for why we obey.
- Explain when charismatic leaders are likely to attract followers.
- Describe how research on obedience and charismatic leaders helps us to understand events such as the Holocaust.

Obedience An action engaged in to fulfill a direct order or command of another person.

(a)

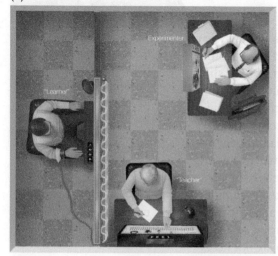

(b)

Figure 7.7

Milgram's Obedience Studies

The drawing in part (a) depicts the setup in one variant of Milgram's studies. Here the learner is in a private room, while the teacher sits in a room with the shock generator (b) and the experimenter.

[Part (b): Stanley and Alexandra Milgram]

Achieve
Video: Obedience: Examining the Milgram Experiment

Achieve
Video: Social Influence: Obedience

---

no matter what happened from that point on. He and another apparent participant were greeted by an experimenter, who explained that the study concerned the effects of punishment on learning. However, the apparent participant was actually a confederate working with the experimenter. The participant and the confederate chose slips of paper, ostensibly to determine randomly who would be assigned to be the teacher and who would be assigned to be the learner. This drawing was actually rigged so the participant would always be the teacher.

The learner was then strapped into a chair, with an electrode attached to his wrist. The experimenter explained that the electrode was attached to a shock generator in the next room. The teacher's task was to read pairs of words to the learner and then test whether the learner could remember which words were paired together by choosing the correct paired word from four possible words. The learner would choose his answer by pressing one of four switches in front of him; his responses would be indicated by a light in an answer box in the adjacent room (see **FIGURE 7.7a**). The participant was then escorted into that room, which housed the shock generator and the answer box. The generator had 30 switches, labeled from 15 to 450 volts from left to right, in 15-volt increments (see **FIGURE 7.7b**). The switches for voltage levels above 180 were labeled "Very Strong Shock"; those above 240 were labeled "Intense Shock"; those above 300 were labeled "Extreme Intensity Shock"; and those above 360 were labeled "Danger: Severe Shock."

The participant was instructed to read the word pairs and then test the learner for each word pair. Whenever the learner made an error, the participant was to give a shock to the learner. With each error, he was to increase the shock by 15 volts. Thus, the participant would administer a 15-volt shock for the first error, a 30-volt shock for the second error, a 45-volt shock for the third error, and so forth. The participant was given a sample shock of 45 volts to convince him that the shock generator was real. What the participant didn't know was that the shock generator was not connected to the electrode attached to the learner's wrist. How long the participant would continue administering escalating levels of shock before refusing to continue was the indicator of level of obedience.

As the study proceeded, the learner used a predetermined set of three wrong answers to every correct one. In this initial study, the learner was silent when the shocks were administered, but if the participant continued to the point of delivering 300 volts, the learner pounded on the wall. In subsequent variations of the study, the learner grunted, complained, and screamed as the shocks escalated, but these reactions did not affect the level of obedience exhibited by the participants. After the 300-volt shock, the participant was confronted with silence as the learner no longer provided any answers. At this point, participants usually asked the experimenter for guidance. The experimenter told them to treat no responses after 10 seconds as a wrong answer and to continue with the appropriate level of shock. If the participant expressed unwillingness to continue, the experimenter used a set of four verbal prompts ranging from "Please continue" to "You have no other choice, you must continue." But, of course, the point is that participants *did* have a choice: Should they obey these commands, given by respected researchers at Yale University? Or should they refuse and perhaps ruin the experiment but save the learner from additional pain?

How do you think you would respond if you were the teacher in this study? What about other people? What percentage of participants do you think would go along with administering what they believed to be even the most dangerous shocks? Take a moment to think about it.

Milgram asked Yale senior psychology majors, graduate students, faculty, and psychiatrists to predict whether they would continue obeying all the way to 450 volts (about four times the voltage of a standard electrical outlet). He also asked people from these same groups to predict the percentage of participants in the study who would do so. No one predicted that they would do so themselves, and each of these groups predicted that fewer than 2% of participants would obey fully by continuing to administer shocks until the maximum voltage was reached.

They were quite wrong in their predictions. In fact, 26 of the 40 participants (65%) obeyed fully to the point of agreeing to deliver a dangerous 450-volt shock to the learner. Furthermore, not a single participant refused to continue until the shock level reached 315 volts. The level of obedience went far beyond what anyone predicted. As Milgram noted, this was a particularly remarkable level of obedience to engage in morally reprehensible actions because, unlike in many real-life situations, the authority figure here (the experimenter) had no real power to enforce his commands, and no significant penalty would be incurred from disobedience.

In subsequent studies, Milgram used the same shock-the-learner paradigm with one or more aspects changed each time. (See **FIGURE 7.8** for rates of obedience in some of Milgram's different variations.) From this series of follow-up studies, Milgram learned about variables that contributed to the high level of obedience found in the original study. The most important variable was the extent to which the person giving commands was perceived to be a legitimate authority figure. For example, if the study was run in an unimpressive-looking building in downtown New Haven rather than at the prestigious Yale University, full obedience was reduced to 47.5%. If the person directing the real participant to deliver the shocks seemed to be another participant in the study instead of the experimenter (who left, supposedly to take a telephone call), full obedience dropped to 20%.

These findings help explain why so many Germans contributed to the heinous actions during the Nazi era once Hitler became a legitimate authority figure in 1933. However, Milgram (1974) emphasized two points to make it clear that

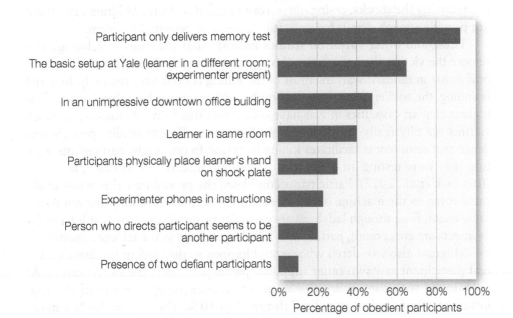

Figure 7.8

Factors Affecting Obedience

Distance and legitimacy are two important factors that influence obedience. When the "teacher" is more removed from the "learner," the rate of obedience is higher. When the experimenter is more removed from the teacher, the rate of obedience is lower. When the authority is seen as being more legitimate, the rate of obedience is higher.

[Data from Milgram, 1974]

this proclivity to obey authority is a potential danger in any culture and in any era. First, he pointed out that horrific acts are not limited to dictatorships and fascist states. Once in power, duly elected officials in democracies are legitimate authorities who often demand actions that conflict with conscience. Second, he noted that the Nazi era was far from the first or the last time that obedience has led people to engage in egregious, destructive actions:

> The destruction of the American Indian population, the internment of Japanese Americans, the use of napalm against civilians in Vietnam, all are harsh policies that originated in the authority of a democratic nation, and were responded to with the expected obedience. . . . When lecturing . . . I faced young men who were aghast at the behavior of experimental subjects and proclaimed they would never behave in such a way, but who, in a matter of months, were brought into the military and performed without compunction actions that made shocking the victim seem pallid. In this respect, they are no better and no worse than human beings of any other era who lend themselves to the purposes of authority and become instruments in its destructive processes. (MILGRAM, 1974, PP. 179–180)

Other Variables That Play Roles in Obedience

One factor Milgram examined is the role of the physical closeness of the authority figure. If the experimenter phoned in the instructions from a distant location, full obedience was reduced to 22.5%. So the more physically distant the authority figure, the lower the percentage of obedience. This suggests that a salient authority figure will minimize disobedience, something to keep in mind when obedience is a good thing.

In addition, Milgram explored the closeness of the victim. Recall that in the original study, the victim was in a different room and could be heard but not seen. In a variation in which the victim was in the same room, full obedience dropped to 40%. And in another version of the study where participants had to physically place the learner's hand on a shock plate, obedience dropped to 30%. This is a substantial decrease in obedience, but it is also quite remarkable and disturbing that 3 in 10 participants would obey the repeated commands even when doing so meant physically compelling the shock. The plausibility of this particular variation could be called into question, however, because the confederate had to act out receiving the shocks, crying out, screaming, and so forth. Milgram (1974) did not provide enough details for us to fully assess this potential problem.

These and other variation studies indicate that the more psychologically remote the victim, the greater the obedience to doing the victim harm. It is interesting that in modern warfare, most of the killing is done very remotely. In aerial bombing, the soldiers launching the bombs neither see nor hear their victims. The highest civilian casualties in war have come from this form of violence, in which victims are physically and psychologically remote. Recent studies provide evidence that remoteness facilitates killing behavior. In one study, participants were told they were testing an apparatus used to kill insects—in this case, ladybugs (Rutchick et al., 2017). Participants completed the procedure either while in the same room as the machine or via video conference, with the machine not in the same room. Even though ladybugs are generally positively regarded (at least as far as insects are concerned), participants killed more bugs in the remote condition.

Milgram also wondered what would happen to the level of obedience if the real participant saw two other supposed participants defy the experimenter. As Asch found with conformity, this seemed to reduce greatly the impact of social influence; the full obedience level dropped to 10%. Those who disobey make it easier for others to disobey, which is something the Nazis seemed to understand.

Thus, psychological distance from the authority, psychological closeness to the victim, and witnessing defiance all reduced obedience. But one important variation led to even more obedience than the original Milgram study. In this version, the real participant didn't physically flip the switch on the shock generator. Rather, the real participant delivered the memory test, and another supposed participant dutifully delivered shocks up to 450 volts. In this version, 92.5% of the participants obeyed fully. This is an especially chilling finding. Very few Germans actually pushed Jews and other "undesirables" into the gas chambers or shot them, but many, many people participated in indirect ways, conducting the trains, spreading hatred of Jews and other groups, arresting them, processing paperwork, building the camps, designing mobile gas chambers at the Volkswagen automobile plants, and so on.

▲ The 1993 film *Schindler's List* portrayed how the Nazis would brutally squelch disobedience before it could spread.

[Universal Pictures/Photo 12/Alamy]

We can see from the Milgram research that at least a minority of people will eventually disobey when they feel that their own actions are physically causing harm. But when people contribute to but are not physically causing the harm, virtually all resistance to participating in atrocities sanctioned by authorities seems to vanish. Consistent with this reluctance to be directly responsible for causing sanctioned harm, it is common practice during executions for more than one individual to pull the lever, inject the serum, flip the switch, or take aim and fire. Thus no single individual knows for sure if he or she was actually physically responsible for executing the person condemned to death. The willingness to obey when one is not certain that one is physically causing the actual harm seems virtually limitless.

The lesson here is reminiscent of the oft-quoted adage (attributed to the statesman Edmund Burke), "The only thing necessary for the triumph of evil is for good men to do nothing."

In addition, if the harm is not severe physical pain and won't occur until after the participant leaves the situation, resistance to obedience again is virtually absent. In a series of studies in the Netherlands, when participants were commanded to give negative evaluations of a job applicant's test performance that would result in the applicant's not being hired at a later date, more than 90% of the participants obeyed these instructions (Meeus & Raaijmakers, 1995).

Anticipating Your Questions

No doubt you have found the obedience studies discussed in this section both fascinating and disturbing. The studies also may have raised some questions. Let's begin with some simple ones.

Males were used exclusively in the initial set of Milgram studies. Perhaps they are more likely to engage in extreme acts of violence. Would females show a similar level of obedience? The answer is "yes." Milgram's eighth study used only females and found a similar rate of obedience.

What would levels of obedience be in other countries? Although the rate of obedience was actually a bit higher in Germany (85%; Mantell, 1971), levels of obedience similar to those in the United States were observed in a variety of other countries, ranging from relatively individualistic to relatively collectivistic ones (Blass, 2000; Doliński et al., 2017; Milgram, 1974; Shanab & Yahya, 1978). This suggests that the explanation for obedience does not lie primarily in the specific features of a culture but in something about being human.

What is known about who fully obeys and who doesn't? Not much. Researchers have examined a variety of potential personality and demographic differences between the obedient and defiant participants, and most have not distinguished the two groups (Blass, 2000). But some studies have provided relevant insights regarding factors that play a small role. Burger (2009) found that people who are high in empathy for others tended to need a prod sooner than less empathetic people, but they were ultimately just as likely to be fully obedient. There is also some evidence that the defiant participants are lower in authoritarianism. *Authoritarianism* is a broad personality trait that is characterized by a "submissive, uncritical attitude toward idealized moral authorities of the ingroup" (Adorno et al., 1950, p. 228). So a submissive attitude toward authority is associated with greater obedience. Milgram (1974) also reported that more educated people and those higher in moral development were less likely to obey fully. There is some evidence suggesting that after the experiments were over, those who fully obeyed reported somewhat more suspicion about whether the learner was really being shocked (Perry et al., 2020). However, that could be because those participants were most motivated to paint their behavior in a less negative light. In addition, if high obedience was due partly to suspicion, it would be hard to explain why variations like phoned-in instructions and having the learner in the room reduced obedience instead of increasing it.

What about now? The original studies were done during the early 1960s, a time when people perhaps had more faith in science and authority and before the civil unrest that characterized the later part of the decade had arisen. Would obedience levels be lower now? Before addressing this question, we should note that only with very careful attention do institutional review boards now allow people to use the Milgram paradigm. When Milgram published his initial research, there was quite an uproar over the ethicality of commanding study participants to engage in behaviors that they believed would seriously harm another person (e.g., Baumrind, 1964). Some critics focused on the stress that was imposed on participants; during the task, many displayed signs of stress, such as twitches and nervous laughter. Other critics contended that the most egregious ethical problem was that the study led most participants to discover something about themselves that could harm their self-image: that they were capable of seriously harming another human being simply because they were told to do so.

Milgram responded to these concerns first by noting his elaborate and thorough debriefing procedures. He described how, at the conclusion of each session, participants met the learner, saw that he was unharmed, and were fully informed of the study's purpose in examining the powerful effects of the situation on behavior. Milgram also conducted a follow-up study, which showed that more than 83% of participants were glad that they had been in the experiment and fewer than 1% of participants were sorry they had been in it. He also had participants examined by an experienced psychiatrist one year after the study and found no signs that any of the participants had been harmed by the experience. Milgram and others suggested that the ethical uproar might have been a reaction to the unpleasant implications of the findings rather than to the ethicality of the procedures, and some research supports this claim (Schlenker & Forsyth, 1977). Debate regarding this matter continues. In fact, recent archival analysis of Milgram's private notes and other sources of information indicated that Milgram may not have debriefed participants as consistently as he portrayed and that some participants claimed to have sustained serious harm from their involvement (Brannigan et al., 2015). For example, one participant attributed losing his job to an emotional outburst when discussing his participation in the study, and another reported having a heart attack when recalling his participation (Perry, 2013). The validity of these claims is unclear, but if they are valid, then surely the ethicality of the original experiments would be in question. What position would you take on the ethicality of this research?

◄ THINK ABOUT

[Jim Purdum/Getty Images]

Nonetheless, even before these archival analyses, the ethical concerns were such that the full study cannot be replicated in the United States or other countries that adhere to standards of the American Psychological Association. However, Milgram's procedures were replicated in the Netherlands in the early 1990s and showed similarly high levels of obedience (Meeus & Raaijmakers, 1995). Moreover, in 2006, Jerry Burger (2009) obtained permission to replicate Milgram's Study 2, which originally yielded 62.5% full obedience, as long as he had the experimenter stop the study before the participant could flip the switch for 165 volts. In this way, even if the actions of the participants had resulted in actual shocks being delivered, they would not have harmed the learners greatly. Burger also carefully screened potential participants to ensure that they were not especially vulnerable to psychological harm and had a trained psychologist on site to provide counseling, if needed.

Burger found that the percentage of participants willing to proceed past the 150-volt level was no different from what it had been over 40 years earlier. And Milgram found that 79% of those who continued past the 150-volt point were fully obedient through 450 volts. In addition, recently the findings of Milgram's Study 5, a variant in which the "learner" did not have a heart problem, were replicated in Poland (Doliński et al., 2017). Other replications have also been conducted, with some interesting twists made possible by technological advances. In one study in France, instead of having a live confederate act as the learner, Dambrun and Vatiné (2010) used an immersive video environment to simulate the learner via video streaming. This study found not only similar rates of obedience but also that the closeness of the victim similarly influenced rates of obedience. So as best we can surmise, the susceptibility to obedience to legitimate authority has not changed.

Why Do We Obey?

Why is this willingness to obey a part of human nature? Milgram offered some valuable answers to this question. First, he proposed that from an evolutionary perspective, groups with a single leader and people willing to do what they are told may have operated more effectively as small groups in obtaining food and other resources and defending the group from threats. Thus, a capacity to obey may have been selected for among group-living animals. In situations in which individuals feel that they are in the presence of a legitimate higher authority, they view themselves as agents executing the wishes of that authority figure, thereby abdicating personal responsibility for their actions.

Some neuroscience research supports this agentic state account. In a situation resembling Milgram's, participants in Belgium were either ordered by an experimenter to administer electric shocks to another participant or were given the choice to administer shocks (Caspar et al., 2016). Participants actually inflicted harm on each other; thus, there can be no doubting that the participants believed the shocks were real. The researchers measured electrical activity in the brain often associated with feeling responsible. When participants obeyed commands to inflict harm, they showed neurological signs of a lower sense of personal agency, as if the cause for their action came from outside themselves.

However, Milgram (1974) himself reported that his participants often exhibited signs of stress and internal conflict, including nervous laughter. This suggests that participants struggled with what was the right thing to do rather than simply entirely abdicating responsibility for their actions. As Gibson and colleagues (2018) have pointed out, based on archival analyses of transcripts from Milgram's studies, participants' claims of being agents of the authority may have been in part a way to excuse their behavior. And, of course, a substantial minority of participants eventually refused to go on even after being forcefully prodded to continue (Reicher et al., 2014).

Another explanation begins by noting that a considerable portion of the socialization process involves teaching children to obey first their parents and then teachers, other adults, doctors, police, and a host of other legitimate authority figures within the culture. So we all have been taught to obey legitimate authority figures. And by and large, we are rewarded when we do obey, and we are punished, often severely, when we don't. Obedience is the norm in all cultures and becomes a remarkable and negative phenomenon only when authority figures tell us to do things that end up causing great harm.

Besides the innate predispositions and learning experiences we humans share, Milgram also pointed to some specific factors in the paradigm he created that may have contributed to the levels of obedience. One is the gradual increase in the severity of the actions in which the participants were commanded to engage. Fifteen volts is barely a noticeable tickle, a 30-volt shock is very tolerable, and so on. Thus, one aspect of the process was its gradual nature. Once the participant delivered 30 volts, why not proceed to 45? Once 45, why not 60? And if one has delivered 330 volts, why resist moving on to 345?

Can you think of any theories that could explain how actions once taken can increase commitment to further actions along similar lines? Recall self-perception theory, which suggests that we infer our attitudes from our own actions, and cognitive dissonance theory, which proposes that people often shift their attitudes to justify their prior actions. Either or both of these theories could help explain why someone who has delivered 315-volt shocks likely would be okay with delivering 330 volts. Such processes are even more likely to be involved in harmful real-life examples of obedience. Imagine being a non-Jewish German during the early 1930s. Perhaps a friend coaxes you into going to a Hitler rally. Once you are there, others greet you with "Heil, Hitler." You find yourself following suit. Sometime later, the Nazi propaganda machine exhorts you to boycott Jewish shops. If you support that, why not support the deportation of Jews to concentration camps, where they will have to work for the Third Reich? The point is that historically significant atrocities often start with small acts that escalate to more severe ones over time.

Another aspect of this paradigm that Milgram noted was that, in the studies with the highest levels of obedience, the participants had to tell the authority figure to his face that they refused to continue. Milgram posited that it is very difficult to defy a legitimate authority figure in this manner. Why? Milgram based his explanation on Goffman's (1959) analysis of self-presentation. Defying legitimate authorities challenges the definition of the situation and disrupts the working consensus by which we all live. The participants had agreed to take part in the Milgram study, and they may have viewed their agreement as a contract they needed to honor. Another, broader way to view the difficulty of defying authority is that legitimate authority figures are valued representatives of the prevailing cultural worldview (Solomon et al., 1991). In fact, the legitimacy of their authoritative position is given to them by the culture. In this vein, Haslam and colleagues (2015, 2016) argued that participants both identify strongly with the experimenter and the goals of the study and lack such identification with the learner. So to defy a scientist running a study, a doctor in an examination room, a police officer who has pulled you over, or a teacher in a classroom is to go against the very worldview and social identifications on which you predicate your meaningful view of the world and your own self-worth. So for this reason as well, we obey.

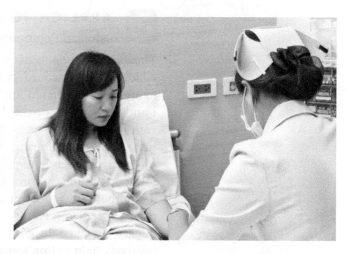

▲ Nursing is one context in which socialization to obedience can occur. In fact, one study found that 21 of 22 nurses who received a phone call from a supposed doctor they did not know would have, without hesitation, administered an excessive level of medication (Hofling et al., 1966). Once obedience becomes routine, it can occur virtually automatically.

[yanyong/iStock/Getty Images]

The Role of Charisma in the Rise to Power

So now we know that people are likely to obey far beyond what our intuitions would lead us to believe. And we know some reasons people obey. That humans have a proclivity to obey helps to explain the historical phenomenon of Nazi Germany. But another major aspect is understanding whom we obey. Obviously, we obey people in various authoritative roles whom the culture tells us to obey. One important set of such individuals is the people we view as leaders. But the remaining question regarding the Nazi phenomenon is How in the world did someone as vile as Adolf Hitler become the revered leader of Germany?

The existential perspective provides some answers. New leaders emerge when the prevailing worldview of a culture no longer provides its members with compelling bases of meaning and self-worth (Becker, 1973; Greenberg et al., 2008). In such a context, people need a more secure belief system that provides them with a sense of enduring significance, especially if death-related concerns are heightened by prevailing political or economic factors. In such circumstances, an individual who takes bold action and who very confidently espouses an alternative worldview that seems to offer a better basis of meaning and self-worth can gain followers. A worldview that portrays the ingroup as representing the greater good and as being on a heroic mission to vanquish evil is particularly suited to providing such a sense of purpose and enduring significance. A leader who exhibits these attributes—boldness, self-confidence, and a vision that inspires and meets the psychological needs of followers—is known as a **charismatic leader**.

Charismatic leader An individual in a leadership role who exhibits boldness and self-confidence and emphasizes the greatness of the ingroup.

APPLICATION
Historical Perspectives

The existential analysis just described seems to fit many historical instances in which charismatic leaders, including Hitler, emerge and rise to great power. Germany was humiliated and economically devastated by the loss of World War I and the signing of the Treaty of Versailles in 1919, which was very disadvantageous to Germany. In the wake of all these events, it did not feel good to be a German. During the early 1920s, Hitler began his crusade to oust the ruling government and rid Germany of what he called the impure evil others—Jews, communists, homosexuals, and other supposedly inferior peoples. After a bold but failed attempt to overthrow the government by violence, Hitler was tried for treason. He became a well-known figure as he confidently and eloquently attacked the government during his well-publicized trial. He was given a relatively light prison sentence, despite his treasonous actions. While in prison, he wrote *Mein Kampf* ("My Struggle"), a book in which he outlined his worldview, which espoused the superiority of the Aryan people and his desire to lead Germany back to greatness. When he got out of prison, he organized the National Socialist Party and began gaining followers in an atmosphere of fears of economic and political instability. When Germany experienced a severe economic depression in 1929, Hitler's message began to gain considerable ground. In 1933, the former fringe figure was elected chancellor as part of a coalition government. Once in office, he seized total power. The rest was a very tragic chapter in human history.

SOCIAL PSYCH OUT IN THE WORLD

Death in the Voting Booth

On September 10, 2001, polls showed that President George W. Bush's approval rating was at a dismal 49% (Pyszczynski et al., 2003). On September 13, his approval rating soared to 94%. Why did the events of 9/11 have such a powerful effect on support for Bush? Landau, Solomon, and colleagues (2004) proposed that the dramatic spike in support for President George W. Bush and his policies following the deadly terrorist attacks of September 11, 2001, could be traced in part to the massive reminder of mortality the attacks provided and people's corresponding need for a charismatic leader.

Bush fit the characteristics of a charismatic leader in that he exuded calm self-confidence and espoused the greatness of America and the importance of vanquishing "evildoers." In contrast, his opponent in the upcoming Presidential election, Democratic candidate John Kerry, did not emphasize the need to triumph over evil and was painted by well-publicized political ads as an untrustworthy waffler who continually changed his positions. Landau and colleagues posited that the attacks heightened Americans' awareness of death on a mass scale and that people sought to avoid death-related fears by supporting Bush's message of triumphing over evil

and ensuring America's legacy. Supporting this analysis, a series of studies indicated that reminders of death and reminders of the 9/11 attacks both increased Americans' support for President Bush and his political policies prior to the 2004 presidential election and reduced support for Kerry. These effects were found among both liberal and conservative Americans, indicating that Bush's charismatic leadership quelled death concerns for Americans, regardless of their political orientation. This research suggests that the many reminders of the attacks of 9/11 and threats of additional terrorist attacks leading up to the election, including a video of Osama bin Laden shown on television just one day before the polls opened, may have tipped the scales in favor of Bush, who won a second term as U.S. president.

Interestingly, months before the 2016 American presidential election, Cohen and colleagues (2017) proposed that Republican candidate Donald Trump was similarly charismatic, with his bold vision to "Make America Great Again," whereas Democratic candidate Hillary Clinton did not fit the charismatic style; her motto, "Stronger Together," better reflects a relationship-oriented leadership style. Moreover, the 2016 campaign occurred in the context of an increasingly vulnerable climate, with 2015 labeled as "the Year of

Similar contributing factors have been observed in the rise of admired leaders as well as vilified ones. For example, the Indian leader Mohandas K. ("Mahatma") Gandhi firmly and boldly engaged in acts of nonviolent resistance and espoused a philosophy of national empowerment in his early efforts to free India from subjugation to Great Britain. He became the leader of this large nation during its process of liberation from British control without election to any government position. Similar analyses can be applied to the emergence of leaders of small cults, such as the Reverend Jim Jones, and large cults, such as the Reverend Sun Yung Moon, as well as many other religious and political leaders.

Of course, all of these historical phenomena are complex and involve many potential causal factors that are difficult to disentangle. However, studies support the role of charismatic qualities in binding people to a particular leader. Experiments inspired by social identity theory show that participants are more willing to stand behind leaders who affirm the value of their shared social identity and contribute to the ingroup's collective interests (Haslam & Platow, 2001). Leaders who are "one of us" and exemplify what makes the group distinct and special are seen as more charismatic (Steffens et al., 2015). And leaders who have a vision for how the group can achieve great things are better able to inspire followers, especially in times of crisis (Halevy et al., 2011).

Other studies have supported the specific role of concerns with mortality in the appeal of such charismatic leaders (Solomon & Thompson, 2019). In a study by Cohen and colleagues (2004), participants were led to think about

Mass Shootings" (Oldham, 2016) and concerns rising over immigration reform, health care, and other domestic and international geopolitical instabilities. Cohen and colleagues thus wondered: Would reminders of mortality increase support for Trump just as they had over a decade earlier for Bush?

In a series of pre-election studies, they found exactly that. Reminders of mortality increased support for Trump but not for Clinton (see **FIGURE 7.9**). It may not be a coincidence that, as in the case of Bush in 2004, the charismatic candidate who better assuaged mortality concerns won the 2016 presidential election.

Clearly, voter decisions are complex judgments influenced by a range of different existential factors and values (Burke et al., 2013). In many contexts, people's need to manage existential insecurity push them to support candidates who charismatically offer a vision of national superiority and certainty. Yet we can also manage existential insecurity by supporting leaders who charismatically speak to other values if those values are especially salient. For example, leading up to the 2008 presidential election, Vail and colleagues (2009) found that reminders of mortality increased support for Democratic candidate Barack Obama when participants were first primed with the importance of compassionate values.

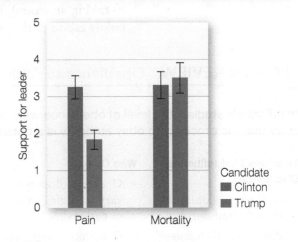

Figure 7.9

The Effects of Mortality Salience on Liking for the 2016 Presidential Candidates

Reminders of mortality increased support and intentions to vote for Donald Trump.

[Data from Cohen et al., 2017]

Looking forward, whether Democrat or Republican, the key may be to encourage people to look to their most important values when heading to the voting booth.

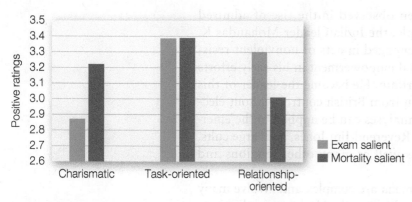

Figure 7.10

The Effects of Mortality Salience and Leader Characteristics on Liking for a Leader

When reminded of mortality, participants' attitudes toward a charismatic candidate for governor who promotes the greatness of the state became more favorable.

[Data from Cohen et al., 2004]

their own deaths or another aversive topic, an upcoming exam. They then read campaign statements purportedly written by three political candidates in a hypothetical gubernatorial election. Each candidate was modeled to fit the profile of either a charismatic, task-oriented, or relationship-oriented leader (Ehrhart & Klein, 2001). The charismatic leader was bold, self-confident, and visionary, promising citizens, "You are not just an ordinary citizen, you are part of a special state and a special nation, and if we work together we can make a difference." The task-oriented candidate emphasized effectiveness at solving practical problems. The relationship-oriented candidate promised to promote positive relationships and portrayed everyone as an equal contributor to a better future for the state. Finally, participants were asked how much they admired each leader and which of the three leaders they would vote for.

In **FIGURE 7.10**, you can see that after people thought about an upcoming exam, their attitudes toward the charismatic leader were less favorable than they were toward the other two leaders. However, after people thought about their own deaths, they were significantly more attracted to the charismatic leader. This effect was also reflected in their voting intentions. Whereas exam-primed participants gave the charismatic leader a paltry 4 votes (out of 94), death-primed participants gave the charismatic leader a third of the votes, a significant increase. These results support the terror management analysis by showing that when people are led to think about their own deaths (as opposed to taking an exam), they are especially attracted to a charismatic leader who boldly espouses the greatness of the group. ■

SECTION REVIEW Obedience to Authority

In Milgram's studies, the level of obedience went far beyond what anyone had predicted and made it clear that the proclivity to obey authority is a potential danger in any culture and in any era.

Variables That Influence Obedience	Who Obeys	We Obey Because	The Role of Charisma
• Psychological distance from the authority • Psychological closeness to the victim • Witnessing defiance • Not personally causing the harm	• Obedience does not vary according to sex or nationality. • Obedience is influenced by whether the participant has a submissive attitude. • More recent research suggests that rates of obedience have not changed.	• We evolved a propensity to follow those in power. • We are socialized to obey authority. • Small acts may escalate such that once an action is begun, we gradually become more and more committed to continuing. • It is difficult to defy a legitimate authority.	• When the prevailing worldview no longer provides members of society with compelling bases of meaning and self-worth, charismatic leaders are likely to gain followers. • Reminders of mortality increase the appeal of charismatic leaders.

CRITICAL LEARNING EXERCISES

1. Imagine that you're a television executive charged with creating a show, based on the principles of Bandura's social learning theory, to help reduce excessive teenage drug and alcohol use. What kind of characters, plot lines, or situations would you create to attract teenage viewers and discourage their risky behavior?

2. Think about how you acted your first couple of weeks in college. What were instances where you conformed to others? Did you conform for normative or informational reasons? In hindsight, do you wish you had acted differently? If so, what advice would you give to someone just starting college?

3. Devise a three-step plan of action to increase compliance with recycling on your campus or in your neighborhood. Which of the compliance techniques that you've read about might be most effective in your community? Why do you think they would be effective?

4. Imagine you were in charge of a military unit and had a set of leaders for each platoon of soldiers who will soon be off to war. What kind of rules or guidelines would you implement to ensure obedience but also ensure that, unlike what happened in the My Lai massacre in Vietnam and in Abu Ghraib prison in Iraq, soldiers do not obey commands that run contrary to the Geneva Convention or a reasonable code of ethics?

Don't stop now! Check out our videos and additional resources located at www.macmillanlearning.com

WOMEN on the verge of a

WHERE MAXIMUM PERFORMANCE LIVES

NERVOUS

YOU ALREADY KNOW YOU'RE GONN

CHAPTER 8

Persuasion, Attitudes, and Behavior

The next time you walk across campus, take some time to count how many commercial messages you see. It will probably be a lot. In the 10 minutes it took your current author (Mark) to walk to the student union this morning, he recorded 43 commercial messages posted on T-shirts, posters, packages, and even across people's buttocks! Efforts to persuade are all around us. Any time we turn on the television, listen to a streaming music station, watch a movie, surf the Net, or browse a magazine, advertisers rush to persuade us to prefer certain products and services.

Does this mean persuasion is insidious, beguiling and entrapping us to harmful or unnecessary ends? Not necessarily. When a 2010 earthquake utterly destroyed Port au Prince, the capital of Haiti, news of the tragedy and donation opportunities were widely circulated on pop-up ads, social networking sites, and cell phones. As a result, millions of people gave more money through private and corporate donations than any individual nation's government and even more than the World Bank emergency grant (Evans, 2010). Similar generosity occurred in 2017, as Houston and surrounding areas of Texas sought to recover from Hurricane Harvey, and again in 2019, as the Bahamas sought to recover from Hurricane Dorian.

Persuasion appears in every corner of social life, so it is important to understand this direct form of social influence. Let's start with the basics. **Persuasion** refers to the ways in which people try to change other's minds by changing their attitudes. **Attitudes** are evaluations that range from positive to negative. People can have attitudes about pretty much anything in their social world, ranging from consumer products (e.g., air freshener) to people (e.g., themselves, presidential candidates) to social issues (e.g., global warming). Because people's attitudes often predict how they intend to behave (though not always, as we'll see later on), the goal of persuasion is to change attitudes in the hope of eventually changing behavior.

Persuasion Intentional effort to change other people's attitudes in order to change their behavior.

Attitude Evaluation of a stimulus; can range from positive to negative.

What have social psychologists discovered about what makes some attempts at persuasion more effective than others in changing attitudes? In this chapter we focus on:

- The two routes to persuasion: changing attitudes either from the central merits of a message or from peripheral cues

- The effect of the persuasive message, depending on *who* says *what* to *whom* — that is, the characteristics of the source, the message, and the audience

- The ability to resist persuasion

- How changing someone's attitudes changes his or her behavior

- Explain the two routes to persuasion proposed by the elaboration likelihood model, including circumstances for and durability of each.

Elaboration likelihood model
A theory of persuasion which proposes that persuasive messages can influence attitudes by two different routes: central or peripheral.

Central route to persuasion A style of processing a persuasive message by a person who has both the ability and the motivation to think carefully about the message's argument. Attitude change depends on the strength of the argument.

Argument The true merits of the person, object, or position being advocated in a message.

Peripheral route to persuasion A style of processing a persuasive message by a person who is not willing or able to put effort into thinking carefully about the message's argument. Attitude change depends on the presence of peripheral cues.

Peripheral cues Aspects of communication that are irrelevant (that is, *peripheral*) to the true merits of the person, object, or position advocated in a message (e.g., a speaker's physical attractiveness when attractiveness is irrelevant to the position).

Achieve
Social Psych in Everyday Life: Austin

Elaboration Likelihood Model: Central and Peripheral Routes to Persuasion

In earlier chapters, you learned that people often are unwilling or unable to think deeply about every decision they make and every piece of information they encounter. Although they sometimes engage in controlled, deliberate thinking, often they think in a more automatic and superficial manner. (For a refresher, see the section "Dual Process Theories" in chapter 3.) The **elaboration likelihood model** (Petty & Cacioppo, 1986), or ELM, is a theory of persuasion that builds on this distinction. This theory proposes that persuasive messages can influence attitudes in two different ways, or *routes*. Which route a person takes depends on his or her motivation and ability to elaborate on—or think carefully about—the information to which he or she is exposed.

People follow the **central route to persuasion** when they think carefully about the information that is pertinent, or *central*, to the true merits of the person, object, or position being advocated in the message. This information is referred to as the **argument**. For example, people who follow the central route while listening to a political candidate's speech attend closely to the candidate's arguments concerning why he or she will make a good leader, and they consider whether those arguments are factual and cogent. Thus, when people follow the central route, their attitudes are influenced primarily by the strength of the argument. Strong arguments change attitudes; weak arguments do not.

In contrast, people follow the **peripheral route to persuasion** when they are not willing or able to put effort into thinking carefully about the argument. In these cases, people's attitudes are influenced primarily by **peripheral cues**, which are aspects of the communication that are irrelevant (that is, *peripheral*) to the true merits of the person, object, or position advocated in the message. For example, people following the peripheral route while listening to a candidate's speech might focus not on the candidate's arguments but on the candidate's physical attractiveness. People taking the peripheral route also tend to base their attitudes on *heuristics*—mental shortcuts, such as "A person who speaks for a long time must have a valid point" (see chapter 3) (Chaiken, 1987).

Whether people follow the central route or the peripheral route does not necessarily lead them to have more positive or more negative attitudes. In our example, a person who is diligently considering the candidate's arguments and another person who is wowed by the surrounding pageantry may both report the same increase or decrease in liking for the candidate. Instead, which route people follow determines which aspects of the persuasive message have the strongest influence on their attitudes. (**FIGURE 8.1** presents a summary of the two routes to persuasion.)

Why do people take one or the other route? According to the ELM, the key factors are the individual's motivation and ability to think deeply about the message. When motivation and ability to process the message are high, the person usually takes the central route. But a person who lacks either the motivation or the ability to process the message is more likely to take the peripheral route.

Motivation to Think

Imagine the following couple: Jill is highly motivated to eat healthy food, whereas her husband, Bill, is less health conscious. Jill asks Bill to pick up a healthy cereal for the family when he is at the store. He sees that both Kellogg's Raisin Bran and

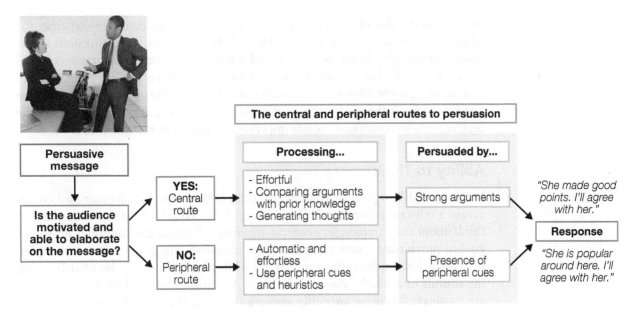

Figure 8.1

The Elaboration Likelihood Model

The central and peripheral routes are two distinct pathways of persuasion.
[Digital Vision/Getty Images]

a new Scooby-Doo cereal are on sale. Which to choose? Because he's been asked to grab a healthy choice, Bill assumes that the bran in one name means all-natural nutrition and that the kids' cartoon character in the other name means empty calories. But such a decision would likely reflect more heuristic processing. The next time you're at a grocery store, check out nutritional data on different cereals. You'll see that one cup of a "healthy" cereal often has more calories and sugar, and less of some important vitamins, than a cup of a "sugary" cereal.

Effectively communicating calorie information can lead to healthier choices (Lim et al., 2018), but only if people take the time to process that information. If Jill had been faced with the same choice, her deeper commitment to healthy eating might have led her to spend the time and effort to scrutinize the nutritional labels to make a more informed decision through central route processing. People who are highly motivated in a topic concentrate more attention on the quality of an *argument*, or pros and cons for one product over another.

An influential study by Rich Petty and colleagues (1983) shows us how a message's relevance to people's goals influences which persuasion route they take. People were told that as a reward for participating in a study on consumer attitudes, they could choose from among different brands of either razor blades or toothpaste. Later, when all participants were asked to flip through some ads, they came upon an ad for Edge razor blades. This ad was relevant for participants expecting to choose a brand of razor blades but not for those expecting to choose a toothpaste. The researchers introduced two other variables. First, participants either read strong arguments for the Edge razor's quality, such as "Special chemically formulated coating eliminates nicks and cuts and prevents rusting," or weak arguments, such as "Designed with the bathroom in mind." Second, one version of the ad featured an attractive celebrity endorsing the Edge razor, whereas the other version featured anonymous, average-looking people endorsing it.

What influenced participants' attitudes toward the Edge razor? When participants expected to choose a razor later on—that is, when the Edge ad was relevant to their decision—the most influential factor was the strength of the ad's arguments for the Edge brand's quality. If the arguments were weak, participants disliked the Edge razor; if the arguments were strong, they liked it. But a different picture emerged among the participants who did not expect to choose a razor—that is, those to whom the ad was not relevant. They were *not* influenced by whether the ad's arguments were strong or weak. Instead, their attitudes were influenced by the spokesperson: They liked the Edge brand if it was endorsed by an attractive celebrity spokesperson but not when it was endorsed by the average Joe. Note, though, that among people who were motivated to think carefully about the message, the attractiveness of the spokesperson did not influence attitudes: People taking the central route to persuasion are not impressed by those kinds of peripheral cues.

Ability to Think

Let's revisit Jill, who is now contemplating buying a new computer and comes across a relevant commercial. Other things being equal, Jill will be motivated to think about the commercial's central arguments because they are relevant to her goal of purchasing a new computer. But, of course, things are not always equal: Perhaps Jill is watching the commercial while she is hungry or bombarded with the sounds of a nearby construction site. According to the ELM, even if people are motivated to think carefully about a message, they may be unable to do so because of distractions and other demands on their attention. Under these conditions, people tend to take the peripheral route to persuasion.

How the ability to think influences routes to persuasion is demonstrated in another study by Petty and colleagues (1976). Participants listened to a recorded message arguing that the tuition at their university should be cut in half. Participants heard either strong arguments (such as "The currently high tuition prevents high school students from going to college") or weak arguments ("Cutting tuition would lead to increased class size"). While they listened to the message, participants repeatedly were asked to record the location of an X that appeared at various spots on a screen in front of them. For some participants, the Xs flashed every 15 seconds. You can imagine that this would be mildly distracting. But other participants had to identify the X every 5 seconds—which was very distracting. As you can see in **FIGURE 8.2**, there was an interesting interaction between argument strength and level of distraction: Participants who were mildly distracted agreed with the tuition cut if they heard strong arguments for it but not if they heard weak arguments. But participants who were highly distracted were less influenced by the strength of the argument and generally saw the tuition cut as a good idea.

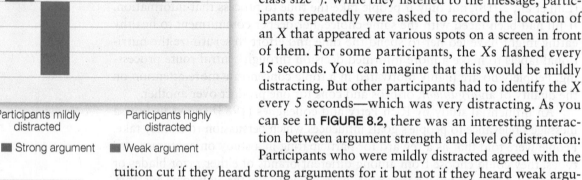

Figure 8.2

The Effects of Distraction on Persuasion

In this study, people who were only mildly distracted were persuaded through the central route; they agreed more with a planned tuition cut if the arguments they heard were strong, and they disagreed with it if the arguments were weak. But being highly distracted switched them to the peripheral route, and their agreement with the proposal was unaffected by the strength of the argument.

[Data from Petty et al., 1976]

Why It Matters

Why does it matter whether people take the central route or the peripheral route to persuasion if either one can lead them to change their attitudes? Compared with attitudes formed through the peripheral route, attitudes formed through the central route are stronger—more durable and resistant to contrary information and more likely to determine how people behave (Chaiken, 1980; Petty & Cacioppo, 1986). Think about it: If you form an attitude through the central route, you are elaborating on the arguments relevant to the issue, rehearsing them in your head, and considering them in light of other evidence. The resulting attitude is therefore more likely to be supported by a range of knowledge. This means the attitude is likely to remain in your memory even if one piece of evidence in support of that attitude is forgotten or contradicted by other evidence. Attitudes formed through the peripheral route, in contrast, are usually supported by a single, simple association or inference ("My favorite celebrity uses this product, so I do, too") and therefore may decay over time.

For example, in one study, students were presented with a proposal to require psychology majors to participate in research. (You might recall such experiences from your own introduction to psychology class.) Those who formed their attitudes through central route processing were more likely to sustain those attitudes three weeks later and, moreover, were also more likely to engage in behavior consistent with their attitudes a month later (and actually participate in studies if they had positive attitudes) (Pierro et al., 2012). Thus, attitudes formed through the central and the peripheral routes to persuasion might be equally favorable or unfavorable immediately following a persuasive message, but which route was used influences whether a change in attitude persists over time.

Now that we've introduced the idea that following the central route or the peripheral route to persuasion orients people toward different aspects of a persuasive message, next we'll consider those aspects in more detail. We'll group them into three categories: *who* says *what* to *whom*. First, we'll see how attitudes are influenced by characteristics of the individual or group communicating the message (the *who*, or **source**). Then we'll look at the characteristics of the message itself (the *what*). Finally, we'll consider characteristics of the person or group receiving the message *(whom*, or the **audience**).

Source The person or group communicating a message.

Audience The person or group receiving a message.

SECTION REVIEW   Elaboration Likelihood Model: Central and Peripheral Routes to Persuasion

The elaboration likelihood model proposes that a persuasive message can influence attitudes by two different routes, depending on a person's motivation and ability to think carefully about the message.

Motivation	Ability	Persistence
• When people are motivated to think carefully about a message, they take the central route, basing their attitudes on argument strength. • If people are less motivated, they take the peripheral route, basing their attitudes on emotional and other such cues.	• When people have the mental resources to think carefully about a message, they take the central route. • If people are cognitively busy, they take the peripheral route.	• Attitude change produced by central route processing is more durable and resistant to other influences than change produced by peripheral route processing.

Characteristics of the Source

Learning Outcomes

Logic suggests that a good argument should be persuasive, regardless of who delivers it. Although this view is admirable, messages delivered by likable, attractive, powerful, and famous sources are more often met with approval than are the same messages delivered by sources lacking these characteristics (Chaiken, 1979, 1980; French & Raven, 1959; Whittler & Spira, 2002).

How a message is delivered matters, too. Schroeder and Epley (2015) found that potential employers were more interested in hiring a job candidate when

- Identify the factors that influence *who* best delivers a message persuasively.
- Describe why persuasive impact can change over time.

▲ You can often be more persuasive in person than in writing. Even brief "elevator conversations" can help convey a more thoughtful and intelligent person than can the written word.

[kate_sept2004/E+/Getty Images]

Source credibility The degree to which the audience perceives a message's source as expert and trustworthy.

▲ After learning about the strategies that advertisers use to market their goods, you are smart to be skeptical of some of the claims and endorsements you read or hear.

[SDI Productions/Getty Images]

they heard, rather than read, a brief pitch by the candidate, even though the content of the pitch was the same. Similarly, Roghanizad and Bohns (2017) found that people often overestimate how much people agree to email requests compared to face-to-face requests. And it's not just what you say that matters but how you say it. People tend to be more persuaded by speakers who, for example, adjust their pitch and tone—using *paralinguistic cues*—than they are by speakers who talk normally (Guyer et al., 2019; Van Zant & Berger, 2020). These linguistic flourishes help the person pitching the message seem more confident and thus more credible. Let's consider credibility in a bit more detail.

Communicator Credibility

Messages are especially persuasive when they are delivered by a person (or a group) perceived to have **source credibility**—that is, someone who is both *expert* and *trustworthy*. For example, in one study, people were more likely to agree with an article advocating that antihistamine drugs should be sold without a doctor's prescription when told the article came from the *New England Journal of Biology and Medicine* (an expert source) than when it came from a popular magazine such as those you see in the supermarket (a nonexpert source) (Hovland & Weiss, 1951). We tend to be more persuaded by expert sources than by nonexpert sources (Pornpitakpan, 2004).

The Appearance of Expertise and Trustworthiness Although real expertise can convey strong arguments that persuade people through central route processing, the *appearance* of expertise often persuades through the peripheral route. For example, a commercial advertising mouthwash may feature a spokesperson wearing a white lab coat and a stethoscope around his neck, giving him the appearance of a medical expert when in reality he is most likely an actor. Indeed, speakers can appear more credible, and thus be more persuasive, simply by speaking with confidence, quoting statistics, or even just speaking quickly—none of which necessarily means they have expert knowledge (Erickson et al., 1978; Miller et al., 1976; von Hippel et al., 2016).

The source of a message can also gain credibility by being perceived as trustworthy or unbiased in his or her views. Imagine that you overhear some people at a coffee shop praising a new restaurant. You have no reason to believe that these people are biasing their opinions to influence you (they don't even know you're eavesdropping!); research suggests that you will find their overheard opinions believable (Walster & Festinger, 1962). The power of overheard messages hasn't been lost on advertisers. Just think of all the commercials you've seen that attempt to portray a private conversation between two people ("Gee, Tyler, your glasses really do sparkle! What dish detergent do you use?"). In fact, advertising and public relations agencies often pay writers to masquerade online as delighted consumers and to write positive reviews of their products or services on web sites such as Amazon.com (Dellarocas, 2006).

Another way in which a communicator increases trustworthiness (and persuasiveness) is by arguing in favor of a position that seems to be *opposed* to self-interest. Imagine that you, like participants in a classic study by Walster, Aronson, and Abrahams (1966), hear "Joe 'The Shoulder' Napolitano," a habitual criminal and drug dealer, arguing for more lenient court proceedings. Even if he is making some good arguments, you might not be very persuaded because you know that he personally has something to gain from convincing you of his position. Indeed, participants in the study were completely unconvinced. But if the same alleged criminal argues for stricter court proceedings, how do you think you would respond? Participants in the study were much more likely to agree with his position.

Other tactics can decrease trustworthiness and arouse suspicion that the actor is being inauthentic. Imagine that Richard compliments you at a party and then asks you out on a date. In many ways, this is a persuasive appeal; Richard is hoping to convince you he is date-worthy. After being initially flattered and positively inclined, you later overhear Richard make the same compliment (or sales pitch) to a friend of yours! Your reaction is likely to be that he is just using a line, and you would doubt the authenticity of his interest. Indeed, people are viewed as inauthentic when they are found using the same pitch to persuade different audiences (Gershon & Smith, 2020). Drawing from our discussion of self-presentation in chapter 6, it is as if observing the repetition pierces the façade of a sincere performance and leads people to view the would-be persuader as untrustworthy.

The Sleeper Effect Credibility can be a peripheral cue when people are not focused on the persuasive message. It's a handy heuristic simply to decide "She's an expert, I'll believe her" or "I'm not buying anything that sleazeball says." However, this kind of peripheral influence of source credibility may not last long. The decay of source effects can happen when, over time, people forget the source of the message but remember the message content, a concept known as the **sleeper effect.** Suppose that while waiting in line at the grocery checkout, you scan the front page of a sensationalistic gossip magazine, which claims that new evidence calls global warming into question. A few weeks later, the topic of global warming comes up in a conversation, and you remark that you read a story arguing that global warming may in fact not be happening, but you can't remember where you read it. Might that argument be more compelling now that you've forgotten that it came from a not-so-credible source?

Hovland and Weiss (1951) found the first evidence of the sleeper effect. Recall the experiment showing that people were more likely to agree with high-credibility sources (e.g., a medical journal) than with low-credibility sources. When the researchers again measured participants' attitudes four weeks after they were first exposed to the arguments, participants who initially had agreed with a position advocated by a high-credibility source showed less agreement, and those who had disagreed with a low-credibility source had come to agree with the position (see **FIGURE 8.3**). Subsequent research has clarified that such sleeper effects are most likely when people learn about the credibility of the source *after* they have been exposed to the arguments (Pratkanis, 2007). When people know in advance that an argument comes from a low-credibility source, they are better able to discount the argument. At the same time, source credibility can also give rise to a sleeper effect. If people don't recall that a particular argument was weak but do recall that it came from a credible source, persuasion can increase over time (Albarracín et al., 2017).

Sleeper effect The phenomenon whereby people can remember a message but forget where it came from; thus, source credibility has a diminishing effect on attitudes over time.

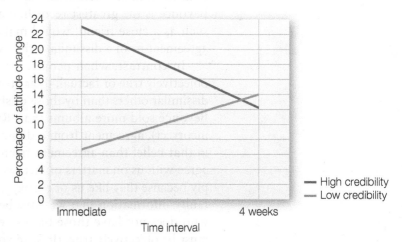

Figure 8.3

The Sleeper Effect

In this study, people were more likely to change their attitude to agree with arguments if the author was an expert and therefore credible. But four weeks later, the credibility of the source no longer mattered, and arguments made by less credible sources were equally likely to have changed people's minds.

[Data from Hovland & Weiss, 1951]

Communicator Attractiveness

As you most likely know already, communicators can be persuasive when they are *attractive*, even if their credibility is low (Chaiken, 1979; Mills & Aronson, 1965). When a communicator's attractiveness is irrelevant to the true merits of a position—as when a supermodel graces a billboard for an energy drink—it influences the audience's attitudes through the peripheral route. It is important to note, though, that the communicator's attractiveness also can influence attitudes through the central route when the product or service is intended to boost physical attractiveness (Shavitt et al., 1994).

Consider an attractive, muscled spokesperson for a rather odd-looking exercise machine who says, "If you use the Abdominator for just 20 minutes every day, you will have rock-hard abs like mine." Is the spokesperson's physique relevant information for evaluating whether the exercise machine works? What if the spokesperson were sporting a bit of a belly (perhaps more of a keg than a six pack)? What reason would you have to believe that the machine works?

THINK ABOUT

[MSPhotographic/Shutterstock]

Communicator Similarity

If we tend to be persuaded by those who are trustworthy, likable, and attractive, we must also be persuaded by people who are similar to us, right? Here the answer depends on whether the persuasive appeal pertains to a subjective preference or to objective facts (Goethals & Nelson, 1973). For issues dealing primarily with subjective preference—that is, when there is no "correct" answer—people are more confident in their attitude when similar others agree with them than when dissimilar others agree with them. So if you believe that Beyoncé is the greatest recording artist alive, agreement from a similar other, such as a close friend, would make you more confident in that attitude than agreement from a dissimilar other, such as a foreign exchange student.

In contrast, when people are trying to determine whether something is objectively true or factual, their attitudes are influenced more by the opinions of dissimilar others than by those of similar others. For instance, if you believe that Beyoncé sold more albums than Rihanna (which is either factually correct or incorrect), agreement from a dissimilar other would make you more confident in that belief than agreement from a similar other. Why? When similar others agree with us on matters of fact, we are often uncertain whether they agree simply because they like us or perhaps because they have been exposed to the same faulty information that we have been exposed to. But when a dissimilar other who does not have those biases verifies our belief, we assume that the belief must be objectively true. (In case you were wondering, at least as of June 2018, Rihanna had sold more albums than Beyoncé [Moore, 2018].)

 APPLICATION
Similarity and Morality in Politics

Understanding the influence of communicator similarity gives us some insight into why appeals to morality in political rhetoric often fall on deaf ears and fail to change attitudes. Some research shows that liberals and conservatives have somewhat different moral priorities (Graham et al., 2009; see chapter 2). Conservatives, more than liberals, for example, value loyalty to the group and respect for authority as moral principles. From this cultural perspective, morals are more subjective than objective, and our perceptions of them are colored by our motivational biases. For example, we're more likely to forgive someone who lies if that lie supports our own moral concerns. In fact, we forgive politicians who make up facts if they are arguing for a position that we support (Mueller & Skitka, 2018).

When it comes to persuasion, the problem, according to Feinberg and Willer (2015), is that political candidates often advocate their positions based on their own sense of morality, when they would be more persuasive if they focused on the moral principles of their audience. Indeed, across such issues as military spending, same-sex marriage, and English as the official language of the United States, Feinberg and Willer found that framing the issue in terms of liberal morals (e.g., fairness) better persuades liberal audiences, whereas framing the same message with conservative morals (e.g., loyalty) better persuades conservative audiences. This can be seen as a specific example of a broader tendency for communicators to be more effective when they present audiences with messages that fit with values the audience finds personally important (Blankenship & Wegener, 2008). ■

SECTION REVIEW Characteristics of the Source

The power of a message to influence attitudes depends, in part, on *who* is delivering that message or its source.

Credibility	Attractiveness	Similarity
• Credible communicators are both expert and trustworthy. • Legitimate expertise persuades through the central route. • The *appearance* of expertise persuades through the peripheral route.	Communicators can be persuasive when they are attractive, even if their credibility is low.	• Attitudes about subjective preferences are influenced more by a similar source than by a dissimilar source. • Attitudes about objective facts are more influenced by a dissimilar source. • People are more persuaded by sources that share their values than by sources with different values.

Characteristics of the Message

Attitudes are influenced not only by the source of the message but by the content and style of the message. Here we consider some characteristics of the message, including approaches you can take to enhance your own ability to persuade.

Thinking Differently: What Changes Our Minds

It is not just what you say but how you say it. Different features of persuasive communications can more or less successfully change people's minds.

Argument Strength   Earlier we said that when people take the central route to persuasion, their attitudes are influenced primarily by the strength of the arguments. But what makes an argument strong or weak?

First, to be strong, a message needs to be comprehensible. For example, people are more convinced by arguments arranged in a logical order than by the same arguments presented in a jumbled order (Eagly, 1974).

> **Learning Outcomes**
>
> • Identify characteristics of a message that are most likely to get us to change our minds.
>
> • Explain the relationship between our emotions and our tendencies to be persuaded.

Argument strength is also influenced by the length of the message, but the nature of the effect depends on how people are processing the message. If the audience takes the central route, message length can increase persuasion if this length adds supportive arguments. But if the added arguments are weak or repetitive or prevent the person from thinking about them, length can backfire (Cacioppo & Petty, 1979; Calder et al., 1974; Eagly, 1974). As a result, longer messages with arguments of varying quality can be *less* persuasive than messages containing only a few, highly convincing arguments (Anderson, 1974; Harkins & Petty, 1987). Sometimes less is more.

If the audience is taking the peripheral route, longer messages tend to be more persuasive than shorter ones (Petty & Cacioppo, 1984; Wood et al., 1985). Why? Imagine reading a newspaper editorial that lists 19 bullet-pointed arguments in support of increasing the local property tax. Even if you didn't have the motivation or the energy to digest this long article, you might think, "A person who has that many reasons must have a valid point." This heuristic, or mental rule of thumb, ignores the fact those 19 reasons may be totally biased, redundant, or just plain wrong.

Confident Thoughts About the Message   People often step back and think about their own thoughts—a process called *metacognition*. The more confident people are that their thoughts about a message are correct, the more powerfully those thoughts guide their attitudes (Petty et al., 2002). Confidence can be influenced by some surprisingly subtle factors. Consider how people move their heads. Usually, if you are talking and the people listening are nodding their heads up and down, it means they agree with you, and that is likely to boost your confidence in what you are saying.

Briñol and Petty (2003) hypothesized that if people were to nod their *own* heads while generating thoughts about a message, those thoughts would feel more valid and would therefore strongly guide their attitudes. To test this hypothesis, they had college students put on a pair of headphones and listen to a speech advocating that students be required to carry personal identification cards. Participants were also told that the headphones were specially designed for use during exercise and other bodily movement. Thus, to test the headphones' performance, participants were asked to move their heads while listening to the speech. Half the participants were asked to move their heads up and down (as if nodding "yes"); the other participants were asked to shake their heads from side to side (as if saying "no"). Even though this head-nodding exercise was unrelated to the persuasive communication, it had a potent effect (see **FIGURE 8.4**). When presented with strong arguments for why they should carry identification cards, the head-nodding participants were more confident in their positive attitudes and more likely to agree. But when presented with weak arguments, they were more confident in the negative attitudes they formed and less likely to agree with the communication. In contrast, when participants shook their heads, they felt less confident about their positive or negative thoughts, and so those thoughts had less influence on whether they agreed with the message.

These findings suggest that sometimes it is our *perceptions* of confidence in our attitudes that are especially important (Barden & Petty, 2008). Just think of how you say "Now that I've thought about it a lot . . . ," which conveys a

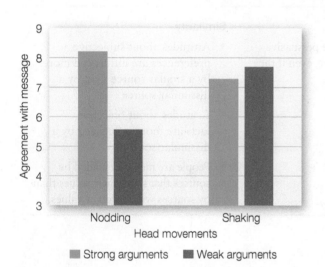

Figure 8.4

Nod If You Agree

Nodding is a subtle signal of endorsement and can magnify your response to an argument by making you more confident of your (either positive or negative) opinion. In this study, participants who were instructed to nod their heads while listening to a persuasive message were more likely to agree with the message if the arguments were strong than if the arguments were weak. But if they were instructed to shake their heads from side to side, they were not affected by the strength of the argument.

[Data from Briñol & Petty, 2003]

confident, well-thought-out attitude. When we're less sure, we often preface with "I haven't given it much thought, but . . . ," and this conveys more doubt and uncertainty (Barden & Tormala, 2014). Most people believe that when they've thought deeply about an issue, they have a more informed attitude. Sometimes, however, giving an issue a lot of thought simply allows us to become more certain of our initial hunches and intuitions, even if those hunches are no more informed than they were initially.

Statistical Trends Versus Vivid Instances   Persuasive messages often feature statistics ("Four in five dentists agree.") or vivid examples ("Extreme mayhem strikes . . . better be insured"). Which is more persuasive? Consider this scenario: You're tentatively planning to move to Chicago after graduation, based on a comparison of statistics such as per capita crime rates and housing market trends. But then a friend tells you in vivid detail about her purse being stolen in Chicago. Of course, rationally speaking, that person's experience is one out of millions and should have little influence on your decision. Nevertheless, a single vivid example can have a surprisingly strong impact on attitudes, even when it conflicts with one's knowledge of what is generally or statistically true. Why? Because a vivid instance entices the audience to connect the message to their own experience and emotions (Strange & Leung, 1999). In this example, your friend's experience may trigger your own memories of times you felt unsafe in a big city or of other negative things you've heard about Chicago.

In one demonstration of this, Hamill and colleagues (1980) had participants read an article that described in vivid detail how a welfare recipient had spent the past couple years abusing the welfare system by making dishonest purchases and neglecting her adult responsibilities. After reading the article, some participants (those in the "typical" condition) were told that the woman described in the article was typical of welfare recipients and had been receiving welfare for an average length of time. In contrast, participants in the "atypical" condition were told the opposite—that the woman had been on welfare much longer than was common. The researchers also had a third group of participants who did not read about the woman's situation.

Afterward, all participants reported their attitudes toward the entire population of welfare recipients, answering questions such as "How hard do people on welfare work to improve their situations?" As you can see in **FIGURE 8.5**, participants exposed to the vivid description of just one person abusing the welfare system reported less favorable attitudes toward the entire population of welfare recipients than did those who did not read the description. It didn't matter if she was presented as typical or atypical of welfare recipients. A vivid description of a single case can have a powerful influence on attitudes, even when it's not representative of a larger population of people or experiences.

The Order of Presentation: Primacy Versus Recency   Imagine that you get a phone call in early December, in which you learn that you're one of two final applicants for a great job. The employer asks if you would like to be the first person interviewed or the second. During the interview, you'll be given time to make your case about why the employers should hire you rather than the other applicant. Other things being equal, should you opt to go first or second?

Achieve
Video: How can you convince a skeptic?

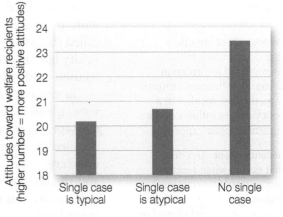

Figure 8.5

The Persuasive Power of Anecdotes

In this study, a single vivid story of a person who abuses the welfare system decreased the positivity of people's attitudes toward welfare. This striking effect occurred regardless of whether people were told that this person was typical or atypical of welfare recipients.

[Data from Hamill et al., 1980]

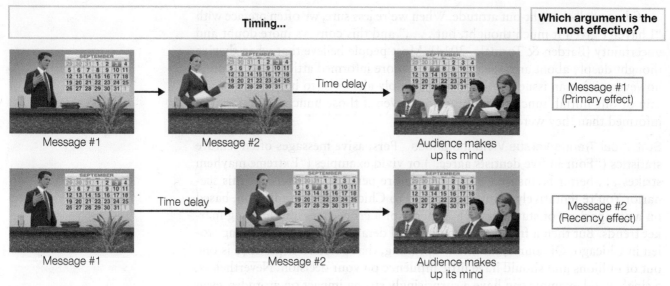

Figure 8.6

Getting Time on Your Side

When making a persuasive appeal, it is better to go first if the audience will be making its decision after hearing both arguments and then taking a break. But it is better to go last if the audience will make their decision immediately after hearing your presentation.

Primacy effect An effect that occurs when initially encountered information primarily influences attitudes (e.g., the first speaker in a policy debate influences the audience's policy approval).

Recency effect An effect that occurs when recently encountered information primarily influences attitudes (e.g., a commercial viewed just before shopping influences a shopper's choices).

Will the person who is interviewed first be more persuasive because she has the chance to make the critical first impression, or will the person who interviews second have the advantage because her arguments will be fresher in the employers' memory when they make their hiring decision?

What should you do? We suggest that it would behoove you to ask the employers, "When do you plan to decide who you're going to hire—before or after the holiday break?" This is an important piece of knowledge because the timing of the overall situation makes a big difference (Miller & Campbell, 1959; see **FIGURE 8.6**). If the two messages (or interviews) happen back to back followed by a delay before a judgment is made, then the first message will be more persuasive than the second (other things being equal, of course). This is called the **primacy effect**. Under these circumstances, the audience has more difficulty learning the arguments in the second message because their mind is still focused on the first, so you should volunteer to go first.

In contrast, if there is a time delay separating the two messages (or interviews), and if the audience makes up its mind immediately after the second message, then the second message will be more persuasive than the first. This is called the **recency effect**. Under these conditions, the first message does not interfere so much with the audience's ability to learn the second argument, and the second argument is fresher in the audience's memory when making a decision. You should volunteer to go second if the two interviews will be spaced out.

Emotional Responses to Persuasive Messages

Persuading people involves changing their thoughts, but it also involves changing how they feel about something at a deeper, "gut" level. A message that gets the audience to associate a position or a product with positive feelings and the avoidance of negative feelings can help to persuade. And people implicitly know this. When we want to persuade others, we tend to use more emotional language in how we communicate (Rocklage et al., 2018). Generally, this below-the-cortex approach to persuasion takes the peripheral route. Conscious deliberation about the message is not needed and might even interfere with the effectiveness of such strategies.

Repetition and Familiarity   One of the most basic strategies of persuasion is repetition. The more we hear an argument, the more we think it is true (Unkelback et al., 2019). Repetition also helps to increase positive feelings about a message or product. The **mere exposure effect** shows that the more we are exposed to a novel stimulus, the more we tend to like it (Zajonc, 1968). The mere exposure effect occurs even when people are unaware of having been frequently exposed to a stimulus. In fact, research suggests that the mere exposure effect actually might be strongest when exposure happens outside of awareness (Bornstein, 1989). There are two likely explanations for why we prefer things we have been exposed to frequently (Chenier & Winkielman, 2007). First, as novel stimuli become familiar, they seem less strange and more safe. Second, familiar stimuli are easier to perceive and grasp fully.

The mere exposure effect has been demonstrated for a host of different types of stimuli, including people, music, and geometric figures, but it has limits. For one, the effect generally plateaus at around 20 exposures; further exposures have only minimal impact on attitudes (Chenier & Winkielman, 2007). Furthermore, the complexity of the stimulus influences the optimal number of exposures (Cacioppo & Petty, 1979). Simpler stimuli sometimes may be liked more quickly, but the liking also turns to boredom more quickly. Think of songs that you hear repeatedly and initially enjoy, but after a few weeks of hearing the station playing the song all the time, you want to stuff your ears with cotton. Another exception is captured by the idea of attitude polarization (see chapter 9) (Tesser & Conlee, 1975). Research demonstrating the mere exposure effect focuses on changing people's attitudes toward something that is initially neutral. But if we dislike something initially, we dislike it even more if we are exposed to it over and over.

Mere exposure effect An effect that occurs when people hold a positive attitude toward a stimulus simply because they have been exposed to it repeatedly.

APPLICATION
Should Universities Be Selling Beer to Students?

Advertisers often use group affiliation to create positive feelings about products. As you've read in a number of chapters (and will read about more in the next chapter), people generally think positively of their group memberships. Advertisers capitalize on such affiliative feelings in ways that range from the innocuous to the concerning. Consider the problem that many college campuses have with binge drinking and excessive alcohol use. Now consider that some universities directly market alcoholic beverages with university-themed beer cans. Concerned? Bruce Bartholow and colleagues (2018) were, so they examined whether associating beer with a university would increase students' desire for that particular brand of beer. They showed some college students images of a brand of beer against their university's logo while recording the electrical signals in the students' brains; other students saw the same brand of beer against the logo from another university. Students reported greater interest in the brand of beer paired with their university logo, and these reports of greater desire were also reflected in the unique electrical signals in their brains. Such findings raise concerns about whether marketing beer by affiliating with students' universities might actually increase alcohol consumption on college campuses. ▪

Cognitive Balance and Positive Associations   Fritz Heider's **balance theory** gives us another way of understanding how messages can link products or positions with positive things effectively, even without repeated exposure.

Balance theory A theory which proposes that the motivation to maintain consistency among one's thoughts colors how people form new attitudes and can also drive them to change existing attitudes.

Figure 8.7

Balance Theory

According to Heider's balance theory, if you like Jennifer Aniston and she likes Smart Water, then you are inclined to like Smart Water, too.

[Adam Nemser-PHOTOlink.net/PHOTOlink/ Newscom]

(a)

(b)

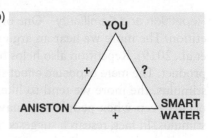

Heider (1946) posited that people have a strong tendency to maintain consistency among their thoughts (an idea that should be familiar from our discussion of cognitive dissonance in chapter 6). This perspective helps to explain why the magazine ad in **FIGURE 8.7a** might be effective. The ad assumes that you, as the magazine reader, already have a positive attitude toward Jennifer Aniston (hence the plus sign connecting you and Aniston in **FIGURE 8.7b**). The ad informs you that Aniston is positively inclined toward Smart Water. This leaves only your relationship to Smart Water undetermined. According to balance theory, the audience would experience an internal pressure to evaluate Smart Water positively in order to maintain a harmonious state in which all the elements (themselves, Aniston, Smart Water) are consistent with each other. If people were *not* naturally inclined to prefer balanced over imbalanced relationships between their thoughts, then we wouldn't expect them to feel any motivation to like Smart Water because they would be perfectly comfortable if some of the elements in this system didn't quite fit together.

Positive Mood Another way to create positive feelings toward a message is to deliver it when people are in a good mood. A classic study by Janis and colleagues (1965) found that participants given peanuts and soda to snack on while reading messages on topics such as the armed forces and 3-D movies were more convinced by the messages than participants who were not snacking. Since this study was conducted, research has shown that people more readily agree with messages when they experience success, hear pleasant music, or view beautiful scenery (Schwarz, Bless, & Bohner, 1991). The influence of positive mood on persuasion has not been lost on people. You probably know that businesspeople often take clients to lunch at a fancy restaurant, or you may have experienced a salesperson opening up a conversation with a funny story. If you are in a good mood while receiving a message, you will be more likely to agree with it, even if the reason for your good mood has nothing to do with the message itself.

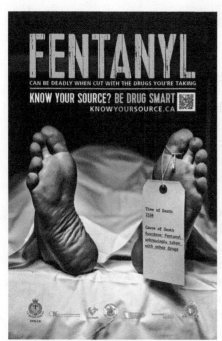

▲ Graphic warning labels try to persuade people by conveying how to avoid a feared outcome.

[RMCP/Contraband Collection/Alamy]

Negative Emotions Sometimes messages try to persuade the audience that by doing something or acquiring something, they can avoid negative consequences or punishments. In such cases, the designer of the message is hoping to arouse negative emotions. Graphic warning labels displaying the negative health consequences of smoking are one example. These ads can arouse negative emotions, increase feelings of risk, and increase intentions to quit (Evans et al., 2017). Graphic warning labels have also been used to highlight health consequences of drinking lots of sugary soda, including obesity, tooth decay, and diabetes. One study found that displaying such labels reduced the percentage of sugary drinks purchased at a cafeteria during a two-week period (Donnelly et al., 2018).

But these fear-based messages don't always work and can sometimes even backfire (Evans et al., 2017; Janis & Feshbach, 1953; Leventhal, 1970). When people are told simply that they will suffer some threatening outcome, they feel distressed or helpless, and they often tune out entirely. But if you provide them with a clear means of protecting themselves from that threatening outcome, they are more likely to be persuaded (Rogers & Prentice-Dunn, 1997; Ruiter et al., 2014; Tannenbaum et al., 2015; Witte & Allen, 2000). In addition, how a message is pitched can make a big difference (Rothman & Salovey, 1997). People are more likely to comply with a message that frames a health behavior in gain-related terms ("Use sunscreen to help your skin stay healthy") when they don't see themselves as being particularly at risk for that condition (Updegraff et al., 2015). However, a message that frames a health behavior in loss-related terms ("Without regular mammograms, breast cancer can go undetected until it's too late") is more effective when people think their risk is particularly high (Ferrer et al., 2012).

 APPLICATION

Is Death Good for Your Health?

So far, we've assumed that fear-arousing messages are effective because they motivate people to avoid threats to their physical health. But arousing fear may have opposite effects when it motivates people to care more about their self-images than about their health. From the existential perspective, recall that people strive to maintain self-esteem as a way of protecting themselves from concerns about vulnerability and mortality.

Thus, although arousing fears about death may motivate people to avoid unhealthy behavior that threatens their survival, increasing people's death awareness might motivate them to enhance their self-esteem. This can be problematic if unhealthy behaviors help to confer self-esteem. The question, then, is What determines whether increasing people's awareness of their mortality increases or decreases risky but self-esteem-bolstering health behaviors?

Goldenberg and Arndt (2008; Arndt & Goldenberg, 2017) proposed that one key factor is whether people are consciously thinking about death. When people are explicitly concerned about death, they are more motivated to take practical steps to reduce or avoid threats to their physical health if they think they can do so effectively (Cooper et al., 2014). But when death thoughts are activated outside conscious attention, people can be motivated to enhance their self-esteem, even if it means engaging in unhealthy behaviors. For example, if you are headed to the beach on a sunny day, you might be more likely to drive slowly, slather on sunscreen, and pass when offered a cigarette if you are consciously thinking about your mortality and ways to prolong your life. But if death is primed only subtly below conscious attention, you might instead prioritize ways to feel and look good by putting the pedal to the floor, taking a drag on a cigarette, and getting that socially valued but nonetheless skin-damaging suntan (Hansen et al., 2010; Jessop & Wade, 2008; Routledge et al., 2004). ■

SECTION REVIEW Characteristics of the Message

Attitudes are influenced by the content and style of a message.

What Changes Our Minds	What Creates an Effective Emotional Response
• Comprehensible messages	• Repetition and familiarity
• Confident thoughts about the message	• Learned associations with positive stimuli
• Vivid instances that connect with personal experience	• The need to maintain consistent ideas about related people or things
• The order in which competing arguments are presented as they relate to the timing of the overall situation	• Positive mood
	• Use of fear to avoid negative consequences if paired with strategies to reduce the negative consequences
	• Thoughts of death, although unconscious thoughts of death create the need to boost self-esteem and may result in unhealthy behaviors

 SOCIAL PSYCH OUT IN THE WORLD

This Is Like That: Metaphor's Significance in Persuasion

Many times, we come across persuasive messages that, strictly speaking, make no sense. Consider the statement made by opponents of a mandatory seatbelt law being contested in California some years ago: "We don't want Governor Deukmejian sitting in our bathtub telling us to wash behind our ears."

This is an example of a *metaphoric message*, a communication that compares one type of thing with another type of thing. Aristotle and many scholars since his time have noted metaphor's power to persuade. Let's return to the bathtub metaphor: Even though people know that enacting a seatbelt law does not *literally* mean having the governor in the bathtub with them, hearing the bathtub metaphor guides them to think about the seatbelt law as the same type of thing—a disgusting violation of personal privacy. In fact, study volunteers randomly assigned to read the bathtub statement evaluated the seatbelt legislation more negatively than those who didn't (Read et al., 1990).

From immigration to health care decisions, other common metaphoric messages try to change how people understand social problems and thus evaluate certain solutions. Is the sun *attacking* your skin? If so, then sunscreen can be your *shield*

of protection (Landau et al., 2018). Many real-world problems, such as crime and cancer, are abstract, complex, and difficult to comprehend fully. A metaphor comparing an abstract problem with a more familiar problem suggests what solutions are more and less likely to work. For example, one television ad advocated cutting government spending on social programs by comparing the federal budget with a household budget. The ad aimed to get the audience thinking, "In my house we don't buy goodies that we cannot afford. Therefore, the best solution to our economic problems is to stop the government from funding programs."

Do such messages work? To find out, Thibodeau and Boroditsky (2011) asked participants to read different stories about a city with a serious crime problem. For some participants, crime was compared with a "beast" that was "preying upon" the innocent citizens of the town. For other participants, it was described as a "disease" that "plagued" the town. After participants compared crime with a wild animal, they were more likely to generate solutions based on increased enforcement (e.g., calling in the National Guard, imposing harsher penalties). In contrast, participants given the virus analogy strongly preferred solutions that were more diagnostic and reform oriented (e.g., finding the root cause of the crime wave, improving the economy). In other words, the solutions that participants generated to solve the crime

Characteristics of the Audience

In addition to the source of a persuasive message and the nature of the message itself, a message's impact on an audience also depends on the characteristics of the audience members. Whether a given audience member responds favorably or unfavorably to a message is influenced by his or her age, sex, personality, socioeconomic status, education level, and habitual way of living, as well as the events and experiences of his or her life. For example, we discussed earlier that whether a person processes a persuasive message through the central route or the peripheral route depends in part on his or her motivation to attend to the message. So we would expect individual differences in interests, values, and prior knowledge to influence who finds certain messages worthy of attention. Let's consider how audiences differ according to a number of characteristics.

Persuadability

People differ in their overall *persuadability*, their susceptibility to persuasion. People high in persuadability are more likely to yield to persuasive messages,

problem were consistent with the metaphors they read: If they thought crime was like a beast, they thought they should control it, but if they likened crime to a disease, they thought they should treat it.

Metaphoric messages change attitudes, but can they change behavior? Maybe you recall seeing warning videos that are sometimes played before a movie. These videos aim to provide a lesson in the legality of downloading movies from torrent web sites on the Internet. The words "You wouldn't steal a car" appear on the screen, followed by a dramatic reenactment of a car theft. Then, "You wouldn't steal a purse." After reminding you of other objects you presumably do not intend to steal, the message concludes: "Downloading pirated films is stealing." Pilfering a woman's purse and downloading a pirated film are obviously similar situations in some respects, but they differ in others (e.g., the woman is left without the purse, whereas the movie's owner still has it). Given what you've learned about social psychology research, how would you design an experiment to test whether this metaphor changes people's behavior?

▲ [Mike Luckovich/Cartoonist Group]

▲ [Gary Varvel/Cartoonist Group]

whereas low-persuadability individuals are less likely to be influenced. There are three key determinants of persuadability:

- *Age*: Between the ages of 18 to 25, people are usually in the process of forming their attitudes, and so they are more likely to be influenced by persuasive messages. As they move into their late 20s and beyond, their attitudes tend to solidify and become more resistant to change (Koenig et al., 2008; Krosnick & Alwin, 1989).

- *Self-esteem*: People with low self-esteem are more likely to be influenced by persuasive messages than are those with high self-esteem (Wood & Stagner, 1994; Zellner, 1970). People with low self-esteem view themselves as generally less capable than others and, as you might expect, do not regard their own attitudes very highly. They are therefore likely to give up their current attitudes and go along with the position advocated in a message. People with high self-esteem are generally more confident in their attitudes and are therefore less likely to yield to influence.

- *Education and intelligence*: Audience members who are more educated and intelligent are less persuadable than those with normal to low intelligence (McGuire, 1968). We can interpret this finding in a similar way as the self-esteem finding: People who are highly intelligent are more confident in their ability to think critically and form their own attitudes.

Initial Attitudes

An important audience characteristic is the attitude that audience members already have toward the position advocated in a message. Imagine that you are trying to persuade your parents that you should be allowed to study in Spain for a semester through a foreign exchange program. Should you present only arguments favoring a semester abroad and ignore any arguments opposed to your position—a *one-sided* message? Or should you bring up and then refute arguments opposing the trip—a *two-sided* message? The answer depends on your parents' initial attitudes (Hovland et al., 1949). If your parents are already inclined to oppose the semester abroad, they probably have some reasons (e.g., it is too dangerous). Thus, if your message ignores the opposing arguments, your parents will conclude that you are biased, uninformed, or manipulative. But if they are inclined to support you, they are less likely to be aware of opposing arguments. Therefore, simply mentioning those opposing arguments may lead them to question your proposal ("Hmm, I was all for the semester abroad, but now that you mention it, the trip *would* be awfully expensive.") In this case, you would be more persuasive if you focused only on arguments favoring your position.

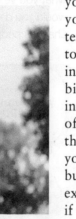

▲ Perspective taking can backfire as a persuasive strategy, such as when it leads those from different sides of the political aisle to realize they have different values.
[Cameron Whitman/Shutterstock]

Perspective taking is another strategy for considering two different sides of an issue. You might implore someone "to put yourself in my shoes," under the assumption that the person will then see the situation from your perspective and appreciate your arguments. But perspective taking can backfire as a strategy to change attitudes (Catapano et al., 2019). If a person whose shoes you are putting on is very different from you, you might see those reasons as being less relevant and reflecting very different values. For example, with perspective taking, a political conservative might understand why a liberal argues for higher taxes on the wealthy, but in so doing, the conservative might be reminded that the liberal has very different values about wealth and responsibility. In such situations, perspective taking can work against persuasion. When it comes to persuasion, sometimes another person's shoes just don't fit.

Need for Cognition and Self-Monitoring

Think back to the study we discussed earlier in this chapter, involving attitudes toward Edge razor blades (Petty et al., 1983). That study showed that a person's motivation to think about a message varies depending on whether the message pertains to his or her current goals and interests (e.g., anticipating a choice between razors or toothpastes). But you may have noticed that, across different situations, some people are generally more interested in thinking deeply about issues, whereas others are not. According to Cacioppo and Petty (1982), individuals high in **need for cognition** tend to think about things critically and analytically and enjoy solving problems. They tend to agree strongly with statements such as "I really enjoy a task that involves coming up with new solutions to problems." Individuals low in need for cognition are less interested in effortful cognitive activity and agree with statements such as "I think only as hard as I have to." With your knowledge of the elaboration likelihood model (ELM), do you suspect that individuals with high need for cognition would tend to take the central route or the peripheral route to persuasion?

Need for cognition Differences between people in their need to think about things critically and analytically.

If you think individuals with high need for cognition would tend to take the central route, you're right. This was shown recently by Luttrell and colleagues (2017). They measured college students' need for cognition and then asked them to read an editorial arguing that all seniors be required to pass a rigorous comprehensive exam to graduate. Thus, in this experiment, the message was relevant to all the participants. But for half the participants, the editorial contained fairly strong arguments in favor of the exam ("The quality of undergraduate teaching has improved at schools with the exams"), whereas the other participants read fairly unconvincing arguments for the exam ("The risk of failing the exam is a challenge more students would welcome"). Overall, as you might expect, participants were more favorable toward the exam requirement when it was supported by strong rather than weak arguments. But participants with high need for cognition were especially likely to approve of the proposal when it was supported by strong arguments and to disapprove of the proposal when it was supported by weak arguments (see **FIGURE 8.8**). So even though the message was equally relevant to all participants, some of them were inherently motivated to pay close attention to the arguments, whereas others were content merely to skim the message.

Just as some people are motivated to think in greater depth, people high in self-monitoring (introduced in chapter 6) are motivated to make a good impression and present a desired social image. Snyder and DeBono (1985) reasoned that because high self-monitors are concerned with projecting the right image, they should be more susceptible to image-focused peripheral route cues. In one study, not only were high self-monitors more persuaded by image-oriented ads, they also were willing to put their money where their mouths were. For example, high

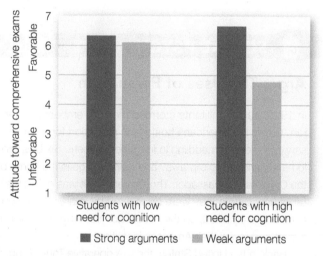

Figure 8.8

Need for Cognition

People who have a high need for cognition like to think deeply and tend to be affected by central route factors such as argument strength. In this study, students high in need for cognition were more positive toward a proposed comprehensive exam if the arguments for it were strong than if the arguments were weak. Those low in need for cognition were less sensitive to argument strength.

[Data from optimal replication conditions in Luttrell et al., 2017]

self-monitors were willing to pay more for a bottle of Canadian Club whisky if it was pitched as enhancing one's status ("Canadian Club Whisky: You're not just moving in, you're moving up"). Low self-monitors, in contrast, were willing to pay more in response to a message focused on the quality of the whisky rather than the status it would bring. So just as certain people can be differentially motivated to think carefully about a message, others may be motivated more by the power of the images—and the peripheral cues—that a message presents.

Regulatory Focus

Promotion focus A general tendency to think and act in ways oriented toward achieving positive outcomes.

Prevention focus A general tendency to think and act in ways oriented toward avoiding negative outcomes.

Earlier we noted that in certain situations, people are influenced by thinking about what they might gain, whereas in other situations, they are influenced by thinking about what they could lose (Rothman, 2000). Consider Frank, who works out and watches what he eats so that he can look more like Ryan Reynolds. Frank has a strong *growth motivation*. Other people are oriented more toward the prevention of negative outcomes. They are motivated to maintain *security* (see chapter 2). Consider Stephen, who works out and watches what he eats so he can avoid looking like Jabba the Hutt. Note that Frank and Stephen engage in the same types of behavior, but they regulate their behavior according to two very different endpoints. We would say that Frank is high in **promotion focus**, whereas Stephen is high in **prevention focus**.

 SOCIAL PSYCH AT THE MOVIES

Argo: The Uses of Persuasion

In 1979, Iranian militants stormed the U.S. embassy in Tehran, taking 52 Americans hostage in retaliation for what they saw as American meddling in Iran's government. Six U.S. diplomats managed to slip away and found refuge in the home of the Canadian ambassador. They feared that it was only a matter of time before they were discovered by Iranian revolutionaries and likely killed, so they could not just arrive at Tehran's airport and reveal their American identities.

Back in the United States, the CIA operative Tony Mendez came up with a plan to get the diplomats safely out of the country: Convince the Iranians that the diplomats were Canadian filmmakers who were in Iran scouting exotic locations for a sci-fi adventure movie along the lines of *Star Wars*. Although all of this sounds like a crazy premise cooked up by a screenwriter dreaming of a box office smash, the movie *Argo* (Affleck, 2012), directed by and starring Ben Affleck in the role of Mendez, actually tells a gripping true story of rescue and persuasion.

In the movie, Mendez first has to persuade the higher-ups in Washington to authorize and fund his rescue operation. He lays out the plan using strong arguments, describing the operation in detail and carefully explaining why it is the most promising idea considered so far. But they're not convinced because they are processing Mendez's message through the peripheral route to persuasion. Maybe they feel pressed for time, but they have difficulty getting past a simple heuristic: On the face of it, the idea of staging a fake movie sounds insane.

Eventually Mendez gets the green light and works with the Hollywood makeup artist John Chambers (John Goodman) and the producer Lester Siegel (Alan Arkin) to set up a phony movie production company with the pretense of developing a sci-fi flick called *Argo*. If they are going to convince the Iranians that they are making a Hollywood movie, they need all the trappings of a film crew on a scouting mission, including a glossy poster, a script and storyboards, press releases, and an office phone if and when the Iranians decide to check things out (which they do). With all of these peripheral cues to back up their story, they create a convincing cover for the trip.

The next group that needs to be persuaded is the people whose lives are on the line. Posing as *Argo*'s producer, Mendez meets the diplomats who are in hiding and provides them with Canadian passports and fake identities. He also gives them a crash course in the film industry and Canadian citizenship. After all, if they have any chance of making it past the authorities and getting on the plane, they need to play their roles convincingly. But they too are skeptical of Mendez's scheme and reluctant to go along with it. At first Mendez tries to persuade them by presenting himself as a trustworthy source, a powerful peripheral cue when audiences take the peripheral route.

APPLICATION
Using Regulatory Focus to Get the Most Out of a Message

Individual differences in promotion focus and prevention focus can determine which types of persuasive messages are influential. This has been found when persuading people to lead healthier lifestyles (Fuglestad et al., 2008; Updegraff et al., 2015), to engage in environmental behaviors (White et al., 2011), and to get the most out of an educational program (Cesario et al., 2004). For example, in the study by Cesario and colleagues, participants read an argument in favor of a new afterschool program. For some participants, the program was billed as catering to a positive end state (facilitating children's progress and graduation). For other participants, it was billed as preventing a negative end state (ensuring that fewer children failed). For participants who were promotion focused, the promotion-oriented articulation of the program was a better fit to their current motivation and, as a result, these participants were more likely to support it. However, those who were prevention focused experienced a better fit with the avoidance message of reducing failures and thus were more likely to support the program when it was framed in prevention-oriented terms. ■

But the diplomats aren't processing information peripherally. The outcome of what happens is incredibly relevant to them, and that elicits central route processing. Shifting gears, Mendez takes the time to deliver a strong argument for why they should trust him. He reveals his true identity and describes his training and his record of successful rescue missions. He also reminds them that he is risking his own life, too. He knows that the source of a message can gain credibility by being perceived as having nothing to gain by deception or manipulation. His willingness to risk his own life is evidence that he firmly believes that the plan can work, and the diplomats begin getting into character.

In the movie's suspenseful climax, we watch the "film crew" slowly making their way through security checkpoints in Tehran's airport. Gun-toting Iranian soldiers suspect them of being American and lock them in a room to interrogate them just as their flight is boarding. The soldiers have very strong initial attitudes of mistrust toward Americans, in large part because of being repeatedly exposed to this message by revolutionaries who give impassioned speeches on America as the enemy of Iran. As the tensions rise in the interrogation room, one of the diplomats steps in and tries a new persuasive strategy. He lays out the movie storyboards on a table and improvises a stirring synopsis of the film they are supposed to be making. He is appealing to the soldiers by applying the principle of balance. He knows that the soldiers have a very strong positive attitude toward revolution, so he's showing that the film crew is equally excited to be capturing a fictional story about a triumphant revolution on film. He's hoping that the soldiers will seek to bring those two cognitions into balance: If *we* like revolution, and *you* like revolution, then it follows that we like you. Is he persuasive? Do the Americans make it out of Iran? You'll have to watch to find out.

▲ [Warner Bros./Photofest]

SECTION REVIEW Characteristics of the Audience

A message's influence on attitudes and behavior depends on who receives it.

Three Determinants of Persuadability	Initial Attitudes	How People Think and Self-Monitor	Regulatory Style
• Age • Self-esteem • Education and intelligence	• One-sided arguments obscure counterarguments and appeal to audiences leaning toward agreement. • Two-sided arguments avoid the perception of bias and appeal to audiences leaning toward disagreement.	• People with a high need for cognition prefer the central route. • Those motivated to make a good impression are more susceptible to peripheral route cues.	• For audiences high in promotion focus, influential messages highlight positive outcomes. • Prevention-focused people are persuaded by messages about avoiding negative outcomes.

Learning Outcome

• Prepare a strategic list of ways to resist persuasion while retaining the ability to recognize legitimate efforts to persuade.

Resistance to Persuasion

Throughout this book, we have discussed how, as motivated animals, people are far from objective consumers of information. Rather, we filter information through our own preconceptions and biases. These motivated biases give us a measure of resistance when we encounter persuasion attempts that conflict with our preexisting beliefs (Lord et al., 1979).

Further, when we're exposed to mixed evidence on a given issue, we often focus on the information that supports, and as a consequence bolsters, our preexisting beliefs (Pyszczynski & Greenberg, 1987b). This is why it can be so hard to convince people of something they are set against. Just think about the resistance that scientists encounter when arguing to some government officials that the mounting evidence for global climate change threatens the future viability of life as we know it. Of course, in many situations, we may not have strong preexisting beliefs that arm us with skepticism about persuasive appeals. Nonetheless, resistance is not always futile. But successfully resisting persuasion depends on a few factors: We need to know what to resist, be motivated to resist it, and have strategies that will be effective.

Knowing What to Resist

In Steven Spielberg's classic film *E.T. the Extra-Terrestrial*, a boy named Elliott tries to lure an alien from a hiding place by laying out a trail of Reese's Pieces. Shortly after the release of this blockbuster movie in 1982, sales of these peanut-butter snacks in a crisp candy shell boomed. This is an example of the widespread advertising technique of product placement in TV shows and movies (York, 2001), which capitalizes on our tendency to be influenced by what we see in the media. Whether it's Eleven on *Stranger Things* eating Eggo waffles or Tony Stark (aka Iron Man) in the Marvel superhero movies driving an Audi, product decisions in the media are far from

▲ Television shows and movies, such as Tony Stark driving an Audi in the Iron Man films, use product placement to advertise their corporate sponsors.
[Paramount Pictures/Photofest]

coincidental. The influence of celebrities or other TV or movie characters using a product extends to behavior that can be downright deadly. For example, the more children see movies in which grownups smoke, the more positive their attitudes are toward smoking and the more likely they are to start smoking (Sargent et al., 2002; Wills et al., 2008).

Product placement works for a number of reasons. These images make a product accessible and lead us to associate positive feelings with that product, particularly when we identify with the character using the product. Indeed, the more people identify with a character who is smoking, the more likely they are to develop positive associations with smoking (Dal Cin et al., 2007). Narrative transportation theory (Green & Brock, 2000) helps us understand this process, not just with tobacco use but also with attitudes about other consumer products and even racial prejudice (Green & Clark, 2013; Murrar & Brauer, 2019). When audiences are transported into a story, whether on the screen or in the pages of a book, they are immersed in the imaginative world and more open to adopting the attitudes and preferences of the characters with whom they identify. Placing particular products in movies is an especially effective form of advertising because people most often do not realize they are being targeted with a persuasive appeal. Recall our discussion earlier in this chapter about source credibility and persuasive intent. If you are unaware that you're the target of persuasion, there is little resistance for advertisers to overcome, and so positive attitudes toward the product are free to develop.

But the effectiveness of product placement also gives us important insight into factors opposing persuasion. If we're aware that a persuasive appeal is coming our way, we're better able to deflect its impact. In fact, such knowledge arouses motivations and cognitions that not only bolster our ability to withstand a persuasive message but can actually provoke us to do the very opposite of what the would-be persuader is trying to get us to do.

Being Motivated to Resist

As we've noted, persuasion can come from many sources. Our parents, for example, often try to persuade us to act in accord with cultural values. This socialization process is a vital ingredient in the recipe for a smoothly functioning society. But sometimes our parents also impose their own idiosyncratic—and maybe outdated—preferences on how we style our hair, or what we wear, or whom we date. Perhaps you've had the experience of introducing your parents to your new boyfriend or girlfriend, only to face a later barrage of comments of the "I forbid you to see that person!" sort. Did those admonitions increase or decrease your attraction to the new partner? If your experiences are similar to those of many research participants, chances are that your parents' restrictions backfired. The *Romeo and Juliet effect* shows that parental opposition to a relationship partner is typically associated with deeper romantic love for that partner (Driscoll et al., 1972). The more our parents say "no way," the more we often say "yes way."

Why is forbidden fruit so tempting? Jack Brehm's (1966; Brehm & Brehm, 1981) seminal **psychological reactance theory** explains why forceful, demanding efforts to compel obedience, compliance, or persuasive attitude change can backfire. This theory is based on the assumption that people experience an uncomfortable emotional state, called *reactance*, when they feel a threat to their freedom to think, feel, or act in the way they would like. People are motivated to reduce reactance and restore their sense of freedom by doing or expressing

Psychological reactance theory A theory which proposes that people value thinking and acting freely. Therefore, situations that threaten their freedom arouse discomfort and prompt efforts to restore freedom.

Figure 8.9

Reactance

When our freedoms are threatened, we experience reactance and engage in behavior to reassert our independence.

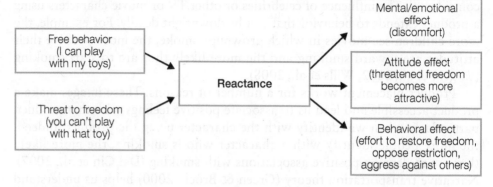

Free behavior (I can play with my toys)

Threat to freedom (you can't play with that toy)

Reactance

Mental/emotional effect (discomfort)

Attitude effect (threatened freedom becomes more attractive)

Behavioral effect (effort to restore freedom, oppose restriction, aggress against others)

THINK ABOUT

[parema/E+/Getty Images]

the very thing that they are told they shouldn't do. In fact, the motivation to reduce reactance can be so strong that it leads people to act aggressively against the person threatening their freedom (see **FIGURE 8.9**).

Have you ever tried your hand at the popular notion of *reverse psychology*, whereby you tell someone to do something in the hope that they'll do the opposite? If so, you've taken advantage of reactance and how people respond to it. How did it turn out? In one of the first demonstrations of reactance, Brehm and colleagues (1966) invited students to participate in a study on marketing musical recordings. The students rated a few sample recordings and were told that they would receive one of the records as a gift. In one condition, participants were told that they would get to choose whichever record they wanted. In another condition, participants were also given the opportunity to choose, but the options were rigged. Participants were told that their third-rated record inadvertently had been excluded from the shipment and was unavailable. Thus, in this condition, a restriction was placed on the participants' freedom to choose what they wanted. All participants were then asked again to indicate their ratings of the different musical samples, and it was these changed attitudes that revealed reactance. Among subjects who were given a choice but denied the freedom to choose their third-most-highly rated selection, 67% increased their ratings of this selection, compared with 42% of participants' increasing their rating of this record when they had no restriction on their freedom.

So we can think about reactance as pushback against attempts to restrict our freedom to have, do, or think what we want. The amount of pushback depends on how important that freedom is to us as well as how forceful the threat is. Efforts by outside sources to control our thoughts, even more than our behaviors, are especially likely to arouse reactance (Ma et al., 2019). People don't want others messing with what's in their heads.

Looking at reactance from a cultural perspective, we find that culture plays a big role in determining the importance people place on freedom, whose freedoms are most important, and thus how strong their reactance is. In our discussion of cultural variation in chapter 2, we saw that individual agency and a sense of personal freedom are more important to people in Western, individualistic cultures. A sense of group harmony is more important to those from collectivistic cultures, and as a result, reactance might play out differently for people from such cultures. Indeed, European American students (who tend to value individualism) tend to show more reactance when their personal freedoms are threatened, whereas Asian Americans and Latin Americans (who tend to value collectivism) generally show more reactance when the freedoms of their fellow students are threatened (Jonas et al., 2009).

APPLICATION
Reactance in Jury Decision Making

The research on reactance can be applied to a fairly common occurrence in jury trials. Consider the following scenario: As a witness faces intense questioning from the opposing attorney, he blurts out some off-limits comment about the defendant's prior criminal record. The judge quickly intervenes, declaring, "The jury is to disregard that testimony." When framed in terms of reactance theory, this directive can be viewed as an attempt to restrict what you are allowed to think about. And in light of what you now know about reactance, you won't be surprised to learn that such instructions often backfire and produce a boomerang effect (Lieberman & Arndt, 2000).

In an experiment by Wolf and Montgomery (1977), mock jurors were presented with a simulated trial in which specific testimony was ruled either admissible or inadmissible. An important aspect of the inadmissible conditions was that the ruling was accompanied by a weak admonition or a strong admonition. The weak admonition simply instructed the jurors not to consider that testimony, whereas the strong admonition declared, "I want to remind you that the testimony . . . was ruled inadmissible. Therefore, it must play no role in your consideration of the case. You have no choice but to disregard it" (p. 211). After considering other testimony and arguments, the mock jurors were asked to give their verdicts. Participants receiving a strong admonition actually were more influenced by the inadmissible evidence than participants in either the weak-admonition condition or the admissible control condition. Thus, forceful instructions to ignore information may arouse reactance, leading jurors to reestablish their freedom by more heavily weighing precisely the information they have been told to disregard. To avoid reactance, subtle suggestions work better than forceful directives. ■

Resisting Strategically: Attitude Inoculation

Think about what people do to protect themselves from a virus. A weak dose of a virus is administered in the form of a vaccination. The dose is strong enough to trigger the body's production of resistant antibodies but weak enough that it does not overwhelm the body's resistance. The body can then more effectively marshal defenses to ward off stronger exposure to the virus that may come later.

William McGuire (1964) applied the logic of vaccination against disease to increase resistance to persuasion. He was inspired by the alarming decision of nine U.S. Army prisoners to remain with their captors in the aftermath of the Korean War, and the popular theory that they must have been brainwashed. He reasoned that, prior to their capture, the soldiers had rarely if ever been exposed to anticapitalist or procommunist arguments. Therefore, they were unprepared and had no ready defenses or counterarguments when their North Korean captors launched their persuasive attack. This led McGuire to the idea of attitude inoculation as a strategy that enables people to resist persuasion. The basic idea behind attitude inoculation is that exposing people to weak forms of a persuasive argument, much like inoculating people with a small amount of a virus, should motivate them to produce the cognitive equivalent of antibodies—that is, counterarguments—against this weakly advocated position. When later exposed to strong forms of the persuasive attempt, people already possess the motivation and counterarguments to use in their defense and thus more effectively resist the persuasive appeal (McGuire & Papageorgis, 1961).

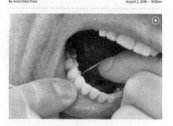

Flossing is a complete waste of time

By Associated Press

August 2, 2016 | 9:08am

▲ Would you be persuaded by this headline? It might depend on whether you've already been exposed to arguments against flossing.
[New York Post]

For example, most people are told and typically unquestioningly believe that flossing is one of the best ways to fight gum disease. But in 2016, the press reported a large meta-analysis that failed to provide clear and convincing support for this belief. How might people be inoculated against suddenly throwing away their floss after reading these headlines? McGuire's research suggests that if people are first given weak arguments against the health benefits of flossing ("flossing can be painful"), they will easily refute these claims (*yes, but the more you floss, the less painful it is*). The act of having to argue against a weak claim then puts them in a better position to argue against stronger evidence. In this example, those who in the past have argued against rather silly excuses not to floss might be more likely to dismiss those headlines about flossing's inability to prevent tooth decay.

Attitude inoculation has been widely studied across a variety of domains, such as politics, advertising, and health care, and it has been shown to be a potent means of strengthening resistance to persuasion (Wan & Pfau, 2004). The power of inoculation is greater when people play an active role in generating counterarguments (Bernard et al., 2003). In one study (Banerjee & Greene, 2007), junior high students participated in one of two workshops on resisting smoking advertisements or in a third group that did not participate in a workshop. In both of the resistance workshops, students discussed and analyzed antismoking ads. But one workshop went further, encouraging students to create their own antismoking ads. Although both workshop groups were effective in reducing students' intentions to smoke, the group of students who also created their own ads (and thus their own counterarguments) showed the lowest intentions to start smoking. Indeed, we often find the arguments that we generate more compelling than arguments generated by others (Gascó et al., 2018).

Consequences of Forewarning

One of the catchphrases used to summarize the literature on resistance to persuasion is "Forewarned is forearmed." When we know persuasion is going to attack, we can better arm ourselves. However, a number of interesting consequences can stem from these efforts. Some bode well for our ability to process and reason about persuasion attempts more carefully; others, however, offer a less optimistic forecast.

Recognizing Legitimate Appeals   Whereas inoculation gives us a taste of the arguments a would-be persuader will use so that we can better resist them, other types of forewarning help us to pierce the deceptions some persuaders try to use. This can enable us to resist persuasion that relies on deception and increase our openness to legitimate appeals. This is important because sometimes people try to persuade us to do things that are good for us, and it behooves us to listen to such messages with an open mind.

Sagarin and colleagues (2002) showed this potential. They trained some of their participants to be suspicious of advertisers' manipulative intent. For example, students were taught clues to diagnose whether a spokesperson in a television commercial is an actual expert or a model posing as an expert. ("Is that an actor pretending to be a doctor or an actual doctor promoting a brand of pain reliever?") Other participants were not given this training. Afterward, participants were presented with persuasive appeals by both legitimate and illegitimate authorities and were asked to indicate how much they agreed with the messages.

As you can see in **FIGURE 8.10**, participants who were given the training were not only more resistant to deceptive persuasion (i.e., when the authority was not actually an authority, such as a model dressed as a stockbroker pitching the *Wall Street Journal*) but also were more likely to be persuaded by commercials by legitimate authorities (e.g., the president of a financial institution pitching an investment fund).

This research makes two critical points. First, people are most likely to resist persuasion when (a) their motivation to resist is increased (i.e., by being told that advertisers will try to deceive them) and (b) when given the means to do so (i.e., strategies for recognizing illegitimate authorities). Second, when people are armed with the means to resist persuasion, they are also more open to appeals by legitimate authorities.

Making the Effort to Resist Finally, as much as we might want to resist persuasion in certain contexts, we should recognize that it takes cognitive effort to do so. Recall from chapter 6 our discussion of self-regulatory depletion. From this perspective, people's ability to control their thoughts, desires, and intentions can be weakened with repeated use. Although there is much discussion in the literature about whether these "ego-depletion" effects replicate well (Carter et al., 2015), a number of studies suggest that resisting persuasion is an effortful process that is challenging to motivate and sustain (e.g., Burkley, 2008; Clarkson et al., 2010; Petrocelli et al., 2015). Of course, changing attitudes when people's self-control resources are taxed is one thing, but changing actual behavior is another. Changing behavior is more challenging because when we're tired, we often fall back to our habitual routines (Itzchakov et al., 2018).

The idea that resistance to persuasion takes cognitive or motivational effort offers an interesting way of understanding considerably more dramatic forms of intense indoctrination or interviewing, from police interrogation to more unsavory tactics of torture. The subjects may be deprived of basic sustenance needs such as food or sleep in an effort to wear them down—that is, to make them more open to the examiner's questions. This can be considered the ultimate way of breaking down resistance to persuasion, paving the way for changing someone's attitude.

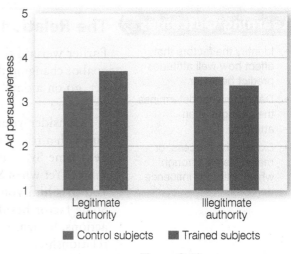

Figure 8.10

Knowledge Is Power

When participants in this study were trained to spot deceptive advertising tactics, they were less persuaded by testimonials given by actors (illegitimate authorities) than were control participants not given this training. They were also more persuaded than untrained participants by testimonials given by legitimate authorities.

[Data from Sagarin et al., 2002]

SECTION REVIEW   Resistance to Persuasion

Resistance is not always futile.

Awareness	Motivation	Inoculation	Consequences of Forewarning
If we're aware of a persuasive appeal, we're better able to resist it.	• Reactance theory explains why people resist persuasion attempts that infringe on their freedom. • Culture influences how much people value freedom and, thus, how strongly they react to persuasion attempts.	As with a vaccine, people can build up resistance by defending themselves against weaker arguments first.	• Given the motivation and the means to resist opens people's minds to legitimate appeals. • The motivation to resist persuasion can be undermined.

- Identify the factors that affect how well attitudes predict behavior.
- Describe what determines the strength of an attitude.
- Explain the process, or mechanisms, through which attitudes influence behavior.

The Relationship Between Attitudes and Behavior

Earlier we said that attempts at changing people's attitudes have the ultimate goal of changing their behavior—for example, getting them to purchase a product, go on a date, or wear a seatbelt. But how well do attitudes really predict behavior?

Consider your own experience. For instance, in anticipation of hanging out with a friend who constantly borrows your things, you might think, "The next time Sven asks to borrow my car, I'm going to tell him what I really think." Yet when Sven subsequently and predictably asks to borrow your ride, you toss him your keys with perhaps only a fleeting glance of disapproval. Some factor besides your attitude toward Sven's mooching determined your actions. It turns out that a number of factors complicate the attitude–behavior relationship.

The first hint of such complicating factors was uncovered by the sociologist Richard LaPiere in 1934. He traveled across the United States with a young Chinese couple, visiting 251 different hotels and restaurants. At that time, there was rather strong anti-Chinese prejudice in the United States, and there were no broadly enforced laws against ethnic, racial, or gender discrimination. LaPiere was curious to see how many of the places they visited would refuse service to the Chinese couple. As it turned out, they were refused service only in one case.

What makes this finding particularly surprising is that, six months later, LaPiere wrote letters to each establishment he had visited, asking if its employees would serve Chinese individuals. Of the establishments that wrote back, 92% said that they would not. But of course, only one actually did refuse service. Although LaPiere acknowledged a number of problems with this study (e.g., different employees might have answered his letter than those he encountered when visiting in person), the findings were striking in their total lack of support for the notion that verbal reports of attitudes guide behavior. Decades later, the relevant literature continued to reveal surprisingly limited support for the influence of attitudes on behavior (e.g., Wicker, 1969).

Why Attitudes Often Don't Predict Behavior

One reason attitudes often are poor predictors of behavior is that sometimes people do not know what their attitudes are, or at least they don't know exactly why they feel the way they do. As we saw in chapter 5, people can easily verbalize the reasons one *might* hold a particular attitude, but those reasons may not reflect their personal, gut-level feelings (Nisbett & Wilson, 1977b); thus, they can be poor predictors of behavior.

A second reason is that even when people do have a clear attitude that is relevant to a behavior, other factors can pull them in other directions (Fishbein & Ajzen, 1975). For example, have you ever found yourself sitting through a movie that you initially had no interest in seeing? Although you had a negative attitude toward the movie, you may have had other attitudes, such as your desire to please your significant other, who was interested in the movie. In this example, your attitudes toward your relationship won out over your attitude toward the movie to influence your movie-going behavior. Or consider two individuals who both have proenvironment attitudes. Research suggests that the everyday challenges of having lower socioeconomic status will make it more difficult for people from lower-income backgrounds to act in accordance with their environmental beliefs (Eom et al., 2018). In contrast, those from wealthier backgrounds have greater freedom and a greater sense of control over their future; this sense of freedom and self-efficacy make it easier for them to act in line with their attitudes.

Factors That Affect How Well Attitudes Predict Behavior

Understanding why attitudes don't always predict behavior gives us important clues about when attitudes *do* predict behavior (Glasman & Albarracín, 2006).

Matching the Attitude to the Behavior   When LaPiere asked hotel and restaurant employees whether they would serve Chinese individuals, he did not mention the specific details of his visit six months earlier; for example, he didn't say that the Chinese couple was well dressed and in the company of an American university professor. Thus, the employees' general attitude toward serving Chinese patrons may have been *too* general to predict their behavior in that specific situation. This highlights an important point: Although general attitudes are poor predictors of specific behaviors, more specific attitudes fare much better; conversely, general attitudes are better predictors of more general classes of behavior.

In a classic illustration of this point, Davidson and Jaccard (1979) asked a sample of married women about their attitudes toward birth control. Two years later, they interviewed the women again and asked how often they had used the birth control pill in the preceding two years (see **FIGURE 8.11**). In the first condition, the researchers asked women, "What is your attitude toward birth control?" They found that responses correlated .08 with Pill-taking behavior. This means there was practically no relationship between the women's attitude and their behavior.

Why do you think this relationship was so small? Obviously, the question was quite general, glossing over many ways of thinking about the Pill. For example, people might have a positive attitude toward birth control in general but feel that the Pill is not the best method. Still others might be trying to get pregnant, so although they might advocate birth control for other people, they are not using birth control themselves.

In the second condition, the researchers asked a more specific question: "What is your attitude toward the birth control pill?" Here they found that the correlation between women's attitude and their behavior improved to .32. This means women who reported having more positive attitudes toward the Pill were somewhat more likely to be taking it. But the relationship between attitude and behavior still was not very strong. In the third condition, women were asked about their attitudes "toward *using* birth control pills," and in the fourth condition, they were asked about their attitudes about "using the birth control pill in the next two years." In these conditions, the correlations increased to .53 and .57, respectively. These findings show that attitudes more specifically relevant to a behavior are better predictors of that behavior.

However, in situations where you are trying to predict a general set of behaviors, more general attitudes do a much better job. For instance, if you're trying to predict whether people will behave in environmentally friendly ways,

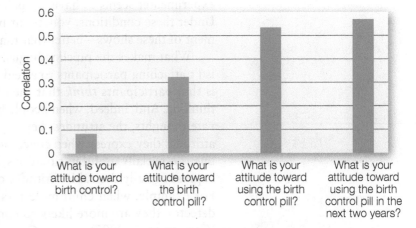

Figure 8.11

Predicting Behavior

Attitudes predict behavior better when they are phrased in a very specific way. In 1979, women's use of the Pill was unrelated to their general attitudes toward birth control but was correlated with their attitudes toward the Pill and toward taking the Pill.

[Data from Davidson & Jaccard, 1979]

you're better off getting their attitudes about environmental protection in general than getting one specific attitude. Rather than ask them how they feel about recycling soda cans, you should measure attitudes toward a range of proenvironment practices (e.g., support for hybrid cars and protecting endangered species) and combine them into an overall environmentalism attitude (Weigel & Newman, 1976).

Self-Presentational Concerns   Another reason that attitudes poorly predicted behavior in LaPiere's study may be that when hotel and restaurant employees were responding in the moment to LaPiere and the couple's visit, they were probably under self-presentational pressures that were absent when they later described in a letter what they would hypothetically do. In the lobby of a hotel, for example, the employees were most likely concerned with appearing professional and avoiding an unpleasant scene, self-presentational concerns that may have influenced their behavior more than their private attitudes toward Chinese people. In a private letter, though, they could express their negative attitudes without being concerned about public scrutiny.

The distinction between what one is willing to express in public and what one will express in private highlights the importance of knowing people's *true* attitudes for predicting their behavior. One technique for learning these attitudes is the *bogus pipeline* (Jones & Sigall, 1971). Imagine that you're participating in a psychology study, and the researcher asks you—in front of your peers, who disdain reality shows—whether you like to watch reality TV shows. Even if you actually enjoy settling in on the sofa and watching the trials and tribulations of people testing their singing voices or trying to fall in love with a stranger, you might be reluctant to reveal this attitude in front of the other students. But now imagine that the experimenter hooks you up to a polygraph machine—that is, a "lie detector"—and asks you the same question. Now the experimenter seems to have a pipeline, or a direct route, to your true attitudes. Under these conditions, you might be much more likely to confess your enjoyment of these shows—better that than to be caught lying!

What makes the pipeline bogus, so to speak, is that often the experimenter isn't attaching participants to a real mind-reading machine. What is important is that participants *think* that the experimenter knows exactly what they are thinking. And, indeed, when people believe that there is a pipeline into their private thoughts, the attitudes they express predict their behavior better than the attitudes they express when concerned about self-presentation. The bogus pipeline is especially useful in situations where people are under strong pressures to express socially desirable attitudes or to inhibit socially undesirable attitudes. For example, when child molesters are attached to what appears to be a lie detector, they are more likely to confess their sexual thoughts about children (Gannon et al., 2007).

Implicit Attitudes   Another approach to avoiding seeing merely what is socially desirable is to measure people's *implicit attitudes*, which we introduced in chapter 3. These are attitudes people have but are not consciously aware they have. Implicit attitudes predict some forms of behavior better than explicit attitudes—those that people can report consciously—because they are less influenced by self-presentational concerns about how they should and should not feel. Social psychologists have developed a number of techniques to measure implicit attitudes. For example, they often present participants with a word or an image (e.g., a picture of an African American face) and then observe how quickly the subjects recognize positive or negative words. If the word or image triggers negative feelings, participants should recognize negative words more quickly.

We will talk about this work in much greater detail when we discuss prejudice in chapter 10. But as you might imagine, it often is undesirable to admit to having a prejudiced attitude toward African Americans, or Hispanics, or physically disabled people. Yet many people clearly possess these prejudiced attitudes (Devine, 1989), as recent events make all too apparent. But because many people tend to underreport their level of prejudice on explicit measures, the correlation between implicit and explicit racial attitudes is often weak (Charlesworth & Banaji, 2019; Dovidio et al., 2001). Because implicit attitudes lurk beneath people's conscious awareness, they can predict subtle social behaviors that the people themselves do not recognize (Kurdi et al., 2019). For example, a person claims to have no prejudice toward African Americans, but when talking to African Americans, his body language tells a different story: He makes little eye contact, sits farther away, and interrupts the others' sentences. These behaviors are poorly predicted by his explicit attitude ("I thought the conversation went great!") but correlate highly with his implicit attitude (Dovidio et al., 2002).

Implicit attitudes also predict other types of behavior. For example, implicit attitudes toward smoking do a better job than explicit attitudes at predicting whether teens start smoking (Sherman et al., 2009), and implicit attitudes toward drinking better predict drinking behavior (Houben & Wiers, 2007). You may notice that both of these examples pertain to behaviors that are often engaged at the spur of the moment. And indeed, whereas explicit attitudes often do a better job of predicting more deliberate and reasoned behavior, implicit attitudes often fare better in predicting spontaneous behavior (Rydell & McConnell, 2006).

The Strength of the Attitude   Let's return to our example of holding a negative attitude toward a certain movie while, at the same time, holding a positive attitude toward a romantic partner who wants to see the movie. Which attitude will win out, so to speak, and exert a greater influence on your behavior? In general, whichever attitude is stronger, or held more firmly, will exert a more potent influence. So if you really detest this kind of movie, and your liking for your partner is not especially strong, you might be more likely to bail on the movie outing. Stronger attitudes not only influence behavior more, they are also represented more strongly in memory, and they are more enduring over time and resistant to change (Nayakankuppam et al., 2018; Petty & Krosnick, 1995).

What determines the strength of an attitude? There are a number of factors to consider.

Personal Experience.   An attitude tends to be stronger when it stems from a person's own experiences than when it is based on secondhand experiences heard about from others. Thus, if you see the trailer for a particular movie and think, "This stinks," your attitude toward that movie is likely to be stronger than if you hear from an acquaintance that the movie is not even worth renting.

Because attitudes stemming from firsthand experience are stronger than those based on secondhand experience, they do a better job of predicting behavior. This effect was shown in a study that took advantage of a severe housing shortage at Cornell University during the 1970s (Regan & Fazio, 1977). In the throes of this shortage, many first-year students had to make do with temporary accommodations, such as sleeping on a cot in a dormitory lounge. Others were fortunate enough to be assigned permanent housing. Regan and Fazio contacted students from both groups and assessed their attitudes toward the housing crisis, asking them, for example, how much they had suffered and whether they thought the university was dealing with the situation effectively. Later, the experimenters gave participants an opportunity to take action, such as signing a petition. Although the two groups of students had roughly equivalent attitudes toward the housing crisis, those who had to suffer through it personally (rather than simply hearing about it) had a stronger connection between their attitudes and their behavior. The more negative their attitudes, the more likely they were to engage in behavior to try to correct the situation. For those without the personal experience, the connection between their attitudes and their behavior was much weaker.

Vested Interest in the Attitude.   Another factor that contributes to attitude strength is the extent to which the individual has a vested interest in the attitude. The greater our vested interest in an attitude, or the more it connects to the self, the stronger the attitude, and thus the better the attitude predicts behavior (Zunick et al., 2017). Consider, for example, the current drinking age where you live. How bummed would you be if a law were passed that raised the drinking age by a couple of years? Would you do anything to prevent such a law from passing? Do you think that it might depend on how old you currently are? Sivacek and Crano (1982) studied just this situation in Michigan in the late 1970s, when a ballot was proposed to raise the minimum drinking age from 18 to 21. Among students who were over 21, and thus had little vested interest in the drinking age issue, there was only a small relationship between their attitudes and their behavior. However, among those under 21, who would have been affected personally by the proposal, there was a much tighter relationship between their attitudes and behavior. The more against the proposal they were, the more likely they were to volunteer to work against it.

Attitude Domain.   A final factor that influences attitude strength is the importance of the *attitude domain*. Two people may hold a similar attitude, but for one person the domain in question may be much more important. Here's a personal example from your current author (Jamie). He and his wife, though both liking Thai food in general, dislike a particular local Thai restaurant in their area. But whereas you couldn't drag Jamie there with a pack of wild horses, his wife will concede to going there if others have already chosen that location. For Jamie, food quality is more important, whereas for his wife, being socially amiable is more important. Their dislike is the same, but the importance of the domain (food quality versus socializing) varies. When a domain is important to us, our attitude about it is more likely to influence our behavior. In a study of political attitudes and voting behavior, for example, Krosnick (1988) showed that the political policies that were most important to people exerted the strongest influence on their actual voting behavior.

The Accessibility of the Attitude   In situations in which we have multiple attitudes that are relevant to a given behavior, the attitude that is most accessible will be the one most likely to guide behavior. A number of factors influence attitude accessibility, including our emotions. The more an attitude is based on emotion, the more accessible it is in memory (Rocklage & Fazio, 2018). This makes sense when we remember that our emotions often signal what we find important.

We see the influence of attitude accessibility in a classic study by Fazio and Williams (1986). They examined whether more accessible attitudes toward the then U.S. presidential candidates Ronald Reagan and Walter Mondale would predict people's actual voting behavior. They assessed how quickly American citizens indicated their attitudes toward Reagan and Mondale, reasoning that the more quickly a person indicates her attitude when asked, the more accessible that attitude is. A few months later, after the election, they called those people and asked who they had voted for. What did the researchers find? The more quickly a participant had indicated her attitude, the better that attitude predicted her voting behavior. For example, someone who had more quickly said she had a positive attitude toward Reagan was more likely to vote for Reagan than someone who indicated the same positive attitude but took longer to do so.

▲ How are you going to vote in the next election? You're likely to be strongly influenced by your most accessible political attitudes.

[Hill Street Studios/DigitalVision/Getty Images]

The fact that accessible attitudes predict behavior gives us important insights into why attitudes may at times fail to predict behavior. As we go about our daily affairs and interact with the world, we're often focused on what is happening around us, and we're not thinking of our attitudes. And unless we think about our attitudes, they are not accessible and thus have little influence on our behavior.

Can you recall a theory discussed in chapter 5 that explains what kinds of situations might make our attitudes accessible and thus more likely to influence our behavior? If you came up with *self-awareness theory* (Duval & Wicklund, 1972), you hit the nail on the head. To recap, this theory explains that people's attention can be focused internally on the self or externally on the environment. When people are self-aware, they compare their current behavior with the standard, or attitude, that is relevant to their situation. If possible, they then adjust their behavior so that it matches that salient attitude.

Recall, for example, the study by Carver (1975) (see chapter 5, p. 174) that initially measured participants' attitudes toward the use of punishment in teaching. When participants were not self-aware, their preexisting attitude about punishment did a poor job of predicting the level of punishment they administered when trying to teach another person a vocabulary list. However, when participants were made self-aware by looking in a mirror, their preexisting attitudes toward punishment were much better predictors of their willingness to dispense punishment. The interpretation here is that self-awareness made the preexisting attitude more influential.

Along with heightened self-awareness, simply priming an attitude or making it salient can also make it more likely to affect behavior. In one study, Snyder and Kendzierski (1982) first measured participants' attitudes toward sex discrimination. Weeks later, they had participants read a case regarding sex discrimination and render their own verdicts. Before they did, half of them were instructed, "You may want to think about how you feel about sex discrimination before rendering your verdict." For participants not reminded to consider their attitudes, their prior attitude had virtually no influence on their verdicts. However, for those who were reminded, their prior attitude was a good predictor of their verdicts. So, if you went camping and had a great time with friends, and awoke the next morning and saw a bunch of cans and bottles on the ground, would simply reminding your friends of their proenvironment attitudes (presuming they have them) motivate them to help you clean up the campsite?

◀ **THINK ABOUT**

[Pixel Youth Movement 3/Alamy]

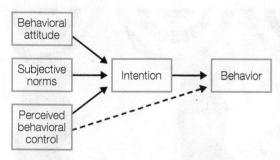

Figure 8.12

Theory of Planned Behavior

Attitudes, norms, and perceived control all shape people's intentions to engage in behavior.

Theory of planned behavior
A theory which proposes that attitudes, subjective norms, and perceived behavioral control interact to shape people's behavioral intentions.

Prototype/willingness model of health behavior A model that explains how, when it comes to opportunistic behaviors, a person's willingness to be influenced by a situation is a key predictor of behavior.

How Attitudes Influence Behavior

How is it that our attitudes actually guide our behavior? Do we just feel positively or negatively about something and then act accordingly? Or is there an intermediary step along the way? One influential theory proposes that our attitudes do not influence our behavior directly; rather, they do so through our *intentions*. According to the **theory of planned behavior** (Ajzen, 1985), attitudes are one of three ingredients in the intentions that we form (see **FIGURE 8.12**). The other two ingredients are subjective norms and perceived behavioral control. *Attitude* is your positive or negative evaluation of performing the behavior. *Subjective norms* are your perceptions of approval or disapproval of performing the behavior—that is, how much you perceive that others in your life think that a given behavior is a good or bad thing to do. Finally, *perceived behavioral control* is how much control you think you have over the behavior—whether you think you can do it or not. These three ingredients combine to shape your intentions, which in turn directly influence your behavior.

 APPLICATION

Understanding Risky Behavior

For an illustration of how the theory of planned behavior works, consider whether someone chooses to practice safe sex. If the person has a positive attitude about using condoms, thinks that others view them as important to use (a positive norm perception), and believes that he can in fact buy them and put them on (a strong sense of behavioral control), then he should have a strong intention to use condoms. This intention will be more likely to translate to behavior, and the person should in fact use a condom when having sex. But let's say, for example, that the individual's peer group or partner thinks wearing condoms is not cool. In this case, despite the individual's positive attitude, he may develop weaker intentions and thus make the (potentially deadly) mistake of not wearing a condom during sex. Indeed, research has examined just these kinds of decisions (Albarracín et al., 2001; Sheeran & Taylor, 1999), as well as many others in a variety of different domains from health to environmental behavior to consumer purchasing.

The picture gets more complicated, though, when we recognize that many types of behaviors—particularly risky behaviors such as starting to smoke, having unsafe sex, and drinking and driving—rarely are planned in advance. Rather, these behaviors are often more reactive to the situation. People find themselves in situations where these behaviors are options that they—unfortunately and far too frequently—can't turn down (Gibbons et al., 2006). This is often especially the case with risky behavior among adolescents. In such situations, intentions are not the most relevant factor to consider. Instead, it is more informative to consider people's *willingness* to engage in the behavior (Gibbons & Gerrard, 1997). As described in Rick Gibbons and Meg Gerrard's **prototype/willingness model of health behavior**, the distinction between willingness and intention is rather subtle but important. Like intention, willingness is influenced by one's attitudes and the norm and images of what one thinks is good to do, but willingness refers more specifically to a person's openness to being influenced by social circumstances. Thus, a young man may have no plans to drive drunk, but when drunk and with the opportunity to drive himself home, he may be more likely to do so. The point here is that attitudes often indirectly influence our behavior, and when it comes to "opportunistic" behaviors—such as risky behaviors that are often unplanned—it can be our willingness that best enables prediction about whether we will partake. ■

SECTION REVIEW   The Relationship Between Attitudes and Behavior

A number of factors complicate the attitude–behavior relationship.

Attitudes Don't Always Predict Behavior	Factors Affecting the Attitude–Behavior Link	How Attitudes Influence Behavior
• Attitudes may not reflect gut-level feelings. • One attitude may be trumped by other attitudes.	• Attitudes that are directly relevant are better predictors of behavior than are attitudes that are less relevant. • Self-presentation may mask the influence of attitudes on behavior. • Implicit attitudes better predict subtle or spontaneous behavior than deliberative behavior. • Strong and accessible attitudes are most likely to guide behavior.	• The theory of planned behavior proposes that attitudes, along with subjective norms and perceived behavioral control, form our intentions, which motivate behavior. • Attitudes also influence willingness to engage in a behavior, which plays a key role in decisions to engage in risky health behaviors.

CRITICAL LEARNING EXERCISES

1. Imagine that your TV show goes to commercial, showing a driver deliberately sliding on leather gloves and then excitedly gripping the steering wheel. She revs the engine, and a powerful roar complements the dramatic music playing in the background. She then puts the car into gear and races around twisting mountain roads with a confident and satisfied expression. As the commercial winds down, a narrator discusses the car's performance ratings, gas mileage, and dependability, comparing it to other cars in its class. Which elements of this message are targeting the central route to persuasion, and which are targeting the peripheral route? What elements of the commercial do you find most compelling? How does this fit with what we know about when people follow the central route or the peripheral route?

2. Today the political climates of many nations are characterized by strong and intolerant attitudes among people from both sides of the aisle (e.g., liberals and conservatives). Do you think this is a problem in the national government of the country where you live? If you were a politician now, how would you approach this problem? How would you address the particular concern that people tend to visit social media and news sites that reinforce their political views? How would you get people to change their minds?

3. Imagine that you graduate from college and take a job with an advertising company. Your first assignment is to come up with a commercial for a new basketball sneaker. Considering the different elements of persuasion, who would you want to appear in your commercial, what would you want the message to be, and who would you be targeting as the audience? What different aspects of persuasion would you incorporate into your commercial?

4. Imagine that you are a parent with a teenager who is just starting to go to high school parties. You want to teach your kid how to resist peers' attempts to persuade him to engage in risky behavior. You also want to make sure the attitudes you've taught about responsibility actually predict behavior in these party situations. What kind of things might you tell your kid in this situation?

Don't stop now! Check out our videos and additional resources located at: www.macmillanlearning.com

TOPIC OVERVIEW

CHAPTER 9

Group Processes

In the history of rock and roll, few bands have had such devoted fans as the Grateful Dead. When the band began touring in the late 1960s, die-hard fans, known affectionately as "deadheads," piled in their vans and followed along, knowing that the band's improvisational style meant that no two concerts would be the same. Over the next 30 years, a growing number of deadheads traveled with the band from city to city, some of them spending decades on the road.

To say that deadheads are a bunch of people who like the Grateful Dead misses the strong sense of community that binds them together. Before the invention of social networking, deadheads shared personal stories with one another through newsletters such as the *Grateful Dead Almanac*, and they created their own economy at concerts, buying and selling veggie burritos, T-shirts, and other essentials.

As a community, deadheads expected each other to behave in certain ways and socialized newcomers to conform to those expectations. As an example, following the release of the band's 1987 album *In the Dark*, concerts were flooded by younger fans whose belligerent behavior disrupted the mellow atmosphere. To restore order, senior deadheads organized a mass distribution of flyers, instructing everyone to "cool out." Deadheads also organized substance-abuse programs and worship services. Even today, more than two decades after the band's guitarist and frontman Jerry Garcia died, deadheads continue to interact and help each other by sharing travel stories on fan web sites and exchanging recordings of live performances free of charge. The group is much more than a collection of people who happen to like the same band.

▲ Deadheads are more than just a collection of people who like the Grateful Dead; they are a cultural group with their own norms and rituals.
[Barry Brecheisen/AP Images]

Deadheads are just one example of a group. Virtually every human on the planet identifies with at least one cultural group, whether it is a small tribe or a billion-person nation. People also identify with groups based on common genes (family), geography (neighborhood associations, gangs), ideology (Catholics, Young Republicans), causes (Black Lives Matter, the #MeToo movement), goals (the Senate Committee on Homeland Security, the NCAA Division I Basketball Committee), broad social interests (sororities and fraternities), shared experiences (Alcoholics Anonymous, alumni groups), and hobbies (Garden Club of America, Comic-Con).

In this chapter, we explore how group membership defines our self-concept and shapes our everyday life. We'll consider:

- What a group is and why people join groups

- When and why people cooperate in groups, as well as how they perform around others

- How groups make decisions and interact with leaders

- Why people sometimes leave groups

- Identify features of cohesive groups.

Entitativity The degree to which a collection of people feels like a cohesive group.

What Is a Group?

This question may seem strange at first because you probably have an intuitive sense of what a group is, but sometimes it is difficult to say for sure whether a collection of individuals constitutes a group. Are Canadians a group? Are strangers in line at the movies a group? What about the students in your social psychology class?

If you ask people to define groups, they generally agree that groups come in four types: intimacy groups (e.g., family, romantic partners, or friends), task groups (committees, orchestras, teams), social categories (women, North Americans, Jewish people), and loose associations (people in the same neighborhood, people who like classical music) (Lickel et al., 2000, 2001).

People also share the intuition that some groups are more, well, *group-y* than others. The formal (and hard to pronounce!) term is **entitativity**, which refers to the degree to which a collection of people feels like a cohesive group (Campbell, 1958); the term comes from groups feeling like real, solid *entities*.

What features of groups make them feel more or less cohesive? One feature is the presence of a *common bond*, the degree to which group members interact with and depend on each other to meet their needs and attain their goals (Johnson et al., 2006; Prentice et al., 1994; Rabbie & Horwitz, 1988; Shaw, 1981). Sometimes these interactions are based on *communal sharing*—the sense that "What's mine is yours" (Fiske, 1990). (For a refresher on this concept, see chapter 2.) You probably interact in this way when you hang out with your closest group of friends from high school. Other types of interactions are based on *market pricing*: "I will wash your back if you wash mine." This might be how you interact with classmates on an assignment, for example. In both types of interactions, a common bond creates a sense of entitativity, or cohesion (Cartwright & Zander, 1960; Clark & Mills, 1979; Lickel et al., 2006). As we'll see later, cohesion has both upsides and downsides.

A second feature of groups that increases their entitativity is a *common identity*. Groups often form among individuals who share similar characteristics, and people also come to feel a certain "we-ness," or shared attachment, to groups that they belong to (Prentice et al., 1994; Rabbie & Horwitz, 1988; Turner et al., 1987). Sharing the same gender, race, or even appearance can create a sense of common identity (Ip et al., 2006). So, too, can sharing a symbol like a flag or a mascot (Callahan & Ledgerwood, 2016). A common identity can also stem from supporting the same cause or working on a goal. For instance, a team of medical researchers might form a strong group identity while collaborating to develop a new medicine.

A common identity is especially likely to arise when individuals face a shared threat or challenge (Allport, 1954; James, 1906). Families often experience a renewed sense of unity in the face of adversity; school spirit spikes during athletic contests with rival schools; and citizens of a nation often come together in solidarity during times of war. For example, when United Airlines Flight 93 took off for San Francisco on the morning of September 11, 2001, the 37 passengers were just a loose collection of people. But when 4 men on board hijacked the plane with plans to crash it into either the White House or the U.S. Capitol, the other passengers began thinking and behaving in terms of "we" instead of "I." Their coordinated assault against the hijackers successfully diverted the plane from its intended target. The group-binding power of a common enemy is so powerful that leaders sometimes invent an enemy figure—a "them"—to cement the perception of "us" and transform a collective into a group (Silverstein, 1992).

▲ The movie *United 93* tells the story of how passengers on board this hijacked airliner came together as a group to thwart the terrorists' plan to fly the plane into the White House or the U.S. Capitol on September 11, 2001.

[Universal/The Kobal Collection/Shutterstock]

SECTION REVIEW What Is a Group?

The term *entitativity* describes the degree to which a group feels cohesive.

A group is cohesive when its members:

- Share a common bond because they interact and depend on one another.
- Share a common identity based on similar characteristics, goals, or challenges.

Why Do People Join and Identify with Groups?

> **Learning Outcome**
>
> - Outline reasons people benefit from being in groups.

For the better part of human history, the groups into which people were born—such as family and caste—largely defined what a person could be and do, and it was not possible to voluntarily exit those groups and join different ones. Even in the most progressive of modern societies, ethnicity, social class, nationality, family, and gender are ascribed by others to people at birth and still influence how people think and behave.

Today we have more freedom to decide which groups to join. Most of us have opportunities to join intramural sports teams and social clubs, committees, religious groups, and political parties. We can move up the career ladder to join a higher social class. And many people are now resisting traditional cultural categories such as gender and generation. When the *New York Times* asked readers to pick a new name for the generation after millennials, thousands of young people replied, "Don't call us anything" (Bromwich, 2018).

Whether by birth or by choice, groups are a central aspect of being human. Why? Let's take a look at a few important reasons.

Promoting Survival and Achieving Goals

Belonging to groups has been crucial to the development and survival of humans as a species. Over the course of evolution, humans depended on social networks to acquire and share food, transmit information, rear children, and avoid predators and other threats (Brewer & Caporael, 2006). Within this environment, individuals with characteristics that helped them get along with others—such as the desire for social acceptance, cooperativeness, and loyalty—had better chances of living long enough to pass on their genes to future generations. Through the natural selection process, modern humans might possess an innate desire to belong to groups and to avoid being kicked out of them (Baumeister & Leary, 1995).

This evolutionary perspective helps us understand why people have a generally positive view of their hometown, local region, and country, despite not having chosen them. People form close bonds within kinship groups and with non-kin in the vicinity because they would not survive very long without the cooperation of others (Kurzban & Neuberg, 2005).

People also form and join groups to accomplish goals they would be unlikely to accomplish on their own (Sherif, 1966). Most human achievements—from making a movie to incarcerating criminals—require the coordination of many people working in groups. At school or at work, people are more successful when they work in tight-knit groups of friends rather than with acquaintances (Chung et al., 2018). In fact, merely bringing to mind one's membership in a group causes people to feel more in control of their lives and capable of acting effectively (Greenaway et al., 2015), especially if the group is stable rather than constantly in flux (Proudfoot & Kay, 2018). What's more, the sense of personal control gained from group identification improves people's satisfaction with life and wards off unhealthy feelings of helplessness and depression. Shifting one's thinking from "me" to "we" boosts confidence that one can attain goals.

Reducing Uncertainty

Life is filled with uncertainties, from the location of your keys to the content of next week's physics exam. People generally dislike being uncertain about themselves. They also don't like being uncertain about who other people are and how they might behave. As you may recall from chapter 2, **uncertainty-identity theory** (Hogg, 2007) proposes that people join and identify with groups to reduce these negative feelings of uncertainty about themselves and others.

How does belonging to groups reduce uncertainty? Groups reinforce people's faith in their *cultural worldview* and their valued place within it. Most beliefs about reality can never be proven through personal experience. Even scientific facts—such as that the earth revolves around the sun—are not things that people see firsthand. Rather, confidence in these beliefs comes from social consensus: As more people share a belief, the truer it seems to be (Berger & Luckmann, 1967; Festinger, 1954). Being in a group provides this consensus through explicit routes (e.g., formal codes of conduct) and implicit routes (e.g., value-laden rituals), helping group members feel certain about how the world works.

A second way groups reduce uncertainty is by prescribing norms and roles. As we discussed in chapter 2, *norms* are rules for how all group members ought to behave. Most norms are unspoken agreements about what behavior is acceptable or unacceptable, but they can also be made explicit. Students told that most students at their university limit how much junk food they eat were then less interested in chowing down on junk food (Liu et al., 2019). *Roles* are

Uncertainty-identity theory The theory that people join and identify with groups in order to reduce negative feelings of uncertainty about themselves and others.

expectations for how people who hold certain positions in the group ought to behave. The captain of a soccer team can typically make decisions that other team members are not allowed to make.

Because a group's norms and roles tell its members how to behave and even how to think, group members do not have to wonder how they'll act in a given situation. This perspective leads to a hypothesis: In situations in which people feel uncertain about who they are, they will identify more with groups, particularly cohesive groups that offer a clear identity.

To test this hypothesis, Hogg and colleagues (Hogg et al., 2007) formed small groups of participants who had not previously known each other. Some participants were told they and the other members of their group had all responded very similarly on a series of questionnaires and that their group was very different from other groups. As we saw earlier, two ways of increasing entitativity, or cohesion, is perceiving "us" as the same and "them" as different. The other participants were told there wasn't much similarity in how the members of their group had responded and that all the groups were similar. This information should have made their group seem low in entitativity.

Then, in what seemed to be an unrelated task, participants wrote about either ways in which they felt uncertain about who they are and what their future holds or about more certain aspects of their life. Finally, all participants were asked how much they identified with the group they had just become part of in the study. Check out **FIGURE 9.1**. Increasing uncertainty about the self increased group identification—but only when the group was high in entitativity. Later studies showed that feeling different from others increased self-uncertainty, which then increased group identification (Hohman et al., 2017). Think back to when you first started college or university. Did you quickly identify with a new group in order to manage the uncertainty of such a major life transition?

Norms and roles reduce uncertainty about other people, too. Even if you know nothing about certain individuals, if you know what groups they belong to, you can expect them to behave in line with the norms and roles set out by those groups. Of course, as we will see later, such group-based expectations can also lead to harmful stereotyping.

The uncertainty perspective helps us to understand radicalization, or falling under the influence of extremist groups such as cults, hate groups, and terrorist organizations. When threats to personal significance make people feel uncertain about themselves, they become especially attracted to ideologies that promise clear-cut guidelines for how to live (Webber et al., 2018). In the face of this kind of uncertainty, a recipe for how to act and think can be especially comforting.

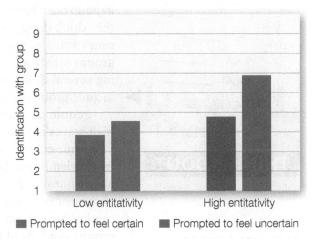

Figure 9.1

Group Identification Reduces Uncertainty

When participants were made to feel uncertain about themselves, they identified more strongly with a new group that was high in entitativity.

[Data from Hogg et al., 2007]

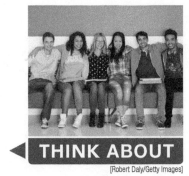

◀ **THINK ABOUT**

[Robert Daly/Getty Images]

Achieve
Social Psych in Everyday Life: Lyla

Bolstering Self-Esteem

According to **social identity theory**, belonging to groups is an important source of self-esteem (Tajfel & Turner, 1979; Turner et al., 1987). The theory says that a person's understanding of *who they are* is shaped by group memberships. If groups are a source of identity, and if people are motivated to view themselves in a positive light, then it follows that people would be motivated to view their groups positively as well. That explains why people generally show strong

Social identity theory The theory that group identities are an important part of self-definition and a key source of self-esteem.

THINK ABOUT

Ingroup bias A tendency to favor groups we belong to more than those that we don't.

ingroup bias, behaving more favorably toward groups they belong to than those they don't (Hogg, 2006). In the next chapter we look at how ingroup bias sometimes leads people to dislike outgroups. But for now, we can see that social groups satisfy a person's motivation to view the self in a positive light. Try listing several things that make you the person you are. Chances are your list will include group identities that help you feel good about yourself.

People can enhance their self-esteem by identifying with successful or high-status groups. For instance, when the Kansas City Chiefs won Super Bowl LIV, your current author (Mark), who lives in Kansas City, received messages from friends and family saying, "So proud of you!" This made him feel great about himself, even though he had no responsibility for that group's accomplishment (see chapter 6) (Cialdini et al., 1976). By belonging to groups, people can bolster self-esteem without lifting a finger (Kyprianides et al., 2019). In fact, groups don't need to be big or successful to bolster self-esteem; being part of small groups rich with supportive interactions can make people feel good about themselves (Postmes et al., 2019). This is seen, for example, in the use of social media. When people use social networking sites to make meaningful social connections, their self-esteem gets a boost (Clark et al., 2018). But be careful: When people simply view profiles without interacting with other users, they often end up comparing their lives with others and feeling lower in self-esteem.

Managing Mortality Concerns

As you'll recall from chapter 2, the existential perspective explains how people cope with the threatening knowledge of their mortality by maintaining faith in a cultural worldview and a sense of self-esteem. Belonging to groups strengthens these resources by allowing people to feel connected to something bigger and longer-lasting than their personal existence. While death is inevitable, people can take solace from belonging to an ancestral line, a national or religious group, a political movement, a scientific or artistic field, or some other enduring group that provides a sense that some part of them will live on in a symbolic sense. Indeed, people who are reminded of their death (in comparison to other negative topics) tend to view their country, religious organization, and other groups to which they belong more favorably and as higher in entitativity and longevity (Castano & Dechesne, 2005; Sani et al., 2009).

SECTION REVIEW Why Do People Join and Identify with Groups?

People are born into some groups and join others voluntarily. People can strongly identify with both types of groups. Here is why.

Promoting Survival and Achieving Goals	Reducing Uncertainty	Bolstering Self-Esteem	Managing Mortality Concerns
• During human evolution, group cooperation benefited survival and reproduction. • Hence, modern humans have an innate desire to join groups and identify with groups they're born into.	• People dislike feeling uncertain about themselves and others. • Belonging to a group reduces negative feelings of uncertainty.	• Groups are a source of self-esteem. • By viewing their group in a positive light, people feel better about themselves.	• Groups connect people to something bigger and longer-lasting than their own existence. • In this way, group identification eases mortality concerns.

Cooperation in Groups

Learning Outcomes

Why study cooperation? Historically, cooperation enabled our species to populate the entire globe and construct complex civilizations and technology. At an everyday level, your food, shelter, clothing, and physical safety—not to mention roads, electric power, waste management, intricate electronics, mass transit systems, institutions of higher education, and social welfare programs—are all available to you thanks to the cooperation of many people. What's more, the big challenges facing humanity today boil down to problems of group cooperation: How do conflicting groups come to trust each other? How can groups with competing interests make compromises and reach agreements?

- Explain the role of trust in the Prisoner's Dilemma.
- Explain why environmental conservation issues are examples of the commons dilemma.
- Identify evidence that people value fairness.
- Explain the role of physiology in cooperation.
- Explain the role of culture in cooperation.

Social Dilemmas and the Science of Cooperation

Because cooperation is critical for groups to develop trade and build economic relationships, the ones to study the psychology of cooperation and trust are often researchers interested in behavioral economics and decision making. The method often used in this research is to have people make decisions that pit their self-interest against a larger social goal. These types of decisions are called *social dilemmas* because they occur in situations in which what is good for the individual (and in the short term) might not be good for the group or within a larger social context.

The prisoner's dilemma The best-known social dilemma is the *prisoner's dilemma*. **FIGURE 9.2** depicts a typical setup. Imagine that you and your partner in crime have been apprehended after committing a burglary and hiding your loot. The detectives are interrogating you and your partner in separate rooms. They know you did the crime, but they need to build their case. They offer you a lighter charge if you confess to the heist and rat on your friend. The dilemma is that you know that your partner is being offered the same deal. If you cooperate with each other and remain silent, the prosecution's case will be flimsy, and you'll both get light sentences. But the best-case scenario for you personally would be to confess and squeal on your partner, assuming that he's faithfully keeping quiet. By adopting this more competitive strategy—sometimes called *defection*—you walk away with a fine, whereas he does a long stretch behind bars. Then again, if he's thinking the same thing, you might both end up confessing and then both being locked up. So maybe you should just keep your mouth shut and hope he does the same. Such a decision requires trust, and if your partner violates that trust and confesses, you'll be the one doing time. What would you do?

When people are paired with partners to play this game over a series of trials, they often end up adopting a *tit-for-tat strategy*, reciprocating whatever their partners did on the last trial. A cooperative move on one trial cues the partner to make a cooperative move on the next trial. Of course, competition will also be reciprocated with

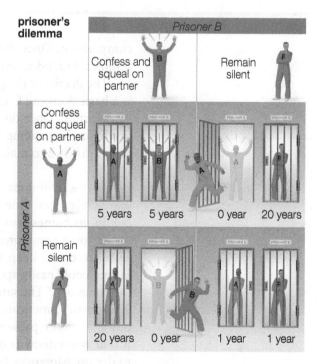

prisoner's dilemma

Figure 9.2

The prisoner's dilemma

In the prisoner's dilemma, you decide between cooperating and competing with a partner. Your decision depends on how much you trust your partner to cooperate with you.

SOCIAL PSYCH OUT IN THE WORLD

When Cooperation Is the Key to Economic Growth and Stability

Have you ever stopped to consider how the money we use is itself a form of cooperation? If you didn't agree to the value of your nation's currency, any purchase you made would involve an intense debate over the value of the $5 bill you are offering in exchange for a sandwich. Not only is it an act of cooperation to agree on the value of currency, it also can be an act of cooperation to defend it. Two national case studies make these points clear.

First, consider the case of Barbados, a former British colony. During the early 1990s, Barbados experienced an economic crisis that threatened to cripple the country. One proposed solution was to devalue the Barbadian currency, just as neighboring Jamaica had done in 1978. But the government refused and instead used persuasion techniques such as appealing to national pride to orchestrate cooperation among employers, labor unions, and the workers themselves.

As a result, employees agreed to accept a one-time 9% reduction in their wages, and businesses agreed to keep price increases at a minimum while the economy weathered the storm and began growing again (Henry & Miller, 2009). All the Barbadians took a temporary hit to their own economic self-interest,

but in doing so, they protected the value of their nation's currency, and the country quickly bounced back from its recession. If they hadn't had a strong shared belief that the currency had value, people would not have been willing to sacrifice their own personal self-interest to preserve the value of their currency.

Brazil also faced an economic crisis in recent history. After decades of printing money, inflation skyrocketed in the early 1990s. Imagine that one day you could buy a carton of eggs

▲ [Glyn Thomas/Alamy]

competition. Once one player begins playing competitively, the other person responds in kind to avoid getting penalized in future trials.

The details of the prisoner's dilemma may seem complicated, but at its heart is a basic decision: Can I trust you, or can't I? If I can't, I'd better protect myself by defecting. Once distrust is there, the two sides compete with each other. This is why nations racing to have the largest armed forces and weapons stockpiles find it difficult to make a cooperative pact for disarmament.

Resource Dilemmas Social dilemmas sometimes involve competition for scarce resources. One such dilemma is called the *commons dilemma*. The term *commons* comes from medieval times, when people would bring their herds to the town commons to graze (Hardin, 1968). Although it was in everyone's self-interest to keep the commons healthy, overgrazing by each individual farmer could easily spell the destruction of the resource, creating the "tragedy of the commons." The same dilemma arises in people's modern lives. For example, in 2020, many Americans responded to the coronavirus pandemic by thinking, "If I buy a few more packs of toilet paper, not much harm will be done." The problem is that when many people or groups think this way, the common resources start to dry up. Moreover, because these problems are caused by groups, the solutions also require groups. For example, although you might take pro-environmental actions like eating less meat and biking to work, you will not see the impact of those choices on climate change. A solution requires group members to identify with the group and change norms together (Fritsche et al., 2018).

for $1, but by the end of the year, a carton of eggs would cost you $1,000! The rate of inflation was so high that shopkeepers increased the prices of their goods every single day. As a result, people lost all trust in their government and in the value of their currency. As you know by now, trust is the key to cooperation.

How did Brazil turn its economy around so that today it is poised to become a global leader? A group of economists formulated a scheme to create a new currency that everyone could believe in. This new currency initially existed only as a name—the *unidade real de valor*, or unit of real value (URV). It was fixed to be the equivalent of one U.S. dollar. Although people still were paying for things with the old, inflated currency, they got used to *thinking* of prices in terms of this new, more stable form of money because products and services were all labeled in URVs. On July 1, 1994, all banks across the country began using newly printed *real* notes in place of the old currency. Within six months, faith in the economy was completely restored, and inflation ended (Joffe-Walt, 2010).

As these stories make clear, people can cooperate both in belief and in behavior. Trust is the linchpin in making cooperation succeed. In both examples, though, people also were cooperating with others who shared a common national identity. Their identification with their country and its currency as a

symbol of cultural value might also have played a role in fostering cooperation.

Earlier in this chapter, we discussed four factors that motivate people to identify with their groups: achieving goals, reducing uncertainty, bolstering self-esteem, and managing mortality concerns. How do you think each of these factors might have played a role in facilitating cooperation in Barbados and Brazil?

▲ [John W Banagan/Getty Images]

Another resource dilemma is called the *public goods dilemma*. A valued resource can continue to exist only if everyone contributes something to it. Local blood banks, libraries, and public radio and television are all examples of public goods that endure only because enough people chip in to keep them going. Solving a public goods dilemma requires cooperation of contributions so that the resource can be maintained. Indeed, taxes are society's solution to this dilemma: Although you might not like to see those taxes come out of your weekly paycheck, they do help pay for the roads you drive on, the schooling you have received, and the parks where you vacation.

Both kinds of resource dilemmas face the problem of *free riders*. These are individuals who take more than their fair share from the common pool or refuse to contribute to the public good, even while enjoying the same benefits as those who do contribute. Free riders serve their own self-interest instead of cooperating for the larger social goal.

Distribution Games Researchers can study cooperation by looking at how people behave when faced with distribution games. Distribution games are set up so that one person or group has the power to decide how resources get

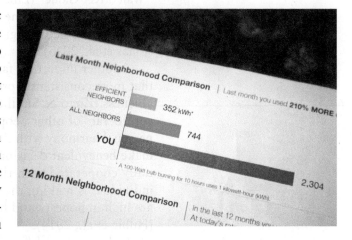
▲ In the *commons dilemma*, gobbling up a scarce resource benefits you but hurts the group. Some public utility companies have begun making people more aware of this trade-off. How would you react to an electric bill showing that you use more electricity than your neighbors?
[Max Whittaker/The New York Times/Redux]

distributed. In the *ultimatum game*, one person, called the "decider," is given a real sum of money and told she can decide how much to keep and how much to give to another person. The other person, the "recipient," then chooses to either accept or reject this offer; if the recipient rejects the offer, *no one* gets money. Researchers can use this game to look at whether people are more or less likely to distribute outcomes equally. The *dictator game* is similar, except the recipient doesn't have the option of "punishing" the decider by rejecting his or her offer. This game allows researchers to look at people's reactions to unfair distribution of resources.

In both games, people put in the role of decider often distribute money equally, even though it clearly would be in their self-interest to take the whole pot and give nothing to the recipient (Camerer, 2003). People value fairness. Still, deciders occasionally make unfair offers. In these cases, recipients usually punish them by rejecting the offer, even when such punishment comes at a cost to themselves. If your partner offers you only $2 and chooses to keep $8 for himself, you might reject the offer and forfeit your two bucks to send a clear message to your partner: Your unfairness is unacceptable.

When Do People Cooperate?

Although cooperation can be a great way to achieve goals, the research on social dilemmas shows that people sometimes choose what's good for themselves over what's good for the group. Can we predict when people will cooperate? Yes—by appreciating the role of the situation, the person, and culture.

To appreciate the importance of the situation, consider what happens when different norms are salient in the person's immediate context. When a prisoner's dilemma was labeled the "Community Game," participants chose to cooperate on twice the number of trials as when the same dilemma was called the "Wall Street Game" (Liberman et al., 2004). When deciders playing the dictator game are primed with the concept of fairness and thus motivated to do the right thing, they sometimes give away more money than they keep for themselves (Jonas et al., 2013).

Another important factor is the person's personality. The personality trait that most consistently predicts more cooperative and fair decisions is agreeableness (Zhao & Smillie, 2014). People who are high in agreeableness are considerate of other people's needs and feelings, and they try to foster interpersonal harmony with their actions. Thus, it is not surprising that they would make benevolent decisions, especially when interacting with others who initially cooperated with them. But what about when instead of reacting, the individual is making the first move? In these types of contexts, people who are high in honesty and humility tend to open with more generous proposals (Hilbig et al., 2014).

Culture also plays a role in cooperative tendencies. On the surface, it might seem that individuals from collectivist (versus individualist) cultures would generally be more cooperative. After all, what better way to achieve social harmony than through cooperation? The full picture is more complex. People from collectivist cultures do cooperate more, but only when they are interacting with friends (Leung, 1988); when interacting with strangers, collectivists can be more competitive. We see this in studies that prime different cultural identities. When Chinese Americans were primed to think about their Chinese identity (rather than their American identity), they were more cooperative when playing with friends but not when playing with strangers (Wong & Hong, 2005).

Why Do People Cooperate?

The neuroscience perspective provides some clues as to why people cooperate. One line of research looks at the biological basis of trust, which we saw is crucial for cooperation. The hormone *oxytocin* is a biological marker of trust as well as other prosocial feelings (Porges, 1998). When other people place their trust in you, your levels of oxytocin rise and increase your willingness to act in a trustworthy way (Zak et al., 2005). Perceiving more trust also increases oxytocin levels, greasing the wheels of further trust and cooperation.

You can see oxytocin at work in a study by Kosfeld and colleagues (Kosfeld et al., 2005). Participants were randomly assigned to receive an injection of either oxytocin or a placebo. They then played the *trust game*, in which they decided how much money they wanted to invest with another player (called the trustee). The experimenter tripled whatever was invested, but much as in the dictator game, the trustee got to decide how much of that money would be paid back to the investor. Check out **FIGURE 9.3**. Those who had received the boost in oxytocin were twice as likely to make the maximum investment as those in the placebo group. People are not, however, blindly controlled by biochemical secretions. If the social basis for trusting others is absent, as when an interaction partner appears unreliable, an oxytocin boost does not increase trust (Mikolajczak et al., 2010). Oxytocin seems to signal that others are trustworthy, but it does not simply make people more gullible.

If trust influences people's tendency to be fair, what about their reactions to being treated unfairly? Take away a child's toy on the playground, and you will get a clear taste of an immediate, negative, and probably loud reaction to unfairness. We get a quieter indication of this negative reaction in neuroimaging studies. When people receive low offers in the ultimatum game—like $2 out of $10—they show activation in the anterior insula region of the brain, which is associated with an automatic emotional response. But they also show activation of the dorsolateral prefrontal cortex, which is linked to thinking carefully about what to do (Sanfey et al., 2003). Why are both brain areas responding? In response to a low offer, people feel an initial impulse to take anything profitable that comes their way, but then they override that impulse and reject the offer as unfair. In fact, if people's right dorsolateral prefrontal cortex is temporarily deactivated, they become more likely to accept unfair offers, even while acknowledging that they are getting the short end of the stick (Knoch et al., 2006).

Fairness Norms: Evolutionary and Cultural Perspectives

When people reject a low offer in the ultimatum game, they are asserting that fairness is more important than getting a few dollars. This concern with fairness is culturally

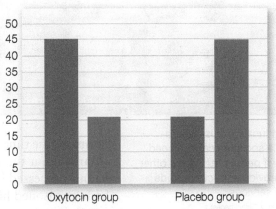

Percentage of participants who invested all their money, reflecting high trust

Percentage who made smaller, less trusting investments

Figure 9.3

The Trust Game

In this *trust game*, participants decide how much money to invest in an exchange with someone who might abuse their trust and make off with everything. Participants who received a dose of oxytocin (versus a placebo) were more trusting. They were twice as likely to invest all their money.

[Data from Kosfeld et al., 2005]

▲ TV talk show host Jimmy Kimmel asked parents to videotape their children's reactions to learning that Mom or Dad had eaten all their Halloween candy. The resulting videos show people's extreme emotional reactions when others violate their trust.

[Kevin Mazur/Getty Images for SiriusXM]

widespread and is even shared by our primate relatives. When chimpanzees play a version of the ultimatum game and one partner makes an unfair offer, the recipient hisses and spits at the other chimp, even while grudgingly accepting it (Proctor et al., 2013). Even nonhuman animals get outraged when they have been shortchanged.

Given this evidence, it is possible that evolution endowed our species with a tendency to agree on norms for fairness (Fehr & Gächter, 1998; Hoffman et al., 1998). How might this have happened? Treating others fairly is beneficial to each of us because people tend to reciprocate how they are treated. Those who are fair are treated better by others in return, thereby improving the chances that the genes associated with a propensity for fairness will be represented in future generations.

To get the full picture, though, we also need to look at culture. Cultures differ in how strongly they enforce the norm of fairness. In large-scale industrialized societies, people playing the ultimatum game typically offer a 50–50 split of the resources. If they are in the role of recipient, they usually reject any offer below 20 or 30% of the total (Henrich & Henrich, 2007). But when members of small-scale societies consider the same decision, they show much more variability in their responses. In some communities where almost all interaction takes place face to face, people make very low offers to others and are willing to accept even the most unbalanced proposal (Henrich et al., 2010).

▲ In tuna we trust. Large-scale societies can succeed only if people trust each other to provide expected goods and services.

[Tim Boyle/Getty Images]

At first glance, you might think that small-scale, face-to-face agrarian cultures would be more cooperative and concerned with fairness than urban cultures whose interactions tend to be less intimate and are reliant on remote electronic communication. Henrich and his colleagues (2010) argued, though, that when society grows beyond the reach of family and known reputations, norms of fairness and cooperation develop to help govern the needs of an expanding network of relationships. Put more simply, the big societies filled with strangers are the ones that *need* strong fairness norms in order to hold together. We rely on fairness norms all the time in our everyday life. For example, when your current author (Mark) ate a tuna sandwich an hour ago, he had to trust that the cannery hadn't processed spoiled fish and that the clerk who assembled the sandwich hadn't poisoned him.

Cultural factors can also erode trust, with consequences for economic development. Nathan Nunn (2008), an economist at Harvard, has observed that the African countries that were most affected by the slave trade have seen the least amount of economic development and also exhibit the lowest levels of trust (Nunn & Wantchekon, 2011). His theory is that because people in former African slave-trading countries worried about being tricked or sold into slavery, sometimes even by acquaintances and friends, a culture of mistrust developed that has impeded political and economic cooperation even long after the demise of the slave trade. How might these ideas help us understand current problems in the world? Do you think mistrust has contributed to the racially charged incidents involving law enforcement in the United States in the past few years?

THINK ABOUT ▶

[Joshua Lott/Getty Images]

SECTION REVIEW Cooperation in Groups

To survive and thrive, individuals in a group must cooperate, balancing their personal interests with others' interests.

Studying Cooperation

- The Prisoner's Dilemma demonstrates how distrust escalates competition.
- Resource dilemmas demonstrate how cooperation is essential to providing or maintaining valuable shared resources.
- Distribution games assess whether people distribute resources fairly or unfairly and others' reactions to those decisions.

Cooperation: When and Why

- Social norms, personality traits, and culture all play roles in determining when people will cooperate.
- Oxytocin signals trust.
- We respond negatively to unfairness.

Evolution and Culture

- A desire for fairness and cooperation is culturally widespread and likely evolved.
- Still, cultures vary in their norms of fairness.

Performance in a Social Context

Learning Outcomes

So far, we've explored the benefits of living in groups and the cooperation needed to navigate group life. But group living also means performing actions in the presence of others or alongside them. If you are like most other students, you probably groan at the thought of group projects or having to give a speech to the class. If humans evolved to live in groups, why is performing in a group often so unpleasant and inefficient? Let's hit the court to find out.

- Identify when performing in a social context is likely to improve performance and when it is likely to impair performance.
- List situations in which people might fall prey to social loafing.
- Explain why hiding behind masks can increase aggression.

Performing in Front of Others: Social Facilitation

It was 2008, and the NCAA men's basketball championship trophy was on the line. With just under two minutes left to play, the Memphis Tigers had a 9-point lead over the Kansas Jayhawks. That lead quickly started to vanish after a key player fouled out of the game. The Tigers' defense broke down, and the team missed several key free throws in a row that would have clinched the title for them. These missteps allowed the Jayhawks to tie the score at the buzzer and then trounce the beleaguered Tigers in overtime. With so much on the line and so much talent on the team, why did Memphis choke?

Interest in questions like this goes back more than a century and motivated one of the first experiments in social psychology. In this study, though, the question was why performance sometimes gets better, rather than worse, in the presence of others.

▲ Athletes have to learn to perform in front of huge crowds, but sometimes even the best players and teams choke under pressure.
[Bill Shettle/Cal Sport Media/AP Images]

Social Facilitation Theory, Take 1: When Others Improve Performance At the end of the 19th century, Norman Triplett did what most psychology researchers do best: He observed a phenomenon, developed a theory he thought might explain it, and designed experiments to test his idea. The observation was that cyclists were able to ride 20 to 30 seconds per mile faster when they were racing with other cyclists than when they were racing alone. Triplett speculated that the mere presence of other competitors heightens arousal, which in turn improves performance.

To test his idea, Triplett (1898) asked children to reel in a cord on a fishing rod as fast as they could while he recorded their time. Sometimes they performed this task alone, and other times they competed with each other. Most of the kids tested were faster at reeling in the cord when they were competing than when they were performing alone—a finding that supported an early version of *social facilitation theory*.

Triplett's paper sparked a flurry of research exploring how an individual's performance is affected not only by a competitive environment but also by the mere presence of other people watching. Many studies showed that performance improves when an audience is watching. The problem was that other studies began showing the opposite effect: Performance worsened when others were watching. To make sense of these mixed results, Robert Zajonc proposed an updated version of social facilitation theory.

Social Facilitation Theory, Take 2: Others Facilitate One's Dominant Response

Social facilitation theory
The theory that the presence of others increases a person's dominant response—that is, the response that is most likely for that person for the task at hand.

Zajonc (1965) refined **social facilitation theory** by suggesting that the mere presence of others does not always improve or hurt performance; rather, it increases one's *dominant response*—the response that is most likely for that person for that particular task. If that task is a simple motor task (reeling in a fishing line) or something that you've practiced very well (playing a piano sonata for the thousandth time), your dominant or automatic response is to reel fast and play accurately. In these cases, having an audience likely will *improve* your performance. But if the task is a complex one (finding the logical inconsistencies in a philosophical treatise) or one that you are only just beginning to learn (playing a piano sonata for the first time), the dominant response will be to make mistakes; therefore, an audience will most likely *impair* your performance. What is it about an audience that increases the dominant response?

The Role of Arousal

Zajonc proposed that simply being in the presence of others heightens arousal, which can improve performance but can also make it hard to focus. In fact, he said, every animal is aroused by the presence of other members of its species. Does this mean that other animals will show social facilitation effects?

To find out, Zajonc carried out what is the only social psychology study performed on cockroaches (Zajonc et al., 1969). Cockroaches were timed as they ran a maze to escape a bright light for a dark corner. Two aspects of the situation were varied. First, the cockroaches either ran the maze alone or in the presence of other cockroaches placed in clear Plexiglas boxes alongside the runways. In addition, the route to the darkened goal box was either easy (just a straight shot down a runway) or relatively difficult (requiring a choice of paths and a 90-degree turn to find the goal box) (see **FIGURE 9.4**). Just as others had found with humans, when the task was easy, the cockroaches reached their goal more quickly in the presence of other cockroaches than when they were alone. But when the task was difficult, it took the cockroaches longer to reach their goal with other cockroaches lurking about. Because

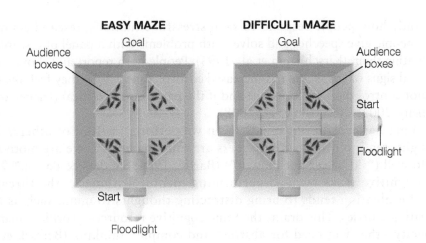

Figure 9.4

Do Other Species Get Aroused by an Audience?

Even cockroaches exhibit a social facilitation effect. When around other cockroaches (compared with being alone), they do better on an easy maze but worse on a difficult maze.

[Research from Zajonc et al., 1969]

the psychology of a cockroach is pretty stripped down compared with our own, these findings suggest that social facilitation effects are due to a very basic biological process: feeling aroused when in the presence of others. (In a recent replication, cockroaches took longer to complete both the difficult and easy mazes in the presence of other cockroaches, suggesting that arousal may inhibit performance in general; Halfmann et al., 2020.)

However, human psychology is more complex than cockroach psychology. Modern research has revealed that the type of arousal humans feel in the presence of others also depends on their interpretation of the situation. In chapter 6 we introduced the idea that people's reaction to a stressful situation depends on whether they feel they have the resources to meet the demands of the task at hand (Blascovich & Tomaka, 1996). A person with the necessary resources, perhaps because the task is well practiced, tends to show a *challenge response*: The heart pumps harder with each beat, and arteries and veins expand to accommodate the rush of blood to vital organs and extremities. But when people feel *threatened* because they think they might not have what it takes to meet the demands of the task, the physiological profile is different. The heart still beats harder, but now the arteries and veins constrict in a way that makes it more difficult to move oxygenated blood through the body. This is the pattern that people exhibit when trying to do a new and difficult task with an audience watching. Perhaps it's no surprise that their performance also suffers (Blascovich et al., 1999).

Let's return to the example of the NCAA championship. When Memphis's All-American Chris Douglas-Roberts approached the free throw line with a chance to wrap up the title by sinking a couple of free throws, the stakes had changed. The additional elements of the high-pressure situation, Kansas's mounting comeback, and the fact that commentators actually had forecast that Memphis's overall weak free throw shooting might be the team's undoing could have shifted the moment from a challenge to a threat, making the task much more difficult. To the Memphis fans' dismay, Chris Douglas-Roberts's performance at the free throw line suffered.

The Role of Evaluation   The description of the NCAA championship game reveals that, for humans, the social context includes more than just heightened arousal; it also carries the potential for social judgment. When all eyes are on you and a lot is at stake, the concern about social evaluation is heightened.

▲ The comedian Jerry Seinfeld remarks on the common fear of public scrutiny: "According to most studies, people's number-one fear is public speaking. Number two is death. Death is number two. Does that sound right? This means to the average person, if you go to a funeral, you're better off in the casket than doing the eulogy."

[Theo Wargo/Getty Images Entertainment/Getty Images]

To study how people respond to such stressful situations, researchers often have people give speeches and solve math problems with a panel of researchers evaluating them (Kirschbaum et al., 1993). People both report and show physiological signs of stress, such as increased cortisol, especially if they feel like they cannot control their performance and if the panel is very critical (Dickerson & Kemeny, 2004; Dickerson et al., 2008).

What happens in our minds when we perform in front of others? Our thoughts tend to drift to what others are thinking even as we are motivated to do well ("I'd better not blow it") (Baron, 1986; Sanders & Baron, 1975). On cognitive tasks such as performing mental arithmetic, the threat of social evaluation tends to bring distracting thoughts to mind, such as self-defeating worries. This drains the same cognitive resource—working memory capacity—that you need for abstract and complex thinking (Beilock et al., 2004; Schmader et al., 2008). With this resource hijacked by worries about your performance, you simply have less mental capacity to focus on the task at hand—an effect even seen at the level of activation of different types of neurons (Belletier et al., 2019).

Other kinds of performance don't rely on working memory capacity. Becoming an expert in a domain such as basketball, piano, or a video game means practicing to the point that certain actions become automatic. When you reach that point, you no longer need to focus your conscious stream of attention on the step-by-step elements of a task. When people feel the threat of social evaluation and doubts creep in, they slip out of the routine performance they have practiced and begin mentally micromanaging their movements—dooming themselves to failure (Beilock & Carr, 2001). Thus, a professional tennis player who gets nervous and thinks, "I have to remember to get my racket back, step into my shot, shift my weight, and follow through" is likely to have found that Rafael Nadal's blistering forehand has whizzed right by him before he can set up for the shot.

So how do you go about preventing what happened to Memphis from happening to you? Perhaps we can find wisdom in the advice of the basketball legend Charles Barkley, who said, "I know I'm never as good or bad as one single performance. I've never believed in my critics or my worshippers, and I've always been able to leave the game at the arena." By disengaging his own self-evaluation from a single game, from the audience in the stands, and from the court more generally, he became less vulnerable to the disruptive pressures of being in the spotlight.

Performing with Others: Social Loafing

Research on social facilitation reveals how performance is affected when people perform in front of others. But what about performing *with* other people on a common task? Those who coach teams or manage organizations know that it can be challenging to get group performance to equal or exceed the sum of its parts. Part of the problem is simply coordinating behavior among two or more people (Latané et al., 1979). But another challenge to optimizing group performance is a phenomenon called **social loafing**, in which an individual exerts less effort when performing as a part of a collective or group than when performing as an individual.

Social loafing A tendency to exert less effort when performing as part of a collective or group than when performing as an individual.

Consider this study: Participants were asked to clap or cheer as loudly as they could in what was described as a study of sound perception (Latané et al., 1979). They had to be as loud as possible either alone, in pairs, in a group of four, or in a group of six. What would you do in these different contexts? If the social context doesn't matter, then you would probably clap as loudly when alone as when you are in a big group. But that's not what the researchers found. Instead, the sound generated per person was highest when people were clapping and cheering alone and decreased each time the group size was increased. This slacking off occurred even when people were doing their clapping and shouting in individual sound-proof chambers and believed that the sound they generated would be combined with the sounds of other group members in separate chambers.

The social loafing effect has been found for tasks as varied as rope pulling, swimming, cheering, brainstorming, and maze solving. How often have you found yourself slacking off when in a group? Looking deeper, why are people less likely to give their all when they are part of a group?

THINK ABOUT

[stock_colors/coloroftime/iStock/Getty Images]

Low Accountability The biggest reason that people slack off in groups is that they feel less accountable. This means they feel that their contribution to the group's outcome will not be recognized. If, in contrast, people feel solely responsible for a task, they put forth more effort. For example, when the clapping study was repeated so that participants believed their contribution to the total noise could be traced back to them, the social loafing effect disappeared (Williams et al., 1981).

This finding helps to explain why managers and teachers can increase productivity and performance on group projects by establishing incentives for both individual and group efforts. Is this Big Brother approach of external evaluation the only solution to social loafing? Happily, the answer is "no." Simply giving people a way to monitor and evaluate their own performance reduces loafing (Harkins & Szymanski, 1988; Szymanski & Harkins, 1987).

Low Expected Effort from Others People also hold back effort because they believe others will do the same. After all, who wants to be the sucker who does all the work for only a piece of the credit? If people are instead led to believe that others will work hard for the duration of a task, they loaf less (Jackson & Harkins, 1985).

If you find yourself working in a group and are concerned that others might start slacking off, asserting the level of effort you intend to put forth can encourage others to make a greater effort.

High Perceived Dispensability A third reason for social loafing is that people in a group can feel that their own efforts are not particularly important to the group's outcome (Kerr & Bruun, 1983). For example, many people don't vote in elections because they feel that their one individual vote will not have much impact. However, feelings of dispensability depend on the type of task. In *disjunctive tasks*, the most skilled members of the group determine the outcome. Imagine a team quiz show or a debate team in which one genius can carry the team to group success. On *conjunctive tasks*, the group will do only as well as the worst performer. For example, in mountain climbing, the team can get up the mountain only as fast as its slowest member. Research shows that when group tasks are disjunctive, the most skilled members of the group make the greatest effort, whereas the least skilled members slack off. On conjunctive tasks, however, the least skilled members exert the greatest effort, and the most skilled members slack off.

If you're leading a group and want maximum effort from everyone, you can capitalize on these effects by encouraging your best performers to view the task as disjunctive and your lesser performers to perceive it to be conjunctive. In this way, all group members will believe that their efforts are indispensable.

Caring Decreases Loafing   You'll notice that in many of the studies mentioned in this chapter, people were performing tasks they didn't normally do, like clapping in a sound booth. In these situations, they probably didn't care much about what the group accomplished. No wonder, then, that they slacked off. But in the real world, people belong to groups that they value, and they perform group activities that feel like extensions of their identity. In these situations, people loaf less (Karau & Williams, 1997). Similarly, people who highly value relationships loaf less. For example, women and East Asians—groups that both tend to focus on maintaining relationships—are less likely to loaf than are more agentic and individualistic groups, such as North American males (Karau & Williams, 1993). People also loaf less when they find the task interesting, personally meaningful, or rewarding (Brickner et al., 1986; Zaccaro, 1984).

Competition between groups also decreases loafing, most likely by increasing group value. When construction on the Petronas Towers in Malaysia began in 1993, the towers were planned to be the tallest structure in the world. The plan called for two identical towers to be built simultaneously, and each tower was contracted to a different company: Tower One to a Korean corporation and Tower Two to a Japanese firm. Whether by design or by happy accident, the pace of building soon became a matter of national pride for the construction workers, who marked their progress by comparing the heights of two flags that steadily rose higher as the build advanced. (The Korean team won the race.) With such a visible way to measure progress toward the group goal, social loafing probably was kept to a minimum. If only all construction projects could be so speedy!

▲ The twin Petronas Towers in Malaysia were constructed by workers from two different countries who competed against one another to finish their tower first.

[Martin Puddy/Getty Images]

Social Facilitation and Social Loafing Compared

At this point, you might be thinking that social loafing and social facilitation contradict one another. According to social facilitation theory, performing in a social context heightens people's concern with being evaluated, improving their performance on an easy task and impairing performance on a difficult task. But research on social loafing shows that performing in a social context can reduce people's concern with being evaluated, impairing performance on an easy task and sometimes improving performance when the task is challenging. What gives? It's important to remember that the nature of the social context in these two effects is very different. With social facilitation, others stand by watching you perform, and you feel yourself in the spotlight. With social loafing, others are working alongside you toward a common goal, and your own individual efforts feel anonymous.

Another difference is that, in most studies of social loafing, task performance is mostly a matter of motivation. You don't need special skills to clap or to pull a rope, and your performance is simply a function of how much effort you put in. On tasks such as these, being accountable or watched increases effort and boosts performance. But for other, more complicated tasks, effort alone doesn't guarantee success. You cannot ace your college boards merely if you are motivated enough; you also need to have the knowledge to solve complex problems. The threat of being negatively evaluated on these tasks can impair performance even when motivation is high (Forbes & Schmader, 2010).

Deindividuation: Getting Caught Up in the Crowd

Sometimes when individuals are in groups or crowds, they lose their sense of individuality. This psychological state is known as **deindividuation**. Deindividuation is the opposite of heightened self-awareness. As we discussed in chapter 5, when people are highly aware of themselves as individuals, their actions tend to be guided by their personal attitudes, moral standards, and goals. But when people feel deindividuated, as they do in a large crowd, they are more likely to do what others around them are doing, even when those actions run counter to their personal attitudes and standards (Postmes & Spears, 1998).

People are most likely to feel deindividuated when they are overstimulated by sights and sounds, when they are high in cognitive load, and when there are few if any cues distinguishing them from the crowd. In these circumstances, people often behave in more extreme ways than they otherwise would. In one study, participants who dressed identically and wore hoods over their heads were more aggressive toward a stranger than participants who could be identified at a glance (Zimbardo, 1970).

Deindividuation may help account for especially egregious actions that people sometimes engage in during wars, riots, lynchings, and large-scale public crowding. For example, in cultures where warriors tend to hide their identities with paint or masks, killing, torture, and mutilation of captives is more common (Watson, 1973). A review of newspaper accounts of 60 lynchings of African Americans in the United States between 1899 and 1946 revealed that the most savage and vicious killings were carried out by large crowds and hooded mobs (Mullen, 1986). Fast forward to 2017, when demonstrators assembled in Charlottesville, Virginia, and far-right White supremacists turned up wearing a uniform of white polo shirts and tan khakis; among them was neo-Nazi James Fields, who wore this uniform as he mowed down a crowd of protesters, killing Heather Heyer in the process.

Although deindividuation likely contributes to many instances of horrifying behavior in crowds, bad behavior is not an inevitable consequence of being in a large group of people. If the salient cues in the situation are to do something positive, then deindividuation can foster prosocial behavior. In one study, female participants were asked to wear the same nurses' uniform rather than the ominous robes and hoods that participants wear in similar studies. In this case, deindividuation led to *less* aggression toward a stranger (Johnson & Downing, 1979). Wearing the uniform may have obscured the participants' individual identities, but it also cued them to treat others with care. In addition, whereas deindividuation can increase cheating and theft when we see others committing crimes, it can also increase donations to charity if that's what the crowd is doing (Nadler et al., 1982).

Deindividuation A tendency to lose one's sense of individuality when in a group or crowd.

▲ White supremacists arrived at a 2017 rally wearing polo shirts and khakis. When group members wear a uniform, they feel deindividuated and thus behave in more extreme ways than they otherwise would.

[Jason Andrew/Redux]

SECTION REVIEW   Performance in a Social Context

Social context influences performance.

Social Facilitation Theory (individual performance with an audience)	Social Loafing (performing together)	Deindividuation
• Early research showed that an audience improves task performance, but further research clarified that having an audience increases one's dominant response to a task. • Across animal species, the presence of others increases arousal and thus dominant responses. • In humans, feeling challenged can boost performance, but feeling threatened can impair performance. • The threat of social evaluation can absorb working memory capacity, leaving fewer cognitive resources for the task at hand. • On well-learned motor tasks, social evaluation leads people to overthink their actions, impairing performance.	The individual exerts less effort when performing as part of a group than as an individual. To avoid social loafing: • Monitor and evaluate performance. • Declare your own level of effort. • Distinguish disjunctive and conjunctive tasks. • Make the task more interesting or rewarding. • Maintain intragroup cohesion and intergroup competition.	When people feel anonymous, they are more likely to do what others around them are doing, for better or for worse.

Learning Outcomes

- Describe the causes of group polarization.
- Explain the role of group harmony in groupthink.
- Identify the ways that groupthink undermines effective decision making.
- List steps that improve group decision making.

Group Decision Making

Earlier we noted that groups are able to accomplish goals that individuals cannot accomplish on their own. One important goal of groups is to make decisions—hopefully, *good* decisions. Indeed, many important decisions are made by groups rather than individuals: the Canadian Senate, the United Nations, juries, political action committees, hiring committees, boards of directors, city councils, award committees, and so forth. Two (or more) heads are better than one, right? For instance, if four doctors are discussing a difficult medical problem, they can combine their unique knowledge and experience, consider diverse perspectives, and analyze alternative courses of action to determine which is best. However, the benefits of group decision making can be subverted by two psychological processes that get in the way of clear thinking: group polarization and groupthink.

Group Polarization

Imagine that, as part of a psychology experiment, you are asked to read scenarios describing people making decisions. One scenario describes a man deciding between taking a new job that pays a lot but that may not last (a risky alternative) or keeping his current job, which pays less but is more stable (a conservative alternative). After reading each scenario, you are asked which alternative you personally would choose. Next, you are asked to discuss the same scenarios with a group of participants and come to a joint decision about each scenario.

Do you think you would make riskier decisions when thinking about the scenarios alone or when discussing them with others as a group? When Stoner (1961) conducted a study like the one just described, he found that participants made riskier decisions as a group than they did on their own. This tendency came to be known as *risky shift* (Cartwright, 1971).

The story gets more interesting, though. Researchers who followed up on these findings showed that, for some decisions, groups did in fact take more conservative, middle-of-the-road positions than did individuals. Why do groups, compared to individuals, sometimes make riskier decisions and other times make less risky ones? Do you remember how research on social facilitation initially found one thing, then the opposite, and eventually resolved the paradox and arrived at a broader understanding? The same happened with research on group decision making.

Researchers eventually discovered that when people discuss their opinions with like-minded others, the discussion exaggerates their initial leanings, leading the group to take a more extreme position than the individual group members held initially. This broader phenomenon (which came to replace the risky shift) is known as **group polarization**, meaning that group discussion shifts group members toward an extreme position, or pole (Moscovici & Zavalloni, 1969; Myers, 1982).

Group polarization A tendency for group discussion to shift group members toward an extreme position.

For example, if each individual member of the group initially leans toward a risky alternative prior to the group discussion, they shift toward an even riskier position after group discussion. But if group members initially prefer a more conservative alternative, group discussion shifts them toward extreme caution (Lamm et al., 1976).

If group polarization exaggerates group members' initial leanings, then we would expect group discussion to intensify attitudes about a variety of topics, not just decisions about risk. This is indeed the case: When women who were moderately feminist discussed gender issues with each other, they became strongly feminist (Myers, 1975). French students who initially liked their president and disliked North Americans felt stronger in both directions after group discussion (Moscovici & Zavalloni, 1969). And Americans on the extremes of political orientation—both liberal and conservative—use more negative, angry language, most likely because they communicate and signal a social identity with like-minded others (Frimer et al., 2019).

Part of what makes group polarization interesting is that it seems to contradict the research on norm formation. If you look back at our discussion of conformity in chapter 7, you'll recall Sherif's (1936) finding that when individuals were put together to voice their opinions about something (in that case, the movement of a point of light), they made middle-of-the-road judgments that canceled out their own, sometimes extreme, judgments. Group polarization research seems to show exactly the opposite: Groups produce more extreme decisions, sometimes even more extreme than any of the group members' initial individual ratings. Sherif's studies are different because there was no group discussion to arrive at some consensus. This raises the question: What happens during group discussions that shifts the group toward more extreme positions? Let's look at two theories (Isenberg, 1986; Myers & Lamm, 1976).

Person A   3/10, 9:16pm
So we need to figure out where we're going for spring break. Im kinda leaning toward Austin. Just an idea.

Person B   3/10, 11:05pm
I could see Austin working cuz the music scene

Person C   3/11, 10:20am
yeah the music scene is obvious but it also has amazing restaurants so austin sounds great to me!

Person B   3/11, 11:10am
oh that's good! I didn't know about the food there. Thatreminds me that the bars there are open all night :)
I'm getting really excited about Austin!

Person D   3/11, 7:30pm
what's perfect about Austin that you guys are forgetting is the shopping. I was there a couple years ago on a class trip and they've got evvvvery thing.

Person A   3/11, 8:47pm
oh good I've been meaning to go shopping. Austin is definitely my number one choice, no doubt about that

Person C   3/11, 11:18pm
Grab your cowboy hats, folks—we're going to Austin!

Figure 9.5

Polarization Through New Arguments

When others add new arguments to support an opinion, the group's initial attitude becomes more extreme.

Exposure to New Persuasive Arguments The *persuasive arguments theory* (Burnstein & Vinokur, 1977) explains group polarization through the concept of *informational influence*, which occurs when you conform to others' actions or attitudes because you believe they know something that you don't (chapter 7). The theory assumes that people begin with at least one good argument to support their initial opinion or attitude (e.g., Mary likes Candidate X because of his immigration policy), but they probably have not considered *all* the relevant arguments (e.g., Candidate X's environmental policy). During group discussion, group members learn new arguments from each other that reinforce the position they already preferred (**FIGURE 9.5**). As a result, the group as a whole adopts a more extreme position.

In line with this theory, polarization doesn't require face-to-face interaction. People adopt more extreme positions than they initially held after simply overhearing a group discussion among like-minded others (Lamm, 1967) or even after merely reading a list of persuasive arguments generated by others (Burnstein et al., 1973).

How do we know that informational social influence is at work here? In one study (Liu & Latané, 1998), participants discussed a topic as a group and then were asked two weeks later how they felt about the topic. Their individual position lined up with their group's extreme position, not with the less extreme position that they had endorsed prior to the discussion. This suggests that learning new arguments from the group changed how these individuals perceived the world, not just what they said to fit in.

 APPLICATION
Polarization and Social Media

The rising popularity of social media raises the stakes of polarization. Social networking sites like Twitter and Facebook give us unprecedented access to information and viewpoints about the major issues facing society. In an ideal world, this online media environment would resemble a "national conversation" in which individuals are exposed to information from diverse ideological perspectives and circulate those opinions to others. But in reality, this environment more resembles an echo chamber, in which individuals selectively take in and share ideas that reinforce what they already believe. When Barberá et al. (2015) analyzed nearly 150 million tweets shared by almost 4 million Twitter users in the United States, they found that people preferred to connect with and share the opinions of like-minded others. This was especially true for politically charged events and issues like the federal budget, marriage equality, and the minimum wage, as compared with less politicized events like the Winter Olympics. Once individuals embed themselves in an ideologically homogenous media environment, it's all too easy for them to gorge on a steady diet of arguments that persuade them that their attitudes are correct. The result?

An increasingly segregated and polarized nation. There is hope, though: Sometimes when people share views on controversial topics with politically like-minded others, their beliefs become *more* accurate and less polarized (Becker et al., 2019). Exchanging information in politically segregated "echo chamber" networks can amplify partisan bias, but it can also help you see the world more accurately. Why do you think it can go one way and the other? ◼

▲ In theory, social media sites connect us to diverse viewpoints; in reality, however, they often create an echo chamber, where users encounter only the viewpoints they already hold. This can exaggerate attitudes, but under some conditions can improve accuracy.

Trying to Be a "Better" Group Member If we apply *social comparison theory* (Festinger, 1954), discussed in chapter 5, we can explain group polarization as a result of *normative social influence*, which occurs when you conform to others' actions or attitudes to be liked (Myers et al., 1980).

When individuals get together to make a decision, they often look around to figure out where the other group members stand on the topic. Once it becomes clear what position the group is leaning toward, a cycle of comparison and amplification is set in motion: One person in the group tries to compare herself favorably with other group members. She wants to be a "better" group member, so she advocates the group's position but takes it a little further than everyone else: "You guys seem to like this idea, but I *love* it!" Seeing this, another group member tries to present himself to the group even more favorably, so he amplifies the group's position even more: "Oh yeah? I will fight tooth and nail for this idea!!"

The net effect of this cycle is that the group shifts toward a more extreme position. As we would expect from this theory, group discussion is more likely to result in polarized positions when group members are motivated to be liked by other group members (Spears et al., 1990).

Groupthink

In many of the studies we've discussed, individuals were making decisions in relatively casual groups and even about hypothetical situations. In these contexts, it's not surprising that processes like group polarization can get in the way of clear thinking. What *is* surprising is when smart people have formal discussions about important topics and still end up making really disastrous decisions.

Consider this example. On January 28, 1986, NASA launched the space shuttle *Challenger*. There was special public interest and excitement about the launch because one of the seven crew members was a private citizen and teacher, Christa McAuliffe. She was the first representative of the Teacher in Space Project, a NASA program designed to inspire students, honor teachers, and spur interest in mathematics, science, and space exploration. Consequently, students in schools around the country watched the launch on TV. However, there were warning signs that the shuttle could malfunction. Despite these warnings, NASA insisted on moving forward with the scheduled launch. The shuttle indeed broke apart 73 seconds into its flight, and all seven crew members were killed.

With so much on the line, why would smart people working together make such a bad decision? Irving Janis (1982) had begun asking such questions just a few years earlier. He analyzed notoriously bad foreign policy decisions made by top U.S. officials, including the Bay of Pigs fiasco in 1961 (when President Kennedy and his inner circle launched an ill-fated attempt to overthrow the communist government of Fidel Castro in Cuba) and the decision in 1964 to escalate U.S. military involvement in Vietnam.

▲ Groupthink was to blame for the 1986 malfunction and crash of the space shuttle *Challenger*.

[Steve Liss/Time & Life Pictures/Getty Images]

🅰 Achie/e

Video Activity: Group Think: The Challenger

What does groupthink feel like?

- Group members feel strong pressure to agree with the majority view.
- They feel that if they were to voice concerns about the majority view or challenge the group's assumptions, they would be criticized by other group members as stupid, weak, or evil.
- Thus, they remain silent, censoring their doubts and questions. This results in the illusion that the group is in total agreement.
- Consensual agreement without debate also gives the illusion that the group is invulnerable and morally infallible.

Why do groups fall prey to groupthink?

Because group members are too focused on reaching consensus. This is more likely when:

- Group members are motivated to be liked by the group or by an opinionated group leader.
- They want to keep the group together, particularly if they fear that external threats or recent failures will break the group apart.
- They close themselves off to new information, opinions, or perspectives.

How does groupthink affect decision making?

- Group members do not gather enough information before making their decision.
- They do not fully consider alternative perspectives or courses of action.
- They fail to examine the risks of their preferred course of action.
- As a result, they do not make adequate plans for what to do in the event that their decisions and actions turn out badly.

Figure 9.6

Harmony at All Costs?

Groupthink results in faulty group thinking.

Groupthink A tendency toward flawed group decision making when group members are so intent on preserving group harmony that they fail to analyze a problem completely.

Janis concluded that these bad decisions suffered from a common problem called **groupthink**, a kind of faulty group thinking that occurs when group members are so intent on preserving group harmony and cohesion that they fail to analyze a problem completely (**FIGURE 9.6**). Groupthink is similar to group polarization but taken to the extreme, as if the group has become of one mind. Group members start to focus their attention on information that supports their position and ignore information that contradicts it. They stop testing their assumptions against reality, and they stop generating new perspectives on the problem at hand. Eventually they become convinced of the absolute truth and morality of their preferred course of action. They don't stop to think what would happen if they made an error in reasoning.

Janis described groupthink using the metaphor of a syndrome that afflicts the group, and he specified several symptoms of groupthink. One hallmark symptom is suppression of dissent: When group members express doubts about the majority's preferred position, they are harshly criticized and pressured to fall back in line with the majority view. For example, when NASA engineers charged with understanding the safety parameters of equipment pointed out one of the *Challenger* shuttle's mechanical flaws, they were harshly rebuked and pressured to stay silent by those overseeing the launch (Esser & Lindoerfer, 1989; Vaughan, 1996). To avoid being reprimanded or excluded, group members begin to censor themselves, giving the outward impression of agreement even though privately they think that the group is on the wrong track. This results in an illusion of unanimity: It *appears* that everyone is in agreement, although some group members may have serious misgivings.

Groupthink is especially likely to occur when group members view group cohesion as being more important than anything else. For example, when one person in a group complains about people outside the group ("Our enemy is so stupid"), other group members are motivated to be liked, so they agree wholeheartedly ("Totally. They are *so* stupid"). Although that support gives group members a warm feeling of belonging, it exaggerates negative attitudes toward outgroups and reduces willingness to resolve group conflicts (Lemay et al., 2019). In contrast, if group members are less concerned with reaching consensus or being disliked by other group members, they are more likely to consider alternative courses of action and express their doubts about the majority view. Groupthink is also more likely when the group is isolated from outside sources of information and when a group's powerful leader voices his or her views. Knowing the leader's views, the other members want to reinforce those views to win the leader's approval.

 APPLICATION
How to Improve Group Decision Making

Our discussion of group polarization and groupthink seems to suggest that making decisions as a group is often a bad idea. And sometimes it is. Yet in many cases groups do solve problems and make decisions more effectively than separate individuals can. This is especially true when groups work together on tasks that require the contribution of different knowledge. For example, groups perform better than individuals on analogy problems because each group member has knowledge about word meaning and other trivia that other group members do not; put everyone together, and you have a larger knowledge base to draw on (Laughlin et al., 2003).

Still, the unfortunate reality is that group polarization and groupthink often force groups into an isolated universe where prior beliefs are reinforced and the status quo is justified. Fortunately, there are strategies groups can use to avoid these pitfalls.

Increase Group Diversity   Recall that group polarization happens when all or most of the group members enter the discussion already leaning toward a certain position (Van Swol, 2009). Also remember that in Asch's (1956) conformity studies and Milgram's (1974) obedience studies (chapter 7), the presence of a single nonconforming other significantly reduced conformity and obedience (Allen & Levine, 1968). In much the same way, the presence of a dissenting voice in a group discussion is a powerful antidote to group polarization. For example, when members of the same political party discuss votes, they tend to take more extreme positions than they would individually. (Democrats cast less conservative votes; Republicans cast more conservative votes.) But if just one member of the opposite party joins the discussion, group votes become less extreme (Schkade & Sunstein, 2003). If the group cannot find someone who genuinely disagrees with the majority view, designating a "devil's advocate," someone given free license to search for flaws in the group's thinking, will help the group consider the relevant information more carefully before deciding on a course of action (Nemeth, Brown, & Rogers, 2001).

Group diversity is also a powerful safeguard against groupthink. Although we may feel more comfortable discussing decisions in groups of like-minded others, including people with diverse perspectives and opinions is likely to result in more vigorous discussion, fresh perspectives, and creative ideas (Nemeth & Ormiston, 2007; Page, 2007). Racial diversity is one means to increase cognitive diversity, which is the key ingredient in helping groups make wiser decisions (de Oliveira & Nisbett, 2018). For example, racially diverse juries made better decisions than all-White juries (Sommers, 2006). Racially diverse jurors exchanged a wider range of information and facts and were less likely to misremember

▲ Diverse groups can make better decisions than homogeneous groups because they bring together unique viewpoints and past experiences that provide a broader framework for a problem.

[sanjeri/Getty Images]

THINK ABOUT ▶

[Zachary Scott/Getty Images]

evidence as they discussed the case. In fact, when members of the White majority simply *expected* to make a decision in a racially diverse group, they took a broader perspective on the evidence at hand (Sommers et al., 2008).

Reinterpret Group Cohesion Stressing the importance of group cohesion can create a breeding ground for group polarization and groupthink. This doesn't necessarily mean, however, that improving group decision making requires squelching group cohesion. Rather, group members can reinterpret what it means to be a cohesive group. Rather than think of cohesion as pushing the group toward consensus, think about it as a promise to reach the best possible outcome, share constructive criticism, and prevent the group from doing something harmful (Packer, 2009; Postmes et al., 2001).

Encourage Individuality Recall that according to the social comparison theory of group polarization, groups shift toward more extreme positions because group members are concerned with other group members liking them. Thus, they exaggerate their agreement with the group's position. It seems that group polarization would be reduced if group members focused on themselves as individuals and cared less about how they are evaluated by the group. Indeed, one study showed that group discussion did not polarize group members' initial attitudes if, prior to the discussion, group members were primed to focus on their unique individual qualities (Lee, 2007).

The same holds true for groupthink, which occurs in large part because group members fail to break from the group norm and voice their doubts about ideas they perceive as wrong or harmful. If group members are led to believe that they are personally responsible for the outcome of their group's decision, they are less likely to fall victim to groupthink tendencies (Kroon et al., 1991). Consider this research on groupthink and individuality side-by-side with our previous discussions of deindividuation and social loafing. What themes do they have in common?

Plan to Be Objective Another safeguard against bad decision making is to schedule some "distancing" into your group interactions—step back, cool down, and take the perspective of a neutral observer on the process of decision making. But to do this effectively, research suggests, it's not enough to simply set the goal "We want to take an outsider's viewpoint." Your intention may be good, but it's likely that as the group's discussion whips up enthusiasm, the opportunity to act on that goal will slip by. What is needed is an implementation intention, which we introduced in chapter 5. This is an intention that specifies when, where, and how the group will act to avoid getting too committed to a course of action. This intention might look like: "IF we encounter such-and-such situation, THEN we will take an outsider's viewpoint." When study participants put into discussion groups formed implementation intentions to engage in distancing, they were more likely to follow through, and they made better decisions, compared to groups that simply promised to get around to distancing at some point (Wieber et al., 2015). ■

SECTION REVIEW Group Decision Making

In theory, groups have more resources than do individuals for making decisions, but two psychological processes, group polarization and groupthink, can subvert good group decision making.

Group Polarization	Groupthink	Groups Can Avoid Problems of Group Decision Making By:
After group discussion, group members' initial leanings are intensified. This is caused by learning new information and trying to fit in.	Group members intent on preserving group harmony fail to analyze a problem completely and often make disastrous decisions.	• Encouraging group diversity and allowing dissent • Focusing on achieving the best outcome rather than group harmony • Encouraging members to take individual responsibility • Making specific plans to take the perspective of a neutral observer on group decision making

Leadership, Power, and Group Hierarchy

Most groups have leaders—individuals with extra power, status, and responsibility. Cultures have presidents, chiefs, or sovereigns. Armies have generals. Sports teams have captains. Committees have chairpersons or heads. Let's look at how groups respond to leaders and what happens to a group when leaders assume power.

What Makes a Leader Effective?

Conventional wisdom holds that effective leaders are those who possess certain personality traits; thus, they are effective regardless of what kind of situation they and their followers are in. There is some limited evidence that effective leaders tend to be high in the traits of extraversion, openness to experience, and conscientiousness (Judge et al., 2002), and they are more confident in their own leadership abilities (Chemers et al., 2000). However, these correlations are small, meaning that knowing a person's personality traits tells you surprisingly little about whether that person is or will become an effective leader. Indeed, Simonton (1987) analyzed 100 attributes of past U.S. presidents, including dozens of personality variables, and found no correlation between personality traits and historians' assessments of their leadership effectiveness. We need a more sophisticated picture of how leaders interact with their followers and the broader social situation.

▲ German Chancellor Angela Merkel knows that effective leadership requires a sensitivity to followers' psychological needs.

[Bloomberg/Getty Images]

> ### Learning Outcomes
>
> • Explain what leadership styles are effective for various situations.
>
> • Identify potential pitfalls of having power.
>
> • Explain reasons people regard hierarchies as legitimate.
>
> • Explain the social factors that prompt collective action.

The most effective leaders focus on the needs of their followers (Bass, 1985), but these needs can be quite different from situation to situation (Fiedler, 1967). As we discussed in chapter 7, *charismatic* leaders emphasize bold actions and inspire belief in the greatness of the group. *Task-oriented* leaders are more practical, focusing on achieving the group's goals. *Relationship-oriented* leaders focus on fostering equality, fairness, harmony, and participation among group members (Hogg, 2010).

None of these leadership types is more effective than the others in every context; rather, leadership effectiveness depends on a match between leadership type and the situation. For example, in some work situations, group members have clearly defined tasks and are relatively free from conflict. Task-oriented leaders are most effective in these highly structured situations because there is less need to attend to interpersonal dynamics and a greater need to keep everyone on track toward common goals. In other work situations, group members are confused about what they should be doing and often have a difficult time

 SOCIAL PSYCH AT THE MOVIES

Milk: Charismatic Leadership Style

Milk (Van Sant, 2008) is a moving biopic about Harvey Milk, an influential figure in the movement for gay civil rights. In depicting Milk's rise to leadership, the movie illustrates a number of features of an effective leadership style. The story begins in the Castro district of San Francisco in the early 1970s. Milk, played by Sean Penn, has just moved from New York, and although he is enamored of his neighborhood's charm, he is outraged by everyday acts of discrimination against gays in his new city. Police harassment and murderous gay-bashing are common, and Milk is told that his camera shop cannot join local business associations on account of his "unholy" lifestyle.

Fed up, Milk stands on top of a wooden crate and announces to his neighbors that it's time to fight back. So begins his rise into the political spotlight from a grassroots activist—referred to by his neighbors as the mayor of Castro Street—to being one of the first openly gay men elected to major public office in North America. In the mere 11 months that he was on the Board of Supervisors of San Francisco before being fatally shot, he made major strides for gay civil rights. What made him an effective leader?

To answer this question, let's unpack the concept of *charisma*, introduced as one of the qualities of an effective leader. Charisma is that special magnetism that we've all seen in larger-than-life celebrities and leaders, but it is difficult to define. According to Ernest Becker (1975), a charismatic leader is one who with great self-confidence offers people a heroic vision, a grand mission to triumph over evil and bring about a better future.

Early in his career, Milk is a *relationship-oriented* leader who focuses on making sure that his staff members feel included and enjoy their work on his campaign. But his career really takes off after he follows the advice given to him by another politician: If you want to win over the people, you have to give them hope for a better life and a better tomorrow. Eventually Milk embodies charisma. His heroic vision can be seen in three messages that he gives to the people.

First, he tells people that the gay rights movement is big—a social movement on a grand scale with far-reaching implications. One way he does this is to connect the gay rights movement to the broader idea that America is a free country in which people have a fundamental right to live without bigotry. In this way, he presents himself as fighting for the rights of everyone, from union workers to senior citizens to small-business owners. In one impassioned speech, he notes that the gay rights movement is "not about personal gain, not about ego, not about power . . . it's about the 'us's' out there. Not only gays, but the Blacks, the Asians, the disabled, the seniors, the us's. Without hope, the us's give up. I know you cannot live on hope alone, but without it, life is not worth living. So you, and you, and you. . . . You gotta give 'em hope . . . you gotta give 'em hope."

Second, he tells people that, by supporting the gay rights movement, they have an opportunity to be part of a lasting legacy that will make a mark on history. For example, he says to members of his campaign, "If there should be an assassination, I would hope that five, ten, one hundred, a thousand would rise. I would like to see every gay lawyer, every gay architect come out—If a bullet should enter my brain, let that working together. Relationship-oriented leaders are the most effective in these types of situations because they can attend to people's feelings and relationships and ultimately get the group to work together more smoothly (Schriesheim et al., 1994).

Power Changes People

History is replete with scandals involving powerful people abusing their advantages and turning a blind eye toward the suffering of others. In an oft-told (but apparently unsubstantiated) story, Marie Antoinette, the queen of France, supposedly responded to news of bread shortages among the under-class with the flippant remark *"Qu'ils mangent de la brioche"* ("Let them eat cake"). The implication is that living with an abundance of resources might make it difficult to comprehend how others might be lacking. Through such cultural legends, we see the idea that power, if it doesn't corrupt, might at least

bullet destroy every closet door. . . . And that's all. I ask for the movement to continue." This message is attractive to people because, as we've noted in this chapter, they join groups in part to cope with the fear of death. Belonging to a group means that one's life does not end with death but continues on as long as the group survives.

A third message in Milk's heroic vision is that there is a clear enemy out there who is holding society back from progress. In 1978, Anita Bryant, a former singer and model, starts advocating for a proposition that would ban gays from teaching in schools. Armed with moral rhetoric and the support of the Christian community, she gets this legislation passed in Florida and is gaining traction in other states. Milk initially feels defeated by Anita Bryant's success, but when he walks into the street, he finds that it is exactly what was needed to bring the gay community's anger to the boiling point. Now hundreds of citizens are ready to take action. Milk seizes the moment, grabs a bullhorn, and says, "I know you're angry. I'm angry. Let's march the streets of San Francisco and share our anger."

He leads the march to the steps of City Hall, where he gives the people the enemy they want: "I am here tonight to say that we will no longer sit quietly in the closet. We must fight. And not only in the Castro, not only in San Francisco, but everywhere the Anitas go. Anita Bryant cannot win tonight. Anita Bryant brought us together! She is going to create a national gay force!"

Because of Milk's charismatic leadership style, he is remembered today as a major figure in the continuing struggle for equal human rights.

▲ Guided by the charismatic leadership of Harvey Milk (portrayed by Sean Penn in the movie *Milk*), gay rights supporters felt united in a grand mission to overcome discrimination.

[Focus Features/Photofest]

enable one to lose sight of how the other half (or 99%) lives. Let's consider some evidence for this idea.

Loosened Inhibitions   Just as people with power have greater access to and control over resources, they also have greater freedom to do as they please. In contrast, those with little power and low socioeconomic status face many constraints on what they can do and be. Dacher Keltner and colleagues (Keltner et al., 2003) argue that this creates a mind-set of *behavioral approach* for those in greater power positions but a mind-set of *behavioral inhibition* for those in lesser power positions. In general, *approach* motivation orients the person toward achieving positive outcomes and reward. When powerful people adopt a behavioral approach orientation, they pursue their goals without too much concern for the obstacles that might stand in their way (Whitson et al., 2013). In contrast, inhibition or avoidance motivation orients the person toward avoiding negative outcomes and punishments.

Having power even changes how we talk. When undergraduates were randomly assigned a high (versus low) rank in a negotiation exercise, their voices suddenly became higher pitched and more variable in loudness, perhaps because they felt less inhibited about talking as loudly as they pleased from moment to moment. What's more, perceivers used those acoustic cues to accurately infer that the speakers were high in rank (Ko et al., 2015).

Other research suggests that a sense of power can create a feeling of distance between the self and others, allowing for the kind of abstract thought needed to make complex decisions (Smith & Trope, 2006; Smith et al., 2008). This can make it easier for those in power to achieve more and solve thorny problems that face the group, but it can also disinhibit people from harming people with less power (Galinsky et al., 2006; Guinote, 2007; Keltner et al., 2003).

For example, in one study, four members of a fraternity were brought into the lab and encouraged to tease each other (Keltner et al., 1998). In each group, two individuals were relatively new to the fraternity and thus had lower status, whereas two were higher-status members of the group. It won't surprise you that these guys had little difficulty sitting around the room teasing one another. (They took turns so that each fraternity member had the opportunity to tease every other fraternity member who took part in the study.) More interesting, though, is that the type of teasing varied depending on who was teasing whom. Higher-status fraternity brothers teased others (regardless of their status) with little concern for whether they might humiliate them or display their dominance over them. But lower-status brothers were more prosocial in the way they teased high-status brothers. They would try to tease their big brothers in ways that acknowledged their status or flattered their strengths. For example, when asked to come up with a nickname for a person using two initials, 30% of lower-status brothers gave higher-status brothers names that were essentially flattering (e.g., MM = Muscle Machine). In contrast, only 7% of higher-status brothers gave these positive teases to their lower-status brothers. Most of the time these higher-status brothers gave insulting teases (e.g., PP = Pimple Party).

Does this mean that the powerful are more unethical than those lacking power? Not necessarily. Dubois and colleagues (2015) found that upper-class individuals—those with money and power—were more unethical than poor individuals, but only in situations in which acting unethically would benefit them personally. If you look instead at situations in which acting unethically can benefit other people, such as stealing medicine for a sick child, the relationship between power and ethicality flip-flops: Now *lower*-class individuals are prone to behave more unethically than are upper-class individuals. Having high power doesn't make you unethical, per se; it just makes you more willing to do whatever serves your selfish interest.

It's also important to consider the cultural context. Most studies showing that power numbs people to others have looked at people from Western cultural contexts, where the norm is to focus on the self. But in East Asian countries, where the norm is to orient to others, high socioeconomic status is associated with more concern for others (Miyamoto et al., 2018).

Less Empathy   The findings from the fraternity study just mentioned partly reflect subordinates being extra cautious around their leaders, but they also raise the possibility that people in positions of power are less compassionate toward their subordinates or those who are disadvantaged. More direct evidence for this comes from studies showing that people from higher socioeconomic backgrounds (high SES) can be less generous and charitable than people from lower social classes (Piff et al., 2010). In one study, people who were simply *reminded* of how they are financially better off than others recommended that people give about 3% of their income to charity, whereas those led to think about their disadvantage in society recommended giving away almost 5% of one's income. Moreover, people led to feel high in status were less supportive of redistributive policies aimed at reducing economic inequality in society than were people led to feel low in status (Brown-Iannuzzi et al., 2015). They even shifted to a more conservative political ideology to justify their stingier policy attitudes. This finding seems counterintuitive because we would expect the people with more resources and status to be in a better position to give more to others. However, having lower status can make people more generous because it cues a sense of compassion and egalitarian values.

Related findings show that people in power positions tend to be insensitive toward less powerful others. Greater power decreases empathy (Galinsky et al., 2006; Gwinn et al., 2013; van Kleef et al., 2008), increases the tendency to treat others as objects (Gruenfeld et al., 2008), and leads individuals raised in both Western and Asian cultures to endorse harsher punishment of others (Kuwabara et al., 2016; Wiltermuth & Flynn, 2012). In addition, people in power are more likely to use stereotypes to form impressions of lower-status individuals (Goodwin et al., 2000), devalue or take credit for the contributions of their underlings (Kipnis, 1972), and bring to mind implicit prejudices toward outgroups (Guinote et al., 2010). But those in power will be mindful of their subordinates' individuating characteristics when doing so is relevant to what they are trying to accomplish (Overbeck & Park, 2001).

High-power individuals are not only less able to empathize with those lacking power, they also have difficulty coordinating with others who also hold power. Why does this matter? In many real-world cases, important decisions and problems are addressed not by single leaders but by groups of leaders. We see this, for example, when corporate executives try to work out a merger, heads of state draft environmental policies, and leaders of sororities and fraternities come together to agree on a budget. The hope is that concentrating all that talent and confidence in one room will result in optimal decisions and solutions.

But the problem is that each leader is accustomed to possessing power and being followed. Hence, they have difficulty listening to each other, questioning their own ideas, and putting aside their selfish interests for the common good. In one study, individuals randomly assigned higher power and then asked to work together as a team performed worse than did other groups (Hildreth & Anderson, 2016). They were less creative and less likely to reach agreement on a difficult negotiation task.

Hierarchy in Social Groups

Social dominance theory
The theory that large societies create hierarchies and that people tend to endorse beliefs that legitimatize hierarchy.

Many groups are organized hierarchically, meaning that some members have higher status than others. How does hierarchy come about? According to **social dominance theory** (Sidanius & Pratto, 1999), a key step occurs when human societies grow large enough to produce a surplus of food and other basic resources. The division of labor then expands beyond fixed roles stemming from biological characteristics to the creation of *arbitrary sets*, groups of people distinguished by culturally defined roles, attributes, or characteristics. In addition to those who cultivate food, care for children, and offer physical security, our society includes people who specialize in providing spiritual guidance, entertaining us with music and stories, hauling away our trash, and teaching us about the complexities of our own society. Depending on the cultural values of a society, some of these groups are afforded higher status, and their activities are deemed more valuable than those of groups afforded lower status.

Legitimizing Hierarchy A central idea we have touched on throughout this textbook is that much of our social reality is based on a cultural worldview—a socially constructed view of reality. This means that for advantaged groups to stay in power and for group hierarchies to persist, individuals across society need to believe in the legitimacy of their leaders and the institutions that keep them in power. In cases where belief in the existing hierarchy crumbles, people rebel, sometimes violently, as seen in the 2019 protests in Hong Kong. But these are exceptions, and researchers have discovered how most people maintain faith that the existing hierarchy is real and legitimate.

Legitimizing Myths. One strategy is to believe in *legitimizing myths*—overly simplistic beliefs about why people succeed or fail in society. One myth is that anyone can get ahead in life by simply working hard enough. Because of this myth, people who are advantaged in society may, ironically, be more likely than underprivileged groups to claim that they are unfairly discriminated against (Thomsen et al., 2010). Consider the following experiment, in which college students were asked to role-play a situation in which they were applying for a managerial position (Major et al., 2002). White participants who learned that they had been passed over for the job by a Latino manager who favored a Latino applicant were more likely to claim discrimination than were Latino participants passed over by a White manager who favored a White applicant.

System justification theory
The theory that negative stereotypes get attached to groups partly because they help explain and justify why some individuals are more advantaged than others.

System justification theory (Jost & Banaji, 1994) highlights another way people maintain faith in hierarchy: believing in stereotypes that seem to explain why some individuals are more advantaged than others. For example, if someone high in power stereotypes homeless people as being dim-witted, lazy, and dangerous, then it's possible to explain why they suffer without questioning that the hierarchy is fair and good. Without those stereotypes, one might have to face the harsh reality that the hierarchy is biased or flawed and that people do not always get what they deserve.

Idealizing High Status. It's easy to understand why members of advantaged groups would want to maintain their legitimizing beliefs. As we noted in our discussion of social identity theory earlier in this chapter, it's quite common for individuals to show *ingroup bias*, a preference for their own group over outgroups. The more remarkable observation is that some members of disadvantaged groups actually show a preference for the higher-status group over their own group (Sidanius & Pratto, 1999). For instance, some studies show that Arabs living in Israel and Latinos living in Los Angeles (who both value group hierarchy and believe that the hierarchy in their respective societies is legitimate) were more favorably disposed toward the higher-status majority group than toward their own (Levin et al., 2002).

Mitigating Comparisons. Disadvantaged groups also justify hierarchy by believing in **complementary stereotypes** that portray groups with a mix of positive and negative characteristics (Kay & Jost, 2003; Kay et al., 2007). For example, after reading stories about people who are poor yet happy (versus sad), or rich yet corrupt (versus honest), people saw the system as fairer. We seem to like it when groups that are socially disadvantaged appear satisfied with their lives and when groups that are especially well off look miserable or untrustworthy. (Consider how wealthy individuals are often depicted in popular movies.) This means that when members of disadvantaged groups endorse seemingly positive stereotypes for their own group—"We're broke but we're kind!"—they may be inadvertently promoting the very social system that keeps them in their disadvantaged place.

> **Complementary stereotypes** Both positive and negative stereotypes that are ascribed to a group as a way of justifying the status quo.

To acknowledge instead a sense of disadvantage requires a comparison with others who are more advantaged. Karl Marx famously wrote:

> A house may be large or small; as long as the neighboring houses are likewise small, it satisfies all social requirement for a residence. But let there arise next to the little house a palace, and the little house shrinks to a hut. . . . [T]he occupant of the relatively little house will always find himself more uncomfortable, more dissatisfied, more cramped within his four walls." (MARX, 1847)

As Marx's quote suggests, we tend to compare ourselves with similar others or with those who are close by. Because societies tend to segregate themselves socially and physically on the basis of class membership and other similarities, we most often compare ourselves with people like us—people who might be disadvantaged in the same way. According to **relative deprivation theory**, these comparisons can keep lower-status groups in the dark about their disadvantage. They are focused on how their life compares to that of their neighbors, and they don't see the larger societal patterns that constrain them. We see this process in a survey of soldiers in the U.S. Army (Stouffer et al., 1949). Despite the fact that a job in the air corps afforded twice as many opportunities for promotion as did a job in the military police, soldiers in the military police reported much higher satisfaction with their access to promotion opportunities than did those in the air corps. Why? Because soldiers in the air corps were more likely to come into

> **Relative deprivation theory** A theory which states that disadvantaged groups are less aware of and bothered by their lower status because of a tendency to compare their outcomes only with others who are similarly deprived.

▲ The black power movement of the 1960s was promoted by prominent and successful African Americans, such as Tommie Smith and John Carlos, medalists at the 1968 Summer Olympics.

[John Dominis/Time & Life Pictures/ Getty Images]

Collective action Efforts by groups to resist and change the status quo in the service of group goals.

Identity fusion A profound feeling of oneness with a group and a perception that one's personal identity and group identity are essentially the same. It is a strong motivator of collective action.

contact with their promoted peers and feel unhappy about their own subordinate status.

What Causes Collective Action? We've seen that lower-status groups at times convince themselves that it's right and good that they are on society's bottom rung. But clearly sometimes people take **collective action**—action aimed at changing the status quo in the service of advancing the group's survival and goals. When do we see this?

The higher people are in system justification—that is, the higher their motivation to defend the status quo—the less willing they are to engage in collective action that challenges the existing regime, such as joining protests (Osborne et al., 2019). People are more likely to take collective action when they see the system as not only illegitimate but also unstable—and hence capable of change. Also, people are more likely to fight for their group when they believe the boundaries between groups are *impermeable*. That means that they don't see many opportunities to exit their disadvantaged group and get into a more advantaged group. As a result, they identify more strongly with the ingroup, which motivates them to take actions to raise that group's status (DeWeerd & Klandermans, 1999; Ellemers et al., 1988; Tajfel & Turner, 1979). Consider, for example, the fight for civil rights spearheaded by the black power movement during the 1960s. Most of the members of this movement were not the poorest and most disadvantaged Blacks, as one might expect. Instead, they were members of the emerging Black middle and upper classes (Caplan, 1970). Although individual mobility efforts can allow people to rise within their group, sometimes a move to collective action does not happen until relatively advantaged members of a lower-status group run up against a barrier that seems to prevent further success. It might be only at this point that the system seems rigged against them, and something in addition to their individual efforts toward individual goals is needed for further advancement.

Another potent spur to pro-group behavior is **identity fusion**—a strong feeling of "oneness" with the group. To understand this idea, recall that the social identity perspective says people distinguish between their personal identity (aspects of the self that make people unique) and their social identity (aspects of the self that align people with groups). The salience of these two identities ebbs and flows depending on the context. But for strongly fused individuals, the boundary between "me" and "we" dissipates; they feel "fused" to their group like a stone fused to a wall. To measure identity fusion, researchers adapted the Inclusion of Other in the Self Scale (Aron et al., 1992), originally developed to measure attachment in close relationships (chapter 15). The scale asks people to choose from among a series of pictures that represent varying degrees of overlap between two circles representing the self and their group (e.g., their nation or political party). People who report high overlap of self and group identities are more willing to act for the good of their group, even if that means sacrificing their own well-being (Fredman et al., 2015; Swann & Buhrmester, 2015).

APPLICATION
The Power of Influencers

Collective action doesn't always come with a bang. Sometimes it happens quietly, through a subtle changing of norms. This can occur through the power of "influencers." People in a group often pay particular attention to the behavior of certain individuals. Group members look to these individuals to figure out what is socially normative and to adjust their own behaviors. In this way, the influencers' attitudes and behavior slowly spread throughout the group. We see this in one study where researchers asked select middle school students—those identified as being popular in their school—to take a stand against bullying. Compared to control schools, those with anti-bullying influencers saw a significant drop in bullying behavior throughout the school year (Paluck et al., 2016). Just having a few influential people take a stand can spread out to change a group's culture. ■

▲ [Pacific Press/Getty Images]

SECTION REVIEW   Leadership, Power, and Group Hierarchy

Most groups have leaders who wield power and are at the top of a hierarchy.

Leadership Style	Effects of Power	Hierarchies
• In general, effective leaders match their approach to the needs of their followers. • Depending on followers' needs, effective leaders can be charismatic, task oriented, or relationship oriented.	• Power leads people to be more approach oriented and less inhibited. • People in power tend to have less empathy and can be less generous to those in need. They also act less ethically, but only if doing so serves themselves.	• As societies grow, work shifts from basic divisions of labor to culturally defined roles. • People tend to regard existing hierarchies as legitimate, even when they are disadvantaged by them. • Collective action toward social change occurs when successful members of disadvantaged groups encounter barriers, when a person's identity is fused with the group, and when high-status influencers change group norms.

Why Do People Leave and Disidentify with Groups?

Please accept my resignation. I don't want to belong to any club that will accept people like me as members.

—Groucho Marx, in a telegram to the Friars Club of Beverly Hills (1959)

We've seen how living in groups, although at times frustrating and dysfunctional, benefits the individual in several ways. It satisfies four basic psychological needs: promoting survival, reducing uncertainty, enhancing self-esteem, and managing the potential terror of being mortal. This raises a new question: Given the benefits of being in a group, why would individuals ever leave or distance themselves from their groups? What groups have you left? Why?

Often people leave a group because the group no longer successfully serves one or more psychological needs. Sometimes groups can make us feel unworthy, incapable, and stressed out (Wakefield et al., 2019).

Learning Outcome

• Identify reasons that leaving a group may offer more benefits than staying with a group.

THINK ABOUT

[Masterfile]

Promoting Survival

Every year in the United States, hundreds of thousands of boys and girls as young as 12 years join gangs (Snyder & Sickmund, 2006). Although the gang expects them to join for life, about two thirds of new initiates leave the gang after one or two years. Contrary to popular myth, those who wish to leave do not generally face the threat of death from fellow gang members. However, leaving often means facing the worst of two worlds. On the one hand, their fellow gang members reject them. On the other, because of their past criminal activities as gang members, they struggle to find legitimate employment and to be accepted by mainstream social institutions (Decker & Lauritsen, 2002). So why do they leave?

In interviews with former gang members in cities such as Rochester, Denver, and St. Louis, researchers found that the reason most often cited for the decision to leave a gang is fear of injury and death after being injured or after witnessing fellow gang members fall prey to violence (Decker & Van Winkle, 1996; Thornberry et al., 2004). Former gang members often said things such as, "Well after I got shot. . . . You know how your life just flash? It like did that so I stopped selling dope, got a job, stayed in school, just stopped hanging around cause one day I know some other gang member catch me and probably kill me" (Decker & Van Winkle, 1996, p. 269).

This is surprising given that, as we said earlier, group members become more committed to the group when they face a common threat. We might therefore expect the threat of violence to *strengthen* solidarity among gang members. This is indeed the case when there is a threat of violence—when violence seems to loom on the horizon. But when individuals experience violence themselves or observe their own friends and family members being harmed, they think twice about staying in the group. Thus, young boys and girls join the gang in order to seek safety from harm, but if they realize belonging to the gang poses risks to their lives rather than protecting them, they often leave (Decker & Van Winkle, 1996; Peterson et al., 2004). The need to survive has the power both to draw people toward groups and to push them to leave.

Reducing Uncertainty

Recall that uncertainty-identity theory says that people join and identify with groups to reduce negative feelings of uncertainty. Does this mean that leaving groups always increases uncertainty about oneself and the broader world?

No. Sometimes leaving is exactly what the person or subgroup needs to do to maintain certainty in the cultural worldview. For example, when the individual perceives that the group has changed or has acted in a way that violates an important value or norm, belonging to that group is no longer useful in validating that individual's worldview, and it may even increase uncertainty. The individual may therefore disidentify with the group or leave it altogether in order to uphold the norm.

This can result in *schisms*, which occur when a subgroup of people break away from the larger parent group and form their own group or join a different parent group. A schism happens when a subgroup feels that the parent group has forgotten or violated its own core values (Sani & Todman, 2002). For example, in 2020, a separate "traditionalist" denomination was proposed to split from the more inclusive-leaning United Methodist Church as a means of accommodating a group opposed to repealing the ban on same-sex marriage and LGBTQ clergy. In such cases, people sacrifice the certainty of being in an established group for the certainty of maintaining their values.

Bolstering Self-Esteem

We've seen that people join and identify with groups to bolster their self-esteem. But what happens when a person feels incapable of living up to the group's standards of value? Under such circumstances, the person may seek alternative groups whose worldviews seem to provide more attainable standards of self-worth. This happens when people convert to new religions or join cults. Cults generally target people struggling economically and young people searching for a positive identity and sense of purpose. People who join cults and experience religious conversions are generally under stress and have shaky self-esteem. After joining these new groups, they experience increases in self-esteem and purpose in life, as well as a reduced fear of death (Levine, 1981; Paloutzian, 1981; Ullman, 1982).

▲ Ruslan Tsarni, the uncle of the suspected bombers at the 2013 Boston Marathon, reacted to the news that his nephews might have committed the bombings by distancing himself and the rest of his family from them.
[Allison Shelley/Getty Images]

What happens when members cannot view the group positively, perhaps because a rival group is more successful? In these situations, belonging to a group threatens to *decrease* self-esteem. Sometimes group members stick with their group through the rough times, but in some situations, they distance themselves from the group to protect their own self-esteem. In one study (Snyder et al., 1986), participants led to believe that their group failed on a task (compared to succeeding on a task) were less interested in continuing to work with their group or wearing a badge indicating they were part of the group. In other studies, people were less likely to feel fused with their country after thinking of just a couple ways that fellow citizens acted poorly (Gómez et al., 2019).

In fact, people occasionally disidentify with their group even if just one other group member does something negative (Eidelman & Biernat, 2003). Why? In general, we assume that members of a group share similar beliefs and characteristics. Thus, when a member of your own group does something embarrassing or immoral, you may fear that you will be found guilty by association simply because you are in the same group as that person (Cooper & Jones, 1969). When the group identity is very important, however, and the behavior is seen as being out of character for the group, another strategy is to oust the perpetrator from the group psychologically. Ruslan Tsarni, the uncle of the Tsarnaev brothers, the two men believed to be responsible for the bombings at the 2013 Boston Marathon, described them as "losers" and said they brought shame on their family and their Chechen ethnic group. In this way, he clearly distanced not only himself but also the rest of the family and Chechens in general from them and the brothers' alleged misdeeds.

Managing Mortality Concerns

As noted earlier, reminding people of their mortality generally increases their identification with the groups to which they belong. From the perspective of terror management theory, this happens because these groups help validate people's worldview, self-worth, and sense that they are part of something larger that will continue after their death. However, when a given group identification no longer serves one of these functions, reminders of death lead people to jump ship and shift their identification to other groups that are better at providing these psychological resources.

For example, when Latinos or women are reminded of their mortality and led to think of negative aspects of the group membership (for Latinos the stereotype that Latinos tend to be drug dealers; for women, the stereotype that women are not good at math), they respond by distancing themselves from their ethnic or gender identification (Arndt, Greenberg et al., 2002). Latino participants, for example, disliked artwork that was attributed to Latino artists. Female participants emphasized how they were in fact different from other women.

Whether people defend or distance themselves from their group when mortality is salient depends on how permanent they consider group identity to be. When Dutch students were exposed to criticism of their university, and they were led to think that university affiliation was a permanent identification, mortality salience led them to reject that criticism as false. However, if students were led to think that university affiliation was temporary and were reminded of death, they instead responded to the criticism by identifying less with their university (Dechesne et al., 2000).

SECTION REVIEW Why Do People Leave and Disidentify with Groups?

The same psychological motives that drive people to join and identify with groups also can drive them to leave when group membership itself threatens to undermine those needs.

Promoting Survival	Reducing Uncertainty	Bolstering Self-Esteem	Managing Mortality Concerns
When people sense that belonging to a group increases the risk of being harmed or killed, they tend to break away from the group.	Subgroups may break away from a parent group when they believe the group is violating a core value that provides certainty.	When a group member cannot view the group positively, membership may decrease self-esteem, prompting the person to leave.	When a group no longer buffers mortality concerns by providing meaning and value, group members may disidentify, especially if they regard the group as temporary.

CRITICAL LEARNING EXERCISES

1. We mentioned that a group creates norms that tell its members how to act and even how to think. But many people identify with several groups, and those groups can prescribe different and even incompatible norms. As a result, most of us have to adjust our behavior, speech, and appearance as we move in and out of group settings (e.g., family dinners versus sorority parties). What does this switching of group identities mean for *authenticity*? Many of us believe that we have a "true," or authentic, self, and we place a lot of importance on expressing it. But can we be authentic when we're wearing different masks from one group setting to the next?

2. Imagine that you are a psychotherapist, and you take on a client who experiences debilitating anxiety when he is asked to perform a task in front of other people. Drawing on what you have learned about performance in a group context, how might you help him overcome his problem?

How would you break down the problem in terms of the person, the task, and the audience?

3. Imagine that you are the leader of a new start-up. Your goal is to develop an effective company that is driven by engaged employees. Given what you have learned about the power of groupthink to impede decision making, what steps would you take to prevent groupthink from arising in your team?

4. In the American political system, members of a political party may find themselves increasingly at odds with positions advocated by their traditional party affiliation. Given what you've learned in this chapter about system justification and group identification, explain when and why people might stick with a party that seems to act against their personal interests.

 Achieve

Don't stop now! Check out our videos and additional resources located at: www.macmillanlearning.com

CHAPTER 10

Understanding Prejudice, Stereotyping, and Discrimination

We live in families, tribes, and nations. Our groups help us survive and provide our lives with structure. They give us bases of self-worth and imbue life with meaning and purpose. But one major problem is inherent in living within groups: It separates us from other human beings who live within other groups. Prejudice is the all-too-common consequence of this distinction between us (the ingroup) and them (the outgroup). Virtually every known culture has been hostile to members of some other culture or oppressed certain segments of its society. Indeed, recorded history is riddled with the bloody consequences of a seemingly endless parade of oppression, persecution, colonization, crusades, wars, and genocides. The violent heritage of our species led a character from James Joyce's classic novel *Ulysses* to comment, "History . . . is a nightmare from which I am trying to awake" (Joyce, 1961, p. 28).

We will explore the many reasons that history has been and continues to be such a nightmare of intergroup hatred and violence in two chapters, this one and chapter 11. In chapter 11, we will consider how prejudice, stereotyping, and discrimination affect those targeted by these biases. We will also consider ways in which we might hope someday to awaken from this nightmare to an egalitarian reality in which people treat each other fairly, regardless of their differences.

In this chapter, we focus on:

- The nature of prejudice

- Three basic causes of prejudice

- Who is prone to prejudice

- Prejudice in the modern world

- How stereotyping arises and affects the way people perceive others and behave toward them

The Nature of Prejudice: Pervasiveness and Perspective

Virtually every person currently living on this planet has been profoundly affected by prejudice. In most if not all cultures, women are to varying degrees targets of violence and restricted in their freedoms and opportunities. Likewise, every ethnic and cultural group has been powerfully influenced by historical intergroup conflicts and oppression. As of this writing, millions of refugees have been displaced because of a violent civil war in Syria, China has been accused of human rights abuses against the Uyghurs, and Russia launched a full-scale military attack against Ukraine. Pick a group, and you could read volumes about how that group has been affected by prejudice.

In social psychology, **prejudice** is defined as a negative attitude toward an individual based solely on that person's presumed membership in a particular group. Thus the person is disliked not because of personal attributes or actions but simply because of being perceived to be in some supposedly undesirable group.

An interesting aspect of prejudice is that, on the one hand, many if not most people seem to be prejudiced against some group—and they usually feel that their particular prejudice is justified. On the other hand, social psychologists generally assume that prejudice against a person based simply on membership in a group is never justified. This assumption is based on three characteristics of prejudice.

▲ Intergroup conflicts have affected every nation. Millions of Syrians became displaced refugees because of a violent civil war in their homeland.
[Photo by United Nation Relief and Works Agency via Getty Images]

First, prejudice involves judging an individual negatively without considering the person's actual attributes or actions. Social psychologists follow the hope famously articulated by Dr. Martin Luther King, Jr. (1963/1992): "I have a dream that my four little children will one day live in a nation where they will not be judged by the color of their skin but by the content of their character." If someone harms you or someone you care about, you are justified in disliking that person. If a person simply practices a religion different from your own, has a different skin tone, or comes from a different country, you are not justified in disliking that person.

Second, any large category of people will include tremendous variability in virtually every possible attribute by which one might judge another person positively or negatively (Allport, 1954). There may be a group mean (what the average member of a group is like), but there also is always a normal distribution that captures the range along which most people vary from that mean. Think of members of your own extended family—siblings, parents, aunts, uncles, cousins, grandparents. Can you think of some who are generous, some who are cheap; some who are likable, some who are unpleasant; some who are smart, some not so much; some who are honest, some who are deceitful; some who are ambitious, some who are not? If you can find variability in such a small group, imagine the variability in the many millions of people who are identified as Americans, Muslim, Hispanic, or gay. Because of this variation, assuming anything about all members of such groups will necessarily lead to many errors. To use an example where measurable data are available, consider that although the average American (male, 5'9½", female,

THINK ABOUT ▶
[Blend Images-Hill Street Studios/Brand XPictures/DigitalVision/Getty Images]

5′4″) is taller than the average Chinese person (male, 5′7″; female, 5′2½″) (Yang et al., 2005), literally millions of Americans are shorter than the average Chinese person, and millions of Chinese people are taller than the average American (**FIGURE 10.1**).

The third reason social psychologists judge prejudice negatively is that it has all too often led to appalling acts of violence against innocent people—including children—who happened or were presumed to be members of particular groups. Many early social psychologists were inspired to focus on prejudice because of one of the most egregious examples of what prejudice can lead to: the Nazi Holocaust, which resulted in the deaths of an estimated 6 million Jews and 5 million members of other groups despised by the Nazis (e.g., Slavs and physically disabled individuals).

So that's the case for prejudice being a bad thing. People who hold prejudices usually justify them with **stereotypes**—overgeneralized beliefs about the traits and attributes of members of a particular group, such as "Black Americans are violent," "Jewish people are cheap," "White men are racist," "Latinos are lazy," and so forth. Not all stereotypic traits attributed to a group are negative, but overall, stereotypes of outgroups tend to be negative. Later in this chapter, we will consider where these stereotypes come from, how they affect us, and how they are perpetuated. As we will learn, stereotypes provide justifications for prejudice and lead to biases against outgroups.

People holding prejudices and stereotypes often leads to **discrimination**—negative behavior toward an individual solely on the basis of membership in a particular group. Discrimination comes in many forms, ranging from cold behavior at a party to declining someone's loan application to torture and genocide. Discrimination is often the consequence of the negative attitudes (prejudice) and beliefs (stereotypes) a person holds. But because of laws, norms, and values to be egalitarian, people's behaviors are not always biased by their prejudice and stereotypes.

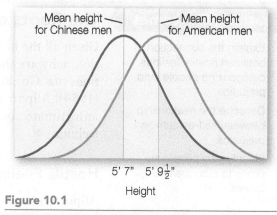

Figure 10.1

Overlapping Normal Distributions of Two Groups with Different Mean Heights

The normal distribution of Chinese and American males' heights, based on the group means, might look something like this. The blue areas represent cases in which we would be incorrect if we simply assumed that an American male was taller than the average Chinese male or that a Chinese male was shorter than the average American male.

Stereotype Overgeneralized beliefs about the traits and attributes of members of a particular group.

Discrimination Negative behavior toward an individual solely on the basis of that person's membership in a particular group.

SECTION REVIEW The Nature of Prejudice: Pervasiveness and Perspective

Prejudice has been a pervasive destructive force over the course of human history and continues to be so.

Prejudice is a negative *attitude* toward an individual based solely on that person's presumed membership in a particular group, without consideration of the unique individual, group variability, or potential for violence against the innocent.	Stereotypes are overgeneralized *beliefs* about the traits and attributes of members of a particular group.	Discrimination is negative *behavior* toward an individual based solely on that person's presumed membership in a particular group.

- Explain the connection between hostile feelings, categorizing people, and prejudice.
- Describe the relationship between self-esteem and prejudice.
- Identify why people are prone to ethnocentric biases.

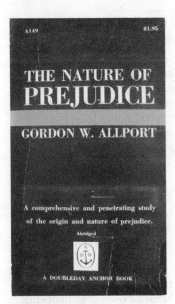

▲ Gordon Allport's book *The Nature of Prejudice* launched decades of research on the subject.

The Roots of Prejudice: Three Basic Causes

Given all the harm that has come from prejudice, stereotypes, and discrimination, why are these phenomena so prevalent? This is one of the central questions that Gordon Allport addressed in his classic book *The Nature of Prejudice* (1954). Allport proposed three basic causes of prejudice, each of which is an unfortunate consequence of some very basic aspects of human thought and feeling.

Hostile Feelings Linked to a Category

Allport viewed the first fundamental cause of prejudice to be a result of two basic human tendencies. First, people are likely to feel hostility when they are frustrated or threatened, or when they witness things they view as unpleasant or unjust. Second, just as we routinely categorize objects (see chapter 3), we also categorize other people as members of social groups, such as *women*, *Asians*, and *teenagers*, often within milliseconds of encountering them (Dickter & Bartholow, 2007; Fiske, 1998; Ito & Bartholow, 2009). Prejudice often results from linking hostile feelings to such salient categories of people (e.g., Crandall et al., 2011; O'Donnell et al., 2019). Hostile attitudes toward a group can result from various negative emotions associated with that group. For example, recent research on Islamophobia showed that the emotions of fear, anger, and disgust independently predicted anti-Muslim prejudice (Uenal et al., 2021).

Let's consider a few examples of how this might occur. Imagine a French man robbed at gunpoint by another French man in Marseilles. The victim will likely experience fear and anger, hate the robber, and hope the thief is caught and imprisoned. Now imagine a French man who is robbed by an Algerian man. He will experience the same emotions but is more likely to direct his hatred toward Algerians and may therefore want all Algerians expelled from his country. Why? When we encounter outgroup members, what is salient to us is their group membership rather than their individual characteristics. So in the latter example, the victimized individual views his experience as being mugged by an *Algerian*; thus, his negative feelings are overgeneralized to the category rather than applied only to the individual mugger whose actions caused his negative experience. In a similar vein, an Afghan woman whose niece was killed by an American guided missile is likely to hate Americans. A European American kid hassled by a Mexican American kid in a middle school restroom may decide he hates "Mexicans." In each of these examples, negative experiences with a single individual or a small sample of individuals leads to a sweeping negative feeling that is applied to literally millions of people who are perceived to be members of the salient group. In a finding consistent with these examples, Rosenfield and colleagues (1982) showed that when White participants were asked for money by a shabbily dressed Black panhandler, they were later less willing to volunteer to help promote a racial brotherhood week compared to those who were initially approached by either a well-dressed Black graduate student or a shabbily dressed White panhandler.

This idea of negative feelings generalized to an entire group can help explain sudden increases in prejudice after particularly threatening circumstances arise. For example, after the terrorist attacks of September 11, 2001, Americans exhibited more negative attitudes and behavior toward Muslim and Arab Americans. Although these reactions were sadly predictable, they are classic examples of prejudice: The Arab and Muslim Americans targeted had nothing to do with the attacks on the United States but were judged negatively because of their perceived group membership. Similarly, in the United States during the COVID-19 pandemic, there was a three-fold increase in verbal and physical attacks directed at Asian Americans (Yam, 2022). The negative feelings associated with the virus were linked to China because the first major outbreak occurred there, and then President Trump reinforced this association by referring to it as the "Chinese virus." With the category linked to the negative feelings, prejudice and discrimination became all too predictable consequences.

Sometimes, frustrations people experience fuel negative feelings and actions toward outgroups even in the absence of any inciting behavior by a member of that group. This is known as *displaced aggression*, and it can explain why in tough economic times, prejudice, stereotyping, and discrimination tend to increase (e.g., Hepworth & West, 1988; Hovland & Sears, 1940; Krosch et al., 2017). Experimental research confirms this process. When White American participants are led to believe resources are scarce, their brain activity indicates that they engage in less processing of Black American faces, and they reduce their resource allocations to Black Americans but not White Americans (Krosch & Amodio, 2019; Krosch et al., 2017).

Realistic group conflict theory (Levine & Campbell, 1972) adds to Allport's idea of hostility generalized to a group by arguing that the initial negative feelings between groups are often based on a real conflict or competition over scarce resources. If individuals in one group think that their access to land, water, jobs, or other resources is being threatened or blocked by another group, the resulting sense of threat and frustration is likely to generate negative emotions about the perceived rival group. People are more likely to harbor and express prejudice toward a particular outgroup when they view their own group as cohesive and as having collective interests possibly threatened by that outgroup (Effron & Knowles, 2015). How can this theory explain why prosperous people are often prejudiced against low-status groups? It's important to consider not just wealth, but also beliefs about the stability of one's position on the socioeconomic "ladder." In one recent study, wealthy individuals made to feel secure in their advantaged status were tolerant of immigrants and open to immigration. But those people led to fear that positions of high wealth are unstable and always changing showed greater opposition to immigrants and immigration (Jetten et al., 2021).

Also, negative feelings stemming from resource competition are often culturally transmitted from generation to generation so that intergroup hostilities are perpetuated even after the initial conflict is no longer pertinent. As a result of protracted intergroup conflict, members of the conflicting groups come to feel anxious around each other, and that intergroup anxiety can further fuel prejudice toward the outgroup (Stephan & Stephan, 1985).

Realistic group conflict theory A theory which asserts that the initial negative feelings between groups are often based on a real conflict or competition regarding scarce resources.

▲ Many Asian Americans, including these two Chinese American high school students, have experienced increased prejudice against them ever since COVID-19 took hold in the United States.

[Craig F. Walker/The Boston Globe via GettyImages]

Ingroup Bias: We Like Us Better Than Them

The second cause of prejudice, according to Allport, is the tendency to prefer what is familiar over what is not. As the mere exposure effect discussed in chapter 8 shows, the more familiar we are with a stimulus, the more we like it. We like—indeed, usually love—our own families, our own towns, our own stuff, and our own group. In contrast, outgroups are less familiar, stranger, less known. They make us feel uneasy, anxious. They are harder to predict and understand. This sense of unfamiliarity is amplified when people assume that because the outgroup differs from "us" on one dimension, such as political orientation, they probably differ from us in many other ways as well (Stern & Crawford, 2021).

Taking an evolutionary perspective, some psychologists have argued that a preference for familiar others is probably something adaptive that has been selected for (e.g., Park et al., 2003). Our ancestors, living in small groups, were probably safer if they stayed close to their own. If they ventured away from their own group and encountered other groups, they may have experienced peril, including exposure to germs. In fact, when thoughts of disease are made salient, people become particularly negative toward ethnically different others (Faulkner et al., 2004). A recent study of identical twins suggested that how prone an individual is to favor their ingroup is partly genetically determined (Lewis & Bates, 2017). Allport noted that because of common backgrounds, it's also just easier to know what to say and how to behave around those who are members of the ingroup.

In addition to this familiarity-based preference for the ingroup over outgroups, most of us like ourselves and demonstrate a self-serving bias, as you'll recall from our coverage of self-esteem (chapter 6). So if I am great, then my group must be great also. Surely groups I am *not* a member of can't be as great as those to which I belong! Indeed, research has shown that ingroup pronouns such as *us* are associated automatically with positive feelings and that outgroup pronouns such as *them* are associated automatically with negative ones (Perdue et al., 1990). So pride in one's own group and preference for one's own group over others may be a natural extension of self-serving bias.

Social identity theory (see chapter 9) (Tajfel & Turner, 1986) looks at the relationship between self-esteem and groups the other way around, reversing the causal direction. This theory proposes that a considerable portion of our self-esteem actually derives from our group memberships. Not only is my group great because I'm in it, but I am great because I am in this group! So I gain self-esteem by thinking highly of my own group and less highly of outgroups. And sure enough, wherever you travel, you meet people who are proud of their own cultures and ethnicities and think more highly of them than they do of other cultures and ethnicities.

A large body of experimental research supports the existence of ingroup bias and the validity of social identity theory. One important line of inquiry has examined whether arbitrarily formed groups immediately exhibit ingroup bias. This idea was anticipated in Jonathan Swift's (1726/2001) classic satire *Gulliver's Travels*, which describes wars breaking out between those who believe eggs should be cracked at the big end and those who believe they should be cracked at the small end.

Henri Tajfel and colleagues demonstrated this phenomenon in a seminal study in which high school students were asked to estimate how many dots were displayed on a screen (Tajfel et al., 1971). The researchers told one random set of students that they were "overestimators" and the other set that they were "underestimators." Even in such minimal newly formed groups, researchers found bias in favor of distributing more resources to members of one's own group than to the outgroup (Tajfel & Turner, 1986). We should note, however, that recent replication efforts (Kerr et al., 2018) have shown that this bias may not even occur in some cases: if it is clear to the participants

▲ During World Cups and the Olympics, we can see the basic truth that social identity theory captures: People derive self-worth from their ingroup identifications.

[Sebastian Gollnow/picture alliance via Getty Images]

▲ On which side would you crack the egg? Would you prefer people who pick the side you would choose over those who would pick the other side?

that the groups were formed randomly; if people make their resource allocations in private rather than in the presence of their group members; and in collectivist cultures, like Japan, as well as in cultures that highly value equality, like Australia.

Theory and research also suggest that liking for the ingroup is usually stronger than disliking of the outgroup (e.g., Allport, 1954; Brewer, 1979). However, this "love prejudice" often has negative consequences for outgroups. A Black American woman who is having trouble finding employment would feel little comfort in knowing that it's not so much that White employers are biased against Black Americans but just that they prefer to hire their "own kind." In addition, if we view an outgroup as threatening our beloved ingroup, our ingroup love can fuel outgroup hate.

Research also supports social identity theory's claim that ingroup bias serves self-esteem needs. From a social identity perspective, people should be especially likely to laud their own group and derogate outgroups after a threat to their personal self-esteem. In a series of studies (**FIGURE 10.2**), Fein and Spencer (1997) gave non–Jewish American participants positive or negative feedback on a test of social and verbal skills and then had them evaluate a woman after seeing a résumé and a videotape. For half the participants, the job candidate was depicted as Italian American; for the other half, she was depicted as Jewish American. Participants given self-esteem-threatening negative feedback rated the woman more negatively if they thought she was Jewish. In addition, participants given negative feedback and who had the opportunity to derogate the Jewish American woman showed an increase in self-esteem. And the more negatively they evaluated the Jewish American woman, the more their self-esteem increased. Subsequent studies have provided further support for the role of self-esteem threat in prejudice and stereotyping, showing, for example, that threatening Whites' self-esteem brings negative stereotypes of Black and Asian Americans closer to mind (Spencer et al., 1998). When people feel bad about themselves, they seem to compensate through downward comparison by thinking more harshly of outgroups. Another example of this kind of self-esteem-protecting prejudice is *scapegoating*, a phenomenon whereby people who feel inferior, guilty, anxious, or unsuccessful blame an outgroup for their troubles (Allport, 1954; Jung, 1945/1970; Miller & Bugelski, 1948). The Nazis blamed the Jews, and unsuccessful North Americans blame immigrants. Studies show that when people feel as though they lack control over their life, they compensate by blaming some outgroup (Rothschild et al., 2012; Sullivan et al., 2010).

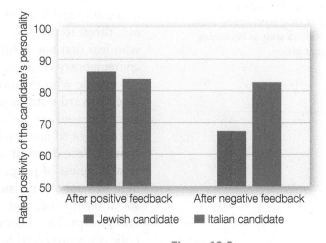

Figure 10.2

The Role of Self-Esteem Threat in Prejudice

After receiving negative feedback, American participants rated a woman more negatively if she was described as Jewish American than if she was described as Italian American.

[Data from Fein & Spencer, 1997]

Ethnocentrism, the Cultural Worldview, and Threat

The third basic cause of prejudice identified by Allport stems from the fact that each of us is raised within a particular cultural worldview and therefore has specific beliefs about what is good and what is bad. The cultural worldview may explicitly disparage particular groups, or it may implicitly disparage them by prioritizing certain values and goals. We can see such cultural differences at a cross-national level. For example, nations that endorse collectivist values of family harmony show less bias against older adults than nations that

Ethnocentrism Viewing the world through our own cultural value system and thereby judging actions and people based on our own culture's views of right and wrong and good and bad.

THINK ABOUT

[Janine Wiedel Photolibrary/Alamy]

Symbolic racism A tendency to view members of a racial outgroup as a threat to one's way of life and to express this view by rejecting social policies seen as benefiting that group.

value individual achievement (Ackerman & Chopik, 2021). Zooming in, we see regional variation within a nation, such as state-level differences in the acceptability of racial discrimination within the United States (Pettigrew, 1958). Looking even closer, we see fluctuations within a culture over time in the acceptability of prejudice. For instance, a sharp increase in bias-related incidents in 2016 may have resulted in part from Donald Trump's harsh rhetoric focused on immigrants (Crandall et al., 2018).

The internalized worldview contributes to prejudice in another important way. Because this worldview determines our view of what is right and good, we can't help but judge others on the basis of those cultural values. This kind of judgment, called **ethnocentrism** (Sumner, 1906), often leads us to hold negative attitudes about others who were raised in different cultures. An American who finds out that people in culture Z believe in bathing only twice a year is going to have a hard time not judging the members of that culture negatively: "They're dirty and primitive!" By the same token, members of culture Z may observe the American tendency to bathe or shower virtually every day as bizarre: "They're wasteful and compulsive!" These kinds of judgments often get more serious, such as when North Americans learn of cultures that practice female circumcision or believe that women should never leave the house without covering every part of their bodies. When are right and wrong merely matters of cultural preference? When are they a legitimate basis for judging members of another group negatively? It is very hard to say because our sense of right and wrong is intertwined with the cultural worldview in which we were raised.

Symbolic Racism   The theory of **symbolic racism** (Sears & Kinder, 1971) posits that the tendency to reject groups that don't conform to one's own view of the world underlies much of the racial prejudice that White Americans have against Black Americans. From this perspective, many White Americans have internalized traditional, conservative Eurocentric moral values and view Black Americans as a threat to the American way of life. "White Replacement Theory" advocates who fear that non-Whites will take over and replace White American values are contemporary symbolic racists (Garcia-Navarro, 2021).

People who exhibit signs of symbolic racism don't think they are prejudiced toward outgroups. Rather, their negative attitudes toward these groups are expressed symbolically as opposition to policies that are seen as giving advantages to marginalized groups. They might deny that those groups continue to face discrimination and believe that racial disparities result from the unwillingness of people in those groups to work hard enough. Those who are high in symbolic racism feel justified in opposing social programs that rectify social inequalities and supporting those that might curtail civil liberties of certain groups. The theory of symbolic racism has shown how prejudice is symbolically represented in diverging political opinions (Sears & Henry, 2005). In these studies, those who score high on measures of symbolic racism are more likely to support punitive anticrime policies that discriminate against marginalized groups (e.g., the death penalty or "three strikes and you're out" laws; Green et al., 2006).

Terror Management Theory   We've seen that people tend to think poorly of those who seem different. But why can't people just leave it at "Different strokes for different folks"? According to the existential perspective of terror management theory, one reason is that people must sustain faith in the validity of their own cultural worldview so that it can continue to offer psychological security in the face of our personal vulnerability and mortality. Other cultures threaten that faith: "One culture is always a potential menace to another because it is a living example that life can go on heroically within a value framework totally alien to one's own" (Becker, 1971, p. 140).

Basing their work on this idea, terror management researchers have tested the hypothesis that raising the problem of mortality would make people especially positive toward others who support their worldview and especially negative to others who implicitly or explicitly challenge it (Greenberg et al., 2016). In the first study testing this notion, when reminded of their own mortality, American Christian students became more positive toward a fellow Christian student and more negative toward a Jewish student (Greenberg et al., 1990). Similarly, when reminded of death, Italians and Germans became more negative toward other cultures (Castano et al., 2002; Jonas et al., 2005) and non-atheists became more negative toward atheists (Cook et al., 2015). Hirschberger and colleagues (2005) found that reminders of mortality increased prejudice against physically disabled individuals because they reminded people of their own physical vulnerabilities.

In the first of a pair of studies particularly pertinent to the ongoing tensions in the Middle East, researchers found that when reminded of their own mortality, Iranian college students expressed greater support for suicidal martyrdom against Americans (Pyszczynski et al., 2006). The second study showed that politically conservative American college students who were reminded of their mortality similarly supported preemptively bombing countries that might threaten the United States, regardless of "collateral damage" (Pyszczynski et al., 2006). And in yet another troubling study, Hayes, Schimel, and colleagues (2008) found that Christian Canadians who were reminded of their mortality were better able to avoid thoughts of their own death if they imagined Muslims dying in a plane crash.

SECTION REVIEW   The Roots of Prejudice: Three Basic Causes

Gordon Allport proposed three basic causes of prejudice, each based on fundamental ways that people think, feel, and are influenced by the cultures they live within.

Hostility plus Categorization

- We tend to feel hostility when we are frustrated or threatened.

- When negative feelings are associated with a member of an outgroup, we tend to overgeneralize those negative feelings and associated beliefs to the entire group.

Ingroup Bias

- We prefer what is familiar, including people like us.

- A portion of our self-esteem comes from group membership, biasing us against those in outgroups.

- When our self-worth is threatened, we tend to derogate and blame members of other groups.

Threats to One's Worldview

- Ethnocentrism leads people to judge people from different cultures more negatively.

- Cultural worldviews teach norms and values that encourage viewing certain groups more negatively than others.

- Ethnocentric biases are more severe when we feel vulnerable or when we see another's worldview as threatening to our own.

Learning Outcomes

- Describe right-wing authoritarianism.
- Describe social dominance orientation.

Right-wing authoritarianism (RWA) An ideology which holds that the social world is inherently dangerous and that maintaining security requires upholding society's order and tradition. It predicts prejudice against groups seen as socially deviant or dangerous.

Social dominance orientation (SDO) An ideology in which the world is viewed as a ruthlessly competitive jungle where it is appropriate and right for powerful groups to dominate weaker ones.

Figure 10.3

Social Dominance Orientation

These items are used to measure social dominance orientation. How would you rate your attitude toward each of them?

[Data from Pratto et al., 1994]

The Prejudiced Personality

Prejudice is common in most if not all known cultures. However, within a culture, some people are far more prone to prejudice, stereotyping, and discriminating against outgroups than others. What accounts for these differences? One set of answers can be derived from the causes of prejudice we have already discussed. For example, people have different direct experiences with outgroups and are exposed to different kinds of information about them. They also vary in their level of self-esteem and the lessons they learn growing up about how groups differ and what those differences mean. However, research shows that there are particular kinds of people who are especially prone to being prejudiced and that people who tend to be prejudiced against one outgroup also tend to be prejudiced against other outgroups (Meeusen et al., 2018).

In response to the Nazi era, Theodor Adorno and colleagues (1950) sought to understand the roots of anti-Semitism; they found that individuals who were prejudiced against Jews were also prejudiced against other groups. Adorno and colleagues determined that these overlapping biases reflected an *authoritarian personality*. People with this prejudiced personality style possess a cluster of traits including uncritical acceptance of authority, preference for well-defined power arrangements in society, adherence to conventional values and moral codes, and a tendency to think in rigid, black-and-white terms. More modern researchers have refined this idea with a measure of **right-wing authoritarianism (RWA)** (Altemeyer, 1981, 1998; De Keersmaecker et al., 2018). Individuals high in RWA believe that the social world is inherently dangerous and unpredictable, and the best way to maintain a sense of security in both their personal and social lives is to preserve society's order, cohesion, and tradition. High RWA people dislike ethnic outgroups as well as groups they perceive to threaten traditional norms, such as feminists and lesbians.

Other contemporary personality approaches to prejudice focus on some features related to the authoritarian personality. **Social dominance orientation (SDO)**, which was mentioned in chapter 9 (Pratto et al., 1994; Sidanius & Pratto, 1999), taps into beliefs that some people and groups are essentially better than others, and so society should be structured hierarchically, with some individuals and groups having higher social and economic status than others. SDO more strongly than RWA predicts dislike of disadvantaged groups that are perceived to be inferior, such as those who are physically disabled, those who are unemployed, and homemakers (Duckitt, 2006; Duckitt & Sibley, 2007; **FIGURE 10.3**).

Items on the social dominance orientation scale

1. Some groups of people are simply not the equals of others.
2. Some people are just more worthy than others.
3. This country would be better off if we cared less about how equal all people are.
4. Some people are just more deserving than others.
5. It is not a problem if some people have more of a chance in life than others.
6. Some people are just inferior to others.
7. To get ahead in life, it is sometimes necessary to step on others.
8. Increased economic equality.
9. Increased social equality.
10. Equality.
11. If people were treated more equally, we would have fewer problems in this country.
12. In an ideal world, all nations would be equal.
13. We should try to treat one another as equals as much as possible. (All humans should be treated equally.)
14. It is important that we treat other countries as equals.

All items are measured on a *very negative* (1) to *very positive* (7) scale. Responses to 8–14 are reverse-coded before being averaged so that higher numbers on that averaged composite imply higher levels of social dominance orientation.

SECTION REVIEW The Prejudiced Personality

Researchers have developed two useful measures of proneness to prejudice.

Right-Wing Authoritarianism (RWA)	Social Dominance Orientation (SDO)
High-RWA individuals:	High-SDO individuals:
• view the social world as dangerous.	• are competitively driven to maintain the dominance of some groups over others.
• are motivated to maintain collective security (societal order, cohesion, stability, tradition).	• are therefore prejudiced against groups that they perceive as being lower in society's status hierarchy.
• are prejudiced against groups that they perceive to threaten to disrupt collective security because they appear dangerous or deviant.	

Has Prejudice Become Less Prevalent over Time?

Learning Outcomes

Dial back time to 1954. The U.S. Supreme Court had just announced the historic decision *Brown v. Board of Education*, which struck down state laws enforcing racial segregation in the public schools. The Court ruled that "separate but equal" schools for Black and White students were inherently *un*equal. The ruling was met with stark and at times violent opposition in a number of states.

In the decades since then, Americans have enacted antidiscrimination laws and elected (2008) and reelected (2012) a Black man as president of the United States. In some respects at least, the United States has made tremendous strides in race relations. In 1958, 94% of Americans surveyed opposed interracial marriage, but that number dropped to 17% by 2007 (**FIGURE 10.4a**; Carroll, 2007) and recently has been found to be only 6% (McCarthy, 2021). And, an analysis of millions of American Internet respondents found that explicit and implicit attitudes regarding race became less negative between 2007 and 2016 (**FIGURE 10.4b**; Charlesworth & Banaji, 2019).

- Give evidence of both steps forward in the fight against discrimination and areas where we have room to grow.
- Define *ambivalent racism* and *aversive racism*.
- Explain how implicit racism can be revealed.

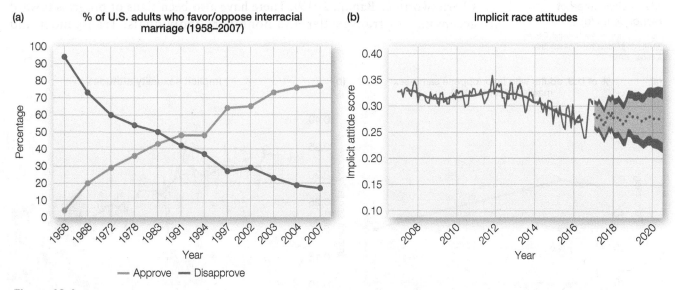

Figure 10.4

Progress Against Racial Prejudice

Disapproval of interracial marriage dropped significantly between 1958 and 2007 (a). Implicit prejudice against Black individuals is also declining, according to analysis of millions of American Internet respondents (b).

[Part (a): data from Carroll, 2007; part (b): data from Charlesworth & Banaji, 2019]

▲ President Barack Obama
gives the pen he used to sign
the Matthew Shepard Act
on October 28, 2009, to the
parents of Matthew Shepard,
Dennis Shepard, left, and
Judy Shepard, third left.

[Manuel Balce Ceneta/AP Images]

Figure 10.5

**Progress Against LGBTQ
Prejudice**

Today more Americans
approve of same-sex
marriage than disapprove (a).
Implicit prejudice against
gay and lesbian people is
also declining, according
to analysis of millions
of American Internet
respondents (b).

[Part (a): data from Pew Research Center,
2019; part (b): data from Charlesworth
& Banaji, 2019]

Similar changes can be seen with other prejudices. Countries such as Germany and Great Britain have elected female leaders over the past few decades. A study of questionnaire responses of more than 15,000 New Zealanders found that sexism was reduced between 2009 and 2016 (Huang et al., 2019). In 2016—almost 100 years after the 19th Amendment (1920) guaranteed women the right to vote—a major political party in the United States nominated a female presidential candidate, Hillary Clinton. In 2020, Kamala Harris was elected Vice President. The #MeToo movement, which is associated with bringing to justice powerful and wealthy men who have harassed and abused women, has also brought much-needed progress in fighting mistreatment of women (Bennett, 2020; MacKinnon, 2019). Despite these and other indications that treatment and status of women in the United States has steadily improved, many people viewed the June 24th, 2022 overturning of Roe vs. Wade by the U.S. Supreme Court as a major backwards step, as it eliminated federal protection for women to have the freedom to choose whether or not to have an abortion, a freedom that had been theirs since 1973.

What about prejudice against LGBTQ people? In 2009, the United States added perceived gender, gender identity, sexual orientation, and disability to the federal definition of hate crimes through the Matthew Shepard Act. In 2010, the U.S. Senate voted to repeal the "Don't Ask, Don't Tell" policy and struck down the ban on openly gay men and women serving in the military. In 2013, the U.S. Supreme Court decided a landmark case that opened the door for same-sex couples to qualify for federal benefits previously only extended to heterosexual couples (*U.S. v. Windsor*, 2013). Evidence suggests that states making same-sex marriages legal may have contributed to these reductions in antigay bias (Ofosu et al., 2019). In 2001, 43% of Americans supported same-sex marriage, but in 2019, 61% said they supported it (**FIGURE 10.5a**; Masci et al., 2019), a figure which is now up to 70% (McCarthy, 2021). And from 2007 to 2016, American Internet respondents exhibited a reduction in explicit and implicit bias against gay and lesbian people (**FIGURE 10.5b**; Charlesworth & Banaji, 2019). There have also been signs of progress toward acceptance of transgender and nonbinary individuals. Transgender and

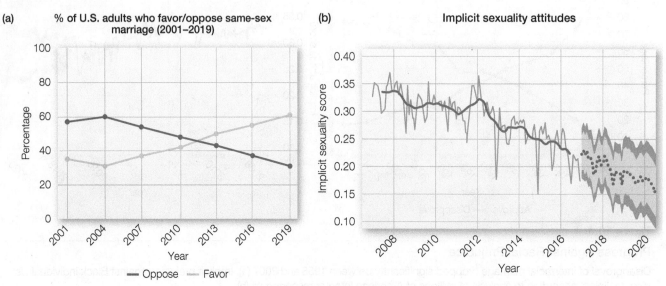

(a) **% of U.S. adults who favor/oppose same-sex marriage (2001–2019)**

— Oppose — Favor

(b) **Implicit sexuality attitudes**

nonbinary actors are being increasingly cast in American television series, including the shows *Big Sky* and *General Hospital*.

Perhaps because of this relative progress, many Americans believe that prejudice, especially against Black people in the United States, is a thing of the past (Norton & Sommers, 2011). However, in a Pew survey, nearly half of Black Americans surveyed said that they have had the experience of others treating them as if they are suspicious or unintelligent compared to only about 10% of White Americans reporting having had this experience. Black individuals were also six times as likely as Whites to report having been stopped unfairly by police (Pew Research Center, 2016). So reports of the death of prejudice have been greatly exaggerated. Let's consider some of the evidence.

Even though segregation is against the law, we still live in a society that is quite segregated. Think back to high school. Did Black students sit mainly in one part of the cafeteria, Whites in another, Hispanics in another, and Asians in yet another? Did you even attend a school or live in an area that was ethnically diverse? If people are still clustering by race and ethnicity, we might wonder whether biases still shape our preferences in whom to approach and whom to avoid.

While attitudes toward some groups have become more favorable over time, social and political contexts can bring about new hostilities. Whereas Jews were the most salient target of religious prejudice in the United States when Allport wrote his book in 1954, in 2010 "only" about 15% of Americans surveyed reported having even a little prejudice against Jews, compared with nearly 43% who reported having at least some prejudice toward Muslims (Gallup Center for Muslim Studies, 2010). Anti-Semitism is far from gone, however. In 2020, according to the FBI, Jews were targeted by 683 hate crimes in the United States, more than any other religious group (ADL, 2022). And, anti-Semitism has long been quite prevalent in many European and Asian countries (Baum et al., 2016).

Although overt expressions of discrimination and racial injustice are certainly declining, they are far from absent. Consider, for example, the well-publicized killings of Black Americans, such as the video recorded murder of George Floyd in 2020, the choking to death of Eric Garner, and the fatal shootings of Tamir Rice, Breonna Taylor, and Ahmaud Arbery. These tragic killings have spurred the development of the Black Lives Matter movement, many protests, and intensified efforts to improve diversity, equity, and inclusion, and political and legal actions around the country. The goal is better social justice, fairer policing, and a more truly egalitarian society.

In addition, there is ample evidence of less visible forms of discrimination that are harder to see. Beginning in the late 1950s, the civil rights campaign brought to public awareness the problem of **institutional discrimination**, unfair restrictions on the opportunities of certain groups of people by institutional policies, structural power relations, and formal laws (e.g., a height requirement for employment as a police officer that excludes most women). This form of discrimination has been so deeply embedded in the fabric of American society that it has often taken place without people even being aware that institutional practices had discriminatory effects (Pettigrew, 1958).

THINK ABOUT

[timsa/iStock/Getty Images]

📺 Achieve
Video Activity: Prejudice Against Gays and Lesbians (ABC What Would You Do Series)

Institutional discrimination Unfair restrictions on opportunities for certain groups of people through institutional policies, structural power relations, and formal laws.

▲ The Black Lives Matter movement makes clear that America continues to struggle with racial tension and conflict.

▲ Women are overrepresented in many lower paid occupations, such as preschool teacher, while being underrepresented in higher paid occupations like airline pilot.

[DGLimages/iStock/Getty Images]

At a broader cultural level, despite the obvious importance to societies of many occupations traditionally held more by women, such as nursing and child education, they are generally less economically rewarded than those traditionally held by men, with the net result that women earn less than their male contemporaries (Alksnis et al., 2008). Particularly in higher-paying jobs (e.g., hospital administrator), equally qualified women may earn only about 79 cents to every dollar that men earn (Eagly & Carli, 2007; Semega, 2009). Are women paid less than men for the same jobs? Sometimes that is the case. But even when it is not, keep in mind that women are more likely to be represented in jobs that have lower earning potential (**FIGURE 10.6**). Other below-awareness evidence of the greater valuing of males was brought to light in a recent study of more than 600,000 social media posts from St. Petersburg, Russia, in which parents mentioned their sons more than their daughters, and posts of sons received more likes than posts of daughters (Sivak & Smirnov, 2019).

Clear signs of racial discrimination can also be found in everything from employment to housing, credit markets, the justice system, and consumer pricing (Pager & Shepherd, 2008). For example, the way in which lawyers

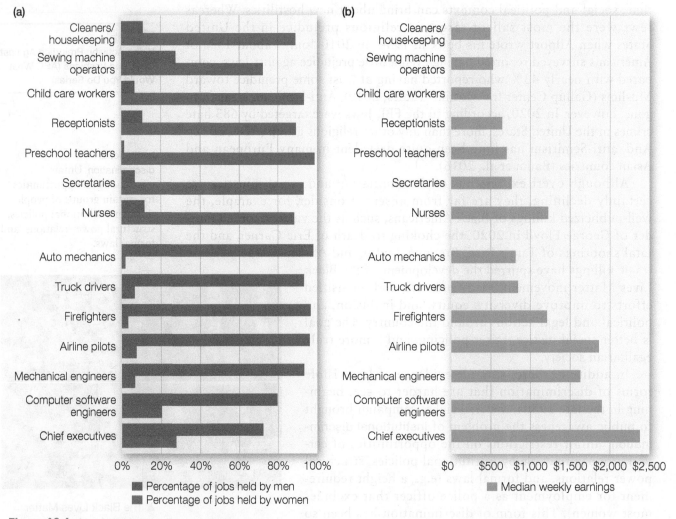

Figure 10.6

Women Are Underrepresented in Higher-Paying Jobs

Women are underrepresented in some of the highest-paid fields, which perpetuates gender inequality in overall earnings.

[Data from U.S. Bureau of Labor Statistics (a) https://www.bls.gov/cps/cpsaat11.htm; (b) https://www.bls.gov/cps/cpsaat39.htm]

select or exclude jury members can lead to juries that are biased against a Black defendant (Morrison et al., 2016). Once convicted, the more a Black male has "Afrocentric" facial features—in other words, the more they look like Whites' stereotypes of Black people—the harsher their prison sentences for the same crime tend to be (Blair et al., 2004; Kleider-Offutt et al., 2017), and the more likely they are to receive the death penalty for capital offenses when the victim was White (Eberhardt et al., 2006).

These findings indicate that in the contemporary world, we often see these subtler—or what are termed *modern*—forms of prejudice that disadvantage minoritized groups. Because of America's sordid history with slavery and explicit discrimination against Black Americans, the study of modern forms of prejudice in the United States has focused largely on racial prejudice.

Complexities of Modern Prejudice

Social psychologists have developed a number of related concepts to explain the subtler, more complex forms of prejudice that have emerged. Each in its own way emphasizes the need to understand how and why people might explicitly reject prejudiced attitudes but still harbor subtle biases. The idea of **ambivalent racism** is that many White Americans embrace both one belief that leads to negativity toward Blacks and another that leads to more favorable views of them (Katz & Hass, 1988). Specifically, the belief that people will be successful if they just work hard enough leads to a negative view of Blacks. On the other hand, the belief that all people should have equal opportunities to succeed leads to a more sympathetic, positive view of Blacks.

A related idea is **aversive racism**, which proposes that many White Americans have subtle, often early learned negative feelings about Blacks, but also support racial equality (Gaertner & Dovidio, 1986). People who score high in aversive racism outwardly support fair treatment of Blacks, but when angry or when they can discriminate against Blacks without it being obvious they are doing so, a negative bias emerges (e.g., Gaertner & Dovidio, 2000; Hodson et al., 2002). These two concepts have contributed to an explosion of interest in subtle ways that bias operates focused on the concept of implicit prejudice.

Ambivalent racism The influence of two clashing sets of values on White Americans' racial attitudes: a belief in individualism and a belief in egalitarianism.

Aversive racism Negative, often unconscious, feelings and beliefs about Black people held by White people who otherwise support racial equality and do not knowingly discriminate.

Implicit Prejudice

The term **implicit prejudice** refers to negative attitudes toward a group of people for which the individual has little or no conscious awareness. Some people may choose not to admit their prejudices, whereas others may not be aware of them. Measures of implicit prejudice tap into attitudes that lie beneath the surface of what people report (Nosek et al., 2011). And, indeed, whereas a majority of White Americans don't report being prejudiced on explicit measures, most do show signs of having biases when their attitudes are assessed implicitly with either cognitive measures of implicit associations or physiological measures of affective responding (Cunningham, Johnson et al., 2004; Dovidio et al., 2001; Hofmann et al., 2005; Mendes et al., 2002). Recent studies have shown that negative stereotypes about a group contribute to implicit prejudice against the group (Phills et al., 2020).

Implicit prejudice Negative attitudes or affective reactions associated with an outgroup for which the individual has little or no conscious awareness and that can be automatically activated in intergroup encounters.

Physiological Measures of Bias Measures of implicit prejudice tap into people's automatic affective response to a person or a group. Some measures do this by indexing an immediate physiological reaction that people are unlikely to control or may find difficult to control. For example, when

Whites are asked to imagine working on a project with a Black partner or a White partner, they often report a stronger preference for working with the Black partner. But their faces tell a different story. Electrodes connected to their brows and cheeks pick up subtle movements of the facial muscles that reveal a negative attitude when they think about working with a Black partner (Vanman et al., 2004). Similarly, when Whites are actually paired up to work with a Black partner, they show a cardiovascular response that is associated with threat: Their hearts pump more blood, and their veins and arteries contract (Mendes et al., 2002).

The brain also registers the threat response. The amygdala is the brain region that signals negative emotional responses, especially fear, to things in our environment. Whites who have a strong racial bias exhibit an especially pronounced amygdala response when they view pictures of Black men (Amodio, 2014; Phelps et al., 2000). Interestingly, however, if given more time, this initial negative attitude tends to get downregulated by the more rational dorsolateral prefrontal cortex (Cunningham, Johnson et al., 2004; Forbes et al., 2012). We'll further discuss why and how people go about controlling their prejudiced attitudes and emotions in chapter 11. For now, the primary point is that automatic negative bias leaks out in people's physiological responses.

Cognitive Measures of Implicit Bias   Cognitive measures also tell us something about people's implicit attitudes. These measures take different forms, but they all rely on the same assumption: If you like a group, then you will quickly associate that group with good stuff; if you don't like a group, you will quickly associate that group with bad stuff. To assess such implicit

SOCIAL PSYCH OUT IN THE WORLD

Do Americans Live in a Postracial World?

History was made in 2008, when the United States elected its first Black president. Less than 50 years after Martin Luther King, Jr. spoke of his dream that his children would be judged not by the color of their skin but by the content of their character, this dream seemed much closer to reality. With a multiracial president having served two terms in the White House, many Americans began to wonder: Do we now finally live in a postracial world?

Probably not. Granted, the research we've reviewed in this chapter demonstrates that racial prejudice has changed considerably over time. However, we've also learned in this chapter that in the contemporary world, prejudice often is ambivalent and manifests in subtle ways. Elections might be times when people try to set aside biases to weigh the more established merits of different candidates. However, among undecided voters, implicit biases seem to play a stronger role in predicting decisions at the polls (Galdi et al., 2008;

see also Greenwald, Smith, et al., 2009). Such findings suggest that negative biases still lie beneath the surface of people's consciously held values, beliefs, and intentions.

On the other hand, Barack Obama's presidency meant that every American citizen had a highly visible exemplar of a successful Black political leader. In this way, he may have tilted Americans' implicit associations of Blacks in a more positive direction. Indeed, there is some evidence that the election of Obama and exposure to his campaigns helped to reduce people's implicit racial bias, in part by providing a positive example of a Black individual that may counter many of the negative stereotypes that are so pervasive in mass media (Columb & Plant, 2011; Plant et al., 2009). When President Obama was the example that people brought to mind when they thought of Black people, they were less likely to be racially prejudiced.

However, we must be careful not to look at data like these and feel that we need do no more to rectify racial inequality or to change the disparities that do exist. For example, in one study (Effron et al., 2009), participants who varied in their level of racial prejudice indicated associations, researchers prime people with members of different groups and measure how fast it takes them to identify good stuff and bad stuff (Dovidio et al., 2002; Fazio et al., 1995).

For example, Fazio and colleagues (1995) reasoned that if Whites experience an automatic negative reaction to Blacks, then exposure to photographs of Black individuals should speed up evaluations of negative words and slow down evaluations of positive words. To test this hypothesis, they presented participants with positive words (e.g., *wonderful*) and negative words (e.g., *annoying*) and then asked them to indicate as fast as they could whether each was good or bad by pressing the appropriate button. Each word was immediately preceded by a brief presentation of a photograph of a Black person or a White person. The results revealed substantial individual differences in White participants' automatic reactions: For many White participants, being primed with Black faces significantly sped up reactions to negative words and slowed down reactions to positive words. Other White participants did not show this pattern, and some even showed the opposite. More importantly, the more closely these people seemed to associate "Black" with "bad," the less friendly they were during a later 10-minute interaction with a Black experimenter.

Since the late 1990s, the most commonly used measure of implicit attitudes has been the *implicit association test*, or *IAT* (Greenwald et al., 1998), which we introduced in chapter 3. The basic logic of this test is that if you associate group A with "bad," then it should be pretty easy to group together instances of group A and instances of bad stuff, and it should be relatively difficult to group together instances of group A and instances of good stuff. This basic paradigm can be used to assess implicit associations with any group you can think of, but it has most commonly been used for race, so let's take

whether they would vote for Obama or McCain in the 2008 election or indicated whether they would have voted for Bush or Kerry in 2004. (This condition was included to control for priming political orientation.) Subsequently, participants imagined that they were on a community committee with a budget surplus that could be allocated to two community organizations: one that primarily served a White neighborhood and one that primarily served a Black neighborhood.

When participants indicated that they would vote for Obama, especially those higher in prejudice turned around and allocated significantly less money to the organization that would serve the Black neighborhood and more money to the organization that would serve the White neighborhood. For people with strong racial biases, acknowledging and endorsing the success of a single outgroup member seems to come at a cost to broader policies that could benefit more people. The visible success of one person does not imply the success of the group as a whole. Certainly more progress was made when biracial Kamala Harris became the first female and BIPOC vice president of the United States. At the same time, both before and since her election, Vice President Harris has been subject to many racist and sexist attacks online (Bierman, 2021). Clearly, more work needs to be done to fully realize Dr. King's dream.

▲ In 2021, Kamala Harris made history when she became the first woman, first Black American, and first Asian American to become the vice-president of the United States.

[Kent Nishimura/Los Angeles Times via GettyImages]

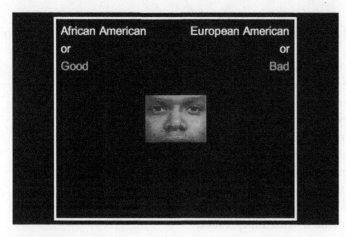

Figure 10.7

A Classic Measure of Implicit Racism

The Implicit Association Test can be used to measure the relative difficulty people can have in automatically associating Black faces with good thoughts.

[Data from Greenwald et al. (1998)]

📚 Achieve
Science of Everyday Life: Implicit Association Test

---

that example. (You can take this and other versions of the IAT yourself by visiting the Project Implicit website, at www.projectimplicit.com.)

In the Race IAT, people are instructed to do some basic categorization tasks (**FIGURE 10.7**). The first two rounds are just practice getting used to the categories. For the first round, you are presented with White and Black faces one at a time, and you just need to click on one button if the face is Black and another button if the face is White. In the second round, you categorize positive ("rainbow," "present") and negative ("vomit," "cancer") words by clicking on one button if the word is positive and a different button if the word is negative. In the third round, the task becomes more complicated as you are presented with faces or words, one at a time. Deciding as quickly as possible, you must then click one button if what you see is either a Black face or a positive word but a different button if you see either a White face or a negative word. When your cognitive network links "Black" with "bad," it's relatively hard to use the same button to categorize Black faces along with positive words without either slowing down or making lots of category errors. In contrast, if "Black" and "bad" are closely associated in your cognitive network, you should find it much easier to use the same button to indicate that you see either a Black face or negative word, the task required in a fourth round. If you're faster with "Black" and "bad" than "Black" and "good," you're showing associations that are predictive of implicit bias.

What We've Learned from Measuring Implicit Bias.   Research using the race-related version of the IAT has shown that although implicit bias has been trending down (Charlesworth & Banaji, 2019), as of 2015, 48% of White and 42% of Biracial adults showed at least a slight implicit bias toward Whites, whereas 45% of Black adults showed at least a slight bias toward Blacks (Morin, 2015). What is less clear is what these associations mean. Some researchers have criticized the measure for confounding the tendency to associate "Black" and "bad" with the tendency to associate "White" and "good" (Blanton & Jaccard, 2006; Blanton et al., 2006). However, other evidence suggests that IAT scores do reliably assess responses that are predictive of behavior (Greenwald, Smith et al., 2009; Greenwald et al., 2015; Kurdi et al., 2019; LeBel & Paunonen, 2011). Even if we grant that the race-related IAT is a reliable measure, some dispute continues about what it taps into. For example, people actually show stronger racial biases when they know the measure is supposed to reveal their racial biases (Frantz et al., 2004). Anxiety about being labeled racist might actually make it more difficult for people to perform the task. In addition, some researchers have noted that an association of "Black" with "bad" could mean a variety of things, such as the acknowledgment that Blacks are mistreated and receive bad outcomes or simply cultural stereotypes that might have little to do with one's personal attitudes (Andreychik & Gill, 2012; Olson & Fazio, 2004). Other theorists suggest that implicit associations primarily tap into biases in the surrounding cultural context more than in the minds of individuals (Payne et al., 2017).

Even if we set aside the debate about the IAT in particular, a broader pattern emerges from the literature examining both implicit and explicit measures of prejudiced attitudes. Most notably, although they can be correlated, they are often quite distinct. In other words, people who have an implicit negative attitude toward a group might still explicitly report having positive feelings. But even more interesting is that people's implicit attitudes seem to predict different kinds of behavior than their explicit attitudes. Explicit prejudice predicts overt or controllable expression of prejudice, whereas implicit prejudice better predicts subtler negative reactions to outgroup members.

For example, when researchers have analyzed interracial interactions between strangers, they have found that Whites' explicit prejudice predicts *what* they say to a Black partner, but it's their implicit prejudice that predicts *how* they say it (Dovidio et al., 2002). What this means is that even when explicitly well-intentioned Whites might try to say the right thing, their body language may communicate discomfort and avoidance (see also Amodio & Devine, 2006; McConnell & Leibold, 2001).

Although the IAT has been primarily used to measure racial attitudes, researchers are increasingly using it to study other forms of prejudice. For example, recent studies utilized the IAT to measure implicit transgender attitudes, which predicted transphobia and transgender-related policy support over and above explicit transgender attitudes (Axt et al., 2021)

SECTION REVIEW   Has Prejudice Become Less Prevalent over Time?

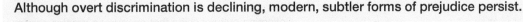

Although overt discrimination is declining, modern, subtler forms of prejudice persist.

Complexities of Modern Prejudice	Ambivalent and Aversive Racism	Implicit Prejudice
• While there are examples of strides forward when considering overt expressions of prejudice, evidence of institutional discrimination reveals how biases can be so embedded in the structure of our society that discrimination can occur without intention.	• *Ambivalent racism* is the coexistence of positive and negative attitudes about Blacks resulting from clashing beliefs in individualism and egalitarianism. • *Aversive racism* occurs when people have nonconscious, negative feelings even when they consciously support racial equality.	• *Implicit prejudice* refers to automatically activated negative associations with outgroups. • These associations can be revealed through physiological or cognitive measures, such as the IAT.

Stereotyping: The Cognitive Companion of Prejudice   ◀ Learning Outcomes

A *stereotype* is a cognitive schema containing knowledge about and associations with a social group (Dovidio et al., 1996; Hamilton & Sherman, 1994). For example, our stereotype of the group *librarians* may contain our beliefs about the traits shared by members of that group (e.g., librarians are smart and well read), theories about librarians' preferences and attitudes (e.g., librarians probably like quiet), and examples of librarians we have known (e.g., Ms. Smith, from my school library). We may not want to admit it, but we all probably have stereotypes about dozens of groups, such as lawyers, gays, lesbians, truckers, grandmothers, goths, Russians, immigrants, and overweight individuals.

- Explain reasons that stereotypes develop.
- Identify reasons that people use stereotypes.
- Describe how stereotypes can skew a person's judgment.

People around the globe often openly endorse certain stereotypes about various groups, but because stereotypes are so prominently promoted in cultures, even people who explicitly reject them may have formed implicit associations between groups and the traits their culture attributes to those groups. At a conscious level, you might recognize that not all librarians, if any at all, really fit the mold of being bookish, quiet women who wear glasses. But simply hearing the word *librarian* is still likely to bring to mind these associated attributes, even if you're not consciously aware of it.

Finally, although we commonly refer to stereotyping as having false negative beliefs about members of a group, it should be clear from the librarian example that stereotypes don't have to be negative. They don't even have to be entirely false (Jussim et al., 2015). Being well-read is a positive trait, and the average librarian probably has read more than your average nonlibrarian. But even if we grant this possible difference in averages of these two groups, the assertion that *all* librarians are better read than *all* nonlibrarians is certainly false. So stereotyping goes awry because people typically overgeneralize a belief about a group to make a blanket judgment about virtually every member of that group.

 SOCIAL PSYCH AT THE MOVIES

Gender Stereotypes in Animated Films, Then and Now

Have you ever stopped to think about how the stories you learned as a child might have formed a foundation for the gender stereotypes you hold today? Children become aware of their own gender and begin showing a preference for gender-stereotypical toys and activities between two and three years of age (Encyclopedia of Children's Health, n.d.). Some of these beliefs and preferences are learned from observing their parents, peers, and siblings (e.g., Tenenbaum & Leaper, 2002), but children's books, movies, and other media also play roles in reinforcing cultural messages about gender.

Consider some popular pre–women's movement children's movies. In the classic 1959 film *Sleeping Beauty*, the protagonist, Aurora, pretty and kind, cannot even regain consciousness without the love and assistance of her prince (Geronimi, 1959). Snow White cheerily keeps house and cleans up after the seven dwarfs in the 1937 animated film (Hand, 1937) until her status is elevated through marriage to a prince. *Cinderella*, released in 1950, feels more obviously oppressed by the forced domestic labor and humiliation by her stepmother and stepsisters, but again, she can only escape her fate through the love of a wealthy prince (Geronimi et al., 1950).

The common theme in these films is that beauty and innocence are the qualities a young woman should possess to achieve her Happily Ever After, which can happen only through marriage to a handsome and well-heeled man. And older,

unmarried, or widowed women are often cast as the villains in these stories, spurred to evil acts by jealousy of their younger rivals.

Reflecting cultural shifts that encourage greater agency in women, princess characters in films released more recently have become noticeably more assertive. Ariel, from *The Little Mermaid* (Clements & Musker, 1989), is willful and adventurous, eager to explore the world beyond her ocean home. But even so, she needs the permission of her authoritative father and the love of a man to realize her dreams. Along the way, she even trades her talent (her voice) to undergo severe changes to her body (legs instead of a tail) for the opportunity to woo her love interest.

In other modern animated films, the portrayals of princesses have become more complex and counterstereotypic. First, there has been an effort to present characters from different cultures, with protagonists who are Middle Eastern (Jasmine in *Aladdin*, 1992), Native American (*Pocahontas*, 1995), Chinese (*Mulan*, 1998), Black (Tiana, *The Princess and the Frog*, 2009), Scottish (Merida, *Brave*, 2012), and Pacific Islander (*Moana*, 2016).

Second, the modern princesses in animated films are more often cast as heroic. In *Mulan*, the protagonist disguises herself as male so that she can use her fighting skills to save and rescue the male characters in the movie. In *Moana*, the titular character is an adventurous teenager who leaves the safety of her island to embark on a treacherous journey to save her people. Finally, the two *Frozen* films (2013 and 2019) tell the story of two strong and determined sisters. Elsa, the

Moreover, even though some stereotypes are positive, they can still have negative effects. Stereotypes can be benevolent on the surface but ultimately patronize the stereotyped group and suggest that negative stereotypes are not far behind (Siy & Cheryan, 2016). We discuss one example of this in the Social Psych at the Movies box.

Where Do People's Stereotypic Beliefs Come From?

The cultural perspective suggests that we learn stereotypes over the course of socialization as they are transmitted by parents, friends, and the media. These stereotypes are often quite blatant in the media, but they may be represented subtly as well. For example, in American print ads, men tend to be higher in the page, and this positioning contributes to perceiving men as more dominant than women (Lamer & Weisbuch, 2019). Even small children have been shown to grasp the prevailing stereotypes of their culture (e.g., Aboud, 1988; Williams et al., 1975). People who don't endorse stereotypes about other ethnic groups can still report on what those cultural stereotypes are

older sister, embraces her power to control ice and become a strong leader to Arendelle, and her little sister Anna bravely risks her own life to find and save Elsa. These newer princess stories highlight autonomy, strength, and independence for young women.

Of course, before we get too encouraged by these messages of equality, we might ponder whether these modern fairy tales reflect lower levels of hostile sexism toward women (gone are the evil witches and stepmothers in these more contemporary films) but still reinforce benevolent sexist beliefs about women. The female characters are still young, beautiful, and good, and their Happily Ever After still often involves getting the guy.

In fact, these benevolent views of women are manifested in children's movies more generally—if girls and women are portrayed at all, that is. Studies of G-rated family films have found that only about 30% of the speaking characters are female (Smith et al., 2010), a disparity that is also evident in prime-time television and has remained largely unchanged over 15 years (Sink & Mastro, 2017). Female characters are more likely to wear sexy or revealing clothing than their male counterparts (Sink & Mastro, 2017). Whereas male characters are more often portrayed as having power and/or being funny, female characters are more

[Elisabeth LHOMELET/Getty Images]

commonly portrayed as having good motives and being attractive, although in an encouraging trend, they are also portrayed as being equally or even more intelligent (Smith et al., 2010).

It's likely that these stereotypic portrayals shape our gender schemas. A meta-analysis of more than 30 studies suggested that up to the mid-1990s, children and adults who watched more television also had more traditional views about gender (Herrett-Skjellum & Allen, 1996). Longitudinal studies have suggested that the causal arrow goes from exposure to television to gender stereotypes because the more television children watch, the more they accept gender stereotypes when they are much older (e.g., Kimball, 1986). Increasing scrutiny of these subtle ways that stereotypes are perpetuated raises questions for policy makers. Should films, television shows, and other media be rated on the basis of their stereotypic messages? The Swedish Film Institute thought so back in 2013. Swedish theaters began employing a feminist rating system known as the Bechdel test (Rising, 2013), which awards an A rating to films that portray two female characters talking to each other about something other than a man. It's not a perfect system, but it's a start in calling needed attention to gender bias at the movies.

(Devine, 1989). So, even if we try not to accept stereotypes ourselves, we are likely to learn cultural stereotypes through prior exposure. For example, people who watch more news programming—which tends to overreport crime by marginalized groups—are more likely to perceive Blacks and Latinos in stereotypic ways as poor and violent (Dixon, 2008a, 2008b; Mastro, 2003). This process of social learning explains how an individual picks up stereotypes both consciously and unconsciously. But how do these beliefs come to exist in a culture in the first place?

A Kernel of Truth   Even when stereotypes are broad overgeneralizations of what a group is like, some (but not all) stereotypes may be based on actual differences in the average traits or behaviors associated with two or more groups. This is what Allport called the *kernel of truth hypothesis*. Even though this kernel might be quite small, with much more overlap between groups than there are differences, as perceivers, we tend to exaggerate any differences that might exist and apply them to virtually all members of the groups; indeed, the most prominent stereotypic attributes ascribed to a group are sometimes the most exaggerated (Eyal & Epley, 2017). However, Lee Jussim and colleagues (2015) have been particularly active in making the provocative case that many of the stereotypes people hold about groups *that have to do with specific facts*, such as the percentage of Asian Americans who complete college relative to the percentage other Americans who do so, are often quite accurate. In fact, they sometimes even underestimate (rather than overestimate) group differences. Consistent with the idea of stereotypes reflecting some level of accuracy, a recent large sample study of Americans showed that the Black-violent stereotype is stronger in states in which Blacks have a higher rate of having been convicted of violent crimes (Johnson & Chopik, 2019). However, this is just a correlation, and the causality could run the other way. It's possible that in states in which Blacks are viewed more negatively, they experience more poverty and prejudice, which contributes to their being convicted of more violent crimes.

But when it comes to personality traits, there is little support for the kernel of truth hypothesis. Consider a set of studies by Robert McCrae and colleagues (Terracciano et al., 2005). They assessed actual personalities in samples from 49 nations and then assessed the stereotypes about the personalities of people from those nations. There was good agreement across nations about what each nationality is like (e.g., Italians, Germans, Canadians). But the researchers found no correspondence between these stereotypes and the actual personalities of the people in those nations! You might think that Germans are more conscientious than Italians, but there's no evidence from the personality data that this is actually the case.

A complicating factor with the kernel of truth hypothesis is that even when facts seem to support an overall group difference, those facts don't necessarily imply innate differences. For example, it may be true that a disproportionate percentage of Black American males are convicted of crimes. However, this does not mean that Black men are more violent by nature. In most cultures, groups that are economically disadvantaged and targets of discrimination are more likely to get in trouble with the law. Members of groups who are low in socioeconomic status also tend to do less well in school, but again, an attribution of innate intellectual inferiority is an unwarranted leap. So even in cases in which there is a kernel of truth, the stereotype usually leads to an unjustified jump to assumptions about essential differences in traits and abilities. This is problematic because attributing negative attributes to genetic differences increases prejudice (e.g., Suhay et al., 2017).

Social Role Theory   If stereotypes don't arise from real differences in the underlying traits of different groups, where do they come from? One possibility is that they come from the roles and behaviors that societal pressures may impose on a particular group. Because of the fundamental attribution error, when people see us in a role, they jump to the conclusion that we have the traits implied by the behaviors we enact in that role. This is the basic assumption of Alice Eagly's (1987) social role theory: We infer stereotypes that describe who people are from the roles that we see people play.

Social role theory primarily has been used to explain the existence of persistent stereotypes about men and women. Men are stereotyped to be *agentic*—assertive, aggressive, and achievement oriented. Women are stereotyped to be *communal*—warm, empathic, and emotional. Are these stereotypes supported by gender differences in behavior? Yes. Men are more likely tobe the CEOs of Fortune 500 companies. Women are more likely to be the primary caregivers of children. If we look only at these statistics, we will find more than a kernel of truth to the stereotype. But does this gender segregation in the boardroom and at the playground really imply biological differences in traits? Not necessarily. **FIGURE 10.8** shows what happened when people were asked to rate the traits listed in a brief description of an average man or an average woman, with either no information about the person's occupation, role as a full-time employee, or role as a full-time homemaker (Eagly & Steffen, 1984). With no information, people readily applied their stereotypes, assuming that a woman is more communal than a man and that a man is more agentic than a woman. But this may just result from assumptions about social roles of men and women because occupation completely trumps anatomy: A homemaker is judged to be more communal and less agentic than an employee, regardless of that person's gender. More recent research shows a similar effect in the context of language use (Senden et al., 2020). When participants freely created sentences from assorted pronouns and traits, they described women as more communal and men as more agentic. However, if they were also asked to use occupation labels in their sentences, they described women and men in the same occupation as similarly agentic or communal. For example, they created sentences portraying a nurse as having communal traits regardless of whether the nurse was a "he" or a "she." These findings support the idea from social role theory that stereotypes about social roles partly motivate gender stereotypes.

Social pressures can shape the roles in which various groups find themselves, and differences in stereotypes follow suit (Croft et al., 2015). The traditional

Figure 10.8

How Social Roles Can Determine Stereotypes

With no other information, people assume that (a) women are more communal than men and that (b) men are more agentic than women. But social roles might explain these stereotypes: Homemakers (either male or female) are assumed to be more communal than employees, and employees (either male or female) are assumed to be more agentic.

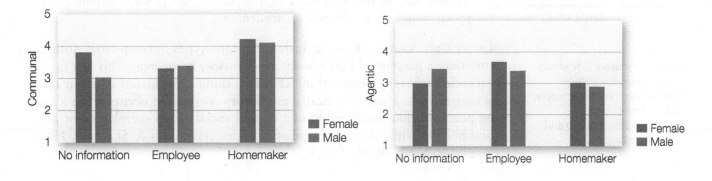

stereotype of Black Americans as lazy and ignorant was developed in the pre-Civil War South, when the vast majority of them were forced to work as slaves and excluded from schools. Similarly, Jews have been stereotyped as money hungry or cheap, a stereotype that developed in Europe at a time when Jews were not allowed to own land, and they needed to become involved in trade and commerce in order to survive economically. The particular stereotypes attached to groups are often a function of such historical and culturally embedded social constraints.

The Stereotype Content Model   The stereotype content model posits that stereotypes develop on the basis of how groups relate to one another along two basic dimensions (Fiske et al., 2002). The first is status: Is the group perceived as having relatively low or high status in society, relative to other groups? The second is cooperation in a very broad sense that seems to encompass likability: Is the group perceived to have a cooperative/helpful or a competitive/harmful relationship with other groups in that society?

The answers to these questions lead to predictions about the traits that are likely to be ascribed to the group. Higher status brings assumptions about competence, prestige, and power, whereas lower status leads to stereotypes of incompetence and laziness. These two dimensions of evaluation, *warmth* and *competence,* have long been acknowledged to be fundamental to how we view others. When we consider that these dimensions are largely independent, we see that stereotypes can cluster together in one of four quadrants in a warmth-by-competence space (**FIGURE 10.9**). For example, groups that are seen as cooperative/helpful within the society are seen as warm and trustworthy, whereas groups that are viewed as competitive/harmful within the larger society are seen as cold and conniving (Cuddy et al., 2008).

People have different emotional reactions to groups whose stereotypes fit into one of these quadrants (Cuddy, Fiske, & Glick, 2007). Groups that are stereotyped as personally warm but incompetent (e.g., elderly people, physically disabled people) elicit pity and sympathy. Groups perceived as low in warmth but high in competence (e.g., rich people, Asians, Jews, professionals from underrepresented groups) elicit envy and jealousy. Groups stereotyped in purely positive terms as both warm and competent tend to be ingroups or groups that are seen as the cultural norm in a society. To the degree that these groups are valued, they generally elicit pride and admiration. Finally, groups stereotyped in purely negative terms as both cold and incompetent (e.g., homeless people, drug addicts, welfare recipients) elicit disgust and scorn. Researchers have argued that this model is too simplistic because it fails to consider another fundamental dimension of stereotyping: perceptions of morality (Leach et al., 2007). In addition, stereotypes are often more complex than the model implies; for example, a group may be stereotyped as high in competence in some domains (e.g., sports) and low in others (e.g., academics).

Illusory Correlations   In some instances, stereotypes develop from nothing more than a perceptual bias known as an **illusory correlation**. This is a faulty perception whereby people think that two things are related when in reality they are not. More specifically, an illusory correlation occurs when a person perceives that membership in a certain social group correlates—or goes hand in hand with—a certain type of behavior (Hamilton & Sherman, 1989; Costello & Watts, 2019).

Figure 10.9

The Stereotype Content Model

According to the stereotype content model, the stereotypes we have of different groups can range along two dimensions: competence and warmth. As a result, we have different emotional reactions to different types of groups.

[Data from Fiske et al., 2002]

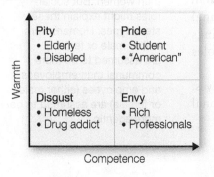

Illusory correlation A tendency to assume an association between two rare occurrences, such as being in an underrepresented group and performing negative actions.

These kinds of illusory correlations occur when two things that are generally rare or distinctive co-occur in close proximity to one another. When strange or unusual things happen, our attention is drawn to them because they stand out. And when two unusual things co-occur, our mind automatically assumes a connection. For most ingroup members, outgroup members are distinctive. Also, most people, regardless of their group membership, tend to find socially undesirable behaviors distinctive. (Fortunately, most of the time, people do good things rather than bad things!) So when ingroup members see outgroup members acting negatively—for example, in news reports about Black men accused of violent crimes—two distinctive features of the situation, an outgroup member and an undesirable behavior, grab their attention. This doubly distinctive perception results in believing the two attributes go together, even when the outgroup is no more likely than the ingroup to engage in bad behavior (Hamilton et al., 1985).

Why Do We Apply Stereotypes?

We have looked at where stereotypes come from, and now we consider why we apply and maintain them. Research reveals that stereotypes have four primary psychological functions.

1. Stereotypes Are Cognitive Tools for Simplifying Everyday Life   People rely on stereotypes to simplify social perception. It would take a lot of effort to assess every person we interact with solely on the basis of individual characteristics and behaviors. Stereotypes allow people to draw on their beliefs about the traits that characterize typical group members to make inferences about what a given group member is like or how the person is likely to act. Imagine that you have two neighbors, one a librarian and the other a veterinarian. If you had a book title on the tip of your tongue, you would more likely consult the librarian than the vet—unless it was a book about animals! In other words, stereotyping is a cognitive shortcut that allows people to draw social inferences quickly and conserve limited cognitive resources while navigating a pretty complex social environment (Taylor, 1981). If stereotyping does in fact conserve mental resources, then people should be more likely to fall back on their stereotypes when they are stressed, tired, under time pressure, or otherwise cognitively overloaded. Many lines of research have shown that this indeed is the case (e.g., Kruglanski & Freund, 1983; Macrae et al., 1993).

2. Stereotypes Justify Prejudice and Discrimination   Stereotypes aren't mere by-products of our limited cognitive capacities. People also are sometimes motivated to hang on to beliefs to justify their prejudices. One example is that once a country has declared war on another nation, stereotypes of that nation become more negative. In addition, encountering members of outgroups sometimes automatically elicits potent negative feelings, such as fear and disgust (e.g., Esses et al., 1993). People may generate a negative stereotype of a group to justify their feelings.

According to the **justification suppression model** of prejudice expression (Crandall & Eshleman, 2003), stereotypes can provide people with supposedly acceptable explanations for having negative feelings about a group. If, for example, a person stereotypes all Hispanics as aggressive, then he can justify why he feels frightened around Hispanics. From this perspective, the negative

▲ The idea that stereotypes are mental heuristics that we fall back on to save time in social perception has been turned into a tongue-in-cheek T-shirt message.

Justification suppression model The idea that people endorse and freely express stereotypes in part to justify their own negative affective reactions to outgroup members.

feelings sometimes come first, and the stereotypes make those feelings seem acceptable—or even rational.

To test this idea, Chris Crandall and colleagues (2011) set up a situation in which they induced some people to have a negative feeling toward a group *prior* to forming a stereotype about that group. They did this by repeatedly pairing a group that participants knew nothing about—people from the country Eritrea—with unrelated negative words or images (e.g., sad faces) to create an implicit negative reaction to the group. In this way, half of the participants developed a negative affective association toward Eritreans, whereas those in a control group did not. Afterward, participants were given a list of traits, such as *dangerous*, *violent*, and *unfriendly*, and asked to indicate whether those traits were descriptive of people from Eritrea. Participants trained to have a negative affective reaction toward Eritreans were more likely than those in the control condition to stereotype Eritreans as cold and threatening. After all, if the people of Eritrea are perceived as cold and threatening, then one's negative feelings suddenly seem justified.

Dehumanization The tendency to hold stereotypic views of outgroup members as animals rather than as humans.

Dehumanization. Stereotypes justify negative behavior as well as negative feelings. One common way people justify negative behavior is by dehumanizing outgroup members. **Dehumanization** is viewing outgroup members as less than fully human. The most extreme form of dehumanization is to compare outgroup members directly with nonhuman animals. Blatant examples of this can be seen in the way that nations portray groups they intend to kill. During World War II, Nazi propaganda portrayed European Jews as disease-carrying rats, Americans portrayed the Japanese as vermin (**FIGURE 10.10a**), and the Japanese portrayed Americans as bloodthirsty eagles mauling innocent Japanese civilians. One of our students who served in the U.S. military during the 1991 Persian Gulf War showed us a flyer dehumanizing Iraqi people (**FIGURE 10.10b**) that was circulated among the soldiers. In two studies of actual police officers, Goff and colleagues (2014) found that the more an officer implicitly associated Black people with apes, the more likely that officer was to have a record of using force on Black children more than on children of other groups.

Figure 10.10

Propaganda used by Americans during World War II (a) and during the 1991 Persian Gulf War (b) to dehumanize Japanese and Iraqi people, respectively.

[Part (a): U.S. National Archives and Records Administration]

These tendencies to think about members of outgroups as nonhuman animals have likely been partly responsible for fueling many historical examples of horrible treatment of outgroups, such as slavery, bombings, and genocide (Kteily & Bruneau, 2017). One study, for example, showed that hearing about acts of terrorism by Muslims against American and British targets in 2013 made American and British participants more likely to dehumanize Muslims and support violent countermeasures such as bombing entire countries believed to be harboring terrorists (Kteily et al., 2015).

As we discussed in our coverage of cognitive dissonance (chapter 6), when people act in ways that fall short of their moral standards, they often attempt to seek justifications. In times of extreme intergroup conflict, when innocent people are being killed, perpetrators of that violence—and even those standing by—often reduce the dissonance by regarding the victims as subhuman and therefore less deserving of moral consideration. Indeed, Castano and Giner-Sorolla (2006) found that when people were made to feel a sense of collective responsibility for their ingroup's mass killing of an outgroup, they viewed members of that outgroup as less human.

Once the outgroup has been reduced to animals who do not deserve moral consideration, the perpetrators feel less inhibited about committing further violence (Kelman, 1976; Kteily et al., 2015; Staub, 1989; Viki et al., 2013). Indeed, in one study, people were more likely to administer a higher intensity of shock to punish people described in dehumanizing (i.e., animalistic) terms than people described in distinctively human terms (Bandura et al., 1975).

Infrahumanization. A subtler form of dehumanization is **infrahumanization** (Leyens, Paladino et al., 2000). When people infrahumanize outgroup members, they do not compare them directly with nonhuman animals. Rather, they perceive those outgroup members as lacking qualities viewed as being unique to humans. These qualities include complex human emotions such as hope, humiliation, nostalgia, and sympathy. People attribute these uniquely human emotions more to members of their ingroup than to outgroup members (Gaunt et al., 2002; Leyens et al., 2001).

Infrahumanization has important repercussions for people's treatment of outgroup members. Cuddy, Rock, and Norton (2007) looked at people's desire to help with relief efforts in the aftermath of Hurricane Katrina, which caused massive destruction to parts of the southeastern United States in 2005. Participants in their study were less likely to infer that racial outgroup members who suffered from the hurricane were experiencing uniquely human emotions, such as remorse and mourning, than were racial ingroup members. The more participants infrahumanized the hurricane victims in this way, the less likely they were to report that they intended to take actions to help those individuals recover from the devastation. These effects mirror other evidence indicating that Whites assume that Blacks who have faced hardships feel less pain than Whites who have faced similar hardships (Hoffman & Trawalter, 2016; Hoffman et al., 2016).

Sexual Objectification. Women as a group are subject to a specific form of dehumanization known as **sexual objectification**, which consists of thinking about women in a narrow way, as if their physical appearance were all that matters. Based on early theorists such as the psychoanalyst Karen Horney and the philosopher Simone de Beauvoir, Barbara Fredrickson and Tomi-Ann Roberts's (1997) **objectification theory** notes that in most if not all societies, women are objectified by being judged primarily on the basis of their physical appearance. Although objectification does not involve equating women with animals, it is a way of denying that women possess the psychological characteristics that make them fully human, such as a unique point of view and a complex mental life.

In assessing this idea, researchers found that well-known women, but not men, were perceived more like objects—cold, incompetent, and without morality—when participants were asked to focus on the women's appearance than when they were asked to focus on the women as people (Heflick & Goldenberg, 2009; Heflick et al., 2011). For example, in studies carried out during Barack Obama's first term as president, they found that the first lady, Michelle Obama, was perceived as lower in warmth, competence, and morality when participants focused on her appearance. In contrast, focusing on President Obama's appearance did not have a similar effect on ratings of him.

Infrahumanization The perception that outgroup members lack qualities viewed as being unique to human beings, such as language, rational intelligence, and complex social emotions.

Sexual objectification The tendency to think about women in a narrow way as objects rather than as full humans, as if their physical appearance were all that matters.

Objectification theory A theory which proposes that the cultural value placed on women's appearance leads people to view women more as objects than as full human beings.

Objectification of women can help justify exploitation of them. Integrating objectification theory and terror management theory, Jamie Goldenberg and colleagues proposed that objectification also may help people avoid acknowledging the fact that we humans are animals and therefore mortal (e.g., Goldenberg et al., 2009). Portraying women in an idealized (often airbrushed) way and only as objects of beauty or sexual appeal reduces their connection to animalistic physicality. Supporting this view, Goldenberg and colleagues have shown that reminding both men and women of their mortality, or of the similarities between humans and other animals, increases negative reactions to women who exemplify the creaturely nature of the body: women who are overtly sexual, menstruating, pregnant, or breast-feeding. This line of research suggests that objectifying women as idealized symbols of beauty and femininity and rejecting women who seem to fall short of those ideals helps both men and women deny their own animal nature.

3. Stereotypes Justify the Status Quo Stereotypes don't justify only our emotions and behavior; they also justify the status quo. Evidence suggests that the stereotypes we have of groups are often *ambivalent*—including positive traits alongside negative traits. High-status groups that are assumed to be competent are also more likely to be stereotyped as cold. Lower-status groups might be stereotyped as being less intelligent or successful but are also often seen as warm and friendly. According to *system justification theory*, these ambivalent stereotypes help maintain the status quo by justifying the way things are (Jost & Banaji, 1994). In some ways, this is the flip side of social role theory: We not only assume the traits people have by the roles they enact, we also assert that they *should* be in those roles because they have the traits that are needed for those roles.

System justification theory suggests that those who have high status in a society will often come to view those with lower status as being less intelligent and industrious than their own group to justify their own superior economic position. If advantaged members of a society didn't generate such justifications, they would have to admit that deep injustices exist that they should all be working to rectify; such rectification would alter the status quo, with advantaged groups potentially losing their advantages and everyone experiencing upheaval. Indeed, subtly priming people with economic inequality makes them more likely to endorse the stereotype that wealthy individuals are smart and deserving (Connor et al., PSPB, 2021), an effect that may reflect a desire to justify a system that divides the rich and the poor.

Although higher-status people show a stronger tendency to justify the status quo, those who are disadvantaged sometimes do so as well. For example, when people are made to feel that the stability of their nation is in question, members of both lower- and higher-status ethnic groups more strongly endorse the belief that the higher-status group is relatively more competent and that the lower-status group is relatively warmer (Jost et al., 2005).

How do these complementary stereotypes play into the motivation to justify existing status differences among groups? By favoring ambivalent stereotypes, groups that are disadvantaged in terms of their status in society can still pride themselves on their warmth. With that positive stereotype to hold on to, the negative stereotypes don't seem so bad. Similarly, groups with power and status can assuage any guilt by acknowledging the warmth of those with lower status. We see this most strikingly with gender. Modern theories of gender bias point to **ambivalent sexism** (Glick & Fiske, 1996), which

Ambivalent sexism The pairing of *hostile* beliefs about women with *benevolent* but patronizing beliefs about them.

pairs *hostile* beliefs about women (that women are incompetent or push too hard for gender equality) with *benevolent* beliefs (that women are pure and more compassionate than men). Although women primed to think about hostile sexism are motivated to fight for greater gender equality, reminders of benevolent sexism seem to only encourage their support for the status quo (Becker & Wright, 2011).

Research also suggests that people prefer outgroup members to conform to prevailing stereotypes. Women who are assertive and direct are often judged negatively, whereas the same actions by men lead to admiration (Rudman, 1998). Terror management researchers (Schimel et al., 1999) have shown that reminding people of their mortality, which motivates people to want their worldviews upheld, leads heterosexual White Americans to prefer Germans, Black Americans, and gay men who conform to prevailing American stereotypes of these groups over those who behave counterstereotypically.

4. Stereotypes Are Self-Esteem Boosters As described previously, self-esteem threats not only increase negative feelings about outgroup members but also lead to negative beliefs about them and make negative stereotypes of such groups more accessible to consciousness (Spencer et al., 1998). Viewing members of outgroups as stupid, lazy, cowardly, or immoral can help people feel better about themselves (Fein & Spencer, 1997). Other evidence also supports the role of stereotyping in boosting the perceiver's self-esteem. For example, if a member of a disliked outgroup praises us, we shouldn't be too motivated to apply a negative stereotype. But what happens when that person gives us negative feedback?

Research by Lisa Sinclair and Ziva Kunda (1999) showed that we selectively focus on different ways of categorizing people, depending on these self-serving motivations. After all, people belong to myriad different social categories, and the intersectionality of multiple identities means that motivation can play a determining role in shaping when a person is categorized in one group or another. In their study, White Canadian participants imagined receiving either praise or criticism from a Black doctor or a White doctor. The researchers measured whether stereotypic knowledge was automatically brought to mind. Participants who were praised by the Black doctor activated positive stereotypes of doctors but not negative stereotypes about Blacks. However, participants who were criticized by the Black doctor activated the negative stereotype of Blacks and not the positive stereotype of doctors.

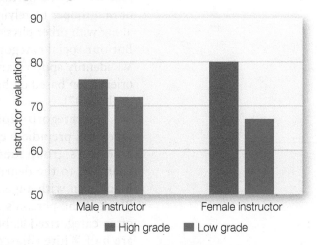

Further research suggests that once activated, these stereotypes likely bias people's judgments. In one study, for example, female and male faculty members received similar course evaluations from students who did well in their courses, but students who received lower grades evaluated female instructors as less competent than their male peers (**FIGURE 10.11**; Sinclair & Kunda, 2000).

How Do Stereotypes Come into Play?

So far, we have covered where stereotypes come from and why we tend to rely on them. But how do they actually work? Take a look at the guy in the

Figure 10.11

Self-Esteem Threat and Gender Bias

Although student evaluations of male and female instructors are equivalent among students who perform well, students who receive a lower grade rate female instructors as less competent than male instructors.

[Data from Sinclair & Kunda, 1999]

THINK ABOUT

Achieve
Science of Everyday Life:
Self-Esteem Threats

photo. What's your impression of him? How did you form that impression? You might see the jacket, collared shirt, and neatly trimmed hair and think he's a young, attractive, professional man. You've just categorized him on the basis of age, appearance, educational level, and gender. He looks to be White, so we can throw a racial categorization in as well. From this, you are likely to activate some relevant stereotypes—intelligent, competent, well liked. Because you have no reason not to, you will probably be happy to apply these judgments to him. In general, we love sizing people up, and this guy seems approachable. If he asked you to help him load a dresser into his van, you would, right?

Unfortunately, many young women did just that. They categorized him as you probably did. They had no way of knowing one additional group he belonged to—serial killers. The man in the photo is Ted Bundy, who brutally raped and murdered more than 30 women, mostly college students, during the 1970s. It is likely that the categorizations activated by his appearance helped him carry out his heinous crimes.

Research has delved into the process by which we initially *categorize* a person as belonging to a group, *activate* stereotypes associated with that group, and then *apply* those stereotypes in forming judgments of that person. Let's learn more about how this process works.

Categorization   The categories we attend to most readily for people are gender, age, and other cues that might signal how we should treat one another (Fiske & Taylor, 2008; Kurzban et al., 2001). Because telling friend from foe was a life-or-death decision for our evolutionary ancestors, our brains have also adapted to form these categorizations using whatever cues will quickly do the job. We may be particularly likely to categorize an individual as an ingrouper or outgrouper by relying on cues such as accent, mode of dress, and adornment, along with other physical features, such as skin tone, body shape, and hair color. But our social categories are flexible enough to be cued by a host of things. We identify sports teams using different-colored uniforms and can guess sexual orientation based on how a person walks (Johnson & Tassinary, 2005; Johnson et al., 2007).

The categorization process isn't entirely objective. A perceiver's stereotypes and prejudices can shape how someone is categorized, especially when a person's group identity is ambiguous (Freeman & Johnson, 2016). For example, to the degree that people tend to stereotypically associate young Black men with anger, they are quicker to categorize an angry face as being Black if the person's race is rather ambiguous. Mixed-race individuals are often categorized as being members of the stigmatized group even when they are half White (Blascovich et al., 1997; Halberstadt et al., 2011; Ho et al., 2011).

Once we categorize a person as an outgroup member, we tend to view that person in stereotypic ways. One reason this happens is that the very act of categorizing makes us more likely to assume that all members of the outgroup category are alike. Merely by categorizing people into outgroups, we tend to view those individuals as being more similar to each other—that is, more homogeneous—than they really are and as being more similar to each other than ingroup members are to each other (Linville et al., 1989; Park & Rothbart, 1982; Quattrone, 1986). This tendency is called the **outgroup homogeneity effect.** If you've ever heard someone say "Those people are all alike," you have probably witnessed this effect.

Outgroup homogeneity effect The tendency to view individuals in outgroups as being more similar to each other than they really are.

The primary explanation for the outgroup homogeneity effect is that we are very familiar with members of our own group and therefore tend to see them as unique individuals. We have less detailed knowledge about members of outgroups, so it's easier simply to assume that they are all alike. In addition, we often know outgroup members only in a particular context or role. For example, a suburban White American might know Black Americans mainly as sports figures, hip-hop artists, and criminals on TV. This role-restricted knowledge also encourages viewing outgroup members as being less diverse than they actually are.

In one demonstration of the outgroup homogeneity effect, psychologists (Quattrone & Jones, 1980) asked university students to watch a video of a student from the participant's own university or from a different university make a decision (e.g., between listening to rock or classical music). The participants were then asked to estimate what percentage of people from that person's university would make the same decision. They estimated that a higher percentage of the person's fellow students would have the same musical preference when they were from a different university than when they were from the participants' own university. So when you assume that "they are all alike," you can infer that what one likes, they all like, but you probably also like to believe that "we" are a diverse assortment of unique individuals.

I don't know officer: They all look alike to me...

[Hagen/Cartoonstock]

The outgroup homogeneity effect not only extends to the inferences we make about a person's attitudes but also leads to very real perceptual confusions. We actually do *see* outgroup members as looking more similar to each other, a phenomenon that can have profound consequences for the accuracy of eyewitness accounts (Wells et al., 2006). This type of perceptual bias was first illustrated in a series of studies in which participant ingroup and outgroup members interacted in a group discussion (Taylor et al., 1978). When later asked to remember who said what—that is, to match a comment with a person—the participants made an interesting pattern of errors. They were more accurate at remembering ingroup statements than outgroup statements. But more telling, they were likelier to mistake one outgroup member for another. These confusions happen when we group other people together on the basis of visible categories, such as gender, race, age, skin tone, and attractiveness, but they even happen when we group others on the basis of nonvisible categories, such as sexual orientation and attitudes (e.g., Klauer & Wegener, 1998; van Knippenberg & Dijksterhuis, 2000).

Stereotype Activation After we make an initial categorization, the stereotypes that we associate with that category are often automatically brought to mind, or *activated*, whether we *want* them to be or not. Sure, some folks have blatant negative beliefs about others that they are happy to bend your ear about. Others want to believe that they never ever judge people on the basis of stereotypes. Most of us probably are somewhere in the middle. Individuals raised and exposed to the same cultural information all have knowledge of which stereotypes are culturally associated with which groups (Devine, 1989). This information has made it into those mental file folders in our head, even if we have tried to flag it as false and malicious. When we meet someone from Wisconsin, we mentally pull up our Wisconsin folder on the state to be better prepared for discussing the intricacies of cheese making and the Green Bay Packers. We do this unconsciously and without necessarily intending to; the association is ingrained and automatic, based on cultural learning.

Patricia Devine (1989) provided an early and influential demonstration of automatic stereotype activation. She reasoned that anything that reminds White Americans of Black Americans would activate the trait *aggressive* because it is strongly associated with the Black American stereotype. To test this hypothesis, she subliminally exposed White participants to 100 words. Each word was presented so briefly (for only 80 milliseconds) that participants could not detect the words and experienced them as mere flashes of light. Depending on which condition participants were in, 80% (or 20%) of the words—some very explicit—were related to the Black American stereotype (e.g., *lazy, ghetto, slavery, welfare, basketball, unemployed*), while the rest of the words were neutral.

Then, as part of an apparently separate experiment, participants read a paragraph describing a person named Donald, who behaved in ways that could be seen as either hostile or merely assertive. Participants primed with the Black stereotype interpreted Donald's ambiguous behaviors as more hostile than did those who didn't get this prime. Even though *aggressive* was not primed outright, because it is part of the stereotype schema for Black Americans, priming that stereotype cued people to perceive the next person they encountered as being aggressive.

Importantly, this effect was the same for those who reported low and high levels of prejudice toward Black Americans. However, it is important to clarify that Devine's study primed people directly with stereotypes about Blacks, not simply with the social category "Blacks" or a photo of a Black individual. Other research suggests that some people are less likely to activate stereotypic biases automatically. For example, Lepore and Brown (1997) showed that people with stronger prejudices activate a negative stereotype about Blacks when they are simply exposed to the category information (i.e., the word *Blacks*), whereas those who are low in prejudice don't show this activation at all.

Additional research has suggested that the goal of being egalitarian can itself be implicitly activated when people encounter an outgroup and can help keep negative stereotypes from coming to mind (Moskowitz, 2010; Moskowitz & Li, 2011; Sassenberg & Moskowitz, 2005). The takeaway message seems to be that although low-prejudice individuals may be aware of culturally prevalent stereotypes about outgroups, they often do not activate those stereotypes.

How Do Stereotypes Contribute to Bias?

Once stereotypes are activated, we use them to perceive and make judgments about others in ways that confirm, rather than disconfirm, them. Stereotypes influence information processing at various stages, from the first few milliseconds of perception to the way we remember actions years in the future. Let's take a closer look at how stereotypes color people's understanding of others in ways that can have very important consequences.

APPLICATION
Stereotypes Influence Perception

Just after midnight on February 4, 1999, four New York City police officers were in pursuit of a serial rapist believed to be Black. They approached a

23-year-old African immigrant, Amadou Diallo, in front of his Bronx apartment building. Assuming that the police would want to see his identification, Diallo reached into his jacket and pulled out his wallet. One of the officers saw the situation differently and called out, "Gun!" The officers fired 41 bullets, 19 of which struck Diallo, killing him. Bruce Springsteen wrote a song about the incident, "American Skin (41 Shots)." The officers were acquitted of any wrongdoing by a jury in Albany, New York (about 150 miles from New York City), a decision that sparked public protest. The city eventually settled a wrongful-death lawsuit by Diallo's family for $3 million. Many factors likely played roles in the tragedy, but one thing is clear: In his hand Diallo held a wallet that was mistaken for a gun. Can research on stereotyping help us understand how this could happen?

Yes. In fact, this event inspired a line of research on what has come to be called the **shooter bias**. This bias has to do with the stereotyped association of Blacks with violence and crime (e.g., Eberhardt et al., 2004; Payne, 2001). We know that people process stereotype-consistent information more quickly than stereotype-inconsistent information, all else being equal. What is surprising is how quickly stereotypes can exert this influence on perception.

In three studies (Correll et al., 2002), White American participants played a video game in which they were shown photographs of Black and White men holding an object (sample images appear in **FIGURE 10.12**) and were asked to press the "shoot" button if the individual was holding a gun and the "don't shoot" button if the individual was not holding a gun. The experimenters predicted that White participants would be faster to shoot an armed person if he were Black than if he were White. In addition, they should be faster to make the correct decision to not shoot an unarmed person if he was White rather than

Shooter bias The tendency to mistakenly see objects in the hands of Black men as guns.

Figure 10.12

The Shooter Bias

In studies that document the shooter bias, participants play a video game in which they are instructed to shoot at anyone who is armed but to avoid shooting anyone who is unarmed.

[Photos: Bernd Wittenbrink, University of Chicago, Center for Decision Research]

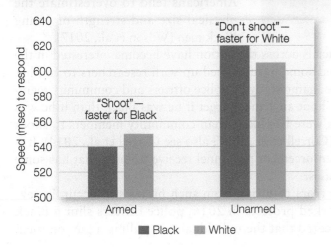

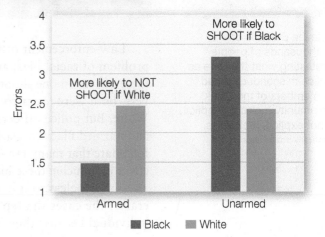

Black. The bar graph on the left in **FIGURE 10.12** shows that this is just what happened. When in another study (shown in the right graph of **FIGURE 10.12**) participants were forced to make decisions under more extreme time pressure, they made the same kind of error that the police made when they shot Diallo. That is, participants were more likely to shoot an unarmed Black man than they were to shoot an unarmed White man. Evidence from these studies suggests that these effects resulted more from the individual's knowledge of the cultural stereotype that Blacks are dangerous than from personal prejudice toward Blacks. In fact, in a follow-up study, the researchers found that even Black participants showed these same shooter biases.

Further studies using the same shooter-game paradigm have revealed that the shooter bias is affected by a number of additional factors. People show a stronger shooter bias if the context itself is threatening—say, a dark street corner rather than a sunlit church (Correll et al., 2011). It's also stronger when the Blacks in the photos look more prototypically Black—in other words, when they have darker skin and more typically Afrocentric features (Ma & Correll, 2010). This finding reveals part of a general tendency for stereotypes to be applied more strongly to those who seem most prototypical of a group. In fact, anything that reinforces, justifies, or increases the accessibility of a racial stereotype strengthens the likelihood that the stereotype will be applied (Correll et al., 2007). Research suggests that people make these mistakes of misidentifying an object as a gun when it's in the hands of someone who is Black rather than White even when perceiving 5-year-old children (Todd et al., 2016). No wonder women like Iesha Evans, a 28-year-old mother of a 5-year-old son, came out to protest police brutality in the wake of several high-profile police shootings of Black men in the summer of 2016.

The stereotype of Black American men as threatening leads to another erroneous perception that may contribute to police overreacting to Black American men they encounter. A series of studies has shown that non-Black Americans tend to overestimate the physical size and strength of young Black men (Wilson et al., 2017).

▲ Iesha Evans is one of thousands of people protesting what they see as police misconduct aimed at members of the Black community fueled by implicit, if not explicit, racial bias.
[REUTERS/Jonathan Bachman]

Law-enforcement officials across the nation have become interested in the problem of racial bias, and some have teamed up with researchers to combat these effects. In one shooter-game study of police officers and community members, both were faster to shoot an armed target if he was Black than if he was White. But police officers were less likely than community members to shoot an unarmed Black target (Correll et al., 2007; also see Correll et al., 2014). It is fortunate that many law-enforcement personnel receive training that has some effect in reducing these biases.

Nevertheless, tragic errors resulting from such biases still occur. In several of the cases that sparked protests in 2016, police officers shot a Black individual because they feared that the individual was pulling a gun on them or might do so. For example, in 2014, 12-year-old Tamir Rice was shot dead by a police officer who mistook the Black child's pellet gun for a handgun (Almasy, 2015). In another incident, a police officer shot a 47-year-old Black therapist, Charles Kinsey, who was trying to assist his severely autistic patient who had wandered away from a group home and was sitting in the middle of the street playing with a toy truck. Lying on the ground with his hands in the air and a bullet in his leg, Kinsey asked the officer why he had just shot him. The officer responded, "I don't know" (Silva, 2017). Given the many incidents that have been documented over the last decade, it is not surprising that Black Americans react to images of police officers with more anticipated anxiety and greater flight-or-fight intentions than White Americans do (Lloyd et al., 2020). ■

Interpreting Behavior If stereotypes actually can lead us to sometimes see something that isn't there, it should come as no surprise that they also affect how we interpret ambiguous information and behaviors (e.g., Kunda & Thagard, 1996).

Research shows that people interpret the same behavior differently when it is performed by individuals who belong to stereotyped groups. In one study (Duncan, 1976), White students watched a videotape of a discussion between two men that ended just after one of the men shoved the other. Was the shove harmless horseplay, or was it an act of aggression? If participants (who were White) watched a version of the tape in which the man delivering the shove was White, only 17% described the shove as violent, and 42% said it was playful. However, if they watched a version in which the same shove was delivered by a Black man, 75% said it was violent, and only 6% said it was playful.

In fact, stereotypes influence the interpretation of ambiguous behaviors even when those stereotypes are primed outside conscious awareness. When police and probation officers were primed beneath conscious awareness with words related to the Black stereotype and then read a vignette about a shoplifting incident, they rated the offender as being more hostile and deserving of punishment if he was Black than if he was White (Graham & Lowery, 2004).

Many other studies have similarly shown that stereotypes associated with race, social class, gender, or profession can lend different meanings to the same ambiguous information (e.g., Chaxel, 2015; Darley & Gross, 1983; Dunning & Sherman, 1997). Evidence indicates that stereotypes set up a hypothesis about a person, but because of the confirmation bias, we interpret ambiguous information as evidence supporting that hypothesis.

The Ultimate Attribution Error Stereotypes also bias our explanations of interpretation after events have played out. You may remember that we tend to make self-serving attributions for our own experiences: Good things happen because of us, and bad things happen because of the situation. We show a similar bias when we make attributions for fellow ingroup members and exactly the opposite tendency when explaining the behavior of outgroup members (Hilton & von Hippel, 1996). This is called the **ultimate attribution error** (Hewstone, 1990; Pettigrew, 1979). When an outgroup member does something negative, or when an ingroup member does something positive, this is consistent with our automatic preference for ingroups over outgroups (Perdue et al., 1990). We infer that it's the dispositional character of the groups that caused the behaviors: *We* do good things because *we* are good people. *They* do bad things because *they* are bad people.

Ultimate attribution error The tendency to believe that bad actions by outgroup members occur *because of their internal dispositions* and good actions by them occur *because of the situation*, while believing the reverse for ingroup members.

Of course, every now and again, we might be forced to admit that an outgroup member performed well or behaved admirably and an ingroup member performed or behaved poorly. But in such cases, the attribution veers toward the situation. Attributing negative outgroup behavior to the person but positive outgroup behavior to the situation reinforces negative stereotypes about the outgroup and belief in the superiority of the ingroup. Not surprisingly, this tendency is strongest in ingroup members highest in prejudice against the outgroup (e.g., Greenberg & Rosenfield, 1979).

The ultimate attribution error has been applied primarily to ethnic prejudice, but stereotypes also influence how people make attributions for men's and women's behavior (e.g., Deaux, 1984). When men succeed on a stereotypically masculine task, observers tend to attribute that success to the men's dispositional ability, but when women perform well on the same task, observers tend to attribute that success to luck or effort. Likewise, men's failures on stereotypically masculine tasks are often attributed to bad luck and lack of effort, whereas women's failures on the same tasks are attributed to their lack of ability. In this research, both men and women often exhibit this pattern of attributions: Regardless of their gender, people tend to explain men's and women's behaviors in ways that fit culturally widespread stereotypes.

Stereotypes Distort Memory   Finally, stereotypes bias how we recall information. Back in chapter 3, we described a study in which White participants were shown a picture of a Black man in a business suit being threatened by a young White man holding a straight razor (Allport & Postman, 1947). As that participant described the scene to another participant, who described it to another participant, and so on, the story tended to shift to the razor being in the Black man's hand and the business suit being on the White man. Rumors often can distort the facts because our stereotypes bias what we recall (and what we retell) in ways that fit our expectations. Since that initial demonstration, similar findings have also been shown even when the stereotype isn't evoked until *after* the information has been encoded—and for a wide range of stereotypes regarding ethnicity, occupation, gender, sexual orientation, and social class (e.g., Dodson et al., 2008; Frawley, 2008).

 APPLICATION
Stereotypes Tend to Be Self-Confirming

The phenomena we've discussed are just a few of the many ways in which stereotypes systematically bias how we think and make judgments about other individuals and groups. A harmful consequence of this influence is that stereotypes reinforce themselves, which makes them relatively impervious to change (Darley & Gross, 1983; Fiske & Taylor, 2008; Rothbart, 1981). Stereotypes lead us to attend to information that fits those stereotypes and to ignore information that does not. When we do observe behaviors that are inconsistent with our stereotypes, we tend to explain them away as isolated instances or exceptions to the rule (Allport, 1954). Because stereotypes can be activated unconsciously, people may not even be aware that stereotypes are biasing what they perceive. Instead, they believe that their reactions to and interpretations of stereotyped individuals are free of prejudice because they assume that they are looking at the world objectively. When it comes to stereotypes, believing is seeing. ■

SECTION REVIEW Stereotyping: The Cognitive Companion of Prejudice

Stereotypes can help promote and justify prejudice, even if they are positive.

Where Do Stereotypes Come From?

- A kernel of truth that is overblown and overgeneralized
- Assumptions about group differences in traits inferred from group differences in social roles
- Generalizations about a group's warmth and competence that are based on judgments of cooperativeness and status
- Illusory correlations that make unrelated things seem related

Why Do We Apply Stereotypes?

- To simplify the process of social perception and to conserve mental energy
- To justify prejudice and discrimination, including by dehumanizing, infrahumanizing, or objectifying others
- To justify the status quo and to maintain a sense of predictability
- To maintain and bolster self-esteem

How Do Stereotypes Affect Judgment?

- Categorization increases the perceived homogeneity of outgroup members, thereby reinforcing stereotypes.
- Stereotypes can be activated automatically, coloring how we perceive, interpret, and communicate about the characteristics and behaviors of outgroup (and ingroup) members.
- Stereotypes influence how we perceive and interpret behavior, as well as how we remember information.
- Because of these biases, stereotypes tend to be self-perpetuating, even in the face of disconfirming information.

CRITICAL LEARNING EXERCISES

1. Think about a relative or friend who has a prejudice against a particular group. How would the theories and research in this chapter explain the person's prejudice? Can you think of any factors involved that are not covered in the chapter?

2. Go to www.projectimplicit.com. Take the IAT regarding your implicit associations with three of the social identities available there (e.g., Black, old, disabled). If you seemed to have negative associations with any of them, why do you think that might be? And if not, why not?

3. Think of two stereotypes that are prevalent in your culture. Do you think they are based on kernels of truth? If so, why? If not, what other factors discussed in the chapter could account for those particular stereotypes? Can you think of any factors not covered in the chapter that also contribute to stereotypes?

4. Given the four psychological functions of stereotypes, what do you think could be done at a societal level to reduce both their prevalence and their role in biased judgments and behavior against stereotyped groups?

Don't stop now! Check out our videos and additional resources located at: www.macmillanlearning.com

FilippoBacci/E+/Getty Images

CHAPTER 11

Responding to and Reducing Prejudice

History is littered with examples of the harm that prejudice can cause. This harm can be obvious and severe, as in atrocities such as genocide, enslavement, and colonization. These atrocities often continue to affect the targeted groups many generations after their occurrence (Salzman, 2001). But prejudice can also lead to less visible discrimination in hiring, career advancement, health care, legal proceedings, and loan opportunities that exacerbate social problems (Nelson, 2009; Riach & Rich, 2004; Stangor, 2009). Psychologically, prejudice can lead members of targeted groups to feel devalued within their culture (Frable et al., 1990; Inzlicht et al., 2006). Chronically feeling socially devalued can have detrimental effects on health and well-being (Major & Schmader, 2017). In all these ways, prejudice, stereotyping, and discrimination contribute to poverty, physical, behavioral, and mental health problems, as well as a sense of being excluded from mainstream society (e.g., Anderson & Armstead, 1995; Kessler et al., 1999; Klonoff et al., 1999; Schmader & Sedikides, 2018; Williams, 1999; Williams et al., 1999).

In this chapter, we focus on:

- What happens psychologically to people who are targeted by prejudice and how they cope

- The processes that influence how and whether people perceive prejudice and how they respond to it

- How even subtle encounters with prejudice and stereotypes can affect one's health, behavior, and performance and how members of stigmatized groups can remain resilient despite bias and discrimination

- Some promising strategies for reducing prejudice

Prejudice from a Target's Perspective

Perceiving Prejudice and Discrimination

Master status The perception that a person will be seen only in terms of a stigmatizing attribute rather than as the total self.

Stigma consciousness The expectation of being perceived by other people, particularly those in the majority group, in terms of one's group membership.

Membership in a group that is viewed or treated negatively by the larger society is bound to affect people in some way (Allport, 1954). Yet, as you learned in the previous chapter, for many stigmatized groups in the United States, prejudice is sometimes a lot subtler and harder to detect than it was 50 years ago. Although this might be a sign of progress, it makes it harder to pinpoint when one is the target of prejudice. Anyone who feels marginalized in society has probably faced this dilemma. Take the following quote from Erving Goffman's classic 1963 book *Stigma*: "And I always feel this with straight people [people who are not ex-convicts]—that whenever they're being nice to me, pleasant to me, all the time really, underneath they're only assessing me as a criminal and nothing else" (p. 14).

This individual's reflection reveals the **master status** that can accompany stigmatizing attributes—the perception that others will see a person solely in terms of one aspect rather than appreciating the person's total self. As a result, stigmatized individuals are persistently aware of what sets them apart in their interactions with others. For example, when asked to describe themselves, students from an ethnic-minoritized background are more likely to make mention of their group identity than are students from the ethnic majority (McGuire et al., 1978).

When people are conscious of being stigmatized, they become more attuned to signs of prejudice. In one study, women expecting to interact with a sexist man were quicker to detect sexism-related words (e.g., *harassment, hooters, bitch*) during a computer task and were more likely to judge ambiguous facial expressions as showing criticism (Inzlicht et al., 2008; Kaiser et al., 2006).

Individual Differences in Perceiving Prejudice As you might suspect, not all minoritized group members share equally the expectation of being the target of prejudice. People's sensitivity to perceiving bias depends on the extent to which they identify with their stigmatized group. If people normally don't think about themselves as being members of disadvantaged groups, then discrimination might not seem like something that happens to them. In contrast, people who are highly identified with their stigmatized group are more likely to recognize when prejudice and discrimination might affect their lives (Major et al., 2003; Operario & Fiske, 2001).

Members of minoritized groups also differ in their **stigma consciousness**—their expectation that other people, particularly those in the majority group, will perceive them in terms of their group membership (Pinel, 1999). People higher in stigma consciousness are more likely to expect their interactions with others to go poorly. Unfortunately, these expectations can sometimes lead to self-fulfilling prophecies. For example, when women particularly high in stigma consciousness had reason to think that a male stranger might be sexist, they evaluated an essay he had written more negatively, which then led him

▲ Birding while Black. In May 2020, Christian Cooper, an avid birdwatcher, described the racism he experienced when a White woman called the police, claiming that he was threatening her. In fact, he had merely asked her to leash up her dog, as the park rules require. Cooper said in an interview, "You know, the simple fact of my skin color means that I run the risk of being perceived as a menace or a threat despite the fact that I'm doing the exact same thing as anybody else in that park" (Chang, 2020).
[BRITTAINY NEWMAN/The New York Times/Redux Pictures]

to evaluate *their* essays more negatively (Pinel, 2002). The negative evaluations they received might have confirmed their assumption of the man's sexism, yet his evaluations might have been more positive if they had not criticized his essay first. But as we will discuss shortly, self-fulfilling prophecies are a two-way street. They also affect how those who are nonstigmatized perceive and interact with stigmatized targets.

Motivations to Avoid Perceptions of Prejudice   Although stigma consciousness might lead people to sometimes overestimate their experience of prejudice, this is not the norm. Instead, it is more common for people to estimate that they personally experience less discrimination than does the average member of their group (Taylor et al., 1990). This effect, called the **person–group discrimination discrepancy,** has been documented in many groups, including women reporting on their experience of sexism and racial-marginalized people reporting on their experience of racism. This effect has even been found among low-income Black American men, a group that is probably most likely to experience actual discrimination in employment, housing, and interactions with police (Taylor et al., 1994). Why is the tendency to avoid seeing prejudice and discrimination directed at oneself so pervasive?

Person–group discrimination discrepancy The tendency for people to estimate that they personally experience less discrimination than is faced by the average member of their group.

People may fail to see the prejudice targeted at them because they are motivated to deny that prejudice and discrimination affect their lives. Why? For one thing, this denial may be part of a more general tendency to be optimistic. Experiencing discrimination, having health problems, and being at risk for experiencing an earthquake all are negative events, and people are generally overly optimistic about their likelihood of experiencing such outcomes (Lehman & Taylor, 1987; Taylor & Brown, 1988). It might be beneficial to one's own psychological health to regard discrimination as something that happens to *other* people.

Another reason is that people may be motivated to sustain their faith that the way society is set up is inherently right and good, thereby justifying the status quo (Jost & Banaji, 1994). Buying into the status quo brings a sense of stability and predictability, but it can lead stigmatized individuals to downplay their experience of discrimination. In one experiment, White and Latinx students were put in the same situation of feeling that they had been passed over for a job that was given to someone of another ethnicity (Major et al., 2002). To what extent did they view this as discrimination? The results depended on the students' ethnicity. Among White people those most convinced that the social system in America is fair and that hard work pays off thought it was quite discriminatory for a Latinx employer to pass them over to hire another Latinx candidate. After all, if the system is fair, and Whites have been very successful in the system, an employer has no justification for choosing a minoritized group member over themselves. But among Latinx participants, those who saw the social system as fair were least likely to feel that it was discriminatory for a White employer to pass them over in favor of a White participant. Believing the system is fair might keep people motivated to do their best, but for members of minoritized groups in society, it can reduce the likelihood of recognizing discrimination when it does occur.

APPLICATION
Is Perceiving Prejudice Bad for Your Health?

Living in a society that devalues you because of your ethnicity, gender, sexual preferences, or religious beliefs can take a toll on both your mental and physical health. People who report experiencing more prejudice in their daily lives also show evidence of poorer psychological health (Branscombe et al., 1999; Schmitt et al., 2014; Sutin et al., 2015). In one study of 392 African Americans, an increase in their experience of discrimination over a 10-year time period predicted chromosomal changes (i.e., shortening of telomeres) that are indicative of early aging and a shortened life expectancy (Chae et al., 2020). The intersection of two or more devalued identities can be particularly associated with negative health outcomes (Lewis & Van Dyke, 2018). Negative consequences, such as increased depression and lower life satisfaction, are especially extreme when people blame themselves for their stigma or the way people treat them. Such adverse mental health effects of discrimination are also seen among children and young adults (Bernard et al., 2021).

▲ After many years of complaints about the racist nature of Washington D.C.'s NFL football team's name and logo, in 2021, the name was finally changed to "Commanders."

[Rob Carr/Getty Images]

Because our culture is infused with stereotypic portrayals of various groups, these negative effects on mental health can be quite insidious. For example, in the United States the use of Native American images as mascots for school and sports teams is contentious because of the accumulating research that exposure to these mascots generally reinforces people's stereotypes of Native Americans (Angle et al., 2017; Fryberg & Eason, 2017) and had negative effects on Native Americans. When Native American children and young adults were primed with these images, their self-esteem was reduced, they felt worse about their community, and they imagined themselves achieving less in the future (Fryberg et al., 2008).

In response to the evidence that mascots might have insidious effects on well-being, in 2014, the U.S. Patent and Trademark Office canceled the trademark that the Washington Redskins had on the football team's name and logo because both were deemed to be disparaging to Native Americans (Vargas, 2014). The team discontinued using the name, and after going by the Washington Football Team in 2020–2021, are now the Washington Commanders. Note, however, that removing such mascots can be threatening to some majority group members and risk prejudicial backlash. White participants exposed to information about the removal of a Native American mascot punished a Native American more than participants not exposed to such information in a hypothetical legal scenario (Jimenez et al., 2022). Moreover, this effect was mirrored in societal trends. Using regional level implicit bias data, Jimenez and colleagues also found that prejudice against Native Americans increased in Illinois the year following the removal of "Chief Illiniwek" (the former mascot of the University of Illinois) and in Ohio following the removal of "Chief Wahoo" (the former mascot of baseball's Cleveland Indians). To effectively reduce prejudice, then, efforts to change offensive team names need to be accompanied by other strategies.

Prejudice can have long-term consequences for physical health as well (Contrada et al., 2000). Like any other chronic stressor, the experience of prejudice elevates the body's physiological stress response. For example, women who report being frequent targets of sexism show a greater physiological stress response (i.e., increases in cortisol, a stress-related hormone) when they believe they personally might have been targeted by bias (Townsend et al., 2011). Over time, this stress response can predict poorer cardiovascular functioning, the buildup of plaque in the arteries, and artery calcification, which increase the risk for coronary heart disease (Brondolo et al., 2018; Guyll et al., 2001; Lewis et al., 2006; Troxel et al., 2003).

Although perceiving frequent discrimination predicts poorer well-being, this correlation also implies that those who do not perceive frequent experiences of prejudice fare much better psychologically. Later, we will discuss how particular ways of perceiving and reacting to discrimination can sometimes buffer people against its negative psychological consequences (Crocker & Major, 1989). ∎

The Harmful Impact of Stereotypes on Behavior

Being the target of prejudice also affects how people behave and perform. When you hold a stereotypic expectation about another person (because of group membership, for example), you may act in a way that leads the stereotyped person to behave just as you expected. For example, say that you suspect that the clerk at the café is going to be rude, so you are curt with her. She responds by being curt back to you. Voilà! Your initial judgment seems to be confirmed. Yet you may be ignoring the fact that, had you approached the interaction with a different expectation in mind, the clerk might not have acted rudely.

This was demonstrated in a classic study of self-fulfilling prophecy, a topic we introduced in chapter 3 (Word et al., 1974). In the first of a pair of studies, White participants were asked to play the role of an interviewer with two different job candidates, one White and the other Black. When the job candidate was Black, the interviewer chose to sit farther away from him, was more awkward in his speech, and conducted a shorter interview than when the candidate was White. The racial identity of the candidate affected the way in which the interview was conducted. But does this difference in the interviewer's manner affect how the job candidate comes across during the interview? The answer is "yes."

▲ Teachers' expectations of students' abilities can subtly shape their interactions with those students in ways that confirm their stereotypes.

[nano/E+/Getty Images]

In a second study, the researchers trained their assistants to conduct an interview either using the "good interviewer" style that was more typical of the interviews with White candidates (e.g., sitting closer) or the "bad interviewer" style that was more typical of the interviews with Black candidates (e.g., sitting farther away). When the trained assistants interviewed unsuspecting White job candidates, an interesting pattern emerged: The job candidates assigned to a "bad" interviewer came across as less calm and composed than those assigned to the "good" interviewer.

Research now considers these types of effects as forms of "microaggressions" and reveals how they can be both subtle and impactful (Williams, 2021). In one set of studies, when female engineering students were paired with male peers to work together on a project, a male partner's implicit sexist attitudes about women predicted the female partner's poorer performance on an engineering test (Logel et al., 2009). What were the more implicitly sexist guys doing? They were not more hostile or dismissive toward their female partners. Rather, they were more flirtatious with them, and in fact the women reported liking these men. Yet the men's flirtatious behavior led women to perform more poorly on the engineering test. Other research has shown that self-fulfilling prophecy effects are stronger when more people hold the stereotypes (Madon et al., 2018). What might be a small effect when considering the stereotyped expectations of just one perceiver becomes much larger when aggregated across many perceivers and experiences.

Confirming Stereotypes to Get Along   The findings just discussed point to a powerful dilemma. Stereotypes are schemas. You'll remember from chapter 3

Figure 11.1

Conforming to Stereotypes

Women who were motivated to get along with others (high in affiliative motivation) acted more stereotypically during a conversation with a man the more they believed that he had sexist views about women.

[Data from Sinclair, Huntsinger et al., 2005]

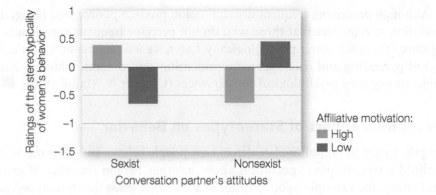

Self-objectification

A phenomenon whereby intense cultural scrutiny of the female body leads many girls and women to view themselves as objects to be looked at and judged.

▲ What if we objectified men in the same way as we objectify women?

[Photography by Alicia Mariah Elfving for MotoCorsa]

that schemas help social interactions run smoothly. People get along better when each individual confirms the other person's expectations. This suggests that the more motivated people are to be liked, the more they might behave in ways that are consistent with the other person's stereotypes, a form of self-stereotyping.

In one study of self-stereotyping (Sinclair, Huntsinger et al., 2005), women had a casual conversation with a male student whom they were led to believe had sexist or nonsexist attitudes toward women. In actuality, he was a member of the research team trained to act in a similar way with each woman and to rate his perceptions of her afterward. Those women who generally had a desire to get along with others and make new friends (i.e., they were high in affiliative motivation) rated themselves in more gender-stereotypic ways when interacting with the guy they believed to be sexist, and as shown in **FIGURE 11.1**, he also rated their behavior to be more stereotypically feminine. Women who were low in this general motivation to affiliate with others did just the opposite: If they thought their conversation partner would be sexist, they rated themselves as being more counterstereotypic, and the researcher also rated them as coming across in less stereotypical ways during their interaction. The motivation to get along can sometimes lead people to act in stereotypical ways.

Objectification Although the consequences of being stigmatized often apply broadly to different groups, some are more specific. One important example is the objectification that can result from the strong focus in many cultures on women's bodies. In chapter 10, we discussed how the sexual objectification of women promotes certain stereotypes and prejudice against them. But Fredrickson and Robert's (1997) objectification theory also proposes that this intense cultural scrutiny of the female body leads many girls and women to view themselves as objects to be looked at and judged, a phenomenon that the researchers called **self-objectification**. Being exposed to sexualizing words or idealized media images of women's bodies, hearing other women criticizing their own bodies, and undergoing men's visual scrutiny of their bodies all prompt self-objectification, which increases negative emotions such as body shame, appearance anxiety, and self-disgust (e.g., Aubrey, 2007; Calogero, 2004; Gapinski et al., 2003; Roberts & Gettman, 2004). The more shame they feel, the more vulnerable they are to disordered eating, depression, and sexual dysfunction (Fredrickson & Roberts, 1997). These effects of self-objectification have likely contributed to the obsession with weight that has led 73% of American women to make some serious effort at some point to lose weight, compared with only 55% of men (Saad, 2011).

Self-objectification also disrupts concentration and interferes with cognitive performance (Fredrickson et al., 1998). In one study, male and female college students were first asked to try on and evaluate either a swimsuit or a sweater. Then, wearing the particular garment while alone in a makeshift dressing room, they completed a short math test. Men were unaffected by what they were wearing, but women who were wearing the swimsuit were drawn to monitoring their appearance and consequently performed worse than if they were wearing a sweater.

Stereotype Threat   Self-fulfilling prophecies and self-stereotyping are examples of how stereotypes affect behavior of members of stereotyped groups during social interactions. Other research shows that even when a person is not interacting with someone, the immediate context can bring to mind stereotypes that can interfere with a person's ability to perform at their best. This was the discovery made by the Stanford researchers Claude Steele and Joshua Aronson (1995) when they conducted pioneering work on what they called *stereotype threat*, a phenomenon you were first introduced to in chapter 1, when we covered research methods.

Stereotype threat is the concern that one might do something to confirm a negative stereotype about one's group either in one's own eyes or in the eyes of someone else. Although this phenomenon has far-reaching consequences for a variety of situations, it has been studied primarily as an explanation for racial and ethnic differences in academic performance and for gender differences in standardized math test scores. Other explanations for these performance gaps have focused on whether nature (genetics, hormones, even brain size) or nurture (upbringing, educational values, access to educational resources) offers a better explanation of these performance gaps (Nisbett, 2009). Research on stereotype threat takes a distinctly social psychological view, indicating that performance can be influenced by aspects of the situation, such as the person's experience of the classroom in which they are taking a test.

> **Stereotype threat** The concern that one might do something to confirm a negative stereotype about one's group either in one's own eyes or the eyes of someone else.

In one of their original studies, Steele and Aronson (1995) gave Black and White undergraduates a challenging set of verbal problems to solve. For half of the sample, the problems were described as a diagnostic test of verbal intelligence (similar to the SAT or GRE). For the other half, the same problems were described as a simple lab exercise. Although White students were unaffected by how the task was described, Black students performed significantly worse when the task was presented as a diagnostic test of intelligence (see **FIGURE 11.2**). When Black students were reminded of the stereotype that their group is intellectually inferior, they performed more poorly on the test.

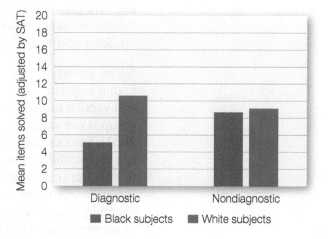

Figure 11.2

Stereotype Threat

In research on stereotype threat, Black college students performed significantly worse when a task was framed as a diagnostic test of verbal ability than as a nondiagnostic laboratory exercise.

[Data from Steele & Aronson, 1995]

In addition to undermining performance on tests of math, verbal, or general intellectual ability of minoritized groups, women, and those of lower socioeconomic status (Croizet & Claire, 1998), stereotype threat has also been shown to impair memory performance of older adults (Chasteen et al., 2005); driving performance of women (Yeung & von Hippel, 2008); athletes' performance in the face of racial stereotypes (Stone et al., 2012); men's performance on an emotional sensitivity task (Leyens et al., 2000); and women's negotiation skills (Kray et al., 2001). As mentioned in chapter 1, meta-analyses suggest that these effects are small to medium in size (Armstrong et al., 2017;

Doyle & Voyer, 2016; Gentile et al., 2018; Liu et al., 2021; Nadler & Clark, 2011; Picho et al., 2013).

Theoretically, stereotype threat is thought to impair performance under some conditions more than others (Schmader et al., 2008). The effect is strongest when:

- The stigmatized identity is salient either because of the situation (e.g., being the only women in a high-level math class) or due to stigma consciousness or group identification.
- The task is characterized as a diagnostic measure of an ability for which one's group is stereotyped as being inferior (as in Steele & Aronson, 1995).
- Individuals are led to believe that their performance is going to be compared with that of members of the group stereotyped as superior on the task.
- Individuals are aware of the stereotype and are concerned that others (or even themselves) might believe it to be true.

Researchers also have learned a great deal about the processes that contribute to the deleterious effects of stereotype threat. First, it's important to point out that those who care the most about being successful feel stereotype threat most acutely (Steele, 1997). In fact, it's partly because people are trying so hard to prove the stereotype wrong that their performance suffers (Jamieson & Harkins, 2007). When situations bring these stereotypes to mind, anxious thoughts and feelings of self-doubt are more likely to creep in (Bosson et al., 2004; Cadinu et al., 2005; Johns et al., 2008; Spencer et al., 1999). Efforts to push these thoughts away and to stay focused on the task can hijack the very same cognitive resources that people need to do well on tests and in other academic pursuits (Johns et al., 2008; Logel et al., 2009; Schmader et al., 2008). For other kinds of activities (e.g., trying to sink a golf putt, shoot a basket, or parallel park), becoming proficient means relying on skills that have become automatic over hours or even years of practice. When the situation reminds people of a negative group stereotype about those activities, they end up scrutinizing the behaviors that they normally do automatically; as a result, they trip themselves up (Schmader & Beilock, 2011).

Social Identity Threat   Research on stereotype threat reveals that it's mentally taxing to perform under the pressure of presumed incompetence. A more general version of this threat is called *social identity threat,* the feeling that your group is not valued in a domain and that you do not belong there (Steele et al., 2002). For example, women working in engineering report greater social identity threat and job burnout on days when they feel their male colleagues do not respect their contributions (Hall et al., 2019). To cope with social identity threat, people might find themselves trying to juggle their various identities. For example, women who go into male-dominant domains find themselves having to suppress their more feminine qualities (Pronin et al., 2004; von Hippel et al., 2011) and some even psychologically distance themselves from other women (Veldman et al., 2021). A minoritized student who excels in academics can be accused of "acting White" (Fordham & Ogbu, 1986). Older adults struggle to feel committed to their job when their age feels at odds with their identity as an employee (Manzi et al., 2019).

On the one hand, repeated exposure to stereotype threat and social identity threat can eventually lead to **disidentification**, which occurs when people no longer feel that their performance in a domain is an important part of themselves, and they stop caring about being successful (Steele, 1997). This can be a serious problem if, for example, minoritized children disidentify with

Disidentification The process of disinvesting in any area in which one's group traditionally has been underrepresented or negatively stereotyped.

◄ Women sitting at the computer scientist's desk on the left (with the *Star Trek* poster) expressed less interest in computer science as a major than did women sitting at the computer scientist's desk on the right. The geek stereotype of computer scientists might prevent women from becoming interested in this field.

[Cheryan et al., 2010]

school. In fact, being the target of negative stereotypes can steer people away from certain opportunities if those stereotypes lead them to assume they will experience a lack of fit and belonging (Aday & Schmader, 2019; Schmader & Sedikides, 2018).

For example, women continue to be underrepresented in science, technology, engineering, and math, and this is particularly true in computer science, where the percentage of women has actually decreased over the past three decades. One factor is that students have a very specific stereotype of what a computer scientist is like, and women are much more likely than men to think that it isn't like them. In one study, women expressed far less interest in majoring in computer science when they completed a survey in a computer scientist's office filled with reminders of the computer-geek stereotype than did those who completed the same questionnaire in a room that did not reinforce the conventional stereotype of computer scientists (Cheryan et al., 2009, 2017). Other research has shown that girls experience greater feelings of fit in science when they interact with successful female role models in the field (O'Brien et al., 2017). The take-away message is that the ability to identify with the field (Chen et al., 2021) and with similar others plays an important role in attracting women and minorities to fields where they have been historically underrepresented.

Achie∕e
Social Psych in Everyday Life:
Gaylean

SECTION REVIEW Prejudice from a Target's Perspective

Regardless of how accurately prejudice is perceived, being a target of bias can have negative consequences for psychological and physical health.

Perceiving Prejudice

- Because prejudice is less overt today than it once was, it is difficult to know if and when one is the target of prejudice.
- People differ in their sensitivity to prejudice, but people commonly underestimate personal discrimination.
- People may be motivated to deny discrimination out of optimism or out of a desire to justify the social system.
- Prejudice can take a toll on a person's mental and physical health.

The Harmful Impact of Stereotypes

- Holding a stereotype can change how observers interact with targets, sometimes causing targets to act stereotypically.
- Targets sometimes inadvertently act stereotypically to get along with others.
- Self-objectification—viewing the self as an object to be looked at—can undermine health and performance.
- Stereotype threat—the fear of confirming a negative stereotype—can undermine performance.
- Social identity threat—the feeling that a group does not belong in a domain—can repel people from that domain.

What's a Target to Do? Coping with Stereotyping, Prejudice, and Discrimination

The evidence we've reviewed on the effects of prejudice and stereotyping might lead us to expect targets of bias to feel rather lousy about themselves. Interestingly, a review of the literature revealed surprisingly little evidence that people stigmatized based on race, ethnicity, physical disability, or mental illness report lower levels of self-esteem than those who are not normally stigmatized (Crocker & Major, 1989). Even in the face of negative treatment and social devaluation, people can be remarkably resilient. Let's look at a few of the ways people cope with the daily jabs of stereotyping and prejudice, as well as the trade-offs these strategies can have.

Coping with Stereotype and Social Identity Threat

Research has pointed to several ways in which the negative psychological effects of prejudice and stereotypes can be reduced. These findings have important implications for educational and social policies.

Identifying with Positive Role Models   When individuals are exposed to role models—people like themselves who have been successful—the stereotype is altered, and they feel inspired to do well (Dasgupta & Asgari, 2004; Marx & Roman, 2002; McIntyre et al., 2003; O'Brien et al., 2017; Stout et al., 2011). In one study (Stout et al., 2011), college students were randomly assigned to either a female or a male calculus professor, and their performance over the course of the semester was tracked. The gender of the professor had no effect on men's attitudes or behavior. But women with a female professor participated more in class over the course of the semester and became more confident in their ability to do well.

Reappraising Anxiety   When stereotypes are difficult to change, targets can reinterpret what the stereotypes mean. For example, often when people think that they are stereotyped to do poorly, they are more likely to interpret difficulties and setbacks as evidence that the stereotype is true and that they do not belong. They perform better, though, if they reinterpret difficulties as normal challenges faced by anyone. In one remarkable study, minoritized college students who read testimonials about how everyone struggles and feels anxious when beginning college felt a greater sense of belonging in academics, did better academically, and were less likely to drop out of school (Walton & Brady, 2020; Walton & Cohen, 2007, 2011). Similarly, other studies have found that getting instructions to reappraise anxiety as a normal part of test-taking improved women's and minoritized groups' performance (Liu et al., 2021). In one study, these effects persisted even months later, when students took an actual high-stakes test such as the GRE (Jamieson et al., 2010). In fact, Johns and colleagues (2005) found that simply being able to interpret test anxiety as resulting from stereotype threat improved women's performance on a math test.

Affirming Broader Values   Another possible coping strategy is *self-affirmation*. Self-affirmation theory (for a refresher, see chapter 6) posits that people need to view themselves as good and competent. When they encounter a threat to their positive self-view in one area of life, they can compensate

▲ One of us currently has a graduate student who noted that when he was growing up in India, he saw a photo of famous Indian-born social psychologist Mahzarin Banaji, pictured here, and when he did, he realized he could become a social psychologist and was inspired to go to grad school.

[Astrid Stawiarz/Getty Images for The Leakey Foundation]

by affirming other deeply held values. On the basis of this theory, people who are reminded of their core values might be protected from the negative effects of stereotypes. This hypothesis has been supported in several longitudinal studies (Cohen et al., 2006; Cohen et al., 2009; Miyake et al., 2010). In one study (Cohen et al., 2006; Cohen et al., 2009), students were assigned to write about either a personally cherished value or a value that others might care about but that was not central to their own lives. The researchers then tracked students' grades. This simple affirmation task had no effect on White students' academic performance. But Black students who affirmed their values were far less likely to earn low grades over the course of that semester. The positive effects on their academic performance persisted up to two years later (see **FIGURE 11.3**). Although other researchers have not always replicated this effect (Hanselman et al., 2017), recent evidence suggests that self-affirmation works best for students who take the affirmation task seriously and are most at risk of experiencing stereotype threat (Borman et al., 2018).

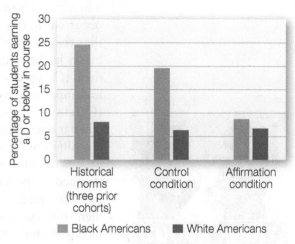

Figure 11.3

The Power of Self-Affirmation

When middle school students spent just 15 minutes at the start of the school year reflecting on their core values, the percentage of Black American students who earned a D or lower at the end of the semester was reduced.

[Data from Cohen et al., 2006]

Coping with Prejudice and Discrimination: Social Strategies

Just as there are a number of ways to counter the effects of stereotype threat, there are also a number of behavioral response options for dealing with interpersonal encounters with prejudice.

Confronting Those with Biases   Consider the following scenario: You are working on a class project as part of a small group, and you and your team members have to take turns choosing what kinds of people you would want with you on a deserted island. One young man in the group consistently makes sexist choices (e.g., "Let's see, maybe a chef? No, one of the women can cook."). Would you say anything to him? In a study that presented women with this scenario, most said they would confront the guy in some way, probably by questioning his choice or pointing out how inappropriate it is (Swim & Hyers, 1999). But when women were actually put in this situation, more than half of them did nothing at all. People often find it difficult to confront episodes of prejudice or discrimination they observe or experience.

This "do-nothing effect" isn't limited to targets put in the position of confronting an outgroup member (Crosby, 2015). White Americans often stay silent when they overhear another White person use a racial slur when referring to a Black person (e.g., Greenberg & Pyszczynski, 1985b; Kawakami et al., 2009). Confronting those who express prejudice is a lot harder than we might imagine it to be. Being silent in these situations is particularly troubling because expressions of prejudice can rub off on the observer. In one study, White participants who heard a racial slur used to describe a Black American became more negative in their evaluation of the person targeted by the slur, despite the fact that in debriefings, the participants reported being appalled by the remark (Greenberg & Pyszczynski, 1985b).

Why do racist and sexist remarks often go unchallenged? One reason is because those who do the confronting are often viewed as complainers (Kaiser & Miller, 2001). This kind of "blame the victim" reaction happens even when the evidence supports the student's claim that discrimination actually occurred! In other research, when Whites were confronted with the possibility that they were biased in their treatment of others, they tried to correct their biases in the future but also felt angry and disliked the person who confronted them (Czopp et al., 2006). Even members of your own stigmatized group can be unsympathetic when you point to the role of discrimination in your outcomes (Garcia et al., 2005). These social costs can make it difficult to address bias when it does occur, particularly if you are the person targeted by the bias and in a position of relatively little power. On the other hand, members of advantaged groups can confront bias while facing fewer social costs, but can also feel constrained in speaking up. For example, people tend to underestimate the degree to which men support gender equality and these misconceptions can inhibit men from confronting sexist statements (De Souza & Schmader, 2022). When have you confronted someone who was biased against you or another person? What was the cost?

THINK ABOUT

[wdstock/iStock/Getty Images]

Compensating for Other's Biases Targets of prejudice also cope with stigma by compensating for the negative stereotypes or attitudes they think other people have toward them. For example, when overweight women were making a first impression on a person and were led to believe that that person could see them (and thus knew their weight), they acted in a more extraverted way than if they were told that they could not be seen. They compensated for the weight-based biases they expected others to have by being extra-friendly. And it worked: Those who thought they were visible were rated as friendlier by the person with whom they were interacting (Miller et al., 1995).

In a similar finding, Black college freshmen who expected others to have racial biases against them and their group reported spending more time disclosing information about themselves when talking with their White dormitory mates (Shelton et al., 2005). Self-disclosure is a powerful way of establishing trust and liking, so it is not surprising that Black participants who self-disclosed a great deal were liked more by their White roommates. Unfortunately, these kinds of compensation strategies can come with costs. Black students who reported engaging in a lot of self-disclosure with a White roommate also reported feeling inauthentic in this relationship. By trying to put their White roommates at ease, they might feel unable to be true to themselves.

Another potential cost of compensation is that it can disrupt the smooth flow of social interaction as people work to manage the impressions they are making (Bergsieker et al., 2010; Shelton & Richeson, 2006). For people who belong to the more advantaged group, interactions with outgroup members can bring to mind concerns about appearing prejudiced and may lead them to increase their efforts to come across as likable and unbiased (Vorauer et al., 1998). People who belong to the disadvantaged group might be most concerned about being stereotyped as incompetent and compensate by trying to self-promote. The problem here is that interactions tend to go more smoothly when people's impression-management goals are matched. If one person cracks jokes to show how warm and likable she is while the other wants to have an intellectual conversation to bolster her perceived competence, each party might walk away from the interaction feeling misunderstood, disconnected from

▲ To ease interracial tension, minoritized students self-disclose more to White roommates. Such disclosure is effective in reducing racial biases but does not always allow people to be themselves.

[cglade/iStock/Getty Images]

the other, and a bit cognitively exhausted (Richeson et al., 2003; Richeson & Shelton, 2003; Richeson & Trawalter, 2005).

APPLICATION
The Costs of Concealing

When people are concerned about being discriminated against, they sometimes choose to cope by concealing their stigma, if this is an option. This strategy is common for those who identify as gay, lesbian, bisexual, or transgender. For example, Jason Collins played professional basketball in the NBA for 12 years before coming out of the closet in April 2013. He described his experience concealing his sexual orientation in an interview with *Sports Illustrated*:

> It takes an enormous amount of energy to guard such a big secret. I've endured years of misery and gone to enormous lengths to live a lie. I was certain that my world would fall apart if anyone knew. And yet when I acknowledged my sexuality I felt whole for the first time. (COLLINS, 2013)

When Jason Collins joined the Brooklyn Nets in the spring of 2014, he became a true trailblazer—the first openly gay male athlete actively playing a major professional sport in the United States. Yet some retired players have noted that they are sure they played with gay teammates over the years. An ESPN story from 2011 quoted the Hall of Famer and basketball analyst Charles Barkley as saying, "It bothers me when I hear these reporters and jocks get on TV and say: 'Oh, no guy can come out in a team sport. These guys would go crazy.' . . . I'd rather have a gay guy who can play than a straight guy who can't play" (ESPN.com news services, 2011).

For those who are particularly aware of and worried about how others judge them, concealment can sometimes be a beneficial way to cope (e.g., Cole et al., 1997), but as Jason Collins's quote reveals, concealment comes with its own costs. Those who conceal an important aspect of their identity might struggle with the inability simply to be their authentic selves. Also, the effort it takes to be vigilant about what you say and how you act and to monitor whether others have figured out your secret can be emotionally and cognitively draining (Frable et al., 1990; Smart & Wegner, 1999). So although concealing a stigma might be one way to sidestep discrimination, it's often not an optimal solution.

Fortunately, highly publicized examples of people living more authentically can help others feel they can do the same. In 2020, former NBA star, Dwyane Wade, announced that his 12-year-old daughter, Zaya, is transgender (i.e., born as a male, now identifying as female) saying, "She's known it for nine years. She's known since she was 3 years old. Along this way we've asked questions and we've learned. But she's known" (Wells, 2020). Wade's motivation for publicizing Zaya's gender identity is to

▲ NBA basketball player Dwyane Wade demonstrates acceptance and support for transgender children by publicly introducing his transgender daughter Zaya to the world.

[Rich Fury/Getty Images for Gucci]

help other families support their own children who identify as transgender or nonbinary.

Public examples of support and acceptance are perhaps an important reason suicide attempts among adolescents who identify as LGBTQIA+ persons have been decreasing in recent years (Raifman et al., 2020). Still, gay, lesbian, and bisexual teens are three times more likely to attempt suicide than their straight peers, and a 2018 study in the United States suggested that 30 to 50% of transgender and nonbinary adolescents had attempted suicide (Raifman et al., 2020; Toomey et al., 2018). Because stigma is a threat to one's very sense of identity, it might not be a coincidence that the negative consequences of prejudice are particularly high during adolescence and young adulthood, when people are still forming an identity (Erikson, 1968). The It Gets Better Project (www.itgetsbetter.org), started by the columnist and author Dan Savage and his partner, Terry Miller, is an effort to communicate to LGBTQIA+ teens that the stress of embracing their sexual identity, coming out to others, and experiencing bias will get better over time. In fact, research suggests that attitudes toward LGBTQIA+ individuals are generally becoming more positive over time (Charlesworth & Banaji, 2019). At the same time, as of this writing, a number of states are introducing legislation that risks exacerbating stigma and mental health issues for sexual minorities (Tensley, March 2022). ■

Seeking Social Support At the other end of the spectrum from concealment is creating and celebrating a shared identity with others who are similarly stigmatized. Earlier we mentioned that those who report encountering frequent or ongoing discrimination show signs of psychological distress. But according to **rejection identification theory**, the negative consequences of being targeted by discrimination can be offset by a strong sense of identification and pride with a stigmatized group (Branscombe et al., 1999; DeMarco & Newheiser, 2019; Postmes & Branscombe, 2002).

Rejection identification theory The idea that people can offset the negative consequences of being targeted by discrimination by feeling a strong sense of identification with their stigmatized group.

Although pride in one's ethnic identity is likely supported by one's family and social circle, other identities can be stigmatized even by parents, siblings, and friends. That is why gay pride and similar movements can be so critical to a feeling of social support. In certain cases, marginalized groups band together to form broader coalitions against bias and discrimination (Craig & Richeson, 2016). For example, the term *people of color* (POC) is increasingly a label preferred by members of non-White groups because it creates a common identity united by shared experience of bias in America. When minoritized groups become allies, they not only gain greater social support, they also become a more powerful force for social change.

▲ In 2020, members of First Nations tribes in northwestern Canada banded together to support the hereditary chiefs of the Wet'suwet'en Nation who oppose the construction of an oil pipeline on their territory.

[Erik McGregor/LightRocket via Getty Images]

Coping with Prejudice and Discrimination: Psychological Strategies

The social strategies discussed above offer examples of how those who are stigmatized can manage their interpersonal interactions in ways that minimize their experience of bias and discrimination. But in addition to directly altering interpersonal interactions, people also rely on a host of psychological strategies that can help them remain resilient in the face of social devaluation.

Blaming the Bias, Not Oneself   As mentioned earlier, the dilemma of modern-day prejudice is that it can be very subtle. Consider an instance in which a woman is passed over for a promotion in favor of a male colleague. Is that discrimination? Or is she simply less qualified? There are times when it is difficult to know, and this situation puts those who are targeted by bias in a state of **attributional ambiguity** (Crocker et al., 1991). Crocker and her colleagues pointed out that attributing a negative outcome to prejudice can in some situations allow one to shift blame onto the biases of others and escape some of the negative feelings that might otherwise result. For example, if the woman in the example can dismiss the boss who rejected her as a sexist bigot, then she can maintain her opinion of herself as competent and intelligent. In one experiment, when Black college students learned that a White student was not that interested in becoming friends with them, their self-esteem was reduced when they didn't think the other person knew their race but was buffered when they believed their race was known (Crocker et al., 1991).

> **Attributional ambiguity**
> A phenomenon whereby members of stigmatized groups often can be uncertain whether negative experiences are based on their own actions and abilities or are the result of prejudice.

Discrimination has reverberating negative effects as we have reviewed. Yet there can be situations where such attributions afford some measure of psychological protection. When is this likely to occur? First, attributing an isolated incident to prejudice might buffer self-esteem from negative outcomes, but when that incident seems indicative of pervasive patterns of discrimination, it can have more harmful effects (Eliezer et al., 2010; McCoy & Major, 2003; Schmitt et al., 2003).

Second, when people blame themselves for their stigmatizing condition in the first place, they get no comfort from being the target of bias. When overweight female college students learned that a man wasn't interested in meeting them, they felt worse, not better, if they thought their weight played a factor in his evaluation (Crocker et al., 1993). Because society continues to perceive weight as something that can be controlled, these women felt responsible for being rejected. Finally, acknowledging that prejudice exists can reduce the shock when it happens to you. In one set of studies, women and minorities who generally believed that the world is unfair (compared with those who didn't) showed less physiological threat when they met and interacted with someone who was prejudiced against their group (Townsend et al., 2010).

People can also protect their self-esteem more effectively by claiming discrimination when they can be certain that discrimination did occur (Major et al., 2003). In 2017, dozens of actresses, including Gwyneth Paltrow, Ashley Judd, Rose McGowan, and Angelina Jolie, publicly shared their stories of sexual harassment and abuse by Hollywood film producer Harvey Weinstein. The power in numbers has given other women the certainty and support to come forward to tell their horrific stories of casting calls with Weinstein. One of these women, Tomi-Ann Roberts, was an aspiring actress in her 20s when she met with Weinstein about a possible film role. She was shocked and appalled to find him naked in a bathtub, insisting that she would need to remove her top to be considered for the role. Roberts not only left the hotel suite, she gave up her plan to go into acting and instead pursued a successful career as a social psychologist studying objectification and sexism. In March 2020, Weinstein was found guilty of criminal sexual assault and rape in New York State and sentenced to 23 years in prison.

▲ The social psychologist Tomi-Ann Roberts is one of dozens of women who have publicly shared their stories of sexual harassment by the Hollywood film producer Harvey Weinstein. Roberts has spent her career researching the harmful effects of objectification and sexism, work you have learned about in chapters 10 and 11.
[Dr. Tomi-Ann Roberts]

Devaluing the Domain Another coping strategy that people turn to in dealing with discrimination is to devalue areas of life where they face pervasive experiences of prejudice and discrimination. If you decide that you really don't care about working on a naval submarine, then you might be relatively unaffected by the U.S. Navy's long-standing ban (not repealed until 2010) on women serving on submarines.

The tendency to devalue those areas where your group doesn't excel seems like a pretty effective strategy for managing bad outcomes. But the whole story is more complicated. It turns out that it is not so easy to devalue those domains in which higher-status groups are more accomplished. For example, on learning that women score higher on a new personality dimension described only by the name *surgency*, men readily devalue this trait as something that is not important to them personally (Schmader, Major, Eccleston, & McCoy, 2001). But when women learn that men score higher in surgency, they assume that this trait is at least as valuable as when women are higher on it. This pattern is reflective of a general asymmetry in how stereotypes constrain men's and women's interests (Croft et al., 2015). Although women are increasingly fighting to be respected in traditionally high-status male-dominated domains, men are generally less concerned that they are underrepresented in what are more likely to be lower-status female-dominated domains (Block et al., 2019).

These pressures on groups with lower status can leave them with a difficult choice: Continue to strive for success in arenas where they are socially

---

SOCIAL PSYCH OUT IN THE WORLD

One Family's Experience of Religious Prejudice

In this chapter, we are considering the scholarly evidence on how people experience, cope with, and try to deflect discrimination. But personal experience with prejudice can cut very deep. Let's examine prejudice from the perspective of one family's account, told as part of the radio program *This American Life* (Spiegel, 2006, 2011).

We begin with a love story in the West Bank in the Middle East. A young Muslim American woman named Serry met and fell in love with a Muslim man from the West Bank. As they got to know one another, he told her how difficult it was for him and everyone he knew to grow up in the middle of the deep religious and political conflict between Israel and the West Bank. So when they decided to marry and make a life together, she convinced him that their children would have a better life in the United States, a country where she spent a much happier childhood and where people from different religious backgrounds easily formed friendships.

They settled down in the suburbs of New York City, had five children, and became a very typical American family. But when terrorists attacked the World Trade Center and the Pentagon on September 11, 2001, their lives changed forever. Like everyone around them, they were horrified and deeply saddened by what had happened. But their friends, neighbors, and even strangers on the street began to treat them differently. Drivers would give Serry the finger, and someone put a note on her minivan, telling her family to leave the country. The situation escalated when their fourth-grade daughter came home from school in tears on the one-year anniversary of 9/11, after the school district presented a lesson for all fourth-graders, explaining that 9/11 happened because Muslims hate Christians and also hate Americans. From that day on, their once-popular daughter was the target of taunting and bullying by other kids. The situation grew worse when her teacher told the class that non-Christians and nonbelievers would burn in hell. Her nine-year-old classmates began calling her "Loser Muslim" after her teacher said that she should be transferred to another classroom. Soon her younger siblings stigmatized because these are the domains that society considers important or call into question the very legitimacy of that society by devaluing those domains (e.g., making the decision to drop out of school). For example, although Black and Latinx college students get lower grades on average than their White and Asian peers, they report valuing education at least as much if not more (Major & Schmader, 1998; Schmader, Major, & Gramzow, 2001). However, those who regard the ethnic hierarchy in the United States as unfair and illegitimate are more likely to call into question the value and utility of getting an education (Schmader, Major, & Gramzow, 2001). If the deck is stacked against you, you might very well decide to leave the game.

One extreme form of devaluing is to create a group identity that opposes the majority group and its characteristic behaviors, ideas, and practices, in what is labeled an *oppositional culture* (Ogbu & Simons, 1998). For example, researchers have suggested that ethnic minoritized students (e.g., African Americans, Mexican Americans, Native Americans) may consider doing well in school or conforming to school rules as "acting White" (Fordham & Ogbu, 1986). If they are concerned about facing opposition from their peers or community for engaging in these "White" behaviors, minoritized students might instead devalue or avoid doing well in school. Although this has been a widely cited idea, a recent review of the evidence finds little support that an oppositional culture explains existing academic disparities (Tyson & Lewis, 2021). Structural inequalities in educational resources, not a widespread tendency to devalue academic success, is what seems to create racial and ethnic disparities in educational outcomes.

were targeted by bullying, too. Eventually even her best friend turned her back on her.

This heart-wrenching story reveals how prejudice can flare up when people feel that their worldview has been threatened. As we discussed in chapter 10, because the events of 9/11 were viewed as an attack on American values by Islamic extremists, the attacks led some Americans to view all Muslims with hate and suspicion—even those with whom they had previously been friendly. But this story also reveals how different people in the same family can respond very differently to others' prejudice.

The oldest daughter's response was to renounce her religion, to try to escape that part of her identity that her peers and her teacher so clearly devalued. When she moved to a new school, she chose to *conceal* her religious background to try to avoid further discrimination.

For Serry, the mother of the family, her religion was deeply important to her, but being American was even more central to her identity. She was shocked and saddened to find that she was no longer viewed as an American, but she still believed that American values of freedom would win out in the end. As Serry explained, "I was born and raised in this country, and I'm aware of what makes this country great, and I know that what happened to our family, it doesn't speak to American values. And I feel like this is such a fluke. I have to believe this is not what America is about. I know that." In line with *system justification theory*, her belief in American values led her to minimize these events as aberrations.

Serry's husband found his vision of America as a land free of religious prejudice shattered. Like every other immigrant before him in the history of the United States, he had traveled to a new and different culture in the hope of making a better life for himself and his family. Once a very happy man with a quick sense of humor, he slipped into depression and eventually decided to return to the West Bank, where he died a few years later. Not much is said about his death, so it's not known how his experience with anti-Islamic prejudice might have eroded his health. But his choice was to return to his homeland, a place that is far from being free of discrimination from religious intolerance but where at least he could live among others who share the same stigmatized identity. Consistent with *rejection identification theory*, his identification as a Muslim from the West Bank seemed to offer him a source of psychological security.

SECTION REVIEW What's a Target to Do? Coping with Stereotyping, Prejudice, and Discrimination

People can take steps to mitigate the consequences of stereotyping, prejudice, and discrimination.

- Ways to overcome stereotype threat include identification with role models, reappraisal of anxiety as normal, and self-affirmation.

- To address or minimize their experience of prejudice in social interactions, stigmatized targets use confrontation, compensation, concealment, and coming together.

- To minimize the negative psychological effects of social devaluation, stigmatized targets can discount negative outcomes or devalue domains where they experience discrimination. These strategies can benefit targets in some situations, but they can also backfire or create new problems.

Learning Outcomes

- Identify how institutional changes can have a positive impact on a disadvantaged group.

- Describe how preventing prejudice in intergroup relationships can work and how it can also backfire.

- Explain conditions that make optimal contact effective at reducing prejudice.

- Outline ways that prejudice can be reduced without contact.

Reducing Prejudice

Reducing prejudice essentially entails changing the values and beliefs by which people live. This is tricky for a number of reasons. One is that people's values and beliefs are often a long-standing basis of their psychological security. Another is that prejudice often serves specific psychological functions for people, such as allowing them to displace their hostile feelings or buttress their shaky self-esteem. A third difficulty arises because, once established, prejudiced views and stereotypes constitute schemas, and like other schemas, they tend to bias perceptions, attributions, and memories in ways that are self-perpetuating. Finally, people sometimes are not even aware of their prejudices and their influence. All these factors make prejudice difficult to combat.

However, although there is no one-size-fits-all solution, a number of encouraging approaches are available. We will start from the top, so to speak, and examine how prejudice can be reduced at the societal or institutional level. Given that the effectiveness of institutional change sometimes hinges on people controlling their expressions of prejudice, we will turn next to whether and when people are able to effectively do so. Finally, we discuss how to go beyond controlling the expression of prejudice to actually change people's prejudiced attitudes and ease intergroup conflict.

Working from the Top Down: Changing the Culture

Prejudice exists within a cultural context, legitimized (albeit subtly at times) by the laws, customs, and norms of a society (Hatzenbuehler, 2014; Salter et al., 2018). Thus, one of the great challenges in reducing prejudice lies in changing these laws, customs, and norms. One dramatic example occurred when the Supreme Court's 1954 decision in *Brown v. Board of Education* declared public school segregation unconstitutional. Desegregation fostered integration and reduced prejudice (Pettigrew, 1961). As we discussed in chapter 6, a change in behavior (in this case, by law) often can lead to a change in attitudes because people strive for consistency between the two.

Changing public attitudes can also lead to institutional change. In June 2020, at a time when public support of LGBTQIA+ rights had never been higher, the Supreme Court ruled that it is unconstitutional to be fired for one's sexual orientation or transgender status. Around the same time, thousands of Americans across the country were coming together to protest policing practices that systematically and tragically disadvantage Black Americans (Hetey & Eberhardt,

2018). These protests have led to some changes, but also some evidence of backlash to that change. For example, there has been a dramatic shift in public opinion, and a majority of Americans believe that there is a larger problem of racial bias in law enforcement (Voytko, 2020). Although this has led many states to pass legislation to reform policing, it remains to be seen if this will lead to true changes in outcomes (Subramanian & Arzy, 2021). At the same time we see increased acknowledgment of transgender rights, legislation in Texas and Florida seems aimed at denying the experience and rights of transgender youth (Keveney, 2022). These episodes remind us that institutional change often happens with two steps forward, one step back.

▲ At age 15, Eric Adams, a gang member, was arrested for criminal trespassing and beaten by the police, only to be saved by a Black officer's intervention. This experience helped motivate Adams to join the NYPD himself, hoping to be a force for change. After serving for over 20 years, Adams became a politician, and was elected mayor of New York in 2021.

[Jeenah Moon/Bloomberg via Getty Images]

Institutional changes not only stem from changing attitudes but can help break down stereotypes. After desegregation, when the educational structure became somewhat more (though not completely) equal, many more Black Americans were able to be successful. The more such *counterstereotypic* narratives pervade the cultural landscape, the more people encounter those who defy their preconceived ideas about certain groups. As discussed in chapter 10, when President Obama is the example that people bring to mind when thinking of Black people, they are less likely to be prejudiced (Columb & Plant, 2011; Plant et al., 2009). By increasing the diversity of different groups, affirmative action policies can help change stereotypes (Allport, 1954; Morgenroth & Ryan, 2018). The less a group is associated with poorer neighborhoods and jobs, lower academic performance, increased crime, and the like, the better.

Recognizing this cycle of group images and prejudice, we see how powerfully the mass media affect how majority group members perceive minoritized group members. *The Jeffersons* in the 1970s and 1980s, *Murphy Brown* in the early 1990s, and Glee in 2010 were important in bringing into mainstream awareness the issues faced by Black American families, single working moms, and gay teenagers. Similarly, in 2017, the television show *Billions* introduced a nonbinary character played by a nonbinary actor, Asia Kate Dillon. And research confirms that the more people are exposed to counterstereotypic fictional examples of marginalized groups, the less they show automatic activation of stereotyped associations (Blair et al., 2001; Dasgupta & Greenwald, 2001). In fact, an ambitious field experiment in Rwanda exposed people to one of two radio shows over the course of a year: either a soap opera with health messages or a soap opera about reducing intergroup prejudice (Paluck, 2009). Those exposed to the show about reducing prejudice displayed more positive attitudes about and behavior toward interracial marriage.

▲ In 2022, Ketanji Brown Jackson was confirmed as the first Black woman United States Supreme Court Judge.

[Bill O'Leary/The Washington Post via Getty Images]

Connecting Across a Divide: Controlling Prejudice in Intergroup Interactions

As society's laws change, popular portrayals of groups become less stereotypic, and individuals within that society feel a greater responsibility to control their biased attitudes and beliefs. Indeed, research finds that people are less likely to express their prejudice publicly if they believe that people in general will disapprove of such biases (Crandall et al., 2002). As students were faced with the reality of desegregation during the 1960s and 1970s, they were also faced with the reality of needing to control, at least to some extent, their prejudicial biases and stereotypic assumptions about outgroups. To bring it closer to home, imagine

THINK ABOUT
[Fuse/Corbis/Getty Images]

that on your first day at college, you move into your dorm room and meet your roommate. Your roommate is of a different ethnic group than you, and cultural norms and your own internal attitudes say that you should not be prejudiced. But you worry that underlying uneasiness may creep into your interactions. Will you be able to set aside any prejudices you might have and avoid stereotyping?

A Dual Process View of Prejudice The issue of controlling prejudice takes us back to the *dual process* approach (Devine, 1989; Fazio, 1990), first introduced in chapter 3. In Process 1, stereotypes and biased attitudes are brought to mind quickly and automatically through a *reflexive* or *experiential process* (sometimes called System 1). In Process 2, people employ *reflective* or *cognitive processes* (sometimes called System 2) to regulate or control the degree to which those thoughts and attitudes affect their behavior and judgment.

Because prejudicial thoughts are often reinforced by a long history of socialization and cues in one's environment, they can come to mind easily, but this does not mean they cannot be controlled. For one thing, controlling one's biases requires an awareness that those biases are present, and some people are more aware of their biases than are others (Perry et al., 2015). Education can also raise awareness. Although interventions are mostly unsuccessful at changing people's implicit biases (Forscher et al., 2019; Lai et al., 2016), research is beginning to show that teaching people cognitive strategies to control their biases can improve their attitudes and intentions (Burns et al., 2017; Devine et al., 2017). Such education efforts can only be successful, however, if individuals are motivated to control their biases, which isn't always the case (Forscher et al., 2015). Even when people are motivated, their motivations can stem from different goals. When a motivation to avoid being biased stems from an internalized goal of being nonprejudiced, people can proactively keep implicit biases from influencing their decisions and judgment (Amodio & Swencionis, 2018). In many cases, though, the motivation to control prejudice stems from the perception of external pressures, such as the pressure to be politically correct or to avoid making others angry (Plant & Devine, 1998, 2009). Those who have little internal motivation to control their biases but feel externally coerced to keep quiet end up being resentful about having to censor themselves and have a stronger motivation to express their prejudice (Forscher et al., 2015; Plant & Devine, 2001). Research now suggests that Donald Trump's election as president of the United States in 2016 marked a shift in prejudicial attitudes. Although many social prejudices have generally been decreasing over time, those who supported Trump's presidency have shown a different pattern. Perhaps as a function of feeling justified in expressing explicit prejudice, Trump supporters have shown an increase in explicit prejudice against Blacks, Hispanics, Muslims, Jews, and immigrants (Ruisch & Ferguson, 2022).

Given the negative consequences of extrinsically motivated efforts to suppress prejudice, how is it possible to increase people's intrinsic motivation to control prejudice? One way is to impress on them the necessity of cooperating with those with whom they are working. When people realize that they need to cooperate with an outgroup person, they can be motivated to be nonbiased in their interactions with the outgroup and even show improved memory for the unique or individual aspects of that person (Neuberg & Fiske, 1987). At some level, people realize that falling back on stereotypes to form impressions might not provide the most accurate assessment of another person's character and abilities. The need to work together on a common goal helps to cue this motivation to be accurate and allows people to set aside their biases.

Research taking a neuroscience perspective has uncovered the neurological mechanisms that support these two processes (Amodio & Cikara, 2021;

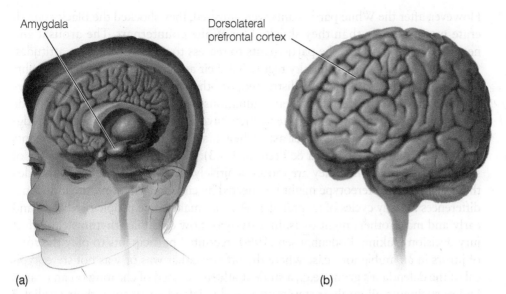

Amygdala

Dorsolateral prefrontal cortex

(a)　　　　　　　　　　　　　　　　(b)

Figure 11.4

Downregulating Prejudice

Social neuroscience research suggests that the immediate amygdala responses (a) that Whites sometimes exhibit to Black faces can be downregulated by the dorsolateral prefrontal cortex (DLPFC) (b).

Lieberman et al., 2002). Bartholow and colleagues (2006) examined specific electrical signals emitted from the brain that are indicative of efforts at cognitive control. They found that when White participants were presented with pictures of Black targets, the more of these signals that their brains emitted, the lower the accessibility of stereotypic thoughts. However, this occurred only when people's cognitive-control abilities were intact. When they were impaired through the consumption of alcohol, fewer of these specific signals were emitted, and participants were less able to control their tendency to stereotype others.

Additional research shows that when White participants were exposed very briefly (for only 30 milliseconds) to pictures of Black faces, they showed increased activation in the amygdala (the fear center of the brain) that correlated with the degree to which they associated "Black American" with "bad" on an implicit association test (**FIGURE 11.4**) (Cunningham, Johnson et al., 2004; Phelps et al., 2000). With such a brief exposure, people can do little to override knee-jerk reactions. What is interesting is that lengthening exposure to the faces to 250 milliseconds increased activation in the dorsolateral prefrontal cortex (DLPFC), the region of the brain responsible for more effortful and controlled processes of judgment and decision making. Furthermore, the more DLPFC activation people experienced, the lower the amygdala activation they exhibited. Additional studies point to the right posterior insula as playing a potentially important role in controlling the application of stereotypes (Jia, Sung & Wang, 2022). These findings suggest that automatic negative attitudes that might have sprung to mind initially can be modified by more controlled processes (Cunningham, Johnson et al., 2004).

Prejudice Isn't Always Easily Controlled The research just described sounds pretty encouraging, but marshalling resources for mental control takes effort and energy. As a result, people face a few limitations when they attempt to control their biases.

The first limitation is that sometimes people make judgments of others when they are already aroused or upset. In these situations, cognitive control is impaired, so people likely will fall back on their prejudices and stereotypes. Consider, for example, a study in which White participants were asked to deliver shocks (that were not actually administered) to a White or Black confederate under the pretext of a behavior-modification study (Rogers & Prentice-Dunn, 1981). Half the White participants were angry about an overheard insult directed toward them by the confederate. When not angered, the White participants actually chose a less severe shock for the Black confederate than they did for the White confederate.

However, after the White participants were angered, they shocked the Black confederate more strongly than they shocked his White counterpart. The arousal and negative emotion caused the participants to regress to gut-level negative attitudes.

People also can have difficulty regulating their automatically activated thoughts when they are pressed for time, distracted, or otherwise cognitively busy. Teachers are more likely to be biased in their evaluations of students if they have to grade essays under time pressure. If instead they have ample time to make their judgments, they are better able to set aside their biases to provide fairer assessments of students' work (Kruglanski & Freund, 1983). People are also more capable of setting aside biases when they are most cognitively alert. This fact leads to the idea that a tendency to stereotype might be affected by circadian rhythms, the individual differences in daily cycles of mental alertness that make some people rise bright and early and make others night owls. In a study of how circadian rhythms can affect jury decision making, Bodenhausen (1990) recruited participants to play the roles of jurors in an ambiguous case where the offense either was or was not stereotypical of the defendant's group (e.g., a student athlete accused of cheating on an exam). Did participants allow their stereotypes of the defendant to sway their verdicts? Not if they were participating in the study during their optimal time of day. But if morning people were participating in the evening or evening people were participating early in the morning, their verdicts were strongly colored by stereotypes.

The Downsides of Control Strategies   Even when people succeed in controlling their biases, some downstream consequences of these efforts can be negative. First, exerting mental effort in one context might make people less willing or able to exert effort afterward in another context. For example, when White college students had any kind of conversation with a Black peer, regardless of whether the conversation was even about race, they performed more poorly on a demanding computer task right afterward than when they had this conversation with another White student (Richeson et al., 2003; Richeson & Shelton, 2003; Richeson & Trawalter, 2005). In addition, trying to push an unwanted thought out of mind often has the ironic effect of activating that thought even more. As a result, the more people try not to think of a stereotypic bias, the more it can eventually creep back in, especially when cognitive resources are limited (Follenfant & Ric, 2010; Gordijn et al., 2004; Macrae, Bodenhausen et al., 1994).

Failure of control strategies can happen even when it seems that one has gotten past initial stereotypes to appreciate the outgroup person's individual qualities. In one study, participants who watched a video of a stigmatized student talking showed stereotype activation within the first 15 seconds, but after 12 minutes, the stereotype was no longer active or guiding judgment (Kunda et al., 2002). This might seem to be good news. However, if participants later learned that the person in the video disagreed with them, the stereotype was reactivated. The implication is that, in our own interactions, we might often succeed in getting past initial stereotypes, but those stereotypes still might lurk just offstage, waiting to make an appearance if the situation prompts negative or threatening feelings toward that person.

We've seen that conscious efforts to control prejudice, although well intentioned, can fail or backfire completely. The implication is that reducing prejudice requires more than employing strategies to control prejudice; it also requires going to the source and changing people's prejudicial attitudes. How do we do this?

Setting the Stage for Positive Change: The Contact Hypothesis

One strategy that seems to be an intuitive way to foster more positive intergroup attitudes is to encourage people actually to interact with those who are the targets of their prejudice. In the late 1940s and the 1950s, as American society started to break down barriers of racial segregation, some interesting effects on racial prejudice were observed. For example, the more White and Black merchant marines served together in racially mixed crews, the more positive their racial attitudes became (Brophy, 1946). Such observations suggest that if people of different groups interact, prejudice should be reduced. There is certainly some truth to this. Research on the mere exposure effect (see chapters 8 and 14) shows that familiarity does increase liking, all other things being equal.

The problem with this strategy is that only rarely are all other things equal! If you look around the world and back in history, you quickly notice countless examples of people of different groups having extensive contact—yet their prejudices remain and even intensify (Kotzur & Wagner, 2021). For example, in states where a high proportion of residents are Black, both White and Black participants have a stronger tendency to favor their own racial group over the other, as measured by an implicit association test (IAT; Rae et al., 2015; see **FIGURE 11.5**).

Why did interracial contact in the merchant marines reduce prejudice, whereas other forms of contact do not? In considering such questions, Allport (1954) proposed that contact between groups can reduce prejudice only if it occurs under optimal conditions. According to Allport's original recipe, four principal ingredients are necessary for positive intergroup contact:

1. *Equal status* between groups in the situation
2. Contact that is intimate and varied, allowing people to get *acquainted*
3. Contact involving intergroup cooperation toward a **superordinate goal**—that is, a goal that is beyond the ability of any one group to achieve on its own
4. *Institutional support*, or contact that is approved by authority, law, or custom

In the time since Allport laid out this recipe for reducing prejudice, hundreds of studies with thousands of participants have examined whether intergroup contact that meets these requirements can reduce prejudices based on such distinctions as race and ethnicity, sexual orientation, age, and physical and mental disabilities. These studies range from archival studies of historical situations to controlled

Superordinate goal A common problem or shared goal that groups work together to solve or achieve.

Figure 11.5

Implicit Racial Bias in the United States

Living in a diverse world doesn't guarantee a reduction in intergroup bias. In fact, in U.S. states where there is a higher ratio of Black to White residents, both White and Black respondents show a larger implicit bias in favor of their own racial group.

[Data from Rae et al., 2015]

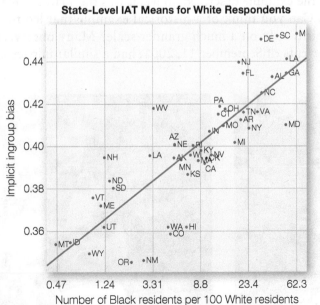

State-Level IAT Means for White Respondents

Implicit ingroup bias

Number of Black residents per 100 White residents

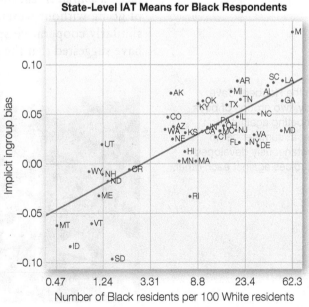

State-Level IAT Means for Black Respondents

Implicit ingroup bias

Number of Black residents per 100 White residents

interventions that manipulate features of the contact setting. Despite the diversity of methodologies, research generally finds that the more closely the contact meets Allport's requirements, the more effectively it reduces a majority group's prejudice against marginalized groups (Pettigrew & Tropp, 2006; Tropp & Pettigrew, 2005).

The Robbers Cave Study   To examine these ingredients for change in more detail, let's consider a classic study by Sherif and colleagues (Harvey et al., 1961), which dramatically demonstrates both how to create a prejudice and how to use the power of superordinate goals to reduce it. Sherif and colleagues invited 22 psychologically healthy boys to participate in a summer camp in Oklahoma. Because the camp was at the former hideout of the noted Old West outlaw Jesse James, this study has come be known as the Robbers Cave study. As the boys arrived at the camp, Sherif assigned them to one of two groups: the "Rattlers" or the "Eagles." During the first week, the groups were kept separate, but as soon as they learned of each other's existence, the seeds of prejudice toward the other group began to grow (thus showing how mere categorization can breed prejudice).

During the second week, Sherif set up a series of competitive tasks between the groups. As realistic group conflict theory would predict, this competition quickly generated remarkable hostility, prejudice, and even violence between the groups as they competed for scarce prizes. In the span of a few days, the groups were stealing from each other, using derogatory labels to refer to each other (calling the rival group sissies, communists, and stinkers; the study was conducted during the 1950s!), and getting into fistfights. Was all lost at the Robbers Cave?

It certainly appeared that way until, during the third week, Sherif introduced different types of challenges. In one of these challenges, he sabotaged the camp's water supply by clogging the faucet of the main water tank. The camp counselors announced that there was in fact a leak and that to find the leak, *all* 22 boys would need to search the pipes running from the reservoir to the camp. Thus, the campers were faced with a common goal that required their cooperation. As the Eagles and Rattlers collaborated on this and other such challenges, their hostilities disintegrated. They were no longer two groups warring with each other but rather one united group working together. Successfully achieving common goals effectively reduced their prejudice.

Another way of looking at these challenges is that the Rattlers and Eagles faced a *shared threat*. In the example described above, it was the shared threat of going without water. Can you think of a historical example that led to a similarly cooperative spirit, only on a much grander scale? Many observers have suggested that the events of September 11, 2001, had a similar impact in

► In the Robbers Cave study, two groups of boys competing against each other at summer camp spontaneously developed prejudices against each other.

reducing some types of intergroup biases in America. During and after this tragedy, the American people were confronted with the shared threat of terrorism at the hands of Osama bin Laden and al Qaeda. How did they react? In a rousing display of patriotism and goodwill, they united. Although prejudice against Muslims and Arab Americans increased, previous divisions among other groups of people were set aside—at least for a time. Research shows that the shared threat of global warming can also reduce prejudice against outgroups (Pyszczynski et al., 2012). As people think about the fate they share with others, a sense of common humanity can help reduce prejudice.

▲ In response to Russia's invasion of Ukraine in February 2022, Ukrainian president Volodymyr Zelensky called on the European Union and NATO to unite in their support of Ukrainian independence and military resistance.
[LUDOVIC MARIN/POOL/AFP via Getty Images]

Why Does Optimal Contact Work?   Although the Robbers Cave experiment is usually described as an example of how superordinate goals can help break down intergroup biases, Allport's other key ingredients for optimal contact were present as well: The boys had equal status, the cooperative activities were sanctioned by the camp counselors, and there were plenty of activities where the boys could get to know one another. But knowing that these factors reduce prejudice doesn't tell us much about why. Other research has isolated a few key mechanisms by which optimal contact creates positive change:

Reducing stereotyping. Consider that one of the most effective forms of contact involves members of different groups exchanging intimate knowledge about each other. This allows the once-different other to be *decategorized*. As a result, people are less likely to stereotype members of the outgroup (Kawakami et al., 2000).

Reducing anxiety. Optimal contact also reduces anxiety that people may have about interacting with people who are different from themselves (Stephan & Stephan, 1985). The unfamiliar can be unsettling, so by enhancing familiarity and reducing anxiety, contact helps to reduce prejudice.

Fostering empathy. Finally, optimal contact can lead someone to adopt the other person's perspective and increase feelings of empathy. This helps people to look past group differences to see what they have in common with others (e.g., Galinsky & Moskowitz, 2000).

When Do the Effects of Contact Generalize Beyond the Individual?   Does contact reduce only prejudice toward individuals whom you get to know? Or do these effects generalize to that person's group? If Frank, a Christian, develops a friendship with a Muslim roommate, Ahmed, during a stay at summer camp, will this contact generalize and reduce Frank's prejudice against other Muslims when he goes back to school? Here, too, the answer is not a simple "yes" or "no." Rather, it depends on a sequence of stages that play out over time (**FIGURE 11.6**) (Pettigrew, 1998; Pettigrew & Tropp, 2006).

In an initial stage, as two people become friends, their sense of group boundaries melts away. Perhaps you have had this experience of talking to other people and simply forgetting that they are from a different group. This is decategorization at work. When sharing their love of music, Frank and Ahmed are not Christian and Muslim; they are simply two roommates and friends. Their liking for each other replaces any initial anxiety they might have felt about interacting with a member of another group.

Figure 11.6

Stages for Intergroup Contact

Positive contact with an individual from an outgroup is most likely to generalize to the outgroup as a whole when group categorization processes are initially reduced but then reintroduced over time.

[mediaphotos/E+/Getty Images]

STAGE 1
Initial contact
Decategorization
Initial anxiety, but can lead to liking of the individual

STAGE 2
Established contact
Salient categorization
Can lessen prejudice against the outgroup

STAGE 3
Common ingroup identity
Recategorization
Maximum reduction in prejudice and fosters cooperation

Time

But if Frank is to generalize his positive impression of Ahmed to other Muslims, and if Ahmed is to generalize his positive impression of Frank to other Christians, those different social categories must again become salient during a second stage, after contact has been established (Brown & Hewstone, 2005). Also, Frank's overall impression of Muslims is more likely to change if he regards Ahmed as representative of the outgroup as a whole (Brown et al.,

 SOCIAL PSYCH AT THE MOVIES

Remember the Titans

Capturing the complexities of racial integration on film is no easy feat. Many movies tackle themes of racial prejudice, but the 2000 film *Remember the Titans* (Yakin, 2000) provides what might be the best cinematic example of how to reduce prejudice by applying Allport's formula for successful intergroup contact. This movie is based on the true story of separate high schools in Alexandria, Virginia, that were forced to merge in 1971 as part of a rather delayed effort to desegregate Virginia's public schools. Integrating the student body

▲ [Disney Enterprises, Inc/Photofest]

also meant integrating the football teams, and the movie chronicles the growing pains of this newly diversified group and its struggle to put together a winning season.

The film centers around the head coach of the Titans, Herman Boone, played by Denzel Washington, who faces an uphill battle in training a unified team of White and Black players who previously attended separate schools, played on rival teams, and still hold deeply entrenched racial prejudices. The film clearly depicts the conflict on the football field as a microcosm of the conflict in American culture in the immediate aftermath of the civil rights movement. The movie just as effectively portrays how Coach Boone pulls his team together to clinch the state championship in 1971.

Recall that one of the elements for effective intergroup contact is the presence of *institutional support*. In the movie, this support is established at the outset when the school board decides to give the head coaching job to the former coach of the Black high school rather than to the coach of the White high school (played by Will Patton). This decision sends a clear message to the players and their parents that the school board has good intentions to integrate not only the school and the athletic programs but also the staff. Although tensions occasionally flare among the coaches, they generally work together for successful integration.

The second element for effective contact is establishing *equal status*. Coach Boone makes his hard-as-nails coaching

1999). If Frank views Ahmed as being quite unlike other Muslims, then his positive feelings toward his new friend might never contribute to his broader view of Muslims. But if the category differences between them become salient and each considers the other to be representative of his religious group, then both Frank and Ahmed will develop more positive attitudes toward the respective religious outgroup more broadly.

You might be noticing a few rubs here. Effective contact seems to require getting to know an outgroup member as an individual, but this process of decategorization can prevent people from seeing that person as also being a representative of their group. There is a tension between focusing on people's individual characteristics and recognizing the unique vantage point of their group or cultural background. But understanding others' group identities is a key step in reducing prejudice against the group as a whole. This might be part of the reason that members of minoritized groups often prefer and feel more empowered by an ideology of *multiculturalism*, which endorses seeing the value of different cultural identities, over an ideology of being *colorblind*, whereby people simply pretend that group membership doesn't exist or doesn't matter (Plaut et al., 2009; Plaut et al., 2018; Vorauer & Quesnel, 2017).

Another potential pitfall is that although this second stage of established contact might reduce intergroup prejudice, there is no guarantee that it will promote intergroup cooperation. For this reason, researchers have suggested that a stage

style crystal clear to the players' parents, to the other members of his coaching staff, and to his team. But perhaps most importantly, he quite visibly metes out punishment equally to Black players and to White players. As a result, the players quickly learn that earning a starting position on the team will have nothing to do with the color of their skin. Anyone who wants to play on the team will have to work hard.

Still, the players struggle to get past their mistrust of one another. Seeing how his team continues to default to self-segregation by race, Coach Boone intervenes. When the team heads off to a training camp in two buses, he divides the players not by race but by offensive or defensive positions. To encourage contact further, he pairs White and Black players to room together for the duration of the intensive training. The overall message is that all the players, regardless of race, need to work together as a team to achieve the same *superordinate goal* of winning games.

Does this strategy of forcing players to room together work? Not at first. A White player objects to his Black roommate's iconic poster of the track and field champions Tommie Smith and John Carlos giving the raised-fist black power salute during the medal ceremony at the 1968 Olympic Games. Not surprisingly, tempers flare, and a fight breaks out. Sharing a room in the dormitory also doesn't translate into socializing during meal times. Realizing that an important ingredient—*intimate and varied contact*—is still missing,

▲ [Walt Disney/Bruckheimer Films/The Kobal Collection/Bennett, Tracy]

Coach Boone mandates that each player interview his roommate to further break down the barriers of misunderstanding and mistrust. As Allport would have predicted, the players finally begin to cooperate as a unified team after this final element of friendship is established.

Remember the Titans shows these important components of contact at work. If any of these components were missing, do you think that T. C. Williams High School still would have won the state championship in 1971? Why or why not? What lessons can we learn for creating more effective integration today?

Common ingroup identity A recategorizing of members of two or more distinct groups into a single, overarching group.

of recategorizing outgroups into a unified group, or **common ingroup identity**, will further reduce prejudice by harnessing the biases people have in favor of their ingroups (Gaertner & Dovidio, 2000). If Frank and Ahmed see each other and other members of their respective religious groups as all being part of the same camp or the same nation, then they are all in the same overarching ingroup. Perhaps this is the final dash of spice needed in the recipe of contact that will not only end intergroup prejudices but also lead to peace and cooperation.

Is this vision just pie in the sky? There are hopeful signs that having a common ingroup identity can effectively reduce some manifestations of prejudice. A few years ago, a school district in Delaware instituted the Green Circle program for elementary school students. Over the course of a month, first- and second-graders in this program participated in exercises that encouraged them to think of their social world—which they designated their "green circle"—as getting bigger and bigger to underscore the idea that all people belong to one family, the human family. Students who participated in the program were more likely later to want to share and play with other children who were of different genders, weights, and races than were students in the same school who had not yet gone through the program (Houlette et al., 2004). Studies suggest that adults also can become less prejudiced, more tolerant, and more open to immigration when the common humanity among members of different groups is made salient (Kunst et al., 2015; Motyl et al., 2011; Pavetich & Stathi, 2021; Syropoulos et al., 2022).

▲ Combating climate change to preserve the natural environments we all cherish and rely on is the kind of superordinate goal that can help make salient our common humanity and bridge across the many sub-identities that so often divide us.

[Busakorn Pongparnit/Moment/Getty Images]

Although these findings are surely encouraging, Allport (1954) was skeptical about people's ability to stay focused on the superordinate identity of humans, as opposed to more circumscribed national, regional, and family identities. For example, some theorists suggest that we are most likely to identify with groups that provide *optimal distinctiveness* (Brewer, 1991). Such groups are large enough to foster a sense of commonality but small enough to allow us to feel distinct from others. Geographic differences mean different languages, customs, arts, values, styles of living—all useful ways to define what feels like a shared but unique identity. Keeping salient the more abstract identity we all share is no easy chore, but superordinate goals and concerns can help.

Does Contact Increase Positive Attitudes Toward the Majority Group? It should be noted that our discussion so far has focused largely on how contact can help members of more advantaged social groups develop more positive intergroup attitudes and become invested in working toward equality (Tropp & Barlow, 2018). What about the other side of the coin? Does optimal contact also improve intergroup attitudes for the marginalized group member, such as the Black American woman or the gay man put into contact with members of the majority group? A small body of research on this question shows that contact is more of a mixed bag for those from the marginalized group (Tropp & Pettigrew, 2005). Contact situations often are framed from the perspective of reducing biases held by a majority group. The risk is that marginalized-group members can feel stripped of an important identity. Furthermore, when marginalized-group individuals are exposed to prejudice against their group, which is more likely to occur in the initial stages of contact, this prejudice can intensify their negative attitudes toward the majority group (Tropp, 2003). Contact situations might need to be designed specifically to reduce marginalized-group members' own biases against the majority.

APPLICATION

Implementing Optimal Contact in a Jigsaw Classroom

Although each of Allport's conditions can improve racial attitudes (at least among the majority group), the best recipe for success is to combine all the ingredients in the contact setting (Pettigrew & Tropp, 2006). Because the desegregation of schools seldom included all of these components for effective contact, initial evaluations of school desegregation found little success in reducing prejudice and intergroup conflict (Stephan, 1978). For example, school settings tend to emphasize competition rather than cooperation; authority figures are often mainly from the majority group, and the minoritized students don't feel they have equal status; and ethnic groups often segregate within the school, minimizing the opportunity for intimate contact and cooperation.

How can schools do better? Consider a cooperative learning technique developed by Elliot Aronson and colleagues called the *jigsaw classroom* (**FIGURE 11.7**) (Aronson et al., 1978). In this approach, the teacher creates a lesson that can be broken down into several subtopics. For example, if the topic is the presidency of the United States, the subtopics might include influential presidents, how the executive branch relates to other branches of the government, how the president is elected, and so on. The class is also subdivided into racially mixed groups, and one person in each group is given the responsibility of learning one of the subtopics of the lesson. This student meets with other students from other groups assigned to that subtopic so that they can all review, study, and become experts in that topic and create some kind of artifact such as a poster or a presentation to summarize their newly gained knowledge. The experts then return to their original group and take turns teaching the others what they have learned.

The power of this approach is its potential for embodying all of Allport's conditions for optimal contact. First, because the task is assigned by the teacher,

Achieve
Video Profile: The Life and Work of Elliot Aronson

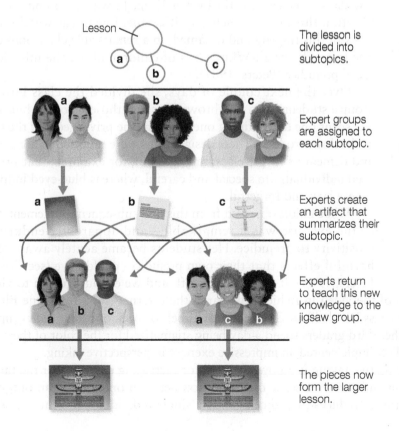

Figure 11.7

Jigsaw Classroom

In a jigsaw classroom assignment, a lesson is divided into different subtopics, and students in diverse groups are given the assignment of mastering one subtopic. These expert groups work together to create an artifact (e.g., a joint summary or poster). Then members of each expert group return to teach their newfound knowledge to the jigsaw group, where each member has now learned a piece that makes up the larger lesson. By giving every student equal status and encouraging cooperation toward a common goal, the jigsaw classroom is an effective way to reduce prejudice.

Lesson

The lesson is divided into subtopics.

Expert groups are assigned to each subtopic.

Experts create an artifact that summarizes their subtopic.

Experts return to teach this new knowledge to the jigsaw group.

The pieces now form the larger lesson.

it is authority sanctioned. Second, because the students are all in charge of their own subtopics, all the kids become experts and thus have equal status. Third, the group is graded both individually (recall our discussion from chapter 9 on accountability and social loafing) and as a group. Thus, the students share a common goal. And fourth, to do well and reach that common goal, they must cooperate in intimate and varied ways, both teaching and learning from each other. All the pieces must fit together, like the pieces in a jigsaw puzzle.

Is the jigsaw classroom successful? On the one hand, recent studies do not find better learning outcomes for students who go through the jigsaw classroom compared to traditional methods (Stanczak et al., 2022). However, compared with children in traditional classrooms, children who go through the program show increased self-esteem, intrinsic motivation for learning, and, most crucially, increased peer liking across racial and ethnic groups (Blaney et al., 1977; Hänze & Berger, 2007; Slavin, 2012). ■

Reducing Prejudice Without Contact

As we've just seen, Allport provided us with an excellent playbook for reducing intergroup prejudices through positive and cooperative contact. But sometimes people hold prejudices about groups with which they never interact. When the opportunities for contact are infrequent, can other psychological strategies reduce intergroup biases? The answer is "yes."

Perspective Taking and Empathy Earlier, we mentioned that one of the reasons optimal contact can be so effective is that it creates opportunities to take the perspective of members of the other group and see the world through their eyes. Direct contact isn't the only way for people to learn this lesson. To see why, let's go back in time to 1968, just a few days after Dr. Martin Luther King, Jr. was assassinated. Jane Elliott, a third-grade teacher in Riceville, Iowa, was watching the news of this tragedy and dreamed up a remarkable classroom exercise to teach her all-White class of children about the injustice of racial prejudice (Peters, 1987).

Over the next couple of days, she divided the class into two groups: students who had brown eyes and those who had blue eyes. She spent one day defining one group as the privileged and the other as the downtrodden. These designations were reflected in her actions and demeanor to the class, telling them, for example, that brown-eyed individuals are special and careful, whereas blue-eyed individuals are lazy and forgetful.

What Elliott observed from this and subsequent implementations of the exercise was a remarkable—and apparently enduring—sensitivity to prejudice. Her students became acutely aware of the harmful effects that their own prejudices could have (see Cobb & Peters, 1985). It is powerful stuff, and we encourage you to view a portion of the video in Achieve or search the Internet (look for "Jane Elliott" plus "A Class Divided" on Google or YouTube) to check out some video clips. In having her third-graders spend a day being stigmatized for the color of their eyes, Jane Elliott implemented an impressive exercise in perspective taking.

Perspective taking is a powerful tool for increasing empathy for the target's situation and creates a sense of connection between oneself and an outgroup. This strategy reduces prejudice against a single individual, and those positive

Achieve
Video: Eye of the Storm Parts I & II (Jane Elliott's Blue-Eyed/Brown-Eyed Experiment)

▲ In the aftermath of the assassination of Dr. Martin Luther King, Jr., Jane Elliott taught her third-grade class about prejudice by having them feel what it is like to be targeted by negative stereotypes.

[Charlotte Button, Photographer, courtesy of Jane Elliott]

feelings are often likely to generalize to other members of the outgroup (Dovidio et al., 2004; Galinsky & Moskowitz, 2000; Vescio et al., 2003; Vorauer & Sasaki, 2009). For example, in one study, participants who were asked to imagine vividly the experiences of a young woman who had been diagnosed with AIDS (as opposed to taking a more objective viewpoint toward her plight) felt more empathy for AIDS victims in general as well as for her (Batson et al., 1997).

Perspective taking not only reduces explicit types of prejudice but also might reduce more implicit and subtle forms of bias we described earlier. For example, imagine that you are White and that you are asked to write about a day in the life of a young Black man (Todd et al., 2011). If you are in the perspective-taking condition, you will be told to visualize what the young man might be thinking and feeling as he goes about his day. If you are in the control condition, you will be told to take a more objective approach to writing about his day. After doing your respective assignment as well as some other unrelated surveys, you are led to a different room and asked to grab two chairs from a stack and set them up for a mock-interview task between you and an assistant named either "Jake," a typical White name, or "Tyrone," a typical Black name.

Unknown to the participants who actually were in this study, the researchers measured the distance between the two chairs as an implicit measure of prejudice. They reasoned that if people had a more positive attitude toward the interviewer, they would set the chairs closer together. As you can see in **FIGURE 11.8**, participants in the control condition elected to sit farther away from Tyrone than from Jake. But if they first had to take the perspective of another young Black man during the earlier task, they sat at the same distance from the assistant, regardless of his race.

Members of majority groups can often be blind to the privilege they enjoy (e.g., "I am never asked to speak for all the people of my racial group", McIntosh, 1988). But lessons in White privilege can increase empathy for those who experience racial bias (Cooley et al., 2019). In fact, in one very clever study conducted in Barcelona, Spain, researchers used virtual reality to have light-skinned female participants see and feel what it would look like to walk around with darker skin. Participants who spent about 20 minutes inhabiting a virtual body with darker skin subsequently exhibited a weaker implicit negative attitude toward Black people on an IAT than did participants who had a light-skinned virtual body; those who had an alien-looking, purple-skinned virtual body; or those who did not have a virtual body and merely saw a dark-skinned person walk in the background of their virtual world (Peck et al., 2013).

These benefits of perspective taking are impressive, but it is important to note that although perspective taking can reduce prejudicial attitudes, it is not always effective at changing people's stereotypes (Huang et al., 2021; Skorinko & Sinclair, 2013; Sun et al., 2016). One reason might be that people often do not accurately guess how others truly feel (Eyal et al., 2018). To become accurate in perceiving others, it's better to take the time to learn what they feel and think than to assume that we can imagine what their experience is truly like.

Reducing Prejudice by Bolstering the Self Perspective taking reduces prejudice by changing the way people think about others. But can we also reduce

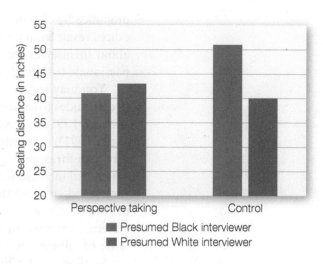

Figure 11.8

Reducing Prejudice with Perspective Taking

Although White participants in a control condition chose to keep their distance from a Black interviewer, after having vividly imagined the day in the life of a young Black man, this implicit form of bias was eliminated.

[Data from Todd et al., 2011]

prejudice by changing how people think about themselves? Because some prejudices result from people's deep-seated feelings of insecurity, when their feelings about themselves are bolstered, they often can become more tolerant and compassionate toward those who are different.

You may recall a couple of theories suggesting that people take on negative attitudes toward others to protect their positive view of themselves (Fein & Spencer, 1997). For example, according to terror management theory (Solomon et al., 1991), encountering someone who holds a very different cultural worldview can threaten the belief system that upholds one's sense of personal value, which can increase fears about death. When people feel that their self-esteem is threatened, or when they are reminded of their mortality, they cling more tightly to their own worldview, which can mean derogating those with a different belief system. Therefore, one remedy for prejudice might be to bolster an individual's sense of self-esteem (Harmon-Jones et al., 1997; Schmeichel et al., 2009).

Similarly, self-affirmation theory (Steele, 1988) also predicts that prejudice can be a defensive reaction to feelings of personal insecurity. In the Fein and Spencer (1997) study discussed in chapter 10, participants who received negative feedback were more likely to derogate a Jewish student. However, if participants first had the chance to think about how they lived up to their own values, they showed no such pattern of discrimination.

Although bolstering a person's self-esteem can reduce prejudice, there is one caveat to this effect: If the value system being bolstered is the cultural worldview threatened by the outgroup, then the effects of self-affirmation can backfire (Arndt & Greenberg, 1999). For example, although you might be able to reduce antigay prejudice by affirming people's values and abilities in areas such as athletics or sense of humor, an affirmation of their traditional family values will do little to decrease this prejudice (Lehmiller et al., 2010; Vescio & Biernat, 2003).

Reducing Prejudice with a More Multicultural Ideology   In part, bolstering how people see themselves reduces prejudice because it makes people more open minded and less defensive (Sherman & Cohen, 2006). This leads us to consider perhaps a more straightforward strategy for reducing prejudice: reminding people of their tolerant values so that they are more willing to accept, if not embrace, others' differences (Greenberg, Simon et al., 1992; Vail et al., 2019).

Sometimes people believe that the best way to be tolerant is to embrace a **colorblind ideology**—that is, view people only on their individual merits and avoid any judgment based on group membership. One concern with the colorblind approach is that it encourages efforts simply to control any biases or prejudices that one has toward an outgroup. Although this can sometimes be an effective way to avoid engaging in discrimination, our earlier discussion of controlling prejudice revealed that these efforts can also backfire.

Another criticism of the colorblind approach is that it can imply that everyone should conform to the status quo and act as if ethnic differences don't matter (Plaut et al., 2018). As we alluded to previously, the colorblind approach is a much more comfortable stance for the advantaged majority group than for currently disadvantaged minoritized groups. Whites in the United States tend to take this to the extreme, sometimes failing to mention a person's race, even when doing so is simply stating a descriptive fact about an individual that could help describe the person to whom they are referring (Apfelbaum et al., 2008; Norton et al., 2006).

An alternative is to embrace cultural pluralism, or a **multicultural ideology**, which acknowledges and appreciates different cultural viewpoints. This view emphasizes not just tolerating but actively embracing diversity. To understand

Colorblind ideology A worldview in which group identities are ignored and people are judged solely on their individual merits, thereby avoiding any judgment based on group membership.

Multicultural ideology A worldview in which different cultural identities and viewpoints are acknowledged and appreciated.

the distinction between these two ideologies, consider the metaphors used in the United States and Canada, two countries that were formed largely as a result of immigration. The United States is typically referred to as a melting pot, a place where people of different ethnicities and former nationalities might converge and blend to form a single group. In Canada, the prevailing metaphor is the salad bowl, where citizens form an integrated collective while still maintaining their distinct ethnic heritage. These two approaches can have distinct effects for marginalized groups. When institutions signal that they value the diverse perspectives and contributions from minoritized students, for example, those students tend to feel a greater sense of belonging and perform better (Brannon et al., 2015).

▲ Diversity can be described through metaphor. The melting pot depicts a colorblind approach, whereas the salad bowl emphasizes multiculturalism.

From a psychological perspective, these different ideologies suggest different ways of approaching intergroup relations. A colorblind approach suggests that we should *avoid* focusing on group identity, whereas multiculturalism suggests that we should *approach* group differences as something to be celebrated (Chen et al., 2016). Members of advantaged groups who endorse a multicultural ideology tend to be less implicitly and explicitly prejudiced and are more likely to seek out contact with other groups (Leslie et al., 2020; Plaut et al., 2018; Rosenthal & Levy, 2013; Whitley & Webster, 2019). Furthermore, going into an interaction with a multicultural mind-set might sidestep all of the problems we see when people are focused on avoiding being biased. This is just what Trawalter and Richeson (2006) have found. When White participants were told to avoid being biased during an interaction with Black students, they became cognitively depleted from the effort and probably less receptive to future intergroup interactions. But when they were instead told to approach the interaction as an opportunity to have a positive interracial exchange, those effects weren't present, and the interaction went more smoothly.

In a clever application of a similar idea, Kerry Kawakami and her colleagues (Kawakami et al., 2007) showed that these approach tendencies can be trained quite subtly. In one of their studies, participants completed an initial task in which they simply had to pull a joystick toward them when they saw the word *approach* displayed on a screen or push it away from them when they saw the word *avoid*. Unknown to the participants, faces were subliminally presented just before the target words appeared. Some individuals always were shown a Black face when they were cued to approach; others were shown a Black face when they were cued to avoid. After completing this task, participants had an unconscious association to approach or avoid Blacks. When they were asked to engage in an interracial interaction with a Black confederate, those in the approach condition behaved in a friendlier and more open way than those in the avoid condition. These results show that our goals for interactions can be cued and created unconsciously as well as consciously and that an approach orientation toward diverse others can be quite beneficial.

Although these findings are encouraging, embracing diversity is not without challenges. Even majority group members who try to take a multicultural approach run the risk of being ham-handed in their efforts (*You're Asian, do you know of a good sushi restaurant I could try?*, Zou & Cheryan, 2015). Promoting diversity also makes salient both group categories and differences between groups. And in cultural-diversity training, the line between teaching about valid cultural differences and promoting unwarranted stereotypes is sometimes crossed. Fortunately, recent research shows that multiculturalism is not generally viewed as a "zero-sum" situation that inherently threatens the majority group (Ballinger & Crocker, 2021).

Final Thoughts

Social psychology has taught us a lot about where prejudice comes from and how it is activated, and it has also shown us how it affects others and how it can be reduced. Yes, there is a long and varied list of cures, but that's because bias has many different causes and manifestations. Our interest in being egalitarian can motivate us to control our biases and become more tolerant of diversity in society (Verkuyten & Yogeeswaran, 2017). However, moving beyond a "live and let live" brand of tolerance to embracing the value of different viewpoints and perspectives may be the most effective way of achieving intergroup harmony.

Embracing the value of diversity assumes that people *want* to achieve intergroup harmony. Broader changes in cultural norms can play a powerful role in helping people internalize these motivations. The more we see others behave and interact in an egalitarian way, the more we follow suit (MacInnis et al., 2017). Reducing prejudice doesn't happen overnight. All of us will suffer relapses on the way, but cultures can shift gradually toward equality. Reducing prejudice against a segment of the population can benefit everyone in the end. For example, cross-national data from the World Bank reveals a strong positive correlation between equivalent educational opportunities for both girls and boys and the economic prosperity of a country (Chen, 2004). We can all benefit from maximizing the well-being and opportunities of everyone in society.

SECTION REVIEW Reducing Prejudice

Prejudice does not have a single cause. Various strategies are available to reduce it.

Changing the Culture	Controlling Prejudice in Interactions	The Contact Hypothesis	Reducing Prejudice Without Contact
Long-term, systematic reduction of prejudice requires changing laws, customs, and norms.	• Individuals can prevent their automatically activated prejudices from affecting their behavior. • However, controlling prejudice is not always easy and can backfire.	• According to Allport's conditions, optimal intergroup contact can reduce prejudice when it involves: 1. Equal status 2. Potential to make friends 3. Cooperation toward shared goals 4. Buy-in from those in power • Optimal contact reduces stereotyping, decreases intergroup anxiety, and increases empathy for the outgroup. • Positive effects of contact are often weaker for members of the minoritized group. • The jigsaw classroom is an application of optimal contact to education.	• Perspective taking increases empathy and decreases negative stereotypes. • Bolstering people's good feelings about themselves helps them feel less threatened by those who hold different views. • Multiculturalism is perhaps the most effective ideology for reducing biases held by the majority while also valuing diverse perspectives held by minoritized groups.

CRITICAL LEARNING EXERCISES

1. Do you have some identity that is negatively stereotyped or socially devalued in some domain or aspect? Can you think about a time when someone perceived you through the lens of this identity? How did it make you feel or react, and how did you cope with it?

2. When people experience instances of subtle bias, is it better to try to downplay the experience in the interest of having a smooth interaction or to confront the person who has displayed the bias? When are people likely to do one or the other?

3. Compare and contrast the difference between treating people the same regardless of their identity (i.e., being blind to their identity) and valuing the different cultural backgrounds of people (i.e., multiculturalism). Is one of these ideologies more effective for reducing bias?

4. If you had to lead, manage, or teach a diverse group of people, how would you apply research regarding intergroup contact to reduce the possible biases those people might have against one another?

Don't stop now! Check out our videos and additional resources located at: www.macmillanlearning.com

TOPIC OVERVIEW

CHAPTER 12

Interpersonal Aggression

Nonviolence means avoiding not only external physical violence but also internal violence of spirit. You not only refuse to shoot a man, but you refuse to hate him.

—Martin Luther King Jr. (1992, p. 102)

Mass shootings used to be a very rare occurrence in the United States. In 2019, however, more than 400 mass shootings (defined in this case as at least 4 people being shot by a single individual) occurred in the United States (Gun Violence Archive, 2019). For example, a man was fired from his job one August morning, and a few hours later he went on a shooting spree with an assault rifle in Texas, killing 7 people and wounding many others (CBS News, 2019). But mass shootings haven't just happened in the United States. On July 22, 2016, a depressed teenager obsessed with violent video games went on a shooting spree in Munich, Germany, killing 9 people and leaving three dozen injured (Jahn & Rising, 2016). This attack was partly inspired by the fifth anniversary of an incredibly deadly attack. On July 22, 2011, a 32-year-old Norwegian man, Anders Behring Breivik, first set off a bomb near a government building in Oslo, killing 8 people, then went to a youth summer camp, where he shot and killed 69 young people and camp counselors (Mala & Goodman, 2011). Although some observers have suggested that mental health problems contributed to Breivik's horrendous actions, many of the specific factors known to contribute to aggression likely played roles as well. He was an isolated man, full of hostile feelings, who had experienced failure and frustration in his life. He was also a fan of violent electronic media and hate-filled right-wing websites (Schwirtz & Saltmarsh, 2011).

Although mass shootings have become an increasing threat in recent years and are certainly of great concern, the majority of gun-related murders in the United States in 2019 were not related to mass shootings (Gun Violence Archive, 2019). In addition, many less direct acts of aggression lead to tragedy. On December 1, 2016, 18-year-old Brandy Vela shot herself in the chest in her Texas home while her family pleaded with her not to. She had experienced months of relentless cyberbullying regarding her weight on Facebook and in texts to her cell phone. As her father put it, "I feel like these people are cowards, these people hiding behind the texts and fake pages. They're the ones who pushed her to this point. She lost all her self-esteem, lost all her self-worth" (Gullo, 2016). The cyberbullying even continued after her death.

Cyberbullying can involve behaviors such as posting rumors and insults and uploading embarrassing photos, videos, and computer viruses. It is a particularly invasive form of bullying because it can follow the victim home or anywhere with Internet access. Given repeated instances of tragedies such as this, many states have enacted

▲ All humans are capable of aggression, and monsters often don't look like monsters. Does this man look like a mass murderer? Maybe not, but in 2011, he set off a bomb in an office building before committing mass murder at a summer camp.

[DANIEL SANNUM LAUTEN/AFP/Getty Images]

laws against cyberbullying (Donnerstein, 2011). But it can be difficult to apprehend the perpetrators, such as those who drove Brandy to suicide, as they often use apps that protect their anonymity.

Fortunately, horrific acts such the ones we have just recounted are relatively rare. On the other hand, who among us has never insulted, pushed, snapped at, punched, or kicked another individual (or wanted to) sometime in our lives? Almost all of us have engaged in at least minor acts of aggression. To get a sense of how pervasive aggression is, consider these statistics: There were almost 700,000 incidents of child abuse in the United States in 2015 (National Children's Alliance, n.d.). In addition, 20 to 30% of American romantic partners report that acts of aggression have occurred in their relationships. On average, a woman in the United States is raped every six minutes, and more than 70% of those rapes are committed by someone the woman knows; about 4% of male inmates in U.S. prisons report having been sexually assaulted (Federal Bureau of Investigation [FBI], 2015). Some American cities average more than one murder per day (Truman & Morgan, 2016). During the July 4 holiday period from June 30 to July 5 in 2017 in Chicago, more than 100 people were shot, 15 fatally (Nickeas et al., 2017).

How can we understand such interpersonal aggression? This chapter covers theories and research that provide some answers:

■ We define aggression and look at how researchers measure it.

■ We look at biological factors that underlie human aggression.

■ We map out the situational and cultural factors that make aggression more likely.

■ We examine the role of individual difference variables, including gender, intelligence, and personality.

■ We provide coverage of two specific topics because of their prevalence: the role of alcohol and drugs and violence against women.

■ We conclude by applying our knowledge of the causes of aggression to steps to take to reduce interpersonal violence in society.

▲ Tina Meier gazes at a picture of her daughter, Megan Meier, who committed suicide on October 16, 2007, after being victimized by cyberbullies. Tina created the Megan Meier foundation (meganmeierfoundation.org) to teach others about the harmful effects of Internet harassment.
[Sarah Conard/AP Images]

- Define aggression from a social psychology point of view.
- Explain the importance of intention.
- Describe the different types of harm that aggression can cause.
- Compare the two types of aggression.

Aggression Any physical or verbal behavior that is intended to harm another person or persons (or any other living thing).

Defining Aggression

Defining aggression is difficult because the word is used to describe many different things, from a persistent salesperson to a rude comment. Let's start by defining **aggression** as any physical or verbal behavior that is intended to harm another person or persons (or any other living thing). This definition implies that an aggressive act may be intended to cause physical harm (a punch) or psychological harm (e.g., posting hurtful comments on Twitter) or both. We generally reserve the term *violence* for acts of aggression with more severe or lasting consequences.

The Role of Intention

Our definition of aggression emphasizes the intention of the person committing the act. If a person intends to harm another person but isn't successful (e.g., throws a punch but misses), we would consider that an aggressive act. Likewise, aggression can be a deliberate *failure* to act (e.g., not telling someone that he is about to embarrass himself because you want to see him humiliated). When a lifeguard applies painful pressure to someone's chest in order to help her breathe, we wouldn't call this aggression because the intention is to save a life.

The Harm Caused by Aggression

When acts of aggression are physical, the harm can be in the form of pain, suffering, injury, or death. Nonlethal types of physical violence, such as rape and assault, can be psychologically traumatic for the victim, leading to general feelings of anxiety, hypervigilance, sleeplessness, nightmares, rumination, irritability, self-blame, emotional detachment (dissociation), difficulty concentrating, and humiliation. An act of violence can shatter a person's normally secure feeling that the world is a safe and orderly place (Coker et al., 2002; Janoff-Bulman & Yopyk, 2004; Winkel & Denkers, 1995). In extreme cases, posttraumatic stress disorder (PTSD) may occur, and it may extend these negative reactions over many years (Keane et al., 1990). In short, many acts of violence change the victim's life forever.

As the story of Brandy Vela's suicide illustrates, verbal insults, social rejection, and cyberbullying can also have grave consequences. These acts cause feelings of frustration, humiliation, anxiety, anger, social isolation, helplessness, and despair. In children, they can result in reduced self-esteem, poorer grades, and depression (e.g., Donnerstein, 2011). These negative feelings also can lead to aggressive acts of retaliation, resulting in a vicious cycle of violence. One such incident was the mass shooting at Columbine High School in Colorado in 1999, a shocking and highly publicized act that probably sparked the alarming increase in frequency of mass shootings in the years since then. The killers, Dylan Klebold and Eric Harris, felt rejected and bullied, and they reacted by killing 12 students and a teacher before turning their weapons on themselves (Chua-Eoan, 2007). Seung-Hui Cho, who killed 32 people at Virginia Tech University in 2009, was also the target of verbal aggression in high school and regarded the Columbine killers as heroes standing up for the oppressed. According to a student in his English class, "As soon as he started reading, the whole class started laughing and pointing and saying, 'Go back to China'" (NBC News, 2007). People stripped of a sense of significance and value in the world, whether due to being victims of aggression or other life circumstances, sometimes perceive lashing out violently as their only recourse to enact revenge and to have a lasting impact on the world (Greenberg, 2015).

Acts of aggression that lead to serious harm or death also have wide-ranging effects on those who care about the victim (e.g., Parkes & Weiss, 1983). For example, after 49 people at an Orlando nightclub were fatally shot by an angry gunman in 2016, about 50,000 people gathered in public parks to mourn the victims (Turkewitz, 2016). The community's pain was so great, in fact, that charity groups sent in the K-9 Comfort Dogs team—12 golden retrievers trained to provide emotional support to the families of those killed, emergency medical workers, and anyone else who could use unconditional canine affection following that horrific shooting (Bromwich, 2016).

Finally, we should note that the collateral damage from aggression extends to those who witness it (Davis & Carlson, 1987). They often experience symptoms of trauma. Those who survive attacks such as the Norway and Orlando shootings also often experience survivor guilt, the haunting sense that there is

▲ People all over the world held vigils in honor of the victims of the mass shooting in an Orlando, Florida, nightclub on June 12, 2016.
[BRENDAN SMIALOWSKI/AFP/Getty Images]

something unjust in their own survival when those equally innocent did not survive (Erikson, 1968).

Affective and Instrumental Aggression

Affective aggression Harm-seeking done to another person that is elicited in response to some negative emotion.

Instrumental aggression Harm-seeking done to another person that serves some other goal.

Social psychologists distinguish between two types of aggression (Geen, 2001). With **affective aggression**, a person intends to harm the other person simply for the sake of doing so. Such behavior is motivated by a strong affective, or emotional, state. Affective aggression often is impulsive, as when a fight breaks out at a bar, but it can be delayed and calculated, as in the case of a premeditated plan to seek revenge by throwing a rock through someone's window. **Instrumental aggression** occurs when someone intends to harm another person in order to serve some other goal. Take the school bully who hits a classmate to get his lunch, or a professional hit man who murders for a fee. Instrumental aggression is not triggered by strong emotions, but it's still intended to harm. Although it's useful to distinguish these two types of aggression, they often blend together to fuel aggressive acts. A husband may punch his wife in anger but also to maintain control over her.

Although instrumental aggression certainly is important, most of the theory and research we will discuss deals with the "hot," affective type of aggression because it appears to characterize a majority of the aggressive acts committed. For example, in 2018, more than half of murders were committed by a current or former romantic partner, a family member, or a friend (FBI, 2018).

Measuring Aggression

As illustrated by the previously mentioned statistics, researchers have precise ways to categorize types of aggression and quantify aggressive acts. These data allow them to chart how aggression correlates with factors like violent TV watching and economic conditions. But if researchers want to go deeper and examine what *causes* aggression, they need ways to measure the behavior without assaults and shootings breaking out in their labs. Fortunately, laboratory paradigms have been developed that lead participants to believe they are causing physical harm to someone else without actually doing so (Geen, 2001). For example, participants have been given opportunities to administer electric shocks to supposed other participants (e.g., Buss, 1961) or dole out a dose of painfully spicy hot sauce (e.g., Lieberman et al., 1999). Although not typical, these are forms of aggression; in fact, hot sauce has been used in numerous cases of child abuse (Koppel, 2011; Lieberman et al., 1999).

SECTION REVIEW Defining Aggression

Aggression is any physical or verbal behavior—or deliberate failure to act—that is intended to harm another person(s) or any living thing.

| This definition emphasizes the *intention* to harm rather than the consequences of the behavior. | Harm from aggression affects not only the victim but also loved ones, witnesses, and sometimes the broader community. | Aggression can take two forms.

• Affective: emotionally driven actions where the intent is to harm.
• Instrumental: actions that do harm but the intention is to achieve another goal. |

Biology and Human Aggression

Before World War I, Sigmund Freud (1921/1955) maintained that people are motivated by an inborn instinct to seek pleasure and to create, which he called **eros**. But after observing how willing and even eager people were to torture, maim, and murder one another during the war, he proposed that humans are also born with an aggressive instinct, which he called **thanatos**, that seeks to destroy life. Was Freud right? Is aggressiveness biologically programmed into human nature? There is no simple answer to this question. Some evidence on the "yes" side comes from comparisons of humans with other animal species.

An Ethological Perspective

Ethology, or behavioral biology, is the study of animal behavior in its natural context. Konrad Lorenz, a Nobel Prize–winning Austrian ethologist, posited that if we observe humans and other species displaying similar aggressive behaviors under roughly similar situations, we can infer that those behaviors helped humans and other species alike to survive and reproduce (Lorenz, 1966). Such evidence would suggest that we are innately prepared to aggress under certain conditions.

In fact, we do observe interesting parallels in the aggressive behavior of humans and other animal species. For example, in species as diverse as chimpanzees, crayfish, and bald eagles, an organism will usually aggress against another organism that attempts to acquire or gain control over material resources that are necessary for survival, such as food, nesting sites, and feeding sites (Enquist & Leimar, 1983). Similarly, humans display anger and aggression when others attempt to take control of their territory or property (Worchel & Teddie, 1976).

Animal species also show signs of threat and aggression when they or their offspring are attacked, tendencies that are also seen in humans. Indeed, laws in most cultures formally recognize that aggression in defense of self or others is justified. Aggression in the animal world is also commonly seen in competition over social status. In many social species, such as monkeys, apes, and hyenas, members of a group are organized in a dominance hierarchy. Lower-status group members (particularly males) sometimes try to achieve a higher status to gain access to more material resources, sexual partners, and control over others' behavior. Of course, high-status group members are reluctant to relinquish their dominant position and respond to a competitor with overt displays of anger. If the competitor doesn't back down, physical combat may ensue.

In humans, too, threats to status are a primary trigger for aggression. From the tribal communities of Highland New Guinea (Sargent, 1974) to the Jivaro people of the western Amazon (Karsten, 1935) to the street gangs of America's cities (Toch, 1969), threats to one's honor or status often trigger violent or even homicidal aggressive acts among young men. Also consistent with the idea that anger and aggression function to maintain one's reputation, people are especially likely to retaliate against someone who insults them when they know that an audience has witnessed the insult (Brown, 1968; Felson, 1982; Kim et al., 1998).

Across species, aggression is often triggered by the perception that others are making one's life difficult, either by imposing costs (e.g., direct threats to survival, stealing resources) or denying benefits (e.g., preventing a rise in status). In addition, anger and aggression seem to have similar functions across species. Anger displays (e.g., baring one's teeth) deter others who might challenge one's

- Explain how aggression in animals relates to aggression in humans.
- Identify regions of the brain that respond to threat.
- Describe the uniquely human aspects of aggression.

Eros Freud's term for what he proposed is the human inborn instinct to seek pleasure and to create.

Thanatos Freud's term for what he proposed is the human inborn instinct to aggress and to destroy.

▲ Many social species have dominance hierarchies. These animals use the threat of aggression to achieve and maintain a position of status within the group.

[Danita Delimont/Gallo Images/Getty Images]

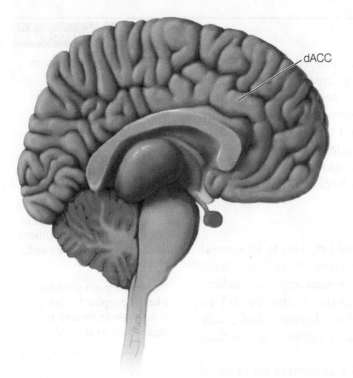

dACC

Figure 12.1

The Dorsal Anterior Cingulate Cortex (dACC)

This brain area is active when people detect actions and outcomes that interfere with their goals, including social threats.

▲ Driving is one situation in which our expectations can be violated (e.g., when another car veers in front of us). When this happens, the dorsal anterior cingulate cortex is activated and prepares us to act, sometimes aggressively.

[Sean Murphy/Getty Images]

status (Sell, 2011). If displays of anger are not effective at changing others' behavior, aggression is a way to reinforce the message (Clutton-Brock & Parker, 1995). Given these parallels, it seems likely that the human mind has inherited a propensity to respond to certain situations with anger and, in some cases, aggression.

The Physiology of Aggression

If the human mind evolved to respond to certain situations with anger and aggression, then these adaptations should be reflected in our physiology. Research has indeed discovered physiological mechanisms involved in the detection of social threat, the experience of anger, and engaging in aggressive behavior.

Brain Regions One region of the brain involved in the detection of social threat is the *dorsal anterior cingulate cortex*, or dACC (see **FIGURE 12.1**). This region responds when there is a conflict between our expectations and the situation we are in (Bush et al., 2000).

Insults and other provocations have been shown to activate the dACC because those situations create conflict between how we feel we should be treated and how we actually are treated. To see how this works, consider a study by Denson and colleagues (2009). Participants were asked to complete difficult puzzles and to state their answers to the puzzles out loud to the experimenter. The experimenter pretended not to hear the participants and politely prompted them to speak louder. But on the third such "mishearing," the experimenter insulted the participants by saying in an irate and condescending tone, "Look, this is the third time I've had to say this! Can't you follow directions?" Relative to the baseline measure taken earlier, participants showed increased activation in the dACC after the insult. This activation was positively correlated with how much anger they felt toward the experimenter. Related research shows that the dACC is activated when we feel rejected by others (Eisenberger & Lieberman, 2004). Rejection is an important cause of aggressive behavior, as we will see later in this chapter. Krämer and colleagues (2007) found that the more people showed dACC activation in response to a provocation by another person, the more willing they were to retaliate against that person by subjecting him or her to blasts of painful noise.

The *hypothalamus* and the *amygdala* (see **FIGURE 12.2**) are two other brain regions involved in the experiences of fear and anger, which often elicit aggressive behaviors. When we are faced with threat, the hypothalamus kicks into high-arousal mode, preparing our body for "fight or flight"—that is, fleeing from danger or preparing to aggress against the threatening stimulus. The amygdala responds to threatening stimuli with processes generating fear or anger. When the emotion is fear, the behavior is avoidance, or "flight." When the emotion is anger, the behavior is aggression, or "fight." In experiments with cats and monkeys, a lesion to the amygdala leads them to be excessively tame, whereas stimulation to the amygdala leads them to display signs of anger such as shrieks and hisses. Neuroimaging studies show that our limbic system revs up in response to displays of anger in others, such as menacing faces (Murphy et al., 2003; Pezawas et al., 2005), and provocations such as unfair treatment by a peer (Meyer-Lindenberg et al., 2006).

Body Chemistry A number of hormones play roles in the experience of anger and aggressive behavior. The most widely studied of them is the sex hormone testosterone. The more people secrete testosterone, the more likely they are to aggress. For example, in one study, men who committed assault and other aggressive crimes showed higher concentrations of testosterone in their blood than did men who committed nonaggressive crimes (Dabbs et al., 1995). Of course, such correlational findings don't prove causation. What happens when testosterone levels change? Although testosterone level predicts aggression in both sexes (Dabbs & Hargrove, 1997; Sapolsky, 1998), males secrete more testosterone and they commit more serious acts of physical aggression than females do (Archer, 2004). Evidence from experimental studies with humans in which testosterone levels are altered is limited, but one such study showed that for men with a combination of proneness to dominance, independent self-construal, and low self-control, increasing their testosterone level did increase aggressive tendencies (Geniole et al., 2019).

Testosterone levels most clearly correlate with aggressiveness in situations involving provocation and interpersonal conflict. One study showed that Swedish boys with higher testosterone levels were more physically and verbally aggressive, especially in response to provocations (Olweus et al., 1980). A similar study showed that in response to mounting intensity of provocation by another participant, men with high levels of testosterone were more physically aggressive than were those with lower levels of testosterone (Berman et al., 1993). Why is testosterone linked to retaliation? Some researchers say that testosterone increases people's efforts to preserve their social status (Josephs et al., 2006).

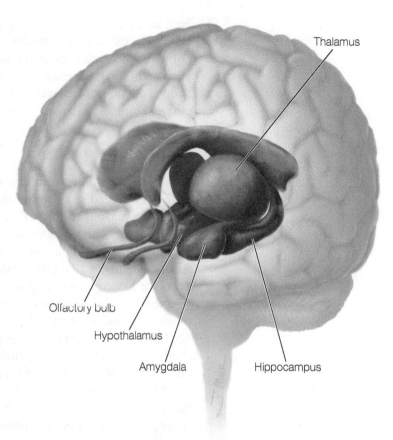

Figure 12.2

Fight or Flight

The hypothalamus and the amygdala are two brain regions in the limbic system that play a key role in people's emotional experiences of fear and anger and that prepare them for a fight-or-flight response.

 **APPLICATION**

The Hazards of Puberty

Between the ages of 15 and 30, males show a dramatic spike in the rate of violent criminal offending. For instance, the prototypical homicide perpetrator is 27 years old (FBI, 2009). One reason for this spike in physical aggression from adolescence forward is that this is also when testosterone levels peak.

After early adulthood, there is a dramatic decline in interpersonal aggression and rates of violent criminal offenses, even among men. One reason is that men are secreting less testosterone after they reach age 25. In addition, by adulthood both men and women are using more verbal means of aggression (Björkqvist et al., 1994). Of course, these developmental trends are also affected by the social norms of the society in question, but at least among adult middle-class European and North American males, physical aggression in middle and late adulthood is commonly believed to be acceptable only in self-defense or in defense of others (Holm, 1983). ■

Natural-Born Pacifists

Before we conclude from this biological evidence that humans are born to aggress, we need to examine the other side of the biological coin. There are numerous reasons to think that both humans and other animals have evolved *not* to be particularly aggressive. For one, even if an animal ends up dominating another animal in a competition, it probably will suffer injuries, some fatal. Also, those prone to aggress risk getting a bad reputation. We see this in monkeys, for example, when group members known to be aggressive are usually rejected by other members (Higley et al., 1994). In humans, people who are overly aggressive—either by physically attacking others or by trying to damage others' peer relationships (e.g., by spreading hateful gossip)—increase their chances of being rejected by their peers in the future and often of being imprisoned (Crick & Grotpeter, 1995; Dishion et al., 1994; Dodge, 1983).

Also, although aggressing against someone who harmed us may deter them in the future, it usually damages our relationship with that person. As a result, we miss out on any benefits that might have come from that relationship. Therefore, some theorists argue that natural selection may have shaped the human mind to *forgive* valued relationship partners despite the harm they have caused us (McCullough, 2008). If ancestral humans forgave an offending relationship partner and reconciled after interpersonal conflict, they could restore relationships that, on average, would have increased their chances of surviving and reproducing.

Uniquely Human Aspects of Aggression

Two differences between humans and animals stand out when comparing aggressive behavior in humans and other species. One makes us more aggressive than other animals, the other makes us less.

Technology Outstrips Natural Controls on Aggression   When two nonhuman animals of the same species fight, they have evolved strategies to avoid unnecessary injury and death. For example, if two dogs get in a fight, once one has clearly dominated the other, the loser assumes a subordinate position, such as lying on its back or baring its throat. "All right, you win," the loser communicates, "Let's both walk away with minimal injuries." At that point, the dominant animal does not go in for the kill. In fact, it may even make a friendly gesture to the loser (Lorenz, 1966).

Human aggression doesn't seem to work by these rules. Whereas other species have natural controls that restrain violence before it gets out of hand, humans seem to have far fewer qualms about killing each other. Why is this? An important part of the answer proposed by Lorenz (1966) is that our technological capacity for violence has outstripped any inhibitions against killing that we may have. The ability to pull triggers, hire hit men, plant bombs, and launch missiles means we can cause lethal harm so quickly, and from such a distance, that evolved controls over violence, such as empathy and signs of submission and suffering, have no opportunity to intercede and limit the damage. Consistent with this idea, Rutchick and colleagues (2017) found that people were more willing to kill bugs remotely via videoconference software than when in the same room with the bugs. Because our technological proficiency in killing is so great, we humans kill more members of our own species because of how we are different from other animals rather than because of how we are similar to them.

The Human Mind Specializes in Self-Control A second uniquely human aspect of aggression is that, compared to other species, humans are especially good at regulating their emotions and controlling their behavior. We have the ability to think abstractly and to reflect on and learn from our past experiences and future possibilities, reappraise emotional events, empathize with others, and internalize morals. So for humans, moral values that forbid hurting others, feelings of empathy for others, and consideration of possible aversive consequences for oneself, such as prison or retaliation, all play roles in inhibiting aggression, particularly when the capacity for self-control is high (e.g., Geen, 2001). However, high cognitive load can interfere with such inhibitors of aggression, and people differ in the strength of these inhibitors; as a result, some people are more prone to aggression than others.

Earlier we saw that brain regions such as the dACC and the limbic system act as a neural alarm system that alerts us when something is wrong. In some circumstances, these regions produce an impulsive desire to retaliate aggressively to perceived hostile treatment. But obviously we don't act on every aggressive impulse that we experience. Rather, these impulses are regulated by regions of our **prefrontal cortex**—in particular the *medial prefrontal cortex*, or MPFC, and the *dorsolateral prefrontal cortex*, or DLPFC, which we discussed in chapter 11 (**FIGURE 12.3**) (Davidson et al., 2000; Raine, 2008; Siever, 2008). These regions of the prefrontal cortex are active when we consider our morals and the consequences of our actions, reflect on our emotional responses to distressing stimuli, and control our behavior. Also, they share many neural connections with the dACC and the "hot" limbic structures such as the amygdala. Through these connections, prefrontal regions can "put the brakes on" aggressive impulses (Inzlicht & Gutsell, 2007). That's why individuals who suffer injury to the prefrontal cortex become dramatically more irritable, hostile, and aggressive (Grafman et al., 1996).

What's more, our prefrontal cortex has many receptors for a neurotransmitter called **serotonin**, which dampens our angry and aggressive impulses. *Neurotransmitters* are chemicals that carry messages between brain cells. Serotonin, often called the "feel-good" neurotransmitter, helps the prefrontal cortex control impulsive responses to distressing events (Soubrié, 1986). In humans and other animals, high levels of serotonin are correlated with low levels of aggression (Ferris et al., 1997; Suarez & Krishnan, 2006). Experimentally boosting serotonin's activity reduces aggression (Berman et al., 2009; Carrillo et al.,

Prefrontal cortex The region of the brain that regulates impulsive behavior.

Serotonin A neurotransmitter that regulates our experience of negative affect.

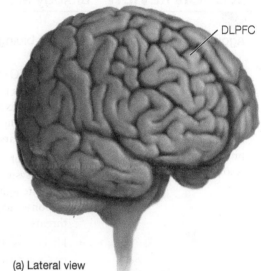

(a) Lateral view

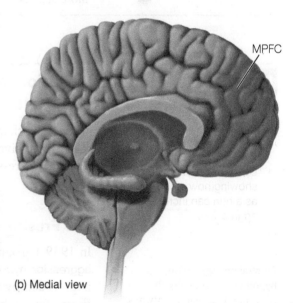

(b) Medial view

Figure 12.3

Impulse Regulation

The prefrontal cortex (PFC) is the brain area involved in controlling impulses and emotions. When our impulse is to lash out aggressively, the prefrontal cortex can help us restrain that impulse. The figure shows the dorsolateral region (a) and the medial region (b) of the PFC.

2009; Cleare & Bond, 1995), and reducing serotonin leads to more aggressive responses to distressing events such as unfair treatment (Crockett et al., 2008).

Clearly then, although humans experience impulses to harm, they have sophisticated abilities to stop, think, and find alternative means to resolve the situation. But as we'll see, certain factors can cause such self-regulation to fail.

SECTION REVIEW Biology and Human Aggression

Aggressiveness may be part of our biology, but so is pacifism.

There are parallels between humans and other species when it comes to using aggression to gain advantages and protect oneself and one's resources.	• The dACC region of our brains is activated when we experience injustice, insults, and other threats. • Regions of the limbic system help generate fight-or-flight responses to perceived threats. • Higher testosterone levels correlate with more aggression.	There are many advantages to being nonaggressive, and humans have many evolved cognitive and emotional capacities that often curtail aggressive impulses.	• Humans have the greatest capacity to kill because of our technology. • Conversely, humans also have the greatest capacity for self-control. Morals, empathy, and consideration of consequences can inhibit our aggressive impulses.

Learning Outcomes

- Explain the role of frustration and stressors in direct and displaced aggression.
- Describe the evidence showing how a cue such as a gun can increase aggression.

Frustration-aggression hypothesis Originally the idea that aggression is always preceded by frustration and that frustration inevitably leads to aggression. Revised to suggest that frustration produces an emotional readiness to aggress.

Situational Triggers of Aggression: The Context Made Me Do It

We've seen that people are biologically prepared to both lash out and control their aggressive impulses. But what kinds of situations make us more or less likely to aggress? Researchers have found that everyday *frustrations* are powerful triggers.

The Frustration-Aggression Hypothesis

In 1939 a group of psychologists at Yale University first proposed the **frustration-aggression hypothesis** (Dollard et al., 1939), which posits that aggression always is preceded by frustration and that frustration inevitably leads to aggression. Frustration is the consequence of a blockage of a desired goal. For example, when participants were prevented from obtaining a desired prize—that is, frustrated—by a bumbling partner, and then given the opportunity to shock their partner during a subsequent learning task, they chose to give this partner stronger shocks than did participants not expecting an attractive prize (Buss, 1963). Subsequent studies have found that the more frustrated people are, the more likely they are to aggress. For example, it's nearly always frustrating when someone cuts in front of you when you've been standing in line for a while. But the closer you are to the front of the line and to your goal, the more frustrating this injustice is. With increased frustration, we see a stronger aggressive response (Harris, 1974).

This hypothesis helps to explain some patterns of aggression in the real world. For example, during the first half of the 20th century, there were more lynchings of African Americans by Whites in the American South in years when the value of cotton was low and the southern economy was suffering (Hovland & Sears, 1940). Why? One explanation is that as the price of cotton went down, southern Whites became more frustrated at their economic misfortunes. This frustration led to more aggression against African Americans. Other findings fit this explanation. Across diverse cultures, aggressive behaviors (e.g., homicide, road rage, child abuse) increase with increased prevalence of various sources of frustration and stressors, including shrinking workforce, unemployment, increase in population density, low economic status, and economic hardship (Geen, 1998).

Displaced Aggression In many cases, frustration-based aggression is directed at targets that didn't cause the frustration. Dollard and colleagues (1939) labeled this phenomenon **displaced aggression**. Imagine someone coming home after a stressful workday and grueling commute and shoving their cat, Georgie, who was just lying there. Generally, people will displace aggression when something prevents them from aggressing against the original source of the frustration. The source of frustration may be something intangible, such as a downturn in the economy. Other times the original source is high in status, such as one's boss or parents, so one refrains from direct aggression to avoid punishment. In such cases, the aggressive impulse often is instead directed at a safer, often innocent target. But in other cases, the alternative target adds a bit to the level of frustration, leading to what is known as *triggered displaced aggression.*

Displaced aggression
Aggression directed to a target other than the source of one's frustration.

Triggered displaced aggression occurs when someone does not respond to an initial frustration but later is faced with a second event that elicits a more aggressive response than would be warranted by only the relatively minor affront on its own. Now imagine that the stressed-out person from our earlier example comes home to find that Georgie tipped over a house plant. They might react more harshly to this minor infraction than they normally would. What is really going on in such cases? The original provocation produces anger and aggressive thoughts. However, because the individual is prevented from retaliating, or decides not to retaliate, against the original provocation, the hostile feelings and thoughts remain. Then, when the individual is confronted with a second, actually minor, frustrating event, the preexisting hostility biases how he or she interprets and emotionally responds to that event (Miller et al., 2003). The more the provoked person ruminates about the initial aversive event, the more likely triggered displaced aggression is to occur (Bushman, Bonacci et al., 2005).

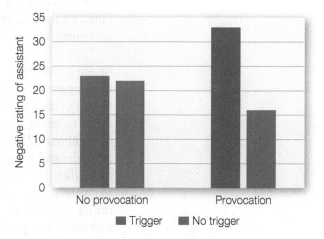

Figure 12.4

Triggered Displaced Aggression

When rating a somewhat bumbling assistant (in the trigger condition), participants made the harshest evaluations if they had been insulted earlier by someone else. This situation illustrates triggered displaced aggression because insulted participants derogated the assistant only if he or she did something to trigger the aggressive response.

[Data from Pedersen et al., 2000]

A study by Pedersen and colleagues (2000) illustrates how this works. Participants were initially given either insulting feedback about their performance on a task or no such feedback. Later in the study, they were given another task by a different assistant. In one condition, the assistant was somewhat annoying and incompetent, whereas in the other condition the participants had no such minor trigger. Participants were then given the opportunity to rate the assistant's qualifications for a job. As can be seen in **FIGURE 12.4**, in the absence of an initial provocation, participants were not especially critical of the bumbling assistant. However, when participants had initially been insulted and were then exposed to the annoying assistant, they evaluated the assistant much more negatively.

What this and other studies reveal is that we don't displace our aggression against just anyone. Rather, we are most likely to lash out at targets who do something mildly annoying, are dislikable, are relatively low in social status and power, or resemble the person with whom we actually are angry (e.g., Marcus-Newhall et al., 2000; Pedersen et al., 2008).

Arbitrariness of the Frustration Although the studies we've reviewed so far support a role for frustration in aggression, other studies showed that the original hypothesis was too absolute. Although frustrated people sometimes aggress, they often do not. Can you think of times when frustration led you to aggress? What about times when you were frustrated but did not aggress? The questions for social psychologists become: When do frustrating circumstances lead to aggression? When do they not?

One factor that researchers discovered very quickly is that sometimes frustration seems to be justified and other times arbitrary (e.g., Ohbuchi, 1982; Pastore, 1952). Imagine stepping up to the refreshment counter at a movie theater and being denied a large container of buttered popcorn. If the snack bar attendant says you can't have any because the popcorn machine is broken, your goal is frustrated but in a way that is justifiable, so you would be unlikely to aggress. But if the attendant says you can't have any but you can see plenty of popcorn behind the counter, the frustration seems to be arbitrary, and a disturbance in the theater is far more likely. In one study (Fishman, 1965), participants were promised $2 if they succeeded on a task but then were denied the $2, either despite having succeeded (arbitrary frustration) or after being told they had failed on the task (nonarbitrary frustration). When the frustration was arbitrary, participants were more aggressive toward the experimenter.

Attacks, Insults, and Social Rejection Perhaps the most reliable provocation of an aggressive response is the belief that one has been or will be attacked intentionally, either physically or verbally (Geen, 2001). What could be more frustrating than being attacked or insulted? For example, in one study (Harmon-Jones & Sigelman, 2001), participants wrote an essay that an evaluator (actually a confederate) rated either positively ("I can understand why someone would think like this") or negatively ("I can't believe an educated person would think like this"). In a later part of the experiment, participants were given an opportunity to pick the type and quantity of beverage the evaluator would have to sample. When participants previously had been insulted, they were more likely to pick an unpleasant beverage (e.g., water mixed with vinegar) and to administer more of that beverage. Moreover, this aggressive reaction was related to how much each participant's brain was emitting electrical signals that typically reflect anger-related motivation: greater activation of the left prefrontal cortex and diminished activation of the right prefrontal cortex.

Although it is not surprising that physical attack often leads to counterattack, if only for self-defense, why aggress against someone who has insulted us? One answer is that insults threaten our self-esteem and sense of significance. When James Averill (1982) asked participants to recall situations that made them angry, he found that the causes often boiled down to threats to self-esteem. Because our sense of significance in the world is so important to us and it depends so heavily on validation from others, insults and social rejection can arouse anger and an impulse to aggress, often in an attempt to restore wounded pride (Tangney, Wagner et al., 1996). Indeed, when Leary and colleagues (2003) examined well-documented cases of school shootings between 1995 and 2001, they found that in 13 of the 15 cases, the perpetrator had been subjected to often malicious bullying, teasing, and rejection. Although a host of factors certainly contribute to these horrific acts, an attempt to restore a sense of significance in response to social rejection or humiliation is clearly one of them.

The sting of rejection has also been observed in the lab. In one study (Twenge et al., 2001), groups of participants had a 15-minute conversation before voting for the person they wanted to interact with further. But the voting was rigged: Some participants were told that everyone wanted to interact with them (the "accepted" condition), but others were told that no one wanted to interact with them (the "rejected" condition). Each participant then was directed to play a computer game with another participant and told that the loser of the game would be punished by the winner with noise blasts through a pair of headphones. Performance on the game was also rigged such that the (rejected or accepted) participant won and was thus allowed to choose the volume and duration of the unpleasant noise that the loser had to listen to. Compared with those participants who had experienced acceptance, participants who had experienced rejection blasted their opponents with louder and longer noises.

When Do Hostile Feelings Lead to Aggression? The Cognitive Neoassociationism Model

Of course, people don't always respond to rejection by becoming more aggressive. Sometimes they become withdrawn and despondent. Sometimes they seek acceptance (Leary et al., 2006). When will aggression become a more likely reaction? Berkowitz (1989) provided a particularly valuable answer to this question with his **cognitive neoassociationism model**. This model expands on the frustration-aggression hypothesis in three important ways. First, it proposes that a wide range of unpleasant, stressful conditions can prompt hostile feelings. Second, it posits that these hostile feelings are central contributors to affective aggression. Third, the model specifies that when people have hostile feelings, features of situations that prime aggressive cognitions make aggression more likely. Let's discuss these developments in more detail.

Cognitive neoassociationism model A model of aggression that emphasizes three causal factors: stressors, hostile feelings, and cues associated with aggression.

Physical Pain and Discomfort   It turns out that when people are hurt physically as well as emotionally, they are more likely to lash out. In one study that made this point, Berkowitz and colleagues (1981) had participants immerse one hand either in a bucket of freezing-cold ice water or in a bucket of comfortably tepid water as they were told to administer noise blasts to someone they thought was another participant in the study. Participants who experienced the pain of cold-water immersion administered a greater number of loud noise blasts to the other person.

Excessive heat can also cause discomfort that triggers hostile feelings. Craig Anderson and colleagues (Anderson, 1989; Anderson et al., 1997; Bushman, Bonacci et al., 2005) have shown that as the temperature goes up, so do signs of aggression. We see this based on location, as violent crimes (but not nonviolent crimes) are more frequent in the hottest regions of countries (Anderson et al., 1996), and also with regard to time periods, as hotter years, months, and days have more violent crimes (Anderson et al., 1997). We also see this relationship in field studies. When Kenrick and MacFarlane (1986) stalled a car at a green light at an intersection in Phoenix, Arizona, they found that people were much more likely to honk the horn—often continuously and with aggressive fervor—on hotter days than on cooler days. Another study analyzing four Major League

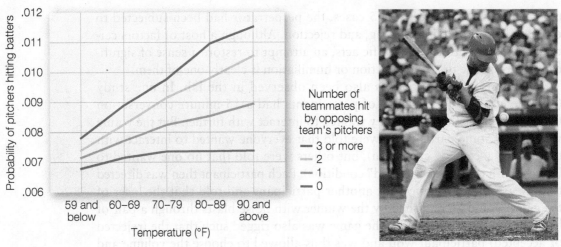

Figure 12.5

It's Getting Hot in Here

When temperatures are especially hot, tempers also rise. Major League Baseball pitchers were more likely to hit batters the hotter the temperature, especially if their teammates had been hit earlier in the game.

[Left: Data from Larrick et al., 2011; right: Dilip Vishwanat/Getty Images]

Baseball seasons revealed that pitchers were more likely to hit batters on days when the temperature reached or surpassed 90 degrees Fahrenheit (Reifman et al., 1991). The relationship between heat and plunking the batter holds up even after the researchers took into account other indices of the pitchers' accuracy (e.g., walks, wild pitches). More recent research shows that perceived provocations intensify these effects. That is, pitchers are more likely to throw at opposing batters on hot days when one of their own teammates previously has been hit by a pitch (Larrick et al., 2011; see **FIGURE 12.5**). Even spicy food may make people more prone to aggression (Batra et al., 2017).

The Role of Arousal in Aggression   According to Zillmann's (1971) *excitation transfer theory* (chapter 5), when people are still physiologically aroused by an initial event but are no longer thinking about what made them aroused, this residual (or unexplained) excitation can be transferred and interpreted in the context of some new event. As a result, people who are already aroused are likely to overreact to subsequent provocations with intensified anger and aggression. This is different from triggered displaced aggression because for the latter phenomenon, the initial event causes frustration and hostile feelings. In the case of excitation transfer, the initial event can be a neutral cause of arousal.

Consider the following demonstration (Zillmann & Bryant, 1974). Participants were told they would be playing a game with an opponent who was actually a confederate. Some participants were asked to ride an exercise bike, while others performed a less vigorous activity. Two minutes later, a confederate either insulted them or treated them in a neutral manner. Then, about six minutes after the first activity, when participants were still aroused by the exercise but no longer aware of their own arousal, they were given the opportunity to deliver a punishing noxious noise to the person who had previously angered them. Do you think you might be more or less aggressive after exercising? Though the idea of catharsis or "blowing off steam" might lead you to think the exercise would provide a release, purging you of aggressive inclinations, the results were quite the opposite. In accordance with excitation transfer theory, those participants who engaged in exercise and were insulted actually delivered more of the noxious noise than the other participants. The excitation provided by exercise intensified their anger at the insulter and thus intensified their aggressive behavior. A follow-up study (Zillmann et al., 1975) showed that when highly aroused, people are unable or unwilling to reduce their aggressive response even when apprised of mitigating circumstances for the provocation. Exercise is, of course, not the only source of such arousal; research shows that other sources of arousal also can exacerbate aggression in provoking situations (e.g., Zillmann, 1971).

Priming Aggressive Cognitions

Taking the social cognitive perspective, Berkowitz's model also proposes that hostile feelings will be especially likely to lead to aggression when hostile cognitions are primed by cues in the person's situation. What are some of the most common environmental cues that prime violence and aggression? One big category that stands out is firearms. This leads us to a discussion of one of the seminal studies of aggression—the study that introduced what is known as the **weapons effect** (Berkowitz & LePage, 1967).

Weapons effect The tendency for the presence of firearms to increase the likelihood of aggression, especially when people are frustrated.

Imagine that you show up for a study and are told that the study is exploring the connection between physiology and stress. You're informed that another participant (actually a confederate) will be grading ideas that you come up with for a task by administering electric shocks to you (1 shock = good answers, 7 shocks = bad answers). After generating your ideas, you get hit with 7 shocks—an outcome likely to anger most people. Other participants in the study are randomly assigned to receive just the minimal 1 shock and likely feel less angry as a result. After this, you're brought to the room with the shock generator and given the chance to retaliate by administering electric shocks to the person who just shocked you. The second independent variable is whether people administered these shocks with a neutral object (e.g., a badminton racquet) sitting on the desk next to the shock generator, with nothing else on the desk, or—in the critical condition—with a 12-gauge shotgun and a .38-caliber revolver sitting on the desk. Participants were told that these objects were left over from a previous study and that they should ignore them. How do you think you would respond?

Check out **FIGURE 12.6**. If participants were not previously made angry, the presence of weapons had no effect on their level of aggression. Similarly, if participants were angry but not in the presence of weapons, they were more aggressive—but not overly so. A very different effect emerged when participants were both made angry and in the presence of weapons. In this condition, they administered the greatest number of intense electric shocks.

The weapons effect can also influence what happens when we get behind the wheel. Researchers (Bushman et al., 2017) put university students into a driving simulator and had them drive through frustrating events such as being cut off and driving through construction. In one condition, there was a training pistol on the passenger seat that looked like a real 9 mm semiautomatic handgun; in the other condition, there was a tennis racket on the seat. The mere presence of a gun in the vehicle caused students to drive more aggressively. They were more likely to tailgate, speed, honk the horn, and give the finger. In fact, one participant even grabbed the unloaded gun and shot it at another (virtual) driver!

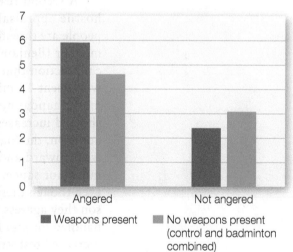

Legend: ■ Weapons present ■ No weapons present (control and badminton combined)

Figure 12.6

The Weapons Effect

Berkowitz and LePage's (1967) classic weapons-effect study shows that participants became the most aggressive when they were in a condition in which they were both angered and in the presence of a gun and a rifle; under these circumstances, they administered an especially large number of shocks to another person.

[Data from Berkowitz & LePage, 1967]

You might be wondering whether something like this could happen outside the laboratory. You bet it could. In one field study, researchers got a pickup truck with a gun rack and had it stall at a traffic light (Turner et al., 1975). In one condition, there were two cues associated with violence: a military rifle in the gun rack and a bumper sticker that read "VENGEANCE." In another condition, there was one cue—the rifle—along with a bumper sticker that read "FRIEND." In a third condition, there was neither a rifle nor a bumper sticker. Drivers behind the stalled truck were most likely to honk the horn when hostile cognitions were primed by the rifle and the "VENGEANCE" bumper sticker and least likely to honk when there were no cues priming such cognitions. This is a powerful demonstration when you consider that if participants had been thinking rationally about their behavior, someone with a rifle and a "VENGEANCE" bumper sticker would be the last person they would want to mess with.

Why does the weapons effect occur? One reason is that merely seeing a weapon primes aggressive thoughts in one's memory, which in turn makes it more likely an angered person will think of aggressive ways to deal with that anger. In one recent study (Bushman, 2018), participants who saw photos of people holding guns (compared to viewing police in street clothes without guns) were more likely to complete word fragments to form aggressive words (e.g., the fragment KI_ _ completed as KILL rather than KISS). Also, guns primed aggressive thoughts regardless of whether they were held by "good guys" (i.e., police officers, soldiers) or "bad guys" (i.e., criminals).

A second reason is that the mere presence of weapons can also increase hostile appraisals. That is, weapons can lead people to believe that other people are threatening, which prepares the person to respond in an aggressive manner (Benjamin et al., 2018). Finally, weapons can induce a physiological reaction that prepares the person to lash out. In one study, participants who spent 15 minutes handling a pellet gun that looked a lot like an automatic handgun, as opposed to handling the children's game Mousetrap, showed increases in their level of testosterone (Klinesmith et al., 2006). In addition, the bigger their increase in testosterone, the more aggressive they were toward another supposed participant, spiking that person's water with more hot sauce. An interesting result was that these hostile acts occurred even though these participants had not been frustrated or insulted by the person they aggressed against. The researchers suggest that because participants handled the gun for 15 minutes, their extended time with a weapon may have increased testosterone levels and aggression even though they had not been provoked or frustrated. Such findings support Berkowitz's (1968, p. 22) suggestion that "the finger pulls the trigger but the trigger may also be pulling the finger."

Stimuli other than firearms also can become associated with violence and therefore can prime cognitions that encourage aggression. In one study, participants who watched a violent film scene involving the actor Kirk Douglas were later more aggressive toward a provoking confederate if he was named Kirk than if he was named Bob (Berkowitz & Geen, 1967). In another study, seven- to nine-year-old boys watched either a neutral show or a violent TV show in which walkie-talkies were used. Later they played a game of floor hockey. Boys who had seen the violent show and then saw walkie-talkies at the beginning of the game were the most aggressive during the game (Josephson, 1987).

Is it always true that guns are cues to aggression? It largely depends on the thoughts that a person associates with guns. Although for many people guns have an associative history with violence and aggression, this is not the case for everyone. People who hunt for sport may see guns in a different light. As a result, they don't tend to show activation of aggressive cognitions and are not more aggressive toward those who provoke them when exposed to pictures of guns; in contrast, nonhunters are (Bartholow et al., 2005). For hunters, pictures of guns actually arouse warm and pleasant cognitions (perhaps reflecting the enjoyable times with family while they've hunted). But when hunters are shown pictures of assault rifles, which have no connection to recreational sport, they do show increased aggressive cognitions and behavior. Thus, the weapons effect critically depends on the person's prior learning and experiences.

Of course, most Americans are not recreational hunters. Thus these weapons-effect findings prompt us to pause when we think about the influence that rampant exposure and accessibility of guns have on violence in the United States. Consider the following statistics. In the United States, just shy of 40,000 people died from gun-related injuries in 2016 compared to roughly 250 in the United Kingdom, where gun ownership is banned (**FIGURE 12.7**; JAMA, 2018). Although the homes of gun owners differ in a variety of ways from non–gun owners' homes, researchers point out that people in homes with guns are 2.7 times more likely to be murdered than those in homes without guns (Kellermann et al., 1993; Wiebe, 2003).

Also, there is an escalating cycle of violence and gun ownership. After highly publicized tragic shootings, Americans actually purchase more guns, making it even more likely that another shooting will occur (Wallace, 2015). A more recent study shows that right after a mass shooting, guns are more attractive to people who feel that their personal goals are being thwarted (Leander et al., 2019). Guns might seem to be a repellant reminder of suffering to those closest to a mass shooting, but for many individuals who feel frustrated, mass shootings make guns more appealing.

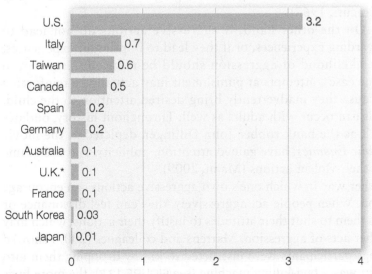

NOTE: List includes countries with a per capita GDP of more than $30,000 and a population of 20 million or more; all data for the most recent year available

* Does not include Northern Ireland

Figure 12.7

Gun-Related Homicides

Gun-related homicides occur at a much higher rate in the United States than in other industrialized nations.

[Data from United Nations Office on Drugs and Crime, 2013; Photo: Mr.Nikon/Shutterstock]

SECTION REVIEW Situational Triggers of Aggression: The Context Made Me Do It

Unpleasant, frustrating experiences arouse hostile affect, which makes us prone to aggression, particularly when situational cues prime aggressive cognitions.

Frustration-Aggression Hypothesis

- Frustration produces an emotional readiness to aggress.
- Conditions of the situation can then trigger an aggressive response.
- Displaced aggression is aggression directed at targets other than the original source of the frustration.
- Triggered displaced aggression is targeted against a secondary, even minor, source of frustration.

Factors That Increase Aggressive Responses

- The frustration seems arbitrary rather than justified.
- There is an expectation of physical or verbal attack, insult, or social rejection.
- The individual is experiencing physical pain, heat, or discomfort.
- The individual has residual arousal from prior events.
- There is a situational cue, such as a nearby weapon, that primes aggressive cognitions.

Learning Outcomes

- Outline evidence that media violence increases the incidence of aggression.
- Explain factors in family life that influence the tendency to aggress.
- Give examples of how culture influences proneness to aggression.

▲ Sometimes the punishment for and media attention on violent actions can make them rewarding, as was the case with the bank robber John Dillinger, who was glamorized by newspapers in his day, and in the film *Public Enemies*, in which Johnny Depp played him.

[© Universal Pictures Photographer: Peter Mountain/Photofest]

Learning to Aggress

One of the great adaptive features of our species is our capacity for learning. But this capacity means that people can learn to aggress. Some learning of aggression is based on operant conditioning. Beginning in early childhood, we all engage in some aggressive acts, such as biting, hitting, shoving, kicking, and verbal aggression. If these actions garner desired attention or specific rewards, or if they alleviate negative feelings, they will become more likely (Dengerink & Covey, 1983; Geen, 2001; Geen & Pigg, 1970; Geen & Stonner 1971; Loew, 1967). If Taylor hits Tim to get his lollipop, Taylor's aggression will be reinforced if the consequence is successfully enjoying a tasty lollipop. If kids hassle and make fun of a child and that child finds that aggressive action alleviates the hassling, the child is likely to learn that physical aggression is a way to get relief from being bothered by others. In gang subcultures, members may win admiration for engaging in violence (Wolfgang & Ferracuti, 1967).

On the other hand, if aggressive actions do not lead to rewarding experiences, or if they lead to unpleasant experiences, the likelihood of aggression should be reduced. However, in some cases, attempts at punishment may actually be reinforcing because they inadvertently bring desired attention to the child. This can occur with adults as well. Throughout history, outlaws such as the bank robber John Dillinger, depicted in the movie *Public Enemies*, have gained attention, publicity, and even fame for their violent actions (Mann, 2009).

There is another way in which one's own aggressive actions can encourage further aggression. When people act aggressively, they can feel dissonance or guilt, which leads them to shift their attitudes to justify their actions, which may then lead to further acts of aggression. Martens and colleagues (2007) showed that the more bugs participants were instructed to kill by dropping them into what they thought was a bug-killing machine (see **FIGURE 12.8**), the more bugs they voluntarily chose to kill later on. Interestingly, this escalation of killing occurred only in people who believed there was some similarity between bugs and humans and therefore were likely to feel guilty about those first bugs they killed. This process of escalating killing mirrors many historical examples of initial acts of aggression being followed by more severe acts of aggression (Kressel, 1996).

In addition to learning to aggress through their own actions, people also learn to aggress by watching the actions of others. Humans have a great capacity for imitation and observational learning (Bandura, 1973). Indeed, most children probably learn more about aggression from the media, from watching their parents and peers, and from their cultural upbringing than they do from their own actions. So let's take a careful look at how the media, family life, and culture contribute to aggression.

Media and Aggression

A large body of research shows that exposure to violent media increases the prevalence of aggression in a society (e.g., Bushman & Huesmann, 2010). In fact, the relationship between exposure to media depictions of violence and aggressive behavior is stronger than many other relationships that are considered very well established, including, for example, the extent to which condom use predicts likelihood of contracting HIV and the extent to which calcium intake is related to bone mass (see **FIGURE 12.9**) (Bushman & Anderson, 2001). Despite this evidence, violent content is pervasive in modern television programming, films, and video games and on the Internet (Donnerstein, 2011).

Bushman and Anderson (2001) argued that one reason these research findings are largely ignored is that violent media are very popular and therefore profitable. Consequently, news media outlets, which often are connected to the businesses that gather these profits, tend to be biased in their reporting of the evidence. To illustrate the profitability of film violence, as this textbook goes to press, all of the top 10 highest-grossing films of all time worldwide feature a great deal of violence: *Avengers: Endgame, Avatar, Titanic, Star Wars: The Force Awakens, Avengers: Infinity War, Jurassic World, The Lion King, The Avengers, Furious 7*, and *Avengers: Age of Ultron* (Box Office Mojo, 2019). Similarly, the most popular show on American television is *NCIS*, which typically begins with a murder. Other popular violent television shows include *The Walking Dead, Game of Thrones, Orange Is the New Black*, and *Blue Bloods*. The current most popular video game series include such violent offerings as *Call of Duty: Black Ops 4, Grand Theft Auto V*, and *Red Dead Redemption 2*. Given that the average American 12-year-old spends more time consuming media than attending

Figure 12.8

Does Killing Beget Killing?

When participants believed they were grinding up bugs in this modified coffee grinder, those who initially killed five bugs justified their aggression by killing even more later (Martens et al., 2007).

[Jeff Greenberg]

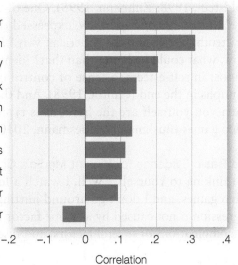

Figure 12.9

Does Media Violence Matter?

The effect of media violence on actual aggression seems to be just as strong as, and in many cases stronger than, a number of influences that go unquestioned in society.

[Data from Bushman & Anderson, 2001]

school (Bushman & Huesmann, 2010) and that by age 18 the typical American child has viewed more than 200,000 acts of violence on television, including more than 16,000 murders (Strasburger, 2007), young people have plenty of opportunities to learn how to be aggressive.

What Is the Appeal of Media Violence?

Violence and smut are of course everywhere on the airwaves. You cannot turn on your television without seeing them, although sometimes you have to hunt around.

—Dave Barry (1996)

Why is violent entertainment so popular? From an evolutionary perspective, it's likely been adaptive for humans to be innately vigilant to viewing, and be physiologically aroused by, instances of violence (e.g., Beer, 1984). As the old journalism cliché goes, "If it bleeds, it leads." If there is potential danger, we want to know what, where, how, and why. And well we should, so that we can prepare for fight or flight. The entertainment industry takes advantage of these innate tendencies. Although people don't like it directed at themselves, they do enjoy seeing violence in movies on TV or enacting it in video games—where they are not in any real danger (McCauley, 1998). This is especially true of people who are high in sensation seeking or who feel bored (Cantor, 1998; Tamborini & Stiff, 1987).

The other easy way to make viewers excited is with sexually appealing images, another feature of much popular entertainment, as Dave Barry noted. But in American culture, younger viewers are shielded much more strictly from sexual content than they are from violent content. For example, in movie ratings, nudity or even use of the F-word virtually guarantees an R rating, whereas massive amounts of killing can now be found in many PG-13 movies. Back in 1985, PG-13 movies had about the same amount of gun violence as did G-rated movies; but since 2009, levels of gun violence in these adolescent-friendly PG-13 pictures now match or even exceed those in R-rated films (Bushman et al., 2013). Pop culture commentator Chris Eggertsen (2016) noted the hypocrisy of the system that "rates a film like Mike Birbiglia's *Don't Think Twice* an 'R' for 'language and some drug use' . . . while awarding a film like *Suicide Squad*, which features almost wall-to-wall gun violence . . . a PG-13." Eggertsen rightly wondered why a few curse words and grown-ups smoking a joint are viewed as worse for kids to see than relentless amounts of gun violence and other forms of killing. Aside from the arousal and excitement, media violence is also appealing because it commonly portrays heroic victories over evil and injustice (e.g., Goldstein, 1998; Zillmann, 1998). One of the first violent American TV shows, *The Adventures of Superman*, expressed this very succinctly: Superman fights for "truth, justice and the American way." For American children watching that show, what could be better than that? Identifying with such heroes may provide a boost in self-esteem, a sense of control over threats, and a feeling that good triumphs in the end (Cantor, 1998). And these feelings may be especially strong when you yourself are the hero, as is typically the case for players of violent video games (Bushman & Huesmann, 2010).

The Basic Evidence for Violent Media's Contribution to Aggression You may be thinking to yourself, "Well, I watch a lot of violent entertainment and play video games, and I don't go around hurting other people." As we noted earlier, aggression is not caused by any one factor in isolation but results from particular combinations of several factors, and researchers debate the impact of violent video games (Hilgard et al., 2017). Still, evidence strongly indicates that exposure to violent video games, movies, and TV shows contributes to aggression (Kepes et al., 2017; Prescott et al., 2018) not only in North America but also in China, Germany, Japan, and other nations (Anderson et al., 2017).

Studies have shown that the more violence an individual watches, the more aggressive that person is (e.g., Singer & Singer, 1981), and the more violent video games children play, the more aggressive they tend to be (Ferguson, 2015). Of course, these findings are merely correlations and so could mean either that violent entertainment encourages aggression or that viewers who like aggression are more likely to watch violent entertainment. Longitudinal evidence (i.e., studies that follow people over time) suggests that the former causal pathway provides the more likely explanation (Huesmann, Lagerspetz et al., 1984; Huesmann et al., 2003; Lefkowitz et al., 1977). The more violent programs an individual watches as a child, the more likely that individual is to be violent up to 22 years later. In contrast, a person's level of aggressiveness as a child does not similarly predict that person's interest in watching violent programs as an adult. Similar findings are emerging for violent video game play as well (Anderson et al., 2008).

The best way to test for cause and effect is to conduct field and lab experiments in which some participants are randomly assigned to watch violent or nonviolent content (Berkowitz, 1965; Geen & Berkowitz, 1966). The findings of many such studies show that exposure to media violence through watching videos or playing video games increases aggression (Bushman & Huesmann, 2010; Geen, 2001). Let's consider two examples that illustrate these effects.

In a home for juvenile delinquent boys, Leyens and colleagues (1975) had boys in two of the cottages watch five nights of violent movies. Boys in two other cottages watched five nights of nonviolent movies. The boys were observed each night for frequency of hitting, slapping, choking, and kicking their cottage mates. The boys who watched the violent films engaged in more such aggressive behavior than those who watched the nonviolent films. In another study, Konijn and colleagues (2007) randomly assigned Dutch adolescent boys to play a violent or nonviolent video game for 20 minutes and then play a competitive game with another study participant. The winner got the privilege of blasting the loser with noise at a volume of their choosing, ranging from a tolerable 60 decibels to a potentially hearing-damaging 105 decibels. The adolescents who played the violent video game chose potentially harmful noise levels more often.

It's important to note that the majority of the laboratory experiments show these effects of violent media primarily when participants are frustrated or provoked (e.g., Geen & Stonner, 1973) and for viewers who are generally above average in aggressive tendencies (e.g., Anderson & Dill, 2000; Bushman, 1995). So your hunch that media violence doesn't lead to aggression for everyone, or all the time, is correct (Ferguson, 2015). However, in people experiencing stress and hostile feelings, media violence increases the likelihood of aggressive action (Anderson & Dill, 2000; Berkowitz, 1993; Bushman & Huesmann, 2006; Kepes et al., 2017).

▲ As first-person shooter games become increasingly realistic and popular, research suggests that they can prime and promote aggression at least in some individuals.

[Doug Steley A/Alamy]

How and Why Does Watching Violence Contribute to Aggression in Viewers? How and why does media violence have the effects just described? From the perspective of the cognitive neoassociationism model, media violence makes aggressive scripts more accessible in people's minds. In stressed people, this makes aggressive actions more likely. Social learning theory and research provide additional important answers. People tend to imitate the behaviors they observe in others and learn new behaviors from them. As the Bobo doll studies showed (Bandura, 1973; see chapter 7), frustrated children who observed an adult model attacking a Bobo doll became more aggressive toward the doll, often in the same specific way that they saw the adult aggress. They also aggressed more if they identified with the adult model and if they observed the model being rewarded for his or her aggression.

Many subsequent experiments with both children and adults further support the role of social learning in the effects of observed violence in general and violence portrayed in films and video material in particular. The more people identify with the character they see engaging in filmed violence, the more they are likely to aggress (Perry & Perry, 1976; Turner & Berkowitz, 1972). In addition, filmed violence is more likely to be imitated if the violence is rewarded rather than punished, if it seems justified rather than unjustified, and if the harm caused by the aggression is deemphasized or sanitized (Donnerstein, 2011; Geen & Stonner, 1972, 1973). The common television and film scenario in which the hero uses weapons to defeat the villains fits these conditions perfectly: The likable protagonist, easy to identify with, engages in aggression that is justified and leads to a rewarding outcome. Bushman and Huesmann (2010) suggest that these conditions are even more common in violent video games in which the gamer's character is him- or herself the hero who is rewarded for aggression.

Further evidence of the effects of media violence is provided by instances in which very specific forms of violence depicted in films have been imitated in the real world. In just one of many examples, in 1971, Stanley Kubrick's disturbing, ultraviolent, dystopian science-fiction film classic *A Clockwork Orange* opened in British theaters to great controversy. After its release, the British press chronicled a series of copycat crimes, including the beating to death of a homeless man, leading Kubrick to ban the film in the United Kingdom in 1973. In one scene from the film, a gang of teens rape a woman while singing "Singin' in the Rain." Shortly after the film was banned, a gang of British teens raped a teenage girl while singing the same song (Travis, 1999). Social Psych at the Movies discusses another historically important film that inspired violence.

The sociologist David Phillips (1979, 1982) demonstrated a similar imitative tendency by examining frequencies of suicides and car accidents in communities following exposure to news coverage of real-life celebrity suicides and fictional soap opera depictions of suicides. He also examined homicides after highly publicized heavyweight boxing matches (Phillips, 1983; Phillips & Hensley, 1984). In all of these cases, he found significant increases in suicides and homicides a few days after these media depictions. The more these events were publicized in a community, the greater the increase in corresponding violent actions.

Besides teaching aggressive scripts to model, a steady diet of violent media leads people to believe that violence is common in the real world (Gerbner et al., 1980, 1982). This sense that the world is unsafe

Being the adventures of a young man whose principal interests are rape, ultra-violence and Beethoven.

STANLEY KUBRICK'S CLOCKWORK ORANGE

▲ Stanley Kubrick's 1971 film *A Clockwork Orange* is one of many examples in which media violence seems to have inspired real-life violence.

[Warner Bros./Photofest]

Achieve
Video Activity: Observational Learning of Aggression: Bandura's Bobo Doll Study Animation

also may contribute to aggression by increasing a sense of threat and encouraging the idea that aggression is normative. Furthermore, the more children and adults watch media violence, the less they become disturbed by it (Drabman & Thomas, 1974; Linz et al., 1989; Thomas et al., 1977) and the less empathy they have for victims of harm (Anderson et al., 2017). One study that takes the social neuroscience perspective showed that playing a violent video game leads to a reduced physiological reaction in the brain called the P3 response, which indicates a lack of surprise in response to viewing aggression. Furthermore, this neural desensitization helps explain why violent video games tend to increase aggression (Engelhardt et al., 2011). The lower participants' P3 response to violent stimuli, the more aggressive they were when administering noise blasts to an opponent.

In sum, both theory and research suggest a disturbing conclusion. If 10 million people watch a violent television show or movie, play a violent video game, or listen to violent music lyrics, the vast majority surely won't be moved to engage in aggression. However, just as surely, a minority of them—those with hostile feelings or dispositional aggressiveness, or both—will be. And even if that minority were a mere one tenth of 1% of the viewing or gaming audience, that still would be 10,000 people moved by violent media toward engaging in aggression.

 ## APPLICATION
Family Life and Aggression

Mass-media entertainment is not the only source of aggressive models and thoughts. Aggression is an all too common part of family life (Gelles, 2007; Green, 1998; Straus et al., 1980), whether between parents, between siblings, or between parents and their children. Just as people who are exposed to a great deal of media violence are more likely to aggress, so are children who are exposed to a great deal of physical aggression and conflict at home (Geen, 2001; Huesmann, Eron et al., 1984; Straus et al., 1980). In fact, exposure to family violence is likely an especially impactful contributor to subsequent aggression.

What causes family violence? The same factors that contribute to aggression in general play roles in family violence. All relationships inevitably involve frustration at some times, and our family relationships can be especially aggravating because we are so invested in them. Raising children is very challenging, and frustration is an inevitable aspect of that experience. Moreover, family members are also closest at hand, and thus they are likely targets of displaced aggression for those who are frustrated by their bosses, teachers, or other life stressors.

How does domestic aggression affect children growing up in such circumstances? A violent family atmosphere generates negative affect and disrupts the psychological security that a consistently loving upbringing would provide. Sibling rivalry, conflicts between parents, lack of affection, and inconsistent discipline by parents all can increase frustration and stress in both toddlers and older children (e.g., Cummings et al., 1981, 1985).

Violence in the family also reinforces and models aggression. Aggressive parents often give children approval for responding aggressively to perceived slights and provocations. Parents who employ corporal punishment to discipline their children also are implicitly teaching that physical aggression is an appropriate way to respond to those perceived as wrongdoers and portrays violence as normative to the child. These lessons also communicate that the world is a dangerous place in which most people have negative intentions, which encourages children to see hostile intent in others' actions (e.g., Dodge, Bates, & Pettit, 1990).

SOCIAL PSYCH AT THE MOVIES

Violence on Film: *Taxi Driver*

The 1976 classic Martin Scorsese film *Taxi Driver* (Scorsese, 1976), starring Robert De Niro as the cabbie Travis Bickle and Jodie Foster as the underage prostitute Iris, was one of the most violent films of its time. The film has one of the most famous and most quoted scenes in movie history. And it is referenced in the recent film *Joker* in numerous ways. It depicts much of what we know about the causes of aggression and the kind of explosive gun violence that has become much more common since the release of the film.

As a former marine who served in Vietnam, Travis has had training in violence (*social learning*). He is stressed by insomnia, stomach pains, and a sense of alienation and loneliness. He drinks heavily (and therefore might be more *disinhibited*) and takes amphetamines (which might elevate his *arousal*). He drives the streets of New York in his cab, witnessing aggression and violent conflict on a nightly basis (*violent cues and scripts*). He is looking for some way to feel heroic, like a person of significance in the world (*low self-esteem with touches of narcissism*). He is deeply frustrated when he is rejected by an attractive political campaign volunteer named Betsy, whom he had viewed as an angel amid the filth and ugliness around him. One of his customers primes him with the idea of getting a .44 Magnum and avenging himself against Betsy. He subsequently attempts in vain to shoot a presidential candidate whom Betsy worked for. He eventually goes on a bloody rampage, intending to strike out at those he perceives as evil and to save Iris from a life of prostitution.

A few years after the film came out, a socially inhibited and lonely young man named John Hinckley Jr. became obsessed with the film, watched it 15 times, and photographed himself in Travis Bickle poses. He eventually decided that he needed to save Jodie Foster, at the time an undergraduate at Yale University. He made contact with her and sent her flowers. Foster soon recognized Hinckley as an unstable stalker and cut off communication with him. He decided he needed to impress her and wrote her a letter explaining as much. His misguided effort resulted in his attempt to assassinate President Ronald Reagan in 1981. He got close enough to Reagan to seriously wound him with a pistol. He also wounded Reagan's press secretary James Brady, who was paralyzed by the shooting.

Hinckley's act of violence, inspired in part by *Taxi Driver*, caused great physical harm to major government officials

Stress, disrupted attachment, distrust in other people, and training in and modeling of aggression in violent families have both short-term and long-term consequences (Straus et al., 1980). In the short term, these conditions of family life lead children to become more aggressive. For example, Rohner (1975) found that across 60 different cultures, rejected children were more aggressive than accepted children. In a study of American preadolescent and adolescent boys, Loeber and Dishion (1984) found that those whose family lives were characterized by marital conflict, rejection, and inconsistent discipline were especially aggressive both at home and in school.

In the long term, children who are exposed to a violent family life are more prone to become aggressive adults (Eron et al., 1991; Hill & Nathan, 2008; McCord, 1983). Longitudinal studies have found that children subjected to witnessing domestic violence or victimized by abuse are more likely as adults to become spousal abusers and child abusers themselves, creating a vicious cycle perpetuated across generations (Hotaling & Sugarman, 1990; MacEwen & Barling, 1988; Widom, 1989). Even though only 2 to 4% of the general population of parents is physically abusive, approximately 30% of abused children grow up to be abusive parents (Gelles, 2007; Kaufman & Zigler, 1987). ▪

Culture and Aggression

As we've considered the cultural perspective throughout this book, we've seen how culture shapes our values, beliefs, and behavior. Aggression is no exception.

but also eventually led to the Brady bill, which requires a three-day waiting period and a background check for anyone in the United States to purchase a firearm. The Brady Handgun Violence Prevention Act, enacted in 1993, has stopped many convicted felons and people deemed mentally unfit from purchasing such weapons, although it does not catch everyone due to inadequate resources devoted to enforcement. Seung-Hui Cho, who killed 32 people and wounded 25 others on the campus of Virginia Tech University in 2007, was able to purchase multiple weapons despite having been declared mentally ill by a judge and ordered to get treatment one year earlier.

The other major long-term effect the Hinckley shooting had was on the legal system. Hinckley eventually was found not guilty by reason of insanity, a verdict that outraged many Americans and led to changes in the insanity plea. Currently, in most states, the plea is guilty but insane rather than not guilty by reason of insanity. Thirty-five years after his arrest, in 2016, Hinckley was released from St. Elizabeth's Hospital to live with his mother (Boburg, 2016).

▲ [Columbia Pictures/Photofest]

As we grow up, we are socialized with particular expectations and into particular roles. Along the way, we also learn how, when, and to what extent aggressive behavior is an acceptable or normative response to certain situations. Some cultures and subcultures may socialize us to "turn the other cheek," whereas others emphasize an "eye for an eye" or not backing down from a fight. Cultures further teach us what responses are appropriate in the face of frustration or insult. Culture thus has a profound influence on not only the extent of aggression but also the forms it can take. We see this influence when we compare national cultures as well as regions and cultural subgroups within a nation.

Comparing National Cultures   Across nations, we find striking differences in the prevalence of serious acts of aggression. In the United States, for example, one murder occurs every 31 seconds. This dwarfs the murder rates in other industrialized nations such as Canada, Australia, and Great Britain and is approximately double the world average (Barber, 2006). Although some countries in Eastern Europe, Africa, and Asia have higher rates, much of the violence in those nations is between groups and results from political instability, whereas violent crimes in the United States tend to be committed by individuals against other individuals. One likely factor is that Americans have a particularly strong tendency to resort to aggressive solutions to interpersonal conflicts (Archer & McDaniel, 1995).

As we noted earlier, the high murder rate in the United States also stems in part from the ready availability of firearms (e.g., Archer, 1994; Archer & Gartner, 1984). Firearms not only prime aggression-related thoughts, they also increase the lethality of violence. People looking to aggress use whatever is available. Aggression with firearms leads to death 1 in 6 times; aggression with knives, 1 in 30 times (Goldstein, 1986). Consider the 2016 Orlando nightclub shooting spree. The killer used a semiautomatic rifle that holds 30 rounds and a semiautomatic gun that holds 17 (Jensen, 2016). He would have done far less harm if he hadn't been able to obtain such semiautomatic weapons. As noted earlier, mass shootings, rather than making Americans more leery of firearms, make them more interested in buying guns—and often the specific guns used in the shooting (Leander et al., 2019; Wallace, 2015).

In trying to understand how and why cultures differ in aggression, some researchers focus on individualism versus collectivism. As we first discussed in chapter 2, individualistic cultures place greater value on independence and self-reliance, whereas collectivistic cultures place greater value on cooperation and maintaining harmonious relationships with others. Perhaps as a consequence, individualistic cultures tend to have more interpersonal aggression than collectivistic cultures. For example, the United States is more individualistic than Poland, which in turn is more individualistic than China. These differences in individualism mirror the rates of violence. The United States has more violence than Poland, which in turn has more violence than China (Forbes et al., 2009). Nevertheless, there are many exceptions. Some fairly collectivistic African and Latin American cultures have homicide rates considerably higher than the more individualistic United States. There is no single or simple set of variables that can account for a given nation's record of violence.

Cultures of Honor   Imagine that you are walking down a narrow hallway toward your psychology classroom as another student approaches you. As you pass by, you bump shoulders. Apparently prompted by this contact, the other student mutters "asshole" under his breath before stepping into another room. How would you react? Do you think you might react differently if you grew up in the northern United States as opposed to the South?

THINK ABOUT ▶

[Ryan McVay/Getty Images]

Research on regional variations in a culture of honor suggests that the answer might be "yes." In places that have a *culture of honor*, people (especially men) are highly motivated to protect their status or reputations. Daly and Wilson (1988, p. 128) describe it this way:

> A seemingly minor affront . . . must be understood within a larger social context of reputations, face, relative social status, and enduring relationships. Men are known by their fellows as "the sort who can be pushed around" or "the sort who won't take any shit," as people whose words mean action, or as people who are full of hot air, as guys whose girlfriends you can chat up with impunity or guys you don't want to mess with.

This mentality is a recipe for conflict. Honor, masculinity, and a tough-guy reputation are not the kind of things that a person can achieve and then forget about. They are *precarious*, meaning that the person has to constantly maintain his honor in others' eyes, and if he loses that honor, it's almost impossible to get it back. As a result, even minor affronts—a stepped-on toe at the bar or a stranger walking across the backyard—take on enormous significance as threats that must be confronted (Berke & Zeichner, 2016; Vandello & Bosson, 2013).

Dov Cohen and Richard Nisbett (Cohen & Nisbett, 1994; Nisbett, 1993) have documented a strong culture of honor in the southern and western United States. Recall the scenario of someone bumping into you in a hallway and then cursing (presumably about your being in his way). Cohen and his colleagues

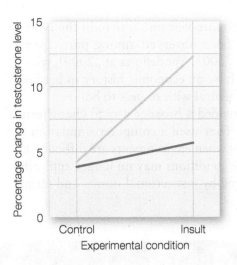

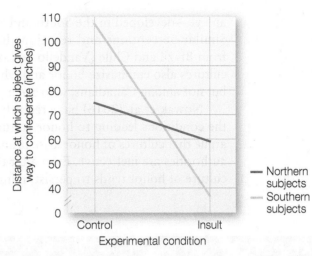

— Northern subjects
— Southern subjects

Figure 12.10

Culture of Honor

After being insulted, students from the South showed greater increases in testosterone than those from the North, and they were subsequently less likely to back down when approaching a confederate of the researchers in a narrow hallway.

[Data from Cohen et al., 1996]

(1996) put unsuspecting male college students from either the North or the South in that very situation. Students from the North did not have much of a reaction to the insult, but students from the South showed comparative increases in aggressive feelings, thoughts, and physiology. They were more likely to think their masculine reputations had been threatened and were more upset and primed for an aggressive response, as indicated by higher levels of cortisol, testosterone, and aggressive cognitions. Later on, they were more likely to act in a hyper-macho way to restore their bruised honor. For example, they were slower to move out of the way when walking toward a confederate of the researchers in a narrow hallway through which only one person could pass at a time (see **FIGURE 12.10**). And this person was 6 feet, 3 inches tall and weighed 250 pounds—no small dude!

Homicide rates among White men living in rural or small-town settings in the southern and western United States are higher than corresponding rates in similar settings in other regions of the country. Southern White men are also more likely than northern White men to believe that lethal violence is justified as a means of defending life, family, property, or reputation when they're threatened. Why did the culture of honor develop primarily in the South and West? Cohen and Nisbett (1994; Nisbett & Cohen, 1996) theorized that the answer goes back to the environmental and economic conditions in the places the American settlers came from and in the regions where they settled. Many southern settlers came from pastoral, herding societies, such as Scotland. Settlers who migrated to the arid western regions of the country became economically more dependent on cattle ranching and sheepherding than on farming. In contrast, the North largely was settled by farmers and developed a more agricultural, as opposed to herding, economy. Because people from a herding-based culture are more vulnerable to having their livelihood (e.g., livestock) rustled away, norms developed whereby men cultivated a rough, tough affect, responding harshly and violently to even the smallest threat or slight. These aggressive responses were intended to discourage theft of their means of sustenance. In contrast, because it is more difficult to steal a whole crop than a single sheep, such norms did not develop in the more agricultural North.

Another factor is that because much of the South and West remained frontier land with widely scattered, less effective law enforcement, it became even more important to protect one's own property. Because of the need to take matters into one's own hand, norms for retributive justice—that is, an eye for

▲ Herding cultures are associated with cultures of honor.

[Gianluca68/iStock/Getty Images]

an eye—developed in the South and West more vigorously than in the North. Similar perceptions and reactions have been observed among participants from Brazil and Chile (Vandello & Cohen, 2003; Vandello et al., 2009), whose cultures also emphasize honor and which have an economic history of herding, but not among Canadians, who are more neutral with respect to honor.

Nowak et al. (2016) have recently provided a broader way to characterize the conditions leading to honor cultures. They used a computer simulation to argue that cultures of honor arise primarily when environments are difficult and authorities are ineffective. Even after these conditions may no longer apply, the culture of honor tends to persist, reinforced by institutional norms and scripts

SOCIAL PSYCH OUT IN THE WORLD

Race and Violence in City Neighborhoods

On July 4, 2009, a 16-year-old boy named Terrance Green was shot and killed in Englewood, an economically disadvantaged and predominantly African American neighborhood on the South Side of Chicago (Glass, 2013a). It is also a neighborhood terrorized by gang violence. Presumably because of the stressors and lack of opportunity that come with poverty, poorer neighborhoods generally have high rates of gang activity and crime (Berkowitz, 1993; Short, 1997).

On the surface, Terrance Green's murder seems like another statistic in a larger and disturbing pattern: In the United States, violence is more prevalent in Black neighborhoods than other American neighborhoods. For example, although African Americans comprise approximately 13% of the U.S. population, according to the FBI (2018), they accounted for 38.7% of homicide offenders in 2018. Young Black males are also more likely than White males to be victims of violence. You may have heard such statistics before, but let's probe further to get a better idea of what might lie beneath these cycles of

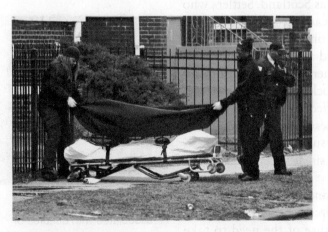

▲ [Scott Olson/Getty Images]

violence. It's true that Terrance was a gang member and that he was killed by a rival gang. But although these facts about Terrance's death conform to the general beliefs people have about gang violence, many others do not. For example, children reared in fatherless homes tend to be more violent and aggressive than children in two-parent families (Lykken, 2000; Staub, 1996; Vaden-Kiernan et al., 1995), and Black kids are often raised by single moms without the help of a father (Kids Count, 2013). While Terrance grew up in Chicago's toughest neighborhood, he came from a loving, two-parent household. He was the youngest of five kids; his oldest brother is a pastor. With such a stable and supportive home life, how did Terrance end up in a gang?

Many social psychological processes lie beneath the cycle of violence (Anderson, 2000). In a place like Englewood, students often don't join gangs by choice. Instead, the gang you end up in depends on the block you live on. By the time Terrance and his friends hit puberty, they were bullied by older kids for merely walking down a street in another gang's territory. By default, Terrance was assumed to be part of the gang in his neighborhood, even though he'd never been recruited or agreed to be a member. He was an athlete and a natural leader, and he found himself having to defend his friends as well as himself.

Not knowing what else to do, Terrance and his teenage friends banded together for protection and called themselves Yung Lyfe (Young Unique Noble Gentlemen Live Youthful and Fulfilled Everyday)—not exactly a name designed to strike fear in the minds of others. Terrance's father didn't realized that his son had been backed into being a gang member. And after Terrance was killed, he was shocked to learn that a 23-block section of his neighborhood was named TG City after his son, not just to memorialize Terrance but to establish a new and bigger gang territory for those kids who rallied together to avenge Terrance's death. In the three years after Terrance Green was murdered, at least 10 shootings and 7 additional murders occurred as part of a string of retaliatory attacks.

of action that people learn through socialization processes and extending to their attitudes and behavior. People from the South have a more lenient attitude toward crimes—even murder—when they believe the perpetrator is acting to protect honor, such as killing to defend his family (Vandello et al., 2008). Indeed, when employers were sent a job application from a fictitious applicant who admitted that he had impulsively killed a man who had had an affair with his wife and then publicly taunted him about it, southern employers responded more sympathetically than did those in the North (Cohen & Nisbett, 1997). However, no such differences emerged with respect to an applicant who admitted that he had stolen a car because he had needed the money. Honor cultures

If you want to learn more about Terrance's story and those of other teenagers in his community, check out a two-part story called "Harper High School" that was broadcast on *This American Life* in February 2013 (Glass, 2013a).

Stories like Terrance's reveal the bind that teens can find themselves in when they live within a gang culture in which many people have guns and aren't afraid to use them to terrorize others and settle even the smallest of arguments. What would you do in this situation? Maybe you are thinking *Why not go to your parents, your teachers, or the police?* Unfortunately, you'd be unlikely to tell them anything they didn't already know. It's no secret that gang violence is a problem in these neighborhoods, but effective solutions are lacking. A large-scale study of more than 100 U.S. cities suggests that in cities with a greater proportion of Black residents, *fewer* arrests are made of violent Black offenders (Stucky, 2012). In such cases, the local police might lack either the resources or the motivation to bring an end to the violence. Instead, kids accept the belief voiced by one gang member: "There's no solution to the violence. Killing, killing is the solution" (Jacobson, 2012).

Breaking the cycle of violence in places like Englewood means confronting and looking beyond the racial stereotypes that feed the cycle. Gangs often form in the first place to regulate a market of illegal activities, such as drugs and prostitution. Without ready access to a good education, job training, or job opportunities, illegal behavior can seem like the only choice for survival. As one young Englewood man said in the previously cited interview with Walter Jacobson, "We've got to eat. We want to. We want money. . . . In our neighborhood, I ain't going to lie to you. [Selling drugs] . . . that's where the money comes from."

Because neither the police nor the government can regulate these illegal activities, gangs rely on a culture of honor and code of the street to police each other and enforce norms. Once people outside this life start seeing an increased prevalence of gang behavior and violence among members of a specific ethnic or racial group, a stereotyped association of Black = violent begins to form (Dixon, 2008a). African Americans are more prevalent in gangs than European Americans (National Gang Center, 2016). However, although any given gang member is more likely to be Black than White, television, movies, and news reporting often exaggerate this association even further (Dixon & Linz, 2000).

From learning about schematic processing in chapter 4 and stereotyping in chapter 10, we know that once such stereotypes are established, they can bias our perceptions. In a study of prison inmates convicted of violent crimes, those inmates who looked more Black (i.e., darker skin tone and more Afrocentric features) were more likely to have been sentenced to death, even when the crime was no more severe than one committed by a White inmate (Blair et al., 2004; Eberhardt et al., 2006). With such strong associations of "Black" with "violence," self-fulfilling prophecies are likely to occur. For example, if Whites see a young Black (versus White) male with a neutral expression on his face, they're more likely to think he is angry (Hugenberg & Bodenhausen, 2003). But how well will his interactions go if people assume he is angry and likely to be violent? It's hard not to feel angry when people seem to assume that you are angry anyway.

As we try to understand the disturbing cycles of violence that plague lower-income African American urban communities, social psychology has much to teach us. Although gang subcultures and fatherless homes play a role, the reasons for these situations, and the stereotypes and norms they conjure up and perpetuate, also can fuel an escalating violent lifestyle. Perhaps because these factors are still quite prevalent, homicide is still common. Shootings and homicides remain a serious problem in Chicago, as well as other American cities. Over Father's Day weekend in Chicago in 2020, there were 104 shootings, including 15 fatalities; 5 of the victims were children (Sun-Times Wire, 2020). Much will need to be accomplished before victims like Terrance become a rare tragedy.

do not consider just any aggressive or criminal action acceptable; they single out those that involve matters of honor.

Another factor is that herding cultures tend to have greater status disparities between the haves and the have-nots, leading lower-status men to become especially sensitive to status threats (e.g., insults) (Henry, 2009). People with high status are not similarly bothered by status threats because they have various material signs of their status (e.g., luxury cars, nice houses). Indeed, Greitemeyer and Sagioglou (2016) have found that people who perceive themselves to be of low socioeconomic status and therefore disadvantaged are higher in aggressive inclinations. This is true when perceived socioeconomic status is simply measured and correlated with aggressiveness and also when people are led by an experimental manipulation to think they are lower versus higher in socioeconomic status.

Finally, the ideas of a culture of honor and the protection of tenuous self-worth can help explain gang-related violence. In 1967, Wolfgang and Ferracuti developed the very similar concept of *subcultures of violence* to explain big-city gang-related violence. A number of factors contribute to gang-related violence, including the strain of poverty and attempts by poor teenagers to exert control over their lives (Goldstein, 1994). Corey Pegues (2016, p. 233) recounted in his book *Once a Cop* how he went from teen gang member and drug dealer to one of the highest-ranking African American officers in the NYPD. He observed that "you feel like you don't have any power, any control. . . . Kids join gangs and do drugs because at least it gives them the feeling they are . . . making money, asserting themselves." But it is also important to consider the subcultural norms and expectations that develop within economically disadvantaged city neighborhoods, which sociologist Elijah Anderson (2000) has dubbed "the code of the street." In this subculture, violence and aggression are means of maintaining one's honor and status. The code of the street sets up the rules for being someone of value not to be trifled with. Social Psych Out in the World takes a closer look at an example of gang violence in the African American community.

SECTION REVIEW Learning to Aggress

As a species, we excel at social learning, sometimes including how to aggress.

Electronic Media	Family Life	Culture
• Experimental and longitudinal research shows that watching media violence contributes to aggression.	• A violent family life disrupts psychological security and models aggression.	• Individualistic cultures tend to have higher levels of aggression than collectivistic ones.
• This is especially true when the hero is easy to identify with and is triumphant.	• Rejected or abused children are more likely to become aggressive themselves.	• A culture of honor or code of the street may encourage aggression that is regarded as necessary to protect one's livelihood or status.
• Aggressive and frustrated people are more susceptible to the influence of media violence than are others.		

Individual Differences in Aggression

Learning Outcomes

We've seen how learning experiences and situations partly determine a person's anger, hostility, and aggression. Now let's consider some factors of the individual him- or herself that make a difference.

- Differentiate the likelihood and style of aggression in men and women.
- Explain the role of socialization experiences and genes in the likelihood to aggress.
- List reasons intelligence is a factor in aggressive behavior.
- Identify the personality traits that foster aggression.

Gender Differences in Aggression

Over the course of history and around the globe today, men are more likely than women to be physically aggressive (Archer, 2004; Card et al., 2008). Men commit the vast majority of violent and homicidal aggressive acts, such as murder, armed robbery, and aggravated assault (Daly & Wilson, 1988). However, women are more likely than men to engage in acts of verbal aggression by spreading malicious rumors and gossip, excluding others from desirable events and groups, and threatening to end friendships (Archer, 2004; Card et al., 2008; Crick & Grotpeter, 1995). Men and women do not differ in their overall level of aggression as much as they do in their preferred mode of aggression—physical for men, verbal for women.

Verbal aggression can be extremely harmful, and victims of verbal aggression are at a high risk for depression and anxiety (Crick & Grotpeter, 1996). The distress and humiliation they experience can even lead them to take their own lives, as in the cyberbullying case of Brandy Vela, described earlier in this chapter. Still, because the consequences of physical aggression are usually more apparent and severe, research has so far focused on understanding why men are more physically aggressive than women.

One theory traces this gender difference back to physiological differences between men and women (Maccoby & Jacklin, 1974). Recall that testosterone level is correlated with aggressive behavior, particularly in response to provocation, and that men secrete more testosterone than women. Men injected with testosterone are more aggressive, especially if they are predisposed to dominance and impulsivity (Geniole et al., 2019). Another factor may be that men are generally larger and physically stronger than women. A third factor is that men are more likely than women to interpret other people's actions as intended to provoke them—for example, by insulting their reputations (Crick & Dodge, 1994; Dodge & Coie, 1987).

But why aren't women more physically aggressive? According to Eagly and Steffen (1986), boys and girls are socialized with different normative expectations; a certain amount of physical aggression is acceptable among young boys but not as much among young girls (Björkqvist et al., 1992). As a result, women are more prone to inhibit their aggressive impulses (Brock & Buss, 1964; Eagly & Steffen, 1986; Wyer et al., 1965). Consistent with this explanation, research shows that when women are in situations where they feel less constrained by traditional gender-role norms, they are less likely to inhibit themselves from being physically aggressive (Bettencourt & Miller, 1996).

Trait Aggressiveness

Some people demonstrate trait aggressiveness. They are more likely than others to aggress over time and across situations, are susceptible to hostile thoughts, are likely to express anger, and tend to engage in physical and verbal aggression.

Achieve

Video: Mean Girls (ABC What Would You Do Series)

▲ Words do hurt. Victims of verbal aggression are at increased risk of depression and anxiety. In some cases, they commit suicide.
[omgimages/iStock/Getty Images]

▲ Conflicts between parents are very stressful for children, making them more prone to aggression and antisocial behavior later in life.

[Stuart Pearce/AGE Fotostock]

Hostile attribution bias The tendency to attribute hostile intent to others' actions, even when others' intentions are innocent.

Researchers often measure trait aggressiveness in adults by giving them questionnaires that ask how much they agree with statements such as "Once in a while I can't control the urge to strike another person" and "I sometimes feel like a powder keg ready to explode" (Buss & Perry, 1992).

Individual differences in trait aggressiveness emerge as early as age three (Olweus, 1979). These differences are stable across the life span, with trait aggressiveness in childhood correlating highly with aggressiveness as much as 40 years later (Huesmann et al., 2009). Indeed, the continuity of aggression across the life span is as stable as the continuity of IQ. Laboratory studies show that individuals who are high in trait aggressiveness engage in higher levels of aggressive behavior under both neutral and provoking conditions (Bettencourt et al., 2006; Bushman, 1995).

Why are some people high in trait aggressiveness? A complete answer to this question would likely involve virtually all the factors we have already discussed in this chapter. But let's take a brief look at two influences.

Bad Parenting Coercive parenting styles, inconsistent discipline, physical abuse, and exposure to family conflicts all contribute to a child's tendency to behave in an aggressive and antisocial manner later in life (Rhee & Waldman, 2002). In fact, bad parenting can set into motion a chain of aggressiveness that spans three generations (Capaldi et al., 2003; Conger et al., 2003; Hops et al., 2003; Thornberry et al., 2003).

From the social cognitive perspective, part of what children learn from more aggressive parents is not just aggressive behavior but also aggressive interpretations of social information. When a person is provoked, the degree to which he or she infers that another's actions were committed with hostile intent is called a *hostile attribution*. Inferring hostile attributions (e.g., "He stepped on my sneakers to disrespect me") strongly predicts whether the person will react aggressively. If the same person infers that the action in question was not intended to harm (e.g., "He stepped on my sneakers because he didn't see me"), the probability of an aggressive reaction is much lower (Dodge, 1980). The link between hostile attributions and aggressive behavior holds across ages, demographic and cultural groups, and social contexts (de Castro et al., 2003). Children classified as highly aggressive by their peers and teachers are more likely than their less aggressive peers to attribute hostile intent to others' actions, even when others' intentions are benign (Dodge, 1980; Nasby et al., 1980). This has been called the **hostile attribution bias** (Crick & Dodge, 1994). In hostile family environments, children quickly learn to attribute hostile motives to others. The experience of physical and/or psychological abuse by one's parents during the first five years of life predicts a tendency toward the hostile attribution bias, which in turn predicts aggressive behavior years later (Dodge et al., 1990; Weiss et al., 1992; Zhu et al., in press). Childhood maltreatment also predicts a tendency toward anger and ruminating about that anger, which also contributes to aggression (Zhu et al., in press).

Genetic Factors The clearest evidence for the role of genetic influences on aggressiveness comes from studies of twins (Miles & Carey, 1997; Rhee & Waldman, 2002). In one study (Rushton et al., 1986), monozygotic twin pairs (twins who are genetically identical) were more similar in aggressiveness than were dizygotic twin pairs (those who on average share only half of their genes). In another study (Eley et al., 2003), researchers looked at more than 1,000 identical and fraternal pairs of Swedish twins and had parents rate their children's aggressiveness first as children (ages 8 to 9) and then again as adolescents (ages 13 to 14). Twins' aggressiveness over time was highly correlated, particularly when they were identical, suggesting that aggressive behavior might be influenced by genetic factors.

Although there have been few successes so far in identifying any single gene that makes people aggressive, studies have found interesting links between aggressiveness and genes involved in the production of serotonin. As noted earlier, serotonin is a neurotransmitter that helps regulate stress. Low levels of serotonin are associated with high levels of aggression. For the body to metabolize and secrete serotonin, it needs an enzyme called monoamine oxidase A, or MAO-A for short. A rare genetic variant that causes low levels of MAO-A has been linked to violent and antisocial behavior (Brunner et al., 1993; Munafò et al., 2003), perhaps because individuals with this genetic variant have greater difficulty metabolizing serotonin to help deal with stress (Meyer-Lindenberg et al., 2006).

It's important to keep in mind that this genetic factor—referred to by some researchers as the *warrior gene*—does not universally predict aggressive behavior. It does so largely in response to enduring and situational stressors. For example, the genetic variant causing low MAO-A levels predicts aggressive behavior only among people who were exposed to high levels of maltreatment and stress during childhood (Caspi et al., 2002; Kim-Cohen et al., 2006). But for an individual reared in an environment that was nurturing and supportive, this genetic variant does not predict aggressiveness.

The genetic variant indicating low MAO-A also predicts higher levels of aggression when people are currently provoked. McDermott and colleagues (2009) showed that, in the absence of provocation, MAO-A levels did not predict aggression. However, when participants were told that another person had taken money from them, those with low levels of MAO-A forced that person to consume more painful hot sauce. Thus, we should consider this genetic factor a biological predisposition that interacts with the person's environment rather than as a strict determinant of the person's behavior.

Intelligence

Poor intellectual functioning is linked to high aggressiveness, especially in children (e.g., Pitkanen-Pulkinen, 1979). Why? For one, if people are less able to process the subtleties of a social situation and the intentions behind other people's actions, they may be more likely to infer automatically that other people are deliberately trying to offend them (Guerra et al., 1994).

Poor intellectual functioning also makes it more likely that people will feel frustrated in their lives. This may be especially evident in school, where students with deficits in reading comprehension and mathematical reasoning may be continually frustrated by the tasks assigned to them. Intellectual deficits may also make it difficult to understand the inappropriateness of aggression, consider future consequences, or think of nonaggressive means of responding in frustrating situations (Geen, 2001; Slaby & Guerra, 1988).

Finally, not only does poor intellectual functioning lead to aggression but aggression can impair intellectual functioning (Huesmann, 1988). Children who tend to lash out aggressively often end up disrupting good relationships with their teachers and peers, and they miss out on opportunities to learn problem-solving skills and advance intellectually. One 22-year longitudinal study showed that aggressiveness in children at age 8 predicted poor intellectual functioning at age 30 better than intellectual functioning at age 8 predicted adult aggressiveness (Huesmann & Eron, 1984).

Personality Traits and Reactivity to Provocation

We've seen that perceived provocation is a major trigger of aggressive behavior. A number of personality traits predict how strongly people react to provocation and, thus, how likely they are to retaliate with anger and aggression.

Narcissism and Deficits in Self-Esteem   A long-standing belief of many researchers and lay individuals alike is that low self-esteem contributes to aggression. Research backs this up. Physically abusive parents and spouses and aggressive children tend to have lower self-esteem than their nonaggressive counterparts (Anderson & Lauderdale, 1982; Burdett & Jensen, 1983; Goldstein & Rosenbaum, 1985; Tangney et al., 2011). Given that provocations are often threats to self-esteem, those who have lower self-esteem also react more emotionally than others to failure, negative social feedback, and social rejection.

Researchers have also found links between aggression and narcissism and unstable self-esteem. Narcissists have a grandiose but fragile view of themselves and tend to agree with statements such as "If I ruled the world, it would be a much better place" and "I get upset when people don't notice how I look when I go out in public" (Baumeister et al., 1996; Thomaes & Bushman, 2011). Narcissists often exhibit low self-esteem when it is measured implicitly (e.g., Gregg & Sedikides, 2010). Individuals with unstable self-esteem have views of themselves that fluctuate radically in response to social events (Kernis et al., 1989).

People high in narcissism or with unstable self-esteem respond to provocations with higher levels of aggressive behavior than those who are comparatively low in these traits (Bushman & Baumeister, 1998). Unlike trait aggressiveness, which predicts aggressive behavior under both neutral and provocation conditions, narcissism and unstable self-esteem seem to make people particularly reactive to threats to their self-views (Bettencourt et al., 2006). Further implicating self-esteem deficits in aggression, research by Krizan and Johar (2015) shows that it is the feeling of vulnerability of narcissists, not their grandiosity, which underlies their hostility and aggressiveness in response to perceived slights.

Individual Differences in Impulsivity   People differ in their ability to control their thoughts and behaviors, which affects how well they can inhibit an impulse to aggress. Individuals who are high in impulsivity tend to react to situations without thinking through the consequences of their actions (Barratt, 1994). They respond affirmatively to questions such as "Do you do things on the spur of the moment?" They also tend to respond to insults, attacks, and frustrations with angry outbursts, whereas low-impulsivity individuals tend to stay calm, refrain from overt signs of anger, and inhibit their urge to behave aggressively after being provoked (Caprara et al., 2002). For example, high- and low-impulsivity individuals can experience equivalent levels of anger in response to a provocation, but high-impulsivity individuals are less able to resist the urge to lash out aggressively (e.g., Hynan & Grush, 1986). Consequently, high impulsivity is correlated with aggressive behaviors and has, in fact, been found to be one of the best predictors of criminal behavior (Pratt & Cullen, 2000).

▲ People high in impulsivity have difficulty controlling their aggressive impulses.

[Christopher Robbins/Getty Images]

Research taking the social neuroscience perspective looks at the brain regions involved in impulsive aggression (Davidson et al., 2000; Raine, 2008). Recall that the *prefrontal cortex* is the part of the brain that governs our ability to monitor and control our behavior. Research has shown that convicted murderers display less glucose metabolism in their prefrontal regions than do their less violent counterparts (Raine et al., 1997). Differences in prefrontal functioning also predict aggressive responses to provocation. Lau and colleagues (1995) found that participants with weak frontal lobe functioning tended to be more aggressive (administering painful electric shocks) toward a confederate who previously provoked them. In contrast, the effect of provocation was found to be substantially weaker among individuals with strong frontal-lobe functioning.

It is interesting to note that a certain subgroup of violent criminals does not fit this high-impulsivity pattern. On the one hand, studies of violent criminals reveal one group of individuals who often have an extensive history of impulsive actions and assaults (D'Silva & Duggan, 2010; Du Toit & Duckitt, 1990; Megargee, 1966). These individuals seem to have *undercontrolled* aggressive impulses. But a second group of violent criminals often have no prior assaultive history; they seem to be low in impulsivity and have rigid inhibitions against expressing anger. Researchers suggest that these *overcontrolled* offenders allow their frustrations and hostilities to build up until they boil over into an extreme act of aggression. Consistent with this idea, many of the mass shooters from the Columbine killers to the present day have had no history of violence before their sudden deadly outbursts.

Sadism

Individuals high in dispositional *sadism* perceive that harming others is a way to get pleasure. Those high in sadism are motivated to aggress by the *enjoyment* they expect to get from inflicting suffering on others. Chester and colleagues (2019) found that self-reported sadism was positively associated with making others listen to loud noise blasts, eat painfully spicy hot sauce, and view gruesome images. The associations between sadism and aggressive behavior held even when controlling for impulsivity, trait aggression, and narcissism. Ironically, however, sadists did not feel positive affect after aggressive acts. For some people, others' suffering may seem enjoyable, but in the end, it is their own mood that suffers.

SECTION REVIEW   Individual Differences in Aggression

Individual differences affect a person's tendency toward aggression.

Gender Differences	Trait Aggressiveness	Intelligence	Personality Traits
• Men and women differ more in their mode than in their overall level of aggression. • These differences are influenced by both social roles and biology (e.g., testosterone).	• Some people are high in trait aggressiveness. • Maltreatment and stress during childhood may also exacerbate genetic predispositions toward aggression.	• Frustration and misunderstanding may contribute to aggression in low-intellect individuals. • Aggression can also impair future intellectual functioning.	• Narcissists and those with low and/or unstable self-esteem are more likely to retaliate with aggression. • People high in impulsivity also react aggressively. • People who tend to overcontrol their impulses sometime engage in aggression when hostility boils over. • People high in sadism anticipate that they will enjoy harming others.

- Identify possible consequences of criminalization of recreational drugs.
- List reasons alcohol increases aggressive behavior.

The Roles of Alcohol and Other Drugs in Aggression

In most if not all known cultures, many people have engaged in activities that alter their state of consciousness, whether through meditation, trances, or the use of mind-altering substances such as alcohol, marijuana, cocaine, opiates, MDMA (ecstasy), methamphetamine, and hallucinogens (McKenna, 1993; Rosen & Weil, 2004; Weil, 1972). Although drugs can be appealing for a variety of reasons, both the resulting altered states and the desire for these drugs can contribute to aggression in a variety of ways.

Some theorists have argued that the criminalization of recreational drugs and the quite ineffective "war on drugs" play a substantial role in gang activity, crime, and violence. In poor communities, the lure of easy drug money is hard to resist. As former dealer Corey Pegues (2016, p. 23) put it, "that extra bit of money . . . to take your girl out. . . . You're young, you're black, you don't see any prospects. Then you see these dealers, and they're living the American Dream." The drugs generate huge profits that legitimate authorities are unable to regulate and that bankroll other illegal activities (Goldstein, 1986). Both small-time drug dealers and large-scale drug cartels must therefore devise their own means of protection. As a result, the illegal drug trade contributes to a large percentage of violent crimes, ranging from assault to homicide, in countries such as the United States (Roth, 1994) and Mexico (Miroff & Booth, 2010). For example, Mexican drug cartels hire *sicarios*, assassins who protect their turf and business interests, leaving casualties in their wake (e.g., Molloy & Bowden, 2011).

The effects of drugs on users also can contribute to violence. Although a common belief is that addicts turn to crimes such as muggings and burglary to support their addiction, at least for heroin, evidence for this link is not clear (Kretschmar & Flannery, 2007). However, drugs can increase physiological arousal, heightening emotional reactions to provocations and reducing higher-order cognition and impulse control. Some drugs can create a sense of paranoia, which also intensifies feelings of being threatened. Unfortunately, experimental research on the effects of illegal drugs on aggression is rare because of the ethical and practical difficulty of giving such drugs to participants. More research is needed before strong conclusions can be drawn about the direct effects of such drugs on aggression.

The vast majority of studies on the effects of drugs on aggression have focused on alcohol (Kretschmar & Flannery, 2007; Kruesi, 2007). This is partly because alcohol is a legal recreational drug and partly because it is the most commonly used (and abused) recreational drug in the United States and most other large cultures. Imagine that you are at a sporting event, a party, or a concert, and a fight breaks out. How likely do you think it would be that at least one of the combatants is drunk? Correlational research indicates that it would be pretty likely. Alcohol is involved in about half of all violent crimes and sexual assaults worldwide (Beck & Heinz, 2013; Chermack & Giancola, 1997). Some studies show even higher rates. In one study of 882 persons arrested in Ohio for felonies, over 75% of offenders who were arrested for violent crimes, ranging from assault to murder, were legally intoxicated (Shupe, 1954).

Experimental research further supports a causal role of alcohol use in aggression. When given an opportunity to deliver electric shocks or aversive noise to another person, participants who have consumed alcohol under conditions of threat or competition engage in more aggression than do sober participants. The higher

▲ Clearly, alcohol use is positively associated with aggression. This is especially true for people with aggressive dispositions and low impulse control (Geen, 2001).

[Epoxydude/Getty Images]

the dose of alcohol, the greater the aggression (Bushman & Cooper, 1990; Taylor & Leonard, 1983). In contrast, threatened participants who have consumed the psychoactive ingredients in marijuana generally have been found to be less rather than more aggressive than sober participants (e.g., Taylor & Leonard, 1983). Why is alcohol intoxication such a significant contributor to aggression?

One reason is that alcohol impairs higher-order thinking such as self-awareness and therefore reduces inhibitions and impulse control (e.g., Hull et al., 1983; Ito et al., 1996). A minor slight or insult that a sober person would likely ignore or deflect is more likely to provoke aggression in a drunk person. In addition, this cognitive impairment makes it less likely that drunk people will consider the consequences of their actions (Steele & Josephs, 1990; Taylor & Leonard, 1983). Neuroscience research further shows that patterns of electrical activity in the brains of intoxicated people indicate that they are less distressed than sober participants by the mistakes they make (Bartholow et al., 2012). All these factors highlight alcohol's tendency to reduce the self-regulatory controls with which we ordinarily inhibit aggressive impulses.

A second reason that alcohol increases aggression is that we *expect* alcohol use to lead to aggression. Participants who drank a placebo beverage that they believed contained alcohol (but actually did not) showed increased behavioral signs of aggression compared with those who knew they were not drinking alcohol (Rohsenow & Bachorowski, 1984). In fact, simply exposing participants to alcohol-related pictures (e.g., a beer bottle or martini glass) or even subliminal flashes of alcohol-related words on a computer screen leads participants to interpret a person's behavior as more aggressive and leads to more hostile evaluations of another person in the face of frustration (Bartholow & Heinz, 2006; Friedman et al., 2007). These effects tend to be stronger the more strongly people believe that alcohol use causes aggression.

Although the bulk of the experimental research has focused on the effects of aggression on perpetrators, some research suggests that victims of violent crimes are also more likely to be drunk (e.g., Chermack & Giancola, 1997). One explanation for the latter finding is suggested by research showing that when people have consumed alcohol, they become less able to read social cues such as the emotions on the face of another person (Steele & Josephs, 1990; Taylor & Leonard, 1983), a phenomenon Steele and Josephs refer to as *alcohol myopia*. So in a bar or at a party, a drunk person may, because of alcohol's disinhibiting effects, become increasingly annoying to another person, but because of their insensitivity to facial and social cues, they are insufficiently aware of how much they are angering that person. Consequently, alcohol consumption not only makes a person a more likely perpetrator of violence but also a more likely victim of it. Worth keeping in mind!

SECTION REVIEW The Roles of Alcohol and Other Drugs in Aggression

Altered states can contribute to aggression.

Drugs contribute to aggression because:	The most commonly used drug is alcohol, and research supports its causal role in aggression because:
• Illegal business activities are often regulated through violence. • Drugs can increase arousal and create a sense of paranoia.	• It impairs higher-order thinking. • We *expect* it to lead to aggression. • It impedes a potential victim's ability to read social cues.

-
-
-

Violence Against Women

Some forms of male aggression are directed primarily at women. Men are on average more physically aggressive, larger in size, and have greater power and status in society, giving them a clear advantage in physical altercations. Furthermore, because women can block some of men's specific desires (or may be perceived to be blocking them), women have been common targets of male aggression in many places and times over the course of history (Brownmiller, 1975; Gelles, 2007). Thus, substantial theory and research have focused on two common forms of violence directed at women: domestic violence and sexual coercion.

Domestic Violence

You hit me once
I hit you back
You gave a kick
I gave a slap
You smashed a plate
Over my head
Then I set fire to our bed. . . .
A kiss with a fist is better than none

—Florence and the Machine (2009), "Kiss with a Fist"

Domestic violence is violence between current or former romantic partners. Most of the time we can safely avoid those who would harm us. We steer clear of angry people on the street, and we don't waltz into the middle of a fight between rival gangs. But in the case of partner violence, the perpetrator and the victim of violence interact frequently and feel bound to each other. In fact, Arriaga and colleagues (2016) found that for men and women who were highly committed to their romantic partner, but not for those less committed, experiencing aggression from their partner made them more tolerant of additional acts of aggression. These findings suggest that, over time, people allow themselves to take more and more abuse from the very person who should be caring for and protecting them.

Although some self-report survey research suggests that in heterosexual relationships, the frequency of physical aggression by males and females is actually the same (Straus, 2005), males clearly engage in more injurious and lethal physical aggression against their partners than females do (Gelles, 2007). Many of the causal contributors to aggression that we have already discussed also contribute to domestic violence against women (e.g., Hamberger & Hastings, 1991; MacEwen & Barling, 1988; O'Leary & Vivian, 1990). **FIGURE 12.11** details how some of these factors fit together. In addition, macho cultures of honor often promote attitudes that are particularly accepting of violence against women (Vandello & Cohen, 2003). Male abusers tend to hold beliefs that condone violence against women, such as the belief that marital violence is acceptable (Stith & Farley, 1993). Men who feel low power in their relationships and who are high in hostile sexism are especially likely to be abusive, especially if they fear their female partners may leave them (Cross et al., 2017, 2019).

Research on the personalities of male domestic violence offenders has revealed three types, each characterizing about a third of total offenders (Dutton, 1998; Geen, 2001). The first type, the *psychopathic abuser*, is likely to employ physical aggression both inside and outside the relationship. These men

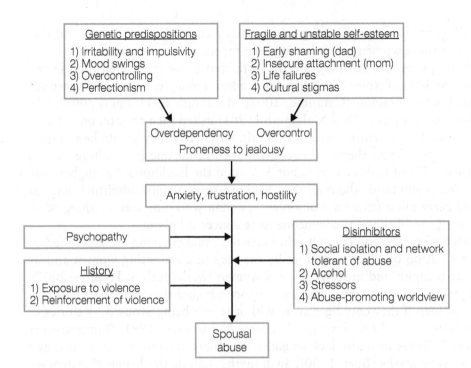

Figure 12.11

What Predicts Spousal Abuse?
Different factors contribute to male domestic violence against women.
[Research by Jeff Greenberg]

are bullies with low impulse control and often a history of violent incidents. The second type, the *overcontrolled abuser*, is a man who generally is not violent but builds up resentments from various aspects of his life and eventually uses his relationship partner as a target for his displaced aggression.

The third and perhaps best-understood type, the *borderline abuser*, is narcissistic and likely to have a borderline personality organization, which entails an uncertain, insecure sense of self, a proclivity for defensiveness, abandonment issues, anger, and impulsivity (Dutton, 2002). These men tend to have experienced disordered childhood attachment with one or both parents that involved neglect or abuse and to have been shamed in childhood, typically by their fathers. They are overly dependent on their relationship partner for psychological security and consequently use jealous outbursts to control their partner. This type of offender often traps a woman in a cyclical pattern of escalating tension, hostility, and abuse followed by contrition (e.g., "Baby, please don't leave me. I promise I'll quit drinking and never do that again.") (Dutton, 2002; Walker, 1979). The 1984 award-winning film *The Burning Bed* portrays the true story of a woman caught in this cycle who endured over 15 years of on-again, off-again abuse. Finally, as the title implies, she did something drastic about it (Greenwald, 1984).

Sexual Coercion and Rape

Sexual coercion occurs when an individual forces sexual behavior such as kissing, fondling, or sexual penetration on another person. The most severe form of sexual coercion is rape, forcing individuals to engage in sexual intercourse against their will. Rape is generally more traumatic for the victim than are other forms of physical assault (Malamuth & Huppin, 2007). The great majority of rapes of women are committed by men who know their female victims. Date rape, which occurs in the context of dating or an ongoing romantic relationship, is more common than rape by a stranger (Sinozich & Langton, 2014). Almost half of college women report having been sexually coerced at least once, and 6 to 15% of college women report having been raped.

Perhaps more disturbing are the data that come from men themselves. Fifteen to 30% of American college men admit having engaged in at least one act of sexual coercion (Catanese, 2007; Malamuth & Huppin, 2007). The pioneering researcher Neil Malamuth (1981) asked men to rate, on a 1 to 5 scale (with 1 representing zero likelihood), how likely they would be to rape a woman if they knew they could get away with it. In American college student samples, 65% of males chose 1, but 35% said the likelihood was higher than zero. When you think about all the social pressures against admitting that one would carry out a felony act of violence, a man who indicates anything other than a 1 (zero likelihood) is someone to be concerned about.

Men who rape and commit other acts of sexual coercion are motivated by a combination of being turned on by the idea of dominating women and by insecurity about and hostility toward women (Malamuth & Huppin, 2007). Both convicted rapists and men who report a higher than 0% chance of raping a woman if they could get away with it report being aroused by stories of women being forced to have sex (Barbaree & Marshall, 1991; Donnerstein et al., 1987). These men also lack empathy for others, tend to be narcissistic, and believe rape myths (Burt, 1980). Such myths include the beliefs that women like to be dominated, are aroused by the idea of being raped, and bring the attacks on themselves. **TABLE 12.1** lists some common rape myths and statements that researchers have used to measure men's endorsement of them (Payne et al., 1999).

Sexually aggressive men also associate sex with power. When men prone to sexual aggression (but not other men) were subtly primed with power-related stimuli, such as the words *authority* and *control*, they rated a female confederate as more attractive (Bargh et al., 1995). Research also suggests that men who perceive low power in their lives are prone to use sexual aggression to try to compensate for their inadequacies (Williams et al., 2017). Sexually aggressive

Table 12.1 Sample Items Used to Measure Rape Myths

Rape Myth	Measuring Statement
She asked for it	When women go around wearing low-cut tops or short skirts, they're just asking for trouble.
It wasn't really rape	If a woman doesn't physically resist sex—even when protesting verbally—it really can't be considered rape.
He didn't mean to	Men don't usually intend to force sex on a woman, but sometimes they get too sexually carried away.
She wanted it	Although most women wouldn't admit it, they generally find being physically forced into sex a real turn-on.
She lied	Many so-called rape victims are actually women who had sex willingly and changed their minds afterward.
Rape is a trivial event	Women tend to exaggerate how much rape affects them.
Rape is a deviant event	Men from nice, middle-class homes almost never rape.

[Research by Payne et al., 1999]

men also tend to view friendliness from a female as a sexual invitation and to view female assertiveness as hostility (Murphy et al., 1986; Zurbriggen, 2000).

Malamuth (2007) has labeled the combination of hostile sexism, belief in rape myths, insecurity about one's masculinity and power, and sexual arousal linked to dominating women the *hostile masculinity syndrome*. Men with this syndrome are likely to engage in acts of sexual coercion, especially if they are sexually promiscuous. They are also likely to abuse their female partners. Convicted rapists display this syndrome, but in addition, they are more likely than other sexually aggressive males to have a general history of aggressiveness (Malamuth & Huppin, 2007).

The prevalence of this syndrome has led some evolutionary theorists to speculate that it occurs in some present-day men because sexual coercion is a strategy that, though abhorrent, may have in the past been an effective means of perpetuating one's genes into future generations (Buss & Malamuth, 1996; Thornhill & Thornhill, 1992).

In contrast, more feminist and socially oriented theorists and researchers (e.g., Brownmiller, 1975; Donnerstein et al., 1987) have focused on the ways that cultural environments promote beliefs in rape myths, make domination of women seem normative, and objectify women, portraying them as mere objects of sexual pleasure for men (as we discussed in chapters 10 and 11). For example, a substantial body of research supports a strong learning component to a propensity to engage in sexual aggression. Mainstream films often depict sexual coercion and sometimes even rape as pleasing to women, and male participants randomly assigned to watch such films (compared with control films) reported an increased belief in rape myths and acceptance of violence against women (Malamuth & Check, 1981). In other experiments, men assigned to watch pornographic films that depict violence against women became more aggressive toward a female confederate who insulted them (e.g., Donnerstein et al., 1987). Although nonviolent pornography depicting consensual sex doesn't have this same effect, long-term exposure to even nonviolent sex scenes predicts greater acceptance of violence against women and increases the likelihood of sexual aggression (Donnerstein et al., 1987; Geen, 2001; Hald et al., 2010).

Taken together, the experimental and correlational research suggests that media that reinforce rape myths and portray women as victims of violence or sex objects may indeed contribute to aggression against women in the real world. Furthermore, this is especially likely for men with hostile masculinity syndrome (Vega & Malamuth, 2007).

SECTION REVIEW Violence Against Women

Women have been targets of male aggression in many places and times over the course of history.

- Male abusers of current or former romantic partners tend to believe that marital violence is acceptable.
- There are three categories of domestic violence offenders: psychopathic, overcontrolled, and borderline.

- Men who commit acts of sexual coercion are insecure about and hostile toward women, are turned on by the idea of dominating them, and tend to believe myths about rape.
- Evidence suggests that films which portray women as targets of violence promote aggression against women and more tolerance of it.

- Summarize ways to reduce aggression at three levels: societal, relationship, and personal.

▲ In *The Purge*, the government designates one day a year when most forms of violence are allowed. The idea was that this would produce a catharsis, leading to peace the rest of the year. Research indicates that this would actually cause more violence rather than less.

[Universal Pictures/Photofest]

 Achieve
Video: Moral Disengagement

Reducing Aggression

It would be an overstatement to say that all types of aggression are bad for individuals and for society in general. Appropriate expressions of anger and aggression can help a person avoid being harmed, treated unjustly, or blocked from worthwhile goals (DaGloria, 1984; Felson & Tedeschi, 1993; Netzer et al., 2015). Also, in many cultures, people value others who are willing and able to be aggressive, from military and law enforcement personnel to professional athletes. Nevertheless, interpersonal aggression causes a great deal of harm and often has tragic consequences. How can we reduce, if not prevent, such harmful aggression?

When this question is put to psychologists and laypeople alike, a frequent answer is *catharsis*, or allowing people to "blow off steam" or otherwise vent their aggressive impulses. These ideas are generally incorrect. Catharsis—whether it is vicarious (like watching a violent film) or direct (punching a pillow)—has side effects that make it not only ineffective but also likely to exacerbate aggression. These side effects include making violence seem acceptable, reinforcing aggressive scripts and actions, and increasing arousal that can be misattributed as anger in response to provocation (Bandura, 1973; Geen, 2001; Zillmann, 1979). If vicarious catharsis worked, people would be less aggressive after watching hockey, football, wrestling matches, and violent films than before seeing them. But quite the opposite is true: Crowds are more aggressive after such events than before them (Geen, 2001).

So what *does* work? Because aggression has so many causes, there is no easy answer. Fortunately, though, there are some effective interventions that address society, relationships, and individuals.

Societal Interventions

1. **Reduce frustration by improving the quality of life.** Aggression can be curbed by reducing the prevalence and severity of conditions that trigger frustration and hostility. Although it is impossible to eliminate all frustrations in life, we can improve the economy and provide healthier, more pleasant living conditions, especially in low socioeconomic status communities that are often plagued by aggression. Police use of excessive force has long been a major source of frustration in African American, Hispanic, and Native American communities. This problem became a focal point for massive protests after the police killings of unarmed African Americans in the spring of 2020. In response, reforms have been enacted to try to create fairer and less violent policing toward members of these groups. Another approach to reducing frustration is to teach aggressive children better problem-solving, communication, and negotiating skills. If they learn these skills, they will experience less frustration in their lives and use more constructive strategies for dealing with day-to-day challenges (Goldstein, 1986).

2. **Better control access to weapons.** We know that the mere presence of firearms can prime aggressive thoughts and that interacting with guns can boost testosterone, further fueling aggressive behavior. We also know that firearms make aggression more lethal. And assault weapons and extended magazines make it much easier for a single individual to kill and wound many people in a short period of time, which allows mass shooters to do extensive harm before law enforcement officials arrive to intervene. Limiting access to these products could greatly reduce the harm individuals can inflict on others.

Another approach is to enact extreme risk laws, also known as red flag laws, as at least 18 U.S. states have done. These laws establish that if individuals show clear signs of crisis or violent intent in their daily lives or on social media, they can be blocked from purchasing firearms and other potential weapons (Everytown for Gun Safety, 2020). Enacting these laws and controlling the number and kinds of weapons that are available may not only prevent people from causing unnecessary death and pain but also make it less likely for people's thoughts to turn to aggression in the first place.

3. **More effectively punish aggression.** In most societies, efforts to curb aggression involve punishing aggressive offenders. This can be effective. In one study (Fitz, 1976), participants were less likely to aggress against someone if they knew that they would suffer severe consequences as a result. However, many forms of punishment also model aggression and can increase the recipients' frustration, thus having the opposite of the intended effect. For example, children who are physically punished at home are more aggressive outside the home later in life (e.g., Gershoff, 2002; Lefkowitz et al., 1978). Given these conflicting findings, researchers have investigated the specific conditions under which punishment is effective (Baron, 1977; Berkowitz, 1993). To be effective, punishment must be (1) severe (without modeling aggression); (2) delivered promptly, before the aggressors benefit from or change their behavior; (3) perceived as justified; and (4) administered consistently. The American legal system rarely meets the second and fourth criteria (Goldstein, 1986). Typically there is a lot of time between an arrest and sentencing, and laws and sentencing are often inconsistent within and between states. In addition, there is bias against minority group members in prosecution and sentencing (e.g., Kleider-Offutt et al., 2017). Because the legal system often fails to meet these criteria, the system's punishments have limited success deterring aggressive behavior.

These criteria also help explain why the death penalty has not been effective in deterring violent crime. In fact, as **FIGURE 12.12** shows, murder rates tend to be higher in states with the death penalty than in those without it. When the death penalty is introduced, the murder rate actually tends to increase (Goldstein, 1986). Capital punishment makes aggression salient and communicates the idea that killing is sometimes justified. Executions

▲ Gun shows like this one illustrate how popular and available firearms such as semiautomatic assault rifles are in the United States.

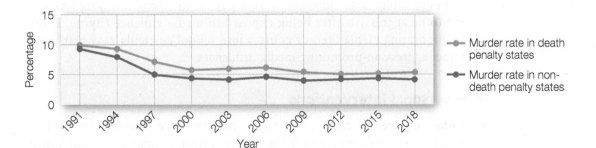

Figure 12.12

Murder Rates in States With and Without the Death Penalty

The death penalty is intended as both punishment and deterrent, but statistics (here, the total number of murders per 100,000 people in the two kinds of states) show that murder rates are higher in states with the death penalty than in those without it (Death Penalty Information Center, n.d.).

tend to happen many years after the murder that they are intended to punish. In addition, most murders are committed in a fit of rage, when people are unlikely to be thinking of consequences.

What forms of treatment would work to decrease violence in an individual? One promising alternative approach is *multisystematic therapy*, which addresses what drives individuals to aggress in specific contexts in which they are embedded, such as school and neighborhood (Borduin et al., 2009; Henggeler et al., 1998). Courses and other training programs that focus on rehabilitation, as opposed to deterrence or retribution, also hold promise. But American penal institutions spend very few of their resources on rehabilitation (Goldstein, 1986), a fact that probably contributes to the high recidivism rate. A U.S. Department of Justice study (Alper et al., 2018) found that 83% of prisoners released in 2005 were rearrested within nine years.

4. **Reduce or reframe media depictions of aggression.** With all the evidence indicating that exposure to violence in the media can prime and model violent thoughts and actions, we might reduce aggression by minimizing people's exposure to such media depictions. Of course, censorship carries its own costs, but there is no question that American society can do a better job of limiting exposure of young children to violence in the media. Another approach is to direct people to media that model prosocial behavior or depict the negative consequences of aggression. The media frequently portray people as benefiting from aggressive behavior. Viewing such portrayals increases aggression. In contrast, exposure to scenes showing punishment of aggressive behavior inhibits viewers from aggressing (Betsch & Dickenberger, 1993). Just as playing violent video games can increase aggressive cognitions and behavior, playing prosocial video games can decrease hostile attributions and aggressive cognitions (Greitemeyer & Osswald, 2009). The more children play prosocial video games, the more they also engage in prosocial behavior (Gentile et al., 2009; discussed more in chapter 13). Thus, there is potential for reducing aggression in exposing people, and especially children, to different types of media depictions.

Another useful approach is to educate people about how to interpret violent media depictions. Rosenkoetter and colleagues (2009) designed a seven-month media literacy program in which children were encouraged to distinguish between "pretend" aggression and aggression in the real world and to admire and imitate people who contribute peacefully to solving problems. Children who took part in this program were less willing to be aggressive after being exposed to media violence (Byrne, 2009). Incorporating media literacy courses into school curricula may help counteract aggression-promoting media influences.

Interpersonal Interventions

1. **Improve parental care.** Training parents in more effective methods of raising their children often leads to a reduction in aggressive and antisocial behavior in the children (Patterson et al., 1982). Goldstein and colleagues (1998) found that training juvenile offenders and their parents to communicate better with each other helped reduce violent activity among aggressive youth. Given that most children will eventually become parents, why aren't courses on appropriate parenting routinely included in school curricula?

2. **Strengthen social connections.** A greater sense of communal connection, more cooperation and less competition, and fewer experiences of social rejection would reduce aggression in society. Improving people's social skills is likely to lead to more positive social interactions and has been shown to be effective in reducing aggression in children (Pepler et al., 1995). Connecting with others, even if only briefly, helps to reduce aggression that stems from feeling rejected (e.g., Twenge et al., 2007).

3. **Enhance empathy.** Aggressive behaviors seem to reflect a low awareness of or concern for others' pain and suffering. *Empathy* is the ability to take another person's point of view and to experience vicariously the emotions that the person is feeling. Results of many studies conducted with children and adults show that as empathy increases, aggression decreases (Richardson et al., 1994). Programs that teach juvenile delinquents how to take other people's perspective also have been found to be beneficial (Goldstein, 1986). However, recent studies indicate that empathy and compassion for a victim of injustice could lead to moral outrage–fueled aggression toward the perceived perpetrator of that injustice (Pfatthiecher et al., 2019).

Individual Interventions

1. **Improve emotional self-awareness.** Berkowitz and Troccoli (1990) proposed that people can become aware of what makes them feel unpleasant or stressed and choose not to let that distress trigger aggressive behavior. In addition, self-awareness tends to bring internalized morals and standards to mind and increase their influence on behavior. Berkowitz and Troccoli designed a study to test this idea. Some of the participants were put through an uncomfortable physical activity, and others were not. Half the participants in each of these conditions were then distracted with an irrelevant task, whereas the remaining participants were asked to attend to their inner feelings. Immediately afterward, all participants rated another student's personality. As you can see from **FIGURE 12.13**, when participants were distracted, the more discomfort they felt, the more unfavorably they rated the target. In contrast, participants prompted to attend to their emotional states did not verbally aggress, and they even became *more* reluctant to say negative things about the target person (perhaps to correct for the possible influence of their negative mood).

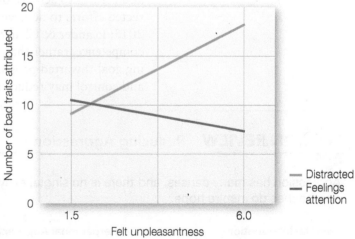

2. **Increase self-regulatory strength.** If we can improve people's self-regulatory abilities, they will be better able to control their aggressive impulses. This can be facilitated by minimizing obstacles to self-awareness and self-control, such as alcohol use, environmental stressors such as noise, and conditions that foster deindividuation (described in chapter 9).

   People can also be encouraged to practice controlling their behavior. In one study (Finkel et al., 2009), participants who took part in a two-week regimen designed to bolster self-regulatory strength (e.g., by brushing their teeth with the nondominant hand or by making sure that they did not begin

Figure 12.13

Self-Awareness of Feelings and Aggression

If people focus their awareness on their feelings, they are less likely to view others negatively. This is one promising avenue toward reducing aggression.

[Data from Berkowitz & Troccoli, 1990]

sentences with "I") reported a reduced likelihood of being physically aggressive toward their romantic partner.

3. **Teach how to minimize hostile attributions.** Hudley and Graham (1993) developed a 12-week program designed to prevent aggressive children from lashing out by reducing their tendency to attribute hostile intent to others. Through games, role-play exercises, and brainstorming sessions, they taught children about the basic concepts of intention in interpersonal interactions and helped them to decide when someone's actions (e.g., spilling milk on them in the lunchroom) are deliberate or accidental. Compared with boys who went through an equally intensive program that did not focus on attributions of intent, boys who received the attribution training were less likely to presume that their peers' actions (real and imagined) were hostile in intent, they were less likely to engage in verbally hostile behaviors, and they were rated as less aggressive by their teachers.

4. **Improve people's sense of self-worth and control.** When people have high, stable self-esteem, they respond to threats with lower levels of hostility and anger (e.g., Kernis et al., 1989). One source for such a foundation is a stable, secure attachment with a close other. Indeed, studies show that, among troubled and delinquent adolescents in residential treatment programs, those who formed secure attachment bonds with staff members exhibited less aggressive and antisocial behavior (Born et al., 1997). As Corey Pegues (2016, p. 272) noted from his experiences mentoring kids, "the single biggest deterrent to gang violence was giving children a sense of self-worth and self-esteem, breaking the cycle of anger and negativity that fuels violence in the first place." More broadly, a society that provides a wide range of attainable ways of developing and maintaining self-esteem should foster less aggressive people.

Closely related to self-esteem is the sense of having enough competence and control to achieve one's goals in life. Acts of aggression are often misdirected efforts to achieve a sense of competence and control (Landau et al., 2015; Leander & Chartrand, 2017). If the overarching psychological goal is competence, rather than aggression per se, then we should find that providing goal-thwarted people with alternative means of establishing competence and control may reduce the tendency to turn to aggression as a substitute.

SECTION REVIEW Reducing Aggression

Aggression has many causes, and there is no single, easy way to reduce its prevalence. However, some approaches do inspire hope.

Societal Interventions	Interpersonal Approaches	Individual Approaches
• Improve quality of life.	• Improve parental care.	• Improve self-awareness and self-regulatory control.
• Better control access to weapons.	• Strengthen social connections.	• Reduce hostile attribution bias.
• Punish aggression more effectively.	• Promote empathy.	• Promote stable bases of self-worth and competence.
• Better address media violence.		

CRITICAL LEARNING EXERCISES

1. Find a recent example of interpersonal violence in the news. What ideas from the chapter could help explain it? Can you think of any factors that played causal roles in the violence that are not covered in the chapter?

2. Social psychology has amassed a lot of evidence showing that guns and media violence contribute to aggression. However, in the United States, very little has been done to control either one of these factors. Why do you think that is, and how do you feel about it?

3. Can you think of an example of aggression from a romantic relationship you or a relative or friend has been in? How well can it be explained by the research on domestic violence that is covered in this chapter?

4. The chapter presents a variety of strategies for possibly reducing violence in society. Which of these do you think is most realistic, and how could it be implemented? Can you think of any other approaches not discussed in the chapter?

 Achieve

Don't stop now! Check out our videos and additional resources located at: www.macmillanlearning.com

TOPIC OVERVIEW

CHAPTER 13

Prosocial Behavior

In our exploration of prejudice and aggression, we have encountered some of the darker sides of human nature. But as social animals, human beings also are drawn to help each other. Examples abound of both extraordinary and ordinary acts of kindness carried out for the benefit of others. Consider the many acts of altruism people have engaged in during the global COVID-19 pandemic. Nurses, doctors, and other care workers have put their own health at risk to care for those fighting the infection. Some who have recovered have volunteered to donate plasma that might boost the immunity of others. Neighbors have reached out to elderly people in the communities, offering to bring them groceries. Musicians have collaborated in online concerts or performed from their balconies to provide a sense of hope and community. Citizens have followed public health guidelines to stay at home, wear masks, and severely limit their normal routines as part of a global strategy to suppress the spread of infection and protect the health of those most at risk. Large and small, these acts remind us that people sometimes go out of their way to help and care for others in need, even when it means making personal sacrifices or putting themselves in harm's way.

If people *always* helped others, we would not have much to cover in this chapter. Just as we can bring to mind uplifting stories of helping, we can also recollect instances when someone could have been saved from danger or a social problem that could have been alleviated if people had intervened. Consider an incident in which a 15-year-old girl was raped and beaten by several teenage boys in a dark alley outside their school's homecoming dance (Chen, 2009). More than 20 other students were said to have watched—some even recording the horrific event on their cell phones—yet no one called the police.

Which of these examples better captures human nature? Are we the devoted volunteers and brave at heart who elevate the needs of others above our own? Or are we the apathetic bystanders who look on and do nothing as harm is carried out? We are, of course, both, and one of the questions that social psychology examines is why this is the case. In this chapter, we will consider:

- The biological and sociocultural bases for helping others

- The question of whether true altruism exists

- Social and emotional reasons for helping others and how to promote them

- Reasons people sometimes fail to help

- Who is most likely to help

▶ During the COVID 19 pandemic in 2020, people around the world put their own self-interest aside to help others in need and minimize the spread of the virus.

[South_agency/E+/Getty Images]

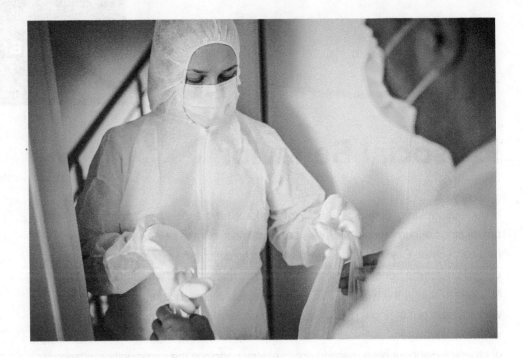

Learning Outcomes

- Explain the foundation of prosocial behavior from an evolutionary perspective.
- Cite evidence that points to a biological basis for prosocial behavior.
- Identify ways that prosocial behavior is learned.

Prosocial behavior Action by an individual that is intended to benefit another individual or set of individuals.

The Basic Motives for Helping

Before we get any further, let's define what we mean by prosocial behavior. **Prosocial behavior** is action by an individual that is intended to benefit another individual or set of individuals. By this definition, many of the actions of artists, entertainers, scientists, and political figures can be considered prosocial behavior. After all, many people have benefited from their artistic creations, scientific discoveries, and social changes. Although these forms of prosocial behavior are important, theory and research on prosocial behavior generally have not focused on people with extraordinary talent. Instead, most of this work studies the factors that influence whether ordinary people choose to help or not help each other from day to day. Sometimes the help people give is quite minor, such as stopping to help someone pick up a bag of groceries that has spilled. Other times, it can be much more dramatic, such as providing CPR to someone who has collapsed. Some instances of helping come at a personal cost or physical risk. Other times, the person giving help benefits as much as, if not more than, the person receiving help.

Psychologists often assume that people's actions are motivated at least in part by some degree of self-interest. Consequently, even though prosocial behavior is directed toward the benefit of someone else, theorists have often posited self-serving or *egoistic* motivations for helping. As Ralph Waldo Emerson claimed, "It is one of the most beautiful compensations of this life that no man can sincerely try to help another without helping himself." In terms of broad motivations that guide human behavior, helping others can make people feel good about themselves and their value in the larger scheme of things. Prosocial behavior also can serve more circumscribed goals, such as making the helper better liked or socially accepted in a group. We might help a teacher so we can get a letter of recommendation for graduate school; an attractive individual so we can get a date; or a high-status person so we can get a job, entry into a club, or some other favor in return.

However, being social animals, we also genuinely care about those with whom we form emotional attachments—our families, our relationship partners, our friends, our group members, our pets, and perhaps anyone in distress with whom we identify. The staunchest advocate of this position, the social psychologist Dan Batson (e.g., 1991), asserts that helping is often the result of a desire to help another person purely for the other person's benefit, regardless of whether there is any benefit to the self. He argues that when we feel *empathy* for another person, we help not to serve our own needs but rather to serve the needs of the other. This kind of helping is known as **altruism.**

Dramatic examples of altruism occur when people risk their lives to help unrelated others. During the Nazi occupation of Europe, a substantial number of non-Jewish individuals protected Jews whom the Nazis would have killed outright or sent to concentration camps. When asked in interviews why they put their own lives on the line to protect others, many of them complete strangers, these rescuers reported being motivated by either of two factors (Fogelman & Wiener, 1985):

Altruism The desire to help another purely for the other person's benefit, regardless of whether we derive any benefit.

- They wanted to live up to deeply held *moral values* passed down to them by their parents and learned through their religious upbringing.
- They were motivated by feelings of empathy, either because members of their own group also had been persecuted or because they had personal affection for the victims. For example, the German journalist Gitta Bauer described her experience protecting Ilse Mosle, the 17-year-old daughter of Jewish friends, by saying, "It took me nine months to deliver her to freedom, so I consider Ilse my baby" (Fogelman & Wiener, 1985, p. 63).

Human Nature and Prosocial Behavior

If you take an evolutionary perspective on human behavior, you might think that people who risk their lives to save others from the Nazis or who throw themselves into raging rivers to save a stranger are acting very strangely. After all, evolutionary theory assumes that new traits and behavioral tendencies are selected for when those attributes benefit the propagation of an organism's genes to the next generation. We might therefore expect people to care only about their own well-being and reproductive opportunities. But our inherited propensities are far more complicated than that and encourage prosocial behavior in a variety of ways.

Kin Selection: Hey, Nice Genes! A propensity for helping close relatives, or *kin*, may have been selected for over the course of hominid evolution through a process known as **kin selection** (Hamilton, 1964). The principle underlying kin selection is that because close relatives share many genes with an individual, when the individual helps close kin, those shared genes are more likely to be passed on to offspring. In this way, genes promoting the propensity for helping close kin become more prevalent in future generations. In support of this idea, people across a variety of cultural contexts report that they are more likely to help another person the closer their genetic relationship (Burnstein et al., 1994; Madsen et al., 2007). Regardless of whether they are risking their lives or merely lending a hand, people report being more helpful to parents and siblings than to cousins, aunts, and uncles. Also, they are more likely to help distant relatives than acquaintances or strangers.

Kin selection The idea that natural selection led to greater tendencies to help close kin than to help those with whom we have little genetic relationship.

The role of kin selection in human prosocial behavior, however, is difficult to isolate empirically. Cultures invariably teach people that they are obligated to help close relatives, so we don't know how much of the preference for helping close kin is innate and how much is culturally learned. In addition, many examples of human helping cannot be explained by kin selection. These include devoted parents who raise adopted children; people from developed countries who give to charities such as CARE and UNICEF; individuals who would more readily help a good friend than a disliked first cousin; and good Samaritans who, at great personal risk, help complete strangers and unrelated friends.

Sociability, Attachment, and Helping Evolutionary theory can help to explain altruism even if culture plays a role in shaping when and toward whom we act altruistically. Our evolutionary history likely selected for not just a tendency to help close kin but also a general proclivity to be helpful. This inherited propensity can lead to behaviors that sometimes prevent the transmission of an individual's genes but that, on average, across people and situations, may have adaptive value. As we noted in chapter 2, our hominid ancestors lived in small groups in which members were successful by caring about others: emotionally attaching to them, caring for and cooperating with them, fitting in with the group, trying to be liked and to live up to internalized morals. These bonds with others connect to the innate capacity humans have for emotions such as sympathy, empathy, compassion, and guilt. These emotions are the bases for the human propensity to engage in prosocial behavior. We help because we care.

Reciprocal Helping Evolutionary psychologists have suggested that the human propensity for cooperation offers another explanation of why helping is such a prominent aspect of human behavior. In fact, cooperation itself can be viewed as a form of prosocial behavior. Cooperating with others for a common goal means placing a certain amount of trust in someone else. If I help you today, you might be more likely to help me tomorrow, and that, my friends, could give me a genetic advantage over the grumpy lout who never does anything for anyone else. This pattern of *you scratch my back, I'll scratch yours* is referred to as the **norm of reciprocity**. Evolutionary theory suggests that patterns of reciprocity

Norm of reciprocity An explanation for why we give help: If I help you today, you might be more likely to help me tomorrow.

 SOCIAL PSYCH OUT IN THE WORLD

A Real Football Hero

During the 1980s, Joe Delaney was a star running back, jersey no. 37 for the NFL's Kansas City Chiefs. Many thought he was on his way to a Hall of Fame career. In 1983, he was the best young running back in the American Football Conference. He was also happily married, with three young daughters. However, his bright future was cut tragically short by his own heroic actions (Chiefs Kingdom, 2013; Reilly, 2003).

On a hot and sunny afternoon in 1983, Joe Delaney was relaxing at a park in Monroe, Louisiana. After hearing cries for help from a nearby pond, he bounded into action. Three young boys had waded into the pond to cool off in the hot Louisiana sun. The boys—two brothers, Harry and LeMarkits Holland, and their cousin Lancer Perkins—were all aged 10

or 11. None of them knew how to swim, but they had unexpectedly stepped into deep water and were struggling to stay above the surface. Joe did not stop to consider if someone else should be attempting this rescue. Although he knew that his own swimming skills were weak, Joe felt an immediate obligation to try to save these children. He managed to grab LeMarkits just as water began to enter the boy's lungs, saving his life. But his attempt to save the other two failed, and the boys and Joe drowned.

The park was crowded that day with people enjoying the summer afternoon, but only this man, celebrated for his speed and agility, rushed into action. In a documentary on the event, Deron Cherry, Delaney's teammate, described Joe's heroic actions that day, "You ask yourself, what would you do in that situation? And if you have to think about it, then you know you

▲ People are motivated to reciprocate the generosity shown by prior generations by paying that generosity forward to the future.

[Terry Vine/Blend Images/Getty Images]

⧉ Achie√e
Social Psych in Everyday Life: Samantha

can provide individuals or even groups with an adaptive advantage (Trivers, 1971). Reciprocity need not even be direct. People are motivated to reciprocate the generosity shown by prior generations by paying that generosity forward to the future (Bang et al., 2017). Indeed, this might be how a norm of reciprocity develops and is maintained. Reciprocity can even be more powerful than conformity in motivating cooperative behavior (Romano & Balliet, 2017).

Reciprocal helping can be found in numerous animal species, including (as we noted in chapter 7) vampire bats, impalas, capuchin monkeys, and chimps (Brosnan & de Waal, 2002). For example, if baboon A grooms baboon B,

are not going to do the right thing. But he never thought about it. The thing that was on his mind was, 'I need to save these kids'" (Chiefs Kingdom, 2013).

As you will learn in this chapter, being in a crowd of people can often immobilize individuals, preventing them from stepping up to help. But Joe Delaney's story offers a powerful exception to the rule. People do sometimes help others—even at extraordinary costs to themselves. Joe continued to help kids after his death. A foundation started in his honor, the 37 Forever Foundation, spent the next two decades offering free swimming lessons to children (Reilly, 2003).

▲ [DAN PEAK/Tribune News Service/KANSAS CITY/MO/USA/Newscom]

baboon B is more likely to later share food with baboon A. In humans, we automatically feel obligated to return favors even to people we don't know or don't like (Regan, 1971). That said, reciprocity has its limits and cannot explain all prosocial behavior. The impulse to reciprocate is strongest right away and can fade over time (Chuan et al., 2018). Humans are also generous to others when the likelihood that they will reciprocate is low (Delton et al., 2011) and even without a tit-for-tat agreement that they will receive help in the future (de Waal, 1996). Thus, the instinctive drive to help might be indicative of a broader evolved tendency to be prosocial.

Biological Bases of Helping   If helpfulness has a genetic basis, there should be some evidence of gene-based variability in this trait. Consistent with this idea, studies have found evidence of the heritability of prosocial tendencies (Knafo & Plomin, 2006). When pairs of seven-year-old twins were rated by parents for prosocial behavior, identical twins showed correlations greater than .60, whereas fraternal twins showed correlations lower than .40. Keep in mind that identical twins share 100% of their genes and that fraternal twins share only about 50%. But both types of twins are typically raised together in the same household by the same parents and go to the same school. So when behavioral geneticists observe higher correlations among identical (monozygotic) twins than among fraternal (dizygotic twins), they conclude that the trait has some genetic component. In this case, 62% in the variation among the children in prosociality was attributed to genetic factors. This is suggestive evidence, but it is not definitive because identical twins' similar levels of helpfulness could result from their being treated especially similarly by others because their personalities and physical attributes are so similar.

Other evidence suggestive of a biological basis for helpfulness can be found in the study of nonhuman social animals. Chimpanzees have been observed quickly and spontaneously engaging in a range of prosocial tasks (Rosati et al., 2018), such as helping out their human caretaker by getting something that she cannot reach (Warneken & Tomasello, 2006). Researchers have also found that they share food with other chimps and help other chimps who have helped them in the past or with whom they have formed friendships or alliances (Brosnan & de Waal, 2002). Such examples of helping are not confined to primates. Scientists monitoring a group of killer whales near Patagonia observed that when an elderly female had damaged her jaw and could not eat properly, her companions fed her and kept her alive (Mountain, 2012). Similarly, researchers found that rats who first shared a cage with another rat for a couple of weeks worked to free their cage mate when they found he was trapped behind a closed door (Bartal et al., 2011). Without any prior learning about how to open the door or any clear reward for doing so, the rats figured out how to free their buddy. If a pile of delicious chocolate chips was placed behind a second closed door, the rats were as likely to free their cage mate as free the chocolate chips. And when both doors had been opened, the two rats tended to share the chocolate. Who knew rats could make such good roommates! Of course, nonhuman animals are occasionally stingy, keeping food for themselves even when another is visibly begging for a snack (Vonk et al., 2008), but a good deal of evidence shows that species other than humans can and do engage in prosocial behavior.

If prosocial behavior is an inherent part of our nature, then we might see evidence of it at a very young age. In fact, babies

▼ As shown in laboratory research by Bartal and colleagues (2011), even rats will work to free a trapped cage mate without prior learning or obvious reward.
[Courtesy of Inbal Ben-Ami Bartal and University of Chicago]

have a pretty keen sense of who's naughty and who's nice. Infants as young as three months prefer others who are helpful rather than hurtful (Hamlin et al., 2007, 2010; Hamlin & Wynn, 2011). If we come into the world ready to evaluate people on the basis of their good or bad behavior, perhaps we come preequipped to carry out good behavior ourselves. In one study, toddlers less than two years old helped an experimenter pick up something she had dropped (Warneken & Tomasello, 2006). What's more, the toddlers did not help simply because they were interested in picking up stuff when it fell. They picked up a fallen item only if it seemed to have been dropped by accident and not when the experimenter intentionally dropped it. Young kids do not help just anyone but selectively help those who have been helpful in the past (Dunfield & Kuhlmeier, 2010). Taken together, this research points to an innate prosocial proclivity in our species.

Learning to Be Good

Humans are no doubt genetically predisposed toward helping, but we also are predisposed to learn helpful behaviors from others. Positive parenting practices, for example, predict greater prosocial behavior in children even after controlling for any shared genetic relationship (Knafo & Plomin, 2006). Culture and learning also shape when and for whom any genetic inclinations are cued (Becker, 1962; Hoffman, 1981). People's prosocial behavior is, therefore, jointly influenced by both genes and environment (Eisenberg & Mussen, 1989; Knafo et al., 2011).

A learning-theory account of prosocial development suggests that people learn to be helpful in a series of three stages:

- At a young age, children learn to be helpful to get things they want. Parents facilitate this mind-set with charts that award a star every time the child shares toys, says "Please" and "Thank you," or makes the bed.
- Later in development, people learn to help because social rewards come from the approval they receive from others. A child might learn that other kids are more likely to play with her when she has helped them in the past.
- And finally, in stage three, people help because they adhere to internalized values (Bar-Tal, 1976; Cialdini et al., 1981). That means they are listening to the voice of their moral conscience rather than pursuing material goodies or approval from others.

Taken together, we can conclude that people's propensity for prosocial behavior comes online early in development, but these learning stages shape how this propensity is expressed and reinforced (Dahl & Brownell, 2019). Like other forms of social learning, learning to be helpful comes from a variety of cultural sources. Sometimes, parents and teachers explicitly reinforce prosocial behavior. Parents might give children chores to do around the house to teach them ways they can help the family. In an effort to extend the prosocial orientation beyond close family members and friends, many elementary and secondary schools offer programs to encourage community service or fund-raising efforts for local and international charities. In 1993, President Bill Clinton signed into law the National Community Service Trust Act, a program that provides students the opportunity to receive academic credit, money toward college tuition, and/or job training for the time they spend volunteering with community agencies (Lee, 1993).

▲ When they are quite young, children show a desire to help others.

[PeopleImages/E+/Getty Images]

▲ Practicing helping can make you more prosocial. Immediately after people play the video game *Lemmings*, which requires them to keep the little lemmings from leaping to their deaths, they are more helpful to other people.

[ArcadeImages/Alamy]

Just as children learn specific behaviors and acts of charity from the people around them, so too do these people influence children's emotional responses to those in need. For example, parents who display more emotional warmth themselves tend to have children who show an increasing ability to empathize with others, independent of their level of empathy two years earlier (Zhou et al., 2002). Children also can learn to be more prosocial if they are encouraged to integrate helpfulness into their personal identities. In one study, second-graders who were labeled helpful when they shared were more likely to be helpful later than those who shared but weren't labeled helpful (Eisenberg et al., 1987).

People also learn prosocial tendencies from the media. Consider video games. In chapter 12 we noted some evidence that violent video games can encourage aggressive responses, but evidence also suggests that playing video games that reward prosocial behavior might increase that behavior (Greitemeyer, 2011a). When study participants first played *Lemmings*, a video game whose primary goal is to keep your little group of lemmings alive, they were later almost three times more likely to help the experimenter pick up spilled pencils than were those who had played *Tetris*. Of course, picking up pencils poses no great sacrifice. But what about a more dangerous situation? When the experimenters constructed a scenario in which the participants witnessed the female experimenter being harassed by her hostile ex-boyfriend, 56% of those who had just played the prosocial video game *City Crisis* intervened to help her, compared with only 22% who had played *Tetris* (Greitemeyer & Osswald, 2010). In these cases, the prosocial video games primed prosocial thoughts and behavioral scripts, which remained accessible in people's minds and influenced their behavior when they interacted with others later on. If only the sales of prosocial video games were higher than those of their more violent counterparts.

SECTION REVIEW The Basic Motives for Helping

Prosocial behavior is action by an individual that benefits another.

Genetic Influences

- People may be helpful because prosocial behavior might have been generally adaptive in the history of our species.
- Although the propensity for helping is especially strong among close kin, it is not restricted to them.
- Prosocial emotions contribute to helping.
- Norms of reciprocity contribute to prosocial behavior, even among strangers.
- Research with twins, toddlers, and nonhuman animals points to an inherited biological basis of prosocial behavior.

Learned Behavior

- Parents greatly influence prosocial behavior in children.
- Children learn prosocial behavior in stages: to get things (e.g., gold stars), for social rewards, and to satisfy internal moral values.
- Media can encourage prosocial behavior by making helping-related thoughts more accessible.

Does Altruism Exist?

In an episode of the popular 1990s television show *Friends,* the good-hearted Phoebe and her struggling actor friend Joey debate whether it is possible to engage in truly altruistic behavior (Jensen, 1998). Phoebe claims that she constantly acts for the benefit of others. But when Joey catches Phoebe admitting that it makes her feel good to put smiles on other people's faces, it highlights a seemingly selfish side to Phoebe's benevolence. If helping makes us feel good, we could argue that it benefits us as well as the recipient of the help. Is Joey right? Recall the distinction we made earlier between egoistic and altruistic motivations for helping. Is every act of helping inherently egoistic in some way? Or is true altruism possible? Fortunately, we don't have to rely on sitcoms to answer this question. Researchers have developed theories and carried out studies to try to differentiate selfish from selfless acts of helping.

Social Exchange Theory: Helping to Benefit the Self

Helping others can bring material benefits. Strong reciprocity norms all but guarantee that giving a little help to others might mean that you can count on them for help down the road. A **social exchange theory** approach to helping focuses on such egoistic motivations. It maintains that people help someone else when the benefits of helping and the costs of not helping (either to oneself or the other person) outweigh the potential costs of helping and the benefits of not helping (Thibaut & Kelley, 1959). It may sound like the kind of theory an accountant would dream up, but it is not difficult to imagine carrying out this kind of mental calculation in some situations.

If you saw a stranger collapsed in a subway car or another public place, and he seemed to need help, would you come to his aid? Sure, you might be able to help the person (a clear benefit to helping), but maybe the person is merely taking a nap on a long journey. He might see it as a cost (to his naptime) if you tried to help. If the person were in distress, you would feel good about yourself for having intervened (another benefit), but maybe the person has a contagious disease and could get you sick (a clear cost).

Researchers have actually used variants of this situation to study the mental trade-offs people make when deciding whether or not to help. If you're like the participants in these studies, your response might depend on aspects of the situation. When the confederate who was seemingly collapsed carried a cane, he was helped within one minute in nearly 90% of the trials. When he appeared to be drunk, he was helped in fewer than 20% of the trials (Piliavin et al., 1969). Piliavin and colleagues argued that the reason we help is to reduce the arousal we feel when we see someone in distress. The costs of not helping an invalid seem much higher than the costs of not helping someone who is drunk. But the fact that someone needs help also can be offset by our aversion to situations or people we find disgusting or disturbing. In another subway collapse study, people were slower to act, if they helped at all, if the person who had collapsed had blood trickling out of his mouth (Piliavin & Piliavin, 1972). Although the victim's need for help was quite clear, people were reluctant to step forward when they might get bloody. And when it's a question of helping someone who is in physical danger, we might worry about our own welfare if we intervene to break up an argument or prevent an attack. Perceived costs need not be so dramatic. A cost to time or money or our worries that it will make the person

- Explain the social exchange theory perspective on helping.
- Defend the idea that people can have truly altruistic motives.

▲ In an episode of the television show *Friends,* Phoebe is challenged by her friend Joey to find a way to help others that doesn't in some way benefit her.
[Everett Collection, Inc]

THINK ABOUT
[Uriel Sinai/Getty Images]

Social exchange theory A theory which maintains that people provide help to someone else when the benefits of helping and the costs of not helping outweigh the potential costs of helping and the benefits of not helping.

▲ According to the Dalai Lama, "If you want others to be happy, practice compassion. If you want to be happy, practice compassion."

[TORU YAMANAKA/AFP via Getty Images]

Empathy-altruism model The idea that the reason people help others depends on how much they empathize with them. When empathy is low, people help others when benefits outweigh costs; when empathy is high, people help others even at costs to themselves.

in need feel embarrassed or ashamed (Sandstrom et al., 2019) can also weigh against helping when someone is in need.

On the other side of the scale are the possible benefits of helping. Obviously the person in need stands to benefit from what you actually do. But there are other, less tangible benefits to helping. When the Dalai Lama received the Nobel Peace Prize in 1989, he included these words of wisdom in his acceptance speech: "If you want others to be happy, practice compassion. If you want to be happy, practice compassion." Research backs up these words. A meta-analysis of studies in which people were instructed to carry out acts of kindness reveals small but significant boosts to well-being for helping (Curry et al., 2018). People who generally feel compassion for others also feel better about themselves (Crocker et al., 2010). When people help others for intrinsic reasons—that is, reasons that align with their core values (see the discussion of self-determination theory in chapter 6)—both they and the recipients of their help feel a boost to their well-being (Weinstein & Ryan, 2010). People report feeling somewhat happier after spending money on others than after spending the same amount on themselves (Aknin et al., 2020; Dunn et al., 2008), an effect that's been replicated even with people who exhibit antisocial tendencies (Hanniball et al., 2019). These effects are larger when we help someone we feel close to (Aknin et al., 2011). These are exactly the kinds of benefits that Phoebe derives from helping other people, but the question remains: Does that make her selfless acts actually selfish?

Empathy: Helping to Benefit Others

According to Daniel Batson's **empathy-altruism model** (Batson et al., 1981), people might very well provide help to others to get certain psychological payoffs. But this rational approach to helping applies only when one feels no real connection to another person. When your next-door neighbor is stressed out over moving, you might pitch in and pack a few boxes because you have the afternoon free and you know you would feel guilty if you didn't. But you might not skip your favorite class or switch a shift at work to load her things onto a moving van—unless, that is, you feel a true sense of empathy for her situation. When people empathize with someone in need, they take the other's perspective and may even vicariously experience their pain or negative emotions. If your neighbor is moving out because of a difficult breakup similar to one you've experienced yourself, you can easily imagine what she is going through and even feel her sadness. If this is the case, you are more likely to be motivated to reduce her sense of suffering. As Batson would say, the road to true altruism is paved with empathy. Empathy allows people to truly understand someone else's distress and motivates a desire to help, regardless of their own selfish interests. Is this true?

Research shows that empathy can be an emotionally powerful experience. When people vicariously feel another person's emotion, their brains show activation in the same areas that are activated when they themselves feel the same emotion (Brethel-Haurwitz et al., 2018; de Vignemont & Singer, 2006; Preston & de Waal, 2002). Studies also show strong correlations between empathy and helping. For example, people are particularly likely to help others whom they feel similar to and like, especially those who seem to see the world the same way (Huneke & Pinel, 2016). These feelings of similarity make it easier to empathize with others (Batson et al., 2007; Coke et al., 1978). Also, recall that exposure to prosocial media, such as helping-oriented video games, can promote prosocial behavior. Follow-up research points to empathy as the key factor explaining this effect (Prot et al., 2014). The more adolescents and young adults engaged with prosocial movies, TV shows, and video games, the more empathy they felt for others and, as a result, the more likely they were to help others. Indeed, this finding held true for men and women of all ages and across seven different countries. And it's not just empathy for people's suffering that predicts prosocial behavior. Being able to share in other people's joys and successes is also linked to a stronger desire to help (Morelli et al., 2015).

Thus, empathy is a powerful spur to prosocial behavior. But remember that the empathy-altruism model makes a stronger claim: Empathy will encourage helping even when the costs to the helper are high. Imagine that you are a participant in an early study by Batson and colleagues (1981). You arrive at a laboratory along with another participant, named Elaine. After completing an initial preference survey, you learn that the two of you either do or do not share the same tastes in magazines and other preferences. Elaine is randomly assigned to complete a performance task under stressful circumstances; you are assigned to observe. But your observation role will either last the entire study or only the first set of trials. It sounds pretty straightforward until you learn that Elaine will be exposed to a series of mild but painful electric shocks. After her first round of shocks, Elaine is obviously anxious and explains that she is unusually fearful of electricity. The experimenter isn't sure what to do but, after giving it some thought, turns to you and suggests that perhaps you could switch places with Elaine. Would you volunteer? Would it matter whether you feel similar to or dissimilar to Elaine? Would it matter if you were not going to have to watch her take any more shocks or if the study procedure called for you to observe a second round of trials?

THINK ABOUT
[PeopleImages/E+/Getty Images]

Look at the two bars on the left of **FIGURE 13.1**. When people didn't feel especially similar to Elaine and so were not likely to feel empathy for her, 64% volunteered to trade places with her if they would otherwise have to watch her endure another set of shocks. However, if they didn't have to watch her take any more shocks, it was easy for them simply to leave the study, and in fact only 18% stayed to help. In the absence of empathy, these participants relied on a cost–benefit analysis to decide whether to help, and they determined that by not helping and simply removing themselves from the situation, they wouldn't suffer costs. But now look at the two bars on the right. When participants were made to feel similar to Elaine, a situation we know can increase empathy, 80 to 90% of participants stayed and took her place, regardless of whether they had an easy means of escape. This is one of many experiments in which Batson and colleagues have demonstrated that feelings of empathy lead to helping even when the cost of not helping is low—that is, even when it would be easy simply to ignore the person in need (Batson, 2011).

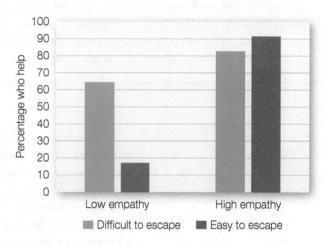

Figure 13.1

People Help When Either Empathy or the Cost of Not Helping Is High

This study by Batson and colleagues shows us that empathy is a key catalyst for helping. When people were low in empathy (on the left), they helped only if they would suffer by not helping. However, people high in empathy (on the right) helped regardless of the costs of not helping.

[Data from Batson et al., 1981]

Feeling empathy for someone in need is an important precursor to providing help, and as we just saw, it leads people to step up even at some cost to themselves. In fact, the obligatory impact of empathy is so strong that if people perceive the costs as being too high, they will sometimes choose to avoid experiencing empathy in the first place. For example, in one study, participants avoided exposing themselves to a heart-tugging story about a homeless man, preferring a more objective description of his plight, when they knew they would later have to decide to help the person or not (Shaw et al., 1994). Empathy can be such a powerful emotion that people sometimes actively avoid situations that would lead them to empathize with others.

SOCIAL PSYCH AT THE MOVIES

Prosocial Behavior in *The Hunger Games*

Imagine this: You and 23 other people are competing in the biggest reality TV show ever created. The stakes are life and death, and only the strongest survive. Worse yet, you are forced to play, and there can be only one winner. What would you do?

This is the premise of the film *The Hunger Games* (Ross, 2012), based on the popular novel, the first of a trilogy by Suzanne Collins (2008). The time is the distant future. The Capitol government rules over the nation of Panem. To punish lower-class citizens for a past uprising, the Capitol forces each of its 12 districts to offer up a teenage boy and girl, chosen by lottery, to compete in the annual Hunger Games, a nationally televised event in which these young Tributes must fight one another to the death, until a sole survivor remains. In these cutthroat circumstances, we might expect the characters to have little capacity for prosocial behavior. Yet acts of kindness and care do occur. The concepts outlined in this chapter help explain why.

The story's first remarkable prosocial act occurs when the protagonist, Katniss Everdeen (played by Jennifer Lawrence), steps forward to take the place of her beloved 12-year-old sister, Prim (played by Willow Shields), who was initially selected to be District 12's female Tribute. Why would Katniss volunteer

to be thrust into a situation in which she is almost certain to die? The idea of kin selection provides one answer: We are innately predisposed to help those who share many of our genes.

We also witness characters who are not genetically closely related helping one another. In one scene, Katniss has been chased up a tree by an alliance of vicious, highly trained Tributes from other districts. Her goose appears to be cooked until 12-year-old Rue (played by Amandla Stenberg), a Tribute who is hiding in a nearby tree, gives her a tip: Break a branch to drop a nest of poisonous wasps on the assailants. Rue also

▲ [Lionsgate/Photofest]

So does true altruism really exist? Batson has been a champion of altruism, but critics have argued that empathy is not always about what another person feels. They grant that when people empathize with someone in need, they feel that person's pain. But they point out that the pain becomes *their* pain, such that the motivation to help really traces back to reducing one's own pain—that is, egoistic motivation (Cialdini et al., 1987). For example, people who donate a kidney to a stranger (compared to a sample of non-donors) show a stronger neural signal of empathetic pain—that is, they are truly more likely to feel the pain of someone else (Brethel-Haurwitz et al., 2018)—so perhaps they are motivated by a selfish instinct to reduce this experience of pain. However, donating a kidney seems like such an extreme way to reduce empathetically experienced pain that one would be hard pressed to reframe such behavior as selfishly motivated. Researchers considered this question and ultimately did not find much support for this egoistic alternative (Carlson & Miller, 1987; Miller & Carlson, 1990). Although we sometimes might support Joey's position—helping others just to make ourselves feel better when we don't empathize with others—studies like these suggest that we can also be like Phoebe and show a genuine altruistic concern with the welfare of others.

cares for Katniss after she is subsequently stung by one of the wasps. Why does Rue choose to help another competitor, knowing that it could mean her disadvantage, or death, later in the Games? Kin selection probably is not the answer: Katniss and Rue have different ethnic backgrounds, and their homelands are far apart, making it unlikely that they are close genetic relatives. More likely, Rue anticipates that Katniss will reciprocate by providing help in the future. In this case, reciprocal helping may have been stronger than the situational pressure to kill everyone in sight. And it pays off: Later, Katniss shares food with Rue and does her best to protect her. When Rue is fatally wounded, Katniss shows tremendous empathy for her, easing her dying and paying respect to her after her death in numerous ways and at considerable risk to herself.

Another scene illustrates the power of empathy to spur altruism. Prior to entering the arena, Katniss is mentored by Haymitch Abernathy (Woody Harrelson). Later, while watching the Hunger Games on TV, Haymitch sees Katniss in agonizing pain after she is injured in battle. This prompts him to petition a sponsor from Panem's elite class to have a healing balm delivered to Katniss. Why does he take the time and energy to do this? He does not personally benefit, and Katniss had done nothing special to deserve his favor. Empathy seems to be the answer. Because Haymitch is a former victor in the Hunger Games, he can easily put himself in Katniss's shoes and feel her pain and fear. When he sees her wince in pain, he winces too. He may help simply to stop feeling bad, but he could just as easily distract himself from Katniss's plight to do so. So his actions more likely result from empathy, a genuine concern for another's well-being.

Perhaps the most profound displays of prosocial action occur between Katniss and Peeta Mellark (Josh Hutcherson), the male Tribute from District 12. Throughout the Hunger Games, Katniss and Peeta put their own lives in great danger to help and protect one another. One basis for this may be their shared social identity of being from the same District. But beyond that, Peeta is clearly in love with Katniss. Katniss's feelings for Peeta are more ambivalent, but their affection and consequent empathy is increasingly reciprocated over the course of the Games. As the research on rescuers of Jews during the Nazi era found, affection is a common basis for empathy and helping, and this may be especially true when feelings of romantic love are involved. In addition, such feelings may signal the possibility of reproduction. If so, we may be prepared to offer help to those with whom we fall in love.

The ultimate problem for Katniss and Peeta is that there can be only one survivor of the Games. In case you are one of the few who haven't seen this film, we won't reveal how that dilemma is resolved.

SECTION REVIEW   Does Altruism Exist?

Researchers have studied whether genuine altruism exists or whether individuals engage in prosocial behavior for their own benefit.

The Social Exchange Theory

People do a quick cost–benefit analysis to determine whether to help someone.

The Empathy-Altruism Model

People can feel empathy, and this empathy leads to genuinely altruistic acts.

The Social and Emotional Triggers of Helping

Learning Outcomes

Our discussion of evolution and social learning, or the nature and nurture of altruism, examines the *why* of helping—that is, the motivations that underlie prosocial behavior. Let's take a closer look at *when* and *whom* we help. By definition, helping is a social process, one that is influenced by how we think and feel about our relationships to other people. In this section, we'll consider the social and emotional processes that trigger our prosocial tendencies.

- Explain the relationship between similarity and willingness to help.
- Describe factors that may reduce the feeling of empathy.

THINK ABOUT

[Viacheslav Nikolaenko/Shutterstock]

Similarity and Prejudice

Stop and think about the last few times you helped someone else. How would you describe the person you helped? We've already mentioned that most of the time, people help those who are close or similar to them. After all, it is easier for us to imagine ourselves in the shoes of people like us, to take their perspective, and feel a sense of empathy for their situation (Krebs, 1975). Let's take a closer look at this important influence on helping. In one study conducted in the 1970s, research assistants dressed either like hippies (think bell bottoms, sandals, flowered shirts, and long, flowing hair) or more conservatively (pressed slacks, polished shoes, short hair) (Emswiller et al., 1971). They positioned themselves in the campus student union, approached passing students, and asked to borrow a dime (which, at the time, was the amount it would cost to make a call in a phone booth). Some of the students they asked were themselves dressed like hippies; others were dressed more conservatively. What did the researchers find? People were more likely to help if the other person dressed the way they did. When it comes to helping, birds of a feather most definitely do flock together.

The notion that people are more likely to help similar others has a pleasant ring to it, but the dark underbelly of this effect is people's tendency to walk past those who are dissimilar or against whom they are prejudiced. Many studies of helping have revealed that people are less likely to help members of socially devalued groups (Saucier et al., 2005). In one set of experiments, 92% of White college students came to the aid of another White student who had fallen and seemed to be injured in the next room, compared with only 70% when the victim was Black (Kunstman & Plant, 2008). And those who did offer help to the Black victim were about a minute slower to respond. When Black participants were faced with the same situation, they were equally likely to help the victim, regardless of his or her race. In follow-up studies, Whites reported that when the victim was Black, the situation seemed less severe, and they felt less responsible for intervening. Indeed, according to the meta-analysis by Saucier and colleagues (2005), Whites are especially unlikely to help a Black individual when they can claim nonracial justifications for their inaction, evidence of what has been called *aversive racism*, a topic you might remember learning about in chapter 10.

Race isn't the only dimension on which prejudice plays a role in the failure to help. Even families aren't immune. Parents are less likely to pay tuition for their overweight children than for their normal-weight children (Crandall, 1991), an effect that is typical of a general bias against those who are overweight (Crandall, 1994; Major et al., 2018). Even when people do not actively harm members of socially stigmatized groups, the tendency to withhold help and assistance can be a subtle but pervasive form of discrimination. This type of discrimination is especially likely when people have a convenient excuse for their inaction. For example, as we reviewed in chapter 10 as well, a White participant is less likely to help a Black victim if it is plausible that someone else might intervene (Gaertner & Dovidio, 1977). These biases against people based on race and weight can even affect the quality of health care people receive, contributing to poorer health outcomes for those who are stigmatized (Major et al., 2018).

Although our prejudices can sometimes make it more challenging to feel similar to others, we are able to overcome these biases if we are motivated to do so. Increasingly, members of more advantaged groups act alone or with others to be allies to those who are disadvantaged or discriminated against (Louis et al., 2019). By working for the benefit of those who are stigmatized, and even in solidarity with them, people's prosocial tendencies can help to break down social barriers and increase inclusion.

The Empathy Gap

We've already described how people are more likely to help those they feel similar to because they find it easier to empathize with their plight. One factor that works against developing empathy is that people tend to underestimate other people's experience of physical pain (Loewenstein, 2005) as well as the pain of social rejection (Nordgren, Banas, & MacDonald, 2011). In fact, some of the racial biases in who people help might stem from a disturbing tendency among both Whites and Blacks to perceive Black faces as experiencing less pain and to assume that Black people have a higher pain threshold (Mende-Siedlecki et al., 2019; Trawalter & Hoffman, 2015). Because of the **empathy gap**, people often fail to give help when help is needed. Asking people to experience pain or rejection actually can help close this gap. In one study, middle school teachers were more favorable to antibullying programs at their school after they were first asked to imagine in vivid detail the pain of being rejected (Nordgren et al., 2011).

Empathy gap The underestimation of other people's experience of physical pain as well as the pain of social rejection.

Another way to close the empathy gap is to take the perspective of the person in need—that is, to imagine what that person is experiencing from his or her point of view. For example, after students listened to and took the perspective of a drug addict recounting his struggles with addiction, they were more likely to support funding a campus agency that would help fight addiction. Those who merely listened objectively to the same man's experience were less willing to fund this new group (Batson et al., 2002). When people feel empathy for someone who is disadvantaged in society, they are also more likely to support policies that would help his or her group. Although those who have suffered the same misfortune are often in the best position to take a person's perspective, there is one caveat to note: People who have endured some prior hardship are less sympathetic to others who seem to be failing to cope with the same ordeal (Ruttan et al., 2015).

An interesting by-product of empathy is that it makes people more likely to help when they focus on the suffering of a single individual than when they consider a tragedy that befalls a large group. In the aftermath of the tsunami that leveled many coastal communities in Japan in 2011, humanitarian groups rallied to raise money to meet the basic needs of the survivors and to repair the massive damage that had been done. When such a disaster happens, the enormous scale of suffering is almost beyond comprehension. People can find it so emotionally overwhelming to contemplate that they actually downregulate their reaction to avoid distress (Cameron & Payne, 2011). In an ironic consequence, they are less likely to help in situations where help is most sorely needed. This is why many fund-raising organization such as UNICEF, Save the Children, and the Animal Legal Defense Fund often feature the suffering of a representative child or animal to elicit most effectively the kinds of empathy that trigger helping.

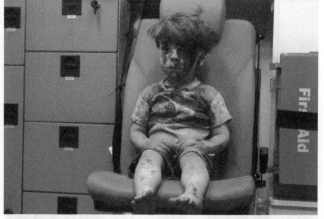

▲ Over the course of 2016, a bloody civil war in Syria displaced and killed tens of thousands of people. It was this tragic photo of a young boy rescued from a bombed building in Aleppo that aroused the strongest sense of compassion.

[Mahmud Rslan/Anadolu Agency/Getty Images]

The Role of Causal Attributions

One factor that often contributes to people's decision to help is whether or not they believe the person in need deserves her or his misfortune. This is where attribution theory enters the scene. You'll recall from chapter 4 that people—especially those in individualistic cultures—have a tendency to make dispositional attributions. They infer that another person's condition is the result of his or her own personality or freely chosen actions, not the result of the situation. In addition, you may recall that we have a desire to believe in a just world where people generally get what they deserve. Because of these tendencies, people are quick to assume that others deserve their suffering. Even children as young as three years assume that if a random bad thing happens to a person, that person must not be very nice (Olson et al., 2008). This means that if you are hoping to get some help when you find yourself in a bind, you might be fighting an uphill battle.

We are less likely to help those we believe are responsible for their current need. If we think their present position is something they could have controlled, we are more likely to turn our backs on them. If a classmate asks to borrow your notes from a class he missed, you are less likely to help him out if the reason for his absence was completely within his control (Weiner, 1980). On the other hand, when something uncontrollable happens, our response is to feel sympathy rather than disgust or anger, and this emotional response activates our desire to help out (Reisenzein, 1986). Thinking back to the studies where a confederate collapsed in a crowded subway car, we might wonder whether attributions played a role in people's willingness to help someone who seemed disabled or their apathy about the person who seemed drunk.

The attributions people make also affect their decision to help groups of people. When a group is socially stigmatized due to factors out of its control, people feel sympathy and offer their support for policies that would benefit its members (Weiner et al., 1988). For example, we might expect people to support charities more that help those with cancer or heart disease than those suffering from obesity or drug abuse, which tend to be viewed as more within a person's control. Indeed, some groups in society that might be most in need of help, such as homeless people and drug addicts, actually elicit disgust rather sympathy. When observing these groups, people show reduced activation in areas of the brain, such as the medial prefrontal cortex, where perceptions and impressions of human beings are formed (Bernard et al., 2018; Harris & Fiske, 2006). That is, their brains react as though they were observing objects rather than people.

Other Prosocial Feelings

We have focused on the role of empathy in helping, but other feelings also play roles in motivating a tendency to help. Among these are guilt, communal feelings, gratitude, and feeling socially secure.

Guilt Sometimes people offer help because they feel personally responsible for another person's plight. When we have treated another person or group badly, feelings of guilt elicit a need to repair that damaged social relationship (Baumeister et al., 1994; Rank, 1932/1989). Guilt is a bit like a Bat-Signal beamed into the sky, but instead of calling for the Caped Crusader, it calls the person into action to right some wrong. Many studies have demonstrated that inducing people to feel guilty increases their tendency to help others (Cunningham et al., 1980). In one staged experiment, when shoppers at a mall were made to believe that they had broken a confederate's camera (rather than being told that the camera was malfunctioning), they later were more than three times as likely to help a passerby whose

▲ People are less likely to offer help to a homeless person if they attribute the person's need to his or her own lack of effort.

[DebbiSmirnoff/Getty Images]

bag full of candy was spilling on the ground (Regan et al., 1972). In such situations, helping someone (even if it is not the person who was harmed) can help people alleviate guilt.

Even when people do not feel personally responsible for harm done to another person or group, they can nevertheless feel *collective guilt* for the role their group might have played in past or present harms (Ferguson & Branscombe, 2014). For example, when people identify with a group that is socially advantaged over others, they can feel collective guilt about a less fortunate outgroup, especially if they see that the outgroup's disadvantaged position in society is illegitimate (Miron et al., 2006). Collective guilt motivates a desire to make reparations to victims of past injustice or otherwise support policies that level the playing field (J. W. Regan, 1971). This relationship has been found in many circumstances: among U.S. and British students reflecting on the harm to the Iraqi people during their countries' occupation of Iraq (Iyer et al., 2007); Chileans reflecting on Chile's disadvantaged indigenous people (Brown et al., 2008); South Africans reflecting on their country's history of apartheid (Klandermans et al., 2008); men reflecting on gender inequality (Gunn & Wilson, 2011); and White Americans reflecting on racial disadvantage in the United States (Iyer et al., 2003).

Although research shows that guilt is effective at motivating helping, this effect may be short-lived. When people help out of guilt—over either personal or collective actions—they can be focused on trying to make themselves feel better (Iyer et al., 2003). The problem with this kind of helping is that it sometimes leads only to token forms of help that actually reduce the likelihood of providing more significant help at a later time (Dutton & Lennox, 1974). This work leads back to the conclusion that the best forms of helping are motivated by true empathy and compassion rather than guilt.

A Communal Feeling   All this talk of guilt and empathy reminds us that one of the strongest motivators of our behavior is to form, strengthen, and maintain close relationships with others (Baumeister & Leary, 1995; Bowlby, 1973). Guilt lets us know when we might be falling down on that job and prompts us to restore a close relationship, but compassion and empathy motivate lasting change. In romantic relationships, being willing to make sacrifices for your partner is a strong predictor of the health of your relationship (van Lange, Rusbult, et al., 1997).

In close relationships, people are more likely to adopt a **communal orientation** where they don't distinguish between what is theirs and what is someone else's. When a "you and I" becomes a "we," the person attends to his or her partner's needs regardless of whether that partner ever will be able to reciprocate (Clark et al., 1986). People become more sensitive to the partner's sadness and more likely to help when the partner is feeling down (Clark et al., 1987). Family relationships—especially the relationship between a parent and child—are the prototypical communal relationship. Think of all the ways in which your parents have helped you over the years. (Now might be a good time to send a thank-you note!) How have you returned the favor?

Even our relationships with friends and acquaintances can take on these communal characteristics when we treat a friend to lunch without keeping track of whether she pays us back. In fact, the happiness we feel when we get something ourselves fades more quickly than the happiness we feel when we give to others (O'Brien & Kassirer, 2019). In our communal relationships, helping someone else feels a lot like helping ourselves. Maybe this is why we feel the largest boost in mood when we help someone we feel communally connected to and the biggest drop in mood when we turn our back on that person (Williamson & Clark, 1989, 1992).

Communal orientation A frame of mind in which people don't distinguish between what's theirs and what is someone else's.

THINK ABOUT

[Wong Sze Yuen/Shutterstock]

The Recipient's Gratitude It is not surprising that when the people we help express their gratitude, we are more likely to help again—and we are not just more likely to help the person who thanked us but anyone else in need (Grant & Gino, 2010; Ma et al., 2017). This effect of gratitude on prosociality doesn't happen only because being thanked makes us feel good or cues a norm of reciprocity (Bartlett & DeSteno, 2006). Rather, people who express their gratitude to us make us feel more communal and enhance our feelings of social value. When we feel like a valued part of a community, we are more likely to keep helping that community. Before you draw the conclusion that gratitude is only about appreciating others, keep in mind that gratitude also has benefits for us. People who count their blessings feel happier, become more optimistic, exercise more, and sleep better (Emmons & McCullough, 2003). And people who score higher in gratitude are rated by their friends as engaging in more helpful behavior (McCullough et al., 2002).

Feeling Socially Secure Evidence suggests that a focus on how others help you is beneficial because it emphasizes that you are a part of a social *ecosystem*, which is a lot better for mental health than an emphasis on your own self-interested *egosystem* (Crocker, 2011). In fact, people who suffer from feelings of insecurity in their social relationships—especially those who avoid becoming too close to others—find it more difficult to feel compassion for someone in distress and are less likely to come to that person's aid. People who are either dispositionally more secure in their relationships or who are primed with a sense of relationship security feel more compassionate and behave more prosocially toward both family members and distant acquaintances (Mikulincer et al., 2005; van Lange, De Bruin et al., 1997).

SECTION REVIEW The Social and Emotional Triggers of Helping

Helping is a social process that is influenced by how we think and feel about our relationships with other people.

Similarity and Prejudice	The Empathy Gap	Causal Attributions	Other Prosocial Feelings
• People are most likely to help those who are similar to them. • This can lead to prejudicial behavior when people ignore the plight of those who are different.	• People tend to underestimate others' pain. • This can result in an empathy gap and reduced likelihood of offering help.	• Because of attributional processes and a desire to see the world as just, people may convince themselves a person bears responsibility for his or her own troubles. • This feeling can reduce empathy and thus helping.	• People are motivated to help by feelings of guilt, communal connections, and others' gratitude. • A clear sense of one's own relational security can also facilitate helping.

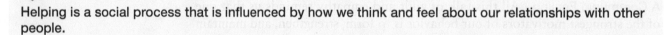

Learning Outcome

- Identify the situational factors that increase prosocial behavior.

Priming Prosocial Feelings and Behavior

Evolutionary perspectives on helping provide insight into how prosocial tendencies and associated emotions may have become part of human nature. Social learning perspectives provide insight into how helpfulness is learned and transmitted within a given culture or social environment. We might think of evolutionary processes as giving us the basic machinery to be helpful and of social learning as providing us with culturally specific scripts for how to be helpful. But we still need situational accounts to provide insight into when we enact these scripts and when we do not. The story of when we help is based partly on our relationships with others and partly on the emotions triggered in social situations. For example, when we see another person perform a virtuous act, it can inspire us to be more prosocial ourselves (Van de Vyver & Abrams, 2015). But as we've seen in several places throughout this book, even very subtle situational cues can activate behavioral scripts outside our conscious awareness. The same is true of prosocial behaviors. For example, eating from a shared plate seems to automatically cue cooperation among people (Woolley & Fishbach, 2019). Let's review a few of the other subtle ways in which people can be primed with prosocial scripts.

▲ Prosociality can sometimes be primed automatically. Eating from a shared plate with others can put people in a cooperative mindset.
[Boone Rodriguez/Corbis/VCG/Getty Images]

Positive Affect

One of the earliest lines of studies examining what primes people to be prosocial looked at the effect of positive mood. If your intuition tells you that you'll be more helpful in a positive mood, research by Alice Isen suggests that you are right. Whether participants' positive mood arose from succeeding in a difficult task, receiving cookies, or unexpectedly finding money, they were more likely to help afterward. They gave more money to charities, offered more assistance to others who had spilled their belongings, and were more likely to buy a stamp and mail a letter that had been left behind (Isen, 1970; Isen & Levin, 1972; Levin & Isen, 1975). Like most other priming effects, these can be transient, dissipating once people's mood returns to baseline (Isen et al., 1976).

What is it about being in a good mood that makes people more prosocial? Several processes might be in play (Carlson et al., 1988). On the one hand, good moods are inherently rewarding, making people loath to do anything that might knock them out of that mood. Consequently, when people are in a good mood, they may help to avoid the guilt that would arise if they turned their backs on someone in need. In addition to this rather selfish influence, happy moods make people see the best in other people. With this more positive frame of reference on humanity comes a more prosocial orientation and a tendency to see the inherent good that comes from lending a helping hand (Carlson et al., 1988).

Not only do positive moods encourage helping but so too can more intense feelings of awe. Think about the last time you happened to catch an especially mesmerizing sunset that seemed to airbrush the sky with a kaleidoscope of color or a time when you stood in a towering grove of trees in a tranquil forest. How and why might this sense of wonder and amazement affect your propensity to aid others? Feelings of awe inspire us to think beyond ourselves and see ourselves as small players in a much grander, more expansive drama. As a result, when we experience awe, we are more likely to act prosocially. In support of this idea, when study participants recollected experiences of awe, saw video clips intended to elicit awe, or stood among the towering eucalyptus trees in northern California, they showed more prosocial tendencies and behavior (Piff et al., 2015).

▲ Does this make you feel small? When Piff and colleagues (2015) had research participants stand in this grove of eucalyptus trees in northern California, they found that it induced feelings of awe, made participants feel part of something bigger than themselves, and elicited more prosocial behavior.
[David Ponton/AGE Fotostock]

Priming Prosocial Roles

Social roles and relationships come with certain norms that tell us how to behave. When you take the role of friend, that role carries the norm that you will help more than when you take the role of stranger or coworker. If people commit themselves to a helping profession such as teaching, nursing, or customer service, taking on that role should also prepare them to be helpful. These prosocial roles and relationships can be primed in surprising and subtle ways. In one study, people at an airport were asked to do a quick survey in which they recalled and answered a few questions about either a close friend or a coworker. Afterward, they were merely asked to rate their interest in helping the experimenter by completing a second, longer survey. Only 19% agreed when they were first primed to think of a coworker, but 53% agreed when first primed with a friend (Fitzsimons & Bargh, 2003). You might say that thinking about friendship puts us in a friendly state of mind and readies us to act in a friendly, helpful way. We might even be more likely to incorporate these subtle cues into our behavior when we otherwise feel deindividuated or disinhibited (Hirsh et al., 2011). Just as people can become more aggressive when they feel deindividuated but are primed with an aggressive role, they can become more prosocial when they feel deindividuated and are primed with a caregiving role, such as being a nurse (Johnson & Downing, 1979). These learning outcomes, taken from the syllabus of an introductory nursing course, show how central the concept of caring for others is to the profession of nursing (Roach, 2002):

1. Examine the concept of caring in nursing practice.
2. Describe the integration of caring into nursing processes.
3. Discuss the issues associated with caring and power.
4. Discuss the relationship between caring and safety and quality.

Priming Mortality

A pale light . . . fell straight upon the bed; and on it . . . was the body of this man. . . . Oh cold, cold, rigid, dreadful death! . . . But of the loved, revered, and honoured head, thou canst not turn one hair to thy dread purposes. . . . It is not that the hand is heavy and will fall down when released . . . but that the hand was open, generous, and true; the heart brave, warm, and tender. . . . [S]ee his good deeds springing up from the wound, to sow the world with life immortal!

—Charles Dickens, *A Christmas Carol* (1843/1950, pp. 115–116)

Most of us are socialized to try to do the right thing. Cultural worldviews usually if not always promote helping as the way to be a good, valuable person. Consequently, helping behaviors normally contribute to our sense of significance in the world and of creating a legacy of positive impact into the future—even beyond our own lives. By applying an existential perspective, terror management theory suggests that our awareness of our mortality should promote prosocial behavior. In the classic Charles Dickens tale *A Christmas Carol*, the stingy Ebenezer Scrooge is ultimately moved to become a charitable person by the Ghost of Christmas Future, which shows him his fate: to be forgotten after his death. He realizes that generosity will ensure that he has a positive impact and will be remembered beyond his physical death.

Do reminders of mortality make people more generous? In support of this "Scrooge effect," studies by Jonas and colleagues (2002) have shown that making people think about death increases donations to valued charities. Such studies help us understand why real-world reminders of death, such as the terrorist attacks of September 11, 2001, generally increase charitable giving, volunteerism, and blood donations (Glynn et al., 2003; Penner et al., 2005; Yum & Schenck-Hamlin, 2005). Reminders of mortality are especially likely to increase

▲ In the classic Charles Dickens tale *A Christmas Carol*, the stingy Ebenezer Scrooge is ultimately moved to become a charitable person by the Ghost of Christmas Future, which shows him his fate: to be forgotten after his death.

[Charles Phelps Cushing/ClassicStock/Alamy]

social behavior when the charitable action helps to connect the person's identity to entities that transcend one's death (Dunn et al., in press) and when prosocial cultural values have also been primed (Gailliot et al., 2008; Jonas et al., 2008). For example, Jonas et al. (2013) gave people $10 to split with an anonymous other person and told them they could keep as much as they wanted. If reminded of their mortality and then prompted to think about fairness, they actually gave more than half to the other person! However, these prosocial effects of reminders of mortality may be blocked or even reversed if the prosocial actions themselves remind people of death—for example, if the request is for organ donation (Hirschberger et al., 2008). Prosocial behavior can give us the reassuring feeling that some aspect of us continues beyond death.

Priming Religious Values

When it comes to priming moral behavior, some of the most potent concepts come from religion. Religion, like culture more generally, gives people a set of rules that help regulate their behavior. Religious teachings explain what it is to be a good and moral person and almost invariably preach kindness and compassion. Indeed, the notion that we should do unto others as we would have them do unto us captures our basic prosocial norm for positive reciprocity and can be found in all of the major world religions (Batson et al., 1993). The problem is that true reciprocity works best with people we see and interact with on an ongoing basis. When societies got big, people found themselves having more and more one-time interactions with complete strangers. These large societies function better if we expand our notion of reciprocity to people we do not know. Big religions help do this by incorporating the message of reciprocity as a general principle, a "golden rule" (Norenzayan, 2013; Norenzayan & Shariff, 2008; Shariff et al., 2010).

Does this then imply that those who are religious act more prosocially? Not necessarily. It's true that people who report high levels of religiosity also report being more altruistic, but in laboratory settings designed to measure the likelihood of helping, religiosity is unrelated to the actual likelihood of prosocial actions (Batson et al., 1993). Other work points to competing values associated with religiosity, at least in the United States (Malka et al., 2011). On the one hand, religiosity in America is associated with conservative ideologies that tend to oppose social welfare policies. Religious individuals also tend to make dispositional attributions (Jackson & Esses, 1997), which, as we discussed earlier, can make people less likely to help a person. However, religiosity is also associated with prosocial values that predict increased support for social welfare. These competing cultural messages indicate that the relationship of religiosity to helping is not so clear-cut.

Even if we can't always count on religious adherence to predict prosocial practices, the mere idea of religion can still prime more positive acts (Shariff et al., 2016). In one study, participants who first unscrambled sentences that primed them with concepts such as "divine" and "sacred" were more generous to a stranger than were those primed with neutral concepts (Shariff & Norenzayan, 2007). This effect was present even for those who reported being atheists, although it is interesting that priming people with other ways that society promotes justice ("courts" and "contracts") had the same effect. In fact, one of the ways that concepts of deities might help us keep on the moral path is by giving us the sense that someone is always watching what we do, keeping track of when we are naughty or nice (Gervais & Norenzayan, 2012; Norenzayan, 2013).

SECTION REVIEW Priming Prosocial Feelings and Behavior

Situations can trigger helping behaviors, even without our awareness. Prosocial behavior is increased by:

| Positive moods and emotions, such as awe, that put people in a prosocial mind-set | Friends and primes of friendship that cue a communal orientation | Reminders of mortality that lead people to help someone who supports their worldview | Priming religion or religious values, although the relationship between dispositional religiosity and helping is rather complicated |

Learning Outcomes

- Define the *bystander effect*.
- List the steps to take when making a decision about whether to help.
- Compare the evidence of helpfulness in small versus large population areas.

▲ Kitty Genovese was brutally murdered in 1964. News accounts claimed that witnesses heard the attack take place but did not help, spurring researchers to study the bystander effect.

[New York Daily News Archive/Getty Images]

Why Do People Fail to Help?

We like to think of ourselves as good, moral people, capable of empathy and compassion. But we can probably think of times when we have passed by a panhandler without giving him money, closed the door on a solicitor seeking donations for a local charity, or made excuses to a friend looking for a ride to the airport. The fact of the matter is that we don't always give or receive help. The flip side of looking at variables that elevate our helpful tendencies is to consider those that inhibit helping.

The Bystander Effect

Every month or so in countries around the world, you can find a story in the news of a horrible tragedy that could have been prevented by a mere phone call, such as the story we noted earlier of a girl who was gang-raped outside a homecoming dance while other students stood by and watched. When such events happen, we read about them with horror but also confusion. How could someone stand by and do *nothing* to help? Is this evidence of a callous generation of youth, desensitized by a lifetime of online interactions or violent video games? Probably not. The sad truth is that such events have happened for generations. In fact, social psychologists first took an interest in studying the complexities of prosocial behavior after just such an incident made headlines in 1964.

In the early morning hours on a cold day in March, Kitty Genovese returned home after work. As she walked toward her apartment building in Queens, New York, she was attacked from behind and stabbed in the back. The perpetrator continued to assault and stab her in a brutal attack that lasted over 30 minutes. During this time, Genovese cried for help, screamed that she had been stabbed, and tried to fight off her assailant. A New York newspaper reported that 38 people had witnessed the attack from their apartment windows but that no one called the police until after the attack had ended. Unfortunately, by then it was too late. Genovese died on the way to the hospital (Gansberg, 1964).

At the time, people took this horrific episode as evidence of the moral disintegration of New Yorkers—not just the murderer but also the witnesses who did not act. Although there has been some recent debate about whether the newspaper report exaggerated the number of witnesses (Manning et al., 2007), there were clearly more than enough witnesses to expect someone to have picked up the phone and called the police, yet no one did. This event inspired John Darley and Bibb Latané (1968) to engage in a groundbreaking set of studies documenting the bystander effect. The **bystander effect** generally refers to a phenomenon in which a person who witnesses another in need is less likely to help when there are other bystanders present to witness the event. On the surface, this idea seems ironic. Shouldn't the presence of other witnesses encourage individuals to help? The interesting fact of psychology is that sometimes the presence of others can make an individual inactive.

To see how this works, put yourself in the shoes of one of Darley and Latané's (1968) participants. You think you are going to be having a conversation over an intercom system about the challenges of being at college. You learn that it will be just you and another student or that you will be part of a group of either three or six, with each of you in separate rooms. As the discussion gets under way, one of the other participants discloses his history of having seizures and talks about how disruptive and stressful it can be. Later during the discussion, this same student seems to be having a seizure. The transcript of what people actually heard included:

> I-er-um-I think I-I need-er-if-if could-er-er-somebody er-er-er-er-er-er-er give me a little-er-give me a little help here because-er-I-er-I'm-er-er—having a-a-a real problem-er-right now and I-er-if somebody could help me out it would-it would- er-er s-s-sure be-sure be good. (p. 379)

Clearly, this person is having a hard time and is explicitly asking for help. If you were like the students who participated in this study over 50 years ago, you probably would get up to find the experimenter if you thought you had been having a private conversation with this person. Every single participant in that condition got up to help, and 85% of them did so within a minute and before the victim's apparent seizure had ended. When participants believed instead that four other people were listening, only 31% tried to help by the time the seizure had ended.

In another study (Latané & Darley, 1968), participants completed questionnaires in a waiting room, either alone or with two others who were sometimes confederates of the study or sometimes other naive participants. As they dutifully answered surveys, smoke began to stream into the room through a wall vent. In the group condition, the two confederates both looked up at the smoke briefly and then went back to their questionnaires. If participants

Bystander effect A phenomenon in which a person who witnesses another in need is less likely to help when there are other bystanders present to witness the event.

WHAT'S BYSTANDER INTERVENTION?

Choosing to take action when you see behavior that puts others at risk for violence, victimization, or perpetration. These include speaking out against rape myths & sexist language, supporting victim/survivors, & intervening in potentially violent situations.

LIKE THIS

▲ This poster from the University of Kansas shows how universities provide information about bystander intervention as a way to enlist students' help to prevent episodes of sexual harassment and violence.

[University of Kansas, Sexual Assault Prevention and Education Center]

were alone, 75% of them got up and alerted the experimenters to the smoke. But this dropped to fewer than 40% when three naive participants were in the room and only 10% if the participant sat alongside confederates who remained inactive.

A meta-analysis of 50 years of research shows the bystander effect to be a reliable phenomenon (Fischer et al., 2011). A tendency toward inaction even increases as the number of bystanders gets larger. The effect has also been shown in kids as young as five years old (Plötner et al., 2015). Although people clearly fail to act sometimes when the victim is in great peril, they are even less likely to act if the need for help is minor and others might be expected to intervene (Fischer et al., 2011). The bystander effect also is more likely to occur among strangers than among friends (Gottlieb & Carver, 1980). But even among strangers, feeling a sense of connection to those around you can turn a mere collection of inactive individuals into a powerful collective. You'll be happy to know that learning about the bystander effect, as you are right now, can prompt people into action when they face a crisis in the midst of a crowd (Beaman et al., 1978). In fact, universities are increasingly providing training on bystander intervention as a way to enlist students' help to prevent episodes of sexual violence, which occur all too frequently on college campuses (Coker et al., 2015).

APPLICATION

Steps to Helping—or Not!—in an Emergency

What is it about being in a group that immobilizes us? When we break down an event into its component parts, we can see that the decision to provide help in an emergency situation requires several steps. As shown in **FIGURE 13.2**, at each step—whether it be noticing the situation, interpreting it as an emergency, taking responsibility, deciding how to help, or actually providing help—something in the situation can waylay the process, causing us to keep going and ignore those who are in need.

Let's take a closer look at each of these steps.

Step 1: Notice the situation. The first step on the path to helping is to notice that something is amiss and that help might be needed. Although the seizure study was designed to make the victim's plight quite obvious, in the real world, we often go about our day immersed in our egocentric bubble, somewhat oblivious to the needs of those around us. We don't like to think that something as simple as being rushed for time would prevent us from offering assistance to someone in need. But this is exactly what Darley and Batson (1973) found in one intriguing experiment using what should be some of the most compassionate folks around—students studying to be priests. The researchers even put half the participants in a compassionate frame of mind by having them prepare to give a sermon on the parable of the Good Samaritan. In this biblical story, a

Achieve
Video: Bystander Intervention: Baby in a Hot Car (ABC's What Would You Do series)

Figure 13.2

Steps to Helping . . . or Not

When encountering a potential emergency situation, people must take multiple steps in deciding whether to offer help. At each step, we can make a judgment about ourselves or the situation that prevents us from helping.

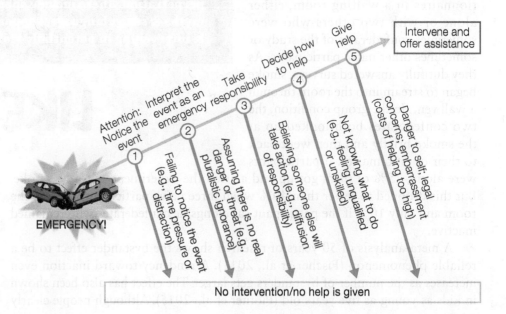

EMERGENCY!

1 Attention: Notice the event
2 Interpret the event as an emergency
3 Take responsibility
4 Decide how to help
5 Give help
Intervene and offer assistance

Failing to notice the event (e.g., time pressure or distraction)

Assuming there is no real danger or threat (e.g., pluralistic ignorance)

Believing someone else will take action (e.g., diffusion of responsibility)

Not knowing what to do (e.g., feeling unqualified or unskilled)

Danger to self; legal concerns; embarrassment (costs of helping too high)

No intervention/no help is given

Jewish man is attacked by robbers and lies, injured and suffering, on the side of the road. Several high-status individuals pass by, ignoring him. Only a low-status Samaritan stops to help, an act that is particularly significant given the hostility between the Jews and the Samaritans.

After rehearsing this story of goodwill and compassion, the experimenter explained that participants would give their sermon in another building and that they either had plenty of time to get there or that they were running late. As these unwitting participants followed a map to the assigned location, they passed a person hunched over and moaning in a doorway—a modern-day version of the very parable they were about to preach on! Surely every single one of them would stop to help this poor man in pain. Alas, that was not what happened. Of those participants who were in a rush, only 10% stopped to provide help, compared with 63% of those on a leisurely stroll. Many of those rushing to preach about compassion seemed not to have noticed passing a person who needed help. Leading a moral life involves stopping to notice when others need help.

Step 2: Interpret the situation as an emergency. Assuming that you notice that something is not quite right, stepping in to provide help requires you to interpret the event as one in which help is needed. If you were in the study where smoke started wafting through an air vent, you would also probably feel uncertain about whether this was cause for alarm. If you recall our discussion of *informational social influence* in chapter 7, you'll remember that when situations are ambiguous, we take our cues from other people. So when two confederates look at the smoke and then turn back to their questionnaires, it is not too surprising that only 10% of people bother to go alert the experimenter to the growing haze in the room. Even when the situation includes other naive bystanders like yourself, if you are all glancing at each other, trying to decide whether there is anything to be worried about, then no one is actually doing anything. What occurs in this situation is known as **pluralistic ignorance**. The inaction of all the members of the group can itself contribute to a collective ignorance of anything being amiss. In such situations, when bystanders are instead able and encouraged to communicate with one another, they are not paralyzed by pluralistic ignorance (Darley et al., 1973). So if you're in a group and think something is wrong but are not sure, communicate with others about it!

Step 3: Take responsibility. In some of our examples, bystanders should sail through the first two steps. When you hear someone tell you outright that he needs help after just informing you of his tendency toward seizures, it is a bit hard to imagine that you wouldn't notice or be aware that he was in trouble. Nevertheless, the presence of others can prevent us from helping. This is because of another powerful effect that groups can have on us, known as **diffusion of responsibility**. For a victim to receive help, someone needs to decide that it will be his or her responsibility to act. When you are the only witness, the moral burden clearly rests on your shoulders. But when others are present, it is easy to imagine that someone else should or has already taken action. In fact, even being primed to think about being part of a group can make people feel less personally accountable and less likely to donate money or stay to help out the experimenter (Garcia et al., 2002). If you ever need help and there are multiple witnesses, you can solve the problem of diffusion of responsibility by picking out—talking or pointing to—a specific individual and asking that person to help.

Step 4: Decide how to help. In this day and age, many people can help by using their cell phones to call 911. But in some situations, a specific kind of help is needed. If you feel that you lack the expertise, it is particularly easy to imagine that someone else might be better qualified to give help. A student having a

Pluralistic ignorance A situation in which individuals rely on others to identify a norm but falsely interpret others' beliefs and feelings, resulting in inaction.

Diffusion of responsibility A situation in which the presence of others prevents any one person from taking responsibility (e.g., for helping).

seizure might need someone with medical training, so a witness in the presence of others could hope that someone else is more knowledgeable than he or she would be. In the subway collapse study we talked about earlier, the researchers actually had to exclude two trials that they conducted when a nurse was on the train and immediately rushed to help. When people are trained to handle emergency situations, they are more likely to burst the bubble of inaction and rush to the aid of a person in need even as others stand by and watch (Pantin & Carver, 1982). Newer research from a social neuroscience perspective also suggests that for some people, the presence of others during an emergency automatically increases the level of distress in the situation. This distress can cause people to freeze reflexively, which makes any action difficult (Hortensius & de Gelder, 2018). Having prior training helps people overcome this freeze reflex.

Step 5: Decide whether to give help. You've noticed the event, interpreted it as an emergency, and taken responsibility, and you know what needs to be done. At this point, the only thing that might still prevent you from providing help is a quick calculation of the risks and other costs involved. When people witness a violent attack, they might be afraid to intervene for fear of getting hurt themselves. When someone has collapsed and needs CPR, witnesses might be worried that they could injure the person when performing chest compressions or could otherwise make the situation worse and get sued. To counter these concerns, all 50 states and all the Canadian provinces have enacted "Good Samaritan" laws that protect people from liability for any harm they cause when they act in good faith to save another person. ■

Population Density

THINK ABOUT ▶

[Michael Shake/Shutterstock; AMzPhoto/Shutterstock]

Social psychologists most often concern themselves with the effects of immediate situations on our behavior. But broader social contexts also can influence how we act. Think about where you live. Is it a small, rural community, a large urban area, or a suburban neighborhood? If you fall and break your leg, are you more likely to get help depending on the city where you take your tumble? We tend to assume that smaller communities are friendlier places and that large cities bring an inevitable sense of anonymity and indifference to others' needs (Simmel, 1903/2005). But is that the case?

In a unique study, Levine and colleagues (2008) traveled to 24 different U.S. cities and staged the following three helping opportunities. In one situation, a research assistant dropped a pen and acted as though he or she did not notice. In a second situation, he or she appeared to have an injured leg and struggled to pick up a pile of dropped magazines. In a third situation, the assistant approached people and asked if they could provide change for a quarter. The cities they chose varied from small (Chattanooga, Tennessee, population 486,000), to medium (Providence, Rhode Island, population 1,623,000), to large (New York City, population 18,641,000). Across the cities, the researchers consistently found that they received less help in larger, denser cities (**FIGURE 13.3**). For example, the correlation between the population density of the city and likelihood of receiving help was –0.55 when the assistant dropped the pen, –0.54 when the assistant needed help picking up magazines, and –0.47 when the assistant was trying to make change for a quarter. Notice that those correlations are negative, meaning that the bigger the city, the less likely people were to help. There is a kernel of truth to the stereotypical image of small-town friendliness.

One caveat, however, is that it is always a bit difficult to know what to make of correlations. Do these patterns tell us something about the personalities of the people living in these different parts of the country or about local cultural

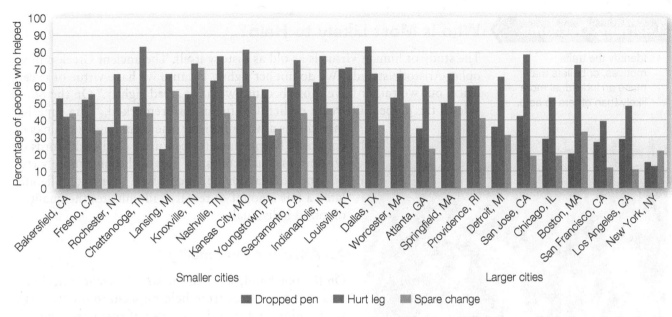

Figure 13.3

Where's the Help?

Do many hands mean people are less likely to lend a hand? Studies of helping suggest that strangers receive more help in smaller cities than in larger ones.

[Data from Levine et al., 2008]

norms? Are New Yorkers unhelpful contrarians? Or does living in an urban environment like New York work against whatever help-giving tendencies you might have? The jury is still out on that one. At least some research suggests that where you currently live better predicts how helpful you are than where you were born and raised (Korte, 1980). But this could mean either that the local norms of a culture change our behavior or that people choose to live in places that best reflect their personalities.

Milgram (1970) speculated that living in a dense urban area exposes people to greater stimulation or noise pollution. Living in a city apartment, you get used to the sounds of sirens, crying babies, car alarms, late-night partiers, and impatient drivers honking their horns. To deal with the din that comes with population density, people might learn to cope by shutting out these sounds. If this **urban overload hypothesis** is true, then city dwellers might sometimes find it difficult to distinguish between real cries of help and a normal night in the city.

Urban overload hypothesis The idea that city dwellers avoid being overwhelmed by stimulation by narrowing their attention, making it more likely that they overlook legitimate situations where help is needed.

SECTION REVIEW Why Do People Fail to Help?

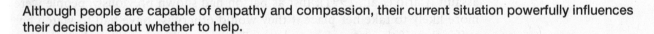

Although people are capable of empathy and compassion, their current situation powerfully influences their decision about whether to help.

The Bystander Effect	Helping—or Not—in an Emergency	Population Density
The greater the number of witnesses to a situation requiring help, the less likely any one of the witnesses will help.	Helping behavior results from several steps in sequence: • Attending to and interpreting the situation as an emergency • Taking responsibility for helping • Deciding how to help • Conducting a cost–benefit analysis At any step, some aspect of the situation (e.g., the presence of others) can short-circuit helping.	In bigger cities, despite a denser population, people tend to be less willing to help strangers.

- Identify the traits, motives, or beliefs that make an individual more likely than others to help.

▲ The study of human virtue can be traced back to ancient philosophers such as Confucius and Aristotle (shown here to the right of his mentor, Plato).

[Godong/Universal Images Group via Getty Images]

Altruistic personality A collection of personality traits, such as empathy, that render some people more helpful than others.

Who Is Most Likely to Help?

The study of human virtue is as old as history itself. The ancient Greek philosopher Aristotle stated, "We do not act rightly because we have virtue or excellence, but we rather have those because we have acted rightly." On the other side of the globe, 200 years earlier, Confucius had remarked, "The superior man thinks always of virtue; the common man thinks of comfort." People have for centuries used such words of wisdom as touchstones for how to become more virtuous and compassionate. Today, well over two millennia later, a fair amount of research illuminates the qualities of moral individuals.

An Altruistic Personality?

On the one hand, some of the social psychological factors that prevent us from helping seem to question the very notion of a moral character. If seminary students rush by a moaning person as they prepare a sermon on the Good Samaritan, what hope do any of the rest of us have in following the advice of Confucius and Aristotle? Other research, however, suggests that we can measure meaningful individual differences in what is known as the **altruistic personality**. Whether measured as behaviors (giving someone directions, donating blood; Rushton et al., 1981) or tendencies (to take another person's perspective, to experience empathy; Eisenberg et al., 1989), these differences can be pretty stable across one's life. Teenagers who score higher in empathy when they are 13 still view themselves as prosocially oriented a decade later (Eisenberg et al., 2002). Even their moms agree: Those teens who later scored highest in prosociality in their early 20s tended to be seen as pretty helpful kids by their moms a decade earlier.

Furthermore, although strong situational forces can constrain people's behavior, keeping them from acting in line with their underlying values and traits, personality characteristics shine through when situations are more ambiguous. Remember the study in which participants decided whether to switch places and receive mild shocks instead of watching the electricity-phobic Elaine suffer? In a variation of that study, participants could choose to trade places with a woman who was visibly upset about having to read about a physical assault (Carlo et al., 1991). Just as Batson had shown previously, people were more likely to take her place if they would otherwise have had to watch her suffer than if they were free to leave. When the situation was relatively easy to escape, people tended to take that option. But it was in this easy-to-escape condition that moral character mattered. Those who scored highest on a measure of altruism, or other personality variables associated with altruism, were more likely to take the other person's place (Eisenberg et al., 1989; Graziano et al., 2007).

In a more dramatic example of personality predicting altruism, research has shown that those who risked their lives to save others during the Holocaust can be distinguished from those who did nothing by a constellation of relevant traits such as strong moral reasoning, a sense of social responsibility, and empathy (Midlarsky et al., 2005). Together, these research results describe a profile of more specific traits that likely combine to make some of us more altruistic than others.

Individual Differences in Motivations for Helping

Some research has tackled the question of who is most likely to help by examining the motivations people generally have for helping. For example, people who score high on a measure of trait agreeableness or humility are thought to be motivated by prosocial concerns (Graziano et al., 2007; Hilbig et al., 2014). People who are agreeable and/or humble are sensitive to the needs of others and motivated to adapt their behavior to meet those needs. Although our dispositional agreeableness doesn't predict whether we will help family members, it is a useful predictor of who will help a stranger. The motivation to act prosocially seems to broaden our scope of social connection.

There are also added benefits to being intrinsically motivated to help other people—that is, when being altruistic is an important aspect of your identity. When you see a child share a toy with a classmate who is feeling sad, is he being helpful for external reasons ("I help because others tell me to") or internal reasons ("I help because I think it is important to"). Those who help for more intrinsic reasons show higher levels of empathy and report feeling a stronger connection to others (Ryan & Connell, 1989). In fact, because helping others can satisfy a basic need to feel connected to others, helping for these intrinsic reasons seems to have the most emotional benefits for both the giver and the receiver of help (Weinstein & Ryan, 2010). All this talk of intrinsic motivations brings up the idea that some people stake their sense of identity on being moral (Aquino & Reed; Aquino et al., 2011). People who say that being a moral, helpful person is central to their sense of identity respond to prosocial primes by being more helpful than those who don't define themselves along these prosocial lines (Aquino et al., 2009).

Being oriented toward others and incorporating that role into one's sense of identity also bodes well for sustaining prosocial behavior over time. For example, in one study, the best predictor of whether people volunteered for AIDS organizations was the extent to which they were motivated toward others rather than toward the self (Omoto et al., 2010). Once people begin volunteering, experiences of social validation and personal satisfaction lead people to keep at it (Kiviniemi et al., 2002; Omoto & Snyder, 2002; Penner & Finkelstein, 1998). For example, when volunteer experiences are positive and rewarding, helping becomes part of one's identity, leading to a sustained investment in time and effort toward helping others (Piliavin et al., 2002). In fact, any time people feel that what they give is a part of themselves, they are more committed to keep giving (Koo & Fishbach, 2016).

▲ Is the child being helpful because this is merely what he has been told to do or because he knows he might be praised for being helpful or because he truly wants to make his friend feel better? People have both internal and external reasons for being helpful.
[Dave Clark Digital Photo/Shutterstock]

The Role of Political Values

We've seen that morality clearly plays a role in helping, but at least in the United States, different moral domains are important to people, depending on their political orientation. In American political culture, liberals are sometimes seen as "bleeding hearts," but what is the evidence that people's political leanings predict a more prosocial orientation? One way to answer this question is to look at how people's ideologies relate to the kinds of policies they support (Kluegel & Smith, 1986). Whereas conservatives are more likely to withhold public assistance to people whom they view as responsible for their own predicament, liberals tend to support providing assistance to people regardless of how they got there (Skitka, 1999; Skitka & Tetlock, 1992; Skitka et al., 1991; Weiner et al., 2011). But this liberal generosity only extends so far. If resources are scarce and belts need to be tightened, both liberals and conservatives choose to help those who are least to blame for being in a bind.

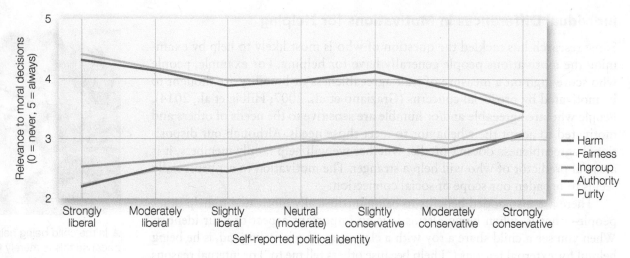

Figure 13.4

Political Differences in Moral Foundations

Although Americans generally place the highest value on being fair and doing no harm, conservatives also base their moral decisions on ingroup loyalty, respect for authority, and purity, whereas liberals want to help those who are suffering unnecessarily.

[Data from Graham et al., 2009]

What accounts for these differences in political proclivities of helpfulness? Are liberals more empathic and less inclined to make "us versus them" distinctions? Are conservatives simply savvier in making financial investments that pay off for society as a whole? Some evidence points to the different motivations of liberals and conservatives in making policy decisions (Skitka & Tetlock, 1993). Conservatives are more motivated to maintain traditional values and norms. When they see people violating those norms, they are more inclined to punish than to help them. Liberals, on the other hand, are more motivated by egalitarian values and don't like to see a price tag put to anyone's pain and suffering.

We can also gain insight into the role of political ideology in moral reasoning by turning to research on moral foundations theory, which we introduced back in chapter 2 (e.g., Graham et al., 2009). This work finds that people take into account five guiding principles when they prioritize whom and when to help or how to be virtuous: preventing harm to others, ensuring fair treatment to all, being loyal to one's group, respecting authority, and maintaining purity in one's actions (Haidt & Joseph, 2007).

In **FIGURE 13.4**, you can see that across the political spectrum, Americans generally make moral decisions with an eye toward avoiding harm and maintaining fairness (Graham et al., 2009). The graph also shows that conservatives prioritize respecting authority, maintaining purity, and protecting the ingroup—but liberals do not. These different moral foundations suggest that liberals will tend to reach out primarily to those who seem to be suffering unnecessarily or as a result of unfair disadvantage, whereas conservatives will be more likely to help individuals and groups they see as conforming to traditional moral and religious norms and values and generally upholding the social order.

 APPLICATION

Using Political Values to Protect the Environment

Throughout this chapter, we've been talking about prosocial behavior as helping other people. But one way to help humanity as a whole is to protect and preserve the planet that is our home. In fact, environmental conservation presents a classic social dilemma that requires people to put aside their own self-interest of today to prioritize global interests for future generations. Although the very future of humanity could be at stake, environmental concern has become a politically loaded topic. For example, according to a 2016 Pew survey, 82% of liberals think that stricter environmental laws and regulations are

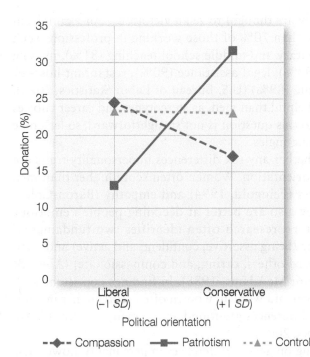

Compassion Frame on Conservation Message

Show your love for all of humanity and the world in which we live by helping to care for our vulnerable natural environment. Help to reduce the harm done to the environment by taking action. By caring for the natural world you are helping to ensure that everyone around the world gets to enjoy fair access to a sustainable environment. Do the right thing by preventing the suffering of all life-forms and making sure that no one is denied their right to a healthy planet. SHOW YOUR COMPASSION.

Patriotism Frame on Conservation Message

Show you love your country by joining the fight to protect the purity of America's natural environment. Take pride in the American tradition of performing one's civic duty by taking responsibility for yourself and the land you call home. By taking a tougher stance on protecting the natural environment, you will be honoring all of Creation. Demonstrate your respect by following the examples of your religious and political leaders who defend America's natural environment. SHOW YOUR PATRIOTISM!

Figure 13.5

Which Message Do You Find More Convincing?

When researchers varied which message people received (compared to a control condition with no message), people with different political orientations reacted differently to each message. Liberals were more likely to donate money to the Environmental Defense Fund after reading about conservation framed as an act of compassion, and conservatives were more likely to donate after reading about conservation framed as an act of patriotism.

[Data from Wolsko et al., 2016]

worth the possible costs to the economy compared to only 29% of conservatives (Bialik, 2016). Can understanding of the moral foundations that conservatives value be applied to motivate support for environmental policies? Research suggests that it can. As shown in **FIGURE 13.5**, tying environmental messages to different moral values can change the way liberals and conservatives react (Wolsko et al., 2016). When environmental conservation is framed in terms of harm to the environment and a need to show compassion for the suffering that climate change has caused and will cause, liberals were more persuaded to donate money to the Environmental Defense Fund. But when environmental conservation was framed in terms of civic duty, protecting the land, respecting leaders, and showing one's patriotism, conservatives were much more willing to donate than were liberals. ■

The Role of Gender

What are little boys made of?

Snips and snails and puppy dogs tails,

That's what little boys are made of.

What are little girls made of?

Sugar and spice and everything nice,

That's what little girls are made of.

—Traditional nursery rhyme

We've all heard this nursery rhyme and its chipper little message about sex differences. This cultural clipping reflects an assumption that boys are rough and tumble, girls sweet and good. Although discussions of sex differences and stereotypes often turn on ways in which women are thought to be weaker, more submissive, and less competent than their male peers, prosocial behavior is one arena in which women usually are thought to reign victorious. For example, in 2019, women made up more than 70% of those working in professions such as social work (82%), elementary and middle school teaching (81%), nursing (89%), medical assistance (93%), legal assistance (90%), restaurant host- or hostessing (82%), and cleaning (89%) (U.S. Bureau of Labor Statistics, 2020). But are women in fact more helpful than men, as stereotypes and career choices would suggest? The answer to this question is not straightforward, so let's take a look at it from a few different angles.

First, we can consider whether any sex differences in personality traits are associated with a prosocial orientation. Women often score higher than men on measures of agreeableness (Feingold, 1994) and empathy (Baron-Cohen & Wheelwright, 2004). They also are better at decoding people's emotions (McClure, 2000). Furthermore, research often identifies two fundamental dimensions of identity: agency (being assertive, confident, and active) and communion (being oriented toward others, caring, and compassionate) (Abele & Wojciszke, 2007; Bakan, 1966; McAdams, 1988). In findings consistent with the common stereotypes of men and women, women often score higher in communion than do men. These differences are found across many cultures (Costa et al., 2001; Schwartz & Rubel, 2005).

One problem with focusing on gender differences in personality, however, is that personality is most often measured with surveys. This means that what we really learn is whether women *think about themselves* as being more helpful and prosocial compared with how men think of themselves. We might think about whether these gender differences in self-perceptions are backed up by actual behavior. A meta-analysis of the kinds of helping studies conducted back in the heyday of helping research suggests that there is a reliable gender difference in a tendency to provide help, but it's not the difference you might have expected. In 62% of the studies that Eagly and Crowley analyzed, men were more likely to help than were women (Eagly & Crowley, 1986). For example, recall the studies in which someone collapsed on a subway. In those field experiments, men were more likely than women to step in and assist the collapsed stranger (Piliavin et al., 1975). **FIGURE 13.6** shows approximately every sixth study reported in the meta-analysis, rank ordered by the size of the effect. Positive effect sizes indicate that men were more likely to help than were women; effects shown in blue were statistically significant. Negative effect sizes mean that women were more likely to help than were men; effects shown in red were examples of significantly greater prosocial behavior from women. Studies shown in green did not find significant sex differences between men and women. Notice any patterns?

Eagly and Crowley (1986) coded these studies for various characteristics and noted that men are more likely to help in situations that call for chivalrous behavior or taking action despite possible danger. Men are more likely to help a woman with heavy packages, hold a door open (especially for a woman), or be willing to take the risk of picking up a hitchhiker or letting a stranger into their home. Men are also more likely to help when others will *know* that they have helped, suggesting that men more than women might act prosocially as a way to boost their own social status. They might be smart to do this: It turns out that women report being more attracted to men who behave prosocially (Jensen-Campbell et al., 1995). Women, on the other hand, are more likely to volunteer their time for others or go out of their way to mail a letter that has been left behind. In other words, both men and women are prosocially oriented in some ways, but gender roles suggest who should help in which kinds of situations.

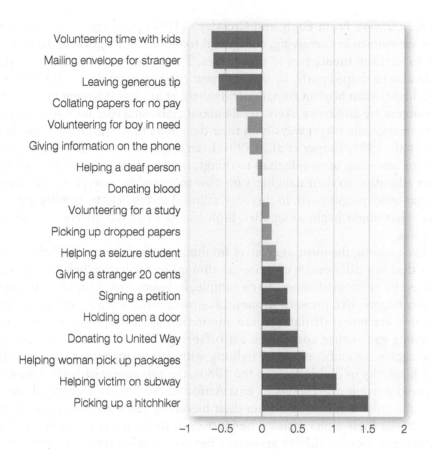

Figure 13.6

Gender Differences in How We Help

A review of studies on helping reveals that men and women help in different ways. Women are more likely to volunteer time to provide care for others (red bars), sometimes on an ongoing basis, whereas men are more likely to help in potentially dangerous situations or when norms for chivalry are present (blue bars).

[Data from Eagly & Crowley, 1986]

If there are some average differences in prosocial orientation between men and women, are these differences really a function of "what little boys and girls are made of," as the poem would suggest? Or are they passed along from one generation to the next through such poetry? As in most other nature versus nurture disputes, both elements likely factor in. On the side of biology, Shelly Taylor and her colleagues have argued that in addition to the typical fight-or-flight response to acutely stressful situations, women might also exhibit a "tend-and-befriend" response to stressors (Taylor et al., 2000). In other words, in stressful situations, a suite of hormonal responses, including increases in oxytocin, spur women to seek safety and comfort for both themselves and close others, especially their offspring, and to build social networks. From this perspective, evolved biological differences in hormonal responses might lead women more than men to reach out to others and offer a helping hand.

Developmental and comparative studies also provide compelling evidence for sex differences. In babies who are less than a year old, boys look longer at a truck than at a doll, whereas girls look longer at a doll than at a truck (Alexander et al., 2009; Ruble et al., 2006). Because these same sex-typed preferences show up in nonhuman primates (Alexander & Hines, 2002; Hassett et al., 2008), some researchers have argued that females have an inherent preference for people over things, whereas males show interest in things before people (Lippa, 1998). These biologically based differences might set the stage for girls and women to be more prosocially attuned than boys and men and to help out of a concern for alleviating the suffering of others.

Other perspectives layer on top of these initial differences the role of socialization and cultural influences in magnifying gendered behavior (Bussey &

Bandura, 2004). From Eagly and Crowley's (1986) perspective, because we so often see women in caregiving, communal roles, little girls grow up to be better able to envision themselves in those roles. Those communal personality traits might also be shaped partly by our environment. For example, grade school girls score higher than boys in empathy (Eisenberg et al., 1991; Knight et al., 1994), but parents are also more likely to talk about emotional reactions and behave in more emotionally warm ways with their daughters than with their sons (Eisenberg et al., 1991; Leaper et al., 1998). Even if girls show some greater preference for attending to people than to things, it seems that parents also provide a richer education to their daughters on how to attend to, interpret, and respond to what other people need. In this way, cultural forces help to amplify and reinforce what might begin as smaller, biologically disposed differences between the sexes.

Even among the most aggressive nonhuman primates, some evidence indicates that sex differences in more communal or affiliative behaviors can be reduced by cultural changes. For example, baboons are thought to be one of the most aggressive primate species. Like most other female primates, female baboons are more affiliative than the males, spending more of their time grooming each other and caring for offspring. The male baboons are much more aggressive and combative, fighting with competing troops and establishing a hierarchy of dominance. In the 1980s, the primatologist Robert Sapolsky observed a troop of baboons in East Africa whose behavior changed entirely when the most dominant males in their hierarchy suddenly died of tuberculosis. Without these alpha males around, the remaining males in the troop began to engage in more affiliative grooming behavior—grooming both females and other males alike, a behavior that was nearly unprecedented. More amazing, six years later Sapolsky discovered that the troop had maintained this new norm of prosociality. By that time, new adolescent males had joined the troop but apparently had learned to adopt this kinder, gentler lifestyle (Sapolsky & Share, 2004). Even among baboons, changes in social dynamics can narrow the gap between the sexes in prosocial tendencies.

Think about your own experiences. In what ways do you feel culture has influenced how you help others?

THINK ABOUT
[John Fedele/Getty Images]

 APPLICATION
Toward a More Prosocial Society

Our tour through the research on prosocial behavior has taught us that humans, along with many other social species, have an innate capacity for helping. It is important to note, however, that there is also variation in this tendency and the degree to which we act on it. It might not even be realistic to expect individuals to engage in prosocial behavior all the time. But there is undoubtedly room for most if not all of us, in one way or another, to be a little more giving and helpful to each other. This chapter offers a useful blueprint for creating a more prosocially oriented society. In a nutshell, it looks something like this: Raise our children to be adults who have a great capacity for empathy and a strong moral identity. Model how to show warmth and take the perspective of others, especially of those others who seem most different from ourselves. Teach children to view various forms of prosocial behavior as an important basis for being a good, valued person in the world; this can help them become adults who strongly value their identity as generous, helpful people. Parents, teachers, and peers all can enact these changes. Through television shows, movies, and video games, the mass media also can facilitate them by depicting more prosocial role models. It would help further if these media resources reinforced the rewarding nature of prosocial behavior. These changes will be more likely the more we foster a communal orientation in how we think about our families, friends, communities, culture, humanity, and even perhaps all living things. ■

SECTION REVIEW Who Is Most Likely to Help?

Although situations matter, there are meaningful individual differences in prosocial tendencies.

Altruism	Individual Differences	Political Values	Gender
Personality traits such as moral reasoning, sense of social responsibility, and empathy predict altruism.	People who identify themselves as being moral and helpful generally are more prosocial.	Political conservatives and liberals endorse different moral foundations, making them more or less likely to help depending on their moral interpretation of the situation.	Women are generally seen as being more prosocial, but in some situations men are more willing to help.

CRITICAL LEARNING EXERCISES

1. Are people born to be good, or is this something they learn? Can you think about a way that parents or teachers in your life have tried to teach you to help others? Do you think their efforts have had an effect on your own altruistic behavior? Why or why not?
2. Think about a time you helped someone else even though doing so posed some cost or risk to you. Using the ideas and theories discussed in this chapter, describe what you believe were your motivations for helping.
3. During the COVID-19 epidemic in the winter and spring of 2020, people often helped others at great risk to themselves. Using the steps to deciding to help in an emergency, outline the process by which someone might have decided to help a neighbor in need during this global pandemic.

Don't stop now! Check out our videos and additional resources located at: www.macmillanlearning.com

E+/wundervisuals/Getty Images

CHAPTER 14

Interpersonal Attraction

At the beginning of the sci-fi film *Passengers* (Tyldum, 2016), Jim Preston (played by Chris Pratt) wakes up 90 years too early from suspended animation on a spaceship heading toward a distant new planet. With the other 7,000 passengers and crewmembers still in suspended animation, Jim has all the food, drink, and entertainment he would ever need. He can even interact with an android bartender. But over the course of a year, the lack of human companionship and the prospect of living out his whole life alone brings him to the brink of despair. After almost committing suicide, Jim makes a desperate, selfish decision to end his unbearable isolation.

Passengers joins earlier movies including *I Am Legend* (2007), *The Martian* (2015), and *Castaway* (2000) in exploring a question that has gripped people's imaginations for ages: What would it be like to be cut off from others? This question intrigues us because relationships—however frustrating and disappointing at times—play a central role in living a significant and satisfying life.

◄ Chris Pratt stars in the movie *Passengers*, which touches on a question that has long captured our interest: What would life be like without any human contact? Why are we so intrigued by this question, and what does that tell us about our need for other people?

[Columbia Pictures/Photofest]

In this chapter, we focus on:

- The basic human need to connect with other people

- What it takes to get relationships off the ground

- Who people find attractive and choose to connect with

- Sex and its many meanings

- Describe evidence that humans have a need to belong.
- Explain the evolutionary basis for this need.

Psychological need A mechanism for regulating behavior to acquire the tangible or intangible resources necessary for survival and well-being.

The Need to Belong

The desire to form social relationships is a fundamental part of human nature. We *need* to be part of stable, healthy bonds with family members, romantic partners, and friends to function normally.

Why Do We Need to Belong?

It may seem obvious to you that we have a need to belong. But although we use the word *need* loosely in everyday language, the stakes are higher when we claim that something is a **psychological need**. It could be that close relationships are just nice, not necessary. (Consider: People may seek frequent, pleasant interactions with their computers, but they don't *need* them.) What evidence is there that the need to belong is inherent to our nature?

The Need to Belong Can Be Satisfied Biologically based needs work on the principle of homeostasis: You experience a deficiency (e.g., you're hungry) that motivates thoughts and behaviors (you eat) until the need is satisfied (you're full and stop eating). The same principle applies to close relationships. People do not need hundreds of relationships, just a few that are lasting and caring, and when they have them, they are less motivated to form additional relationships. People may have hundreds of followers on social media, but they find deeper satisfaction in interacting face-to-face with a few close others (Dwyer et al., 2018; Kushlev & Heintzelman, 2018; Manago et al., 2012; Wheeler & Nezlek, 1977).

The need to belong also resembles physiological needs in that it can be satisfied in flexible ways. If your hunger pangs motivate you to get up and search for cereal, and you discover that you are out of milk, you'll find something else to eat. Similarly, when people are unable to satisfy their need to belong in their existing relationships, they find substitutes. For example, people in prison cope with the stressful separation from their biological family by forming temporary "families" with other prisoners (Burkhart, 1973).

When the Need to Belong Is Satisfied, People Thrive When people receive proper nutrition, shelter, and sleep, they feel good psychologically and physically. In the same way, feeling connected to others promotes an individual's mental and physical health. Compared with people who live more isolated lives, people who have pleasant interactions with a network of close friends, lovers, family members, and coworkers have higher self-esteem (Denissen et al., 2008; Leary & Baumeister, 2000), feel happier and more satisfied with their lives (Diener et al., 1999), and have better mental health (Kim & McKenry, 2002). Across different cultures, people who marry and stay married are happier overall than are those who are less committed to an intimate partnership (Diener et al., 2000). With regard to physical health, people who feel socially connected have stronger cardiovascular, immune, and endocrine systems, and they are less likely to die prematurely (Cacioppo & Patrick, 2008; House et al., 1988; Uchino, 2006).

 APPLICATION

When the Need to Belong Is Unmet, Health Suffers

A hallmark of a need is that if it goes unsatisfied for a long time, people suffer negative consequences. It is in this respect that we see the strongest evidence for the claim that the need to belong qualifies as a true psychological need. When people are isolated for long periods, studies show, their mental and physical health deteriorates.

Many of these studies look at the experience of **loneliness**—the feeling that one is deprived of human social connections (Cacioppo & Patrick, 2008). Although people can choose to be alone without experiencing loneliness (Pepping et al., 2018), generally they find it very stressful to be alone for a long time (Schachter, 1959). To ease the pain of loneliness, people strive to connect. For example, when stay-at-home orders were issued to stem the coronavirus pandemic in 2020, people scrambled to find means—from using remote meeting apps to making old-fashioned phone calls—to feel connected (Kang, 2020). Occasionally people take more extreme measures to numb the pain of loneliness, such as bingeing on alcohol or drugs (Rook, 1984) and staying in unhappy relationships (Kamp Dush & Amato, 2005). Over time, loneliness can take a toll on mental and physical health. It contributes to depression, eating disorders, and schizophrenia (Cacioppo et al., 2006; Segrin, 1998). During times of loneliness, college students have weaker immune systems, which means they are especially vulnerable to catching a cold or flu (Pressman et al., 2005). In fact, when it comes to predicting people's physical health, loneliness is as significant a risk factor as smoking and obesity (Hawkley et al., 2009).

Like loneliness, rejection undermines mental and physical health (S. Cohen, 2004; Ryff & Singer, 2000). After being rejected, people feel distressed and find it hard to concentrate (Baumeister et al., 2002; Smart Richman & Leary, 2009; Williams, 2007). After a divorce, the sting of rejection increases vulnerability to psychological problems (Bloom et al., 1979), physiological stress (Kiecolt-Glaser & Newton, 2001), and early death (Sbarra et al., 2011). It's no wonder that many people seek to remarry after divorce or the death of their spouse (Livingston, 2014). Much like rejection, feeling that you've been forgotten can hurt. Being remembered is a sign of importance, so when David says, "nice to meet you" even though you've hung out with him at, like, *two* parties before, it can make you feel unimportant (Ray et al., 2019).

Everyone experiences loneliness or rejection at some point. How can you protect your health and reestablish a sense of belonging? It can help to bring to mind the people you know that you can turn to for help. Even better, find someone to give you a hug. In one study, people who received a hug from someone else were less likely to develop cold symptoms after exposure to the cold virus (Cohen et al., 2015). ■

Loneliness The feeling that one is deprived of human social connections.

▲ When people were ordered to stay home to slow the spread of Covid-19, they fended off loneliness by connecting with people online.
[Alistair Berg/Getty Images]

Where Did This Need Come From?

So relationships are essential for a good, long life, but where did this need for relationships originate? Why do virtually all of us care so much about forming and maintaining relationships? To answer these questions, let's consider the evolution of our species.

From an evolutionary perspective, early humans who formed close social bonds were more likely to survive and reproduce than were loners and outcasts. To appreciate how beneficial social relationships were, try to envision yourself in the environments of our hominid ancestors—environments very different from the ones we live in today. Imagine being in a desert or forested area, and every day you're scrambling to find food (no food delivery apps), looking out for dangerous predators, and protecting yourself from illness and harsh climates. In such environments, being embedded in a network of relationships helped people survive, have children, and see that their children grew to maturity and reproduced (Fehr, 1996; Trivers, 1971).

Another feature of our species is that children depend on years of care and protection to survive until they can function on their own. Infants born with a tendency to connect to caregivers would have been more likely than antisocial infants to receive that care (Bowlby, 1980; Buss, 1994).

In short, early ancestors who attended to others and cared for them were more likely to enjoy the benefits of stable, affectionate connections. As a result, more and more humans were born with a genetic predisposition to get along with others. In this way, over thousands of generations, the need to belong came to be an inherited characteristic of our species (Baumeister & Leary, 1995; Buss & Schmitt, 1993; Simpson & Kenrick, 1997).

Proponents of this evolutionary account note that it helps to explain four observations:

■ *The motive to belong is universal*: In every culture that has been examined, people care deeply about forming and maintaining romantic bonds, parent–offspring attachments, and close relationships with siblings, friends, and group members (e.g., Eibl-Eibesfeldt, 1989).

■ *Affiliation behaviors are innate*: Soon after human infants exit the womb, they instinctively engage with other people (Murray & Trevarthen, 1986). They pay special attention to other people's faces, and they delight in mimicking others' facial expressions (Meltzoff & Moore, 1977). They also pay particular attention to human voices, especially when others use baby talk (Cooper & Aslin, 1990). These tendencies are seen in children all over the world, and they are not seen in other species.

■ *Rejection hurts—literally*: Earlier we noted that the experience of social rejection is distressing. Here we add that rejection causes the same stress responses as physical pain. Even minor forms of rejection—such as hearing someone spread unkind gossip about oneself—increase stress-related heart activity and a flood of stress hormones. Being ignored or rejected also activates the anterior cingulate cortex, a brain region that processes physically painful stimuli (Eisenberger et al., 2003).

   The similarity of the stress responses to physical pain and social rejection makes perfect sense if we think about the need to belong as an evolved tendency (MacDonald & Leary, 2005). Individuals who felt horrible pain when they were rejected were presumably more motivated to alleviate that pain by repairing their relationships, thereby increasing their chances of reproducing. Those who were less rattled by social rejection may have gone off on their own, making it less likely that they would survive and ultimately contribute to the human gene pool.

■ *Reproductive success is fostered in relationships*: Adults who form stable close relationships are more likely to reproduce than those who fail to form them. Long-term relationships tend to increase the chances that the offspring will survive and reach maturity (Buss & Schmitt, 1993).

SECTION REVIEW The Need to Belong

The desire to form social relationships is a fundamental part of human nature.

Evidence of a Fundamental Need to Belong	Evidence That the Need to Belong Has an Evolutionary Basis
• Like other needs, the need to belong can be satisfied in flexible ways.	• People of all cultures share the need to belong.
• Belonging promotes mental and physical health.	• Newborn infants instinctively engage other people.
• Loneliness, rejection, and feeling forgotten take a toll on mental and physical health.	• Social rejection activates the same stress responses as physical pain.
	• Long-term relationships promote successful procreation and raising of offspring.

The Basics of Interpersonal Attraction

Learning Outcomes

- Explain why proximity is important to initiating relationships.
- Outline the reward model of liking.
- Identify the attributes of another person that increase attraction.
- Explain the interrelationship between attraction and the needs for meaning and self-esteem.

We've seen that relationships are important, but how do we choose who to be in a relationship with? Some people might say, "Each case is special. Science cannot tell us who we'll be attracted to." Although there is some evidence that each of us has a "type" that we're attracted to over time (Bredow & Hames, 2019; Park & MacDonald, 2019), the research in this section shows that there are reliable patterns in attraction. It's important to note that most of the research in this area has focused on attraction between heterosexual men and women, but we will also highlight the emerging interest in studying patterns of attraction among same-sex couples.

Proximity: Like the One You're Near

One factor in interpersonal attraction is **proximity**, or the physical nearness of others. You can't form a relationship with people unless you meet them, and the more proximal you are to someone, the more likely you are to meet. Some of the coolest evidence of proximity's importance comes from a study by Festinger and colleagues (1950). They interviewed residents in a new apartment complex. These residents had been assigned their apartments in an essentially random fashion, allowing the researchers to study whether proximity influences who makes friends with whom. People were nearly twice as likely to form a friendship with the person in the next-door apartment as they were to form a friendship with the person who lived two doors away. Also, people who lived in first-floor apartments were more likely to make friends on the second floor if they lived near the stairwell rather than far away, presumably because they were more likely to encounter second-floor residents on a daily basis. We like to believe we choose our friends carefully, on the basis of their unique attributes, but these findings suggest that some of our choices are based largely on who happens to be nearby.

Even a small increase in spatial proximity can amplify liking. Shin and colleagues (2019) asked single, heterosexual men to watch a video clip of a young woman. Depending on condition, the woman stood close to the camera (60 centimeters) or far away (150 cm). Although it was the same woman across both conditions, when she was closer, men found her to be more approachable and likable.

Proximity The physical nearness of others. It is a major factor determining who we form relationships with.

▲ The power of proximity. In many contexts, such as apartment complexes, you are randomly placed near some people and far from others. Nevertheless, physical location powerfully predicts who you are attracted to and form relationships with.

[Lisa Werner/Alamy]

Reward model of liking A model which proposes that people like other people whom they associate with positive stimuli and dislike people whom they associate with negative stimuli.

One reason proximity makes a difference is that we tend to like things better the more we are exposed to them—a phenomenon called the *mere exposure effect* (chapter 8; Zajonc, 1968). People are initially wary of unfamiliar others, but with repeated exposure, they generally feel more at ease and willing to reach out. To examine this effect in the lab, Reis and colleagues (2011) arranged it so that strangers chatted with each other between one and eight times. The more chats people had, the more they liked each other. This is because more conversation increased comfort and a sense that the other person was responsive. The increased frequency of exposures increased familiarity, which then increased attraction. In fact, when we're frequently exposed to people, we not only like them more but also judge them as happier (Carr et al., 2017) and as having a stronger moral character (Bocian et al., 2018).

Of course, there are important exceptions to the proximity effect: the roommates who grate on each other, the annoying neighbor, the cultural groups that share a border and can't get along. Indeed, the mere exposure effect does not occur if the stimulus is initially disliked or is associated with negative outcomes (e.g., Swap, 1977). If repeated exposure to others due to close proximity only reminds people of ways that they differ from one another, they can like one another less rather than more (Norton et al., 2007). This brings us to our first broad theory of attraction.

The Reward Model of Liking

The core idea of the **reward model of liking** is simple: We like people we associate with positive feelings and dislike people we associate with negative feelings (e.g., Byrne & Clore, 1970; Lott & Lott, 1974). Recall from chapter 8 that advertisers often pair their product with an uplifting jingle or a cute image in an attempt to foster a positive association with the product. The reward model is based on the same principle of classical conditioning: A new person begins as a relatively neutral stimulus. If exposure to the person is paired with a second stimulus you already like, the positive feelings evoked by the second stimulus start to become evoked by the person. If, however, the second stimulus evokes negative feelings, those feelings can be linked to the person.

This model challenges our commonsense wisdom. If we're asked why we like someone, we usually respond by noting qualities of that person. That is certainly part of the total picture, but the reward model suggests that we could come to like (or dislike) people not because of any quality they have but because they happened to be around when we were feeling good (or bad). One early test of this idea had participants sit in a room for 45 minutes and fill out some questionnaires. One of the questionnaires described a stranger's attitudes on various issues. The experimenter varied the temperature in the room so that it was either comfortable or unpleasantly hot. Participants were then asked how they felt about the stranger. As the reward model predicts, participants liked the stranger better if the room was comfortable (Griffitt, 1970). Other studies reveal the same basic effect using different methods. In one, participants overheard bad or good news on a radio broadcast just before evaluating a stranger (Veitch & Griffitt, 1976). They liked the stranger better if they had just heard good news. So sometimes, we may like or dislike people because they just happen to be there when something pleasant or unpleasant happens to occur.

Others' Attributes Can Be Rewarding

Having acknowledged the role of situational factors, we next consider: What attributes of people themselves evoke the positive feelings that increase our attraction to them?

Transference   First, some attributes may evoke positive feelings because we associate them with people we like or positive experiences we had in the past. For example people are often drawn to romantic partners who have a caregiving style similar to that of their parents (Collins & Read, 1990). More generally, in a finding consistent with the Freudian concept of **transference** (Freud, 1912/1958), Susan Andersen and colleagues discovered that if a new acquaintance resembles a significant other in your life whom you like or dislike, you may carry over those feelings to the new person (Andersen & Baum, 1994; Andersen et al., 1996). Often these associations can be subtle, such as sharing the same birthday or wearing a similar style of eyeglasses.

Transference A tendency to map on, or transfer, feelings for a person who is known onto someone new who resembles that person in some way.

▲ Research on transference suggests that if you already have positive feelings about Courteney Cox, then you'll like Demi Moore simply because they look alike.
[Gregg DeGuire/WireImage/Getty Images]

Culturally Valued Attributes and Personality Traits   As cultural animals, we also are drawn to people who have talents or have achieved things that our culture values (e.g., Fletcher et al., 2000). If you happened to meet a celebrity at the airport or in a bar, you would probably tell everyone about it. Why? Being connected to, or basking in the reflected glory of, another person with culturally valued attributes can enhance our own self-esteem (Cialdini et al., 1976). This form of attraction extends not only to the extremes of celebrity but also to any attributes or talents that are culturally valued. For example, one of your authors (Jeff) had a roommate in college who was brilliantly talented in music. He read symphony scores for fun and, on hearing a song once, could play it on the piano. Your author recalls taking great pride in his friend's ability, even though he himself entirely lacked that ability!

In addition to talents, people are attracted to culturally valued personality traits such as friendliness, honesty, intelligence, and a good sense of humor (e.g., Sprecher & Regan, 2002). However, which traits people desire in others depends to some extent on the kind of relationship they have. For example, people value traits like agreeableness and emotional stability when looking for a close friend more than a study group partner, whereas they value intelligence in a study partner more than in a close friend (Cottrell et al., 2007). In another example, people are attracted to individuals with a strong moral identity—those who follow strict standards of right and wrong—because they seem trustworthy. At the same time, however, morally upstanding individuals can seem to lack a sense of humor, making them less attractive overall (Yam et al., 2019).

Note that, in studies like these, researchers asked people to report what traits they *think* they like, not those that they actually like (Eastwick et al., 2014).

Why is this important? Because the cultural worldview people learn as children teaches them that kindness, intelligence, honesty, and so forth are good qualities. Thus, people's self-reports are likely to mimic these teachings. In fact, when we examine what traits people in different cultures claim to like, their responses mirror aspects of the culture. This was observed in a large Internet survey of participants from 53 nations. When they were asked to rate the importance of various attributes of a romantic partner, participants from modern, individualistic nations rated humor and kindness higher, and dependability lower, than did participants from more collectivistic nations (Lippa, 2007). Perhaps individuals in different cultures really do find different attributes attractive. But a more provocative interpretation is that culture teaches people what qualities they *think* they should like in others rather than the qualities that they genuinely like.

▲ All of these people likely came into the speed-dating context with ideas of what qualities they like in a partner. Turns out, however, that those preferences tell us little about who they end up being attracted to.

[CB2/ZOBWENN/New York City/United States/Newscom]

How can you tease apart people's reported preferences from their actual preferences? One method is to create a situation that resembles speed dating. Eastwick and colleagues (Eastwick, Eagly, et al., 2011; Eastwick, Finkel, & Eagly, 2011) had heterosexual men and women sit at individual tables as a parade of potential partners (or "dates") rotated through, spending about four minutes with each participant. Later, the participants were asked whom they would have liked to see again. The findings might surprise you: The traits the participants said mattered in a prospective romantic partner *failed* to predict how interested they were in others who had or did not have those qualities when they met them face-to-face.

Of course, speed-dating studies have their own limitations. One is that they don't tell us which traits people like in others whom they have known for a long time. In fact, one study of middle-aged participants currently in relationships showed that the match between their reported ideal traits in a romantic partner and their perceptions of their current partners was in fact a good predictor of how positively they viewed their partner and the relationship (Eastwick, Finkel, & Eagly, 2011).

Still, the point remains that what people *think* they find attractive is not always what they *do* find attractive. This discovery helps to explain why finding a date or friend on Tinder or Bumble might not work (Finkel et al., 2012b). You get some information about what the person is like before you even meet, which can seem very handy. But that information may not tell you whether things will go smoothly when you meet that person face-to-face and learn more about each other. For example, you might think you'd like someone who is extraverted, the life of the party, and open to experiences, but when you actually sit down with that person, you might find him or her to be obnoxious or exhausting.

Attraction to Those Who Fulfill Needs

Beyond being attractive because of their talents, achievements, and desirable traits, people can be attractive because they help to satisfy our psychological needs. One is the need to sustain faith in a worldview that gives meaning to life. Another is to maintain a strong sense of self-esteem. We like people who help validate these psychological resources. These include people who seem similar to us, who like us, and who flatter us. Let's look more closely at each.

Similarity in Attitudes and Personality   One of the strongest determinants of attraction is perceived similarity. As the old saying goes, "Birds of a feather flock together." People who become friends, lovers, and spouses tend to be similar in several dimensions, including socioeconomic status, age, geographic location, ethnic identity, looks, and personality (Byrne et al., 1966; Caspi & Herbener, 1990; Hinsz, 1989; Youyou et al., 2017). Let's look first at the power of similarity in attitudes and overall worldview.

Imagine Lana, a Republican Christian young woman who is against abortion and is a supporter of low taxes, a strong military, and gun rights. She likes country music, skiing, tennis, action movies, fine wine, and Italian food. She meets Rosa and Erica at a party. Rosa is a conservative Christian who supports the same issues and likes country music, tennis, action movies, fine clothes, and (OMG) Italian food. Erica is a liberal agnostic who is prochoice and antigun, and she likes hip-hop, basketball, independent art movies, kombucha tea, and gluten-free vegan cuisine. Which of these two is Lana going to like better and perhaps see as a potential new friend to hang out with? Rosa, of course. She validates Lana's beliefs about the way the world works, what good music sounds like, what makes for a good meal, and so forth. Erica, in contrast, challenges the validity of Lana's beliefs and preferences, threatening her worldview and self-esteem. Studies indeed show that people with similar attitudes are better liked and are more likely to become friends and romantic partners (Byrne, 1971; Griffitt & Veitch, 1974; Newcomb, 1956). In one early study, Newcomb (1956) found that when transfer students moved into a college dorm, those with similar attitudes were the most likely to end up getting along. Married couples who perceive their attitudes to be similar are likely to have more satisfying, longer-lasting marriages (Bentler & Newcomb, 1978; Cattell & Nesselroade, 1967; Houts et al., 1996). People are especially attracted to others who share their rare attitudes—that is, attitudes not shared by many others (Alves, 2018). Similarity in attitudes is so attractive that, if people feel like their values don't fit with the values of their community, they are motivated to pack up and move to another community (Motyl et al., 2014).

A few interesting notes about similarity. One is that casual friends and very close friends show the same level of similarity (Bahns et al., 2017). This finding suggests that once people have found someone who is "similar enough," the level of similarity matters less for their closeness and commitment. Another interesting finding is that the causal arrow works both ways. Just as perceived similarity increases attraction, attraction increases perceived similarity. If we like someone, we also tend to assume that we share similar attitudes (Miller & Marks, 1982). A third observation is that couples tend to think their attitudes are more similar than they actually are (Kenny & Acitelli, 2001; Murray, Holmes, et al., 2002). In fact, several studies show that what is important for attraction and relationship commitment is how much people *perceive* that they are similar to one another and not necessarily how similar they are from an objective point of view (Montoya et al., 2008). For example, people's initial

▼ We like to be around people who share our attitudes and interests because it validates our view of the world and ourselves.

[From left to right: © Tommy (Louth)/Alamy; Roger Cracknell 16/Glastonbury/Alamy; MARK RALSTON/Getty Images]

attraction in a speed-dating context and their satisfaction in long-term relationships are better predicted by perceived similarity than by actual similarity (Dyrenforth et al., 2010; Tidwell et al., 2013).

Do Opposites Ever Attract? At this point you might think, "Yeah, we like similar others. Who doesn't know that?" But isn't it sometimes the case that "opposites attract"? This idea has some intuitive appeal. Shouldn't someone who likes to make decisions get along with someone who doesn't? Shouldn't someone prone to emotional ups and downs fit with someone very even-keeled? Of course, dissimilar people sometimes do hit it off as friends or romantic partners, but most evidence suggests that this is more the exception than the rule.

However, a few studies show ways in which opposites may attract. One way is that highly masculine men tend to be attracted to highly feminine women (Orlofsky, 1982). In addition, Dryer and Horowitz (1997) found that, after a brief interaction, female students high in dominance (e.g., assertiveness) preferred a submissive (e.g., shy) partner, and females high in submissiveness preferred a dominant partner. These findings suggest that when it comes to the traits of dominance and submission, in particular, people are more attracted to those who complement them—that is, who are opposite—than to those who are similar. The same applies to fiscal habits: People who tend to scrimp and save often marry people who like to spend. Still, their different spending styles contribute to conflicts over finances, which reduce marital well-being (Rick et al., 2011). Other studies show that people partner up with a dissimilar other if they are looking for a short-term, low-commitment relationship, presumably because they find their differences to be novel and exciting (Amodio & Showers, 2005).

Tesser's (1988) self-evaluation maintenance model (described in chapter 6) suggests another way that dissimilarity can help a relationship. Friends or partners who are both strong in the same domains of abilities and accomplishments sometimes experience threatening social comparisons and friction. People may find it easier to get along if they are invested in different types of activities—if, for example, one partner is all about cooking and the other is into playing guitar. That way, each person can take pride in the other's accomplishments rather than experiencing self-esteem threat from them (Pilkington et al., 1991). One study supporting this idea showed that scientists had better relationships with their sons if the sons went into a field different from their own (Tesser, 1980).

Similarity in Perceptions So far, we've been talking about similarity (perceived or actual) in personality traits, demographic characteristics, behavioral preferences, and attitudes. These are all features of the self that William James called the "Me." But recall from chapter 5 that James divided the self into the *Me*—beliefs about ourselves—and the *I*—your experience of reality from moment to moment. According to Liz Pinel and colleagues (Pinel et al., 2004), we "Me-share" with others when we feel that we are the same kind of person, whereas we "I-share" with others when we believe that our subjective experiences of the world are the same, even if our "Me's" seem very different.

By way of example, your current author (Jeff) once joined a crew tasked with painting the interior of non-air-conditioned dorms in one blazingly hot summer in Dallas, Texas. Being an introverted liberal from New York, he developed a strong dislike for a boisterous, politically conservative crew member from Georgia. However, about two weeks into the job, this odd couple came to realize that they shared a rare love of Italian opera. They spent the rest of their time as fast friends, joyfully singing tunes from Verdi's *Aida* while painting, probably high on paint fumes.

This story illustrates how I-sharing can connect people so strongly that it can even lead them to look past the external differences that normally keep them separated. Research backs this up. In one study (Pinel & Long, 2012), heterosexual men were shown nonsensical associations between famous people and objects (e.g., "If Oprah Winfrey were a plant, what would she be?") and four possible responses (in this case: "Dried flower, Venus fly trap, Kudzu, or Red rose"). They were instructed to "go with their gut" and select the response that made sense to them. Immediately after making their response, they learned how two other participants—one straight, one gay—responded to the same association. In truth, there were no other participants. The feedback was set up to make it appear that one of the two others I-shared with the participant, picking the same "gut-level" responses nearly every time. Finally, they were asked which other participant they wanted to interact with. Without an opportunity to I-share, heterosexual men generally preferred to interact with the heterosexual man. This is unsurprising, since sexual orientation is an attribute of the "Me" and, as we've seen, similarity in "Me's" is normally appealing. In contrast, participants led to believe that they I-shared with the gay man instead preferred to hang out with *him*, despite having a dissimilar sexual orientation. They didn't care if he had a dissimilar "Me" if he seemed to experience reality in the same way that they do.

The idea that similarity can vary on both the "Me" level and the "I" level connects to an idea called **existential isolation**—the sense that one is alone in one's experience and that others cannot understand one's perspective. People may be physically surrounded by close others, so they don't seem to be alone, yet may feel existentially isolated if they sense that no one else shares their inner experience of the world (Helm et al., 2019; Pinel et al., 2017). Much like loneliness, existential isolation is distressing, so it's not surprising that we're attracted to people who seem to understand how we see the world.

If You Like Me, I'll Like You!   It's hard not to like people when they are willing to like you back. This is application of the norm of reciprocity (chapter 13) to liking. All else being equal, if you find out that someone else likes you (more than he or she likes others), it makes you more likely to like that person, too (Condon & Crano, 1988; Curtis & Miller, 1986; Eastwick et al., 2007). In one study, people's reports of how they fell in love or formed a friendship with a person indicated that a key factor was realizing that the other person liked them (Aron et al., 1989). Why do we reciprocate liking with liking? Think about the reward model mentioned earlier: Being liked bolsters our self-esteem, which feels good, thereby leading us to like those who like us. Another reason is that we expect someone who likes us to treat us well, so the anticipation of rewards enhances our liking for that person (Montoya & Insko, 2008).

Flattery   You might also suspect that we like those who compliment us, even to the point of flattery, and you would be right. The more nice things someone says about us, the more we like that person (Gordon, 1996; Jones, 1990). The benefits of flattery even extend to computers. When participants received randomly generated positive performance evaluations from a computer, they liked the computer better—even if they knew the positive evaluations were randomly generated and had nothing to do with their actual performance (Fogg & Nass, 1997).

Flattery doesn't always work, however. Think about times when flattery has made you feel uncomfortable or annoyed. What was different about those instances that made you react negatively? If it's obvious that a flatterer has

Achieve
Social Psych in Everyday Life:
Faqryza

Existential isolation The sense that one is alone in one's experience and that others cannot understand one's perspective. One can feel existentially isolated even with many social interactions.

THINK ABOUT

an ulterior motive, compliments from that person are not attractive (Gordon, 1996; Matsumura & Ohtsubo, 2012). Still, we generally prefer someone who says nice things about us (even if that person's motives are suspect) to someone who doesn't have anything nice to say at all (Drachman et al., 1978). This is because any compliment will still make us feel good (Chan & Sengupta, 2010). We usually are more motivated to embrace positive feedback than to question its validity (Jones, 1964, 1990; Vonk, 2002).

Aronson and Linder's **gain-loss theory** (1965) added an interesting twist to our tendency to like those who flatter us. They observed that in some contexts, a compliment from someone who has criticized you in the past is more surprising and thus more potent than a compliment from a friend or spouse who has had only good things to say about you. Aronson and Linder tested this hypothesis by having participants overhear a series of evaluations of them by a discussion partner (in reality, a confederate). Depending on which condition they were randomly assigned to, participants received evaluations that fell into one of four patterns: consistently positive, consistently negative, initially negative and then becoming positive (gain), and initially positive and becoming negative (loss). The participants liked the confederate best in the "gain" condition, second best in the consistently positive condition, even less in the consistently negative condition, and least in the "loss" condition.

Aronson and Linder noted that this phenomenon may put a long-term spouse at a disadvantage relative to new people the spouse meets: The spouse's compliments will have less impact, but criticisms will have more impact. Married 10 years, Rondae may compliment his wife, Renée, on how nice she looks to little apparent effect as they head to a party, and then observe that she is quite overtly pleased when someone at the party says the same thing.

Gain-loss theory A theory of attraction which posits that liking is highest for others when they increase their positivity toward you over time.

SECTION REVIEW The Basics of Interpersonal Attraction

Several factors affect how we choose others with whom we form close relationships.

Proximity	The Reward Model of Liking	Attributes of the Person	Our Psychological Needs
• Physical proximity is an important factor in developing relationships. Proximity's power is due in part to the mere exposure effect.	• People like others whom they associate with positive feelings and dislike those associated with negative feelings.	• People like those who remind them of others they like. • People like those with culturally valued attributes and personality traits. • People's self-reports of personal traits they prefer are surprisingly weak predictors of liking.	People tend to like others who fulfill their needs for meaning and self-esteem. Specifically, those who: • Are perceived as similar to the self in attitudes, personality, and subjective experience, though opposites can attract under particular conditions • Reciprocate liking • Flatter them

Physical Attractiveness

In 2010, the CNN correspondent and blogger Jack Cafferty posed the following question: "What does it mean that despite the worst recession since the Great Depression, Americans spent more than $10 billion on cosmetic procedures last year?" Although many Americans worried about health care costs, employment, and the like, they still managed to spend what money they had on tucking their tummies, enlarging their breasts, and chiseling their cheekbones—in short, making themselves appear more physically attractive. In fact, Americans collectively spent the same amount that some economists estimate it would cost to provide universal schooling. So to answer Cafferty's question: Clearly, physical attractiveness is important to people.

The Importance of Physical Appearance

Just how important are people's looks to liking someone? Is it important enough to influence who we decide to put in charge of leading our country? Todorov and colleagues (2005) showed students photographs of two of the major political candidates from each of 95 different Senate races and 600 different races for the House of Representatives in the United States (see **FIGURE 14.1**). Simply by viewing these candidates' pictures and judging how competent they looked, students correctly guessed the winner of each contest in 72% of the Senate races and 67% of the House races.

If physical appearance can have such a potent influence on political decisions, just imagine how important it is for our interpersonal decisions. As you

Which person is the more competent?

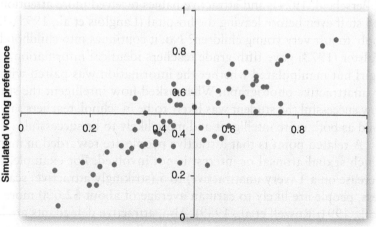

Inferred competence from faces

Figure 14.1

Looks Like a Winner

Here are some pictures of politicians, chosen at random. Does their appearance tell you anything about their competence? The graph underneath, adapted from Todorov and colleagues (2005), shows that political candidates judged to look more competent by one group of participants were more likely to be chosen in a mock election by another group of participants.

[Data from Todorov et al., 2005]

probably would guess, people who are more physically attractive are also more popular and date more frequently (Berscheid et al., 1971; Reis et al., 1980). But is physical attractiveness more important than other factors in determining whether a relationship gets off the ground? The short answer, at least in terms of the spark that gets the relationship going, is "yes." For most people heading off to a blind date, the physical attractiveness of their partner is going to be the most important factor influencing whether they want to have a second date. However, as we will see later, after we meet and get to know another person, attractiveness matters less for sustaining our interest over time.

Physical attractiveness is important for a variety of reasons. From the perspective of the reward model, it may be simply more pleasant to look at attractive people. In fact, even infants gaze more at attractive adult faces (Langlois et al., 1991). Another reason is that physical appearance is typically the first attribute we come to know about a person. It takes much less time to assess someone's looks—as little as 0.15 seconds—than his or her honesty, intelligence, and other qualities (Zajonc, 1998). Also, the more attractive is the person we're with, the more likely it is that other people will form positive impressions of us (Sigall & Landy, 1973).

The Physical Attractiveness Stereotype, AKA the Halo Effect

Another reason we might care about someone's attractiveness is that we assume it will mean that they have other positive characteristics. Despite the cultural maxim to "never judge a book by its cover," in Western cultures people see beautiful people (compared with those of average attractiveness) as happier, warmer, more dominant, mature, mentally healthy, and more outgoing, intelligent, sensitive, confident, and successful—though not more honest, concerned for others, or modest (e.g., Eagly et al., 1991; Feingold, 1992b; Langlois et al., 2000). This tendency to see attractive people as having positive traits, to see beautiful as good in a global sense, is referred to as a *physical attractiveness stereotype*, or **halo effect** (Anderson & Nida, 1978; Cash & Trimer, 1984; Dion et al., 1972). For example, people evaluated an essay purportedly written by an attractive person more positively than the same essay when it was purportedly written by an unattractive person (Landy & Sigall, 1974).

Halo effect A tendency to assume that people with one positive attribute (e.g., who are physically attractive) also have other positive traits.

The Reach of the Attractive Advantage   Is it simply that people judge attractive people more positively because they want to hook up with them? No, the halo effect biases how people perceive and treat pretty much anyone. Studies show that cuter premature infants were treated better in hospitals and consequently fared better than their less cute fellow preemies (Badr & Abdallah, 2001); young children showed preferences for other attractive children (Dion & Berscheid, 1974); and attractive babies received more attention from parents and staff even before leaving the hospital (Langlois et al., 1995). Does the effect apply to just very young children? No, it continues into childhood. Clifford and Walster (1973) gave fifth-grade teachers identical information about a boy or a girl but manipulated whether the information was paired with an attractive or unattractive photograph. When asked how intelligent the student was and how successful the student was likely to be in school, teachers saw the attractive child as both more intelligent and more likely to be successful.

A related point is that attractive people are rewarded in many contexts in which sexual arousal or interest is not involved. For example, for each point increase on a 1 (very unattractive) to 5 (strikingly attractive) scale of attractiveness, people are likely to earn an average of about $2,000 more a year (Frieze et al., 1991; Roszell et al., 1989). Also, attractive defendants are less likely than unattractive defendants to be found guilty when accused of a crime (Efran,

1974), and when they are found guilty, they are given lighter sentences (Stewart, 1980). This bias is strongest in jurors who rely on their emotions and gut-level reactions in their decision making (Gunnell & Ceci, 2010).

In an interesting twist, stereotypes about attractive people can sometimes cause them to be discriminated against. Many people believe that attractive individuals have a greater sense of entitlement, meaning that they expect good things to come to them. That might be why, when people are making hiring decisions for undesirable jobs, they are less likely to hire attractive (versus less attractive) candidates. People making employment decisions may assume that an attractive candidate will feel entitled to positive conditions and treatment, so when the job is menial, they think an attractive candidate will be dissatisfied and complain (Lee et al., 2018).

Is the Attractiveness Stereotype True? The answer to this question is complex. On the one hand, attractive people are not higher in self-esteem, life satisfaction, or mental health (Diener et al., 1995; Major et al., 1984; Sparacino & Hansell, 1979). Nor is there strong evidence that physically attractive people are more intelligent (Feingold, 1992b).

However, there is one way in which the attractiveness stereotype is somewhat true: attractive people are generally more outgoing, popular, and socially skilled (Feingold, 1992b; Langlois et al., 2000). For example, when researchers conducted phone interviews with attractive versus unattractive people, more attractive people were rated by interviewers as more likable and socially skilled, despite the fact that the interviewers did not know what they looked like (Goldman & Lewis, 1977).

But why? Is it because attractive people are, in fact, more socially skilled? Or is it because those who are beautiful get special treatment that then makes them more socially skilled? Snyder and colleagues (1977) set up a study to find out. They had male and female participants talk to one another over an intercom without having met first in person. Before a conversation, a male participant was given some information about a female participant, including a photograph. The photograph depicted either a very attractive or a rather unattractive woman, but in actuality, the photograph was of a different person. The woman's recorded responses were later coded by independent judges who did not know what the study was about. The researchers wondered whether men treated women differently depending on how they thought the women looked, and whether the women would respond by acting differently.

When the male participant thought he was talking to an attractive woman, the independent judges rated her more positively (e.g., friendlier and more open). Thinking that he was talking to an attractive woman, the male participant was more pleasant and elicited pleasantness in return. This effect occurred when women conversed with men they thought were attractive or unattractive (Andersen & Bem, 1981). Indeed, meta-analyses have found that people are equally positive in their treatment of attractive men and women (Eagly et al., 1991; Feingold, 1992b; Langlois et al., 2000).

Why Do We Associate Beautiful with Good? Where does the beautiful-is-good stereotype come from? One source of this stereotype is the culture in which we live (Dion et al., 1972). From our earliest moments in life, we are bombarded with images, stories, and fairy tales that convey a clear and simple message: Good people are good looking; bad people are ugly. Overwhelmingly the good princess is beautiful and the hero handsome, whereas the evil witch and villain are ugly. In *Star Wars*, when Anakin Skywalker chooses the dark side of the Force, his good looks are masked in robotic, menacing armor. Think about your favorite childhood movie or fairy tale book. How were the principal characters portrayed?

◀ **THINK ABOUT**

[RKO Radio Pictures/Photofest]

Analyses of popular movies support this cultural media explanation. Smith and colleagues (1999) found a positive correlation between how physically attractive a movie's main character was and how virtuous and successful the character was. In a second study, they showed college students a film reinforcing the beautiful-is-good stereotype. Subsequently, the students were asked to give their impression of two people they thought were applicants to graduate school. They thought more highly of the physically attractive applicant than the less attractive applicant, even though the two applicants had similar academic credentials.

If the physical attractiveness stereotype is at least partly a product of our culture, then we should expect it to vary along cultural lines. And to a certain extent it does. People associate beauty with traits that their culture generally defines as positive and valuable. So in North America and other Western cultures, this means seeing beautiful people as friendly, independent, and assertive. But when researchers gave Korean students pictures of attractive Koreans, they did not see them as having characteristics such as potency, which Americans value (Wheeler & Kim, 1997). Rather, Korean students judged attractive Koreans as being more honest and concerned for others—precisely the traits that are valued in that culture.

Common Denominators of Attractive Faces

"Beauty is in the eye of the beholder." This popular saying suggests that people have very different notions of who is physically attractive. Is it true? There are some important differences among individuals, cultures, and historical periods in perceptions of what is attractive (Darwin, 1872; Landau, 1989; Newman, 2000; Wiggins et al., 1968). Just look at magazines such as *People* and *Maxim*, which select the year's most attractive celebrities and models, and you will see that the rankings change substantially from year to year, depending on passing trends and pop-cultural events.

On the other hand, research shows that people agree about who is (and isn't) physically attractive much more than they disagree (Langlois et al., 2000; Marcus & Miller, 2003). This consensus holds both across cultures and within a culture over time. For example, when Latino, Asian, Black, and White men rated the attractiveness of different women in pictures, there was some variability in preferred body shape, but in general, the correlations across the groups exceeded 0.90 (Cunningham et al., 1995). This indicates strong agreement in perceptions of who is hot and who is not. What's more, newborn infants—too young to be aware of their culture's local beauty standards—prefer to gaze longer at the faces that adults find attractive than at those adults find unattractive (Langlois et al., 1987, 1991; Slater et al., 2000). But what exactly makes those faces so lovely?

Facial "Averageness" and Symmetry Beautiful faces seem to stand out from the crowd, so we might infer that attractive faces have unique features. Think again. To be attractive is actually to have quite average facial features. Researchers studying attraction have used computer-imaging software to superimpose images of faces on top of each other, thereby creating composite faces that represent the digital "average" of the individual faces (see **FIGURE 14.2**). Both men and women rate these composite faces as more attractive than nearly all of the individual faces that make them up, leading to what is known as the **averageness effect** (Langlois & Roggman, 1990; Rhodes, 2006). Also, the more faces that are combined to create a composite face, the more attractive that face is perceived to be.

Averageness effect The tendency to perceive a composite image of multiple faces that have been photographically averaged as more attractive than any individual face included in that composite.

Figure 14.2

The Allure of "Average" Faces

If you digitally average original photos of faces (like the three farthest left), the result is a composite face (the fourth photo on the right). The more real faces that are used to create the composite face, the more attractive the composite face is deemed to be. Evolutionary psychologists argue that we are attracted to these "average" faces because they signal good health and thus good mating potential.

[David Ian Perrett, University of St. Andrews]

Do these findings mean that to be attractive is to have bland, ordinary looks? Not at all. These composite faces are actually quite unusual (that's why we put "average" in quotes): Their features are all proportional to one another; no nose is remarkably big or small; no cheeks are puffy or sunken. In short, nothing about these composite faces is exaggerated, underdeveloped, or odd.

Another similar feature of faces that both men and women find attractive is bilateral symmetry (Thornhill & Gangestad, 1993). Symmetry occurs when the two sides of the face are mirror images of one another (**FIGURE 14.3**). You might think that you have a symmetrical face; after all, you probably have one eye on the right side of your face and another eye on the left. Yes, but look more closely—perhaps with the help of a computer, as researchers have done—and you will find numerous asymmetries: Your eyes are slightly different in shape, size, and position on your face, your cheekbones are at slightly different angles, and, if you are like the current author, one of your nostrils has a bigger circumference than the other. All things being equal, the more symmetrical a face, the more people find it attractive.

The preference for "average" and symmetrical faces is universal. Men and women from all over the world—North America, China, Nigeria, India, and Japan—agree that "average," symmetrical faces are more attractive than faces with exaggerated features or asymmetries (Rhodes et al., 2002). Why do we see such widespread agreement? One influential answer comes from evolutionary psychology. Throughout human evolution and up to the present day, a big challenge to successful reproduction is finding a healthy person with whom to mate. Because diseases and developmental disorders can be passed on genetically, our ancestors who mated with healthy (versus unhealthy) partners were more likely to have healthy offspring, who themselves went on to reproduce and populate the gene pool.

But how can we tell whether a potential mate is in good health? One indicator may be facial features. When people are developing *in utero* (in the womb) before birth, their genes are normally set up to create a symmetrical face and body, with no feature badly out of proportion. Yet if people are exposed to pathogens, parasites, or viruses during development, they can be born with irregular and asymmetric features of the face and body. For example, the more infectious diseases experienced by a mother during pregnancy, the more likely her infant is to have asymmetries in the face and body (Livshits & Kobyliansky, 1991). Research also shows that men and women with more symmetrical faces are, indeed, healthier (e.g., suffer from fewer infections) and more fertile than are people whose faces are less symmetrical (Jasienska et al., 2006; Soler et al., 2003; Thornhill & Gangestad, 2006; although see Kalick et al., 1998, and Rhodes et al., 2001).

Figure 14.3

The Importance of Symmetry

Which of these faces do you find most attractive? People tend to rate more symmetrical faces as more attractive. Some psychologists say that this preference stems from an innate tendency to search for healthy mates.

[Republished with permission of SAGE Publications, from Rhodes, G., Sumich, A., & Byatt, G. (1999). Are average facial configurations attractive only because of their symmetry? Psychological Science, 10(1), 52-58. doi: 10.1111/1467-9280.00106. Permission conveyed through Copyright Clearance Center, Inc.]

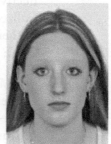

Asymmetrical   Original   Symmetrical

Although this evolutionary perspective on the allure of averageness and symmetry has some appeal, another explanation is that more average-appearing and symmetrical faces simply seem more familiar. Remember the mere exposure effect? Well, in a sense, an "average" face is the one you've been exposed to most often, and so, all else equal, you should like it. In fact, people who grew up around each other tend to agree more in their ratings of facial attractiveness than do people from different regions (Bronstad & Russell, 2007). These differences make sense if we think about attraction as being shaped by who we are commonly exposed to, but they are hard to explain from the perspective that everyone is born with the same innate preference. More recent studies show that computer-generated "typical" faces are perceived as more trustworthy— that is, as safer and less hostile (Sofer et al., 2015). So maybe the preference for "average" faces reflects a general liking of familiarity rather than an evolved sensitivity to signals of health.

Do Men and Women Differ in What They Find Attractive? An Evolutionary Perspective

Up to this point, we've mostly been talking about the attributes and characteristics that are generally seen as attractive. But of course, because attraction is often about finding a romantic partner, it's important to consider the role of a person's sex, sexual orientation, and gender identity in what characteristics people are attracted to. In this section, we'll focus on the different features and attributes that heterosexual women and men tend to find attractive in a partner. Most of the research has focused on attraction among **cis-gender** heterosexual individuals, people who identify with the gender that is consistent with their assigned sex at birth. Researchers are beginning to examine attraction among those who are attracted to partners of the same sex, and this newer work will be summarized later in this chapter. More work needs to be done examining attraction among **transgender** individuals. An interesting question to consider is whether the differences in what people find attractive are more a function of their designated sex at birth (e.g., female, male), their gender identity (e.g., identifying as a woman or a man), or the sex or gender of the target of their attraction. As you read though this next section summarizing heterosexual relationships, give this some thought.

The psychologist David Buss (1989) asked thousands of men and women in 37 cultures what they found attractive in a romantic partner. Across these cultures, men and women gave their highest rating—and equally high ratings—to kindness, dependability, a good sense of humor, and a pleasant disposition. But there were some gender differences. An evolutionary perspective sheds light on these differences. It suggests that, over the course of evolutionary history, males and females both were motivated to reproduce, but they faced different reproductive challenges. As a result, men and women evolved to have different, specialized preferences in their mates that favor the conception, birth, and survival of their offspring (Buss & Schmitt, 1993; Gangestad & Simpson, 2000; Geary, 2010; Trivers, 1972).

For Men, Signs of Fertility An evolutionary perspective suggests that the challenge men face when attempting to reproduce is finding a mate who is *fertile*—put simply, capable of producing offspring. This is difficult, however, because in humans, fertility does not involve outward signs, such as reddened skin, as it does in some other species. It needs to be inferred, and one useful

Cis-gender Heterosexual individuals who identify with the gender that is consistent with their assigned sex at birth.

Transgender People who identify with a gender that is different from their assigned sex at birth.

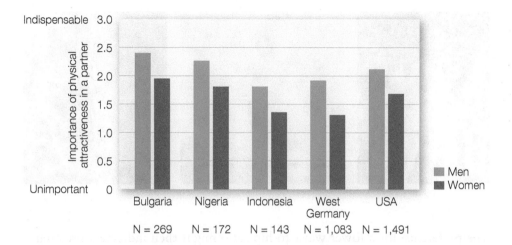

Figure 14.4

Gender Differences in Desire for Physically Attractive Partners

Across 37 cultures, men reported desiring physical attractiveness in a romantic partner more than women did.
[Data from Buss & Schmitt, 1993]

clue is a woman's age. Women are not fertile until puberty, and their fertility ends after they reach menopause around age 50. As our species evolved, men who were attracted to features of women's faces and bodies that signal that they are young (but not too young) were more likely to find a fertile mate and successfully reproduce. Those attracted to women with other features were less successful in populating the gene pool. As a result, those preferences may be built into modern heterosexual men's genetic inheritance (Buss, 1989, 2016). Indeed, across many cultures, men are attracted to cues to youth and fertility (Walter et al., 2020). They not only prefer their sexual partners to be younger than themselves, they also like youthful facial features: large eyes, a small nose, a small chin, and full lips (Cunningham et al., 2002; Jones, 1995). In addition, men, more than women, prefer their partners to be physically attractive (Buss, 2008; Buss & Schmitt, 1993; Feingold, 1992a; Geary, 2010; see **FIGURE 14.4**). When men were given pictures of and background information on potential dating partners, they were more likely than women to base their preferences on appearance, selecting the more attractive women (Feingold, 1990).

Another physical feature that serves as a cue to fertility in women is waist-to-hip ratio (**FIGURE 14.5**). If you measure the circumference of your waist at its narrowest point and divide that by the circumference of your hips at your broadest point, the number you get is your waist-to-hip ratio. Men are most attracted to women's bodies with a waist-to-hip ratio of 0.7—a very curvy "hourglass" figure in which the waist is 30% narrower than the hips (Furnham et al., 2005; Singh, 1993). This preference seems to hold even in cultures and time periods where people were or are generally more attracted to voluptuous women (Pettijohn & Jungeberg, 2004; Silverstein et al., 1986; Singh & Luis, 1995; Wiseman et al., 1992).

Some research has suggested that this lower waist-to-hip ratio might indicate a particular mix of hormones (estradiol and progesterone) that allows women to become pregnant more easily and to enjoy better physical health than do women with less curvy bodies (Lassek & Gaulin, 2008). However, newer work puts a different spin on waist-to-hip ratio as a cue to fertility. Across societies, and controlling for women's age and overall size, women have a larger waist-to-hip ratio as they give birth to more children (Butovskaya et al., 2017).

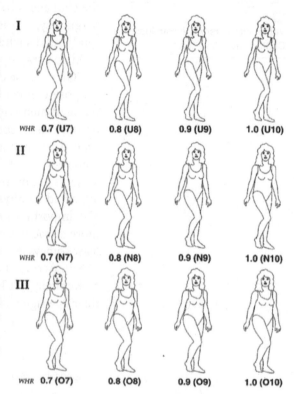

Figure 14.5

Waist-to-Hip Ratio

When people are asked to judge which of these women is most attractive, the average preference is usually a woman with a 0.7 ratio of waist to hip.

▶ Over time, standards of attractiveness for the overall size of women's bodies have changed, but the ideal of a 0.7 waist-to-hip ratio has remained fairly constant. Today, films like *Wonder Woman* (Jenkins, 2017) try to draw large audiences by featuring actresses like Gal Gadot wearing outfits that highlight this ideal waist-to-hip ratio.

[From left to right: Art Media/Print Collector/Getty Images; Hulton Archive/Getty Images; Warner Bros./Photofest]

 Achieve
Video: Interpersonal Attraction: Clothes that Make the Man

The preference for a lower waist-to-hip ratio might then indicate a preference for women who have not yet had children over those who have.

For Women, Signs of Masculinity and Power   From an evolutionary perspective, women do not need to be as concerned as men are with finding a youthful partner because men's fertility is less bound to their age. What, then, were the challenges to reproduction that women faced? During the many months of pregnancy, it was more difficult for them to go out on their own to forage for food, build shelters, and fend off predators. What's more, they had to nurse the child and stay by its side to ensure that it didn't die.

Given these challenges to survival and reproduction, what attributes do you suppose women looked for when evaluating potential mates? They might have pursued men with good financial status and resources who could be counted on to invest resources in protecting and providing for them and their offspring. Indeed, women around the globe say that a man's income is very important in who they are attracted to (see **FIGURE 14.6**). In studies of online dating, wealthier guys get more e-mails from the ladies (Hitsch et al., 2010). Women are also attracted to physical features they associate with physical strength. Height is also important in standards of male attractiveness. Taller men tend to be seen as more attractive, and for many women, it's especially important that a man be at least somewhat taller than she if he is a dating prospect (Shepperd & Strathman, 1989). Across cultures, women look for men who are slightly older (Grøntvedt & Kennair, 2013; Kenrick & Keefe, 1992; Walter et al., 2020), perhaps because their age signals social power.

Figure 14.6

Gender Differences in Desire for Partners with Good Financial Prospects

Across cultures, women were more likely than men to say that they look for romantic partners with financial status and resources.

[Data from Buss & Schmitt, 1993]

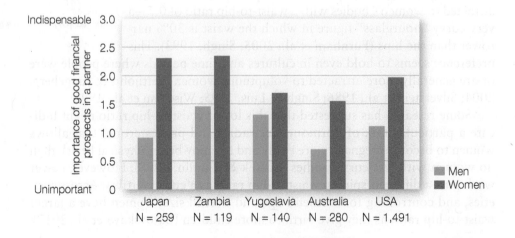

The strongest evidence of the evolutionary perspective can be found in studies on women's mate preferences at different times of their monthly menstrual cycle. Women are fertile for only a few days preceding ovulation each month. This is the time when they are most likely to conceive if they have sex (except where the Pill and other forms of contraception are used), and so it also is the time when issues of genetic transmission are most relevant. During the ovulatory phase of the menstrual cycle (compared to other phases), women report preferring more masculine faces—that is, faces with strong jaws and broad foreheads (think George Clooney) rather than youthful boyishness (think Tobey Maguire) (Penton-Voak et al., 1999). They also prefer men who have deeper, more masculine voices (Puts, 2005) and who present themselves as more assertive, confident, and dominant (Gangestad et al., 2004, 2007; Macrae et al., 2002).

▲ When women are at their peak fertility, they are more attracted to men with very masculine features (e.g., George Clooney) than to men with baby-faced features (e.g., Tobey Maguire).
[Left: Elisabetta A. Villa/WireImage/Getty Images; right: Jean-Paul Aussenard/WireImage/Getty Images]

The theoretical explanation for these ovulatory shifts in women's mate preferences is that, over the millennia, women who mated with men who were more dominant were more successful at propagating their genes. Men also seem to pick up on women's fertility unconsciously and play the part of the dominant man. Men who sniffed T-shirts worn by women who were in the fertile phase of their cycle showed a bigger spike in their testosterone levels than did men who sniffed T-shirts worn by women who were not fertile (Miller & Maner, 2010). This boost in testosterone is thought to prompt men to engage in more dominant and risk-taking behaviors that might increase their chance of being attractive to and mating with fertile women. Women might also use subtle cues to pick up on other women's fertility, helping them to guard their guys. After viewing photographs of other ovulating or non-ovulating women, women with desirable partners felt like avoiding women who were in the fertile phase of their menstrual cycle (Krems et al., 2016).

Questions and Controversies About the Evolutionary Perspective Do findings like those just discussed mean that there are fundamental, built-in, or hardwired differences between men and women in the characteristics they find attractive in potential partners? Not necessarily. This is a very strong claim, and you might not be surprised to hear that the evolutionary perspective on mate preferences has sparked considerable controversy. Researchers debate the role of innate mechanisms and other influences. Here are some points to keep in mind when critically evaluating claims about innate attraction preferences:

- *Inconsistent data*: The evidence supporting the gender differences we've discussed is sometimes mixed. There is disagreement, for example, about whether women's mate preferences vary by ovulatory cycle. In 2014, two different meta-analyses drew quite different conclusions about the strength of the evidence for these effects (Gildersleeve et al., 2014; Wood et al., 2014). A large preregistered study published in 2018, however, found evidence that women are in fact most interested in sex during the fertile peak of their ovulatory cycle (Arslan et al., 2018). However, these changes were not strongly related to her partner's behavior or attractiveness, as some past theorists have presumed. Other researchers have criticized the methods used in this area of research, leading to debate in the literature about how robust these ovulatory effects on mate preferences really are (Jones et al., 2019).

■ *Differences can be small*: Although there very well may be some biologically driven components to attraction that differentiate the sexes, it's important to remember that men and women are far more similar than they are different in terms of the attributes they rate as highly preferable in a romantic partner. In every culture, both sexes look for partners who are warm and loyal, and these qualities are rated as more important than physical attractiveness and status (Buss, 1989; Tran et al., 2008). Men's and women's preferences get even more similar in cultures with greater gender equality (Conroy-Beam et al., 2015; Walter et al., 2020). If we focus solely on the differences, we risk losing the broader perspective on human attraction (Hanel et al., 2019). When evaluating a potential mate, we don't judge the person on any single attribute; rather, we consider lots of qualities that make up the person as a whole. Attraction stems from an intricate web of influences derived from each person's biology, culture, and immediate social context.

■ *Limits of self-report*: In many studies on gender differences, men and women indicate the attributes they *think* they find attractive. It turns out that when people actually meet and interact face-to-face, they don't always show the same differences in their likes and dislikes (Walster, Aronson, Abrahams, & Rottman, 1966). Eastwick and Finkel (2008) had participants take part in a speed-dating paradigm where each had very brief face-to-face interactions with several interaction partners. Before the session, men more than women *said* they valued physical attractiveness, but when it came to choosing a live dating partner, men and women were *equally* influenced by physical attractiveness. In fact, a recent meta-analysis confirms that once live interaction occurs with a potential romantic partner, physical attractiveness is equally predictive of liking and interest for men and women (Eastwick et al., 2014). The same is true for the gender difference in focus on wealth and status. Once live interaction with a potential partner occurs, the wealth and status of a potential partner are only slightly influential, and they are equally influential for women and men (Eastwick et al., 2014). As we've seen throughout this textbook, people don't always know what they really want.

■ *Alternative explanations*: Even when there is good evidence to support certain differences in what men and women find attractive, remember that an evolutionary perspective provides only one explanation for them. Take, for example, the finding that women say they prefer men of higher status. Why else might that be? Women's preference for higher-status men makes rational sense in a historic or cultural context in which women rely on men for protection and support (Eagly & Wood, 1999; Wood & Eagly, 2002, 2007). But although it historically has been the case that men have had disproportionate if not exclusive control over material resources and economic and political power, women have gained greater access to equal opportunities in recent decades. The sociocultural perspective suggests that in societies with greater gender equality—that is, societies in which women's occupation of powerful positions and their earning capacity are similar to men's—the greater female emphasis on finding a mate with status and economic resources should be reduced, and in fact it is (Conroy-Beam et al., 2015; Eagly & Diekman, 2003; Stanik & Ellsworth, 2010; Walter et al., 2020; Wood & Eagly, 2002; Zentner & Mitura, 2012). And although men and women both prefer physically attractive mates for a short-term fling (Li & Kenrick, 2006), more economically successful women also report prioritizing men's physical attractiveness when considering them for a long-term relationship (Eagly & Wood, 1999; Gangestad, 1993). It's difficult to explain this cross-cultural variability in patterns with a purely evolutionary account focused on innate preferences that evolved over thousands of years. It seems instead that women report caring more than men do about pursuing desirable resources through their partners when they expect to have relatively lower social and economic status.

Attraction in Same-Sex Relationships

I was wild for her. I don't know how to describe it. It was everything. It was just more so. . . . We had very different passions, but we both had enormous love for each other's passions. She played the violin. She played golf. And she did them both obsessively. With golf I had to make certain rules, because if she came home talking her head off about every shot, I would say, "The idea is for you to go and enjoy it and discuss it completely and *then* come home." (HICKLIN, 2011)

▲ Edith Windsor, holding a picture of herself and her wife, Thea Spyer.
[Chester Higgins Jr/The New York Times/Redux Pictures]

Edith Windsor (1929–2017) was an influential gay-rights activist who helped bring about the 2015 Supreme Court ruling for marriage equality. In this quote, she describes her attraction to her late wife Thea Spyer. When Thea died of multiple sclerosis in 2009, Edith was denied the federal inheritance-tax exemptions typically afforded with heterosexual marriages. She was the plaintiff in a landmark lawsuit that ultimately led to the repeal of the Defense of Marriage Act (*United States v. Windsor*, 2013).

Edith's description of her attraction to Thea reveals many of the same factors that influence heterosexual attraction. In fact, the factors that predict attraction in gay and lesbian relationships are often quite similar to those that predict attraction in heterosexual relationships (Diamond, 2018). People, whether they are gay, straight, or bisexual, generally are attracted to people who provide affection, are dependable, and have shared interests (Peplau & Fingerhut, 2007).

The overall similarity between heterosexual and same-sex attraction is evident in other ways as well. Whereas men, regardless of sexual orientation, tend to report emphasizing physical attractiveness, women, regardless of sexual orientation, are more likely to report emphasizing personality characteristics (Peplau & Spalding, 2000). This gender difference notwithstanding, there are interesting nuances in what gay men and lesbians consider attractive. Studies of personal ads reveal that many gay men look for masculine traits and partners who adopt what are typically masculine roles (Bailey et al., 1997). For gay men, physical appearance (in particular, a lean, muscular build) is especially important when evaluating prospects for short-term as opposed to long-term relationships (Varangis et al., 2012).

In contrast, whereas lesbians look for partners with feminine characteristics, they don't necessarily want partners who assume what are typically feminine roles (Bailey et al., 1997). Indeed, perhaps because lesbians eschew typical gender roles, the physique they report as being most attractive is less close to the thin ideal promoted by the mass media and often preferred by heterosexual men (Swami & Tovee, 2006).

There are a couple of points of caution in drawing conclusions from research in this area. One is simply that little research has been carried out on same-sex attraction. There is a great need for more research on the topic (Diamond, 2018).

▲ Cultures vary in the kind of ornamentation people use to enhance their attractiveness.

[From left to right: Veronique DURRUTY/ Gamma-Rapho via Getty Images; Angelo Giampiccolo/Shutterstock; Dan Kitwood/Getty Images; Trinette Reed/Blend Images/Alamy]

Second, sexuality researchers have noted that both men and women show some degree of fluidity in their sexual orientation. In longitudinal studies, between 25 and 65% of participants have reported some change in their attraction to same- or other-gender partners across a 10- to 15-year time period (Diamond, 2016). Women often report greater fluidity in their sexual attraction, although it's not clear if this is simply because same-gender attraction is viewed as more stigmatizing for men than for women (Herek & McLemore, 2013). As an increasing number of people identify as non-binary or gender fluid, the science of attraction will need to expand its traditional approach to contrasting women's and men's preferences.

Cultural and Situational Influences on Attractiveness

Despite the cross-cultural consistency in what people find physically attractive, there is also plenty of variability. As you've likely noticed, there are considerable cultural and subcultural differences in what people find fetching (e.g., Darwin, 1872; Fallon, 1990; Ford & Beach, 1951; Hebl & Heatherton, 1998). In some cultures, people like nose rings, in other cultures filed teeth; lily-white skin and stretched necks are turn-ons in some cultures but distasteful in others. The list goes on.

Standards of beauty also vary within the same culture over time. For example, a study of *Playboy* centerfolds from 1953 to 2001 showed a trend toward thinner figures and a lower bust-to-waist ratio (Voracek & Fisher, 2002).

How can we explain cultural variations in preferences?

Status and Access to Scarce Resources Attributes that are associated with having high status in a given culture are often seen as more attractive. Consider the current preference for tanned skin among Caucasian Americans (Chung et al., 2010). In days gone by, those lower in socioeconomic status worked outside as manual laborers. As a result, they tended to be more tanned than their financially well-off counterparts, and it seems, at least for the upper class, pale skin tones were culturally valued and considered attractive. But the Industrial Revolution and the consequent proliferation of factories changed those standards by moving many low-paying jobs indoors. Today, tan skin isn't a sign that you labor outdoors; it says that you are high enough in status to get out of your cubicle and vacation in the Caribbean. Put differently, pale or tan skin may not be inherently attractive; they may simply be signals to others that one is high status. Take a look at the two images of the young woman and think about which one you find more attractive.

THINK ABOUT ▶

[Alberto Zornetta/Shutterstock]

Body size and weight are similarly influenced by cultural trends and values. In cultures and societies in which resources such as food are scarce, men tend to prefer heavier women, but in cultures and societies with an abundance of resources, men prefer thinner women (Anderson et al., 1992; Sobal & Stunkard, 1989). These examples illustrate a useful way to understand cultural variations: People are attracted to whatever happens to be scarce or in high demand at that time in their society. As those conditions change, so do preferences.

Nelson and Morrison (2005) took this idea one step further. They reasoned that scarcity would influence attraction not only across cultures but from one situation to the next. They interviewed heterosexual men either before they entered or after they came out of the dining hall at their university. Walking into the cafeteria and presumably hungry, men estimated that an ideal partner would weigh about 125.5 pounds. After they had chowed down and were no longer hungry, their preferences were more in the ballpark of 123 pounds (a small but statistically reliable difference).

Media Effects   Perhaps the most potent source of cultural influences on perceptions of attractiveness is the media. Billboards, television shows, movies, magazines, and the Internet all routinely expose us to an endless parade of images of attractive people, especially women. In an interesting twist, women are less likely to be represented in some mass media such as feature films and television, but when they are, they are more likely to be physically attractive and dressed in revealing clothing (Smith et al., 2013). This raises questions about how such exposure affects how we view others and ourselves.

In 1980, not many people had cable or satellite television, most people had just a handful of channels, there were no DVRs, and there were no shows streaming over the Internet (and, well, there was no Internet)— let alone handheld devices to watch them on. (Yes, it was a bleak time.) You watched what was on one of the three or four channels you could tune in, and you got up to turn a knob when you wanted to surf those several channels. Maybe you've seen the 2019 movie *Charlie's Angels*, but did you know that it was a remake of a one of the most popular TV shows from the 1980s? The original show centered on the adventures of three very attractive crime-solving women. It also formed the basis for a naturalistic study by Kenrick and Gutierres (1980). The researchers sent two confederates to the common TV areas in dorms (as practically no students had their own TVs in their rooms; as we said, a bleak time) either just before the show was scheduled to start or while the episode was on the air. Check out **FIGURE 14.7** for a transcript of what the confederates said to the groups of people who either were or were not watching *Charlie's Angels*. In a nutshell, they had students rate the attractiveness of a purported blind date for one of their friends while those students were watching

> *Confederate A:* Listen, could I just interrupt you guys for 30 seconds? We're having a major philosophical dispute here and we need to do an informal survey to resolve the question. You see, we have a friend coming to town this week and we want to fix him up with a date, but we can't decide whether to fix him up with her or not, so we decided to conduct a survey.
>
> *Confederate B:* You see, I don't think she looks very good.
>
> *Confederate A:* But I think she looks pretty good. At any rate, we want you to give us your vote on how attractive you think she is. (Confederate A begins to hold up the picture, but is faced away from the subjects so they can't see it.)
>
> *Confederate B:* Right, on a scale of 1 to 7, with 1 being very unattractive, 4 being exactly average, and 7 being beautiful.
>
> *Confederate A:* (turns over photo) Now, nobody say anything until everyone makes up his own mind, and be honest—give your honest opinion.
>
> *Confederate B:* Remember, 1 is very unattractive, 4 is right in the middle, and 7 is very attractive.

Figure 14.7

Angels?

When college students were asked to rate an average-looking woman, they rated her as less attractive if they had just been watching a television show featuring extremely attractive women.

[Research from Kenrick et al., 1989]

SOCIAL PSYCH OUT IN THE WORLD

Living Up to Unrealistic Ideals

We've discussed evidence that mass media depictions of beauty can negatively affect how we perceive the people we encounter in everyday life. For example, after looking at *Playboy* centerfolds, men tended to see other women and even their own wives as less attractive (Kenrick et al., 1989).

Here we add that it is not only men's perceptions that are affected; women's own self-perceived attractiveness also suffers (Thornton & Maurice, 1997). Mass media can be downright harmful to women's self-images. A meta-analysis of about 140 studies revealed that media depictions of women—often falling under the rubric of the modern thin ideal we noted earlier—cause women to have problems coming to terms with their own body shapes and sizes, sometimes contributing to the development of serious eating disorders such as anorexia and bulimia (Grabe et al., 2008).

The emphasis on the thin ideal is one facet of the broader tendency to objectify women, which we discussed in chapter 11 (Fredrickson & Roberts, 1997). As part of the objectification

of women—whereby women are socialized to see themselves as objects of sexual utility—they are held to a ridiculously unrealistic standard of what constitutes beauty. Physical attractiveness, both in body shape and facial features, becomes equated with a woman's value as a person.

We refer to these standards as ridiculously unrealistic because even the people whose faces and figures appear on billboards, in magazines, and in movies cannot actually meet the standards of their media-fostered images. Media designers use special effects, such as body or body-part doubles in films, Photoshop manipulation, and graphical rearrangements, to make even the "beautiful people" look more "beautiful" than they actually are. In 1990, Michelle Pfeiffer's face appeared on the cover of *Esquire* with the caption "What Michelle Pfeiffer needs . . . is absolutely nothing." It turned out that *Esquire* apparently felt that she needed over a thousand dollars' worth of photo alterations to make her image acceptably beautiful (DeVoss & Platt, n.d.). Reports suggest that more recent subjects of elaborate Photoshopping include Jessica Alba, Mischa Barton, Anne Hathaway, Kiera Knightley, Kate Middleton,

Charlie's Angels or while they were not watching the show. Students watching *Charlie's Angels* rated the blind date as less physically attractive than did those not watching the show. Although this study was methodologically limited (note that participants were not randomly assigned to conditions of watching the show or not), subsequent studies using more tightly controlled laboratory procedures have replicated this effect (Kenrick et al., 1989). What we find attractive is influenced by factors as temporary as what media depictions we just came across. For women, especially, the media's focus on appearance can lead to unrealistic ideals that can damage their well-being, a topic discussed in the Social Psych out in the World section.

APPLICATION
Online Dating and Attraction

Up until very recently, people met dating partners at work, through mutual friends, or through other traditional routes. Today they are increasingly turning to online dating sites such as Match.com, Tinder, and OkCupid (Finkel et al., 2012a; Rosenfeld & Thomas, 2012). These sites offer unique advantages. Many of them use computer algorithms to find compatible matches from a larger pool of people than users could ever meet in person (Finkel et al., 2012b).

But because online dating requires quickly sifting through information about large numbers of people in an anonymous way, it can also alter people's approach to dating. For example, people are less afraid of being rejected online and more willing to contact possible partners whom they might normally consider

Katy Perry, Andy Roddick, Britney Spears, and Kate Winslet (Weber, n.d.). Dove Soap's *Evolution* campaign video made the public aware that beauty standards are often unattainable fabrications (Dove, 2007). The video reveals that not only are the model's hair and makeup meticulously styled but also that photo-editing software was used to raise her cheekbones, enlarge her eyes, and align her nose and ears to enhance her facial symmetry. Until young girls are no longer bombarded with extremely thin and otherwise unrealistic images of "beauty," the media will continue to contribute to body-image issues and the psychological and physical problems that result from them.

We can be thankful that some contemporary celebrities are beginning to resist these trends. Lena Dunham, Natalie Portman, Kelly Clarkson, Tyra Banks, Amy Poehler, Tina Fey, and Jennifer Lawrence are just a few of the famous women who have spoken out against public and professional pressures to present an unrealistic ideal of women's bodies. Some organizations are putting these principles into policy. For example, Victoria's Secret canceled its annual televised fashion show of supermodels in lingerie, stating that it's time for the brand to evolve (Collie & Hensley, 2020).

▲ Notice the progression in the model's unrealistic attractiveness as makeup and then various computer enhancements are applied.

to be out of their league (Kreager et al., 2014). With sites like Tinder, users spend only a fraction of a second deciding whether a possible mate is swiped to the right or the left (Wotipka & High, 2016). In this fast-paced environment, where image is everything, how do people present themselves? And what do viewers find attractive?

Not surprisingly, people are strategic in how they present themselves online. Many present an idealized profile about themselves, especially to highly attractive mates (Ellison et al., 2011; Lo et al., 2013). Men tend to lie about their height, while women tend to lie about their weight (Toma & Hancock, 2010; Toma et al., 2008). Although women are somewhat more likely to bend the truth in their profiles (Lo et al., 2013), men are more likely to represent themselves as kind and emotionally stable partners (Guadagno et al., 2012). When it comes to choosing a profile picture, people seem to be aware of what evolutionary psychology teaches us about attraction. Women try to appear younger by disguising their gray hair and exposing more skin than men. Men are more likely to tilt the camera to seem taller and use photos that highlight their physique and athleticism (Ellison et al., 2006; Gallant et al., 2011).

Online daters are generally aware of and wary about misleading information on profiles, perhaps because they've embellished their own. Although most online daters post carefully posed pictures that present themselves in an attractive light, viewers actually prefer people who use candid pictures that make a person seem genuine and sincere (Berger & Barasch, 2015; Lo et al., 2013). When searching for partners in an online environment fraught with deception, sometimes too beautiful seems too good to be true.

⧉ Achie√e
Social Psych in Everyday Life: Ruairidh

Indeed, trustworthiness is a key concern when dating online, and many users are especially attuned to assessing how authentic people are. Profiles that display more self-enhancing information (e.g., graduated *with honors*) are perceived to be *less* attractive and trustworthy than profiles that do not (e.g., graduated *from college*) (Wotipka & High, 2016). Profile pics that show the person in everyday life were rated as more trustworthy and attractive than pics that show the person partying like a rock star (Jin & Martin, 2015).

In addition to caring about trustworthiness, online daters are clearly concerned about finding someone similar to themselves. In one study, the best predictor for people to both send and receive messages was similar educational status (Skopek et al., 2011). Divorced users are more attracted to other divorcees, and users with children are attracted to each other (Hitsch et al., 2010). People are also attracted to others who share their current relational goals, whether that means enjoying a short-term fling or finding a soul mate. They also use different apps depending on their relational goals (Wotipka & High, 2016).

Finally, some patterns in online daters' preferences align with the evolutionary perspective. For example, men with higher reported incomes received 10 times more profile visits from women than did those with low incomes. Men, in contrast, showed no preference for income when visiting the profiles of women (Ong & Wang, 2015). Still, don't let the evolutionary perspective obscure the ways men and women are alike. When researchers examined how first impressions of online dating profile pictures influenced perceived personality traits and online dating success, they found that *both* men and women were attracted to those whose profile pictures gave the impression that they were outgoing, emotionally stable, open to new experiences, and kind (Oliviola et al., 2015). Should you smile? Although smiles can be attractive (Brand et al., 2012), it depends on your cultural background. European Americans believe that the best emotions are high in arousal (think the excitement of being on a roller coaster), so on social media they're attracted to people with big, excited smiles. In contrast, Hong Kong Chinese don't value high arousal positive states as much, and they are not as attracted to a big grin (Tsai et al., 2019).

A lot of effort and money are put into using online dating sources, but are they any more effective at helping people find a mate? The evidence is surprisingly mixed. Some studies show that couples who met online have better and longer relationships than those who met offline; others show just the reverse (Cacioppo et al., 2013; Paul, 2014). ■

Is Appearance Destiny? Even though some physical attributes are considered universally attractive, people's perceived attractiveness is not set in stone at birth. A person's perceived attractiveness at age 17 does not predict the same person's perceived attractiveness at ages 30 and 50 (Zebrowitz, 1997). People's attractiveness increases when others view them positively or become more familiar with them (Gross & Crofton, 1977; Lewandowski et al., 2007; Price & Vandenberg, 1979). And the happier a couple is with their relationship, the more physically attractive they view each other as being (Murray & Holmes, 1997). We learn from social psychology that perceptions of physical attractiveness are highly malleable and vary across individuals, cultures, historical eras, and even the person's social situation in the moment.

SECTION REVIEW Physical Attractiveness

Research reveals the importance of physical attractiveness, what people find physically attractive (and why), and the consequences for relationships.

The Importance of Physical Attractiveness	Common Denominators of Attractive Faces	Gender Differences in What Is Attractive	Attraction in Same-Sex Relationships	Cultural and Situational Factors
• Sexual and aesthetic appeal predict liking. • Attractive people are stereotyped to have positive traits.	• Composite and symmetrical faces are rated as more attractive, perhaps as a reflection of good health or because they seem familiar.	• Men universally prefer a waist-to-hip ratio that signals fertility. • At times of peak fertility, women are more attracted to more masculine faces. • Men report an ideal preference for attractiveness; women report an ideal preference for social and financial status. • In actual relationships, men and women are equally influenced by physical attractiveness and, to a lesser extent, partner status. • Women's stated preference for higher-status men might also be changing as women achieve greater equality. • Both men and women rank personality traits such as warmth and loyalty above all other factors.	• Gay men tend to emphasize the physical attributes and masculine traits of a partner. • Lesbians show more complexity in what they find attractive in a partner.	• Standards of beauty vary across cultures and over time. • Scarcity and status influence trends. • Attractiveness can change across time and place, and perceptions of attractiveness are highly flexible.

Gender Differences in Sexual Attitudes and Behaviors ⟨ Learning Outcomes

We've seen how men and women can differ in what they find attractive. It turns out they differ in attitudes and behavior regarding sex as well. Most of us are familiar with the common stereotypes: Men, it is often said, want sex all the time, whereas women typically play the role of gatekeeper, deciding if and when sex begins in a relationship. Is there some truth to these stereotypes? Although there is variation within each gender, many findings support the idea that, compared with women, men have more permissive attitudes about sexuality in and out of relationships:

■ Men are much more likely than women to say that they would enjoy casual sex outside the context of a committed relationship, whereas women prefer to engage in sexual activities as part of an emotionally intimate relationship (Hendrick et al., 2006; Oliver & Hyde, 1993; Ostovich & Sabini, 2004). Also, men are quick to interpret a woman's behavior as signaling that she wants to

- Explain the evolutionary perspective differentiating male and female attitudes on sexual behavior.
- Identify ways that culture influences attitudes toward sex.
- Describe the evidence for and against the evolutionary perspective on attitudes toward infidelity.

have sex with them, even when that's the furthest thing from her mind (Haselton & Buss, 2009; Perilloux & Kurzban, 2015).

■ If you ask teenagers how they feel about having sex for the first time, most of the young men cannot wait to lose their virginity, and only one third of them view the prospect with a mix of positive and negative feelings. Young women have a different view: Most are ambivalent about having sex, some are opposed, and only a third of them are looking forward to their first experience of sex (Abma et al., 2004).

■ If you went on a date with someone and *didn't* have sex, would you regret it? Men report regretting not pursuing a sexual opportunity much more often than women do (Roese et al., 2006).

■ Once in a romantic relationship, men want to begin having sex sooner than women do, they want sex more often, and they are more likely to express dissatisfaction with the amount of sex they have (Sprecher, 2002).

The differences between men and women go beyond what they say. When we look at what people are actually doing, men on average have higher sex drives than women do:

■ Men experience sexual desire more frequently and intensely than do women, and they are more motivated to seek out sexual activity (Vohs et al., 2004). Young men experience sexual desire on average 37 times per week, whereas women experience sexual desire only about 9 times per week (Regan & Atkins, 2006). Men also spend more time fantasizing about sex than women do: Sex crosses men's minds about 60 times per week; for women, only about 15 times (Leitenberg & Henning, 1995; Regan & Atkins, 2006).

■ 71% of men admit to exaggerating the depth of their feeling for a woman in order to have sex with her, whereas only 39% of women admitted to having done so (Buss, 2016).

■ Men spend more money on sex. Not only do men spend a lot of money on sexual toys and pornography (Laumann et al., 2004), they are much more likely than women to pay for sex. One study found that, among Australians, 23% of men said that they had paid for sex at least once, but almost none of the women had (Pitts et al., 2004).

■ Men masturbate more frequently than women do (Oliver & Hyde, 1993). Among people who have a regular sexual partner, about half of the men still masturbate more than once a week, whereas only 16% of women pleasure themselves as frequently (Klusmann, 2002).

■ Men are more likely to be sexually unfaithful to their romantic partners. Although most husbands and wives never have sex with someone other than their partner after they marry, about one out of every three husbands, compared with only one out of five wives, has an extramarital affair (Tafoya & Spitzberg, 2007).

These and other facts paint a clear picture: On average, men are more sex driven than women. A big question, of course, is why these differences exist.

An Evolutionary Perspective

Again we find useful insights from evolutionary psychology. Robert Trivers (1972) proposed that reproductive success means different things to men and women because the sexes differ in their **parental investment**—the time and effort that they have to invest in each child they produce. Men's parental investment can be relatively low. If a man has sex with 100 different women in

WOODY ALLEN   DIANE KEATON

ANNIE HALL

▲ The following scene from the movie *Annie Hall* (Allen, 1977) satirizes how men and women can view sex differently.

[Alvy and Annie are seeing their therapists at the same time on a split screen]

Alvy Singer's Therapist: How often do you sleep together?

Annie Hall's Therapist: Do you have sex often?

Alvy Singer [lamenting]: Hardly ever. Maybe three times a week.

Annie Hall [annoyed]: Constantly. I'd say three times a week.

[United Artists/AF archive / Alamy Stock Photo]

Parental investment The time and effort that parents must invest in each child they produce.

a year, he can, in theory, father 100 or more children with little more time and effort than it takes to ejaculate. Women have a much higher level of parental investment. The number of children they can bear and raise in a lifetime is limited, and they have to commit enormous time and energy to each child to keep it alive.

Trivers argued that because men and women differ in their parental investment, they evolved to have different **mating strategies,** or overall approaches to mating, that helped them to reproduce successfully (Buss, 2016; Geary, 2010). For men, there may be some benefit to a *short-term mating strategy* of pursuing many sexual opportunities with little commitment. If a man mates with many women in short-term relationships, he probably won't be able to provide high-quality parenting to every child he fathers, and so many of those children will not thrive as well as they would with high investment from both parents (Allen & Daly, 2007). But what a man lacks in parental quality he might make up in sheer quantity: Chances are that at least some of those children will survive to propagate the man's genes.

Women, in contrast, would get no reproductive benefit from being highly promiscuous. They would not be able to produce any more children than they would by having sex with only one fertile man for a lifetime. Instead, women would benefit from a *long-term mating strategy* of choosing their mates carefully, seeking out partners with good genes who would contribute resources to protect and feed their offspring.

This evolutionary perspective could explain many of the gender differences in sexual attitudes and behavior that we listed above (Buss, 2017). It helps to explain why men all over the world show a greater desire than women for brief affairs with a variety of partners (Schmitt, 2005). What's more, women are indeed more careful and deliberate than men in their choice of sexual partners. They are less interested than men are in casual, uncommitted sex (Gangestad & Simpson, 1990). They will not have sex with a partner unless he meets a fairly high bar of intelligence, friendliness, prestige, and emotional security, whereas men set the bar much lower for the personal qualities they look for in a potential sexual partner (Kenrick et al., 1990).

It is important to note, however, that the evolutionary perspective does not imply that men and women use a single mating strategy across all situations and periods in their lives. It also doesn't mean that all men and women will use the same strategy. For one thing, the mating strategies that men and women adopt depend on whether they are looking for a short-term fling or a long-term partnership (Buss & Schmitt, 1993). For example, when men look for a committed, long-term relationship, they look for qualities like warmth and not just interest in having sex (Buss, 2000).

It is also important to emphasize that any strategy has costs and benefits. The social, cultural, and physical environment can make a strategy more or less advantageous in the long run (Geary, 2010). For example, in contexts where infant mortality is high, men benefit more from increasing their parental investment (Pollet & Nettle, 2008). In fact, in some cultural contexts, a short-term strategy can get men into a lot of trouble, as when it increases the chances of violent conflict with other men. Thus, even if certain mating strategies were adaptive in our distant evolutionary past, they should not be viewed as "natural" or preferable ways to act.

Consider today's modern world. Do you think these strategies would be advantageous in the contemporary mating landscape? In the modern environment we inhabit now, male promiscuity and female chastity might not

Mating strategies Approaches to mating that help people reproduce successfully. People prefer different mating strategies depending on whether they are thinking about a short-term pairing or a long-term commitment.

Achieve
Video: Evolutionary Psychology and Sex Differences

necessarily help people reproduce more effectively. For one thing, many women now use birth control to prevent fertility. Also, many casual sexual encounters involve the use of prophylactics to prevent the spread of sexually transmitted diseases (as well as pregnancy). In fact, in this environment, men might be able to reproduce more successfully if, instead of pursuing multiple partners, they consistently showed love and commitment to one partner and increased their parental investment (Geary, 2010). Furthermore, as women gain more equal footing with men in terms of economic and social power, and because technology has potentially reduced the burdens of infant care (e.g., formula as a substitute for breast milk, the ability to pump and store breast milk), women may benefit from a less selective approach (Schmitt, 2005). Let's look at some other cultural factors influencing people's views of sex and their sexual behavior.

Cultural Influences

Although sex obviously serves the biological function of reproduction, many psychological motives influence people's decisions to have sex or not. When college students were asked to list all of the reasons they or someone they know had recently engaged in sexual intercourse, they mentioned 237 reasons (Meston & Buss, 2007). Most of these reasons had to do with seeking positive states such as pleasure, affection, love, emotional closeness, adventure, and excitement. Students also mentioned more calculating and callous reasons, albeit less frequently. Some used sex as a way to aggress against someone ("I was mad at my partner, so I had sex with someone else"), to gain some advantage ("I wanted a raise"), or to enhance their social status ("I wanted to impress my friends").

Culturally Shaped Motives   Many of the reasons for sex boil down to five core motives (Cooper, Shapiro, & Powers, 1998). Among both college-student and community samples, the most frequently endorsed motives for sex are (in descending order) to enhance physical or emotional pleasure, to foster intimacy, to affirm one's sense of self-worth, to cope with negative emotions, and to gain partner or peer approval. These motives are closely connected to culturally learned beliefs about what makes us valuable, happy, and part of the group.

Cultural Norms   Sexual attitudes and behavior are also shaped by the prevailing cultural norms for what is and what is not permissible. Cultures vary in how permissive they are about several sexual topics, such as sex before marriage and same-sex relations (Widmer et al., 1998). The strength of people's religious beliefs also predicts their attitudes toward their own and others' sexual conduct (Moon et al., 2019). Also, within a given culture, norms change over time. For example, chances are good that you are more accepting of premarital sexual intercourse than your grandparents were. In the first half of the 20th century, most Americans disapproved of sex before marriage; these days, fewer than a third of Americans think that premarital sex is wrong (Wells & Twenge, 2005; Willetts et al., 2004). Although on average American men and women do not marry until their mid- to late 20s, they usually have sex for the first time around age 17. In fact, by the time Americans reach 20 years of age, only 15% have not yet had sex (Fryar et al., 2007).

If we look more closely, though, we see that today's norms surrounding casual sex are complicated. People polled in the past 20 or so years generally disapprove of sex between unmarried partners who are not emotionally committed to each other, and they look more favorably on sexually active partners who are in a "serious" rather than a "casual" relationship (Bettor et al., 1995; Willetts et al., 2004). And yet, over the past 60 years we see a cultural trend, at least in the West, toward more acceptance of "hooking up"—brief sexual encounters among individuals who are not in a committed romantic relationship (Garcia et al., 2012). So, although most people still believe—or say they believe—that sex outside marriage is more acceptable if it occurs in the context of a committed, affectionate relationship (Sprecher et al., 2006), uncommitted "hookups" are becoming more engrained in popular culture. Even so, people are conflicted about hookup culture (Garcia et al., 2012). Young men and women often say that while they enjoy some aspects of casual sex, they are disturbed by the lack of emotional connection and commitment. They seem to be juggling two cultural "scripts" for interpreting appropriate sexual behavior: the "no-strings attached" script portrayed in pop culture and the traditional valuing of romance and finding the "right one."

Norms and Reporting of Attitudes and Behavior   Cultural norms influence not only whether people engage in sex but how comfortable they feel about *reporting* permissive sexual attitudes and behavior. Consider this puzzle: Among heterosexuals, the average middle-aged man reports that he has had seven sexual partners during his lifetime, whereas the average woman has had only four (Fryar et al., 2007). Shouldn't these numbers be the same? If a partner were required for sex, it would seem that each time a man engages in heterosexual sex, his female partner does, too. There are several possible explanations for this common sex difference. For example, men are more likely than women to have sex with prostitutes, but prostitutes rarely respond to these surveys. Also, men and women tend to hold different definitions of what constitutes "sex." For example, in heterosexual couples, men are more likely than women to say that oral sex qualifies as sex (Sanders & Reinisch, 1999).

Another explanation is that men tend to exaggerate the number of partners they've been with, whereas women tend to minimize that number (Willetts et al., 2004). When men are asked about their number of partners, they tend to estimate the number rather than counting diligently, and when in doubt, they round up. As a result, they usually report round numbers, such as 10 or 30, and almost never provide seemingly exact counts such as 14 or 27 (Brown & Sinclair, 1999). Women, on the other hand, respond to researchers' inquiries into their sex lives by counting their partners more accurately and then fudging by subtracting a partner or two from their reported total (Wiederman, 2004).

How do we know that norms play a role in men's and women's biased reporting? You might expect that if, for impression-management purposes, men exaggerate their numbers to appear like studs, and women downplay their numbers to appear chaste, then the difference between men and women would be especially pronounced if they expected that other people would view their responses. That is exactly what a study by Alexander and Fisher (2003) found. This study produced an even more interesting result: If men and women were put into a "bogus pipeline" condition in which they were led to believe that lying could be detected, sex differences in reported sexual behavior became less pronounced.

One general point to take from all this is that although some of the reasons people pursue sex certainly involve biological tendencies toward pleasure seeking and reproduction, many others reflect how a person is shaped by, and interacts with, his or her social and cultural environment.

Your Cheating Heart: Reactions to Infidelity

Let's do a little thought experiment, shall we? Imagine that you are in a committed relationship with someone whom you love very deeply. (If you are lucky, maybe you already are there, and not much imagination is required.) Now imagine that you learn that your partner has been secretly carrying on with another person. In one version of this dark scenario, you learn that the affair is about wild, passionate sex. In an alternative version, it is about a deep emotional attachment. If you were forced to choose between these two tragic turns in your relationship, which would seem to be the lesser of two evils?

Early Research   When researchers first examined how people react to infidelity, they found evidence of a significant difference between men and women. In an early set of studies, 49% of men but only 19% of women said they would be more upset if they caught their partner sleeping around than if their partner had fallen in love with another person (Buss et al., 1992). Of course, this means that 81% of women, compared with only 51% of men, said they would be more bothered by learning that their partner had fallen in love with someone else. Do men and women really have such different views of disloyalty? If so, why? The next two decades of research sought to answer these questions.

If we take the evolutionary perspective, we can see that people have a lot to lose if their partner is unfaithful. Jealousy might have evolved to be an emotional "warning light" signaling our partner's real or imagined indiscretions. Jealousy might cue us to be alert to possible rivals who could catch our partner's eye and woo him or her away (Buss, 2000). An evolutionary perspective goes further, suggesting that infidelity carries different meanings for men and women because it affects their ability to reproduce in different ways.

Romantic attachments provide the emotional glue to bond couples together and keep caregivers committed to providing offspring with resources and protection (Geary, 2010). Women could have evolved a greater sensitivity than men to threats to that emotional bond because, if their partner left, they would be stuck with the burden of child rearing. As a result, they may have evolved to experience jealousy primarily in response to emotional, rather than sexual, infidelity. For a man, when a partner has sex with someone else, it can lead to a situation where he unwittingly invests his resources into raising another man's offspring. From an evolutionary perspective, this is one of the worst ways to botch your entire life. Hence, men may have evolved **mate guarding** efforts to keep their partner from sleeping around, and they therefore experience jealousy primarily in response to sexual infidelity.

Mate guarding Efforts to prevent one's sexual partner from mating with someone else in order to avoid the costs of rearing offspring that do not help to propagate one's genes.

Modern Perspectives   The evolutionary argument for gender differences in jealousy fits the findings of those early studies, but theorists soon raised questions about whether the gender differences in infidelity attitudes actually exist and, if so, what they really mean.

Research in Support of the Evolutionary Perspective   Some researchers who followed up on Buss's original research found the same effect across several different cultures: Men worried more about their partner's sexual infidelity, while women were worried about their partner's emotional infidelity (Buss et al., 1999; Buunk et al., 1996; Geary et al., 1995). More recent studies have replicated the effect with regard to online relationships (Groothof et al., 2009). A meta-analysis of studies that have presented participants with the choice between sexual and emotional infidelity shows this sex difference to be of moderate size, although it is stronger among college-age, heterosexual participants (Harris, 2003). The sex difference goes beyond what people say. When male and female college students imagined these two types of infidelity, their bodies reacted somewhat differently. Male participants imagining their partners sexually cheating on them had elevated skin conductance, indicative of an increased sympathetic response of the fight-or-flight type. Women showed higher levels of skin conductance when imagining that their partners had become emotionally attached to someone else (Buss et al., 1992).

Critiques The story might have ended here, with the field concluding that men and women evolved to have different triggers for jealousy. However, other researchers noted that the evidence for this sex difference is overstated (Harris, 2003). Forcing people to choose between a love affair and a lustful liaison is a rather artificial scenario—a bit like asking whether someone would prefer a kick in the head or a punch in the stomach. Neither is particularly desirable, and by focusing on sex differences in preferring one choice over the other, we might be ignoring an obvious but important point: that both sexes would experience jealousy in either case. When people are asked about each kind of infidelity independently rather than being forced to choose between one or the other, the sex difference disappears (DeSteno & Salovey, 1996; Harris, 2003; Sagarin et al., 2003).

Researchers pointed to other flaws in the methods used in the earlier studies. For example, studies of actual infidelity rather than imagined infidelity do not always replicate the sex difference (Edlund et al., 2006; Harris, 2002). It also might be difficult to draw conclusions about the greater sympathetic activation when men imagine sexual versus emotional infidelity. It turns out that men generally show greater sympathetic activation when imagining their partner having sex instead of becoming emotionally attached, regardless of whether this imagined relationship is with themselves or someone else (Harris, 2000). These critiques of the methods used in the original studies have led some researchers to question how large or meaningful this purported sex difference really is.

Another critique is that sex differences in jealousy might be the result of cultural learning. For example, women tend to assume that a man in love will also be having sex, whereas men assume that a woman having sex will also be in love (DeSteno & Salovey, 1996; Harris & Christenfeld, 1996). So women might be more bothered than men by emotional infidelity because they are more likely to assume that their partner has or is very likely to consummate the affair (DeSteno et al., 2002).

Another culturally based argument is that men derive more self-esteem from their sex lives than women do, whereas women derive more self-esteem from being emotionally bonded to a partner than men do (Goldenberg et al., 2003). Therefore, it's no surprise that a partner's emotional disloyalty would trigger greater self-esteem concerns for women, whereas a partner's sexual disloyalty would trigger greater self-esteem concerns for men. For example, when participants are asked to think about death, a condition known to elevate efforts to defend self-esteem, men become even more threatened by imagining their partner sleeping with someone else, whereas women become even more threatened by imagining their partner falling in love with someone else. In further support of a self-esteem-based argument, research that induces jealousy in the laboratory (as opposed to measuring it by having participants imagine hypothetical scenarios) finds that situations that increase jealousy do so by threatening self-esteem (DeSteno et al., 2006).

A third critique is that certain aspects of the data just don't seem to fit with an evolutionary account. For example, if differences in jealous reactions truly are sex linked, then gay men should show the same patterns of response found in straight men but with regard to their same-sex partners (Symons, 1979). This does not appear to be the case. In a study of both gay and straight men and women, straight men reported greater relative concern about sexual than about emotional infidelity, but gay men did not. In addition, every group reported greater concerns about emotional infidelity. When asked to recollect a time when a partner actually cheated on them, people were more upset about the emotional aspects of the affair than about the sexual aspects (Harris, 2002). In fact, most studies using the "choose your infidelity" method have found that the percentage of men (typically straight) who say they would be more bothered by sexual infidelity is at or near 50% (DeSteno & Salovey, 1996). If a specific mechanism had evolved such that men could detect and react to sexual infidelity

---

 SOCIAL PSYCH AT THE MOVIES

Attraction in *Best in Show*

At first glance, the movie *Best in Show* (Guest, 2000) might seem like an odd choice for a discussion of human attraction. What does a mockumentary about a dog show have to do with how people partner up? It provides the perfect satirical account of the various factors that attract people to one another. The movie (directed by Christopher Guest) follows the trials and tribulations of several dogs on their journey toward the title Best in Show at the annual Mayflower Kennel Club Dog Show. But the movie really centers around the owners of these dogs and their quirky personalities and relationships.

As the movie begins, we get to know each set of dog owners in an interview-type format typical of true documentaries. Many of these introductions involve a brief retelling of how the couple met, and it is in these brief scenes that we see various patterns of attraction on display. The couples are as different as the breeds of dogs represented in the show, and their stories reflect many of the themes discussed throughout this chapter.

One couple's story shows the importance of *proximity*. Hamilton and Meg Swan met at Starbucks. Not at the same Starbucks, mind you, but at two different Starbucks that were just across the street from each other. After noticing each other, they soon realized that their shared yuppie interests extended far beyond soy chai lattes to Apple computers and J. Crew. Clearly these two thirtysomethings are meant for each other! Or, at least, they have similar attitudes. Unfortunately, as we get to know Hamilton and Meg a bit more, we learn that they also share a tendency to crack under pressure. One gets the sense that this shared disposition for being hot tempered

Some pets deserve a little more respect than others.

A comedy from the director of *Waiting for Guffman*.

▲ [Warner Bros./Photofest]

is bound to doom this couple. When their Weimaraner's favorite squeaky toy goes missing, their frantic search for it leads to an early disqualification from the competition.

in their mates, wouldn't you would expect men's aversion to sexual infidelity to be stronger than a coin toss?

A Final Thought on the Evolutionary Perspective Throughout this chapter, we've seen that many aspects of relationships—from initial attraction to lust to jealousy—can be understood in part by looking back on the evolution of our species and considering how our psychology was shaped by natural selection. At the same time, we noted that this perspective ignites fierce debates about human nature and that the evidence for evolutionary explanations is sometimes open to alternative explanations. On the one hand, this controversy is part of what makes research on relationships so interesting. On the other, we acknowledge that all these questions about theories and methods can be overwhelming. So let's back up and get a broader perspective on this controversy.

Another couple, Leslie and Sherri Ann Cabot, pushes evolutionary theorizing on sex differences in *mating strategies* to its limits. Leslie is very old but very wealthy. Sherri Ann is much younger and obviously spends a lot of time on her appearance. But in their interview (during which he merely blankly gums his dentureless mouth), she insists that what really makes their relationship work is his very high sex drive and all the interests they have in common: "We both love soup. We love the outdoors. We love snow peas. And, uh, talking and not talking. We could not talk or talk forever and still find things to not talk about."

But as the movie continues, it's clear that their relationship contains no true attraction. Instead, Sherri Ann is having an affair with her dog's handler, Christy. When Sherri Ann and Christy discuss their relationship to each other and to their poodle, Rhapsody in White, we see that they are attracted by complementary characteristics—reflecting the idea that "opposites attract" (see text for more discussion). Sherri Ann, who generally seems to need someone else to be in charge, describes Christy as the disciplinarian. Christy, on the other hand, values Sherri Ann's tendency to provide unconditional love, just as her mother had (note the effect of *transference*).

The one couple whose source of attraction to each other is the most difficult to identify is Jerry and Cookie Fleck. Cookie is an energetic and not unattractive middle-aged woman who spent the earlier years of her adult life pursuing what we've labeled a short-term mating strategy of having many, many one-night stands. Throughout the movie, she repeatedly runs into old flames, which only ignites feelings of jealousy in her husband, Jerry. And Jerry, it must be said,

[Warner Bros./Photofest]

is neither highly attractive nor financially secure. In fact, he literally has two left feet, a cinematic device that could hardly scream "Hey, I'm asymmetrical" any louder. So what does this woman who had "hundreds of boyfriends" in her past see in this man, whose nickname used to be Loopy because his two left feet made him always walk in circles? It can only be their shared love for their pooch, little Winky, who is the underdog (no pun intended) contender for the Best in Show title.

Although no one in this quirky cast of characters fits anyone's ideal notion of a partner, they all manage in the end to find some degree of happiness with each other. Perhaps it's their shared love of dogs and the dog-show lifestyle that really sustains these relationships, whereas other sources of attraction were only fleeting factors that initially brought them together.

If you think about our relationship psychology as a pie, one slice of that pie is our evolved tendencies. Another slice might be cultural upbringing. Yet other slices might be gender differences in other relevant personality traits or the person's experiences in the immediate social context. So one way to approach the controversy is to figure out which theoretical perspectives account for which pieces of the total pie, not whether the entire pie belongs to evolution, culture, or any other single source.

If you want to explore these topics at a deeper level, there is another, more ambitious approach. Rather than think about culture or evolution as gobbling up separate pieces of the pie, we can figure out how different factors *interact* to shape our relationship lives. As just one example, women more than men may react negatively to emotional infidelity because of an evolved mating strategy, but that strategy guides women's behavior only to the extent that they organize their lifestyle around childbearing. Cultural influences such as changing norms and technology make it increasingly possible for women to pursue other goals . . . and to tell their genes to go jump in a lake. This and many similar examples illustrate a key point: Whatever evolutionary mechanisms we're born with do not govern our behavior in simple, rigid ways. Rather, they are a set of sensitivities and tendencies that respond flexibly to what's happening in the person's life *right now*, not 3 million years ago, when they might have first been adaptive.

SECTION REVIEW   Gender Differences in Sexual Attitudes and Behaviors

Men and women differ in behavior and attitudes toward sex. Explaining those differences requires a diversity of perspectives.

An Evolutionary Perspective	**Cultural Influences**	**Men, Women, and Infidelity**
• Men's attitudes reflect the reproductive advantages of mating with multiple women, while women's attitudes reflect the need to find one mate to help support child rearing.	• Motives to have sex are shaped by culturally informed beliefs about personal value and fitting in. • Cultural norms also affect attitudes, as evidenced by changing attitudes toward premarital sex across generations as well as among cultures.	• There is some evidence that men and women view sexual and emotional infidelity from different perspectives. • Researchers debate the relative role of evolved mechanisms and cultural influences in creating these differences.

CRITICAL LEARNING EXERCISES

1. Over the past few decades, a dominant message in North American culture has been *assert your individuality*. Consumer messages tell people to stand out from the crowd, college orientation materials encourage first-year students to blaze their own path, and the trending message in spirituality is to let go of others' influence and focus on one's inner core. Compare this influence to this chapter's claim that humans have an innate need to belong. Does the message to "stand out" conflict with our need to "fit in"? Or is there a way to live up to the cultural ideal of individuality while satisfying the need to belong?

2. Recall that *existential isolation* is a nagging feeling that other people do not share our experience of reality. Do you think it's possible to share your "I" with someone else's? Can you ever truly know what the world is like from another person's perspective? Think about times in your own life when you *I-shared*: What, if anything, made those encounters special?

3. We read about the halo effect, a pervasive tendency to assume (perhaps even unconsciously) that physically attractive people have other valued traits and abilities. Although it is a positive judgment, it can still lead to biased

and unfair treatment. Try to imagine an intervention to prevent or at least attenuate the halo effect. For example, how could you instruct teachers or managers to avoid unfairly benefiting attractive students or job candidates and neglecting or underestimating those who are less attractive?

4. The chapter introduced the study of infidelity in social psychology. We saw that men and women sometimes show different reactions to different types of infidelity, although there is some debate as to when and why. But in all the studies we discussed, people are asked to react to the real or imagined cheating of their romantic partner with another *real* person. But now consider how people respond when they discover their romantic partner privately views pornography. If Susan and Dave are dating, and Susan finds pornography on Dave's laptop, will she interpret that as infidelity or not? If Susan is upset, how could we explain her reaction from an evolutionary perspective? After all, there are no real sexual or emotional consequences that would impact Susan's chances of reproduction . . . or are there?

CHAPTER 15

Close Relationships

A few days before beginning this chapter, one of your authors (Jeff) glanced at a fascinating article about a couple who were married for over 60 years and passed away together. After a 63-year marriage, Henry and Jeanette De Lange both died on July 31. Jeanette died first, at 5:10 p.m., and 20 minutes later, Henry died, too. According to their children, they couldn't bear to be apart. Many similar stories pop up.

Life is tough, so having a long-term life partner to support you in the rough times and share the good times can be of great value. Good close relationships even contribute to physical health (Slatcher & Selcuk, 2017). In this chapter we focus on such close relationships, their benefits, the feelings of love that bind them, the difficulties of sustaining them, and strategies for making them satisfying over the long haul. Specifically, in this chapter we consider the following:

- The value of close relationships and the nature and functions of love

- Models of romantic relationships and the roles of interdependence and commitment in romantic relationships

- The time course of romantic relationships, sources of relationship difficulties, and relationship dissolution

- Strategies for optimizing satisfaction and longevity in relationships

What Makes Close Relationships Special?

We all have a sense that close relationships are different from our casual inter-actions with strangers and acquaintances, but what exactly makes them special? According to both scholars and laypersons, closeness involves six components: *knowledge*, *caring*, *interdependence*, *mutuality*, *trust*, and *commitment* (Laurenceau et al., 2004; Marston et al., 1998; Parks & Floyd, 1996). Let's look at each of these.

People in close relationships *know* a lot about each other and are com-fortable sharing intimate information about their personal histories, feelings, and desires that they do not share with casual friends. They also feel more *care*, or affection, for one another than they do for most others. The closer people are, the more they experience **interdependence**: What each person does significantly influences what the other person does over long periods of time (Berscheid et al., 2004). Close relationships are also characterized by a high

Learning Outcomes

- List the components of close relationships.
- Define parasocial relationships.
- Explain why close relationships are important.

Interdependence A situation in which what each person does significantly influences what the partner does over long periods of time.

Mutuality Partners' acknowledgment that their lives are intertwined and thinking of themselves as a couple ("us") instead of as two separate individuals ("me" and "you").

Commitment Partners' investment of time, effort, and resources in their relationship, with the expectation that it will continue indefinitely.

degree of **mutuality**: Partners acknowledge that their lives are intertwined, and they think of themselves as a couple ("us") instead of as two separate individuals ("me" and "you") (Fitzsimons & Kay, 2004; Levinger & Snoek, 1972). People in close relationships also *trust* each other, meaning that they expect their partners to treat them with fairness, to be responsive to their needs, and not to cause them unnecessary harm (Reis et al., 2004; Simpson, 2007). Finally, closeness is defined by a high degree of **commitment**, meaning that partners invest time, effort, and resources in their relationship, with the expectation that it will continue indefinitely.

Relationships that include all six of these components are the most satisfying and feel the closest to us. Nevertheless, closeness can exist to varying degrees when only some of these components are present. For instance, roommates who frequently influence each other (interdependence) and treat each other fairly (trust) are likely to feel closer to each other than they do to acquaintances, but not as close as they feel in relationships that include more components.

Parasocial Relationships

Parasocial relationships Individuals' relationships with people in the media, including celebrities, television characters, and athletes.

Breaking down closeness into these components helps us to understand a curious but common phenomenon: People can feel surprisingly close to others whom they've never met face-to-face, and even to fictional others: celebrities, television characters, talk-show hosts, athletes, and characters in soap operas and novels. These are called **parasocial relationships** (Horton & Wohl, 1956). They are one-sided, lacking interdependence, but can include three other components of closeness: Fans believe that they *know* the media personalities, they *care* what happens to them, and they are *committed* to following and supporting them.

Because parasocial relationships involve some components of closeness, we can understand why they are so important and satisfying for many people. In fact, people report turning to their favorite television programs when they feel lonely. Merely bringing to mind a favorite television program buffers people from feeling rejected when their real relationships are threatened (Derrick et al., 2009). What's more, a parasocial breakup, such as when a favorite television character is killed off or otherwise taken off the air, can be as emotionally distressing as the breakup of a real relationship (J. Cohen, 2004; Giles, 2002). And as some celebrities know too well, parasocial relationships have led some mentally unstable fans to stalking and even worse. For example, in chapter 12's movie box, we described how John Hinckley Jr. became obsessed with and a stalker of actress Jodie Foster.

Of course, most close relationships involve real people mutually interacting. And those close relationships are the focus of this chapter.

▲ Parasocial relationships with celebrities such as Taylor Swift can include some core components of closeness but usually lack interdependence.
[Brendon Thorne/Getty Images]

Why Are Close Relationships So Important?

Because close relationships involve a high degree of care, interdependence, and commitment, they can be very demanding. Your friends, family members, and romantic partners all expect you to respond to their needs in various ways, and often that means sacrificing your desires and even some of your aspirations. Partly as a result, close relationships can be the source of extreme stress, frustration, and emotional pain. So why do people care so deeply about forming and maintaining close relationships?

Despite their potential costs, close relationships facilitate our day-to-day activities. They allow us to pool resources and share labor. For example, while one of your authors (Mark) sits on the couch writing this chapter, his partner is braving the snow to pick up groceries, thus saving him time and effort. Also, when we face a problem that is difficult to understand, others can provide much-needed advice and consolation. Indeed, if something threatening is about to happen or has happened, people are especially desirous of contact with others, particularly those facing a similar threat (Kulik et al., 1994; Schachter, 1959).

But pointing out practical benefits takes us only so far. To see why, imagine that a devious genie appears and offers you a team of personal assistants devoted to satisfying all your daily needs. *But* this will happen only on the condition that you'll never again experience a close emotional connection with someone. Would you accept the offer? Most of us wouldn't choose such a carefree but solitary life. People want—indeed *need*—love in their lives. Why is that?

SECTION REVIEW What Makes Close Relationships Special?

Closeness in relationships involves knowledge, caring, interdependence, mutuality, trust, and commitment.

Closeness in Relationships	Parasocial Relationships	The Importance of Close Relationships
Relationships feel the closest when they include all six components, but they can exist to varying degrees when only some are present.	Parasocial relationships are those in which, for example, fans feel close to a fictional character or media personality.	Relationships have practical benefits, such as sharing responsibilities. They also are the basis of emotional support.

This Thing Called Love

To this crib I always took my doll; human beings must love something, and, in the dearth of worthier objects of affection, I contrived to find a pleasure in loving and cherishing a faded graven image, shabby as a miniature scarecrow.

—Charlotte Brontë, *Jane Eyre* (1847/1992, p. 27)

The British novelist Charlotte Brontë captured a basic truth not only about humans but about other primates as well. Over a hundred years later, the psychologist Harry Harlow discovered that when he separated infant monkeys from their moms and put them in cages by themselves, they became intensely attached to cheesecloth baby blankets he included in their cages; when the blankets were removed for laundering, the poor little monkeys became distressed (Harlow, 1959).

In its most general sense, love is a strong, positive feeling we have toward someone or something we care deeply about (Berscheid, 2006). The object of our love is of great value to us. We feel possessive toward it, and if it is a living being, we usually want the love object to love us back. Indeed, in the romantic context,

Learning Outcomes

- Identify characteristics of romantic love.
- Explain how culture shapes aspects of love.
- Describe each of the theories that explain the psychological functions of love: attachment theory, terror management theory, and the self-expansion model.
- Explain the theories that describe the experiences of love: two-factor theory and the triangular model of love.

unrequited love causes damage to self-esteem and hostility in the rebuffed lover and guilt in the nonreciprocating beloved (Baumeister et al., 1993). We typically love our parents, our children, our siblings, our pets, and our romantic partners. We also may love other relatives, friends, our car, our flat-screen TV, our hometown, and our country. Although all of these forms of love can be important, social psychologists have focused primarily on love between adults that includes sexual attraction and which is commonly referred to as romantic love.

Romantic Love

When people are asked to name the person they feel closest to, the most popular choice is one's romantic partner (Berscheid et al., 1989). What is it like to experience romantic love? Answers have been provided by many observers over human history: ancient philosophers, poets, and storytellers; Renaissance writers such as Shakespeare; 19th-century poets such as Keats and Shelley and novelists such as Austen and Brontë; early psychologists such as Freud and Karen Horney; and present-day poets, songwriters, and novelists. Homer's great epic *The Odyssey* is fundamentally a love story. Shakespeare's *Romeo and Juliet* is perhaps the most famous love story of all. Romantic love is often portrayed as inspiring great feelings of joy and wholeness (e.g., Pope, 1980). Romantic love has also been described as a madness or a disease and a cause of great suffering, pain, and discord (Pope, 1980). And indeed, when love is unrequited or a romantic relationship doesn't work out, some resort to stalking, abuse, murder, and suicide (Daly & Wilson, 1988; Fisher, 2004).

Social psychologists began focusing on love with Zick Rubin's seminal 1973 book *Liking and Loving*. Rubin developed scales to distinguish feelings of liking, which characterize many types of relationships, from feelings of loving, which characterize romantic relationships. As the sample questionnaire items in **FIGURE 15.1** show, Rubin assessed positive evaluations of, and perceived similarity to, another person as the core of liking but attachment, caring, and intimacy as the key aspects of romantic love. In support of the validity of his loving scale, Rubin found that the higher people scored on loving, the more they thought marriage to their partner was likely, the more eye contact they made when with their romantic partner, and the more the relationship had progressed in intensity six months later (Rubin, 1973; for more recent love scales, see Hatfield & Sprecher, 1986; Hendrick & Hendrick, 1986).

The culture theorist Kenneth Pope described the subjective experience of romantic love this way, consistently with Rubin's scale:

> A preoccupation with another person. A deeply felt desire to be with the loved one. A feeling of incompleteness without him or her. Thinking of the loved one often, whether together or apart. Separation frequently provokes feelings of genuine despair or else tantalizing anticipation of reuniting. Reunion is seen as bringing feelings of euphoric ecstasy or peace and fulfillment. (POPE, 1980, P. 4)

This description captures what researchers have found out about people who are in the throes of love. Anthropologist Helen Fisher (2004) noted some recurring themes from a survey about romantic love administered in the United States and Japan. Among these were that the beloved becomes the focus of the

Liking

I have great confidence in _____'s good judgment.
I think that _____ and I are quite similar to one another.
_____ is the sort of person whom I myself would like to be.

Loving

It would be hard for me to get along without _____.
One of my primary concerns is _____'s welfare.
I feel that I can confide in _____ about virtually everything.

Figure 15.1

Sample Items from Rubin's Liking and Loving Scales

Rubin's liking and loving scales were among the first to assess two different kinds of attraction: romantic love and liking.

[Research from Rubin, 1973]

person's attention, feelings, and sexual desire and a central source of meaning and value. Fisher also noted that feelings may swing from joy to despair, with jealousy sprinkled in.

Supporting the desire and joy that accompany love, neuroscience research reveals that when people in love contemplate their beloved, there is increased activation of the dopamine-rich ventral tegmental area and the caudate nucleus—areas of the brain associated with reward, motivation, and pleasure (e.g., Aron et al., 2005; Fisher, 2004).

Of course, love may not be experienced in this way (or at all) by all people or in all cultures. Some people and cultures may see this kind of love as too dramatic or reflecting codependency, but evidence suggests both that when one falls in love and when one is in a love relationship for a decade or more, emotional dependence is pretty likely. This is why people sometimes resort to violence when they perceive a threat to their relationship or if it is ended (Fisher, 2004) and why people mourn, often to the point of depressive symptoms, when they lose a romantic partner (Bowlby, 1980). And the opening story about the De Langes suggests that perhaps losing a loved one can even shut down the urge to continue living.

We can consider such a high level of emotional investment healthy or unhealthy, but evidence suggests that it occurs in many, if not the majority of, committed romantic relationships. From this perspective, love is a leap, a risk, with individuals investing their happiness partly in their partner and the relationship. If you love someone—whether a parent, child, friend, pet, or romantic partner—you care about the loved one's fortunes as well as your own. So your emotions are partly dependent on the loved one's feelings and situation. If you don't want to risk that, don't love someone else. That way, your emotions will be based only on your own fortunes. Yet most people do take those risks—as children, parents, friends, pet owners, and lovers. Of these loves, romantic love is probably the most unstable and the most likely to lead to heartache. Most of us take the plunge anyway, often multiple times. Let's consider some perspectives on this fascinating phenomenon.

Culture and Love

Romantic love seems to exist in the vast majority of cultures and perhaps all of them. In a survey of cultures around the globe, anthropologists found clear evidence of romantic love in 147 out of 166 cultures (Jankowiak & Fischer, 1992). In the 19 other cultures, this aspect of people's lives was not necessarily absent but had not been studied (Fisher, 2006).

Although prevalent across cultures, romantic love is partly shaped by a person's culture. The culture we are raised in tells us what love is like, whom we should love and when, and how to act on our feelings (Hatfield & Rapson, 1993; Landis & O'Shea, 2000; Rubin, 1973). To gain insight into how the nature of love is portrayed, researchers examined the use of words and songs to express love in the United States and China. Although they found similar levels of passion expressed, the Chinese were more likely to incorporate suffering and sadness as part of the love experience (Rothbaum & Tsang, 1998; Shaver et al., 1992).

Cultures also vary in whether they associate love with marriage. Many contemporary cultures, such as the United States and Japan, consider love a primary basis for deciding whom to marry. But in some cultures, such as those prevalent in many parts of India and Pakistan, marriages are arranged; in fact,

▲ Attesting to the great/ lasting/global appeal of the story of Romeo and Juliet, tourists from around the world flock to this balcony in Verona, Italy, believed by many to be the inspiration for the famous balcony scene.

[Jeff Greenberg]

basing a marriage on love is considered inappropriate and foolhardy (Hatfield et al., 2015; Levine et al., 1995). Even in European cultures, until well into the 19th century, love generally was not considered a basis for marriage (Coontz, 2005; Finkel et al., 2014). Rather, marriage was a pragmatic arrangement that served social and economic goals of the bride's and groom's families.

In many stories, romantic love emerges in opposition to cultural forces that control who marries whom. In the well-known Chinese story of the Butterfly Lovers, which is over 1,000 years old (Idema, 2010), society blocks young lovers from marrying. As a result, the man eventually pines away and dies, and the woman subsequently commits suicide by throwing herself into his grave. The good news is that they reemerge as butterflies. Stories like this, along with *Romeo and Juliet* and countless others dating back over 4,000 years (Fisher, 2006; Wolkstein, 1991), attest to the universality of romantic love and to the fact that it often persists despite opposition from society.

Psychological Theories of Love

We've seen that culture shapes some features of romantic love, but what explains the widespread existence of the phenomenon and the power it often holds over people? Let's consider three broad theoretical perspectives that help clarify why romantic love and relationships are so important to people.

Attachment Theory: Love's Foundation

The greatest thing you'll ever learn
Is just to love and be loved in return

—eden ahbez, "Nature Boy" (1948)

From an evolutionary perspective, love may be advantageous because it generally helps us focus on courting and mating with a single individual at a time. This focus conserves energy and motivates lengthy pair bonding, which aids a couple's effective raising of their offspring (e.g., Fisher, 2004). However, evolutionary adaptations don't spring out of nowhere; they build on preexisting tendencies and structures. Any compelling theory of love must combine insights from human evolution, human development, and adult psychological functioning. Attachment theory provides just such an integrative perspective on love.

The Basics of Attachment: Infancy and Childhood Attachment theory is rooted in the ideas of early psychoanalytic theorists such as Otto Rank, Karen Horney, and Melanie Klein, and it was formally developed by John Bowlby in his three-volume classic *Attachment and Loss* (1969, 1973, 1980). He combined insights from the psychoanalytic tradition, studies of primate behavior, developmental psychology, and his firsthand studies of children separated from their parents (Mikulincer & Shaver, 2007).

Attachment theory posits that the prototypical experience of love is the young child's bond with the primary caretaker, typically the child's mother. The importance of this bond is rooted in our primate heritage, but it is particularly essential for humans, whose newborns are the most helpless and dependent of all mammalian species and need the longest period of care before reaching adulthood. Human newborns lack the capacity to roll over, let alone find food, feed themselves, or defend themselves against predators. They only survive by relying on close attachments to parental figures who can provide care and protection. In fact, infants come into the world with a number of evolved techniques for assuring proximity to attachment figures (Berry & McArthur, 1986; McArthur & Baron, 1983). For instance, their cries guarantee that no one (their parents or anyone else!) can ignore them in times of need.

When infants feel close to an available and responsive attachment figure, they feel comfort and reassurance. Parents who are consistently responsive and supportive provide a safe haven when the child is fearful and a secure base from which the child can venture forth, explore, and grow.

The developmental psychologist Mary Ainsworth studied attachment before and independently of Bowlby. However, after working with Bowlby, she became the primary researcher to study infant attachment systematically. Along with conducting naturalistic observation studies of infants and mothers in their homes, she developed a set of *strange situation tests* to examine the early attachment bond between mothers and their children (Ainsworth & Bell, 1970). Through this research, Ainsworth and colleagues demonstrated the role of attachment in providing young children with psychological security. They also established three major forms of attachment that are associated with particular patterns of child–maternal interaction (Ainsworth et al., 1978):

▲ Infants lack the physical and cognitive abilities to survive in the world on their own. But they have a number of characteristics that we adults seem to find irresistible. These characteristics help to ensure that grown-ups will attend to and care for them.

[Anneka/Shutterstock]

- *Secure attachment style.* In the initial version of the strange situation test, a mother and her nearly one-year-old child enter an unfamiliar room with toys and chairs. After a short time, a female stranger enters the room and sits down. The mother eventually leaves for a few minutes and then returns. In the typical case, the child is attentive to her mother but then happily turns to exploring the toys. When the stranger enters, the child exhibits distress and relieves that distress by returning to her mother. When the mother leaves, distress returns. When the mother returns, the child greets her, becomes relaxed, and resumes exploring the toys. The mother is a secure base for the child's explorations and play. About 60% of the children displayed this form of secure attachment. The other 40% of the children were split about evenly between two insecure attachment styles, described next.

- *Anxious-ambivalent attachment style.* Children who exhibit the anxious-ambivalent attachment style are overly clingy while the mom is there, but they do explore the toys. When the mom leaves the room, they cry and protest. When she returns, they seem angry and resistant (ambivalent) and have difficulty calming down and returning to play with the toys. Parents of these anxious-ambivalent children tend to be very inconsistent, fluctuating between unresponsive and overly intrusive.

- *Avoidant attachment style.* Children who exhibit the avoidant attachment style are not very affectionate with the mom there. They play with the toys but not very enthusiastically. When the mother leaves, they show little distress, and when she returns, they often turn away or avoid her. Parents of avoidant children tend to reject or deflect the child's bids for comfort and closeness.

Subsequent research has confirmed this general distribution of attachment styles. For example, Campos and colleagues (1983) found that among American samples, 62% of infants were secure, 23% were avoidant, and 15% were anxious-ambivalent.

Attachment Style, Genes, and Parental Caregiving   Research on attachment theory has addressed the extent to which a child's temperament and genetic inheritance contribute to the child's attachment style (Kagan, 1994). Findings regarding the role of genes are mixed. Some studies have found that genes have a negligible influence (e.g., Bokhorst et al., 2003). Other research suggests that DNA associated with low dopamine levels is linked to high levels of attachment anxiety, and DNA associated with low serotonin levels is linked to high levels of attachment avoidance (Gillath et al., 2008). This latter work suggests that about 20% of variability in attachment anxiety and attachment avoidance may result from genetic factors.

As attachment theory proposes, the variability in attachment style depends primarily on how attachment figures interact with the child (Fraley, 2002; Main, 1995; Waller & Shaver, 1994). In one particularly ambitious study, Dymphna van den Boom (1994) showed that when a random half of mothers of temperamentally difficult six-month-old infants were trained for three months in sensitive responding to the child, by 12 months of age, 62% of the infants were securely attached, whereas only 22% of the children whose parents weren't so trained exhibited secure attachment. A follow-up study found that the children whose mothers had received training were still benefiting from it when the children were three (van den Boom, 1995).

Working models of relationships Global feelings about the nature and worth of close relationships and other people's trustworthiness.

The Enduring Influence of Attachment: Adult Romantic Relationships   So what does attachment during childhood have to do with adult romantic relationships? The nature of this initial love relationship influences the close relationships individuals have over the course of their lives, including adult love relationships. Just as attachment to the parents is central to a child's psychological security, attachment to the romantic partner is central to psychological security for most adults (e.g., Mikulincer, 2006; Simpson et al., 1992). Attachment theorists explain that childhood experiences result in **working models of relationships**—that is, global feelings about the nature and worth of close relationships and other people's trustworthiness and ability to provide security—that extend into adulthood (Baldwin et al., 1996; Collins & Read, 1994; Pietromonaco & Barrett, 2000).

To determine if attachment styles do endure into adulthood, Cindy Hazan and Phil Shaver (1987) recruited community participants of various ages in their first study and college students in their second study. They created three descriptions of how people think and feel about getting close to others that corresponded to the secure, anxious-ambivalent, and avoidant attachment styles established by Ainsworth. These are depicted in **FIGURE 15.2**. Which best fits you? Hazan and Shaver hypothesized that if childhood attachment styles are stable and affect adult relationships, the percentages of people who picked one of the three different paragraphs should be similar to the percentages that Ainsworth and colleagues found with very young children. And indeed it was: Across the two studies, roughly 56% reported the secure style, 20% the anxious-ambivalent style, and 24% the avoidant style. Subsequent studies have found similar frequencies of these attachment styles (Mickelson et al., 1997). Further supporting the stability of attachment styles, longitudinal studies have been conducted, and they generally suggest considerable stability of attachment style from infancy to adulthood (Fraley, 2002; Simpson et al., 2007).

A. I am somewhat uncomfortable being close to others; I find it difficult to trust them completely, difficult to allow myself to depend on them. I am nervous when anyone gets too close, and often, others want me to be more intimate than I feel comfortable being.

B. I find it relatively easy to get close to others and am comfortable depending on them and having them depend on me. I don't worry about being abandoned or about someone getting too close to me.

C. I find that others are reluctant to get as close as I would like. I often worry that my partner doesn't really love me or won't want to stay with me. I want to get very close to my partner, and this sometimes scares people away.

Figure 15.2

Attachment Style Questionnaire

Hazan and Shaver developed these descriptions to capture three basic attachment styles. Which one best fits your view of close relationships?

[Research from Hazan & Shaver, 1987]

However, early attachment style is not entirely set in stone. As Bowlby (1980) proposed, experiences with attachment figures throughout one's life can alter one's predominant working model of attachment. A horrible relationship, full of betrayal, could make a securely attached person insecure; a happy, stable relationship might shift an insecure person toward a secure style. Indeed, in a four-year longitudinal study of adults, Kirkpatrick and Hazan (1994) found that 30% of the adults overall changed their attachment style. Secures were more stable than others, with only 17% changing. In other words, the anxious and avoidant-attached adults were more likely to change styles over the four years (also see Baldwin & Fehr, 1995).

Over the years, researchers have specified two dimensions that underlie these styles of attachment (Bartholomew & Horowitz, 1991; Brennan et al., 1998). One dimension is referred to as attachment-related *anxiety*. People high in attachment-related anxiety are overly concerned with whether the partner is attentive and responsive. The other dimension is labeled attachment-related *avoidance* and refers to a reluctance to depend on others. People can be high or low in either or both dimensions. As shown in **FIGURE 15.3**, this yields what many researchers now recognize as four possible styles.

Research using this dimensional approach provides further insight into how people's attachment feelings relate to the nature of their most important romantic relationship, their views of romantic love, their approach to sex, and their reports of how their parents raised them. Let's consider some of these findings.

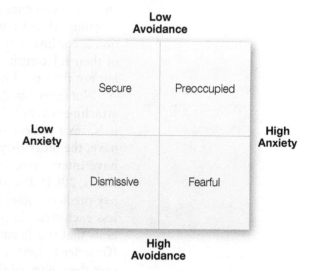

Figure 15.3

Attachment Dimensions

Expanding on the categorical approach of distinct attachment styles, research uncovered two attachment dimensions. People can be high or low on attachment avoidance and attachment anxiety, which when crossed yield four attachment styles.
[Research from Brennan et al., 1998]

Low Avoidance/Low Anxiety: Securely Attached Adults Participants who are **securely attached** are low in both attachment anxiety and attachment avoidance. They tend to report the longest-lasting, most satisfying romantic relationships. They believe that love can endure, and they tend to be self-confident and trusting of others. They recall having warm relationships with both of their parents while growing up. Moreover, securely attached people are generally psychologically well adjusted (Mikulincer & Shaver, 2007). When their relationship partners need care or comfort, they are very responsive in providing it. This is important, as when one's partner is perceived to be responsive, people are less anxious and sleep better (Selcuk et al., 2017). Also, securely attached people react less negatively than insecurely attached people to unflattering feedback from their partners (Collins & Feeney, 2004). Those with a more secure attachment style are also more comfortable with their sexuality and generally enjoy sex (Tracy et al., 2003). They are also more likely to have sex within a committed relationship (Feeney et al., 1993) and to see sex as a way to enhance intimacy in the relationship and express their love for their partner (Cooper et al., 2006).

Securely attached An attachment style characterized by a positive view of self and others, low anxiety and avoidance, and stable, satisfying relationships.

Low Avoidance/High Anxiety: Anxious-Ambivalent Adults Anxious-ambivalent (or preoccupied) individuals tend to have a negative view of themselves (i.e., low or unstable self-esteem) but a positive view of others. They have short, intense relationships but with many emotional highs and lows (Hazan & Shaver, 1987), featuring frequent feelings of passion, jealousy, anger, and smothering (e.g., Davis et al., 2004; Shaver et al., 2005). They tend to fall in love very easily but at the same time are skeptical of how long love can last, and they are dissatisfied with the attentiveness of romantic partners. When people high in attachment

Anxious-ambivalent An attachment style characterized by a negative view of the self but a positive view of others, high anxiety, low avoidance, and intense but unstable relationships.

anxiety become parents, they become especially concerned with their children "stealing" time from their romantic partner (Jones et al., 2015). They give affection according to their own needs, as opposed to being responsive to the needs of their relationship partners. They fulfill their partners' need for relatedness but not their need for autonomy (Hadden et al., 2016).

Not surprisingly, they also use and see sex differently from those with other attachment types. Like many other aspects of relationships for these individuals, sex can become riddled with anxiety. The more attachment anxiety men have, the older they are when they first have sex, and the less frequently they have intercourse and with fewer partners (Feeney et al., 1993; Gentzler & Kerns, 2004). But among anxious-ambivalent women, greater attachment anxiety predicts higher likelihood of having sex, earlier age at first intercourse, and less exclusivity in partners (Cooper, Shapiro, & Powers, 1998). Research suggests that this is partly because such women succumb to pressures to have sex (Gentzler & Kerns, 2004) and use sex to avoid partner disapproval and to reassure themselves of their self-worth (Cooper et al., 2006).

High Avoidance/High or Low Anxiety: Avoidantly Attached Adults   Participants who report higher levels of avoidance tend to have relatively short relationships that lack intimacy (Hazan & Shaver, 1987). They recall their mothers as being cold and rejecting. They don't believe love endures, are fearful of closeness, and lack trust in romantic partners. Avoidantly attached people perceive their intimate partners as feeling more negative emotions about the relationship than the partners actually experience. These biased perceptions in turn lead them to act in hostile, defensive ways in daily life (Overall et al., 2015). They are also more sensitive to their partners' negative communication, which escalates conflict (Kuster et al., 2015). They seem not to want to get much from their romantic relationships, are emotionally distant, and tend to ignore their partners' needs for care and intimacy (Collins & Feeney, 2000). They allow their partners to fulfill their need for autonomy but don't fulfill their need for relatedness (Hadden et al., 2016).

People who are high in attachment avoidance are more likely to delay having sex, and when they do, they do so in contexts that limit intimacy, such as having more casual as well as solitary sex (Cooper, Shapiro, & Powers, 1998). This is partly because avoidant people tend to use sex to affirm their desirability and to cope with negative emotions rather than to seek pleasure or enhance intimacy. And research suggests this preference for casual sex leads to less satisfying and less long-lasting marriages (French et al., 2019). Avoidantly attached people are also less motivated to have children, which reflects their valuing of independence (Jones et al., 2015).

Avoidant styles can come in one of two forms (Bartholomew & Horowitz, 1991). High levels of avoidance can be paired with high levels of anxiety (referred to as a fearful avoidant style) and reflect negative views of both self and others. So the **fearfully avoidant** person doesn't feel worthy, doesn't trust others, and fears rejection. People high in avoidance and high in anxiety seem to have a lot of ambivalence about and low commitment to their romantic relationships (Park et al., 2019). High levels of avoidance can also be paired with low levels of anxiety. Those with this **dismissive avoidant** attachment style tend to show a positive view of the self but a negative view of others. Dismissive avoidant people are more self-satisfied and appear not to need closeness with others. They hide their vulnerability, deny their desire for intimacy, and tend to be sexually promiscuous (Gjerde et al., 2004; Mikulincer et al., 2004).

Fearfully avoidant An avoidant attachment style characterized by a negative view of both self and others, high avoidance and high anxiety, and distant relationships, in which the person doesn't feel worthy, doesn't trust others, and fears rejection.

Dismissive avoidant An avoidant attachment style characterized by a negative view of others but a positive view of the self, high avoidance but low anxiety, and distant relationships.

As previously mentioned, one reason people high in attachment avoidance push their partners away is that they don't trust that the support they're receiving can be counted on to last. Backing up this idea, research shows that when partners provide low to moderate levels of support (e.g., helping out with daily hassles), highly avoidant individuals react negatively. However, if partners' support shifts from moderate to high levels, avoidant individuals become receptive and experience better psychological functioning (Girme et al., 2015). Consistently high levels of support offer convincing evidence that the partner can be relied on, which relaxes the defenses that avoidant individuals typically put up when others try to care for them.

Combinations of Attachment Styles and Long-Term Relationships   Clearly the best bet for a stable and satisfying long-term relationship is for both members of a couple to have a secure attachment style (Kane et al., 2007; Senchak & Leonard, 1992; Shaver & Mikulincer, 2010; Simpson, 1990). Other combinations of attachment styles yield less mutual satisfaction and stability, with one interesting exception. Over a four-year period, Kirkpatrick and Davis (1994) found that anxious women and avoidant men had relationships as stable as those of secure couples, although they were far less satisfying. Kirkpatrick and Davis suggested that this is because women who are highly invested in relationships and men who are distant and less invested fit the prevailing gender stereotypes. In these relationships, the women put up with the men and vice versa, even though neither of them is very satisfied. In fact, some studies of heterosexual couples have found that women's dissatisfaction increases the more avoidant their male partners are, and men's dissatisfaction increases the more anxious their female partners are (Collins & Read, 1990; Kane et al., 2007).

Love, the Ultimate Security Blanket   As we wrap up our discussion of attachment theory and research, we want to close by reiterating this theory's central insight regarding love. From the perspective of attachment theory, we seek and maintain love for significant others to garner a sense of support, comfort, relief, trust, and security, particularly when we are confronted with threats from the outside world or distressing thoughts and emotions (e.g., Mikulincer et al., 2001). The sense of warmth and physical protection that we experience as infants when we are close to a responsive caregiver lays the foundation for the comforting experience we have as adults when we feel a secure bond with our romantic partners. It may seem odd that the same basic emotional needs that tie children to their parents also tie adults to their romantic partners, but that's a central message of attachment theory: Even when we're grown up, we crave the security of being close to someone who cares for us.

Terror Management Theory: Love and Death

Unable are the Loved to die
For Love is Immortality

—Emily Dickinson (1864/1960, p. 394)

In the weeks following the terrorist attacks of September 11, 2001, Americans showed an increased tendency to solidify their close relationships, expressed more commitment, spent more time with family members and friends, and sought more intimate sexual encounters with their romantic partners (e.g., Ai et al., 2009). Various newspapers and magazines such as *Newsweek* also reported similar trends in the wake of the Oklahoma City bombing in 1995 and Hurricane

Katrina in 2005, as well as among military units facing more combat and higher levels of violence (e.g., Mitchell, 2009). Why?

One answer comes from the existential perspective offered by terror management theory. Terror management theory is highly compatible with attachment theory in its focus on how children develop security and how that sets the stage for adults' bases of psychological security. From this theoretical perspective, romantic partners help each other manage the threat of mortality by giving life meaning and reinforcing self-worth (Kosloff, Greenberg, Sullivan, & Weise, 2010; Solomon et al., 1991). Thus, even in situations in which a person faces no immediate threat to her survival, the knowledge that life is fragile and destined to end—a fact made salient, for example, by media reports of terrorist attacks—helps fuel feelings of love by driving people to cling to close relationships for security.

According to Otto Rank (1936), as Western societies became more secular during the 20th century, romantic relationships largely replaced religion as the primary source of meaning and value, the basis for how people feel protected from death. Rank suggested that as this occurred in Western cultures, the romantic relationship became viewed increasingly as a magical, eternal bond of love with a soul mate. Thus, romantic relationships became a central basis of feeling that one's life is meaningful and enduringly significant. You know you are valued because you are loved. A life partner knows your life story and cares about the minute details of your life, thus bearing witness to and validating your existence and its value. Though perhaps particularly prevalent in modern Western societies, this idea has been around for many centuries and has been expressed in many cultures. A Hindu song put it this way: "My lover is like God: if he accepts me my existence is utilized" (Becker, 1973, p. 161). Eli Finkel and colleagues (Finkel, Cheung et al., 2015) have recently made similar observations, suggesting that people in North America increasingly view having romantic relationships as a way to meet the needs for self-esteem and self-actualization.

Studies have supported the idea that romantic partners enhance people's self-worth and validate their worldviews. Aron and colleagues (1995) tracked people who did and did not fall in love over time. One of their findings was that people who fell in love showed an increase in self-esteem. And even more directly, studies have shown that thinking of our mortality leads us to be more committed to lovers who positively regard us and make us feel good about ourselves. In addition, when participants were reminded of death, the more highly committed they were to the relationship, the more positively they viewed their romantic partners and the more positively they felt that their romantic partners viewed them (Cox & Arndt, 2012).

Further support for the role of romantic relationships in terror management has been provided by a series of studies conducted in Israel by Mario Mikulincer and colleagues, who noted that such relationships may be especially important for managing fear of death because they provide the same type of physical and emotional closeness we all relied on as children when we were scared (see Mikulincer et al., 2003). They have found that for people in committed relationships, threats to the relationship or thoughts of being away from their partners increase the accessibility of death-related thoughts. In addition, reminders of mortality increase the desire for closeness in the romantic relationship. In people lacking a romantic relationship, reminders of mortality increase the desire to have one. Finally, romantic relationships help securely attached people manage their concerns about mortality, but they don't do so for those who are insecurely attached. Additional evidence suggests that insecurely attached young adults still rely on their parents, rather than their romantic partners, for existential security (Cox et al., 2008).

Terror management theory also helps us understand the desire for and love of one's children, as having children can be one way to feel that a part of the self lives on beyond one's own death. Indeed, death reminders increase desire for offspring among Dutch, German, and Chinese individuals (Fritsche et al., 2007; Wisman & Goldenberg, 2005; Zhou et al., 2008). They also increase interest in naming future children after oneself (Vicary, 2011). Furthermore, for young married adults without children, death reminders increase positive thoughts of parenthood, and thinking about becoming parents reduces the accessibility of death-related thoughts (Yaakobi et al., 2014). Taken together, this work suggests that the idea of having children, and thereby continuing to live on in some way, helps to quell concerns about personal mortality.

The Self-Expansion Model: Love as a Basis of Growth

To get the full value of joy you must have someone to divide it with.

—Mark Twain

So far we've been focusing on theories that portray love primarily as a basis for feeling safe and secure in the world. But this is undoubtedly an incomplete picture of why we pursue love relationships. Recall from chapter 6 that humanistic psychology and self-determination theory emphasize the person's potential to grow and change. These theories view the person as inherently motivated to cultivate inner potentialities, seek out optimal challenges, and master new experiences.

According to Art Aron's **self-expansion model of relationships**, one way that people satisfy this motive is through romantic relationships. The self-expansion model proposes that a central human motive is the desire to expand the self and that loving another person is an important way to do so (Aron et al., 2001). From this perspective, the romantic partner becomes incorporated as part of the self, thus helping to expand the self, making the self more complex. When you fall in love, you start to care about the things your partner cares about. You may start doing different activities, eating different foods, listening to different music, reading different books, and so forth.

Self-expansion model of relationships The idea that romantic relationships serve the desire to expand the self and grow.

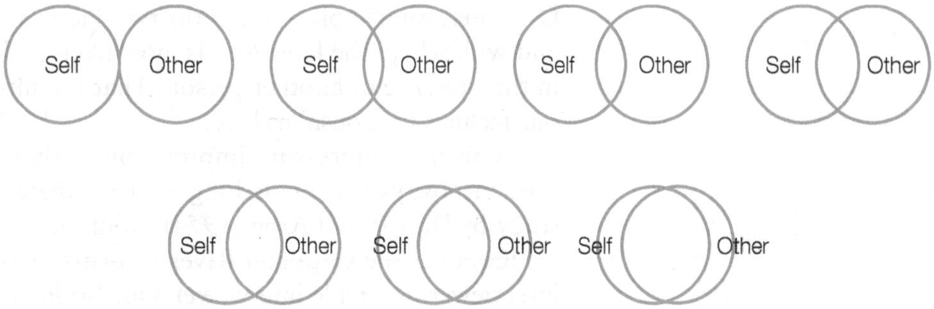

In this way, love can enhance growth. In support of this idea, Aron and colleagues (1995) found that when people fell in love, their self-concept did indeed become more complex.

To assess the idea that people incorporate their partners partly into the self, Aron and colleagues (1992) developed the Inclusion of Other in the Self (IOS) scale. As depicted in **FIGURE 15.4**, the scale consists of seven pairs of circles that represent varying degrees of overlap between self and partner. Individuals are asked to select the pair that best describes their relationship with their partners. This simple scale has proven very useful for assessing relationship closeness (Agnew et al., 2004). People who choose more overlapping circles

Figure 15.4

The Inclusion of Other in the Self Scale

How much mutuality do people feel in a relationship? Asking people to choose the pair of overlapping circles that best portrays their relationship with their partner provides a measure of the closeness they feel.

[Research from Aron et al., 1992]

have more satisfying relationships and use more plural pronouns in describing their relationship. They are also more likely to blur the line between their sense of who they are and who their partner is. After rating some traits for self and other traits for their partners, they were more likely to mistake traits they rated for self for those they rated for others (Aron & Fraley, 1999).

The self-expansion model also posits that the experience of self-expanding adds pleasure and excitement to relationships (Aron & Aron, 2006). On the basis of this idea, Aron and colleagues proposed that early in relationships, during the "honeymoon period," people are getting to know each other. This stimulates a great deal of rapid self-expansion and exhilaration. Over time, however, the self-expanding aspect of a relationship tends to slow down as the relationship falls into routine. The challenge then is to keep the process of mutual self-expansion going over the long haul, an idea we will return to later in this chapter.

Models of the Experience of Love

Attachment theory, terror management theory, and the self-expansion model help explain why love is a virtually universal and very important aspect of human experience. Other social psychological models of love provide insights into the subjective experience of love and the various forms romantic love can take.

Schachter's Two-Factor Theory: Love as an Emotion   Falling in love and being in love can be intense feelings. Where do these feelings come from? Berscheid and Walster (1974) applied Schachter's (1964) two-factor theory of emotion to understanding love as a felt emotion. As you'll recall from chapter 5, Schachter's theory proposed that emotions result from the combination of two factors: physiological arousal and a label for that arousal based on cues present when the arousal is being felt. This theory suggests that when an individual is aroused in the presence of a member of the preferred sex and in a context that cultural learning suggests is romantic, that arousal may be interpreted as love (or lust). One interesting implication of the two-factor theory is that cultures direct when and with whom the label *love* is most likely to be applied to arousal that occurs in the presence of another person. That is, cultural scripts tell us when to label our feelings of arousal as love.

A second interesting implication is that the real source of the arousal doesn't always matter, as long as it is labeled *attraction* or *love*. Consider a study by Dutton and Aron (1974). Adult males were interviewed on one of two bridges over the Capilano River in British Columbia by an attractive female interviewer or a male interviewer. One bridge was a very wide, safe bridge, only 10 feet over a small rivulet. The other bridge was a wobbly, narrow 450-foot suspension bridge over a 230-foot gorge, with shallow rapids below. Dutton and Aron assumed that the narrow bridge over the deep drop would generate some physiological arousal because of the possibility of danger (and perhaps also the spectacular setting), whereas the small footbridge would not. Applying the two-factor theory, they thus proposed that men interviewed over the scary bridge by the female interviewer would attribute some of their arousal to their feelings of attraction to and perhaps romantic interest in her. They therefore predicted that men would be more attracted to the female interviewer on the scary bridge than on the safe bridge.

Dutton and Aron used two clever dependent variables to test this idea. First, while on the bridge, the interviewer showed the interviewees an ambiguous picture of a young woman covering her face with one hand and reaching out with the other and asked them to write a brief story about it. Dutton and Aron had the stories coded for sexual content. They expected more sexual content in the stories by the men who were interviewed by the female on the scary bridge. Second, they had the interviewer give the interviewees her phone number in case they wanted to learn more about the study. Dutton and Aron figured that if the scary bridge interviewees were more attracted to the female interviewer, they would be more likely to call her. Both hypotheses were supported. The scary bridge interviewees made more calls and wrote more sexual stories. For example, 50% of these interviewees called, whereas only about 20% called in the other three conditions tested (female interviewer on safe bridge or male interviewer on either bridge).

The idea that love and attraction can be fueled by external sources of arousal has been supported in other ways as well (e.g., Valins, 1966; White et al., 1981; White & Kight, 1984). For example, working with the excitation transfer paradigm developed by Zillmann (1971) and described in chapter 5, White and colleagues (1981) showed that arousal from both exercise and funny or disturbing audiotapes increased men's romantic attraction to a female confederate. In a study conducted at an amusement park, individuals found a photographed member of the opposite sex more desirable as a date after exiting a roller coaster than before getting on the roller coaster—unless they were with a romantic partner on the roller coaster (Meston & Frohlich, 2003).

How much of our attraction to, and even love for, a romantic partner may have been fueled or intensified by external sources of arousal without our awareness? It is hard to say in any specific case. But the research supporting the two-factor theory suggests that initial attraction to or feelings of love for a romantic partner may indeed be affected by external sources of arousal. And think of what people do when they date others they are interested in: They often do exciting, physiologically arousing things—go dancing, watch exciting or scary movies, go on amusement-park rides or hikes, play sports or watch sporting events, or visit exciting places. Coincidence?

▲ Don't look down! But if you do, do you think the arousal you experience might influence your affection for an attractive person you meet on a narrow suspension bridge overlooking the Capilano River in British Columbia? When Dutton and Aron (1974) interviewed people on such a bridge, they found that the answer is "yes."

[toos/iStock Unreleased/Getty Images]

Sternberg's Triangular Model of Love Think about all the couples you have known in your life as well as your own relationships. Has the love involved always been the same? Chances are each love relationship has a somewhat different flavor. This observation has led researchers to look into different types of love. Perhaps the most basic distinction is between passionate love and companionate love (e.g., Hatfield, 1988). Passionate love involves an emotionally intense and erotic desire to be absorbed in another person; it is the kind of love Schachter's theory applies to best. With companionate love, there is still great affection, trust, and a sense that the relationship is important, but passion is much diminished or absent.

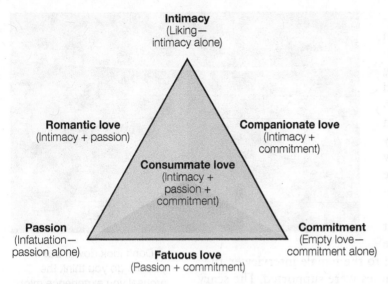

Figure 15.5

Triangular Model of Love Relationship

Robert Sternberg proposes that we can break down love into three main facets, which when combined with one another yield seven different types of love. Think about where some of the most important close relationships in your life fit within this triangle.

[Research from Sternberg, 1997]

Robert Sternberg's triangular model of love relationships (depicted in **FIGURE 15.5**) elegantly captures not only these two kinds of love but five others as well. The model posits three basic components of love relationships that in different combinations describe different kinds of relationships (Aron & Westbay, 1996): passion, intimacy, and commitment. Passion is the excitement about, sexual attraction to, and longing for the partner. Intimacy involves liking, sharing, knowing, and emotional support of the partner. Commitment is the extent to which the individual is invested in maintaining the relationship.

People generally describe their ideal romantic relationship as high on all three factors—what is called consummate love (Sternberg, 1997). But what makes the model elegant is that it also describes forms of love that center around a single component or combine just two components. A relationship with only passion is an infatuation; there is strong attraction and arousal, but the partner is not well known, and there is no commitment to a relationship. Intimacy alone can characterize a close acquaintanceship or friendship. Sternberg labeled commitment alone as empty love; there is investment in maintaining the relationship, but there is no sharing, and there is no passion. This sometimes occurs in older couples for whom the passion and even the sense of liking for the partner are no longer present, but commitment persists—out of habit, familiarity, or fear of being alone. The relationship still helps the individual feel secure, but there is no growth or stimulation.

Sternberg labeled the combination of passion and intimacy as romantic, or passionate, love; people are in love and share knowledge of each other but haven't made a real commitment to sustaining the relationship over time. Romantic love often is a step toward consummate love, but in some cases that commitment is never made. The combination of passion and commitment is called fatuous love and is exemplified by young adults who have developed a strong infatuation and jump to the commitment of marriage before they really know each other well. These kinds of relationships often don't turn out well because, lacking intimacy, partners don't know what they are getting into. Each partner will tend to idealize the other at first, but they may discover less-than-ideal surprises as they get to know each other better.

Finally, the combination of intimacy and commitment without passion is companionate love, a kind of love often found in older couples who have been together a very long time (like the couple introduced at the beginning of this chapter). Stimulation and sexual attraction have died out, but the positive feelings, sharing, and commitment have remained strong. Though passion in relationships does tend to diminish somewhat in intensity over time, it still can be found in many long-standing relationships (Acevedo & Aron, 2009; Acker & Davis, 1992). If consummate love is the ideal, keeping passion alive over the long haul is one of the biggest challenges of long-term relationships, and we will address this challenge later in the chapter.

SECTION REVIEW   This Thing Called Love

Social scientists have made great strides in understanding the motivations underlying romantic love, its components, and factors that shape the experience of it.

Romantic Love	Culture and Love	Theories of Love's Psychological Functions	Models of the Components of Love
Early research distinguished between liking and loving. Loving typically involves intense caring, intimacy, and a deep emotional investment.	The capacity to experience romantic love is likely universal but is partly shaped by culture.	• Attachment theory proposes that most people seek security from their romantic relationships much as they once did from their parents. The nature of that original child–parent bond affects the nature of subsequent adult close relationships. • Terror management theory suggests that love and close relationships help us to buffer the dread of being aware of our mortality. • The self-expansion model of relationships suggests that love relationships often are valuable paths to personal growth.	• The two-factor theory posits that love is partly a label we apply to feelings of arousal on the basis of contextual cues. • The triangular model of love suggests that love is based on combinations of three basic components: passion, intimacy, and commitment.

Cost–Benefit Perspectives on Relationships

No doubt you have heard people refer to the dating scene as a meat market. This rather blunt expression is a nod to the ways in which romantic relationships are like commodities to be negotiated and bartered on the open market. We bring certain strengths to the table, try to tuck our baggage under our chair, and look to make a good deal with a partner. With the advent of online dating sites and apps such as Match.com, eHarmony, OkCupid, Tinder, Bumble, and Grindr, this shopping metaphor has taken on an even more literal dimension. When we take this market-driven approach to studying how people form relationships, we are applying the social exchange model.

The Social Exchange Model

The **social exchange model** (Thibaut & Kelley, 1959) takes an economic perspective and assumes that people approach relationships with the underlying motivation of self-interest: relationships have value when both people perceive that they have more to gain than to lose from being in a partnership. The benefits of a relationship can be financial, emotional, sexual, and social. But entering into any relationship also carries certain costs that need to be negotiated along the way.

Clearly, this is not the most romantic view of love. But a social exchange approach to relationships does make intuitive sense. Every relationship has ups and downs, but as long as the ups outnumber the downs, the outcome of the relationship is generally positive (Hicks & McNulty, 2019). Several studies have confirmed that people are more satisfied in a relationship to the extent that they see the benefits as outweighing the costs (Duffy & Rusbult, 1986; Rusbult, 1980, 1983; Rusbult & Martz, 1995; Rusbult et al., 1986).

Learning Outcome

• Identify how the social exchange model, equity theory, and the matching phenomenon address love from a cost–benefit perspective.

Achieve
Video Activity: Online Dating

Social exchange model A model which takes an economic perspective and assumes that people approach relationships with an underlying motivation of self-interest.

▲ The social exchange model takes an economic perspective on relationships in which prospective and actual partners are assessed on the basis of costs and benefits.

[IPGGutenbergUKLtd/Getty Images]

Comparison level The expectation of how rewarding a relationship should be.

Equity theory The idea that people are motivated to maintain a sense of fairness or equity, whereby both partners feel that the proportion of outcomes (rewards) to inputs (costs) that each receives is roughly equal.

But not everyone is equally happy with the same relationship outcome. If you were brought up in a harmonious, two-parent home, watched a steady diet of Disney movies, or paid a lot of attention to online matchmaking sites advertising the importance of finding your soul mate (Finkel et al., 2012b), you might have internalized ideals of happily ever after and one true love. These cultural standards can set a high **comparison level**, or expectation of how rewarding a relationship should be. A relationship that merely delivers more benefits than costs might not quite live up to the ideal of finding your soul mate. At the other extreme, if you were raised in a home characterized by marital strife and domestic violence, your comparison level for a satisfying relationship would likely be much lower and thus more easily met or exceeded. A relationship with a given set of rewards and costs would seem much more satisfying to a person with the very low comparison level than to a person with the very high one (Rusbult, 1983). We can express this in a formal equation:

$$\text{SATISFACTION} = (\text{REWARDS} - \text{COSTS}) - \text{COMPARISON LEVEL}$$

Do people really use this kind of calculus to judge their relationships? Some evidence shows that people who believe in the idea of a soul mate (a rather high comparison level) are satisfied in their current relationship only to the extent that they see the partner as an ideal mate (Franiuk et al., 2002; Franiuk et al., 2004; Knee, 1998).

Still, for something as deeply emotional and prosocial as our close relationships, is it fair to say that our selfish desire for benefits is the only driving force in how we form and maintain strong bonds with each other? Critics of the social exchange model have said, "No!" They point out that this model does not explain the sense of fairness that is so important in our relationships (Clark & Mills, 1979; Fiske, 1991). We generally don't keep a ledger of who contributes what to the relationship, and we generally don't try to maximize our own outcomes at the expense of our partner—at least not if we want the relationship to last!

Equity Theory

Equity theory addresses the fairness shortcoming of the social exchange model. It proposes that people are motivated to maintain a sense of fairness or equity, where both partners feel that the proportion of rewards or outcomes (benefits) to inputs (costs) that each receives is roughly equal (Adams, 1963; Hatfield et al., 1978). The equity formula looks like this, with "O" standing for outcomes and "I" standing for inputs:

$$\text{O/I FOR SELF} = \text{O/I FOR PARTNER}$$

When we feel that our partner is getting a higher proportion of outcomes relative to inputs than we are, we feel angry and resentful. But the partner who feels unfairly advantaged in a relationship also can feel a sense of guilt that can motivate effort to balance the scales (Sprecher, 1986, 1992). How is equity restored? You can either increase the inputs or decrease the outcomes for the advantaged partner. Alternatively, you can decrease the inputs or increase the outcomes of the person who is disadvantaged.

To see how equity works, let's consider an example from a popular television show. In the sitcom *Modern Family*, the clean freak Mitchell works full-time as an attorney. He resists the urge to clean up the house in order to send a message to his stay-at-home, less tidy husband, Cameron, that perhaps he should help with the housework (Koch, 2011). In this example, the overburdened

Mitchell has reduced his cleaning inputs to try to restore a sense of equity. At the same time, he hopes that this reduction in input—his no longer cleaning up the mess—will prompt Cameron to increase his input. These two strategies are adjustments to inputs, but adjustments also can be made to outcomes. The overworked partner might withhold other, you know, "benefits" of the relationship. Or the person doing less housework might surprise his or her partner with a weekend trip to a spa.

These little adjustments in relationships happen all the time as partners try to maintain a sense of equity. Even when equity isn't achieved objectively, just *feeling* as if things are equitable can make a difference. In the *Modern Family* example, we imagine that Cameron might not permanently change his sloppier habits, but maybe he'll make up for his low inputs in cleaning by being especially appreciative of the hard work that Mitchell puts into the house. Gratitude actually can go a long way toward making the scales seem more balanced. Perceived equity is an important determinant of the progress and quality of relationships. When people feel that the proportion of costs to benefits is roughly equivalent for both themselves and their partners, they are more likely to have sex, fall in love, commit to a long-term relationship, and be satisfied in that relationship (Buunk & van Yperen, 1989; Sprecher, 1998; van Yperen & Buunk, 1990).

Assortative Mating

The motivation for fairness in our relationships helps explain **assortative mating,** people's tendency to seek relationships with others who are similar to them in some kind of social hierarchy. Pairing up with those who are similar in social value helps to equate partners on what rewards or resources they bring to the relationship (Hatfield & Rapson, 1993). For example, on the website hotornot .com, people can post pictures of themselves to be rated by others on attractiveness, and they can also use this website to contact other people to strike up conversations. Although there is strong agreement in who is rated as most attractive, people still generally contact others who are similar to themselves in attractiveness (Lee et al., 2008)—those in their own league, so to speak. This is known as the **matching phenomenon,** and it helps ensure a certain balance of outcomes in the relationship. People generally seek and end up in romantic relationships with someone similar to them in physical attractiveness (Feingold, 1988).

This matching phenomenon only holds for people who start dating not long after they became acquainted with each other (Hunt et al., 2015). For people who knew each other for nine months or more before dating, and for people who were friends before they began dating, there was no evidence that people who ended up in relationships were similar in physical attractiveness. Presumably this is because if you're acquainted with someone for a while before deciding to date, the person's unique idiosyncratic qualities are better known and become the more influential factors in dating and mating choices.

It's also worth noting that when assortative mating does occur, the exchange of relationship rewards can cross currencies: One person (more often a woman) might trade on her youth and good looks to attract a mate who can provide financial resources and security (Baumeister & Vohs, 2004). For example, the late Hugh Hefner, the famed and wealthy impresario of all things *Playboy*, had a string of beautiful girlfriends decades younger than himself.

Think back to the discussion of evolution and mating strategies from chapter 14. How does that help us explain such trade-offs in assortative mating?

▲ The TV show *Modern Family* depicts some of the dynamics of maintaining close relationships. In one episode, Cameron and Mitchell make adjustments to try to maintain equitable contributions to their relationship.
[ABC-TV/Shutterstock]

Assortative mating The idea that people are attracted to others who are similar to them in some kind of social hierarchy.

Matching phenomenon The idea that people seek romantic relationships with others who are similar to themselves in physical attractiveness.

◄ **THINK ABOUT**
[David Livingston/Getty Images]

SECTION REVIEW Cost–Benefit Perspectives on Relationships

People evaluate relationships according to the costs and benefits to themselves and their partners.

Social Exchange Model	Equity Theory	Assortative Mating
The social exchange model is based on the idea that relationship satisfaction depends on both the rewards received minus the costs and expectations about the relationship (comparison level).	Equity theory is based on the idea that partners look for fairness within a relationship both for themselves and for their partners. This desire for a fair relationship may help account for people's tendency to form relationships with others of similar perceived social value.	People tend to seek partners who are similar in some kind of social hierarchy.

Learning Outcome

- Identify how romantic commitment varies between individualistic and collectivistic cultures.

THINK ABOUT

[Eamonn M. McCormack/Getty Images]

Responses:	Yes	No	Undecided
India	49.0%	24.0%	26.9%
Pakistan	50.4%	39.1%	10.4%
Thailand	18.8%	33.8%	47.5%
United States	3.5%	85.9%	10.6%
England	7.3%	83.6%	9.1%
Japan	2.3%	62.0%	35.7%
Philippines	11.4%	63.6%	25.0%
Mexico	10.2%	80.5%	9.3%
Brazil	4.3%	85.7%	10.0%
Hong Kong	5.8%	77.6%	16.7%
Australia	4.8%	80.0%	15.2%

Figure 15.6

Love and Marriage in Different Countries

Responses to the question "If a man (woman) had all the other qualities you desired, would you marry this person if you were not in love with him (her)?"

[Data from Levine et al., 1995].

Cultural and Historical Perspectives on Relationships

Suppose that a man (woman) had all the qualities you desired in a partner. Think about it. Would you marry this person if you were not in love with him (her)? Chances are that you answered "no." In today's Western world, love typically is viewed as the reason for getting hitched and for staying committed to the relationship. We're bombarded with stories and songs that exalt love as the glue that binds people together and leads us into the happily ever after (Jackson et al., 2006). It is part of our cultural fabric. In fact, when American students were asked this question in 1995, only 3.5% of men and women said "yes" to the prospect of a loveless but otherwise satisfying marriage (Levine et al., 1995). But it's not just Americans who are romantics. As **FIGURE 15.6** shows, respondents from only 2 of 11 countries were fine with choosing to marry without love—India and Pakistan, where arranged marriages have remained common (Epstein et al., 2013; Hatfield et al., 2015).

But love has not always played such a central role in marriage, even in the United States. When the same question was presented to American students in 1967, only 65% of men and 24% of women said "no" (Kephart, 1967). Such studies tell us that in different eras and countries, people have been more receptive to entering into, and staying in, a marriage for reasons other than being in love. Let's take a look at this cross-cultural variability.

Cross-Cultural Differences in Romantic Commitment

Differences between individualistic and collectivistic cultures shape the way people view intimate commitments. In collectivistic cultures, family considerations and opinion have a much stronger influence than they do in individualistic cultures in determining whom people decide to marry, as well as whether or not they stay in the relationship (Dion & Dion, 1996).

Take China as an example. In Chinese culture, two fundamental values are *xiao* (loosely translated as "filial piety"—respect for and devotion to family) and *guanxi* ("network," referring to broader social interdependence). Both strongly drive decisions about intimate relationships. Chinese students are more likely to report family disapproval as an obstacle to marriage than are U.S. students. In China, judgments about whether the partner will support one's parents are more important factors in decisions to marry and stay together than in the United States (Zhang & Kline, 2009).

The fairy-tale themes of romantic bliss that pervade the Western conception of a lifelong commitment to another are much less prevalent in Chinese culture (Jackson et al., 2006). If the basis of commitment to another person is not one's own personal fulfillment, then one's own satisfaction, or lack thereof, in a relationship is not a compelling reason to get divorced. In collectivistic cultures, as long as the relationship fulfills the cultural expectation of maintaining communal cohesion and family unity, it is likely to be maintained. This is partly how cultural psychologists explain the negative correlation between collectivism and divorce rates (**FIGURE 15.7**). In fact, this correlation appears even when comparing U.S. states that vary in their valuing of collectivism (Toth & Kemmelmeier, 2009; Vandello & Cohen, 1999). In India, where arranged marriages are the cultural norm, the divorce rate is around 5%, compared with a rate of 30% or higher in many individualistic cultures.

Does this mean that people are more happily married in India or other countries where arranged marriages are prevalent? Not necessarily: Evidence suggests it can go either way. In China and Turkey, for example, partner-selected marriages appear to be happier both initially and over the long term than arranged marriages (e.g., Demir & Fışıloğlu, 1999). In contrast, partner-selected marriages in India are often happier initially, whereas arranged marriages grow happier as the years go by (e.g., Yelsma & Athappilly, 1988). Researchers speculate that these differences may reflect different cultural expectations for marital satisfaction. As Bradbury and Karney (2010) explain, given the typically more formalized structure of arranged marriages in India, spouses may expect it to take time for intimacy and satisfaction to develop, and they nurture these qualities over the years. But those in partner-selected marriages may be surprised and unprepared when their initial passion fades over the years.

▲ Different cultures, different customs. Marriage and weddings are often construed very differently in different cultures. The relatively collectivistic culture of China prescribes different norms and expectations for both entering and staying committed to a close relationship.

[somethingway/E+/Getty Images]

Figure 15.7

Divorce Rates in Different Countries

Why do different countries have different rates of divorce? Some research suggests that a critical factor is the level of individualism or collectivism of a culture. Individualistic cultures, such as the United States, tend to have higher divorce rates than more collectivistic cultures, such as Mexico. *Note:* Divorce rate is per 1,000. In the Hofstede Individualism/Collectivism Index, higher numbers indicate more individualistic countries.

[Data sources: Divorce rate: Data from U.S. Census Bureau, 2012; for Turkey, Mexico, and Chile: Data from Maps of World, 2017; and for Hofstede Individualism/Collectivism Index: https://clearlycultural.com/geert-hofstede-cultural-dimensions/individualism/]

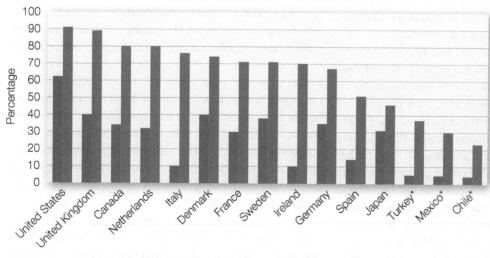

Divorce rate (per 1,000)   ■ Hofstede Ind/Col Index

SECTION REVIEW Cultural and Historical Perspectives on Relationships

Differences in Romantic Commitment

- Historical differences in the United States and cultural differences around the world suggest that love is not always the central basis of marriage.
- In collectivistic cultures, family considerations have more influence on choice of marriage partners than in individualistic cultures.

Learning Outcomes

- Identify the factors that make the early stages of a relationship a "honeymoon period."
- Explain how interdependence can either strengthen or weaken a relationship.
- List the factors that can create marital *dis*satisfaction.
- Identify the personal characteristics that speed recovery after a breakup.

Self-disclosure The sharing of information about oneself.

The Time Course of Romantic Relationships

Although romantic relationships progress in a variety of ways, there are commonalities in how relationships change over time. As we have done throughout this chapter, we will generally discuss these issues without focusing on the sexual orientation of the partners in the relationship. To date, the vast majority of relationship research has been conducted with heterosexual couples, and this can be an important factor to keep in mind. However, the factors that influence relational commitment and satisfaction have generally been found to be similar among same-sex and heterosexual couples (e.g., Balsam et al., 2008; Ducharme & Kollar, 2012; Kurdek, 2004; Roisman et al., 2008).

Self-Disclosure

Imagine two people meeting for the first time. During this initial stage of a relationship, people engage in varying degrees of **self-disclosure,** sharing information about themselves. Self-disclosure plays a key role in the formation and maintenance of close relationships and in the intimacy developed between two

SOCIAL PSYCH OUT IN THE WORLD

Historical Differences in Long-Term Commitment

Like the study of cross-cultural differences in intimate commitment, the historical record reveals the powerful influence of cultural expectation and norms. You live in a very different world than did your grandparents. Marriage (and staying in that marriage) is now much more of a choice than it used to be.

Marriage has become somewhat less popular in recent years in the U.S. Fewer people are getting married than ever before, and those who do marry wait longer to do so (Horowitz et al., 2019). More and more couples are living together without being married (Graf, 2019). People are increasingly having or adopting babies without being married (Livingston, 2018). In fact, after steadily rising for five decades, the number of children born to unmarried women has crossed a critical threshold: More than half of births to American women under 30 occur outside marriage. This is especially true for those who don't go to college and among certain minority groups: 73% of Black children are born outside marriage, compared with 53% of Latino children and 29%

of White children. In the United States, relationships in which couples have children are more than twice as likely to dissolve if they are not married than if they are. In one study, two thirds of cohabitating couples split up by the time their child turned 10 years old (Smock & Greenland, 2010).

Thus, what was once viewed as deviant and illegitimate is now becoming more commonplace and turning into a cultural norm. Such changes are important because we rely on cultural norms to interpret what is normal and how we should conduct a relationship. But some of the changing norms can lead to erroneous expectations about relationships. For example, high school seniors now believe that it is a good idea for a couple to cohabitate for a while before marriage. Yet research shows that cohabitation does not make it more likely that a subsequent marriage will be successful. If anything, cohabitation prior to marriage is associated with a greater likelihood of divorce, although the reasons for this remain unclear (Dush et al., 2003; McGinnis, 2003).

Of course, cultural change does not occur in isolation but in the context of, and in part because of, changes in the economic, technological, and population landscape. For example, people. When people first meet, they usually engage in superficial forms of self-disclosure that generally go no deeper than the weather or where they are from. If both find these initial encounters rewarding, they tend to open up, communicating about a broader range of topics and revealing deeper, more intimate information (Altman & Taylor, 1973). Typically, smooth, enjoyable conversations in early stages tend to involve exchanges of self-disclosure at the same depth. Too much self-discourse too soon is viewed as bizarre and off-putting (think of the colloquial abbreviation TMI—too much information); too little self-disclosure can interfere with the progress of trust and intimacy.

It turns out that relationship partners share different types of information about themselves at different stages of the relationship. According to Bernard Murstein's (1987) *stimulus-value-role theory* (**FIGURE 15.8**), when partners first meet, their attraction to each other is primarily based on *stimulus* information—conspicuous attributes such as age and physical appearance. If the relationship progresses beyond these first impressions, partners enter the *value* stage, in which they share their attitudes and beliefs (e.g., about religion and sex). This stage helps them decide whether they are sufficiently compatible to continue the relationship. It is generally only later, after partners have been committed to each other for a while, that they begin communicating about their roles, meaning their attitudes and plans when it comes to major life tasks such as parenting and establishing a career.

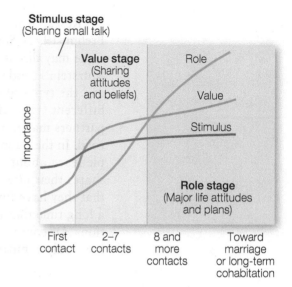

Figure 15.8

Self-Disclosing Different Types of Personal Information at Three Different Phases of Relationship Development

Murstein's stimulus-value-role theory suggests that as time goes by and romantic partners continue to self-disclose, they share three types of information that influence the relationship. However, it is not until late in the developing relationship—in some cases, after marriage—that partners learn about their role incompatibility.

[Data from Murstein, 1987]

whereas marriage traditionally was fueled in part by economic concerns, this is now less the case. Women's role in the workplace is changing the relationship context, and women are now less reliant on a husband's financial contributions than they were in the past. As a consequence, divorce becomes more common as nations become more industrialized and the gender disparities in the workplace decrease (e.g., Wang, 2001).

Cultural, economic, and technological changes have contributed to what Finkel and colleagues (Finkel, Cheung et al., 2015) characterize as three dominant models of marriage. They argue that from the late 1700s to the mid-1800s, marriage was geared primarily toward resolving practical concerns and meeting pragmatic goals, such as economic self-sufficiency. They refer to this model as practical marriage. From the mid-1800s to the mid-1960s, the breadwinner model dominated. During this time, a wife's labor became less essential to the household's economic self-sufficiency, and consistent with Rank's (1936) idea that romantic love became more important in the 20th century, marriages focused more on love, passion, and intimacy. Finkel and colleagues suggest that from the mid-1960s

to the present time, marriages have increasingly become a forum for trying to experience a greater sense of satisfaction from life and self-growth and actualization. This self-expressive model can put a lot of pressure on the relationship if it is not built to support those kinds of goals. In fact, Finkel and colleagues use the metaphor that such a reliance often sets people up to climb Mount Maslow (referring to the famous psychologist who introduced the concept of self-actualization; see chapter 6) without enough oxygen.

▲ [Blazej Lyjak/Shutterstock]

Research suggests that these stages are not really discrete or orderly (e.g., Brehm, 1992). Some couples get into values and roles early in the relationship; some may discuss roles before getting to know each other's values. However, Murstein's model is useful when we think about how relationships progress and the types of shared knowledge that matter. One consequence of sharing different types of information at different stages of the relationship is that partners may not be aware of differences that can create problems down the road. In the budding stages of a new relationship, during the value stage, people learn about each other's likes and dislikes. Having found someone who shares their interests in cuisine, entertainment, and politics, they may believe that they have finally found *the* one. It may not be until they are together for a long time that they learn of incompatibilities in, for example, role expectations. Of course, for some couples, this can be a time when partners discover how truly compatible they are.

Rose-Colored Lenses?

People all over the world want to have a romantic partner who is warm and trustworthy, loyal and passionate, attractive and exciting, and smart and competent (Tran et al., 2008). What we usually end up with, however, is someone with less than the total package. How is it, then, that we can be satisfied with the partner we're with? As dissonance theory predicts, once we choose a partner knowing they have some suboptimal attributes, we tend to put emphasis on the partner's positive qualities and minimize the person's negative qualities.

Positive illusions Idealized perceptions of romantic partners that highlight their positive qualities and downplay their faults.

Indeed, people show a powerful tendency—at least early in a relationship—to construct idealized perceptions of their romantic partners that highlight their positive qualities and downplay their faults. These idealized perceptions are called **positive illusions** (Murray et al., 1996). They are not full-blown illusions in the sense that partners are completely blind to the truth about each other's virtues and faults. Rather, they are illusions in the sense that individuals interpret facts about their partners in a more benevolent fashion than other people would (Gagné & Lydon, 2004); recent research suggests that high levels of the hormone oxytocin are associated with more proneness to such rosy views of one's partner (Algoe et al., 2017).

Consider some common positive illusions. People judge their partner's faults to be less important than outside observers judge them to be (Murray & Holmes, 1993, 1999). For example, a woman might say that although her boyfriend gets upset easily, that behavior reflects his exceptionally passionate and vivacious personality. People may even at times downplay verbal and physical abuse, viewing it as being due to stress or joking around (Arriaga et al., 2018). People offer "yes, but" interpretations of their partner's faults— that is, they recognize their partner's faults but focus on the positive repercussions. People also perceive their partner's faults as affecting the relationship less than the partner's many positive qualities (Neff & Karney, 2003).

Is it really such a good idea to put our lovers up on a pedestal? The answer hinges on just how removed from reality a positive illusion is (Neff & Karney, 2005). People who project onto their partners positive qualities that the partners simply don't have are likely setting themselves up for disappointment (Miller, 1997). On the other hand, if people are aware of their partner's positive and negative qualities but interpret them positively, such illusions can benefit the relationship. Sandra Murray and her colleagues have shown that people who idealize their romantic partners are more satisfied and feel stronger love and trust (Murray & Holmes, 1993, 1997; Murray et al., 2000; Neff & Karney, 2002). In one study (Murray et al., 1996), married couples and dating partners were asked to rate themselves and their partners on their positive and negative qualities. Positive illusion was measured by the participants' tendency to overestimate their partner's positive qualities and underestimate their faults compared with their self-ratings. The more participants idealized their romantic partners, the more satisfied they were in the relationship.

By idealizing them, we are likely to view our partner's qualities and behaviors as all the more rewarding—so much so, in fact, that it seems inconceivable that someone else out there could provide us with the same rewards. In fact, people who are highly satisfied in their relationships tend to view other potentially appealing prospects as less attractive than do less satisfied people and single people (Cole et al., 2016). Although perhaps illusory, such perceptions have the beneficial consequence of strengthening commitment.

Furthermore, a self-fulfilling prophecy often occurs such that these positive perceptions can motivate people to reach for the positive image their partner has of them and thus grow and develop toward matching that positive image. When Murray and colleagues (1996) followed couples over time, they found that in more satisfied relationships, the partners came to perceive themselves more as they initially were idealized to be. And the more one's partner seems to approach their ideal self in the relationship, the more authentic people feel in their relationship (Gan & Chen, 2017). Such findings led Murray and colleagues to suggest that love can be more prescient than blind.

Adjusting to Interdependence

Romantic relationships usually start off with a rapid increase in satisfaction as partners are overtaken with the excitement and passion of new love. But soon after this initial state of bliss, most dating relationships—even those that eventually result in marriage—hit a plateau in which satisfaction levels off for a while (Eidelson, 1980) (see **FIGURE 15.9**).

Why? According to the **model of relational turbulence** proposed by Solomon and Knobloch (2004) (**FIGURE 15.10**), in the early stage of a relationship, there is little conflict, largely because partners do not interfere with each other's routines or goals. But as partners make the transition from casual dating to more serious involvement in the relationship, they often go through a turbulent period of adjustment and turmoil (Knobloch & Donovan-Kicken, 2006; Knobloch et al., 2007). As they spend more time together and become dependent on each other, partners start to interfere with each other's daily routines, which take up the time the partners previously devoted to the activities they enjoyed before the relationship began. For example, perhaps Jane had plans to hang out with her friends this weekend, but her long-term boyfriend assumed that she was going to hang out with him, and now she is stressed out by the competing demands on her time.

If the partners stay together and learn how to adjust to their increasing interdependence, coordinating their routines and accommodating each other's personal needs and plans, the period of turmoil quiets down. ("Honey, let's agree

Model of relational turbulence The idea that as partners make the transition from casual dating to more serious involvement in the relationship, they go through a turbulent period of adjustment.

Level of involvement

Figure 15.9

Relationship Satisfaction Changes with Level of Involvement

The beginning of a romantic relationship typically is marked by a rapid rise in satisfaction. Soon after, though, satisfaction levels off, most likely because the partners are adjusting to their increasing interdependence. If the relationship survives this turbulent period and the partners accommodate to each other's needs and lives, the couple enjoys even more satisfaction, albeit at a more gradual rate.

[Data from Eidelson, 1980]

Figure 15.10

The Relational Turbulence Model

The level of turbulence in a new relationship increases as the partners become more interdependent, spending more time together and interfering with each other's routines. If the partners stay together and negotiate how to facilitate each other's goals, turbulence declines.

[Data from Knobloch & Donovan-Kicken, 2006]

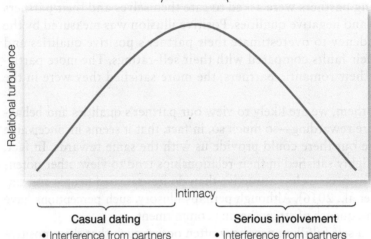

Transition from casual dating to serious involvement
• Interference from partners is high because partners are influencing each other's routines without expertise.

Relational turbulence

Intimacy

Casual dating
• Interference from partners is low because individuals are autonomous.

Serious involvement
• Interference from partners is low because partners are skilled at helping each other accomplish goals.

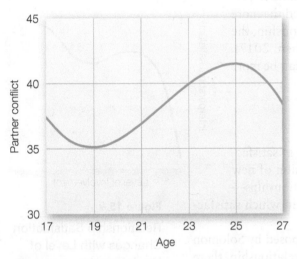

Partner conflict

Age

Figure 15.11

Romantic Conflict in Young Adulthood

Many people begin romantic relationships in their mid-20s, but this is also a time when people typically struggle to establish their careers and pursue their personal goals. As a result, conflict in romantic relationships tends to spike. After a while, though, perhaps because people feel more secure in their careers, conflict gradually diminishes.

[Data from Chen et al., 2006]

that Friday is my 'friend night.'") This can result in another, albeit subtler, increase in satisfaction (see **FIGURE 15.9**).

This model helps explain why conflict in romantic relationships is particularly high during the period of young adulthood. As you can see in **FIGURE 15.11**, the frequency of conflict increases as people go from their late teens to their mid-20s, when people are starting romantic relationships while simultaneously choosing what occupational roles to pursue. Things become more peaceful after that (Chen et al., 2006).

Let's say a couple has made it through the turbulence caused by adjusting to interdependence, and they have struck a workable balance between their motives for independence and belonging. They decide to get married, pledging to spend the rest of their lives together. We can now expect that they will live happily ever after, right?

Marital Satisfaction?

Unfortunately, research shows that the prognosis for the course of the marital relationship is not as blissful as most couples expect it will be when they tie the knot. In one comprehensive study of marital satisfaction, Huston and colleagues (2001) followed dozens of spouses who married in 1981. Relationship satisfaction steadily declined for both husbands and wives as the years ticked by (see **FIGURE 15.12**). A similar pattern has been reported for the majority of couples in other studies (Karney & Bradbury, 2000; Kurdek, 1999), but a substantial number of couples don't experience this decline (Kurdek, 2005).

Marital satisfaction tends to take a particularly steep dive at two points: after the first year of marriage and after the eighth year (Kovacs, 1983). The big question, of course, is what causes the decline in marital satisfaction once the honeymoon is over. Let's consider six of the many factors.

Partners Start with Unrealistic Expectations   Good relationships demand a great deal more work and sacrifice than is typically portrayed in movies. If a couple weds with unrealistically high expectations about marriage, they can feel cheated and disappointed later on, even if their relationship is healthy according to objective criteria (Amato et al., 2007). As we mentioned when discussing social exchange, satisfaction in close relationships depends on how well the partners' current outcomes match their comparison level—the outcomes they expected to have when they married.

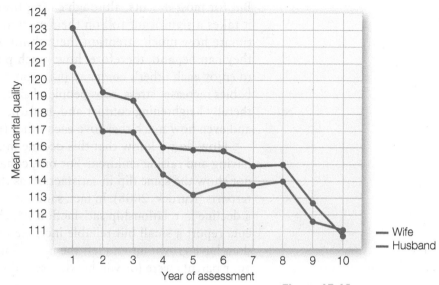

Figure 15.12

The Trajectory of Marital Satisfaction

Most newlyweds presume that their marriages will become more and more satisfying over time, but statistics suggest that, on average, satisfaction actually tends to decline over time.

[Data from Kurdek, 1999]

Slacking Off   When two people start dating, they go to a lot of trouble to be—or at least appear to be—polite and thoughtful. They suppress their burps, hold the door open, and put on makeup. But once this initial courtship phase has passed and the ink on the marriage certificate is dry, people may stop trying so hard to be consistently courteous and charming (Miller, 2001). One study showed that acts of kindness and expressions of affection dropped by half within the first two years of marriage (Huston et al., 2001).

Small Issues Get Magnified   Interdependence acts as a magnifying glass, exaggerating conflicts that do not exist in more casual relationships. Why? Because we spend so much time with our romantic partners and depend so heavily on them for valuable rewards, they have the power to cause us more frustration than anyone else can. For example, people are more negatively affected by their intimate partner's cranky moods (Caughlin et al., 2000) and work-related stress (Lavee & Ben-Ari, 2007) than they are by the similar tribulations of their friends. In addition, frequent interaction can lead to a partner's grating quirks gradually building up to real annoyance (Cunningham et al., 2005).

Sore Spots Are Revealed   As a relationship grows, partners reveal more and more of themselves to each other. Although opening up to another person can be very exciting (Archer & Cook, 1986; Taylor et al., 1981), it also means that partners know a lot of not-so-pleasant information about each other, including their secrets, foibles, and weaknesses. This means that when conflict occurs, our romantic partners have at their disposal an arsenal of emotional weaponry that they can use to wound us in ways others can't. In fact, even if partners do not intend to cause harm, their access to this sensitive information suggests that they can, sooner or later, accidently reveal our secrets (Petronio et al., 1989), hurt our feelings (Kowalski, 2003), or embarrass us in public (Miller, 1996).

The Challenges of Parenthood   The realities of parenthood and money problems are the biggest sources of marital conflict (Stanley et al., 2002). Most newlyweds, if they plan to have children, presume that parenthood will be enjoyable and bring them closer together. And evidence suggests that spending time with one's children does enhance joy and meaning for many parents (Nelson et al., 2013).

But for most parents, although caring for one's children is wonderful at times, it takes a significant toll on their marital satisfaction. Parents often underestimate how much attention their children will demand and how frustrating they can be, and, therefore, how much parenting interferes with quality time to enjoy each other's company (Claxton & Perry-Jenkins, 2008). The arrival of babies increases stress, robs people of sleep, and introduces new responsibilities, thereby heightening conflict and, in turn, decreasing how satisfied partners are and even how much they love each other (Lawrence et al., 2008).

How do we know that this decline in satisfaction is related to the stress of having and raising children? For one, cohabitating couples without children do not show the same dip in satisfaction as their heterosexual, child-raising counterparts (Kurdek, 2008). In fact, same-sex couples who have children also report a decline in relationship satisfaction (Ducharme & Kollar, 2012). Second, parents report a small but reliable increase in marital satisfaction once their children have grown up and left the nest (Gorchoff et al., 2008). And you thought your parents were (or will be) devastated when you move out.

Passionate Love Loses Steam A final reason satisfaction declines during the first years of marriage is that passionate love tends to diminish over time (Sprecher & Regan, 1998; Tucker & Aron, 1993). Whereas early on, husbands and wives claim that they feel an urgent longing for each other and that they melt when they look into each other's eyes, pretty soon the intensity dissipates. Indeed, the decrease in a couple's romantic love can happen rapidly. As noted earlier, by the end of the first two years of marriage, expressions of affection typically become less and less frequent (Huston & Chorost, 1994). This may be one reason that, around the globe, divorces occur most frequently in the fourth year of marriage, when married couples complain that the "magic" has died (Fisher, 1995).

Part of the reason for this dwindling of romance is that, over time, what was novel becomes less so. The sheer novelty of new love makes the partners especially arousing and exciting (Foster et al., 1998). Partners may continue to view each other with affection and sexual interest, but the intensity of the arousal—a principal ingredient in passionate love—inevitably diminishes somewhat (Acker & Davis, 1992). **FIGURE 15.13** displays some of the results from a broad survey of American sexuality. Here we see that the average couple has intercourse less and less frequently over the course of their marriage. Although this may be due partly to advancing age, other studies show that people who remarry—and thus experience the novelty of a new partner—increase their frequency of intercourse, at least

Figure 15.13

Frequency of Sexual Intercourse over the Course of Marriages in the United States

As the years tick by in a marriage, the frequency with which the partners have sex tends to decline.

[Data from Call et al., 1995]

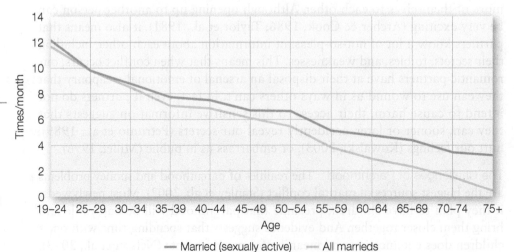

Married (sexually active) — All marrieds

for a while (Call et al., 1995). Think about how these findings compare with the evidence, discussed in chapter 14, that more proximity and interaction tends to increase attraction. Why might proximity, and associated processes like the mere exposure effect, affect marital quality differently than initial attraction?

When the Party's Over . . . The Breakup

Breakups can be devastating. Even for the "dumper" as opposed to the "dumpee," a breakup often exacts a severe toll on overall well-being (Sbarra, 2006).

THINK ABOUT

[UpperCut Images/Alamy]

The two major emotions that people experience during a breakup are anger and sadness. Of course, the strength of these emotions depends on the importance of the relationship, the circumstances of the breakup, and how quickly the individual can accept it. Those who maintain love for the partner and are unable to accept the dissolution of the relationship recover much more slowly from these negative emotions (Sbarra, 2006). Recall our discussion of self-regulatory perseveration from chapter 5. Staying invested in a goal, such as being with another person, that is unattainable perpetuates a cycle of negativity (Pyszczynski & Greenberg, 1987a).

Who is least able to come to terms with the dissolution of a relationship? Those who are higher in attachment anxiety cling more tightly to the relationship. The hope of rekindling the extinguished flame allows the negative emotions to persist. In contrast, more securely attached people generally are better able to accept the breakup and so recover from sadness more quickly (Mikulincer & Shaver, 2007).

A breakup can also jar our sense of who we are, blurring our sense of self. Research by Slotter and colleagues (2010) found that when people recalled or imagined a breakup, they reported changes in their self-concept and reduced self-concept clarity. This lack of self-concept clarity plays a key role in the reduced well-being that people experience after a breakup. During a six-month window, the more self-concept confusion people experienced, the more distress they experienced (Mason et al., 2012). This kind of dynamic occurs, for example, when the person reflects back and says something such as "Now that I'm not with Carol, I just don't know who I am anymore."

 APPLICATION

So What Can You Do to Facilitate the Recovery Process?

Perhaps when getting dumped by an ex, you've heard the line that your now ex-partner would rather "just be friends." Do you think this is a good idea? For the person whose love has dissipated, it may not be that bad, but for the person who just got jilted, it can be difficult. Indeed, in one study that followed college students for a month after they broke up, recurring contact with an ex was associated with persisting love and sadness (Sbarra & Emery, 2005). After a breakup, absence makes the heart grow less fond, and that might be exactly what you need to move on with your life. Investing in alternative pursuits, such as other relationships or challenges at school or work, can be precisely the catalyst that helps people disengage from the failed relationship (Pyszczynski & Greenberg, 1992).

Research suggests that you also should strive to have compassion for yourself. When Dave Sbarra and colleagues (2012) studied divorcing couples, they audiotaped the participants talking about the divorce for four minutes and later had judges rate the participants' levels of self-compassion. Even this short snippet of observation was informative. The more self-compassion judges saw in a participant, the better the participant's emotional recovery in the nine months following the divorce. ∎

Are We All Doomed?

All of this can seem depressing, but it shouldn't be. The processes we've described—the trials and tribulations, the inevitable decline in novelty, and so on—are normal and happen to most married couples. But people can mitigate the negative impact of these processes simply by being well informed. Studies show that spouses who began with unrealistically positive expectations of marital bliss are the least satisfied as the years tick on. Conversely, after four years of marriage, the happiest couples are those who started out with realistic outlooks about what married life would be like (McNulty & Karney, 2004). Simply by being aware of these processes and starting marriage with reasonable expectations, couples can enjoy their relationships long after the honeymoon is over (Srivastava et al., 2006).

Of course, some committed romantic relationships end in a few years, some last but become less and less satisfying, and others remain satisfying and passionate for a lifetime. Even in marriages where the passion has dwindled, older couples sometimes continue to express deep companionate love for each other that can keep them genuinely happy (Hecht et al., 1994; Lauer & Lauer, 1985). Next, we'll take a close look at factors that contribute to romantic relationships that dissolve and those that thrive.

SECTION REVIEW The Time Course of Romantic Relationships

Relationships change over time in common ways.

Self-Disclosure	Rose-Colored Lenses?	Adjusting to Interdependence	Marital Satisfaction?	The Breakup	Doomed or Not?
Partners share information about themselves gradually, and it may take a long time for some fundamental differences to emerge.	Early on, a romantic partner may be idealized. This may lead to disappointment unless one is aware of—and interprets positively—the partner's full range of qualities.	• As independence evolves into interdependence, conflict may arise. • Adjusting to interdependence creates a firmer footing for the relationship.	On average, marital satisfaction tends to decrease over time, especially after the first and the eighth years of marriage.	Breakups result in anger and sadness, best healed by alternative investments and self-compassion.	The happiest couples start out with realistic outlooks about married life.

Learning Outcomes

- Explain the factors that contribute to the decision to break up a relationship versus stick with it.
- Identify how daily hassles influence relationship stability.
- Outline the responses to problems and identify which are best.
- List the factors that contribute to keeping relationships alive.

Long-Term Relationships: Understanding Those That Dissolve and Those That Thrive

First let me state to you, Alfred, and to you, Patricia, that of the 200 marriages that I have performed, all but seven have failed. So the odds are not good. We don't like to admit it, especially at the wedding ceremony, but it's in the back of all our minds, isn't it? How long will it last?

—Reverend Dupas (played by Donald Sutherland), in the movie *Little Murders* (Arkin, 1971)

A lot of North American marriages don't last "so long as you both shall live." Recent estimates put the divorce rate in the United States at nearly 50% and in Canada at nearly 40%. Moreover, the estimate climbs to between 65% and 75% in the United States for second marriages and even higher for third marriages.

These figures are troubling, given that stable and fulfilling marriages, whether heterosexual or same sex, are associated with better physical and mental health, lower risk of mortality, better educational attainment, and economic achievement for both parents and children (Ducharme & Kollar, 2012; Kiecolt-Glaser & Newton, 2001; Slatcher & Selcuk, 2017; Stavrova, 2019; Thuen et al., 2015; Whisman et al., 2018). Divorce, on the other hand, is linked to a number of negative outcomes, not the least of which is risk of early death. Divorced people are at a 23% greater risk for all causes of mortality (Sbarra et al., 2011), though it is important to note that these data do not permit a causal inference that divorce causes death. It may be that people who are likely to get divorced also have some other characteristics that are likely to contribute to their dying earlier.

Given the benefits of a good long-term relationship, it would be useful to know how to identify when a marriage might find itself on the rocks and how to steer it back to safer waters. On the high seas of marriage, two parts of the journey seem to be most treacherous: the first 7 years and midlife (around 14 to 16 years), typically when couples are dealing with the stress of teenage children. By observing conversations early in marriage and then tracking them over the years, Gottman and colleagues (e.g., Gottman, 1995) have been able to forecast when these storms will hit.

On the basis of observations of hundreds of couples, Gottman (1995) pinpointed a cascading process in which *criticism* (telling the partner his or her faults) by one partner leads to *contempt* (making sarcastic comments about the partner or rolling one's eyes), which in turn leads to *defensiveness* (denying responsibility), which in turn leads to *stonewalling* (withdrawing or avoiding). He refers to these stages as the four horsemen of the (relational) apocalypse because their appearance strongly foreshadows the dissolution of a relationship. Fortunately, as we will see, there are ways of overcoming this cycle of relational doom.

▲ Not a good sign: According to John Gottman's research, eye-rolling is one telltale sign of communication patterns that could forecast the early demise of a relationship.
[cstar55/E+/Getty Images]

Gottman and Levenson (2000) found that by looking at patterns of negative affect and contempt when discussing problems, they could predict which couples were likely to divorce in the first few years and which were more likely to divorce after about 14 years. A high level of negativity—those four horsemen—portends early divorce. In contrast, a lack of strong positive affect in couple conversations predicts divorce in the second decade of marriage. One way to account for these patterns is to think about the security and growth functions of relationships. The early divorces may be predicted by high negative affect, which disrupts the sense of security people seek from romantic relationships. A roller coaster of a relationship—one characterized by intense positivity but also intense negativity—is unlikely to provide much security, so it tends to fail in the first few years. In contrast, a lack of strong positive affect early on may lead to boredom over the long haul. Relationships lacking strong positive affect may provide little growth and stimulation after a decade of marriage.

Should I Stay or Should I Go?

Think about one of the romantic relationships that you've had. Did you stick with it? Or did you head for the door? Some insights into the factors that support or erode commitment come from Caryl Rusbult's (1983)

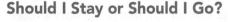
THINK ABOUT
[YaromirM/Shutterstock]

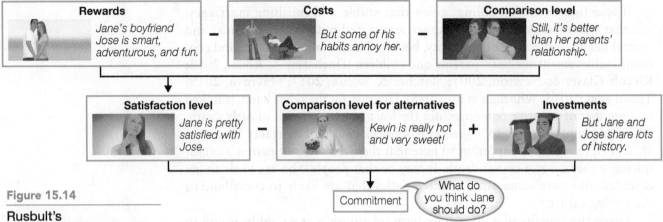

Figure 15.14

Rusbult's Interdependence Model

According to Rusbult, the commitment to a relationship is influenced not just by a person's satisfaction with that relationship but also by how much the person has invested and the quality of the alternatives the person thinks are elsewhere. When satisfaction and investment are high and the quality of alternatives is low, stronger commitment and relationship maintenance generally result.

[Research from Rusbult, 1983]

Interdependence theory The idea that satisfaction, investments, and perceived alternatives are critical in determining commitment to a particular relationship.

Comparison level for alternatives The perceived quality of alternatives to the current relationship.

interdependence theory, which builds on the social exchange model to understand relationship commitment. Recall that the social exchange model posits that rewards, costs, and comparison level determine relationship satisfaction. Interdependence theory proposes that satisfaction is only one of three critical factors that determine commitment to a particular relationship. Check out **FIGURE 15.14**. In addition to the person's satisfaction with the relationship, we also need to consider the person's *investments* in the relationship and the alternatives that the person sees out there in the field.

Part of what keeps people committed to a relationship is the investment of time and resources they have put into building a life together. The greater the sense of investment, the harder it is to walk away from what you have built together. Costs might need to really start outweighing not just current benefits but the sum total of what you've put into the relationship. For example, in one study, among same-sex couples who initially had similar levels of relationship satisfaction, those who went through a legal civil union were less likely three years later to have ended the relationship than those who did not go through this legal process (Balsam et al., 2008).

The third factor that can contribute to overall commitment is an assessment of the alternative options available, the **comparison level for alternatives**. For both men and women, when the comparison level for alternatives is low, commitment remains high, but when alternatives are highly appealing, commitment wavers (Bui et al., 1996; Le & Agnew, 2003). In light of the comparison level for alternatives, it's not too surprising that over a third of marriages that end in divorce involve at least one partner having an extramarital affair (South & Lloyd, 1995). Many people don't think about leaving their current relationship until they have a glimpse of what life could be like in another. Of course, once a partner has been unfaithful, the likelihood of divorce increases (Previti & Amato, 2004).

An interesting implication of interdependence theory is that an individual can be relatively satisfied in a relationship and invest a great deal in it but still decide to leave if he or she suspects that there are better alternatives. For example, perhaps *The Voice* judge Blake Shelton was satisfied with fellow country singer Miranda Lambert but divorced her in 2015 because he came to find then fellow judge Gwen Stefani more appealing. Conversely, this perspective suggests that an individual might decide to stay in a relationship not because he or she is especially satisfied but because there don't seem to be any better options out there. This helps explain why people sometimes stay in relationships that to any outside observer look rather bleak and may even involve abuse. Research has supported this explanation. For example, a study by Rusbult (1983) that followed couples over a seven-month period found that those that stayed together experienced increased costs (e.g., time, effort, loss of freedom) but increased rewards as well (e.g., satisfaction, pleasure). But for couples that broke up, the rewards did not increase as much as the costs did, the alternatives became more appealing, and so commitment declined.

▲ Blake Shelton and Gwen Stefani

[Kevin Mazur/WireImage/Getty Images]

The decision to stick with a relationship also is influenced by how well the relationship meets our psychological needs. As we discussed in chapter 6, self-determination theory argues that people need a basic sense not just of relatedness but also of autonomy and competence. A sense of competence makes us feel secure and valued; a sense of autonomy—feeling that we're taking ownership of what we do—contributes to our growth. And when a relationship doesn't provide a sense of competence and autonomy, and thus doesn't meet these core psychological needs, it is less satisfying, and our commitment wanes (Drigotas & Rusbult, 1992; La Guardia et al., 2000).

Sometimes the decision to break up, though obviously destructive to the relationship, is ultimately good for one or both of the individuals. We all know people—and maybe we've been those people ourselves—who stay in a relationship that is not really in their best interests. It's not meeting their needs and is not especially satisfying, but they think they have no other options and so try to stick it out. Who is most likely to be in this situation? Those who have high attachment anxiety often think they are unworthy of being in a good relationship but are especially dependent on what relationships they do have (Davila & Bradbury, 2001; Mikulincer & Shaver, 2007). Research by Slotter and Finkel (2009) confirms this reasoning. In their first study, they followed couples over six months and found that when people felt that a relationship did not meet their needs, those low in attachment anxiety broke it off, whereas those high in attachment anxiety clung on. The longitudinal aspect of this study is powerful because it reveals how, in this case, attachment anxiety and need satisfaction influenced behavior over time. However, all study designs have weaknesses, and here the weakness is that we can't be sure that attachment anxiety was really the important factor. Because it was just measured, not manipulated, some other variable associated with attachment anxiety might have influenced relationship commitment.

To address this issue, in a second study (**FIGURE 15.15**), Slotter and Finkel (2009) took advantage of the strengths of the experimental method, reasoning that anyone can feel more or less secure in their relationships at various times. Because most people have a mix of good and bad memories, the researchers manipulated whether participants brought to mind ideas related to relational security or insecurity. They first measured how much participants regarded the relationship as meeting psychological needs and then randomly assigned participants to unscramble various words to form a sentence. The list contained either words such as *was, reliable, the,* and *mother* or words such as *was, unreliable, the,* and *mother.* Thus, participants were making sentences that got them thinking about either relational security (e.g., *the mother was reliable*) or insecurity (e.g., *the mother was unreliable*). The results were similar to those in the longitudinal study we just mentioned. When participants were primed with insecurity, they

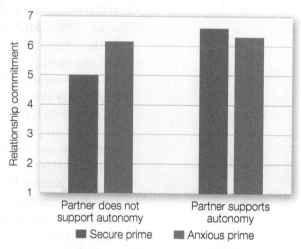

Partner does not support autonomy — Partner supports autonomy

■ Secure prime ■ Anxious prime

Relationship commitment

Figure 15.15

Holding On to an Unfulfilling Relationship

Individuals primed with attachment security were less committed to a relationship if it didn't satisfy their needs for autonomy. In contrast, individuals primed with attachment anxiety were just as committed to a relationship that didn't support as to one that did.

[Data from Slotter & Finkel, 2009]

expressed equally high commitment regardless of whether the relationship met their needs. When primed with security, participants also expressed high commitment if the relationship was satisfying their needs. However, those primed with security expressed less commitment if the relationship was unsatisfying.

In short, more securely attached people are more likely to bolt from a relationship that they do not see as sufficiently fulfilling their psychological needs. Without a strong sense of commitment, such individuals are unlikely to engage in behaviors that help to maintain the relationship, such as making sacrifices for the relationship and responding to betrayals or other problems with forgiveness (Finkel et al., 2002).

 APPLICATION

One Day at a Time: Dealing with the Ups and Downs

Infidelity and emotional and physical abuse are common and rather dramatic causes of relationship problems and breakups. But all long-term relationships, if they are to endure, must also overcome the day-to-day hassles that inevitably occur. Your partner is late getting home from work, fails to notice something that is important to you, or commits to going to dinner with a group of people you find dreadfully boring. How do such events affect your relationship? The cumulative impact of these hassles can contribute to the dissolution of a long-term relationship (Bolger et al., 1989). Thus, a big challenge to maintaining a successful relationship is how the couple deals with the daily events that are a part of life.

Thus, one important factor is how relationship partners interpret the variability—the ups and downs—of the day-to-day events they confront (Jacobson et al., 1982; McNulty & Karney, 2001). When a partner's global perception of the relationship rises and falls with every daily event, the relationship can become more precarious and vulnerable to decline and dissolution (e.g., Arriaga, 2001). Thus, separating overall judgment of the quality of the relationship from day-to-day positive or negative events can lead to more consistent satisfaction (McNulty & Karney, 2001).

How do people separate their overall evaluation of a relationship from the immediate events that they are experiencing? People who are in happier relationships tend to attribute their partner's irritating actions to external factors. So if the partner fails to call to say that he or she will be late, the happily married person tends to attribute that faux pas to the partner being busy at work rather than being inconsiderate. Those who have the most successful relationships develop a priority structure that downplays the importance of their partner's shortcomings and allows them to maintain a positive view of their partner (Neff & Karney, 2003). These optimistic perspectives protect the relationship and maintain a measure of positivity. In contrast, spouses who make internal attributions and blame their partners tend to have unhappier marriages (Bradbury & Fincham, 1990).

Obviously, letting hassles roll off your back will make for a happier relationship both in the short run and over time (McNulty et al., 2008). But what if your partner really is being inconsiderate? The tricky part of relationships is that some of the small stuff really is small, but some of it can be signs of something larger. Couples who ignore the big issues are likely to report lower marital satisfaction as time goes by. The key, then, is to pick your battles wisely: to recognize what are the little things you can let slide and attribute to external factors and what are the bigger issues that you need to address more candidly. Indeed, research shows that

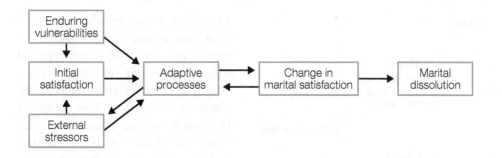

Figure 15.16

Vulnerability Stress Adaptation Model

When does a relationship dissolve? Karney and colleagues' vulnerability stress adaptation model of relationships proposes that the answer depends on how situational stressors interact with personality traits (or vulnerabilities) to create unproductive processes. For example, being insecure and facing stress at work could lead a person to have more maladaptive thoughts about the relationship, which could contribute to dissolution.

[Research from Karney & Bradbury, 1995]

when the problem is not a major one that will fester, avoiding conflict over it can be the best strategy (Cahn, 1992; Canary et al., 1995).

What factors determine whether the daily hassles create problems or are kept in perspective? Benjamin Karney and colleagues' (e.g., Karney & Bradbury, 1995) *vulnerability stress adaptation model* provides some answers to this question. It proposes that there are two key factors that contribute to marital dissolution, as shown in **FIGURE 15.16**. First, in any intimate relationship, some people bring with them vulnerabilities—in their personality, self-conceptions, and so on—that dispose them to have less adaptive conceptions of the relationship. For example, people with low self-esteem (Murray et al., 2002) as well as those with anxious attachment styles (Campbell et al., 2005) tend to be uncertain of their partner's feelings for them and so search for signs of validation. This leads them to put undue weight on daily events. So on days when they perceive more conflict, they feel less close and less optimistic about the relationship. Someone without these vulnerabilities might more easily recognize the small stuff as just small stuff.

The second key factor is external situations that put more strain on the relationship. Imagine a person in sales who faces added work pressure as the economy plummets. As a result, she spends less time at home and is worn out when she is home. So she shows less affection to her relationship partner and shares in fewer mutual activities. This directly adds stress to the relationship (Neff & Karney, 2004). But this stress can also affect the relationship indirectly. It requires effort to engage in adaptive relationship cognitions—to realize, for example, that your partner's not complimenting you on your surprise cleanup of the house is the product of her work distractions and not her general lack of appreciation. Thus, when people encounter outside stress, it can consume the cognitive resources that they would otherwise use to support their relationships. For example, satisfied couples make allowances for a partner's bad behavior and attribute it to external causes (Bradbury & Fincham, 1990), but when under stress, they shift to a less forgiving attributional pattern (Neff & Karney, 2009). Furthermore, stress can hamper executive control, and good executive control contributes to partners being able and willing to make the sacrifices and show the forgiveness that help keep relationships strong (Karremans et al., 2015). ∎

"It's a major fixer-upper. How's your marriage?"

▲ [David Sipress/The New Yorker Collection/ The Cartoon Bank]

And in the Red Corner: Managing Conflict

As if day-to-day stressors and irritations were not enough, all intimate relationships also face a certain amount of actual conflict. Indeed, some conflict in a relationship is healthy (Cahn, 1992; Cloven & Roloff, 1991; Rusbult, 1987). There

Active

Exit	**Voice**
Walking out, physical and/or emotional abuse	Seeking outside help, negotiation, changing own behaviors

Destructive   **Constructive**

Neglect	**Loyalty**
Ignoring and withdrawing from partner, refusing to confront problems	Hoping for conditions to improve, making benign attributions

Passive

Figure 15.17

Managing Conflict: The EVLN Model

Carol Rusbult's work on managing conflict suggests that people can do so in active or passive ways and in constructive or destructive ways. When we combine these two dimensions, we get four kinds of responses. Your best bet if you want to nurture your relationship: Try for the voice response, which is both active and constructive!

[Research from Rusbult et al., 1982]

is no perfect partner who will agree with you about everything. Your partner may prefer different types of movies, music, or sexual activities. They may have different ideas about where to vacation or how to spend disposable income. Issues may arise regarding whether to have children and, if so, when and how to raise them. Resolving such disagreements involves communication and compromise. What separates happy couples from distressed couples is how they deal when conflicts arise. The strategies people apply when conflicts come up vary along two dimensions (Rusbult et al., 1982). Along one dimension are responses ranging from active (e.g., barraging your partner with reasons she was wrong) to passive (e.g., sitting quietly and seething). Along the other dimension are responses ranging from constructive (e.g., sticking by your partner and hoping things will get better) to destructive (e.g., smashing the headlights out of your partner's new car). When we cross these two dimensions with one another (see **FIGURE 15.17**), we see four different types of responses.

An *exit* response is active but destructive to the relationship. It involves separating or threatening to leave. An example of an exit response is "I told him I couldn't take it anymore and it was over." A *voice* response is similarly active but more constructive to the relationship. It involves discussing problems, seeking solutions and help, and attempting to change. For example, with a voice response, one might say, "We talked things over and worked things out."

But not all responses take this active approach. Partners also can respond constructively but in a more passive way. *Loyalty* entails hoping for improvement, supporting a partner, sticking with it, and continuing to wear relationship symbols (e.g., rings): "I just waited to see if things would get better." Although loyalty is generally considered a constructive response, it can be relatively ineffective because it may be difficult for the other partner to notice and pick up on it (Drigotas et al., 1995). And if it does go unnoticed, it is not likely to help the relationship. Finally, a person may respond both passively and destructively with *neglect*, letting things fall apart, and ignoring a partner or drifting away from him or her: "Mostly my response was silence to anything he said."

When Rusbult asked people to recall a time when they had had conflicts with their partner, she found that those in satisfied and committed relationships were more likely to use constructive responses such as voice and loyalty and less likely to turn to exit and neglect responses. People in good relationships are also more likely to accommodate a partner's initially destructive response and respond constructively to it. So what do you do when your partner comes home from a long day, you're excitedly telling him about your day, and he responds, "Just be quiet for a moment"? Whereas some people's first response might be a similarly caustic and disparaging comment—which of course would only further escalate negativity in the relationship—those for whom the relationship is more important will try to inhibit that tit-for-tat strategy and respond constructively (Rusbult et al., 1991). Securely attached people are most likely to rise above and respond well to less-than-constructive remarks from a partner (Collins & Feeney, 2004).

Another characteristic that facilitates more productive accommodation is taking the partner's perspective. The more we can put ourselves in our partner's shoes and see that perhaps a frustrating day at work led her to act that way, the better off our relationship is. Indeed, among both dating and married couples, preexisting tendencies for perspective taking and being induced to take the other's perspective led to more positive emotional reactions and relationship-enhancing attributions (Arriaga & Rusbult, 1998).

Given that voice is the best response to serious or recurring relationship problems, it may be worth considering why voice often isn't how people respond. The first reason is that people often avoid conflict. They are afraid to bring up issues because they don't "want to get into it" or have it "blow up." So instead, they often complain to friends or relatives about what's bothering them. This approach doesn't give the other person a chance to step up and help make things better.

"Don and I rarely fight. Then again, we rarely talk."

▲ [Cartoonstock]

The second reason is that people often approach communicating about problems in the wrong way. Canary and colleagues (Canary & Cupach, 1988; Canary & Spitzberg, 1987) proposed that there are three strategies for conflict management: integrative strategies, distributive strategies, and avoidant strategies. Avoidance can be best when the problem is relatively minor and we can mentally or behaviorally adjust to it. But if it's a problem that must be addressed through some kind of compromise, then it's a matter of how you do it.

An *integrative* strategy works best and is similar to Rusbult's concept of voice. You present the problem as a challenge to shared relational goals—as *our* problem, something we have to solve together. You raise your concern while seeking areas of agreement, express trust and positive regard, and negotiate alternative solutions through frank and positive discussions (Masuda & Duck, 2002). Eli Finkel and colleagues (2013) showed that having couples take about 20 minutes to learn to think about resolving their disagreements in an integrative way improved marital satisfaction over a two-year period.

In contrast, a *distributive* strategy is competitive, emphasizes individual goals, assigns blame, and often devolves into insults and hostility (Masuda & Duck, 2002): "I have a problem with your behavior. You need to change. My needs are not being met." If you are defensive or insecure, or if you've "bitten your lip" for a long time and so are very frustrated, you are more likely to express your concerns in this distributive, accusatory fashion—and your partner is more likely to respond defensively in kind. Try to think about and express problems integratively, as "ours," not distributively, as "yours." And don't apply an *avoidance* strategy by ignoring a problem until you have brooded so long about it that you have lost your sense of positive regard for your partner (Masuda & Duck, 2002).

Booster Shots: Keeping the Relationship and Passion Alive

Managing conflicts and dealing productively with day-to-day hassles can make a relationship more secure, which is critical for the growth of each individual in the relationship. Individuals who view their relationship partner as providing a more secure base spend more time and show greater interest in novel and enriching challenges (Feeney & Thrush, 2010).

Love as Flow   Security is wonderful, and the longer one is with a partner, the more familiar and comfortable a relationship is likely to feel. But a big issue in long-term relationships is how to keep the excitement, fun, stimulation, and passion alive. Csikszentmihalyi (1980) provided some useful insight into this problem by applying his *flow* analysis (introduced in chapter 6) to love relationships. Love relationships are best when people are in flow, when the challenges of a relationship partner are commensurate with one's relationship-related abilities. Early in a relationship, the other person is new, and so there are many challenges that keep things interesting.

If the challenges of satisfying your partner are more than you can handle and it is too difficult to keep your partner satisfied, you experience stress, and the relationship is likely to flame out early. However, if you're in a relationship for a long time, you learn a lot about your partner. It becomes easier to know his or her likes and dislikes, to predict his or her actions, and so forth. The

SOCIAL PSYCH AT THE MOVIES

Husbands and Wives

Although many films focus on romantic relationships, the emphasis usually is on the early stages and rarely on the challenges of maintaining a satisfying marriage over the long haul. One exception is the Woody Allen film *Husbands and Wives* (Allen, 1992), which focuses, almost in documentary style, on two long-married, middle-aged couples having problems: Jack (Sydney Pollack) and Sally (Judy Davis) and Gabe (Woody Allen) and Judy (Mia Farrow). As the film opens, Jack and Sally, married over 20 years, rather casually and apparently amicably announce to their good friends Gabe and Judy that they are getting a divorce.

As the film unfolds, we learn why. Jack becomes dissatisfied with his and Sally's sexual relationship and also feels judged and stifled by Sally. He senses a lack of stimulation and growth. They have intimacy and commitment but little passion. Jack begins engaging the services of a high-priced prostitute. Eventually Sally finds out he is having some sort of affair. Instead of confronting Jack, she keeps quiet about it—an avoidant strategy. Instead of applying the more productive conflict management response of voice, she becomes increasingly neglectful of the relationship. Infidelity is not the kind of small stuff one can easily let go, and she gets more and more bitter. This contributes to her increasingly negative view of Jack and of even small additional problems that arise. Their discussions of their problems become distributive (assigning blame) rather than integrative. All of these issues culminate in their mutual decision to divorce, although we later find out Jack was already seeing

Sam (Lysette Anthony), an aerobics instructor who is into astrology. She is considerably younger than Sally and is more open and less judgmental, so when Jack considered the comparison level of the alternatives to his wife Sally, this further eroded his commitment to the marriage.

Once Jack and Sally break up, Jack is better able to grow in his relationship with Sam. He starts eating right and exercising and can enjoy sports events and movies, activities that would have met with Sally's disapproval. Judy sets Sally up with Michael (Liam Neeson), who is handsome, charming, romantic, and younger. But Sally can't really give him a chance, partly because of the anger she still feels toward Jack. But it's also because she misses the deep sense of psychological security she derived from her marriage and her sense of the investment she had put into it. Eventually, Jack finds out that Sally has begun dating, which makes him jealous. He starts seeing the younger and less sophisticated Sam through the eyes of his friends as an embarrassment that is hurting his stature and self-worth, thereby undermining his own sense of security. Eventually he returns to Sally, and she takes him back. Ultimately they choose the psychological security of their shared life and self-worth from being "Jack and Sally," while recognizing that passion, stimulation, and growth will not be part of their marriage and that rocky times may lie ahead.

Gabe and Judy seem solid as the film opens, but Judy becomes particularly upset when Sally and Jack announce their divorce. It strikes a nerve. Judy begins to reexamine whether she is happy in her marriage, and as she does, we start to see its shortcomings. Meanwhile, Gabe, a professor of English and an accomplished fiction writer, becomes attracted challenges tend to diminish over time, even as your skills increase. But if the challenges become insufficient, flow is impeded, and boredom is likely to set in. Luckily, Csikszentmihalyi (1980) offered a solution. A partner who doesn't grow will become boring. A stagnant partner means a stagnant relationship. So the trick to keeping a long-term relationship alive is for both partners to continue to grow and change so they remain stimulating to each other. One way to accomplish this is for the partners to continue to support each other's growth. Encourage each other to do new things and take on new challenges, both together and separately. Then you are always with someone who is challenging and vibrant. These kinds of efforts can also help relieve some of the pressure that occurs when being with the partner is the only way in which the other gets his or her growth needs met (Finkel, Cheung et al., 2015).

The prospect of change can be scary, though: The same old same old is comfortable and easy. And it's a hassle to support your partner's personal growth; it's easier to maintain the status quo. Thus people are often tempted to squelch their partner's efforts to grow and change. For example, some years back, Liz, the wife of your current author (Jeff), who had been working part-time as a

to one of his much younger students, Rainer (Juliette Lewis). She is a big fan of his work and reciprocates the interest.

It turns out that Judy doesn't feel valued or emotionally supported by Gabe. He dismisses her feedback on his new novel while being intrigued by Rainer's feedback about it. Judy becomes attracted to Michael even though she sets him up with Sally. She shows Michael poems she has written. When Gabe finds out, he asks her why she didn't show him the poems. She says that she wanted some supportive feedback, not the kind of objective critique that Gabe would have offered. Gabe likes the security he gets from his marriage, but a lot of his self-worth and consequent security and all of his growth really seem to come from his career and his budding platonic relationship with Rainer.

After Sally dumps Michael to return to Jack, Judy, seeing a better alternative, ends her marriage and starts seeing Michael. Eventually Judy and Michael marry. Toward the film's conclusion, Gabe rejects a romantic advance from the much younger Rainer, sensing that it would not work out in the long run, and expresses regret that he took Judy for granted. In an interesting twist, soon after this movie came out, Woody Allen, then 56, became committed to a much younger woman, Soon-Yi Previn, 21, the adopted daughter of his then girlfriend, the actress Mia Farrow (OTRC, 2011). Woody and Soon-Yi married in 1997 and, as of this writing, are still together.

During the film, we learn about Gabe's new novel, which discusses Nap and Pepkin, men who live on the same floor of an apartment building. Summing up a major theme of the movie, Gabe writes: "Pepkin married and raised a family. He led a warm domestic life, placid but dull. Nap was a swinger.

He eschewed nuptial ties and bedded five different women a week. . . . Pepkin, from the calm of his fidelity, envied Nap; Nap, lonely beyond belief, envied Pepkin." *Husbands and Wives* thus offers insights into a variety of relationship processes, including how people try to balance the desires for security and for stimulation and growth.

"*Fiercely funny! A groundbreaking film.*"
- Peter Travers, ROLLING STONE

"*One of the finest American films.*"
- Ben Brantley, ELLE MAGAZINE

HUSBANDS AND WIVES

"*A damn fine film.*"
- Richard Corliss, TIME MAGAZINE

"*A masterpiece of invention.*"
- Bob Thomas, ASSOCIATED PRESS

Woody Allen Blythe Danner Judy Davis Mia Farrow Juliette Lewis Liam Neeson Sydney Pollack

▲ [Photo 12 / Alamy Stock Photo]

registered nurse ever since we had gotten married and had children, raised the idea of going back to school to get a PhD in nursing. I instantly realized that this would mean loss of income and years of stress for her (and me); pushing through the challenges of advanced education, such as writer's block; and so on. But Liz felt stagnant in her work and needed this growth experience to meet her professional goals, and so I supported it. By supporting her growth, I gained a more stimulating, fulfilled partner, which served both Liz and our relationship well. Research supports this example. Each partner helping the other partner achieve his or her own self-improvement goals is associated with greater relationship satisfaction (e.g., Drigotas et al., 1999; Overall et al., 2010).

Emotional Support Being a responsive partner is not limited to supporting big-time self-improvement goals. It also involves reacting supportively to the little things. When a partner shares positive news about the day, for example, an active, encouraging, and enthusiastic response is associated with better relationship quality over time (Algoe, 2019; Gable et al., 2004). Even the seemingly mundane things that elicit gratitude, such as taking on more routine household chores if a partner is under stress, enhance relationship quality (Algoe et al., 2010). Overall, mutually responsive partners who offer emotional support and active interest will enhance the relationship for each other (Iida et al., 2008; Lemay & Clark, 2008; Reis et al., 2004). Studies of married and cohabiting couples have also showed that people who are perceived to be responsive—understanding, caring, and appreciative—actually reduce their partner's anxieties, help them sleep better, and improve their physical health by reducing their cortisol levels (Selcuk et al., 2017; Slatcher et al., 2015).

 ## APPLICATION
Keeping the Home Fires Burning

Of course, a big part of nourishing a relationship is keeping passion alive. This can be tough. One of the chief complaints about long-term relationships is a decline in sexual desire (Sprecher & Cate, 2004), and research is clear that sexual activity contributes to relationship satisfaction (Maxwell & McNulty, 2019). The better the relationship, the more likely the couple is having sex at least once a week, and having at least that much sex contributes to relationship satisfaction (Muise et al., 2016). Studies suggest that sexual activity enhances relationship satisfaction at least in part by leading to more expressions of affection and positive affect in the relationship (Debrot et al., 2017). Furthermore, for those in committed relationships, both having sex at least once a week and high relationship satisfaction contribute to partners' happiness and satisfaction with life.

What specific strategies can one utilize to keep fanning the flames? Adopting approach goals can help keep partners turned on. In support of this point, Impett and colleagues (2008) found that people who endorsed more approach than avoidant relationship goals, such as trying to deepen their relationship with their partner as opposed to avoiding disagreements, reported greater sexual desire. Such goals also buffered against declines in sexual desire six months into the relationship.

One of the aspects of approach goals that may facilitate desire is that they lead people to more arousing and exciting activities. Such activities can help to restore the stimulation and novelty of a relationship that typically wanes over time (Aron et al., 2000). There are a number of reasons novel and arousing activities might help to do this. As Aron and colleagues point out, such activities are often intrinsically enjoyable. When they are shared, this enjoyment becomes associated with the relationship. Such activities can also generally increase positive mood, which can, in turn, be a booster shot that makes life, and perhaps the relationship, seem more meaningful (Algoe, 2019; King et al., 2006).

Furthermore, as the two-factor theory of love and related research demonstrates, arousal from exciting activities also can be transferred to feelings of lust and love for the partner. A similar process even seems to hold for nonhuman animals, who exhibit what has come to be known as the Coolidge effect. There is a tendency, first observed in rats but subsequently in all mammals studied, for animals initially to have repeated intercourse with an available mate. The animals will lose interest over time but then have repeated intercourse again when introduced to new sexual partners (Beach & Jordan, 1956; Dewsbury, 1981). One study (Dewsbury, 1981) observed an interesting factor related to the Coolidge effect: Although even a bull's sexual appetite might wane after repeated copulation with the same receptive cow, when the pair was taken to a new enclosure and given a change of scenery, the formerly tired bull's interest was reengaged, and the vigorous sexual activity resumed. The lesson here is that injecting novelty and excitement into a relationship, whether by travel, trying new things like an escape room, rock-climbing, and so forth, can bring new life to a relationship.

Doing novel, fun, exciting things together in new places sounds like a no-lose proposition: Who wouldn't want to do that? However, over the long haul, couples often lose sight of this aspect of their relationship. In early courtship, having fun together—restaurants, dancing, concerts, movies, travel—is a central focus. But as they move in together, take on more and more career responsibilities, and then add pets, kids, financial pressures, and the health issues that come with aging, the partners increasingly focus on just getting through each day. So the trick is to continue to make time to spend alone together doing enjoyable, stimulating things. Indeed, even viewing streams of images in which photos of one's partner subtly appear just before images of positive things like puppies and sunsets has been found to increase marital satisfaction (McNulty et al., 2017).

To explore the potential benefits of such self-expanding novel and enjoyable activities, Aron and colleagues (2000) first conducted some survey studies and found that the more couples reported doing arousing and novel activities together, the more relationship satisfaction they reported. But does participating jointly in stimulating, enjoyable pursuits *causally* increase relational satisfaction? To find out, Aron and colleagues (Aron et al., 2000; Lewandowski & Aron, 2004) conducted a series of experiments in which couples were brought into a lab and engaged either in challenging, novel tasks,

Achieve
Video: Eli Finkel on Romantic Relationships

▲ Early in relationships, couples do a lot of stimulating, fun things together. One key for couples to maintain passion over the long haul is to keep doing such activities, like visiting the Trevi Fountain in Rome.
[Jeff Greenberg]

which should be self-expanding, or in mundane ones. In these studies, when couples first arrived at the lab, they completed measures assessing relationship quality and satisfaction. Then each couple was asked to do either novel physical tasks or more mundane tasks. In one set of studies, the novel, self-expanding task involved the couple's being Velcroed together at the wrists and ankles. They had a limited amount of time to seek a prize by successfully crawling 12 meters over a barrier and pushing a foam cylinder with their heads. In a number of such studies, the couples who combined forces to do challenging and nutty things later reported greater relationship satisfaction than those who did the mundane tasks. These effects were not limited to what the couples reported. Coders who rated videotapes of their interactions observed these benefits as well.

Maintaining passion and enhancing relationship satisfaction takes effort, but these goals can be achieved if we're motivated to do so and keep some basic ideas in mind:

- Have realistic expectations about relationships
- Approach the relationship positively and not just seeking to keep it afloat
- Express love and provide emotional support
- Communicate about problems in an integrative manner toward developing compromise solutions
- Mutually support each other's growth goals
- Preserve quality time alone together
- Inject novelty and arousal

These are all strategies that pay off. We hope they do for those of you seeking an enriching long-term relationship, now or in the future. ■

SECTION REVIEW   Long-Term Relationships: Understanding Those That Dissolve and Those That Thrive

Stay or Go?

- The interdependence theory proposes three factors that determine commitment: satisfaction level, quality of alternatives, and investment.
- Decisions are also based on whether the relationship meets psychological needs.
- Securely attached people are more likely than others to leave an unsatisfying relationship.

Daily Hassles

The ability to let daily hassles roll off one's back makes for a happier relationship. Preexisting vulnerabilities and external stress make this harder to do.

Conflict

- Conflict is inevitable.
- Each partner's ability to use voice constructively facilitates optimal compromise solutions.

Keeping Relationships Alive

- Maintaining a healthy relationship depends on a secure base and mutual support of growth.
- Emotional support also is important, as is sharing novel and stimulating experiences together.

CRITICAL LEARNING EXERCISES

1. Consider attachment theory and research. Thinking back on your childhood and comparing that to your close relationship since then, does your experience fit the theory and findings? If not, how have they been different? If you think your attachment style has changed, why do you think that has happened?

2. This chapter makes strong claims about the value of a good single long-term life partner for physical and mental health and well-being. Do you agree with that? Are there other approaches to close relationships that you think can also help you, or other people, function well over the course of the life span?

3. If a friend came to you about an issue they have in their marriage, based on what you've learned in this chapter, what advice might you offer them for how to communicate about the issue with their spouse? Do you have other ideas about how to raise issues with one's relationship partner?

4. What are some strategies offered in this chapter for keeping passion and stimulation alive over time in a long-term relationship? Which do you think are good ones? Are there any others you can think of?

Don't stop now! Check out our videos and additional resources located at: www.macmillanlearning.com

GLOSSARY

Accessibility The ease with which people can bring an idea into consciousness and use it in thinking.

Acculturation The process whereby individuals adapt their behavior in response to exposure to a new culture.

Action identification theory The theory that explains how people conceive of action—their own or others'—in ways that range from very concrete to very abstract.

Actor–observer effect The tendency to make internal attributions for the behavior of others and external attributions for our own behavior.

Adaptations Attributes that improve an individual's prospects for survival and reproduction.

Affective aggression Harm-seeking done to another person that is elicited in response to some negative emotion.

Affective forecasting Predicting one's emotional reactions to potential future events. These predictions are often inaccurate.

Aggression Any physical or verbal behavior that is intended to harm another person or persons (or any other living thing).

Altruism The desire to help another purely for the other person's benefit, regardless of whether we derive any benefit.

Altruistic personality A collection of personality traits, such as empathy, that render some people more helpful than others.

Ambivalent racism The influence of two clashing sets of values on White Americans' racial attitudes: a belief in individualism and a belief in egalitarianism.

Ambivalent sexism The pairing of *hostile* beliefs about women with *benevolent* but patronizing beliefs about them.

Anxiety buffer The idea that self-esteem allows people to face threats with their anxiety minimized.

Anxious-ambivalent An attachment style characterized by a negative view of the self but a positive view of others, high anxiety, low avoidance, and intense but unstable relationships.

Appraisals What other people think about us.

Argument The true merits of the person, object, or position being advocated in a message.

Assimilation The process whereby people gradually shift almost entirely from their former culture to the beliefs and ways of the new culture.

Associative networks Models for how pieces of information are linked together and stored in memory.

Assortative mating The idea that people are attracted to others who are similar to them in some kind of social hierarchy.

Attitude Evaluation of a stimulus; can range from positive to negative.

Attribution theory The view that people act as intuitive scientists when they observe other people's behavior and infer explanations about why those people acted the way they did.

Attributional ambiguity A phenomenon whereby members of stigmatized groups often can be uncertain whether negative experiences are based on their own actions and abilities or are the result of prejudice.

Audience The person or group receiving a message.

Automatic processes Human thoughts or actions that occur quickly, often without the aid of conscious awareness.

Auto-motive theory The theory that even subtle exposure to goal-related stimuli can automatically activate a goal and guide behavior.

Availability heuristic The tendency to assume that information that comes easily to mind (or is readily available) is more frequent or common.

Averageness effect The tendency to perceive a composite image of multiple faces that have been photographically averaged as more attractive than any individual face included in that composite.

Aversive racism Negative, often unconscious, feelings and beliefs about Black people held by White people who otherwise support racial equality and do not knowingly discriminate.

Balance theory A theory which proposes that the motivation to maintain consistency among one's thoughts colors how people form new attitudes and can also drive them to change existing attitudes.

Basking in reflected glory Associating oneself with successful others to help bolster one's own self-esteem.

Better-than-average effect The tendency to rank oneself higher than most other people on positive attributes.

Bystander effect A phenomenon in which a person who witnesses another in need is less likely to help when there are other bystanders present to witness the event.

Categories Mental "containers" in which people place things that are similar to each other.

Causal attributions Explanations of an individual's behavior.

Central route to persuasion A style of processing a persuasive message by a person who has both the ability and the motivation to think carefully about the message's argument. Attitude change depends on the strength of the argument.

Chameleon effect The tendency to unconsciously mimic the nonverbal mannerisms of someone with whom you are interacting.

Charismatic leader An individual in a leadership role who exhibits boldness and self-confidence and emphasizes the greatness of the ingroup.

Chronically accessible schemas Schemas that are easily brought to mind because they are personally important and used frequently.

Cis-gender Heterosexual individuals who identify with the gender that is consistent with their assigned sex at birth.

Cognitive appraisal theory The idea that our subjective experience of emotions is determined by a two-step process involving a **primary appraisal** of benefit or harm and a **secondary appraisal** that provides a more differentiated emotional experience.

Cognitive dissonance theory The idea that people have such distaste for perceiving inconsistencies in their beliefs, attitudes, and behavior that they will bias their own attitudes and beliefs to try to deny inconsistencies.

Cognitive misers A term that conveys the human tendency to avoid expending effort and cognitive resources when thinking and to prefer seizing on quick and easy answers to questions.

Cognitive neoassociationism model A model of aggression that emphasizes three causal factors: stressors, hostile feelings, and cues associated with aggression.

Cognitive reappraisal The cognitive reframing of a situation to minimize one's emotional reaction to it.

Cognitive system A conscious, rational, and controlled system of thinking.

Collective action Efforts by groups to resist and change the status quo in the service of group goals.

Collectivistic culture A culture in which the emphasis is on interdependence, cooperation, and the welfare of the group over that of the individual.

Colorblind ideology A worldview in which group identities are ignored and people are judged solely on their individual merits, thereby avoiding any judgment based on group membership.

Commitment Partners' investment of time, effort, and resources in their relationship, with the expectation that it will continue indefinitely.

Common ingroup identity A recategorizing of members of two or more distinct groups into a single, overarching group.

Communal orientation A frame of mind in which people don't distinguish between what's theirs and what is someone else's.

Comparison level for alternatives The perceived quality of alternatives to the current relationship.

Comparison level The expectation of how rewarding a relationship should be.

Complementary stereotypes Both positive and negative stereotypes that are ascribed to a group as a way of justifying the status quo.

Conceptual replication The repetition of a study with different operationalizations of the crucial variables but yielding similar results.

Confederate A supposed participant in a research study who, unknown to the real participants, actually is working with experimenters.

Confirmation bias A tendency to seek out information and view events and other people in ways that fit how we want and expect them to be.

Conformity The phenomenon whereby an individual alters beliefs, attitudes, or behavior to bring them in accordance with those of a majority.

Confound A variable other than the conceptual variable intended to be manipulated that may be responsible for the effect on the dependent variable, making alternative explanations possible.

Construal level theory The theory that people focus more on concrete details when thinking about the near future and focus more on abstract meaning when thinking about the distant future.

Construct validity The degree to which a dependent variable assesses what it intends to assess or an independent variable manipulates what it intends to manipulate.

Controlled processes Human thoughts or actions that occur more slowly and deliberatively and that are motivated by some goal that is often consciously recognized.

Conversion theory The explanation that people are influenced by a minority because the minority's distinctive position better captures their attention.

Correlation coefficient A positive or negative numerical value that shows the direction and strength of a relationship between two variables.

Correlational method Research in which two or more variables are measured and analyzed to determine to what extent, if any, they are associated.

Correspondent inference The tendency to attribute to an actor an attitude, desire, or trait that corresponds to the action.

Covariation principle The tendency to see a causal relationship between an event and an outcome when they happen at the same time.

Cover story An explanation of the purpose of a study that is different from the true purpose.

Cultural animals A description of humans as viewing reality through a set of symbols provided by the culture in which they are raised.

Cultural diffusion The transfer of inventions, knowledge, and ideas from one culture to another.

Cultural evolution The process whereby cultures develop and propagate according to systems of belief or behavior that contribute to the success of a society.

Cultural knowledge A vast store of information, accumulated within a culture, that explains how the world works and why things happen as they do.

Cultural perspective A view that focuses on the influence of culture on thought, feeling, and behavior.

Cultural transmission The process whereby members of a culture learn explicitly or implicitly to imitate the beliefs and behaviors of others in that culture.

Cultural traumas Tragic historical examples of cultural disruptions, some of which have led to complete cultural disintegration.

Cultural worldview Human-constructed shared symbolic conceptions of reality that imbue life with meaning, order, and permanence.

Culture A set of beliefs, attitudes, values, norms, morals, customs, roles, statuses, symbols, and rituals shared by a self-identified group, a group whose members think of themselves *as* a group.

Debriefing At the end of a study, the procedure in which participants are assessed for suspicion and then receive a gentle explanation of the true nature of the study in a manner that counteracts any negative effects of the study experience.

Dehumanization The tendency to hold stereotypic views of outgroup members as animals rather than as humans.

Deindividuation A tendency to lose one's sense of individuality when in a group or crowd.

Demand characteristics Aspects of a study that give away its purpose or communicate how the participant is expected to behave.

Descriptive norm A belief about what most people typically do.

Diffusion of responsibility A situation in which the presence of others prevents any one person from taking responsibility (e.g., for helping).

Direct replication The process of reproducing a scientific finding by repeating the same methods and measures used in the original research study.

Discounting principle The tendency to reduce the importance of any potential cause of another's behavior to the extent that other potential causes exist.

Discrimination Negative behavior toward an individual solely on the basis of that person's membership in a particular group.

Disidentification The process of disinvesting in any area in which one's group traditionally has been underrepresented or negatively stereotyped.

Dismissive avoidant An avoidant attachment style characterized by a negative view of others but a positive view of the self, high avoidance but low anxiety, and distant relationships.

Displaced aggression Aggression directed to a target other than the source of one's frustration.

Dispositions Consistent preferences, ways of thinking, and behavioral tendencies that manifest across varying situations and over time.

Domain-general adaptations Attributes that are useful for dealing with various challenges across different areas of life.

Domain-specific adaptations Attributes that evolved to meet a particular challenge but that are not particularly useful when dealing with other types of challenges.

Door-in-the-face effect A phenomenon whereby people are more likely to comply with a moderate request after they have first been presented with and refused to agree to a much larger request.

Downward comparison A comparison of oneself with those who are worse off.

Downward counterfactual An imagined alternative in which the outcome is worse than what actually happened.

Dramaturgical perspective Using the theater as a metaphor, the idea that people, like actors, perform according to a script. If we all know the script and play our parts well, then, like a successful play, our social interactions flow smoothly and seem meaningful, and each actor benefits.

Dual process theories Theories that are used to explain a wide range of phenomena by positing two ways of processing information.

Ease of retrieval effect The process whereby people judge how frequently an event occurs on the basis of how easily they can retrieve examples of that event.

Effort justification The phenomenon whereby people reduce dissonance by convincing themselves that what they suffered for is actually quite valuable.

Ego depletion The idea that ego strength becomes depleted by extended bouts of self-control.

Ego The aspect of self that controls one's thoughts and actions.

Elaboration likelihood model A theory of persuasion which proposes that persuasive messages can influence attitudes by two different routes: central or peripheral.

Emotion differentiation The skills of recognizing fine-grained distinctions between different emotions.

Empathy gap The underestimation of other people's experience of physical pain as well as the pain of social rejection.

Empathy-altruism model The idea that the reason people help others depends on how much they empathize with them. When empathy is low, people help others when benefits outweigh costs; when empathy is high, people help others even at costs to themselves.

Entitativity The degree to which a collection of people feels like a cohesive group.

Equity theory The idea that people are motivated to maintain a sense of fairness or equity, whereby both partners feel that the proportion of outcomes (rewards) to inputs (costs) that each receives is roughly equal.

Eros Freud's term for what he proposed is the human inborn instinct to seek pleasure and to create.

Ethnocentrism Viewing the world through our own cultural value system and thereby judging actions and people based on our own culture's views of right and wrong and good and bad.

Evolution The concept that different species are descended from common ancestors but have evolved over time, acquiring different genetic characteristics as a function of different environmental demands.

Evolutionary perspective A view that humans are a species of animal and that their social behavior is a consequence of particular evolved adaptations.

Excitation transfer theory The theory that leftover arousal caused by an initial event can intensify emotional reactions to a second, unrelated event.

Existential isolation The sense that one is alone in one's experience and that others cannot understand one's perspective. One can feel existentially isolated even with many social interactions.

Existential perspective A view that focuses on the cognitive, affective, and behavioral consequences of basic aspects of the human condition, such as the knowledge of mortality, the desire for meaning, and the precarious nature of identity.

Experiential system An unconscious, intuitive, and automatic system of thinking.

Experimental method A study in which a researcher manipulates a variable, referred to as the **independent variable**, measures possible effects on another variable, referred to as the **dependent variable**, and tries to hold all other variables constant.

Experimenter bias The possibility that an experimenter's knowledge of the condition a particular participant is in could affect her behavior toward the participant and thereby introduce a confounding variable to the independent variable manipulation.

Explicit attitudes Attitudes people are consciously aware of through the cognitive system.

External validity The judgment that a research finding can be generalized to other people, in other settings, at other times.

Facial feedback hypothesis The idea that changes in facial expression elicit emotions associated with those expressions.

False consensus A general tendency to assume that other people share our own attitudes, opinions, and preferences.

Fearfully avoidant An avoidant attachment style characterized by a negative view of both self and others, high avoidance and high anxiety, and distant relationships, in which the person doesn't feel worthy, doesn't trust others, and fears rejection.

Field research Research that occurs outside the laboratory, such as in schools, in office buildings, in medical clinics, at football games, or even in shopping malls or on street corners.

Flow The feeling of being completely absorbed in an activity that is appropriately challenging to one's skills.

Fluid compensation After a blow to self-esteem in one domain, the process of shoring up one's overall sense of self-worth by bolstering how one thinks of oneself in an unrelated domain.

Foot-in-the-door effect A phenomenon whereby people are more likely to comply with a moderate request after having initially complied with a smaller request.

Free choice paradigm A laboratory situation in which people make a choice between two alternatives, and after they do, attraction to the alternatives is assessed.

Frustration-aggression hypothesis Originally the idea that aggression is always preceded by frustration and that frustration inevitably leads to aggression. Revised to suggest that frustration produces an emotional readiness to aggress.

Functional magnetic resonance imagery (fMRI) A scanning technique that provides information about the activity of regions of the brain when people perform certain cognitive or motor tasks.

Fundamental attribution error (FAE) The tendency to attribute behavior to internal or dispositional qualities of the actor and consequently underestimate the causal role of situational factors.

Fusiform face area A region in the temporal lobe of the brain that helps us recognize the people we know.

Gain-loss theory A theory of attraction which posits that liking is highest for others when they increase their positivity toward you over time.

Goals Cognitions that represent outcomes that we strive for in order to meet our needs and desires.

Group polarization A tendency for group discussion to shift group members toward an extreme position.

Groupthink A tendency toward flawed group decision making when group members are so intent on preserving group harmony that they fail to analyze a problem completely.

Halo effect A tendency to assume that people with one positive attribute (e.g., who are physically attractive) also have other positive traits.

Hedonism The human preference for pleasure over pain.

Heuristics Mental shortcuts, or rules of thumb, that are used for making judgments and decisions.

Hierarchy of goals The idea that goals are organized hierarchically from very abstract goals to very concrete goals, with the latter serving the former.

Hostile attribution bias The tendency to attribute hostile intent to others' actions, even when others' intentions are innocent.

Hypothesis An "if-then" statement that follows logically from a theory and specifies how certain variables should be related to each other if the theory is correct.

Identity fusion A profound feeling of oneness with a group and a perception that one's personal identity and group identity are essentially the same. It is a strong motivator of collective action.

Illusion of transparency The tendency to overestimate another's ability to know our internal thoughts and feelings.

Illusory correlation A tendency to assume an association between two rare occurrences, such as being in an underrepresented group and performing negative actions.

Implementation intentions Mental rules reminding us to respond to a cue in a situation with a goal-directed behavior.

Implicit attitudes Automatic associations based on previous learning through the experiential system.

Implicit prejudice Negative attitudes or affective reactions associated with an outgroup for which the individual has little or no conscious awareness and that can be automatically activated in intergroup encounters.

Impressions Schemas people have about other individuals.

Independent self-construal Viewing self as a unique active agent serving one's own goals.

Individualistic culture A culture in which the emphasis is on individual initiative, achievement, and creativity over maintenance of social cohesion.

Induced compliance paradigm A laboratory situation in which participants are induced to engage in a behavior that runs counter to their true attitudes.

Induced hypocrisy paradigm A laboratory situation in which participants are asked to advocate an opinion they already believe in but then are reminded about a time when their actions ran counter to that opinion, thereby arousing dissonance.

Informational influence The process of using others as sources of information about the world.

Infrahumanization The perception that outgroup members lack qualities viewed as being unique to human beings, such as language, rational intelligence, and complex social emotions.

Ingroup bias A tendency to favor groups we belong to more than those that we don't.

Injunctive norm A belief about what behaviors are generally approved of or disapproved of in one's culture.

Institutional discrimination Unfair restrictions on opportunities for certain groups of people through institutional policies, structural power relations, and formal laws.

Instrumental aggression Harm-seeking done to another person that serves some other goal.

Integration The process whereby people retain aspects of their former culture while internalizing aspects of a new host culture.

Interaction A pattern of results in which the effect of one independent variable on the dependent variable depends on the level of a second independent variable.

Interdependence A situation in which what each person does significantly influences what the partner does over long periods of time.

Interdependence theory The idea that satisfaction, investments, and perceived alternatives are critical in determining commitment to a particular relationship.

Interdependent self-construal Viewing self primarily in terms of how one relates to others and contributes to the greater whole.

Internal validity The judgment that for a particular experiment it is possible to conclude that the manipulated independent variable caused the change in the measured dependent variable.

Ironic processing The idea that the more we try *not* to think about something, the more those thoughts enter our mind and distract us from other things.

Just world beliefs The idea that good things will happen to the worthy and bad things will happen to the unworthy.

Justification suppression model The idea that people endorse and freely express stereotypes in part to justify their own negative affective reactions to outgroup members.

Kin selection The idea that natural selection led to greater tendencies to help close kin than to help those with whom we have little genetic relationship.

Literal immortality A culturally shared belief that there is some form of life after death for those who are worthy.

Locus of causality Attribution of behavior to either an aspect of the actor (internal) or to some aspect of the situation (external).

Locus of control The extent to which a person believes that either internal or external factors determine life outcomes.

Loneliness The feeling that one is deprived of human social connections.

Longitudinal studies Studies in which variables are measured in the same individuals over two or more periods of time, typically over months or years.

Long-term memory Information from past experience that may or may not be currently activated.

Looking-glass self The idea that others reflect back to us (much like a looking glass, or mirror) who we are by how they behave toward us.

Lowballing A phenomenon in which after agreeing to an offer, people find it hard to break that commitment even if they later learn of some extra cost to the deal.

Magical thinking The tendency to believe that simply having thoughts about an event before it occurs can influence that event.

Master status The perception that a person will be seen only in terms of a stigmatizing attribute rather than as the total self.

Matching phenomenon The idea that people seek romantic relationships with others who are similar to themselves in physical attractiveness.

Mate guarding Efforts to prevent one's sexual partner from mating with someone else in order to avoid the costs of rearing offspring that do not help to propagate one's genes.

Mating strategies Approaches to mating that help people reproduce successfully. People prefer different mating strategies depending on whether they are thinking about a short-term pairing or a long-term commitment.

Melting pot An ideological view which holds that diverse peoples within a society should converge toward the mainstream culture.

Mere exposure effect An effect that occurs when people hold a positive attitude toward a stimulus simply because they have been exposed to it repeatedly.

Meta-analysis A process of analyzing data across many related studies to determine the strength and reliability of a finding.

Metaphor A cognitive tool that allows people to understand an abstract concept in terms of a dissimilar, concrete concept.

Mindfulness The state of being and acting fully in the current moment.

Minimal deterrence Use of the minimal level of external justification necessary to deter unwanted behavior.

Minority influence The process by which dissenters (or numerical minorities) produce attitude change within a group, despite the risk of social rejection and disturbance of the status quo.

Minority slowness effect An effect that occurs when people who hold the minority position take longer to express their opinions.

Mirror neurons Certain neurons that are activated both when one performs an action oneself and when one observes another person perform that action.

Misattribution of arousal Inadvertent ascription of arousal resulting from one source to a different source.

Misinformation effect The process by which cues that are given after an event can plant false information into memory.

Model of relational turbulence The idea that as partners make the transition from casual dating to more serious involvement in the relationship, they go through a turbulent period of adjustment.

Moderator variables Variables that explain when, where, or for whom an effect is most likely to occur.

Monitor The effortless mental process that is on the lookout for signs of unwanted thoughts.

Mortality salience The state of being reminded of one's mortality.

Motivation The process of generating and expending energy toward achieving or avoiding some outcome.

Multicultural ideology A worldview in which different cultural identities and viewpoints are acknowledged and appreciated.

Multiculturalism (cultural pluralism) An ideological view which holds that cultural diversity is valued and that diverse peoples within a society should retain aspects of their traditional culture while adapting to the host culture.

Mutuality Partners' acknowledgment that their lives are intertwined and thinking of themselves as a couple ("us") instead of as two separate individuals ("me" and "you").

Natural selection The process by which certain attributes are more successful in a particular environment and therefore become more represented in future generations.

Naturalistic fallacy A bias toward believing that biological adaptations are inherently good or desirable.

Need for cognition Differences between people in their need to think about things critically and analytically.

Needs Internal states that drive action that is necessary to survive or thrive.

Norm for social commitment A belief whereby once we make a public agreement, we tend to stick to it even if circumstances change.

Norm of reciprocity An explanation for why we give help: If I help you today, you might be more likely to help me tomorrow.

Normative influence The process of using others to determine how to fit in.

Obedience An action engaged in to fulfill a direct order or command of another person.

Objectification theory A theory which proposes that the cultural value placed on women's appearance leads people to view women more as objects than as full human beings.

Operational definition A specific, concrete method of measuring or manipulating a conceptual variable.

Operator The effortful mental process that pushes any signs of unwanted thoughts out of consciousness.

Outgroup homogeneity effect The tendency to view individuals in outgroups as being more similar to each other than they really are.

Overjustification effect The tendency for salient rewards or threats to lead people to attribute the reason, or justification, for engaging in an activity to an external factor, which thereby undermines their intrinsic motivation for and enjoyment of the activity.

Parasocial relationships Individuals' relationships with people in the media, including celebrities, television characters, and athletes.

Parental investment The time and effort that parents must invest in each child they produce.

Peripheral cues Aspects of communication that are irrelevant (that is, *peripheral*) to the true merits of the person, object, or position advocated in a message (e.g., a speaker's physical attractiveness when attractiveness is irrelevant to the position).

Peripheral route to persuasion A style of processing a persuasive message by a person who is not willing or able to put effort into thinking carefully about the message's argument. Attitude change depends on the presence of peripheral cues.

Person–group discrimination discrepancy The tendency for people to estimate that they personally experience less discrimination than is faced by the average member of their group.

Persuasion Intentional effort to change other people's attitudes in order to change their behavior.

Pluralistic ignorance A situation in which individuals rely on others to identify a norm but falsely interpret others' beliefs and feelings, resulting in inaction.

Positive illusions Idealized perceptions of romantic partners that highlight their positive qualities and downplay their faults.

Possible selves Images of what the self might become in the future.

Prefrontal cortex The region of the brain that regulates impulsive behavior.

Prejudice A negative attitude toward an individual solely on the basis of that person's presumed membership in a particular group.

Prevention focus A general tendency to think and act in ways oriented toward avoiding negative outcomes.

Primacy effect The idea that what we learn early colors how we judge subsequent information.

Priming The process by which exposure to a stimulus in the environment increases the salience of a schema.

Private acceptance Conforming by altering private beliefs as well as public behavior.

Projection Assigning to others those traits that people fear they possess themselves.

Promotion focus A general tendency to think and act in ways oriented toward achieving positive outcomes.

Prosocial behavior Action by an individual that is intended to benefit another individual or set of individuals.

Prosopagnosia The inability to recognize familiar faces.

Prototype/willingness model of health behavior A model that explains how, when it comes to opportunistic behaviors, a person's willingness to be influenced by a situation is a key predictor of behavior.

Proximity The physical nearness of others. It is a major factor determining who we form relationships with.

Psychological need A mechanism for regulating behavior to acquire the tangible or intangible resources necessary for survival and well-being.

Psychological reactance theory A theory which proposes that people value thinking and acting freely. Therefore, situations that threaten their freedom arouse discomfort and prompt efforts to restore freedom.

Public compliance Conforming only outwardly to fit in with a group without changing private beliefs.

Quasi-experimental designs A type of research in which groups of participants are compared on some dependent variable, but for practical or ethical reasons, the groups are not formed on the basis of random assignment.

Random assignment A procedure in which participants are assigned to conditions in such a way that each person has an equal chance of being in any condition of an experiment.

Realistic group conflict theory A theory which asserts that the initial negative feelings between groups are often based on a real conflict or competition regarding scarce resources.

Recency effect An effect that occurs when recently encountered information primarily influences attitudes (e.g., a commercial viewed just before shopping influences a shopper's choices).

Reference group A group with which an individual strongly identifies.

Reflected appraisals What we *think* other people think about us.

Registered report A study that is accepted for publication on the strength of the methods and importance of the question but before results are known.

Rejection identification theory The idea that people can offset the negative consequences of being targeted by discrimination by feeling a strong sense of identification with their stigmatized group.

Relative deprivation theory A theory which states that disadvantaged groups are less aware of and bothered by their lower status because of a tendency to compare their outcomes only with others who are similarly deprived.

Representativeness heuristic The tendency to overestimate the likelihood that a target is part of a category if the person has features that seem representative of that category.

Research The process whereby scientists observe events, look for patterns, and evaluate theories proposed to explain those patterns.

Reverse causality problem The possibility that a correlation between variables x and y may occur because one causes the other, but it is impossible to determine whether x causes y or y causes x.

Reward model of liking A model which proposes that people like other people whom they associate with positive stimuli and dislike people whom they associate with negative stimuli.

Right-wing authoritarianism (RWA) An ideology which holds that the social world is inherently dangerous and that maintaining security requires upholding society's order and tradition. It predicts prejudice against groups seen as socially deviant or dangerous.

Salience The aspect of a schema that is active in one's mind and, consciously or not, colors perceptions and behavior.

Schema A mental structure, stored in memory, that contains prior knowledge and associations with a concept.

Scientific method The process of developing, testing, and refining theories to understand the determinants of social behavior.

Scripts Schemas about an event that specify the typical sequence of actions that take place.

Securely attached An attachment style characterized by a positive view of self and others, low anxiety and avoidance, and stable, satisfying relationships.

Self-affirmation theory The idea that people respond less defensively to threats to one aspect of themselves if they think about another valued aspect of themselves.

Self-awareness theory The theory that aspects of the self—one's attitudes, values, and goals—will be most likely to influence behavior when attention is focused on the self.

Self-compassion Being kind to ourselves when we suffer, fail, or feel inadequate, recognizing that imperfection is part of the human condition, and accepting rather than denying negative feelings about ourselves.

Self-complexity The extent to which an individual's self-concept consists of many different aspects.

Self-concept A person's knowledge about him- or herself, including one's own traits, social identities, and experiences.

Self-concept clarity A clearly defined, internally consistent, and temporally stable self-concept.

Self-determination theory The idea that people function best when they feel that their actions stem from their own desires rather than from external forces.

Self-disclosure The sharing of information about oneself.

Self-discrepancy theory The theory that people feel anxiety when they fall short of how they *ought* to be but feel sad when they fall short of how they ideally *want* to be.

Self-esteem The level of positive feeling one has about oneself.

Self-evaluation maintenance model The idea that people adjust their perceived similarity to successful others to minimize threatening comparisons and maximize self-esteem-supporting identifications.

Self-expansion model of relationships The idea that romantic relationships serve the desire to expand the self and grow.

Self-fulfilling prophecy The phenomenon whereby initially false expectations cause the fulfillment of those expectations.

Self-handicapping Placing obstacles in the way of one's own success to protect self-esteem from a possible future failure.

Self-monitoring A personality variable that indicates the extent to which an individual has the desire and ability to adjust their self-presentations for different audiences.

Self-narrative A coherent life story that connects one's past, present, and possible future.

Self-objectification A phenomenon whereby intense cultural scrutiny of the female body leads many girls and women to view themselves as objects to be looked at and judged.

Self-perception theory The theory that people sometimes infer their attitudes and attributes by observing their behavior and the situation in which it occurs.

Self-regulation A set of processes for guiding one's thoughts, feelings, and behavior to reach desired goals.

Self-regulatory perseveration theory of depression The theory that one way in which people can fall into depression is through persistent self-focus on an unattainable goal.

Self-schema An integrated set of memories, beliefs, and generalizations about a personally important attribute that defines the self.

Self-verification Seeking out other people and social situations that support the way one views oneself in order to sustain a consistent and clear self-concept.

Serotonin A neurotransmitter that regulates our experience of negative affect.

Sexual objectification The tendency to think about women in a narrow way as objects rather than as full humans, as if their physical appearance were all that matters.

Shooter bias The tendency to mistakenly see objects in the hands of Black men as guns.

Short-term memory Information and input that is currently activated.

Sleeper effect The phenomenon whereby people can remember a message but forget where it came from; thus, source credibility has a diminishing effect on attitudes over time.

Social cognition perspective A view that focuses on how people perceive, remember, and interpret events and individuals, including themselves, in their social world.

Social comparison theory The theory that people come to know themselves partly by comparing themselves with similar others.

Social contagion The phenomenon whereby ideas, feelings, and behaviors seem to spread across people like wildfire.

Social dominance orientation (SDO) An ideology in which the world is viewed as a ruthlessly competitive jungle where it is appropriate and right for powerful groups to dominate weaker ones.

Social dominance theory The theory that large societies create hierarchies and that people tend to endorse beliefs that legitimatize hierarchy.

Social exchange model A model which takes an economic perspective and assumes that people approach relationships with an underlying motivation of self-interest.

Social exchange theory A theory which maintains that people provide help to someone else when the benefits of helping and the costs of not helping outweigh the potential costs of helping and the benefits of not helping.

Social facilitation theory The theory that the presence of others increases a person's dominant response—that is, the response that is most likely for that person for the task at hand.

Social identity theory The theory that group identities are an important part of self-definition and a key source of self-esteem.

Social influence The effects of other people on an individual's beliefs, attitudes, values, or behavior.

Social learning The capacity to learn from observing others.

Social loafing A tendency to exert less effort when performing as part of a collective or group than when performing as an individual.

Social neuroscience perspective A view that focuses on understanding the neural processes that underlie social judgment and behavior. Neuroscience involves assessments of brain waves, brain imaging, and cardiovascular functioning.

Social proof A tendency to conform to what we believe respected others think and do.

Social psychology The scientific study of the causes and consequences of people's thoughts, feelings, and actions regarding themselves and other people.

Social role theory The theory that gender differences in behavior, personality, and self-definition arise because of a long history of role distribution between the sexes and error-prone assumptions that those roles are essential to the nature of men and women.

Socialization Learning from parents and others what is desirable and undesirable conduct in a particular culture.

Sociometer model The idea that a basic function of self-esteem is to indicate to the individual how much he or she is accepted by other people.

Solo status A sense that one is unique in some specific manner in relation to other people in the current environment.

Somatic marker hypothesis The idea that changes in the body, experienced as emotion, guide decision making.

Source credibility The degree to which the audience perceives a message's source as expert and trustworthy.

Source The person or group communicating a message.

Spotlight effect The belief that others are more focused on us than they actually are.

Stereotype Overgeneralized beliefs about the traits and attributes of members of a particular group.

Stereotype threat The concern that one might do something to confirm a negative stereotype about one's group either in one's own eyes or the eyes of someone else.

Stigma consciousness The expectation of being perceived by other people, particularly those in the majority group, in terms of one's group membership.

Superordinate goal A common problem or shared goal that groups work together to solve or achieve.

Symbolic immortality A culturally shared belief that, by being part of something greater and more enduring than our individual selves, some part of us will live on after we die.

Symbolic interactionism The perspective that people use their understanding of how others view them as the primary basis for knowing and evaluating themselves.

Symbolic racism A tendency to view members of a racial outgroup as a threat to one's way of life and to express this view by rejecting social policies seen as benefiting that group.

System justification theory The theory that negative stereotypes get attached to groups partly because they help explain and justify why some individuals are more advantaged than others.

Terror management theory A theory which says that to minimize fear of mortality, humans strive to sustain faith that they are enduringly valued contributors to a meaningful world and therefore transcend their physical death.

Thanatos Freud's term for what he proposed is the human inborn instinct to aggress and to destroy.

Theory An explanation for how and why variables are related to each other.

Theory of mind A set of ideas about other peoples' thoughts, desires, feelings, and intentions based on what we know about them and the situation they are in.

Theory of planned behavior A theory which proposes that attitudes, subjective norms, and perceived behavioral control interact to shape people's behavioral intentions.

Theory of symbolic self-completion The idea that when people perceive that a self-defining aspect is threatened, they feel incomplete, and then try to compensate by acquiring and displaying symbols that support their desired self-definition.

Third variable problem The possibility that two variables may be correlated but do not exert a causal influence on one another, and both are caused by some additional variable.

Transference A tendency to map on, or transfer, feelings for a person who is known onto someone new who resembles that person in some way.

Transgender People who identify with a gender that is different from their assigned sex at birth.

Two-factor theory of emotion The theory that people's emotions are the product of both their arousal level and how they interpret that arousal based on contextual cues.

Ultimate attribution error The tendency to believe that bad actions by outgroup members occur *because of their internal dispositions* and good actions by them occur *because of the situation*, while believing the reverse for ingroup members.

Uncertainty-identity theory The theory that people join and identify with groups in order to reduce negative feelings of uncertainty about themselves and others.

Upward comparison A comparison of oneself with those who are better off.

Upward counterfactual An imagined alternative in which the outcome is better than what actually happened.

Urban overload hypothesis The idea that city dwellers avoid being overwhelmed by stimulation by narrowing their attention, making it more likely that they overlook legitimate situations where help is needed.

Weapons effect The tendency for the presence of firearms to increase the likelihood of aggression, especially when people are frustrated.

Working models of relationships Global feelings about the nature and worth of close relationships and other people's trustworthiness.

Working self-concept A set of self-aspects that are currently activated by situational cues and strongly influence thoughts, feelings, and actions in the moment.

Worldview defense The tendency to derogate those who violate important cultural ideals and to venerate those who uphold them.

Aarts, H., & Dijksterhuis, A. (2003). The silence of the library: Environment, situational norm, and social behavior. *Journal of Personality and Social Psychology, 84*(1), 18–28.

Aarts, H., Dijksterhuis, A., & Custers, R. (2003). Automatic normative behavior in environments: The moderating role of conformity in activating situational norms. *Social Cognition, 21*(6), 447–464.

Aarts, H., Gollwitzer, P. M., & Hassin, R. R. (2004). Goal contagion: Perceiving is for pursuing. *Journal of Personality and Social Psychology, 87*(1), 23–37.

Abdel-Khalek, A. M. (1998). The structure and measurement of death obsession. *Personality and Individual Differences, 24*(2), 159–165.

Abele, A. E., & Wojciszke, B. (2007). Agency and communion from the perspective of self versus others. *Journal of Personality and Social Psychology, 93*(5), 751–763.

Abma, J. C., Martinez, G. M., Mosher, W. D., & Dawson, B. S. (2004). *Teenagers in the United States: Sexual activity, contraceptive use, and childbearing, 2002.* National Center for Health Statistics: Vital and Health Statistics. https://www.cdc.gov/nchs/data/series/sr_23/sr23_024.pdf

Aboud, F. (1988). *Children and prejudice.* Basil Blackwell.

Acevedo, B. P., & Aron, A. (2009). Does a long-term relationship kill romantic love? *Review of General Psychology, 13*(1), 59–65.

Acker, M., & Davis, M. H. (1992). Intimacy, passion and commitment in adult romantic relationships: A test of the triangular theory of love. *Journal of Social and Personal Relationships, 9*(1), 21–50.

Ackerman, J. M., Nocera, C. C., & Bargh, J. A. (2010). Incidental haptic sensations influence social judgments and decisions. *Science, 328*(5986), 1712–1715.

Ackerman, L.S., & Chopik, W.J. (2021). Cross-cultural comparisons implicit and explicit age bias. Personality and Social Psychology Bulletin, 47, 953–968.

Adam, M. T. P., Ku, G., & Lux, E. (2018). Auction fever: The unrecognized effects of incidental arousal. *Journal of Experimental Social Psychology, 80,* 52–58.

Adams, J. S. (1963). Towards an understanding of inequity. *Journal of Abnormal and Social Psychology, 67*(5), 422–436.

Aday, A., & Schmader, T. (2019). Seeking authenticity in diverse contexts: How identities and environments constrain "free" choice. *Personality and Social Psychology Compass, 13*(6), e12450.

Adger, W. N., Barnett, J., Brown, K., Marshall, N., & O'Brien, K. (2013). Cultural dimensions of climate change impacts and adaptation. *Nature Climate Change, 3*(2), 112–117.

Adler, A. (1964). *Individual psychology of Alfred Adler.* HarperCollins.

Adler, J. M., Lodi-Smith, J., Philippe, F. L., & Houle, I. (2016). The incremental validity of narrative identity in predicting well-being: A review of the field and recommendations for the future. *Personality and Social Psychology Review, 20*(2), 142–175.

Adler, L. L., & Adler, H. E. (1977). Ontogeny of observational learning in the dog (*Canis familiaris*). *Developmental Psychobiology, 10*(3), 267–271.

Adorno, T. W., Frenkel-Brunswik, E., Levinson, D. J., & Sanford, R. N. (1950). *The authoritarian personality.* Harpers.

Affleck, B. (Director). (2012). *Argo* [Film]. Warner Bros.

Agnew, C. R., Loving, T. J., Le, B., & Goodfriend, W. (2004). Thinking close: Measuring relational closeness as perceived self-other inclusion. In D. J. Mashek & A. Aron (Eds.), *Handbook of closeness and intimacy* (pp. 103–115). Erlbaum.

ahbez, e. (1948). Nature boy [Song]. Capitol.

Ai, A. L., Tice, T. N., & Kelsey, C. L. (2009). Coping after 9/11: Deep interconnectedness and struggle in posttraumatic stress and growth. In M. Morgan (Ed.), *The impact of 9/11 on psychology and education: The day that changed everything?* (pp. 115–138). Palgrave Macmillan.

Ainsworth, M. D. S., & Bell, S. M. (1970). Attachment, exploration, and separation: Illustrated by the behavior of one-year-olds in a strange situation. *Child Development, 41*(1), 49–67.

Ainsworth, M. D. S., Blehar, M. C., Waters, E., & Wall, S. (1978). *Patterns of attachment: A psychological study of the strange situation.* Erlbaum.

Ajzen, I. (1985). From intentions to actions: A theory of planned behavior. In J. Kuhl & J. Beckman (Eds.), *Action-control: From cognition to behavior* (pp. 11–39). Springer.

Aknin, L. B., Dunn, E. W., Proulx, J., Lok, I., & Norton, M. I. (2020). Does spending money on others promote happiness?: A registered replication report. *Journal of Personality and Social Psychology.* Advance online publication.

Aknin, L. B., Sandstrom, G. M., Dunn, E. W., & Norton, M. I. (2011). It's the recipient that counts: Spending money on strong social ties leads to greater happiness than spending on weak social ties. *PloS ONE, 6*(2), e17018.

Albarracín, D., Johnson, B. T., Fishbein, M., & Muellerleile, P. A. (2001). Theories of reasoned action and planned behavior as models of condom use: A meta-analysis. *Psychological Bulletin, 127*(1), 142–161.

Albarracín, D., Kumkale, G. T., & Poyner-Del Vento, P. (2017). How people can become persuaded by weak messages presented by credible communicators: Not all sleeper effects are created equal. *Journal of Experimental Social Psychology, 68,* 171–180.

Alexander, G. M., & Hines, M. (2002). Sex differences in response to children's toys in nonhuman primates (*Cercopithecus aethiops sabaeus*). *Evolution and Human Behavior, 23*(6), 467–479.

Alexander, G. M., Wilcox, T., & Woods, R. (2009). Sex differences in infants' visual interest in toys. *Archives of Sexual Behavior, 38*(3), 427–433.

Alexander, M. G., & Fisher, T. D. (2003). Truth and consequences: Using the bogus pipeline to examine sex differences in self-reported sexuality. *Journal of Sex Research, 40*(1), 27–35.

Algoe, S. B. (2019). Positive interpersonal processes. *Current Directions in Psychological Science, 28*(2), 183–188.

Algoe, S. B., Gable, S. L., & Maisel, N. C. (2010). It's the little things: Everyday gratitude as a booster shot for romantic relationships. *Personal Relationships, 17*(2), 217–233.

Algoe, S. B., Kurtz, L. E., & Grewen, K. (2017). Oxytocin and social bonds: The role of oxytocin in perceptions of romantic partners' bonding behavior. *Psychological Science, 28*(12), 1763–1772.

Alicke, M. D. (1985). Global self-evaluation as determined by the desirability and controllability of trait adjectives. *Journal of Personality and Social Psychology, 49*(6), 1621–1630.

Alksnis, C., Desmarais, S., & Curtis, J. (2008). Workforce segregation and the gender wage gap: Is "women's" work valued as highly as "men's"? *Journal of Applied Social Psychology, 38*(6), 1416–1441.

Allemand, M., Job, V., & Mroczek, D. K. (2019). Self-control development in adolescence predicts love and work in adulthood. *Journal of Personality and Social Psychology, 117*(3), 621–634.

Allen, S., & Daly, K. (2007). *The effects of father involvement: An updated research summary of the evidence inventory.* Centre for Families, Work & Well-Being, University of Guelph. http://www.fira.ca/cms/documents/29/Effects_of_Father_Involvement.pdf

Allen, V. L., & Levine, J. M. (1968). Social support, dissent and conformity. *Sociometry, 31*(2), 138–149.

Allen, V. L., & Levine, J. M. (1969). Consensus and conformity. *Journal of Experimental Social Psychology, 5*(4), 389–399.

Allen, W. (Director). (1977). *Annie Hall* [Film]. Rollins-Joffe Productions.

Allen, W. (Director). (1992). *Husbands and wives* [Film]. TriStar Pictures.

Allen, W. (Director). (2013). *Blue jasmine* [Film]. Sony Pictures Classics.

Allison, S. T., Messick, D. M., & Goethals, G. R. (1989). On being better but not smarter than others: The Muhammad Ali effect. *Social Cognition, 7*(3), 275–295.

Alloy, L. B., & Abramson, L. Y. (1979). Judgment of contingency in depressed and nondepressed students: Sadder but wiser? *Journal of Experimental Psychology: General, 108*(4), 441–485.

Allport, F. H. (1924). *Social psychology.* Houghton Mifflin.

Allport, G. W. (1937). *Personality: A psychological interpretation.* Holt.

Allport, G. W. (1954). *The nature of prejudice.* Addison-Wesley.

Allport, G. W., & Postman, L. J. (1947). *The psychology of rumor.* Henry Holt.

Almasy, S. (2015). *Tamir Rice shooting was "reasonable," two experts conclude.* CNN. http://www.cnn.com/2015/10/10/us/tamir-rice-shooting-reports/

Alper, M., Durose, M. R., & Markman, J. (2018). *2018 update on prisoner recidivism: A 9-year follow-up period (2005–2014).* Bureau of Justice Statistics. https://www.bjs.gov/content/pub/pdf/18upr9yfup0514.pdf

Altemeyer, B. (1981). *Right-wing authoritarianism.* University of Manitoba Press.

Altemeyer, B. (1998). The other "authoritarian personality." In M. P. Zanna (Ed.), *Advances in experimental social psychology* (Vol. 30, pp. 47–92). Academic Press.

Altman, I., & Taylor, D. A. (1973). *Social penetration: The development of interpersonal relationships.* Holt, Rinehart & Winston.

Alves, H. (2018). Sharing rare attitudes attracts. *Personality and Social Psychology Bulletin, 44*(8), 1270–1283.

Alves, H., Koch, A., & Unkelbach, C. (2016). My friends are all alike—The relation between liking and perceived similarity in person perception. *Journal of Experimental Social Psychology, 62*, 103–117.

Alves, H. V., Pereira, C. R., Sutton, R. M., & Correia, I. (2019). The world may not be just for you but you'd better not say it: On the social value of expressing personal belief in a just world. *European Journal of Social Psychology, 49*(2), 270–285.

Amato, P. R., Booth, A., Johnson, D. R., & Rogers, S. J. (2007). *Alone together: How marriage in America is changing.* Harvard University Press.

Ambady, N., & Rosenthal, R. (1992). Thin slices of expressive behavior as predictors of interpersonal consequences: A meta-analysis. *Psychological Bulletin, 111*(2), 256–274.

Ames, D. R., & Lee, A. J. (2015). Tortured beliefs: How and when prior support for torture skews the perceived value of coerced information. *Journal of Experimental Social Psychology, 60*, 86–92.

Amiot, C. E., Doucerain, M. M., Zhou, B., & Ryder, A. G. (2018). Cultural identity dynamics: Capturing changes in cultural identities over time and their intraindividual organization. *European Journal of Social Psychology, 48*(5), 629–644.

Amodio, D. M. (2014). The neuroscience of prejudice and stereotyping. *Nature Reviews Neuroscience, 15*(10), 670–682.

Amodio, D. M., & Cikara, M. (2021). The social neuroscience of prejudice. *Annual Review of Psychology, 72*, 439–469.

Amodio, D. M., & Devine, P. G. (2006). Stereotyping and evaluation in implicit race bias: Evidence for independent constructs and unique effects on behavior. *Journal of Personality and Social Psychology, 91*(4), 652–661.

Amodio, D. M., & Showers, C. J. (2005). "Similarity breeds liking" revisited: The moderating role of commitment. *Journal of Social and Personal Relationships, 22*(6), 817–836.

Amodio, D. M., & Swencionis, J. K. (2018). Proactive control of implicit bias: A theoretical model and implications for behavior change. *Journal of Personality and Social Psychology, 115*(2), 255–275.

Andersen, S. M., & Baum, A. (1994). Transference in interpersonal relations: Inferences and affect based on significant other representations. *Journal of Personality, 62*(4), 459–497.

Andersen, S. M., & Bem, S. L. (1981). Sex typing and androgyny in dyadic interaction: Individual differences in responsiveness to physical attractiveness. *Journal of Personality and Social Psychology, 41*(1), 74–86.

Andersen, S. M., Reznik, I., & Manzella, L. M. (1996). Eliciting facial affect, motivation, and expectancies in transference: Significant-other representations in social relations. *Journal of Personality and Social Psychology, 71*(6), 1108–1129.

Anderson, C. A. (1989). Temperature and aggression: Ubiquitous effects of heat on occurrence of human violence. *Psychological Bulletin, 106*(1), 74–96.

Anderson, C. A., Allen, J. J., Plante, C., Quigley-McBride, A., Lovett, A., & Rokkum, J. N. (2019). The MTurkification of social and personality psychology. *Personality and Social Psychology Bulletin, 45*(6), 842–850.

Anderson, C. A., Anderson, K. B., & Deuser, W. E. (1996). Examining an affective aggression framework: Weapon and temperature effects on aggressive thoughts, affect, and attitudes. *Personality and Social Psychology Bulletin, 22*(4), 366–376.

Anderson, C. A., Bushman, B. J., & Groom, R. W. (1997). Hot years and serious and deadly assault: Empirical tests of the heat hypothesis. *Journal of Personality and Social Psychology, 73*(6), 1213–1223.

Anderson, C. A., & Dill, K. E. (2000). Video games and aggressive thoughts, feelings, and behavior in the laboratory and in life. *Journal of Personality and Social Psychology, 78*(4), 772–790.

Anderson, C. A., Sakamoto, A., Gentile, D. A., Ihori, N., Shibuya, A., Yukawa, S., Naito, M., & Kobayashi, K. (2008). Longitudinal effects of violent video games on aggression in Japan and the United States. *Pediatrics, 122*(5), e1067–e1072.

Anderson, C. A., Suzuki, K., Swing, E. L., Groves, C. L., Gentile, D. A., Prot, S., Lam, C. P., Sakamoto, A., Horiuchi, Y., Krahé, B., Jelic, M., Liuqing, W., Toma, R., Warburton, W. A., Zhang, X.-M., Tajima, S., Qing, F., & Petrescu, P. (2017). Media violence and other aggression risk factors in seven nations. *Personality and Social Psychology Bulletin, 43*(7), 986–998.

Anderson, E. (2000). *Code of the street: Decency, violence and the moral life of the inner city.* W. W. Norton.

Anderson, J. L., Crawford, C. B., Nadeau, J., & Lindberg, T. (1992). Was the Duchess of Windsor right? A cross-cultural review of the socioecology of ideals of female body shape. *Ethology and Sociobiology, 13*(3), 197–227.

Anderson, J. R. (1996). *The architecture of cognition.* Erlbaum.

Anderson, N. B., & Armstead, C. A. (1995). Toward understanding the association of socioeconomic status and health: A new challenge for the biopsychosocial approach. *Psychosomatic Medicine, 57*(3), 213–225.

Anderson, N. H. (1974). Cognitive algebra: Integration theory applied to social attribution. In L. Berkowitz (Ed.), *Advances in experimental social psychology* (Vol. 7, pp. 1–101). Academic Press.

Anderson, R., & Nida, S. A. (1978). Effect of physical attractiveness on opposite and same-sex evaluations. *Journal of Personality, 46*(3), 401–413.

Anderson, S. C., & Lauderdale, M. L. (1982). Characteristics of abusive parents: A look at self-esteem. *Child Abuse & Neglect, 6*(3), 285–293.

Andreychik, M. R., & Gill, M. J. (2012). Do negative implicit associations indicate negative attitudes? Social explanations moderate whether ostensible "negative" associations are prejudice-based or empathy-based. *Journal of Experimental Social Psychology, 48*(5), 1082–1093.

Angle, J. W., Dagogo-Jack, S., Forehand, M. R., & Perkins, A. (2017). Activating stereotypes with brand imagery: The role of viewer political identity. *Journal of Consumer Psychology, 27*(1), 84–90.

Ansfield, M. E., Wegner, D. M., & Bowser, R. (1996). Ironic effects of sleep urgency. *Behaviour Research and Therapy, 34*(7), 523–531.

Apfelbaum, E. P., Sommers, S. R., & Norton, M. I. (2008). Seeing race and seeming racist? Evaluating strategic colorblindness in social interaction. *Journal of Personality and Social Psychology, 95*(4), 918–932.

Aquino, K., Freeman, D., Reed, A., II, Lim, V. K., & Felps, W. (2009). Testing a social-cognitive model of moral behavior: The interactive influence of situations and moral identity centrality. *Journal of Personality and Social Psychology, 97*(1), 123–141.

Aquino, K., McFerran, B., & Laven, M. (2011). Moral identity and the experience of moral elevation in response to acts of uncommon goodness. *Journal of Personality and Social Psychology, 100*(4), 703–718.

Aquino, K., & Reed, A., II. (2002). The self-importance of moral identity. *Journal of Personality and Social Psychology, 83*(6), 1423–1440.

Archer, D., & Gartner, R. (1984). *Violence and crime in cross-national perspective.* Yale University Press.

Archer, D., & McDaniel, P. (1995). Violence and gender: Differences and similarities across societies. In R. B. Ruback & N. A. Weiner (Eds.), *Interpersonal violent behaviors: Social and cultural aspects* (pp. 63–87). Springer.

Archer, J. (1994). *Male violence.* Routledge.

Archer, J. (2004). Sex differences in aggression in real-world settings: A meta-analytic review. *Review of General Psychology, 8*(4), 291–322.

Archer, R. L., & Cook, C. E. (1986). Personalistic self-disclosure and attraction: Basis for relationship or scarce resource. *Social Psychology Quarterly, 49*(3), 268–272.

Arkin, A. (Director). (1971). *Little murders* [Film]. 20th Century Fox.

Armstrong, B., Gallant, S. N., Li, L., Patel, K., & Wong, B. I. (2017). Stereotype threat effects on older adults' episodic and working memory: A meta-analysis. *The Gerontologist, 57*(Suppl. 2), S193–S205.

Arndt, J., & Goldenberg, J. L. (2011). When self-enhancement drives health decisions: Insights from a terror management health model. In M. D. Alicke & C. Sedikides (Eds.), *The handbook of self enhancement and self protection* (pp. 380–398). Guilford Press.

Arndt, J., & Goldenberg, J. L. (2017). Where health and death intersect: Insights from a terror management health model. *Current Directions in Psychological Science, 26*(2), 126–131.

Arndt, J., & Greenberg, J. (1999). The effects of a self-esteem boost and mortality salience on responses to boost relevant and irrelevant worldview threats. *Personality and Social Psychology Bulletin, 25*(11), 1331–1341.

Arndt, J., Greenberg, J., Schimel, J., Pyszczynski, T., & Solomon, S. (2002). To belong or not to belong, that is the question: Terror management and identification with gender and ethnicity. *Journal of Personality and Social Psychology, 83*(1), 26–43.

Arndt, J., Schimel, J., Greenberg, J., & Pyszczynski, T. (2002). The intrinsic self and defensiveness: Evidence that activating the intrinsic self reduces self-handicapping and conformity. *Personality and Social Psychology Bulletin, 28*(5), 671–683.

Aron, A., & Aron, E. N. (2006). Romantic relationships from the perspectives of the self-expansion model and attachment theory. In M. Mikulincer & G. S. Goodman (Eds.), *Dynamics of romantic love: Attachment, caregiving, and sex* (pp. 359–382). Guilford Press.

Aron, A., Aron, E. N., & Norman, C. (2001). Self-expansion model of motivation and cognition in close relationships and beyond. In G. J. O. Fletcher & M. S. Clark (Eds.), *Blackwell handbook of social psychology: Interpersonal processes* (pp. 478–501). Blackwell Publishers Ltd.

Aron, A., Aron, E. N., & Smollan, D. (1992). Inclusion of other in the self scale and the structure of interpersonal closeness. *Journal of Personality and Social Psychology, 63*(4), 596–612.

Aron, A., Dutton, D. G., Aron, E. N., & Iverson, A. (1989). Experiences of falling in love. *Journal of Social and Personal Relationships*, 6(3), 243–257.

Aron, A., Fisher, H., Mashek, D. J., Strong, G., Li, H., & Brown, L. L. (2005). Reward, motivation, and emotion systems associated with early-stage intense romantic love. *Journal of Neurophysiology*, 94(1), 327–337.

Aron, A., & Fraley, B. (1999). Relationship closeness as including other in the self: Cognitive underpinnings and measures. *Social Cognition*, 17(2), 140–160.

Aron, A., Norman, C. C., Aron, E. N., McKenna, C., & Heyman, R. E. (2000). Couples' shared participation in novel and arousing activities and experienced relationship quality. *Journal of Personality and Social Psychology*, 78(2), 273–284.

Aron, A., Paris, M., & Aron, E. N. (1995). Falling in love: Prospective studies of self-concept change. *Journal of Personality and Social Psychology*, 69(6), 1102–1112.

Aron, A., & Westbay, L. (1996). Dimensions of the prototype of love. *Journal of Personality and Social Psychology*, 70(3), 535–551.

Aronofsky, D. (Director). (1998). *Pi* [Film]. Harvest Film Works.

Aronofsky, D. (Director). (2010). *Black swan* [Film]. Fox Searchlight Pictures.

Aronson, E., Blaney, N., Stephin, C., Sikes, J., & Snapp, M. (1978). *The jigsaw classroom*. Sage.

Aronson, E., & Carlsmith, J. M. (1963). Effect of the severity of threat on the devaluation of forbidden behavior. *Journal of Abnormal and Social Psychology*, 66(6), 584–588.

Aronson, E., & Linder, D. (1965). Gain and loss of esteem as determinants of interpersonal attractiveness. *Journal of Experimental Social Psychology*, 1(2), 156–171.

Aronson, E., & Mills, J. (1959). The effect of severity of initiation on liking for a group. *Journal of Abnormal and Social Psychology*, 59(2), 177–181.

Arriaga, X. B. (2001). The ups and downs of dating: Fluctuations in satisfaction in newly formed romantic relationships. *Journal of Personality and Social Psychology*, 80(5), 754–765.

Arriaga, X. B., Capezza, N. M., & Daly, C. A. (2016). Personal standards for judging aggression by a relationship partner: How much aggression is too much? *Journal of Personality and Social Psychology*, 110(1), 36–54.

Arriaga, X. B., Capezza, N. M., Goodfriend, W., & Allsop, K. E. (2018). The invisible harm of downplaying a romantic partner's aggression. *Current Directions in Psychological Science*, 27(4), 275–280.

Arriaga, X. B., & Rusbult, C. E. (1998). Standing in my partner's shoes: Partner perspective taking and reactions to accommodative dilemmas. *Personality and Social Psychology Bulletin*, 24(9), 927–948.

Arslan, R. C., Schilling, K. M., Gerlach, T. M., & Penke, L. (2018). Using 26,000 diary entries to show ovulatory changes in sexual desire and behavior. *Journal of Personality and Social Psychology*. Advance online publication.

Asch, S. E. (1946). Forming impressions of personality. *Journal of Abnormal and Social Psychology*, 41(3), 258–290.

Asch, S. E. (1955). Opinions and social pressure. *Scientific American*, 193(5), 31–35.

Asch, S. E. (1956). Studies of independence and conformity: I. A minority of one against a unanimous majority. *Psychological Monographs: General and Applied*, 70(9), 1–70.

Asendorpf, J. B., Conner, M., de Fruyt, F., De Houwer, J., Denissen, J. A., Fiedler, K., Fiedler, S., Funder, D. C., Kliegl, R., Nosek, B., Perugini, M., Roberts, B. W., Schmitt, M., van Aken, M. A. G., Weber, H., & Wicherts, J. M. (2016). Recommendations for increasing replicability in psychology. In A. E. Kazdin & A. E. Kazdin (Eds.), *Methodological issues and strategies in clinical research* (4th ed., pp. 607–622). American Psychological Association.

Atherton, O. E., Zheng, L. R., Bleidorn, W., & Robins, R. W. (2019). The codevelopment of effortful control and school behavioral problems. *Journal of Personality and Social Psychology*, 117(3), 659–673.

Atir, S., Rosenzweig, E., & Dunning, D. (2015). When knowledge knows no bounds: Self-perceived expertise predicts claims of impossible knowledge. *Psychological Science*, 26(8), 1295–1303.

Attanapola, C. T. (2004). Changing gender roles and health impacts among female workers in export-processing industries in Sri Lanka. *Social Science & Medicine*, 58(11), 2301–2312.

Aubrey, J. S. (2007). The impact of sexually objectifying media exposure on negative body emotions and sexual self-perceptions: Investigating the mediating role of body self-consciousness. *Mass Communication & Society*, 10(1), 1–23.

Auden, W. H. (1950). *Collected shorter poems: 1930–1944*. Faber & Faber.

Averill, J. R. (1982). *Anger and aggression: An essay on emotion*. Springer-Verlag.

Ayduk, O., Mendoza-Denton, R., Mischel, W., Downey, G., Peake, P. K., & Rodriguez, M. (2000). Regulating the interpersonal self: Strategic self-regulation for coping with rejection sensitivity. *Journal of Personality and Social Psychology*, 79(5), 776–792.

Axt, J.R., Conway, M.A., Westgate, E.C., & Buttrick, N.R. (2021). Implicit transgender attitudes independently predict beliefs about gender and transgender people. *Personality and Social Psychology Bulletin*, 47, 257–274.

Badr, L. K., & Abdallah, B. (2001). Physical attractiveness of premature infants affects outcome at discharge from the NICU. *Infant Behavior and Development*, 24(1), 129–133.

Bahns, A. J., Crandall, C. S., Gillath, O., Preacher, K. J. (2017). Similarity in relationships as niche construction: Choice, stability, and influence within dyads in a free choice environment. *Journal of Personality and Social Psychology*, 112(2), 329–355.

Bailey, M. J., Kim, P. Y., Hills, A., & Linsenmeier, J. A. W. (1997). Butch, femme, or straight acting? Partner preferences of gay men and lesbians. *Journal of Personality and Social Psychology*, 73(5), 960–973.

Bakan, D. (1966). *The duality of human existence: Isolation and communion in Western man*. Rand McNally.

Baker, M. (2016). Is there a reproducibility crisis? *Nature*, 533(7604), 452–454.

Baldwin, M. W., Carrell, S. E., & Lopez, D. F. (1990). Priming relationship schemas: My advisor and the Pope are watching me from the back of my mind. *Journal of Experimental Social Psychology*, 26(5), 435–454.

Baldwin, M. W., & Fehr, B. (1995). On the instability of attachment style ratings. *Personal Relationships*, 2(3), 247–261.

Baldwin, M. W., Keelan, J. P. R., Fehr, B., Enns, V., & Koh-Rangarajoo, E. (1996). Social-cognitive conceptualization of attachment working models: Availability and accessibility effects. *Journal of Personality and Social Psychology*, 71(1), 94–109.

Balsam, K. F., Beauchaine, T. P., Rothblum, E. D., & Solomon, S. E. (2008). Three-year follow-up of same-sex couples who had civil unions in Vermont, same-sex couples not in civil unions, and heterosexual married couples. *Developmental Psychology*, 44(1), 102–116.

Ballinger, T., & Crocker, J. (2021). Understanding Whites' perceptions of multicultural policies: A (non) zero-sum framework? *Journal of Personality and Social Psychology*, 120(5), 1231–1260.

Bandura, A. (1965). Influence of models' reinforcement contingencies on the acquisition of imitative responses. *Journal of Personality and Social Psychology*, 1(6), 589–595.

Bandura, A. (1973). *Aggression: A social learning analysis*. Prentice Hall.

Bandura, A. (2009). Social cognitive theory goes global. *The Psychologist*, 22(6), 504–506.

Bandura, A., Ross, D., & Ross, S. A. (1961). Transmission of aggression through imitation of aggressive models. *Journal of Abnormal and Social Psychology*, 63(3), 575–582.

Bandura, A., Ross, D., & Ross, S. A. (1963a). Imitation of film-mediated aggressive models. *Journal of Abnormal and Social Psychology*, 66(1), 3–11.

Bandura, A., Ross, D., & Ross, S. A. (1963b). Vicarious reinforcement and imitative learning. *Journal of Abnormal and Social Psychology*, 67(6), 601–607.

Bandura, A., Underwood, B., & Fromson, M. E. (1975). Disinhibition of aggression through diffusion of responsibility and dehumanization of victims. *Journal of Research in Personality*, 9(4), 253–269.

Banerjee, S. C., & Greene, K. (2007). Antismoking initiatives: Effects of analysis versus production media literacy interventions on smoking-related attitude, norm, and behavioral intention. *Health Communication*, 22(1), 37–48.

Banfield, J. F., Wyland, C. L., Macrae, C. N., Munte, T. F., & Heatherton, T. F. (2004). The cognitive neuroscience of self-regulation. In R. F. Baumeister & K. D. Vohs (Eds.), *Handbook of self-regulation: Research, theory, and applications* (pp. 62–83). Guilford Press.

Bang, H. M., Koval, C. Z., & Wade-Benzoni, K. A. (2017). It's the thought that counts over time: The interplay of intent, outcome, stewardship, and legacy motivations in intergenerational reciprocity. *Journal of Experimental Social Psychology*, 73, 197–210.

Barbaree, H. E., & Marshall, W. L. (1991). The role of male sexual arousal in rape: Six models. *Journal of Consulting and Clinical Psychology*, 59(5), 621–630.

Barber, N. (2006). Why is violent crime so common in the Americas? *Aggressive Behavior*, 32(5), 442–450.

Barberá, P., Jost, J. T., Nagler, J., Tucker, J. A., & Bonneau, R. (2015). Tweeting from left to right: Is online political communication more than an echo chamber? *Psychological Science*, 26(10), 1531–1542.

Barden, J., & Petty, R. E. (2008). The mere perception of elaboration creates attitude certainty: Exploring the thoughtfulness heuristic. *Journal of Personality and Social Psychology*, 95(3), 489–509.

Barden, J., & Tormala, Z. L. (2014). Elaboration and attitude strength: The new meta-cognitive perspective. *Social and Personality Psychology Compass*, 8(1), 17–29.

Bargh, J. A., Bond, R. N., Lombardi, W. J., & Tota, M. E. (1986). The additive nature of chronic and temporary sources of construct accessibility. *Journal of Personality and Social Psychology, 50*(5), 869–878.

Bargh, J. A., Chen, M., & Burrows, L. (1996). Automaticity of social behavior: Direct effects of trait construct and stereotype activation on action. *Journal of Personality and Social Psychology, 71*(2), 230–244.

Bargh, J. A., Raymond, P., Pryor, J. B., & Strack, F. (1995). Attractiveness of the underling: An automatic power --> sex association and its consequences for sexual harassment and aggression. *Journal of Personality and Social Psychology, 68*(5), 768–781.

Barkow, J. H. (1989). *Darwin, sex, and status: Biological approaches to mind and culture*. University of Toronto Press.

Barkow, J. H., Cosmides, L. E., & Tooby, J. E. (Eds.). (1992). *The adapted mind: Evolutionary psychology and the generation of culture*. Oxford University Press.

Barnett, P. A., & Gotlib, I. H. (1988). Psychosocial functioning and depression: Distinguishing among antecedents, concomitants, and consequences. *Psychological Bulletin, 104*(1), 97–126.

Baron, R. A. (1977). *Human aggression*. Plenum.

Baron, R. S. (1986). Distraction-conflict theory: Progress and problems. In L. Berkowitz (Ed.), *Advances in experimental social psychology* (Vol. 19, pp. 1–40). Academic Press.

Baron, R. S., David, J. P., Brunsman, B. M., & Inman, M. (1997). Why listeners hear less than they are told: Attentional load and the teller–listener extremity effect. *Journal of Personality and Social Psychology, 72*(4), 826–838.

Baron-Cohen, S., & Wheelwright, S. (2004). The empathy quotient: An investigation of adults with Asperger syndrome or high functioning autism, and normal sex differences. *Journal of Autism and Developmental Disorders, 34*(2), 163–175.

Baron-Cohen, S., Wheelwright, S., Hill, J., Raste, Y., & Plumb, I. (2001). The "Reading the Mind in the Eyes" test revised version: A study with normal adults, and adults with Asperger syndrome or high-functioning autism. *Journal of Child Psychology and Psychiatry, 42*(2), 241–251.

Baron-Cohen, S. E., Tager-Flusberg, H. E., & Cohen, D. J. (2000). *Understanding other minds: Perspectives from developmental cognitive neuroscience*. Oxford University Press.

Barratt, E. S. (1994). Impulsiveness and aggression. In J. Monahan & H. J. Steadman (Eds.), *Violence and mental disorder: Developments in risk assessment* (pp. 61–78). University of Chicago Press.

Barrett, L. F., Mesquita, B., Ochsner, K. N., & Gross, J. J. (2007). The experience of emotion. *Annual Review of Psychology, 58*, 373.

Barry, D. (1996, March 30). Chipping away those "V" words on TV. *The Free Lance-Star*. http://news.google.com/newspapers?nid=1298&dat=19960330&id=nuoyAAAAIBAJ&sjid=zQcGAAAAIBAJ&pg=3089,5944603

Bar-Tal, D. (1976). *Prosocial behavior: Theory and research*. Hemisphere Publishing Corp.

Bartal, I. B. A., Decety, J., & Mason, P. (2011). Empathy and pro-social behavior in rats. *Science, 334*(6061), 1427–1430.

Barthel, M., Mitchell, A., & Holcomb, J. (2016, December 15). *Many Americans believe fake news is sowing confusing*. Pew Research Center. https://www.journalism.org/2016/12/15/many-americans-believe-fake-news-is-sowing-confusion/

Bartholomew, K., & Horowitz, L. M. (1991). Attachment styles among young adults: A test of a four-category model. *Journal of Personality and Social Psychology, 61*(2), 226–244.

Bartholow, B. D. (2010). Event-related brain potentials and social cognition: On using physiological information to constrain social cognitive theories. *Social Cognition, 28*(6), 723–747.

Bartholow, B. D., Anderson, C. A., Carnagey, N. L., & Benjamin, A. J., Jr. (2005). Interactive effects of life experience and situational cues on aggression: The weapons priming effect in hunters and nonhunters. *Journal of Experimental Social Psychology, 41*(1), 48–60.

Bartholow, B. D., Dickter, C. L., & Sestir, M. A. (2006). Stereotype activation and control of race bias: Cognitive control of inhibition and its impairment by alcohol. *Journal of Personality and Social Psychology, 90*(2), 272–287.

Bartholow, B. D., Fabiani, M., Gratton, G., & Bettencourt, B. A. (2001). A psychophysiological examination of cognitive processing of and affective responses to social expectancy violations. *Psychological Science, 12*(3), 197–204.

Bartholow, B. D., & Heinz, A. (2006). Alcohol and aggression without consumption: Alcohol cues, aggressive thoughts, and hostile perception bias. *Psychological Science, 17*(1), 30–37.

Bartholow, B. D., Henry, E. A., Lust, S. A., Saults, J. S., & Wood, P. K. (2012). Alcohol effects on performance monitoring and adjustment: Affect modulation and impairment of evaluative cognitive control. *Journal of Abnormal Psychology, 121*(1), 173–186.

Bartholow, B. D., Loersch, C., Ito, T. A., Levsen, M. P., Volpert-Esmond, H. I., Fleming, K. A., Bolis, P., & Carter, B. K. (2018). University-affiliated alcohol marketing enhances the incentive salience of alcohol cues. *Psychological Science, 29*(1), 83–94.

Bartlett, M. Y., & DeSteno, D. (2006). Gratitude and prosocial behavior: Helping when it costs you. *Psychological Science, 17*(4), 319–325.

Barasch, A., Diehl, K., Silverman, J., & Zauberman, G. (2017). Photographic memory: The effects of photo-taking on memory for auditory and visual information. *Psychological Science, 28*(8), 1056–1066.

Bass, B. M. (1985). *Leadership and performance beyond expectations*. Free Press.

Bassili, J. N. (2003). The minority slowness effect: Subtle inhibitions in the expression of views not shared by others. *Journal of Personality and Social Psychology, 84*(2), 261–276.

Batra, R. K., Ghoshal, T., & Raghunathan, R. (2017). You are what you eat: An empirical investigation of the relationship between spicy food and aggressive cognition. *Journal of Experimental Social Psychology, 71*, 42–48.

Batson, C. D. (1991). *The altruism question: Toward a social-psychological answer*. Erlbaum.

Batson, C. D. (2011). *Altruism in humans*. Oxford University Press.

Batson, C. D., Chang, J., Orr, R., & Rowland, J. (2002). Empathy, attitudes, and action: Can feeling for a member of a stigmatized group motivate one to help the group? *Personality and Social Psychology Bulletin, 28*(12), 1656–1666.

Batson, C. D., Duncan, B. D., Ackerman, P., Buckley, T., & Birch, K. (1981). Is empathic emotion a source of altruistic motivation? *Journal of Personality and Social Psychology, 40*(2), 290–302.

Batson, C. D., Eklund, J. H., Chermok, V. L., Hoyt, J. L., & Ortiz, B. G. (2007). An additional antecedent of empathic concern: Valuing the welfare of the person in need. *Journal of Personality and Social Psychology, 93*(1), 65–74.

Batson, C. D., Polycarpou, M. P., Harmon-Jones, E., Imhoff, H. J., Mitchener, E. C., Bednar, L. L., Klein, T. R., & Highberger, L. (1997). Empathy and attitudes: Can feeling for a member of a stigmatized group improve feelings toward the group? *Journal of Personality and Social Psychology, 72*(1), 105–118.

Batson, C. D., Schoenrade, P., & Ventis, W. L. (1993). *Religion and the individual: A social-psychological perspective*. Oxford University Press.

Baum, S. K, Kressel, N. K., Cohen, F., & Jacobs, S. L. (Eds.) (2016). *Anti-Semitism in North America*. Brill.

Baumeister, R. F. (in press). Self-control, ego depletion, and social psychology's replication crisis. In A. Mele (Ed.), *Surrounding self-control*. Oxford.

Baumeister, R. F., & Jones, E. E. (1978). When self-presentation is constrained by the target's knowledge: Consistency and compensation. *Journal of Personality and Social Psychology, 36*(6), 608–618.

Baumeister, R. F., & Leary, M. R. (1995). The need to belong: Desire for interpersonal attachments as a fundamental human motivation. *Psychological Bulletin, 117*(3), 497–529.

Baumeister, R. F., Smart, L., & Boden, J. M. (1996). Relation of threatened egotism to violence and aggression: The dark side of high self-esteem. *Psychological Review, 103*(1), 5–33.

Baumeister, R. F., Stillwell, A. M., & Heatherton, T. F. (1994). Guilt: An interpersonal approach. *Psychological Bulletin, 115*(2), 243–267.

Baumeister, R. F., Twenge, J. M., & Nuss, C. K. (2002). Effects of social exclusion on cognitive processes: Anticipated aloneness reduces intelligent thought. *Journal of Personality and Social Psychology, 83*(4), 817–827.

Baumeister, R. F., & Vohs, K. D. (2004). Sexual economics: Sex as female resource for social exchange in heterosexual interactions. *Personality and Social Psychology Review, 8*(4), 339–363.

Baumeister, R. F., & Vohs, K. D. (2016). Misguided effort with elusive implications. *Perspectives on Psychological Science, 11*(4), 574–575.

Baumeister, R. F., Wotman, S. R., & Stillwell, A. M. (1993). Unrequited love: On heartbreak, anger, guilt, scriptlessness, and humiliation. *Journal of Personality and Social Psychology, 64*(3), 377–394.

Baumrind, D. (1964). Some thoughts on ethics of research: After reading Milgram's "Behavioral study of obedience." *American Psychologist, 19*(6), 421–423.

BBC News. (2016, August 12). *Why Simone Manuel's Olympic gold medal in swimming matters*. BBC. https://www.bbc.com/news/world-us-canada-37057236

BBC News. (2017, August 13). *White supremacy: Are US right-wing groups on the rise?* BBC. https://www.bbc.com/news/world-us-canada-40915356

Beach, F. A., & Jordan, L. (1956). Sexual exhaustion and recovery in the male rat. *Quarterly Journal of Experimental Psychology, 8*, 121–133.

Beaman, A. L., Barnes, P. J., Klentz, B., & McQuirk, B. (1978). Increasing helping rates through information dissemination: Teaching pays. *Personality and Social Psychology Bulletin, 4*(3), 406–411.

Beaman, A. L., Klentz, B., Diener, E., & Svanum, S. (1979). Self-awareness and transgression in children: Two field studies. *Journal of Personality and Social Psychology, 37*(10), 1835–1846.

Beauvais, F. (2000). Indian adolescence: Opportunity and challenge. In R. Montemayor, G. R. Adams, & T. P. Gullotta (Eds.), *Adolescent diversity in ethnic, economic, and cultural contexts* (Vol. 1, pp. 110–140). Sage.

Bechara, A., Damasio, H., Tranel, D., & Damasio, A. R. (1997). Deciding advantageously before knowing the advantageous strategy. *Science, 275*(5304), 1293–1295.

Bechara, A., Tranel, D., Damasio, H., & Damasio, A. R. (1996). Failure to respond autonomically to anticipated future outcomes following damage to prefrontal cortex. *Cerebral Cortex, 6*(2), 215–225.

Beck, A., & Heinz, A. (2013). Alcohol-related aggression: Social and neurobiological factors. *Deutsches Ärzteblatt International, 110*(42), 711–715.

Becker, E. (1962). *The birth and death of meaning.* Free Press.

Becker, E. (1971). *The birth and death of meaning: An interdisciplinary perspective on the problem of man* (2nd ed.). Penguin.

Becker, E. (1973). *The denial of death.* Free Press.

Becker, E. (1975). *Escape from evil.* Free Press.

Becker, J., Porter, E., & Centola, D. (2019). The wisdom of partisan crowds. *Proceedings of the National Academy of Sciences, 116*(22), 10717–10722.

Becker, J. C., & Wright, S. C. (2011). Yet another dark side of chivalry: Benevolent sexism undermines and hostile sexism motivates collective action for social change. *Journal of Personality and Social Psychology, 101*(1), 62–77.

Beer, C. (1984). Fearful curiosity in animals. In J. A. Crook, J. B. Haskins, & P. G. Ashton (Eds.), *Morbid curiosity and the mass media: Proceedings of a symposium.* University of Tennessee and the Gannett Foundation.

Beer, J. S. (2002). Implicit self-theories of shyness. *Journal of Personality and Social Psychology, 83*(4), 1009–1024.

Beer, J. S., Heerey, E. A., Keltner, D., Scabini, D., & Knight, R. T. (2003). The regulatory function of self-conscious emotion: Insights from patients with orbitofrontal damage. *Journal of Personality and Social Psychology, 85*(4), 594–604.

Beilock, S. (2011). *Choke: What the secrets of the brain reveal about getting it right when you have to.* Free Press.

Beilock, S. L., & Carr, T. H. (2001). On the fragility of skilled performance: What governs choking under pressure? *Journal of Experimental Psychology: General, 130*(4), 701–725.

Beilock, S. L., Kulp, C. A., Holt, L. E., & Carr, T. H. (2004). More on the fragility of performance: Choking under pressure in mathematical problem solving. *Journal of Experimental Psychology: General, 133*(4), 584–600.

Bélanger, J. J., Schori-Eyal, N., Pica, G., Kruglanski, A. W., & Lafrenière, M.-A. (2015). The "more is less" effect in equifinal structures: Alternative means reduce the intensity and quality of motivation. *Journal of Experimental Social Psychology, 60*, 93–102.

Bell, J. (2009). Why embarrassment inhibits the acquisition and use of condoms: A qualitative approach to understanding risky sexual behaviour. *Journal of Adolescence, 32*(2), 379–391.

Belletier, C., Normand, A., & Huguet, P. (2019). Social-facilitation-and-impairment effects: From motivation to cognition and the social brain. *Current Directions in Psychological Science, 28*(3), 260–265.

Bem, D. J. (1965). An experimental analysis of self-persuasion. *Journal of Experimental Social Psychology, 1*(3), 199–218.

Bem, D. J. (1967). Self-perception: An alternative interpretation of cognitive dissonance phenomena. *Psychological Review, 74*(3), 183–200.

Ben-Ari, O. T., Florian, V., & Mikulincer, M. (1999). The impact of mortality salience on reckless driving: A test of terror management mechanisms. *Journal of Personality and Social Psychology, 76*(1), 35–45.

Benjamin, A. J., Kepes, S., & Bushman, B. J. (2018). Effects of weapons on aggressive thoughts, angry feelings, hostile appraisals, and aggressive behavior: A meta-analytic review of the weapons effect literature. *Personality and Social Psychology Review, 22*(4), 347–377.

Bennett, J. (2020). The #MeToo moment. *The New York Times.* https://www.nytimes.com/series/metoo-moment

Benozio, A., & Diesendruck, G. (2015). From effort to value: Preschool children's alternative to effort justification. *Psychological Science, 26*(9), 1423–1429.

Bentler, P. M., & Newcomb, M. D. (1978). Longitudinal study of marital success and failure. *Journal of Consulting and Clinical Psychology, 46*(5), 1053–1070.

Beresford, B. (Director). (1991). *Black robe* [Film]. Samuel Goldwyn Company.

Berger, J. (1994, February 12). Shattering the silence of autism. *The New York Times.* http://www.nytimes.com/1994/02/12/nyregion/shattering-silence-autism-new-communication-method-hailed-miracle-derided.html

Berger, J., & Barasch, A. (2015). Posting posed, choosing candid: Photo posters mispredict audience preferences. In K. Diehl & C. Yoon (Eds.), *Advances in Consumer Research* (Vol. 43, pp. 51–55). Association for Consumer Research.

Berger, P. L., & Luckmann, T. (1967). *The social construction of reality: A treatise in the sociology of knowledge.* Doubleday Anchor.

Berglas, S., & Jones, E. E. (1978). Drug choice as a self-handicapping strategy in response to noncontingent success. *Journal of Personality and Social Psychology, 36*(4), 405–417.

Bergsieker, H. B., Shelton, J. N., & Richeson, J. A. (2010). To be liked versus respected: Divergent goals in interracial interactions. *Journal of Personality and Social Psychology, 99*(2), 248–264.

Berke, D. S., & Zeichner, A. (2016). Man's heaviest burden: A review of contemporary paradigms and new direction for understanding and preventing masculine aggression. *Social and Personality Psychology Compass, 10*(2), 83–91.

Berkman, E. T., Hutcherson, C. A., Livingston, J. L., Kahn, L. E., & Inzlicht, M. (2017). Self-control as value-based choice. *Current Directions in Psychological Science, 26*(5), 422–428.

Berkowitz, L. (1965). Some aspects of observed aggression. *Journal of Personality and Social Psychology, 2*(3), 359–369.

Berkowitz, L. (1968). Impulse, aggression and the gun. *Psychology Today, 2*(4), 18–22.

Berkowitz, L. (1989). Frustration-aggression hypothesis: Examination and reformulation. *Psychological Bulletin, 106*(1), 59–73.

Berkowitz, L. (1993). *Aggression: Its causes, consequences, and control.* McGraw-Hill.

Berkowitz, L., Cochran, S. T., & Embree, M. C. (1981). Physical pain and the goal of aversively stimulated aggression. *Journal of Personality and Social Psychology, 40*(4), 687–700.

Berkowitz, L., & Geen, R. G. (1967). Stimulus qualities of the target of aggression: A further study. *Journal of Personality and Social Psychology, 5*(3), 364–368.

Berkowitz, L., & LePage, A. (1967). Weapons as aggression-eliciting stimuli. *Journal of Personality and Social Psychology, 7*(2, Pt. 1), 202–207.

Berkowitz, L., & Troccoli, B. T. (1990). Feelings, direction of attention, and expressed evaluations of others. *Cognition and Emotion, 4*(4), 305–325.

Berman, M., Gladue, B., & Taylor, S. (1993). The effects of hormones, type A behavior pattern, and provocation on aggression in men. *Motivation and Emotion, 17*(2), 125–138.

Berman, M. E., McCloskey, M. S., Fanning, J. R., Schumacher, J. A., & Coccaro, E. F. (2009). Serotonin augmentation reduces response to attack in aggressive individuals. *Psychological Science, 20*(6), 714–720.

Bernard, M. M., Maio, G. R., & Olson, J. M. (2003). The vulnerability of values to attack: Inoculation of values and value-relevant attitudes. *Personality and Social Psychology Bulletin, 29*(1), 63–75.

Bernard, P., Gervais, S. J., & Klein, O. (2018). Objectifying objectification: When and why people are cognitively reduced to their parts akin to objects. *European Review of Social Psychology, 29*(1), 82–121.

Bernard, D. L., Smith, Q., & Lanier, P. (2021). Racial discrimination and other adverse childhood experiences as risk factors for internalizing mental health concerns among Black youth. *Journal of traumatic stress.*

Berns, G. S., Chappelow, J., Zink, C. F., Pagnoni, G., Martin-Skurski, M. E., & Richards, J. (2005). Neurobiological correlates of social conformity and independence during mental rotation. *Biological Psychology, 58*(3), 245–253.

Berry, D. S., & McArthur, L. Z. (1986). Perceiving character in faces: The impact of age-related craniofacial changes on social perception. *Psychological Bulletin, 100*(1), 3–18.

Berry, J. W. (1966). Temne and Eskimo perceptual skills. *International Journal of Psychology, 1*(3), 207–229.

Berry, J. W. (1997). *Immigration, acculturation, and adaption.* Psychology Press.

Berry, J. W. (2001). A psychology of immigration. *Journal of Social Issues, 57*(3), 615–631.

Berry, J. W. (2006). Stress perspectives on acculturation. In D. L. Sam & J. W. Berry (Eds.), *The Cambridge handbook of acculturation psychology* (pp. 43–57). Cambridge University Press.

Berscheid, E. (2006). Searching for the meaning of "love." In R. J. Sternberg & K. Weis (Eds.), *The new psychology of love* (pp. 171–183). Yale University Press.

Berscheid, E., Dion, K., Walster, E., & Walster, G. W. (1971). Physical attractiveness and dating choice: A test of the matching hypothesis. *Journal of Experimental Social Psychology, 7*(2), 173–189.

Berscheid, E., Snyder, M., & Omoto, A. M. (1989). The Relationship Closeness Inventory: Assessing the closeness of interpersonal relationships. *Journal of Personality and Social Psychology, 57*(5), 792–807.

Berscheid, E., Snyder, M., & Omoto, A. M. (2004). Measuring closeness: The Relationship Closeness Inventory (RCI) revisited. In D. J. Mashek & A. Aron (Eds.), *Handbook of closeness and intimacy* (pp. 81–101). Erlbaum.

Berscheid, E., & Walster, E. (1974). A little bit about love. In T. Huston (Ed.), *Foundations of interpersonal attraction* (pp. 356–379). Academic Press.

Betsch, T., & Dickenberger, D. (1993). Why do aggressive movies make people aggressive? An attempt to explain short-term effects of the depiction of violence on the observer. *Aggressive Behavior, 19*(2), 137–149.

Bettencourt, B. A., & Miller, N. (1996). Gender differences in aggression as a function of provocation: A meta-analysis. *Psychological Bulletin, 119*(3), 422–447.

Bettencourt, B. A., Talley, A., Benjamin, A. J., & Valentine, J. (2006). Personality and aggressive behavior under provoking and neutral conditions: A meta-analytic review. *Psychological Bulletin, 132*(5), 751–777.

Bettor, L., Hendrick, S. S., & Hendrick, C. (1995). Gender and sexual standards in dating relationships. *Personal Relationships, 2*(4), 359–369.

Bialik, K. (2016). *Most Americans favor stricter environmental laws and regulations.* Pew Research Center. http://www.pewresearch.org/fact-tank/2016/12/14/most-americans-favor-stricter-environmental-laws-and-regulations/

Bierman, N. (2021) Black, female and high-profile, Kamala Harris is a top target in online fever swamps. Los Angeles Times. https://www.latimes.com/politics/story/2021-02-19/kamala-harris-is-the-top-target-of-online-harassment-as-fears-of-political-violence-grow

Birnbach, D. J., Nevo, I., Barnes, S., Fitzpatrick, M., Rosen, L. F. Everett-Thomas, R., Sanko, J. S., & Arheart, K. L. (2012). Do hospital visitors wash their hands? Assessing the use of alcohol-based hand sanitizer in a hospital lobby. *American Journal of Infection Control, 40*(4), 340–343.

Bishop, G. F., Oldendick, R. W., Tuchfarber, A. J., & Bennett, S. E. (1980). Pseudo-opinions on public affairs. *Public Opinion Quarterly, 44*(2), 198–209.

Björkqvist, K., Österman, K., & Kaukiainen, A. (1992). The development of direct and indirect aggressive strategies in males and females. In K. Björkqvist & P. Niemelä (Eds.), *Of mice and women: Aspects of female aggression* (pp. 51–64). Academic Press.

Björkqvist, K., Österman, K., & Lagerspetz, K. M. J. (1994). Sex differences in covert aggression among adults. *Aggressive Behavior, 20*(1), 27–33.

Blackie, L. E. R., Jayawickreme, E., Helzer, E. G., Forgeard, M. J. C., & Roepke, A. M. (2015). Investigating the veracity of self-perceived posttraumatic growth: A profile analysis approach to corroboration. *Social Psychological and Personality Science, 6*(7), 788–796.

Blair, I. V., Judd, C. M., & Chapleau, K. M. (2004). The influence of Afrocentric facial features in criminal sentencing. *Psychological Science, 15*(10), 674–679.

Blair, I. V., Ma, J. E., & Lenton, A. P. (2001). Imagining stereotypes away: The moderation of implicit stereotypes through mental imagery. *Journal of Personality and Social Psychology, 81*(5), 828–841.

Blakeslee, S. (2006, January 10). Cells that read minds. *The New York Times.* http://www.nytimes.com/2006/01/10/science/10mirr.html?pagewanted=all&_r=0

Blaney, N. T., Stephan, C., Rosenfield, D., Aronson, E., & Sikes, J. (1977). Interdependence in the classroom: A field study. *Journal of Educational Psychology, 69*(2), 121–128.

Blankenship, K. L., & Wegener, D. T. (2008). Opening the mind to close it: Considering a message in light of important values increases message processing and later resistance to change. *Journal of Personality and Social Psychology, 94*(2), 196–213.

Blanton, H., & Jaccard, J. (2006). Arbitrary metrics in psychology. *American Psychologist, 61*(1), 27–41.

Blanton, H., Jaccard, J., Gonzales, P. M., & Christie, C. (2006). Decoding the Implicit Association Test: Implications for criterion prediction. *Journal of Experimental Social Psychology, 42*(2), 192–212.

Blascovich, J., & Mendes, W. B. (2000). Challenge and threat appraisals: The role of affective cues. In J. Forgas (Ed.), *Feeling and thinking: The role of affect in social cognition* (pp. 59–82). Cambridge University Press.

Blascovich, J., Mendes, W. B., Hunter, S. B., & Salomon, K. (1999). Social "facilitation" as challenge and threat. *Journal of Personality and Social Psychology, 77*(1), 68–77.

Blascovich, J., Seery, M. D., Mugridge, C. A., Norris, R. K., & Weisbuch, M. (2004). Predicting athletic performance from cardiovascular indexes of challenge and threat. *Journal of Experimental Social Psychology, 40*(5), 683–688.

Blascovich, J., & Tomaka, J. (1996). The biopsychosocial model of arousal regulation. In M. P. Zanna (Ed.), *Advances in experimental social psychology* (Vol. 28, pp. 1–51). Academic Press.

Blascovich, J., Wyer, N. A., Swart, L. A., & Kibler, J. L. (1997). Racism and racial categorization. *Journal of Personality and Social Psychology, 72*(6), 1364–1372.

Blass, T. (Ed.). (2000). *Obedience to authority: Current perspectives on the Milgram paradigm.* Erlbaum.

Bless, H., Bohner, G., Schwarz, N., & Strack, F. (1990). Mood and persuasion: A cognitive response analysis. *Personality and Social Psychology Bulletin, 16*(2), 331–345.

Bless, H., Clore, G. L., Schwarz, N., Golisano, V., Rabe, C., & Wölk, M. (1996). Mood and the use of scripts: Does a happy mood really lead to mindlessness? *Journal of Personality and Social Psychology, 71*(4), 665–679.

Blessing, C., Golden, T. P., Pi, S., Bruyère, S., & Van Looy, S. (2012). Vocational rehabilitation, inclusion, and social integration. In P. Kennedy (Ed.), *Oxford library of psychology. The Oxford handbook of rehabilitation psychology* (p. 453–473). Oxford University Press.

Block, K., Croft, A., De Souza, L., & Schmader, T. (2019). Do people care if men don't care? The asymmetry in support for changing gender roles. *Journal of Experimental Social Psychology, 83*, 112–131.

Bloom, B. L., White, S. W., & Asher, S. J. (1979). Marital disruption as a stressful life event. In G. Levinger & O. C. Moles (Eds.), *Divorce and separation: Context, causes, and consequences* (pp. 184–200). Basic Books.

Boburg, S. (2016, September 10). Would-be Reagan assassin John Hinckley Jr. is freed after 35 years. *The Washington Post.* https://www.washingtonpost.com/local/public-safety/president-reagans-would-be-assassin-is-set-to-be-releasedsaturday/2016/09/09/e1ad0e9e-75ca-11e6-be4f-3f42f2e5a49e_story.html?utm_term=.52080ecdebdd

Bocian, K., Baryla, W., Kulesza, W. M., Schnall, S., & Wojciszke, B. (2018). The mere liking effect: Attitudinal influences on attributions of moral character. *Journal of Experimental Social Psychology, 79*, 9–20.

Bodenhausen, G. V. (1990). Stereotypes as judgmental heuristics: Evidence of circadian variations in discrimination. *Psychological Science, 1*(5), 319–322.

Bodenhausen, G. V., Kramer, G. P., & Süsser, K. (1994). Happiness and stereotypic thinking in social judgment. *Journal of Personality and Social Psychology, 66*(4), 621–632.

Boehm, C. (1999). The natural selection of altruistic traits. *Human Nature, 10*(3), 205–252.

Bokhorst, C. L., Bakermans-Kranenburg, M. J., Fonagy, P., & Schuengel, C. (2003). The importance of shared environment in mother–infant attachment security: A behavioral genetic study. *Child Development, 74*(6), 1769–1782.

Boksem, M. A. S., Meijman, T. F., & Lorist, M. M. (2006). Mental fatigue, motivation, and action monitoring. *Biological Psychology, 72*(2), 123–132.

Bolger, N., DeLongis, A., Kessler, R. C., & Wethington, E. (1989). The contagion of stress across multiple roles. *Journal of Marriage and the Family, 51*(1), 175–183.

Bollich, K. L., Rogers, K. H., & Vazire, S. (2015). Knowing more than we can tell: People are aware of their biased self-perceptions. *Personality and Social Psychology Bulletin, 41*(7), 918–929.

Bond, R., & Smith, P. B. (1996). Culture and conformity: A meta-analysis of studies using Asch's (1952b, 1956) line judgment task. *Psychological Bulletin, 119*(1), 111–137.

Boothby, E. J., Clark, M. S., & Bargh, J. A. (2017). The invisibility cloak illusion: People (incorrectly) believe they observe others more than others observe them. *Journal of Personality and Social Psychology, 112*(4), 589–606.

Boothby, E. J., Cooney, G., Sandstrom, G. M., & Clark, M. S. (2018). The liking gap in conversations: Do people like us more than we think? *Psychological Science, 29*(11), 1742–1756.

Borduin, C. M., Schaeffer, C. M., & Heiblum, N. (2009). A randomized clinical trial of multisystemic therapy with juvenile sexual offenders: Effects on youth social ecology and criminal activity. *Journal of Consulting and Clinical Psychology, 77*(1), 26–37.

Borgida, E., & Brekke, N. (1985). Psycholegal research on rape trials. In A. Burgess (Ed.), *Research handbook on rape and sexual assault* (pp. 313–342). Garland.

Borman, G. D., Grigg, J., Rozek, C. S., Hanselman, P., & Dewey, N. A. (2018). Self-affirmation effects are produced by school context, student engagement with the intervention, and time: Lessons from a district-wide implementation. *Psychological Science, 29*(11), 1773–1784.

Born, M., Chevalier, V., & Humblet, I. (1997). Resilience, desistance and delinquent career of adolescent offenders. *Journal of Adolescence, 20*(6), 679–694.

Bornstein, R. F. (1989). Exposure and affect: Overview and meta-analysis of research, 1968–1987. *Psychological Bulletin, 106*(2), 265–289.

Bosson, J. K., Haymovitz, E. L., & Pinel, E. C. (2004). When saying and doing diverge: The effects of stereotype threat on self-reported versus non-verbal anxiety. *Journal of Experimental Social Psychology, 40*(2), 247–255.

Bosson, J. K., Swann, W. B., & Pennebaker, J. W. (2000). Stalking the perfect measure of implicit self-esteem: The blind men and the elephant revisited? *Journal of Personality and Social Psychology, 79*(4), 631–643.

Bower, G. H., & Forgas, J. P. (2000). Affect, memory, and social cognition. In E. Eich, J. F. Kihlstrom, G. H. Bower, J. P. Forgas, & P. M. Niedenthal (Eds.), *Cognition and emotion* (pp. 87–168). Oxford University Press.

Bowlby, J. (1969). *Attachment and loss, Vol. 1: Attachment.* Basic Books.

Bowlby, J. (1973). *Attachment and loss, Vol. 2: Separation, anxiety and anger.* Basic Books.

Bowlby, J. (1980). *Attachment and loss, Vol. 3: Loss: Sadness and depression.* Basic Books.

Box Office Mojo. (2019). *2019 worldwide box office.* https://www.boxoffice mojo.com/year/world/2019/

Boyd, P., Morris, K. L., & Goldenberg, J. L. (2017). Open to death: A moderating role of openness to experience in terror management. *Journal of Experimental Social Psychology, 71*, 117–127.

Brach, T. (2003). *Radical acceptance*. Bantam Books.

Bradbury, T. N., & Fincham, F. D. (1990). Attributions in marriage: Review and critique. *Psychological Bulletin, 107*(1), 3–33.

Bradbury, T. N., & Karney, B. R. (2010). *Intimate relationships*. W. W. Norton.

Brand, R. J., Bonatsos, A., D'Orazio, R., & DeShong, H. (2012). What is beautiful is good, even online: Correlations between photo attractiveness and text attractiveness in men's online dating profiles. *Computers in Human Behavior, 28*(1), 166–170.

Brannigan, A., Nicholson, I., & Cherry, F. (2015). Introduction to the special issue: Unplugging the Milgram machine. *Theory and Psychology, 25*(5), 551–563.

Brannon, S. M., & Gawronski, B. (2017). A second chance for first impressions? Exploring the context-(in)dependent updating of implicit evaluations. *Social Psychological and Personality Science, 8*(3), 275–283.

Brannon, T. N., Markus, H. R., & Taylor, V. J. (2015). "Two souls, two thoughts," two self-schemas: Double consciousness can have positive academic consequences for African Americans. *Journal of Personality and Social Psychology, 108*(4), 586–609.

Branscombe, N. R., Schmitt, M. T., & Harvey, R. D. (1999). Perceiving pervasive discrimination among African Americans: Implications for group identification and well-being. *Journal of Personality and Social Psychology, 77*(1), 135–149.

Bransford, J. D., & Johnson, M. K. (1973). Considerations of some problems of comprehension. In W. G. Chase (Ed.), *Visual information processing* (pp. 383–438). Academic Press.

Braver, S. L., Linder, D. E., Corwin, T. T., & Cialdini, R. B. (1977). Some conditions that affect admissions of attitude change. *Journal of Experimental Social Psychology, 13*(6), 565–576.

Bredow, C. A., & Hames, N. (2019). Steadfast standards or fluctuating fancies? Stability and change in people's mate criteria over 27 months. *Personality and Social Psychology Bulletin, 45*(5), 671–687.

Brehm, J. W. (1956). Postdecision changes in the desirability of alternatives. *Journal of Abnormal and Social Psychology, 52*(3), 384–389.

Brehm, J. W. (1966). *A theory of psychological reactance*. Academic Press.

Brehm, J. W., & Cohen, A. R. (1962). *Explorations in cognitive dissonance*. Wiley.

Brehm, J. W., Stires, L. K., Sensenig, J., & Shaban, J. (1966). The attractiveness of an eliminated choice alternative. *Journal of Experimental Social Psychology, 2*(3), 301–313.

Brehm, S. S. (1992). *Intimate relationships* (2nd ed.). McGraw-Hill.

Brehm, S. S., & Brehm, J. W. (1981). *Psychological reactance: A theory of freedom and control*. Academic Press.

Brennan, K. A., Clark, C. L., & Shaver, P. R. (1998). Self-report measurement of adult attachment: An integrative overview. In J. A. Simpson & W. S. Rholes (Eds.), *Attachment theory and close relationships* (pp. 46–76). Guilford Press.

Brethel-Haurwitz, K. M., Cardinale, E. M., Vekaria, K. M., Robertson, E. L., Walitt, B., VanMeter, J. W., & Marsh, A. A. (2018). Extraordinary altruists exhibit enhanced self–other overlap in neural responses to distress. *Psychological Science, 29*(10), 1631–1641.

Brewer, M. B. (1979). In-group bias in the minimal intergroup situation: A cognitive-motivational analysis. *Psychological Bulletin, 86*(2), 307–324.

Brewer, M. B. (1991). The social self: On being the same and different at the same time. *Personality and Social Psychology Bulletin, 17*(5), 475–482.

Brewer, M. B., & Caporael, L. R. (2006). An evolutionary perspective on social identity: Revisiting groups. In M. Schaller, J. Simpson, & D. Kenrick (Eds.), *Evolution and social psychology* (pp. 143–161). Psychology Press.

Brickner, M. A., Harkins, S. G., & Ostrom, T. M. (1986). Effects of personal involvement: Thought-provoking implications for social loafing. *Journal of Personality and Social Psychology, 51*(4), 763–769.

Briñol, P., & Petty, R. E. (2003). Overt head movements and persuasion: A self-validation analysis. *Journal of Personality and Social Psychology, 84*(6), 1123–1139.

Brock, T. C., & Brannon, L. A. (1992). Liberalization of commodity theory. *Basic and Applied Social Psychology, 13*(1), 135–144.

Brock, T. C., & Buss, A. H. (1964). Effects of justification for aggression and communication with the victim on postaggression dissonance. *Journal of Abnormal and Social Psychology, 68*(4), 403–412.

Bromwich, J. E. (2016, June 16). In a shaken Orlando, comfort dogs arrive with "unconditional love." *The New York Times*. https://www.nytimes.com/2016/06/17/us/in-a-shaken-orlando-comfort-dogs-arrive-with-unconditional-love.html

Bromwich, J. E. (2018, January 31). We asked Generation Z to pick a name. It wasn't Generation Z. *The New York Times*. https://www.nytimes.com/2018/01/31/style/generation-z-name.html

Broniatowski, D. A., Jamison, A. M., Qi, S., AlKulaib, L., Chen, T., Benton, A., Quinn, S., & Dredze, M. (2018). Weaponized health communication: Twitter bots and Russian trolls amplify the vaccine debate. *American Journal of Public Health, 108*(10), 1378–1384.

Bronstad, P. M., & Russell, R. (2007). Beauty is in the "we" of the beholder: Greater agreement on facial attractiveness among close relations. *Perception, 36*(11), 1674–1681.

Brontë, C. (1992). *Jane Eyre*. Wordsworth Classics. (Original work published 1847)

Brondolo, E., Blair, I. V., & Kaur, A. (2018). Biopsychosocial mechanisms linking discrimination to health: A focus on social cognition. In B. Major, J. F. Dovidio, & B. G. Link (Eds.), *The Oxford handbook of stigma, discrimination, and health*. (pp. 219–240). Oxford University Press.

Brophy, I. N. (1946). The luxury of anti-Negro prejudice. *Public Opinion Quarterly, 9*(4), 456–466.

Brosnan, S. F., & de Waal, F. B. (2002). A proximate perspective on reciprocal altruism. *Human Nature, 13*(1), 129–152.

Brown, B. R. (1968). The effects of need to maintain face on interpersonal bargaining. *Journal of Experimental Social Psychology, 4*(1), 107–122.

Brown, J. C., & Strickland, B. R. (1972). Belief in internal-external control of reinforcement and participation in college activities. *Journal of Consulting and Clinical Psychology, 38*(1), 148.

Brown, K. W., Ryan, R. M., & Creswell, J. D. (2007). Mindfulness: Theoretical foundations and evidence for its salutary effects. *Psychological Inquiry, 18*(4), 211–237.

Brown, M. F. (1986). *Tsewa's gift: Magic and meaning in an Amazonian society*. University of Alabama Press.

Brown, N. R., & Sinclair, R. C. (1999). Estimating number of lifetime sexual partners: Men and women do it differently. *Journal of Sex Research, 36*(3), 292–297.

Brown, R., González, R., Zagefka, H., Manzi, J., & Cehajic, S. (2008). Nuestra culpa: Collective guilt and shame as predictors of reparation for historical wrongdoing. *Journal of Personality and Social Psychology, 94*(1), 75–90.

Brown, R., & Hewstone, M. (2005). An integrative theory of intergroup contact. In M. P. Zanna (Ed.), *Advances in experimental social psychology* (Vol. 37, pp. 255–343). Academic Press.

Brown, R., Vivian, J., & Hewstone, M. (1999). Changing attitudes through intergroup contact: The effects of group membership salience. *European Journal of Social Psychology, 29*(56), 741–764.

Brown-Iannuzzi, J. L., Lundberg, K. B., Kay, A. C., & Payne, B. K. (2015). Subjective status shapes political preferences. *Psychological Science, 26*(1), 15–26.

Brownmiller, S. (1975). *Against our will: Men, women and rape*. Simon & Schuster.

Brownstein, R. J., & Katzev, R. D. (1985). The relative effectiveness of three compliance techniques in eliciting donations to a cultural organization. *Journal of Applied Social Psychology, 15*(6), 564–574.

Bruehlman-Senecal, E., & Ayduk, O. (2015). This too shall pass: Temporal distance and the regulation of emotional distress. *Journal of Personality and Social Psychology, 108*(2), 356–375.

Bruner, J. S. (1957). Going beyond the information given. In J. S. Bruner, E. Brunswik, L. Festinger, F. Heider, K. F. Muenzinger, C. E. Osgood, & D. Rapaport (Eds.), *Contemporary approaches to cognition* (pp. 41–69). Harvard University Press.

Bruner, J. S. (1990). *Acts of meaning*. Harvard University Press.

Brunner, H. G., Nelen, M., Breakefield, X. O., & Ropers, H. H. (1993). Abnormal behavior associated with a point mutation in the structural gene for monoamine oxidase A. *Science, 262*(5133), 578–580.

Bryan, C., Yeager, D. S., & O'Brien, J. (2019). Replicator degrees of freedom allow publication of misleading failures to replicate. *Proceedings of the National Academy of Sciences, 116*(51), pp. 25535–25545.

Buchtel, E. E., Ng, L. C., Norenzayan, A., Heine, S. J., Biesanz, J. C., Chen, S. X., Bond, M. H., Peng, Q., & Su, Y. (2018). A sense of obligation: Cultural differences in the experience of obligation. *Personality and Social Psychology Bulletin, 44*(11), 1545–1566.

Bui, K. V. T., Peplau, L. A., & Hill, C. T. (1996). Testing the Rusbult model of relationship commitment and stability in a 15-year study of heterosexual couples. *Personality and Social Psychology Bulletin, 22*(12), 1244–1257.

Burdett, K., & Jensen, L. C. (1983). The self-concept and aggressive behavior among elementary school children from two socioeconomic areas and two grade levels. *Psychology in the Schools, 20*(3), 370–375.

Burger, J. M. (2009). Replicating Milgram: Would people still obey today? *American Psychologist, 64*(1), 1–11.

Burger, J. M., & Caldwell, D. F. (2003). The effects of monetary incentives and labeling on the foot-in-the-door effect: Evidence for a self-perception process. *Basic and Applied Social Psychology, 25*(3), 235–241.

Burger, J. M., & Petty, R. E. (1981). The low-ball compliance technique: Task or person commitment? *Journal of Personality and Social Psychology, 40*(3), 492–500.

Burke, B. L., Kosloff, S., & Landau, M. J. (2013). Death goes to the polls: A meta-analysis of mortality salience effects on political attitudes. *Political Psychology, 34*(2), 183–200.

Burke, B. L., Martens, A., & Faucher, E. H. (2010). Two decades of terror management theory: A meta-analysis of mortality salience research. *Personality and Social Psychology Review*, 14(2), 155–195.

Burkhart, K. W. (1973). *Women in prison*. Doubleday.

Burkley, E. (2008). The role of self-control in resistance to persuasion. *Personality and Social Psychology Bulletin*, 34(3), 419–431.

Burnette, J. L., O'Boyle, E. H., VanEpps, E. M., Pollack, J. M., & Finkel, E. J. (2012). Mind-sets matter: A meta-analytic review of implicit theories and self-regulation. *Psychological Bulletin*, 139(3), 655–701.

Burns, M. D., Monteith, M. J., & Parker, L. R. (2017). Training away bias: The differential effects of counterstereotype training and self-regulation on stereotype activation and application. *Journal of Experimental Social Psychology*, 73, 97–110.

Burnstein, E., Crandall, C., & Kitayama, S. (1994). Some neo-Darwinian decision rules for altruism: Weighing cues for inclusive fitness as a function of the biological importance of the decision. *Journal of Personality and Social Psychology*, 67(5), 773–789.

Burnstein, E., & Vinokur, A. (1977). Persuasive argumentation and social comparison as determinants of attitude polarization. *Journal of Experimental Social Psychology*, 13(4), 315–332.

Burnstein, E., Vinokur, A., & Trope, Y. (1973). Interpersonal comparison versus persuasive argumentation: A more direct test of alternative explanations for group-induced shifts in individual choice. *Journal of Experimental Social Psychology*, 9(3), 236–245.

Burt, M. R. (1980). Cultural myths and supports for rape. *Journal of Personality and Social Psychology*, 38(2), 217–230.

Burton, C. M., & King, L. A. (2004). The health benefits of writing about intensely positive experiences. *Journal of Research in Personality*, 38(2), 150–163.

Bush, G., Luu, P., & Posner, M. I. (2000). Cognitive and emotional influences in anterior cingulate cortex. *Trends in Cognitive Sciences*, 4(6), 215–222.

Bushman, B. J. (1995). Moderating role of trait aggressiveness in the effects of violent media on aggression. *Journal of Personality and Social Psychology*, 69(5), 950–960.

Bushman, B. J. (2018). Guns automatically prime aggressive thoughts, regardless of whether a "good guy" or "bad guy" holds the gun. *Social Psychological and Personality Science*, 9(6), 727–733.

Bushman, B. J., & Anderson, C. A. (2001). Media violence and the American public: Scientific facts versus media misinformation. *American Psychologist*, 56(6–7), 477–489.

Bushman, B. J., & Baumeister, R. F. (1998). Threatened egotism, narcissism, self-esteem, and direct and displaced aggression: Does self-love or self-hate lead to violence? *Journal of Personality and Social Psychology*, 75(1), 219–229.

Bushman, B. J., Bonacci, A. M., Pedersen, W. C., Vasquez, E. A., & Miller, N. (2005). Chewing on it can chew you up: Effects of rumination on triggered displaced aggression. *Journal of Personality and Social Psychology*, 88(6), 969–983.

Bushman, B. J., & Cooper, H. M. (1990). Effects of alcohol on human aggression: An integrative research review. *Psychological Bulletin*, 107(3), 341–354.

Bushman, B. J., & Huesmann, L. R. (2006). Short-term and long-term effects of violent media on aggression in children and adults. *Archives of Pediatrics & Adolescent Medicine*, 160(4), 348–352.

Bushman, B. J., & Huesmann, L. R. (2010). Aggression. In S. T. Fiske, D. T. Gilbert, & G. Lindzey (Eds.), *Handbook of social psychology* (5th ed., Vol. 2, pp. 833–863). Wiley.

Bushman, B. J., Jamieson, P. E., Weitz, I., & Romer, D. (2013). Gun violence trends in movies. *Pediatrics*, 132(6), 1014–1018.

Bushman, B. J., Kerwin, T., Whitlock, T., & Weisenberger, J. M. (2017). The weapons effect on wheels: Motorists drive more aggressively when there is a gun in the vehicle. *Journal of Experimental Social Psychology*, 73, 82–85.

Buss, A. H. (1961). *The psychology of aggression*. Wiley.

Buss, A. H. (1963). Physical aggression in relation to different frustrations. *Journal of Abnormal and Social Psychology*, 67(1), 1–7.

Buss, A. H., & Perry, M. (1992). The aggression questionnaire. *Journal of Personality and Social Psychology*, 63(3), 452–459.

Buss, D. M. (1989). Sex differences in human mate preferences: Evolutionary hypotheses tested in 37 cultures. *Behavioral and Brain Sciences*, 12(1), 1–49.

Buss, D. M. (1994). The strategies of human mating. *American Scientist*, 82(3), 238–249.

Buss, D. M. (2000). *The dangerous passion: Why jealousy is as necessary as love and sex*. Free Press.

Buss, D. M. (2008). *Evolutionary psychology: The new science of the mind* (3rd ed.). Allyn and Bacon.

Buss, D. M. (2016). *The evolution of desire: Strategies of human mating* (rev. and updated ed.). Basic Books.

Buss, D. M. (2017). Sexual conflict in human mating. *Current Directions in Psychological Science*, 26(4), 307–313.

Buss, D. M., Larsen, R. J., Westen, D., & Semmelroth, J. (1992). Sex differences in jealousy: Evolution, physiology, and psychology. *Psychological Science*, 3(4), 251–255.

Buss, D. M., & Malamuth, N. M. (Eds.). (1996). *Sex, power, conflict: Evolutionary and feminist perspectives*. Oxford University Press.

Buss, D. M., & Schmitt, D. P. (1993). Sexual strategies theory: An evolutionary perspective on human mating. *Psychological Review*, 100(2), 204–232.

Buss, D. M., Shackelford, T. K., Kirkpatrick, L. A., Choe, J. C., Lim, H. K., Hasegawa, M., Hasegawa, T., & Bennett, K. (1999). Jealousy and the nature of beliefs about infidelity: Tests of competing hypotheses about sex differences in the United States, Korea, and Japan. *Personal Relationships*, 6(1), 125–150.

Bussey, K., & Bandura, A. (1999). Social cognitive theory of gender development and differentiation. *Psychological Review*, 106(4), 676–713.

Bussey, K., & Bandura, A. (2004). Social cognitive theory of gender development and functioning. In A. H. Eagly, A. E. Beall, & R. J. Sternberg (Eds.), *The psychology of gender* (2nd ed., pp. 92–119). Guilford Press.

Butovskaya, M., Sorokowska, A., Karwowski, M., Sabiniewicz, A., Fedenok, J., Dronova, D., Negasheva, M., Selivanova, E., & Sorokowski, P. (2017). Waist-to-hip ratio, body-mass index, age and number of children in seven traditional societies. *Scientific Reports*, 7(1), article 1622.

Buunk, B. P., Angleitner, A., Oubaid, V., & Buss, D. M. (1996). Sex differences in jealousy in evolutionary and cultural perspective: Tests from the Netherlands, Germany, and the United States. *Psychological Science*, 7(6), 359–363.

Buunk, B. P., & Van Yperen, N. W. (1989). Social comparison, equality, and relationship satisfaction: Gender differences over a ten-year period. *Social Justice Research*, 3(2), 157–180.

Byrne, D. (1971). *The attraction paradigm*. Academic Press.

Byrne, D., & Clore, G. L. (1970). A reinforcement model of evaluative responses. *Personality: An International Journal*, 1(2), 103–128.

Byrne, D., Clore, G. L., & Worchel, P. (1966). Effect of economic similarity-dissimilarity on interpersonal attraction. *Journal of Personality and Social Psychology*, 4(2), 220–224.

Byrne, S. (2009). Media literacy interventions: What makes them boom or boomerang? *Communication Education*, 58(1), 1–14.

Cacioppo, J. T., Cacioppo, S., Gonzaga, G. C., Ogburn, E. L., & VanderWeele, T. J. (2013). Marital satisfaction and break-ups differ across on-line and offline meeting venues. *Proceedings of the National Academy of Sciences*, 110(25), 10135–10140.

Cacioppo, J. T., Hughes, M. E., Waite, L. J., Hawkley, L. C., & Thisted, R. A. (2006). Loneliness as a specific risk factor for depressive symptoms: Cross-sectional and longitudinal analyses. *Psychology and Aging*, 21(1), 140–151.

Cacioppo, J. T., & Patrick, W. (2008). *Loneliness: Human nature and the need for social connection*. W. W. Norton.

Cacioppo, J. T., & Petty, R. E. (1979). Effects of message repetition and position on cognitive response, recall, and persuasion. *Journal of Personality and Social Psychology*, 37(1), 97–109.

Cacioppo, J. T., & Petty, R. E. (1982). The need for cognition. *Journal of Personality and Social Psychology*, 42(1), 116–131.

Cadinu, M., Maass, A., Rosabianca, A., & Kiesner, J. (2005). Why do women underperform under stereotype threat? Evidence for the role of negative thinking. *Psychological Science*, 16(7), 572–578.

Cadinu, M. R., & Kiesner, J. (2000). Children's development of a theory of mind. *European Journal of Psychology of Education*, 15(2), 93–111.

Cafferty, J. (2010, March 10). *$10 billion spent on cosmetic procedures despite recession*. CNN. http://caffertyfile.blogs.cnn.com/2010/03/10/10-billion-spent-on-cosmetic-procedures-despite-recession/

Cahalan, S. (2019). *The great pretender: The undercover mission that changed our understanding of madness*. Grand Central Publishing.

Cahn, D. D. (1992). *Conflict in intimate relationships*. Guilford Press.

Calder, B. J., Insko, C. A., & Yandell, B. (1974). The relation of cognitive and memorial processes to persuasion in a simulated jury trial. *Journal of Applied Social Psychology*, 4(1), 62–93.

Call, V., Sprecher, S., & Schwartz, P. (1995). The incidence and frequency of marital sex in a national sample. *Journal of Marriage & the Family*, 57(3), 639–652.

Callahan, S. P., & Ledgerwood, A. (2016). On the psychological function of flags and logos: Group identity symbols increase perceived entitativity. *Journal of Personality and Social Psychology*, 110(4), 528–550.

Calogero, R. M. (2004). A test of objectification theory: The effect of the male gaze on appearance concerns in college women. *Psychology of Women Quarterly*, 28(1), 16–21.

Camerer, C. (2003). *Behavioral game theory: Experiments in strategic interaction*. Princeton University Press.

Cameron, C. D., & Payne, B. K. (2011). Escaping affect: How motivated emotion regulation creates insensitivity to mass suffering. *Journal of Personality and Social Psychology*, 100(1), 1–15.

Campbell, D. T. (1958). Common fate, similarity, and other indices of the status of aggregates of persons as social entities. *Behavioral Science, 3*(1), 14–25.

Campbell, J. D. (1986). Similarity and uniqueness: The effects of attribute type, relevance, and individual differences in self-esteem and depression. *Journal of Personality and Social Psychology, 50*(2), 281–294.

Campbell, J. D. (1990). Self-esteem and clarity of the self-concept. *Journal of Personality and Social Psychology, 59*(3), 538–549.

Campbell, L., Simpson, J. A., Boldry, J., & Kashy, D. A. (2005). Perceptions of conflict and support in romantic relationships: The role of attachment anxiety. *Journal of Personality and Social Psychology, 88*(3), 510–531.

Campbell, W. K., & Sedikides, C. (1999). Self-threat magnifies the self-serving bias: A meta-analytic integration. *Review of General Psychology, 3*(1), 23–43.

Campos, J. J., Barrett, K. C., Lamb, M. E., Goldsmith, H. H., & Stenberg, C. (1983). Socioemotional development. In M. M. Haith & J. J. Campos (Eds.), *Handbook of child psychology, Vol. 2: Infancy and developmental psychobiology* (4th ed., pp. 783–915). Wiley.

Canary, D. J., & Cupach, W. R. (1988). Relational and episodic characteristics associated with conflict tactics. *Journal of Social and Personal Relationships, 5*(3), 305–325.

Canary, D. J., Cupach, W. R., & Messman, S. J. (1995). *Relationship conflict: Conflict in parent–child, friendship, and romantic relationships.* Sage Publications, Inc.

Canary, D. J., & Spitzberg, B. H. (1987). Appropriateness and effectiveness perceptions of conflict strategies. *Human Communication Research, 14*(1), 93–120.

Cantor, J. (1998). Children's attraction to television programming. In J. H. Goldstein (Ed.), *Why we watch: The attractions of violent entertainment* (pp. 88–115). Oxford University Press.

Cantor, J. R., Bryant, J., & Zillmann, D. (1974). Enhancement of humor appreciation by transferred excitation. *Journal of Personality and Social Psychology, 30*(6), 812–821.

Cantor, J. R., & Zillmann, D. (1973). The effect of affective state and emotional arousal on music appreciation. *Journal of General Psychology, 89*(1), 79–108.

Capaldi, D. M., Pears, K. C., Patterson, G. R., & Owen, L. D. (2003). Continuity of parenting practices across generations in an at-risk sample: A prospective comparison of direct and mediated associations. *Journal of Abnormal Child Psychology, 31*(2), 127–142.

Caplan, N. (1970). The new ghetto man: A review of recent empirical studies. *Journal of Social Issues, 26*(1), 59–73.

Caprara, G. V., Regalia, C., & Bandura, A. (2002). Longitudinal impact of perceived self-regulatory efficacy on violent conduct. *European Psychologist, 7*(1), 63–69.

Card, N. A., Stucky, B. D., Sawalani, G. M., & Little, T. D. (2008). Direct and indirect aggression during childhood and adolescence: A meta-analytic review of gender differences, intercorrelations, and relations to maladjustment. *Child Development, 79*(5), 1185–1229.

Carlo, G., Eisenberg, N., Troyer, D., Switzer, G., & Speer, A. L. (1991). The altruistic personality: In what contexts is it apparent? *Journal of Personality and Social Psychology, 61*(3), 450–458.

Carlson, E. N., Vazire, S., & Furr, R. M. (2011). Meta-insight: Do people really know how others see them? *Journal of Personality and Social Psychology, 101*(4), 831–846.

Carlson, M., Charlin, V., & Miller, N. (1988). Positive mood and helping behavior: A test of six hypotheses. *Journal of Personality and Social Psychology, 55*(2), 211–229.

Carlson, M., & Miller, N. (1987). Explanation of the relation between negative mood and helping. *Psychological Bulletin, 102*(1), 91–108.

Carlson, S. M., Shoda, Y., Ayduk, O., Aber, L., Schaefer, C., Sethi, A., Wilson, N., Peake, P. K., & Mischel, W. (2018). Cohort effects in children's delay of gratification. *Developmental Psychology, 54*(8), 1395–1407.

Carr, E. W., Brady, T. F., & Winkielman, P. (2017). Are you smiling, or have I seen you before? Familiarity makes faces look happier. *Psychological Science, 28*(8), 1087–1102.

Carrillo, M., Ricci, L. A., Coppersmith, G. A., & Melloni, R. H. (2009). The effect of increased serotonergic neurotransmission on aggression: A critical metaanalytical review of preclinical studies. *Psychopharmacology, 205*(3), 349–368.

Carroll, J. (2007, August 16). *Most Americans approve of interracial marriages.* Gallup News Service. http://www.gallup.com/poll/28417/most-americans-approve-interracial-marriages.aspx

Carstensen, L. L. (2009). *A long bright future: An action plan for a lifetime of happiness, health, and financial security.* Broadway Books.

Carstensen, L. L., Isaacowitz, D. M., & Charles, S. T. (1999). Taking time seriously: A theory of socioemotional selectivity. *American Psychologist, 54*(3), 165–181.

Carter, E. C., Kofler, L. M., Forster, D. E., & McCullough, M. E. (2015). A series of meta-analytic tests of the depletion effect: Self-control does not seem to rely on a limited resource. *Journal of Experimental Psychology: General, 144*(4), 796–815.

Cartwright, D. (1971). Risk taking by individuals and groups: An assessment of research employing choice dilemmas. *Journal of Personality and Social Psychology, 20*(3), 361–378.

Cartwright, D., & Zander, A. (1960). Group cohesiveness: Introduction. In D. Cartwright & A. Zander (Eds.), *Group dynamics: Research and theory* (2nd ed., pp. 69–94). Row, Peterson.

Carver, C. S. (1975). Physical aggression as a function of objective self-awareness and attitudes toward punishment. *Journal of Experimental Social Psychology, 11*(6), 510–519.

Carver, C. S., Blaney, P. H., & Scheier, M. F. (1979). Reassertion and giving up: The interactive role of self-directed attention and outcome expectancy. *Journal of Personality and Social Psychology, 37*(10), 1859–1870.

Carver, C. S., & Scheier, M. P. (1981). *Attention and self-regulation: A control theory approach to human behavior.* Springer-Verlag.

Cash, T. F., & Trimer, C. A. (1984). Sexism and beautyism in women's evaluations of peer performance. *Sex Roles, 10*(1–2), 87–98.

Cash Cash, P. (2006). *The ecology of Nez Perce names* [Paper presentation]. Plateau Conference, Plateau Center for American Indian Studies, Washington State University, Pullman, WA.

Caspar, E. A., Christensen, J. F., Cleeremans, A., & Haggard, P. (2016). Coercion changes the sense of agency in the human brain. *Current Biology, 26*(5), 585–592.

Caspi, A., & Herbener, E. S. (1990). Continuity and change: Assortative marriage and the consistency of personality in adulthood. *Journal of Personality and Social Psychology, 58*(2), 250–258.

Caspi, A., McClay, J., Moffitt, T., Mill, J., Martin, J., Craig, I. W., Taylor, A., & Poulton, R. (2002). Role of genotype in the cycle of violence in maltreated children. *Science, 297*(5582), 851–854.

Castano, E., & Dechesne, M. (2005). On defeating death: Group reification and social identification as immortality strategies. *European Review of Social Psychology, 16*(1), 221–255.

Castano, E., & Giner-Sorolla, R. (2006). Not quite human: Infrahumanization in response to collective responsibility for intergroup killing. *Journal of Personality and Social Psychology, 90*(5), 804–818.

Castano, E., Yzerbyt, V., Paladino, M. P., & Sacchi, S. (2002). I belong, therefore, I exist: Ingroup identification, ingroup entitativity, and ingroup bias. *Personality and Social Psychology Bulletin, 28*(2), 135–143.

Catanese, K. (2007). Date rape. In R. Baumeister & K. Vohs (Eds.), *Encyclopedia of social psychology* (pp. 217–219). Sage.

Catapano, R., Tormala, Z. L., & Rucker, D. D. (2019). Perspective taking and self-persuasion: Why "putting yourself in their shoes" reduces openness to attitude change. *Psychological Science, 30*(3), 424–435.

Cattell, R. B. (1971). *Abilities: Their growth, structure, and action.* Houghton Mifflin.

Cattell, R. B., & Nesselroade, J. R. (1967). Likeness and completeness theories examined by sixteen personality factor measures on stably and unstably married couples. *Journal of Personality and Social Psychology, 7*(4, Pt. 1), 351–361.

Caughlin, J. P., Huston, T. L., & Houts, R. M. (2000). How does personality matter in marriage? An examination of trait anxiety, interpersonal negativity, and marital satisfaction. *Journal of Personality and Social Psychology, 78*(2), 326–336.

CBS News. (2019, September 2). *Motive sought for latest Texas mass shooting.* CBS. https://www.cbsnews.com/news/shooting-in-texas-odessa-midland-at-least-6-dead-3-police-injured-mass-shooting-latest-news-2019-09-01/

Cesario, J., Grant, H., & Higgins, E. T. (2004). Regulatory fit and persuasion: Transfer from "feeling right." *Journal of Personality and Social Psychology, 86*(3), 388–404.

Cesario, J., Plaks, J. E., Hagiwara, N., Navarrete, C. D., & Higgins, E. T. (2010). The ecology of automaticity: How situational contingencies shape action semantics and social behavior. *Psychological Science, 21*(9), 1311–1317.

Cesario, J., Plaks, J. E., & Higgins, E. T. (2006). Automatic social behavior as motivated preparation to interact. *Journal of Personality and Social Psychology, 90*(6), 893–910.

Chae, D. H., Wang, Y., Martz, C. D., Slopen, N., Yip, T., Adler, N. E., Fuller-Rowell, T. E., Lin, J., Matthews, K. A., Brody, G. H., Spears, E. C., Puterman, E., & Epel, E. S. (2020). Racial discrimination and telomere shortening among African Americans: The Coronary Artery Risk Development in Young Adults (CARDIA) Study. *Health Psychology, 39*(3), 209–219.

Chaiken, S. (1979). Communicator physical attractiveness and persuasion. *Journal of Personality and Social Psychology, 37*(8), 1387–1397.

Chaiken, S. (1980). Heuristic versus systematic information processing and the use of source versus message cues in persuasion. *Journal of Personality and Social Psychology*, 39(5), 752–766.

Chaiken, S. (1987). The heuristic model of persuasion. In M. Zanna, J. Olson, & C. Herman (Eds.), *Social influence: The Ontario Symposium* (Vol. 5, pp. 3–39). Erlbaum.

Chan, E., & Sengupta, J. (2010). Insincere flattery actually works: A dual attitudes perspective. *Journal of Marketing Research*, 47(1), 122–133.

Chandler, J. J., Reinhard, D., & Schwarz, N. (2012). To judge a book by its weight you need to know its content: Knowledge moderates the use of embodied cues. *Journal of Experimental Social Psychology*, 48, 948–952.

Chang, A. (Host). (2020, May 26). An avid birder talks about his conflict in Central Park that went viral [Audio podcast episode]. *All Things Considered*. NPR. https://www.npr.org/2020/05/26/862838384/an-avid-birder-talks-about-a-conflict-in-central-park-he-taped-and-went-viral

Chapman, L. J., & Chapman, J. P. (1967). Genesis of popular but erroneous psychodiagnostic observations. *Journal of Abnormal Psychology*, 72(3), 193–204.

Chapman, L. J., & Chapman, J. P. (1969). Illusory correlation as an obstacle to the use of valid psychodiagnostic signs. *Journal of Abnormal Psychology*, 74(3), 271–280.

Charlesworth, T. E., & Banaji, M. R. (2019). Patterns of implicit and explicit attitudes: I. Long-term change and stability from 2007 to 2016. *Psychological Science*, 30(2), 174–192.

Chartrand, T. L., & Bargh, J. A. (1999). The chameleon effect: The perception–behavior link and social interaction. *Journal of Personality and Social Psychology*, 76(6), 893–910.

Chartrand, T. L., & Bargh, J. A. (2002). Nonconscious motivations: Their activation, operation, and consequences. In A. Tesser, D. A. Stapel, & J. V. Wood (Eds.), *Self and motivation: Emerging psychological perspectives* (pp. 13–41). American Psychological Association.

Chasteen, A. L., Bhattacharyya, S., Horhota, M., Tam, R., & Hasher, L. (2005). How feelings of stereotype threat influence older adults' memory performance. *Experimental Aging Research*, 31(3), 235–260.

Chatard, A., Bocage-Barthélémy, Y., Selimbegovic, L., & Guimond, S. (2017). The woman who wasn't there: Converging evidence that subliminal social comparison affects self-evaluation. *Journal of Experimental Social Psychology*, 73, 1–13.

Chaxel, A. S. (2015). How do stereotypes influence choice? *Psychological Science*, 26(5), 641–645.

Chemers, M. M., Watson, C. B., & May, S. T. (2000). Dispositional affect and leadership effectiveness: A comparison of self-esteem, optimism, and efficacy. *Personality and Social Psychology Bulletin*, 26(3), 267–277.

Chen, D. H. C. (2004). *Gender equality and economic development: The role for information and communication technologies*. The World Bank. http://info.worldbank.org/etools/docs/library/117321/35079_wps3285.pdf

Chen, H., Cohen, P., Kasen, S., Johnson, J. G., Ehrensaft, M., & Gordon, K. (2006). Predicting conflict within romantic relationships during the transition to adulthood. *Personal Relationships*, 13(4), 411–427.

Chen, S. (2009, October 30). *Gang rape raises questions about bystanders' role*. CNN. http://www.cnn.com/2009/CRIME/10/28/california.gang.rape.bystander/index.html?_s=PM:CRIME

Chen, S. X., Lam, B. P., Hui, B. H., Ng, J. K., Mak, W. S., Guan, Y., Buchtel, E. E., Tang, W., & Lau, V. (2016). Conceptualizing psychological processes in response to globalization: Components, antecedents, and consequences of global orientations. *Journal of Personality and Social Psychology*, 110(2), 302–331.

Chen, S., Binning, K. R., Manke, K. J., Brady, S. T., McGreevy, E. M., Betancur, L., . . . & Kaufmann, N. (2021). Am I a science person? A strong science identity bolsters minority students' sense of belonging and performance in college. *Personality and Social Psychology Bulletin*, 47(4), 593–606.

Cheng, C. M., & Chartrand, T. L. (2003). Self-monitoring without awareness: Using mimicry as a nonconscious affiliation strategy. *Journal of Personality and Social Psychology*, 85(6), 1170–1179.

Chenier, T., & Winkielman, P. (2007). Mere exposure effect. In R. Baumeister & K. Vohs (Eds.), *Encyclopedia of social psychology* (Vol. 2, pp. 556–558). Sage.

Chermack, S. T., & Giancola, P. R. (1997). The relation between alcohol and aggression: An integrated biopsychosocial conceptualization. *Clinical Psychology Review*, 17(6), 621–649.

Cheryan, S., Plaut, V. C., Davies, P. G., & Steele, C. M. (2009). Ambient belonging: How stereotypical cues impact gender participation in computer science. *Journal of Personality and Social Psychology*, 97, 1045–1060.

Cheryan, S., Ziegler, S. A., Montoya, A., & Jiang, L. (2017). Why are some STEM fields more gender balanced than others? *Psychological Bulletin*, 143(1), 1–35.

Chester, D. S., DeWall, C. N., & Enjaian, B. (2019). Sadism and aggressive behavior: Inflicting pain to feel pleasure. *Personality and Social Psychology Bulletin*, 45(8), 1252–1268.

Chiefs Kingdom. (2013, September 28). *Joe Delaney*. http://www.kcchiefs.com/media-center/videos/Chiefs_Kingdom_Joe_Delaney/0cb246318c8a-41fa-a2ab-ea04fc495990

Chien, Y., Wegener, D. T., Petty, R. E., & Hsiao, C. (2014). The flexible correction model: Bias correction guided by naïve theories of bias. *Social and Personality Psychology Compass*, 8(6), 275–286.

Choi, I., & Nisbett, R. E. (1998). Situational salience and cultural differences in the correspondence bias and actor-observer bias. *Personality and Social Psychology Bulletin*, 24(9), 949–960.

Chua-Eoan, H. (2007, March 1). Columbine massacre, 1999. *Time*. http://content.time.com/time/specials/packages/article/0,28804,1937349_1937350_1937526,00.html

Chuan, A., Kessler, J. B., & Milkman, K. L. (2018). Field study of charitable giving reveals that reciprocity decays over time. *Proceedings of the National Academy of Sciences of the United States of America*, 115(8), 1766–1771.

Chung, S., Lount, R. B., Jr., Park, H. M., & Park, E. S. (2018). Friends with performance benefits: A meta-analysis on the relationship between friendship and group performance. *Personality and Social Psychology Bulletin*, 44(1), 63–79.

Chung, V. Q., Gordon, J. S., Veledar, E., & Chen, S. C. (2010). Hot or not—Evaluating the effect of artificial tanning on the public's perception of attractiveness. *Dermatologic Surgery*, 36(11), 1651–1655.

Church, A. T. (1982). Sojourner adjustment. *Psychological Bulletin*, 91(3), 540–572.

Cialdini, R. B. (2003). Crafting normative messages to protect the environment. *Current Directions in Psychological Science*, 12(4), 105–109.

Cialdini, R. B. (2006). *Influence: The psychology of persuasion*. HarperCollins.

Cialdini, R. B., Baumann, D. J., & Kenrick, D. T. (1981). Insights from sadness: A three-step model of the development of altruism as hedonism. *Developmental Review*, 1(3), 207–223.

Cialdini, R. B., Borden, R. J., Thorne, A., Walker, M. R., Freeman, S., & Sloan, L. R. (1976). Basking in reflected glory: Three (football) field studies. *Journal of Personality and Social Psychology*, 34(3), 366–375.

Cialdini, R. B., Cacioppo, J. T., Bassett, R., & Miller, J. A. (1978). Low-ball procedure for producing compliance: Commitment then cost. *Journal of Personality and Social Psychology*, 36(5), 463–476.

Cialdini, R. B., Demaine, L. J., Sagarin, B. J., Barrett, D. W., Rhoads, K., & Winter, P. L. (2006). Managing social norms for persuasive impact. *Social Influence*, 1(1), 3–15.

Cialdini, R. B., & Goldstein, N. J. (2004). Social influence: Compliance and conformity. *Annual Review of Psychology*, 55(1), 591–621.

Cialdini, R. B., Schaller, M., Houlihan, D., Arps, K., Fultz, J., & Beaman, A. L. (1987). Empathy-based helping: Is it selflessly or selfishly motivated? *Journal of Personality and Social Psychology*, 52(4), 749–758.

Cialdini, R. B., Vincent, J. E., Lewis, S. K., Catalan, J., Wheeler, D., & Darby, B. L. (1975). Reciprocal concessions procedure for inducing compliance: The door-in-the-face technique. *Journal of Personality and Social Psychology*, 31(2), 206–215.

Cialdini, R. B., Wosinska, W., Barrett, D. W., Butner, J., & Gornik-Durose, M. (1999). Compliance with a request in two cultures: The differential influence of social proof and commitment/consistency on collectivists and individualists. *Personality and Social Psychology Bulletin*, 25(10), 1242–1253.

Cimino, M. (Director). (1978). *The deer hunter* [Film]. Universal Pictures.

Clark, J. L., Algoe, S. B., & Green, M. C. (2018). Social network sites and well-being: The role of social connection. *Current Directions in Psychological Science*, 27(1), 32–37.

Clark, M. S., & Mills, J. (1979). Interpersonal attraction in exchange and communal relationships. *Journal of Personality and Social Psychology*, 37(1), 12–24.

Clark, M. S., Mills, J., & Powell, M. C. (1986). Keeping track of needs in communal and exchange relationships. *Journal of Personality and Social Psychology*, 51(2), 333–338.

Clark, M. S., Oullette, R., Powell, M. C., & Milberg, S. (1987). Recipient's mood, relationship type, and helping. *Journal of Personality and Social Psychology*, 53(1), 94–103.

Clarkson, J. J., Hirt, E. R., Jia, L., & Alexander, M. B. (2010). When perception is more than reality: The effects of perceived versus actual resource depletion on self-regulatory behavior. *Journal of Personality and Social Psychology*, 98(1), 29–46.

Claxton, A., & Perry-Jenkins, M. (2008). No fun anymore: Leisure and marital quality across the transition to parenthood. *Journal of Marriage and Family*, 70(1), 28–43.

Cleare, A. J., & Bond, A. J. (1995). The effect of tryptophan depletion and enhancement on subjective and behavioural aggression in normal male subjects. *Psychopharmacology*, 118(1), 72–81.

Clements, R., & Musker, J. (Directors). (1989). *The little mermaid* [Film]. Walt Disney Pictures.

Clifford, M. M., & Walster, E. (1973). The effect of physical attractiveness on teacher expectations. *Sociology of Education, 46*(2), 248–258.

Cloven, D. H., & Roloff, M. E. (1991). Sense-making activities and interpersonal conflict: Communicative cures for the mulling blues. *Western Journal of Communication, 55*(2), 134–158.

Clutton-Brock, T. H., & Parker, G. A. (1995). Punishment in animal societies. *Nature, 373*(6511), 209–216.

Coan, R. W. (1977). *Hero, artist, sage, or saint?* Columbia University Press.

Cobb, C. (Writer), & Peters, W. (Director). (1985, March 26). A class divided [TV series episode]. In D. Fanning & M. Kirk (Producers), *Frontline*. PBS. http://www.pbs.org/wgbh/pages/frontline/shows/divided/etc/view.html

Cohen, A. B. (2015). Religion's profound influences on psychology morality, intergroup relations, self-construal, and enculturation. *Current Directions in Psychological Science, 24*(1), 77–82.

Cohen, C. E. (1981). Person categories and social perception: Testing some boundaries of the processing effect of prior knowledge. *Journal of Personality and Social Psychology, 40*(3), 441–452.

Cohen, D., & Nisbett, R. E. (1994). Self-protection and the culture of honor: Explaining southern violence. *Personality and Social Psychology Bulletin, 20*(5), 551–567.

Cohen, D., & Nisbett, R. E. (1997). Field experiments examining the culture of honor: The role of institutions in perpetuating norms about violence. *Personality and Social Psychology Bulletin, 23*(11), 1188–1199.

Cohen, D., Nisbett, R. E., Bowdle, B. F., & Schwarz, N. (1996). Insult, aggression, and the southern culture of honor: An "experimental ethnography." *Journal of Personality and Social Psychology, 70*(5), 945–960.

Cohen, F., Solomon, S., & Kaplin, D. (2017). You're hired! Mortality salience increases Americans' support for Donald Trump. *Analyses of Social Issues and Public Policy, 17*(1), 339–357.

Cohen, F., Solomon, S., Maxfield, M., Pyszczynski, T., & Greenberg, J. (2004). Fatal attraction: The effects of mortality salience on evaluations of charismatic, task oriented, and relationship-oriented leaders. *Psychological Science, 15*(12), 846–851.

Cohen, G. L., Garcia, J., Apfel, N., & Master, A. (2006). Reducing the racial achievement gap: A social-psychological intervention. *Science, 313*(5791), 1307–1310.

Cohen, G. L., Garcia, J., Purdie-Vaughns, V., Apfel, N., & Brzustoski, P. (2009). Recursive processes in self-affirmation: Intervening to close the minority achievement gap. *Science, 324*(5925), 400–403.

Cohen, J. (2004). Parasocial break-up from favorite television characters: The role of attachment styles and relationship intensity. *Journal of Social and Personal Relationships, 21*(2), 187–202.

Cohen, S. (2004). Social relationships and health. *American Psychologist, 59*(8), 676–684.

Cohen, S., Janicki-Deverts, D., Turner, R. B., & Doyle, W. J. (2015). Does hugging provide stress-buffering social support? A study of susceptibility to upper respiratory infection and illness. *Psychological Science, 26*(2), 135–142.

Coke, J. S., Batson, C. D., & McDavis, K. (1978). Empathic mediation of helping: A two-stage model. *Journal of Personality and Social Psychology, 36*(7), 752–766.

Coker, A. L., Davis, K. E., Arias, I., Desai, S., Sanderson, M., Brandt, H. M., & Smith, P. H. (2002). Physical and mental health effects of intimate partner violence for men and women. *American Journal of Preventive Medicine, 23*(4), 260–268.

Coker, A. L., Fisher, B. S., Bush, H. M., Swan, S. C., Williams, C. M., Clear, E. R., & DeGue, S. (2015). Evaluation of the Green Dot bystander intervention to reduce interpersonal violence among college students across three campuses. *Violence Against Women, 21*(12), 1507–1527.

Cole, S., Trope, Y., & Balcetis, E. (2016). In the eye of the betrothed: Perceptual downgrading of attractive alternative romantic partners. *Personality and Social Psychology Bulletin, 42*(7), 879–892.

Cole, S. W., Kemeny, M. E., & Taylor, S. E. (1997). Social identity and physical health: Accelerated HIV progression in rejection-sensitive gay men. *Journal of Personality and Social Psychology, 72*(2), 320–335.

Coleridge, S. T., & Fenby, T. (1877). *Aids to reflection in the formation of a manly character on the several grounds of prudence, morality and religion* (Rev. ed.). Edward Howell. (Original work published 1825)

Coles, N. A., Larsen, J. T., & Lench, H. C. (2019). A meta-analysis of the facial feedback literature: Effects of facial feedback on emotional experience are small and variable. *Psychological Bulletin, 145*(6), 610–651.

Collie, M., & Hensley, L. (2020, March 6). Victoria's Secret 2019 fashion show officially cancelled. *Global News*. https://globalnews.ca/news/6200843/victorias-secret-fashion-show-cancelled/

Colligan, M., Pennebaker, J., & Murphy, P. (Eds.). (1982). *Mass psychogenic illness: A social psychological analysis*. Erlbaum.

Collins, A. M., & Loftus, E. F. (1975). A spreading-activation theory of semantic processing. *Psychological Review, 82*(6), 407–428.

Collins, J. (2013, April 29). Why NBA center Jason Collins is coming out now. *Sports Illustrated*. https://www.si.com/more-sports/2013/04/29/jason-collins-gay-nba-player

Collins, N. L., & Feeney, B. C. (2000). A safe haven: An attachment theory perspective on support seeking and caregiving in intimate relationships. *Journal of Personality and Social Psychology, 78*(6), 1053–1073.

Collins, N. L., & Feeney, B. C. (2004). Working models of attachment shape perceptions of social support: Evidence from experimental and observational studies. *Journal of Personality and Social Psychology, 87*(3), 363–383.

Collins, N. L., & Read, S. J. (1990). Adult attachment, working models, and relationship quality in dating couples. *Journal of Personality and Social Psychology, 58*(4), 644–663.

Collins, N. L., & Read, S. J. (1994). Cognitive representations of attachment: The structure and function of working models. In K. Bartholomew & D. Perlman (Eds.), *Advances in personal relationships, Vol. 5: Attachment processes in adulthood* (pp. 53–90). Jessica Kingsley.

Collins, S. (2008). *The hunger games*. Scholastic, Inc.

Colman, D. E., Letzring, T. D., & Biesanz, J. C. (2017). Seeing and feeling your way to accurate personality judgments: The moderating role of perceiver empathic tendencies. *Social Psychological and Personality Science, 8*(7), 806–815.

Columb, C., & Plant, E. A. (2011). Revisiting the Obama Effect: Exposure to Obama reduces implicit prejudice. *Journal of Experimental Social Psychology, 47*(2), 499–501.

Condon, J. W., & Crano, W. D. (1988). Inferred evaluation and the relation between attitude similarity and interpersonal attraction. *Journal of Personality and Social Psychology, 54*(5), 789–797.

Conger, R. D., Neppl, T., Kim, K. J., & Scaramella, L. (2003). Angry and aggressive behavior across three generations: A prospective, longitudinal study of parents and children. *Journal of Abnormal Child Psychology, 31*(2), 143–160.

Connor, P., Varney, J., Keltner, D., & Chen, S. (2021). Social class competence stereotypes are amplified by socially signaled economic inequality. *Personality and Social Psychology Bulletin, 47*, 89–105.

Conroy-Beam, D., Buss, D. M., Pham, M. N., & Shackelford, T. K. (2015). How sexually dimorphic are human mate preferences? *Personality and Social Psychology Bulletin, 41*(8), 1082–1093.

Contrada, R. J., Ashmore, R. D., Gary, M. L., Coups, E., Egeth, J. D., Sewell, A., Ewell, K., Goyal, T. M., & Chasse, V. (2000). Ethnicity-related sources of stress and their effects on well-being. *Current Directions in Psychological Science, 9*(4), 136–139.

Cook, C. L., Cohen, F., & Solomon, S. (2015). What if they're right about the afterlife? Evidence of the role of existential threat on anti-atheist prejudice. *Social Psychological and Personality Science, 6*(7), 840–846.

Cooley, C. H. (1902). *Human nature and the social order*. Charles Scribner's Sons.

Cooley, E., Brown-Iannuzzi, J., & Cottrell, D. (2019). Liberals perceive more racism than conservatives when police shoot Black men—But, reading about White privilege increases perceived racism, and shifts attributions of guilt, regardless of political ideology. *Journal of Experimental Social Psychology, 85*. https://doi.org/10.1016/j.jesp.2019.103885

Coontz, S. (2005). *Marriage, a history: From obedience to intimacy, or how love conquered marriage*. Viking.

Cooper, D. P., Goldenberg, J. L., & Arndt, J. (2014). Perceived efficacy, conscious fear of death, and intentions to tan: Not all fear appeals are created equal. *British Journal of Health Psychology, 19*(1), 1–15.

Cooper, J. (1980). Reducing fears and increasing assertiveness: The role of dissonance reduction. *Journal of Experimental Social Psychology, 16*(3), 199–213.

Cooper, J., & Fazio, R. H. (1984). A new look at dissonance theory. In L. Berkowitz (Ed.), *Advances in experimental social psychology* (Vol. 17, pp. 229–266). Academic Press.

Cooper, J., & Jones, E. E. (1969). Opinion divergence as a strategy to avoid being miscast. *Journal of Personality and Social Psychology, 13*(1), 23–30.

Cooper, M. L., Pioli, M., Levitt, A., Talley, A. E., Micheas, L., & Collins, N. L. (2006). Attachment styles, sex motives, and sexual behavior: Evidence for gender-specific expressions of attachment dynamics. In M. Mikulincer & G. S. Goodman (Eds.), *Dynamics of romantic love: Attachment, caregiving, and sex* (pp. 243–274). Guilford Press.

Cooper, M. L., Shapiro, C. M., & Powers, A. M. (1998). Motivations for sex and risky sexual behavior among adolescents and young adults: A functional perspective. *Journal of Personality and Social Psychology, 75*(6), 1528–1558.

Cooper, R. P., & Aslin, R. N. (1990). Preference for infant-directed speech in the first month after birth. *Child Development, 61*(5), 1584–1595.

Coopersmith, S. (1967). *The antecedents of self-esteem*. W. H. Freeman.

Correll, J., Hudson, S. M., Guillermo, S., & Ma, D. S. (2014). The police officer's dilemma: A decade of research on racial bias in the decision to shoot. *Social and Personality Psychology Compass, 8*(5), 201–213.

Correll, J., Park, B., Judd, C. M., & Wittenbrink, B. (2002). The police officer's dilemma: Using ethnicity to disambiguate potentially threatening individuals. *Journal of Personality and Social Psychology, 83*, 1314–1329.

Correll, J., Park, B., Judd, C. M., Wittenbrink, B., Sadler, M. S., & Keesee, T. (2007). Across the thin blue line: Police officers and racial bias in the decision to shoot. *Journal of Personality and Social Psychology, 92*(6), 1006–1023.

Correll, J., Wittenbrink, B., Park, B., Judd, C. M., & Goyle, A. (2011). Dangerous enough: Moderating racial bias with contextual threat cues. *Journal of Experimental Social Psychology, 47*(1), 184–189.

Costa, P., Jr., Terracciano, A., & McCrae, R. R. (2001). Gender differences in personality traits across cultures: Robust and surprising findings. *Journal of Personality and Social Psychology, 81*(2), 322–331.

Costa, P. T., Jr., & McCrae, R. R. (1994). Stability and change in personality from adolescence through adulthood. In C. F. Halverson, Jr., G. A. Kohnstamm, & R. P. Martin (Eds.), *The developing structure of temperament and personality from infancy to adulthood* (pp. 139–150). Erlbaum.

Costello, F., & Watts, P. (2019). The rationality of illusory correlation. *Psychological Review, 126*(3), 437–450.

Cottrell, C. A., Neuberg, S. L., & Li, N. P. (2007). What do people desire in others? A sociofunctional perspective on the importance of different valued characteristics. *Journal of Personality and Social Psychology, 92*(2), 208–231.

Cox, C. R., & Arndt, J. (2012). How sweet it is to be loved by you: The role of perceived regard in the terror management of close relationships. *Journal of Personality and Social Psychology, 102*(3), 616–632.

Cox, C. R., Arndt, J., Pyszczynski, T., Greenberg, J., Abdollahi, A., & Solomon, S. (2008). Terror management and adults' attachment to their parents: The safe haven remains. *Journal of Personality and Social Psychology, 94*(4), 696–717.

Craig, M. A., & Richeson, J. A. (2016). Stigma-based solidarity: Understanding the psychological foundations of conflict and coalition among members of different stigmatized groups. *Current Directions in Psychological Science, 25*(1), 21–27.

Crandall, C. S. (1991). Do heavy-weight students have more difficulty paying for college? *Personality and Social Psychology Bulletin, 17*(6), 606–611.

Crandall, C. S. (1994). Prejudice against fat people: Ideology and self-interest. *Journal of Personality and Social Psychology, 66*(5), 882–894.

Crandall, C. S., Bahns, A. J., Warner, R., & Schaller, M. (2011). Stereotypes as justifications of prejudice. *Personality and Social Psychology Bulletin, 37*(11), 1488–1498.

Crandall, C. S., & Eshleman, A. (2003). A justification-suppression model of the expression and experience of prejudice. *Psychological Bulletin, 129*(3), 414–446.

Crandall, C. S., Eshleman, A., & O'Brien, L. (2002). Social norms and the expression and suppression of prejudice: The struggle for internalization. *Journal of Personality and Social Psychology, 82*(3), 359–378.

Crandall, C. S., Miller, J. M., & White, M. H., II. (2018). Changing norms following the 2016 U.S. presidential election: The Trump effect on prejudice. *Social Psychological and Personality Science, 9*(2), 186–192.

Crandall, C. S., & Sherman, J. W. (2016). On the scientific superiority of conceptual replications for scientific progress. *Journal of Experimental Social Psychology, 66*, 93–99.

Crano, W. D., & Chen, X. (1998). The leniency contract and persistence of majority and minority influence. *Journal of Personality and Social Psychology, 74*(6), 1437–1450.

Crick, N. R., & Dodge, K. A. (1994). A review and reformulation of social information-processing mechanisms in children's social adjustment. *Psychological Bulletin, 115*(1), 74–101.

Crick, N. R., & Grotpeter, J. K. (1995). Relational aggression, gender, and social-psychological adjustment. *Child Development, 66*(3), 710–722.

Crick, N. R., & Grotpeter, J. K. (1996). Children's treatment by peers: Victims of relational and overt aggression. *Development and Psychopathology, 8*(2), 367–380.

Critcher, C. R., & Dunning, D. (2015). Self-affirmations provide a broader perspective on self-threat. *Personality and Social Psychology Bulletin, 41*(1), 3–18.

Crivelli, C., Jarillo, S., Russell, J. A., & Fernández-Dols, J. M. (2016). Reading emotions from faces in two indigenous societies. *Journal of Experimental Psychology: General, 145*(7), 830–843.

Crocker, J. (2011). Safety in numbers: Shifting from egosystem to ecosystem. *Psychological Inquiry, 22*(4), 259–264.

Crocker, J., Canevello, A., Breines, J. G., & Flynn, H. (2010). Interpersonal goals and change in anxiety and dysphoria in first-semester college students. *Journal of Personality and Social Psychology, 98*(6), 1009–1024.

Crocker, J., Cornwell, B., & Major, B. (1993). The stigma of overweight: Affective consequences of attributional ambiguity. *Journal of Personality and Social Psychology, 64*(1), 60–70.

Crocker, J., & Major, B. (1989). Social stigma and self-esteem: The self-protective properties of stigma. *Psychological Review, 96*(4), 608–630.

Crocker, J., & Park, L. E. (2004). The costly pursuit of self-esteem. *Psychological Bulletin, 130*(3), 392–414.

Crocker, J., Voelkl, K., Testa, M., & Major, B. (1991). Social stigma: The affective consequences of attributional ambiguity. *Journal of Personality and Social Psychology, 60*(2), 218–228.

Crocker, J., & Wolfe, C. T. (2001). Contingencies of self-worth. *Psychological Review, 108*(3), 593–623.

Crockett, M. J., Clark, L., Tabibnia, G., Lieberman, M. D., & Robbins, T. W. (2008). Serotonin modulates behavioral reactions to unfairness. *Science, 320*(5884), 1739.

Croft, A., Schmader, T., & Block, K. (2015). An underexamined inequality: Cultural and psychological barriers to men's engagement with communal roles. *Personality and Social Psychology Review, 19*(4), 343–370.

Croizet, J. C., & Claire, T. (1998). Extending the concept of stereotype threat to social class: The intellectual underperformance of students from low socioeconomic backgrounds. *Personality and Social Psychology Bulletin, 24*(6), 588–594.

Crosby, J. R. (2015). The silent majority: Understanding and increasing majority group responses to discrimination. *Social and Personality Psychology Compass, 9*(10), 539–550.

Cross, E. J., Overall, N. C., Hammond, M. D., & Fletcher, G. J. (2017). When does men's hostile sexism predict relationship aggression? The moderating role of partner commitment. *Social Psychological and Personality Science, 8*(3), 331–340.

Cross, E. J., Overall, N. C., Low, R. S., & McNulty, J. K. (2019). An interdependence account of sexism and power: Men's hostile sexism, biased perceptions of low power, and relationship aggression. *Journal of Personality and Social Psychology, 117*(2), 338–363.

Cross, K. P. (1977). Not can, but will college teaching be improved? *New Directions for Higher Education, 1977*(17), 1–15.

Cross, S. E., Hardin, E. E., & Gercek-Swing, B. (2010). The what, how, why, and where of self-construal. *Personality and Social Psychology Review, 15*(2), 142–179.

Crutchfield, R. S. (1955). Conformity and character. *American Psychologist, 10*(5), 191–198.

Csikszentmihalyi, M. (1980). Love and the dynamics of personal growth. In K. S. Pope (Ed.), *On love and loving* (pp. 306–326). Jossey-Bass.

Csikszentmihalyi, M. (1990). *Flow: The psychology of optimal experience*. Harper & Row.

Csikszentmihalyi, M. (1996). *Creativity: Flow and the psychology of discovery and invention*. HarperCollins.

Cuddy, A. J., Fiske, S. T., & Glick, P. (2007). The BIAS map: Behaviors from intergroup affect and stereotypes. *Journal of Personality and Social Psychology, 92*(4), 631–648.

Cuddy, A. J., Fiske, S. T., & Glick, P. (2008). Warmth and competence as universal dimensions of social perception: The stereotype content model and the BIAS map. In M. P. Zanna (Ed.), *Advances in experimental social psychology* (Vol. 40, pp. 61–149). Academic Press.

Cuddy, A. J., Rock, M. S., & Norton, M. I. (2007). Aid in the aftermath of Hurricane Katrina: Inferences of secondary emotions and intergroup helping. *Group Processes & Intergroup Relations, 10*(1), 107–118.

Cummings, E. M., Iannotti, R. J., & Zahn-Waxler, C. (1985). Influence of conflict between adults on the emotions and aggression of young children. *Developmental Psychology, 21*(3), 495–507.

Cummings, E. M., Zahn-Waxler, C., & Radke-Yarrow, M. (1981). Young children's responses to expressions of anger and affection by others in the family. *Child Development, 52*(4), 1274–1282.

Cunningham, M. R., Barbee, A. P., & Philhower, C. L. (2002). Dimensions of facial physical attractiveness: The intersection of biology and culture. In G. Rhodes & L. A. Zebrowitz (Eds.), *Facial attractiveness: Evolutionary, cognitive, and social perspectives* (pp. 193–238). Ablex.

Cunningham, M. R., Roberts, A. R., Barbee, A. P., Druen, P. B., & Wu, C. H. (1995). "Their ideas of beauty are, on the whole, the same as ours": Consistency and variability in the cross-cultural perception of female physical attractiveness. *Journal of Personality and Social Psychology, 68*(2), 261–279.

Cunningham, M. R., Shamblen, S. R., Barbee, A. P., & Ault, L. K. (2005). Social allergies in romantic relationships: Behavioral repetition, emotional sensitization, and dissatisfaction in dating couples. *Personal Relationships, 12*(2), 273–295.

Cunningham, M. R., Steinberg, J., & Grev, R. (1980). Wanting to and having to help: Separate motivations for positive mood and guilt-induced helping. *Journal of Personality and Social Psychology, 38*(2), 181–192.

Cunningham, W. A., Johnson, M. K., Raye, C. L., Gatenby, J. C., Gore, J. C., & Banaji, M. R. (2004). Separable neural components in the processing of Black and White faces. *Psychological Science, 15*(12), 806–813.

Curry, O. S., Rowland, L. A., Van Lissa, C. J., Zlotowitz, S., McAlaney, J., & Whitehouse, H. (2018). Happy to help? A systematic review and meta analysis of the effects of performing acts of kindness on the well-being of the actor. *Journal of Experimental Social Psychology, 76,* 320–329.

Curtis, R. C., & Miller, K. (1986). Believing another likes or dislikes you: Behaviors making the beliefs come true. *Journal of Personality and Social Psychology, 51*(2), 284–290.

Curtiz, M. (Director). (1942). *Casablanca* [Film]. Warner Bros. Pictures, Inc.

Czopp, A. M., Monteith, M. J., & Mark, A. Y. (2006). Standing up for a change: Reducing bias through interpersonal confrontation. *Journal of Personality and Social Psychology, 90*(5), 784–803.

Dabbs, J. M., Carr, T. S., Frady, R. L., & Riad, J. K. (1995). Testosterone, crime, and misbehavior among 692 male prison inmates. *Personality and Individual Differences, 18*(5), 627–633.

Dabbs, J. M., & Hargrove, M. F. (1997). Age, testosterone, and behavior among female prison inmates. *Psychosomatic Medicine, 59*(5), 477–480.

DaGloria, J. (1984). Frustration, aggression, and the sense of justice. In A. Mummendey (Ed.), *Social psychology of aggression: From individual behavior to social interaction* (pp. 127–141). Springer.

Dahl, A., & Brownell, C. A. (2019). The social origins of human prosociality. *Current Directions in Psychological Science, 28*(3), 274–279.

Dal Cin, S., Gibson, B., Zanna, M. P., Shumate, R., & Fong, G. T. (2007). Smoking in movies, implicit associations of smoking with the self, and intentions to smoke. *Psychological Science, 18*(7), 559–563.

Daly, M., & Wilson, M. (1988). *Homicide.* Aldine de Gruyter.

Damasio, A. (1999). *The feeling of what happens: Body and emotion in the making of consciousness.* Harcourt College Publishers.

Damasio, A. R. (2001). Fundamental feelings. *Nature, 413*(6858), 781–782.

Damasio, H., Grabowski, T., Frank, R., Galaburda, A. M., & Damasio, A. R. (1994). The return of Phineas Gage: Clues about the brain from the skull of a famous patient. *Science, 264*(5162), 1102–1105.

Dambrun, M., & Vatiné, E. (2010). Reopening the study of extreme social behaviors: Obedience to authority within an immersive video environment. *European Journal of Social Psychology, 40*(5), 760–773.

Darley, J. M., & Batson, C. D. (1973). "From Jerusalem to Jericho": A study of situational and dispositional variables in helping behavior. *Journal of Personality and Social Psychology, 27*(1), 100–108.

Darley, J. M., & Gross, P. H. (1983). A hypothesis-confirming bias in labeling effects. *Journal of Personality and Social Psychology, 44*(1), 20–33.

Darley, J. M., & Latané, B. (1968). Bystander intervention in emergencies: Diffusion of responsibility. *Journal of Personality and Social Psychology, 8*(4, Pt. 1), 377–383.

Darley, J. M., Teger, A. I., & Lewis, L. D. (1973). Do groups always inhibit individuals' responses to potential emergencies? *Journal of Personality and Social Psychology, 26*(3), 395–399.

Darwin, C. (1860). *On the origin of species by means of natural selection: Or the preservation of the favoured races in the struggle for life.* John Murray.

Darwin, C. (1872). *The expression of the emotions in man and animals.* John Murray.

Dasen, P. (1994). Culture and cognitive development from a Piagetian perspective. In W. J. Lonner & R. S. Malpass (Eds.), *Psychology and culture* (pp. 37–63). Allyn & Bacon.

Dasgupta, N. (2011). Ingroup experts and peers as social vaccines who inoculate the self-concept: The stereotype inoculation model. *Psychological Inquiry, 22*(4), 231–246.

Dasgupta, N., & Asgari, S. (2004). Seeing is believing: Exposure to counterstereotypic women leaders and its effect on the malleability of automatic gender stereotyping. *Journal of Experimental Social Psychology, 40*(5), 642–658.

Dasgupta, N., & Greenwald, A. G. (2001). On the malleability of automatic attitudes: Combating automatic prejudice with images of admired and disliked individuals. *Journal of Personality and Social Psychology, 81*(5), 800–814.

Davidson, A. R., & Jaccard, J. J. (1979). Variables that moderate the attitude–behavior relation: Results of a longitudinal survey. *Journal of Personality and Social Psychology, 37*(8), 1364–1376.

Davidson, R. J., Putnam, K. M., & Larson, C. L. (2000). Dysfunction in the neural circuitry of emotion regulation—A possible prelude to violence. *Science, 289*(5479), 591–594.

Davila, J., & Bradbury, T. N. (2001). Attachment insecurity and the distinction between unhappy spouses who do and do not divorce. *Journal of Family Psychology, 15*(3), 371–393.

Davis, B. P., & Knowles, E. S. (1999). A disrupt-then-reframe technique of social influence. *Journal of Personality and Social Psychology, 76*(2), 192–199.

Davis, C. G., Lehman, D. R., Wortman, C. B., Silver, R. C., & Thompson, S. C. (1995). The undoing of traumatic life events. *Personality and Social Psychology Bulletin, 21*(2), 109–124.

Davis, D., Shaver, P. R., & Vernon, M. L. (2004). Attachment style and subjective motivations for sex. *Personality and Social Psychology Bulletin, 30*(8), 1076–1090.

Davis, D. E., Rice, K., Van Tongeren, D. R., Hook, J. N., DeBlaere, C., Worthington, E. L., Jr., & Choe, E. (2016). The moral foundations hypothesis does not replicate well in Black samples. *Journal of Personality and Social Psychology, 110*(4), e23–e30.

Davis, K. E., & Jones, E. E. (1960). Changes in interpersonal perception as a means of reducing cognitive dissonance. *Journal of Abnormal and Social Psychology, 61*(3), 402–410.

Davis, L. V., & Carlson, B. E. (1987). Observation of spouse abuse: What happens to the children? *Journal of Interpersonal Violence, 2*(3), 278–291.

Dearing, R. L., Stuewig, J., & Tangney, J. P. (2005). On the importance of distinguishing shame from guilt: Relations to problematic alcohol and drug use. *Addictive Behaviors, 30*(7), 1392–1404.

Death Penalty Information Center. (n.d.). *Murder rate of death penalty states compared to non-death penalty states.* https://deathpenaltyinfo.org/facts-and-research/murder-rates/murder-rate-of-death-penalty-states-compared-to-non-death-penalty-states

Deaux, K. (1984). From individual differences to social categories: Analysis of a decade's research on gender. *American Psychologist, 39*(2), 105–116.

De Brigard, F., & Parikh, N. (2019). Episodic counterfactual thinking. *Current Directions in Psychological Science, 28*(1), 59–66.

Debrot, A., Meuwly, N., Muise, A., Impett, E. A., & Schoebi, D. (2017). More than just sex: Affection mediates the association between sexual activity and well-being. *Personality and Social Psychology Bulletin, 43*(3), 287–299.

de Castro, B. O., Bosch, J. D., Veerman, J. W., & Koops, W. (2003). The effects of emotion regulation, attribution, and delay prompts on aggressive boys' social problem solving. *Cognitive Therapy and Research, 27*(2), 153–166.

Dechesne, M., Janssen, J., & van Knippenberg, A. (2000). Derogation and distancing as terror management strategies: The moderating role of need for closure and permeability of group boundaries. *Journal of Personality and Social Psychology, 79*(6), 923–932.

Deci, E. L., & Ryan, R. M. (2000). The "what" and "why" of goal pursuits: Human needs and the self-determination of behavior. *Psychological Inquiry, 11*(4), 227–268.

Deci, E. L., & Ryan, R. M. (Eds.). (2002). *Handbook of self-determination research.* University of Rochester Press.

Decker, S. H., & Lauritsen, J. L. (2002). Breaking the bonds of membership: Leaving the gang. In C. R. Huff (Ed.), *Gangs in America III* (pp. 103–122). Sage.

Decker, S. H., & Van Winkle, B. (1996). *Life in the gang: Family, friends, and violence.* Cambridge University Press.

DeCoster, J., & Claypool, H. M. (2004). A meta-analysis of priming effects on impression formation supporting a general model of informational biases. *Personality and Social Psychology Review, 8*(1), 2–27.

De Dreu, C. K. W., & De Vries, N. K. (1993). Numerical support, information processing, and attitude change. *European Journal of Social Psychology, 23*(6), 647–663.

De Keersmaecker, J., Bostyn, D. H., Fontaine, J. R., Van Hiel, A., & Roets, A. (2018). Toward an integrated cognition perspective on ethnic prejudice: An investigation into the role of intelligence and need for cognitive closure. *Social Psychological and Personality Science, 9*(6), 719–726.

Dellarocas, C. (2006). Strategic manipulation of Internet opinion forums: Implications for consumers and firms. *Management Science, 52*(10), 1577–1593.

Delton, A. W., Krasnow, M. M., Cosmides, L., & Tooby, J. (2011). Evolution of direct reciprocity under uncertainty can explain human generosity in one-shot encounters. *Proceedings of the National Academy of Sciences, 108*(32), 13335–13340.

DeMarco, T. C., & Newheiser, A. (2019). When groups do not cure: Group esteem moderates the social cure effect. *European Journal of Social Psychology, 49*(7), 1421–1438.

Demir, A., & Fisiloglu, H. (1999). Loneliness and marital adjustment of Turkish couples. *Journal of Psychology, 133*(2), 230–240.

Dengerink, H. A., & Covey, M. K. (1983). Implications of an escape-avoidance theory of aggressive responses to attack. In R. G. Geen & E. I. Donnerstein (Eds.), *Aggression: Theoretical and empirical reviews* (Vol. 1, pp. 163–188). Academic Press.

Denissen, J. J., Penke, L., Schmitt, D. P., & van Aken, M. A. (2008). Self-esteem reactions to social interactions: Evidence for sociometer mechanisms across days, people, and nations. *Journal of Personality and Social Psychology, 95*(1), 181–196.

Denson, T. F., Pedersen, W. C., Ronquillo, J., & Nandy, A. S. (2009). The angry brain: Neural correlates of anger, angry rumination, and aggressive personality. *Journal of Cognitive Neuroscience, 21*(4), 734–744.

de Oliveira, S., & Nisbett, R. E. (2018). Demographically diverse crowds are typically not much wiser than homogeneous crowds. *Proceedings of the National Academy of Sciences of the United States of America, 115*(9), 2066–2071.

DePaulo, B. M., & Kashy, D. A. (1998). Everyday lies in close and casual relationships. *Journal of Personality and Social Psychology, 74*(1), 63–79.

DePaulo, B. M., Kashy, D. A., Kirkendol, S. E., Wyer, M. M., & Epstein, J. A. (1996). Lying in everyday life. *Journal of Personality and Social Psychology, 70*(5), 979–995.

Deri, S., Davidai, S., & Gilovich, T. (2017). Home alone: Why people believe others' social lives are richer than their own. *Journal of Personality and Social Psychology, 113*(6), 858–877.

Derrick, J. L., Gabriel, S., & Hugenberg, K. (2009). Social surrogacy: How favored television programs provide the experience of belonging. *Journal of Experimental Social Psychology, 45*(2), 352–362.

Derryberry, D., & Tucker, D. M. (1994). Motivating the focus of attention. In P. M. Niedenthal & S. Kitayama (Eds.), *The heart's eye: Emotional influences in perception and attention* (pp. 167–196). Academic Press.

DeSteno, D., Bartlett, M. Y., Braverman, J., & Salovey, P. (2002). Sex differences in jealousy: Evolutionary mechanism or artifact of measurement? *Journal of Personality and Social Psychology, 83*(5), 1103–1116.

DeSteno, D., Bartlett, M. Y., & Salovey, P. (2006). Constraining accommodative homunculi in evolutionary explorations of jealousy: A reply to Barrett et al. (2006). *Journal of Personality and Social Psychology, 91*(3), 519–523.

DeSteno, D. A., & Salovey, P. (1996). Jealousy and the characteristics of one's rival: A self-evaluation maintenance perspective. *Personality and Social Psychology Bulletin, 22*(9), 920–932.

Deutsch, M., & Gerard, H. B. (1955). A study of normative and informational social influences upon individual judgment. *Journal of Abnormal and Social Psychology, 51*(3), 629–636.

De Souza, L., & Schmader, T. (2022). The misjudgment of men: Does pluralistic ignorance inhibit allyship? *Journal of Personality and Social Psychology, 122*(2), 265–285. https://doi.org/10.1037/pspi0000362.supp (Supplemental)

de Vignemont, F., & Singer, T. (2006). The empathic brain: How, when and why? *Trends in Cognitive Sciences, 10*(10), 435–441.

Devine, P. G. (1989). Stereotypes and prejudice: Their automatic and controlled components. *Journal of Personality and Social Psychology, 56*(1), 5–18.

Devine, P. G., Forscher, P. S., Cox, W. T. L., Kaatz, A., Sheridan, J., & Carnes, M. (2017). A gender bias habit-breaking intervention led to increased hiring of female faculty in STEMM departments. *Journal of Experimental Social Psychology, 73*, 211–215.

DeVoss, D. N., & Platt, J. (n.d.). *Image manipulation and ethics in a digital visual world.* http://www2.bgsu.edu/departments/english/cconline/ethics_special_issue/DEVOSS_PLATT

De Vries, M., Fagerlin, A., Witteman, H., & Scherer, L. D. (2013). Combining deliberation and intuition in patient decision support. *Patient Education and Counseling, 91*(2), 154–160.

de Waal, F. B. (1996). *Good natured: The origins of right and wrong in humans and other animals.* Harvard University Press.

DeWall, C. N., Baumeister, R. F., Chester, D. S., & Bushman, B. J. (2016). How often does currently felt emotion predict social behavior and judgment? A meta-analytic test of two theories. *Emotion Review, 8*(2), 136–143.

DeWeerd, M., & Klandermans, B. (1999). Group identification and political protest: Farmers' protest in the Netherlands. *European Journal of Social Psychology, 29*(8), 1073–1095.

Dewey, J. (1922). *Human nature and conduct: An introduction to social psychology.* Carlton House.

Dewsbury, D. A. (1981). Effects of novelty of copulatory behavior: The Coolidge effect and related phenomena. *Psychological Bulletin, 89*(3), 464–482.

Diamond, J., & Bellwood, P. (2003). Farmers and their languages: The first expansions. *Science, 300*(5619), 597–603.

Diamond, L. M. (2016). Sexual fluidity in males and females. *Current Sexual Health Reports, 8*, 249–256.

Diamond, L. M. (2018). *Contemporary theory in the study of intimacy, desire, and sexuality.* In N. K. Dess, J. Marecek, & L. C. Bell (Eds.), *Gender, sex, and sexualities: Psychological perspectives* (p. 271–294). Oxford University Press.

Dickens, C. (1950). *A Christmas carol in prose: Being a ghost story of Christmas.* Grabhorn Press/Ransohoffs. (Original work published 1843)

Dickerson, C. A., Thibodeau, R., Aronson, E., & Miller, D. (1992). Using cognitive dissonance to encourage water conservation. *Journal of Applied Social Psychology, 22*(11), 841–854.

Dickerson, S. S., & Kemeny, M. E. (2004). Acute stressors and cortisol responses: A theoretical integration and synthesis of laboratory research. *Psychological Bulletin, 130*(3), 355–391.

Dickerson, S. S., Mycek, P. J., & Zaldivar, F. (2008). Negative social evaluation, but not mere social presence, elicits cortisol responses to a laboratory stressor task. *Health Psychology, 27*(1), 116–121.

Dickinson, E. (1960). *The complete poems of Emily Dickinson* (T. H. Johnson, Ed.). Little, Brown. (Original work published 1864)

Dickter, C. L., & Bartholow, B. D. (2007). Racial ingroup and outgroup attention biases revealed by event-related brain potentials. *Social Cognitive and Affective Neuroscience, 2*(3), 189–198.

Diekelmann, S., & Born, J. (2010). The memory function of sleep. *Nature Reviews: Neuroscience, 11*(2), 114–126.

Diener, E., Gohm, C. L., Suh, E., & Oishi, S. (2000). Similarity of the relations between marital status and subjective well-being across cultures. *Journal of Cross-Cultural Psychology, 31*(4), 419–436.

Diener, E., Kanazawa, S., Suh, E. M., & Oishi, S. (2015). Why people are in a generally good mood. *Personality and Social Psychology Review, 19*(3), 235–256.

Diener, E., Suh, E. M., Lucas, R. E., & Smith, H. L. (1999). Subjective well-being: Three decades of progress. *Psychological Bulletin, 125*(2), 276–302.

Diener, E., & Wallbom, M. (1976). Effects of self-awareness on antinormative behavior. *Journal of Research in Personality, 10*(1), 107–111.

Diener, E., Wolsic, B., & Fujita, F. (1995). Physical attractiveness and subjective well-being. *Journal of Personality and Social Psychology, 69*(1), 120–129.

Dienstbier, R. A., Kahle, L. R., Willis, K. A., & Tunnell, G. B. (1980). The impact of moral theories on cheating. *Motivation and Emotion, 4*(3), 193–216.

Dion, K., Berscheid, E., & Walster, E. (1972). What is beautiful is good. *Journal of Personality and Social Psychology, 24*(3), 285–290.

Dion, K. K., & Berscheid, E. (1974). Physical attractiveness and peer perception among children. *Sociometry, 37*(1), 1–12.

Dion, K. K., & Dion, K. L. (1996). Cultural perspectives on romantic love. *Personal Relationships, 3*(1), 5–17.

Dishion, T. J., Patterson, G. R., & Griesler, P. C. (1994). Peer adaptations in the development of antisocial behavior: A confluence model. In L. R. Huesmann (Ed.), *Aggressive behavior: Current perspectives* (pp. 61–95). Plenum Press.

Dixon, T. L. (2008a). Crime news and racialized beliefs: Understanding the relationship between local news viewing and perceptions of African Americans and crime. *Journal of Communication, 58*(1), 106–125.

Dixon, T. L. (2008b). Network news and racial beliefs: Exploring the connection between national television news exposure and stereotypical perceptions of African Americans. *Journal of Communication, 58*(2), 321–337.

Dixon, T. L., & Linz, D. (2000). Overrepresentation and underrepresentation of African Americans and Latinos as lawbreakers on television news. *Journal of Communication, 50*(2), 131–154.

Dodge, K. A. (1980). Social cognition and children's aggressive behavior. *Child Development, 51*(1), 162–170.

Dodge, K. A. (1983). Behavioral antecedents of peer social status. *Child Development, 54*(6), 1386–1399.

Dodge, K. A., Bates, J. E., & Pettit, G. S. (1990). Mechanisms in the cycle of violence. *Science, 250*(4988), 1678–1683.

Dodge, K. A., & Coie, J. D. (1987). Social-information-processing factors in reactive and proactive aggression in children's peer groups. *Journal of Personality and Social Psychology, 53*(6), 1146–1158.

Dodge, K. A., Price, J. M., Bachorowski, J. A., & Newman, J. P. (1990). Hostile attributional biases in severely aggressive adolescents. *Journal of Abnormal Psychology, 99*(4), 385–392.

Dodson, C. S., Darragh, J., & Williams, A. (2008). Stereotypes and retrieval provoked illusory source recollections. *Journal of Experimental Psychology: Learning, Memory, and Cognition, 34*(3), 460–477.

Dolinński, D., Grzyb, T., Folwarczny, M., Grzybała, P., Krzyszycha, K., Martynowska, K., & Trojanowski, J. (2017). Would you deliver an electric shock in 2015? Obedience in the experimental paradigm developed by Stanley Milgram in the 50 years following the original studies. *Social Psychological and Personality Science, 8*(8), 927–933.

Dollard, J., Miller, N. E., Doob, L. W., Mowrer, O. H., & Sears, R. R. (1939). *Frustration and aggression.* Yale University Press.

Donnelly, G. E., Zatz, L. Y., Svirsky, D., & John, L. K. (2018). The effect of graphic warnings on sugary-drink purchasing. *Psychological Science, 29*(8), 1321–1333.

Donnerstein, E. (2011). The media and aggression: From TV to the Internet. In J. P. Forgas & A. W. Kruglanski (Eds.), *The psychology of social conflict and aggression* (pp. 267–284). Psychology Press.

Donnerstein, E., Linz, D., & Penrod, S. (1987). *The question of pornography: Research findings and policy implications.* Free Press.

Doré, B. P., Zerubavel, N., & Ochsner, K. N. (2015). Social cognitive neuroscience: A review of core systems. In M. Mikulincer, P. R. Shaver, E. Borgida, J. A. Bargh. *APA handbook of personality and social psychology,* Vol 1: Attitudes and social cognition. American Psychological Association.

Dorfman, H. M., Bhui, R., Hughes, B. L., & Gershman, S. J. (2019). Causal inference about good and bad outcomes. *Psychological Science*, 30(4), 516–525.

Dove. (2007). Evolution [TV commercial]. Ogilvy & Mather.

Dovidio, J. F., Brigham, J. C., Johnson, B. T., & Gaertner, S. L. (1996). Stereotyping, prejudice, and discrimination: Another look. In C. N. Macrae, C. Stangor, & M. Hewstone (Eds.), *Stereotypes and stereotyping* (pp. 276–322). Guilford Press.

Dovidio, J. F., Kawakami, K., & Beach, K. (2001). Implicit and explicit attitudes: Examination of the relationship between measures of intergroup bias. In R. Brown & S. L. Gaertner (Eds.), *Blackwell handbook of social psychology* (Vol. 4, pp. 175–197). Blackwell.

Dovidio, J. F., Kawakami, K., & Gaertner, S. L. (2002). Implicit and explicit prejudice and interracial interaction. *Journal of Personality and Social Psychology*, 82(1), 62–68.

Dovidio, J. F., ten Vergert, M., Stewart, T. L., Gaertner, S. L., Johnson, J. D., Esses, V. M., Riek, B. M., & Pearson, A. R. (2004). Perspective and prejudice: Antecedents and mediating mechanisms. *Personality and Social Psychology Bulletin*, 30(12), 1537–1549.

Doyle, R. A., & Voyer, D. (2016). Stereotype manipulation effects on math and spatial test performance: A meta-analysis. *Learning and Individual Differences*, 47, 103–116.

Drabman, R. S., & Thomas, M. H. (1974). Does media violence increase children's toleration of real-life aggression? *Developmental Psychology*, 10(3), 418–421.

Drachman, D., DeCarufel, A., & Insko, C. A. (1978). The extra credit effect in interpersonal attraction. *Journal of Experimental Social Psychology*, 14(5), 458–465.

Draganich, C., & Erdal, K. (2014). Placebo sleep affects cognitive functioning. *Journal of Experimental Psychology: Learning, Memory, and Cognition*, 40(3), 857–864.

Drigotas, S. M., & Rusbult, C. E. (1992). Should I stay or should I go? A dependence model of breakups. *Journal of Personality and Social Psychology*, 62(1), 62–87.

Drigotas, S. M., Rusbult, C. E., Wieselquist, J., & Whitton, S. W. (1999). Close partner as sculptor of the ideal self: Behavioral affirmation and the Michelangelo phenomenon. *Journal of Personality and Social Psychology*, 77(2), 293–323.

Drigotas, S. M., Whitney, G. A., & Rusbult, C. E. (1995). On the peculiarities of loyalty: A diary study of responses to dissatisfaction in everyday life. *Personality and Social Psychology Bulletin*, 21(6), 596–609.

Driscoll, R., Davis, K. E., & Lipetz, M. E. (1972). Parental interference and romantic love: The Romeo and Juliet effect. *Journal of Personality and Social Psychology*, 24(1), 1–10.

Dryer, D. C., & Horowitz, L. M. (1997). When do opposites attract? Interpersonal complementarity versus similarity. *Journal of Personality and Social Psychology*, 72(3), 592–603.

D'Silva, K., & Duggan, C. (2010). Revisiting the overcontrolled–undercontrolled typology of violent offenders. *Personality and Mental Health*, 4(3), 193–205.

Du, H., & Chi, P. (2016). War, worries, and religiousness. *Social Psychological and Personality Science*, 7(5), 444–451.

Duarte, J., Crawford, J., Stern, C., Haidt, J., Jussim, L., & Tetlock, P. (2015). Political diversity will improve social psychological science. *Behavioral and Brain Sciences*, 38, E130.

Dubois, D., Rucker, D. D., & Galinsky, A. D. (2015). Social class, power, and selfishness: When and why upper and lower class individuals behave unethically. *Journal of Personality and Social Psychology*, 108(3), 436–449.

Ducharme, J. K., & Kollar, M. M. (2012). Does the "marriage benefit" extend to same-sex union? Evidence from a sample of married lesbian couples in Massachusetts. *Journal of Homosexuality*, 59(4), 580–591.

Duckitt, J. (2006). Differential effects of right wing authoritarianism and social dominance orientation on outgroup attitudes and their mediation by threat from and competitiveness to outgroups. *Personality and Social Psychology Bulletin*, 32(5), 684–696.

Duckitt, J., & Sibley, C. G. (2007). Right wing authoritarianism, social dominance orientation and the dimensions of generalized prejudice. *European Journal of Personality*, 21(2), 113–130.

Duckworth, A. L., Gendler, T. S., & Gross, J. J. (2016). Situational strategies for self-control. *Perspectives on Psychological Science*, 11(1), 35–55.

Duffy, S. M., & Rusbult, C. E. (1986). Satisfaction and commitment in homosexual and heterosexual relationships. *Journal of Homosexuality*, 12(2), 1–23.

Duffy, S., & Verges, M. (2009). It matters a hole lot: Perceptual affordances of waste containers influencing recycling compliance. *Environment and Behavior*, 41(5), 741–749.

Duncan, B. L. (1976). Differential social perception and attribution of intergroup violence: Testing the lower limits of stereotyping of Blacks. *Journal of Personality and Social Psychology*, 34(4), 590–598.

Duncker, K. (1945). On problem-solving (L. S. Lees, Trans.). *Psychological Monographs*, 58(5), i–113.

Dunfield, K. A., & Kuhlmeier, V. A. (2010). Intention-mediated selective helping in infancy. *Psychological Science*, 21(4), 523–527.

Dunn, E. W., Aknin, L. B., & Norton, M. I. (2008). Spending money on others promotes happiness. *Science*, 319(5870), 1687–1688.

Dunn, E. W., Wilson, T. D., & Gilbert D. T. (2003). Location, location, location: The misprediction of satisfaction in housing lotteries. *Personality and Social Psychology Bulletin*, 29, 1421–1432.

Dunn, L., White, K., & Dahl, D. W. (in press). A little piece of me: When mortality reminders lead to giving to others. *Journal of Consumer Research*.

Dunning, D., Johnson, K., Ehrlinger, J., & Kruger, J. (2003). Why people fail to recognize their own incompetence. *Current Directions in Psychological Science*, 12(3), 83–87.

Dunning, D., & Sherman, D. A. (1997). Stereotypes and tacit inference. *Journal of Personality and Social Psychology*, 73(3), 459–471.

Dupree, C. H., & Fiske, S. T. (2019). Self-presentation in interracial settings: The competence downshift by White liberals. *Journal of Personality and Social Psychology*, 117(3), 579–604.

Dush, C. M. K., Cohan, C. L., & Amato, P. R. (2003). The relationship between cohabitation and marital quality and stability: Change across cohorts? *Journal of Marriage and Family*, 65(3), 539–549.

Dutcher, J. M., Creswell, J. D., Pacilio, L. E., Harris, P. R., Klein, W. P., Levine, J. M., Bower, J., Muscatell, K., & Eisenberger, N. I. (2016). Self-affirmation activates the ventral striatum: A possible reward-related mechanism for self-affirmation. *Psychological Science*, 27(4), 455–466.

Du Toit, L., & Duckitt, J. (1990). Psychological characteristics of over and undercontrolled violent offenders. *Journal of Psychology*, 124(2), 125–141.

Dutton, D. G. (1998). *The abusive personality: Violence and control in intimate relationships*. Guilford Press.

Dutton, D. G. (2002). Personality dynamics of intimate abusiveness. *Journal of Psychiatric Practice*, 8(4), 216–228.

Dutton, D. G., & Aron, A. P. (1974). Some evidence for heightened sexual attraction under conditions of high anxiety. *Journal of Personality and Social Psychology*, 30(4), 510–517.

Dutton, D. G., & Lennox, V. L. (1974). Effect of prior "token" compliance on subsequent interracial behavior. *Journal of Personality and Social Psychology*, 29(1), 65–71.

Duval, S., & Wicklund, R. A. (1972). *A theory of objective self awareness*. Academic Press.

Dweck, C. S. (1975). The role of expectations and attributions in the alleviation of learned helplessness. *Journal of Personality and Social Psychology*, 31(4), 674–685.

Dweck, C. S. (2012). Implicit theories. In P. A. M. Van Lange, A. W. Kruglanski, & E. T. Higgins (Eds.), *Handbook of theories in social psychology* (Vol. 2, pp. 43–61). Sage.

Dweck, C. S., Davidson, W., Nelson, S., & Enna, B. (1978). Sex differences in learned helplessness: II. The contingencies of evaluative feedback in the classroom and III. An experimental analysis. *Developmental Psychology*, 14(3), 268–276.

Dwyer, R. J., Kushlev, K., & Dunn, E. W. (2018). Smartphone use undermines enjoyment of face-to-face interactions. *Journal of Experimental Social Psychology*, 78, 233–239.

Dyrenforth, P. S., Kashy, D. A., Donnellan, M. B., & Lucas, R. E. (2010). Predicting relationship and life satisfaction from personality in nationally representative samples from three countries: The relative importance of actor, partner, and similarity effects. *Journal of Personality and Social Psychology*, 99(4), 690–702.

Eagly, A. H. (1974). Comprehensibility of persuasive arguments as a determinant of opinion change. *Journal of Personality and Social Psychology*, 29(6), 758–773.

Eagly, A. H. (1987). *Sex differences in social behavior: A social role interpretation*. Erlbaum.

Eagly, A. H., Ashmore, R. D., Makhijani, M. G., & Longo, L. C. (1991). What is beautiful is good, but . . . : A meta-analytic review of research on the physical attractiveness stereotype. *Psychological Bulletin*, 110(1), 109–128.

Eagly, A. H., & Carli, L. L. (1981). Sex of researchers and sex-typed communications as determinants of sex differences in influenceability: A meta-analysis of social influence studies. *Psychological Bulletin*, 90(1), 1–20.

Eagly, A. H., & Carli, L. L. (2007). *Through the labyrinth: The truth about how women become leaders*. Harvard Business School Press.

Eagly, A. H., & Crowley, M. (1986). Gender and helping behavior: A metaanalytic review of the social psychological literature. *Psychological Bulletin*, 100(3), 283–308.

Eagly, A. H., & Diekman, A. B. (2003). The malleability of sex differences in response to changing social roles. In L. G. Aspinwall & U. M. Staudinger (Eds.), *A psychology of human strengths: Fundamental questions and future directions for a positive psychology* (pp. 103–115). American Psychological Association.

Eagly, A. H., & Steffen, V. J. (1984). Gender stereotypes stem from the distribution of women and men into social roles. *Journal of Personality and Social Psychology, 46*(4), 735–754.

Eagly, A. H., & Steffen, V. J. (1986). Gender and aggressive behavior: A meta-analytic review of the social psychological literature. *Psychological Bulletin, 100*(3), 309–330.

Eagly, A. H., & Wood, W. (1999). The origins of sex differences in human behavior: Evolved dispositions versus social roles. *American Psychologist, 54*(6), 408–423.

Earp, B. D., Everett, J. C., Madva, E. N., & Hamlin, J. K. (2014). Out, damned spot: Can the "Macbeth Effect" be replicated? *Basic and Applied Social Psychology, 36*(1), 91–98.

Eastwick, P. W., Eagly, A. H., Finkel, E. J., & Johnson, S. E. (2011). Implicit and explicit preferences for physical attractiveness in a romantic partner: A double dissociation in predictive validity. *Journal of Personality and Social Psychology, 101*(5), 993–1011.

Eastwick, P. W., & Finkel, E. J. (2008). Sex differences in mate preferences revisited: Do people know what they initially desire in a romantic partner? *Journal of Personality and Social Psychology, 94*(2), 245–264.

Eastwick, P. W., Finkel, E. J., & Eagly, A. H. (2011). When and why do ideal partner preferences affect the process of initiating and maintaining romantic relationships? *Journal of Personality and Social Psychology, 101*(5), 1012–1032.

Eastwick, P. W., Finkel, E. J., Mochon, D., & Ariely, D. (2007). Selective versus unselective romantic desire: Not all reciprocity is created equal. *Psychological Science, 18*(4), 317–319.

Eastwick, P. W., Luchies, L. B., Finkel, E. J., & Hunt, L. L. (2014). The predictive validity of ideal partner preferences: A review and meta-analysis. *Psychological Bulletin, 140*(3), 623–665.

Eberhardt, J. L., Davies, P. G., Purdie-Vaughns, V. J., & Johnson, S. L. (2006). Looking deathworthy: Perceived stereotypicality of Black defendants predicts capital-sentencing outcomes. *Psychological Science, 17*(5), 383–386.

Eberhardt, J. L., Goff, P. A., Purdie, V. J., & Davies, P. G. (2004). Seeing Black: Race, crime, and visual processing. *Journal of Personality and Social Psychology, 87*(6), 876–893.

Edlund, J. E., Heider, J. D., Scherer, C. R., Fare, M., & Sagarin, B. J. (2006). Sex differences in jealousy in response to actual infidelity. *Evolutionary Psychology, 4*(1), 462–470.

Effron, D. A., Bryan, C. J., & Murnighan, J. K. (2015). Cheating at the end to avoid regret. *Journal of Personality and Social Psychology, 109*(3), 395–414.

Effron, D. A., Cameron, J. S., & Monin, B. (2009). Endorsing Obama licenses favoring Whites. *Journal of Experimental Social Psychology, 45*(3), 590–593.

Effron, D. A., & Knowles, E. D. (2015). Entitativity and intergroup bias: How belonging to a cohesive group allows people to express their prejudices. *Journal of Personality and Social Psychology, 108*(2), 234–253.

Efran, M. G. (1974). The effect of physical appearance on the judgment of guilt, interpersonal attraction, and severity of recommended punishment in a simulated jury task. *Journal of Research in Personality, 8*(1), 45–54.

Eggersten, C. (2016, August 5). *Shame on the MPAA.* Uproxx. https://uproxx.com/hitfix/suicide-squad-the-mpaa-and-americas-toxic-obsession-with-violence/

Ehrhart, M. G., & Klein, K. J. (2001). Predicting followers' preferences for charismatic leadership: The influence of follower values and personality. *Leadership Quarterly, 12*(2), 153–179.

Eibl-Eibesfeldt, I. (1989). *Human ethology.* Aldine de Gruyter.

Eidelman, S., & Biernat, M. (2003). Derogating black sheep: Individual or group protection? *Journal of Experimental Social Psychology, 39*(6), 602–609.

Eidelson, R. J. (1980). Interpersonal satisfaction and level of involvement: A curvilinear relationship. *Journal of Personality and Social Psychology, 39*(3), 460–470.

Einhorn, H. J., & Hogarth, R. M. (1986). Judging probable cause. *Psychological Bulletin, 99*(1), 3–19.

Eisenberg, N., Cialdini, R. B., McCreath, H., & Shell, R. (1987). Consistency based compliance: When and why do children become vulnerable? *Journal of Personality and Social Psychology, 52*(6), 1174–1181.

Eisenberg, N., Guthrie, I. K., Cumberland, A., Murphy, B. C., Shepard, S. A., Zhou, Q., & Carlo, G. (2002). Prosocial development in early adulthood: A longitudinal study. *Journal of Personality and Social Psychology, 82*(6), 993–1006.

Eisenberg, N., Miller, P. A., Schaller, M., Fabes, R. A., Fultz, J., Shell, R., & Shea, C. L. (1989). The role of sympathy and altruistic personality traits in helping: A reexamination. *Journal of Personality, 57*(1), 41–67.

Eisenberg, N., Miller, P. A., Shell, R., McNalley, S., & Shea, C. (1991). Prosocial development in adolescence: A longitudinal study. *Developmental Psychology, 27*(5), 849–857.

Eisenberg, N., & Mussen, P. H. (Eds.). (1989). *The roots of prosocial behavior in children.* Cambridge University Press.

Eisenberger, N. I., & Lieberman, M. D. (2004). Why rejection hurts: A common neural alarm system for physical and social pain. *Trends in Cognitive Sciences, 8*(7), 294–300.

Eisenberger, N. I., Lieberman, M. D., & Williams, K. D. (2003). Does rejection hurt? An fMRI study of social exclusion. *Science, 302*(5643), 290–292.

Eisenberger, R., & Armeli, S. (1997). Can salient reward increase creative performance without reducing intrinsic creative interest? *Journal of Personality and Social Psychology, 72*(3), 652–663.

Ekman, P. (1980). *The face of man: Expressions of universal emotions in a New Guinea village.* Garland STPM Press.

Ekman, P., & Cordaro, D. (2011). What is meant by calling emotions basic. *Emotion Review, 3*(4), 364–370.

Ekman, P., Friesen, W. V., & Ellsworth, P. (1972). *Emotion in the human face: Guidelines for research and an integration of findings.* Pergamon Press.

Eley, T. C., Lichtenstein, P., & Moffitt, T. E. (2003). A longitudinal behavioral genetic analysis of the etiology of aggressive and nonaggressive antisocial behavior. *Development and Psychopathology, 15*(2), 383–402.

Eliade, M. (1959). *Cosmos and history: The myth of the eternal return.* Harper.

Eliezer, D., Major, B., & Mendes, W. B. (2010). The costs of caring: Gender identification increases threat following exposure to sexism. *Journal of Experimental Social Psychology, 46*(1), 159–165.

Eliot, T. S. (1964). *T. S. Eliot: Selected poems.* Harcourt, Brace & World. (Original work published 1917)

Ellemers, N., van Knippenberg, A., De Vries, N., & Wilke, H. (1988). Social identification and permeability of group boundaries. *European Journal of Social Psychology, 18*(6), 497–513.

Elliot, A. J., & Devine, P. G. (1994). On the motivational nature of cognitive dissonance: Dissonance as psychological discomfort. *Journal of Personality and Social Psychology, 67*(3), 382–394.

Ellison, N. B., Hancock, J. T., & Toma, C. L. (2011). Profile as promise: A framework for conceptualizing veracity in online dating self-presentations. *New Media and Society, 14*(1), 45–62.

Ellison, N., Heino, R., & Gibbs, J. (2006). Managing impressions online: Self-presentation processes in the online dating environment. *Journal of Computer-Mediated Communication, 11*(2), 415–441.

Elmore, K. C., & Luna-Lucero, M. (2017). Light bulbs or seeds? How metaphors for ideas influence judgments about genius. *Social Psychological and Personality Science, 8*(2), 200–208.

Emmons, R. A., & McCullough, M. E. (2003). Counting blessings versus burdens: An experimental investigation of gratitude and subjective well-being in daily life. *Journal of Personality and Social Psychology, 84*(2), 377–389.

Emswiller, T., Deaux, K., & Willits, J. E. (1971). Similarity, sex, and requests for small favors. *Journal of Applied Social Psychology, 1*(3), 284–291.

Encyclopedia of Children's Health. (n.d.). *Gender identity.* Advameg, Inc. http://www.healthofchildren.com/G-H/GenderIdentity.html

Engelhardt, C. R., Bartholow, B. D., Kerr, G. T., & Bushman, B. J. (2011). This is your brain on violent video games: Neural desensitization to violence predicts increased aggression following violent video game exposure. *Journal of Experimental Social Psychology, 47*(5), 1033–1036.

Enquist, M., & Leimar, O. (1983). Evolution of fighting behaviour: Decision rules and assessment of relative strength. *Journal of Theoretical Biology, 102*(3), 387–410.

Eom, K., Kim, H. S., & Sherman, D. K. (2018). Social class, control, and action: Socioeconomic status differences in antecedents of support for proenvironmental action. *Journal of Experimental Social Psychology, 77*, 60–75.

Epley, N., & Dunning, D. (2000). Feeling "holier than thou": Are self-serving assessments produced by errors in self or social prediction? *Journal of Personality and Social Psychology, 79*(6), 861–875.

Epstein, R., Mayuri, P., & Mansi Thakar, M. (2013). How love emerges in arranged marriages: Two cross-cultural studies. *Journal of Comparative Family Studies, 44*(3), 341–360.

Epstein, S. (1980). The self-concept: A review and the proposal of an integrated theory of personality. In E. Staub (Ed.), *Personality: Basic issues and current research.* Prentice Hall.

Epstein, S. (1990). Cognitive–experiential self-theory. In L. Pervin (Ed.), *Handbook of personality: Theory and research* (2nd ed., pp. 165–192). Guilford Press.

Epstein, S. (1994). Integration of the cognitive and the psychodynamic unconscious. *American Psychologist, 49*(8), 709–724.

Epstude, K., & Roese, N. J. (2008). The functional theory of counterfactual thinking. *Personality and Social Psychology Review, 12*(2), 168–192.

Epton, T., Harris, P. R., Kane, R., van Koningsbruggen, G. M., & Sheeran, P. (2015). The impact of self-affirmation on health-behavior change: A meta-analysis. *Health Psychology, 34*(3), 187–196.

Erb, H. P., Hilton, D. J., Bohner, G., & Roffey, L. (2015). The minority decision— A risky choice. *Journal of Experimental Social Psychology, 57*, 43–50.

Erickson, B., Lind, E. A., Johnson, B. C., & O'Barr, W. M. (1978). Speech style and impression formation in a court setting: The effects of "powerful" and "powerless" speech. *Journal of Experimental Social Psychology, 14*(3), 266–279.

Erikson, E. H. (1959). *Identity and the life cycle.* W. W. Norton.

Erikson, E. H. (1963). *Childhood and society.* W. W. Norton.

Erikson, E. H. (1968). *Identity: Youth and crisis.* W. W. Norton.

Eron, L. D., Huesmann, L. R., & Zelli, A. (1991). The role of parental variables in the learning of aggression. In D. J. Pepler & K. H. Rubin (Eds.), *The development and treatment of childhood aggression* (pp. 169–188). Erlbaum.

ESPN.com news services. (2011, May 18). *Charles Barkley: I had gay teammates.* ESPN. http://sports.espn.go.com/nba/news/story?id=6563128

Esser, J. K., & Lindoerfer, J. S. (1989). Groupthink and the space shuttle *Challenger* accident: Toward a quantitative case analysis. *Journal of Behavioral Decision Making, 2*(3), 167–177.

Esses, V. M., Haddock, G., & Zanna, M. P. (1993). Values, stereotypes, and emotions as determinants of intergroup attitudes. In D. M. Mackie & D. L. Hamilton (Eds.), *Affect, cognition, and stereotyping: Interactive processes in group perception* (pp. 137–166). Academic Press.

Evans, A. T., Peters, E., Shoben, A. B., Meilleur, L. R., Klein, E. G., Tompkins, M. K., Romer, D., & Tusler, M. (2017). Cigarette graphic warning labels are not created equal: They can increase or decrease smokers' quit intentions relative to text-only warnings. *Nicotine & Tobacco Research, 19*(10), 1155–1162.

Evans, L. (2010, January 14). Haiti earthquake aid. *The Guardian.* http://www.theguardian.com/news/datablog/2010/jan/14/haiti-quake-aid-pledges-country-donations

Everytown for Gun Safety. (2020). *Extreme risk laws save lives.* https://everytownresearch.org/extreme-risk-laws-save-lives/

Eyal, T., & Epley, N. (2017). Exaggerating accessible differences: When gender stereotypes overestimate actual group differences. *Personality and Social Psychology Bulletin, 43*(9), 1323–1336.

Eyal, T., Steffel, M., & Epley, N. (2018). Perspective mistaking: Accurately understanding the mind of another requires getting perspective, not taking perspective. *Journal of Personality and Social Psychology, 114*(4), 547–571.

Eyink, J., Hirt, E. R., Hendrix, K. S., & Galante, E. (2017). Circadian variations in claimed self-handicapping: Exploring the strategic use of stress as an excuse. *Journal of Experimental Social Psychology, 69*, 102–110.

Fallon, A. (1990). Culture in the mirror: Sociocultural determinants of body image. In T. Cash & T. Pruzinsky (Eds.), *Body images: Development, deviance, and change* (pp. 80–109). Guilford Press.

Farber, P. D., Khavari, K. A., & Douglass, F. M. (1980). A factor analytic study of reasons for drinking: Empirical validation of positive and negative reinforcement dimensions. *Journal of Consulting and Clinical Psychology, 48*(6), 780–781.

Faulkner, J., Schaller, M., Park, J. H., & Duncan, L. A. (2004). Evolved disease-avoidance mechanisms and contemporary xenophobic attitudes. *Group Processes & Intergroup Relations, 7*(4), 333–353.

Fausset, R. (2020, May 5). 2 suspects charged with murder in Ahmaud Arbery shooting. *The New York Times.* https://www.nytimes.com/2020/05/07/us/ahmaud-arbery-shooting-arrest.html

Fazio, R. H. (1990). Multiple processes by which attitudes guide behavior: The MODE model as an integrative framework. In M. P. Zanna (Ed.), *Advances in experimental social psychology* (Vol. 23, pp. 75–109). Academic Press.

Fazio, R. H., Jackson, J. R., Dunton, B. C., & Williams, C. J. (1995). Variability in automatic activation as an unobtrusive measure of racial attitudes: A bona fide pipeline? *Journal of Personality and Social Psychology, 69*(6), 1013–1027.

Fazio, R. H., & Williams, C. J. (1986). Attitude accessibility as a moderator of the attitude-perception and attitude-behavior relations: An investigation of the 1984 presidential election. *Journal of Personality and Social Psychology, 51*(3), 505–514.

Federal Bureau of Investigation. (2009). *2008 crime in the United States.* http://www2.fbi.gov/ucr/cius2008/offenses/violent_crime/murder_homicide.html

Federal Bureau of Investigation. (2015). *Crime in the United States 2015: Expanded offense.* https://ucr.fbi.gov/crime-in-the-u.s/2015/crime-in-the-u.s.-2015/offenses-known-to-law-enforcement/expanded-offense

Federal Bureau of Investigation. (2018). *2018 crime in the United States: Expanded homicide data table 3.* https://ucr.fbi.gov/crime-in-the-u.s/2018/crime-in-the-u.s.-2018/tables/expanded-homicide-data-table-3.xls

Feeney, B. C., & Thrush, R. L. (2010). Relationship influences on exploration in adulthood: The characteristics and function of a secure base. *Journal of Personality and Social Psychology, 98*(1), 57–76.

Feeney, J. A., Noller, P., & Patty, J. (1993). Adolescents' interactions with the opposite sex: Influence of attachment style and gender. *Journal of Adolescence, 16*(2), 169–186.

Fehr, B. (1996). *Friendship processes.* Sage.

Fehr, E., & Gächter, S. (1998). Reciprocity and economics: The economic implications of *Homo Reciprocans. European Economic Review, 42*(3), 845–859.

Fein, S., & Spencer, S. J. (1997). Prejudice as self-image maintenance: Affirming the self through derogating others. *Journal of Personality and Social Psychology, 73*(1), 31–44.

Feinberg, M., & Willer, R. (2015). From gulf to bridge: When do moral arguments facilitate political influence? *Personality and Social Psychology Bulletin, 41*(12), 1665–1681.

Feingold, A. (1988). Matching for attractiveness in romantic partners and same-sex friends: A meta-analysis and theoretical critique. *Psychological Bulletin, 104*(2), 226–235.

Feingold, A. (1990). Gender differences in effects of physical attractiveness on romantic attraction: A comparison across five research paradigms. *Journal of Personality and Social Psychology, 59*(5), 981–993.

Feingold, A. (1992a). Gender differences in mate selection preferences: A test of the parental investment model. *Psychological Bulletin, 112*(1), 125–139.

Feingold, A. (1992b). Good-looking people are not what we think. *Psychological Bulletin, 111*(2), 304–341.

Feingold, A. (1994). Gender differences in personality: A meta-analysis. *Psychological Bulletin, 116*(3), 429–456.

Feldman, R. S., & Prohaska, T. (1979). The student as Pygmalion: Effect of student expectation on the teacher. *Journal of Educational Psychology, 71*(4), 485–493.

Felson, R. B. (1982). Impression management and the escalation of aggression and violence. *Social Psychology Quarterly, 45*(4), 245–254.

Felson, R. B., & Tedeschi, J. T. (Eds.). (1993). *Aggression and violence: Social interactionist perspectives.* American Psychological Association.

Fenigstein, A., Scheier, M. F., & Buss, A. H. (1975). Public and private self-consciousness: Assessment and theory. *Journal of Consulting and Clinical Psychology, 43*(4), 522–527.

Ferguson, C. J. (2015). Do angry birds make for angry children? A meta-analysis of video game influences on children's and adolescents' aggression, mental health, prosocial behavior, and academic performance. *Perspectives on Psychological Science, 10*(5), 646–666.

Ferguson, M. A., & Branscombe, N. R. (2014). The social psychology of collective guilt. In C. von Scheve & M. Salmela (Eds.), *Collective emotions: Perspectives from psychology, philosophy, and sociology.* (pp. 251–265). Oxford University Press.

Ferguson, M. J., Mann, T. C., Cone, J., & Shen, X. (2019). When and how implicit first impressions can be updated. *Current Directions in Psychological Science, 28*(4), 331–336.

Ferrer, R. A., Klein, W. M., Zajac, L. E., Land, S. R., & Ling, B. S. (2012). An affective booster moderates the effect of gain and loss-framed messages on behavioral intentions for colorectal cancer screening. *Journal of Behavioral Medicine, 35*(4), 452–461.

Ferris, C. F., Melloni, R. H., Jr., Koppel, G., Perry, K. W., Fuller, R. W., & Delville, Y. (1997). Vasopressin/serotonin interactions in the anterior hypothalamus control aggressive behavior in golden hamsters. *Journal of Neuroscience, 17*(11), 4331–4340.

Festinger, L. (1954). A theory of social comparison processes. *Human Relations, 7*(2), 117–140.

Festinger, L. (1957). *A theory of cognitive dissonance.* Stanford University Press.

Festinger, L., & Carlsmith, J. M. (1959). Cognitive consequences of forced compliance. *Journal of Abnormal and Social Psychology, 58*(2), 203–210.

Festinger, L., Schachter, S., & Back, K. (1950). *Social pressures in informal groups: A study of human factors in housing.* Harper.

Fiedler, F. E. (1967). *A theory of leadership effectiveness.* McGraw Hill.

Finkel, E. J., Cheung, E. O., Emery, L. F., Carswell, K. L., & Larson, G. M. (2015). The suffocation model: Why marriage in America is becoming an all-or-nothing institution. *Current Directions in Psychological Science, 24*(3), 238–244.

Finkel, E. J., DeWall, C. N., Slotter, E. B., Oaten, M., & Foshee, V. A. (2009). Self-regulatory failure and intimate partner violence perpetration. *Journal of Personality and Social Psychology, 97*(3), 483–499.

Finkel, E. J., Eastwick, P. W., Karney, B. R., Reis, H. T., & Sprecher, S. (2012a). Dating in a digital world. *Scientific American Mind, 23*, 26–33.

Finkel, E. J., Eastwick, P. W., Karney, B. R., Reis, H. T., & Sprecher, S. (2012b). Online dating: A critical analysis from the perspective of psychological science. *Psychological Science in the Public Interest, 13*(1), 3–66.

Finkel, E. J., Eastwick, P. W., & Reis, H. T. (2015). Best research practices in psychology: Illustrating epistemological and pragmatic considerations with the case of relationship science. *Journal of Personality and Social Psychology, 108*(2), 275–297.

Finkel, E. J., Hui, C. M., Carswell, K. L., & Larson, G. M. (2014). The suffocation of marriage: Climbing Mount Maslow without enough oxygen. *Psychological Inquiry, 25*, 1–41.

Finkel, E. J., Rusbult, C. E., Kumashiro, M., & Hannon, P. A. (2002). Dealing with betrayal in close relationships: Does commitment promote forgiveness? *Journal of Personality and Social Psychology, 82*(6), 956–974.

Finkel, E. J., Slotter, E. B., Luchies, L. B., Walton, G. M., & Gross, J. J. (2013). A brief intervention to promote conflict reappraisal preserves marital quality over time. *Psychological Science, 24*(8), 1595–1601.

Fiorito, G., & Scotto, P. (1992). Observational learning in *Octopus vulgaris. Science, 256*(5056), 545–547.

Fischer, P., Krueger, J. I., Greitemeyer, T., Vogrincic, C., Kastenmüller, A., Frey, D., Heene, M., Wicher, M., & Kainbacher, M. (2011). The bystander-effect: A meta-analytic review on bystander intervention in dangerous and non-dangerous emergencies. *Psychological Bulletin, 137*(4), 517–537.

Fishbein, M., & Ajzen, I. (1975). *Belief, attitude, intention, and behavior: An introduction to theory and research.* Addison-Wesley.

Fisher, H. (1995). The nature and evolution of romantic love. In W. Jankowiak (Ed.), *Romantic passion: A universal experience?* (pp. 23–41). Columbia University Press.

Fisher, H. (2004). *Why we love: The nature and chemistry of romantic love.* Henry Holt.

Fisher, H. (2006). The drive to love: The neural mechanism for mate selection. In R. J. Sternberg & K. Weis (Eds.), *The new psychology of love* (pp. 87–115). Yale University Press.

Fishman, C. G. (1965). Need for approval and the expression of aggression under varying conditions of frustration. *Journal of Personality and Social Psychology, 2*(6), 809–816.

Fiske, A. P. (1990). Relativity within Moose ("Mossi") culture: Four incommensurable models for social relationships. *Ethos, 18*(2), 180–204.

Fiske, A. P. (1991). *Structures of social life: The four elementary forms of human relations: Communal sharing, authority ranking, equality matching, market pricing.* Free Press.

Fiske, S. T. (1998). Stereotyping, prejudice, and discrimination. In D. T. Gilbert, S. T. Fiske, & G. Lindzey (Eds.), *The handbook of social psychology* (4th ed., Vol. 2, pp. 357–411). McGraw-Hill.

Fiske, S. T., Cuddy, A. J., Glick, P., & Xu, J. (2002). A model of (often mixed) stereotype content: Competence and warmth respectively follow from perceived status and competition. *Journal of Personality and Social Psychology, 82*(6), 878–902.

Fiske, S. T., & Neuberg, S. L. (1990). A continuum model of impression formation, from category based to individuating processes: Influence of information and motivation on attention and interpretation. In M. P. Zanna (Ed.), *Advances in experimental social psychology* (Vol. 23, pp. 1–74). Academic Press.

Fiske, S. T., & Taylor, S. E. (2008). *Social cognition: From brains to culture.* McGraw-Hill.

Fitz, D. (1976). A renewed look at Miller's conflict theory of aggression displacement. *Journal of Personality and Social Psychology, 33*(6), 725–732.

Fitzsimons, G. M., & Bargh, J. A. (2003). Thinking of you: Nonconscious pursuit of interpersonal goals associated with relationship partners. *Journal of Personality and Social Psychology, 84*(1), 148–164.

Fitzsimons, G. M., & Finkel, E. J. (2018). Transactive-goal-dynamics theory: A discipline-wide perspective. *Current Directions in Psychological Science, 27*(5), 332–338.

Fitzsimons, G. M., & Kay, A. C. (2004). Language and interpersonal cognition: Causal effects of variations in pronoun usage on perceptions of closeness. *Personality and Social Psychology Bulletin, 30*(5), 547–557.

Fleischman, J. (2002). *Phineas Gage: A gruesome but true story about brain science.* Houghton Mifflin.

Fleming, J. H., Darley, J. M., Hilton, J. L., & Kojetin, B. A. (1990). Multiple audience problem: A strategic communication perspective on social perception. *Journal of Personality and Social Psychology, 58*(4), 593–609.

Fleming, J. H., & Rudman, L. A. (1993). Between a rock and a hard place: Self-concept regulating and communicative properties of distancing behaviors. *Journal of Personality and Social Psychology, 64*(1), 44–59.

Fletcher, G. J., Simpson, J. A., & Thomas, G. (2000). Ideals, perceptions, and evaluations in early relationship development. *Journal of Personality and Social Psychology, 79*(6), 933–940.

Flore, P. C., & Wicherts, J. M. (2015). Does stereotype threat influence performance of girls in stereotyped domains? A meta-analysis. *Journal of School Psychology, 53*(1), 25–44.

Florence and the Machine. (2009). Kiss with a fist [Song]. On *Lungs.* Universal International.

Flores, A. J., Chavez, T. A., Bolger, N., & Casad, B. J. (2019). Cardiovascular and self-regulatory consequences of SES-based social identity threat. *Personality and Social Psychology Bulletin, 45*(5), 700–714.

Florian, V., & Mikulincer, M. (1998). Symbolic immortality and the management of the terror of death: The moderating role of attachment style. *Journal of Personality and Social Psychology, 74*(3), 725–734.

Focella, E. S., Bean, M. G., & Stone, J. (2015). Confrontation and beyond: Examining a stigmatized target's use of a prejudice reduction strategy. *Social and Personality Psychology Compass, 9*(2), 100–114.

Fogelman, E., & Wiener, V. L. (1985). The few, the brave, the noble. *Psychology Today, 19*(8), 60–65.

Fogg, B. J., & Nass, C. (1997). Silicon sycophants: The effects of computers that flatter. *International Journal of Human-Computer Studies, 46*(5), 551–561.

Fointiat, V. (2004). "I know what I have to do, but . . ." When hypocrisy leads to behavioral change. *Social Behavior and Personality, 32*(8), 741–746.

Follenfant, A., & Ric, F. (2010). Behavioral rebound following stereotype suppression. *European Journal of Social Psychology, 40*(5), 774–782.

Forbes, C. E., Amey, R., Magerman, A. B., Duran, K., & Liu, M. (2018). Stereotype-based stressors facilitate emotional memory neural network connectivity and encoding of negative information to degrade math self-perceptions among women. *Social Cognitive and Affective Neuroscience, 13*(7), 719–740.

Forbes, C. E., Cox, C. L., Schmader, T., & Ryan, L. (2012). Negative stereotype activation alters interaction between neural correlates of arousal, inhibition, and cognitive control. *Social Cognitive and Affective Neuroscience, 7*(7), 771–781.

Forbes, C. E., & Leitner, J. B. (2014). Stereotype threat engenders neural attentional bias toward negative feedback to undermine performance. *Biological Psychology, 102*, 98–107.

Forbes, C. E., & Schmader, T. (2010). Retraining attitudes and stereotypes to affect motivation and cognitive capacity under stereotype threat. *Journal of Personality and Social Psychology, 99*(5), 740–754.

Forbes, G., Zhang, X., Doroszewicz, K., & Haas, K. (2009). Relationships between individualism–collectivism, gender, and direct or indirect aggression: A study in China, Poland, and the US. *Aggressive Behavior, 35*(1), 24–30.

Ford, B. Q., Feinberg, M., Lam, P., Mauss, I. B., & John, O. P. (2019). Using reappraisal to regulate negative emotion after the 2016 U.S. Presidential election: Does emotion regulation trump political action? *Journal of Personality and Social Psychology, 117*(5), 998–1015.

Ford, B. Q., & Gross, J. J. (2019). Why beliefs about emotion matter: An emotion-regulation perspective. *Current Directions in Psychological Science, 28*(1), 74–81.

Ford, C. S., & Beach, F. A. (1951). *Patterns of sexual behavior.* Harper & Row.

Fordham, S., & Ogbu, J. U. (1986). Black students' school success: Coping with the "burden of 'acting White.'" *Urban Review, 18*(3), 176–206.

Forgas, J. P. (1995). Mood and judgment: The affect infusion model (AIM). *Psychological Bulletin, 117*(1), 39–66.

Forgas, J. P. (1998). On feeling good and getting your way: Mood effects on negotiator cognition and bargaining strategies. *Journal of Personality and Social Psychology, 74*(3), 565–577.

Forgas, J. P., Laham, S. M., & Vargas, P. T. (2005). Mood effects on eye-witness memory: Affective influences on susceptibility to misinformation. *Journal of Experimental Social Psychology, 41*, 574–588.

Forscher, P. S., Cox, W. T., Graetz, N., & Devine, P. G. (2015). The motivation to express prejudice. *Journal of Personality and Social Psychology, 109*(5), 791–812.

Forscher, P. S., Lai, C. K., Axt, J. R., Ebersole, C. R., Herman, M., Devine, P. G., & Nosek, B. A. (2019). A meta-analysis of procedures to change implicit measures. *Journal of Personality and Social Psychology, 117*(3), 522–559.

Foster, C. A., Witcher, B. S., Campbell, W. K., & Green, J. D. (1998). Arousal and attraction: Evidence for automatic and controlled processes. *Journal of Personality and Social Psychology, 74*(1), 86–101.

Frable, D. E., Blackstone, T., & Scherbaum, C. (1990). Marginal and mindful: Deviants in social interactions. *Journal of Personality and Social Psychology, 59*(1), 140–149.

Fraley, R. C. (2002). Attachment stability from infancy to adulthood: Metaanalysis and dynamic modeling of developmental mechanisms. *Personality and Social Psychology Review, 6*(2), 123–151.

Franiuk, R., Cohen, D., & Pomerantz, E. M. (2002). Implicit theories of relationships: Implications for relationship satisfaction and longevity. *Personal Relationships, 9*(4), 345–367.

Franiuk, R., Pomerantz, E. M., & Cohen, D. (2004). The causal role of theories of relationships: Consequences for satisfaction and cognitive strategies. *Personality and Social Psychology Bulletin, 30*(11), 1494–1507.

Frantz, C. M., Cuddy, A. J., Burnett, M., Ray, H., & Hart, A. (2004). A threat in the computer: The race Implicit Association Test as a stereotype threat experience. *Personality and Social Psychology Bulletin, 30*(12), 1611–1624.

Frawley, T. J. (2008). Gender schema and prejudicial recall: How children misremember, fabricate, and distort gendered picture book information. *Journal of Research in Childhood Education, 22*(3), 291–303.

Fredman, L. A., Buhrmester, M. D., Gomez, A., Fraser, W. T., Talaifar, S., Brannon, S., & Swann, W. B. (2015). Identity fusion, extreme pro-group behavior, and the path to defusion. *Social and Personality Psychology Compass, 9*(9), 468–480.

Fredrickson, B. L. (2001). The role of positive emotions in positive psychology: The broaden-and-build theory of positive emotions. *American Psychologist, 56*(3), 218–226.

Fredrickson, B. L., & Branigan, C. (2005). Positive emotions broaden the scope of attention and thought-action repertoires. *Cognition & Emotion, 19*(3), 313–332.

Fredrickson, B. L., & Roberts, T.-A. (1997). Objectification theory. *Psychology of Women Quarterly, 21*(2), 173–206.

Fredrickson, B. L., Roberts, T.-A., Noll, S. M., Quinn, D. M., & Twenge, J. M. (1998). That swimsuit becomes you: Sex differences in self-objectification, restrained eating, and math performance. *Journal of Personality and Social Psychology, 75*(1), 269–284.

Frehse, R. (2020, January 7). *Anti-Semitic hate crimes rise in 2019, overall crime at record low, NYPD says.* CNN. https://www.cnn.com/2020/01/07/us/newyork-crime-stats-anti-semitic-hate-crimes/index.html

Freedman, J. L. (1965). Long-term behavioral effects of cognitive dissonance. *Journal of Experimental Social Psychology, 1*(2), 145–155.

Freedman, J. L., & Fraser, S. C. (1966). Compliance without pressure: The foot-in-the-door technique. *Journal of Personality and Social Psychology, 4*(2), 195–202.

Freeman, J. B., & Johnson, K. L. (2016). More than meets the eye: Split-second social perception. *Trends in Cognitive Sciences, 20*(5), 362–374.

French, J., & Raven, B. H. (1959). The bases of social power. In D. Cartwright (Ed.), *Studies in social power* (pp. 150–167). Institute for Social Research.

French, J. F., Altgelt, F. F., & Meltzer, A. L. (2019). The implications of socio-sexuality for marital satisfaction and dissolution. *Psychological Science, 30*, 1460–1472.

Freud, S. (1950). *Totem and taboo* (J. Strachey, Trans.). Routledge. (Original work published 1913)

Freud, S. (1955). *Group psychology and the analysis of the ego.* In J. Strachey (Ed. and Trans.), *The standard edition of the complete psychological works of Sigmund Freud* (Vol. 18, pp. 67–143). Hogarth Press. (Original work published 1921)

Freud, S. (1958). *The dynamics of transference.* In J. Strachey (Ed. and Trans.), *The standard edition of the complete psychological works of Sigmund Freud* (Vol. 12, pp. 97–108). Hogarth Press. (Original work published 1912)

Freud, S. (1961). *Beyond the pleasure principle* (J. Strachey, Ed. & Trans.). W. W. Norton. (Original work published 1920)

Frey, D. (1982). Different levels of cognitive dissonance, information seeking, and information avoidance. *Journal of Personality and Social Psychology, 43*(6), 1175–1183.

Friedman, R. S., McCarthy, D. M., Bartholow, B. D., & Hicks, J. A. (2007). Interactive effects of alcohol outcome expectancies and alcohol cues on nonconsumptive behavior. *Experimental and Clinical Psychopharmacology, 15*(1), 102–114.

Fries, A., & Frey, D. (1980). Misattribution of arousal and the effects of self-threatening information. *Journal of Experimental Social Psychology, 16*(5), 405–416.

Friese, M., Loschelder, D. D., Gieseler, K., Frankenbach, J., & Inzlicht, M. (2019). Is ego depletion real? An analysis of arguments. *Personality and Social Psychology Review, 23*(2), 107–131.

Frieze, I. H., Olson, J. E., & Russell, J. (1991). Attractiveness and income for men and women in management. *Journal of Applied Social Psychology, 21*(13), 1039–1057.

Frimer, J. A., Brandt, M. J., Melton, Z., & Motyl, M. (2019). Extremists on the left and right use angry, negative language. *Personality and Social Psychology Bulletin, 45*(8), 1216–1231.

Frith, C. D., & Frith, U. (1999). Interacting minds—A biological basis. *Science, 286*(5445), 1692–1695.

Fritsche, I., Barth, M., Jugert, P., Masson, T., & Reese, G. (2018). A social identity model of pro-environmental action (SIMPEA). *Psychological Review, 125*(2), 245–269.

Fritsche, I., Jonas, E., Fischer, P., Koranyi, N., Berger, N., & Fleischmann, B. (2007). Mortality salience and the desire for offspring. *Journal of Experimental Social Psychology, 43*(5), 753–762.

Fryar, C. D., Hirsch, R., Porter, K. S., Kottiri, B., Brody, D. J., & Louis, T. (2007, June 28). *Drug use and sexual behaviors reported by adults: United States, 1999–2002.* Centers for Disease Control and Prevention. http://www.cdc.gov/nchs/data/ad/ad384.pdf

Fryberg, S. A., Markus, H. R., Oyserman, D., & Stone, J. M. (2008). Of warrior chiefs and Indian princesses: The psychological consequences of American Indian mascots. *Basic and Applied Social Psychology, 30*(3), 208–218.

Fryberg, S. A., & Eason, A. E. (2017). Making the invisible visible: Acts of commission and omission. *Current Directions in Psychological Science, 26*(6), 554–559. https://doi.org/10.1177/0963721417720959

Fuglestad, P. T., Rothman, A. J., & Jeffery, R. W. (2008). Getting there and hanging on: The effect of regulatory focus on performance in smoking and weight loss interventions. *Health Psychology, 27*(3S), S260–S270.

Furnham, A., & Bochner, S. (1986). *Culture shock: Psychological reactions to unfamiliar environments.* Methuen.

Furnham, A., & Gunter, B. (1984). Just world beliefs and attitudes towards the poor. *British Journal of Social Psychology, 23*(3), 265–269.

Furnham, A., Petrides, K. V., & Constantinides, A. (2005). The effects of body mass index and waist-to-hip ratio on ratings of female attractiveness, fecundity, and health. *Personality and Individual Differences, 38*(8), 1823–1834.

Gable, S. L., Hopper, E. A., & Schooler, J. W. (2019). When the muses strike: Creative ideas of physicists and writers routinely occur during mind wandering. *Psychological Science, 30*(3), 396–404.

Gable, S. L., Reis, H. T., Impett, E. A., & Asher, E. R. (2004). What do you do when things go right? The intrapersonal and interpersonal benefits of sharing positive events. *Journal of Personality and Social Psychology, 87*(2), 228–245.

Gaertner, S. L., & Dovidio, J. F. (1977). The subtlety of White racism, arousal, and helping behavior. *Journal of Personality and Social Psychology, 35*(10), 691–707.

Gaertner, S. L., & Dovidio, J. F. (1986). The aversive form of racism. In J. F. Dovidio & S. L. Gaertner (Eds.), *Prejudice, discrimination, and racism.* Academic Press.

Gaertner, S. L., & Dovidio, J. F. (2000). *Reducing intergroup bias: The common ingroup identity model.* Psychology Press.

Gagné, F. M., & Lydon, J. E. (2004). Bias and accuracy in close relationships: An integrative review. *Personality and Social Psychology Review, 8*(4), 322–338.

Gagné, M., & Deci, E. L. (2005). Self-determination theory and work motivation. *Journal of Organizational Behavior, 26*(4), 331–362.

Gailliot, M. T., Stillman, T. F., Schmeichel, B. J., Maner, J. K., & Plant, E. A. (2008). Mortality salience increases adherence to salient norms and values. *Personality and Social Psychology Bulletin, 34*(7), 993–1003.

Gaither, S. E. (2015). "Mixed" results: Multiracial research and identity explorations. *Current Directions in Psychological Science, 24*(2), 114–119.

Galdi, S., Arcuri, L., & Gawronski, B. (2008). Automatic mental associations predict future choices of undecided decision-makers. *Science, 321*(5892), 1100–1102.

Galinsky, A. D., Magee, J. C., Inesi, M. E., & Gruenfeld, D. H. (2006). Power and perspectives not taken. *Psychological Science, 17*(12), 1068–1074.

Galinsky, A. D., & Moskowitz, G. B. (2000). Perspective-taking: Decreasing stereotype expression, stereotype accessibility, and in-group favoritism. *Journal of Personality and Social Psychology, 78*(4), 708–724.

Gallant, S., Williams, L., Fisher, M., & Cox, A. (2011). Mating strategies and self-presentation in online personal advertisement photographs. *Journal of Social, Evolutionary, and Cultural Psychology, 5*(1), 106–121.

Gallup. (2018). *U.S. media trust continues to recover from 2016 low.* https://news.gallup.com/poll/243665/media-trust-continues-recover-2016-low.aspx

Gallup Center for Muslim Studies. (2010, January 21). *In U.S., religious prejudice stronger against Muslims.* www.gallup.com/poll/125312/religious-prejudice-stronger-against-muslims.aspx

Gan, M., & Chen, S. (2017). Being your actual or ideal self? What it means to feel authentic in a relationship. *Personality and Social Psychology Bulletin, 43*(4), 465–478.

Gan, M., Heller, D., & Chen, S. (2018). The power in being yourself: Feeling authentic enhances the sense of power. *Personality and Social Psychology Bulletin, 44*(10), 1460–1472.

Gangestad, S. W. (1993). Sexual selection and physical attractiveness. *Human Nature, 4*(3), 205–235.

Gangestad, S. W., Garver-Apgar, C. E., Simpson, J. A., & Cousins, A. J. (2007). Changes in women's mate preferences across the ovulatory cycle. *Journal of Personality and Social Psychology, 92*(1), 151–163.

Gangestad, S. W., & Simpson, J. A. (1990). Toward an evolutionary history of female sociosexual variation. *Journal of Personality, 58*(1), 69–96.

Gangestad, S. W., & Simpson, J. A. (2000). The evolution of human mating: Tradeoffs and strategic pluralism. *Behavioral and Brain Sciences, 23*(4), 573–644.

Gangestad, S. W., Simpson, J. A., Cousins, A. J., Garver-Apgar, C. E., & Christensen, P. N. (2004). Women's preferences for male behavioral displays change across the menstrual cycle. *Psychological Science, 15*(3), 203–206.

Gannon, T. A., Keown, K., & Polaschek, D. L. (2007). Increasing honest responding on cognitive distortions in child molesters: The bogus pipeline revisited. *Sexual Abuse: A Journal of Research and Treatment, 19*(1), 5–22.

Gansberg, M. (1964, March 27). 37 who saw murder didn't call the police. *The New York Times.* http://www.nytimes.com/1964/03/27/37-who-saw-murder-didnt-call-the-police.html?_r=0

Gapinski, K. D., Brownell, K. D., & LaFrance, M. (2003). Body objectification and "fat talk": Effects on emotion, motivation, and cognitive performance. *Sex Roles, 48*(9–10), 377–388.

Garcia, D. M., Reser, A. H., Amo, R. B., Redersdorff, S., & Branscombe, N. R. (2005). Perceivers' responses to in-group and out-group members who blame a negative outcome on discrimination. *Personality and Social Psychology Bulletin, 31*(6), 769–780.

Garcia, J. R., Reiber, C., Massey, S. G., & Merriwether, A. M. (2012). Sexual hookup culture: A review. *Review of General Psychology, 16*(2), 161–176.

Garcia, S. M., Weaver, K., Moskowitz, G. B., & Darley, J. M. (2002). Crowded minds: The implicit bystander effect. *Journal of Personality and Social Psychology, 83*(4), 843–853.

Garcia-Navarro, L. (2021, September 26) What Is White Replacement Theory? Explaining The White Supremacist Rhetoric [Interview]. NPR. https://www.npr.org/2021/09/26/1040756471/what-is-white-replacement-theory-explaining-the-white-supremacist-rhetoric

Gardner, W. L., Gabriel, S., & Dean, K. K. (2004). The individual as "melting-pot": The flexibility of bicultural self-construals. *Cahiers de Psychologie Cognitive/Current Psychology of Cognition, 22*(2), 181–201.

Gardner, W. L., Gabriel, S., & Lee, A. Y. (1999). "I" value freedom, but "we" value relationships: Self-construal priming mirrors cultural differences in judgment. *Psychological Science, 10*(2), 321–326.

Garrison, K. E., Finley, A. J., & Schmeichel, B. J. (2019). Ego depletion reduces attention control: Evidence from two high-powered preregistered experiments. *Personality and Social Psychological Bulletin, 45*(5), 728–739.

Gascó, M., Briñol, P., Santos, D., Petty, R. E., & Horcajo, J. (2018). Where did this thought come from? A self-validation analysis of the perceived origin of thoughts. *Personality and Social Psychology Bulletin, 44*(11), 1615–1628.

Gasiorowska, A., Zaleskiewicz, T., & Kesebir, P. (2018). Money as an existential anxiety buffer: Exposure to money prevents mortality reminders from leading to increased death thoughts. *Journal of Experimental Social Psychology, 79*, 394–409.

Gasper, K., & Clore, G. L. (2002). Attending to the big picture: Mood and global versus local processing of visual information. *Psychological Science, 13*(1), 34–40.

Gaunt, R., Leyens, J. P., & Demoulin, S. (2002). Intergroup relations and the attribution of emotions: Control over memory for secondary emotions associated with the ingroup and outgroup. *Journal of Experimental Social Psychology, 38*(5), 508–514.

Gawronski, B., & Bodenhausen, G. V. (2006). Associative and propositional processes in evaluation: An integrative review of implicit and explicit attitude change. *Psychological Bulletin, 132*(5), 692–731.

Gawronski, B., & Bodenhausen, G. V. (2014). Implicit and explicit evaluation: A brief review of the associative–propositional evaluation model. *Social and Personality Psychology Compass, 8*(8), 448–462.

Gawronski, B., & Bodenhausen, G. V. (2015). Social-cognitive theories. In B. Gawronski & G. V. Bodenhausen (Eds.), *Theory and explanation in social psychology* (pp. 65–83). Guilford Press.

Geary, D. C. (2010). *Male, female: The evolution of human sex differences* (2nd ed.). American Psychological Association.

Geary, D. C., Rumsey, M., Bow-Thomas, C., & Hoard, M. K. (1995). Sexual jealousy as a facultative trait: Evidence from the pattern of sex differences in adults from China and the United States. *Ethology & Sociobiology, 16*(5), 355–383.

Geen, R. G. (1968). Effects of frustration, attack, and prior training in aggressiveness upon aggressive behavior. *Journal of Personality and Social Psychology, 9*(4), 316–321.

Geen, R. G. (1998). Aggression and antisocial behavior. In D. T. Gilbert, S. T. Fiske, & G. Lindzey (Eds.), *The handbook of social psychology* (4th ed., Vol. 2, pp. 317–356). McGraw-Hill.

Geen, R. G. (2001). *Human aggression* (2nd ed.). Open University Press.

Geen, R. G., & Berkowitz, L. (1966). Name-mediated aggressive cue properties. *Journal of Personality, 34*(3), 456–465.

Geen, R. G., & Pigg, R. (1970). Acquisition of an aggressive response and its generalization to verbal behavior. *Journal of Personality and Social Psychology, 15*(2), 165–170.

Geen, R. G., & Stonner, D. (1971). Effects of aggressiveness habit strength on behavior in the presence of aggression-related stimuli. *Journal of Personality and Social Psychology, 17*(2), 149–153.

Geen, R. G., & Stonner, D. (1972). The context of observed violence: Inhibition of aggression through displays of unsuccessful retaliation. *Psychonomic Science, 27*(6), 342–344.

Geen, R. G., & Stonner, D. (1973). Context effects in observed violence. *Journal of Personality and Social Psychology, 25*(1), 145–150.

Geller, J., Johnston, C., Madsen, K., Goldner, E. M., Remick, R. A., & Birmingham, C. L. (1998). Shape and weight-based self-esteem and the eating disorders. *International Journal of Eating Disorders, 24*(3), 285–298.

Gelles, R. J. (2007). The politics of research: The use, abuse, and misuse of social science data—The cases of intimate partner violence. *Family Court Review, 45*(1), 42–51.

Gendron, M., Crivelli, C., & Barrett, L. F. (2018). Universality reconsidered: Diversity in making meaning of facial expressions. *Current Directions in Psychological Science, 27*(4), 211–219.

Geniole, S. N., Procyshyn, T. L., Marley, N., Ortiz, T. L., Bird, B. M., Marcellus, A. L., Welker, K. M., Bonin, P. L., Goldfarb, B., Watson, N. V., & Carré, J. M. (2019). Using a psychopharmacogenetic approach to identify the pathways through which—and the people for whom—testosterone promotes aggression. *Psychological Science, 30*(4), 481–494.

Genschow, O., & Brass, M. (2015). The predictive chameleon: Evidence for anticipated social action. *Journal of Experimental Psychology: Human Perception and Performance, 41*, 265–268.

Gentile, A., Boca, S., & Giammusso, I. (2018). "You play like a woman!" Effects of gender stereotype threat on women's performance in physical and sport activities: A meta-analysis. *Psychology of Sport and Exercise, 39*, 95–103.

Gentile, D. A., Anderson, C. A., Yukawa, S., Ihori, N., Saleem, M., Ming, L. K., Shibuya, A., Liau, A. K., Khoo, A., Bushman, B. J., Huesmann, L. R., & Sakamoto, A. (2009). The effects of prosocial video games on prosocial behaviors: International evidence from correlational, longitudinal, and experimental studies. *Personality and Social Psychology Bulletin, 35*(6), 752–763.

Gentzler, A. L., & Kerns, K. A. (2004). Associations between insecure attachment and sexual experiences. *Personal Relationships, 11*(2), 249–265.

Gerber, P. J., Steinfeld, H., Henderson, B., Mottet, A., Opio, C., Dijkman, J., & Tempio, G. (2013). *Tackling climate change through livestock: A global assessment of emissions and mitigation opportunities*. Food and Agriculture Organization of the United Nations. http://www.fao.org/3/a-i3437e.pdf

Gerbner, G., Gross, L., Morgan, M., & Signorielli, N. (1980). The "mainstreaming" of America: Violence profile no. 11. *Journal of Communication, 30*(3), 10–29.

Gerbner, G., Gross, L., Morgan, M., & Signorielli, N. (1982). Charting the mainstream: Television's contributions to political orientations. *Journal of Communication, 32*(2), 100–127.

Gergen, K. J., & Gergen, M. M. (1988). Narrative and the self as relationship. In L. Berkowitz (Ed.), *Advances in experimental social psychology* (Vol. 21, pp. 17–56). Academic Press.

Geronimi, C. (Director). (1959). *Sleeping beauty* [Film]. Walt Disney Pictures.

Geronimi, C., Luske, H., & Jackson, W. (Directors). (1950). *Cinderella* [Film]. Walt Disney Pictures.

Gerrard, M., Gibbons, F. X., Houlihan, A., Stock, M. L., & Pomery, E. A. (2008). A dual-process approach to health risk decision making: The prototype willingness model. *Developmental Review, 28*(1), 29–61.

Gerrard, M., Gibbons, F. X., Stock, M. L., Vande Lune, L. S., & Cleveland, M. J. (2005). Images of smokers and willingness to smoke among African American pre-adolescents: An application of the prototype/willingness model of adolescent health risk behavior to smoking initiation. *Pediatric Psychology, 30*, 305–318.

Gershoff, E. T. (2002). Corporal punishment by parents and associated child behaviors and experiences: A meta-analytic and theoretical review. *Psychological Bulletin, 128*(4), 539–579.

Gershon, R., & Smith, R. K. (2020). Twice-told tales: Self-repetition decreases observer assessments of performer authenticity. *Journal of Personality and Social Psychology, 118*(2), 307–324.

Gervais, W. M., & Norenzayan, A. (2012). Like a camera in the sky? Thinking about God increases public self-awareness and socially desirable responding. *Journal of Experimental Social Psychology, 48*(1), 298–302.

Gibbons, F. X., & Gerrard, M. (1997). Health images and their effects on health behavior. In B. P. Buunk & F. X. Gibbons (Eds.), *Health, coping, and wellbeing: Perspectives from social comparison theory* (pp. 63–94). Erlbaum.

Gibbons, F. X., Gerrard, M., Reimer, R. A., & Pomery, E. A. (2006). Unintentional behavior: A subrational approach to health risk. In D. T. M. de Ridder & J. B. F. de Wit (Eds.), *Self-regulation in health behavior* (pp. 45–70). John Wiley & Sons Ltd.

Gibson, C. E., Losee, J., & Vitiello, C. (2014). A replication attempt of stereotype susceptibility (Shih, Pittinsky, & Ambady, 1999): Identity salience and shifts in quantitative performance. *Social Psychology, 45*(3), 194–198.

Gibson, S., Blenkinsopp, G., Johnstone, E., & Marshall, A. (2018). Just following orders? The rhetorical invocation of "obedience" in Stanley Milgram's post-experiment interviews. *European Journal of Social Psychology, 48*(5), 585–599.

Gigerenzer, G., & Garcia-Retamero, R. (2017). Cassandra's regret: The psychology of not wanting to know. *Psychological Review, 124*(2), 179–196.

Gilbert, D. T., Morewedge, C. K., Risen, J. L., & Wilson, T. D. (2004). Looking forward to looking backward: The misprediction of regret. *Psychological Science, 15*(5), 346–350.

Gilbert, D. T., Pelham, B. W., & Krull, D. S. (1988). On cognitive busyness: When person perceivers meet persons perceived. *Journal of Personality and Social Psychology, 54*(5), 733–740.

Gilder, T. S. E., & Heerey, E. A. (2018). The role of experimenter belief in social priming. *Psychological Science, 29*(3), 403–417.

Gildersleeve, K., Haselton, M. G., & Fales, M. R. (2014). Do women's mate preferences change across the ovulatory cycle? A meta-analytic review. *Psychological Bulletin, 140*(5), 1205–1259.

Giles, D. C. (2002). Parasocial interaction: A review of the literature and a model for future research. *Media Psychology, 4*(3), 279–305.

Gillath, O., Shaver, P. R., Baek, J. M., & Chun, D. S. (2008). Genetic correlates of adult attachment style. *Personality and Social Psychology Bulletin, 34*(10), 1396–1405.

Gilovich, T. (1987). Secondhand information and social judgment. *Journal of Experimental Social Psychology, 23*(1), 59–74.

Gilovich, T., Kerr, M., & Medvec, V. H. (1993). Effect of temporal perspective on subjective confidence. *Journal of Personality and Social Psychology, 64*(4), 552.

Gilovich, T., & Medvec, V. H. (1994). The temporal pattern to the experience of regret. *Journal of Personality and Social Psychology, 67*(3), 357–365.

Gilovich, T., Medvec, V. H., & Savitsky, K. (2000). The spotlight effect in social judgment: An egocentric bias in estimates of the salience of one's own actions and appearance. *Journal of Personality and Social Psychology, 78*(2), 211–222.

Gilovich, T., Savitsky, K., & Medvec, V. H. (1998). The illusion of transparency: Biased assessments of others' ability to read one's emotional states. *Journal of Personality and Social Psychology, 75*(2), 332–346.

Girme, Y. I., Overall, N. C., Simpson, J. A., & Fletcher, G. J. O. (2015). "All or nothing": Attachment avoidance and the curvilinear effects of partner support. *Journal of Personality and Social Psychology, 108*(3), 450–475.

Gjerde, P. F., Onishi, M., & Carlson, K. S. (2004). Personality characteristics associated with romantic attachment: A comparison of interview and self-report methodologies. *Personality and Social Psychology Bulletin, 30*(11), 1402–1415.

Glasman, L. R., & Albarracín, D. (2006). Forming attitudes that predict future behavior: A meta-analysis of the attitude-behavior relation. *Psychological Bulletin, 132*(5), 778–822.

Glass, I. (Host). (2009, March 27). Scenes from a recession [Radio broadcast]. *This American life.* Chicago Public Media. http://www.thisamericanlife.org/radio-archives/episode/377/transcript

Glass, I. (Host). (2013a, February 22). Harper high school, part two [Radio broadcast]. In I. Glass (Producer). *This American life.* Chicago Public Media & Ira Glass. http://www.thisamericanlife.org/radio-archives/episode/488/transcript

Glass, I. (Host). (2013b, April 12). Dr. Gilmer & Mr. Hyde [Radio broadcast]. In I. Glass (Producer), *This American life.* Chicago Public Media & Ira Glass. http://www.thisamericanlife.org/radio-archives/episode/492/dr-gilmer-and-mr-hyde

Glick, P., & Fiske, S. T. (1996). The ambivalent sexism inventory: Differentiating hostile and benevolent sexism. *Journal of Personality and Social Psychology, 70*(3), 491–512.

Glynn, S. A., Busch, M. P., Schreiber, G. B., Murphy, E. L., Wright, D. J., Tu, Y., & Kleinman, S. H. (2003). Effect of a national disaster on blood supply and safety. *The Journal of the American Medical Association, 289*(17), 2246–2253.

Goethals, G. R., & Nelson, R. E. (1973). Similarity in the influence process: The belief-value distinction. *Journal of Personality and Social Psychology, 25*(1), 117–122.

Goff, P. A., Jackson, M. C., Di Leone, B. A. L., Culotta, C. M., & DiTomasso, N. A. (2014). The essence of innocence: Consequences of dehumanizing Black children. *Journal of Personality and Social Psychology, 106*(4), 526–545.

Goffman, E. (1959). *The presentation of self in everyday life.* Doubleday.

Goffman, E. (1963). *Stigma: Notes on the management of spoiled identity.* Prentice Hall.

Goldenberg, J., Heflick, N., Vaes, J., Motyl, M., & Greenberg, J. (2009). Of mice and men, and objectified women: A terror management account of infrahumanization. *Group Processes & Intergroup Relations, 12*(6), 763–776.

Goldenberg, J. L., & Arndt, J. (2008). The implications of death for health: A terror management health model for behavioral health promotion. *Psychological Review, 115*(4), 1032–1053.

Goldenberg, J. L., Landau, M. J., Pyszczynski, T., Cox, C. R., Greenberg, J., Solomon, S., & Dunnam, H. (2003). Gender-typical responses to sexual and emotional infidelity as a function of mortality salience induced self-esteem striving. *Personality and Social Psychology Bulletin, 29*(12), 1585–1595.

Goldman, W., & Lewis, P. (1977). Beautiful is good: Evidence that the physically attractive are more socially skillful. *Journal of Experimental Social Psychology, 13*(2), 125–130.

Goldschmidt, W. R. (1990). *The human career: The self in the symbolic world.* Blackwell.

Goldstein, A. P. (1994). Delinquent gangs. In L. R. Huesman (Ed.), *Aggressive behavior: Current perspectives* (pp. 255–273). Plenum Press.

Goldstein, A. P., Glick, B., & Gibbs, J. C. (1998). *Aggression replacement training: A comprehensive intervention for aggressive youth* (Rev. ed.). Research Press.

Goldstein, D. (2020, January 12). Two states. Eight textbooks. Two American stories. *New York Times.* https://www.nytimes.com/interactive/2020/01/12/us/texas-vs-california-history-textbooks.html

Goldstein, D., & Rosenbaum, A. (1985). An evaluation of the self-esteem of maritally violent men. *Family Relations, 34*(3), 425–428.

Goldstein, J. H. (1986). *Aggression and crimes of violence.* Oxford University Press.

Goldstein, J. H. (Ed.). (1998). *Why we watch: The attractions of violent entertainment.* Oxford University Press.

Gollwitzer, P. M. (1999). Implementation intentions: Strong effects of simple plans. *American Psychologist, 54*(7), 493–503.

Gollwitzer, P. M., & Bargh, J. A. (2005). Automaticity in goal pursuit. In A. J. Elliot & C. S. Dweck (Eds.), *Handbook of competence and motivation* (pp. 624–646). Guilford Press.

Gollwitzer, P. M., Marquardt, M. K., Scherer, M., & Fujita, K. (2013). Identity goal threats: Engaging in distinct compensatory efforts. *Social Psychological and Personality Science, 4*(5), 555–562.

Gollwitzer, P. M., Sheeran, P., Michalski, V., & Seifert, A. E. (2009). When intentions go public: Does social reality widen the intention–behavior gap? *Psychological Science, 20*(5), 612–618.

Gollwitzer, P. M., & Wicklund, R. A. (1985). Self-symbolizing and the neglect of others' perspectives. *Journal of Personality and Social Psychology, 48*(3), 702–715.

Gollwitzer, P. M., Wicklund, R. A., & Hilton, J. L. (1982). Admission of failure and symbolic self-completion: Extending Lewinian theory. *Journal of Personality and Social Psychology, 43*(2), 358–371.

Gómez, A., Vázquez, A., López-Rodríguez, L., Talaifar, S., Martínez, M., Buhrmester, M. D., & Swann, W. B., Jr. (2019). Why people abandon groups: Degrading relational vs. collective ties uniquely impacts identity fusion and identification. *Journal of Experimental Social Psychology, 85*, 103853.

Gommans, R., Sandstrom, M. J., Stevens, G. W., ter Bogt, T. F., & Cillessen, A. H. (2017). Popularity, likeability, and peer conformity: Four field experiments. *Journal of Experimental Social Psychology, 73*, 279–289.

Goode, W. J. (1960). A theory of role strain. *American Sociological Review, 25*(4), 483–496.

Goodwin, G. P. (2015). Moral character in person perception. *Current Directions in Psychological Science, 24*(1), 38–44.

Goodwin, S. A., Gubin, A., Fiske, S. T., & Yzerbyt, V. Y. (2000). Power can bias impression processes: Stereotyping subordinates by default and by design. *Group Processes & Intergroup Relations, 3*(3), 227–256.

Gorchoff, S. M., John, O. P., & Helson, R. (2008). Contextualizing change in marital satisfaction during middle age: An 18-year longitudinal study. *Psychological Science, 19*(11), 1194–1200.

Gordijn, E. H., Hindriks, I., Koomen, W., Dijksterhuis, A., & Van Knippenberg, A. (2004). Consequences of stereotype suppression and internal suppression motivation: A self-regulation approach. *Personality and Social Psychology Bulletin, 30*(2), 212–224.

Gordon, R. A. (1996). Impact of ingratiation on judgments and evaluations: A meta-analytic investigation. *Journal of Personality and Social Psychology, 71*(1), 54–70.

Gorman, B. J. (1999). Facilitated communication: Rejected in science, accepted in court—A case study and analysis of the use of FC evidence under *Frye* and *Daubert. Behavioral Sciences & the Law, 17*(4), 517–541.

Gosling, S. D., Ko, S. J., Mannarelli, T., & Morris, M. E. (2002). A room with a cue: Personality judgments based on offices and bedrooms. *Journal of Personality and Social Psychology, 82*(3), 379–398.

Gottlieb, J., & Carver, C. S. (1980). Anticipation of future interaction and the bystander effect. *Journal of Experimental Social Psychology, 16*(3), 253–260.

Gottman, J. M. (1995). *Why marriages succeed or fail.* Simon & Schuster.

Gottman, J. M., & Levenson, R. W. (2000). The timing of divorce: Predicting when a couple will divorce over a 14-year period. *Journal of Marriage and Family, 62*(3), 737–745.

Grabe, S., Ward, L. M., & Hyde, J. S. (2008). The role of the media in body image concerns among women: A meta-analysis of experimental and correlational studies. *Psychological Bulletin, 134*(3), 460–476.

Gräf, M., & Unkelbach, C. (2016). Halo effects in trait assessment depend on information valence: Why being honest makes you industrious, but lying does not make you lazy. *Personality and Social Psychology Bulletin, 42*(3), 290–310.

Graf, N. (2019, November 6). *Key findings on marriage and cohabitation in the U.S.* Pew Research Center. https://www.pewresearch.org/fact-tank/2019/11/06/key-findings-on-marriage-and-cohabitation-in-the-u-s/

Grafman, J., Schwab, K., Warden, D., Pridgen, A., Brown, H. R., & Salazar, A. M. (1996). Frontal lobe injuries, violence, and aggression: A report of the Vietnam Head Injury Study. *Neurology, 46*(5), 1231–1238.

Graham, J., Haidt, J., & Nosek, B. A. (2009). Liberals and conservatives rely on different sets of moral foundations. *Journal of Personality and Social Psychology*, 96(5), 1029–1046.

Graham, S., & Lowery, B. S. (2004). Priming unconscious racial stereotypes about adolescent offenders. *Law and Human Behavior*, 28(5), 483–504.

Grant, A. M., & Gino, F. (2010). A little thanks goes a long way: Explaining why gratitude expressions motivate prosocial behavior. *Journal of Personality and Social Psychology*, 98(6), 946–955.

Graziano, W. G., Habashi, M. M., Sheese, B. E., & Tobin, R. M. (2007). Agreeableness, empathy, and helping: A person × situation perspective. *Journal of Personality and Social Psychology*, 93(4), 583–599.

Green, A. H. (1998). Factors contributing to the generational transmission of child maltreatment. *Journal of the American Academy of Child & Adolescent Psychiatry*, 37(12), 1334–1336.

Green, E. G. T., Staerkle, C., & Sears, D. O. (2006). Symbolic racism and Whites' attitudes towards punitive and preventive crime policies. *Law and Human Behavior*, 30(4), 435–454.

Green, M. C., & Brock, T. C. (2000). The role of transportation in the persuasiveness of public narratives. *Journal of Personality and Social Psychology*, 79(5), 701–721.

Green, M. C., & Clark, J. L. (2013). Transportation into narrative worlds: Implications for entertainment media influences on tobacco use. *Addiction*, 108(3), 477–484.

Greenaway, K. H., Haslam, A., Cruwys, T., Branscombe, N. R., Ysseldyk, R., & Heldreth, C. (2015). From "we" to "me": Group identification enhances perceived personal control with consequences for health and well-being. *Journal of Personality and Social Psychology*, 109(1), 53–74.

Greenaway, K. H., Kalokerinos, E. K., & Williams, L. A. (2018). Context is everything (in emotion research). *Social and Personality Psychology Compass*, 12(6), e12393.

Greenberg, J. (2015). The psychological worm at the core of mass shootings. *Psykologisk Tidsskrift*, 19(1), 28–33.

Greenberg, J., Landau, M. J., Kosloff, S., Soenke, M., & Solomon, S. (2016). How our means for feeling transcendent of death foster prejudice, stereotyping, and intergroup conflict: Terror management theory. In T. D. Nelson (Ed.), *Handbook of prejudice, stereotyping, and discrimination* (2nd ed., pp. 107–148). Psychology Press.

Greenberg, J., & Pyszczynski, T. (1985a). Compensatory self-inflation: A response to the threat to self-regard of public failure. *Journal of Personality and Social Psychology*, 49(1), 273–280.

Greenberg, J., & Pyszczynski, T. (1985b). The effect of an overheard ethnic slur on evaluations of the target: How to spread a social disease. *Journal of Experimental Social Psychology*, 21(1), 61–72.

Greenberg, J., Pyszczynski, T., & Paisley, C. (1984). Effect of extrinsic incentives on use of test anxiety as an anticipatory attributional defense: Playing it cool when the stakes are high. *Journal of Personality and Social Psychology*, 47(5), 1136–1145.

Greenberg, J., Pyszczynski, T., & Solomon, S. (1986). The causes and consequences of a need for self-esteem: A terror management theory. In R. F. Baumeister (Ed.), *Public self and private self* (pp. 189–212). Springer-Verlag.

Greenberg, J., Pyszczynski, T., Solomon, S., Rosenblatt, A., Veeder, M., Kirkland, S., & Lyon, D. (1990). Evidence for terror management theory II: The effects of mortality salience on reactions to those who threaten or bolster the cultural worldview. *Journal of Personality and Social Psychology*, 58(2), 308–318.

Greenberg, J., & Rosenfield, D. (1979). Whites' ethnocentrism and their attributions for the behavior of Blacks: A motivational bias. *Journal of Personality*, 47(4), 643–657.

Greenberg, J., Simon, L., Solomon, S., Chatel, D., & Pyszczynski, T. (1992). Terror management and tolerance: Does mortality salience always intensify negative reactions to others who threaten one's cultural worldview? *Journal of Personality and Social Psychology*, 63(2), 212–220.

Greenberg, J., Solomon, S., & Arndt, J. (2008). A basic but uniquely human motivation: Terror management. In J. Y. Shah & W. L. Gardner (Eds.), *Handbook of motivation science* (pp. 114–134). Guilford Press.

Greenberg, J., Solomon, S., Pyszczynski, T., Rosenblatt, A., Burling, J., Lyon, D., & Pinel, E. (1992). Why do people need self-esteem? Converging evidence that self-esteem serves an anxiety-buffering function. *Journal of Personality and Social Psychology*, 63(6), 913–922.

Greenberg, J., Vail, K., & Pyszczynski, T. (2014). Terror management theory and research: How the desire for death transcendence drives our strivings for meaning and significance. In A. J. Elliot, *Advances in motivation science, Vol. 1* (p. 85–134). Elsevier Academic Press.

Greenwald, A. G., Banaji, M. R., & Nosek, B. A. (2015). Statistically small effects of the Implicit Association Test can have societally large effects. *Journal of Personality and Social Psychology*, 108(4), 553–561.

Greenwald, A. G., McGhee, D. E., & Schwartz, J. L. (1998). Measuring individual differences in implicit cognition: The Implicit Association Test. *Journal of Personality and Social Psychology*, 74(6), 1464–1480.

Greenwald, A. G., Smith, C. T., Sriram, N., Bar-Anan, Y., & Nosek, B. A. (2009). Implicit race attitudes predicted vote in the 2008 U.S. presidential election. *Analyses of Social Issues and Public Policy*, 9(1), 241–253.

Greenwald, A. G., Spangenberg, E. R., Pratkanis, A. R., & Eskenazi, J. (1991). Double-blind tests of subliminal self-help audiotapes. *Psychological Science*, 2(2), 119–122.

Greenwald, R. (Director). (1984). *The burning bed* [Film]. Tisch/Avnet Productions Inc.

Gregg, A. P., & Sedikides, C. (2010). Narcissistic fragility: Rethinking its links to explicit and implicit self-esteem. *Self and Identity*, 9(2), 142–161.

Gregory, R. L. (1968). Visual illusions. *Scientific American*, 219(5), 66–76.

Greitemeyer, T. (2011a). Effects of prosocial media on social behavior: When and why does media exposure affect helping and aggression? *Current Directions in Psychological Science*, 20(4), 251–255.

Greitemeyer, T. (2011b). Exposure to music with prosocial lyrics reduces aggression: First evidence and test of the underlying mechanism. *Journal of Experimental Social Psychology*, 47(1), 28–36.

Greitemeyer, T., & Osswald, S. (2009). Prosocial video games reduce aggressive cognitions. *Journal of Experimental Social Psychology*, 45(4), 896–900.

Greitemeyer, T., & Osswald, S. (2010). Effects of prosocial video games on prosocial behavior. *Journal of Personality and Social Psychology*, 98(2), 211–221.

Greitemeyer, T., & Sagioglou, C. (2016). Subjective socioeconomic status causes aggression: A test of the theory of social deprivation. *Journal of Personality and Social Psychology*, 111(2), 178–194.

Griffitt, W. (1970). Environmental effects on interpersonal affective behavior: Ambient effective temperature and attraction. *Journal of Personality and Social Psychology*, 15(3), 240–244.

Griffitt, W., & Veitch, R. (1974). Preacquaintance attitude similarity and attraction revisited: Ten days in a fall-out shelter. *Sociometry*, 37(2), 163–173.

Grøntvedt, T. V., & Kennair, L. E. O. (2013). Age preferences in a gender egalitarian society. *Journal of Social, Evolutionary, and Cultural Psychology*, 7, 239–249.

Groothof, H. K., Dijkstra, P., & Barelds, D. H. (2009). Sex differences in jealousy: The case of Internet infidelity. *Journal of Social and Personal Relationships*, 26(8), 1119–1129.

Gross, A. E., & Crofton, C. (1977). What is good is beautiful. *Sociometry*, 40(1), 85–90.

Gross, J. J. (1998). Antecedent and response-focused emotion regulation: Divergent consequences for experience, expression, and physiology. *Journal of Personality and Social Psychology*, 74(1), 224–237.

Gross, J. J. (2001). Emotion regulation in adulthood: Timing is everything. *Current Directions in Psychological Science*, 10(6), 214–219.

Gross, J. J. (2002). Emotion regulation: Affective, cognitive, and social consequences. *Psychophysiology*, 39(3), 281–291.

Grossmann, I., & Varnum, M. E. (2015). Social structure, infectious diseases, disasters, secularism, and cultural change in America. *Psychological Science*, 26(3), 311–324.

Grover, S. S., Ito, T. A., & Park, B. (2017). The effects of gender composition on women's experience in math work groups. *Journal of Personality and Social Psychology*, 112(6), 877–900.

Gruenfeld, D. H., Inesi, M. E., Magee, J. C., & Galinsky, A. D. (2008). Power and the objectification of social targets. *Journal of Personality and Social Psychology*, 95(1), 111–127.

Guadagno, R. E., Okdie, B. M., & Kruse, S. A. (2012). Dating deception: Gender, online dating, and exaggerated self-presentation. *Computers in Human Behavior*, 28(2), 642–647.

Guéguen, N., Martin, A., Silone, F., & David, M. (2016). Foot-in-the-door technique and reduction of driver's aggressiveness: A field study. *Transportation Research Part F: Traffic Psychology and Behaviour*, 36, 1–5.

Guendelman, M. D., Cheryan, S., & Monin, B. (2011). Fitting in but getting fat: Identity threat and dietary choices among U.S. immigrant groups. *Psychological Science*, 22(7), 959–967.

Guerra, N. G., Nucci, L., & Huesmann, L. R. (1994). Moral cognition and childhood aggression. In L. R. Huesmann (Ed.), *Aggressive behavior: Current perspectives* (pp. 13–33). Plenum Press.

Guest, C. (Director). (2000). *Best in show* [Film]. Castle Rock Entertainment.

Guinote, A. (2007). Power and goal pursuit. *Personality and Social Psychology Bulletin*, 33(8), 1076–1087.

Guinote, A., Willis, G. B., & Martellotta, C. (2010). Social power increases implicit prejudice. *Journal of Experimental Social Psychology*, 46(2), 299–307.

Gullo, J. (2016, December 15). *Teen who killed herself in front of her parents is still being bullied*. News 10. http://news10.com/2016/12/15/teen-who-killed-herself-in-front-of-her-parents-is-still-being-bullied/

Gunaydin, G., Selcuk, E., & Zayas, V. (2017). Impressions based on a portrait predict, 1-month later, impressions following a live interaction. *Social Psychological and Personality Science*, 8(1), 36–44.

Gunn, G. R., & Wilson, A. E. (2011). Acknowledging the skeletons in our closet: The effect of group affirmation on collective guilt, collective shame, and reparatory attitudes. *Personality and Social Psychology Bulletin*, 37(11), 1474–1487.

Gunnell, J. J., & Ceci, S. J. (2010). When emotionality trumps reason: A study of individual processing style and juror bias. *Behavioral Sciences & the Law*, 28(6), 850–877.

Gun Violence Archive. (2019). https://www.gunviolencearchive.org

Guyer, J. J., Fabrigar, L. R., & Vaughan-Johnston, T. I. (2019). Speech rate, intonation, and pitch: Investigating the bias and cue effects of vocal confidence on persuasion. *Personality and Social Psychology Bulletin*, 45(3), 389–405.

Guyll, M., Matthews, K. A., & Bromberger, J. T. (2001). Discrimination and unfair treatment: Relationship to cardiovascular reactivity among African American and European American women. *Health Psychology*, 20(5), 315–325.

Gwinn, J. D., Judd, C. M., & Park, B. (2013). Less power = less human? Effects of power differentials on dehumanization. *Journal of Experimental Social Psychology*, 49(3), 464–470.

Hadden, B. W., Rodriguez, L. M., Knee, C. R., DiBello, A. M., & Baker, Z. G. (2016). An actor–partner interdependence model of attachment and need fulfillment in romantic dyads. *Social Psychological and Personality Science*, 7(4), 349–357.

Hafer, C. L., & Bègue, L. (2005). Experimental research on just-world theory: Problems, developments, and future challenges. *Psychological Bulletin*, 131(1), 128–167.

Hagger M. S., Chatzisarantis N. L. D., Alberts, H., Anggono, C. O., Batailler, C., Birt, A. R., Brand, R., Brandt, M., Brewer, S., Bruyneel, S., Calvillo, D., Campbell, W. K., Cannon, P., Carlucci, M., Carruth, N., Cheung, T., Crowell, A., Ridder, D., Dewitte, S., . . . Zwienenberg, M. (2016). A multilab preregistered replication of the ego-depletion effect. *Perspectives on Psychological Science*, 11(4), 546–573.

Haidt, J., & Joseph, C. (2007). The moral mind: How 5 sets of innate moral intuitions guide the development of many culture-specific virtues, and perhaps even modules. In P. Carruthers, S. Laurence, & S. Stich (Eds.), *The innate mind* (Vol. 3, pp. 367–391). Oxford University Press.

Haidt, J., & Kesebir, S. (2010). Morality. In S. T. Fiske, D. T. Gilbert, & G. Lindzey (Eds.), *Handbook of social psychology* (5th ed., pp. 797–832). Wiley.

Haimovitz, K., & Dweck, C. S. (2016). What predicts children's fixed and growth intelligence mind-sets? Not their parents' views of intelligence but their parents' views of failure. *Psychological Science*, 27(6), 859–869.

Halberstadt, J., Sherman, S. J., & Sherman, J. W. (2011). Why Barack Obama is Black: A cognitive account of hypodescent. *Psychological Science*, 22(1), 29–33.

Hald, G. M., Malamuth, N. M., & Yuen, C. (2010). Pornography and attitudes supporting violence against women: Revisiting the relationship in nonexperimental studies. *Aggressive Behavior*, 36(1), 14–20.

Halevy, N., Berson, Y., & Galinsky, A. D. (2011). The mainstream is not electable: When vision triumphs over representativeness in leader emergence and effectiveness. *Personality and Social Psychology Bulletin*, 37(7), 893–904.

Halfmann, E., Bredehöft, J., & Häusser, J. A. (2020). Replicating roaches: A preregistered replication of Zajonc, Heingartner, and Herman's (1969) social-facilitation study. *Psychological Science*, 31(3), 332–337.

Hall, E. (1984). *The dance of life: The other dimension of time*. Anchor Books.

Hall, W. M., Schmader, T., Aday, A., & Croft, E. (2019). Decoding the dynamics of social identity threat in the workplace: A within-person analysis of women's and men's interactions in STEM. *Social Psychological and Personality Science*, 10(4), 542–552.

Hamberger, L. K., & Hastings, J. E. (1991). Personality correlates of men who batter and nonviolent men: Some continuities and discontinuities. *Journal of Family Violence*, 6(2), 131–147.

Hamill, R., Wilson, T. D., & Nisbett, R. E. (1980). Insensitivity to sample bias: Generalizing from atypical cases. *Journal of Personality and Social Psychology*, 39(4), 578–589.

Hamilton, D. L., Driscoll, D. M., & Worth, L. T. (1989). Cognitive organization of impressions: Effects of incongruency in complex representations. *Journal of Personality and Social Psychology*, 57(6), 925–939.

Hamilton, D. L., Dugan, P. M., & Trolier, T. K. (1985). The formation of stereotypic beliefs: Further evidence for distinctiveness-based illusory correlations. *Journal of Personality and Social Psychology*, 48(1), 5–17.

Hamilton, D. L., & Sherman, J. W. (1994). Stereotypes. In R. S. Wyer & T. K. Srull (Eds.), *Handbook of social cognition* (2nd ed., Vol. 2, pp. 1–68). Erlbaum.

Hamilton, D. L., & Sherman, S. J. (1989). Illusory correlations: Implications for stereotype theory and research. In D. Bar-Tal, C. F. Graumann, A. W. Kruglanski, & W. Stroebe (Eds.), *Stereotypes and prejudice: Changing conceptions* (pp. 59–82). Springer-Verlag.

Hamilton, W. D. (1964). The genetical evolution of social behaviour. II. *Journal of Theoretical Biology*, 7(1), 17–52.

Hamlin, J. K., & Wynn, K. (2011). Young infants prefer prosocial to antisocial others. *Cognitive Development*, 26(1), 30–39.

Hamlin, J. K., Wynn, K., & Bloom, P. (2007). Social evaluation by preverbal infants. *Nature*, 450(7169), 557–559.

Hamlin, J. K., Wynn, K., & Bloom, P. (2010). Three-month-olds show a negativity bias in social evaluation. *Developmental Science*, 13(6), 923–939.

Hand, D. (Director). (1937). *Snow White and the seven dwarfs* [Film]. Walt Disney Pictures.

Hanel, P. H. P., Maio, G. R., & Manstead, A. S. R. (2019). A new way to look at the data: Similarities between groups of people are large and important. *Journal of Personality and Social Psychology*, 116(4), 541–562.

Haney, C., Banks, C., & Zimbardo, P. (1973). Interpersonal dynamics in a simulated prison. *International Journal of Criminology and Penology*, 1(1), 69–97.

Hanniball, K. B., Aknin, L. B., Douglas, K. S., & Viljoen, J. L. (2019). Does helping promote well-being in at-risk youth and ex-offender samples? *Journal of Experimental Social Psychology*, 82, 307–317.

Hanselman, P., Rozek, C. S., Grigg, J., & Borman, G. D. (2017). New evidence on self-affirmation effects and theorized sources of heterogeneity from large-scale replications. *Journal of Educational Psychology*, 109(3), 405–424.

Hansen, J., Winzeler, S., & Topolinski, S. (2010). When the death makes you smoke: A terror management perspective on the effectiveness of cigarette on-pack warnings. *Journal of Experimental Social Psychology*, 46(1), 226–228.

Hänze, M., & Berger, R. (2007). Cooperative learning, motivational effects, and student characteristics: An experimental study comparing cooperative learning and direct instruction in 12th grade physics classes. *Learning and Instruction*, 17(1), 29–41.

Hardin, G. (1968). The tragedy of the commons. *Science*, 162(3859), 1243–1248.

Harkins, S. G., & Petty, R. E. (1987). Information utility and the multiple source effect. *Journal of Personality and Social Psychology*, 52(2), 260–268.

Harkins, S. G., & Szymanski, K. (1988). Social loafing and self-evaluation with an objective standard. *Journal of Experimental Social Psychology*, 24(4), 354–365.

Harlow, H. F. (1959). Love in infant monkeys. *Scientific American*, 200(6), 68–86.

Harmon-Jones, E. (2003). Clarifying the emotive functions of asymmetrical frontal cortical activity. *Psychophysiology*, 40(6), 838–848.

Harmon-Jones, E., & Allen, J. J. B. (1998). Anger and frontal brain activity: EEG asymmetry consistent with approach motivation despite negative affective valence. *Journal of Personality and Social Psychology*, 74(5), 1310–1316.

Harmon-Jones, E., Brehm, J. W., Greenberg, J., Simon, L., & Nelson, D. E. (1996). Evidence that the production of aversive consequences is not necessary to create cognitive dissonance. *Journal of Personality and Social Psychology*, 70(1), 5–16.

Harmon-Jones, E., Harmon-Jones, C., & Amodio, D. M. (2012). A neuroscientific perspective on dissonance, guided by the action-based model. In B. Gawronski & F. Strack (Eds.), *Cognitive consistency: A fundamental principle in social cognition* (pp. 47–65). Guilford Press.

Harmon-Jones, E., & Sigelman, J. (2001). State anger and prefrontal brain activity: Evidence that insult-related relative left-prefrontal activation is associated with experienced anger and aggression. *Journal of Personality and Social Psychology*, 80(5), 797–803.

Harmon-Jones, E., Simon, L., Greenberg, J., Pyszczynski, T., Solomon, S., & McGregor, H. (1997). Terror management theory and self-esteem: Evidence that increased self-esteem reduced mortality salience effects. *Journal of Personality and Social Psychology*, 72(1), 24–36.

Harris, C. R. (2000). Psychophysiological responses to imagined infidelity: The specific innate modular view of jealousy reconsidered. *Journal of Personality and Social Psychology*, 78(6), 1082–1091.

Harris, C. R. (2002). Sexual and romantic jealousy in heterosexual and homosexual adults. *Psychological Science*, 13(1), 7–12.

Harris, C. R. (2003). A review of sex differences in sexual jealousy, including self-report data, psychophysiological responses, interpersonal violence, and morbid jealousy. *Personality and Social Psychology Review*, 7(2), 102–128.

Harris, C. R., & Christenfeld, N. (1996). Gender, jealousy, and reason. *Psychological Science*, 7(6), 364–366.

Harris, C. R., Coburn, N., Rohrer, D., & Pashler, H. (2013). Two failures to replicate high-performance-goal priming effects. *PLoS ONE* 8(8), e72467.

Harris, L. T., & Fiske, S. T. (2006). Dehumanizing the lowest of the low: Neuroimaging responses to extreme out-groups. *Psychological Science*, 17(10), 847–853.

Harris, M. (2001). *Cultural materialism: The struggle for a science of culture.* AltaMira Press. (Original work published 1979)

Harris, M. B. (1974). Mediators between frustration and aggression in a field experiment. *Journal of Experimental Social Psychology, 10*(6), 561–571.

Harris, M. J., & Rosenthal, R. (1985). Mediation of interpersonal expectancy effects: 31 meta-analyses. *Psychological Bulletin, 97*(3), 363–386.

Harris, P. R., Mayle, K., Mabbott, L., & Napper, L. (2007). Self-affirmation reduces smokers' defensiveness to graphic on-pack cigarette warning labels. *Health Psychology, 26*(4), 437–446.

Harter, S. (1998). The development of self-representations. In W. Damon & N. Eisenberg (Eds.), *Handbook of child psychology* (5th ed., Vol. 3, pp. 553–617). Wiley.

Harvey, O. J., White, B. J., Hood, W. R., & Sherif, C. W. (1961). *Intergroup conflict and cooperation: The Robbers Cave experiment.* University Book Exchange.

Haselton, M. G., & Buss, D. M. (2009). Error management theory and the evolution of misbeliefs. *Behavioral & Brain Sciences, 32*(6), 522–523.

Haslam, S. A., & Platow, M. J. (2001). The link between leadership and followership: How affirming social identity translates vision into action. *Personality and Social Psychology Bulletin, 27*(11), 1469–1479.

Haslam, S. A., Reicher, S. D., & Birney, M. E. (2016). Questioning authority: New perspectives on Milgram's "obedience" research and its implications for intergroup relations. *Current Opinion in Psychology, 11*, 6–9.

Haslam, S. A., Reicher, S. D., & Millard, K. (2015). Shock treatment: Using immersive digital realism to restage and re-examine Milgram's "obedience to authority" research. *PLoS ONE, 10*(3), e109015.

Hassett, J. M., Siebert, E. R., & Wallen, K. (2008). Sex differences in rhesus monkey toy preferences parallel those of children. *Hormones and Behavior, 54*(3), 359–364.

Hastorf, A. H., & Cantril, H. (1954). They saw a game: A case study. *Journal of Abnormal and Social Psychology, 49*(1), 129–134.

Hatfield, E. (1988). Passionate and companionate love. In R. Sternberg & M. L. Barnes (Eds.), *The psychology of love* (pp. 191–217). Yale University Press.

Hatfield, E., Cacioppo, J. T., & Rapson, R. L. (1993). Emotional contagion. *Current Directions in Psychological Science, 2*(3), 96–99.

Hatfield, E., Mo, Y.-M., & Rapson, R. L. (2015). Love, sex, and marriage across cultures. In Lene Jensen (Ed.), *The Oxford handbook of human development and culture: An interdisciplinary perspective.* Oxford University Press.

Hatfield, E., & Rapson, R. L. (1993). *Love, sex, and intimacy: Their psychology, biology, and history.* HarperCollins.

Hatfield, E., & Sprecher, S. (1986). Measuring passionate love in intimate relationships. *Journal of Adolescence, 9*(4), 383–410.

Hatfield, E., Walster, G. W., & Berscheid, E. (1978). *Equity: Theory and research.* Allyn & Bacon.

Hatvany, T., Burkley, E., & Curtis, J. (2018). Becoming part of me: Examining when objects, thoughts, goals, and people become fused with the self-concept. *Social and Personality Psychology Compass, 12*(1), e12369.

Hatzenbuehler, M. L. (2014). Structural stigma and the health of lesbian, gay, and bisexual populations. *Current Directions in Psychological Science, 23*(2), 127–132.

Hawkley, L. C., Thisted, R. A., & Cacioppo, J. T. (2009). Loneliness predicts reduced physical activity: Cross-sectional & longitudinal analyses. *Health Psychology, 28*(3), 354–363.

Hayes, J., Schimel, J., Arndt, J., & Faucher, E. H. (2010). A theoretical and empirical review of the death-thought accessibility concept in terror management research. *Psychological Bulletin, 136*(5), 699–739.

Hayes, J., Schimel, J., Faucher, E. H., & Williams, T. J. (2008). Evidence for the DTA hypothesis II: Threatening self-esteem increases death-thought accessibility. *Journal of Experimental Social Psychology, 44*(3), 600–613.

Hayes, J., Schimel, J., & Williams, T. J. (2008). Fighting death with death: The buffering effects of learning that worldview violators have died. *Psychological Science, 19*(5), 501–507.

Hazan, C., & Shaver, P. (1987). Romantic love conceptualized as an attachment process. *Journal of Personality and Social Psychology, 52*(3), 511–524.

Heatherton, T. F., & Baumeister, R. F. (1991). Binge eating as escape from self-awareness. *Psychological Bulletin, 110*(1), 86–108.

Hebl, M. R., & Heatherton, T. F. (1998). The stigma of obesity in women: The difference is black and white. *Personality and Social Psychology Bulletin, 24*(4), 417–426.

Hecht, M. L., Marston, P. J., & Larkey, L. K. (1994). Love ways and relationship quality in heterosexual relationships. *Journal of Social and Personal Relationships, 11*(1), 25–43.

Heflick, N. A., & Goldenberg, J. L. (2009). Objectifying Sarah Palin: Evidence that objectification causes women to be perceived as less competent and less fully human. *Journal of Experimental Social Psychology, 45*(3), 598–601.

Heflick, N. A., Goldenberg, J. L., Cooper, D. P., & Puvia, E. (2011). From women to objects: Appearance focus, target gender, and perceptions of warmth, morality and competence. *Journal of Experimental Social Psychology, 47*(3), 572–581.

Heider, F. (1946). Attitudes and cognitive organisations. *Journal of Psychology, 21*, 107–112.

Heider, F. (1958). *The psychology of interpersonal relations.* Wiley.

Heider, F., & Simmel, M. (1944). An experimental study of apparent behavior. *American Journal of Psychology, 57*(2), 243–259.

Heine, S. J., Proulx, T., & Vohs, K. D. (2006). The meaning maintenance model: On the coherence of social motivations. *Personality and Social Psychology Review, 10*(2), 88–110.

Helm, P. J., Greenberg, J., Park, Y. C., & Pinel, E. C. (2019). Feeling alone in your subjectivity: Introducing the State Trait Existential Isolation Model. *Journal of Theoretical Social Psychology, 3*(3), 146–157.

Hendrick, C., & Hendrick, S. (1986). A theory and method of love. *Journal of Personality and Social Psychology, 50*(2), 392–402.

Hendrick, C., Hendrick, S. S., & Reich, D. A. (2006). The brief sexual attitudes scale. *Journal of Sex Research, 43*(1), 76–86.

Henggeler, S. W., Schoenwald, S. K., Borduin, C. M., Rowland, M. D., & Cunningham, P. B. (1998). *Multisystemic treatment of antisocial behavior in children and adolescents: Treatment manuals for practitioners.* Guilford Press.

Hennes, E. P., Ruisch, B. C., Feygina, I., Monteiro, C. A., & Jost, J. T. (2016). Motivated recall in the service of the economic system: The case of anthropogenic climate change. *Journal of Experimental Psychology: General, 145*(6), 755–771.

Henrich, J., Heine, S. J., & Norenzayan, A. (2010). The weirdest people in the world. *Behavioral and Brain Sciences, 33*(2–3), 61–83.

Henrich, N., & Henrich, J. (2007). *Why humans cooperate: A cultural and evolutionary explanation.* Oxford University Press.

Henry, P. B., & Miller, C. (2009). Institutions vs. policies: A tale of two islands. *American Economic Review, 99*(2), 261–267.

Henry, P. J. (2009). Low-status compensation: A theory for understanding the role of status in cultures of honor. *Journal of Personality and Social Psychology, 97*(3), 451–466.

Hepworth, J. T., & West, S. G. (1988). Lynchings and the economy: A time-series reanalysis of Hovland and Sears (1940). *Journal of Personality and Social Psychology, 55*(2), 239–247.

Herek, G. M., & McLemore, K. A. (2013). Sexual prejudice. *Annual Review of Psychology, 64*, 309–333.

Herold, E. S. (1981). Contraceptive embarrassment and contraceptive behavior among young single women. *Journal of Youth and Adolescence, 10*(3), 233–242.

Herrett-Skjellum, J., & Allen, M. (1996). Television programming and sex stereotyping: A meta-analysis. In B. R. Burleson (Ed.), *Communication yearbook* (pp. 157–185). Sage Publications, Inc.

Heslin, P. A., & Vandewalle, D. (2008). Managers' implicit assumptions about personnel. *Current Directions in Psychological Science, 17*(3), 219–223.

Hetey, R. C., & Eberhardt, J. L. (2018). The numbers don't speak for themselves: Racial disparities and the persistence of inequality in the criminal justice system. *Current Directions in Psychological Science, 27*(3), 183–187.

Hewstone, M. (1990). The "ultimate attribution error"? A review of the literature on intergroup causal attribution. *European Journal of Social Psychology, 20*(4), 311–335.

Hicklin, A. (2011, January 9). Edie Windsor and Thea Spyer: When Edie met Thea. *Out.* http://www.out.com/entertainment/2011/01/09/edie-windsor-and-thea-spyer-when-edie-met-thea?page=0,1

Hicks, L. L., & McNulty, J. K. (2019). The unbearable automaticity of being . . . in a close relationship. *Current Directions in Psychological Science, 28*(3), 254–259.

Higgins, E. T. (1989). Self-discrepancy theory: What patterns of self-beliefs cause people to suffer? In L. Berkowitz (Ed.), *Advances in experimental social psychology* (Vol. 22, pp. 93–136). Academic Press.

Higgins, E. T. (1996). Knowledge activation: Accessibility, applicability, and salience. In E. T. Higgins & A. W. Kruglanski (Eds.), *Social psychology: Handbook of basic principles* (pp. 133–168). Guilford Press.

Higgins, E. T. (2012). Accessibility theory. In P. A. M. Van Lange, A. W. Kruglanski, & E. T. Higgins (Eds.), *Handbook of theories of social psychology* (Vol. 1, pp. 75–96). Sage.

Higgins, E. T., & Brendl, C. M. (1995). Accessibility and applicability: Some "activation rules" influencing judgment. *Journal of Experimental Social Psychology, 31*(3), 218–243.

Higgins, E. T., King, G. A., & Mavin, G. H. (1982). Individual construct accessibility and subjective impressions and recall. *Journal of Personality and Social Psychology, 43*(1), 35–47.

Higgins, E. T., Rhodewalt, F., & Zanna, M. P. (1979). Dissonance motivation: Its nature, persistence, and reinstatement. *Journal of Experimental Social Psychology, 15*(1), 16–34.

Higgins, E. T., Rholes, W. S., & Jones, C. R. (1977). Category accessibility and impression formation. *Journal of Experimental Social Psychology, 13*(2), 141–154.

Higley, J. D., Linnoila, M., & Suomi, S. J. (1994). Ethological contributions. In M. Hersen, R. T. Ammenman & L. A. Sisson (Eds.), *Handbook of aggressive and destructive behavior in psychiatric patients* (pp. 17–32). Plenum Press.

Hilbig, B. E., Glöckner, A., & Zettler, I. (2014). Personality and prosocial behavior: Linking basic traits and social value orientations. *Journal of Personality and Social Psychology, 107*(3), 529–539.

Hildreth, J. A., & Anderson, C. (2016). Failure at the top: How power undermines collaborative performance. *Journal of Personality and Social Psychology, 110*(2), 261–286.

Hilgard, J., Engelhardt, C. R, & Rouder, J. N. (2017). Overstated evidence for short-term effects of violent games on affect and behavior: A reanalysis of Anderson et al. (2010). *Psychological Bulletin, 143*(7), 757–774.

Hill, J., & Nathan, R. (2008). Childhood antecedents of serious violence in adult male offenders. *Aggressive Behavior, 34*(3), 329–338.

Hilton, J. L., & Darley, J. M. (1985). Constructing other persons: A limit on the effect. *Journal of Experimental Social Psychology, 21*(1), 1–18.

Hilton, J. L., & von Hippel, W. (1996). Stereotypes. *Annual Review of Psychology, 47*(1), 237–271.

Hinsz, V. B. (1989). Facial resemblance in engaged and married couples. *Journal of Social and Personal Relationships, 6*(2), 223–229.

Hirschberger, G., Ein-Dor, T., & Almakias, S. (2008). The self-protective altruist: Terror management and the ambivalent nature of prosocial behavior. *Personality and Social Psychology Bulletin, 34*(5), 666–678.

Hirschberger, G., Florian, V., & Mikulincer, M. (2005). Fear and compassion: A terror management analysis of emotional reactions to physical disability. *Rehabilitation Psychology, 50*(3), 246–257.

Hirsh, J. B., Galinsky, A. D., & Zhong, C. B. (2011). Drunk, powerful, and in the dark: How general processes of disinhibition produce both prosocial and antisocial behavior. *Perspectives on Psychological Science, 6*(5), 415–427.

Hirsh, J. B., & Kang, S. K. (2016). Mechanisms of identity conflict: Uncertainty, anxiety, and the behavioral inhibition system. *Personality and Social Psychology Review, 20*(3), 223–244.

Hitsch, G. J., Hortaçsu, A., & Ariely, D. (2010). What makes you click?—Mate preferences in online dating. *Quantitative Marketing and Economics, 8*(4), 393–427.

Ho, A. K., Sidanius, J., Levin, D. T., & Banaji, M. R. (2011). Evidence for hypodescent and racial hierarchy in the categorization and perception of biracial individuals. *Journal of Personality and Social Psychology, 100*(3), 492–506.

Hobson, P. (2004). Symbol minded. *Nature, 431*(7005), 127–128.

Hodges, B. H., & Geyer, A. L. (2006). A nonconformist account of the Asch experiments: Values, pragmatics, and moral dilemmas. *Personality and Social Psychology Review, 10*(1), 2–19.

Hodson, G., Dovidio, J. F., & Gaertner, S. L. (2002). Processes in racial discrimination: Differential weighting of conflicting information. *Personality and Social Psychology Bulletin, 28*(4), 460–471.

Hoffman, E., McCabe, K. A., & Smith, V. L. (1998). Behavioral foundations of reciprocity: Experimental economics and evolutionary psychology. *Economic Inquiry, 36*(3), 335–352.

Hoffman, K. M., & Trawalter, S. (2016). Assumptions about life hardship and pain perception. *Group Processes & Intergroup Relations, 19*(4), 493–508.

Hoffman, K. M., Trawalter, S., Axt, J. R., & Oliver, M. N. (2016). Racial bias in pain assessment and treatment recommendations, and false beliefs about biological differences between Blacks and Whites. *Proceedings of the National Academies of Science, 113*(16), 4296–4301.

Hoffman, M. L. (1981). Is altruism part of human nature? *Journal of Personality and Social Psychology, 40*(1), 121–137.

Hofling, C. K., Brotzman, E., Dalrymple, S., Graves, N., & Pierce, C. M. (1966). An experimental study in nurse-physician relationships. *Journal of Nervous and Mental Disease, 143*(2), 171–180.

Hofmann, W., Gawronski, B., Gschwendner, T., Le, H., & Schmitt, M. (2005). A meta-analysis on the correlation between the Implicit Association Test and explicit self-report measures. *Personality and Social Psychology Bulletin, 31*(10), 1369–1385.

Hogg, M. A. (2006). Social identity theory. In P. J. Burke (Ed.), *Contemporary social psychological theories* (pp. 111–136). Stanford University Press.

Hogg, M. A. (2007). Uncertainty-identity theory. In M. P. Zanna (Ed.), *Advances in experimental social psychology* (Vol. 39, pp. 69–126). Academic Press.

Hogg, M. A. (2010). Influence and leadership. In S. T. Fiske, D. T. Gilbert, & G. Lindzey (Eds.), *Handbook of social psychology* (5th ed., Vol. 2, pp. 1166–1207). Wiley.

Hogg, M. A., Sherman, D. K., Dierselhuis, J., Maitner, A. T., & Moffitt, G. (2007). Uncertainty, entitativity, and group identification. *Journal of Experimental Social Psychology, 43*(1), 135–142.

Hohman, Z. P., Gaffney, A. M., & Hogg, M. A. (2017). Who am I if I am not like my group? Self-uncertainty and feeling peripheral in a group. *Journal of Experimental Social Psychology, 72*, 125–132.

Holan, A. D. (2016, December 13). *2016 lie of the year: Fake news*. PolitiFact. https://www.politifact.com/article/2016/dec/13/2016-lie-year-fake-news/

Hollis-Walker, L., & Colosimo, K. (2011). Mindfulness, self-compassion, and happiness in nonmeditators: A theoretical and empirical examination. *Personality and Individual Differences, 50*(2), 222–227.

Holm, O. (1983). Four factors affecting perceived aggressiveness. *Journal of Psychology, 114*(2), 227–234.

Hong, Y. Y., Chiu, C., & Dweck, C. S. (1995). Implicit theories of intelligence: Reconsidering the role of confidence in achievement motivation. In M. H. Kernis (Ed.), *Efficacy, agency, and self-esteem. Plenum Series in Social/Clinical Psychology* (pp. 197–216). Plenum Press.

Hong, Y. Y., Chiu, C., Dweck, C. S., Lin, D., & Wan, W. (1999). Implicit theories, attributions, and coping: A meaning system approach. *Journal of Personality and Social Psychology, 77*(3), 588–599.

Hong, Y. Y., Chiu, C. Y., & Kung, T. M. (1997). Bringing culture out in front: Effects of cultural meaning system activation on social cognition. In K. Leung, Y. Kashima, U. Kim, S. Yamaguchi, & Y. Kashima (Eds.), *Progress in Asian social psychology* (Vol. 1, pp. 135–146). Wiley.

Hops, H., Davis, B., Leve, C., & Sheeber, L. (2003). Cross-generational transmission of aggressive parent behavior: A prospective, mediational examination. *Journal of Abnormal Child Psychology, 31*(2), 161–169.

Horney, K. (1937). *The neurotic personality of our time*. W. W. Norton.

Hornsey, M. J., Bain, P. G., Harris, E. A., Lebedeva, N., Kashima, E. S., Guan, Y., González, R., Chen, S. X., & Blumen, S. (2018). How much is enough in a perfect world? Cultural variation in ideal levels of happiness, pleasure, freedom, health, self-esteem, longevity, and intelligence. *Psychological Science, 29*(9), 1393–1404.

Hornsey, M. J., Faulkner, C., Crimston, D., & Moreton, S. (2018). A microscopic dot on a microscopic dot: Self-esteem buffers the negative effects of exposure to the enormity of the universe. *Journal of Experimental Social Psychology, 76*, 198–207.

Horowitz, J. M., Graf, N., & Livingson, G. (2019, November 6). *Marriage and cohabitation in the U.S.* Pew Research Center. https://www.pewsocialtrends.org/2019/11/06/marriage-and-cohabitation-in-the-u-s/

Hortensius, R., & de Gelder, B. (2018). From empathy to apathy: The bystander effect revisited. *Current Directions in Psychological Science, 27*(4), 249–256.

Horton, D., & Wohl, R. R. (1956). Mass communication and para-social interaction: Observations on intimacy at a distance. *Psychiatry, 19*(3), 215–229.

Horton, R. (1967). African traditional thought and Western science. *Africa, 37*, 155–187.

Hotaling, G. T., & Sugarman, D. B. (1990). A risk marker analysis of assaulted wives. *Journal of Family Violence, 5*(1), 1–13.

Houben, K., & Wiers, R. W. (2007). Personalizing the alcohol-IAT with individualized stimuli: Relationship with drinking behavior and drinking-related problems. *Addictive Behaviors, 32*(12), 2852–2864.

Houlette, M. A., Gaertner, S. L., Johnson, K. M., Banker, B. S., Riek, B. M., & Dovidio, J. F. (2004). Developing a more inclusive social identity: An elementary school intervention. *Journal of Social Issues, 60*(1), 35–55.

House, J. S., Landis, K. R., & Umberson, D. (1988). Social relationships and health. *Science, 241*(4865), 540–545.

Houts, R. M., Robins, E., & Huston, T. L. (1996). Compatibility and the development of premarital relationships. *Journal of Marriage and the Family, 58*(1), 7–20.

Hovland, C. I., Lumsdain, A. A., & Sheffield, F. D. (1949). *Experiments in mass communication*. Princeton University Press.

Hovland, C. I., & Sears, R. R. (1940). Minor studies of aggression: VI. Correlation of lynchings with economic indices. *Journal of Psychology, 9*(2), 301–310.

Hovland, C. I., & Weiss, W. (1951). The influence of source credibility on communication effectiveness. *Public Opinion Quarterly, 15*(4), 635–650.

Hu, X., Bergström, Z. M., Bodenhausen, G. V., & Rosenfeld, J. P. (2015). Suppressing unwanted autobiographical memories reduces their automatic influences: Evidence from electrophysiology and an implicit autobiographical memory test. *Psychological Science, 26*(7), 1098–1106.

Huang, Q., Peng, W., & Simmons, J. V. (2021). Assessing the evidence of perspective taking on stereotyping and negative evaluations: a p-curve analysis. *Group Processes & Intergroup Relations, 24*(8), 1306–1334.

Huang, Y., Osborne, D., & Sibley, C. G. (2019). The gradual move toward gender equality: A 7-year latent growth model of ambivalent sexism. *Social Psychological and Personality Science, 10*(3), 335–344.

Hudley, C., & Graham, S. (1993). An attributional intervention to reduce peer-directed aggression among African-American boys. *Child Development, 64*(1), 124–138.

Huesmann, L. R. (1988). An information processing model for the development of aggression. *Aggressive Behavior, 14*(1), 13–24.

Huesmann, L. R., Dubow, E. F., & Boxer, P. (2009). Continuity of aggression from childhood to early adulthood as a predictor of life outcomes: Implications for the adolescent-limited and life-course-persistent models. *Aggressive Behavior, 35*(2), 136–149.

Huesmann, L. R., & Eron, L. D. (1984). Cognitive processes and the persistence of aggressive behavior. *Aggressive Behavior, 10*(3), 243–251.

Huesmann, L. R., Eron, L. D., Lefkowitz, M. M., & Walder, L. O. (1984). Stability of aggression over time and generations. *Developmental Psychology, 20*(6), 1120–1134.

Huesmann, L. R., Lagerspetz, K., & Eron, L. D. (1984). Intervening variables in the TV violence–aggression relation: Evidence from two countries. *Developmental Psychology, 20*(5), 746–775.

Huesmann, L. R., Moise-Titus, J., Podolski, C. L., & Eron, L. D. (2003). Longitudinal relations between children's exposure to TV violence and their aggressive and violent behavior in young adulthood: 1977–1992. *Developmental Psychology, 39*(2), 201–221.

Hugenberg, K., & Bodenhausen, G. V. (2003). Facing prejudice: Implicit prejudice and the perception of facial threat. *Psychological Science, 14*(6), 640–643.

Hughes, R. (2010). *A high wind in Jamaica.* Chatto & Windus. (Original work published 1929)

Hull, J. G., Levenson, R. W., Young, R. D., & Sher, K. J. (1983). Self-awareness reducing effects of alcohol consumption. *Journal of Personality and Social Psychology, 44*(3), 461–473.

Hull, J. G., & Young, R. D. (1983). Self-consciousness, self-esteem, and success–failure as determinants of alcohol consumption in male social drinkers. *Journal of Personality and Social Psychology, 44*(6), 1097–1109.

Hull, J. G., Young, R. D., & Jouriles, E. (1986). Applications of the self-awareness model of alcohol consumption: Predicting patterns of use and abuse. *Journal of Personality and Social Psychology, 51*(4), 790–796.

Humberg, S., Dufner, M., Schönbrodt, F. D., Geukes, K., Hutteman, R., Küfner, A. C., Zalk, M., Denissen, J., Nestler, S., & Back, M. D. (2019). Is accurate, positive, or inflated self-perception most advantageous for psychological adjustment? A competitive test of key hypotheses. *Journal of Personality and Social Psychology, 116*(5), 835–859.

Huneke, M., & Pinel, E. C. (2016). Fostering selflessness through I-sharing. *Journal of Experimental Social Psychology, 63*, 10–18.

Hunt, L. L., Eastwick, P. W., & Finkel, E. J. (2015). Leveling the playing field: Longer acquaintance predicts reduced assortative mating on attractiveness. *Psychological Science, 26*(7), 1046–1053.

Huston, T. L., Caughlin, J. P., Houts, R. M., Smith, S. E., & George, L. J. (2001). The connubial crucible: Newlywed years as predictors of marital delight, distress, and divorce. *Journal of Personality and Social Psychology, 80*(2), 237–252.

Huston, T. L., & Chorost, A. F. (1994). Behavioral buffers on the effect of negativity on marital satisfaction: A longitudinal study. *Personal Relationships, 1*(3), 223–239.

Hyde, J. S. (2005). The gender similarities hypothesis. *American Psychologist, 60*(6), 581–592.

Hynan, D. J., & Grush, J. E. (1986). Effects of impulsivity, depression, provocation, and time on aggressive behavior. *Journal of Research in Personality, 20*(2), 158–171.

Iacoboni, M. (2009). Imitation, empathy, and mirror neurons. *Annual Review of Psychology, 60*, 653–670.

Iati, M., Kornfield, M., Hauslohner, A., Sonmez, F., Flynn, M., Chiu, A., Shepherd, K., Armus, T., & Laurent, O. (2020). Protesters clash with police after former officer is charged in George Floyd's death. *The Washington Post.* https://www.washingtonpost.com/nation/2020/05/29/george-floyd-minneapolis-protests-live-updates/

Ichiyama, M. A. (1993). The reflected appraisal process in small-group interaction. *Social Psychology Quarterly, 56*(2), 87–99.

Idema, W. L. (Ed. and Trans.). (2010). *The butterfly lovers: The legend of Liang Shanbo and Zhu Yingtai: Four versions, with related texts.* Hackett Publishing Company.

Iida, M., Seidman, G., Shrout, P. E., Fujita, K., & Bolger, N. (2008). Modeling support provision in intimate relationships. *Journal of Personality and Social Psychology, 94*(3), 460–478.

Impett, E. A., Strachman, A., Finkel, E. J., & Gable, S. L. (2008). Maintaining sexual desire in intimate relationships: The importance of approach goals. *Journal of Personality and Social Psychology, 94*(5), 808–823.

internetlivestats.com. (2020). *Tweets sent in 1 second.* https://www.internetlivestats.com/one-second/

Inzlicht, M., & Berkman, E. T. (2015). Six questions for the resource model of control (and some answers). *Social & Personality Psychology Compass, 9*(10), 511–524.

Inzlicht, M., & Gutsell, J. N. (2007). Running on empty: Neural signals for self-control failure. *Psychological Science, 18*(11), 933–937.

Inzlicht, M., Kaiser, C. R., & Major, B. (2008). The face of chauvinism: How prejudice expectations shape perceptions of facial affect. *Journal of Experimental Social Psychology, 44*(3), 758–766.

Inzlicht, M., McKay, L., & Aronson, J. (2006). Stigma as ego depletion: How being the target of prejudice affects self-control. *Psychological Science, 17*(3), 262–269.

Inzlicht, M., Schmeichel, B. J., & Macrae, C. N. (2014). Why self-control seems (but may not be) limited. *Trends in Cognitive Sciences, 18*(3), 127–133.

Ip, G. W. M., Chiu, C. Y., & Wan, C. (2006). Birds of a feather and birds flocking together: Physical versus behavioral cues may lead to trait versus goal-based group perception. *Journal of Personality and Social Psychology, 90*(3), 368–381.

Ipsos/Reuters. (2011, April 25). *Ipsos global @dvisory: Supreme being(s), the afterlife and evolution.* http://www.ipsos-na.com/download/pr.aspx?id=10670

Isen, A. M. (1970). Success, failure, attention, and reaction to others: The warm glow of success. *Journal of Personality and Social Psychology, 15*(4), 294–301.

Isen, A. M. (1987). Positive affect, cognitive processes, and social behavior. In L. Berkowitz (Ed.), *Advances in experimental social psychology* (Vol. 20, pp. 203–253). Academic Press.

Isen, A. M., Clark, M., & Schwartz, M. F. (1976). Duration of the effect of good mood on helping: "Footprints on the sands of time." *Journal of Personality and Social Psychology, 34*(3), 385–393.

Isen, A. M., Daubman, K. A., & Nowicki, G. P. (1987). Positive affect facilitates creative problem solving. *Journal of Personality and Social Psychology, 52*(6), 1122–1131.

Isen, A. M., & Levin, P. F. (1972). Effect of feeling good on helping: Cookies and kindness. *Journal of Personality and Social Psychology, 21*(3), 384–388.

Isen, A. M., Shalker, T. E., Clark, M., & Karp, L. (1978). Affect, accessibility of material in memory, and behavior: A cognitive loop? *Journal of Personality and Social Psychology, 36*(1), 1–12.

Isenberg, D. J. (1986). Group polarization: A critical review and meta-analysis. *Journal of Personality and Social Psychology, 50*(6), 1141–1151.

Ismail, I., Martens, A., Landau, M. J., Greenberg, J., & Weise, D. R. (2012). Exploring the effects of the naturalistic fallacy: Evidence that genetic explanations increase the acceptability of killing and male promiscuity. *Journal of Applied Social Psychology, 42*(3), 735–750.

Ito, T. A., & Bartholow, B. D. (2009). The neural correlates of race. *Trends in Cognitive Sciences, 13*(12), 524–531.

Ito, T. A., Larsen, J. T., Smith, N. K., & Cacioppo, J. T. (1998). Negative information weighs more heavily on the brain: The negativity bias in evaluative categorizations. *Journal of Personality and Social Psychology, 75*(4), 887–900.

Ito, T. A., Miller, N., & Pollock, V. E. (1996). Alcohol and aggression: A meta-analysis on the moderating effects of inhibitory cues, triggering events, and self-focused attention. *Psychological Bulletin, 120*(1), 60–82.

Itzchakov, G., Uziel, L., & Wood, W. (2018). When attitudes and habits don't correspond: Self-control depletion increases persuasion but not behavior. *Journal of Experimental Social Psychology, 75*, 1–10.

Iyer, A., Leach, C. W., & Crosby, F. J. (2003). White guilt and racial compensation: The benefits and limits of self-focus. *Personality and Social Psychology Bulletin, 29*(1), 117–129.

Iyer, A., Schmader, T., & Lickel, B. (2007). Why individuals protest the perceived transgressions of their country: The role of anger, shame, and guilt. *Personality and Social Psychology Bulletin, 33*(3), 572–587.

Izard, C. E. (1977). *Human emotions.* Plenum Press.

Izuma, K., Kennedy, K., Fitzjohn, A., Sedikides, C., & Shibata, K. (2018). Neural activity in the reward-related brain regions predicts implicit self-esteem: A novel validity test of psychological measures using neuroimaging. *Journal of Personality and Social Psychology, 114*(3), 343–357.

Jackson, J. M., & Harkins, S. G. (1985). Equity in effort: An explanation of the social loafing effect. *Journal of Personality and Social Psychology, 49*(5), 1199–1206.

Jackson, L. M., & Esses, V. M. (1997). Of scripture and ascription: The relation between religious fundamentalism and intergroup helping. *Personality and Social Psychology Bulletin, 23*(8), 893–906.

Jackson, T., Chen, H., Guo, C., & Gao, X. (2006). Stories we love by: Conceptions of love among couples from the People's Republic of China and the United States. *Journal of Cross-Cultural Psychology, 37*(4), 446–464.

Jacobs, R. C., & Campbell, D. T. (1961). The perpetuation of an arbitrary tradition through several generations of a laboratory microculture. *Journal of Abnormal and Social Psychology, 62*(3), 649–658.

Jacobson, N. S., Follette, W. C., & McDonald, D. W. (1982). Reactivity to positive and negative behavior in distressed and nondistressed married couples. *Journal of Consulting and Clinical Psychology, 50*(5), 706–714.

Jacobson, W. (Host). (2012, September 27). *"Killing is the solution," gang member tells Walter Jacobson.* CBS Chicago. http://chicago.cbslocal.com/2012/09/27/killing-is-the-solution-gang-member-tells-walter-jacobson/

Jahn, G., & Rising, D. (2016, July 24). Police: Munich shooter as loner, planned attack. *Arizona Daily Star (Associated Press)*, p. 10.

JAMA. (2018). Original investigations, global mortality from firearms, 1990–2016. *Journal of the American Medical Association, 320*(8), 792–814.

James, W. (1890). *The principles of psychology.* Henry Holt and Company.

James, W. (1906). *The moral equivalent of war* [Address to Stanford University]. http://www.constitution.org/wj/meow.htm

Jamieson, J. P., & Harkins, S. G. (2007). Mere effort and stereotype threat performance effects. *Journal of Personality and Social Psychology, 93*(4), 544–564.

Jamieson, J. P., Mendes, W. B., Blackstock, E., & Schmader, T. (2010). Turning the knots in your stomach into bows: Reappraising arousal improves performance on the GRE. *Journal of Experimental Social Psychology, 46*(1), 208–212.

Janis, I. L. (1982). *Groupthink: Psychological studies of policy decisions and fiascoes.* Houghton Mifflin.

Janis, I. L., & Feshbach, S. (1953). Effects of fear-arousing communications. *Journal of Abnormal and Social Psychology, 48*(1), 78–92.

Janis, I. L., Kaye, D., & Kirschner, P. (1965). Facilitating effects of "eating-while-reading" on responsiveness to persuasive communications. *Journal of Personality and Social Psychology, 1*(2), 181–186.

Jankowiak, W. R., & Fischer, E. F. (1992). A cross-cultural perspective on romantic love. *Ethnology, 31*(2), 149–155.

Janoff-Bulman, R., & Yopyk, D. J. (2004). Random outcomes and valued commitments: Existential dilemmas and the paradox of meaning. In J. Greenberg, S. L. Koole, & T. Pyszczynski (Eds.), *Handbook of experimental existential psychology* (pp. 122–138). Guilford Press.

Jasienska, G., Lipson, S. F., Ellison, P. T., Thune, I., & Ziomkiewicz, A. (2006). Symmetrical women have higher potential fertility. *Evolution and Human Behavior, 27*(5), 390–400.

Jaynes, J. (1976). *The origin of consciousness in the breakdown of the bicameral mind.* Houghton Mifflin.

Jenkins, P. (Director). (2017). *Wonder woman* [Film]. DC Films.

Jensen, B. (2016, June 14). Weapons gunman used in Orlando shooting are high-capacity, common. *USA Today.* http://www.usatoday.com/story/news/2016/06/14/guns-used-kill-49-orlando-high-capacity-common-weapons/85887260/

Jensen, S. (Director). (1998, October 18). The one where Phoebe hates PBS [Television series episode]. *Friends.* Bright/Kauffman/Crane Productions.

Jensen-Campbell, L. A., Graziano, W. G., & West, S. G. (1995). Dominance, prosocial orientation, and female preferences: Do nice guys really finish last? *Journal of Personality and Social Psychology, 68*(3), 427–440.

Jessop, D. C., & Wade, J. (2008). Fear appeals and binge drinking: A terror management theory perspective. *British Journal of Health Psychology, 13*(4), 773–788.

Jetten, J., Mols, F., & Steffens, N.K. (2021). Prosperous but fearful of falling: The wealth paradox, collective angst, and opposition to immigration. *Personality and Social Psychology Bulletin, 47*, 766-780.

Jimenez, T., Arndt, J., & Helm, P.J. (in press). Prejudicial reactions to the removal of Native American Mascots. *Group Processes & Intergroup Relations.*

Ji, L. J., Zhang, Z., & Nisbett, R. E. (2004). Is it culture or is it language? Examination of language effects in cross-cultural research on categorization. *Journal of Personality and Social Psychology, 87*(1), 57–65.

Jiang, T., Chen, Z., & Sedikides, C. (2019). Self-concept clarity lays the foundation for self-continuity: The restorative function of autobiographical memory. *Journal of Personality and Social Psychology.* https://doi.org/10.1037/pspp0000259

Jia, L., Sung, B., & Wang, J. (2022). The role of right insula and its functional connectivity in the regulation of negative implicit stereotypes against rural migrant workers. *Cognitive, Affective, & Behavioral Neuroscience*, 1–15.

Jin, S. V., & Martin, C. (2015). "A match made . . . online?" The effects of user-generated online dater profile types (free-spirited versus uptight) on other users' perception of trustworthiness, interpersonal attraction, and personality. *Cyberpsychology, Behavior, and Social Networking, 18*(6), 320–327.

Job, V., Dweck, C., & Walton, G. (2010). Ego depletion: Is it all in your head? Implicit theories about willpower affect self-regulation. *Psychological Science, 21*(11), 1686–1693.

Joffe-Walt, C. (2010, October 4). How fake money saved Brazil [Radio broadcast]. In A. Blumberg & A. Davidson, *All things considered: Planet money.* National Public Radio. http://www.npr.org/blogs/money/2010/10/04/130329523/how-fake-money-saved-brazil

Johns, M., Inzlicht, M., & Schmader, T. (2008). Stereotype threat and executive resource depletion: Examining the influence of emotion regulation. *Journal of Experimental Psychology: General, 137*(4), 691–705.

Johns, M., Schmader, T., & Martens, A. (2005). Knowing is half the battle: Teaching stereotype threat as a means of improving women's math performance. *Psychological Science, 16*(3), 175–179.

Johnson, A. L., Crawford, M. T., Sherman, S. J., Rutchick, A. M., Hamilton, D. L., Ferreira, M. B., & Petrocelli, J. V. (2006). A functional perspective on group memberships: Differential need fulfillment in a group typology. *Journal of Experimental Social Psychology, 42*(6), 707–719.

Johnson, D. J., & Chopik, W. J. (2019). Geographic variation in the black-violence stereotype. *Social Psychological and Personality Science, 10*(3), 287–294.

Johnson, K. L., Gill, S., Reichman, V., & Tassinary, L. G. (2007). Swagger, sway, and sexuality: Judging sexual orientation from body motion and morphology. *Journal of Personality and Social Psychology, 93*(3), 321–334.

Johnson, K. L., & Tassinary, L. G. (2005). Perceiving sex directly and indirectly: Meaning in motion and morphology. *Psychological Science, 16*(11), 890–897.

Johnson, R. D., & Downing, L. L. (1979). Deindividuation and valence of cues: Effects on prosocial and antisocial behavior. *Journal of Personality and Social Psychology, 37*(9), 1532–1538.

Joireman, J., & King, S. (2016). Individual differences in the consideration of future and (more) immediate consequences: A review and directions for future research. *Social and Personality Psychology Compass, 10*(5), 313–326.

Jolley, D., & Douglas, K. M. (2014). The effects of anti-vaccine conspiracy theories on vaccination intentions. *PLoS ONE, 9*(2), e89177.

Jonas, E., Fritsche, I., & Greenberg, J. (2005). Currencies as cultural symbols—An existential psychological perspective on reactions of Germans toward the euro. *Journal of Economic Psychology, 26*(1), 129–146.

Jonas, E., Graupmann, V., Kayser, D. N., Zanna, M., Traut-Mattausch, E., & Frey, D. (2009). Culture, self, and the emergence of reactance: Is there a "universal" freedom? *Journal of Experimental Social Psychology, 45*(5), 1068–1080.

Jonas, E., Martens, A., Niesta Kayser, D., Fritsche, I., Sullivan, D., & Greenberg, J. (2008). Focus theory of normative conduct and terror-management theory: The interactive impact of mortality salience and norm salience on social judgment. *Journal of Personality and Social Psychology, 95*(6), 1239–1251.

Jonas, E., Schimel, J., Greenberg, J., & Pyszczynski, T. (2002). The Scrooge effect: Evidence that mortality salience increases prosocial attitudes and behavior. *Personality and Social Psychology Bulletin, 28*(10), 1342–1353.

Jonas, E., Sullivan, D., & Greenberg, J. (2013). Generosity, greed, norms, and death—Differential effects of mortality salience on charitable behavior. *Journal of Economic Psychology, 35*, 47–57.

Jonas, K. J. (2013). Automatic behavior—Its social embedding and individual consequences. *Social and Personality Psychology Compass, 7*(9), 689–700.

Jones, B. C., Hahn, A. C., & DeBruine, L. M. (2019). Ovulation, sex hormones, and women's mating psychology. *Trends in Cognitive Sciences, 23*(1), 51–62.

Jones, D. (1995). Sexual selection, physical attractiveness, and facial neoteny: Cross-cultural evidence and implications. *Current Anthropology, 36*(5), 723–748.

Jones, E. E. (1964). *Ingratiation.* Appleton-Century-Crofts.

Jones, E. E. (1990). *Interpersonal perception.* Freeman.

Jones, E. E., & Davis, K. E. (1965). A theory of correspondent inferences: From acts to dispositions. In L. Berkowitz (Ed.), *Advances in experimental social psychology* (Vol. 2, pp. 219–266). Academic Press.

Jones, E. E., & Harris, V. A. (1967). The attribution of attitudes. *Journal of Experimental Social Psychology, 3*(1), 1–24.

Jones, E. E., Jones, R. G., & Gergen, K. J. (1963). Some conditions affecting the evaluation of a conformist. *Journal of Personality, 31*(2), 270–288.

Jones, E. E., & Nisbett, R. E. (1971). *The actor and the observer: Divergent perceptions of the causes of behavior.* General Learning Press.

Jones, E. E., & Pittman, T. S. (1982). Toward a general theory of strategic self-presentation. In J. Suls (Ed.), *Psychological perspectives on the self* (Vol. 1, pp. 231–262). Erlbaum.

Jones, E. E., & Sigall, H. (1971). The bogus pipeline: A new paradigm for measuring affect and attitude. *Psychological Bulletin, 76*(5), 349–364.

Jones, E. E., & Wortman, C. B. (1973). *Ingratiation: An attributional approach.* General Learning Press.

Jones, J. D., Cassidy, J., & Shaver, P. R. (2015). Parents' self-reported attachment styles: A review of links with parenting behaviors, emotions, and cognitions. *Personality and Social Psychology Review, 19*(1), 44–76.

Jones, J. H. (1981). *Bad blood: The Tuskegee syphilis experiment.* Free Press.

Jones, T. F., Craig, A. S., Hoy, D., Gunter, E. W., Ashley, D. L., Barr, D. B., Brock, J. W., & Schaffner, W. (2000). Mass psychogenic illness attributed to toxic exposure at a high school. *The New England Journal of Medicine, 342*(2), 96–100.

Jordan, C. H., Spencer, S. J., Zanna, M. P., Hoshino-Browne, E., & Correll, J. (2003). Secure and defensive high self-esteem. *Journal of Personality and Social Psychology, 85*(5), 969–978.

Josephs, R. A., Sellers, J. G., Newman, M. L., & Mehta, P. H. (2006). The mismatch effect: When testosterone and status are at odds. *Journal of Personality and Social Psychology, 90*(6), 999–1013.

Josephson, W. L. (1987). Television violence and children's aggression: Testing the priming, social script, and disinhibition predictions. *Journal of Personality and Social Psychology, 53*(5), 882–890.

Jost, J. T. (2019). The IAT is dead, long live the IAT: Context-sensitive measures of implicit attitudes are indispensable to social and political psychology. *Current Directions in Psychological Science, 28*(1), 10–19.

Jost, J. T., & Banaji, M. R. (1994). The role of stereotyping in system-justification and the production of false consciousness. *British Journal of Social Psychology, 33*(1), 1–27.

Jost, J. T., Kivetz, Y., Rubini, M., Guermandi, G., & Mosso, C. (2005). System-justifying functions of complementary regional and ethnic stereotypes: Cross-national evidence. *Social Justice Research, 18*(3), 305–333.

Jostmann, N. B., Lakens, D., & Schubert, T. W. (2009). Weight as an embodiment of importance. *Psychological Science, 20*(9), 1169–1174.

Joyce, J. (1961). *Ulysses*. Random House.

Judge, T. A., Bono, J. E., Ilies, R., & Gerhardt, M. W. (2002). Personality and leadership: A qualitative and quantitative review. *Journal of Applied Psychology, 87*(4), 765–780.

Jung, C. G. (1970). *After the catastrophe*. In G. Adler & R. F. C. Hull (Eds. And Trans.), *Collected works of C. G. Jung: Vol. 10. Civilization in transition*. Princeton University Press. (Original work published 1945)

Jung, C. G., & von Franz, M. L. (Eds.). (1968). *Man and his symbols*. Random House.

Jussim, L. (1986). Self-fulfilling prophecies: A theoretical and integrative review. *Psychological Review, 93*(4), 429–445.

Jussim, L., Crawford, J. T., & Rubinstein, R. S. (2015). Stereotype (in)accuracy in perceptions of groups and individuals. *Current Directions in Psychological Science, 24*(6), 490–497.

Kabat-Zinn, J. (1990). *Full catastrophe living: Using the wisdom of your body and mind to face stress, pain, and illness*. Delacorte.

Kagan, J. (1994). *Galen's prophecy: Temperament in human nature*. Basic Books.

Kahneman, D. (2011). *Thinking, fast and slow*. Farrar, Straus and Giroux.

Kahneman, D., & Tversky, A. (1973). On the psychology of prediction. *Psychological Review, 80*(4), 237–251.

Kahneman, D., & Tversky, A. (1982). The simulation heuristic. In D. Kahneman, P. Slovic, & A. Tversky (Eds.), *Judgment under uncertainty: Heuristics and biases* (pp. 201–208). Cambridge University Press.

Kaiser, C. R., Drury, B. J., Spalding, K. E., Cheryan, S., & O'Brien, L. T. (2009). The ironic consequences of Obama's election: Decreased support for social justice. *Journal of Experimental Social Psychology, 45*(3), 556–559.

Kaiser, C. R., & Miller, C. T. (2001). Stop complaining! The social costs of making attributions to discrimination. *Personality and Social Psychology Bulletin, 27*(2), 254–263.

Kaiser, C. R., Vick, S. B., & Major, B. (2006). Prejudice expectations moderate preconscious attention to cues that are threatening to social identity. *Psychological Science, 17*(4), 332–338.

Kalick, S. M., Zebrowitz, L. A., Langlois, J. H., & Johnson, R. M. (1998). Does human facial attractiveness honestly advertise health? Longitudinal data on an evolutionary question. *Psychological Science, 9*(1), 8–13.

Kamp Dush, C. M., & Amato, P. R. (2005). Consequences of relationship status and quality for subjective well-being. *Journal of Social and Personal Relationships, 22*(5), 607–627.

Kane, H. S., Jaremka, L. M., Guichard, A. C., Ford, M. B., Collins, N. L., & Feeney, B. C. (2007). Feeling supported and feeling satisfied: How one partner's attachment style predicts the other partner's relationship experiences. *Journal of Social and Personal Relationships, 24*(4), 535–555.

Kang, C. (2020, April 9). The humble phone call has made a comeback. *The New York Times*. https://www.nytimes.com/2020/04/09/technology/phone-calls-voice-virus.html

Kann, L., O'Malley Olsen, E., McManus, T., Harris, W. A., Shanklin, S. L., Flint, K. H., Queen, B., Lowry, R., Chyen, D., Whittle, L., Thornton, J., Lim, C., Yamakawa, Y., Berner, N., & Zaza, S. (2016). Sexual identity, sex of sexual contacts, and health-related behaviors among students in grades 9–12—United States and selected sites, 2015. *Morbidity and Mortality Weekly Report, 65*, 1–81.

Kantola, S. J., Syme, G. J., & Campbell, N. A. (1984). Cognitive dissonance and energy conservation. *Journal of Applied Psychology, 69*(3), 416–421.

Kanwisher, N., McDermott, J., & Chun, M. M. (1997). The fusiform face area: A module in human extrastriate cortex specialized for face perception. *Journal of Neuroscience, 17*(11), 4302–4311.

Karau, S. J., & Williams, K. D. (1993). Social loafing: A meta-analytic review and theoretical integration. *Journal of Personality and Social Psychology, 65*(4), 681–706.

Karau, S. J., & Williams, K. D. (1997). The effects of group cohesiveness on social loafing and social compensation. *Group Dynamics: Theory, Research, and Practice, 1*(2), 156–168.

Kardas, M., & O'Brien, E. (2018). Easier seen than done: Merely watching others perform can foster an illusion of skill acquisition. *Psychological Science, 29*(4), 521–536.

Karney, B. R., & Bradbury, T. N. (1995). The longitudinal course of marital quality and stability: A review of theory, methods, and research. *Psychological Bulletin, 118*(1), 3–34.

Karney, B. R., & Bradbury, T. N. (2000). Attributions in marriage: State or trait? A growth curve analysis. *Journal of Personality and Social Psychology, 78*(2), 295–309.

Karremans, J. C., Tila, M., Pronk, T. M., & Wal, R. C. (2015). Executive control and relationship maintenance processes: An empirical overview and theoretical integration. *Social and Personality Psychology Compass, 9*(7), 333–347.

Karsten, R. (1935). *The head-hunters of western Amazonas*. Societas Scientiarum Fennica.

Kashdan, T. B., Barrett, L. F., & McKnight, P. E. (2015). Unpacking emotion differentiation transforming unpleasant experience by perceiving distinctions in negativity. *Current Directions in Psychological Science, 24*(1), 10–16.

Kaspar, K. (2013). A weighty matter: Heaviness influences the evaluation of disease severity, drug effectiveness, and side effects. *PLoS ONE, 8*(11), e78307.

Kasser, T., & Ryan, R. M. (1993). A dark side of the American dream: Correlates of financial success as a central life aspiration. *Journal of Personality and Social Psychology, 65*(2), 410–422.

Kassin, S. M., Bogart, D., & Kerner, J. (2012). Confessions that corrupt evidence from the DNA exoneration case files. *Psychological Science, 23*(1), 41–45.

Katz, I., & Hass, R. G. (1988). Racial ambivalence and American value conflict: Correlational and priming studies of dual cognitive structures. *Journal of Personality and Social Psychology, 55*(6), 893–905.

Kaufman, J., & Zigler, E. (1987). Do abused children become abusive parents? *American Journal of Orthopsychiatry, 57*(2), 186–192.

Kaur, H., & Mack, J. (2020). *The cities, states, and countries finally putting an end to police neck restraints*. CNN. https://www.cnn.com/2020/06/10/world/police-policies-neck-restraints-trnd/index.html

Kawakami, K., Dovidio, J. F., Moll, J., Hermsen, S., &Russin, A. (2000). Just say no (to stereotyping): Effects of training in the negation of stereotypic associations on stereotype activation. *Journal of Personality and Social Psychology, 78*(5), 871–888.

Kawakami, K., Dunn, E., Karmali, F., & Dovidio, J. F. (2009). Mispredicting affective and behavioral responses to racism. *Science, 323*(5911), 276–278.

Kawakami, K., Phills, C. E., Steele, J. R., & Dovidio, J. F. (2007). (Close) distance makes the heart grow fonder: Improving implicit racial attitudes and interracial interactions through approach behaviors. *Journal of Personality and Social Psychology, 92*(6), 957–971.

Kay, A. C., & Jost, J. T. (2003). Complementary justice: Effects of "poor but happy" and "poor but honest" stereotype exemplars on system justification and implicit activation of the justice motive. *Journal of Personality and Social Psychology, 85*(5), 823–837.

Kay, A. C., Jost, J. T., Mandisodza, A. N., Sherman, S. J., Petrocelli, J. V., & Johnson, A. L. (2007). Panglossian ideology in the service of system justification: How complementary stereotypes help us to rationalize inequality. In M. P. Zanna (Ed.), *Advances in experimental social psychology* (Vol. 39, pp. 305–358). Academic Press.

Keane, T. M., Litz, B. T., & Blake, D. D. (1990). Post-traumatic stress disorder in adulthood. In M. Hersen & C. G. Last (Eds.), *Handbook of child and adult psychopathology: A longitudinal perspective*. Pergamon Press.

Keinan, G. (1994). The effects of stress and tolerance of ambiguity on magical thinking. *Journal of Personality and Social Psychology, 67*(1), 48–55.

Keinan, G. (2002). The effects of stress and desire for control on superstitious behavior. *Personality and Social Psychology Bulletin, 28*(1), 102–108.

Keller, J., & Bless, H. (2008). Flow and regulatory compatibility: An experimental approach to the flow model of intrinsic motivation. *Personality and Social Psychology Bulletin, 34*(2), 196–209.

Kellermann, A. L., Rivara, F. P., Rushforth, N. B., Banton, J. G., Reay, D. T., Francisco, J. T., Locci, A. B., Prodzinski, J., Hackman, B. B., & Somes, G. (1993). Gun ownership as a risk factor for homicide in the home. *The New England Journal of Medicine, 329*(15), 1084–1091.

Kelley, D. E. (Writer). (2008). Tabloid nation [Television series episode]. *Boston legal*. 20th Century Fox Television.

Kelley, H. H. (1967). Attribution theory in social psychology. *Nebraska Symposium on Motivation, 17*, 192–238.

Kelley, H. H. (1971). *Attribution in social interaction*. General Learning Press.

Kelley, H. H. (1973). The processes of causal attribution. *American Psychologist, 28*(2), 107–128.

Kelman, H. C. (1976). Violence without restraint: Reflections on the dehumanization of victims and victimizers. In G. M. Kren & L. H. Rappoport (Eds.), *Varieties of psychohistory* (pp. 282–314). Springer.

Keltner, D., Gruenfeld, D. H., & Anderson, C. (2003). Power, approach, and inhibition. *Psychological Review, 110*(2), 265–284.

Keltner, D., Young, R. C., Heerey, E. A., Oemig, C., & Monarch, N. D. (1998). Teasing in hierarchical and intimate relations. *Journal of Personality and Social Psychology, 75*(5), 1231–1247.

Kenny, D. A., & Acitelli, L. K. (2001). Accuracy and bias in the perception of the partner in a close relationship. *Journal of Personality and Social Psychology, 80*(3), 439–448.

Kenrick, D. T., Griskevicius, V., Neuberg, S. L., & Schaller, M. (2010). Renovating the pyramid of needs: Contemporary extensions built upon ancient foundations. *Perspectives on Psychological Science, 5*(3), 292–314.

Kenrick, D. T., & Gutierres, S. E. (1980). Contrast effects and judgments of physical attractiveness: When beauty becomes a social problem. *Journal of Personality and Social Psychology, 38*(1), 131–140.

Kenrick, D. T., Gutierres, S. E., & Goldberg, L. L. (1989). Influence of popular erotica on judgments of strangers and mates. *Journal of Experimental Social Psychology, 25*(2), 159–167.

Kenrick, D. T., & Keefe, R. C. (1992). Age preferences in mates reflect sex differences in human reproductive strategies. *Behavioral and Brain Sciences, 15*, 75–91.

Kenrick, D. T., & MacFarlane, S. W. (1986). Ambient temperature and horn honking: A field study of the heat/aggression relationship. *Environment and Behavior, 18*(2), 179–191.

Kenrick, D. T., Sadalla, E. K., Groth, G., & Trost, M. R. (1990). Evolution, traits, and the stages of human courtship: Qualifying the parental investment model. *Journal of Personality, 58*(1), 97–116.

Kenworthy, J. B., Hewstone, M., Levine, J. M., Martin, R., & Willis, H. (2008). The phenomenology of minority–majority status: Effects on innovation in argument generation. *European Journal of Social Psychology, 38*(4), 624–636.

Kepes, S., Bushman, B. J., & Anderson, C. A. (2017). Violent video games remain a societal concern: Reply to Hilgard, Engelhardt & Rouder (2017). *Psychological Bulletin, 143*(7), 775–782.

Kephart, W. M. (1967). Some correlates of romantic love. *Journal of Marriage and the Family, 29*(3), 470–474.

Kernis, M. H., Grannemann, B. D., & Barclay, L. C. (1989). Stability and level of self-esteem as predictors of anger arousal and hostility. *Journal of Personality and Social Psychology, 56*(6), 1013–1022.

Kernis, M. H., & Waschull, S. B. (1995). The interactive roles of stability and level of self-esteem: Research and theory. In M. P. Zanna (Ed.), *Advances in experimental social psychology* (Vol. 27, pp. 93–141). Academic Press.

Kernis, M. H., Whisenhunt, C. R., Waschull, S. B., Greenier, K. D., Berry, A. J., Herlocker, C. E., & Anderson, C. A. (1998). Multiple facets of self-esteem and their relations to depressive symptoms. *Personality and Social Psychology Bulletin, 24*(6), 657–668.

Kerr, N. L., Ao, X., Hogg, M. A., & Zhang, J. (2018). Addressing replicability concerns via adversarial collaboration: Discovering hidden moderators of the minimal intergroup discrimination effect. *Journal of Experimental Social Psychology, 78*, 66–76.

Kerr, N. L., & Bruun, S. E. (1983). Dispensability of member effort and group motivation losses: Free-rider effects. *Journal of Personality and Social Psychology, 44*(1), 78–94.

Kessler, R. C., Mickelson, K. D., & Williams, D. R. (1999). The prevalence, distribution, and mental health correlates of perceived discrimination in the United States. *Journal of Health and Social Behavior, 40*(3), 208–230.

Keveney, B. (2022) 'We're going to fight': Trans people express outrage over anti-*LGBTQ* measures in Texas, Florida. USA Today. https://www.usatoday.com/story/news/nation/2022/03/12/texas-florida-lgbt-restrictions-stire-anger-resolve-trans-people/9441847002/?gnt-cfr=1

Kids Count. (2013). *Children in single-parent families by race.* http://datacenter.kidscount.org/data/acrossstates/Rankings.aspx?ind=107

Kiecolt-Glaser, J. K., & Newton, T. L. (2001). Marriage and health: His and hers. *Psychological Bulletin, 127*(4), 472–503.

Kihlstrom, J. F. (1994). Hypnosis, delayed recall, and the principles of memory. *International Journal of Clinical and Experimental Hypnosis, 42*(4), 337–345.

Kihlstrom, J. F. (2019). The motivational unconscious. *Social and Personality Psychology Compass, 13*(5), e12470.

Kim, H. K., & McKenry, P. C. (2002). The relationship between marriage and psychological well-being: A longitudinal analysis. *Journal of Family Issues, 23*(8), 885–911.

Kim, H. Y., & Pettit, N. C. (2019). A cross-cultural review and perspective on status striving. *Social and Personality Psychology Compass, 13*(7), e12488.

Kim, J. Y., Fitzsimons, G. M., & Kay, A. C. (2018). Lean in messages increase attributions of women's responsibility for gender inequality. *Journal of Personality and Social Psychology, 115*(6), 974–1001.

Kim, S. H., Smith, R. H., & Brigham, N. L. (1998). Effects of power imbalance and the presence of third parties on reactions to harm: Upward and downward revenge. *Personality and Social Psychology Bulletin, 24*(4), 353–361.

Kimball, M. M. (1986). Television and sex-role attitudes. In T. M. Williams (Ed.), *The impact of television: A natural experiment in three communities* (pp. 265–301). Academic Press.

Kimble, C. E., & Hirt, E. R. (2005). Self-focus, gender, and habitual self-handicapping: Do they make a difference in behavioral self-handicapping? *Social Behavior and Personality: An International Journal, 33*(1), 43–56.

Kim-Cohen, J., Caspi, A., Taylor, A., Williams, B., Newcombe, R., Craig, I. W., & Moffitt, T. E. (2006). MAOA, maltreatment, and gene-environment interaction predicting children's mental health: New evidence and a meta-analysis. *Molecular Psychiatry, 11*(10), 903–913.

King, D., Vlaev, I., Everett-Thomas, R., Fitzpatrick, M., Darzi, A., & Birnbach, D. J. (2016). "Priming" hand hygiene compliance in clinical environments. *Health Psychology, 35*(1), 96–101.

King, L. A., Hicks, J. A., Krull, J. L., & Del Gaiso, A. K. (2006). Positive affect and the experience of meaning in life. *Journal of Personality and Social Psychology, 90*(1), 179–196.

King, M. L., Jr. (1992). I have a dream. In J. M. Washington (Ed.), *I have a dream: Writings and speeches that changed the world* (pp. 101–106). Harper San Francisco. (Original speech given 1963)

Kingdon, J. (1993). *Self-made man: Human evolution from Eden to extinction?* Wiley.

Kipnis, D. (1972). Does power corrupt? *Journal of Personality and Social Psychology, 24*(1), 33–41.

Kirkpatrick, L. A., & Davis, K. E. (1994). Attachment style, gender, and relationship stability: A longitudinal analysis. *Journal of Personality and Social Psychology, 66*(3), 502–512.

Kirkpatrick, L. A., & Epstein, S. (1992). Cognitive-experiential self-theory and subjective probability: Further evidence for two conceptual systems. *Journal of Personality and Social Psychology, 63*(4), 534–544.

Kirkpatrick, L. A., & Hazan, C. (1994). Attachment styles and close relationships: A four-year prospective study. *Personal Relationships, 1*(2), 123–142.

Kirsch, I. (2010). *The emperor's new drugs: Exploding the antidepressant myth.* Basic Books.

Kirschbaum, C., Pirke, K. M., & Hellhammer, D. H. (1993). The 'Trier Social Stress Test'—A tool for investigating psychobiological stress responses in a laboratory setting. *Neuropsychobiology, 28*(1–2), 76–81.

Kitayama, S., & Markus, H. R. (2000). The pursuit of happiness and the realization of sympathy: Cultural patterns of self, social relations, and wellbeing. In E. Diener & E. Suh (Eds.), *Subjective well-being across cultures* (pp. 113–161). MIT Press.

Kitayama, S., Snibbe, A. C., Markus, H. R., & Suzuki, T. (2004). Is there any "free" choice? Self and dissonance in two cultures. *Psychological Science, 15*(8), 527–533.

Kiviniemi, M. T., Snyder, M., & Omoto, A. M. (2002). Too many of a good thing? The effects of multiple motivations on stress, cost, fulfillment, and satisfaction. *Personality and Social Psychology Bulletin, 28*(6), 732–743.

Klandermans, B., Werner, M., & Van Doorn, M. (2008). Redeeming apartheid's legacy: Collective guilt, political ideology, and compensation. *Political Psychology, 29*(3), 331–349.

Klatzky, R. L., & Creswell, J. D. (2014). An intersensory interaction account of priming effects—And their absence. *Perspectives on Psychological Science, 9*(1), 49–58.

Klauer, K. C., & Wegener, I. (1998). Unraveling social categorization in the "Who said what?" paradigm. *Journal of Personality and Social Psychology, 75*(5), 1155–1178.

Kleider-Offutt, H. M., Bond, A. D., & Hegerty, S. E. (2017). Black stereotypical features: When a face type can get you in trouble. *Current Directions in Psychological Science, 26*(1), 28–33.

Klein, R. G., & Edgar, B. (2002). *The dawn of human culture.* Wiley.

Klein, S. B., Sherman, J. W., & Loftus, J. (1996). The role of episodic and semantic memory in the development of trait self-knowledge. *Social Cognition, 14*(4), 277–291.

Kleinfeld, J. S. (1971). *Some instructional strategies for the cross-cultural classroom.* Alaska State Department of Education.

Klinesmith, J., Kasser, T., & McAndrew, F. T. (2006). Guns, testosterone, and aggression: An experimental test of a mediational hypothesis. *Psychological Science, 17*(7), 568–571.

Klonoff, E. A., Landrine, H., & Ullman, J. B. (1999). Racial discrimination and psychiatric symptoms among Blacks. *Cultural Diversity and Ethnic Minority Psychology, 5*(4), 329–339.

Kluegel, J. R., & Smith, E. R. (1986). *Beliefs about inequality: Americans' views of what is and what ought to be.* Aldine de Gruyter.

Klusmann, D. (2002). Sexual motivation and the duration of partnership. *Archives of Sexual Behavior, 31*(3), 275–287.

Knafo, A., Israel, S., & Ebstein, R. P. (2011). Heritability of children's prosocial behavior and differential susceptibility to parenting by variation in the dopamine receptor D4 gene. *Development and Psychopathology, 23*(1), 53–67.

Knafo, A., & Plomin, R. (2006). Prosocial behavior from early to middle childhood: Genetic and environmental influences on stability and change. *Developmental Psychology, 42*(5), 771–786.

Knee, C. R. (1998). Implicit theories of relationships: Assessment and prediction of romantic relationship initiation, coping, and longevity. *Journal of Personality and Social Psychology, 74*(2), 360–370.

Knight, G. P., Johnson, L. G., Carlo, G., & Eisenberg, N. (1994). A multiplicative model of the dispositional antecedents of a prosocial behavior: Predicting more of the people more of the time. *Journal of Personality and Social Psychology, 66*(1), 178–183.

Knobloch, L. K., & Donovan-Kicken, E. (2006). Perceived involvement of network members in courtships: A test of the relational turbulence model. *Personal Relationships, 13*(3), 281–302.

Knobloch, L. K., Miller, L. E., & Carpenter, K. E. (2007). Using the relational turbulence model to understand negative emotion within courtship. *Personal Relationships, 14*(1), 91–112.

Knoch, D., Pascual-Leone, A., Meyer, K., Treyer, V., & Fehr, E. (2006). Diminishing reciprocal fairness by disrupting the right prefrontal cortex. *Science, 314*(5800), 829–832.

Knox, R. E., & Inkster, J. A. (1968). Postdecision dissonance at post time. *Journal of Personality and Social Psychology, 8*(4, Pt. 1), 319–323.

Ko, S. J., Sadler, M. S., & Galinsky, A. D. (2015). The sound of power: Conveying and detecting hierarchical rank through voice. *Psychological Science, 26*(1), 3–14.

Koch, C. (Director). (2011, October 5). Door to door [TV series episode]. In C. Chupack, B. Karlin, J. Morton, J. Richman, C. Smirnoff, B. Walsh, S. Young, D. Zuker, C. Lloyd, P. S. Levitan, P. Corrigan, A. Higginbotham, D. O'Shannon, . . . & B. Wrubel (Producers), *Modern family*. Levitan/Lloyd & 20th Century Fox Television.

Koenig, L. B., McGue, M., & Iacono, W. G. (2008). Stability and change in religiousness during emerging adulthood. *Developmental Psychology, 44*(2), 532–543.

Konijn, E. A., Nije Bijvank, M., & Bushman, B. J. (2007). I wish I were a warrior: The role of wishful identification in the effects of violent video games on aggression in adolescent boys. *Developmental Psychology, 43*(4), 1038–1044.

Koo, M., & Fishbach, A. (2016). Giving the self: Increasing commitment and generosity through giving something that represents one's essence. *Social Psychological and Personality Science, 7*(4), 339–348.

Koppel, N. (2011, August 24). "Hot sauce" mom convicted of child abuse. *The Wall Street Journal.* http://blogs.wsj.com/law/2011/08/24/hotsauce-mom-convicted-of-child-abuse/

Korte, C. (1980). Urban-nonurban differences in social behavior and social psychological models of urban impact. *Journal of Social Issues, 36*(3), 29–51.

Kosfeld, M., Heinrichs, M., Zak, P. J., Fischbacher, U., & Fehr, E. (2005). Oxytocin increases trust in humans. *Nature, 435*(7042), 673–676.

Kosloff, S., & Greenberg, J. (2009). Pearls in the desert: The proximal and distal effects of mortality salience on the appeal of extrinsic goals. *Journal of Experimental Social Psychology, 45*(1), 197–203.

Kosloff, S., Greenberg, J., Dechesne, M., Weise, D., & Schmader, T. (2010). Smearing the opposition: Implicit and explicit stigmatization of the 2008 U.S. presidential candidates. *Journal of Experimental Psychology: General, 139,* 383–398.

Kosloff, S., Greenberg, J., Sullivan, D., & Weise, D. (2010). Of trophies and pillars: Exploring the terror management functions of short-term and long-term relationship partners. *Personality and Social Psychology Bulletin, 36*(8), 1037–1051.

Kovacs, L. (1983). A conceptualization of marital development. *Family Therapy, 10*(3), 183–210.

Kövecses, Z. (2005). *Metaphor in culture: Universality and variation.* Cambridge University Press.

Kövecses, Z. (2010). *Metaphor: A practical introduction.* Oxford University Press.

Kowalski, R. M. (2003). *Complaining, teasing, and other annoying behaviors.* Yale University Press.

Kotzur, P. F., & Wagner, U. (2021). The dynamic relationship between contact opportunities, positive and negative intergroup contact, and prejudice: A longitudinal investigation. *Journal of Personality and Social Psychology, 120*(2), 418–442.

Kramer, R. S., Young, A. W., Day, M. G., & Burton, A. M. (2017). Robust social categorization emerges from learning the identities of very few faces. *Psychological Review, 124*(2), 115–129.

Krämer, U. M., Jansma, H., Tempelmann, C., & Münte, T. F. (2007). Tit-for-tat: The neural basis of reactive aggression. *Neuroimage, 38*(1), 203–211.

Kraus, M. W., Piff, P. K., Mendoza-Denton, R., Rheinschmidt, M. R., & Keltner, D. (2012). Social class, solipsism, and contextualism: How the rich are different from the poor. *Psychological Review, 119*(3), 546–572.

Kraut, R. E., & Johnston, R. E. (1979). Social and emotional messages of smiling: An ethological approach. *Journal of Personality and Social Psychology, 37*(9), 1539–1553.

Kray, L. J., & Haselhuhn, M. P. (2007). Implicit negotiation beliefs and performance: Experimental and longitudinal evidence. *Journal of Personality and Social Psychology, 93*(1), 49–64.

Kray, L. J., Thompson, L., & Galinsky, A. (2001). Battle of the sexes: Gender stereotype confirmation and reactance in negotiations. *Journal of Personality and Social Psychology, 80*(6), 942–958.

Kreager, D. A., Cavanagh, S. E., Yen, J., & Yu, M. (2014). "Where have all the good men gone?" Gendered interactions in online dating. *Journal of Marriage and Family, 76*(2), 387–410.

Krebs, D. (1975). Empathy and altruism. *Journal of Personality and Social Psychology, 32*(6), 1134–1146.

Krems, J. A., Neel, R., Neuberg, S. L., Puts, D. A. (2016). Women selectively guard their (desirable) mates from ovulating women. *Journal of Personality and Social Psychology, 110*(4), 551–573.

Kressel, N. J. (1996). *Mass hate: The global rise of genocide and terror.* Plenum Press.

Kretschmar, J. M., & Flannery, D. J. (2007). Substance use and violent behavior. In D. J. Flannery, A. T. Vazsonyi, & I. D. Waldman (Eds.), *The Cambridge handbook of violent behavior and aggression* (pp. 647–663). Cambridge University Press.

Kreuzbauer, R., & Keller, J. (2017). The authenticity of cultural products: A psychological perspective. *Current Directions in Psychological Science, 26*(5), 417–421.

Krizan, Z., & Johar, O. (2015). Narcissistic rage revisited. *Journal of Personality and Social Psychology, 108*(5), 784–801.

Kroon, M. B., Hart, P. T., & Van Kreveld, D. (1991). Managing group decision making processes: Individual versus collective accountability and groupthink. *International Journal of Conflict Management, 2*(2), 91–115.

Krosch, A. R., & Amodio, D. M. (2019). Scarcity disrupts the neural encoding of Black faces: A socioperceptual pathway to discrimination. *Journal of Personality and Social Psychology, 117*(5), 859–875.

Krosch, A. R., Tyler, T. R., & Amodio, D. M. (2017). Race and recession: Effects of economic scarcity on racial discrimination. *Journal of Personality and Social Psychology, 113*(6), 892–909.

Krosnick, J. A. (1988). The role of attitude importance in social evaluation: A study of policy preferences, presidential candidate evaluations, and voting behavior. *Journal of Personality and Social Psychology, 55*(2), 196–210.

Krosnick, J. A., & Alwin, D. F. (1989). Aging and susceptibility to attitude change. *Journal of Personality and Social Psychology, 57*(3), 416–425.

Krueger, J., & Zeiger, J. S. (1993). Social categorization and the truly false consensus effect. *Journal of Personality and Social Psychology, 65*(4), 670–680.

Kruesi, M. J. (2007). Psychopharmacology of violence. In D. J. Flannery, A. T. Vazsonyi, & I. D. Waldman (Eds.), *The Cambridge handbook of violent behavior and aggression* (pp. 618–635). Cambridge University Press.

Kruger, J., & Dunning, D. (1999). Unskilled and unaware of it: How difficulties in recognizing one's own incompetence lead to inflated self-assessments. *Journal of Personality and Social Psychology, 77*(6), 1121–1134.

Kruglanski, A. W. (1980). Lay epistemologic process and contents: Another look at attribution theory. *Psychological Review, 87*(1), 70.

Kruglanski, A. W. (1989). *Lay epistemics and human knowledge: Cognitive and motivational bases.* Plenum Press.

Kruglanski, A. W. (1996). Motivated social cognition: Principles of the interface. In E. T. Higgins & A. W. Kruglanski (Eds.), *Social psychology: Handbook of basic principles* (pp. 133–168). Guilford Press.

Kruglanski, A. W. (2004). *The psychology of closed mindedness.* Psychology Press.

Kruglanski, A. W., & Freund, T. (1983). The freezing and unfreezing of lay inferences: Effects on impressional primacy, ethnic stereotyping, and numerical anchoring. *Journal of Experimental Social Psychology, 19*(5), 448–468.

Kruglanski, A. W., Schwartz, J. M., Maides, S., & Hamel, I. Z. (1978). Covariation, discounting, and augmentation: Towards a clarification of attributional principles. *Journal of Personality, 46*(1), 176–189.

Krull, D. S., Loy, M. H. M., Lin, J., Wang, C. F., Chen, S., & Zhao, X. (1999). The fundamental fundamental attribution error: Correspondence bias in individualist and collectivist cultures. *Personality and Social Psychology Bulletin, 25*(10), 1208–1219.

Kteily, N. S., & Bruneau, E. (2017). Darker demons of our nature: The need to (re)focus attention on blatant forms of dehumanization. *Current Directions in Psychological Science, 26*(6), 487–494.

Kteily, N., Bruneau, E., Waytz, A., & Cotterill, S. (2015). The ascent of man: Theoretical and empirical evidence for blatant dehumanization. *Journal of Personality and Social Psychology, 109*(5), 901–931.

Kubrick, S. (Director). (1971). *A clockwork orange* [Film]. Warner Bros.

Kulik, J. A., Mahler, H. I., & Earnest, A. (1994). Social comparison and affiliation under threat: Going beyond the affiliate-choice paradigm. *Journal of Personality and Social Psychology*, 66(2), 301–309.

Kunda, Z. (1990). The case for motivated reasoning. *Psychological Bulletin*, 108(3), 480–498.

Kunda, Z. (1999). *Social cognition: Making sense of people*. MIT Press.

Kunda, Z., Davies, P. G., Adams, B. D., & Spencer, S. J. (2002). The dynamic time course of stereotype activation: Activation, dissipation, and resurrection. *Journal of Personality and Social Psychology*, 82(3), 283–299.

Kunda, Z., & Thagard, P. (1996). Forming impressions from stereotypes, traits, and behaviors: A parallel-constraint-satisfaction theory. *Psychological Review*, 103(2), 284–308.

Kunst, J. R., Thomsen, L., Sam, D. L., & Berry, J. W. (2015). "We are in this together": Common group identity predicts majority members' active acculturation efforts to integrate immigrants. *Personality and Social Psychology Bulletin*, 41(10), 1438–1453.

Kunstman, J. W., & Plant, E. A. (2008). Racing to help: Racial bias in high emergency helping situations. *Journal of Personality and Social Psychology*, 95(6), 1499–1510.

Kurdek, L. A. (1999). The nature and predictors of the trajectory of change in marital quality for husbands and wives over the first 10 years of marriage. *Developmental Psychology*, 35(5), 1283–1296.

Kurdek, L. A. (2004). Are gay and lesbian cohabiting couples really different from heterosexual married couples? *Journal of Marriage and Family*, 66(4), 880–900.

Kurdek, L. A. (2005). Gender and marital satisfaction early in marriage: A growth curve approach. *Journal of Marriage and Family*, 67(1), 68–84.

Kurdek, L. A. (2008). Change in relationship quality for partners from lesbian, gay male, and heterosexual couples. *Journal of Family Psychology*, 22(5), 701–711.

Kurdi, B., Seitchik, A. E., Axt, J. R., Carroll, T. J., Karapetyan, A., Kaushik, N., Tomezsko, D., Greenwald, A. G., & Banaji, M. R. (2019). Relationship between the Implicit Association Test and intergroup behavior: A meta-analysis. *American Psychologist*, 74(5), 569–586.

Kurzban, R., & Neuberg, S. (2005). Managing ingroup and outgroup relationships. In D. M. Buss (Ed.), *The handbook of evolutionary psychology* (pp. 653–675). Wiley.

Kurzban, R., Tooby, J., & Cosmides, L. (2001). Can race be erased? Coalitional computation and social categorization. *Proceedings of the National Academy of Sciences*, 98(26), 15387–15392.

Kushlev, K., & Heintzelman, S. J. (2018). Put the phone down: Testing a complement-interfere model of computer-mediated communication in the context of face-to-face interactions. *Social Psychological and Personality Science*, 9(6), 702–710.

Kuster, M., Bernecker, K., Backes, S., Brandstätter, V., Nussbeck, F. W., Bradbury, T. N., Martin, M., Sutter-Stickel, D., & Bodenmann, G. (2015). Avoidance orientation and the escalation of negative communication in intimate relationships. *Journal of Personality and Social Psychology*, 109(2), 262–275.

Kuwabara, K., Yu, S., Lee, A. J., & Galinsky, A. D. (2016). Status decreases dominance in the West but increases dominance in the East. *Psychological Science*, 27(2), 127–137.

Kwon, P., Birrueta, M., Faust, E., & Brown, E. R. (2015). The role of hope in preventive interventions. *Social and Personality Psychology Compass*, 9(11), 696–704.

Kyprianides, A., Easterbrook, M. J., & Brown, R. (2019). Group identities benefit well-being by satisfying needs. *Journal of Experimental Social Psychology*, 84, 103836.

La Barre, W. (1954). *The human animal*. University of Chicago Press.

La Guardia, J. G., Ryan, R. M., Couchman, C. E., & Deci, E. L. (2000). Within-person variation in security of attachment: A self-determination theory perspective on attachment, need fulfillment, and well-being. *Journal of Personality and Social Psychology*, 79(3), 367–384.

Lai, C. K., Skinner, A. L., Cooley, E., Murrar, S., Brauer, M., Devos, T., Calanchini, J., Xiao, Y. J., Pedram, C., Marshburn, C. K., Simon, S., Blanchar, J. C., Joy-Gaba, J. A., Conway, J., Redford, L., Klein, R. A., Roussos, G., Schellhaas, F. M. H., Burns, M., . . . Nosek, B. A. (2016). Reducing implicit racial preferences: II. Intervention effectiveness across time. *Journal of Experimental Psychology: General*, 145(8), 1001–1016.

Laird, J. D. (1974). Self-attribution of emotion: The effects of expressive behavior on the quality of emotional experience. *Journal of Personality and Social Psychology*, 29(4), 475–486.

Lakens, D., & Etz, A. J. (2017). Too true to be bad: When sets of studies with significant and nonsignificant findings are probably true. *Social Psychological and Personality Science*, 8(8), 875–881.

Lakin, J. L., & Chartrand, T. L. (2003). Using nonconscious behavioral mimicry to create affiliation and rapport. *Psychological Science*, 14(4), 334–339.

Lakoff, G., & Johnson, M. (1980). *Metaphors we live by*. University of Chicago Press.

Lamer, S. A., & Weisbuch, M. (2019). Men over women: The social transmission of gender stereotypes through spatial elevation. *Journal of Experimental Social Psychology*, 84, 103828.

Lamm, H. (1967). Will an observer advise higher risk taking after hearing a discussion of the decision problem? *Journal of Personality and Social Psychology*, 6(4, Pt. 1), 467–471.

Lamm, H., Myers, D., & Ochsmann, R. (1976). On predicting group-induced shifts toward risk or caution: A second look at some experiments. *Psychologische Beitrage*, 18(3), 288–296.

Landau, M. J., Arndt, J., & Cameron, L. D. (2018). Do metaphors in health messages work? Exploring emotional and cognitive factors. *Journal of Experimental Social Psychology*, 74, 135–149.

Landau, M. J., Greenberg, J., Sullivan, D., Routledge, C., & Arndt, J. (2009). The protective identity: Evidence that mortality salience heightens the clarity and coherence of the self-concept. *Journal of Experimental Social Psychology*, 45(4), 796–807.

Landau, M. J., Johns, M., Greenberg, J., Pyszczynski, T., Martens, A., Goldenberg, J. L., & Solomon, S. (2004). A function of form: Terror management and structuring the social world. *Journal of Personality and Social Psychology*, 87(2), 190–210.

Landau, M. J., Kay, A. C., & Whitson, J. A. (2015). Compensatory control and the appeal of a structured world. *Psychological Bulletin*, 141(3), 694–722.

Landau, M. J., Kosloff, S., & Schmeichel, B. J. (2011). Imbuing everyday actions with meaning in response to existential threat. *Self and Identity*, 10(1), 64–76.

Landau, M. J., Solomon, S., Greenberg, J., Cohen, F., Pyszczynski, T., Arndt, J., Miller, C. H., Ogilvie, D. M., & Cook, A. (2004). Deliver us from evil: The effects of mortality salience and reminders of 9/11 on support for President George W. Bush. *Personality and Social Psychology Bulletin*, 30(9), 1136–1150.

Landau, T. (1989). *About faces: The evolution of the human face*. Anchor Books.

Landis, D., & O'Shea, W. A. (2000). Cross-cultural aspects of passionate love: An individual differences analysis. *Journal of Cross-Cultural Psychology*, 31(6), 752–777.

Landy, D., & Sigall, H. (1974). Beauty is talent: Task evaluation as a function of the performer's physical attractiveness. *Journal of Personality and Social Psychology*, 29(3), 299–304.

Langer, E. J. (1975). The illusion of control. *Journal of Personality and Social Psychology*, 32(2), 311–328.

Langer, E. J. (1989). *Mindfulness*. Addison-Wesley.

Langer, E. J., Blank, A., & Chanowitz, B. (1978). The mindlessness of ostensibly thoughtful action: The role of "placebo" information in interpersonal interaction. *Journal of Personality and Social Psychology*, 36(6), 635–642.

Langer, E. J., & Moldoveanu, M. (2000). The construct of mindfulness. *Journal of Social Issues*, 56(1), 1–9.

Langlois, J. H., Kalakanis, L., Rubenstein, A. J., Larson, A., Hallam, M., & Smoot, M. (2000). Maxims or myths of beauty? A meta-analytic and theoretical review. *Psychological Bulletin*, 126(3), 390–423.

Langlois, J. H., Ritter, J. M., Casey, R. J., & Sawin, D. B. (1995). Infant attractiveness predicts maternal behaviors and attitudes. *Developmental Psychology*, 31(3), 464–472.

Langlois, J. H., Ritter, J. M., Roggman, L. A., & Vaughn, L. S. (1991). Facial diversity and infant preferences for attractive faces. *Developmental Psychology*, 27(1), 79–84.

Langlois, J. H., & Roggman, L. A. (1990). Attractive faces are only average. *Psychological Science*, 1(2), 115–121.

Langlois, J. H., Roggman, L. A., Casey, R. J., Ritter, J. M., Rieser-Danner, L. A., & Jenkins, V. Y. (1987). Infant preferences for attractive faces: Rudiments of a stereotype? *Developmental Psychology*, 23(3), 363–369.

LaPiere, R. T. (1934). Attitudes vs. actions. *Social Forces*, 13(2), 230–237.

Larrick, R. P., Timmerman, T. A., Carton, A. M., & Abrevaya, J. (2011). Temper, temperature, and temptation: Heat-related retaliation in baseball. *Psychological Science*, 22(4), 423–428.

Lassek, W. D., & Gaulin, S. J. (2008). Waist-hip ratio and cognitive ability: Is gluteofemoral fat a privileged store of neurodevelopmental resources? *Evolution and Human Behavior*, 29(1), 26–34.

Latané, B., & Darley, J. M. (1968). Group inhibition of bystander intervention in emergencies. *Journal of Personality and Social Psychology*, 10(3), 215–221.

Latané, B., Williams, K., & Harkins, S. (1979). Many hands make light the work: The causes and consequences of social loafing. *Journal of Personality and Social Psychology*, 37(6), 822–832.

Lau, M. A., Pihl, R. O., & Peterson, J. B. (1995). Provocation, acute alcohol intoxication, cognitive performance, and aggression. *Journal of Abnormal Psychology*, 104(1), 150–155.

Lauer, J., & Lauer, R. (1985). Marriages made to last. *Psychology Today, 19*(6), 22–26.

Laughlin, P. R., Zander, M. L., Knievel, E. M., & Tan, T. K. (2003). Groups perform better than the best individuals on letters-to-numbers problems: Informative equations and effective strategies. *Journal of Personality and Social Psychology, 85*(4), 684–694.

Laumann, E. O., Ellingson, S., Mahay, J., Paik, A., & Youm, Y. (Eds.). (2004). *The sexual organization of the city.* University of Chicago Press.

Laurenceau, J. P., Rivera, L. M., Schaffer, A. R., & Pietromonaco, P. R. (2004). Intimacy as an interpersonal process: Current status and future directions. In D. J. Mashek & A. Aron (Eds.), *Handbook of closeness and intimacy* (pp. 61–78). Erlbaum.

Laurin, K. (2017). Belief in God: A cultural adaptation with important side effects. *Current Directions in Psychological Science, 26*(5), 458–463.

Lavee, Y., & Ben-Ari, A. (2007). Relationship of dyadic closeness with work-related stress: A daily diary study. *Journal of Marriage and Family, 69*(4), 1021–1035.

Lawrence, E., Rothman, A. D., Cobb, R. J., Rothman, M. T., & Bradbury, T. N. (2008). Marital satisfaction across the transition to parenthood. *Journal of Family Psychology, 22*(1), 41–50.

Lazarus, R. S. (1991). *Emotion and adaptation.* Oxford University Press.

Lazarus, R. S., & Folkman, S. (1984). *Stress, appraisal, and coping.* Springer-Verlag.

Le, B., & Agnew, C. R. (2003). Commitment and its theorized determinants: A meta-analysis of the Investment Model. *Personal Relationships, 10*(1), 37–57.

Leach, C. W., Ellemers, N., & Barreto, M. (2007). Group virtue: The importance of morality (vs. competence and sociability) in the positive evaluation of in-groups. *Journal of Personality and Social Psychology, 93*(2), 234–249.

Leander, N. P., & Chartrand, T. L. (2017). On thwarted goals and displaced aggression: A compensatory competence model. *Journal of Experimental Social Psychology, 72,* 88–100.

Leander, N. P., Stroebe, W., Kreienkamp, J., Agostini, M., Gordijn, E., & Kruglanski, A. W. (2019). Mass shootings and the salience of guns as means of compensation for thwarted goals. *Journal of Personality and Social Psychology, 116*(5), 704–723.

Leaper, C., Anderson, K. J., & Sanders, P. (1998). Moderators of gender effects on parents' talk to their children: A meta-analysis. *Developmental Psychology, 34*(1), 3–27.

Leary, M. R., & Baumeister, R. F. (2000). The nature and function of self-esteem: Sociometer theory. In M. P. Zanna (Ed.), *Advances in experimental social psychology* (Vol. 32, pp. 1–62). Academic Press.

Leary, M. R., & Jones, J. L. (1993). The social psychology of tanning and sunscreen use: Self-presentational motives as a predictor of health risk. *Journal of Applied Social Psychology, 23*(17), 1390–1406.

Leary, M. R., Kowalski, R. M., Smith, L., & Phillips, S. (2003). Teasing, rejection, and violence: Case studies of the school shootings. *Aggressive Behavior, 29*(3), 202–214.

Leary, M. R., Tambor, E. S., Terdal, S. K., & Downs, D. L. (1995). Self-esteem as an interpersonal monitor: The sociometer hypothesis. *Journal of Personality and Social Psychology, 68*(3), 518–530.

Leary, M. R., Tate, E. B., Adams, C. E., Batts Allen, A., & Hancock, J. (2007). Self-compassion and reactions to unpleasant self-relevant events: The implications of treating oneself kindly. *Journal of Personality and Social Psychology, 92*(5), 887–904.

Leary, M. R., Tchividijian, L. R., & Kraxberger, B. E. (1994). Self-presentation can be hazardous to your health: Impression management and health risk. *Health Psychology, 13*(6), 461–470.

Leary, M. R., Twenge, J. M., & Quinlivan, E. (2006). Interpersonal rejection as a determinant of anger and aggression. *Personality and Social Psychology Review, 10*(2), 111–132.

LeBel, E. P., & Paunonen, S. V. (2011). Sexy but often unreliable: The impact of unreliability on the replicability of experimental findings with implicit measures. *Personality and Social Psychology Bulletin, 37*(4), 570–583.

Le Bon, G. (1897). *The crowd: A study of the popular mind.* Macmillan.

LeDoux, J. E. (1996). *The emotional brain.* Simon & Schuster.

Lee, D. S., & Way, B. M. (2019). Perceived social support and chronic inflammation: The moderating role of self-esteem. *Health Psychology, 38*(6), 563–566.

Lee, D. S., Ybarra, O., Gonzalez, R., & Ellsworth, P. (2018). I-through-we: How supportive social relationships facilitate personal growth. *Personality and Social Psychology Bulletin, 44*(1), 37–48.

Lee, E. J. (2007). Deindividuation effects on group polarization in computer-mediated communication: The role of group identification, public-self-awareness, and perceived argument quality. *Journal of Communication, 57*(2), 385–403.

Lee, F. R. (1993, September 20). New York trend: Young urban volunteers. *The New York Times.* http://www.nytimes.com/1993/09/20/nyregion/new-york-trend-young-urban-volunteers.html

Lee, L., Loewenstein, G., Ariely, D., Hong, J., & Young, J. (2008). If I'm not hot, are you hot or not? Physical-attractiveness evaluations and dating preferences as a function of one's own attractiveness. *Psychological Science, 19*(7), 669–677.

Leeming, D. A., & Leeming, M. A. (1994). *A dictionary of creation myths.* Oxford University Press.

Lefkowitz, M. M., Eron, L. D., Walder, L. O., & Huesmann, L. R. (1977). *Growing up to be violent: A longitudinal study of the development of aggression.* Pergamon.

Lefkowitz, M. M., Huesmann, L. R., & Eron, L. D. (1978). Parental punishment: A longitudinal analysis of effects. *Archives of General Psychiatry, 35*(2), 186–191.

Lehman, D. R., & Taylor, S. E. (1987). Date with an earthquake: Coping with a probable, unpredictable disaster. *Personality and Social Psychology Bulletin, 13*(4), 546–555.

Lehmiller, J. J., Law, A. T., & Tormala, T. T. (2010). The effect of self-affirmation on sexual prejudice. *Journal of Experimental Social Psychology, 46*(2), 276–285.

Leitenberg, H., & Henning, K. (1995). Sexual fantasy. *Psychological Bulletin, 117*(3), 469–496.

Lemay, E. P., Jr., & Clark, M. S. (2008). How the head liberates the heart: Projection of communal responsiveness guides relationship promotion. *Journal of Personality and Social Psychology, 94*(4), 647–671.

Lemay, E. P., Jr., Ryan, J. E., Fehr, R., & Gelfand, M. J. (2019). Validation of negativity: Drawbacks of interpersonal responsiveness during conflicts with outsiders. *Journal of Personality and Social Psychology.* Advance online publication.

Lench, H. C., Levine, L. J., Perez, K., Carpenter, Z. K., Carlson, S. J., Bench, S. W., & Wan, Y. (2019). When and why people misestimate future feelings: Identifying strengths and weaknesses in affective forecasting. *Journal of Personality and Social Psychology, 116*(5), 724–742.

Lepore, L., & Brown, R. (1997). Category and stereotype activation: Is prejudice inevitable? *Journal of Personality and Social Psychology, 72*(2), 275–287.

Lepper, M. R., Greene, D., & Nisbett, R. E. (1973). Undermining children's intrinsic interest with extrinsic reward: A test of the "overjustification" hypothesis. *Journal of Personality and Social Psychology, 28*(1), 129–137.

Lerner, M. (1980). *The belief in a just world: A fundamental delusion.* Plenum.

Lerner, M. J., & Simmons, C. H. (1966). Observers' reaction to the "innocent victim": Compassion or rejection? *Journal of Personality and Social Psychology, 4*(2), 203–210.

Leslie, L. M., Bono, J. E., Kim, Y., & Beaver, G. R. (2020). On melting pots and salad bowls: A meta-analysis of the effects of identity-blind and identity-conscious diversity ideologies. *Journal of Applied Psychology, 105*(5), 453–471.

Le Texier, T. (2019). Debunking the Stanford Prison Experiment. *American Psychologist, 74*(7), 823–839.

Leung, A. K. Y., & Chiu, C. Y. (2010). Multicultural experience, idea receptiveness, and creativity. *Journal of Cross-Cultural Psychology, 41*(5–6), 723–741.

Leung, K. (1988). Some determinants of conflict avoidance. *Journal of Cross Cultural Psychology, 19*(1), 125–136.

Leventhal, H. (1970). Findings and theory in the study of fear communications. *Advances in Experimental Social Psychology, 5,* 119–186.

Levin, P. F., & Isen, A. M. (1975). Further studies on the effect of feeling good on helping. *Sociometry, 38*(1), 141–147.

Levin, S., Federico, C. M., Sidanius, J., & Rabinowitz, J. L. (2002). Social dominance orientation and intergroup bias: The legitimation of favoritism for high-status groups. *Personality and Social Psychology Bulletin, 28*(2), 144–157.

Levine, R., Sato, S., Hashimoto, T., & Verma, J. (1995). Love and marriage in eleven cultures. *Journal of Cross-Cultural Psychology, 26*(5), 554–571.

Levine, R. A., & Campbell, D. T. (1972). *Ethnocentrism: Theories of conflict, ethnic attitudes and group behavior.* Wiley.

Levine, R. V., Reysen, S., & Ganz, E. (2008). The kindness of strangers revisited: A comparison of 24 US cities. *Social Indicators Research, 85*(3), 461–481.

Levine, S. V. (1981). Cults and mental health: Clinical conclusions. *Canadian Journal of Psychiatry/La Revue canadienne de psychiatrie, 26*(8), 534–539.

Levinger, G. K., & Snoek, J. D. (1972). *Attraction in relationship: A new look at interpersonal attraction.* General Learning Press.

Lewandowski, G. W., & Aron, A. P. (2004). Distinguishing arousal from novelty and challenge in initial romantic attraction between strangers. *Social Behavior and Personality: An International Journal, 32*(4), 361–372.

Lewandowski, G. W., Aron, A., & Gee, J. (2007). Personality goes a long way: The malleability of opposite-sex physical attractiveness. *Personal Relationships, 14*(4), 571–585.

Lewin, K. (1927). Investigations on the psychology of action and affection. III. The memory of completed and uncompleted actions. *Psychologische Forschung, 9*, 1–85.

Lewin, K. (1935). *A dynamic theory of personality.* McGraw-Hill.

Lewin, K. (1936). *Principles of topographical psychology.* McGraw-Hill.

Lewin, K. (1952). *Field theory in social science: Selected theoretical papers.* (D. Cartwright, Ed.). Tavistock.

Lewis, G. J., & Bates, T. C. (2017). The temporal stability of in-group favoritism is mostly attributable to genetic factors. *Social Psychological and Personality Science, 8*(8), 897–903.

Lewis, T. T., Everson-Rose, S. A., Powell, L. H., Matthews, K. A., Brown, C., Karavolos, K., Sutton-Tyrrell, K., Jacobs, E., & Wesley, D. (2006). Chronic exposure to everyday discrimination and coronary artery calcification in African-American women: The SWAN Heart Study. *Psychosomatic Medicine, 68*(3), 362–368.

Lewis, T. T., & Van Dyke, M. E. (2018). Discrimination and the health of African Americans: The potential importance of intersectionalities. *Current Directions in Psychological Science, 27*(3), 176–182.

Leyens, J. P., Camino, L., Parke, R. D., & Berkowitz, L. (1975). Effects of movie violence on aggression in a field setting as a function of group dominance and cohesion. *Journal of Personality and Social Psychology, 32*(2), 346–360.

Leyens, J. P., Désert, M., Croizet, J. C., & Darcis, C. (2000). Stereotype threat: Are lower status and history of stigmatization preconditions of stereotype threat? *Personality and Social Psychology Bulletin, 26*(10), 1189–1199.

Leyens, J. P., Paladino, P. M., Rodriguez-Torres, R., Vaes, J., Demoulin, S., Rodriguez-Perez, A., & Gaunt, R. (2000). The emotional side of prejudice: The attribution of secondary emotions to ingroups and outgroups. *Personality and Social Psychology Review, 4*(2), 186–197.

Leyens, J. P., Rodriguez-Perez, A., Rodriguez-Torres, R., Gaunt, R., Paladino, M. P., Vaes, J., & Demoulin, S. (2001). Psychological essentialism and the differential attribution of uniquely human emotions to ingroups and outgroups. *European Journal of Social Psychology, 31*(4), 395–411.

Li, N. P., & Kenrick, D. T. (2006). Sex similarities and differences in preferences for short-term mates: What, whether, and why. *Journal of Personality and Social Psychology, 90*(3), 468–489.

Li, N. P., van Vugt, M., & Colarelli, S. M. (2018). The evolutionary mismatch hypothesis: Implications for psychological science. *Current Directions in Psychological Science, 27*(1), 38–44.

Liberman, N., & Trope, Y. (1998). The role of feasibility and desirability considerations in near and distant future decisions: A test of temporal construal theory. *Journal of Personality and Social Psychology, 75*(1), 5–18.

Liberman, V., Samuels, S. M., & Ross, L. (2004). The name of the game: Predictive power of reputations versus situational labels in determining prisoner's dilemma game moves. *Personality and Social Psychology Bulletin, 30*(9), 1175–1185.

Lickel, B., Hamilton, D. L., & Sherman, S. J. (2001). Elements of a lay theory of groups: Types of groups, relational styles, and the perception of group entitativity. *Personality and Social Psychology Review, 5*(2), 129–140.

Lickel, B., Hamilton, D. L., Wieczorkowska, G., Lewis, A., Sherman, S. J., & Uhles, A. N. (2000). Varieties of groups and the perception of group entitativity. *Journal of Personality and Social Psychology, 78*(2), 223–246.

Lickel, B., Miller, N., Stenstrom, D. M., Denson, T. F., & Schmader, T. (2006). Vicarious retribution: The role of collective blame in intergroup aggression. *Personality and Social Psychology Review, 10*(4), 372–390.

Lieberman, D., Oum, R., & Kurzban, R. (2008). The family of fundamental social categories includes kinship: Evidence from the memory confusion paradigm. *European Journal of Social Psychology, 38*(6), 998–1012.

Lieberman, J. D., & Arndt, J. (2000). Understanding the limits of limiting instructions: Social psychological explanations for the failures of instructions to disregard pretrial publicity and other inadmissible evidence. *Psychology, Public Policy, and Law, 6*(3), 677–711.

Lieberman, J. D., Solomon, S., Greenberg, J., & McGregor, H. A. (1999). A hot new way to measure aggression: Hot sauce allocation. *Aggressive Behavior, 25*(5), 331–348.

Lieberman, M. D., Gaunt, R., Gilbert, D. T., & Trope, Y. (2002). Reflexion and reflection: A social cognitive neuroscience approach to attributional inference. In M. P. Zanna (Ed.), *Advances in experimental social psychology* (Vol. 34, pp. 199–249). Academic Press.

Lifton, R. J. (1979). *The broken connection: On death and the continuity of life.* Basic Books.

Lifton, R. J. (1986). *The Nazi doctors: Medical killing and the psychology of genocide.* Basic Books.

Lim, S. L., Penrod, M. T., Ha, O. R., Bruce, J. M., & Bruce, A. S. (2018). Calorie labeling promotes dietary self-control by shifting the temporal dynamics of health- and taste-attribute integration in overweight individuals. *Psychological Science, 29*(3), 447–462.

Lin, Y., Arieli, S., & Oyserman, D. (2019). Cultural fluency means all is okay, cultural disfluency implies otherwise. *Journal of Experimental Social Psychology, 84*, 103822.

Linder, D. E., Cooper, J., & Jones, E. E. (1967). Decision freedom as a determinant of the role of incentive magnitude in attitude change. *Journal of Personality and Social Psychology, 6*(3), 245–254.

Lindquist, C. U., Lindsay, J. S., & White, G. D. (1979). Assessment of assertiveness in drug abusers. *Journal of Clinical Psychology, 35*(3), 676–679.

Lindquist, K. A., Satpute, A. B., & Gendron, M. (2015). Does language do more than communicate emotion? *Current Directions in Psychological Science, 24*(2), 99–108.

Lindquist, K. A., Wager, T. D., Kober, H., Bliss-Moreau, E., & Barrett, L. F. (2012). The brain basis of emotion: A meta-analytic review. *Behavioral and Brain Sciences, 35*(3), 121–143.

Linton, R. (1936). *The study of man: An introduction.* Appleton-Century.

Linville, P. W. (1985). Self-complexity and affective extremity: Don't put all of your eggs in one cognitive basket. *Social Cognition, 3*(1), 94–120.

Linville, P. W., Fischer, G. W., & Salovey, P. (1989). Perceived distributions of the characteristics of in-group and out-group members: Empirical evidence and a computer simulation. *Journal of Personality and Social Psychology, 57*(2), 165–188.

Linz, D., Donnerstein, E., & Adams, S. M. (1989). Physiological desensitization and judgments about female victims of violence. *Human Communication Research, 15*(4), 509–522.

Lippa, R. (1998). Gender-related individual differences and the structure of vocational interests: The importance of the people–things dimension. *Journal of Personality and Social Psychology, 74*(4), 996–1009.

Lippa, R. A. (2007). The preferred traits of mates in a cross-national study of heterosexual and homosexual men and women: An examination of biological and cultural influences. *Archives of Sexual Behavior, 36*(2), 193–208.

Liu, J. H., & Latané, B. (1998). Extremitization of attitudes: Does thought and discussion-induced polarization cumulate? *Basic and Applied Social Psychology, 20*(2), 103–110.

Liu, J., Thomas, J. M., & Higgs, S. (2019). The relationship between social identity, descriptive social norms and eating intentions and behaviors. *Journal of Experimental Social Psychology, 82*, 217–230.

Liu, S., Liu, P., Wang, M., & Zhang, B. (2021). Effectiveness of stereotype threat interventions: A meta-analytic review. *Journal of Applied Psychology, 106*(6), 921–949. https://doi.org/10.1037/apl0000770

Livingston, G. (2014, November 14). *Four-in-ten couples are saying "I do," again.* Pew Research Center. https://www.pewsocialtrends.org/2014/11/14/four-in-ten-couples-are-saying-i-do-again/

Livingston, G. (2018, April 25). *The changing profile of unmarried parents.* Pew Research Center. https://www.pewsocialtrends.org/2018/04/25/the-changing-profile-of-unmarried-parents/

Livingstone, K. M., & Isaacowitz, D. M. (2015). Situation selection and modification for emotion regulation in younger and older adults. *Social Psychological and Personality Science, 6*(8), 904–910.

Livshits, G., & Kobyliansky, E. (1991). Fluctuating asymmetry as a possible measure of developmental homeostasis in humans: A review. *Human Biology, 66*(4), 441–466.

Lo, S. K., Hsieh, A. Y., & Chiu, Y. P. (2013). Contradictory deceptive behavior in online dating. *Computers in Human Behavior, 29*(4), 1755–1762.

Loeber, R., & Dishion, T. J. (1984). Boys who fight at home and school: Family conditions influencing cross-setting consistency. *Journal of Consulting and Clinical Psychology, 52*(5), 759–768.

Loersch, C., & Payne, B. K. (2011). The situated inference model: An integrative account of the effects of primes on perception, behavior, and motivation. *Perspectives on Psychological Science, 6*(3), 234–252.

Loew, C. A. (1967). Acquisition of a hostile attitude and its relationship to aggressive behavior. *Journal of Personality and Social Psychology, 5*(3), 335–341.

Loewenstein, G. (2005). Hot-cold empathy gaps and medical decision making. *Health Psychology, 24*(4S), S49–S56.

Loftus, E. F., Miller, D. G., & Burns, H. J. (1978). Semantic integration of verbal information into a visual memory. *Journal of Experimental Psychology: Human Learning and Memory, 4*(1), 19–31.

Logel, C., Hall, W., Page-Gould, E., & Cohen, G. L. (2019). Why is it so hard to change? The role of self-integrity threat and affirmation in weight loss. *European Journal of Social Psychology, 49*(4), 748–759.

Logel, C., Walton, G. M., Spencer, S. J., Iserman, E. C., von Hippel, W., & Bell, A. E. (2009). Interacting with sexist men triggers social identity threat among female engineers. *Journal of Personality and Social Psychology, 96*(6), 1089–1103.

Lord, C. G., Ross, L., & Lepper, M. R. (1979). Biased assimilation and attitude polarization: The effects of prior theories on subsequently considered evidence. *Journal of Personality and Social Psychology, 37*(11), 2098–2109.

Lorenz, K. (1966). *On aggression*. Harcourt, Brace & World.

Lott, A. J., & Lott, B. E. (1974). The role of reward in the formation of positive interpersonal attitudes. In T. Huston (Ed.), *Foundations of interpersonal attraction* (pp. 171–192). Academic Press.

Louis, W. R., Thomas, E., Chapman, C. M., Achia, T., Wibisono, S., Mirnajafi, Z., & Droogendyk, L. (2019). Emerging research on intergroup prosociality: Group members' charitable giving, positive contact, allyship, and solidarity with others. *Social and Personality Psychology Compass, 13*(3), e12397.

Lowe, M. L., & Haws, K. L. (2019). Confession and self-control: A prelude to repentance or relapse? *Journal of Personality and Social Psychology, 116*(4), 563–581.

Lloyd, E. P., Sim, M., Smalley, E., Bernstein, M. J., & Hugenberg, K. (2020). Good cop, bad cop: Race-based differences in mental representations of police. *Personality and Social Psychology Bulletin, 46*(8), 1205–1218.

Lucas, R. E., & Lawless, N. M. (2013). Does life seem better on a sunny day? Examining the association between daily weather conditions and life satisfaction judgments. *Journal of Personality and Social Psychology, 104*(5), 872–884.

Lumet, S. (Director). (1957). *12 angry men* [Film]. Orion-Nova Productions.

Luttrell, A., Petty, R. E., & Xu, M. (2017). Replicating and fixing failed replications: The case of need for cognition and argument quality. *Journal of Experimental Social Psychology, 69*, 178–183.

Lykken, D. T. (2000). The causes and costs of crime and a controversial cure. *Journal of Personality, 68*(3), 559–605.

Lyubomirsky, S., King, L., & Diener, E. (2005). The benefits of frequent positive affect: Does happiness lead to success? *Psychological Bulletin, 131*(6), 803–855.

Ma, A., Tang, S., & Kay, A. C. (2019). Psychological reactance as a function of thought versus behavioral control. *Journal of Experimental Social Psychology, 84*, 103825.

Ma, D. S., & Correll, J. (2011). Target prototypicality moderates racial bias in the decision to shoot. *Journal of Experimental Social Psychology, 47*(2), 391–396.

Ma, L. K., Tunney, R. J., & Ferguson, E. (2017). Does gratitude enhance prosociality? A meta-analytic review. *Psychological Bulletin, 143*(6), 601–635.

Maass, A., & Clark, R. D. (1983). Internalization versus compliance: Differential processes underlying minority influence and conformity. *European Journal of Social Psychology, 13*(3), 197–215.

Maass, A., & Clark, R. D. (1984). Hidden impact of minorities: Fifteen years of minority influence research. *Psychological Bulletin, 95*(3), 428–450.

Maass, A., Volpato, C., & Mucchi-Faina, A. (1996). Social influence and the verifiability of the issue under discussion: Attitudinal versus objective items. *British Journal of Social Psychology, 35*(1), 15–26.

Maccoby, E. E., & Jacklin, C. N. (1974). *The psychology of sex differences*. Stanford University Press.

MacDonald, G., & Leary, M. R. (2005). Why does social exclusion hurt? The relationship between social and physical pain. *Psychological Bulletin, 131*(2), 202–223.

MacEwen, K. E., & Barling, J. (1988). Multiple stressors, violence in the family of origin, and marital aggression: A longitudinal investigation. *Journal of Family Violence, 3*(1), 73–87.

MacInnis, C. C., Page-Gould, E., & Hodson, G. (2017). Multilevel intergroup contact and antigay prejudice (explicit and implicit): Evidence of contextual contact benefits in a less visible group domain. *Social Psychological and Personality Science, 8*(3), 243–251.

Mackie, D. M., & Worth, L. T. (1989). Processing deficits and the mediation of positive affect in persuasion. *Journal of Personality and Social Psychology, 57*(1), 27–40.

MacKinnon, C. A. (2019). Where #MeToo came from, and where it's going. *The Atlantic*. https://www.theatlantic.com/ideas/archive/2019/03/catharine-mackinnon-what-metoo-has-changed/585313/

Macrae, C. N., Alnwick, K. A., Milne, A. B., & Schloerscheidt, A. M. (2002). Person perception across the menstrual cycle: Hormonal influences on social-cognitive functioning. *Psychological Science, 13*(6), 532–536.

Macrae, C. N., Bodenhausen, G. V., Milne, A. B., & Jetten, J. (1994). Out of mind but back in sight: Stereotypes on the rebound. *Journal of Personality and Social Psychology, 67*(5), 808–817.

Macrae, C. N., Hewstone, M., & Griffiths, R. J. (1993). Processing load and memory for stereotype-based information. *European Journal of Social Psychology, 23*(1), 77–87.

Macrae, C. N., Milne, A. B., & Bodenhausen, G. V. (1994). Stereotypes as energy-saving devices: A peek inside the cognitive toolbox. *Journal of Personality and Social Psychology, 66*(1), 37–47.

Macrae, C. N., Mitchell, J. P., McNamara, D. L., Golubickis, M., Andreou, K., Møller, S., Peytcheva, K., Falben, J. K., & Christian, B. M. (2016). Noticing future me: Reducing egocentrism through mental imagery. *Personality and Social Psychology Bulletin, 42*(7), 855–863.

Madon, S., Jussim, L., Guyll, M., Nofziger, H., Salib, E. R., Willard, J., & Scherr, K. C. (2018). The accumulation of stereotype-based self-fulfilling prophecies. *Journal of Personality and Social Psychology, 115*(5), 825–844.

Madsen, E. A., Tunney, R. J., Fieldman, G., Plotkin, H. C., Dunbar, R. I. M., Richardson, J., & McFarland, D. (2007). Kinship and altruism: A cross cultural experimental study. *British Journal of Psychology, 98*(2), 339–359.

Mahler, H. I., Kulik, J. A., Gerrard, M., & Gibbons, F. X. (2007). Long-term effects of appearance-based interventions on sun protection behaviors. *Health Psychology, 26*(3), 350–360.

Main, M. (1995). Recent studies in attachment: Overview, with selected implications for clinical work. In S. Goldberg, R. Muir, & J. Kerr (Eds.), *Attachment theory: Social, developmental and clinical perspectives* (pp. 407–474). Analytic Press.

Major, B., Carrington, P. I., & Carnevale, P. J. (1984). Physical attractiveness and self-esteem: Attributions for praise from an other-sex evaluator. *Personality and Social Psychology Bulletin, 10*(1), 43–50.

Major, B., Gramzow, R. H., McCoy, S. K., Levin, S., Schmader, T., & Sidanius, J. (2002). Perceiving personal discrimination: The role of group status and legitimizing ideology. *Journal of Personality and Social Psychology, 82*(3), 269–282.

Major, B., Quinton, W. J., & Schmader, T. (2003). Attributions to discrimination and self-esteem: Impact of group identification and situational ambiguity. *Journal of Experimental Social Psychology, 39*(3), 220–231.

Major, B., & Schmader, T. (1998). Coping with stigma through psychological disengagement. In J. K. Swim & C. Stangor (Eds.), *Prejudice: The target's perspective* (pp. 219–241). Academic Press.

Major, B., & Schmader, T. (2017). Stigma, social identity threat, and health. In B. Major, J. Dovidio, & B. Link (Eds.), *The Oxford handbook of stigma, discrimination, and health* (pp. 85–104). Oxford University Press.

Major, B., Tomiyama, A. J., & Hunger, J. M. (2018). The negative and bidirectional effects of weight stigma on health. In B. Major, J. F. Dovidio, & B. G. Link (Eds.), *The Oxford handbook of stigma, discrimination, and health* (pp. 499–519). Oxford University Press.

Ma-Kellams, C., & Blascovich, J. (2012). Enjoying life in the face of death: East–West differences in responses to mortality salience. *Journal of Personality and Social Psychology, 103*(5), 773–786.

Mala, E., & Goodman, J. D. (2011, July 22). At least 80 dead in Norway shooting. *The New York Times*. http://www.nytimes.com/2011/07/23/world/europe/23oslo.html?pagewanted=all&_r=0

Malamuth, N. M. (1981). Rape proclivity among males. *Journal of Social Issues, 37*(4), 138–157.

Malamuth, N. M. (2007). Hostile masculinity syndrome. In R. Baumeister & K. Vohs (Eds.), *Encyclopedia of social psychology* (p. 448). Sage.

Malamuth, N. M., & Check, J. V. (1981). The effects of mass media exposure on acceptance of violence against women: A field experiment. *Journal of Research in Personality, 15*(4), 436–446.

Malamuth, N., & Huppin, M. (2007). Rape. In R. Baumeister, & K. Vohs (Eds.), *Encyclopedia of social psychology* (pp. 723–724). Sage.

Malka, A., Soto, C. J., Cohen, A. B., & Miller, D. T. (2011). Religiosity and social welfare: Competing influences of cultural conservatism and prosocial value orientation. *Journal of Personality, 79*(4), 763–792.

Malle, B. F. (2006). The actor-observer asymmetry in attribution: A (surprising) meta-analysis. *Psychological Bulletin, 132*(6), 895–919.

Malle, B. F., & Hodges, S. D. (Eds.). (2005). *Other minds: How humans bridge the divide between self and others*. Guilford Press.

Malle, B. F., Knobe, J. M., & Nelson, S. E. (2007). Actor-observer asymmetries in explanations of behavior: New answers to an old question. *Journal of Personality and Social Psychology, 93*(4), 491–514.

Manago, A. M., Taylor, T., & Greenfield, P. M. (2012). Me and my 400 friends: The anatomy of college students' Facebook networks, their communication patterns, and well-being. *Developmental Psychology, 48*(2), 369–380.

Mancini, A. D. (2019). When acute adversity improves psychological health: A social–contextual framework. *Psychological Review, 126*(4), 486–505.

Mandler, G. (1984). *Mind and body: Psychology of emotion and stress*. W. W. Norton.

Mangelsdorf, J., Eid, M., & Luhmann, M. (2019). Does growth require suffering? A systematic review and meta-analysis on genuine posttraumatic and postecstatic growth. *Psychological Bulletin, 145*(3), 302–338.

Mann, M. (Director). (2009). *Public enemies* [Film]. Universal Pictures.

Manning, R., Levine, M., & Collins, A. (2007). The Kitty Genovese murder and the social psychology of helping: The parable of the 38 witnesses. *American Psychologist, 62*(6), 555–562.

Mansouri, F. A., Tanaka, K., & Buckley, M. J. (2009). Conflict-induced behavioural adjustment: A clue to the executive functions of the prefrontal cortex. *Nature Reviews Neuroscience, 10*(2), 141–152.

Mantell, D. M. (1971). The potential for violence in Germany. *Journal of Social Issues, 27*(4), 101–112.

Manzi, C., Paderi, F., Benet, M. V., & Coen, S. (2019). Age-based stereotype threat and negative outcomes in the workplace: Exploring the role of identity integration. *European Journal of Social Psychology, 49*(4), 705–716.

Maps of World. (2017). *Top ten countries with lowest divorce rate.* https://www.mapsofworld.com/world-top-ten/countries-with-lowest-divorce-rate.html

Mar, R. A. (2018). Stories and the promotion of social cognition. *Current Directions in Psychological Science, 27*(4), 257–262.

Marcus, D. K., & Miller, R. S. (2003). Sex differences in judgments of physical attractiveness: A social relations analysis. *Personality and Social Psychology Bulletin, 29*(3), 325–335.

Marcus-Newhall, A., Pedersen, W. C., Carlson, M., & Miller, N. (2000). Displaced aggression is alive and well: A meta-analytic review. *Journal of Personality and Social Psychology, 78*(4), 670–689.

Markman, K. D., & Miller, A. K. (2006). Depression, control, and counterfactual thinking: Functional for whom? *Journal of Social and Clinical Psychology, 25*(2), 210–227.

Marks, G., & Miller, N. (1987). Ten years of research on the false-consensus effect: An empirical and theoretical review. *Psychological Bulletin, 102*(1), 72–90.

Markus, H. (1977). Self-schemata and processing information about the self. *Journal of Personality and Social Psychology, 35*(2), 63–78.

Markus, H., & Kunda, Z. (1986). Stability and malleability of the self-concept. *Journal of Personality and Social Psychology, 51*(4), 858–866.

Markus, H., & Nurius, P. (1986). Possible selves. *American Psychologist, 41*(9), 954–969.

Markus, H. R., & Kitayama, S. (1991). Culture and the self: Implications for cognition, emotion, and motivation. *Psychological Review, 98*(2), 224–253.

Marston, P. J., Hecht, M. L., Manke, M. L., McDaniel, S., & Reeder, H. (1998). The subjective experience of intimacy, passion, and commitment in heterosexual loving relationships. *Personal Relationships, 5*(1), 15–30.

Martens, A., Greenberg, J., & Allen, J. B. (2008). Self-esteem and autonomic physiology: Parallels between self-esteem and cardiac vagal tone as buffers of threat. *Personality and Social Psychology Review, 12*(4), 370–389.

Martens, A., Kosloff, S., Greenberg, J., Landau, M. J., & Schmader, T. (2007). Killing begets killing: Evidence from a bug-killing paradigm that initial killing fuels subsequent killing. *Personality and Social Psychology Bulletin, 33*(9), 1251–1264.

Martin, C. L., Eisenbud, L., & Rose, H. (1995). Children's gender-based reasoning about toys. *Child Development, 66*(5), 1453–1471.

Martin, R., Martin, P. Y., Smith, J. R., & Hewstone, M. (2007). Majority versus minority influence and prediction of behavioral intentions and behavior. *Journal of Experimental Social Psychology, 43*(5), 763–771.

Marx, D. M., & Roman, J. S. (2002). Female role models: Protecting women's math test performance. *Personality and Social Psychology Bulletin, 28*(9), 1183–1193.

Marx, G. (1959). *Groucho and me.* Bernard Geis Associates.

Marx, K. (1847). *Wage labour and capital* (F. Engels, Trans.). Marx/Engels Internet Archive. http://www.marxists.org/archive/marx/works/1847/wage-labour/ch06.htm

Masci, D., Brown, A., & Kelly, J. (2019, June 24). *5 facts about same-sex marriage.* Pew Research Center. https://www.pewresearch.org/fact-tank/2019/06/24/same-sex-marriage/

Masicampo, E. J., Martin, S. R., & Anderson, R. A. (2014). Understanding and overcoming self-control depletion. *Social and Personality Psychology Compass, 8*(11), 638–649.

Maslow, A. (1964). *Religion, values and peak experiences.* Viking.

Maslow, A. H., Frager, R., & Fadiman, J. (1970). *Motivation and personality* (Vol. 2). Harper & Row.

Mason, A. E., Law, R., Bryan, A. E. B., Portley, R., & Sbarra, D. A. (2012). Facing a breakup: Electromyographic responses moderate self-concept recovery following a romantic separation. *Personal Relationships, 19*(3), 551–568.

Mastro, D. E. (2003). A social identity approach to understanding the impact of television messages. *Communication Monographs, 70*(2), 98–113.

Masuda, M., & Duck, S. (2002). Issues in ebb and flow: Management and maintenance of relationships as a skilled activity. In J. H. Harvey & A. Wenzel (Eds.), *A clinician's guide to maintaining and enhancing close relationships* (pp. 13–41). Erlbaum.

Mata, A., Sherman, S. J., Ferreira, M. B., & Mendonça, C. (2015). Strategic numeracy: Self-serving reasoning about health statistics. *Basic and Applied Social Psychology, 37*(3), 165–173.

Matsumura, A., & Ohtsubo, Y. (2012). Praise is reciprocated with tangible benefits: Social exchange between symbolic resources and concrete resources. *Social Psychological and Personality Science, 3*(2), 250–256.

Mattingly, B. A., & Lewandowski, G. W. (2014). Broadening horizons: Self-expansion in relational and non-relational contexts. *Social and Personality Psychology Compass, 8*(1), 30–40.

Maxwell, J. A., & McNulty, J. K. (2019). No longer in a dry spell: The developing understanding of how sex influences romantic relationships. *Current Directions in Psychological Science, 28*(1), 102–107.

McAdams, D. P. (1988). Personal needs and personal relationships. In S. Duck (Ed.), *Handbook of personal relationships: Theory, research, and interventions* (pp. 7–22). Wiley.

McAdams, D. P. (1993). *The stories we live by: Personal myths and the making of the self.* William Morrow.

McAdams, D. P. (2001). The psychology of life stories. *Review of General Psychology, 5*(2), 100–122.

McAdams, D. P. (2006). *The redemptive self.* Oxford University Press.

McAdams, D. P., & Guo, J. (2015). Narrating the generative life. *Psychological Science, 26*(4), 475–483.

McArthur, L. Z., & Baron, R. M. (1983). Toward an ecological theory of social perception. *Psychological Review, 90*(3), 215–238.

McCarrey, M., Edwards, H. P., & Rozario, W. (1982). Ego-relevant feedback, affect, and self-serving attributional bias. *Personality and Social Psychology Bulletin, 8*(2), 189–194.

McCarthy, R., Skowronski, J., Verschuere, B., Meijer, E., Jim, A., Hoogesteyn, K., Orthey, R., Acar, O. A., Aczel, B., Bakos, B., Barbosa, F., Baskin, E., Bègue, L., Ben-Shakhar, G., Birt, A., Blatz, L., Charman, S., Claesen, A., & Clay, S., . . . Yıldız, E. (2018). Registered replication report on Srull and Wyer (1979). *Advances in Methods and Practices in Psychological Science, 1*(3), 321–336.

McCarthy, T. (Director). (2015). *Spotlight* [Film]. Open Road Films.

McCarthy, J. (2021) U.S. Approval of Interracial Marriage at New High of 94%. Gallup. https://news.gallup.com/poll/354638/approval-interracial-marriage-new-high.aspx

McCauley, C. (1998). When screen violence is not attractive. In J. H. Goldstein (Ed.), *Why we watch: The attractions of violent entertainment* (pp. 144–162). Oxford University Press.

McClelland, D. C., Atkinson, J. W., Clark, R. A., & Lowell, E. L. (1953). *The achievement motive.* Appleton-Century-Crofts.

McClure, E. B. (2000). A meta-analytic review of sex differences in facial expression processing and their development in infants, children, and adolescents. *Psychological Bulletin, 126*(3), 424–453.

McConnell, A. R., & Leibold, J. M. (2001). Relations among the Implicit Association Test, discriminatory behavior, and explicit measures of racial attitudes. *Journal of Experimental Social Psychology, 37*(5), 435–442.

McConnell, A. R., Renaud, J. M., Dean, K. K., Green, S. P., Lamoreaux, M. J., Hall, C. E., & Rydell, R. J. (2005). Whose self is it anyway? Self-aspect control moderates the relation between self-complexity and well-being. *Journal of Experimental Social Psychology, 41*(1), 1–18.

McCord, J. (1983). A longitudinal study of aggression and antisocial behavior. In K. T. van Dusen & S. A. Mednick (Eds.), *Prospective studies of crime and delinquency* (pp. 269–275). Kluwer-Nijhoff Publishing Company.

McCoy, S. K., & Major, B. (2003). Group identification moderates emotional responses to perceived prejudice. *Personality and Social Psychology Bulletin, 29*(8), 1005–1017.

McCrea, S. M., Hirt, E. R., & Milner, B. J. (2008). She works hard for the money: Valuing effort underlies gender differences in behavioral self-handicapping. *Journal of Experimental Social Psychology, 44*(2), 292–311.

McCullough, M. E. (2008). *Beyond revenge: The evolution of the forgiveness instinct.* Jossey-Bass.

McCullough, M. E., Emmons, R. A., & Tsang, J. A. (2002). The grateful disposition: A conceptual and empirical topography. *Journal of Personality and Social Psychology, 82*(1), 112–127.

McDermott, R., Tingley, D., Cowden, J., Frazzetto, G., & Johnson, D. D. (2009). Monoamine oxidase A gene (MAOA) predicts behavioral aggression following provocation. *Proceedings of the National Academy of Sciences, 106*(7), 2118–2123.

McDougall, W. (1908). *An introduction to social psychology.* Methuen.

McDougall, W. (1923). *An outline of psychology.* Methuen.

McFarland, C., & Ross, M. (1987). The relation between current impressions and memories of self and dating partners. *Personality and Social Psychology Bulletin, 13*(2), 228–238.

McGinnis, S. L. (2003). Cohabitating, dating, and perceived costs of marriage: A model of marriage entry. *Journal of Marriage and the Family, 65*(1), 105–116.

McGuire, W. J. (1964). Inducing resistance to persuasion: Some contemporary approaches. In L. Berkowitz (Ed.), *Advances in experimental social psychology* (Vol. 1, pp. 191–229). Academic Press.

McGuire, W. J. (1968). Personality and attitude change: An information processing theory. In A. G. Greenwald, T. C. Brock, & T. A. Ostrom (Eds.), *Psychological foundations of attitudes* (pp. 171–196). Academic Press.

McGuire, W. J., McGuire, C. V., Child, P., & Fujioka, T. (1978). Salience of ethnicity in the spontaneous self-concept as a function of one's ethnic distinctiveness in the social environment. *Journal of Personality and Social Psychology*, *36*(5), 511–520.

McGuire, W. J., & Papageorgis, D. (1961). The relative efficacy of various types of prior belief-defense in producing immunity against persuasion. *Journal of Abnormal and Social Psychology*, *62*(2), 327–337.

McIntyre, R. B., Paulson, R. M., & Lord, C. G. (2003). Alleviating women's mathematics stereotype threat through salience of group achievements. *Journal of Experimental Social Psychology*, *39*(1), 83–90.

McIntosh, P. (1988). *White privilege: Unpacking the invisible knapsack*. Google Scholar.

McKenna, T. (1993). *True hallucinations: Being an account of the author's extraordinary adventures in the devil's paradise*. HarperCollins.

McNulty, J. K., & Karney, B. R. (2001). Attributions in marriage: Integrating specific and global evaluations of a relationship. *Personality and Social Psychology Bulletin*, *27*(8), 943–955.

McNulty, J. K., & Karney, B. R. (2004). Positive expectations in the early years of marriage: Should couples expect the best or brace for the worst? *Journal of Personality and Social Psychology*, *86*(5), 729–743.

McNulty, J. K., Olson, M. A., Jones, R. E., & Acosta, L. M. (2017). Automatic associations between one's partner and one's affect as the proximal mechanism of change in relationship satisfaction: Evidence from evaluative conditioning. *Psychological Science*, *28*(8), 1031–1040.

McNulty, J. K., O'Mara, E. M., & Karney, B. R. (2008). Benevolent cognitions as a strategy of relationship maintenance: "Don't sweat the small stuff" . . . . But it is not all small stuff. *Journal of Personality and Social Psychology*, *94*(4), 631–646.

McWilliams, L., Bellhouse, S., Yorke, J., Lloyd, K., & Armitage, C. J. (2019). Beyond "planning": A meta-analysis of implementation intentions to support smoking cessation. *Health Psychology*, *38*(12), 1059–1068.

Mead, G. H. (1934). *Mind, self, and society*. University of Chicago Press.

Mead, N. L., & Patrick, V. M. (2016). The taming of desire: Unspecific postponement reduces desire for and consumption of postponed temptations. *Journal of Personality and Social Psychology*, *110*(1), 20–35.

Medvec, V. H., Madey, S. F., & Gilovich, T. (1995). When less is more: Counterfactual thinking and satisfaction among Olympic medalists. *Journal of Personality and Social Psychology*, *69*(4), 603–610.

Meeus, W. H. J., & Raaijmakers, Q. A. W. (1995). Obedience in modern society: The Utrecht studies. *Journal of Social Issues*, *51*(3), 155–176.

Meeusen, C., Meuleman, B., Abts, K., & Bergh, R. (2018). Comparing a variable-centered and a person-centered approach to the structure of prejudice. *Social Psychological and Personality Science*, *9*(6), 645–655.

Megargee, E. I. (1966). Undercontrolled and overcontrolled personality types in extreme antisocial aggression. *Psychological Monographs: General and Applied*, *80*(3), 1–29.

Mehl, M. R. (2017). The Electronically Activated Recorder (EAR): A method for the naturalistic observation of daily social behavior. *Current Directions in Psychological Science*, *26*(2), 184–190.

Mehl, M. R., Vazire, S., Ramírez-Esparza, N., Slatcher, R. B., & Pennebaker, J. W. (2007). Are women really more talkative than men? *Science*, *317*(5834), 82.

Meltzoff, A. N., & Moore, M. K. (1977). Imitation of facial and manual gestures by human neonates. *Science*, *198*(4312), 75–78.

Mendes, W. B., Blascovich, J., Lickel, B., & Hunter, S. (2002). Challenge and threat during social interactions with White and Black men. *Personality and Social Psychology Bulletin*, *28*(7), 939–952.

Mende-Siedlecki, P., Qu-Lee, J., Backer, R., & Van Bavel, J. J. (2019). Perceptual contributions to racial bias in pain recognition. *Journal of Experimental Psychology: General*, *148*(5), 863–889.

Menninghaus, W., Wagner, V., Wassiliwizky, E., Schindler, I., Hanich, J., Jacobsen, T., & Koelsch, S. (2019). What are aesthetic emotions? *Psychological Review*, *126*(2), 171–195.

Mercier, B., Kramer, S. R., & Shariff, A. F. (2018). Belief in God: Why people believe, and why they don't. *Current Directions in Psychological Science*, *27*(4), 263–268.

Merton, R. K. (1948). The self-fulfilling prophecy. *Antioch Review*, *8*(2), 193–210.

Merwin, W. S. (1970). *The carrier of ladders*. Atheneum.

Mesquita, B., & Frijda, N. H. (1992). Cultural variations in emotions: A review. *Psychological Bulletin*, *112*(2), 179–204.

Messick, D. M., & Mackie, D. M. (1989). Intergroup relations. *Annual Review of Psychology*, *40*, 45–81.

Meston, C. M., & Buss, D. M. (2007). Why humans have sex. *Archives of Sexual Behavior*, *36*(4), 477–507.

Meston, C. M., & Frohlich, P. F. (2003). Love at first fright: Partner salience moderates roller-coaster-induced excitation transfer. *Archives of Sexual Behavior*, *32*(6), 537–544.

Meyer, M. L. (2019). Social by default: Characterizing the social functions of the resting brain. *Current Directions in Psychological Science*, *28*(4), 380–386.

Meyer-Lindenberg, A., Buckholtz, J. W., Kolachana, B., Hariri, A. R., Pezawas, L., Blasi, G., Wabnitz, A., Honea, R., Verchinski, B., Callicott, J., Egan, M., Mattay, V., & Weinberger, D. R. (2006). Neural mechanisms of genetic risk for impulsivity and violence in humans. *Proceedings of the National Academy of Sciences*, *103*(16), 6269–6274.

Michotte, A. (1963). *The perception of causality*. Basic Books.

Mickelson, K. D., Kessler, R. C., & Shaver, P. R. (1997). Adult attachment in a nationally representative sample. *Journal of Personality and Social Psychology*, *73*(5), 1092–1106.

Midlarsky, E., Fagin Jones, S., & Corley, R. P. (2005). Personality correlates of heroic rescue during the Holocaust. *Journal of Personality*, *73*(4), 907–934.

Mikolajczak, M., Gross, J. J., Lane, A., Corneille, O., de Timary, P., & Luminet, O. (2010). Oxytocin makes people trusting, not gullible. *Psychological Science*, *21*(8), 1072–1074.

Mikulincer, M. (2006). Attachment, caregiving, and sex within romantic relationships: A behavioral systems perspective. In M. Mikulincer & G. S. Goodman (Eds.), *Dynamics of romantic love* (pp. 23–44). Guilford Press.

Mikulincer, M., Dolev, T., & Shaver, P. R. (2004). Attachment-related strategies during thought suppression: Ironic rebounds and vulnerable self-representations. *Journal of Personality and Social Psychology*, *87*(6), 940–956.

Mikulincer, M., Florian, V., & Hirschberger, G. (2003). The existential function of close relationships: Introducing death into the science of love. *Personality and Social Psychology Review*, *7*(1), 20–40.

Mikulincer, M., Gillath, O., Halevy, V., Avihou, N., Avidan, S., & Eshkoli, N. (2001). Attachment theory and reactions to others' needs: Evidence that activation of the sense of attachment security promotes empathic responses. *Journal of Personality and Social Psychology*, *81*(6), 1205–1224.

Mikulincer, M., & Shaver, P. R. (2007). *Attachment in adulthood: Structure, dynamics, and change*. Guilford Press.

Mikulincer, M., Shaver, P. R., Gillath, O., & Nitzberg, R. A. (2005). Attachment, caregiving, and altruism: Boosting attachment security increases compassion and helping. *Journal of Personality and Social Psychology*, *89*(5), 817–839.

Miles, D. R., & Carey, G. (1997). Genetic and environmental architecture on human aggression. *Journal of Personality and Social Psychology*, *72*(1), 207–217.

Milgram, S. (1963). Behavioral study of obedience. *Journal of Abnormal and Social Psychology*, *67*(4), 371–378.

Milgram, S. (1970). The experience of living in cities. *Science*, *167*(3924), 1461–1468.

Milgram, S. (1974). *Obedience to authority: An experimental view*. Harper & Row.

Milgram, S., Bickman, L., & Berkowitz, L. (1969). Note on the drawing power of crowds of different size. *Journal of Personality and Social Psychology*, *13*(2), 79–82.

Miller, C. T., Rothblum, E. D., Felicio, D., & Brand, P. (1995). Compensating for stigma: Obese and nonobese women's reactions to being visible. *Personality and Social Psychology Bulletin*, *21*(10), 1093–1106.

Miller, D. T., & McFarland, C. (1986). Counterfactual thinking and victim compensation: A test of norm theory. *Personality and Social Psychology Bulletin*, *12*(4), 513–519.

Miller, J. G. (1984). Culture and the development of everyday social explanation. *Journal of Personality and Social Psychology*, *46*(5), 961–978.

Miller, N., & Campbell, D. T. (1959). Recency and primacy in persuasion as a function of the timing of speeches and measurements. *Journal of Abnormal and Social Psychology*, *59*(1), 1–9.

Miller, N., & Carlson, M. (1990). Valid theory-testing meta-analyses further question the negative state relief model of helping. *Psychological Bulletin*, *107*(2), 215–225.

Miller, N., & Marks, G. (1982). Assumed similarity between self and other: Effect of expectation of future interaction with that other. *Social Psychology Quarterly*, *45*(2), 100–105.

Miller, N., Maruyama, G., Beaber, R. J., & Valone, K. (1976). Speed of speech and persuasion. *Journal of Personality and Social Psychology*, *34*(4), 615–624.

Miller, N., Pedersen, W. C., Earleywine, M., & Pollock, V. E. (2003). A theoretical model of triggered displaced aggression. *Personality and Social Psychology Review*, *7*(1), 75–97.

Miller, N. E., & Bugelski, R. (1948). Minor studies of aggression: II. The influence of frustrations imposed by the in-group on attitudes expressed toward outgroups. *Journal of Psychology*, *25*(2), 437–442.

Miller, R. S. (1996). *Embarrassment: Poise and peril in everyday life*. Guilford Press.

Miller, R. S. (1997). We always hurt the ones we love: Aversive interpersonal interactions in close relationships. In R. M. Kowalski (Ed.), *Aversive interpersonal behaviors* (pp. 11–29). Plenum Press.

Miller, R. S. (2001). *Behaving badly: Aversive behaviors in interpersonal relationships*. American Psychological Association.

Miller, S. L., & Maner, J. K. (2010). Scent of a woman: Men's testosterone responses to olfactory ovulation cues. *Psychological Science, 21*(2), 276–283.

Mills, J., & Aronson, E. (1965). Opinion change as a function of the communicator's attractiveness and desire to influence. *Journal of Personality and Social Psychology, 1*(2), 173–177.

Milman, O. (2020, June 8). Minneapolis pledges to dismantle its police department — How will it work? *The Guardian.* https://www.theguardian.com/us-news/2020/jun/08/minneapolis-city-council-police-department-dismantle

Milne, S., Orbell, S., & Sheeran, P. (2002). Combining motivational and volitional interventions to promote exercise participation: Protection motivation theory and implementation intentions. *British Journal of Health Psychology, 7*(2), 163–184.

Miroff, N., & Booth, W. (2010, July 27). Mexican drug cartels bring violence with them in move to Central America. *The Washington Post.* http://www.washingtonpost.com/wp-dyn/content/article/2010/07/26/AR2010072605661.html

Miron, A. M., Branscombe, N. R., & Schmitt, M. T. (2006). Collective guilt as distress over illegitimate intergroup inequality. *Group Processes & Intergroup Relations, 9*(2), 163–180.

Mischel, W. (1977). The interaction of person and situation. In D. Magnusson & N. S. Endler (Eds.), *Personality at the crossroads: Current issues in interactional psychology* (pp. 333–352). Erlbaum.

Mischel, W., & Ayduk, O. (2002). Self-regulation in a cognitive-affective personality system: Attentional control in the service of the self. *Self and Identity, 1*(2), 113–120.

Mischel, W., & Ayduk, O. (2004). Willpower in a cognitive-affective processing system: The dynamics of delay of gratification. In R. F. Baumeister & K. D. Vohs (Eds.), *Handbook of self-regulation: Research, theory, and applications* (pp. 99–129). Guilford Press.

Mischel, W., & Ebbesen, E. B. (1970). Attention in delay of gratification. *Journal of Personality and Social Psychology, 16*(2), 329–337.

Mischel, W., & Peake, P. K. (1982). Beyond déjà vu in the search for cross-situational consistency. *Psychological Review, 89*(6), 730–755.

Mitchell, B. (2009, June 30). *Troops find love in war on web.* Military.com. http://www.military.com/cs/Satellite?c=maArticle&cid=1199422038952&pagename5News%2FnwsLayout

Mitchell, T. R., Thompson, L., Peterson, E., & Cronk, R. (1997). Temporal adjustments in the evaluation of events: The "rosy view." *Journal of Experimental Social Psychology, 33*(4), 421–448.

Mithen, S. (1996). *The prehistory of the mind: A search for the origins of art, religion, and science.* Thames and Hudson.

Mithen, S. (Ed.). (1998). *Creativity in human evolution and prehistory.* Routledge.

Miyake, A., Kost-Smith, L. E., Finkelstein, N. D., Pollock, S. J., Cohen, G. L., & Ito, T. A. (2010). Reducing the gender achievement gap in college science: A classroom study of values affirmation. *Science, 330*(6008), 1234–1237.

Miyamoto, Y., Yoo, J., Levine, C. S., Park, J., Boylan, J. M., Sims, T., Markus, H. R., Kitayama, S., Kawakami, N., Karasawa, M., Coe, C. L., Love, G. D., & Ryff, C. D. (2018). Culture and social hierarchy: Self- and other-oriented correlates of socioeconomic status across cultures. *Journal of Personality and Social Psychology, 115*(3), 427–445.

Moghaddam, F. M. (1988). Individualistic and collective integration strategies among immigrants. In J. W. Berry & R. C. Annis (Eds.), *Ethnic psychology* (pp. 69–79). Swets & Zeitlinger.

Mokdad, A. H., Marks, J. S., Stroup, D. F., & Gerberding, J. L. (2004). Actual causes of death in the United States, 2000. *Journal of the American Medical Association, 291*(10), 1238–1245.

Molden, D. C. (2014). *Understanding priming effects in social psychology.* Guilford Press.

Molloy, M., & Bowden, C. (Eds.). (2011). *El sicario: The autobiography of a Mexican assassin.* Nation Books.

Montoya, R. M., Horton, R. S., & Kirchner, J. (2008). Is actual similarity necessary for attraction? A meta-analysis of actual and perceived similarity. *Journal of Social and Personal Relationships, 25*(6), 889–922.

Montoya, R. M., & Insko, C. A. (2008). Toward a more complete understanding of the reciprocity of liking effect. *European Journal of Social Psychology, 38*(3), 477–498.

Moon, A., Gan, M., & Critcher, C. R. (2020). The overblown implications effect. *Journal of Personality and Social Psychology, 118*(4), 720–742.

Moon, A., & Roeder, S. S. (2014). A secondary replication attempt of stereotype susceptibility (Shih, Pittinsky, & Ambady, 1999). *Social Psychology, 45*(3), 199–201.

Moon, J. W., Krems, J. A., Cohen, A. B., & Kenrick, D. T. (2019). Is nothing sacred? Religion, sex, and reproductive strategies. *Current Directions in Psychological Science, 28*(4), 361–365.

Moore, A. (2018, June 14). Which female artist sold the most records? *Atlanta Black Star.* https://atlantablackstar.com/answer/which-female-artist-sold-the-most-records/

Moreau, D., Macnamara, B. N., & Hambrick, D. Z. (2019). Overstating the role of environmental factors in success: A cautionary note. *Current Directions in Psychological Science, 28*(1), 28–33.

Morelli, G. A., & Rothbaum, F. (2007). Situating the child in context: Attachment relationships and self-regulation in different cultures. In S. Kitayama & D. Cohen (Eds.), *Handbook of cultural psychology* (pp. 500–527). Guilford Press.

Morelli, S. A., Lieberman, M. D., & Zaki, J. (2015). The emerging study of positive empathy. *Social and Personality Psychology Compass, 9*(2), 57–68.

Morgenroth, T., & Ryan, M. K. (2018). Quotas and affirmative action: Understanding group-based outcomes and attitudes. *Social and Personality Psychology Compass, 12*(3), 1–14.

Mori, D., Chaiken, S., & Pliner, P. (1987). "Eating lightly" and the self-presentation of femininity. *Journal of Personality and Social Psychology, 53*(4), 693–702.

Morin, R. (2015, August 16). *Exploring racial bias among biracial and single-race adults: The IAT.* Pew Research Center. https://www.pewsocialtrends.org/2015/08/19/exploring-racial-bias-among-biracial-and-single-race-adults-the-iat/

Morris, M. W., & Peng, K. (1994). Culture and cause: American and Chinese attributions for social and physical events. *Journal of Personality and Social Psychology, 67*(6), 949–971.

Morrison, M., DeVaul-Fetters, A., & Gawronski, B. (2016). Stacking the jury: Legal professionals' peremptory challenges reflect jurors' levels of implicit race bias. *Personality and Social Psychology Bulletin, 42*(8), 1129–1141.

Morrison, M., & Roese, N. J. (2011). Regrets of the typical American: Findings from a nationally representative sample. *Social Psychological and Personality Science, 2*(6), 576–583.

Morse, S., & Gergen, K. J. (1970). Social comparison, self-consistency, and the concept of self. *Journal of Personality and Social Psychology, 16*(1), 148–156.

Moscovici, S. (1980). Toward a theory of conversion behavior. In L. Berkowitz (Ed.), *Advances in experimental social psychology* (Vol. 13, pp. 209–239). Academic Press.

Moscovici, S., Lage, S., & Naffrechoux, M. (1969). Influence of a consistent minority on the responses of a majority in a color perception task. *Sociometry, 32*(4), 365–380.

Moscovici, S., Mungy, G., & Van Avermaet, E. (Eds.). (1985). *Perspectives on minority influence.* Cambridge University Press.

Moscovici, S., & Zavalloni, M. (1969). The group as a polarizer of attitudes. *Journal of Personality and Social Psychology, 12*(2), 125–135.

Moskalenko, S., & Heine, S. J. (2003). Watching your troubles away: Television viewing as a stimulus for subjective self-awareness. *Personality and Social Psychology Bulletin, 29*(1), 76–85.

Moskowitz, G. (2005). *Social cognition.* Guilford Press.

Moskowitz, G. B. (2010). On the control over stereotype activation and stereotype inhibition. *Social and Personality Psychology Compass, 4*(2), 140–158.

Moskowitz, G. B., & Li, P. (2011). Egalitarian goals trigger stereotype inhibition: A proactive form of stereotype control. *Journal of Experimental Social Psychology, 47*(1), 103–116.

Moskowitz, G. B., & Olcaysoy Okten, I. (2016). Spontaneous goal inference (SGI). *Social and Personality Psychology Compass, 10*(1), 64–80.

Motyl, M., Hart, J., Pyszczynski, T., Weise, D., Maxfield, M., & Siedel, A. (2011). Subtle priming of shared human experiences eliminates threat-induced negativity toward Arabs, immigrants, and peace-making. *Journal of Experimental Social Psychology, 47*(6), 1179–1184.

Motyl, M., Iyer, R., Oishi, S., Trawalter, S., & Nosek, B. A. (2014). How ideological migration geographically segregates groups. *Journal of Experimental Social Psychology, 51*, 1–14.

Mountain, M. (2012, February 21). Big step forward for rights of dolphins and whales. Earth in Transition. http://www.earthintransition.org/2012/02/big-step-forward-for-rights-of-dolphins-and-whales/

Moynihan, A. B., Igou, E. R., & van Tilburg, W. A. (2019). Lost in the crowd: Conformity as escape following disbelief in free will. *European Journal of Social Psychology, 49*(3), 503–520.

Mrazek, A. J., Ihm, E. D., Molden, D. C., Mrazek, M. D., Zedelius, C. M., & Schooler, J. W. (2018). Expanding minds: Growth mindsets of self-regulation and the influences on effort and perseverance. *Journal of Experimental Social Psychology, 79*, 164–180.

Mucchi-Faina, A., Maass, A., & Volpato, C. (1991). Social influence: The role of originality. *European Journal of Social Psychology, 21*(3), 183–197.

Mueller, A. B., & Skitka, L. J. (2018). Liars, damned liars, and zealots: The effect of moral mandates on transgressive advocacy acceptance. *Social Psychological and Personality Science, 9*(6), 711–718.

Mueller, C. W., & Donnerstein, E. (1981). Film-facilitated arousal and prosocial behavior. *Journal of Experimental Social Psychology, 17*(3), 1–41.

Muise, A., Schimmack, U., & Impett, E. A. (2016). Sexual frequency predicts greater well-being, but more is not always better. *Social Psychological and Personality Science*, 7(4), 295–302.

Mullen, B. (1986). Atrocity as a function of lynch mob composition: A self-attention perspective. *Personality and Social Psychology Bulletin*, 12(2), 187–197.

Mullen, B., Atkins, J. L., Champion, D. S., Edwards, C., Hardy, D., Story, J. E., & Vanderklok, M. (1985). The false consensus effect: A meta-analysis of 115 hypothesis tests. *Journal of Experimental Social Psychology*, 21(3), 262–283.

Munafò, M. R., Clark, T. G., Moore, L. R., Payne, E., Walton, R., & Flint, J. (2003). Genetic polymorphisms and personality in healthy adults: A systematic review and meta-analysis. *Molecular Psychiatry*, 8(5), 471–484.

Muraven, M., & Slessareva, E. (2003). Mechanism of self-control failure: Motivation and limited resources. *Personality and Social Psychology Bulletin*, 29(7), 894–906.

Muraven, M., Tice, D. M., & Baumeister, R. F. (1998). Self-control as a limited resource: Regulatory depletion patterns. *Journal of Personality and Social Psychology*, 74(3), 774–789.

Murphy, F. C., Nimmo-Smith, I., & Lawrence, A. D. (2003). Functional neuroanatomy of emotions: A meta-analysis. *Cognitive, Affective & Behavioral Neuroscience*, 3(3), 207–233.

Murphy, G., Loftus, E. F., Grady, R. H., Levine, L. J., & Greene, C. M. (2019). False memories for fake news during Ireland's abortion referendum. *Psychological Science*, 30(10), 1449–1459.

Murphy, G., Murphy, L. B., & Newcomb, T. M. (1937). *Experimental social psychology* (Rev. ed.). Harper.

Murphy, M. M., Slavich, G. M., Chen, E., & Miller, G. E. (2015). Targeted rejection predicts decreased anti-inflammatory gene expression and increased symptom severity in youth with asthma. *Psychological Science*, 26(2), 111–121.

Murphy, W. D., Coleman, E. M., & Haynes, M. R. (1986). Factors related to coercive sexual behavior in a nonclinical sample of males. *Violence and Victims*, 1(4), 255–278.

Murrar, S., & Brauer, M. (2019). Overcoming resistance to change: Using narratives to create more positive intergroup attitudes. *Current Directions in Psychological Science*, 28(2), 164–169.

Murray, L., & Trevarthen, C. (1986). The infant's role in mother-infant communications. *Journal of Child Language*, 13(1), 15–29.

Murray, S. L., & Holmes, J. G. (1993). Seeing virtues in faults: Negativity and the transformation of interpersonal narratives in close relationships. *Journal of Personality and Social Psychology*, 65(4), 707–722.

Murray, S. L., & Holmes, J. G. (1997). A leap of faith? Positive illusions in romantic relationships. *Personality and Social Psychology Bulletin*, 23(6), 586–604.

Murray, S. L., & Holmes, J. G. (1999). The (mental) ties that bind: Cognitive structures that predict relationship resilience. *Journal of Personality and Social Psychology*, 77(6), 1228–1244.

Murray, S. L., Holmes, J. G., Bellavia, G., Griffin, D. W., & Dolderman, D. (2002). Kindred spirits? The benefits of egocentrism in close relationships. *Journal of Personality and Social Psychology*, 82(4), 563–581.

Murray, S. L., Holmes, J. G., Dolderman, D., & Griffin, D. W. (2000). What the motivated mind sees: Comparing friends' perspectives to married partners' views of each other. *Journal of Experimental Social Psychology*, 36(6), 600–620.

Murray, S. L., Holmes, J. G., & Griffin, D. W. (1996). The benefits of positive illusions: Idealization and the construction of satisfaction in close relationships. *Journal of Personality and Social Psychology*, 70(1), 79–98.

Murstein, B. I. (1987). A clarification and extension of the SVR theory of dyadic pairing. *Journal of Marriage and Family*, 49(4), 929–933.

Muthukrishna, M., Bell, A., Henrich, J., Curtin, C., Gedranovich, A., McInerney, J., & Thue, B. (2020). *Beyond WEIRD Psychology: Measuring and Mapping Scales of Cultural and Psychological Distance*. http://dx.doi.org/10.2139/ssrn.3259613

Myers, D. G. (1975). Discussion-induced attitude polarization. *Human Relations*, 28(8), 699–714.

Myers, D. G. (1982). Polarization effects of social interaction. In H. Brandstatter, J. H. Davis, & G. Stocher-Kreichgauer (Eds.), *Contemporary problems in group decision-making* (pp. 125–161). Academic Press.

Myers, D. G., Bruggink, J. B., Kersting, R. C., & Schlosser, B. A. (1980). Does learning others' opinions change one's opinions? *Personality and Social Psychology Bulletin*, 6(2), 253–260.

Myers, D. G., & Lamm, H. (1976). The group polarization phenomenon. *Psychological Bulletin*, 83(4), 602–627.

Nadler, A., Goldberg, M., & Jaffe, Y. (1982). Effect of self-differentiation and anonymity in group on deindividuation. *Journal of Personality and Social Psychology*, 42(6), 1127–1136.

Nadler, J. T., & Clark, M. H. (2011). Stereotype threat: A meta-analysis comparing African Americans to Hispanic Americans. *Journal of Applied Social Psychology*, 41(4), 872–890.

Nasby, W., Hayden, B., & DePaulo, B. M. (1980). Attributional bias among aggressive boys to interpret unambiguous social stimuli as displays of hostility. *Journal of Abnormal Psychology*, 89(3), 459–468.

National Children's Alliance. (n.d.) *National statistics on child abuse*. https://www.nationalchildrensalliance.org/media-room/nca-digital-media-kit/national-statistics-on-child-abuse/

National Gang Center. (2016). *National youth gang survey analysis*. https://www.nationalgangcenter.gov/Survey-Analysis/Demographics#anchorregm

National Safety Council. (2020). *Injury facts: Odds of dying*. https://injuryfacts.nsc.org/all-injuries/preventable-death-overview/odds-of-dying/

Nayakankuppam, D., Priester, J. R., Kwon, J. H., Donovan, L. A. N., & Petty, R. E. (2018). Construction and retrieval of evaluative judgments: The attitude strength moderation model. *Journal of Experimental Social Psychology*, 76, 54–66.

NBC News. (2007, April 19). *High school classmates say gunman was bullied*. NBC. http://www.nbcnews.com/id/18169776/

Neff, K. D. (2011). *Self-compassion*. William Morrow.

Neff, K. D., & Vonk, R. (2009). Self-compassion versus global self-esteem: Two different ways of relating to oneself. *Journal of Personality*, 77(1), 23–50.

Neff, L. A., & Karney, B. R. (2002). Judgments of a relationship partner: Specific accuracy but global enhancement. *Journal of Personality*, 70(6), 1079–1112.

Neff, L. A., & Karney, B. R. (2003). The dynamic structure of relationship perceptions: Differential importance as a strategy of relationship maintenance. *Personality and Social Psychology Bulletin*, 29(11), 1433–1446.

Neff, L. A., & Karney, B. R. (2004). How does context affect intimate relationships? Linking external stress and cognitive processes within marriage. *Personality and Social Psychology Bulletin*, 30(2), 134–148.

Neff, L. A., & Karney, B. R. (2005). To know you is to love you: The implications of global adoration and specific accuracy for marital relationships. *Journal of Personality and Social Psychology*, 88(3), 480–497.

Neff, L. A., & Karney, B. R. (2009). Stress and reactivity to daily relationship experiences: How stress hinders adaptive processes in marriage. *Journal of Personality and Social Psychology*, 97(3), 435–450.

Nelson, L. D., & Morrison, E. L. (2005). The symptoms of resource scarcity: Judgments of food and finances influence preferences for potential partners. *Psychological Science*, 16(2), 167–173.

Nelson, R. (1969). *Hunters of the northern ice*. Aldine.

Nelson, S. K., Kushlev, K., English, T., Dunn, E. W., & Lyubomirsky, S. (2013). In defense of parenthood: Children are associated with more joy than misery. *Psychological Science*, 24(1), 3–10.

Nelson, T. D. (Ed.). (2009). *Handbook of prejudice, stereotyping and discrimination*. Psychology Press.

Nemeth, C. (1979). The role of an active minority in intergroup relations. In W. G. Austin & S. Worchel (Eds.), *The social psychology of intergroup relations*. Brooks/Cole.

Nemeth, C., Brown, K., & Rogers, J. (2001). Devil's advocate versus authentic dissent: Stimulating quantity and quality. *European Journal of Social Psychology*, 31(6), 707–720.

Nemeth, C., & Wachtler, J. (1974). Creating the perceptions of consistency and confidence: A necessary condition for minority influence. *Sociometry*, 37(4), 529–540.

Nemeth, C. J. (1986). Differential contributions of majority and minority influence. *Psychological Review*, 93(1), 23–32.

Nemeth, C. J., & Ormiston, M. (2007). Creative idea generation: Harmony versus stimulation. *European Journal of Social Psychology*, 37(3), 524–535.

Netzer, L., Igra, L., Anan, Y. B., & Tamir, M. (2015). When bad emotions seem better: Experience changes the automatic evaluation of anger. *Social Psychological and Personality Science*, 6(7), 797–804.

Neuberg, S. L., & Fiske, S. T. (1987). Motivational influences on impression formation: Outcome dependency, accuracy-driven attention, and individuating processes. *Journal of Personality and Social Psychology*, 53(3), 431–444.

Neuberg, S. L., Kenrick, D. T., & Schaller, M. (2010). Evolutionary social psychology. In S. T. Fiske, D. T. Gilbert, & G. Lindzey (Eds.), *Handbook of social psychology* (5th ed., pp. 761–796). Wiley.

Newby-Clark, I. R., McGregor, I., & Zanna, M. P. (2002). Thinking and caring about cognitive inconsistency: When and for whom does attitudinal ambivalence feel uncomfortable? *Journal of Personality and Social Psychology*, 82(2), 157–166.

Newcomb, T. M. (1943). *Personality and social change: Attitude formation in a student community*. Dryden Press.

Newcomb, T. M. (1956). The prediction of interpersonal attraction. *American Psychologist*, 11(11), 575–586.

Newcomb, T., Koenig, K. E., Flacks, R., & Warwick, D. P. (1967). *Persistence and change: Bennington College and its students after twenty-five years*. Wiley.

Newman, C. (2000, January). The enigma of beauty. *National Geographic*, pp. 94–121.

Newman, D. B., Sachs, M. E., Stone, A. A., & Schwarz, N. (2020). Nostalgia and well-being in daily life: An ecological validity perspective. *Journal of Personality and Social Psychology*, 118(2), 325–347.

Nguyen, H. D., & Ryan, A. M. (2008). Does stereotype threat affect test performance of minorities and women? A meta-analysis of experimental evidence. *Journal of Applied Psychology*, 93(6), 1314–1334.

Nickeas, P., Malagon, E., Cherney, E., & Gorner, J. (2017, July 5). Chicago police express frustration after more than 100 shot in violent fourth of July weekend. *Chicago Tribune*. http://www.chicagotribune.com/news/local/breaking/ct-chicago-july-4-weekend-shootings-violence-20170705-story.html

Nieuwenhuis, S., Aston-Jones, G., & Cohen, J. D. (2005). Decision making, the P3, and the locus coeruleus–norepinephrine system. *Psychological Bulletin*, 131(4), 510–532.

Nisbett, R. E. (1993). Violence and US regional culture. *American Psychologist*, 48(4), 441–449.

Nisbett, R. E. (2003). *The geography of thought: How Asians and Westerners think differently—And why*. Free Press.

Nisbett, R. E. (2009). *Intelligence and how to get it: Why schools and cultures count*. W. W. Norton.

Nisbett, R. E., & Cohen, D. (1996). *Culture of honor: The psychology of violence in the South*. Westview Press.

Nisbett, R. E., & Schachter, S. (1966). Cognitive manipulation of pain. *Journal of Experimental Social Psychology*, 2(3), 227–236.

Nisbett, R. E., & Wilson, T. D. (1977a). The halo effect: Evidence for unconscious alteration of judgments. *Journal of Personality and Social Psychology*, 35(4), 250–256.

Nisbett, R. E., & Wilson, T. D. (1977b). Telling more than we can know: Verbal reports on mental processes. *Psychological Review*, 84(3), 231–259.

Noah, T., Schul, Y., & Mayo, R. (2018). When both the original study and its failed replication are correct: Feeling observed eliminates the facial-feedback effect. *Journal of Personality and Social Psychology*, 114(5), 657–664.

Noor, M., Kteily, N., Siem, B., & Mazziotta, A. (2019). "Terrorist" or "mentally ill": Motivated biases rooted in partisanship shape attributions about violent actors. *Social Psychological and Personality Science*, 10(4), 485–493.

Nordgren, L. F., Banas, K., & MacDonald, G. (2011). Empathy gaps for social pain: Why people underestimate the pain of social suffering. *Journal of Personality and Social Psychology*, 100(1), 120–128.

Nordgren, L. F., Bos, M. W., & Dijksterhuis, A. (2011). The best of both worlds: Integrating conscious and unconscious thought best solves complex decisions. *Journal of Experimental Social Psychology*, 47(2), 509–511.

Norenzayan, A. (2013). *Big gods: How religion transformed cooperation and conflict*. Princeton University Press.

Norenzayan, A., & Shariff, A. F. (2008). The origin and evolution of religious prosociality. *Science*, 322(5898), 58–62.

Norton, M. I., Frost, J. H., & Ariely, D. (2007). Less is more: The lure of ambiguity, or why familiarity breeds contempt. *Journal of Personality and Social Psychology*, 92(1), 97–105.

Norton, M. I., & Sommers, S. R. (2011). Whites see racism as a zero-sum game that they are now losing. *Perspectives on Psychological Science*, 6(3), 215–218.

Norton, M. I., Sommers, S. R., Apfelbaum, E. P., Pura, N., & Ariely, D. (2006). Color blindness and interracial interaction: Playing the political correctness game. *Psychological Science*, 17(11), 949–953.

Nosek, B. A. (2005). Moderators of the relationship between implicit and explicit evaluation. *Journal of Experimental Psychology: General*, 134(4), 565–584.

Nosek, B. A. (2007). Implicit–explicit relations. *Current Directions in Psychological Science*, 16(2), 65–69.

Nosek, B. A., Alter, G., Banks, G. C., Borsboom, D., Bowman, S. D., Breckler, S. J., Buck, S., Chambers, C. D., Chin, G., Christensen, G., Contestabile, M., Dafoe, A., Eich, E., Freese, J., Glennerster, R., Goroff, D., Green, D. P., Hesse, B., Humphreys, M., . . . Yarkoni, T. (2015). Promoting an open research culture: Author guidelines for journals could help to promote transparency, openness, and reproducibility. *Science*, 348(6242), 1422–1425.

Nosek, B. A., Ebersole, C. R., DeHaven, A. C., & Mellor, D. T. (2018). The preregistration revolution. *Proceedings of the National Academy of Sciences of the United States of America*, 115(11), 2600–2606.

Nosek, B. A., Hawkins, C. B., & Frazier, R. S. (2011). Implicit social cognition: From measures to mechanisms. *Trends in Cognitive Sciences*, 15(4), 152–159.

Nowak, A., Gelfand, M. J., Borkowski, W., Cohen, D., & Hernandez, I. (2016). The evolutionary basis of honor cultures. *Psychological Science*, 27(1), 12–24.

Ntoumanis, N., & Sedikides, C. (2018). Holding on to the goal or letting it go and moving on? A tripartite model of goal striving. *Current Directions in Psychological Science*, 27(5), 363–368.

Nunn, N. (2008). The long-term effects of Africa's slave trades. *Quarterly Journal of Economics*, 123(1), 139–176.

Nunn, N., & Wantchekon, L. (2011). The slave trade and the origins of mistrust in Africa. *American Economic Review*, 101(7), 3221–3252.

O'Brien, E. (2019). Enjoy it again: Repeat experiences are less repetitive than people think. *Journal of Personality and Social Psychology*, 116(4), 519–540.

O'Brien, E., & Kassirer, S. (2019). People are slow to adapt to the warm glow of giving. *Psychological Science*, 30(2), 193–204.

O'Brien, L. T., Hitti, A., Shaffer, E., Camp, A. R. V., Henry, D., & Gilbert, P. N. (2017). Improving girls' sense of fit in science: Increasing the impact of role models. *Social Psychological and Personality Science*, 8(3), 301–309.

O'Donnell, A. W., Neumann, D. L., Duffy, A. L., & Paolini, S. (2019). Learning to fear outgroups: An associative learning explanation for the development and reduction of intergroup anxiety. *Social and Personality Psychology Compass*, 13(3), e12442.

Ofosu, E. K., Chambers, M. K., Chen, J. M., & Hehman, E. (2019). Same-sex marriage legalization associated with reduced implicit and explicit antigay bias. *Proceedings of the National Academy of Sciences*, 116(18), 8846–8851.

Ogbu, J. U., & Simons, H. D. (1998). Voluntary and involuntary minorities: A cultural-ecological theory of school performance with some implications for education. *Anthropology & Education Quarterly*, 29(2), 155–188.

Oh, D., Buck, E. A., & Todorov, A. (2019). Revealing hidden gender biases in competence impressions of faces. *Psychological Science*, 30(1), 65–79.

Ohbuchi, K. (1982). Aggressive reaction to arbitrary frustration as a function of causal information. *Japanese Journal of Criminal Psychology*, 19(1–2), 11–20.

Öhman, A., & Mineka, S. (2003). The malicious serpent: Snakes as a prototypical stimulus for an evolved module of fear. *Current Directions in Psychological Science*, 12(1), 5–9.

Oishi, S. (2010). The psychology of residential mobility: Implications for the self, social relationships, and well-being. *Perspectives on Psychological Science*, 5(1), 5–21.

Oishi, S., Ishii, K., & Lun, J. (2009). Residential mobility and conditionality of group identification. *Journal of Experimental Social Psychology*, 45(4), 913–919.

Oishi, S., & Kisling, J. (2009). The mutual constitution of residential mobility and individualism. In R. S. Wyer, C. Chiu, & Y. Hong (Eds.), *Understanding culture: Theory, research, and application* (pp. 223–238). Psychology Press.

Okeowo, A. (2016, November 17). Hate on the rise after Trump's election. *The New Yorker*. https://www.newyorker.com/news/news-desk/hate-on-the-rise-after-trumps-election

Olcaysoy Okten, I., & Moskowitz, G. B. (2018). Goal versus trait explanations: Causal attributions beyond the trait-situation dichotomy. *Journal of Personality and Social Psychology*, 114(2), 211–229.

Olcaysoy Okten, I., Schneid, E. D., & Moskowitz, G. B. (2019). On the updating of spontaneous impressions. *Journal of Personality and Social Psychology*, 117(1), 1–25.

Oldham, A. (2016). *2015: The year of mass shootings*. PBS News Hour. https://www.pbs.org/newshour/nation/2015-the-year-of-mass-shootings

O'Leary, K. D., & Vivian, D. (1990). Physical aggression in marriage. In F. D. Fincham & T. N. Bradbury (Eds.), *The psychology of marriage* (pp. 323–348). Guilford Press.

Oliver, M. B., & Hyde, J. S. (1993). Gender differences in sexuality: A metaanalysis. *Psychological Bulletin*, 114(1), 29–51.

Oliviola, C., Eastwick, P., Finkel, E., Hortaçu, A., Ariely, D., & Todorov, A. (2015). First impressions and consumer mate preferences in online dating and speed-dating. In K. Diehl & C. Yoon (Eds.), *Advances in Consumer Research* (Vol. 43, pp. 51–55). Association for Consumer Research.

Olson, K. R., Dunham, Y., Dweck, C. S., Spelke, E. S., & Banaji, M. R. (2008). Judgments of the lucky across development and culture. *Journal of Personality and Social Psychology*, 94(5), 757–776.

Olson, M. A., & Fazio, R. H. (2004). Reducing the influence of extrapersonal associations on the Implicit Association Test: Personalizing the IAT. *Journal of Personality and Social Psychology*, 86(5), 653–667.

Olweus, D. (1979). Stability of aggressive reaction patterns in males: A review. *Psychological Bulletin*, 86(4), 852–875.

Olweus, D., Mattsson, Å., Schalling, D., & Löw, H. (1980). Testosterone, aggression, physical, and personality dimensions in normal adolescent males. *Psychosomatic Medicine*, 42(2), 253–269.

Omnicore. (2020, January 13). *Facebook by the numbers: Stats, demographics & fun facts*. https://www.omnicoreagency.com/facebook-statistics

Omoto, A. M., & Snyder, M. (2002). Considerations of community: The context and process of volunteerism. *American Behavioral Scientist*, 45(5), 846–867.

Omoto, A. M., Snyder, M., & Hackett, J. D. (2010). Personality and motivational antecedents of activism and civic engagement. *Journal of Personality, 78*(6), 1703–1734.

Ong, D., & Wang, J. (2015). Income attraction: An online dating field experiment. *Journal of Economic Behavior & Organization, 111,* 13–22.

Open Science Collaboration. (2015). Estimating the reproducibility of psychological science. *Science, 349*(6251), aac4716.

Operario, D., & Fiske, S. T. (2001). Ethnic identity moderates perceptions of prejudice: Judgments of personal versus group discrimination and subtle versus blatant bias. *Personality and Social Psychology Bulletin, 27*(5), 550–561.

Orlofsky, J. L. (1982). Psychological androgyny, sex-typing, and sex-role ideology as predictors of male-female interpersonal attraction. *Sex Roles, 8*(10), 1057–1073.

Orne, M. T. (1962). On the social psychology of the psychological experiment: With particular reference to demand characteristics and their implications. *American Psychologist, 17*(11), 776–783.

Orth, U. (2019). The family environment in early childhood has a long-term effect on self-esteem: A longitudinal study from birth to age 27 years. *Journal of Personality and Social Psychology, 114*(4), 637–655.

Orth, U., & Robins, R. W. (2014). The development of self-esteem. *Current Directions in Psychological Science, 23*(5), 381–387.

Osborne, D., Jost, J. T., Becker, J. C., Badaan, V., & Sibley, C. G. (2019). Protesting to challenge or defend the system? A system justification perspective on collective action. *European Journal of Social Psychology, 49*(2), 244–269.

Ostovich, J. M., & Sabini, J. (2004). How are sociosexuality, sex drive, and lifetime number of sexual partners related? *Personality and Social Psychology Bulletin, 30*(10), 1255–1266.

Otgaar, H., Howe, M. L., Patihis, L., Merckelbach, H., Lynn, S. J., Lilienfeld, S. O., & Loftus, E. F. (2019). The return of the repressed: The persistent and problematic claims of long-forgotten trauma. *Perspectives on Psychological Science, 14*(6), 1072–1095.

OTRC. (2011, June 23). *Woody Allen on marriage to Soon-Yi: "What was the scandal?"* OnTheRedCarpet.com. http://abc7.com/archive/8209443/

Ottati, V., Price, E. D., Wilson, C., & Sumaktoyo, N. (2015). When self-perceptions of expertise increase closed-minded cognition: The earned dogmatism effect. *Journal of Experimental Social Psychology, 61,* 131–138.

Otto, A. S., Clarkson, J. J., & Kardes, F. R. (2016). Decision sidestepping: How the motivation for closure prompts individuals to bypass decision making. *Journal of Personality and Social Psychology, 111*(1), 1–16.

Overall, N. C., Fletcher, G. J., & Simpson, J. A. (2010). Helping each other grow: Romantic partner support, self-improvement, and relationship quality. *Personality and Social Psychology Bulletin, 36*(11), 1496–1513.

Overall, N. C., Fletcher, G. J. O., Simpson, J. A., & Fillo, J. (2015). Attachment insecurity, biased perceptions of romantic partners' negative emotions, and hostile relationship behavior. *Journal of Personality and Social Psychology, 108*(5), 730–749.

Overbeck, J. R., & Park, B. (2001). When power does not corrupt: Superior individuation processes among powerful perceivers. *Journal of Personality and Social Psychology, 81*(4), 549–565.

Oyserman, D., Bybee, D., & Terry, K. (2006). Possible selves and academic outcomes: How and when possible selves impel action. *Journal of Personality and Social Psychology, 91*(1), 188–204.

Packer, D. J. (2009). Avoiding groupthink: Whereas weakly identified members remain silent, strongly identified members dissent about collective problems. *Psychological Science, 20*(5), 546–548.

Page, S. E. (2007). *The difference: How the power of diversity creates better groups, firms, schools, and societies.* Princeton University Press.

Pager, D., & Shepherd, H. (2008). The sociology of discrimination: Racial discrimination in employment, housing, credit, and consumer markets. *Annual Review of Sociology, 34,* 181–209.

Paloutzian, R. F. (1981). Purpose in life and value changes following conversion. *Journal of Personality and Social Psychology, 41*(6), 1153–1160.

Paluck, E. L. (2009). Reducing intergroup prejudice and conflict using the media: A field experiment in Rwanda. *Journal of Personality and Social Psychology, 96*(3), 574–587.

Paluck, E. L., Shepherd, H., & Aronow, P. M. (2016). Changing climates of conflict: A social network experiment in 56 schools. *Proceedings of the National Academy of Sciences of the United States of America, 113*(3), 566–571.

Panati, C. (1996). *Sacred origins of profound things: The stories behind the rites and rituals of the world's religions.* Penguin Books.

Pantin, H. M., & Carver, C. S. (1982). Induced competence and the bystander effect. *Journal of Applied Social Psychology, 12*(2), 100–111.

Papies, E. K., Pronk, T. M., Keesman, M., & Barsalou, L. W. (2015). The benefits of simply observing: Mindful attention modulates the link between motivation and behavior. *Journal of Personality and Social Psychology, 108*(1), 148–170.

Park, B., & Rothbart, M. (1982). Perception of out-group homogeneity and levels of social categorization: Memory for the subordinate attributes of in-group and outgroup members. *Journal of Personality and Social Psychology, 42*(6), 1051–1068.

Park, J. H., Faulkner, J., & Schaller, M. (2003). Evolved disease-avoidance processes and contemporary anti-social behavior: Prejudicial attitudes and avoidance of people with physical disabilities. *Journal of Nonverbal Behavior, 27*(2), 65–87.

Park, Y., Debrot, A., Spielmann, S. S., Joel, S., Impett, E., & MacDonald, G. (2019). Distinguishing dismissing from fearful attachment in the association between closeness and commitment. *Social Psychological and Personality Science, 10*(4), 563–572.

Park, Y., & MacDonald, G. (2019). Consistency between individuals' past and current romantic partners' own reports of their personalities. *Proceedings of the National Academy of Sciences, 116*(26), 12793–12797.

Parkes, C. M., & Weiss, R. S. (1983). *Recovery from bereavement.* Basic Books.

Parks, M. R., & Floyd, K. (1996). Meanings for closeness and intimacy in friendship. *Journal of Social and Personal Relationships, 13*(1), 85–107.

Pastore, N. (1952). The role of arbitrariness in the frustration-aggression hypothesis. *Journal of Abnormal and Social Psychology, 47*(3), 728–731.

Patterson, G. R., Chamberlain, P., & Reid, J. B. (1982). A comparative evaluation of a parent-training program. *Behavior Therapy, 13*(5), 638–650.

Paul, A. (2014). Is online better than offline for meeting partners? Depends: Are you looking to marry or to date? *Cyberpsychology, Behavior, and Social Networking, 17*(10), 664–667.

Paunesku, D., Walton, G. M., Romero, C., Smith, E. N., Yeager, D. S., & Dweck, C. S. (2015). Mind-set interventions are a scalable treatment for academic underachievement. *Psychological Science, 26*(6), 784–793.

Pavlov, I. (1927). *Conditioned reflexes.* Oxford University Press.

Pavetich, M., & Stathi, S. (2021). Meta-humanization reduces prejudice, even under high intergroup threat. *Journal of Personality and Social Psychology, 120*(3), 651–671.

Payne, B. K. (2001). Prejudice and perception: The role of automatic and controlled processes in misperceiving a weapon. *Journal of Personality and Social Psychology, 81*(2), 181–192.

Payne, B. K., Brown-Iannuzzi, J. L., & Loersch, C. (2016). Replicable effects of primes on human behavior. *Journal of Experimental Psychology: General, 145*(10), 1269–1279.

Payne, B. K., Vuletich, H. A., & Lundberg, K. B. (2017). The bias of crowds: How implicit bias bridges personal and systemic prejudice. *Psychological Inquiry, 28*(4), 233–248.

Payne, D. L., Lonsway, K. A., & Fitzgerald, L. F. (1999). Rape myth acceptance: Exploration of its structure and its measurement using the Illinois Rape Myth Acceptance Scale. *Journal of Research in Personality, 33*(1), 27–68.

Payne, K., & Lundberg, K. (2014). The affect misattribution procedure: Ten years of evidence on reliability, validity, and mechanisms. *Social and Personality Psychology Compass, 8*(12), 672–686.

Peck, T. C., Seinfeld, S., Aglioti, S. M., & Slater, M. (2013). Putting yourself in the skin of a Black avatar reduces implicit racial bias. *Consciousness and Cognition, 22*(3), 779–787.

Pedersen, W. C., Bushman, B. J., Vasquez, E. A., & Miller, N. (2008). Kicking the (barking) dog effect: The moderating role of target attributes on triggered displaced aggression. *Personality and Social Psychology Bulletin, 34*(10), 1382–1395.

Pedersen, W. C., Gonzales, C., & Miller, N. (2000). The moderating effect of trivial triggering provocation on displaced aggression. *Journal of Personality and Social Psychology, 78*(5), 913–927.

Pegues, C. (2016). *Once a cop.* Atria Books.

Pelham, B. W., Shimizu, M., Arndt, J., Carvallo, M., Solomon, S., & Greenberg, J. (2018). Searching for God: Illness-related mortality threats and religious search volume in Google in 16 nations. *Personality and Social Psychology Bulletin, 44*(3), 290–303.

Pennebaker, J. W., & Beall, S. K. (1986). Confronting a traumatic event: Toward an understanding of inhibition and disease. *Journal of Abnormal Psychology, 95*(3), 274–281.

Pennebaker, J. W., Mayne, T. J., & Francis, M. E. (1997). Linguistic predictors of adaptive bereavement. *Journal of Personality and Social Psychology, 72*(4), 863–871.

Penner, L., Brannick, M. T., Webb, S., & Connell, P. (2005). Effects on volunteering of the September 11, 2001, attacks: An archival analysis. *Journal of Applied Social Psychology, 35*(7), 1333–1360.

Penner, L. A., & Finkelstein, M. A. (1998). Dispositional and structural determinants of volunteerism. *Journal of Personality and Social Psychology, 74*(2), 525–537.

Pennycook, G., Cannon, T. D., & Rand, D. G. (2018). Prior exposure increases perceived accuracy of fake news. *Journal of Experimental Psychology: General, 147*(12), 1865–1880.

Penton-Voak, I. S., Perrett, D. I., Castles, D. L., Kobayashi, T., Burt, D. M., Murray, L. K., & Minamisawa, R. (1999). Menstrual cycle alters face preference. *Nature, 399*(6738), 741–742.

Peplau, L. A., & Fingerhut, A. W. (2007). The close relationships of lesbians and gay men. *Annual Review of Psychology, 58*, 405–424.

Peplau, L. A., & Spalding, L. R. (2000). The close relationships of lesbians, gay men and bisexuals. In C. Hendrick & S. S. Hendrick (Eds.), *Close relationships: A sourcebook* (pp. 111–124), Sage.

Pepler, D. J., King, G., Craig, W., Byrd, B., & Bream, L. (1995). The development and evaluation of a multisystem social skills group training program for aggressive children. *Child and Youth Care Forum, 24*(5), 297–313.

Pepping, C. A., MacDonald, G., & Davis, P. J. (2018). Toward a psychology of singlehood: An attachment-theory perspective on long-term singlehood. *Current Directions in Psychological Science, 27*(5), 324–331.

Perdue, C. W., Dovidio, J. F., Gurtman, M. B., & Tyler, R. B. (1990). Us and them: Social categorization and the process of intergroup bias. *Journal of Personality and Social Psychology, 59*(3), 475–486.

Perilloux, C., & Kurzban, R. (2015). Do men overperceive women's sexual interest? *Psychological Science, 26*(1), 70–77.

Perry, D. G., & Bussey, K. (1979). The social learning theory of sex differences: Imitation is alive and well. *Journal of Personality and Social Psychology, 37*(10), 1699–1712.

Perry, D. G., & Perry, L. C. (1976). Identification with film characters, covert aggressive verbalization, and reactions to film violence. *Journal of Research in Personality, 10*(4), 399–409.

Perry, G. (2013). *Behind the shock machine: The untold story of the notorious Milgram psychology experiments.* The New Press.

Perry, G., Brannigan, A., Wanner, R. A., & Stam, H. (2020). Credibility and incredulity in Milgram's obedience experiments: A reanalysis of an unpublished test. *Social Psychology Quarterly, 83*(1), 88–106.

Perry, S. P., Murphy, M. C., & Dovidio, J. F. (2015). Modern prejudice: Subtle, but unconscious? The role of bias awareness in Whites' perceptions of personal and others' biases. *Journal of Experimental Social Psychology, 61*, 4–78.

Peters, W. (1987). *A class divided: Then and now.* Yale University Press.

Peterson, D., Taylor, T. J., & Esbensen, F. (2004). Gang membership and violent victimization. *Justice Quarterly, 21*(4), 794–815.

Petrocelli, J. V., Williams, S. A., & Clarkson, J. J. (2015). The bigger they come, the harder they fall: The paradoxical effect of regulatory depletion on attitude change. *Journal of Experimental Social Psychology, 58*, 82–94.

Petronio, S., Olson, C., & Dollar, N. (1989). Privacy issues in relational embarrassment: Impact on relational quality and communication satisfaction. *Communication Research Reports, 6*(1), 21–27.

Pettigrew, T. F. (1958). Personality and sociocultural factors in intergroup attitudes: A cross-national comparison. *Journal of Conflict Resolution, 2*(1), 29–42.

Pettigrew, T. F. (1961). Social psychology and desegregation research. *American Psychologist, 16*(3), 105–112.

Pettigrew, T. F. (1979). The ultimate attribution error: Extending Allport's cognitive analysis of prejudice. *Personality and Social Psychology Bulletin, 5*(4), 461–476.

Pettigrew, T. F. (1998). Intergroup contact theory. *Annual Review of Psychology, 49*, 65–85.

Pettigrew, T. F. (2018). The emergence of contextual social psychology. *Personality and Social Psychology Bulletin, 44*(7), 963–971.

Pettigrew, T. F., & Tropp, L. R. (2006). A meta-analytic test of intergroup contact theory. *Journal of Personality and Social Psychology, 90*(5), 751–783.

Pettijohn, T. F., & Jungeberg, B. J. (2004). Playboy Playmate curves: Changes in facial and body feature preferences across social and economic conditions. *Personality and Social Psychology Bulletin, 30*(9), 1186–1197.

Petty, R. E., Briñol, P., & Tormala, Z. L. (2002). Thought confidence as a determinant of persuasion: The self-validation hypothesis. *Journal of Personality and Social Psychology, 82*(5), 722–741.

Petty, R. E., & Cacioppo, J. T. (1984). The effects of involvement on responses to argument quantity and quality: Central and peripheral routes to persuasion. *Journal of Personality and Social Psychology, 46*(1), 69–81.

Petty, R. E., & Cacioppo, J. T. (1986). *Communication and persuasion: Central and peripheral routes to attitude change.* Springer-Verlag.

Petty, R. E., Cacioppo, J. T., & Schumann, D. (1983). Central and peripheral routes to advertising effectiveness: The moderating role of involvement. *Journal of Consumer Research, 10*(2), 135–146.

Petty, R. E., & Krosnick, J. A. (Eds.). (1995). *Attitude strength: Antecedents and consequences.* Erlbaum.

Petty, R. E., Wells, G. L., & Brock, T. C. (1976). Distraction can enhance or reduce yielding to propaganda: Thought disruption versus effort justification. *Journal of Personality and Social Psychology, 34*(5), 874–884.

Pew Research Center. (2016, June 27). *On views of race and inequality, Blacks and Whites are worlds apart.* Pew Research Center. https://www.pewsocial trends.org/2016/06/27/on-views-of-race-and-inequality-blacks-and-whites -are-worlds-apart/

Pew Research Center. (2017, November 15). *Assaults against Muslims in U.S. surpass 2001 level.* Pew Research Center. https://www.pewresearch.org/fact -tank/2017/11/15/assaults-against-muslims-in-u-s-surpass-2001-level/

Pew Research Center. (2019, May 14). *Attitudes on same-sex marriage.* Pew Research Center. https://www.pewforum.org/fact-sheet/changing-attitudes-on-gay-marriage/

Pezawas, L., Meyer-Lindenberg, A., Drabant, E. M., Verchinski, B. A., Munoz, K. E., Kolachana, B. S., Egan, M. F., Mattay, V. S., Hariri, A. R., & Weinberger, D. R. (2005). 5-HTTLPR polymorphism impacts human cingulate-amygdala interactions: A genetic susceptibility mechanism for depression. *Nature Neuroscience, 8*(6), 828–834.

Pfattheicher, S., Sassenrath, C., & Keller, J. (2019). Compassion magnifies third-party punishment. *Journal of Personality and Social Psychology, 117*(1), 124–141.

Phelps, E. A., O'Connor, K. J., Cunningham, W. A., Funayama, E. S., Gatenby, J. C., Gore, J. C., & Banaji, M. R. (2000). Performance on indirect measures of race evaluation predicts amygdala activation. *Journal of Cognitive Neuroscience, 12*(5), 729–738.

Phillips, D. P. (1974). The influence of suggestion on suicide: Substantive and theoretical implications of the Werther effect. *American Sociological Review, 39*(3), 340–354.

Phillips, D. P. (1979). Suicide, motor vehicle fatalities, and the mass media: Evidence toward a theory of suggestion. *American Journal of Sociology, 84*(5), 1150–1174.

Phillips, D. P. (1982). The impact of fictional television stories on U.S. adult fatalities. *American Journal of Sociology, 87*(6), 1340–1359.

Phillips, D. P. (1983). The impact of mass media violence on U.S. homicides. *American Sociological Review, 48*(4), 560–568.

Phillips, D. P., & Hensley, J. E. (1984). When violence is rewarded or punished: The impact of mass media stories on homicide. *Journal of Communication, 34*(3), 101–116.

Phills, C. E., Hahn, A., & Gawronski, B. (2020). The bidirectional causal relation between implicit stereotypes and implicit prejudice. *Personality and social psychology bulletin, 46*(9), 1318-1330.

Picho, K., Rodriguez, A., & Finnie, L. (2013). Exploring the moderating role of context on the mathematics performance of females under stereotype threat: A meta-analysis. *Journal of Social Psychology, 153*(3), 299–333.

Picho, K., & Schmader, T. (2017). When do gender stereotypes impair math performance? A study of stereotype threat among Ugandan adolescents. *Sex Roles: A Journal of Research, 78*(3–4), 295–306.

Pierro, A., Mannetti, L., Kruglanski, A. W., Klein, K., & Orehek, E. (2012). Persistence of attitude change and attitude–behavior correspondence based on extensive processing of source information. *European Journal of Social Psychology, 42*(1), 103–111.

Pietromonaco, P. R., & Barrett, L. F. (2000). The internal working models concept: What do we really know about the self in relation to others? *Review of General Psychology, 4*(2), 155–175.

Piff, P. K., Dietze, P., Feinberg, M., Stancato, D. M., & Keltner, D. (2015). Awe, the small self, and prosocial behavior. *Journal of Personality and Social Psychology, 108*(6), 883–899.

Piff, P. K., Kraus, M. W., Côté, S., Cheng, B. H., & Keltner, D. (2010). Having less, giving more: The influence of social class on prosocial behavior. *Journal of Personality and Social Psychology, 99*(5), 771–784.

Piliavin, I. M., Piliavin, J. A., & Rodin, J. (1975). Costs, diffusion, and the stigmatized victim. *Journal of Personality and Social Psychology, 32*(3), 429–438.

Piliavin, I. M., Rodin, J., & Piliavin, J. A. (1969). Good samaritanism: An underground phenomenon? *Journal of Personality and Social Psychology, 13*(4), 289–299.

Piliavin, J. A., Grube, J. A., & Callero, P. L. (2002). Role as resource for action in public service. *Journal of Social Issues, 58*(3), 469–485.

Piliavin, J. A., & Piliavin, I. M. (1972). Effect of blood on reactions to a victim. *Journal of Personality and Social Psychology, 23*(3), 353–361.

Pilkington, C. J., Tesser, A., & Stephens, D. (1991). Complementarity in romantic relationships: A self-evaluation maintenance perspective. *Journal of Social and Personal Relationships, 8*(4), 481–504.

Pinel, E. C. (1999). Stigma consciousness: The psychological legacy of social stereotypes. *Journal of Personality and Social Psychology, 76*(1), 114–128.

Pinel, E. C. (2002). Stigma consciousness in intergroup contexts: The power of conviction. *Journal of Experimental Social Psychology, 38*(2), 178–185.

Pinel, E. C., & Long, A. E. (2012). When I's meet: Sharing subjective experience with a member of the outgroup. *Personality and Social Psychology Bulletin, 38*(3), 296–307.

Pinel, E. C., Long, A. E., Landau, M., & Pyszczynski, T. (2004). I-sharing, the problem of existential isolation, and their implications for interpersonal and intergroup phenomena. In J. Greenberg, S. Koole, & T. Pyszczynski (Eds.), *Handbook of experimental existential psychology* (pp. 352–368). Guilford Press.

Pinel, E. C., Long, A. E., Murdoch, E. Q., & Helm, P. (2017). A prisoner of one's own mind: Identifying and understanding existential isolation. *Personality and Individual Differences, 105*, 54–63.

Pinel, E. C., Warner, L. R., & Chua, P. P. (2005). Getting there is only half the battle: Stigma consciousness and maintaining diversity in higher education. *Journal of Social Issues, 61*(3), 481–506.

Pinhey, T. K., Rubinstein, D. H., & Colfax, R. S. (1997). Overweight and happiness: The reflected self-appraisal hypothesis reconsidered: Consequences of obesity. *Social Science Quarterly, 78*(3), 747–755.

Pitkanen-Pulkinen, L. (1979). Self-control as a prerequisite for constructive behavior. In S. Feshbach and A. Fraczek (Eds.), *Aggression and behavior change: Biological and social process* (pp. 250–270). Praeger.

Pitts, M. K., Smith, A. M., Grierson, J., O'Brien, M., & Misson, S. (2004). Who pays for sex and why? An analysis of social and motivational factors associated with male clients of sex workers. *Archives of Sexual Behavior, 33*(4), 353–358.

Plant, E. A., & Devine, P. G. (1998). Internal and external motivation to respond without prejudice. *Journal of Personality and Social Psychology, 75*(3), 811–832.

Plant, E. A., & Devine, P. G. (2001). Responses to other-imposed pro-Black pressure: Acceptance or backlash? *Journal of Experimental Social Psychology, 37*(6), 486–501.

Plant, E. A., & Devine, P. G. (2009). The active control of prejudice: Unpacking the intentions guiding control efforts. *Journal of Personality and Social Psychology, 96*(3), 640–652.

Plant, E. A., Devine, P. G., Cox, W. T., Columb, C., Miller, S. L., Goplen, J., & Peruche, B. M. (2009). The Obama effect: Decreasing implicit prejudice and stereotyping. *Journal of Experimental Social Psychology, 45*(4), 961–964.

Plaut, V. C., Thomas, K. M., & Goren, M. J. (2009). Is multiculturalism or color blindness better for minorities? *Psychological Science, 20*(4), 444–446.

Plaut, V. C., Thomas, K. M., Hurd, K., & Romano, C. A. (2018). Do color blindness and multiculturalism remedy or foster discrimination and racism? *Current Directions in Psychological Science, 27*(3), 200–206.

Pliner, P., & Chaiken, S. (1990). Eating, social motives, and self-presentation in women and men. *Journal of Experimental Social Psychology, 26*(3), 240–254.

Plötner, M., Over, H., Carpenter, M., & Tomasello, M. (2015). Young children show the bystander effect in helping situations. *Psychological Science, 26*(4), 499–506.

Pollet, T. V., & Nettle, D. (2008). Driving a hard bargain: Sex ratio and male marriage success in a historical US population. *Biology Letters, 4*(1), 31–33.

Pope, A. (1903). An essay on man. In H. W. Boynton (Ed.), *The complete poetical works of Alexander Pope*. Houghton Mifflin. (Original works published in 1732–1744)

Pope, K. S. (1980). *On love and loving*. Jossey-Bass.

Porges, S. W. (1998). Love: An emergent property of the mammalian autonomic nervous system. *Psychoneuroendocrinology, 23*(8), 837–861.

Pornpitakpan, C. (2004). The persuasiveness of source credibility: A critical review of five decades' evidence. *Journal of Applied Social Psychology, 34*(2), 243–281.

Postmes, T., & Branscombe, N. R. (2002). Influence of long-term racial environmental composition on subjective well-being in African Americans. *Journal of Personality and Social Psychology, 83*(3), 735–751.

Postmes, T., & Spears, R. (1998). Deindividuation and antinormative behavior: A meta-analysis. *Psychological Bulletin, 123*(3), 238–259.

Postmes, T., Spears, R., & Cihangir, S. (2001). Quality of decision making and group norms. *Journal of Personality and Social Psychology, 80*(6), 918–930.

Postmes, T., Wichmann, L. J., van Valkengoed, A. M., & van der Hoef, H. (2019). Social identification and depression: A meta-analysis. *European Journal of Social Psychology, 49*(1), 110–126.

Powers, W. T. (1973). *Behavior: The control of perception*. Aldine.

Pratkanis, A. (2007). Sleeper effect. In R. Baumeister, & K. Vohs (Eds.), *Encyclopedia of social psychology* (pp. 879–881). Sage.

Pratt, T. C., & Cullen, F. T. (2000). The empirical status of Gottfredson and Hirschi's general theory of crime: A meta-analysis. *Criminology, 38*(3), 931–964.

Pratto, F., & John, O. P. (1991). Automatic vigilance: The attention-grabbing power of negative social information. *Journal of Personality and Social Psychology, 61*(3), 380–391.

Pratto, F., Sidanius, J., Stallworth, L. M., & Malle, B. F. (1994). Social dominance orientation: A personality variable predicting social and political attitudes. *Journal of Personality and Social Psychology, 67*(4), 741–763.

Prentice, D. A., Miller, D. T., & Lightdale, J. R. (1994). Asymmetries in attachments to groups and to their members: Distinguishing between common-identity and common-bond groups. *Personality and Social Psychology Bulletin, 20*(5), 484–493.

Prescott, A. T., Sargent, J. D., & Hull, J. G. (2018). Metaanalysis of the relationship between violent video game play and physical aggression over time. *Proceedings of the National Academy of Sciences, 115*(40), 9882–9888.

Pressman, S. D., Cohen, S., Miller, G. E., Barkin, A., Rabin, B. S., & Treanor, J. J. (2005). Loneliness, social network size, and immune response to influenza vaccination in college freshmen. *Health Psychology, 24*(3), 297–306.

Preston, S. D., & de Waal, F. (2002). Empathy: Its ultimate and proximate bases. *Behavioral and Brain Sciences, 25*(1), 1–20.

Previti, D., & Amato, P. R. (2004). Is infidelity a cause or a consequence of poor marital quality? *Journal of Social and Personal Relationships, 21*(2), 217–230.

Price, R. A., & Vandenberg, S. G. (1979). Matching for physical attractiveness in married couples. *Personality and Social Psychology Bulletin, 5*(3), 398–400.

Prinstein, M. J., & Wang, S. S. (2005). False consensus and adolescent peer contagion: Examining discrepancies between perceptions and actual reported levels of friends' deviant and health risk behaviors. *Journal of Abnormal Child Psychology, 33*(3), 293–306.

Proctor, D., Williamson, R. A., de Waal, F. B., & Brosnan, S. F. (2013). Chimpanzees play the ultimatum game. *Proceedings of the National Academy of Sciences, 110*(6), 2070–2075.

Pronin, E., Steele, C. M., & Ross, L. (2004). Identity bifurcation in response to stereotype threat: Women and mathematics. *Journal of Experimental Social Psychology, 40*(2), 152–168.

Pronin, E., Wegner, D. M., McCarthy, K., & Rodriguez, S. (2006). Everyday magical powers: The role of apparent mental causation in the overestimation of personal influence. *Journal of Personality and Social Psychology, 91*(2), 218–231.

Prot, S., Gentile, D. A., Anderson, C. A., Suzuki, K., Swing, E., Lim, K. M., Horiuchi, Y., Jelic, M., Krahé, B., Liuqing, W., Liau, A. K., Khoo, A., Petrescu, P. D., Sakamoto, A., Tajima, S., Toma, R. A., Warburton, W., Zhang, X., & Lam, B. C. (2014). Long-term relations among prosocial-media use, empathy, and prosocial behavior. *Psychological Science, 25*(2), 358–368.

Proudfoot, D., & Kay, A. C. (2018). How perceptions of one's organization can affect perceptions of the self: Membership in a stable organization can sustain individuals' sense of control. *Journal of Experimental Social Psychology, 76*, 104–115.

Proulx, T., & Heine, S. J. (2008). The case of the transmogrifying experimenter: Affirmation of a moral schema following implicit change detection. *Psychological Science, 19*(12), 1294–1300.

Proulx, T., & Heine, S. J. (2009). Connections from Kafka: Exposure to meaning threats improves implicit learning of an artificial grammar. *Psychological Science, 20*(9), 1125–1131.

Proulx, T., & Inzlicht, M. (2012). The five "A"s of meaning maintenance: Finding meaning in the theories of sense-making. *Psychological Inquiry, 23*(4), 317–335.

Provine, R. R. (2004). Laughing, tickling, and the evolution of speech and self. *Current Directions in Psychological Science, 13*(6), 215–218.

Przybylinski, E., & Andersen, S. M. (2015). Systems of meaning and transference: Implicit significant-other activation evokes shared reality. *Journal of Personality and Social Psychology, 109*(4), 636–661.

Puts, D. A. (2005). Mating context and menstrual phase affect women's preferences for male voice pitch. *Evolution and Human Behavior, 26*(5), 388–397.

Pyszczynski, T., Abdollahi, A., Solomon, S., Greenberg, J., Cohen, F., & Weise, D. (2006). Mortality salience, martyrdom, and military might: The great Satan versus the axis of evil. *Personality and Social Psychology Bulletin, 32*(4), 525–537.

Pyszczynski, T., & Greenberg, J. (1987a). Self-regulatory perseveration and the depressive self-focusing style: A self-awareness theory of reactive depression. *Psychological Bulletin, 102*(1), 122–138.

Pyszczynski, T., & Greenberg, J. (1987b). Toward an integration of cognitive and motivational perspectives on social inference: A biased hypothesis testing model. In L. Berkowitz (Ed.), *Advances in experimental social psychology* (Vol. 20, pp. 297–340). Academic Press.

Pyszczynski, T., Greenberg, J., Solomon, S., Arndt, J., & Schimel, J. (2004). Why do people need self-esteem? A theoretical and empirical review. *Psychological Bulletin, 130*(3), 435–468.

Pyszczynski, T., LaPrelle, J., & Greenberg, J. (1987). Encoding and retrieval effects of general person characterizations on memory for incongruent and congruent information. *Personality and Social Psychology Bulletin, 13*(4), 556–567.

Pyszczynski, T., Motyl, M., Vail, K., Hirschberger, G., Arndt, J., & Kesebir, P. (2012). A collateral advantage of drawing attention to global climate change: Increased support for peace-making and decreased support for war. *Journal of Peace Psychology, 18*(4), 354–368.

Pyszczynski, T., Solomon, S., & Greenberg, J. (2003). *In the wake of 9/11: The psychology of terror*. American Psychological Association.

Pyszczynski, T. A., & Greenberg, J. (1981). Role of disconfirmed expectancies in the instigation of attributional processing. *Journal of Personality and Social Psychology, 40*(1), 31–38.

Pyszczynski, T. A., & Greenberg, J. (1992). *Hanging on and letting go: Understanding the onset, progression, and remission of depression*. Springer-Verlag.

Quattrone, G. A. (1986). On the perception of a group's variability. In S. Worchel & W. G. Austin (Eds.), *Psychology of intergroup relations* (2nd ed., pp. 25–48). Nelson-Hall.

Quattrone, G. A., & Jones, E. E. (1980). The perception of variability within in-groups and out-groups: Implications for the law of small numbers. *Journal of Personality and Social Psychology, 38*(1), 141–152.

Rabbie, J. M., & Horwitz, M. (1988). Categories versus groups as explanatory concepts in intergroup relations. *European Journal of Social Psychology, 18*(2), 117–123.

Rae, J. R., Newheiser, A., & Olson, K. R. (2015). Exposure to racial out-groups and implicit race bias in the United States. *Social Psychological and Personality Science, 6*(5), 535–543.

Raghubir, P., & Menon, G. (1998). AIDS and me, never the twain shall meet: The effects of information accessibility on judgments of risk and advertising effectiveness. *Journal of Consumer Research, 25*(1), 52–63.

Raifman, J., Charlton, B., Arrington-Sanders, R., Chan, P., Rusley, J., Mayer, K., Stein, M., Austin, S. B., & McConnell, M. (2020). Sexual orientation and suicide attempt disparities among US adolescents: 2009–2017. *Pediatrics, 145*(3), e20191658.

Raine, A. (2008). From genes to brain to antisocial behavior. *Current Directions in Psychological Science, 17*(5), 323–328.

Raine, A., Buchsbaum, M., & LaCasse, L. (1997). Brain abnormalities in murderers indicated by positron emission tomography. *Biological Psychiatry, 42*(6), 495–508.

Randles, D., Inzlicht, M., Proulx, T., Tullett, A. M., & Heine, S. J. (2015). Is dissonance reduction a special case of fluid compensation? Evidence that dissonant cognitions cause compensatory affirmation and abstraction. *Journal of Personality and Social Psychology, 108*(5), 697–710.

Randles, D., Proulx, T., & Heine, S. J. (2011). Turn-frogs and careful-sweaters: Non-conscious perception of incongruous word pairings provokes fluid compensation. *Journal of Experimental Social Psychology, 47*(1), 246–249.

Rank, O. (1936). *Truth and reality: A life history of the human will*. Knopf.

Rank, O. (1989). *Art and artist: Creative urge and personality development* (C. F. Atkinson, Trans.). W. W. Norton. (Original work published 1932)

Rank, O. (1998). *Psychology and the soul: A study of the origin, conceptual evolution, and nature of the soul* (G. C. Richter & E. J. Lieberman, Trans.). Johns Hopkins University Press. (Original work published 1930)

Ray, D. G., Gomillion, S., Pintea, A. I., & Hamlin, I. (2019). On being forgotten: Memory and forgetting serve as signals of interpersonal importance. *Journal of Personality and Social Psychology, 116*(2), 259–276.

Read, S. J., Cesa, I. L., Jones, D. K., & Collins, N. L. (1990). When is the federal budget like a baby? Metaphor in political rhetoric. *Metaphor and Symbolic Activity, 5*(3), 125–149.

Reeve, J. (2015). Giving and summoning autonomy support in hierarchical relationships. *Social and Personality Psychology Compass, 9*(8), 406–418.

Regan, D. T. (1971). Effects of a favor and liking on compliance. *Journal of Experimental Social Psychology, 7*(6), 627–639.

Regan, D. T., & Fazio, R. H. (1977). On the consistency between attitudes and behavior: Look to the method of attitude formation. *Journal of Experimental Social Psychology, 13*(1), 28–45.

Regan, D. T., Williams, M., & Sparling, S. (1972). Voluntary expiation of guilt: A field experiment. *Journal of Personality and Social Psychology, 24*(1), 42–45.

Regan, J. W. (1971). Guilt, perceived injustice, and altruistic behavior. *Journal of Personality and Social Psychology, 18*(1), 124–132.

Regan, P. C., & Atkins, L. (2006). Sex differences and similarities in frequency and intensity of sexual desire. *Social Behavior and Personality: An International Journal, 34*(1), 95–102.

Reich, T., & Wheeler, S. C. (2016). The good and bad of ambivalence: Desiring ambivalence under outcome uncertainty. *Journal of Personality and Social Psychology, 110*(4), 493–508.

Reicher, S., & Haslam, S. A. (2006). Rethinking the psychology of tyranny: The BBC prison study. *British Journal of Social Psychology, 45*(1), 1–40.

Reicher, S. D., Haslam, S. A., & Miller, A. G. (2014). What makes a person a perpetrator? The intellectual, moral, and methodological arguments for revisiting Milgram's research on the influence of authority. *Journal of Social Issues, 70*(3), 393–408.

Reifman, A. S., Larrick, R. P., & Fein, S. (1991). Temper and temperature on the diamond: The heat-aggression relationship in major league baseball. *Personality and Social Psychology Bulletin, 17*(5), 580–585.

Reilly, R. (2003, July 2). No ordinary Joe: Remembering a heroic act that ended in tragedy. *Sports Illustrated*. http://sportsillustrated.cnn.com/vault/2003/07/07/345894/no-ordinary-joe

Reis, H. T., Clark, M. S., & Holmes, J. G. (2004). Perceived partner responsiveness as an organizing construct in the study of intimacy and closeness. In D. J. Mashek & A. Aron (Eds.), *Handbook of closeness and intimacy* (pp. 201–225). Erlbaum.

Reis, H. T., Maniaci, M. R., Caprariello, P. A., Eastwick, P. W., & Finkel, E. J. (2011). Familiarity does indeed promote attraction in live interaction. *Journal of Personality and Social Psychology, 101*(3), 557–570.

Reis, H. T., Nezlek, J., & Wheeler, L. (1980). Physical attractiveness in social interaction. *Journal of Personality and Social Psychology, 38*(4), 604–617.

Reisenzein, R. (1983). The Schachter theory of emotion: Two decades later. *Psychological Bulletin, 94*(2), 239–264.

Reisenzein, R. (1986). A structural equation analysis of Weiner's attribution–affect model of helping behavior. *Journal of Personality and Social Psychology, 50*(6), 1123–1133.

Reisenzein, R., & Gattinger, E. (1982). Salience of arousal as a mediator of misattribution of transferred excitation. *Motivation and Emotion, 6*(4), 315–328.

Reitz, A. K., Motti-Stefanidi, F., & Asendorpf, J. B. (2016). Me, us, and them: Testing sociometer theory in a socially diverse real-life context. *Journal of Personality and Social Psychology, 110*(6), 908–920.

Rentfrow, P. J., & Gosling, S. D. (2006). Message in a ballad: The role of music preferences in interpersonal perception. *Psychological Science, 17*(3), 236–242.

Rhee, S. H., & Waldman, I. D. (2002). Genetic and environmental influences on antisocial behavior: A meta-analysis of twin and adoption studies. *Psychological Bulletin, 128*(3), 490–529.

Rhodes, G. (2006). The evolutionary psychology of facial beauty. *Annual Review of Psychology, 57*, 199–226.

Rhodes, G., Harwood, K., Yoshikawa, S., Nishitani, M., & McLean, I. (2002). The attractiveness of average faces: Cross-cultural evidence and possible biological basis. In G. Rhodes & L. A. Zebrowitz (Eds.), *Facial attractiveness: Evolutionary, cognitive, and social perspectives* (pp. 35–58). Ablex.

Rhodes, G., Sumich, A., & Byatt, G. (1999). Are average facial configurations attractive only because of their symmetry? *Psychological Science, 10*(1), 52–58.

Rhodes, G., Zebrowitz, L. A., Clark, A., Kalick, S. M., Hightower, A., & McKay, R. (2001). Do facial averageness and symmetry signal health? *Evolution and Human Behavior, 22*(1), 31–46.

Riach, P., & Rich, J. (2004). Fishing for discrimination. *Review of Social Economy, 62*(4), 465–486.

Richardson, D. R., Hammock, G. S., Smith, S. M., Gardner, W., & Signo, M. (1994). Empathy as a cognitive inhibitor of interpersonal aggression. *Aggressive Behavior, 20*(4), 275–289.

Richer, S. F., & Vallerand, R. J. (1995). Supervisors' interactional styles and subordinates' intrinsic and extrinsic motivation. *Journal of Social Psychology, 135*(6), 707–722.

Richeson, J. A., Baird, A. A., Gordon, H. L., Heatherton, T. F., Wyland, C. L., Trawalter, S., & Shelton, J. N. (2003). An fMRI investigation of the impact of interracial contact on executive function. *Nature Neuroscience, 6*(12), 1323–1328.

Richeson, J. A., & Shelton, J. N. (2003). When prejudice does not pay: Effects of interracial contact on executive function. *Psychological Science, 14*(3), 287–290.

Richeson, J. A., & Trawalter, S. (2005). Why do interracial interactions impair executive function? A resource depletion account. *Journal of Personality and Social Psychology, 88*(6), 934–947.

Rick, S. I., Small, D. A., & Finkel, E. J. (2011). Fatal (fiscal) attraction: Spendthrifts and tightwads in marriage. *Journal of Marketing Research, 48*(2), 228–237.

Risen, J. L. (2016). Believing what we do not believe: Acquiescence to superstitious beliefs and other powerful intuitions. *Psychological Review, 123*(2), 182–207.

Rising, M. (2013, November 6). Swedish cinemas launch feminist movie rating. *USA Today*. http://www.usatoday.com/story/news/world/2013/11/06/sweden-cinema-feminist-rating/3451431/

Roach, M. S. (2002). *Caring, the human mode of being: A blueprint for the health professions* (2nd ed.). Canadian Hospital Association Press.

Roberts, T. A., & Gettman, J. Y. (2004). Mere exposure: Gender differences in the negative effects of priming a state of self-objectification. *Sex Roles, 51*(1–2), 17–27.

Rochat, P. (2018). The ontogeny of human self-consciousness. *Current Directions in Psychological Science, 27*(5), 345–350.

Rocklage, M. D., & Fazio, R. H. (2018). Attitude accessibility as a function of emotionality. *Personality and Social Psychology Bulletin, 44*(4), 508–520.

Rocklage, M. D., Rucker, D. D., & Nordgren, L. F. (2018). Persuasion, emotion, and language: The intent to persuade transforms language via emotionality. *Psychological Science, 29*(5), 749–760.

Roese, N. J. (1994). The functional basis of counterfactual thinking. *Journal of Personality and Social Psychology, 66*(5), 805–818.

Roese, N. J., & Epstude, K. (2017). The functional theory of counterfactual thinking: New evidence, new challenges, new insights. In J. M. Olson (Ed.), *Advances in experimental social psychology* (Vol. 56, pp. 1–79). Elsevier Academic Press.

Roese, N. J., Pennington, G. L., Coleman, J., Janicki, M., Li, N. P., & Kenrick, D. T. (2006). Sex differences in regret: All for love or some for lust? *Personality and Social Psychology Bulletin, 32*(6), 770–780.

Rogers, C. R. (1961). *On becoming a person: A psychotherapist's view of psychotherapy*. Houghton Mifflin.

Rogers, R. W., & Prentice-Dunn, S. (1981). Deindividuation and anger-mediated interracial aggression: Unmasking regressive racism. *Journal of Personality and Social Psychology, 41*(1), 63–73.

Rogers, R. W., & Prentice-Dunn, S. (1997). Protection motivation theory. In D. S. Gochman (Ed.), *Handbook of health behavior research* (Vol. 1, pp. 113–132). Plenum.

Rogers, T., & Feller, A. (2016). Discouraged by peer excellence: Exposure to exemplary peer performance causes quitting. *Psychological Science, 27*(3), 365–374.

Roghanizad, M. M., & Bohns, V. K. (2017). Ask in person: You're less persuasive than you think over email. *Journal of Experimental Social Psychology, 69,* 223–226.

Rohner, R. P. (1975). *They love me, they love me not: A worldwide study of the effects of parental acceptance and rejection.* HRAF Press.

Rohrer, J. H., Baron, S. H., Hoffman, E. L., & Swander, D. V. (1954). The stability of autokinetic judgments. *Journal of Abnormal and Social Psychology, 49*(4, Pt. 1), 595–597.

Rohrer, J. M., Egloff, B., Kosinski, M., Stillwell, D., & Schmukle, S. C. (2018). In your eyes only? Discrepancies and agreement between self- and other reports of personality from age 14 to 29. *Journal of Personality and Social Psychology, 115*(2), 304–320.

Rohsenow, D. J., & Bachorowski, J. A. (1984). Effects of alcohol and expectancies on verbal aggression in men and women. *Journal of Abnormal Psychology, 93*(4), 418–432.

Roisman, G. I., Clausell, E., Holland, A., Fortuna, K., & Elieff, C. (2008). Adult romantic relationships as contexts of human development: A multimethod comparison of same-sex couples with opposite-sex dating, engaged, and married dyads. *Developmental Psychology, 44*(1), 91–101.

Romano, A., & Balliet, D. (2017). Reciprocity outperforms conformity to promote cooperation. *Psychological Science, 28*(10), 1490–1502.

Rook, K. S. (1984). Interventions for loneliness: A review and analysis. In L. A. Peplau & S. E. Goldston (Eds.), *Preventing the harmful consequences of severe and persistent loneliness* (pp. 47–79). National Institute of Mental Health.

Rosati, A. G., DiNicola, L. M., & Buckholtz, J. W. (2018). Chimpanzee cooperation is fast and independent from self-control. *Psychological Science, 29*(11), 1832–1845.

Rosen, W., & Weil, A. (2004). *From chocolate to morphine: Everything you need to know about mind-altering drugs* (Rev. ed.). Houghton Mifflin.

Rosenberg, M. (1965). *Society and the adolescent self-image.* Princeton University Press.

Rosenblatt, A., Greenberg, J., Solomon, S., Pyszczynski, T., & Lyon, D. (1989). Evidence for terror management theory: I. The effects of mortality salience on reactions to those who violate or uphold cultural values. *Journal of Personality and Social Psychology, 57*(4), 681–690.

Rosenfeld, M. J., & Thomas, R. J. (2012). Searching for a mate: The rise of the Internet as a social intermediary. *American Sociological Review, 77,* 523–547.

Rosenfield, D., Greenberg, J., Folger, R., & Borys, R. (1982). Effect of an encounter with a Black panhandler on subsequent helping for Blacks: Tokenism or confirming a negative stereotype? *Personality and Social Psychology Bulletin, 8*(4), 664–671.

Rosenhan, D. L. (1973). On being sane in insane places. *Science, 179*(4070), 250–258.

Rosenkoetter, L. I., Rosenkoetter, S. E., & Acock, A. C. (2009). Television violence: An intervention to reduce its impact on children. *Journal of Applied Developmental Psychology, 30*(4), 381–397.

Rosenthal, L., & Levy, S. R. (2013). Thinking about mutual influences and connections across cultures relates to more positive intergroup attitudes: An examination of polyculturalism. *Social and Personality Psychology Compass, 7*(8), 547–558.

Rosenthal, R. (2002). Covert communication in classrooms, clinics, courtrooms, and cubicles. *American Psychologist, 57*(11), 839–849.

Rosenthal, R., & Jacobson, L. (1968). *Pygmalion in the classroom: Teacher expectation and pupils' intellectual development.* Holt, Rinehart and Winston.

Ross, G. (Director). (2012). *The hunger games* [Film]. Lionsgate & Color Force.

Ross, L., Greene, D., & House, P. (1977). The "false consensus effect": An egocentric bias in social perception and attribution processes. *Journal of Experimental Social Psychology, 13*(3), 279–301.

Ross, L. D., Amabile, T. M., & Steinmetz, J. L. (1977). Social roles, social control, and biases in social-perception processes. *Journal of Personality and Social Psychology, 35*(7), 485–494.

Roszell, P., Kennedy, D., & Grabb, E. (1989). Physical attractiveness and income attainment among Canadians. *Journal of Psychology, 123*(6), 547–559.

Roth, J. A. (1994). *Psychoactive substances and violence.* U.S. Department of Justice, Office of Justice Programs, National Institute of Justice.

Rothbart, M. (1981). Memory processes and social beliefs. In D. L. Hamilton (Ed.), *Cognitive processes in stereotyping and intergroup behavior* (pp. 145–181). Erlbaum.

Rothbaum, F., & Tsang, B. Y. P. (1998). Love songs in the United States and China on the nature of romantic love. *Journal of Cross-Cultural Psychology, 29*(2), 306–319.

Rothman, A. J. (2000). Toward a theory-based analysis of behavioral maintenance. *Health Psychology, 19*(1S), 64–69.

Rothman, A. J., & Salovey, P. (1997). Shaping perceptions to motivate healthy behavior: The role of message framing. *Psychological Bulletin, 121*(1), 3–19.

Rothman, A. J., & Schwarz, N. (1998). Constructing perceptions of vulnerability: Personal relevance and the use of experiential information in health judgments. *Personality and Social Psychology Bulletin, 24*(10), 1053–1064.

Rothschild, Z. K., Landau, M. J., Sullivan, D., & Keefer, L. A. (2012). A dual motive model of scapegoating: Displacing blame to reduce guilt or increase control. *Journal of Personality and Social Psychology, 102*(6), 1148–1163.

Rotter, J. B. (1954). *Social learning and clinical psychology.* Prentice Hall.

Routledge, C., Arndt, J., & Goldenberg, J. L. (2004). A time to tan: Proximal and distal effects of mortality salience on sun exposure intentions. *Personality and Social Psychology Bulletin, 30*(10), 1347–1358.

Routledge, C., Arndt, J., Sedikides, C., & Wildschut, T. (2008). A blast from the past: The terror management function of nostalgia. *Journal of Experimental Social Psychology, 44*(1), 132–140.

Routledge, C., Arndt, J., Wildschut, T., Sedikides, C., Hart, C. M., Juhl, J., Vingerhoets, A. J. J. M., & Schlotz, W. (2011). The past makes the present meaningful: Nostalgia as an existential resource. *Journal of Personality and Social Psychology, 101*(3), 638–652.

Routledge, C., & Vess, M. (Eds.). (2018). *Handbook of terror management theory.* Academic Press.

Rozin, P., & Fallon, A. E. (1987). A perspective on disgust. *Psychological Review, 94*(1), 23–41.

Rozin, P., Lowery, L., Imada, S., & Haidt, J. (1999). The CAD triad hypothesis: A mapping between three moral emotions (contempt, anger, disgust) and three moral codes (community, autonomy, divinity). *Journal of Personality and Social Psychology, 76*(4), 574–586.

Rubin, Z. (1973). *Liking and loving: An invitation to social psychology.* Holt, Rinehart & Winston.

Ruble, D. N., Martin, C. L., & Berenbaum, S. A. (2006). Gender Development. In N. Eisenberg, W. Damon, & R. M. Lerner (Eds.), *Handbook of child psychology: Social, emotional, and personality development* (pp. 858–932). John Wiley & Sons Inc.

Ruby, M. B., & Heine, S. J. (2012). Too close to home: Factors predicting meat avoidance. *Appetite, 59*(1), 47–52.

Rudman, L. A. (1998). Self-promotion as a risk factor for women: The costs and benefits of counterstereotypical impression management. *Journal of Personality and Social Psychology, 74*(3), 629–645.

Ruisch, B. C., & Ferguson, M. J. (2022). Changes in Americans' prejudices during the presidency of Donald Trump. *Nat Hum Behav.* https://doi.org/10.1038/s41562-021-01287-2

Ruiter, R. A., Kessels, L. T., Peters, G. J. Y., & Kok, G. (2014). Sixty years of fear appeal research: Current state of the evidence. *International Journal of Psychology, 49*(2), 63–70.

Rusbult, C. E. (1980). Commitment and satisfaction in romantic associations: A test of the investment model. *Journal of Experimental Social Psychology, 16*(2), 172–186.

Rusbult, C. E. (1983). A longitudinal test of the investment model: The development (and deterioration) of satisfaction and commitment in heterosexual involvements. *Journal of Personality and Social Psychology, 45*(1), 101–117.

Rusbult, C. E. (1987). Responses to dissatisfaction in close relationships: The exit-voice-loyalty-neglect model. In D. Perlman & S. Duck (Eds.), *Intimate relationships: Development, dynamics, and deterioration* (pp. 209–237). Sage.

Rusbult, C. E., Johnson, D. J., & Morrow, G. D. (1986). Predicting satisfaction and commitment in adult romantic involvements: An assessment of the generalizability of the investment model. *Social Psychology Quarterly, 49*(1), 81–89.

Rusbult, C. E., & Martz, J. M. (1995). Remaining in an abusive relationship: An investment model analysis of nonvoluntary dependence. *Personality and Social Psychology Bulletin, 21*(6), 558–571.

Rusbult, C. E., Verette, J., Whitney, G. A., Slovik, L. F., & Lipkus, I. (1991). Accommodation processes in close relationships: Theory and preliminary empirical evidence. *Journal of Personality and Social Psychology, 60*(1), 53–78.

Rusbult, C. E., Zembrodt, I. M., & Gunn, L. K. (1982). Exit, voice, loyalty, and neglect: Responses to dissatisfaction in romantic involvements. *Journal of Personality and Social Psychology, 43*(6), 1230–1242.

Rushton, J. P., Chrisjohn, R. D., & Fekken, G. C. (1981). The altruistic personality and the Self-Report Altruism Scale. *Personality and Individual Differences, 2*(4), 293–302.

Rushton, J. P., Fulker, D. W., Neale, M. C., Nias, D. K. B., & Eysenck, H. J. (1986). Altruism and aggression: The heritability of individual differences. *Journal of Personality and Social Psychology, 50*(6), 1192–1198.

Rutchick, A. M., McManus, R. M., Barth, D. M., Youmans, R. J., Ainsworth, A. T., & Goukassian, H. J. (2017). Technologically facilitated remoteness increases killing behavior. *Journal of Experimental Social Psychology, 73*, 147–150.

Rutherford, M. D., Baron-Cohen, S., & Wheelwright, S. (2002). Reading the mind in the voice: A study with normal adults and adults with Asperger syndrome and high functioning autism. *Journal of Autism and Developmental Disorders, 32*(3), 189–194.

Ruttan, R. L., McDonnell, M., & Nordgren, L. F. (2015). Having "been there" doesn't mean I care: When prior experience reduces compassion for emotional distress. *Journal of Personality and Social Psychology, 108*(4), 610–622.

Ryan, R. M., & Connell, J. P. (1989). Perceived locus of causality and internalization: Examining reasons for acting in two domains. *Journal of Personality and Social Psychology, 57*(5), 749–761.

Ryazanov, A. A., & Christenfeld, N. J. (2018). Incremental mindsets and the reduced forgiveness of chronic failures. *Journal of Experimental Social Psychology, 76*, 33–41.

Rydell, R. J., & McConnell, A. R. (2006). Understanding implicit and explicit attitude change: A systems of reasoning analysis. *Journal of Personality and Social Psychology, 91*(6), 995–1008.

Ryff, C. D., & Singer, B. (2000). Interpersonal flourishing: A positive health agenda for the new millennium. *Personality and Social Psychology Review, 4*(1), 30–44.

Saad, L. (2011, November 28). *To lose weight, Americans rely more on dieting than exercise.* Gallup News Service. http://www.gallup.com/poll/150986/Lose-Weight-Americans-Rely-Dieting-Exercise.aspx

Sagarin, B. J., Becker, D., Guadagno, R. E., Nicastle, L. D., & Millevoi, A. (2003). Sex differences (and similarities) in jealousy: The moderating influence of infidelity experience and sexual orientation of the infidelity. *Evolution and Human Behavior, 24*(1), 17–23.

Sagarin, B. J., Cialdini, R. B., Rice, W. E., & Serna, S. B. (2002). Dispelling the illusion of invulnerability: The motivations and mechanisms of resistance to persuasion. *Journal of Personality and Social Psychology, 83*(3), 526–541.

Salmivalli, C., Kaukiainen, A., Kaistaniemi, L., & Lagerspetz, K. M. (1999). Self-evaluated self-esteem, peer-evaluated self-esteem, and defensive egotism as predictors of adolescents' participation in bullying situations. *Personality and Social Psychology Bulletin, 25*(10), 1268–1278.

Salter, P. S., Adams, G., & Perez, M. J. (2018). Racism in the structure of everyday worlds: A cultural-psychological perspective. *Current Directions in Psychological Science, 27*(3), 150–155.

Salzman, M. B. (2001). Cultural trauma and recovery: Perspectives from terror management theory. *Trauma, Violence, & Abuse, 2*(2), 172–191.

Salzman, M. B., & Halloran, M. J. (2004). Cultural trauma and recovery: Cultural meaning, self-esteem, and the reconstruction of the cultural anxiety buffer. In J. Greenberg, S. Koole, & T. Pyszczynski (Eds.), *Handbook of experimental existential psychology* (pp. 231–246). Guilford Press.

Sanders, G. S., & Baron, R. S. (1975). The motivating effects of distraction on task performance. *Journal of Personality and Social Psychology, 32*(6), 956–963.

Sanders, S. A., & Reinisch, J. M. (1999). Would you say you "had sex" if . . .? *JAMA: The Journal of the American Medical Association, 281*(3), 275–277.

Sandstrom, G. M., Schmader, T., Croft, A., & Kwok, N. (2019). A social identity threat perspective on being the target of generosity from a higher status other. *Journal of Experimental Social Psychology, 82*, 98–114.

Sanfey, A. G., Rilling, J. K., Aronson, J. A., Nystrom, L. E., & Cohen, J. D. (2003). The neural basis of economic decision-making in the ultimatum game. *Science, 300*(5626), 1755–1758.

Sani, F., Herrera, M., & Bowe, M. (2009). Perceived collective continuity and ingroup identification as defence against death awareness. *Journal of Experimental Social Psychology, 45*(1), 242–245.

Sani, F., & Todman, J. (2002). Should we stay or should we go? A social psychological model of schisms in groups. *Personality and Social Psychology Bulletin, 28*(12), 1647–1655.

San Martin, A., Schug, J., & Maddux, W. W. (2019). Relational mobility and cultural differences in analytic and holistic thinking. *Journal of Personality and Social Psychology, 116*(4), 495–518.

Santee, R. T., & Maslach, C. (1982). To agree or not to agree: Personal dissent amid social pressure to conform. *Journal of Personality and Social Psychology, 42*(4), 690–700.

Santos, H. C., Varnum, M. E., & Grossmann, I. (2017). Global increases in individualism. *Psychological Science, 28*(9), 1228–1239.

Santos, M. D., Leve, C., & Pratkanis, A. R. (1994). Hey buddy, can you spare seventeen cents? Mindful persuasion and the pique technique. *Journal of Applied Social Psychology, 24*(9), 755–764.

Sapolsky, R. M. (1998). *The trouble with testosterone: And other essays on the biology of the human predicament.* Simon & Schuster.

Sapolsky, R. M., & Share, L. J. (2004). A pacific culture among wild baboons: Its emergence and transmission. *PLoS Biology, 2*(4), e106.

Sargent, F. (Ed.). (1974). *Human ecology.* American Elsevier.

Sargent, J. D., Dalton, M. A., Beach, M. L., Mott, L. A., Tickle, J. J., Ahrens, M. B., & Heatherton, T. F. (2002). Viewing tobacco use in movies: Does it shape attitudes that mediate adolescent smoking? *American Journal of Preventive Medicine, 22*(3), 137–145.

Sassenberg, K., & Moskowitz, G. B. (2005). Don't stereotype, think different! Overcoming automatic stereotype activation by mindset priming. *Journal of Experimental Social Psychology, 41*(5), 506–514.

Saucier, D. A., Miller, C. T., & Doucet, N. (2005). Differences in helping Whites and Blacks: A meta-analysis. *Personality and Social Psychology Review, 9*(1), 2–16.

Savani, K., & Job, V. (2017). Reverse ego-depletion: Acts of self-control can improve subsequent performance in Indian cultural contexts. *Journal of Personality and Social Psychology, 113*(4), 589–607.

Savitsky, K., & Gilovich, T. (2003). The illusion of transparency and the alleviation of speech anxiety. *Journal of Experimental Social Psychology, 39*(6), 618–625.

Sbarra, D. A. (2006). Predicting the onset of emotional recovery following nonmarital relationship dissolution: Survival analyses of sadness and anger. *Personality and Social Psychology Bulletin, 32*(3), 298–312.

Sbarra, D. A., & Emery, R. E. (2005). The emotional sequelae of nonmarital relationship dissolution: Analysis of change and intraindividual variability over time. *Personal Relationships, 12*(2), 213–232.

Sbarra, D. A., Law, R. W., & Portley, R. M. (2011). Divorce and death: A meta-analysis and research agenda for clinical, social, and health psychology. *Perspectives on Psychological Science, 6*(5), 454–474.

Sbarra, D. A., Smith, H. L., & Mehl, M. R. (2012). When leaving your ex, love yourself: Observational ratings of self-compassion predict the course of emotional recovery following marital separation. *Psychological Science, 23*(3), 261–269.

Schachter, S. (1951). Deviation, rejection, and communication. *Journal of Abnormal and Social Psychology, 46*(2), 190–207.

Schachter, S. (1959). *The psychology of affiliation: Experimental studies of the sources of gregariousness.* Stanford University Press.

Schachter, S. (1964). The interaction of cognitive and physiological determinants of emotional state. In L. Berkowitz (Ed.), *Advances in experimental social psychology* (Vol. 1, pp. 48–81). Academic Press.

Schachter, S., & Singer, J. (1962). Cognitive, social, and physiological determinants of emotional state. *Psychological Review, 69*(5), 379–399.

Schacter, D. L. (1996). *Searching for memory: The brain, the mind, and the past.* Basic Books.

Schaller, M., Miller, G. E., Gervais, W. M., Yager, S., & Chen, E. (2010). Mere visual perception of other people's disease symptoms facilitates a more aggressive immune response. *Psychological Science, 21*(5), 649–652.

Schein, C., Goranson, A., & Gray, K. J. (2015). The uncensored truth about morality. *Psychologist, 28*(12), 982–985.

Schimel, J., Arndt, J., Pyszczynski, T., & Greenberg, J. (2001). Being accepted for who we are: Evidence that social validation of the intrinsic self reduces general defensiveness. *Journal of Personality and Social Psychology, 80*(1), 35–52.

Schimel, J., Greenberg, J., & Martens, A. (2003). Evidence that projection of a feared trait can serve a defensive function. *Personality and Social Psychology Bulletin, 29*(8), 969–979.

Schimel, J., Simon, L., Greenberg, J., Pyszczynski, T., Solomon, S., Waxmonsky, J., & Arndt, J. (1999). Stereotypes and terror management: Evidence that mortality salience enhances stereotypic thinking and preferences. *Journal of Personality and Social Psychology, 77*(5), 905–926.

Schkade, D. A., & Kahneman, D. (1998). Does living in California make people happy? A focusing illusion in judgments of life satisfaction. *Psychological Science, 9*(5), 340–346.

Schkade, D. A., & Sunstein, C. R. (2003, June 11). Judging by where you sit. *The New York Times.* http://www.nytimes.com/2003/06/11/opinion/judging-by-where-you-sit.html

Schlenker, B. R., & Forsyth, D. R. (1977). On the ethics of psychological research. *Journal of Experimental Social Psychology, 13*(4), 369–396.

Schlosser, R. W., Balandin, S., Hemsley, B., Iacono, T., Probst, P., & von Tetzchner, S. (2014). Facilitated communication and authorship: A systematic review. *AAC: Augmentative and Alternative Communication, 30*(4), 359–368.

Schmader, T., & Beilock, S. L. (2011). An integration of processes that underlie stereotype threat. In M. Inzlicht & T. Schmader (Eds.), *Stereotype threat: Theory, process, and application* (pp. 34–50). Oxford University Press.

Schmader, T., Johns, M., & Forbes, C. (2008). An integrated process model of stereotype threat effects on performance. *Psychological Review, 115*(2), 336–356.

Schmader, T., & Major, B. (1999). The impact of ingroup vs outgroup performance on personal values. *Journal of Experimental Social Psychology, 35*(1), 47–67.

Schmader, T., Major, B., Eccleston, C. P., & McCoy, S. K. (2001). Devaluing domains in response to threatening intergroup comparisons: Perceived legitimacy and the status value asymmetry. *Journal of Personality and Social Psychology, 80*(5), 782–796.

Schmader, T., Major, B., & Gramzow, R. H. (2001). Coping with ethnic stereotypes in the academic domain: Perceived injustice and psychological disengagement. *Journal of Social Issues, 57*(1), 93–111.

Schmader, T., & Sedikides, C. (2018). State authenticity as fit to environment (SAFE): Implications of social identity for fit, authenticity, and self-segregation. *Personality and Social Psychology Review, 22*(3), 228–259.

Schmeichel, B. J., Gailliot, M. T., Filardo, E. A., McGregor, I., Gitter, S., & Baumeister, R. F. (2009). Terror management theory and self-esteem revisited: The roles of implicit and explicit self-esteem in mortality salience effects. *Journal of Personality and Social Psychology, 96*(5), 1077–1087.

Schmeichel, B. J., & Vohs, K. D. (2009). Self-affirmation and self-control: Affirming core values counteracts ego depletion. *Journal of Personality and Social Psychology, 96*(4), 770–782.

Schmid Mast, M., & Hall, J. A. (2018). The impact of interpersonal accuracy on behavioral outcomes. *Current Directions in Psychological Science, 27*(5), 309–314.

Schmitt, D. P. (2005). Sociosexuality from Argentina to Zimbabwe: A 48-nation study of sex, culture, and strategies of human mating. *Behavioral and Brain Sciences, 28*(2), 247–274.

Schmitt, M. T., Branscombe, N. R., & Postmes, T. (2003). Women's emotional responses to the pervasiveness of gender discrimination. *European Journal of Social Psychology, 33*(3), 297–312.

Schmitt, M. T., Branscombe, N. R., Postmes, T., & Garcia, A. (2014). The consequences of perceived discrimination for psychological well-being: A metaanalytic review. *Psychological Bulletin, 140*(4), 921–948.

Scholer, A. A., & Higgins, E. T. (2013). Dodging monsters and dancing with dreams: Success and failure at different levels of approach and avoidance. *Emotion Review, 5*(3), 254–258.

Schriesheim, C. A., Tepper, B. J., & Tetrault, L. A. (1994). Least preferred co-worker score, situational control, and leadership effectiveness: A meta-analysis of contingency model performance predictions. *Journal of Applied Psychology, 79*(4), 561–573.

Schroeder, J., & Epley, N. (2015). The sound of intellect: Speech reveals a thoughtful mind, increasing a job candidate's appeal. *Psychological Science, 26*(6), 877–891.

Schultz, R. T. (2005). Developmental deficits in social perception in autism: The role of the amygdala and fusiform face area. *International Journal of Developmental Neuroscience, 23*(2), 125–141.

Schwartz, S. H. (1992). Universals in the content and structure of values: Theoretical advances and empirical tests in 20 countries. In M. P. Zanna (Ed.), *Advances in experimental social psychology* (Vol. 25, pp. 1–65). Academic Press.

Schwartz, S. H., & Bardi, A. (2001). Value hierarchies across cultures: Taking a similarities perspective. *Journal of Cross-Cultural Psychology, 32*(3), 270–275.

Schwartz, S. H., Caprara, G. V., Vecchione, M., Bain, P., Bianchi, G., Caprara, M. G., Cieciuch, J., Kirmanoglu, H., Baslevent, C., Lönnqvist, J.-E., Mamali, C., Manzi, J., Pavlopoulos, V., Posnova, T., Schoen, H., Silvester, J., Tabernero, C., Torres, C., Verkasalo, M., . . . Zaleski, Z. (2014). Basic personal values underlie and give coherence to political values: A cross national study in 15 countries. *Political Behavior, 36*(4), 899–930.

Schwartz, S. H., & Rubel, T. (2005). Sex differences in value priorities: Cross-cultural and multimethod studies. *Journal of Personality and Social Psychology, 89*(6), 1010–1028.

Schwartz, S. H., & Sagie, G. (2000). Value consensus and importance: A cross-national study. *Journal of Cross-Cultural Psychology, 31*(4), 465–497.

Schwarz, N., Bless, H., & Bohner, G. (1991). Mood and persuasion: Affective states influence the processing of persuasive communications. In M. P. Zanna (Ed.), *Advances in experimental social psychology* (pp. 161–199). Academic Press.

Schwarz, N., Bless, H., Strack, F., Klumpp, G., Rittenauer-Schatka, H., & Simons, A. (1991). Ease of retrieval as information: Another look at the availability heuristic. *Journal of Personality and Social Psychology, 61*(2), 195–202.

Schwarz, N., & Clore, G. L. (1983). Mood, misattribution, and judgments of well-being: Informative and directive functions of affective states. *Journal of Personality and Social Psychology, 45*(3), 513–523.

Schwarz, N., & Clore, G. L. (2003). Mood as information: 20 years later. *Psychological Inquiry, 14*(3–4), 296–303.

Schwarz, N., Newman, E., & Leach, W. (2016). Making the truth stick and the myths fade: Lessons from cognitive psychology. *Behavioral Science & Policy, 2*(1), 85–95.

Schwirtz, M., & Saltmarsh, M. (2011, July 24). Oslo suspect cultivated parallel life to disguise "martyrdom operation." *The New York Times.* http://www.nytimes.com/2011/07/25/world/europe/25breivik.html?pagewanted=all&_r=0

Scorsese, M. (Director). (1976). *Taxi driver* [Film]. Columbia Pictures.

Sears, D. O., & Henry, P. J. (2005). Over thirty years later: A contemporary look at symbolic racism. *Advances in Experimental Social Psychology, 37*, 95–150.

Sears, D. O., & Kinder, D. R. (1971). Racial tensions and voting in Los Angeles. In W. Z. Hirsch (Ed.), *Los Angeles: Viability and prospects for metropolitan leadership* (pp. 51–88). Praeger.

Sedikides, C., Gaertner, L., & Toguchi, Y. (2003). Pancultural self-enhancement. *Journal of Personality and Social Psychology, 84*(1), 60–79.

Sedikides, C., Gaertner, L., & Vevea, J. L. (2005). Pancultural self-enhancement reloaded: A meta-analytic reply to Heine (2005). *Journal of Personality and Social Psychology, 89*(4), 539–551.

Sedikides, C., Meek, R., Alicke, M. D., & Taylor, S. (2014). Behind bars but above the bar: Prisoners consider themselves more pro-social than non prisoners. *British Journal of Social Psychology, 53*(2), 396–403.

Sedikides, C., & Strube, M. J. (1997). Self-evaluation: To thine own self be good, to thine own self be sure, to thine own self be true, and to thine own self be better. *Advances in Experimental Social Psychology, 29*, 209–269.

Sedikides, C., Wildschut, T., Gaertner, L., Routledge, C., & Arndt, J. (2008). Nostalgia as enabler of self-continuity. In F. Sani (Ed.), *Self-continuity: Individual and collective perspectives* (pp. 227–239). Psychology Press.

Seery, M. D., & Quinton, W. J. (2015). Targeting prejudice: Personal self-esteem as a resource for Asians' attributions to racial discrimination. *Social Psychological and Personality Science, 6*(7), 677–684.

Segall, M. H., Campbell, D. T., & Herskovits, M. J. (1963). Cultural differences in the perception of geometric illusions. *Science, 139*(3556), 769–771.

Segrin, C. (1998). Disrupted interpersonal relationships and mental health problems. In B. H. Spitzberg & W. R. Cupach (Eds.), *The dark side of close relationships* (pp. 327–365). Erlbaum.

Selcuk, E., Stanton, S. C. E., Slatcher, R. B., & Ong, A. D. (2017). Perceived partner responsiveness predicts better sleep quality through lower anxiety. *Social Psychological and Personality Science, 8*(1), 83–92.

Sell, A. (2011). Applying adaptationism to human anger: The recalibrational theory. In P. R. Shaver & M. Mikulincer (Eds.), *Human aggression and violence: Causes, manifestations, and consequences* (pp. 53–70). American Psychological Association.

Sellier, A.-L., Scopelliti, I., & Morewedge, C. K. (2019). Debiasing training improves decision making in the field. *Psychological Science, 30*(9), 1371–1379.

Semega, J. (2009). *Men's and women's earnings by state: 2008 American community survey.* U.S. Census Bureau. http://www.census.gov/library/publications/2009/acs/acsbr08-3.html

Senchak, M., & Leonard, K. E. (1992). Attachment styles and marital adjustment among newlywed couples. *Journal of Social and Personal Relationships, 9*(1), 51–64.

Senden, M.G., Eagly, A., & Sczesny, S. (2020). Of caring nurses and assertive police officers: Social role information overrides gender stereotypes in linguistic behavior. *Social Psychological and Personality Science, 11*, 743–751.

Sezer, O., Gino, F., & Norton, M. I. (2018). Humblebragging: A distinct—and ineffective—self-presentation strategy. *Journal of Personality and Social Psychology, 114*(1), 52–74.

Shah, J. (2003). The motivational looking glass: How significant others implicitly affect goal appraisals. *Journal of Personality and Social Psychology, 85*(3), 424–439.

Shakespeare, W. (1623). Mr. William Shakespeares Comedies, Histories, & Tragedies: Published According to the True Originall Copies. Printed by Isaac Iaggard, and Ed[ward] Blount. p. 194. OCLC 606515358.

Shallice, T. I. M., & Burgess, P. W. (1991). Deficits in strategy application following frontal lobe damage in man. *Brain, 114*(2), 727–741.

Shanab, M. E., & Yahya, K. A. (1978). A cross-cultural study of obedience. *Bulletin of the Psychonomic Society, 11*(4), 267–269.

Shanahan, J., & Morgan, M. (1999). *Television and its viewers: Cultivation theory and research.* Cambridge University Press.

Shanks, D. R., Vadillo, M. A., Riedel, B., Clymo, A., Govind, S., Hickin, N., Tamman, A. J. F., & Puhlmann, L. M. C. (2015). Romance, risk, and replication: Can consumer choices and risk-taking be primed by mating motives? *Journal of Experimental Psychology: General, 144*(6), e142–e158.

Shapira, L. B., & Mongrain, M. (2010). The benefits of self-compassion and optimism exercises for individuals vulnerable to depression. *Journal of Positive Psychology, 5*(5), 377–389.

Shariff, A. F., & Norenzayan, A. (2007). God is watching you: Priming God concepts increases prosocial behavior in an anonymous economic game. *Psychological Science, 18*(9), 803–809.

Shariff, A. F., Norenzayan, A., & Henrich, J. (2010). The birth of high gods: How the cultural evolution of supernatural policing influenced the emergence of complex, cooperative human societies, paving the way for civilization. In M. Schaller, A. Norenzayan, S. J. Heine, T. Yamagishi, & T. Kameda (Eds.), *Evolution, culture, and the human mind* (pp. 119–136). Psychology Press.

Shariff, A. F., & Tracy, J. L. (2011). What are emotion expressions for? *Current Directions in Psychological Science, 20*(6), 395–399.

Shariff, A. F., Willard, A. K., Andersen, T., & Norenzayan, A. (2016). Religious priming: A meta-analysis with a focus on prosociality. *Personality and Social Psychology Review, 20*(1), 27–48.

Sharpe, D., & Faye, C. (2009). A second look at debriefing practices: Madness in our method? *Ethics & Behavior, 19*(5), 432–447.

Shaver, P. R., & Mikulincer, M. (2010). New directions in attachment theory and research. *Journal of Social and Personal Relationships, 27*(2), 163–172.

Shaver, P. R., Schachner, D. A., & Mikulincer, M. (2005). Attachment style, excessive reassurance seeking, relationship processes, and depression. *Personality and Social Psychology Bulletin, 31*(3), 343–359.

Shaver, P. R., Wu, S., & Schwartz, J. C. (1992). Cross-cultural similarities and differences in emotion and its representation. In M. S. Clark (Ed.), *Emotion: Review of personality and social psychology* (Vol. 13, pp. 175–212). Sage.

Shavitt, S., Swan, S., Lowrey, T. M., & Wänke, M. (1994). The interaction of endorser attractiveness and involvement in persuasion depends on the goal that guides message processing. *Journal of Consumer Psychology, 3*(2), 137–162.

Shaw, J., & Porter, S. (2015). Constructing rich false memories of committing crime. *Psychological Science, 26*(3), 291–301.

Shaw, L. L., Batson, C. D., & Todd, R. M. (1994). Empathy avoidance: Forestalling feeling for another in order to escape the motivational consequences. *Journal of Personality and Social Psychology, 67*(5), 879–887.

Shaw, M. E. (1981). *Group dynamics: The psychology of small group behavior.* McGraw-Hill.

Sheeran, P., & Orbell, S. (2000). Using implementation intentions to increase attendance for cervical cancer screening. *Health Psychology, 19*(3), 283–289.

Sheeran, P., & Taylor, S. (1999). Predicting intentions to use condoms: A meta-analysis and comparison of the theories of reasoned action and planned behavior. *Journal of Applied Social Psychology, 29*(8), 1624–1675.

Sheldon, K. M. (2014). Becoming oneself: The central role of self-concordant goal selection. *Personality and Social Psychology Review, 18*(4), 349–365.

Sheldon, K. M., & Elliot, A. J. (1999). Goal striving, need satisfaction, and longitudinal well-being: The self-concordance model. *Journal of Personality and Social Psychology, 76*(3), 482–497.

Sheldon, K. M., & Krieger, L. S. (2007). Understanding the negative effects of legal education on law students: A longitudinal test of self-determination theory. *Personality and Social Psychology Bulletin, 33*(6), 883–897.

Sheldon, K. M., Ryan, R. M., Deci, E. L., & Kasser, T. (2004). The independent effects of goal contents and motives on well-being: It's both what you pursue and why you pursue it. *Personality and Social Psychology Bulletin, 30*(4), 475–486.

Shelton, J. N., & Richeson, J. A. (2006). Interracial interactions: A relational approach. In M. P. Zanna (Ed.), *Advances in experimental social psychology* (Vol. 38, pp. 121–181). Elsevier Academic Press.

Shelton, J. N., Richeson, J. A., & Salvatore, J. (2005). Expecting to be the target of prejudice: Implications for interethnic interactions. *Personality and Social Psychology Bulletin, 31*(9), 1189–1202.

Shepperd, J. A., & Strathman, A. J. (1989). Attractiveness and height: The role of stature in dating preference, frequency of dating, and perceptions of attractiveness. *Personality and Social Psychology Bulletin, 15*(4), 617–627.

Sherif, M. (1936). *The psychology of social norms.* Harper.

Sherif, M. (1966). *In common predicament: Social psychology of intergroup conflict and cooperation.* Houghton Mifflin.

Sherif, M., Harvey, O. J., White, B. J., Hood, W. R., & Sherif, C. W. (1961). *Intergroup conflict and cooperation: The Robbers Cave experiment.* University Book Exchange.

Sherif, M., & Sherif, C. (1969). *Social psychology.* Harper & Row.

Sherman, D. K. (2013). Self-affirmation: Understanding the effects. *Social and Personality Psychology Compass, 7*(11), 834–845.

Sherman, D. K., & Cohen, G. L. (2006). The psychology of self-defense: Self-affirmation theory. In M. P. Zanna (Ed.), *Advances in experimental social psychology* (Vol. 38, pp. 183–242). Elsevier Academic Press.

Sherman, D. K., Kinias, Z., Major, B., Kim, H. S., & Prenovost, M. (2007). The group as a resource: Reducing biased attributions for group success and failure via group affirmation. *Personality and Social Psychology Bulletin, 33*(8), 1100–1112.

Sherman, S. J., Chassin, L., Presson, C., Seo, D. C., & Macy, J. T. (2009). The intergenerational transmission of implicit and explicit attitudes toward smoking: Predicting adolescent smoking initiation. *Journal of Experimental Social Psychology, 45*(2), 313–319.

Sherman, S. J., Presson, C. C., & Chassin, L. (1984). Mechanisms underlying the false consensus effect: The special role of threats to the self. *Personality and Social Psychology Bulletin, 10*(1), 127–138.

Shewach, O. R., Sackett, P. R., & Quint, S. (2019). Stereotype threat effects in settings with features likely versus unlikely in operational test settings: A meta-analysis. *Journal of Applied Psychology, 104*(12), 1514–1534.

Shin, J., Suh, E. M., Li, N. P., Eo, K., Chong, S. C., & Tsai, M.-H. (2019). Darling, get closer to me: Spatial proximity amplifies interpersonal liking. *Personality and Social Psychology Bulletin, 45*(2), 300–309.

Shoda, Y., Mischel, W., & Peake, P. K. (1990). Predicting adolescent cognitive and self-regulatory competencies from preschool delay of gratification: Identifying diagnostic conditions. *Developmental Psychology, 26*(6), 978–986.

Shoham, V., & Rohrbaugh, M. (1997). Interrupting ironic processes. *Psychological Science, 8*(3), 151–153.

Short, J. F. (1997). *Poverty, ethnicity, and violent crime.* Westview Press.

Shrauger, J. S., & Schoeneman, T. J. (1979). Symbolic interactionist view of self-concept: Through the looking glass darkly. *Psychological Bulletin, 86*(3), 549–573.

Shupe, L. M. (1954). Alcohol and crime: A study of the urine alcohol concentration found in 882 persons arrested during or immediately after the commission of a felony. *Journal of Criminal Law, Criminology, and Police Science, 44*(5), 661–664.

Shweder, R. A., Much, N. C., Mahapatra, M., & Park, L. (1997). The "big three" of morality (autonomy, community, and divinity), and the "big three" explanations of suffering. In A. Brandt & P. Rozin (Eds.), *Morality and health* (pp. 119–169). Routledge.

Sidanius, J., & Pratto, F. (1999). *Social dominance: An intergroup theory of social hierarchy and oppression.* Cambridge University Press.

Siever, L. J. (2008). Neurobiology of aggression and violence. *American Journal of Psychiatry, 165*(4), 429–442.

Sigall, H., & Landy, D. (1973). Radiating beauty: Effects of having a physically attractive partner on person perception. *Journal of Personality and Social Psychology, 28*(2), 218–224.

Silva, D. (2017, April 12). *Florida cop charged with attempted manslaughter in shooting of autistic man's unarmed therapist.* NBC News. https://www.nbcnews.com/news/us-news/florida-cop-charged-manslaughter-shooting-autistic-man-s-unarmed-therapist-n745716

Silverstein, B. (1992). The psychology of enemy images. In S. Staub & P. Green (Eds.), *Psychology and social responsibility* (pp. 145–164). New York University Press.

Silverstein, B., Peterson, B., & Perdue, L. (1986). Some correlates of the thin standard of bodily attractiveness for women. *International Journal of Eating Disorders, 5*(5), 895–905.

Simmel, G. (2005). The metropolis and mental life. In J. Lin & C. Mele (Eds.), *The urban sociology reader* (pp. 23–31). Routledge. (Original work published 1903)

Simmons, J. P., Nelson, L. D., & Simonsohn, U. (2011). False-positive psychology: Undisclosed flexibility in data collection and analysis allows presenting anything as significant. *Psychological Science, 22*(11), 1359–1366.

Simon, L., Greenberg, J., & Brehm, J. (1995). Trivialization: The forgotten mode of dissonance reduction. *Journal of Personality and Social Psychology*, 68(2), 247.

Simonovic, B., Stupple, E., Gale, M., & Sheffield, D. (2019). Sweating the small stuff: A meta-analysis of skin conductance on the Iowa gambling task. *Cognitive, Affective & Behavioral Neuroscience*, 19(5), 1097–1112.

Simonton, D. (1987). *Why presidents succeed: A political psychology of leadership*. Yale University Press.

Simpson, J. A. (1990). Influence of attachment styles on romantic relationships. *Journal of Personality and Social Psychology*, 59(5), 971–980.

Simpson, J. A. (2007). Psychological foundations of trust. *Current Directions in Psychological Science*, 16(5), 264–268.

Simpson, J. A., Collins, W. A., Tran, S., & Haydon, K. C. (2007). Attachment and the experience and expression of emotions in romantic relationships: A developmental perspective. *Journal of Personality and Social Psychology*, 92(2), 355–367.

Simpson, J. A., & Kenrick, D. T. (Eds.). (1997). *Evolutionary social psychology*. Erlbaum.

Simpson, J. A., Rholes, W. S., & Nelligan, J. S. (1992). Support seeking and support giving within couples in an anxiety-provoking situation: The role of attachment styles. *Journal of Personality and Social Psychology*, 62(3), 434–446.

Sinclair, L., & Kunda, Z. (1999). Reactions to a Black professional: Motivated inhibition and activation of conflicting stereotypes. *Journal of Personality and Social Psychology*, 77(5), 885–904.

Sinclair, L., & Kunda, Z. (2000). Motivated stereotyping of women: She's fine if she praised me but incompetent if she criticized me. *Personality and Social Psychology Bulletin*, 26(11), 1329–1342.

Sinclair, S., Huntsinger, J., Skorinko, J., & Hardin, C. D. (2005). Social tuning of the self: Consequences for the self-evaluations of stereotype targets. *Journal of Personality and Social Psychology*, 89(2), 160–175.

Sinclair, S., Lowery, B. S., Hardin, C. D., & Colangelo, A. (2005). Social tuning of automatic racial attitudes: The role of affiliative motivation. *Journal of Personality and Social Psychology*, 89(4), 583–592.

Singelis, T. M., Triandis, H. C., Bhawuk, D. P., & Gelfand, M. J. (1995). Horizontal and vertical dimensions of individualism and collectivism: A theoretical and measurement refinement. *Cross-Cultural Research*, 29(3), 240–275.

Singer, J. L., & Singer, D. G. (1981). *Television, imagination and aggression: A study of preschoolers*. Erlbaum.

Singh, D. (1993). Adaptive significance of female physical attractiveness: Role of waist-to-hip ratio. *Journal of Personality and Social Psychology*, 65(2), 293–307.

Singh, D., & Luis, S. (1995). Ethnic and gender consensus for the effect of waist-to-hip ratio on judgment of women's attractiveness. *Human Nature*, 6(1), 51–65.

Sink, A., & Mastro, D. (2017). Depictions of gender on primetime television: A quantitative content analysis. *Mass Communication & Society*, 20(1), 3–22.

Sinozich, S., & Langton, L. (2014). *Rape and sexual assault among college-age females, 1995–2013*. Bureau of Justice Statistics. https://www.bjs.gov/index.cfm?ty=pbdetail&iid=5176

Sirois, F. (1982). Perspective on epidemic hysteria. In M. Colligan, J. Pennebaker, & P. Murphy (Eds.), *Mass psychogenic illness: A social psychological analysis* (pp. 217–236). Erlbaum.

Sirois, F. M. (2014). Procrastination and stress: Exploring the role of self-compassion. *Self and Identity*, 13(2), 128–145.

Sisk, V. F., Burgoyne, A. P., Sun, J., Butler, J. L., & Macnamara, B. N. (2018). To what extent and under which circumstances are growth mind-sets important to academic achievement? Two meta-analyses. *Psychological Science*, 29(4), 549–571.

Sivacek, J., & Crano, W. D. (1982). Vested interest as a moderator of attitude–behavior consistency. *Journal of Personality and Social Psychology*, 43(2), 210–221.

Sivak, E., & Smirnov, I. (2019). Parents mention sons more often than daughters on social media. *Proceedings of the National Academy of Sciences*, 116(6), 2039–2041.

Siy, J. O., & Cheryan, S. (2016). Prejudice masquerading as praise: The negative echo of positive stereotypes. *Personality and Social Psychology Bulletin*, 42(7), 941–954.

Sjåstad, H., & Baumeister, R. F. (2018). The future and the will: Planning requires self-control, and ego depletion leads to planning aversion. *Journal of Experimental Social Psychology*, 76, 127–141.

Skinner, A. L., & Hudac, C. M. (2017). "Yuck, you disgust me!" Affective bias against interracial couples. *Journal of Experimental Social Psychology*, 68, 68–77.

Skitka, L. J. (1999). Ideological and attributional boundaries on public compassion: Reactions to individuals and communities affected by a natural disaster. *Personality and Social Psychology Bulletin*, 25(7), 793–808.

Skitka, L. J., McMurray, P. J., & Burroughs, T. E. (1991). Willingness to provide post-war aid to Iraq and Kuwait: An application of the contingency model of distributive justice. *Contemporary Social Psychology*, 15(4), 179–188.

Skitka, L. J., Mullen, E., Griffin, T., Hutchinson, S., & Chamberlin, B. (2002). Dispositions, scripts, or motivated correction? Understanding ideological differences in explanations for social problems. *Journal of Personality and Social Psychology*, 83(2), 470–487.

Skitka, L. J., & Tetlock, P. E. (1992). Allocating scarce resources: A contingency model of distributive justice. *Journal of Experimental Social Psychology*, 28(6), 491–522.

Skitka, L. J., & Tetlock, P. E. (1993). Providing public assistance: Cognitive and motivational processes underlying liberal and conservative policy preferences. *Journal of Personality and Social Psychology*, 65(6), 1205–1223.

Skopek, J., Schulz, F., & Blossfeld, H. P. (2011). Who contacts whom? Educational homophily in online mate selection. *European Sociological Review*, 27(2), 180–195.

Skorinko, J. L., & Sinclair, S. A. (2013). Perspective taking can increase stereotyping: The role of apparent stereotype confirmation. *Journal of Experimental Social Psychology*, 49(1), 10–18.

Slaby, R. G., & Guerra, N. G. (1988). Cognitive mediators of aggression in adolescent offenders: I. Assessment. *Developmental Psychology*, 24(4), 580–588.

Slatcher, R. B., & Selcuk, E. (2017). A social psychological perspective on the links between close relationships and health. *Current Directions in Psychological Science*, 26(1), 16–21.

Slatcher, R. B., Selcuk, E., & Ong, A. D. (2015). Perceived partner responsiveness predicts diurnal cortisol profiles 10 years later. *Psychological Science*, 26(7), 972–982.

Slater, A., Bremner, G., Johnson, S. P., Sherwood, P., Hayes, R., & Brown, E. (2000). Newborn infants' preference for attractive faces: The role of internal and external facial features. *Infancy*, 1(2), 265–274.

Slavin, R. E. (2012). Classroom applications of cooperative learning. In K. R. Harris, S. Graham, T. Urdan, A. G. Bus, S. Major, & H. Swanson (Eds.), *APA educational psychology handbook* (Vol. 3, pp. 359–378). American Psychological Association.

Sloman, S. A. (1996). The empirical case for two systems of reasoning. *Psychological Bulletin*, 119(1), 3–22.

Slotter, E. B., & Finkel, E. J. (2009). The strange case of sustained dedication to an unfulfilling relationship: Predicting commitment and breakup from attachment anxiety and need fulfillment within relationships. *Personality and Social Psychology Bulletin*, 35(1), 85–100.

Slotter, E. B., Gardner, W. L., & Finkel, E. J. (2010). Who am I without you? The influence of romantic breakup on the self-concept. *Personality and Social Psychology Bulletin*, 36(2), 147–160.

Smart, L., & Wegner, D. M. (1999). Covering up what can't be seen: Concealable stigma and mental control. *Journal of Personality and Social Psychology*, 77(3), 474–486.

Smart Richman, L., & Leary, M. R. (2009). Reactions to discrimination, stigmatization, ostracism, and other forms of interpersonal rejection: A multimotive model. *Psychological Review*, 116(2), 365–383.

Smith, E. R., & Henry, S. (1996). An in-group becomes part of the self: Response time evidence. *Personality and Social Psychology Bulletin*, 22(6), 635–642.

Smith, P. K., Jostmann, N. B., Galinsky, A. D., & van Dijk, W. W. (2008). Lacking power impairs executive functions. *Psychological Science*, 19(5), 441–447.

Smith, P. K., & Trope, Y. (2006). You focus on the forest when you're in charge of the trees: Power priming and abstract information processing. *Journal of Personality and Social Psychology*, 90(4), 578–596.

Smith, S. L., Choueiti, M., Scofield, E., & Pieper, K. (2013). *Gender inequality in 500 popular films: Examining on-screen portrayals and behind-the-scenes employment patterns in motion pictures released between 2007–2012* [Unpublished manuscript]. Annenberg School for Communication & Journalism, University of Southern California. http://annenberg.usc.edu/Faculty/Communication%20and%20Journalism/~/media/A41FBC3E62084AC8A-8C047A9D4A54033.ashx

Smith, S. L., Pieper, K. M., Granados, A., & Choueiti, M. (2010). Assessing gender-related portrayals in top-grossing G-rated films. *Sex Roles*, 62(11–12), 774–786.

Smith, S. M., McIntosh, W. D., & Bazzini, D. G. (1999). Are the beautiful good in Hollywood? An investigation of the beauty-and-goodness stereotype on film. *Basic and Applied Social Psychology*, 21(1), 69–80.

Smock, P. J., & Greenland, F. R. (2010). Diversity in pathways to parenthood: Patterns, implications, and emerging research directions. *Journal of Marriage and Family*, 72(3), 576–593.

Sng, O., Neuberg, S. L., Varnum, M. E., & Kenrick, D. T. (2018). The behavioral ecology of cultural psychological variation. *Psychological Review*, 125(5), 714–743.

Snyder, C. R., Lassegard, M., & Ford, C. E. (1986). Distancing after group success and failure: Basking in reflected glory and cutting off reflected failure. *Journal of Personality and Social Psychology, 51*(2), 382–388.

Snyder, H. N., & Sickmund, M. (2006). *Juvenile offenders and victims: 2006 national report*. U.S. Department of Justice, Office of Justice Programs, Office of Juvenile Justice and Delinquency Prevention. http://eric.ed.gov /?id=ED495786

Snyder, M. (1974). Self-monitoring of expressive behavior. *Journal of Personality and Social Psychology, 30*(4), 526–537.

Snyder, M., & DeBono, K. G. (1985). Appeals to image and claims about quality: Understanding the psychology of advertising. *Journal of Personality and Social Psychology, 49*(3), 586–597.

Snyder, M., & Gangestad, S. (1986). On the nature of self-monitoring: Matters of assessment, matters of validity. *Journal of Personality and Social Psychology, 51*(1), 125–139.

Snyder, M., & Kendzierski, D. (1982). Acting on one's attitudes: Procedures for linking attitude and behavior. *Journal of Experimental Social Psychology, 18*(2), 165–183.

Snyder, M., & Swann, W. B. (1978). Hypothesis-testing processes in social interaction. *Journal of Personality and Social Psychology, 36*(11), 1202–1212.

Snyder, M., Tanke, E. D., & Berscheid, E. (1977). Social perception and interpersonal behavior: On the self-fulfilling nature of social stereotypes. *Journal of Personality and Social Psychology, 35*(9), 656–666.

Snyder, M. L., & Frankel, A. (1976). Observer bias: A stringent test of behavior engulfing the field. *Journal of Personality and Social Psychology, 34*(5), 857–864.

Snyder, M. L., Smoller, B., Strenta, A., & Frankel, A. (1981). A comparison of egotism, negativity, and learned helplessness as explanations for poor performance after unsolvable problems. *Journal of Personality and Social Psychology, 40*(1), 24–30.

Snyder, M. L., Stephan, W. G., & Rosenfield, D. (1976). Egotism and attribution. *Journal of Personality and Social Psychology, 33*(4), 435–441.

Sobal, J., & Stunkard, A. J. (1989). Socioeconomic status and obesity: A review of the literature. *Psychological Bulletin, 105*(2), 260–275.

Sofer, C., Dotsch, R., Wigboldus, D. H., & Todorov, A. (2015). What is typical is good: The influence of face typicality on perceived trustworthiness. *Psychological Science, 26*(1), 39–47.

Soler, C., Núñez, M., Gutiérrez, R., Núñez, J., Medina, P., Sancho, M., Álvarez, J., & Núñez, A. (2003). Facial attractiveness in men provides clues to semen quality. *Evolution and Human Behavior, 24*(3), 199–207.

Solomon, D. H., & Knobloch, L. K. (2004). A model of relational turbulence: The role of intimacy, relational uncertainty, and interference from partners in appraisals of irritations. *Journal of Social and Personal Relationships, 21*(6), 795–816.

Solomon, S., Greenberg, J., & Pyszczynski, T. (1991). A terror management theory of social behavior: On the psychological functions of self-esteem and cultural worldviews. In M. P. Zanna (Ed.), *Advances in experimental social psychology* (Vol. 24, pp. 93–159). Academic Press.

Solomon, S., Greenberg, J., & Pyszczynski, T. (2015). *The worm at the core: On the role of death in life*. Random House.

Solomon, S., & Thompson, S. (2019). Secular cultural worldviews. In C. Routledge & M. Vess (Eds.), *Handbook of terror management theory* (pp. 287–302). Elsevier Academic Press.

Sommers, S. R. (2006). On racial diversity and group decision making: Identifying multiple effects of racial composition on jury deliberations. *Journal of Personality and Social Psychology, 90*(4), 597–612.

Sommers, S. R., Warp, L. S., & Mahoney, C. C. (2008). Cognitive effects of racial diversity: White individuals' information processing in heterogeneous groups. *Journal of Experimental Social Psychology, 44*(4), 1129–1136.

Soubrié, P. (1986). Reconciling the role of central serotonin neurons in human and animal behavior. *Behavioral and Brain Sciences, 9*(2), 319–335.

South, S. J., & Lloyd, K. M. (1995). Spousal alternatives and marital dissolution. *American Sociological Review, 60*(1), 21–35.

Spalding, L. R., & Hardin, C. D. (1999). Unconscious unease and self-handicapping: Behavioral consequences of individual differences in implicit and explicit self-esteem. *Psychological Science, 10*(6), 535–539.

Sparacino, J., & Hansell, S. (1979). Physical attractiveness and academic performance: Beauty is not always talent. *Journal of Personality, 47*(3), 449–469.

Sparkman, G., & Walton, G. M. (2017). Dynamic norms promote sustainable behavior, even if it is counternormative. *Psychological Science, 28*(11), 1663–1674.

Sparkman, G., & Walton, G. M. (2019). Witnessing change: Dynamic norms help resolve diverse barriers to personal change. *Journal of Experimental Social Psychology, 82*, 238–252.

Spears, R., Lea, M., & Lee, S. (1990). De-individuation and group polarization in computer-mediated communication. *British Journal of Social Psychology, 29*(2), 121–134.

Spencer, K. B., Charbonneau, A. K., & Glaser, J. (2016). Implicit bias and policing. *Social and Personality Psychology Compass, 10*(1), 50–63.

Spencer, S. J., Fein, S., Wolfe, C. T., Fong, C., & Duinn, M. A. (1998). Automatic activation of stereotypes: The role of self-image threat. *Personality and Social Psychology Bulletin, 24*(11), 1139–1152.

Spencer, S. J., Logel, C., & Davies, P. G. (2016). Stereotype threat. *Annual Review of Psychology, 67*, 415–437.

Spencer, S. J., Steele, C. M., & Quinn, D. M. (1999). Stereotype threat and women's math performance. *Journal of Experimental Social Psychology, 35*(1), 4–28.

Spencer-Rodgers, J., Boucher, H. C., Mori, S. C., Wang, L., & Peng, K. (2009). The dialectical self-concept: Contradiction, change, and holism in East Asian cultures. *Personality and Social Psychology Bulletin, 35*(1), 29–44.

Spencer-Rodgers, J., Williams, M. J., & Peng, K. (2010). Cultural differences in expectations of change and tolerance for contradiction: A decade of empirical research. *Personality and Social Psychology Review, 14*(3), 296–312.

Spiegel, I. (2006, December 15). Shouting across the divide [Radio broadcast]. In I. Glass (Producer), *This American life*. Chicago Public Media. http://www .thisamericanlife.org/radio-archives/episode/322/shouting-across-the-divide

Spiegel, I. (2011, September 9). Ten years in [Radio broadcast]. In I. Glass (Producer), *This American life*. Chicago Public Media. http://www.thisamerican life.org/radio-archives/episode/445/transcript

Sprecher, S. (1986). The relation between inequity and emotions in close relationships. *Social Psychology Quarterly, 49*(4), 309–321.

Sprecher, S. (1992). How men and women expect to feel and behave in response to inequity in close relationships. *Social Psychology Quarterly, 55*(1), 57–69.

Sprecher, S. (1998). Social exchange theories and sexuality. *Journal of Sex Research, 35*(1), 32–43.

Sprecher, S. (2002). Sexual satisfaction in premarital relationships: Associations with satisfaction, love, commitment, and stability. *Journal of Sex Research, 39*(3), 190–196.

Sprecher, S., & Cate, R. M. (2004). Sexual satisfaction and sexual expression as predictors of relationship satisfaction and stability. In J. H. Harvey, A. Wenzel, & S. Sprecher (Eds.), *The handbook of sexuality in close relationships* (pp. 235–256). Erlbaum.

Sprecher, S., Christopher, F. S., & Cate, R. (2006). Sexuality in close relationships. In A. L. Vangelisti & D. Perlman (Eds.), *The Cambridge handbook of personal relationships* (pp. 463–482). Cambridge University Press.

Sprecher, S., & Regan, P. C. (1998). Passionate and companionate love in courting and young married couples. *Sociological Inquiry, 68*(2), 163–185.

Sprecher, S., & Regan, P. C. (2002). Liking some things (in some people) more than others: Partner preferences in romantic relationships and friendships. *Journal of Social and Personal Relationships, 19*(4), 436–481.

Srivastava, S., McGonigal, K. M., Richards, J. M., Butler, E. A., & Gross, J. J. (2006). Optimism in close relationships: How seeing things in a positive light makes them so. *Journal of Personality and Social Psychology, 91*(1), 143–153.

Stamkou, E., van Kleef, G. A., Homan, A. C., Gelfand, M. J., van de Vijver, F. J. R., van Egmond, M. C., Boer, D., Phiri, N., Ayub N., Kinias, Z., Cantarero, K., Treister, D. E., Figueiredo, A., Hashimoto, H., Hofmann, E. B., Lima, R. P., & Lee, I.-C. (2019). Cultural collectivism and tightness moderate responses to norm violators: Effects on power perception, moral emotions, and leader support. *Personality and Social Psychology Bulletin, 45*(6), 947–964.

Stangor, C. (2009). The study of stereotyping, prejudice, and discrimination within social psychology: A quick history of theory and research. In T. D. Nelson (Ed.), *Handbook of prejudice, stereotyping and discrimination* (pp. 1–22). Psychology Press.

Stanik, C. E., & Ellsworth, P. C. (2010). Who cares about marrying a rich man? Intelligence and variation in women's mate preferences. *Human Nature, 21*(2), 203–217.

Stanley, S. M., Markman, H. J., & Whitton, S. W. (2002). Communication, conflict and commitment: Insights on the foundations of relationship success from a national survey. *Family Process, 41*(4), 659–675.

Stanczak, A., Darnon, C., Robert, A., Demolliens, M., Sanrey, C., Bressoux, P., Huguet, P., Buchs, C., Butera, F., & PROFAN Consortium. (2022). Do jigsaw classrooms improve learning outcomes? Five experiments and an internal meta-analysis. *Journal of Educational Psychology*. Advance online publication. https://doi.org/10.1037/edu0000730

Staub, E. (1989). *The roots of evil: The psychological and cultural origins of genocide and other forms of group violence*. Cambridge University Press.

Staub, E. (1996). Cultural-societal roots of violence: The examples of genocidal violence and of contemporary youth violence in the United States. *American Psychologist, 51*(2), 117–132.

Stavrova, O. (2019). Having a happy spouse is associated with lowered risk of mortality. *Psychological Science*, 30(5), 798–803.

Stavrova, O., Pronk, T., & Kokkoris, M. D. (2019). Choosing goals that express the true self: A novel mechanism of the effect of self-control on goal attainment. *European Journal of Social Psychology*, 49(6), 1329–1336.

Staw, B. M. (1974). Attitudinal and behavioral consequences of changing a major organizational reward: A natural field experiment. *Journal of Personality and Social Psychology*, 29(6), 742–751.

Steele, C. M. (1988). The psychology of self-affirmation: Sustaining the integrity of the self. In L. Berkowitz (Ed.), *Advances in experimental social psychology* (Vol. 21, pp. 261–302). Academic Press.

Steele, C. M. (1997). A threat in the air: How stereotypes shape intellectual identity and performance. *American Psychologist*, 52(6), 613–629.

Steele, C. M., & Aronson, J. (1995). Stereotype threat and the intellectual test performance of African Americans. *Journal of Personality and Social Psychology*, 69(5), 797–811.

Steele, C. M., & Josephs, R. A. (1990). Alcohol myopia: Its prized and dangerous effects. *American Psychologist*, 45(8), 921–933.

Steele, C. M., Southwick, L. L., & Critchlow, B. (1981). Dissonance and alcohol: Drinking your troubles away. *Journal of Personality and Social Psychology*, 41(5), 831–846.

Steele, C. M., Spencer, S. J., & Aronson, J. (2002). Contending with group image: The psychology of stereotype and social identity threat. In M. P. Zanna (Ed.), *Advances in experimental social psychology* (Vol. 34, pp. 379–440). Academic Press.

Steenbarger, B. N., & Aderman, D. (1979). Objective self-awareness as a nonaversive state: Effect of anticipating discrepancy reduction. *Journal of Personality*, 47(2), 330–339.

Steffens, N. K., Schuh, S. C., Haslam, S. A., Perez, A., & Dick, R. (2015). "Of the group" and "for the group": How followership is shaped by leaders' prototypicality and group identification. *European Journal of Social Psychology*, 45(2), 180–190.

Steinman, C. T., & Updegraff, J. A. (2015). Delay and death-thought accessibility: A meta-analysis. *Personality and Social Psychology Bulletin*, 41(12), 1682–1696.

Steinmetz, J., Tausen, B. M., & Risen, J. L. (2018). Mental simulation of visceral states affects preferences and behavior. *Personality and Social Psychology Bulletin*, 44(3), 406–417.

Stephan, W. G. (1978). School desegregation: An evaluation of predictions made in *Brown v. Board of Education*. *Psychological Bulletin*, 85(2), 217–238.

Stephan, W. G., & Stephan, C. W. (1985). Intergroup anxiety. *Journal of Social Issues*, 41(3), 157–175.

Sternberg, R. J. (1997). Construct validation of a triangular love scale. *European Journal of Social Psychology*, 27(3), 313–335.

Stern, C., & Crawford, J.T. (2021). Ideological conflict and prejudice: An adversarial collaboration examining correlates and ideological (a)symmetries. *Social Psychological and Personality Science*, 12, 42–53.

Stewart, J. E. (1980). Defendant's attractiveness as a factor in the outcome of criminal trials: An observational study. *Journal of Applied Social Psychology*, 10(4), 348–361.

Stewart, V. M. (1973). Tests of the "carpentered world" hypothesis by race and environment in America and Zambia. *International Journal of Psychology*, 8(2), 83–94.

Stith, S. M., & Farley, S. C. (1993). A predictive model of male spousal violence. *Journal of Family Violence*, 8(2), 183–201.

Stoet, G., & Geary, D. C. (2018). The gender-equality paradox in science, technology, engineering, and mathematics education. *Psychological Science*, 29(4), 581–593.

Stone, A. A., Hedges, S. M., Neale, J. M., & Satin, M. S. (1985). Prospective and cross-sectional mood reports offer no evidence of a "blue Monday" phenomenon. *Journal of Personality and Social Psychology*, 49(1), 129–134.

Stone, J., Aronson, E., Crain, A. L., Winslow, M. P., & Fried, C. B. (1994). Inducing hypocrisy as a means of encouraging young adults to use condoms. *Personality and Social Psychology Bulletin*, 20(1), 116–128.

Stone, J., Chalabaev, A., & Harrison, C. K. (2012). Stereotype threat in sports. In M. Inzlicht & T. Schmader (Eds.), *Stereotype threat: Theory, process, and application* (pp. 217–230). Oxford University Press.

Stone, J., & Fernandez, N. C. (2008). To practice what we preach: The use of hypocrisy and cognitive dissonance to motivate behavior change. *Social and Personality Psychology Compass*, 2(2), 1024–1051.

Stone, J., Lynch, C. I., Sjomeling, M., & Darley, J. M. (1999). Stereotype threat effects on Black and White athletic performance. *Journal of Personality and Social Psychology*, 77(6), 1213–1227.

Stone, J., Whitehead, J., Schmader, T., & Focella, E. (2011). Thanks for asking: Self-affirming questions reduce backlash when stigmatized targets confront prejudice. *Journal of Experimental Social Psychology*, 47(3), 589–598.

Stoner, J. A. F. (1961). A comparison of individual and group decisions involving risk (Unpublished master's thesis). Massachusetts Institute of Technology, Sloan School of Management.

Storms, M. D. (1973). Videotape and the attribution process: Reversing actors' and observers' points of view. *Journal of Personality and Social Psychology*, 27(2), 165–175.

Storms, M. D., & Nisbett, R. E. (1970). Insomnia and the attribution process. *Journal of Personality and Social Psychology*, 16(2), 319–328.

Stouffer, S. A., Schuman, E. A., DeVinney, L. C., Star, S. A., & Williams, R. B. (1949). *The American soldier: Adjustment during army life* (Vol. 1). Princeton University Press.

Stout, J. G., Dasgupta, N., Hunsinger, M., & McManus, M. A. (2011). STEMing the tide: Using ingroup experts to inoculate women's self-concept in science, technology, engineering, and mathematics (STEM). *Journal of Personality and Social Psychology*, 100(2), 255–270.

Strack, F., Martin, L. L., & Stepper, S. (1988). Inhibiting and facilitating conditions of the human smile: A nonobtrusive test of the facial feedback hypothesis. *Journal of Personality and Social Psychology*, 54(5), 768–777.

Strahan, E. J., Spencer, S. J., & Zanna, M. P. (2002). Subliminal priming and persuasion: Striking while the iron is hot. *Journal of Experimental Social Psychology*, 38(6), 556–568.

Strange, J. J., & Leung, C. C. (1999). How anecdotal accounts in news and in fiction can influence judgments of a social problem's urgency, causes, and cures. *Personality and Social Psychology Bulletin*, 25(4), 436–449.

Strasburger, V. C. (2007). Go ahead punk, make my day: It's time for pediatricians to take action against media violence. *Pediatrics*, 119(6), e1398–e1399.

Straus, M. A. (2005). Women's violence toward men is a serious social problem. In D. R. Loseke, R. J. Gelles, & M. M. Cavanaugh (Eds.), *Current controversies on family violence* (2nd ed., pp. 55–77). Sage.

Straus, M. A., Gelles, R. J., & Steinmetz, S. K. (1980). *Behind closed doors: Violence in the American family*. Doubleday.

Stucky, T. D. (2012). The conditional effects of race and politics on social control: Black violent crime arrests in large cities, 1970 to 1990. *Journal of Research in Crime and Delinquency*, 49(1), 3–30.

Subramanian, R., & Arzy, L. (2021) *State Policing Reforms since George Floyd's Murder*. Brennan Center for Justice. https://www.brennancenter.org/our-work/research-reports/state-policing-reforms-george-floyds-murder

Suarez, E. C., & Krishnan, K. R. R. (2006). The relation of free plasma tryptophan to anger, hostility, and aggression in a nonpatient sample of adult men and women. *Annals of Behavioral Medicine*, 31(3), 254–260.

Sude, D. J., Knobloch-Westerwick, S., Robinson, M. J., & Westerwick, A. (2019). "Pick and choose" opinion climate: How browsing of political messages shapes public opinion perceptions and attitudes. *Communication Monographs*, 86(4), 457–478.

Suh, E. M. (2002). Culture, identity consistency, and subjective well-being. *Journal of Personality and Social Psychology*, 83(6), 1378–1391.

Suhay, E., Brandt, M. J., & Proulx, T. (2017). Lay belief in biopolitics and political prejudice. *Social Psychological and Personality Science*, 8(2), 173–182.

Sullivan, D., Landau, M. J., & Rothschild, Z. K. (2010). An existential function of enemyship: Evidence that people attribute influence to personal and political enemies to compensate for threats to control. *Journal of Personality and Social Psychology*, 98(3), 434–449.

Sullivan, J. (2019). The primacy effect in impression formation: Some replications and extensions. *Social Psychological and Personality Science*, 10(4), 432–439.

Summers, G., & Feldman, N. S. (1984). Blaming the victim versus blaming the perpetrator: An attributional analysis of spouse abuse. *Journal of Social and Clinical Psychology*, 2(4), 339–347.

Sumner, W. G. (1906). *Folkways: A study of the sociological importance of usages, manners, customs, mores, and morals*. Ginn and Co.

Sun, J., & Vazire, S. (2019). Do people know what they're like in the moment? *Psychological Science*, 30(3), 405–414.

Sun, S., Zuo, B., Wu, Y., & Wen, F. (2016). Does perspective taking increase or decrease stereotyping? The role of need for cognitive closure. *Personality and Individual Differences*, 94, 21–25.

Sun-Times Wire. (2020). 104 shot, 15 fatally, over Father's Day weekend in Chicago. *Chicago Sun-Times*. https://chicago.suntimes.com/crime/2020/6/20/21297470/chicago-fathers-day-weekend-shootings-homicide-gun-violence-june-19-22-104-shot

Surowiecki, J. (2004). *The wisdom of crowds*. Doubleday.

Sutin, A. R., Stephan, Y., & Terracciano, A. (2015). Weight discrimination and risk of mortality. *Psychological Science*, 26(11), 1803–1811.

Swami, V., & Tovee, M. J. (2006). The influence of body mass index on the physical attractiveness preferences of feminist and nonfeminist heterosexual women and lesbians. *Psychology of Women Quarterly*, 30(3), 252–257.

Swann, W. B., Jr. (1983). Self-verification: Bringing social reality into harmony with the self. In J. Suls & A. G. Greenwald (Eds.), *Social psychological perspectives on the self* (Vol. 2, pp. 33–66). Erlbaum.

Swann, W. B., Jr., & Buhrmester, M. D. (2015). Identity fusion. *Current Directions in Psychological Science*, 24(1), 52–57.

Swann, W. B., Jr., & Pittman, T. S. (1975). Salience of initial ratings and attitude change in the "forbidden toy" paradigm. *Personality and Social Psychology Bulletin*, 1(3), 493–496.

Swann, W. B., Jr., Wenzlaff, R. M., & Tafarodi, R. W. (1992). Depression and the search for negative evaluations: More evidence of the role of self-verification strivings. *Journal of Abnormal Psychology*, 101(2), 314–317.

Swap, W. C. (1977). Interpersonal attraction and repeated exposure to rewarders and punishers. *Personality and Social Psychology Bulletin*, 3(2), 248–251.

Sweeny, K. (2018). On the experience of awaiting uncertain news. *Current Directions in Psychological Science*, 27(4), 281–285.

Swendsen, J. D., & Merikangas, K. R. (2000). The comorbidity of depression and substance abuse disorders. *Clinical Psychology Review*, 20(2), 173–189.

Swift, J. (2001). *Gulliver's travels*. W. W. Norton (Original work published 1726)

Swim, J. K., & Hyers, L. L. (1999). Excuse me—What did you just say?! Women's public and private responses to sexist remarks. *Journal of Experimental Social Psychology*, 35(1), 68–88.

Symons, D. (1979). *The evolution of human sexuality*. Oxford University Press.

Syropoulos, S., Lifshin, U., Greenberg, J., Horner, D. E., & Leidner, B. (2022, February 17). Bigotry and the human–animal divide: (Dis)Belief in human evolution and bigoted attitudes across different cultures. *Journal of Personality and Social Psychology*. Advance online publication. http://dx.doi.org/10.1037/pspi0000391

Szymanski, K., & Harkins, S. G. (1987). Social loafing and self-evaluation with asocial standard. *Journal of Personality and Social Psychology*, 53(5), 891–897.

Tafoya, M. A., & Spitzberg, B. H. (2007). The dark side of infidelity: Its nature, prevalence, and communicative functions. In B. H. Spitzberg & W. R. Cupach (Eds.), *The dark side of interpersonal communication* (2nd ed., pp. 201–242). Erlbaum.

Tajfel, H., Billig, M. G., Bundy, R. P., & Flament, C. (1971). Social categorization and intergroup behaviour. *European Journal of Social Psychology*, 1(2), 149–178.

Tajfel, H., & Turner, J. C. (1979). An integrative theory of intergroup conflict. In W. G. Austin & S. Worchel (Eds.), *The social psychology of intergroup relations* (pp. 33–47). Brooks/Cole.

Tajfel, H., & Turner, J. C. (1986). The social identity theory of intergroup behavior. In S. Worchel & W. G. Austin (Eds.), *Psychology of intergroup relations* (pp. 7–24). Nelson-Hall.

Talmi, D., Lohnas, L. J., & Daw, N. D. (2019). A retrieved context model of the emotional modulation of memory. *Psychological Review*, 126(4), 455–485.

Tamborini, R., & Stiff, J. (1987). Predictors of horror film attendance and appeal: An analysis of the audience for frightening films. *Communication Research*, 14(4), 415–436.

Tamir, D. I., Templeton, E. M., Ward, A. F., & Zaki, J. (2018). Media usage diminishes memory for experiences. *Journal of Experimental Social Psychology*, 76, 161–168.

Tamir, M., Robinson, M. D., Clore, G. L., Martin, L. L., & Whitaker, D. J. (2004). Are we puppets on a string? The contextual meaning of unconscious expressive cues. *Personality and Social Psychology Bulletin*, 30(2), 237–249.

Tangney, J. P. (1991). Moral affect: The good, the bad, and the ugly. *Journal of Personality and Social Psychology*, 61(4), 598–607.

Tangney, J. P., Miller, R. S., Flicker, L., & Barlow, D. H. (1996). Are shame, guilt, and embarrassment distinct emotions? *Journal of Personality and Social Psychology*, 70(6), 1256–1269.

Tangney, J. P., Stuewig, J., Mashek, D., & Hastings, M. (2011). Assessing jail inmates' proneness to shame and guilt: Feeling bad about the behavior or the self? *Criminal Justice and Behavior*, 38(7), 710–734.

Tangney, J. P., Wagner, P., & Gramzow, R. (1992). Proneness to shame, proneness to guilt, and psychopathology. *Journal of Abnormal Psychology*, 101(3), 469–478.

Tangney, J. P., Wagner, P. E., Hill-Barlow, D., Marschall, D. E., & Gramzow, R. (1996). Relation of shame and guilt to constructive versus destructive responses to anger across the lifespan. *Journal of Personality and Social Psychology*, 70(4), 797–809.

Tankard, M. E., & Paluck, E. L. (2017). The effect of a Supreme Court decision regarding gay marriage on social norms and personal attitudes. *Psychological Science*, 28(9), 1334–1344.

Tannenbaum, M. B., Hepler, J., Zimmerman, R. S., Saul, L., Jacobs, S., Wilson, K., & Albarracín, D. (2015). Appealing to fear: A meta-analysis of fear appeal effectiveness and theories. *Psychological Bulletin*, 141(6), 1178–1204.

Tappin, B. M., & McKay, R. T. (2017). The illusion of moral superiority. *Social Psychological and Personality Science*, 8(6), 623–631.

Tattersall, I. (1998). *Becoming human: Evolution and human uniqueness*. Harcourt Brace.

Tavernise, S., & Oppel, Richard A., Jr. (2020, April 10). Spit on, yelled at, attacked: Chinese-Americans fear for their safety. *The New York Times*. https://www.nytimes.com/2020/03/23/us/coronavirus-asian-americans-attacks.html

Taylor, D. A., Gould, R. J., & Brounstein, P. J. (1981). Effects of personalistic self-disclosure. *Personality and Social Psychology Bulletin*, 7(3), 487–492.

Taylor, D. M., Wright, S. C., Moghaddam, F. M., & Lalonde, R. N. (1990). The personal/group discrimination discrepancy: Perceiving my group, but not myself, to be a target for discrimination. *Personality and Social Psychology Bulletin*, 16(2), 254–262.

Taylor, D. M., Wright, S. C., & Porter, L. E. (1994). Dimensions of perceived discrimination: The personal/group discrimination discrepancy. In M. P. Zanna & J. M. Olson (Eds.), *The psychology of prejudice: The Ontario Symposium* (Vol. 7, pp. 233–255). Erlbaum.

Taylor, S. E. (1981). A categorization approach to stereotyping. In D. L. Hamilton (Ed.), *Cognitive processes in stereotyping and intergroup behavior* (pp. 83–114). Erlbaum.

Taylor, S. E., & Brown, J. D. (1988). Illusion and well-being: A social psychological perspective on mental health. *Psychological Bulletin*, 103(2), 193–210.

Taylor, S. E., & Fiske, S. T. (1975). Point of view and perceptions of causality. *Journal of Personality and Social Psychology*, 32(3), 439–445.

Taylor, S. E., Fiske, S. T., Etcoff, N. L., & Ruderman, A. J. (1978). Categorical and contextual bases of person memory and stereotyping. *Journal of Personality and Social Psychology*, 36(7), 778–793.

Taylor, S. E., Klein, L. C., Lewis, B. P., Gruenewald, T. L., Gurung, R. A., & Updegraff, J. A. (2000). Biobehavioral responses to stress in females: Tend-and-befriend, not fight-or-flight. *Psychological Review*, 107(3), 411–429.

Taylor, S. P., & Leonard, K. E. (1983). Alcohol and human physical aggression. In R. G. Green & E. I. Donnerstein (Eds.), *Aggression: Theoretical and empirical reviews* (Vol. 2, pp. 77–101). Academic Press.

Tenenbaum, H. R., & Leaper, C. (2002). Are parents' gender schemas related to their children's gender-related cognitions? A meta-analysis. *Developmental Psychology*, 38(4), 615–630.

Tensley, B. (2022, March 10). The news out of Florida and Texas exemplifies a larger conservative trend. CNN. https://www.cnn.com/2022/03/10/us/lgbtq-rights-desantis-race-deconstructed-newsletter/index.html

Terracciano, A., Abdel-Khalek, A. M., Adam, N., Adamovova, L., Ahn, C. K., Ahn, H. N., Alansari, B. M., Alcalay, L., Allik, J., Angleitner, A., Avia, M. D., Ayearst, L. E., Barbaranelli, C., Beer, A., Borg-Cunen, M. A., Bratko, D., Brunner-Sciarra, M., Budzinski, L., Camart, N., . . . McCrae, R. R. (2005). National character does not reflect mean personality trait levels in 49 cultures. *Science*, 310(5745), 96–100.

Tesser, A. (1980). Self-esteem maintenance in family dynamics. *Journal of Personality and Social Psychology*, 39(1), 77–91.

Tesser, A. (1988). Toward a self-evaluation maintenance model of social behavior. In L. Berkowitz (Ed.), *Advances in experimental social psychology* (Vol. 21, pp. 181–228). Academic Press.

Tesser, A., & Conlee, M. C. (1975). Some effects of time and thought on attitude polarization. *Journal of Personality and Social Psychology*, 31(2), 262–270.

Thibaut, J. W., & Kelley, H. H. (1959). *The social psychology of groups*. Wiley.

Thibodeau, P. H., & Boroditsky, L. (2011). Metaphors we think with: The role of metaphor in reasoning. *PLoS ONE*, 6(2), e16782.

Thomaes, S., & Bushman, B. J. (2011). Mirror, mirror, on the wall, who's the most aggressive of them all? Narcissism, self-esteem, and aggression. In P. R. Shaver & M. Mikulincer (Eds.), *Human aggression and violence: Causes, manifestations, and consequences* (pp. 203–219). American Psychological Association.

Thomas, M. H., Horton, R. W., Lippincott, E. C., & Drabman, R. S. (1977). Desensitization to portrayals of real-life aggression as a function of television violence. *Journal of Personality and Social Psychology*, 35(6), 450–458.

Thompson, M. M., Naccarato, M. E., Parker, K. C., & Moskowitz, G. B. (2001). The personal need for structure and personal fear of invalidity measures: Historical perspectives, current applications, and future directions. In G. B. Moskowitz (Ed.), *Cognitive social psychology: The Princeton Symposium on the Legacy and Future of Social Cognition* (pp. 19–39). Erlbaum.

Thomsen, L., Green, E. T., Ho, A. K., Levin, S., van Laar, C., Sinclair, S., & Sidanius, J. (2010). Wolves in sheep's clothing: SDO asymmetrically predicts perceived ethnic victimization among White and Latino students across three years. *Personality and Social Psychology Bulletin*, 36(2), 225–238.

Thornberry, T. P., Freeman-Gallant, A., Lizotte, A. J., Krohn, M. D., & Smith, C. A. (2003). Linked lives: The intergenerational transmission of antisocial behavior. *Journal of Abnormal Child Psychology*, 31(2), 171–184.

Thornberry, T. P., Huizinga, D., & Loeber, R. (2004). The causes and correlates studies: Findings and policy implications. *Juvenile Justice, 9*(1), 3–19.

Thorndike, E. L. (1920). A constant error in psychological ratings. *Journal of Applied Psychology, 4*(1), 25–29.

Thornhill, R., & Gangestad, S. W. (1993). Human facial beauty. *Human Nature, 4*(3), 237–269.

Thornhill, R., & Gangestad, S. W. (2006). Facial sexual dimorphism, developmental stability, and susceptibility to disease in men and women. *Evolution and Human Behavior, 27*(2), 131–144.

Thornhill, R., & Thornhill, N. W. (1992). The evolutionary psychology of men's coercive sexuality. *Behavioral and Brain Sciences, 15*(2), 363–375.

Thornton, B., & Maurice, J. (1997). Physique contrast effect: Adverse impact of idealized body images for women. *Sex Roles, 37*(5–6), 433–439.

Thuen, F., Breivik, K., Wold, B., & Ulveseter, G. (2015). Growing up with one or both parents: The effects on physical health and health-related behavior through adolescence and into early adulthood. *Journal of Divorce & Remarriage, 56*(6), 451–474.

Tian, D. A., Schroeder, J., Haubl, G., Risen, J., Norton, M. I., & Gino, F. (2018). Enacting rituals to improve self-control. *Journal of Personality and Social Psychology, 114*(6), 851–876.

Tice, D. M., Baumeister, R. F., Shmueli, D., & Muraven, M. (2007). Restoring the self: Positive affect helps improve self-regulation following ego depletion. *Journal of Experimental Social Psychology, 43*(3), 379–384.

Tidwell, N. D., Eastwick, P. W., & Finkel, E. J. (2013). Perceived, not actual, similarity predicts initial attraction in a live romantic context: Evidence from the speed-dating paradigm. *Personal Relationships, 20*(2), 199–215.

Toch, H. (1969). *Violent men.* Aldine.

Todd, A. R., Bodenhausen, G. V., Richeson, J. A., & Galinsky, A. D. (2011). Perspective taking combats automatic expressions of racial bias. *Journal of Personality and Social Psychology, 100*(6), 1027–1042.

Todd, A. R., Thiem, K. C., & Neel, R. (2016). Does seeing faces of young black boys facilitate the identification of threatening stimuli? *Psychological Science, 27*(3), 384–393.

Todd, D. (2011, February 15). Is there life after death? 71 per cent of Canadians say "yes." *Vancouver Sun.* https://vancouversun.com/news/staff-blogs/is-there-life-after-death-71-per-cent-of-canadians-say-yes

Todorov, A., & Bargh, J. A. (2002). Automatic sources of aggression. *Aggression and Violent Behavior, 7*(1), 53–68.

Todorov, A., Mandisodza, A. N., Goren, A., & Hall, C. C. (2005). Inferences of competence from faces predict election outcomes. *Science, 308*(5728), 1623–1626.

Toma, C. L., & Hancock, J. T. (2010). Looks and lies: The role of physical attractiveness in online dating self-presentation and deception. *Communication Research, 37*(3), 335–351.

Toma, C. L., Hancock, J. T., & Ellison, N. B. (2008). Separating fact from fiction: An examination of deceptive self-presentation in online dating profiles. *Personality and Social Psychology Bulletin, 34*(8), 1023–1036.

Toomey, R. B., Syversten, A. K., & Shramko, M. (2018). Transgender adolescent suicide behavior. *Pediatrics, 142*(4), 1–8.

Topolinski, S., & Strack, F. (2009). The architecture of intuition: Fluency and affect determine intuitive judgments of semantic and visual coherence and judgments of grammaticality in artificial grammar learning. *Journal of Experimental Psychology: General, 138*(1), 3–63.

Tormala, Z. L., Petty, R. E., & Briñol, P. (2002). Ease of retrieval effects in persuasion: A self-validation analysis. *Personality and Social Psychology Bulletin, 28*(12), 1700–1712.

Toth, K., & Kemmelmeier, M. (2009). Divorce attitudes around the world: Distinguishing the impact of culture on evaluations and attitude structure. *Cross-Cultural Research, 43*(3), 280–297.

Townsend, S. S., Major, B., Gangi, C. E., & Mendes, W. B. (2011). From "in the air" to "under the skin": Cortisol responses to social identity threat. *Personality and Social Psychology Bulletin, 37*(2), 151–164.

Townsend, S. S., Major, B., Sawyer, P. J., & Mendes, W. B. (2010). Can the absence of prejudice be more threatening than its presence? It depends on one's worldview. *Journal of Personality and Social Psychology, 99*(6), 933–947.

Tracy, J. L., & Robins, R. W. (2004). Show your pride: Evidence for a discrete emotion expression. *Psychological Science, 15*(3), 194–197.

Tracy, J. L., Shaver, P. R., Albino, A. W., & Cooper, M. L. (2003). Attachment styles and adolescent sexuality. In P. Florsheim (Ed.), *Adolescent romance and sexual behavior: Theory, research, and practical implications* (pp. 137–159). Erlbaum.

Trainor, Z. M., Jong, J., Bluemke, M., & Halberstadt, J. (2019). Death salience moderates the effect of trauma on religiosity. *Psychological Trauma: Theory, Research, Practice, and Policy, 11*(6), 639–646.

Tran, S., Simpson, J. A., & Fletcher, G. J. O. (2008). The role of ideal standards in relationship initiation processes. In S. Sprecher, A. Wenzel, & J. Harvey (Eds.), *The handbook of relationship initiation* (pp. 487–498). Psychology Press.

Travis, A. (1999, September 10). Retake on Kubrick film ban: Family may release A Clockwork Orange as classification board reassesses banned movies for video. *The Guardian.* http://www.theguardian.com/uk/1999/sep/11/alantravis

Trawalter, S., & Hoffman, K. M. (2015). Got pain? Racial bias in perceptions of pain. *Social and Personality Psychology Compass, 9*(3), 146–157.

Trawalter, S., & Richeson, J. A. (2006). Regulatory focus and executive function after interracial interactions. *Journal of Experimental Social Psychology, 42*(3), 406–412.

Triandis, H. C. (1989). The self and social behavior in differing cultural contexts. *Psychological Review, 96*(3), 506–520.

Triandis, H. C. (1994). *Culture and social behavior.* McGraw-Hill.

Triplett, N. (1898). The dynamogenic factors in pacemaking and competition. *American Journal of Psychology, 9*(4), 507–533.

Trivers, R. L. (1971). The evolution of reciprocal altruism. *Quarterly Review of Biology, 46*(1), 35–57.

Trivers, R. L. (1972). Parental investment and sexual selection. In B. Campbell (Ed.), *Sexual selection and the descent of man: 1871–1971* (pp. 136–179). Aldine.

Trope, Y. (1986). Self-enhancement and self-assessment in achievement behavior. In R. M. Sorrentrino & E. T. Higgins (Eds.), *Handbook of motivation and cognition: Foundations of social behavior* (pp. 350–378). Guilford Press.

Trope, Y., & Fishbach, A. (2005). Going beyond the motivation given: Self-control and situational control over behavior. In R. R. Hassin, J. S. Uleman, & J. A. Bargh (Eds.), *Oxford series in social cognition and social neuroscience. The new unconscious* (p. 537–563). Oxford University Press.

Trope, Y., & Liberman, A. (1996). Social hypothesis-testing: Cognitive and motivational mechanisms. In E. T. Higgins & A. W. Kruglanski (Eds.), *Social psychology: Handbook of basic principles* (pp. 239–270). Guilford Press.

Trope, Y., & Liberman, N. (2003). Temporal construal. *Psychological Review, 110*(3), 403–421.

Tropp, L. R. (2003). The psychological impact of prejudice: Implications for intergroup contact. *Group Processes & Intergroup Relations, 6*(2), 131–149.

Tropp, L. R., & Barlow, F. K. (2018). Making advantaged racial groups care about inequality: Intergroup contact as a route to psychological investment. *Current Directions in Psychological Science, 27*(3), 194–199.

Tropp, L. R., & Pettigrew, T. F. (2005). Relationships between intergroup contact and prejudice among minority and majority status groups. *Psychological Science, 16*(12), 951–957.

Tropp, L. R., & Wright, S. C. (2001). Ingroup identification as the inclusion of ingroup in the self. *Personality and Social Psychology Bulletin, 27*(5), 585–600.

Troxel, W. M., Matthews, K. A., Bromberger, J. T., & Sutton-Tyrrell, K. (2003). Chronic stress burden, discrimination, and subclinical carotid artery disease in African American and Caucasian women. *Health Psychology, 22*(3), 300–309.

Trudel, R., & Argo, J. J. (2013). The effect of product size and form distortion on consumer recycling behavior. *Journal of Consumer Research, 40*, 632–643.

Truman, J. L., & Morgan, R. E. (2016). *Criminal victimization.* Bureau of Justice Statistics. https://www.bjs.gov/content/pub/pdf/cv15.pdf

Trzesniewski, K. H., Donnellan, M. B., & Robins, R. W. (2003). Stability of self-esteem across the life span. *Journal of Personality and Social Psychology, 84*(1), 205.

Tsai, J. L. (2007). Ideal affect: Cultural causes and behavioral consequences. *Perspectives on Psychological Science, 2*(3), 242–259.

Tsai, J. L., Blevins, E., Bencharit, L. Z., Chim, L., Fung, H. H., & Yeung, D. Y. (2019). Cultural variation in social judgments of smiles: The role of ideal affect. *Journal of Personality and Social Psychology, 116*(6), 966–988.

Tsai, W., & Lu, Q. (2018). Culture, emotion suppression and disclosure, and health. *Social and Personality Psychology Compass, 12*(3), e12373.

Tucker, P., & Aron, A. (1993). Passionate love and marital satisfaction at key transition points in the family life cycle. *Journal of Social and Clinical Psychology, 12*(2), 135–147.

Tully, S., & Meyvis, T. (2017). Forgetting to remember our experiences: People overestimate how much they will retrospect about personal events. *Journal of Personality and Social Psychology, 113*(6), 878–891.

Turkewitz, J. (2016, June 20). Tens of thousands gather in Orlando to honor shooting victims. *The New York Times.* https://www.nytimes.com/2016/06/21/us/orlando-shooting-nightclub.html

Turner, C. W., & Berkowitz, L. (1972). Identification with film aggressor (covert role taking) and reactions to film violence. *Journal of Personality and Social Psychology, 21*(2), 256–264.

Turner, C. W., Layton, J. F., & Simons, L. S. (1975). Naturalistic studies of aggressive behavior: Aggressive stimuli, victim visibility, and horn honking. *Journal of Personality and Social Psychology, 31*(6), 1098–1107.

Turner, J. C. (1991). *Social influence.* Brooks/Cole.

Turner, J. C., Hogg, M. A., Oakes, P. J., Reicher, S. D., & Wetherell, M. S. (1987). *Rediscovering the social group: A self-categorization theory.* Blackwell.

Tversky, A., & Kahneman, D. (1973). Availability: A heuristic for judging frequency and probability. *Cognitive Psychology, 5*(2), 207–232.

Tversky, A., & Kahneman, D. (1981). The framing of decisions and the psychology of choice. *Science, 211*(4481), 453–458.

Twain, M. (1902). Does the race of man love a lord? *North American Review, 174*, 433–444.

Twenge, J. M., Baumeister, R. F., DeWall, C. N., Ciarocco, N. J., & Bartels, J. M. (2007). Social exclusion decreases prosocial behavior. *Journal of Personality and Social Psychology, 92*(1), 56–66.

Twenge, J. M., Baumeister, R. F., Tice, D. M., & Stucke, T. S. (2001). If you can't join them, beat them: Effects of social exclusion on aggressive behavior. *Journal of Personality and Social Psychology, 81*(6), 1058–1069.

Twenge, J. M., Campbell, W. K., & Gentile, B. (2013). Changes in pronoun use in American books and the rise of individualism, 1960–2008. *Journal of Cross Cultural Psychology, 44*(3), 406–415.

Tyldum, M. (Director). (2016). *Passengers* [Film]. Village Roadshow Pictures.

Tyson, K., & Lewis, A. E. (2021). The "burden" of oppositional culture among Black youth in America. *Annual Review of Sociology, 47*, 459–477. https://doi.org/10.1146/annurev-soc-090420-092123

Uchino, B. N. (2006). Social support and health: A review of physiological processes potentially underlying links to disease outcomes. *Journal of Behavioral Medicine, 29*(4), 377–387.

Uddin, L. Q., Iacoboni, M., Lange, C., & Keenan, J. P. (2007). The self and social cognition: The role of cortical midline structures and mirror neurons. *Trends in Cognitive Sciences, 11*(4), 153–157.

Uenal, F., Bergh, R., Sidanius, J., Zick, A., Kimel, S., & Kunst, J.R. (2021). The nature of Islamophobia: A test of a tripartite view in five countries. *Personality and Social Psychology Bulletin, 47*, 275-292.

Ullman, C. (1982). Cognitive and emotional antecedents of religious conversion. *Journal of Personality and Social Psychology, 43*(1), 183–192.

United Nations Office on Drugs and Crime. (2013). *Global study on homicide. Homicide statistics 2013.* http://www.unodc.org/gsh/en/data.html

Unkelbach, C., Koch, A., Silva, R. R., & Garcia-Marques, T. (2019). Truth by repetition: Explanations and implications. *Current Directions in Psychological Science, 28*(3), 247–253

Updegraff, J. A., Brick, C., Emanuel, A. S., Mintzer, R. E., & Sherman, D. K. (2015). Message framing for health: Moderation by perceived susceptibility and motivational orientation in a diverse sample of Americans. *Health Psychology, 34*(1), 20–29.

U.S. Bureau of Labor Statistics. (2020). *Labor force statistics from the Current Population Survey. Household data, 2019 annual averages.* Bureau of Labor Statistics. https://www.bls.gov/cps/cpsaat11.htm

U.S. Census Bureau. (2012). *Statistical abstract of the United States, 2011, international statistics*, Table 1336, "Marriage and divorce rates by country: 1980 to 2008." http://www.census.gov/compendia/statab/2011/tables/11s1335.pdf

Uziel, L. (2018). The intricacies of the pursuit of higher self-control. *Current Directions in Psychological Science, 27*(2), 79–84.

Vaden-Kiernan, N., Ialongo, N. S., Pearson, J., & Kellam, S. (1995). Household family structure and children's aggressive behavior: A longitudinal study of urban elementary school children. *Journal of Abnormal Child Psychology, 23*(5), 553–568.

Vaidis, D. C., & Bran, A. (2018). Some prior considerations about dissonance to understand its reduction: Comment on McGrath (2017). *Social and Personality Psychology Compass, 12*(9), e12411.

Vail, K. E., Arndt, J., Motyl, M., & Pyszczynski, T. (2009). Compassionate values and presidential politics: Mortality salience, compassionate values, and support for Barack Obama and John McCain in the 2008 presidential election. *Analyses of Social Issues and Public Policy, 9*(1), 255–268.

Vail, K. E., Juhl, J., Arndt, J., Vess, M., Routledge, C., & Rutjens, B. T. (2012). When death is good for life: Considering the positive trajectories of terror management. *Personality and Social Psychology Review, 16*(4), 303–329.

Vail, K. E., Rothschild, Z. K., Weise, D. R., Solomon, S., Pyszczynski, T., & Greenberg, J. (2010). A terror management analysis of the psychological functions of religion. *Personality and Social Psychology Review, 14*(1), 84–94.

Vail, K.E., Courtney, E., & Arndt, J. (2019). The influence of existential threat and tolerance salience on anti-Islamic attitudes in American politics. *Political Psychology, 40*, 1143-1162.

Valins, S. (1966). Cognitive effects of false heart-rate feedback. *Journal of Personality and Social Psychology, 4*(4), 400–408.

Vallacher, R. R., & Wegner, D. M. (1987). What do people think they're doing? Action identification and human behavior. *Psychological Review, 94*(1), 3–15.

van Bavel, J. J., Mende-Siedlecki, P., Brady, W. J., & Reinero, D. A. (2016). Contextual sensitivity in scientific reproducibility. *Proceedings of the National Academy of Sciences, 113*(23), 6454–6459.

Van Boven, L., Kruger, J., Savitsky, K., & Gilovich, T. (2000). When social worlds collide: Overconfidence in the multiple audience problem. *Personality and Social Psychology Bulletin, 26*(5), 619–628.

Vandello, J. A., & Bosson, J. K. (2013). Hard won and easily lost: A review and synthesis of theory and research on precarious manhood. *Psychology of Men & Masculinity, 14*(2), 101–113.

Vandello, J. A., & Cohen, D. (1999). Patterns of individualism and collectivism across the United States. *Journal of Personality and Social Psychology, 77*(2), 279–292.

Vandello, J. A., & Cohen, D. (2003). Male honor and female fidelity: Implicit cultural scripts that perpetuate domestic violence. *Journal of Personality and Social Psychology, 84*(5), 997–1010.

Vandello, J. A., Cohen, D., Grandon, R., & Franiuk, R. (2009). Stand by your man: Indirect prescriptions for honorable violence and feminine loyalty in Canada, Chile, and the United States. *Journal of Cross-Cultural Psychology, 40*(1), 81–104.

Vandello, J. A., Cohen, D., & Ransom, S. (2008). US southern and northern differences in perceptions of norms about aggression: Mechanisms for the perpetuation of a culture of honor. *Journal of Cross-Cultural Psychology, 39*(2), 162–177.

van den Boom, D. C. (1994). The influence of temperament and mothering on attachment and exploration: An experimental manipulation of sensitive responsiveness among lower-class mothers with irritable infants. *Child Development, 65*(5), 1457–1477.

van den Boom, D. C. (1995). Do first-year intervention effects endure? Follow-up during toddlerhood of a sample of Dutch irritable infants. *Child Development, 66*(6), 1798–1816.

Van de Vyver, J., & Abrams, D. (2015). Testing the prosocial effectiveness of the prototypical moral emotions: Elevation increases benevolent behaviors and outrage increases justice behaviors. *Journal of Experimental Social Psychology, 58*, 23–33.

van Kleef, G. A., Oveis, C., Van der Löwe, I., LuoKogan, A., Goetz, J., & Keltner, D. (2008). Power, distress, and compassion: Turning a blind eye to the suffering of others. *Psychological Science, 19*(12), 1315–1322.

van Knippenberg, A. D., & Dijksterhuis, A. (2000). Social categorization and stereotyping: A functional perspective. *European Review of Social Psychology, 11*(1), 105–144.

van Lange, P. A., De Bruin, E., Otten, W., & Joireman, J. A. (1997). Development of prosocial, individualistic, and competitive orientations: Theory and preliminary evidence. *Journal of Personality and Social Psychology, 73*(4), 733–746.

van Lange, P. A., Rusbult, C. E., Drigotas, S. M., Arriaga, X. B., Witcher, B. S., & Cox, C. L. (1997). Willingness to sacrifice in close relationships. *Journal of Personality and Social Psychology, 72*(6), 1373–1395.

Vanman, E. J., Saltz, J. L., Nathan, L. R., & Warren, J. A. (2004). Racial discrimination by low-prejudiced Whites: Facial movements as implicit measures of attitudes related to behavior. *Psychological Science, 15*(11), 711–714.

Van Sant, G. (Director). (2008). *Milk* [Film]. Focus Features.

Van Swol, L. M. (2009). Extreme members and group polarization. *Social Influence, 4*(3), 185–199.

van Tilburg, W. A. P., Sedikides, C., & Vingerhoets, A. J. J. M. (2019). How nostalgia infuses life with meaning: From social connectedness to self-continuity. *European Journal of Social Psychology, 49*(3), 521–532.

van Yperen, N. W., & Buunk, B. P. (1990). A longitudinal study of equity and satisfaction in intimate relationships. *European Journal of Social Psychology, 20*(4), 287–309.

Van Zant, A. B., & Berger, J. (2020). How the voice persuades. *Journal of Personality and Social Psychology, 118*(4), 661–682.

Varangis, E., Lanzieri, N., Hildebrandt, T., & Feldman, M. (2012). Gay male attraction toward muscular men: Does mating context matter? *Body Image, 9*(2), 270–278.

Vargas, T. (2014, June 18). U.S. patent office cancels Redskins trademark registration, says name is disparaging. *Washington Post.* https://www.washingtonpost.com/local/us-patent-office-cancels-redskins-trademark-registration-says-name-is-disparaging/2014/06/18/e7737bb8-f6ee-11e3-8aa9-dad2ec039789_story.html

Vaughan, D. (1996). *The* Challenger *launch decision: Risky technology, culture, and deviance at NASA.* University of Chicago Press.

Vazire, S. (2010). Who knows what about a person? The self–other knowledge asymmetry (SOKA) model. *Journal of Personality and Social Psychology, 98*(2), 281–300.

Vazire, S., & Carlson, E. N. (2011). Others sometimes know us better than we know ourselves. *Current Directions in Psychological Science, 20*(2), 104–108.

Vazire, S., & Gosling, S. D. (2004). e-Perceptions: Personality impressions based on personal websites. *Journal of Personality and Social Psychology, 87*(1), 123–132.

Vázquez, C. A. (1994). A multitask controlled evaluation of facilitated communication. *Journal of Autism and Developmental Disorders, 24*(3), 369–379.

Vega, V., & Malamuth, N. M. (2007). Predicting sexual aggression: The role of pornography in the context of general and specific risk factors. *Aggressive Behavior, 33*(2), 104–117.

Veitch, R., & Griffitt, W. (1976). Good news-bad news: Affective and interpersonal effects. *Journal of Applied Social Psychology, 6*(1), 69–75.

Veldman, J., Van Laar, C., Meeussen, L., & Lo Bue, S. (2021). Daily coping with social identity threat in outgroup-dominated contexts: Self-group distancing among female soldiers. *Personality and Social Psychology Bulletin, 47*(1), 118–130.

Verkuyten, M., & Yogeeswaran, K. (2017). The social psychology of intergroup toleration: A roadmap for theory and research. *Personality and Social Psychology Review, 21*(1), 72–96.

Vescio, T. K., & Biernat, M. (2003). Family values and antipathy toward gay men. *Journal of Applied Social Psychology, 33*(4), 833–847.

Vescio, T. K., Sechrist, G. B., & Paolucci, M. P. (2003). Perspective taking and prejudice reduction: The mediational role of empathy arousal and situational attributions. *European Journal of Social Psychology, 33*(4), 455–472.

Vicary A. (2011). Mortality salience and namesaking: Does thinking about death make people want to name their children after themselves? *Journal of Research in Personality, 45,* 138–141.

Viki, G. T., Osgood, D., & Phillips, S. (2013). Dehumanization and self-reported proclivity to torture prisoners of war. *Journal of Experimental Social Psychology, 49*(3), 325–328.

Vohs, K. D., Catanese, K. R., & Baumeister, R. F. (2004). Sex in "his" versus "her" relationships. In J. H. Harvey, A. Wenzel, & S. Sprecher (Eds.), *The handbook of sexuality in close relationships* (pp. 455–474). Erlbaum.

von Hippel, C., Walsh, A. M., & Zouroudis, A. (2011). Identity separation in response to stereotype threat. *Social Psychological and Personality Science, 2*(3), 317–324.

von Hippel, W., Ronay, R., Baker, E., Kjelsaas, K., & Murphy, S. C. (2016). Quick thinkers are smooth talkers: Mental speed facilitates charisma. *Psychological Science, 27*(1), 119–122.

Vonk, J., Brosnan, S. F., Silk, J. B., Henrich, J., Richardson, A. S., Lambeth, S. P., Schapiro, S. J., & Povinelli, D. J. (2008). Chimpanzees do not take advantage of very low cost opportunities to deliver food to unrelated group members. *Animal Behaviour, 75*(5), 1757–1770.

Vonk, R. (2002). Self-serving interpretations of flattery: Why ingratiation works. *Journal of Personality and Social Psychology, 82*(4), 515–526.

Voracek, M., & Fisher, M. L. (2002). Shapely centrefolds? Temporal change in body measures: Trend analysis. *BMJ: British Medical Journal, 325*(7378), 1447–1448.

Vorauer, J. D., Main, K. J., & O'Connell, G. B. (1998). How do individuals expect to be viewed by members of lower status groups? Content and implications of meta-stereotypes. *Journal of Personality and Social Psychology, 75*(4), 917–937.

Vorauer, J. D., & Quesnel, M. S. (2017). Salient multiculturalism enhances minority group members' feelings of power. *Personality and Social Psychology Bulletin, 43*(2), 259–271.

Vorauer, J. D., & Sasaki, S. J. (2009). Helpful only in the abstract? Ironic effects of empathy in intergroup interaction. *Psychological Science, 20*(2), 191–197.

Voytko, L. (2020, June 9). 74% of Americans support George Floyd protests, majority disapprove of Trump's handling, poll says. *Forbes.* https://www.forbes.com/sites/lisettevoytko/2020/06/09/74-of-americans-support-george-floyd-protests-majority-disapprove-of-trumps-handling/#13b06cbb557c

Wachowski, A., & Wachowski, L. (Directors). (1999). *The matrix* [Film]. Warner Bros.

Wadhwa, M., & Kim, J. C. (2015). Can a near win kindle motivation? The impact of nearly winning on motivation for unrelated rewards. *Psychological Science, 26*(6), 701–708.

Wakefield, J. R. H., Bowe, M., Kellezi, B., McNamara, N., & Stevenson, C. (2019). When groups help and when groups harm: Origins, developments, and future directions of the "Social Cure" perspective of group dynamics. *Social and Personality Psychology Compass, 13*(3), e12440.

Walker, L. E. (1979). *The battered woman.* Harper & Row.

Wallace, L. N. (2015). Responding to violence with guns: Mass shootings and gun acquisition. *The Social Science Journal, 52*(2), 156–167.

Wallas, G. (1926). *The art of thought.* Harcourt-Brace.

Waller, N. G., & Shaver, P. R. (1994). The importance of nongenetic influences on romantic love styles: A twin-family study. *Psychological Science, 5*(5), 268–274.

Walster, E., Aronson, E., & Abrahams, D. (1966). On increasing the persuasiveness of a low prestige communicator. *Journal of Experimental Social Psychology, 2*(4), 325–342.

Walster, E., Aronson, V., Abrahams, D., & Rottman, L. (1966). Importance of physical attractiveness in dating behavior. *Journal of Personality and Social Psychology, 4*(5), 508–516.

Walster, E., & Festinger, L. (1962). The effectiveness of "overheard" persuasive communications. *Journal of Abnormal and Social Psychology, 65*(6), 395–402.

Walter, K. V., Conroy-Beam, D., Buss, D. M., Asao, K., Sorokowska, A., Sorokowski, P., Aavik, T., Akello, G., Alhabahba, M. M., Alm, C., Amjad., N., Anjum, A., Atama, C. S., Atamturk, D. D., Ayebare, R., Batres, C., Bendixen, M., Bensafia, A., Bizumic, B., . . . Zupančič, M. (2020). Sex differences in mate preferences across 45 countries: A large-scale replication. *Psychological Science, 31*(4), 408–423.

Walton, G. M., & Brady, S. T. (2020). The social-belonging intervention. In G. M. Walton & A. J. Crum (Eds.), *Handbook of wise interventions: How social psychology can help people change.* Guilford Press.

Walton, G. M., & Cohen, G. L. (2007). A question of belonging: Race, social fit, and achievement. *Journal of Personality and Social Psychology, 92*(1), 82–96.

Walton, G. M., & Cohen, G. L. (2011). A brief social-belonging intervention improves academic and health outcomes of minority students. *Science, 331*(6023), 1447–1451.

Walton, G. M., & Spencer, S. J. (2009). Latent ability grades and test scores systematically underestimate the intellectual ability of negatively stereotyped students. *Psychological Science, 20*(9), 1132–1139.

Walton, G. M., & Wilson, T. D. (2018). Wise interventions: Psychological remedies for social and personal problems. *Psychological Review, 125*(5), 617–655.

Wan, H.-H., & Pfau, M. (2004). The relative effectiveness of inoculation, bolstering, and combined approaches in crisis communication. *Journal of Public Relations Research, 16*(3), 301–328.

Wang, Q. (2001). China's divorce trends in the transition toward a market economy. *Journal of Divorce & Remarriage, 35*(1–2), 173–189.

Ward, D. S. (Director). (1993). *The program* [Film]. Touchstone Pictures.

Warneken, F., & Tomasello, M. (2006). Altruistic helping in human infants and young chimpanzees. *Science, 311*(5765), 1301–1303.

Warner, W. L. (1959). *The living and the dead: A study of the symbolic life of Americans.* Yale University Press.

Waters, N. L., & Hans, V. P. (2009). A jury of one: Opinion formation, conformity, and dissent in juries. *Journal of Empirical Legal Studies, 6*(3), 513–540.

Watson, D. (1982). The actor and the observer: How are their perceptions of causality divergent? *Psychological Bulletin, 92*(3), 682–700.

Watson, J. (1973). Investigation into deindividuation using a cross-cultural survey technique. *Journal of Personality and Social Psychology, 25*(3), 342–345.

Watson, J. B. (1930). *Behaviorism* (Rev. ed.). Norton.

Watson-Jones, R. E., & Legare, C. H. (2016). The social functions of group rituals. *Current Directions in Psychological Science, 25*(1), 42–46.

Watts, T. W., Duncan, G. J., & Quan, H. (2018). Revisiting the Marshmallow Test: A conceptual replication investigating links between early delay of gratification and later outcomes. *Psychological Science, 29*(7), 1159–1177.

Weary, G., Rich, M. C., Harvey, J. H., & Ickes, W. J. (1980). Heider's formulation of social perception and attributional processes: Toward further clarification. *Personality and Social Psychology Bulletin, 6*(1), 37–43.

Webber, D., Babush, M., Schori-Eyal, N., Vazeou-Nieuwenhuis, A., Hettiarachchi, M., Bélanger, J. J., Moyano, M., Trujillo, H. M., Gunaratna, R., Kruglanski, A. W., & Gelfand, M. J. (2018). The road to extremism: Field and experimental evidence that significance loss-induced need for closure fosters radicalization. *Journal of Personality and Social Psychology, 114*(2), 270–285.

Weber, F. (n.d.). *Is seeing believing?* https://frankwbaker.com/mlc/is-seeing-believing-curriculum/

Wegener, D. T., & Petty, R. E. (1995). Flexible correction processes in social judgment: The role of naive theories in corrections for perceived bias. *Journal of Personality and Social Psychology, 68*(1), 36–51.

Wegner, D. M. (1994). Ironic processes of mental control. *Psychological Review, 101*(1), 34–52.

Wegner, D. M., Connally, D., Shearer, D., & Vallacher, R. R. (1983). Disruption and identifications of the act of eating. Unpublished research data. In R. R. Vallacher & D. M. Wegner (1985), *A theory of action identification.* Erlbaum.

Wegner, D. M., Erber, R., & Zanakos, S. (1993). Ironic processes in the mental control of mood and mood-related thought. *Journal of Personality and Social Psychology, 65*(6), 1093–1104.

Wegner, D. M., Vallacher, R. R., Kiersted, G. W., & Dizadji, D. (1986). Action identification in the emergence of social behavior. *Social Cognition, 4*(1), 18–38.

Wegner, D. M., Wenzlaff, R. M., & Kozak, M. (2004). Dream rebound: The return of suppressed thoughts in dreams. *Psychological Science, 15*(4), 232–236.

Weigel, R. H., & Newman, L. S. (1976). Increasing attitude-behavior correspondence by broadening the scope of the behavioral measure. *Journal of Personality and Social Psychology, 33*(6), 793–802.

Weil, A. (1972). *The natural mind: A new way of looking at drugs and the higher consciousness.* Houghton Mifflin.

Weiner, B. (1980). A cognitive (attribution)-emotion-action model of motivated behavior: An analysis of judgments of help-giving. *Journal of Personality and Social Psychology, 39*(2), 186–200.

Weiner, B., Osborne, D., & Rudolph, U. (2011). An attributional analysis of reactions to poverty: The political ideology of the giver and the perceived morality of the receiver. *Personality and Social Psychology Review*, 15(2), 199–213.

Weiner, B., Perry, R. P., & Magnusson, J. (1988). An attributional analysis of reactions to stigmas. *Journal of Personality and Social Psychology*, 55(5), 738–748.

Weingarten, E., Chen, Q., McAdams, M., Yi, J., Hepler, J., & Albarracín, D. (2016). From primed concepts to action: A meta-analysis of the behavioral effects of incidentally presented words. *Psychological Bulletin*, 142(5), 472–497.

Weingarten, E., & Hutchinson, J. (2018). Does ease mediate the ease-of-retrieval effect? A meta-analysis. *Psychological Bulletin*, 144(3), 227–283.

Weingarten, G. (2007, April 8). Pearls before breakfast. Can one of the nation's great musicians cut through the fog of a D.C. rush hour? Let's find out. *The Washington Post*. http://www.washingtonpost.com/lifestyle/magazine/pearls-before-breakfast-can-one-of-the-nations-great-musicians-cutthrough-the-fog-of-a-dc-rush-hour-lets-find-out/2014/09/23/8a6d46da-433111e4b47c-f5889e061e5f_story.html

Weinstein, N., & Ryan, R. M. (2010). When helping helps: Autonomous motivation for prosocial behavior and its influence on well-being for the helper and recipient. *Journal of Personality and Social Psychology*, 98(2), 222–244.

Weir, K. (2016). Mistaken identity: Is eyewitness testimony more reliable than we think? *APA Monitor on Psychology*, 47(2), 40.

Weiss, B., Dodge, K. A., Bates, J. E., & Pettit, G. S. (1992). Some consequences of early harsh discipline: Child aggression and a maladaptive social information processing style. *Child Development*, 63(6), 1321–1335.

Wells, B. E., & Twenge, J. M. (2005). Changes in young people's sexual behavior and attitudes, 1943–1999: A cross-temporal meta-analysis. *Review of General Psychology*, 9(3), 249–261.

Wells, G. L., Memon, A., & Penrod, S. D. (2006). Eyewitness evidence: Improving its probative value. *Psychological Science in the Public Interest*, 7(2), 45–75.

Wells, G. L., & Petty, R. E. (1980). The effects of overt head movements on persuasion: Compatibility and incompatibility of responses. *Basic and Applied Social Psychology*, 1(3), 219–230.

Wells, V. (2020, February 18). *Dwyane Wade says Zaya knew about her gender identity since she was 3-years-old*. https://madamenoire.com/1133392/dwyane-wade-says-zaya-knew-about-her-gender-identity-since-she-was-3-years-old/

Werner, K. M., & Milyavskaya, M. (2018). We may not know what we want, but do we know what we need? Examining the ability to forecast need satisfaction in goal pursuit. *Social Psychological and Personality Science*, 9(6), 656–663.

Werner, K. M., & Milyavskaya, M. (2019). Motivation and self-regulation: The role of want-to motivation in the processes underlying self-regulation and self-control. *Social and Personality Psychology Compass*, 13(1), e12425.

Wheeler, L., & Kim, Y. (1997). What is beautiful is culturally good: The physical attractiveness stereotype has different content in collectivistic cultures. *Personality and Social Psychology Bulletin*, 23(8), 795–800.

Wheeler, L., & Nezlek, J. (1977). Sex differences in social participation. *Journal of Personality and Social Psychology*, 35(10), 742–754.

Wheelis, A. (1980). *The scheme of things*. Harcourt Brace Jovanovich.

Whisman, M. A., Gilmour, A. L., & Salinger, J. M. (2018). Marital satisfaction and mortality in the United States adult population. *Health Psychology*, 37(11), 1041–1044.

White, G. L., Fishbein, S., & Rutsein, J. (1981). Passionate love and the misattribution of arousal. *Journal of Personality and Social Psychology*, 41(1), 56–62.

White, G. L., & Kight, T. D. (1984). Misattribution of arousal and attraction: Effects of salience of explanations for arousal. *Journal of Experimental Social Psychology*, 20(1), 55–64.

White, K., MacDonnell, R., & Dahl, D. W. (2011). It's the mind-set that matters: The role of construal level and message framing in influencing consumer efficacy and conservation behaviors. *Journal of Marketing Research*, 48, 472–485.

Whitley, B. E., Jr., & Webster, G. D. (2019). The relationships of intergroup ideologies to ethnic prejudice: A meta-analysis. *Personality and Social Psychology Review*, 23(3), 207–237.

Whitman, W. (2001). *Leaves of grass*. Random House (Original work published 1855)

Whitson, J. A., Liljenquist, K. A., Galinsky, A. D., Magee, J. C., Gruenfeld, D. H., & Cadena, B. (2013). The blind leading: Power reduces awareness of constraints. *Journal of Experimental Social Psychology*, 49(3), 579–582.

Whittler, T. E., & Spira, J. (2002). Model's race: A peripheral cue in advertising messages? *Journal of Consumer Psychology*, 12(4), 291–301.

Wicker, A. W. (1969). Attitudes versus actions: The relationship of verbal and overt behavioral responses to attitude objects. *Journal of Social Issues*, 25(4), 41–78.

Wicklund, R. A., & Gollwitzer, P. M. (1982). *Symbolic self-completion*. Erlbaum.

Widmer, E. D., Treas, J., & Newcomb, R. (1998). Attitudes toward nonmarital sex in 24 countries. *Journal of Sex Research*, 35(4), 349–358.

Widom, C. S. (1989). Does violence beget violence? A critical examination of the literature. *Psychological Bulletin*, 106(1), 3–28.

Wiebe, D. J. (2003). Firearms in US homes as a risk factor for unintentional gunshot fatality. *Accident Analysis & Prevention*, 35(5), 711–716.

Wieber, F., Thürmer, L., & Gollwitzer, P. M. (2015). Attenuating the escalation of commitment to a faltering project in decision-making groups: An implementation intention approach. *Social Psychological and Personality Science*, 6(5), 587–595.

Wiederman, M. W. (2004). Self-control and sexual behavior. In R. F. Baumeister & K. D. Vohs (Eds.), *Handbook of self-regulation: Research, theory, and applications* (pp. 525–536). Guilford Press.

Wiggins, J. S., Wiggins, N., & Conger, J. C. (1968). Correlates of heterosexual somatic preference. *Journal of Personality and Social Psychology*, 10(1), 82–90.

Wilding, S., Conner, M., Prestwich, A., Lawton, R., & Sheeran, P. (2019). Using the question–behavior effect to change multiple health behaviors: An exploratory randomized controlled trial. *Journal of Experimental Social Psychology*, 81, 53–60.

Wilkinson, G. S. (1990). Food sharing in vampire bats. *Scientific American*, 262(2), 76–82.

Willetts, M. C., Sprecher, S., & Beck, F. D. (2004). Overview of sexual practices and attitudes within relational contexts. In J. H. Harvey, A. Wenzel, & S. Sprecher (Eds.), *The handbook of sexuality in close relationships* (pp. 57–85). Erlbaum.

Williams, D. R. (1999). Race, socioeconomic status, and health: The added effects of racism and discrimination. *Annals of the New York Academy of Sciences*, 896(1), 173–188.

Williams, D. R., Spencer, M. S., & Jackson, J. S. (1999). Race, stress, and physical health. In R. J. Contrada & R. D. Ashmore (Eds.), *Self, social identity, and physical health: Interdisciplinary explorations* (Vol. 2, pp. 71–100). Oxford University Press.

Williams, J. E., Best, D. L., & Boswell, D. A. (1975). The measurement of children's racial attitudes in the early school years. *Child Development*, 46(2), 494–500.

Williams, K., Harkins, S. G., & Latané, B. (1981). Identifiability as a deterrent to social loafing: Two cheering experiments. *Journal of Personality and Social Psychology*, 40(2), 303–311.

Williams, K. D. (2007). Ostracism. *Annual Review of Psychology*, 58(1), 425–452.

Williams, K. D., & Zadro, L. (2001). Ostracism: On being ignored, excluded, and rejected. In M. R. Leary (Ed.), *Interpersonal rejection* (pp. 21–53). Oxford University Press.

Williams, M. J., Gruenfeld, D. H., & Guillory, L. E. (2017). Sexual aggression when power is new: Effects of acute high power on chronically low-power individuals. *Journal of Personality and Social Psychology*, 112(2), 201–223.

Williams, M. T. (2021). Racial Microaggressions: Critical Questions, State of the Science, and New Directions. *Perspectives on Psychological Science*, 16(5), 880–885.

Williamson, G. M., & Clark, M. S. (1989). Providing help and desired relationship type as determinants of changes in moods and self-evaluations. *Journal of Personality and Social Psychology*, 56(5), 722–734.

Williamson, G. M., & Clark, M. S. (1992). Impact of desired relationship type on affective reactions to choosing and being required to help. *Personality and Social Psychology Bulletin*, 18(1), 10–18.

Wills, T. A. (1981). Downward comparison principles in social psychology. *Psychological Bulletin*, 90(2), 245–271.

Wills, T. A., Sargent, J. D., Stoolmiller, M., Gibbons, F. X., & Gerrard, M. (2008). Movie smoking exposure and smoking onset: A longitudinal study of mediation processes in a representative sample of U.S. adolescents. *Psychology of Addictive Behaviors*, 22(2), 269–277.

Wilson, J. P. (1976). Motivation, modeling, and altruism: A person 3 situation analysis. *Journal of Personality and Social Psychology*, 34(6), 1078–1086.

Wilson, J. P., Hugenberg, K., & Rule, N. O. (2017). Racial bias in judgments of physical size and formidability: From size to threat. *Journal of Personality and Social Psychology*, 113(1), 59–80.

Wilson, J. P., & Rule, N. O. (2015). Facial trustworthiness predicts extreme criminal-sentencing outcomes. *Psychological Science*, 26(8), 1325–1331.

Wilson, J. P., & Rule, N. O. (2016). Hypothetical sentencing decisions are associated with actual capital punishment outcomes: The role of facial trustworthiness. *Social Psychological and Personality Science*, 7(4), 331–338.

Wilson, T. D., Dunn, D. S., Kraft, D., & Lisle, D. J. (1989). Introspection, attitude change, and attitude-behavior consistency: The disruptive effects of explaining why we feel the way we do. In L. Berkowitz (Ed.), *Advances in experimental social psychology* (Vol. 19, pp. 123–205). Academic Press.

Wilson, T. D., & Gilbert, D. T. (2005). Affective forecasting: Knowing what to want. *Current Directions in Psychological Science, 14*(3), 131–134.

Wilson, T. D., & Kraft, D. (1993). Why do I love thee? Effects of repeated introspections about a dating relationship on attitudes toward the relationship. *Personality and Social Psychology Bulletin, 19*(4), 409–418.

Wilson, T. D., Laser, P. S., & Stone, J. I. (1982). Judging the predictors of one's own mood: Accuracy and the use of shared theories. *Journal of Experimental Social Psychology, 18*(6), 537–556.

Wilson, T. D., Reinhard, D. A., Westgate, E. C., Gilbert, D. T., Ellerbeck, N., Hahn, C., Brown, C. L., & Shaked, A. (2014). Social psychology. Just think: The challenges of the disengaged mind. *Science, 345*(6192), 75–77.

Wilson, T. D., Wheatley, T., Meyers, J. M., Gilbert, D. T., & Axsom, D. (2000). Focalism: A source of durability bias in affective forecasting. *Journal of Personality and Social Psychology, 78*(5), 821–836.

Wiltermuth, S., & Flynn, F. (2012). Power, moral clarity, and punishment in the workplace. *Academy of Management Journal, 56*(4), 1002–1023.

Winkel, F. W., & Denkers, A. (1995). Crime victims and their social network: A field study on the cognitive effects of victimisation, attributional responses and the victim-blaming model. *International Review of Victimology, 3*(4), 309–322.

Winkielman, P., & Cacioppo, J. T. (2001). Mind at ease puts a smile on the face: Psychophysiological evidence that processing facilitation elicits positive affect. *Journal of Personality and Social Psychology, 81*(6), 989–1000.

Winkielman, P., Knutson, B., Paulus, M., & Trujillo, J. L. (2007). Affective influence on judgments and decisions: Moving towards core mechanisms. *Review of General Psychology, 11*(2), 179–192.

Winkler-Rhoades, N., Medin, D., Waxman, S. R., Woodring, J., & Ross, N. O. (2010). Naming the animals that come to mind: Effects of culture and experience on category fluency. *Journal of Cognition and Culture, 10*(1–2), 1–2.

Wiseman, C. V., Gray, J. J., Mosimann, J. E., & Ahrens, A. H. (1992). Cultural expectations of thinness in women: An update. *International Journal of Eating Disorders, 11*(1), 85–89.

Wisman, A., & Goldenberg, J. L. (2005). From the grave to the cradle: Evidence that mortality salience engenders a desire for offspring. *Journal of Personality and Social Psychology, 89*(1), 46–61.

Witkower, Z., & Tracy, J. L. (2019). A facial-action imposter: How head tilt influences perceptions of dominance from a neutral face. *Psychological Science, 30*(6), 893–906.

Witte, K., & Allen, M. (2000). A meta-analysis of fear appeals: Implications for effective public health campaigns. *Health Education & Behavior, 27*(5), 591–615.

Wolf, S., & Montgomery, D. A. (1977). Effects of inadmissible evidence and level of judicial admonishment to disregard on the judgments of mock jurors. *Journal of Applied Social Psychology, 7*(3), 205–219.

Wolfgang, M. E., & Ferracuti, F. (1967). *The subculture of violence: Towards an integrated theory in criminology.* Tavistock Publications.

Wolkstein, D. (1991). *The first love stories: From Isis and Osiris to Tristan and Iseult.* HarperCollins.

Wolsko, C., Ariceaga, H., & Seiden, J. (2016). Red, white, and blue enough to be green: Effects of moral framing on climate change attitudes and conservation behaviors. *Journal of Experimental Social Psychology, 65*, 7–19.

Wong, P. T., & Weiner, B. (1981). When people ask "why" questions, and the heuristics of attributional search. *Journal of Personality and Social Psychology, 40*(4), 650–663.

Wong, R. Y. M., & Hong, Y. Y. (2005). Dynamic influences of culture on cooperation in the prisoner's dilemma. *Psychological Science, 16*(6), 429–434.

Wood, W., & Eagly, A. H. (2002). A cross-cultural analysis of the behavior of women and men: Implications for the origins of sex differences. *Psychological Bulletin, 128*(5), 699–727.

Wood, W., & Eagly, A. H. (2007). Social structural origins of sex differences in human mating. In S. W. Gangestad & J. A. Simpson (Eds.), *The evolution of mind: Fundamental questions and controversies* (pp. 383–390). Guilford Press.

Wood, W., Kallgren, C. A., & Preisler, R. M. (1985). Access to attitude-relevant information in memory as a determinant of persuasion: The role of message attributes. *Journal of Experimental Social Psychology, 21*(1), 73–85.

Wood, W., Kressel, L., Joshi, P. D., & Louie, B. (2014). Meta-analysis of menstrual cycle effects on women's mate preferences. *Emotion Review, 6*(3), 229–249.

Wood, W., Lundgren, S., Ouellette, J. A., Busceme, S., & Blackstone, T. (1994). Minority influence: A meta-analytic review of social influence processes. *Psychological Bulletin, 115*(3), 323–345.

Wood, W., & Neal, D. T. (2007). A new look at habits and the habit-goal interface. *Psychological Review, 114*(4), 843–863.

Wood, W., & Ruenger, D. (2016). Psychology of habits. *Annual Review of Psychology, 67*, 289–314.

Wood, W., & Stagner, B. (1994). Why are some people easier to influence than others? In S. Shavitt & T. Brock (Eds.), *Persuasion: Psychological insights and perspectives* (pp. 149–174). Allyn & Bacon.

Woolley, K., & Fishbach, A. (2019). Shared plates, shared minds: Consuming from a shared plate promotes cooperation. *Psychological Science, 30*(4), 541–552.

Worchel, S., & Teddie, C. (1976). The experience of crowding: A two-factor theory. *Journal of Personality and Social Psychology, 34*(1), 30–40.

Word, C. O., Zanna, M. P., & Cooper, J. (1974). The nonverbal mediation of self-fulfilling prophecies in interracial interaction. *Journal of Experimental Social Psychology, 10*(2), 109–120.

Wosinska, W., Dabul, A. J., Whetstone-Dion, R., & Cialdini, R. B. (1996). Self-presentational responses to success in the organization: Costs and benefits of modesty. *Basic and Applied Social Psychology, 18*(2), 229–242.

Wotipka, C. D., & High, A. C. (2016). An idealized self or the real me? Predicting attraction to online dating profiles using selective self-presentation and warranting. *Communication Monographs, 83*(3), 281–302.

Wozniak, J. D., Caudle, H. E., Harding, K., Vieselmeyer, J., & Mezulis, A. H. (2020). The effect of trauma proximity and ruminative response styles on posttraumatic stress and posttraumatic growth following a university shooting. *Psychological Trauma: Theory, Research, Practice, and Policy, 12*(3), 227–234.

Wu, K., Garcia, S. M., & Kopelman, S. (2018). Frogs, ponds, and culture: Variations in entry decisions. *Social Psychological and Personality Science, 9*(1), 99–106.

Wyer, R. S., Weatherley, D. A., & Terrell, G. (1965). Social role, aggression, and academic achievement. *Journal of Personality and Social Psychology, 1*(6), 645–649.

Yaakobi, E., Mikulincer, M., & Shaver, P. (2014). Parenthood as a terror management mechanism: The moderating role of attachment orientations. *Personality and Social Psychology Bulletin, 40*(6), 762–774.

Yakin, B. (Director). (2000). *Remember the Titans* [Film]. Walt Disney Pictures.

Yam, K. (2022) Anti-Asian hate crimes increased 339 percent nationwide last year, report says. NBC News. https://www.nbcnews.com/news/asian-america/anti-asian-hate-crimes-increased-339-percent-nationwide-last-year-repo-rcna14282

Yam, K. C., Barnes, C. M., Leavitt, K., Wei, W., Lau, J., & Uhlmann, E. L. (2019). Why so serious? A laboratory and field investigation of the link between morality and humor. *Journal of Personality and Social Psychology, 117*(4), 758–772.

Yanagisawa, K., Abe, N., Kashima, E. S., & Nomura, M. (2016). Self-esteem modulates amygdala-ventrolateral prefrontal cortex connectivity in response to mortality threats. *Journal of Experimental Psychology: General, 145*(3), 273–283.

Yang, X. G., Li, Y.-P., Ma, G., Wang, J.-Z., Cui, Z. H., Cui, Z.-H., Wang, Z.-H., Yu, W.-T., Yang, Z.-X., & Zhai, F.-Y. (2005). Study on weight and height of the Chinese people and the differences between 1992 and 2002 (in Chinese). *Zhonghua Liu Xing Bing Xue Za Zhi, 26*(7), 489–493.

Yang, Y. (2008). Social inequalities in happiness in the United States, 1972 to 2004: An age-period-cohort analysis. *American Sociological Review, 73*(2), 204–226.

Yang, Y. T., Broniatowski, D. A., & Reiss, D. R. (2019). Government role in regulating vaccine misinformation on social media platforms. *JAMA Pediatrics, 173*(11), 1011–1012.

Yeager, D. S., Hanselman, P., Walton, G. M., Murray, J. S., Crosnoe, R., Muller, C., Tipton, E., Schneider, B., Hulleman, C. S., Hinojosa, C. P., Paunesku, D., Romero, C., Flint, K., Roberts, A., Trott, J., Iachan, R., Buontempo, J., Yang, S. M., Carvalho, C. M., . . . Dweck, C. S. (2019). A national study reveals where a growth mindset improves achievement. *Nature, 573*, 364–369.

Yeager, D. S., Krosnick, J. A., Visser, P. S., Holbrook, A. L., & Tahk, A. M. (2019). Moderation of classic social psychological effects by demographics in the U.S. adult population: New opportunities for theoretical advancement. *Journal of Personality and Social Psychology, 117*(6), e84–e99.

Yelsma, P., & Athappilly, K. (1988). Marital satisfaction and communication practices: Comparisons among Indian and American couples. *Journal of Comparative Family Studies, 19*(1), 37–54.

Yeung, N. C. J., & von Hippel, C. (2008). Stereotype threat increases the likelihood that female drivers in a simulator run over jaywalkers. *Accident Analysis & Prevention, 40*(2), 667–674.

York, A. (2001, April 26). The product placement monster that E.T. spawned. *Salon.* http://dir.salon.com/tech/feature/2001/04/26/product_placement/index.html

Young, J. L., & Hegarty, P. (2019). Reasonable men: Sexual harassment and norms of conduct in social psychology. *Feminism & Psychology, 29*(4), 453–474.

Youyou, W., Stillwell, D., Schwartz, H. A., & Kosinski, M. (2017). Birds of a feather do flock together: Behavior-based personality-assessment method reveals personality similarity among couples and friends. *Psychological Science, 28*(3), 276–284.

Yum, Y. O., & Schenck-Hamlin, W. (2005). Reactions to 9/11 as a function of terror management and perspective taking. *Journal of Social Psychology, 145*(3), 265–286.

Zaccaro, S. J. (1984). Social loafing: The role of task attractiveness. *Personality and Social Psychology Bulletin, 10*(1), 99–106.

Zadro, L., Williams, K. D., & Richardson, R. (2004). How low can you go? Ostracism by a computer is sufficient to lower self-reported levels of belonging, control, self-esteem, and meaningful existence. *Journal of Experimental Social Psychology, 40*(4), 560–567.

Zajonc, R. B. (1965). Social facilitation. *Science, 149*(3681), 269–274.

Zajonc, R. B. (1968). Attitudinal effects of mere exposure. *Journal of Personality and Social Psychology, 9*(2, Pt. 2), 1–27.

Zajonc, R. B. (1998). Emotions. In D. T. Gilbert, S. T. Fiske, & G. Lindzey (Eds.), *The handbook of social psychology* (4th ed., Vol. 1, pp. 591–632). McGraw-Hill.

Zajonc, R. B., Heingartner, A., & Herman, E. M. (1969). Social enhancement and impairment of performance in the cockroach. *Journal of Personality and Social Psychology, 13*(2), 83–92.

Zak, P. J., Kurzban, R., & Matzner, W. T. (2005). Oxytocin is associated with human trustworthiness. *Hormones and Behavior, 48*(5), 522–527.

Zanna, M. P., & Cooper, J. (1974). Dissonance and the pill: An attribution approach to studying the arousal properties of dissonance. *Journal of Personality and Social Psychology, 29*(5), 703–709.

Zanna, M. P., Lepper, M. R., & Abelson, R. P. (1973). Attentional mechanisms in children's devaluation of a forbidden activity in a forced-compliance situation. *Journal of Personality and Social Psychology, 28*(3), 355–359.

Zebrowitz, L. A. (1997). *Reading faces: Window to the soul?* Westview Press.

Zeigarnik, B. (1938). On finished and unfinished tasks. In W. D. Ellis (Ed.), *A sourcebook of Gestalt psychology* (pp. 300–314). Harcourt.

Zell, E., & Alicke, M. D. (2010). The local dominance effect in self-evaluation: Evidence and explanations. *Personality and Social Psychology Review, 14*(4), 368–384.

Zellner, M. (1970). Self-esteem, reception, and influenceability. *Journal of Personality and Social Psychology, 15*(1), 87–93.

Zenger, T. R. (1992). Why do employers only reward extreme performance? Examining the relationships among performance, pay, and turnover. *Administrative Science Quarterly, 37*(2), 198–219.

Zentner, M., & Mitura, K. (2012). Stepping out of the caveman's shadow: Nations' gender gap predicts degree of sex differentiation in mate preferences. *Psychological Science, 23*(10), 1176–1185.

Zestcott, C. A., Lifshin, U., Helm, P. J., & Greenberg J. (2016). He dies he scores: The effects of reminders of death on athletic performance in basketball. *Journal of Sport and Exercise Psychology, 38*(5), 470–480.

Zestcott, C. A., Stone, J., & Landau, M. J. (2017). The role of conscious attention in how weight serves as an embodiment of importance. *Personality and Social Psychology Bulletin, 43*(12), 1712–1723.

Zhang, S., & Kline, S. L. (2009). Can I make my own decisions? A cross cultural study of perceived social network influence in mate selection. *Journal of Cross-Cultural Psychology, 40*(1), 3–23.

Zhao, K., & Smillie, L. D. (2014). The role of interpersonal traits in social decision making: Exploring sources of behavioral heterogeneity in economic games. *Personality and Social Psychology Review, 19*(3), 277–302.

Zhou, H., & Fishbach, A. (2016). The pitfall of experimenting on the web: How unattended selective attrition leads to surprising (yet false) research conclusions. *Journal of Personality and Social Psychology, 111*(4), 493.

Zhou, Q., Eisenberg, N., Losoya, S. H., Fabes, R. A., Reiser, M., Guthrie, I. K., Murphy, B. C., Cumberland, A. J., & Shepard, S. A. (2002). The relations of parental warmth and positive expressiveness to children's empathy-related responding and social functioning: A longitudinal study. *Child Development, 73*(3), 893–915.

Zhou, X., Liu, J., Chen, C., & Yu, Z. (2008). Do children transcend death? An examination of the terror management function of offspring. *Scandinavian Journal of Psychology, 49*(5), 413–418.

Zhu, W., Chen, Y., & Xia, L. X. (in press). Childhood maltreatment and aggression: The mediating roles of hostile attribution bias and anger rumination. *Personality and Individual Differences.*

Zigerell, L. J. (2017). Potential publication bias in the stereotype threat literature: Comment on Nguyen and Ryan (2008). *Journal of Applied Psychology, 102*(8), 1159–1168.

Zillmann, D. (1971). Excitation transfer in communication-mediated aggressive behavior. *Journal of Experimental Social Psychology, 7*(4), 419–434.

Zillmann, D. (1979). *Hostility and aggression.* Erlbaum.

Zillmann, D. (1998). The psychology of the appeal of portrayals of violence. In J. H. Goldstein (Ed.), *Why we watch: The attractions of violent entertainment* (pp. 179–211). Oxford University Press.

Zillmann, D., & Bryant, J. (1974). Effect of residual excitation on the emotional response to provocation and delayed aggressive behavior. *Journal of Personality and Social Psychology, 30*(6), 782–791.

Zillmann, D., Bryant, J., Cantor, J. R., & Day, K. D. (1975). Irrelevance of mitigating circumstances in retaliatory behavior at high levels of excitation. *Journal of Research in Personality, 9*(4), 282–293.

Zillmann, D., & Cantor, J. R. (1976). Effect of timing of information about mitigating circumstances on emotional responses to provocation and retaliatory behavior. *Journal of Experimental Social Psychology, 12*(1), 38–55.

Zillmann, D., Katcher, A. H., & Milavsky, B. (1972). Excitation transfer from physical exercise to subsequent aggressive behavior. *Journal of Experimental Social Psychology, 8*(3), 247–259.

Zimbardo, P. (2007). *The Lucifer effect: Understanding how good people turn evil.* Random House.

Zimbardo, P. G. (1970). The human choice: Individuation, reason, and order versus deindividuation, impulse, and chaos. In W. J. Arnold & D. Levine (Eds.), *Nebraska symposium on motivation* (Vol. 18, pp. 237–307). University of Nebraska Press.

Zou, L., & Cheryan, S. (2015). When Whites' attempts to be multicultural backfire in intergroup interactions. *Social and Personality Psychology Compass, 9*(11), 581–592.

Zunick, P. V., Teeny, J. D., & Fazio, R. H. (2017). Are some attitudes more self-defining than others? Assessing self-related attitude functions and their consequences. *Personality and Social Psychology Bulletin, 43*(8), 1136–1149.

Zurbriggen, E. L. (2000). Social motives and cognitive power–sex associations: Predictors of aggressive sexual behavior. *Journal of Personality and Social Psychology, 78*(3), 559–581.

NAME INDEX